International Business

Introduction and
Essentials

International Business

Introduction and Essentials

DONALD A. BALL
University of Texas—Pan American

WENDELL H. McCULLOCH, JR.
California State University,
Long Beach

Fifth Edition

Homewood, IL 60430
Boston, MA 02116

Senior sponsoring editor: Craig Beytien
Developmental editor: Karen E. Perry
Marketing manager: Kurt Messersmith
Project editor: Jess Ann Ramirez
Production manager: Bette K. Ittersagen
Designer: Maureen McCutcheon
Art manager: Kim Meriwether
Photo research coordinator: Patricia A. Seefelt
Compositor: The Clarinda Co.
Typeface: 10/12 Sabon
Printer: Von Hoffmann Press

Library of Congress Cataloging-in-Publication Data

Ball, Donald A.
    International business : introduction and essentials / Donald A.
Ball, Wendell H. McCulloch, Jr.—5th ed.
        p.   cm.
    Includes bibliographical references (p.   ) and indexes.
    ISBN 0-256-10652-5
        1. International business enterprises—Management.
2. International business enterprises.   3. International economic
relations.   I. McCulloch, Wendell H.   II. Title.
    HD62.4.B34   1993
    658'.049—dc20   92—11278

To Vicky and Sally
Don, Jr., Dulce, Lianne, Susan, Jim,
Kevin, and Malinda

About the Authors

Don Ball is professor of marketing and international business at the University of Texas—Pan American and a consultant to international companies. He has a degree in mechanical engineering from Ohio State University and a Ph.D. in business administration from the University of Florida. Ball has published articles in the *Journal of International Business Studies* and other publications. Before obtaining the doctorate, he spent 15 years in various marketing and production management positions in Latin America and Europe.

Wendell McCulloch is professor of international business, finance, and law at California State University, Long Beach. He earned a bachelor's degree in economics and political science from George Washington University and a J.D. from Yale University. He has published articles in *The Wall Street Journal,* the *Journal of International Business Studies,* and the *Collegiate Forum.* The results of McCulloch's research have appeared in publications by the Joint Economic Committee of the U.S. Congress and the Heritage Foundation. Before beginning his academic career, McCulloch spent 19 years as an executive for American and European multinationals that offered banking, insurance, and investment products in many countries. While teaching and writing, he continues to act as an international business consultant.

A Note to the Student

Throughout the process of preparing the fifth edition of this text, we kept you, the student, uppermost in our minds. The result is a "student-friendly" text with numerous unique features.

1. Students tell us it is eminently readable. You can understand what is written.

2. Each chapter begins with a list of learning objectives and key words and concepts. These help you find the important points that you should understand.

3. The book is practical. Each chapter begins with a Business Incident, each has margin definitions to help you learn the meanings of important terms, and most contain a Worldview reading. Throughout the book, we explain the significance of the material to the businessperson. Many pictures and examples from industry help animate the book.

4. The text contains numerous tables and figures, many of which we constructed so as to present the data in a more useful form for businesspeople. We interpret the tables and graphs to help you understand their importance.

5. Much of a manager's success depends on the ability to find data. We provide long lists of data sources at various points in the book.

6. You will find information in this text that is not usually found in international business books: complete chapters on the international organizations' physical forces, production, and exporting and importing, for example.

7. Because it is so comprehensive, this is a book that you will want to keep for your personal library. Many businesspeople, government officials, international business advisors, and consultants buy it for that reason.

8. Over the life of this book, we have received valuable student feedback. Please continue to send us your comments.

Donald A. Ball
Wendell H. McCulloch, Jr.

Preface

We are pleased with your outstanding response to our fourth edition. As a result, our publisher decided to publish the fifth edition in full color, making Ball & McCulloch the first international business text with this important improvement. We again thank all of you who took time to call us or write us about material and improvements that you and your students wished to see in this edition.

◻ Purpose and Scope of This Text

The text is written for the first course in international business taken either at the undergraduate level or in an M.B.A. program. A growing number of schools are permitting students to take the international business course *before* they have all the required basic courses so they are better prepared to discuss the worldwide aspects of each business function. This enables professors to take a more global approach in the presentation of their material.

In schools that do not yet require an international business course, many professors recommend this text as a supplementary book for international courses in finance, management, marketing, and so forth. Numerous executive seminars include this book as part of their handouts in programs on the various aspects of international business, and many business executives buy it as a reference book.

We begin the text by describing the nature of international business and the three environments in which an international businessperson works. In Section Two, we examine the increasingly important international organizations, the international monetary system, and their impact on business. Next, in Section Three, we discuss the uncontrollable forces that make up the foreign environments and illustrate their effect on business practices. In the final section, we reverse the procedure and deal with the functions of management, showing how managers deal with the uncontrollable forces. The final chapter describes the trends and new directions of international companies. There are many business examples throughout the book.

◻ Changes in the Fifth Edition

Suggestions for improving this edition came from a number of sources: mail questionnaires, detailed chapter-by-chapter reviews by a number of international business professors, calls and letters from professors and students, comments by businesspeople who attended executive seminars or bought the book for their personal libraries, and students in our own classes, both graduate and undergraduate.

Our research confirms that the readability is good, which enables students to read and understand the material. Professors are thus freed of the task of explaining what was read and can use the class time to expand on topics of their choice and to discuss the latest happenings in this rapidly changing field.

We continue to begin each chapter with a quotation, followed by a Business Incident that relates to the material in the chapter. Margin definitions help students learn the language of international business, and the World-views provide readings that are pertinent to the text material.

Reviewers have commented favorably on the use of indented materials as examples, and we have increased their use. Some are our own experiences gathered from a combined 34 years as executives for international firms, both in the United States and in various foreign countries. The supplementary reading list has been expanded. Several new end-of-chapter minicases have been added, and there are new comprehensive cases at the end of the book. You will notice that we have used every effort, including calling government officials, to bring you the latest information. We invite you to compare data in our tables with those of other textbooks published in the same year.

Because the book is now in full color, we are able to place maps right where they are needed rather than in a special section at the end of the book. We are also using more pictures, because they often present a concept more vividly than we can describe it. They also are much more descriptive in full color. Occasionally, we include a cartoon—international business does have its lighter side. There are also more graphs to supplement the tables.

□ Areas of Substantive Change

We have made numerous changes in this edition.

1. In Chapter 1, we introduced an international business model to help explain the relationships among the domestic, international, and foreign environments. We also now have a section on careers in international business located in an appendix to Chapter 1. A new minicase that permits students to use the FT 925 for export market research has been added to Chapter 2. There is now a section on production possibility frontiers to help show the gains from trade in Chapter 3. Graphics to illustrate the product life cycle have been added.

2. In Chapter 4, we describe a new trend in the World Bank and IMF—more encouragement of and support for investment by the private sector. There is expanded coverage of the BIS and an update on the GATT Uruguay Round.

3. Chapter 8 has a new minicase on the protection of the Amazon rain forest, and Chapter 9 now has a description of fung shui.

4. Chapter 10 includes a discussion on developments in the former Soviet Union and its disbanded trade bloc and a privatization update. There is new material on country risk assessment (CRA).

5. A new application of antitrust law is included in Chapter 11, as well as material on intellectual property protection.

6. Chapter 12 contains material on new developments affecting refugee and guest laborers, progress for females in the work force, and new comparative work hours and pay of world's workers.

7. We have added a new case, America Bashing, to Chapter 13. There is also a new minicase utilizing the FT 477 in Chapter 14.

8. Globalization versus localization has been expanded in Chapter 15, and a new case on Black & Decker's brand transfer strategy was added.

9. Chapter 17 has been completely rewritten to deal with the momentous changes taking place in the former Soviet Union, Eastern Europe, and the People's Republic of China.

10. Coverage of currency risk hedging and countertrade has been expanded in Chapter 18.

11. Chapter 19 now includes a discussion of the Malcolm Baldrige quality award and the events in Japan that led to the Deming award.

12. Discussion of the new look in Japanese executive indoctrination programs as well as new material on robotics and labor unions are now in Chapter 20.

13. Considerable new information on both organizational design and strategic planning has been added to Chapter 21. We discuss the horizontal organization. There is a new minicase.

14. Chapter 22 includes information on executives' gross pay and buying power around the world.

15. A completely new Chapter 23 speculates on the future of global and multinational firms and on the world in which they will function.

□ The Advantages of Using This Book in Your Class

This book is the result of teamwork between many professors and their students who have used previous editions. One aspect constantly mentioned is its readability. Because students understand what they read in this book, the professor can spend less time clarifying basic points and more time discussing emerging issues, of which there is no lack in this fast-moving field. However, don't be misled by the writing style. We have compared this book with others and have yet to find one as comprehensive. Note that we have included a complete chapter on the physical forces, to strengthen what is generally a weak area of students' education. There are also complete chapters on exporting-importing and production. We invite comparisons of our treatment of marketing, financial management, and international organizations, all important topics for international business-people. The many tables and their analyses enable students to make important comparisons of markets, and the numerous listed sources of additional information facilitate the research process when you wish to assign them projects.

Our 34 combined years in international business, in both the home offices of worldwide firms and their subsidiaries, have influenced our writing. We wanted a book that would describe what managers have to face in international business and how they respond to the uncontrollable environmental forces; in short, the kind of book people would like to have if they were suddenly told by the boss that they were going overseas. In fact, this happened to one of us—who found no such book at that time.

□ The Ball and McCulloch International Business Package

1. Instructor's Manual.   We have worked to make a manual that will (1) help you save valuable time preparing for the course and (2) provide suggestions for heightening your students' interest in the material. Each chapter-by-chapter discussion presents the learning objectives, an overview, suggestions and comments, student involvement exercises, suggestions for guest lecturers, and a detailed chapter lecture outline, including references to tables when appropriate. Suggestions for videotapes and films are included.

2. Color Teaching Transparencies.   There is now a set of color teaching transparencies available to adopters of the book.

3. Student Resources Manual.   Professor Basel Janavaras of Mankato State University has prepared a *Student Resources Manual* that includes additional questions for review, outlines, summaries, and other material to enrich the study of international business. Some professors require their students to have a manual; others recommend that they have it.

4. Test Bank.   The test bank is available in three formats: (1) a printed manual, (2) Computerized Testing Software—a floppy disk for the extremely rapid preparation of examinations on your own IBM-compatible computer, and (3) Teletest—a customized, phone-in service available from Richard D. Irwin, Inc. The test bank has been improved and expanded for this edition.

5. Video Resources.   Upon request, adopters of the fifth edition will receive a free copy of "Losing the War with Japan," a 90-minute video program produced by Frontline that examines the successful strategies Japan is using to win American markets and the reasons U.S. companies seem unable to compete. The instructor's manual includes lecture notes and discussion questions tying the video to concepts in the text.

6. Annual Updates.   Adopters of the fifth edition will receive updates written by the authors. New, relevant information will be provided that updates the appropriate topics in the text.

□ Acknowledgments

To the long list of people to whom we are indebted, we want to add Professors Robert T. Aubey, University of Wisconsin-Madison; Mark C. Baetz, Wilfrid Laurier University; Rufus Barton, Murray State University; S. A. Billon, University of Delaware; James R. Bradshaw, Brigham Young University; Sharon Browning, Northwest Missouri State University; Dennis Carter, University of North Carolina—Wilmington; Mark Chadwin, Old Dominion University; Refik Culpan, Pennsylvania State University; Peter DeWitt, University of Central Florida; Galpira Eshigi, Illinois State University; Prem Gandhi, State University of New York—Plattsburgh; Stanley D. Guzell, Youngstown State University; Gary Hankem, Mankato State University; Baban Hasnat, State University of New York at Brockport; Paul Jenner, Southwest Missouri State University; Bruce H. Johnson, Gustavus Adolphus College; Michael Kublin, University of New Haven; Eddie Lewis, University of Southern Mississippi; Lois Ann McElroy Lindell, Wartburg College; Carol Lopilato, California State University—Dominguez Hills; Gary Oddon, San Jose

State University; John Setnicky, Mobile College; Jesse S. Tarleton, William and Mary College; John Thanopoulos, Akron University; Kenneth Tillery, Middle Tennessee State University; Hsin-Min Tong, Redford University; Dennis Vanden Bloomen, University of Wisconsin—Stout; and George Westacott, State University of New York—Binghamton. Attorney Mary C. Tolton, Esq., of the law firm Parker, Poe, Adams & Bernstein of Raleigh, North Carolina, provided valuable supplementary readings for the legal forces chapter. Professor Michael Minor, University of Texas—Pan American, made many valuable comments.

We are also indebted to the following reviewers for helping us fine-tune the text to better meet market needs: John Garland, University of Kansas; Mary Howes, Governors State University; Edward R. Raupp, Augsburg College; Frank L. DuBois, The American University; Jan Dunlap, Campbell University; and Kenneth L. Murrell, University of West Florida.

We continue to invite your suggestions for making this a more useful text and thank you for your interest and input.

Donald A. Ball
Wendell H. McCulloch, Jr.

Contents in Brief

Contents

Section One

The Nature of International Business

Section One describes the nature and scope of international business and introduces the three environments in which international business managers must operate. How well they perform in their undertakings will depend in great measure on their understanding of the domestic, international, and foreign environments.

Chapter 1 presents the concept of the three environments and their forces. From the history of international business, we learn that although the international firm existed before the Civil War, it differed markedly from the present-day global company, which is characterized by its explosive growth and closer central control of foreign operations.

In Chapter 2, information is presented to help you comprehend the dynamic growth and the magnitude of both international trade and foreign investment. We discuss why firms go abroad, and we examine the many ways in which they do it.

An overview of the theories of international trade and economic development is given in Chapter 3 because a basic understanding of this material not only will help explain the actions already taken by government officials but also will provide insight into what they plan to do.

Chapter 1

Introduction to International Business

On the need for global awareness . . .

By the year 2000, there will be two types of managers, those with a global awareness and those who are unemployed.

William Simon, former secretary
of U.S. Treasury and investment
banker

There is no longer any such thing as a purely national economy. The rest of the world is just too big to ignore, either as a market or as a competitor. If business schools do nothing other than to train their students to think internationally, they would have accomplished an important task.

John Young, CEO,
Hewlett-Packard

LEARNING OBJECTIVES

In this chapter, you will study:

1. The dramatic internationalization of markets.

2. The various names given to firms that have substantial operations in more than one country.

3. The distinctions between firms of the early 1900s and present-day international companies.

4. Why international business differs from domestic business.

5. The three environments—domestic, foreign, international—in which the international company operates.

KEY WORDS AND CONCEPTS

- Multinational company
- International company
- Global company
- Expropriation
- Host nation
- Environment
- Uncontrollable forces
- Controllable forces
- Domestic environment
- Foreign environment
- International environment
- Self-reference criterion

BUSINESS INCIDENT

In 1989, Xerox celebrated the 25th anniversary of its introduction of the first commercial fax machine. There wasn't much to celebrate, though, because while the inventing company had just 7 percent of the U.S. market, the Japanese had two thirds.[1]

American-owned companies built 80 percent of the cars sold in the United States in 1979, but now their market share has fallen to 63 percent.[2] Imports and production from foreign-owned plants based in the United States supply the rest.

Two decades ago, American firms produced nearly all of the home electronics purchased in the United States; now they make less than 5 percent. In the 1990s, 75 percent of America's goods are expected to face foreign competition, compared with 5 percent in the 1950s.[3]

What does this tell us? That the U.S. market is no longer just for domestic competitors; increasingly, there is global competition. Is this just an American problem? No, Table 1–1 indicates that imports as a percentage of GNP have increased markedly for four out of the five major importing nations over the past 20 years. Only Japan's percentage has decreased.

This huge increase in import penetration, coupled with the massive increases in overseas investment, means that firms of all sizes face competition from companies anywhere in the world. To survive, they too must become

BUSINESS INCIDENT (concluded)

□ **TABLE 1–1**
Merchandise Imports as a Percentage of GNP, 1970 versus 1990 ($ billions)

	Imports		GNP		Imports/GNP (%)	
	1990	**1970**	**1990**	**1970**	**1990**	**1970**
United States	$500	$43	$5,358	$975	9.3%	4.4%
Germany	312	30	1,323	180	23.6	16.6
France	223	19	1,001	157	21.6	12.1
Japan	220	19	3,057	199	7.2	9.5
United Kingdom	218	22	842	127	25.9	17.3

Sources: *World Bank Atlas,* 1971; *UN Statistical Yearbook,* 1988; *World Bank Development Report, 1991; UN Bulletin of Statistics,* December 1990.

international; to do so, they must have managers with an international dimension.

These managers must be able to move easily among the different languages, cultures, and political systems of the world. They need the kind of international experience or education that enables them to operate in the global marketplace that has *already arrived.*

Do the top executives of the major American multinationals regard an international perspective in their managers as important? Apparently Procter & Gamble does, and not only for its managers. The executive vice president states, "P&G management has developed a global perspective, but the globalization of the company is not just a management responsibility. All parts of the company have to support it. And that global perspective is developing in all employees."[4]

Is this belief shared by other top executives? One indication is that they strongly prefer to hire business graduates who have taken programs with a substantial international component. In a recent study of the CEOs of Forbes "100 Largest Multinational Firms" and Fortune's "America's 50 Biggest Exporters," we found that (1) 79 percent believed all business majors should be required to take an "Introduction to International Business" course, (2) over 70 percent felt expertise in various areas such as foreign languages, cultures, investment, and so forth, were important when hiring college graduates, and (3) a majority indicated that a number of international business courses were relevant to their business.

The majority appears to agree with the executive vice president of Texas Instruments who said, "Managers must become familiar with other markets, cultures, and customs. That is because we operate under the notion that it is 'one world, one market,' and we must be able to compete with—and sell to—the best companies around the world."[5]

Business has entered the era of the one-world market. Increasingly, companies are going overseas to attain sales and profits unavailable to them in their home markets. As a result, every firm, including those with purely domestic operations, is facing increased pressure from foreign competitors. As the Business Incident pointed out, the increasing internationalization of business requires managers to have a global business perspective.

What about you? Are you involved in the global economy yet? Think back to how you began your day. After you awoke, you may have looked at your Timex™ watch for the time and turned on your RCA™ TV for the news and weather while you showered. After drying your hair with a Conair™ dryer, you quickly swallowed some Carnation™ Instant Breakfast and Sanka™ coffee, brushed your teeth with Close-Up™ toothpaste, and drove off to class in your Honda™ with its Firestone™ tires and a tank full of Shell™ gasoline.

Meanwhile, on the other side of the world, a group of Japanese students dressed in Lacoste™ shirts, Levi's™ jeans, and Sauçony shoes may be turning off their IBMs™ in the computer lab and debating whether they should stop for hamburgers and Cokes™ at McDonald's™ or coffee and doughnuts at Mister Donut™. They get into their Ford Probe™ with Goodyear™ tires and drive off.

What do you and the Japanese students have in common? You are both consuming products made by *foreign-owned companies*. This is international business.

To further emphasize the point we're making, answer this question: Which of the following companies or brands are foreign owned?

1. Norelco (electric razors).
2. Chesebrough-Pond (Vaseline™).
3. Electrolux (household appliances).
4. Lever Brothers (Lux™, Whisk™, Close-Up).
5. Pearle Eyecare (glasses).
6. Del Monte.
7. BF Goodrich (tires).
8. Burger King.
9. Holiday Inn.
10. Nabisco (crackers and cereal).
11. Scott Paper (Kleenex™).
12. CBS records.
13. General Tire (tires).
14. Manpower (employment agencies).
15. Motel 6.
16. Pillsbury.[6]

Courtesy of Burger King, General Tire, Manpower, and Nabisco Brands

The quotations at the beginning of the chapter, the Business Incident, and all that you have read so far illustrate the dramatic internationalization of markets worldwide. In fact, almost half of the world's economic activity is international.[7] Moreover, business leaders and academicians predict that events such as EC 1992 (when the European Community removes most of the remaining barriers to the free movement of production factors among member-states) and the U.S.–Canada Free Trade Agreement (soon to include Mexico and probably more Latin American states at a later date) will increase the pace of market internationalization. All this points to one salient fact: *There is an emphatic need for all businesspeople to have some knowledge of international business.*

As you increase your knowledge of international business, you will add dozens of words to your vocabulary. Let's look at some important terms.

INTERNATIONAL BUSINESS TERMINOLOGY

International business, like every field of study, has its own terminology. To assist you in learning the special vocabulary, an important function of every introductory course, we've included a glossary at the end of the book and the most important terms are listed at the beginning of each chapter.

◻ Multinational, Global, and International

As with any new discipline, definitions of a number of words vary among users. For example, some people use the words *world* and *global* interchangeably with *multinational;* but increasingly, *global* is being used to describe a firm that attempts to standardize operations in all functional areas but that responds to national market differences when necessary.

A global firm's management:

1. Searches the world for *(a)* market opportunities, *(b)* threats from competitors, *(c)* sources of products, raw materials, and financing, and *(d)* personnel. In other words, it has global vision.
2. Seeks to maintain a presence in key markets.
3. Looks for similarities, not differences, among markets.

multinational company an organization with multicountry affiliates, each of which formulates its own business strategy based on perceived market differences

Those who use *global* in this manner are defining a **multinational company** as a kind of holding company with a number of overseas operations, each of which is left to adapt its products and marketing strategy to what local managers perceive to be unique aspects of their individual markets. *Multidomestic* has also been suggested as a synonym for multinational.[8]

A number of academic writers have recommended another word, *transnational,* as a label for firms doing business in more than one country. For many years, in fact, some UN agencies have used the word in that way. However, businesspeople have defined a transnational as a company formed by a merger (not a joint venture) of two firms of approximately the same size that are from different countries. Four of the largest are (1) Unilever (Dutch-English), (2) Shell (Dutch-English), (3) Azko-Enka (Dutch-German), and (4) ABB, a merger of ASEA (Swedish) and Brown-Bovari (Swiss).

Perhaps the Japanese have the solution to the usage of terms with multiple definitions; they call the technique of adapting to local conditions, *doch-*

akuka, meaning "global localization." The word comes from Japanese agriculture where it means adjusting the planting, fertilizing, and harvesting methods to meet local soil conditions.[9]

To complete this discussion, we need to mention that the term *supranational corporation* was described in a publication of the United Nations as one in which *both* the operation and ownership are multinational; yet many reserve this term for a corporate form that does not now exist—one that would be chartered by an international agency such as the United Nations.

◻ Definitions Used in This Text

In this text, we will employ the definitions listed below, which are generally accepted by businesspeople. Although we primarily use the terms *global, multinational,* and *international* firms or companies, at times we may use multinational enterprise (MNE) interchangeably with **international company** (IC), inasmuch as both terms are employed in the literature and in practice.

international company
either a global or a
multinational company

1. *International business* is business whose activities involve the crossing of national borders. This definition includes not only international trade and foreign manufacturing but also the growing service industry in such areas as transportation, tourism, banking, advertising, construction, retailing, wholesaling, and mass communications.

2. *Foreign business* denotes the domestic operations within a foreign country. This term is sometimes used interchangeably with international business by some writers.

3. *Multinational company (MNC)* is an organization with multicountry affiliates, each of which formulates its own business strategy based on perceived market differences.

4. *Global company (GC)* is an organization that attempts to standardize operations worldwide in all functional areas.

5. *International company (IC)* refers to both global and multinational companies.

While international business as a discipline is relatively new, international business as a business practice is not, as we shall see in the next section, "History of International Business."

HISTORY OF INTERNATIONAL BUSINESS

Well before the time of Christ, Phoenician and Greek merchants were sending representatives abroad to sell their goods. In 1600, the British East India Company, a newly formed trading firm, established foreign branches throughout Asia. At about the same time, a number of Dutch companies, which had organized in 1590 to open shipping routes to the East, joined together to form the Dutch East India Company and also opened branch offices in Asia.[10] American colonial traders began operating in a similar fashion in the 1700s.

Early examples of American foreign direct investment are the English plants set up by Colt Fire Arms and Ford* (vulcanized rubber), which were

---

* This Ford was no relation to Henry Ford.

established before the Civil War. Both operations failed, however, after only a few years.

The first successful American venture into foreign production was the Scotch factory built by Singer Sewing Machine in 1868. By 1880, Singer had become a worldwide organization with an outstanding foreign sales organization and several overseas manufacturing plants. Other firms soon followed, and by 1914, at least 37 American companies had production facilities in two or more overseas locations.

At that time, the U.S. foreign direct investment position measured at historical cost was $2.53 billion, or about 7 percent of the nation's gross national product (GNP).[11] Although this value had risen to $421 billion by 1990, its percentage of the U.S. GNP was still about 7 percent. During the same period, the components of international trade, the other aspect of international business, changed as follows: American exports rose from $2.5 billion to $653 billion, and imports went from $1.89 to $723 billion.[12]

Among those firms already established overseas were National Cash Register and Burroughs, with manufacturing plants in Europe; Parke-Davis, with a plant near London (1902); and Ford Motor Company, which had assembly plants or distribution outlets in 14 countries. General Motors and Chrysler followed soon afterward, so that by the 1920s, all three companies had sizable foreign operations. Interestingly, and quite the reverse of today's situation, in the 1920s, *all* cars sold in Japan were made in the United States by Ford and General Motors and sent to Japan in knocked-down kits to be assembled locally. Another early overseas investor was General Electric, which, by 1919, had plants in Europe, Latin America, and Asia.[13] Other well-known American firms in Europe at that time were Alcoa, American Tobacco, Armour, Coca-Cola, Eastman Kodak, Gillette, Quaker Oats, Western Electric, and Westinghouse.

Interestingly, American business moving overseas caused similar consternation among Europeans that Japanese investments in the United States cause today. One author wrote, "The invasion goes on unceasingly and without noise or show in 500 industries at once. From shaving soap to electric motors, and from shirtwaists to telephones, the American is clearing the field."[14]

Although American firms were by far the largest foreign investors, European companies were also moving overseas. Friedrich Bayer purchased an interest in a New York plant in 1865, two years after setting up his plant in Germany. Then, because of high import duties in his overseas markets, he proceeded to establish plants in Russia (1876), France (1882), and Belgium (1908).[15] Bayer, now one of the three largest chemical companies in the world ($23 billion in sales), has operations in 70 countries. Its annual sales in the United States alone are over $4 billion. Incidentally, Bayer™ aspirin is no longer manufactured by Bayer as this business was expropriated by the United States during World War I.

International firms clearly existed well before World War I. Why then have they only recently become the object of much discussion and investigation? What differences are there between the international company of the early 1900s and the present-day **global company?**

global company an organization that attempts to standardize operations worldwide in all functional areas

□ **TABLE 1–2**
Global FDI and FDI Position in the United States, 1981 versus 1989 ($ billions)

	Global FDI		Increase	FDI in U.S.		Increase	△FDI in U.S. (%)
	1981	1989	1989−1981	1981	1989	1989−1981	△Global FDI (%)
	(1)		(2)	(3)		(4)	(4) ÷ (2)
United Kingdom	$79.4	$191.9	$112.5	$15.6	$105.5	$89.9	79.9%
Germany	37.3	112.6	75.3	7.2	29.0	21.8	29.0
Netherlands*	33.3	88.2	54.9	27.5	56.3	28.8	52.5
France	25.5	55.9	30.4	5.0	16.8	11.8	38.8
Japan	24.5	154.4	129.9	7.0	67.3	60.3	46.4
Canada	23.4	63.9	40.5	9.9	28.7	18.8	46.4
Others	64.8	222.3	157.5	22.6	70.0	47.4	30.1

*1983.

Sources: Keizai Koho Center, *Japan 1992* (Tokyo: December 1991), p. 57, and *Japan 1983*, p. 49; "International Investment Position of the United States in 1990," *Survey of Current Business,* June 1991, p. 32, and August 1984, p. 36.

□ Explosive Growth

One important difference is the explosive growth in both the size and the number of U.S. and foreign multinational concerns. Although no current data on their number and size exist, a good surrogate variable for measuring where and how fast the internationalization of business is taking place is the increase in total foreign direct investment (FDI).* For example, the world *stock* of FDI is estimated to have risen from $105 billion in 1967 to $1,263 billion in 1989, a tenfold increase in just over 20 years.[16] During the same period, U.S. FDI based on historical cost went from $59 billion to $370 billion—6.4 times the 1967 amount. Despite this sizable increase, international firms in Japan and Europe have since the beginning of the 1980s increased their share of total worldwide foreign investment.

Consider this. In 1981, the stock of U.S. FDI amounted to 47.1 percent of all foreign direct investment, yet by 1989 it amounted to just 29.6 percent. During the same period, the Japanese percentage more than doubled (5.1 percent to 12.2 percent), and German foreign investment went from 7.7 percent to 8.9 percent.[17] Table 1–2 is even more revealing.

As you can see, international firms from all these nations have made major investments in the United States. Note the especially high percentages of the total FDI coming from the United Kingdom, Japan, Canada, and the Netherlands. While American international companies were not withdrawing from foreign markets during this period, they seem to have focused more on the U.S. domestic market, in great part because the expansion of Japanese and European firms in the United States increased domestic competition.

We also have estimates of the importance of the globals and multinationals in the world economy. The United Nations Centre on Transnational Corporations states that although most are medium-size companies with annual sales of less than $1 billion, the 56 largest have sales ranging from $10 billion to $100 billion. Moreover, the 600 largest multinational or global firms account for between one fifth and one fourth of the value added in the

---

* *Foreign direct investment* is sufficient investment to obtain significant management control. In the United States, 10 percent of the stockholders' equity is sufficient; in other countries, it is not considered a direct investment until a share of 20 or 25 percent is reached.

production of *all the goods in the world's market economies.* The Centre further states that their importance as exporters and importers is even greater. For example, between 80 and 90 percent of U.S. and U.K. exports are associated with multinational or global firms.[18] In Japan, just nine general trading companies account for 34.9 percent and 63.9 percent of all the country's exports and imports, respectively.[19]

As a result of this expansion, the foreign company's subsidiaries have become increasingly important in the industrial and economic life of many nations, developed and developing. This situation is in sharp contrast to the one that existed when the dominant economic interests were in the hands of local citizens. The expanding importance of foreign-owned firms in local economies is viewed by a number of governments as a threat to their autonomy. However, the 1980s have seen a marked liberalization of government policies and attitudes toward foreign investment in both developed and developing nations. One of the most important reasons for this change in attitude is the realization that most modern commercial technology originates with the multinationals and globals. To be competitive in world markets, firms in these countries must obtain this technology in the form of direct investment, purchase of capital goods, and the right to use the global or multinational firm's expertise.*[20]

Despite this change in attitude, there are still critics of large global firms who cite such statistics as the following to "prove" that host governments are powerless before them:

1. Only 19 nations have gross national products greater than the total annual sales of General Motors, the world's largest international company.
2. GM's total sales surpass the *sum* of the gross national products of 70 nations.[21]

As Table 1–3 illustrates, these statements are certainly true. In fact, when nations and industrial firms are ranked by gross national product and total sales, respectively, 47 of the first 100 on the list are industrial firms. While a nation's GNP and a company's sales are not comparable, they are indicators of potential power, as you shall see in Chapter 10, Political Forces. Also, regardless of the parent company's size, its subsidiaries operate under the authority of the host nation's government. Their affiliates must comply with local laws or be subject to legal action or even **expropriation.**† Notable examples are the loss of Pfizer's and ITT's Chilean subsidiaries and the seizure of Dow Corning's assets in Venezuela. Interestingly, the threat of expropriation diminished in the 1980s. From 1970 through 1975, there were 336 acts of expropriation, but between 1980 and 1985, there were only 15. Most differences are now being settled by arbitration.[22]

expropriation government seizure of foreign-owned assets for which prompt, adequate, and effective compensation must be made

□ Closer Central Control

A second important difference between the modern global firm and the earlier international company is the much closer control now exercised by head-

* Granting the right to use a firm's expertise for a fee is called licensing. See Chapter 2 for more details.
† Expropriation and related subjects are discussed in Chapters 10 and 11.

◻ **TABLE 1–3**
Ranking of International Companies and Nations according to GNP or Total Sales

Ranking	Nation or Firm	GNP or Total Sales for 1989 ($ billions)
1.	United States	$5,237.7
2.	Japan	2,920.3
3.	Germany	1,272.9
4.	France	1,000.9
5.	Italy	872.0
6.	United Kingdom	834.2
7.	Canada	500.3
8.	China	393.0
9.	Brazil	375.1
10.	Spain	358.4
11.	India	287.4
12.	Australia	242.1
13.	Netherlands	237.4
14.	Switzerland	198.0
15.	South Korea	186.5
16.	Sweden	184.2
17.	Mexico	170.1
18.	Belgium	162.0
19.	Austria	131.9
20.	*General Motors*	127.0
21.	Finland	109.7
22.	Denmark	105.3
23.	*Ford Motor*	96.9
24.	Norway	92.1
25.	Saudi Arabia	90.0
26.	Indonesia	87.9
27.	*Exxon*	86.7
28.	South Africa	86.0
29.	*Royal Dutch Shell*	85.5
30.	Turkey	74.7
31.	Argentina	68.8
32.	Poland	67.0
33.	Thailand	64.4
34.	*IBM*	63.4
35.	*Toyota Motor*	60.4
36.	Hong Kong	59.2
37.	Yugoslavia	59.1
38.	*General Electric*	55.3
39.	Greece	53.6
40.	Algeria	53.1
41.	*Mobil*	51.0
42.	*Hitachi*	50.9
43.	*British Petroleum*	49.5
44.	*IRI* (Italy)	49.1

(Continued)

□ **TABLE 1–3 (concluded)**

Ranking	Nation or Firm	GNP or Total Sales for 1989 ($ billions)
45.	Venezuela	$47.2
46.	Israel	44.1
46.	Portugal	44.1
48.	*Matsushita Electric*	43.1
49.	Philippines	42.8
50.	*Daimler-Benz*	40.6
51.	Pakistan	40.1
52.	New Zealand	39.4
53.	*Philip Morris*	39.1
54.	Colombia	38.6
55.	Malaysia	37.0
56.	*Fiat*	36.7
57.	*Chrysler*	36.2
58.	*Nissan Motor*	36.1
59.	*Unilever*	35.3
60.	*Du Pont*	35.2
60.	*Samsung*	35.2
62.	*Volkswagen*	34.7
63.	Kuwait	33.1
64.	*Siemens*	32.7
65.	Egypt	32.5
66.	*Texaco*	32.4
67.	Ireland	30.1
68.	*Toshiba*	29.5
69.	*Chevron*	29.4
69.	*Nestlé*	29.4
71.	United Arab Emirates	28.4
72.	Singapore	28.1
73.	*Renault*	27.5
74.	*ENI*	27.1
74.	Hungary	27.1
76.	*Philips*	27.0
77.	*Honda Motor*	26.5
78.	*BASF*	25.3
79.	*NEC*	24.6
80.	*Hoechst*	24.4
81.	*Amoco*	24.2
82.	*Peugeot*	24.1
83.	*BAT Industries*	23.5
83.	*Elf Aquitane*	23.5
85.	*Bayer*	23.0
85.	Peru	23.0

Note: Does not include nations that do not report GNPs to World Bank.

Source: *The World Bank Atlas 1990,* pp. 6–9; and "Global 500," *Fortune,* July 30, 1990, p. 269.

quarters. Even though the subsidiaries are scattered over the globe, management in the home office coordinates and integrates their activities. Such control has been made possible by fast air travel and by the ability to rapidly transmit and analyze large amounts of information via telephone, telex, and computers.

In earlier days, overseas travel was by ship, communications were handled primarily by letter, and once information arrived in the home office, several days were required for processing before top management could act on it. Under those conditions, there was little possibility of closely coordinating foreign operations and the local subsidiaries had to be given considerable independence. In addition, poor transportation facilities between countries and the presence of tariff and nontariff trade barriers made it difficult for a firm in one country to market its products in another. This meant that there was less need for close integration; thus each subsidiary tended to operate in its own local market.

However, these conditions were changing. The formation of regional marketing groups such as the European Community and the European Free Trade Association and the improvements in transportation facilities made intercountry sales much more feasible. Thus, closer central control became both possible and necessary.

◻ Host Nations' Reaction

host nation nation in which a foreign affiliate is located

As early as the 1950s, **host nation** governments began to realize that the establishment of an increasing number of businesses controlled by managements outside their jurisdictions was resulting in local firms (subsidiaries) that could pursue objectives in conflict with their own. This, they believed, would weaken national sovereignty.

For example, if government leaders believed it necessary to institute a tight monetary policy and thus restrict the amount of capital available for industrial expansion, they feared that foreign-owned subsidiaries might upset their plans by bringing in capital from abroad. If they attempted to raise taxes to reduce purchasing power, absentee owners might shift production elsewhere, and thus sources of employment might be lost.

As governments strove to provide more infrastructure, such as highways, educational facilities, housing, and all the myriad elements of a higher level of living, they required more foreign currency. These efforts would be weakened by anything that reduced the availability of foreign currency, such as fees paid to nonresidents for management services and technological assistance or rules by home offices prohibiting subsidiaries from exporting or buying lower-priced raw materials in the open market rather than from the parent company.

Just how pervasive these practices were was not clear. The multinational company was a new concept, and its operations were not fully understood. To be able to cope with such practices, governments had to know more about them. By the early 1970s, various national and international organizations were studying this new kind of business organization. The United Nations established a Commission on Transnational Corporations and an Information and Research Center at UN headquarters to deal on a continuous basis with issues relating to the activities of international firms. Workshops were set up to train government officials who negotiate with these firms. A U.S. Senate foreign affairs subcommittee conducted an in-depth investigation. All over the world, government technicians, academicians, and business writers were publishing books and studies on the various aspects of the international company.[23]

WHY IS INTERNATIONAL BUSINESS DIFFERENT?

International business differs from domestic business in that a firm operating across borders must deal with the forces of three kinds of environments—domestic, foreign, and international. In contrast, a firm whose business activities are carried out within the borders of one country needs to be concerned essentially with only the domestic environment. However, no domestic firm is entirely free from foreign or international environmental forces because the possibility of having to face competition from foreign imports or from foreign competitors that set up operations in its own market is always present. Let us first examine these forces and then see how they operate in the three environments.

▫ Forces in the Environments

environment all the forces surrounding and influencing the life and development of the firm

uncontrollable forces external forces over which management has no direct control, although it can exert an influence

Environment as used here is the sum of all the forces surrounding and influencing the life and development of the firm. The forces themselves can be classified as *external* or *internal*. Furthermore, management has no direct control over them, though it can exert influences such as lobbying for a change in a law, heavily promoting a new product that requires a change in a cultural attitude, and so on. The external forces are commonly called **uncontrollable forces** and consist of the following:

1. *Competitive*—kinds and numbers of competitors, their locations, and their activities.
2. *Distributive*—national and international agencies available for distributing goods and services.
3. *Economic*—variables (such as GNP, unit labor cost, and personal consumption expenditure) that influence a firm's ability to do business.
4. *Socioeconomic*—characteristics and distribution of the human population.
5. *Financial*—variables such as interest rates, inflation rates, and taxation.
6. *Legal*—the many kinds of foreign and domestic laws by which international firms must operate.
7. *Physical*—elements of nature such as topography, climate, and natural resources.
8. *Political*—elements of nations' political climates such as nationalism, forms of government, and international organizations.
9. *Sociocultural*—elements of culture (such as attitudes, beliefs, and opinions) important to international businesspeople.
10. *Labor*—composition, skills, and attitudes of labor.

11. *Technological*—the technical skills and equipment that affect how resources are converted to products.

The elements over which management does have some command are the internal forces, such as the factors of production (capital, raw material, and people) and the activities of the organization (personnel, finance, production, and marketing). These are the **controllable forces** management must administer in order to adapt to changes in the uncontrollable environmental variables. Look at how one change in the political force—the European Community's passage of the Single European Act in 1986—is affecting *all* the controllable forces of firms worldwide that do business with Western Europe.

This law is intended to eliminate physical (border controls), technical (product standards), and fiscal (different tax and excise duty levels) barriers, thus creating a single internal market of the 320 million inhabitants of the 12 EC member-nations.[24] Although many doubt this goal will be reached by 1992 (the target date), companies are already feeling the impact of this legislation, which some claim is creating a "Fortress Europe."[25]

Hyster Co., a U.S. firm that makes forklift trucks in Europe, had to make changes in its product, suppliers, and shipping pattern to Europe because of a directive on product standards issued to implement the Single European Act. The company was forced to stop shipping certain U.S.-built forklifts directly to its European dealers because the directive requires that they first be certified on EC soil. Now the company must send the forklifts to its Scottish plant to be certified and adorned with a large "E" (for EC) at extra cost. Hyster can no longer use American battery cables because of a required product test—which only one German supplier uses. Altogether, the company has made 15 design changes to conform to the new product standards.[26]

The process of adaptation does not imply that managers must wait passively for changes to occur, to which they then react as Hyster did. As a rule, the most successful administrators are those who are so knowledgeable about the uncontrollable environmental forces that not only are they prepared and waiting, but they may even contribute to these changes. This is, in fact, what the U.S. Department of Commerce has urged businesspeople to do in the case of Europe 1992. They must be so well informed about it that they can alert the government about their problems and concerns, thus enabling officials to discuss those concerns with the EC while there is still time to affect its actions.[27]

☐ The Domestic Environment

The **domestic environment** is composed of all the uncontrollable forces originating in the home country that surround and influence the life and development of the firm. Obviously, these are the forces with which managers are most familiar. Being domestic forces does not preclude their affecting foreign operations, however. For example, if the home country is suffering from a shortage of foreign currency, the government may place restrictions on overseas investment to reduce its outflow. As a result, managements of multinationals find that they cannot expand overseas facilities as they would like to do. In another instance from real life, a labor union striking the home-based plants learned that management was supplying parts from its foreign subsidiaries. The strikers contacted the foreign unions, which pledged not to work

---

controllable forces internal forces that management administers to adapt to changes in the uncontrollable forces

domestic environment all the uncontrollable forces originating in the home country that surround and influence the firm's life and development

"Made in Brazil"
"Made in China"
"Made in Japan"
Domestic firms are always facing the possibility of competition from foreign imports.

overtime to supply what the struck plants could not. The impact of this domestic environmental force was felt overseas as well as at home.

◻ Foreign Environments

foreign environment all the uncontrollable forces originating outside the home country that surround and influence the firm

The forces in the **foreign environment** are the same as those in the domestic environment except that they occur in foreign nations.* However, they operate differently for several reasons, including the following:

Different force values.   Even though the kinds of forces in the two environments are identical, their values often differ widely, and at times they are completely opposed to each other. A good example of diametrically opposed political force values and the bewilderment they create for multinational managers is the case of Dresser Industries and the Soviet pipeline. In June 1982, President Reagan extended the American embargo against shipments of equipment for the pipeline to include foreign companies manufacturing equipment under U.S. license. The Dresser home office instructed its French subsidiary to stop work on an order for compressors. In August, however, the French government ordered Dresser-France to defy the embargo and begin scheduled deliveries under penalty of both civil and criminal sanctions. As Dresser's vice president for finance put it, "The order put Dresser between a rock and a hard place."

---

*   *Foreign* has multiple definitions according to the *American Heritage Dictionary*, including (1) originating from the outside—external, (2) originating from a country other than one's own, and (3) conducted or involved with other nations or governments. *Extrinsic* is a synonym. Note that we are not using another definition—unfamiliar or strange. Some writers have this last definition in mind when they state that overseas markets in which the firm does business are not foreign because their managers know them well. However, according to any of the first three definitions, the degree of familiarity has no bearing.

Changes difficult to assess.   Another problem with the foreign forces is that they are frequently difficult to assess, especially their legal and political elements. A highly nationalistic law may be passed to appease a section of the population. To all outward appearances, a government may appear to be against foreign investment, yet pragmatic leaders may actually encourage it. A good example is Mexico, which, until 1988, had a law prohibiting foreigners from owning a majority interest in a Mexican company. However, a clause permitted exceptions "if the investment contributes to the welfare of the nation." IBM, Eaton, and others were successful in obtaining permission to establish a wholly owned subsidiary under this clause.

Forces interrelated.   In the chapters that follow, it will be evident that the forces are often interrelated. This in itself is no novelty, because the same situation confronts the domestic manager. Often different, however, are the types and degrees of interaction that occur. For instance, the combination of high-cost capital and an abundance of unskilled labor in many developing countries may lead to the use of a lower level of technology than would be employed in the more industrialized nations. In other words, given a choice between installing costly, specialized machinery needing few workers or less expensive, general-purpose machinery requiring a larger labor force, management will frequently choose the latter when faced with high interest rates and a large pool of available workers. Another example is the interaction between physical and sociocultural forces. Barriers to the free movement of a nation's people, such as mountain ranges or deserts, help maintain pockets of distinct cultures within a country.

◻ The International Environment

international environment
interaction between the domestic and foreign environmental forces or between sets of foreign environmental forces

The **international environment** is the interactions (1) between the domestic environmental forces and the foreign environmental forces and (2) between the foreign environmental forces of two countries when an affiliate in one country does business with customers in another. This agrees with the definition of international business—business that involves the crossing of national borders.

For example, personnel at the headquarters of a multinational or global company work in the international environment if they are involved in any way with another nation, whereas those in a foreign subsidiary do not unless they too are engaged in international business through exporting or management of other foreign affiliates. In other words, the sales manager of Goodyear-Chile does *not* work in the international environment if he or she sells tires only in Chile. Should Goodyear-Chile export tires to Bolivia, then the sales manager is affected by forces of both the domestic environment of Chile and the foreign environment of Bolivia and therefore is working in the international environment. International organizations whose actions affect the international environment are also properly part of it. These organizations include (1) worldwide bodies (e.g., World Bank), (2) regional economic groupings of nations (e.g., European Community), and (3) organizations of nations bound by industry agreements (e.g., Organization of Petroleum Exporting Countries).

□ Decision Making More Complex

Those who work in the international environment find that decision making is more complex than it is in a purely domestic environment. Consider managers in the home office who must make decisions affecting subsidiaries in just 10 different countries (many multinationals or globals are in 20 or more countries). They must not only take into account the domestic forces, but they must also evaluate the influence of 10 foreign national environments. Instead of having to consider the effects of a single set of 10 forces, as do their domestic counterparts, they have to contend with 10 sets of 10 forces, *both individually and collectively,* because there may be some interaction.

For example, if management agrees to labor's demands at one foreign subsidiary, chances are it will have to offer a similar settlement at another subsidiary because of the tendency of unions to exchange information across borders. Furthermore, as we shall observe throughout the text, not only are there many sets of forces, but there are also extreme differences among them.

Another common cause of the added complexity of foreign environments is managers' unfamiliarity with other cultures. To make matters worse, they will ascribe to others their own preferences and reactions. Thus, the foreign production manager, facing a backlog of orders, offers the workers extra pay for overtime. When they fail to show up, the manager is perplexed. "Back home, they always want to earn more money." This manager has failed to understand that the workers preferred time off to more money. This *unconscious* reference to the manager's own cultural values, called **self-reference criterion,** is probably the biggest cause of international business blunders. Successful administrators are careful to examine a problem in terms of the local cultural traits as well as their own.

self-reference criterion unconscious reference to one's own cultural values when judging behavioral actions of others in a new and different environment

INTERNATIONAL BUSINESS MODEL

The relationships of the forces in the three environments we have been discussing form the basis for our international business model shown in Figure 1–1. The external or uncontrollable forces in both the domestic and the foreign environments surround the internal forces controlled by management. The domestic environment of the international firm's home country is surrounded by as many sets of foreign environments as there are countries in which the company does business. Solid lines connecting the internal forces at the home office to the internal forces in the foreign affiliates indicate the lines of control. The circles with the broken lines indicate the international environment in which personnel in the headquarters of the international firm work. If, for example, the affiliate in foreign environment A exports to or manages the affiliate in foreign environment B, then its personnel are also working in the international environment, as shown by the straight dashed lines.

We shall be using this model throughout the book. After describing the nature of international business in Section One, we examine the international organizations and the international monetary system in Section Two. In Section Three, we analyze the uncontrollable forces that make up the foreign and domestic environments and illustrate their effect on management functions. Finally, we reverse the procedure in Section Four and deal with the

☐ **FIGURE 1–1   International Business Model**

management functions, demonstrating how they are influenced by the uncontrollable forces.

CENTRAL THEME OF THIS BOOK

A solid understanding of the business concepts and techniques employed in the United States and other advanced industrial nations is a requisite for success in international business. However, because transactions take place across national borders, three environments—domestic, foreign, and interna-

WORLDVIEW
Executives Cite Globalization as Major Concern of U.S. Companies

A recent *Fortune* survey of top American chief executive officers listed progress toward globalization as one of their major concerns.

The United States has been slow in its move toward globalization, however, according to Nolan, Norton & Co., KPMG Peat Marwick's international specialists in information technology. "This lack of progress has occurred despite the fact that the necessary components of the communications infrastructure have been improving rapidly over the past decade," says John L. Daniels, a Nolan Norton principal. "Businesses fail to comprehend that globalization is important, what globalization means, or how to become global."

Doing Business—How, Not Where
Daniels explains that many companies confuse the term "global" with "multinational," "multidomestic," or "worldwide." "Globalization is not an easy idea to grasp because it is more of a business concept—*how* you do business—than a geographic notion—*where* you do business," he says.

"A global company has a sphere of activity and awareness that stretches beyond where it operates to where it earns revenues, where its sources are, and wherever it carries out activities or has a relationship with an outside party. In a global business, relationships with suppliers, distributors, and customers are coordinated across functions and across geographical boundaries."

According to Daniels, recent research on Japanese manufacturing concerns indicates that Japanese firms have an edge over U.S. firms because they tend to coordinate cross-functionally better than their U.S. counterparts. "Canon, of Japan, supplies products to many high tech companies around the world; they also act as distributors to many of these same companies within Japan. They expand their business relationships with one company by sharing the knowledge of their relationship with that company cross-functionally," he explains.

Wired to the World
Daniels and Caroline Frost, a manager at the Nolan Norton Institute, have helped foreign and domestic companies explore global business opportunities offered by information technology.

To be global, businesses shouldn't be concerned about which functions are centralized and which are decentralized, Daniels and Frost point out. While most companies have not yet made the required investment, it is possible today to wire the world to allow members of a company to connect with everyone else in that company, as well as anyone needed outside the company.

Daniels cites the example of IBM. "Its three Nobel prize winners in the past two years were Europeans. Two are working in IBM's Zurich, Switzerland, lab on superconductivity and a powerful new microscope; and Benoit Mendelbroit, a Frenchman, is working in a U.S. lab on fractal geometry. IBM certainly believes that not all good ideas are found within 25 miles of Armonk, New York."

The Nolan Norton team emphasizes that becoming global is one of the most important transformations that companies will make in the information age. Daniels and Frost predict that companies that succeed in globalization will be viable well into the 21st century.

tional—may be involved instead of just one; thus in international business, the international manager has three choices in what to do with a concept or a technique employed in domestic operations: (1) transfer it intact, (2) adapt it to local conditions, or (3) not use it overseas. International managers who have discovered that there are differences in the environmental forces are better prepared to decide which option to follow. To be sure, no one can be an

□ **FIGURE 1–2   Overseas Locations of an International Service Company, the Accounting Firm KPMG**

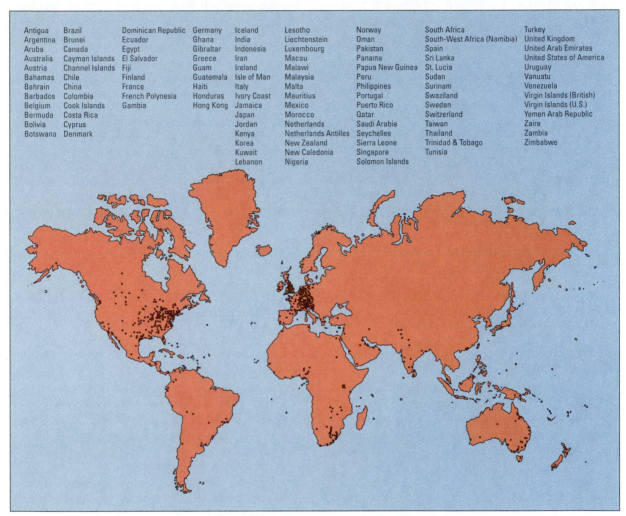

Antigua	Brazil	Dominican Republic	Germany	Iceland	Lesotho	Norway	South Africa	Turkey
Argentina	Brunei	Ecuador	Ghana	India	Liechtenstein	Oman	South-West Africa (Namibia)	United Kingdom
Aruba	Canada	Egypt	Gibraltar	Indonesia	Luxembourg	Pakistan	Spain	United Arab Emirates
Australia	Cayman Islands	El Salvador	Greece	Iran	Macau	Panama	Sri Lanka	United States of America
Austria	Channel Islands	Fiji	Guam	Ireland	Malawi	Papua New Guinea	St. Lucia	Uruguay
Bahamas	Chile	Finland	Guatemala	Isle of Man	Malaysia	Peru	Sudan	Vanuatu
Bahrain	China	France	Haiti	Italy	Malta	Philippines	Surinam	Venezuela
Barbados	Colombia	French Polynesia	Honduras	Ivory Coast	Mauritius	Portugal	Swaziland	Virgin Islands (British)
Belgium	Cook Islands	Gambia	Hong Kong	Jamaica	Mexico	Puerto Rico	Sweden	Virgin Islands (U.S.)
Bermuda	Costa Rica			Japan	Morocco	Qatar	Switzerland	Yemen Arab Republic
Bolivia	Cyprus			Jordan	Netherlands	Saudi Arabia	Taiwan	Zaire
Botswana	Denmark			Kenya	Netherlands Antilles	Seychelles	Thailand	Zambia
				Korea	New Zealand	Sierra Leone	Trinidad & Tobago	Zimbabwe
				Kuwait	New Caledonia	Singapore	Tunisia	
				Lebanon	Nigeria	Solomon Islands		

Note: Some dots represent more than one office.

expert on all these forces for all nations, but just knowing that differences may exist will cause people to "work with their antennas extended." In other words, when they enter international business, they will know they must look out for important variations in many of the forces that they take as given in the domestic environment. It is to the study of the three environments that this text is directed.

SUMMARY

Global competition is mounting. The huge increase in import penetration, plus the massive amounts of overseas investment, means that firms of all sizes face competitors from everywhere in the world. This increasing internationalization of business is requiring managers to have a global business perspective gained through experience, education, or both.

Although the definitions vary among users, a *global company* is an organization that attempts to standardize operations worldwide in all functional areas. A *multinational firm,* on the other hand, is an organization with multicountry affiliates, each of which formulates its own business strategy based on perceived market differences. The term *international company* is often used to refer to both global and multinational firms.

American and foreign multinational companies have existed for more than 100 years, but their explosive growth and much closer central control are a more recent phenomenon. The total stock of foreign direct investment, for example, has risen from $105 billion in 1967 to $1,263 billion in 1989. Since the 1980s, European and Japanese companies have increased their share of worldwide foreign investment, while the U.S. share has fallen from 47.1 percent in 1981 to 29.6 percent in 1989. The United States has become a major recipient of their FDI.

While most international companies are of medium size, when the largest international firms and nations are ranked by sales and GNP, respectively, 47 of the top 100 are companies. Only 19 nations have larger gross national products than General Motors, the world's largest international firm.

International business differs from its domestic counterpart in that it involves three environments—domestic, foreign, and international—instead of one. Although the kinds of forces are the same in the domestic and foreign environments, their values often differ, and changes in the values of foreign forces are at times more difficult to assess. The international environment is defined as the interactions (1) between the domestic environmental forces and the foreign environmental forces and (2) between the foreign environmental forces of two countries when an affiliate in one country does business with customers in another. An international business model helps to explain this relationship.

While international businesspersons must understand business concepts and techniques employed in industrialized nations, they must also know enough about the differences in the environmental forces of the markets in which they operate to be able to decide if a concept or a technique (1) can be transferred to another country as is, (2) must be adapted to local conditions, or (3) cannot be used elsewhere.

QUESTIONS

1. What are the differences between international, global, and multinational companies?

2. Give examples to show how an international business manager might manipulate one of the controllable forces in answer to a change in the uncontrollable forces.

3. A nation whose GNP is smaller than the sales volume of a global firm is in no position to enforce its wishes on the local subsidiary of that firm. True or false? Explain.

4. We know that a number of firms have been active in international business for nearly a century. Why, then, has the international firm attracted so much attention in the last four decades?

5. Business is business, and every firm has to produce and market its goods. Why, then, cannot the managers apply the techniques and concepts they have learned in their own country to other areas of the world?

6. What do you believe makes foreign business activities more complex than purely domestic ones?

7. Discuss some possible conflicts between host governments and foreign-owned companies.

8. Why, in your opinion, do the authors regard the use of the self-reference criterion as "probably the biggest cause of international business blunders?" Can you think of an example?

9. You have decided to take a job after graduation in your hometown. Why should you study international business?

10. Imports as a percentage of GNP have increased, indicating that U.S. firms are facing greater foreign competition in their home market.
    a. Is this occurring in other developed countries as well?
    b. What country received the major part of the United Kingdom's foreign investment in the period from 1981 to 1988? The Netherlands? Japan? Canada?

◻ **MINICASE 1–1**

Dansk Manufacturing (Galawi) Limited

In the developing nation of Galawi,* the president and his cabinet are discussing the results of a meeting with Dick Petersen, managing director of Dansk Manufacturing (Galawi) Limited.

President:

Petersen insists that our proposed law to increase company-paid benefits to employees will raise their costs so much they won't be able to compete in the export market anymore. He says that if they can't export, their sales volume will be so low they won't make enough profit to keep the company going. He thinks the home office may order him to close the Galawi operation down. What's your opinion, Mojabum?

Mr. Mojabum, secretary of labor:

Don't forget—we've promised the leaders of the union that we are going to obtain higher benefits for their people. We can't go back on our word.

President:

Also, Mojabum, have you considered what the reaction of the workers might be if they don't get the benefits that this law will provide?

Mojabum:

That's another concern, Mr. President. This proposed law has received quite a bit of publicity. If it doesn't go into effect, we may face a strike or worse.

President:

Such as?

Mojabum:

Perhaps some civil unrest, even public demonstrations.

Mr. Akam, secretary of commerce:

That could be serious, I admit, but on the other hand, Galawi needs this company. It provides jobs for over 300 people.

Mr. Bonat, secretary of the treasury:

Dansk provides a lot more. We know from their tax return that their total sales were over 25 million Galawi francs (Gf) last year. Even with the special tax concession we offered to get them to locate in Galawi, they still paid 2.5 million Gf. Furthermore, Dansk brought in $1 million from their exports last year, and we need that foreign exchange to help pay for oil imports. Think

about it—that's 5 million Gf worth of dollars they earned for this country.

Mr. Sassou, secretary of the interior:

Yes, but they also consume foreign exchange, don't they? They certainly have to import some raw materials, spare parts, and machinery that they can't find here. How much does that amount to?

Bonat (treasury):

Yes, they do use some of what they earn—about 40 percent. But it is still a net gain for the country. In fact, you may have forgotten that when they asked to come here, we stipulated that they would have to earn, as a minimum, sufficient foreign exchange to cover their import needs *and* any profits they wished to return to Denmark.

Sassou (interior):

Well, I didn't take part in the negotiations so I don't know all of the details. You mentioned profits. You know that some leaders of the opposition are making speeches about the fact that Dansk is bleeding our country with all the money they're taking out of Galawi. This could cause political unrest. As the one responsible for law and order in this country, this bothers me.

Akam (commerce):

That just isn't so. Dansk agreed not to take out any profits for five more years. They're reinvesting their profits as they said they would. Their operation is growing, they're hiring more people, reducing imports because they're making more components of their products locally, and they're expanding their exports.

Bonat (treasury):

Also, their tax concession runs out in five years, and then they'll pay a 50 percent higher rate, the same as our local businesses.

Akam (commerce):

That's good, because I've had a lot of complaints from businesspeople about the tax preference Dansk gets. By the way, another complaint is about the higher wages they pay. A number of local companies say they're losing their good people to Dansk.

Mojabum (labor):

Yes, but the unions love it. Not only do their members at Dansk get better pay, but so do those working in other places because those other firms have been forced to compete in the labor market.

---

*Although Galawi is fictitious, the conditions are not.

President:

Nevertheless, this may be getting out of hand. Akam, you'd better talk to Petersen about keeping his pay scales closer to what others are offering. We don't want an inflation on our hands.

Akam (commerce):

I shall, but I do want to remind you that Dansk is not robbing all of the good people from the others. For example, they bring labor trainers from the home plant to train many unskilled people they hire, and they continuously send young supervisors, technical people, and middle managers to Denmark for training.

Dr. Boya (secretary of education):

Let me remind you of one development that I'm enthusiastic about. Dansk is now going to offer six scholarships annually to sons and daughters of local employees to study engineering or business administration in Denmark. It seems to me, Akam, that Dansk is helping educate our people, many of whom will go to work in the firms that are complaining about losing employees to Dansk. They have also brought in technology that this country had never seen before. One thing, though, we've got to find ways to inform the public about the benefits Dansk is bringing to Galawi. What Sassou told us alarms me.

Akam (commerce):

I agree—it is alarming. By the way, I forgot to tell you about a study our economists finished yesterday. They calculate that every Gf spent by a company such as Dansk has a multiplier effect of almost two; that is, if Dansk is spending locally 13 or 14 million Gf for labor, local purchases, and taxes, this is worth perhaps 25

million Gf to the economy as the workers spend their wages in stores, whose owners in turn make purchases, and so forth. We need to consider this effect when we try to calculate the contribution of companies like Dansk to our economy.

Mojabum (labor):

You're right, and this is something the public needs to know. But let's get back to the proposed labor law. Why, do you suppose, haven't Galawi Manufacturing and Inland Steel Products complained about it?

President:

Probably because they're locally owned and not able to move like Dansk can. Don't forget, Dansk is a subsidiary of a multinational, and Galawi is just one of their markets. Also, these firms don't export either, so they're not worrying about keeping costs down to compete in the world market. Well, that's it, gentlemen. We can (1) get the law passed to satisfy the union and perhaps lose a company that hires 300 workers and earns valuable foreign exchange, among other things, (2) stop the law from being passed so as not to lose Dansk, but damage our relations with the union, or (3) come up with some sort of compromise. Let's meet again next week with your recommendations.

1. What are the advantages and the disadvantages for Galawi of Dansk's presence in the country?

2. Can Dansk do anything to improve its situation in Galawi?

3. What do you recommend the government do with respect to the proposed law?

SUPPLEMENTARY READINGS

Global Competition

"Entering a New Age of Boundless Competition." *Fortune,* March 14, 1988, pp. 40–48.

European Community. *Europe without Frontiers—Completing the Internal Market.* 1988.

Gluck, Frederick W. "Meeting the Challenge of Global Competition." *The McKinsey Quarterly,* Autumn 1982, pp. 2–13.

"Lessons from U.S. Blunders." *Fortune,* April 23, 1990, pp. 128–141.

"The Coming Global Boom." *U.S. News & World Report,* July 16, 1990, pp. 21–28.

"The New American Century." *Fortune,* special issue, Spring–Summer 1991.

"U.S. Should Prepare Now for EC 1992." *Business America,* October 24, 1988, pp. 12–16.

Global, Multinational, International

"Business without Borders." *U.S. News & World Report,* July 16, 1990, pp. 29–31.

"How Coke Markets to the World." *The Journal of Business Strategy,* September–October 1988, pp. 6–9.

"How to Go Global and Why." *Fortune,* August 28, 1989, pp. 70–76.

"Managing in a Borderless World." *Harvard Business Review,* May–June 1989, pp. 152–61.

Prahalad, C. K., and Yves L. Doz. *The Multinational Mission:*

Balancing Local Demands and Global Vision. New York: The Free Press, 1987.

Transnational Corporations in World Development. New York: United Nations Centre on Transnational Corporations, 1988.

History of International Business

"American Business Abroad." *Financial World,* June 25, 1992, pp. 44–47.

"The Growth of Global Industry." *The Wheel Extended,* no. 4, 1989, pp. 11–17.

Tugendhat, Christopher. *The Multinationals.* New York: Random House, 1972.

Wilkins, Mira. *The Emergence of Multinational Enterprise: American Business Abroad from the Colonial Era to 1914.* Cambridge, Mass.: Harvard University Press, 1970.

Wilkins, Mira. *The Maturing of the Multinational Enterprise, 1914–1970.* Cambridge, Mass.: Harvard University Press, 1974.

ENDNOTES

1. "Lessons from U.S. Business Blunders," *Fortune,* April 23, 1990, p. 128.
2. "The New American Century," *Fortune,* Spring–Summer 1991, p. 14.
3. "The Coming Global Boom," *U.S. News & World Report,* July 16, 1990, pp. 21–23.
4. *1990 Annual Report,* Procter & Gamble, p. 6.
5. "Prospects," *The New York Times,* January 3, 1988, p. F1.
6. 1—Philips (Dutch), 2—Unilever (Dutch-English), 3—Electrolux (Swedish) 4—Unilever (Dutch-English), 5—Grand Metropolitan (English), 6—Polly Peak International (English), 7—Michelin (French), 8—Bass PLC (English), 9—Bass PLC (English), 10—American, 11—American, 12—Sony (Japanese), 13—Continental (German), 14—Blue Arrow (English), 15—Accor (French), 16—Grand Metropolitan (English).
7. Warren Keegan, "Global Competition: Strategic Alternatives," paper for the Lubin Graduate School of Business, Pace University, New York, presented on January 24, 1989, pp. 6–13.
8. Thomas Hout, Michael E. Porter, and Eileen Rudden, "How Global Companies Win Out," *Harvard Business Review,* September–October 1982, pp. 98–110.
9. "Business Buzzwords," *International Management,* February 1989, p. 15.
10. "The Growth of Global Industry," *The Wheel Extended,* no. 4, 1989, p. 11.
11. Mira Wilkins, *The Emergence of Multinational Enterprise: American Business Abroad from the Colonial Era to 1914* (Cambridge, Mass.: Harvard University Press, 1974), pp. 1–212. This is a classic history of early multinational firms.
12. Russell B. Scholl, "The International Position of the United States"; and Table 1, "U.S. International Transactions," *Survey of Current Business,* June 1991, pp. 29 and 45.
13. Mira Wilkins, *The Maturing of the Multinational Enterprise, 1914–1970* (Cambridge, Mass.: Harvard University Press, 1974), pp. 1–83.
14. "American Business Abroad," *Financial World,* June 25, 1991, p. 45.
15. Christopher Tugendhat, *The Multinationals* (New York: Random House, 1972), p. 12.
16. *Japan 1992* (Tokyo: Keizai Koho Center, December 1991), p. 57 and Table C–14; *Balance of Payments Statistics Yearbook* (Washington, D.C.: International Monetary Fund, 1990), pp. 68–69.
17. *Japan 1992,* p. 57; and *Japan 1983,* p. 49.
18. *Transnational Corporations in World Development* (New York: United Nations, 1988), p. 16.
19. *Japan 1991,* pp. 42 and 46.
20. *Transnational Corporations in World Development,* pp. 6–10.
21. World Bank, *The World Bank Atlas 1990* (Washington, D.C.: World Bank, 1990), pp. 6–9; and "Global 500," *Fortune,* July 30, 1990, p. 269.
22. Michael Minor, *Changes in Developing Country Regimes for Foreign Direct Investment* (Greenville: University of South Carolina, September 1990), p. 15.
23. There have been dozens of studies made. Among those with a heavy impact were Vernon's *Sovereignty at Bay,* Tugendhat's *Multinationals,* Servan-Schreiber's *American Challenge,* and the continuing reports published by the United Nations Centre on Transnational Corporations.
24. European Community, *Europe without Frontiers—Completing the Internal Market,* 1988, p. 29.
25. "Scrambling for 1992," *Business Marketing,"* February 1988, pp. 12–16.
26. "Obstacle Course," *The Wall Street Journal,* January 19, 1989, p. 1.
27. "U.S. Business Should Prepare Now for EC 1992," *Business America,* October 24, 1988, pp. 12–16.

□ FIGURE 1A–1

The Coca-Cola Company

Job Profile: International Opportunities

- -

COMPANY

The Coca-Cola Company is the world's largest producer and distributor of syrups and concentrates for soft drinks. Company products include Coca-Cola classic, diet Coke, cherry Coke, Sprite, Fanta, and Minute Maid Orange. Independent research confirmed Coca-Cola as far and away the world's best known and most admired trademark. Coca-Cola products are sold in more than 170 countries around the globe. Our international soft drink business has grown at an average annual rate of 9 percent over the last five years and now accounts for 80 percent of the Coca-Cola Company's operating income.

OPPORTUNITIES

The Coca-Cola Company recruits for interns and trainees for each of our international business units: The European Community, Latin America, Northeast Europe/Africa, and the Pacific. International opportunities typically exist for candidates in the areas of marketing research, brand management, financial analysis, accounting, and auditing.

Key Background And Attributes Required

EDUCATION

First year MBA students are recruited for internship opportunities. Recent MBA graduates are recruited for traineeships.

EXPERIENCE

2–5 years of marketing, finance, or technical/engineering experience is preferred.

ATTRIBUTES

Nationalists desired for opportunities in their home countries; multicultural and multilingual candidates preferred; proficiency in English required; willingness to work and travel abroad preferred.

Mail Resume To:

The Coca-Cola Company
Attn: Corporate Staffing
P.O. Drawer 1734
Atlanta, GA   30301

An Equal Opportunity Employer

ENDNOTES

1. Donald A. Ball and Wendell McCulloch, Jr., "International Business Education Programs in American and Non-American Schools: How They Are Ranked by the Academy of International Business," *Journal of International Business Studies,* Summer 1988, pp. 295–99.

2. "Getting a Global M.B.A.," *U.S. News & World Report,* November 11, 1991, p. 87.

Chapter 2

International Trade and Foreign Investment

Exporting isn't always possible . . .

Usually our approach has been to begin with direct export of goods and services. With the EC, we began with direct investment. EC restrictions are very efficient at controlling trade.

> Kim Song Whan, international finance director, Lucky-Goldstar (a Korean conglomerate ranked 32nd in the Fortune International 500 with sales of $14 billion)

Everything here is so cheap!

> Japanese real estate agent visiting Manhattan

LEARNING OBJECTIVES

In this chapter, you will study:

1. The magnitude of international trade and how it has grown.
2. The direction of trade (who trades with whom).
3. The value of analyzing trade statistics.
4. The size, growth, and direction of U.S. foreign direct investment.
5. Who invests and how much is invested in the United States.
6. The reasons for going abroad.
7. The weaknesses in using GNP/capita as a basis for comparing economies.
8. The international market entry methods.
9. The importance of international licensing.
10. The many forms of strategic alliances.

KEY WORDS AND CONCEPTS

- Portfolio investment
- Direct investment
- Preferential trading arrangement
- In-bond plants (maquiladoras)
- Indirect exporting
- Direct exporting
- Sales company
- Joint venture
- Management contract
- Licensing
- Franchising
- Contract manufacturing
- Strategic alliances

BUSINESS INCIDENT

International firms both export and invest overseas . . .

The export machine is still chugging along. After a 21 percent jump in 1988 and a 14 percent gain in 1989, an 8 percent increase in shipments abroad by America's top 50 exporters in 1990 may look sluggish. But U.S. companies scored an important victory last year, moving the country's merchandise trade deficit (excluding oil) to a four-year low. And for those who fear that the United States is losing out in the world technology market, the good news is that the technology component of American exports accounted for 47 percent of all merchandise exports as compared to only 43 percent in 1987.

Foreign investments are also significant for 32 of these companies. The percentages of foreign to total assets ranged from 58.8 percent for Exxon to 10.9 percent for General Electric, with 31 percent being the average for all 32 firms. Every one of this group attained sales of at least $2 billion from overseas operations in 1990. The percentages of foreign sales to total sales ranged from 74.6 percent for Exxon to 12.1 percent for Chrysler, with an average for the group of 42 percent. All sales are to unrelated firms: intergeographic sales between affiliates are not included.

Table 2–1 lists the volumes of exports and foreign sales for the 32 companies that are among the top 50 exporters and also have sizable foreign operations. To see

☐ **TABLE 2–1   Exports and Foreign Sales of Top 50 U.S. Exporters ($ billions)**

Company	U.S. Exports	Rank in Fortune 50	Foreign Sales	Rank in Forbes 100	Total Sales	Rank in Fortune 500	Exports Sales	Foreign Sales Total Sales	Exports + Foreign Sales Total Sales
General Motors	$10.31	2	$37.74	3	$126.02	1	8.2%	29.9%	38.1%
General Electric	7.13	3	8.27	14	58.41	6	12.2	14.2	26.4
Ford	7.10	4	35.88	4	98.27	3	7.2	36.5	43.7
IBM	6.20	5	41.89	2	69.02	4	9.0	60.7	69.7
Chrysler	5.00	6	3.73	42	30.87	11	16.2	12.1	28.3
DuPont	4.35	7	17.41	8	39.84	9	10.9	43.7	54.6
United Tech.	3.61	8	7.84	18	21.78	17	16.6	36.0	52.6
Caterpillar	3.44	10	3.08	51	11.54	39	29.8	26.7	56.5
Eastman Kodak	2.96	11	8.25	15	19.08	20	15.5	43.2	58.7
Philip Morris	2.93	12	10.47	10	44.32	7	6.6	23.6	30.2
Hewlett-Packard	2.82	13	7.21	19	13.23	29	21.3	54.5	75.8
Motorola	2.80	14	5.90	24	10.89	42	25.7	54.2	79.9
Unisys	2.20	15	5.24	28	10.11	49	21.8	55.8	73.6
Digital Equip.	1.92	17	7.12	20	13.08	30	14.7	54.4	69.1
Allied Signal	1.84	18	2.95	56	12.40	36	14.8	23.8	38.6
Dow Chemical	1.34	22	10.28	11	20.01	18	6.7	51.4	58.1
Union Carbide	1.28	23	2.78	61	7.62	23	16.8	36.5	53.3
Minn. Mining & Mfg.	1.20	25	6.22	23	13.02	31	9.2	47.8	57.0
Merck	1.16	28	3.63	44	7.82	63	14.8	46.4	61.2
Compaq Computer	1.12	29	1.94	93	3.63	136	30.9	53.4	84.3
Exxon	1.10	32	79.02	1	105.89	2	1.0	74.6	75.6
International Paper	1.10	33	3.04	54	12.96	32	8.5	23.5	32.0
Monsanto	1.08	35	3.31	50	9.05	53	11.9	36.6	48.5
Alum. Co. of Amer.	0.93	36	4.33	34	10.87	43	8.5	39.8	48.3
Xerox	0.90	37	8.11	17	18.38	22	4.9	44.1	49.0
Rockwell Int'l.	0.84	40	2.41	68	12.44	35	6.7	19.4	26.1
Abbott Lab.	0.81	41	2.25	75	6.21	82	13.1	36.2	49.3
Deere	0.76	42	2.00	90	7.88	62	9.6	25.4	35.0
Honeywell	0.75	43	2.01	89	6.99	69	10.7	28.8	39.5
Amoco	0.74	44	8.03	16	28.28	12	2.6	29.1	31.7
Bristol-Meyer Squibb	0.74	45	4.42	33	10.51	46	7.1	42.1	49.2
Tenneco	0.71	46	4.53	31	14.89	26	4.8	30.4	35.2

Fortune 50 = America's 50 Biggest Exporters from *Fortune.*
Forbes 100 = The 100 Largest U.S. Multinationals from *Forbes.*
Fortune 500 = Fortune 500 Largest Industrial Corporations from *Fortune.*
Source: "Exports: Ship 'Em Out," *Fortune,* Spring–Summer 1991, pp. 58–59; and "The 100 Largest U.S. Multinationals," *Forbes,* July 22, 1991, pp. 286–88.

BUSINESS INCIDENT (concluded)

the importance of international trade and foreign investment for these firms, examine the last column, which
shows the percentages of export sales and foreign sales
to their total sales. Note that Compaq Computer depends
on them for 84 percent of all its sales, and 19 of all 32
companies (59 percent) derive at least half their sales

from international business. Without it, many could not
survive.

Sources: "Exports: Ship 'Em Out," *Fortune,* Spring–Summer 1991, p. 58; and
"U.S. Corporations with the Biggest Foreign Revenues," *Forbes,* July 22,
1991, pp. 286–88.

T he Business Incident illustrates the importance of both aspects of international business—*exporting* and *overseas production*—to many of the
major U.S. corporations. However, these international business activities are
not confined to manufacturing firms. Of the Forbes 100 largest U.S. multinationals, 26 are service companies in banking, finance, construction, insurance,
entertainment, transportation, and retailing. Smaller firms also have overseas
operations. According to a study by the United Nations Centre on Transnational Corporations, "in most home countries, small transnational enterprises
account for over one half of the firms with investments abroad."[1]

In this chapter, we shall examine two topics directly related to exports and
to sales by international companies' foreign affiliates: (1) *international trade,*
which includes exports and imports, and (2) *foreign direct investment,* which
internationals must make to establish and expand their overseas operations.

INTERNATIONAL TRADE

◻ Volume of Trade

By 1990, the volume of international trade in goods and services measured in
current dollars had surpassed $4 trillion.[2] Of this, exports of merchandise
were $3.38 trillion, 26 times what they were in 1960 (see Table 2–2). The
dollar value of total world exports in 1990 was greater than the gross national product of every country in the world except the United States. One
fourth of everything grown or made on earth is exported. True, a large part
of this increase was due to inflation; however, using a quantum index to reflect changes in volume (eliminating the effect of price changes), we find that
the volume of world trade in 1990 was 5.1 times what it was in 1960 (5.5
percent annual increase). Table 2–3 compares the increases in exports measured in current dollars with volume increases measured by quantum indices
for some of the entries in Table 2–2.

How even has this growth been? Have some nations fared better than oth-
ers? There are some differences. All of the major exporting nations shown in
Table 2–2 have exceeded the world average except the United States and
Great Britain. Because of much lower oil prices, the value of OPEC's exports

◻ **TABLE 2–2**
World Trade in
Merchandise Exports (FOB
values; in billions of
current U.S. dollars)

	1960	1970	1980	1986	1990	Average Annual Percentage Increase
Total world exports	$128	$314	$2,003	$2,117	$3,382	11.3%
Developed countries	86	225	1,268	1,471	2,444	11.8
West Germany[a]	12	35	193	246	411	12.5
United States	20	43	221	206	394	10.4
Japan	4	19	129	209	287	15.3
France	7	18	111	119	210	12.0
Great Britain	10	19	110	107	186	10.2
Italy	4	13	78	98	169	13.3
Developing countries[b]	27	56	213	422	767	11.8
OPEC	n.e.	18	307	115	157	7.5[k]
Centrally planned economies						
Europe and U.S.S.R.	13	31	157	190	172	7.7
U.S.S.R.	6	13	76	97	105	10.0
EC	30[c]	88[c]	662[d]	790[e,f]	1,342	13.5
EFTA	18[g]	51[h]	117[i]	133[j]	226	8.8
LAIA	9	13	81	71	107	8.6

Notes: n.e. = Nonexistent.

      EC = European Community.

      EFTA = European Free Trade Association.

      LAIA = Latin American Integration Association (formerly LAFTA).

[a]Includes exports to East Germany.

[b]Defined by the World Bank as low- and middle-level income nations as indicated by GNP/capita.

[c]Original 6 members only (Belgium, Luxembourg, France, West Germany, Italy, and the Netherlands).

[d]Includes original 6 plus Denmark, Ireland, and Great Britain.

[e]And beyond includes Greece.

[f]And beyond includes Spain and Portugal.

[g]Original 7 members (Austria, Denmark, Norway, Portugal, Sweden, Great Britain, and Switzerland).

[h]Includes Finland as associate member.

[i]Includes Iceland and excludes Great Britain and Denmark.

[j]And beyond excludes Portugal.

[k]For years 1970 through 1990.

Sources: United Nations, *Monthly Bulletin of Statistics,* June 1991, pp. 90–111, and various earlier issues.

◻ **TABLE 2–3**
1990/1960 Export Ratios
Based on Current Dollars
and Quantum Indexes

	Current Dollars (1990/1960)	Quantum Indexes (1990/1960)
Total world exports	26.4 times	5.1 times
Developed countries	28.4	6.3
West Germany	34.3	7.3
United States	19.7	4.4
Japan	143.7	18.1
France	30.0	6.4
Great Britain	18.6	3.9
Italy	42.3	9.7
Developing countries	26.0 (1989)	3.6 (1989)
EC	44.7	6.5
EFTA	12.6	5.2

Sources: United Nations, *Monthly Bulletin of Statistics,* June 1991, p. 258; August 1991, pp. 124–54; and various earlier issues.

is only half the 1980 value. Much of the EC's increase has come from the admission of six new members, and the relatively low growth rate of EFTA's exports is the result of losing Denmark, Great Britain, and Portugal to the EC. While the exports of the developing nations as a whole are at the world average, those of the Latin American nations (LAIA) are growing at a much slower pace. Note also that the dollar values of the exports of the former communist nations of Central Europe were actually one third lower in 1990 (U.S.S.R. exports were higher) than they were in 1980.

The quintupling of world exports in only 30 years indicates that opportunities to export continue to grow, but the export growth of individual nations signifies increasing competition from imports in domestic markets. Figure 2–1 shows some of the American industries in which this has occurred. For example, U.S. exports of motor vehicles and car bodies increased by $3.7 billion from 1989 to 1990, but imports increased by $6.8 billion. In other words, even though the volume of American exports of these products increased from 1989 to 1990, so did the deficit in this account. Note, however, that the aerospace and aircraft industries continue to export far more than they import.

❑ Direction of Trade

What are the destinations of these $4 trillion in exports? If you have never examined trade flows, you may believe that international trade consists mainly of industrialized nations exporting manufactured goods to developing nations in return for raw materials. However, Table 2–4 shows that this is not so. Over three fourths of industrialized nations' trade is with each other. Note, though, that the major part (62.5 percent) of developing countries' exports do go to industrialized countries. The main exceptions to this generality have been (1) Japan, (2) the United States, and (3) Central Europe and the Soviet Union.

Japan and the United States.   Japan, being entirely dependent on foreign sources for raw materials, must import to survive. In fact, until the 1980s, Japan behaved more like a resource-poor developing nation than a rich one. It imported raw materials, processed them, and exported the finished products. The distribution system for imports, dominated by large, well-established general trading companies, was designed to provide industry with the raw materials and components it needed and to secure outlets for its production. As other industrialized nations have imposed import restrictions on Japanese exports to protect their home industries, Japanese trading companies have increased their efforts to sell to developing nations.[3] Table 2–4 shows their efforts have succeeded, although long-term indications are that they are shifting their attention back to the industrialized nations. While the developed countries as a whole sent 77.4 percent of their exports to other developed countries (DC) and only 19.3 percent to less developed nations (LDC), Japan sent 59.3 percent of its exports to the DCs and 39.5 percent was sold to LDCs.

The United States also exported a smaller proportion to DCs and more to the developing nations than did developed countries generally, but for somewhat different reasons than Japan. American firms have significantly more

☐ **FIGURE 2–1**
Exports and Imports of
Selected Products, 1989
versus 1990 ($ billions)

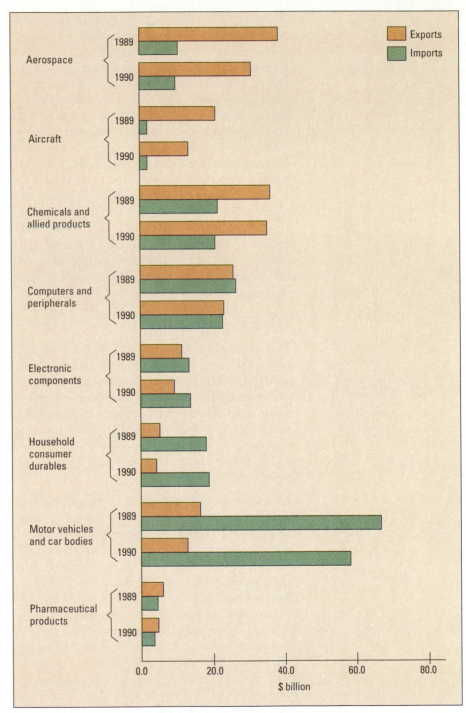

Source: *1991 Industrial Outlook,* U.S. Department of Commerce, January 1991.

Courtesy of Japan National Tourist Organization

Exports have fueled Japan's rapid economic growth. This has resulted in a tremendous growth in Japan's major cities, such as Tokyo.

subsidiaries in developing nations than Japanese companies do; these subsidiaries are captive customers for their American owners. In addition, some buyers in Southeast Asian countries, remembering that Japan was an aggressor nation, prefer to buy from American firms. Notice, also, the high percentage of American exports that go to Latin America. The United States exports to Latin America as much as all of the Latin American nations do to each other.

Central Europe and the U.S.S.R.   With the exception of 1990, the data in Table 2–4 are from when these nations had communist governments that, as a group, attempted to be as self-sufficient as possible, trading with the West only for goods and services unavailable in the East. Even this trade was somewhat restricted because of their lack of foreign exchange. The communist bloc was simply unable to produce the kinds and quality of goods that Western nations were willing to pay for.

Now that these countries are establishing market economies with closer ties to Western Europe, we can expect to see greater trade with the developed nations.

The changing direction of trade.   The percentages in Table 2–4 also indicate how the direction of trade changes. In 1980, only 47.5 percent of Japan's exports went to the developed countries while the LDCs received 45.4 percent. By 1990, 59 percent (25 percent increase) of its exports went to DCs and only 39.5 percent to LDCs. Note, however, that Japan exported more to all categories of developed nations and less to developing nations in Africa and Latin America than did the developed nations generally. The large national debts that many of the developing countries incurred while the industrial economies were expanding were a salient factor.

TABLE 2–4 Direction of Trade for Selected Regions and Countries (Percentage of region's or country's total merchandise exports to regions or country in columns)

Exports from	Year	Exports to											
		DC	U.S.	Can.	Jap.	U.S.S.R.	EC	EFTA	LDC	DA	D. Am.	OPEC	CPE
Developed countries (DC)	1960	70.5%	10.3%	5.7%	2.9%	1.2%	24.4%	18.8%	25.5%	6.2%	11.0%	n.e.	2.9%
	1970	76.9	12.8	5.1	3.9	5.2	39.5	9.4	18.7	4.1	8.3	3.4%	3.1
	1980	71.2	9.7	3.4	3.2	1.9	41.1	9.0	23.3	5.2	6.0	7.9	3.6
	1990	77.4	12.6	4.1	4.2	1.1	46.1	7.9	19.3	2.3	3.8	3.3	2.1
United States (U.S.)	1960	63.8	—	18.3	7.1	0.2	19.3	11.9	34.7	2.4	17.4	n.e.	1.0
	1970	69.5	—	20.7	10.8	0.3	26.6	4.0	29.6	2.3	15.2	4.8	0.8
	1980	59.8	—	15.7	9.5	0.7	24.8	3.7	36.2	2.9	17.6	8.1	1.8
	1990	64.7	—	20.9	12.3	0.8	26.8	2.8	34.0	1.6	14.0	3.6	1.1
Canada (Can.)	1960	91.7	56.6	—	3.3	0.2	8.2	19.5	7.6	0.5	3.5	n.e.	0.7
	1970	90.7	65.4	—	4.7	0.6	16.4	1.8	7.4	0.7	4.3	1.1	0.8
	1980	85.2	63.4	—	5.7	2.0	12.8	1.5	10.5	1.4	5.1	2.9	2.7
	1990	91.1	75.0	—	5.5	0.8	8.1	1.5	8.0	0.7	1.8	1.3	0.9
Japan (Jap.)	1960	47.7	27.4	3.0	—	1.5	4.3	5.7	50.6	8.6	6.8	n.e.	1.6
	1970	54.6	31.1	2.9	—	1.8	11.2	3.0	40.0	5.6	5.8	5.1	2.3
	1980	47.5	24.5	1.9	—	2.1	13.2	2.7	45.4	4.6	6.6	14.2	2.8
	1990	59.3	31.7	2.3	—	0.9	18.8	2.9	39.5	1.3	3.4	4.7	1.2
U.S.S.R.	1960	19.2	0.4	0.1	1.4	—	6.7	6.2	6.6	1.8	1.8	n.e.	56.1
	1970	21.2	0.5	0.1	3.0	—	10.8	4.2	21.0	4.5	5.1	2.9	52.8
	1980	36.1	0.3	neg.	1.9	—	22.6	7.1	25.8	1.8	4.8	2.3	42.2
	1990	36.0	0.9	0.1	2.4	—	27.1	5.5	30.0	2.7	6.1	1.2	34.0
European Community (EC)*	1960	71.9	7.5	1.0	0.7	1.4	34.5	21.7	22.4	9.8	5.2	n.e.	4.1
	1970	80.5	8.1	1.3	1.2	1.2	48.9	16.8	14.0	4.9	3.9	3.4	4.0
	1980	77.7	5.6	0.7	1.0	1.6	53.6	11.9	17.6	6.5	3.0	7.8	3.5
	1990	83.1	12.7	0.9	2.1	1.0	60.7	10.3	12.7	2.8	1.7	3.2	2.2
European Free Trade Association (EFTA)†	1960	71.3	8.7	3.7	0.7	1.2	24.1	21.9	24.6	6.7	4.9	n.e.	3.5
	1970	82.2	6.6	1.3	1.3	2.8	26.4	26.4	10.8	3.5	3.6	1.8	6.6
	1980	79.6	4.9	0.7	1.3	3.4	53.1	15.3	13.3	3.6	2.9	5.0	6.6
	1990	83.6	6.8	1.3	2.6	4.9	57.6	13.4	10.9	1.3	1.6	2.3	4.9
Less developed countries (LDC)	1960	72.3	10.3	1.8	5.1	1.9	22.8	16.2	22.3	3.2	3.9	n.e.	3.5
	1970	72.4	18.4	1.8	10.8	3.1	22.9	3.0	20.2	2.8	6.7	1.9	5.1
	1980	70.2	20.5	1.3	14.0	1.7	27.1	2.7	24.9	2.4	8.0	3.7	2.9
	1990	62.5	22.6	1.5	12.9	2.6	21.8	1.9	32.5	2.2	4.2	3.6	3.9
Developing Africa (DA) (South Africa and Zimbabwe excluded)	1960	79.2	7.9	0.4	1.5	2.7	43.8	21.7	12.8	6.6	0.7	n.e.	5.7
	1970	81.1	6.7	0.7	4.0	4.1	61.4	4.3	10.7	5.6	2.0	1.2	6.5
	1980	83.6	31.1	0.2	2.1	0.8	42.8	2.9	12.6	3.1	6.4	1.1	2.6
	1990	79.7	15.5	0.5	2.3	2.1	59.0	1.5	14.8	6.2	1.6	2.4	4.3
Developing America (D. Am.) (U.S. & Can. excluded)	1960	78.9	42.1	1.7	2.8	1.6	18.5	11.8	18.0	0.7	7.9	n.e.	3.1
	1970	74.2	32.4	3.4	5.4	3.5	26.3	3.3	19.1	0.7	17.3	0.9	5.8
	1980	64.6	32.2	2.6	4.2	4.8	18.9	2.3	26.5	2.2	21.4	3.3	6.5
	1990	70.2	38.1	1.5	5.6	4.4	22.4	1.5	21.1	1.0	14.0	2.6	6.1
Organization of Petroleum Exporting Countries (OPEC)‡	1960	n.e.	n.e.	n.e.	n.e.	n.e.	n.e.	n.e.	n.e.	n.e.	n.e.	n.e.	n.e.
	1970	75.3	9.7	2.5	12.2	0.9	43.5	2.0	19.3	2.3	9.1	0.7	1.6
	1980	75.8	18.4	1.5	17.3	0.3	30.8	3.1	22.2	1.4	8.5	1.3	1.2
	1990	72.6	19.1	1.5	22.2	0.6	27.1	1.8	24.9	2.3	6.1	2.5	1.7
Central Europe and U.S.S.R. (CPE)‖	1960	19.4	0.6	0.1	0.2	17.1	7.2	6.8	6.5	1.9	1.8	n.e.	62.3
	1970	23.0	0.7	0.2	1.5	21.7	12.7	4.6	13.2	3.3	3.1	2.9	60.2
	1980	31.1	0.9	0.2	1.1	17.4	18.7	6.5	14.9	2.8	3.3	3.2	50.7
	1990	38.5	1.3	0.2	1.8	11.6	28.2	5.8	22.7	2.4	4.2	1.7	38.2

Note: n.e. = Nonexistent.
neg. = Negligible.

*1980 data include Denmark, Great Britain, and Ireland. Greece, Spain, and Portugal are included in 1990 data.

†Excludes Denmark and Great Britain and includes Iceland in 1980.

‡OPEC includes Algeria, Ecuador, Gabon, Indonesia, Iran, Iraq, Kuwait, Libya, Nigeria, Qatar, Saudi Arabia, United Arab Emirates, and Venezuela.

‖Includes Albania, Bulgaria, Czechoslovakia, East Germany, Hungary, Poland, Romania, and U.S.S.R.

Sources: *Monthly Bulletin of Statistics* (New York: United Nations, June 1991), pp. 250–54; and *Statistical Yearbook,* 1969 (New York: United Nations), pp. 376–83.

Another interesting observation is that the LDCs as a group are selling a smaller percentage of their exports to the DCs—with the exception of the United States and the centrally planned economies—but more to each other. This is due in part to their increasing ability to export manufactured goods. Their scarcity of convertible currency is also a factor.

◻ Major Trading Partners

An analysis of the major trading partners of the firm's home country and those of the nations where it has affiliates that export can provide valuable insights to management.

Why focus on major trading partners?   There are a number of advantages in focusing attention on a nation that is already a sizable purchaser of goods coming from the would-be exporter's country:

1. Business climate in importing nation is relatively favorable.
2. Export and import regulations are not insurmountable.
3. There should be no strong cultural objections to buying that nation's goods.
4. Satisfactory transportation facilities have already been established.
5. Import channel members (merchants, banks, and customs brokers) are experienced in handling import shipments from the exporter's area.
6. Foreign exchange to pay for the exports is available.
7. The government of a trading partner may be applying pressure on importers to buy from countries that are good customers for that nation's exports. We have seen the efforts of the Japanese, Korean, and Taiwanese governments to persuade their citizens to buy more American goods. They have also sent buying missions to the United States.

Major trading partners of the United States.   Table 2–5 shows the major trading partners of the United States. The data indicate that the United States, an industrialized nation, generally follows the tendency we found in Table 2–4; that is, developed nations trade with one another. Mexico and Canada are major trading partners in great part because they share a common border with the United States. Freight charges are lower, delivery times are shorter, and contact between buyers and sellers is easier and less expensive.

Canada's importance as a trading partner is becoming even greater as a result of the U.S.–Canada Free Trade Agreement, which went into effect in 1989. Although 75 percent of the $170 billion in trade between the partners is already duty free, the progressive removal of import duties from the remaining 25 percent (to be finished by January 1998) will further increase cross-border trade.[4] Mexico's trade with the United States has reached $60 billion ($34 billion in 1987) after Mexico drastically reduced its import duties at the end of 1987. Mexico is now negotiating to become a member of the U.S.–Canada Free Trade Agreement.

Note that in just two decades, there as been a marked change in the ranking of America's trading partners. Not only have the rankings changed, but nations have been added while others have become relatively less important. The newly industrializing nations of Korea, Taiwan, and Singapore are

□ **TABLE 2–5   Major Trading Partners of the United States ($ billions in current dollars)**

1965		1990		1965		1990	
Imports from	**Amount**	**Imports from**	**Amount**	**Exports to**	**Amount**	**Exports to**	**Amount**
1. Canada	$4.83	1. Canada	$91.37	1. Canada	$5.64	1. Canada	$83.87
2. Japan	2.41	2. Japan	89.66	2. Japan	2.08	2. Japan	48.59
3. U.K.	1.41	3. Mexico	30.72	3. W. Germany	1.65	3. Mexico	28.38
4. W. Germany	1.34	4. Germany	28.19	4. U.K.	1.62	4. U.K.	23.48
5. Venezuela	1.02	5. Taiwan	22.67	5. Mexico	1.11	5. Germany	18.75
6. Mexico	0.64	6. U.K.	20.29	6. Netherlands	1.09	6. S. Korea	14.40
7. Italy	0.62	7. S. Korea	18.49	7. France	0.97	7. France	13.65
8. France	0.62	8. China	15.22	8. India	0.93	8. Netherlands	13.02
9. Brazil	0.51	9. France	13.12	9. Italy	0.89	9. Taiwan	11.48
10. Bel. & Lux.	0.49	10. Italy	12.72	10. Australia	0.80	10. Bel. & Lux.	10.45
11. Philippines	0.37	11. Saudi Arabia	9.97	11. Bel. &Lux.	0.65	11. Australia	8.54
12. India	0.35	12. Singapore	9.84	12. Venezuela	0.63	12. Singapore	8.02
13. Hong Kong	0.34	13. Hong Kong	9.49	13. Spain	0.47	13. Italy	7.99
14. Neth.Ant.	0.32	14. Venezuela	9.45	14. S. Africa	0.44	14. Hong Kong	6.84
15. Australia	0.31	15. Brazil	7.98	15. Switzerland	0.37	15. Spain	5.21

Notes: 1. Exports are stated on an f.a.s. (free alongside ship) value basis. Services not included.
2. Imports are stated on CIF (Cost, Insurance, Freight) value basis. Services not included.
3. U.K. = United Kingdom
4. Bel. & Lux. = Belgium and Luxembourg. Their export and import statistics are reported jointly.
5. Neth. Ant. = Netherlands Antilles.

Sources: Department of Commerce, *U.S. Foreign Trade Highlights 1991* (Washington, D.C.: April 1991), pp. 24–35; and *World Almanac 1989*, p. 183.

supplying the United States with huge quantities of electronic products and components and other labor-intensive products, much of which is produced by affiliates of American worldwide companies. China's addition to the list is evidence of the new trade relations with this country. These same countries appear as major importers of American goods as well because (1) their rising levels of living enable their people to afford more imported products, and the countries' export earnings provide the foreign exchange to buy them; (2) they are purchasing large amounts of capital goods to further their industrial expansion; and (3) their governments, pressured by the American government to lower their trade surpluses with the United States, have sent buying missions to this country to look for products to import, as we mentioned in the previous section.

□ Utility of These Data

The analysis of foreign trade that we have described would be helpful to anyone just starting to search outside the home market for new business opportunities. The preliminary steps of (1) studying the general growth and direction of trade (Table 2–4) and (2) analyzing major trading partners (Table 2–5) would provide an idea of where the trading activity is. What kinds of products do these countries import from the United States? The Department of Commerce annual publication, *U.S. Foreign Trade Highlights,* reports the top 40 U.S. exports to and imports from 90 countries. Another Department of Commerce publication, the *FT 925*, details the quantities, dollar values, and destinations of specific products. We shall discuss this in greater detail in Chapter 14.

The topic that we have been examining, international trade, exists because firms export. As you know, however, exporting is only one aspect of international business. The other, overseas production, generally requires foreign investment, our next subject of discussion.

FOREIGN INVESTMENT

portfolio investment the purchase of stocks and bonds to obtain a return on the funds invested

Foreign investment may be divided into two components: **portfolio investment,** which is the purchase of stocks and bonds solely for the purpose of obtaining a return on the funds invested, and **direct investment,** by which the investors participate in the management of the firm in addition to receiving a return on their money.

▫ Portfolio Investment

direct investment the purchase of sufficient stock in a firm to obtain significant management control

Although portfolio investors are not directly concerned with control of a firm, they invest immense amounts in stocks and bonds from other countries. Data from the U.S. Department of Commerce show that persons residing outside the United States hold American stocks and bonds valued at $475 billion ($231 billion in stocks).[5] Of this, 63 percent is owned by European residents, 13 percent by Japanese residents, and 9 percent by Canadian residents.[6] American residents, on the other hand, own $222 billion in foreign securities, of which $93 billion is in corporate stocks.[7] As you can see, foreign portfolio investment is sizable and will continue to grow as more companies list their bonds and equities on foreign exchanges.

▫ Foreign Direct Investment

Volume.   Attempts have been made to estimate the total book value of foreign direct investment by summing yearly totals of new investments, but this procedure understates the present value because of the effects of appreciation and inflation.

In Chapter 1, we stated that the book value of all foreign investments is about $1,200 billion. Table 2–6 indicates how this total is divided among the largest investor nations. Note that the United States has almost double the foreign direct investment of the next largest, the United Kingdom, which in turn has invested 24 percent more than Japan, the third largest. Japan, however, experienced the greatest percentage increase from 1983 to 1989.

Although, in dollar terms, Japan's foreign direct investment increased by 480 percent, it cost Japanese investors much less in Japanese currency because by 1989 the yen was worth nearly twice as much in U.S. dollars as in 1983.

	Yen/US	FDI ($ billions)	FDI (yen billions)	1989/1983
1983	237.52	32.2	7,648	
1989	137.96	154.4	21,301	2.785 = 279%

	1989		1983	
	Amount (US$ billions)	Share (percent)	Amount (US$ billions)	Share (percent)
United States	$ 373.4	29.6%	$226.1	43.9%
United Kingdom	191.9	15.2	91.1	17.7
Japan	154.4	12.2	32.2	6.2
Germany	112.6	8.9	37.3	7.2
Netherlands	88.2	7.0	33.3	6.5
France	55.9	4.4	221.6	4.2
Canada	63.9	5.1	22.0	4.3
Other	222.3	17.6	51.5	10.0
World total	$1,262.6	100.0%	$515.2	100.0%

Sources: *Japan 1992: An International Comparison* (Tokyo: Japan Institute for Social and Economic Affairs, December 20, 1991), p. 58; and *Japan*, 1985, p. 58.

Direction.   Even though it is impossible to make an accurate determination of the present value of foreign investments, we can get an idea of the rate and amounts of such investments and of the places in which they are being made. This is the kind of information that interests managers and government leaders. It is analogous to what is sought in the analysis of international trade. If a nation is continuing to receive appreciable amounts of foreign investment, its investment climate must be favorable. This means that the political forces of the foreign environment are relatively attractive and that the opportunity to earn a profit is greater there than elsewhere. Other reasons for investing exist, to be sure, but if the above are absent, foreign investment is not likely to occur.

In which countries are investments being made, and where do the investments come from? Table 2–7 indicates that the industrialized nations invest primarily in one another just as they trade more with one another.

Actually, foreign investment follows foreign trade. Managements observe that the kinds of products they manufacture are being imported in sizable quantities by a country, and they begin to study the feasibility of setting up production facilities there. They are spurred to action because it is common knowledge that competitors are making similar analyses and may arrive at the same conclusion. Often the local market is not large enough to support local production of all the firms exporting to it, and the situation becomes one of seeing who can become established first. Experienced managers know, too, that governments often limit the number of local firms producing a given product so that those who do set up operations will be assured of having a profitable and continuing business.

□ U.S. Foreign Direct Investment

The United States is by far the largest investor abroad (about one third of the total; see Table 2–6), and as you can see from Table 2–8, American firms have invested much more in the developed than in the developing countries. Also, as with international trade, the relative importance of regions and countries has been changing. In a period of 30 years, the percentage of Amer-

□ **TABLE 2–7**
Direction of Foreign Direct Investment for Selected Regions and Countries (Current US$ billions)

	1973	1979	1989
Where funds originate (net investment)			
World	$23.44	$ 48.37	$190.33*
Industrial nations	23.13	48.08	188.29
United States	11.53	24.84	31.73
United Kingdom	4.01	5.91	31.96
Japan	1.92	2.95	44.16
Germany	1.69	4.73	13.55
France	0.94	2.07	19.05
Netherlands	0.93	2.35	10.16
Canada	0.77	1.89	3.66
Belgium and Luxembourg	0.27	1.36	6.81
Italy	0.26	0.55	2.01
Switzerland	0.30	0.64	6.94
Developing nations (oil export)	0.16	−0.15	0.64
Developing nations (nonoil)	0.15	0.41	1.40
Where funds go (net investment)			
Industrial nations	10.62	24.60	163.24
United States	2.85	9.92	72.23
United Kingdom	1.80	2.76	32.19
France	1.14	2.59	10.29
Spain	0.39	1.43	8.43
Canada	0.83	1.50	2.85
Italy	0.63	0.37	2.54
Belgium and Luxembourg	0.73	1.08	7.06
Netherlands	0.87	1.24	5.94
Germany	2.06	1.13	6.56
Japan	0.21†	0.24	1.06
Developing nations (oil export)	0.27	0.09	3.28
Developing nations (nonoil)	4.04	8.42	15.24
Africa	0.32	0.36	2.57
Asia	0.80	2.14	7.65
People's Republic of China	n.a.	0.43‡	3.39
Singapore	0.39	0.83	4.04
Malaysia	0.17	0.89	1.85
Western hemisphere	2.50	4.38	5.41
Mexico	0.46	0.68	1.85
Brazil	1.39	2.46	2.97‖
Colombia	0.02	0.16	0.58
Argentina	0.01	0.18	1.03

n.a. = Not available.
*Amounts do not coincide because of reporting lag.
†1974.
‡1982.
‖1988.
Sources: International Monetary Fund, *Balance of Payments Yearbook Supplement to Volumes 31 and 33* (Washington, D.C.: December 1980); and *Balance of Payments Statistics Yearbook,* vol. 38, part 2, 1990, pp. 68–69.

☐ **TABLE 2-8   U.S. Direct Investment Position Overseas on a Historical-Cost Basis ($ billions)**

Country or Region	1960		1990							
	Total	Percent of Total	Total	Percent of Total	Manufac-turing	Percent of Manufacturing	Finance[a]	Percent of Finance	Other[b]	Percent of Other
Total	$31.87	100%	$421.49	100%	$168.22	100%	$120.29	100%	$132.98	100%
Developed countries	19.32	61	312.19	74	134.66	80	78.91	66	98.62	74
Canada	11.18	35	68.43	16	33.23	20	13.08	11	22.12	17
Europe[c]	6.69	21	204.20	48	83.99	50	60.91	51	59.30	44
EC[d]	2.65	8	172.94	41	81.26	48	48.22	40	43.46	32
Bel. & Lux.[e]	0.23	0.7	10.58	3	4.87	3	S	—	S	—
France	0.74	2	17.13	4	11.05	7	1.13	<1	4.95	4
Germany	1.01	3	27.72	7	17.49	10	4.56	4	5.67	4
Italy	0.38	1	12.97	3	8.54	5	1.37	1	3.06	2
Netherlands	0.28	0.9	22.78	5	8.14	5	8.81	7	5.83	4
Great Britain	3.23	10	64.98	15	20.64	12	26.65	22	17.69	13
Denmark and Ireland	n.a.	—	8.41	2	5.18	3	S	—	S	—
Greece	n.a.	—	0.30	<1	0.08	<1	S	—	S	—
Japan	0.25	0.8	20.99	5	10.62	6	2.44	2	7.93	6
Aust. and S.A.[f]	1.20	4	18.56	5	6.81	4	2.47	2	9.28	7
Developing countries	11.13	35	105.72	25	33.56	20	41.38	34	30.78	23
Latin America	7.48	23	72.47	17	23.80	14	34.85	29	13.82	10
Brazil	0.95	3	15.42	4	11.29	7	2.20	2	1.93	2
Venezuela	2.57	8	1.58	<1	0.96	<1	0.06	<1	0.56	<1
Mexico and Central America	1.54	5	18.91	5	8.17	5	5.97	5	4.77	4
Other western hemisphere	0.88	3	28.64	7	0.39	<1	25.10	21	3.15	2
Africa[g]	0.64	2	3.78	<1	0.42	<1	.38	<1	2.98	2
Middle East	1.14	4	4.76	<1	0.91	<1	0.94	<1	2.91	2
Other Asia and Pacific	0.98	3	24.72	6	8.43	<1	5.21	4	11.08	8
International[h]	1.42	4	3.54	<1	n.a.	—	n.a.	—	1.04	<1

Notes: n.a. = Not applicable.
    S = Suppressed to avoid disclosure of individual firm.
[a]Includes finance, banking, real estate, and insurance.
[b]Other includes transportation, communications, public utilities, petroleum, mining, and wholesale trade.
[c]No East European investment included.
[d]Great Britain, Ireland, Denmark, and Greece not in EC in 1960. Are included in 1983.
[e]Belgium and Luxembourg.
[f]Australia, New Zealand, and South Africa.
[g]Does not include South Africa.
[h]Shipping companies operating under flags of convenience, primarily those of Panama and Liberia, and investments not allocated to any specific country by reporting firms.
Sources: *Survey of Current Business,* June 1991, p. 29; and *Statistical Abstract of the United States 1977,* p. 755.

☐ **TABLE 2–9**   **Foreign Direct Investment Position in United States on a Historical-Cost Basis, 1990 ($ billions)**

Country	All Industries	Percent of Total	Manufac- turing	Percent of Total	Trade	Percent of Total	Real Estate	Percent of Total	Finance	Percent of Total
Total	$403.71	100.00%	$160.00	100.00%	$62.00	100.00%	$34.63	100.00%	$58.44	100.00%
Europe	256.50	63.54	125.57	78.48	27.18	43.84	11.33	32.72	30.33	51.90
United Kingdom	108.06	26.77	52.96	33.00	7.14	11.52	4.10	11.84	13.14	22.48
Japan	83.50	21.43	15.17	9.48	28.27	45.60	15.86	45.80	16.90	28.92
Netherlands	64.33	15.93	24.45	15.28	24.45	39.44	5.19	14.99	8.36	14.31
Germany	27.77	6.88	15.22	9.51	7.49	12.08	1.05	3.03	2.77	4.73
Canada	27.73	6.87	9.33	5.83	1.72	2.77	3.09	8.92	7.33	12.54
France	19.55	4.84	14.69	9.18	0.69	1.11	0.14	0.40	—	n.a.
Switzerland	17.51	4.34	9.11	5.69	2.03	3.27	0.21	0.61	6.49	11.11
Netherland Antilles	11.15	2.76	4.99	3.12	1.02	1.65	1.22	3.52	S	S
Australia	8.39	2.08	1.89	1.18	S	S	0.35	1.01	S	S
Sweden	5.45	1.35	4.94	3.09	S	S	0.18	0.52	S	S
Belgium	4.23	1.05	1.47	0.92	1.04	1.68	0.07	0.20	S	S
Panama	3.26	0.81	0.07	0.04	0.12	0.19	0.21	0.61	S	S
Venezuela	2.36	0.58	‡	‡	‡	‡	0.03	0.09	S	S
Bermuda	2.24	0.55	0.34	0.21	S	S	0.18	0.52	S	S
Luxembourg	1.83	0.45	0.08	0.05	0.05	0.01	0.14	0.40	S	S
Saudi Arabia	1.79	0.44	S	S	0.01	†	‡	‡	*	†
Finland	1.76	0.44	1.26	0.79	S	S	*	†	S	S
Kuwait	1.58	0.39	S	S	*	†	0.95	2.74	*	†
Italy	1.55	0.38	0.55	0.34	0.12	0.19	0.02	0.06	S	S
Bahamas	1.51	0.37	S	S	S	S	0.02	0.06	S	S

Note: S = Suppressed to avoid disclosure of individual companies.
    N.a. = Not applicable.
*Less than $10 million.
†<0.01%.
‡ = Negative position.
Source: *Survey of Current Business,* August 1991, p. 54.

ican foreign investment in the developed nations has risen from 61 percent to 74 percent. Europe's share has more than doubled, and of the European countries, Great Britain and West Germany have obtained the greatest dollar increase. Note that although the developing nations as a group have suffered a large percentage decrease, the percentage of investment in the Other Asia and Pacific region—which includes newly industrializing countries (NICs) such as Singapore and Hong Kong—has doubled.

☐ Foreign Direct Investment in the United States

Foreign direct investment in the United States has risen rapidly, from about $6.9 billion in 1960 to $403 billion in 1990 (see Table 2–9). Of the 63 percent of the total foreign investment accounted for by Europe, companies in the United Kingdom and the Netherlands owned 27 and 16 percent, respec-

☐ **FIGURE 2–2   Distribution of Japanese Manufacturers' Factory Sites in the United States (September 1990 versus May 1988)**

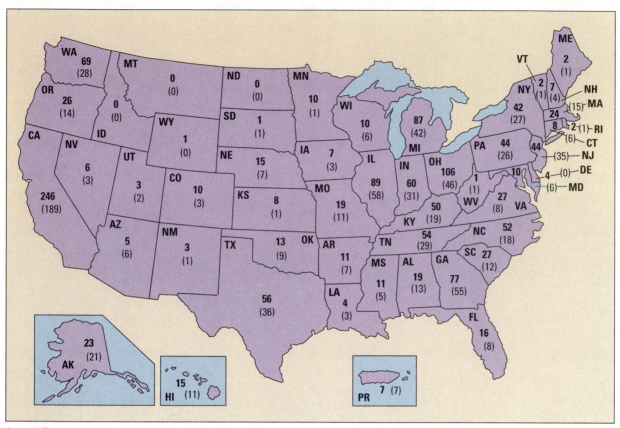

Japanese firms were operating 1,433 plants in the United States as of September 1990 compared to 837 plants in May 1988. The total in 1987 (not shown) was just 530.
Source: JETRO Survey.

tively. Foreign direct investment in the United States is very concentrated, with firms from just four nations—United Kingdom, Japan, the Netherlands, and Germany—owning over 70 percent of the total.

Although the United Kingdom's investments of $108 billion are considerably higher than the Japanese total of $83 billion, Japanese investments in the United States are expanding rapidly. Figure 2–2 illustrates how, in slightly more than two years, the number of Japanese plant sites increased from 837 to 1,433 (1988 data are in parentheses).

The 20 largest investors in the United States are ranked by revenue in Table 2–10. Although a few firms, such as Shell, Nestlé, and Bayer, have been in this country for many years, many of these investments are recent. You can tell from the names of the American affiliates that their major investment strategy has been to acquire existing firms rather than start from the ground up. In 1990, foreign investors spent $56.8 billion on acquisitions and only $7.7 billion to establish new companies.[8]

GNP/Capita

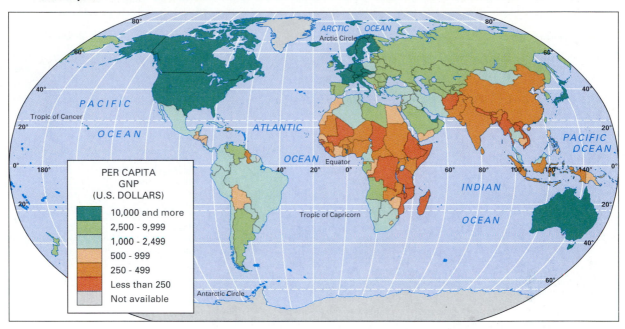

WHY GO ABROAD?

International firms go abroad for a number of reasons, all of which are linked to the desire to either increase profits and sales or protect them from being eroded by competition. Any reason, depending on the firm's situation, may achieve either goal.

◻ Increase Profits and Sales

Enter new markets.   Managers are always under pressure to increase the sales and profits of their firms, and when they face a mature, saturated market at home, they begin to search for new markets outside their home country. They find that (1) a rising GNP/capita and population growth appear to be creating markets that are reaching the "critical mass" necessary to become viable candidates for their operations and (2) the economies of some nations where they are not doing business are growing at a considerably faster rate than is the economy of their own market.

New market creation.   Table 2–11 illustrates the great variety in growth rates among the top and bottom countries ranked by GNP/capita. Note the disparity among and between the two groups.

Although nearly everyone looks to GNP/capita as a basis for making comparisons of nations' economies, extreme care must be exercised to avoid drawing unwarranted conclusions. In the first place, because the statistical systems in many developing nations are deficient, the reliability of the data provided by such nations is questionable.

☐ **TABLE 2–10   Twenty Largest Foreign Investments in the United States ($ millions)**

1990 Rank	Foreign Investor	Country	U.S. Investment	Percent Owned	Industry	Revenue	Assets
1	Seagram Co Ltd	Canada	E I du Pont de Nemours	25	Chemicals, energy	40,047	38,128
			JE Seagram	100	Beverages	3,678	8,935
						43,725	
2	Royal Dutch/Shell Group	Netherlands/U.K.	Shell Oil	100	Energy, chemicals	24,423	28,496
3	British Petroleum Plc	U.K.	BP America	100	Energy	18,620	n.a.
			Standard Oil	100	Energy		
4	Grand Metropolitan Ltd	U.K.	Burger King	100	Fast food	6,100	n.a.
			Grand Metropolitan USA	100	Beverages, retailing	4,120	n.a.
			Pillsbury	100	Food processing	2,600	n.a.
						12,820	
5	Tengelmann Group	Germany	Great A&P Tea	53	Supermarkets	11,391	3,307
6	Campeau	Canada	Federated Dept Stores	100	Retailing	4,576	6,126
			Allied Stores	100	Retailing	2,562	3,024
			Ralphs Grocery	100	Supermarkets	2,800	1,400
						9,938	
7	Petroleos de Venezuela, SA	Venezuela	Citgo Petroleum	100	Refining, marketing	9,049	2,881
8	Unilever NV Unilever Plc	Netherlands U.K.	Unilever United States	100	Food proc, pers prods	8,680	9,039
9	B.hl A.T. Industries Plc	U.K.	Brown & Williamson Tobacco	100	Tobacco	3,050	n.a.
			Farmers Group	100	Insurance	1,297	4,646
	Imasco Ltd	Canada	Hardee's Food Systems	100	Fast food	4,146	n.a.
						8,493	
10	Hanson Plc	U.K.	Hanson Industries	100	Multicompany	6,453	2,027
			Smith Corona	48	Office supplies	471	222
			GR Foods	49	Restaurant	289	202
			Cavenham Forest Inds	100	Timber	276	n.a.
						7,489	

Second, to arrive at a common base of U.S. dollars, the World Bank converts local currencies to dollars. The Bank uses an average of the exchange rate for that year and the previous two years, after adjusting for differences in relative inflation between the particular country and the United States.[9] World Bank economists admit that official exchange rates do not reflect the relative domestic purchasing powers of currencies, but they say, "However, exchange rates remain the only generally available means of converting GNP from national currencies to U.S. dollars."[10]

Finally, you must remember that GNP/capita is merely an arithmetic mean obtained by dividing GNP by the total population. However, a nation with a lower GNP but more evenly distributed income may be a more desirable market than one whose GNP is higher. On the other hand, as you will note in the chapter on the economic forces, a skewed distribution of income in a nation with a low GNP/capita may indicate that there is a viable market, especially for luxury goods. People do drive Cadillacs™ in Bolivia.

The data from Table 2–11 indicate that, from a macro viewpoint, markets around the world are growing, but this does not mean that equally good opportunities exist for all kinds of business. Perhaps surprisingly, economic

☐ **TABLE 2–10   (concluded)**

1990 Rank	Foreign Investor	Country	U.S. Investment	Percent Owned	Industry	Revenue	Assets
11	Sony Corp	Japan	Sony Music Entertainment	100	Music entertainment	7,460	n.a.
			Columbia Pictures	100	Movies		
			Sony Corp of America	100	Consumer electronics		
12	Nestle SA	Switzerland	Nestle USA	100	Food processing	7,225	n.a.
			Alcon Laboratories	100	Pharmaceuticals		
13	Philips NV	Netherlands	North American Philips	100	Electronics	6,119	3,377
14	Franz Haniel & Cie	Germany	Scrivner	100	Food distribution	6,000	1,400
			Gateway Foods	100	Food distribution		
15	Pechiney	France	American National Can	100	Packaging	4,506	6,721
			Howmet	100	Gas turbines	973	
			Other companies	100	Aluminum	459	
						5,938	
16	Bayer AG	Germany	Miles	100	Health care	2,568	2,217
			Mobay	100	Chemicals	2,224	1,891
			Agfa	100	Photography	957	765
			Other companies	100	Chemicals	154	164
						5,903	
17	Hoechst AG	Germany	Hoechst Celanese	100	Chemicals	5,881	6,082
18	Volvo AB	Sweden	Hertz	26	Car rental	2,666	3,852
			Volvo GM Heavy Truck	76	Automotive	999	n.a.
			VME Americas	25	Automotive	360E	n.a.
	Regie Nationale des Usines Renault	France	Mack Trucks	100	Automotive	1,608	n.a.
						5,633	
19	ASEA AB BBC Brown Boveri	Sweden Switzerland					
	ABB Asea Brown Boveri	Switzerland	ABB	100	Power generation	5,600	5,650
20	Delhaize "Le Lion" SA	Belgium	Food Lion	50	Supermarkets	5,584	1,559

n.a. = Not available.

Source: "The 100 Largest Foreign Investors in the U.S.," *Forbes,* July 22, 1991, pp. 280–84.

growth in a nation causes markets for some products to be lost forever while simultaneously markets for other products are being created. Take the case of a country in the initial stage of development. With little local manufacturing, it is a good market for exporters of consumer goods. As economic development continues, however, businesspeople see profit-making opportunities in (1) producing locally the kinds of consumer goods that require simple technology or (2) assembling from imported parts the products that demand a more advanced technology. Given the tendency of governments to protect local industry, the importation of goods being produced in that country will normally be prohibited. Thus, the exporters of the easy-to-manufacture consumer goods, such as paint, adhesives, toilet articles, clothing, and almost anything made of plastic, will begin to lose this market, which now becomes a new market to producers of the inputs to these "infant industries."

Preferential trading arrangements.   The fact that the great majority of nations has experienced population and GNP/capita growth does not necessarily mean they have attained sufficient size to warrant investment by an

□ **TABLE 2-11**
Population (1989),
GNP/Capita (1989), and
Average Growth Rates of
GNP/capita (1965-89) and
Population (1980-1989)
(Countries with populations
of 1 million or more)

| Ranking | Country* | 1989 | | Annual Growth Rates (percentage) | |
		GNP/Capita (current US$)	Population (millions)	GNP/ Capita†	Population
1.	Switzerland	$29,880	6.6	4.6%	0.5%
2.	Japan	23,810	123.1	4.3	0.6
3.	Norway	22,290	4.2	3.4	0.4
4.	Finland	22,120	5.0	3.2	0.4
5.	Sweden	21,570	8.5	1.8	0.2
6.	United States	20,910	248.8	1.6	1.0
7.	Denmark	20,450	5.1	1.8	0.0
8.	Germany‡	20,440	62.0	2.4	0.0
9.	Canada	19,030	26.2	4.0	0.9
10.	United Arab Emirates	18,430	1.5	n.a	4.6
11.	France	17,820	56.2	2.3	0.4
12.	Austria	17,300	7.6	2.9	0.1
13.	Belgium	16,220	10.0	n.a	0.1
14.	Kuwait	16,150	2.0	−4.0	4.4
15.	Netherlands	15,920	14.8	1.8	0.5
16.	Italy	15,120	57.5	3.0	0.2
17.	United Kingdom	14,610	57.2	2.0	0.2
18.	Australia	14,360	16.8	1.7	1.4
19.	New Zealand	12,070	3.3	0.8	0.7
20.	Singapore	10,450	2.7	7.0	1.2
21.	Hong Kong‖	10,350	5.7	6.3	1.5
22.	Israel	9,790	4.5	2.7	1.7
23.	Spain	9,330	38.8	2.4	0.4
24.	Ireland	8,710	3.5	2.1	0.4
25.	Saudi Arabia	6,020	14.4	2.6	5.0

preferential trading
arrangement an agreement
by a small group of nations
to establish free trade among
themselves while maintaining
trade restrictions with all
other nations

international firm in either (1) an organization for marketing exports from the home country or (2) in a local manufacturing plant. For many products, a number of these nations still lack sufficient market potential. However, when such nations have made some kind of a **preferential trading arrangement** (for example, the European Community and the European Free Trade Association), the resultant market has been so much larger that firms frequently have bypassed what is often the initial step of exporting to make their initial market entry with local manufacturing facilities.

Faster-growing foreign markets.   Not only are new markets appearing overseas, but many of these markets are growing at a faster rate than the home market. One outstanding example has been the growth of the Japanese gross national product and GNP/capita, which increased from $43 billion and $458 in 1960 to $2,920 billion and $23,810 in 1989. Table 2–11 shows that Japan's real growth rate averaged 4.3 percent annually, one of the highest among the industrialized nations. Check the annual growth rates of some of the newly industrializing countries (NICs): Singapore, 7.0 percent; Hong Kong, 6.3 percent; and South Korea, 7.0 percent.

□ **TABLE 2–11**
(concluded)

| Ranking | Country* | 1989 | | Annual Growth Rates (percentage) | |
		GNP/Capita (current US$)	Population (millions)	GNP/ Capita†	Population
100.	Benin	$380	4.6%	−0.1%	3.2%
101.	Pakistan	370	109.9	2.5	3.2
102.	Kenya	360	23.5	2.0	3.9
103.	Haiti	360	6.4	0.3	1.9
104.	China	350	1,113.9	5.7	1.4
105.	India	340	832.5	1.8	2.1
106.	Rwanda	320	6.9	1.2	3.2
107.	Burkina Faso	320	8.8	1.4	2.6
108.	Niger	290	7.4	−2.4	3.4
109.	Mali	270	8.2	1.7	2.5
110.	Zaire	260	34.5	−2.0	3.1
111.	Uganda	250	16.8	−2.8	3.2
112.	Nigeria	250	113.8	0.2	3.4
113.	Madagascar	230	11.3	−1.9	2.9
114.	Sierra Leone	220	4.0	0.2	2.4
115.	Burundi	220	5.3	3.6	2.9
116.	Chad	190	5.5	−1.2	2.4
117.	Nepal	180	18.4	0.6	2.6
118.	Malawi	180	8.2	1.0	3.4
119.	Lao, PDR	180	4.1	n.a.	2.7
120.	Bangladesh	180	110.7	0.4	2.6
121.	Somalia	170	6.1	0.3	3.0
122.	Tanzania	130	23.8	−0.1	3.1
123.	Ethiopia	120	49.5	−0.1	3.0
124.	Mozambique	80	15.3	n.a.	2.7

Notes: n.a. = Not available.
*Only countries for which data were reported to the World Bank are listed.
†GNP/capita growth rates are real.
‡Refers to former Federal Republic of Germany.
‖GNP data refer to GDP.
Source: *World Development Report, 1991* (Washington, D.C.: World Bank, 1991).

Another group of high-growth markets—the OPEC nations, especially those of the Middle East—came into being almost overnight when crude oil prices quadrupled in 1980. Managements suddenly found these new markets to be worth billions of dollars. Iran's imports, for example, increased by eight times in only six years. Interestingly, of the 124 nations in the World Bank table on which Table 2–11 is based, 52 had average annual GNP/capita growth rates higher than the American growth rate for the period from 1965 to 1989.

Improved communications.   This might be considered a supportive reason for opening up new markets overseas, because certainly the ability to communicate with subordinates and customers by telex and telephone has given managers confidence in their ability to control foreign operations if they should undertake them. Managers also know that because of improved transportation, they can either send home-office personnel to help with local problems or be there themselves within a few hours if need be.

Good, relatively inexpensive international communication enables large insurance, banking, and software firms to "body shop," that is, transmit computer-oriented tasks worldwide to a cheap but skilled labor force. New York Life, for example, employs 50 people in Ireland to process insurance claims in a computer linked to the firm's computer in New Jersey. American employees coming to work in the morning find the claims processed during the night in Ireland have been transmitted to their computer in the United States. Some computer consultants in the United States are earning $75 an hour while their Indian counterparts are working for the same firms via an overseas telecommunications link for $5 an hour.[11]

Shorter traveling time has also been responsible for numerous business opportunities because foreign businesspersons have come to the home country to look for new products to import or new technology to buy.[12] The Department of Commerce, in *Business America,* regularly publishes a list of arrivals who desire to contact suppliers.

Faster growth in the markets of developing nations frequently occurs for another reason. When a firm that has supplied the market by exports builds a factory for local production, the host government generally prohibits imports. The firm, which may have had to share the market with 10 or 20 competitors during its exporting days, now has the local market all to itself or shares it with only a small number of other local producers. Before General Tire began manufacturing tires in Chile, probably a dozen exporters, including General Tire, were competing in the market. However, once local production got under way, there was only one supplier for the entire market—General Tire. That is growth.

Obtain greater profits.   As you know, greater profits may be obtained by either increasing total revenue or decreasing the cost of goods sold, and often conditions are such that a firm can do both.

Greater revenue.   Rarely will all of a firm's domestic competitors be in every foreign market in which it is located. Where there is less competition, the firm may be able to obtain a better price for its goods or services. For example, General Tire had only three competitors in Spain for its V-belt line when dozens of brands were available in the United States.

Increasingly, firms are obtaining greater revenue by introducing products in overseas markets and their domestic markets simultaneously. This results in greater sales volume while lowering the cost of goods sold.

Lower cost of goods sold.   Going abroad, whether by exporting or by producing overseas, can frequently lower the cost of goods sold. Increasing total sales by exporting will not only reduce R&D costs per unit, but will also make other economies of scale possible. The president of a Westinghouse division stated, "The people who can spread their R&D and engineering and manufacturing development costs across those three markets [Europe, Japan, and North America] have a substantial advantage." Westinghouse, like many companies, obtains lower unit costs through long production runs made possible by having one factory supply one product internationally.[13] The management of Warner-Lambert, a global health care and consumer products manufacturer, evidently agrees as it states, "Warner-Lambert is addressing each new product as a global opportunity, particularly pharmaceuticals. Only in the context of a worldwide marketplace can Warner-Lambert hope to recapture the escalating costs of bringing new drugs to market. Estimates conservatively place development costs at more than $230 million for a single drug."[14]

Another factor that can positively affect the cost of goods sold is the inducements that some governments offer to attract new investment. For example, Greece offers the following to new investors: (1) investment grants of up to 50 percent of the investment, (2) interest subsidies to cover up to 50 percent of the interest cost of bank loans, and (3) reduction of up to 90 percent of a firm's taxes on profits. Incentives such as these are designed to attract prospective investors and generally are not a sufficient motive for foreign investment. Nevertheless, they do have a positive influence on the cost of goods sold.

Higher overseas profits as an investment motive.   There is no question that greater profits on overseas investments were a strong motive for going abroad in the early 1970s and 1980s. *Business International* reported that 90 percent of 140 Fortune 500 companies surveyed had achieved higher profitably on foreign assets in 1974, for example. The survey showed that for the period from 1978 to 1985 the average growth in foreign earnings outpaced foreign sales growth (5.9 percent versus 4.1 percent), whereas domestic earnings were down an average of 27 percent despite a domestic sales growth of 5.2 percent.[15] Many American firms continue to earn greater profits on their foreign sales. In 1990, of the 100 U.S. firms with the biggest foreign revenues, only 21 obtained more than 50 percent of their revenue overseas but 42 earned over 50 percent of their profits overseas.[16]

Acquire products for the home market.   The relative ease of foreign travel has both created markets for new products and facilitated the search for new products to be introduced into the U.S. market. Americans have traveled abroad in unprecedented numbers since World War II, and in their travels they have encountered products and customs previously unknown to them. Those who acquired the European habit of drinking wine with their meals, for example, returned home wanting to continue this custom. American marketers, sensitive to this trend, have sent buyers around the world to bring back these new products, and many manufacturers have begun to produce them here.

> Minnetonka executives were browsing in a German supermarket when they came across an intriguing product—toothpaste in a pump dispenser, which had not yet appeared in the United States—so they contacted the German manufacturer. This was the beginning of Check-Up toothpaste. A marketing vice president stated, "We make grocery shopping a regular part of our business trips to Europe. It helps give us a jump on our bigger competitors."
>
> American firms have found products such as aseptic beverage cartons (which permit storage without refrigeration), hair-styling mousses, and body fragrance sprays. "The search across oceans and borders for new products is heating up," said the president of General Food's international division.[17]

Let's now look at some reasons for going abroad that are more related to the protection of present markets, profits, and sales.

▢ Protect Markets, Profits, and Sales

Protect domestic market.   Frequently, a firm will go abroad to protect its home market.

Follow customers overseas.   Service companies (accounting, advertising, marketing research, banks, law) will establish foreign operations in markets where their principal accounts are, to prevent competitors from gaining access to those accounts. They know that once a competitor has been able to demonstrate to top management what it can do by servicing a foreign subsidiary, it may be able to take over the entire account. Similarly, suppliers to original equipment manufacturers (for example, battery manufacturers to automobile producers) often follow their large customers. These suppliers have an added advantage in that they are moving into new markets with a guaranteed customer base.

This is true for the over 250 Japanese auto parts makers that have come to the United States, the world's largest auto parts producer, to supply the eight Japanese auto plants in this country. For example, Tokyo Seat has established a subsidiary to make seats, exhaust systems, and other parts for Honda, who also asked Nippodenso, a Japanese producer of radiators and heaters, to set up an American plant.

Companies from the Mitsubishi group in Japan created a version of the Japanese supplier network in Ohio to supply the plant of the Mitsubishi-Chrysler joint venture, Diamond Star. In addition, there are captive suppliers that are not part of the Mitsubishi group. Just an hour's drive away from the Diamond Star factory, a cooperative of 16 nonaffiliated Mitsubishi suppliers called Eagle Wing Industries has built a $37 million plant to produce components such as engine mounts and bumpers. "We had a direct request from Mitsubishi to build this project here in the United States," said Eagle Wings president Isamu Kawasaki.[18] According to a University of Michigan study, a similar situation exists in Honda's Ohio plant. The study found that American-owned manufacturers are supplying only 16 percent of the plant's parts requirements; the other 84 percent come either from Japan or Japanese-owned plants in the United States.[19] But not only auto parts manufacturers are involved. Mitsubishi bank, the lead bank for Honda in Japan, opened an office in Columbus, Ohio, to serve Honda's Ohio plant.[20]

Occasionally, a firm will set up an operation in the home country of a major competitor with the idea of keeping it so occupied defending that market that it will have less energy to compete in the home country of the first company. Although Kodak claimed its decision to open a manufacturing plant in Japan had nothing to do with its Japanese competitor (Fuji), its announcement came just 10 days after Fuji began construction of its first manufacturing facility in the United States.[21]

Using foreign production to lower costs.   A company may also go abroad to protect its domestic market when it faces competition from lower-priced foreign imports. By moving part or all of its production facilities to the countries from which its competition is coming, it can enjoy such advantages as less costly labor, raw materials, or energy. Management may decide to produce certain components abroad and assemble them in the home country; or, if the final product requires considerable labor in the final assembly, it may send the components overseas for this final operation.

Zenith Electronics, the last American-owned producer of television sets in the United States, announced in 1992 that it would move its television assembly operations from Missouri to Mexico. Zenith, which has not earned a profit since 1984, expected to save many millions of dollars in annual labor costs from the move. A spokesman said the cutbacks in Missouri should help the company remain competitive in areas such as color picture tubes.[22]

Zenith was able to take advantage of the lower-cost Mexican labor because of the in-bond (*maquiladora* in Mexico) program, a version of the export processing zones that began in the 1960s in Hong Kong, Taiwan, and Singapore. These all pertain to using foreign production to lower costs.

In-bond (maquiladora) industry. **In-bond plants** (**maquiladoras**) came into existence because of an arrangement between Mexico and the United States. The Mexican government permitted plants in the in-bond area to import parts and processed materials to be assembled, packaged, and processed without paying import duties, provided that the finished products were reexported; the American government permitted the finished product containing the American-made parts and materials to be imported with import duty being paid only on the value added in Mexico.

Presently, there are over 2,000 in-bond plants employing nearly one-half million people.[23] Assembly operations now earn more foreign exchange for Mexico than any other export except petroleum. The leading industrial sectors are automobiles, with 112 plants and 90,500 employees; electronics, with 348 plants and 103,500 employees; and textiles, with 245 plants and 39,000 employees. Nearly 90 percent of the in-bond plants are located on the Mexican-U.S. border, but four inland states have important in-bond industries: Jalisco (39), Yucatan (25), Durango (23), and the state of Mexico (18). U.S. in-bond activities range from stuffing junk mail in envelopes and processing supermarkets' discount coupons to building yachts and home appliances. Because of Japanese firms such as Sanyo, Sony, and Matsushita, and the Korean Samsung Electronics, Tijuana has become the TV assembly capital of the world. Estimates are that 70 percent of all television sets sold in the United States are made there.[24]

Caribbean Basin Initiative. This was started by President Reagan to stimulate investment in the Caribbean nations. The advantages are similar to those enjoyed by Mexican in-bond industries, but the Caribbean Basin has more liberal American textile and apparel import quotas. The American apparel industry sends precut pieces to these countries where they are assembled and returned for sale in the United States. This work has created over 100,000 jobs in Haiti, the Dominican Republic, Jamaica, and other nearby countries.[25]

Singapore's growth triangle. To remain competitive in attracting new industry in the face of rising wages, Singapore is promoting a "growth triangle" covering a 30-mile radius around Singapore. The highly technical phases of production will be done in Singapore, where skilled workers earn up to $400 per month; product assembly will be done in the Indonesian island of Batam (12 miles away) or the Malaysian state of Jahore, where wages are about $50 per month.[26]

Export processing zones. Many developing nations have a form of the export processing zone in which firms, mostly foreign manufacturers, enjoy

In-bond plants (maquiladoras) production facilities in Mexico that temporarily import raw materials, components, or parts duty-free to be manufactured, processed, or assembled with less expensive local labor; the finished or semifinished product is then exported almost a complete absence of taxation and regulation of materials brought into the zones for processing and subsequent reexport.[27]

Protect foreign markets.   Changing the method of going abroad from exporting to overseas production is often necessary to protect foreign markets. The management of a firm supplying a profitable overseas market by exports may begin to note some ominous signs that this market is being threatened.

Lack of foreign exchange.   One of the first signs is a delay in payment by the importers. They have sufficient local currency but are experiencing delays in obtaining foreign exchange from the government's central bank. The credit manager, by checking with the firm's bank and other exporters, learns that this condition is becoming endemic—a reliable sign that the country is facing a lack of foreign exchange. In examining the country's balance of payments, the financial manager may find that its export revenue has declined while the import volume remains high. Experienced exporters know that import and foreign exchange controls are in the offing and that there is a good chance of losing the market, especially if they sell consumer products. In times of foreign exchange scarcity, governments will invariably give priority to the importation of raw materials and capital goods.

If the advantages of making the investment outweigh the disadvantages, the company may decide to protect this market by producing locally. Managers know that once the company has a plant in the country, the government will do its utmost to provide foreign exchange for raw materials to keep the plant, a source of employment, in operation. Because imports of competing products are prohibited, the only competition, if any, will have to come from other local manufacturers.

Local production by competitors.   Lack of foreign exchange is not the only reason why a company might change from exporting to manufacturing in a market. Its export business may be growing and payments may be prompt, but still the firm may be forced to set up a plant in the market. The reason is that competitors are also enjoying good profits on a volume that may be reaching a point at which it will support local production.

Should a competing firm decide to put up a factory in the market, management must decide rapidly whether to follow suit or risk losing the market forever. Managers know that many governments, especially those in developing nations, will not only prohibit further imports once the product is produced in the country but will also permit only two or three other companies to enter so as to maintain a sufficient market for these local firms. General Motors tried for years to enter Spain, but the Spanish government, believing there were already enough automobile manufacturers in the country, refused the company entry. Only when Spain joined the European Community was General Motors permitted to enter.

Downstream markets.   A number of OPEC nations have invested in refining and marketing outlets, such as filling stations and heating oil distributors, to guarantee a market for their crude oil at more favorable prices. As shown in Table 2–10, Petroleos de Venezuela, owner of Citgo, is one of the largest foreign investors in the United States. Kuwait bought Gulf Oil's refining and marketing network in three European countries and also owns 20 percent of British Petroleum, which has the third-largest foreign investment in this country. These are just two examples.[28]

WORLDVIEW
Most Television Sets Are Mexican

No matter what the Sony salesperson tells you, the television set he is selling probably came from Mexico, where it was assembled in an in-bond plant on the Mexican side of the Mexican-U.S. border. And Sony is not the only one. Nearly all the Japanese, Korean, and American television manufacturers are moving their plants from the Far East to Mexico. Don Nibbe, publisher of a trade publication for the in-bond industry says, "Mexico has become the television capital of the world." On average, Japanese companies ship nine TV sets a minute across the border.

Zenith Electronics, the only American-owned television manufacturer in the United States, is the latest to announce that it is relocating television assembly to Mexico from Taiwan. The firm already employs 20,000 workers in Mexico in its other businesses. Sony, Panasonic, and others that operate in Mexico are also slowing production in their home countries.

"The movement to Mexico is mainly because of lower wages," claims Professor Sidney Weintraub at the University of Texas. He said that foreign companies had to be lured to Mexico by low wages before Mexicans could have the opportunity to learn high-tech skills. However, once the Mexican workers had them, foreign TV manufacturers changed their production source as if flicking a remote control.

In the space of only six years, Mexico went from fourth to first place among countries supplying TVs to the United States. In 1985, Mexico accounted for 11 percent of U.S. TV imports, but by October 1991, this value had quadrupled. During the same period, the percentage of TVs coming from Japan fell from 25.1 percent to 3 percent, and the combined total from Taiwan and Korea went from 53.6 percent to 22.5 percent.

U.S. Television Imports (Percent of total imports)

	1985		1991
Korea	32.3%	Mexico	43.2%
Japan	25.1	Korea	14.8
Taiwan	21.3	China	9.2
Mexico	11.0	Malaysia	8.8
Singapore	6.2	Taiwan	7.7
Malaysia	1.7	Thailand	6.2
Hong Kong	1.3	Singapore	3.9
Canada	1.0	Others	6.2

The Pacific Rim countries are concerned about what the proposed North American Free Trade Agreement will bring them. Some observers believe the elimination of tariffs among Canada, Mexico, and the United States will further reduce the presence of Asian countries in the U.S. market. "They don't like it one bit because they're afraid they're going to be discriminated against," Weintraub said.

Sources: "Changing Channels," *McAllen Monitor*, December 90, 1991, p. 1A; "Zenith to Shift TV Assembly Work out of U.S. Plant," *The Wall Street Journal*, October 31, 1991, p. A13.

Protectionism.   When a government sees that local industry is threatened by imports, it may erect import barriers to stop or reduce them.* Even threats to do this can be sufficient to induce the exporter to invest in production facilities in the importing country. This and the high-priced yen, which makes it difficult for Japanese exports to compete with American products, are the principal reasons for Japanese investment in the United States.

Guarantee supply of raw materials.   Few developed nations possess sufficient domestic supplies of raw materials. Japan and Europe are almost totally dependent on foreign sources, and even the United States depends on imports for more than half of its aluminum, chromium, manganese, nickel, tin, and zinc. Furthermore, the Department of the Interior estimates that by the end of

* See Chapter 3 for a discussion of import barriers.

the century, iron, lead, tungsten, copper, potassium, and sulfur will be added to the critical list.

To ensure a continuous supply, manufacturers in the industrialized countries are being forced to invest primarily in the developing nations, where most new deposits are being discovered.[29] Japan, for years, has looked to the United States as a source of raw materials. A Japanese deputy general consul stated,

> **The United States offers an abundance of raw materials. Because Japan has long depended on the United States for various materials, such as grain, coking coal, and lumber, it is entirely logical for Japanese firms to establish facilities close to the sources of these essential raw materials.**[30]

Some analysts claim that the Japanese-American trade flows approximate those between an industrialized and a developing country: the industrialized nation sends manufactured goods to the developing nation in return for raw materials. This is something of an exaggeration; nevertheless, in 1990, 97.8 percent of Japan's exports to the United States consisted of manufactured goods and 40 percent of U.S. exports to Japan were foodstuffs, raw materials, and mineral fuels.[31]

Acquire technology and management know-how.   A reason often cited by foreign firms investing in this country is the acquisition of technology and management know-how. Nippon Mining, for example, a copper mining company, came to Illinois and paid $1 billion for Gould Inc. to acquire technology leadership and market share in producing the copper foil used in printed circuit boards.[32] In a similar situation, Taiwan's Acer Inc. wanted to learn about small business computers so it bought Counterpoint Computers in California for just $20 million and saved millions in research.[33]

Geographic diversification.   Many managements have chosen geographic diversification as a means of maintaining stable sales and earnings when the domestic economy or their industry goes into a slump. Generally, when one economy or industry (building materials, for example) is in a trough, it is at its peak elsewhere in the world. In the early 1980s, the foreign operations of American multinationals were outperforming their domestic counterparts. Sunbeam and Ford, for example, reported that their Mexican business was unusually strong, and Twin-Disc, a transmission manufacturer, said that the slowdown in the European market "wasn't nearly as bad as in the United States."[34] In 1987, earnings jumped 32 percent for Hoechst, the German chemical producer, solely because of the earnings of its American subsidiary, Celanese. "Without those earnings, the company would have shown a profit decline," declared Hoechst's chairman.[35]

Satisfy management's desire for expansion.   The faster growth mentioned previously helps fulfill management's desire for expansion. Stockholders and financial analysts also expect firms to continue to grow, and those companies operating only in the domestic market have found it increasingly difficult to sustain that expectation. As a result, many firms have expanded into foreign markets. This, of course, is what companies based in small countries, such as Nestlé (Switzerland), SKF Bearing (Sweden), and Shell (Great Britain and the Netherlands), discovered decades ago.

Another aspect of this reason sometimes motivates a company's top managers to begin searching for overseas markets. Being able to claim that the firm is a "multinational" creates the impression of importance, which can influence its customers. Sun Microsystems, a manufacturer of computer work stations, recently opened a technical center in Germany and is building a factory in Scotland. "To be a major player in the marketplace, you have to be internationally recognized," said the head of Sun's European operations.[36]

We also know of instances where a company has examined and then entered a market because the president brought it to the attention of the market planners after enjoying a pleasant vacation there.

> How else can you explain the fact that in pre-Castro Cuba, there were three American tire factories in Havana, the "fun capital" of the world, with Miami just 90 miles away? Delivery of tires to Cuba could have been made in hours and at better prices. One of the authors found out why when he spent a winter in Akron working for a tire company. That was the time of the year when the Cuban subsidiary customarily had financial, marketing, and production problems that required the presence of Akron executives.

Political stability.   U.S.-based multinationals have not been motivated by political stability to go overseas, although it is often the prime factor in their choice of where to go. However, European and Third World firms may actually make foreign investments (usually in the United States) for that reason. "The U.S. is a very safe place to invest," says Gilbert de Botton, head of London-based Global Asset Management, which manages $1.6 billion. "You are as comfortable there, if not more so, than you are in your own home."[37]

HOW TO ENTER FOREIGN MARKETS

As you learned in Chapter 1, all of the means for becoming involved in overseas business may be subsumed in just two activities: (1) exporting to a foreign market or (2) manufacturing in it.

▫ Exporting

Most firms have begun their involvement in overseas business by exporting—that is, selling some of their regular production overseas. This method requires little in the way of investment and is relatively free of risks. It is an excellent means of getting a feel for international business without committing any great amount of human or financial resources. If management does decide to export, it must choose between *direct* and *indirect* exporting.

indirect exporting the exporting of goods and services through various types of home-based exporters

Indirect exporting.   **Indirect exporting** is simpler than direct exporting because it requires neither special expertise nor large cash outlays. Exporters based in their home country will do the work. Management merely follows instructions. Among the exporters available are (1) *manufacturers' export agents,* who sell for the manufacturer; (2) *export commission agents*, who buy for their overseas customers; (3) *export merchants*, who purchase and sell for their own account; and (4) *international firms,* which use the goods overseas (mining, construction, and petroleum companies are examples).

Indirect exporters, however, pay a price for such service: (1) they will pay a commission to the first three kinds of exporters; (2) foreign business can be lost if exporters decide to change their sources of supply; and (3) firms gain little experience from these transactions. This is why many managements that begin in this manner generally change to direct exporting.

direct exporting the exporting of goods and services by the firm that produces them

sales company a business established for the purpose of marketing goods and services, not producing them

Direct exporting.   To engage in **direct exporting,** management must assign the job of handling the export business to someone within the firm. The simplest arrangement is to give someone, usually the sales manager, the responsibility for developing the export business. Domestic employees may handle the billing, credit, and shipping initially, and if the business expands, a separate export department may be set up. A firm that has been exporting to wholesale importers in an area and servicing them by visits from either home office personnel or foreign-based sales representatives frequently finds that sales have grown to a point that will support a complete marketing organization.

Management may then decide to set up a **sales company** in the area. The sales company will import in its own name from the parent and will invoice in local currency. It may employ the same channels of distribution, though the new organization may permit the use of a more profitable arrangement. This type of organization can grow quite large, often invoicing several millions of dollars annually. Before building a plant in Mexico, for many years Eastman Kodak imported and resold cameras and photographic supplies while doing a large business in local film developing. Many firms that began with local repair facilities later expanded to produce simple components. Gradually, they produced more of the product locally until, after a period of time, they were manufacturing all of the components in the country.

A firm's foreign business may evolve sequentially over the path just traced, or a company may move directly to foreign production (nonsequentially) for any of the reasons discussed previously in the section "Why Go Abroad?"

◻ Foreign Manufacturing

When management does decide to become involved in foreign manufacturing, it generally has five distinct alternatives available, though not all of them may be feasible in a particular country. These are:

1. Wholly owned subsidiary.
2. Joint venture.
3. Licensing agreement.
4. Franchising.
5. Contract manufacturing.

A sixth arrangement, the *management contract,* is utilized by both manufacturing and service companies to earn income by providing management expertise for a fee.

Wholly owned subsidiary.   The company that wishes to own a foreign subsidiary outright may (1) start from the ground up by building a new plant, (2) acquire a going concern, or (3) purchase its distributor, thus obtaining a distribution network familiar with its products. In this case, of course, production facilities will have to be built. American companies certainly prefer wholly owned subsidiaries, but they do not have a marked preference for any of the three means of obtaining them.

However, this is not the case for foreign investors in the United States, who prefer to acquire going concerns for the instant access to the market they provide. Moreover, they also have one less competitor after the purchase.

☐ **TABLE 2–12   Investment Outlays and Number of Investments, 1984–1990**

	Outlays (millions of dollars)							Number						
	1984	1985	1986	1987	1988	1989	1990	1984	1985	1986	1987	1988	1989	1990
Total investments	15,197	23,106	39,177	40,310	72,692	71,163	64,423	764	753	1,040	978	1,424	1,580	1,565
Acquisitions	11,836	20,083	31,450	33,933	64,855	59,708	56,773	315	390	555	543	869	837	796
Establishments	3,361	3,023	7,728	6,377	7,837	11,455	7,651	449	363	485	435	555	743	769

Rather than build a U.S. plant, YKK, a leading Japanese zipper manufacturer, paid $50 million for Universal Fasteners, a competitor based in Kentucky. "They bought instant market share with no headaches," said a banker familiar with the transaction.[38]

In 1990, as in previous years, nearly 90 percent of the $64.4 billion spent by foreign direct investors was for acquiring American firms. Only $7.7 billion was spent to establish new firms.[39] Table 2–12 points out an interesting fact. The average size of an acquisition in 1990 was seven times that of an investment in a new firm ($71.3 million versus $9.95 million).

Sometimes it is not possible to have a wholly owned foreign subsidiary. The host government may not permit it, the firm may lack either capital or expertise to undertake the investment alone, or there may be tax and other advantages that favor a joint venture.

joint venture a cooperative effort among two or more organizations who share a common interest in a business enterprise or undertaking

Joint venture.   A **joint venture** may be (1) a corporate entity between an international company and local owners, (2) a corporate entity between two or more international companies, or (3) a cooperative undertaking between two or more firms of a limited-duration project. Large construction jobs are frequently handled by this last form.

Ford and Volkswagen formed a novel joint venture in which their operations in Argentina and Brazil were merged into a holding company, Autolatina, in an effort to eliminate losses suffered by both. The new company, owned 51 percent by VW and 49 percent by Ford (although the venture is considered by both to be an equal partnership), has $4 billion in sales, 76,600 employees, and 15 plants (10 in Brazil). "While Ford will still be Ford and VW will still be VW," said the president of Ford-Brazil, "the merger will provide greater efficiency and technical capacity, a sort of pooling of resources that will help us both." Autolatina uses the facilities and parts of both partners and is developing a new version of a car produced by VW-Brazil, which is called Fox™ when exported to the United States and Canada.[40]

Another huge joint venture, recently formed by Coca-Cola and Nestlé, is the Coca-Cola Nestlé Refreshments Company, which will make and sell ready-to-serve coffee, tea, and chocolate drinks worldwide. Experts say that by combining Nestlé's well-known trademarks with Coca-Cola's massive global distribution system, the joint venture will bring coffee and tea products to worldwide markets much faster than either company could do it alone.[41]

When the government of a host country requires companies to have some local participation, foreign firms must engage in a joint venture with local owners to do business in that country. In some situations, however, a foreign firm will seek local partners even when there is no local requirement to do so.

Strong nationalism.   Strong nationalistic sentiment may cause the foreign firm to try to lose its identity by joining with local investors. Care must be taken with this strategy, however. Although a large number of people in many developing countries dislike multinationals for "exploiting" them, they still believe, often with good reason, that the products of the foreign companies are superior to the products of purely national firms. One solution to this ambivalence has been to form a joint venture in which the local partners are highly visible, give it an indigenous name, and then advertise that a foreign firm (actually the partner) is supplying the technology. Even wholly owned subsidiaries have followed this strategy.

> Eastman Kodak has eliminated the word *Kodak* from the names of its 100-percent-owned subsidiaries in Venezuela, Mexico, Chile, Peru, and Colombia. Kodak-Venezuela has become Foto Interamericana, and Kodak's large manufacturing company in Mexico is now called Industria Fotografica Interamericana.

Acquire expertise, tax, and other benefits.   Other factors that influence managements to enter joint ventures are the ability to acquire an expertise that is lacking, special tax benefits some governments extend to companies with local partners, or the need for additional capital and experienced personnel.

> Merck, the largest U.S. maker of ethical drugs, spent $313 million to acquire 50.5 percent of Banyu Pharmaceutical in Japan. Management had been dissatisfied with the performance of Merck's Japanese subsidiary in the world's second-largest ethical drug market. With this acquisition, the 600-person sales force of Merck-Japan was augmented by Banyu's 350 sales representatives. Merck's chairman said, "To bring new products effectively to market in Japan required a larger and more effective marketing organization. With a controlling interest in Banyu, I would hope for a better penetration of the Japanese market."[42]
>
> To take advantage of Israel's lower labor costs and the 1985 U.S.–Israel Trade Agreement, which (1) reduced import duties on Israeli-made shirts and (2) permits them quota-free access to the United States, Van Heusen decided to buy the production facilities of an insolvent Israeli clothing manufacturer. When the government refused to sell on Van Heusen's terms, the company formed a joint venture with another Israeli textile-and-apparel conglomerate. Van Heusen will purchase the plant's output for five years, with the option to extend the agreement if satisfied with the local partner's performance, and will have exclusive control over marketing. Although it has trained Israeli engineers and will maintain its own engineers at the operation, the Israeli partner has had to invest all of the capital to expand an existing plant.[43]

Some firms, as a matter of policy, enter joint ventures to reduce investment risk. Their strategy is to enter into a joint venture with either native partners or another worldwide company. Still others, such as Ford and Volkswagen, have joined together to achieve economies of scale. Incidentally, any division of ownership in a joint venture is possible unless there are specific legal requirements.

Disadvantages.   While the joint venture arrangement offers the advantage of less commitment of financial and managerial resources, and thus less risk, there are some disadvantages for the foreign firm. One, obviously, is the fact that profits must be shared. Furthermore, if the law allows the foreign investors to have no more than a 49 percent participation (common in developing countries), they may not have control. This is because the stock markets in these countries are either small or nonexistent, so it is generally impossible to distribute the shares widely enough to permit the foreign firm with its 49 percent to be the largest stockholder.

Lack of control over the joint venture is the reason why many managements resist making such arrangements. They feel that they must have tight control of their foreign subsidiaries to obtain an efficient allocation of investments and production and to maintain a coordinated marketing plan worldwide. For example, local partners might wish to export to markets that the global company serves from its own plants, or they might want to make the complete product locally when the global company's strategy is to produce only certain components there and import the rest from other subsidiaries.[44]

In recent years, numerous governments of developing nations have passed laws requiring local majority ownership for the purpose of giving control of firms within their borders to their own citizens. Despite these laws, control with a minority ownership is still feasible.

Control with minority ownership.   There have been occasions when the foreign partner has been able to circumvent the spirit of the law and ensure its control by taking 49 percent of the shares and giving 2 percent to its local law firm or some other trusted national.

Another method is to take in a local majority partner, such as a government agency, an insurance company, or a financial institution, that is content to invest merely for a return while leaving the venture's management to the foreign partner. If neither arrangement can be made, the foreign company may still control the joint venture, at last in the areas of major concern, by means of a *management contract*.

management contract an arrangement by which one firm provides management in all or specific areas to another firm

Management contract.   The **management contract** is an arrangement under which a company provides managerial know-how in some or all functional areas to another party for a fee that ranges from 2 to 5 percent of sales. International companies make such contracts with (1) firms in which they have no ownership (examples: Hilton Hotel provides management for nonowned overseas hotels that use the Hilton name, and Delta provides management assistance to foreign airlines), (2) joint venture partners, and (3) wholly owned subsidiaries. The last arrangement is made solely for the purpose of allowing the parent to siphon off some of the subsidiary's profits. This becomes extremely important when, as in many foreign exchange–poor nations, the parent firm is limited in the amount of profits it can repatriate. Moreover, because the fee is an expense, the subsidiary receives a tax benefit.

Used in joint ventures.   Management contracts can enable the global partner to control many aspects of a joint venture even when holding only a minority position. If it supplies key personnel, such as the production and technical managers, the global company can be assured of product quality with which its name may be associated as well as be able to earn additional income by selling the joint venture inputs manufactured in the home plant. This is possible because the larger global company is more vertically integrated. A local paint factory, for example, might have to import certain semiprocessed pigments and driers that the foreign partner produces in its home country for domestic operations. If these can be purchased elsewhere at a lower price, the local majority could insist on other sources of supply. This rarely happens, because the production and technical managers can argue that only inputs from their employer will produce a satisfactory product. They are the experts, and they generally have the final word.

Purchasing commission.   There is another source of income that the global or multinational company derives not only from firms with which it has a management contract but also from joint ventures and wholly owned subsidiaries. That source is a commission for acting as purchasing agent of imported raw materials and equipment. This relieves the affiliates of having to establish credit lines with foreign suppliers and assures them that they will receive the same materials used by the foreign partner. The commission received for this service averages about 5 percent of invoice value and is in addition to the management contract fee.

Licensing.   Frequently, worldwide companies are called on to furnish technical assistance to firms that have sufficient capital and management strength. By means of a **licensing** agreement, one firm (the licensor) will grant to another firm (the licensee) the right to use any kind of expertise, such as manufacturing processes (patented or unpatented), marketing procedures, and trademarks for one or more of the licensor's products.

licensing a contractual arrangement in which one firm grants access to its patents, trade secrets, or technology to another for a fee

> **General Tire, before being bought by Continental, the German tire manufacturer, was both a licensor and a licensee. It licensed some firms to use its tire technology and others to use its know-how to produce plastic film. At the same time, it made licensing agreements with manufacturers of conveyor belting, V belting, and car batteries to use their technology in General Tire plants overseas.**

The licensee generally pays a fixed sum when signing the licensing agreement and then pays a royalty of from 2 to 5 percent of sales over the life of the contract (five to seven years, with option for renewal). The exact amount of the royalty will depend on the amount of assistance given and the relative bargaining power of the two parties.

In the past, licensing was not a primary source of income for globals and multinationals. This has changed, however, especially in this country, because (1) the courts are upholding patent infringement claims more than they used to, (2) patent holders are more vigilant in suing violators, and (3) the Reagan and Bush administrations are pressing foreign governments to enforce their patent laws.[45]

This is forcing foreign companies to obtain licenses instead of making illegal copies. Texas Instruments, for instance, expected to collect over $250 million in royalties through 1990—almost as much as the company's 1987 total profit.[46] It is estimated that Union Carbide, which has a special division to sell its technology and services, added 5 percent to its pre-tax profit just by licensing its process to make a single product—polyethylene, a plastic. According to the Department of Commerce, American firms received $15.3 billion from the overseas sale of royalties and license fees in 1990 and paid out only $2.6 billion.[47]

However, more than know-how is licensed. In the fashion industry, a number of designers license the use of their names. Pierre Cardin, the largest such licensor, has 840 licenses worldwide on everything from skis to frying pans. These earn him $75 million annually, including $12 million from 32 American licensees. Even Russia pays him $.75 million every year.

Are you giving Coca-Cola free advertising on your T-shirt? The company's manager for merchandise licensing expects the company to make millions from an agreement with the founder of Gloria Vanderbilt. He says the firm agreed to the arrangement because "clothes enhance our image. The money is not important."

Another industry, magazine publishing, is licensing overseas editions. You can buy *Cosmopolitan* in the native language in over a dozen countries, *Playboy* in 10, and *Penthouse* in 5. For some reason, *High Technology* appears only in Japan.

Despite the opportunity to obtain a sizable income from licensing, many firms, especially those that produce high-tech products, will not grant licenses. They fear that a licensee will become a competitor upon expiration of the agreement or that the licensee will aggressively seek to market the products outside of its territory. At one time, licensors routinely inserted a clause in the licensing agreement that prohibited exports, but most governments will not accept such a prohibition.

Franchising. In recent years, American firms have gone overseas with a new kind of licensing—**franchising.** Franchising permits the franchisee to sell products or services under a highly publicized brand name and a well-proven set of procedures with a carefully developed and controlled marketing strategy. Of the 35,000 overseas outlets operated by 374 American franchising companies, fast-food operations (such as McDonald's, Kentucky Fried Chicken™, and Tastee-Freeze™) are the most numerous—McDonald's alone has about 2,500 outlets in 40 countries (see Figure 2–3). As Table 2–13 indicates, Canada is the dominant market with 9,031 units, Japan is second with 7,366, and Australia is third with 2,816.

Other types of franchisors are hotels (Hilton™, Holiday Inn™), business services (Muzak™, Manpower™), soft drinks (Coca-Cola, Orange Crush™), home maintenance (Servicemaster, Nationwide Exterminating), and automotive products (Midas™).

> **franchising** a form of licensing in which one firm contracts with another to operate a certain type of business under an established name according to specific rules

Contract manufacturing. International firms employ **contract manufacturing** in two ways. One way is as a means of entering a foreign market without investing in plant facilities. The firm contracts with a local manufacturer to produce products for it according to its specifications. The firm's sales organization markets the products under its own brand, just as Montgomery Ward sells washing machines made by Norge.

> **contract manufacturing** an arrangement in which one firm contracts with another to produce products to its specifications but assumes responsibility for marketing

When Gates Rubber licensed its V belt technology to General Tire's Chilean plant, it drew up a novel licensing agreement that included contract manufacturing. General Tire was obliged to produce part of its output with the Gates label. Gates executives knew that in Chile, once General Tire began production, the government would stop the importation of all V belts, including theirs. Gates would gain in a number of ways: (1) it would earn a royalty on all belts made in Chile, (2) it would have belts made in Chile to Gates specifications without making any investment in production facilities, and (3) competition from a dozen importers would be eliminated. There would be only one local competitor, General Tire. General Tire gained because it increased its product mix and offered another product to its present channels of distribution.

The second way is to subcontract assembly work or the production of parts to independent companies overseas. Although the international firm has no equity in the subcontractor, this practice does have some resemblances to

☐ **FIGURE 2–3   International Franchising (U.S. Firms) in 1988**

Asia 2097

Canada 9544

United Kingdom 2843

Continental Europe 4975

Japan 8975

Mexico 684

Caribbean 579

Africa 760

Central America 212

South America 618

Australia 2858

New Zealand 498

Franchising companies–374
Number of franchising outlets–35,046

foreign direct investment. When the international firm is the largest or only customer of the subcontractors, it has in effect created in another country a new company that generates employment and foreign exchange for the host nation. Frequently, the international firm will lend capital to the foreign contractor in the same way that a global or multinational firm will lend funds to its subsidiary. Because of these similarities, this practice has gained the name of "foreign direct investment without investment."

Strategic alliances.   Faced with (1) expanding global competition, (2) the growing cost of research, product development, and marketing, and (3) the need to move faster in carrying out their global strategies, many firms are forming **strategic alliances** with competitors (called competitive alliances), suppliers, and customers. Their aim is to achieve faster market entry and start-up; to gain access to new products, technologies, and markets; and to share costs, resources, and risks.

Alliances include various types of partnerships. Companies wanting to share technology will cross-license their technology (each will license its technology to the other). If their aim is to pool research and design resources, they will form an R&D partnership. For example, Texas Instruments and Hitachi, who have had a technical information exchange since 1988, agreed in 1991 to develop together a common design and manufacturing process for 64-megabit DRAMs. Each firm will handle its own mass production and marketing.[48]

strategic alliance
cooperation between competitors, customers, or suppliers that may take one of various forms

□ **TABLE 2-13   Location of International Franchisees of American Franchisors**

Types of Franchises	Total	Canada	Mexico	Caribbean	U.K.	Other Europe	Australia	Japan	Other Asia	Other
Total	35,046	9,544	684	579	2,843	4,975	2,858	8,975	2,097	2,491
Restaurants (all kinds)	6,996	1,338	146	213	726	772	750	1,827	546	678
Hotels, motels, and campgrounds	518	238	22	19	28	77	13	9	31	81
Recreation, entertainment, and travel	327	194	0	1	17	25	34	41	0	15
Automotive products and services	1,708	683	25	31	15	505	128	143	49	129
Business aids and services	5,851	2,762	8	8	459	732	774	890	103	113
Construction, home improvement, maintenance, and cleaning services	2,813	1,188	0	7	502	104	27	647	17	321
Educational products and services	5,583	520	124	7	106	183	262	1,591	665	43
Laundry and drycleaning services	27	21	0	0	1	0	0	0	5	0
Rental services (auto-truck)	5,548	553	268	265	378	1,682	417	579	471	935
Retailing (nonfood)	3,574	1,378	78	9	548	720	429	227	81	104
Retailing (food, nonconvenience)	2,101	669	13	19	63	175	22	939	129	72

Source: Exhibit 127, *Franchising in the Economy 1988–1990*, p. 100.

Alliances may be joint ventures.   Other companies carry the cooperation further by forming joint ventures in manufacturing and marketing. In 1986, Westinghouse and Toshiba formed an equity joint venture to produce color display tubes for computer terminals and picture tubes for TV sets. Westinghouse, which was making monochrome tubes, formed the alliance to get the technology to produce color tubes. The joint venture gave Toshiba an opportunity to be involved in a manufacturing facility that could supply tubes to its TV plant in Tennessee. The Japanese also expected that another U.S.-based venture would help deflect protectionist pressure from Toshiba.[49] Toshiba provided the technology and Westinghouse provided a factory building and helped arrange financing, including $46 million in low-cost public loans. However, within just two years, Westinghouse had sold its interest to Toshiba, which then became the sole owner of the facility.[50]

Alliances can be mergers and acquisitions.   Swedish ASEA and Swiss Brown Bovari, both energy generation and transmission specialists, merged to form an $18 billion company. The reason, according to the CEO of the new firm, was that the two firms individually were too small to compete with U.S. and Japanese rivals such as Westinghouse, General Electric, Hitachi, and Toshiba.

Future of alliances.   There is no question that some alliances have accomplished what they set out to accomplish. CFM International, the alliance between General Electric and France's Snecma, has been producing jet engines for 17 years. It has taken orders for 10,300 engines worth $38 billion and has delivered over 4,000. Airbus Industrie, an alliance among British, French, German, and Spanish aircraft manufacturers, is now the world's second-largest commercial aircraft producer.

Nevertheless, many alliances fail or are taken over by one of the partners. The management consulting firm, McKinsey & Co., surveyed 150 companies involved in alliances that had been terminated. It found that three quarters of the alliances had been taken over by Japanese partners.[51] Professor Chalmers Johnson, an expert on Japan, warns, "I find the idea of joint ventures no longer makes any sense at all. They are a way for the Japanese to acquire technology."[52]

PATHS TO MULTINATIONALISM

Many large global and multinational firms with numerous manufacturing subsidiaries all over the world began their foreign operations by exporting. As this stage became successful, they established sales companies overseas to market their exports. Where the sales company was able to develop a sufficiently large market, a plant to assemble imported parts was set up. Finally, the complete product was manufactured locally. However, this sequence should not be construed as the only way to become involved in foreign markets. In some countries, conditions may require a complete manufacturing plant as the means of initial entry. International companies today are simultaneously employing all of the methods we have discussed to reach their worldwide markets.

> **Gillette, in its 1990 annual report, states that "manufacturing operations are conducted at 48 facilities in 25 countries, and products are distributed through wholesalers, retailers, and agents in over 200 countries and territories."**

SUMMARY

The volume of international trade in goods and services measured in current dollars has surpassed $4 trillion. Merchandise exports in 1990 were 26 times what they were in 1960. Over three fourths of the industrialized nations' exports are destined for other industrialized nations, and the percentage appears to be growing. The top three U.S. trading partners for both exports and imports are Canada, Japan, and Mexico. Canada's exports to the United States have increased appreciably since the U.S.–Canada Free Trade Agreement went into effect. Mexico is now negotiating to become the third member of the agreement.

Foreign investment also has grown rapidly and now totals about $1 trillion. The foreign direct investment of American firms is almost double that of British firms, the second-largest group of foreign investors. They, in turn, have invested 24 percent more overseas than Japanese firms have. The direction of investment follows the direction of international trade; that is, developed nations invest in each other just as they trade with each other. Foreign direct investment in the United States has risen from $7 billion in 1960 to $403 billion in 1990. Companies from just four nations—Great Britain, Japan, the Netherlands, and Germany—own 70 percent of the total foreign direct investment in the United States.

Companies go abroad (exporting and foreign investment) to increase profits and sales and to protect markets, profits, and sales.[53] A reason often cited by foreign firms that buy American companies is to acquire technology and management know-how. Foreign investment also enables a company to diversify geographically.

The two basic means of going overseas are exporting to markets or producing in them. Exporting may be done directly or indirectly. A firm may become involved in foreign production through various methods: (1) wholly owned subsidiaries, (2) joint ventures, (3) licensing, (4) contract manufacturing, and (5) franchising.

Companies are trying to globalize faster by forming partnerships called strategic alliances with competitors, supplier and customers. Their aim is to achieve faster market entry and start-up; to gain access to new technologies, products, and markets; and to share costs, resources, and risks. Alliances take many forms. They range from mergers and joint ventures to cross-licensing, R&D partnerships, management/marketing agreements, and production agreements. Although some alliances are successful, many fail or are taken over by one of the partners after it has acquired the knowledge from the other partner. A survey of 150 companies involved in terminated alliances found that three quarters of the alliances had been taken over by the Japanese partners.

QUESTIONS

1. The greater part of international trade consists of an exchange of raw materials from the developing nations for the manufactured goods from the developed nations. True or false? Explain.

2. The volume of exports has increased, but the ranking of U.S. trading partners in order of importance remains the same year after year. True or false? Of what use is this information to a businessperson?

3. What should the quintupling of world exports in just 30 years indicate to businesspeople?

4. Knowing that a nation is a major trading partner of another signifies what to a marketing analyst?

5. The value of Japan's foreign direct investment went from $32.2 billion in 1983 to $154.4 billion in 1989, an increase of 480 percent. Did it cost the Japanese investors 480 percent more yen to make these investments in 1989?

6. How can a firm protect its domestic market by investing overseas?

7. Why might management decide to bypass indirect exporting and go to direct exporting right from the start?

8. Under what conditions might a company prefer a joint venture to a wholly owned subsidiary when making a foreign investment?

9. *a.* Why would the foreign partner in a joint venture wish to have a management contract with the local partner?
   b. Why would a global or multinational require a wholly owned foreign subsidiary to sign a management contract when it already owns the subsidiary?

10. *a.* What are in-bond plants?
    b. What simple act by Congress probably would put them out of business?

◻ MINICASE 2–1

Method of Entry for Local Manufacturing—The McGrew Company

The McGrew Company, a manufacturer of peanut combines, has for years sold an appreciable number of machines in Brazil. However, a Brazilian firm has begun to manufacture them, and McGrew's local distributor has told Jim Allen, the president, that if McGrew expects to maintain its share of the market, it will also have to manufacture locally. Allen is in a quandary. The market is too good to lose, but McGrew has had no experience with foreign manufacturing operations. Because Brazilian sales and repairs have been handled by the distributor, no one in McGrew has had any firsthand experience in the country.

Allen has made some rough calculations that indicate the firm can make money by manufacturing in Brazil, but the firm's lack of marketing expertise in the country troubles him. He calls in Joan Beal, the export manager, and asks her to prepare a list of all the options open to McGrew, with their advantages and disadvantages. Allen also asks Beal to indicate her preference.

1. Assume you are Joan Beal. Prepare a list of all the options, and give the advantages of each.
2. Which of the options would you recommend?
3. Assuming the president's calculations are correct and a factory to produce locally the number of machines that McGrew now exports to Brazil will offer a satisfactory return on the investment, what special information about Brazil will you want to gather?

□ MINICASE 2–2

Quick Research—The Stanton Bearing Company

The Stanton Bearing Company is a medium-size manufacturer of tapered, needle, and cylindrical roller bearings. Bill Stanton, the president, is dissatisfied with the company's growth and has been thinking about exporting to increase sales. At a university seminar, Stanton heard about the exporting successes of some small firms whose sales are about the same as those of the Stanton Bearing Company ($25 million annually). He learned that the U.S. Department of Commerce gathers statistics on exports and imports and publishes them in *U.S. Merchandise Trade: Exports, General Imports, and Imports for Consumption,* FT925. A copy is available in the Government Documents section of the local university.

He calls in Jane Anderson, the marketing manager, and asks her to do some quick research. "Jane, perhaps there is a market overseas for our products. I heard that the university has a Department of Commerce publication called

FT925, which gives the monthly and cumulative totals by product for countries importing that product from the United States and for countries exporting it to the United States. The December issue will give you the total for the whole year (see page 73). Please send your assistant to the university to make a copy of the data for our products from this FT925. This will tell us which countries are now buying our American competitors' bearings and which countries are our major competitors here in this market. Of course, I think we already know our competitors. Still, it won't hurt to check."

1. What are the top five importing markets for each category of bearings that the company makes?
2. What are the top five exporting nations for each category of bearings?

SUPPLEMENTARY READINGS

Competitive Alliances

"ABB: The New Energy Powerhouse." *International Management,* June 1988, pp. 24–30.

"ASEA Brown Bovari: Full of Contradictions." *Eurobusiness,* July 1989, pp. 24–27.

"Business without Borders." *U.S. News & World Report,* June 20, 1988, pp. 48–53.

"Collaborative Marketing." *Business Marketing,* April 1987, pp. 33–34.

"Competitive Alliances: Forging Ties Abroad." *International Management,* March 1987, p. 57.

"Competitive Alliances Redefine Companies." *Management Review,* April 1991, pp. 14–18.

"Facing the Realities of Global Alliances." *International Management,* April 1986, pp. 22–30.

"How Business Is Creating Europe, Inc." *Business Week,* September 7, 1987, pp. 40–41.

"Is U.S. Business Giving Away Its Technology—Again?" *Fortune,* September 11, 1989, p. 10.

"Making Global Alliances Work." *Fortune,* December 17, 1990, pp. 121–26.

"Strategic Alliances in LA: New Opportunities for Profit." *Business Latin America,* April 29, 1991, pp. 137–43.

"The Down Side of Competitive Alliances and How to Cut Your Risks." *Business International,* January 12, 1987, p. 15.

"The Latest Business Game." *The Economist,* May 5, 1990, pp. 16–17.

"With Allies Like These." *The Economist,* November 19, 1988, pp. 75–76.

Foreign Investment

"America Still Buys the World." *The Economist,* September 17, 1988, pp. 71–72.

"Are the Japanese Hollowing Out Their Economy?" *International Management,* February 1989, pp. 36–39.

Constantinos, C. Markides, and Norman Berg. "Manufacturing Offshore Is Bad Business." *Harvard Business Review,* September–October 1988, pp. 113–20.

"Foreign Direct Investment in Developing Countries." *Kredietbank Weekly Bulletin,* June 5, 1987, pp. 1–6.

"Foreign Investment Regulations at a Glance." *Business Latin America,* February 29, 1988, pp. 68–69.

"Hunting Heads in the Global Village." *International Management,* May 1990, pp. 52–54.

"Supersonic Boom." *Time,* September 30, 1991, pp. 48–49.

"The International Investment Position of the United States in 1990." *The Survey of Current Business,* June 1991, pp. 24–30.

"The Myth of Economic Sovereignty." *The Economist,* June 23, 1990, p. 67.

"The Rising Power of the Pacific." *Fortune,* Pacific Rim 1990, pp. 8–12.

"U.S. International Transactions, First Quarter 1991." *Survey of Current Business,* June 1991, pp. 36–43.

Table 2. VALUE OF EXPORTS AND GENERAL IMPORTS BY SITC COMMODITY GROUPINGS BY COUNTRY—Con.

[IN THOUSANDS OF DOLLARS. SEE EXPLANATION OF STATISTICS FOR ADDITIONAL INFORMATION ON COVERAGE, DEFINITION OF EXPORT AND IMPORT VALUATIONS, ESTIMATING PROCEDURES, AND SOURCES OF ERROR IN THE DATA.]

74610 BALL BEARINGS—Con.

COUNTRY	CURRENT MONTH EXPORTS F.A.S. VALUE BASIS	CURRENT MONTH GENERAL IMPORTS CUSTOMS VALUE BASIS	CUMULATIVE YEAR TO DATE EXPORTS F.A.S. VALUE BASIS	CUMULATIVE YEAR TO DATE GENERAL IMPORTS CUSTOMS VALUE BASIS
SWITZLD	76	843	540	7 154
THAILND	-	162	1 356	3 772
TURKEY	18	233	755	2 947
U KING	1 057	530	7 674	9 743
VENEZ	214	-	2 552	17
YUGOSLV	-	121	449	2 881
OTH CTY	395	12	4 668	248
TOTAL	10 914	37 516	212 139	509 128

74620 TAPERED ROLLER BEARINGS

COUNTRY	EXPORTS	GENERAL IMPORTS	EXPORTS	GENERAL IMPORTS
ARGENT	112	-	685	692
AUSTRAL	514	-	6 939	1 101
BELGIUM	185	-	3 338	40
BRAZIL	409	79	5 709	1 144
CANADA	3 165	583	45 717	11 175
CHILE	10	-	733	-
CHINA M	9	607	1 078	12 063
CHINA T	31	-	742	158
COLOMB	23	-	2 228	-
FR GERM	945	1 466	15 790	20 008
FRANCE	264	470	6 276	4 692
HG KONG	92	356	553	879
HUNGARY	-	502	-	3 862
INDIA	202	-	2 353	4
ITALY	456	102	5 174	2 102
JAPAN	401	2 357	5 451	41 768
KOR REP	117	2	2 317	143
MEXICO	1 686	247	16 094	2 376
REP SAF	244	-	6 146	120
ROMANIA	-	-	-	992
SINGARP	91	-	2 348	69
SPAIN	132	8	1 416	33
SWEDEN	503	11	1 829	143
THAILND	38	-	603	-
TURKEY	-	-	682	-
U KING	612	317	8 431	4 888
VENEZ	333	-	3 946	7
OTH CTY	457	107	6 133	1 622
TOTAL	11 031	7 211	152 890	110 083

74630 SPHERICAL ROLLER BEARINGS

COUNTRY	EXPORTS	GENERAL IMPORTS	EXPORTS	GENERAL IMPORTS
AUSTRAL	108	-	1 480	132
AUSTRIA	158	47	676	1 149
BRAZIL	116	-	1 112	8
CANADA	735	16	18 400	268
FR GERM	684	1 351	5 919	14 171
FRANCE	24	49	544	1 088
HG KONG	11	33	1 016	33
ITALY	60	527	274	4 935
JAPAN	45	455	963	4 851
MEXICO	170	-	3 027	24
POLAND	-	39	-	932
REP SAF	-	-	668	-
SINGARP	50	-	1 128	-
SWEDEN	179	918	8 451	10 049
U KING	238	479	1 175	3 763
OTH CTY	271	112	2 467	1 764
TOTAL	2 849	4 028	47 299	43 168

74640 NEEDLE ROLLER BEARINGS

COUNTRY	EXPORTS	GENERAL IMPORTS	EXPORTS	GENERAL IMPORTS
AUSTRAL	496	-	975	3
BELGIUM	166	2	1 639	11
BRAZIL	112	33	774	1 393
CANADA	701	71	10 399	282
CHINA T	23	78	457	1 505
FR GERM	1 190	813	10 234	10 042
FRANCE	29	25	310	652
JAPAN	87	968	1 899	10 974
MEXICO	26	-	707	15
SINGARP	52	-	865	11
U KING	241	60	2 101	550
OTH CTY	425	26	2 483	586
TOTAL	3 547	2 075	32 334	26 025

74650 CYLINDRICAL ROLLER BEARINGS NES

COUNTRY	EXPORTS	GENERAL IMPORTS	EXPORTS	GENERAL IMPORTS
AUSTRAL	288	3	1 226	21
AUSTRIA	-	206	26	7 344
BELGIUM	142	-	2 112	10
BRAZIL	64	27	1 040	146
CANADA	1 710	132	22 700	1 893
FR GERM	5	2 133	1 350	24 667
FRANCE	200	737	1 279	4 515
ITALY	68	245	320	889
JAPAN	3	938	984	10 984
KOR REP	7	-	2 550	-
MEXICO	98	-	2 924	7

74650 CYLINDRICAL ROLLER BEARINGS NES—Con.

COUNTRY	EXPORTS	GENERAL IMPORTS	EXPORTS	GENERAL IMPORTS
POLAND	-	40	-	691
SINGARP	50	-	1 043	-
SWEDEN	30	97	116	792
U KING	74	417	1 160	4 209
OTH CTY	222	171	4 230	926
TOTAL	2 962	5 148	43 068	57 094

74680 BALL OR ROLLER BEARINGS NES

COUNTRY	EXPORTS	GENERAL IMPORTS	EXPORTS	GENERAL IMPORTS
AUSTRAL	58	-	628	10
CANADA	1 731	90	26 982	1 236
CHINA M	5	6	688	236
FR GERM	113	419	2 087	6 590
FRANCE	30	41	635	704
JAPAN	48	151	477	2 572
KOR REP	68	-	865	18
MEXICO	182	-	2 039	8
SINGARP	8	58	800	878
SPAIN	39	-	604	10
SWITZLD	23	50	123	2 677
U KING	174	186	1 727	921
OTH CTY	338	86	3 747	1 970
TOTAL	2 816	1 087	41 401	17 830

74691 BALLS, NEEDLES AND ROLLERS (BEARING PARTS)

COUNTRY	EXPORTS	GENERAL IMPORTS	EXPORTS	GENERAL IMPORTS
AUSTRAL	363	-	2 415	-
BELGIUM	25	6	818	24
BRAZIL	19	5	831	273
CANADA	1 036	172	12 567	2 692
CHINA T	4	88	454	705
FR GERM	199	577	3 319	6 942
FRANCE	42	3	1 112	105
ITALY	154	14	1 368	191
JAPAN	338	384	3 170	4 473
KOR REP	420	-	5 946	-
MEXICO	283	-	3 005	-
NETHLDS	60	3	1 066	16
REP SAF	39	-	891	-
SPAIN	117	-	1 001	3
SWITZLD	18	222	95	1 588
U KING	309	13	5 960	589
VENEZ	4	-	775	-
YUGOSLV	-	-	776	-
OTH CTY	480	9	5 225	247
TOTAL	3 911	1 496	50 793	17 849

74699 PTS OF BALL AND ROLLER BEARINGS NES

COUNTRY	EXPORTS	GENERAL IMPORTS	EXPORTS	GENERAL IMPORTS
AUSTRAL	184	1	2 619	989
BELGIUM	17	-	1 087	16
BRAZIL	379	481	5 482	2 918
CANADA	1 545	440	22 086	10 290
CHINA M	-	55	386	2 686
CHINA T	41	26	1 286	688
COLOMB	7	-	837	-
CYPRUS	-	-	-	612
FR GERM	196	713	3 561	14 258
FRANCE	69	477	2 972	4 430
INDIA	511	-	6 708	6
IRELAND	17	-	-	759
ITALY	41	114	614	1 050
JAPAN	119	4 766	2 053	64 122
KOR REP	8	2	2 049	80
MEXICO	520	174	5 390	1 508
REP SAF	526	36	6 877	89
SINGARP	28	102	1 054	194
SWEDEN	19	919	189	3 513
SWITZLD	5	162	32	603
U KING	186	211	2 907	3 074
VENEZ	127	-	1 018	5
OTH CTY	244	-	2 880	1 839
TOTAL	4 767	8 681	72 088	113 729

74710 PRESSURE-REDUCING VALVES

COUNTRY	EXPORTS	GENERAL IMPORTS	EXPORTS	GENERAL IMPORTS
AUSTRAL	124	-	1 075	2
BELGIUM	209	-	2 166	5
CANADA	3 724	613	41 865	4 685
CHILE	54	-	647	3
CHINA T	563	185	1 560	1 546
COLOMB	252	-	909	-
FR GERM	165	400	3 175	4 555
FRANCE	72	7	1 649	304
INDNSIA	68	-	876	-
ITALY	71	58	1 509	478

Foreign Investment in the United States

"A Cash-Rich Europe Finds the U.S. Ripe for Picking." *Business Week,* January 12, 1988, pp. 48–58.

"French Firms Pass British, Japanese as Leading Acquirers of U.S. Concerns." *The Wall Street Journal,* April 24, 1991, p. A4.

"How Japan Will Spend Its Cash." *Fortune,* November 21, 1988, pp. 195–210.

"Japanese Firms Hunt Big Foreign Game." *The Wall Street Journal,* November 10, 1988, p. A20.

"Japanese Investment Drops, Hitting U.S. the Hardest." *Business International,* July 22, 1991, pp. 245–50.

"Still Discovering America." *European Community,* May 1990, pp. 17–19.

"U.S. Affiliates of Foreign Companies: Operations in 1989." *Survey of Current Business,* July 1991, pp. 72–90.

"U.S. Business Enterprises Acquired or Established by Foreign Direct Investment in 1990." *Survey of Current Business,* May 1991, p. 27.

"Who Owns the U.S. and Does It Matter?" *World Monitor,* June 1990, pp. 58–64.

"Why Japan Keeps On Winning." *Fortune,* July 15, 1991, pp. 78–85.

Franchising

"Domino's, Pizza Hut Make a Run for the Border, Continue Their War." *Marketing News,* November 11, 1991, p. 5.

"European Franchisors Go Global." *Europe,* June 1988, pp. 18–19.

International Franchising Association. *Franchising in the Economy, 1980–90.* 1991.

"McDonald's Excellent Soviet Venture." *Canadian Business,* May 1991, pp. 51–69.

"Opportunity Knocks: Franchising in Spain." *Business America,* August 26, 1991, p. 15.

Joint Ventures

"Apple's Japanese Ally." *Fortune,* November 4, 1991, pp. 151–52.

"Don't Merge, Joint Venture." *Forbes,* November 12, 1990, pp. 37–39.

"Europe Cooks Up a Cereal Brawl." *Fortune,* June 3, 1991, pp. 175–79.

"Japan, U.S. Steelmakers Link Up." *The Wall Street Journal,* November 18, 1988, p. A8.

O'Reilly, Anthony. "Establishing Successful Joint Ventures in Developing Nations: A CEO's Perspective." *Columbia Journal of World Business,* Spring 1988, pp. 10–16.

"Strained Alliances." *International Management,* May 1990, pp. 28–34.

"Taking Off—To Taiwan." *Newsweek,* November 25, 1991, p. 52.

"When U.S. Joint Ventures with Japan Go Sour." *Business Week,* July 24, 1989, pp. 30–31.

Licensing

"A Licensing Success Story." *Business International,* June 13, 1988, p. 178.

"How Caterpillar China Coped with Key Obstacles in Major Licensing Deal." *Business International,* July 13, 1987, pp. 217–19.

"How One International Firm Manages a Licensee Network in Latin America." *Business Latin America,* October 3, 1988, p. 314.

"Licensing." *CFO,* June 1987, pp. 43–48.

"Licensing Regulations in 18 Nations." *Business International,* March 7, 1988, pp. 68–69.

"New Profits from Patents." *Fortune,* April 25, 1988, pp. 185–90.

"Running a Licensing Department: The Critical Keys to Success." *Business International,* June 13, 1988, pp. 177–78.

"The Lapse of Luxury." *The Economist,* January 5, 1991, pp. 49–50.

ENDNOTES

1. *Transnational Corporations in World Development* (New York: United Nations, 1988), p. 36.

2. The value of service exports is estimated to be between $700 and $900 billion. Data are very incomplete, and estimates vary according to how they are defined.

3. The nine largest general trading companies, called *sogo shosha,* account for 38.4 percent of Japan's total exports and 71.9 percent of its imports. "Sales of Japan's Nine Sogo Shosha (FY 1990)," *Japan 1992* (Tokyo: Keizai Koho Center, December 1991), Table 4–20, p. 45.

4. "Special Table E," *Monthly Bulletin of Statistics* (Washington, D.C.: United Nations, June 1991), pp. 250–53.

5. "The International Investment Position of the United States in 1990," *Survey of Current Business,* June 1991, p. 24.

6. Ibid., p. 25.

7. Ibid., p. 24.

8. "U.S. Business Enterprises Acquired or Established by Foreign Direct Investment in 1990," *Survey of Current Business,* May 1991, p. 27.

9. "Technical Notes," *World Development Report 1991* (Washington, D.C.: World Bank, 1991), p. 274.

10. Ibid.

11. "Hunting Heads in the Global Village," *International Management,* May 1990, pp. 52–54.

12. Of the eight licensing agreements in which one of the writers was involved, five came about as a result of unexpected visits from foreign businessmen. Vernon, a professor of international business, noted in a 1968 study that U.S. foreign investment in developed nations increased at

the same 10 percent rate as did the arrivals and departures of international travelers in North America and Europe from 1953 to 1965. He suggested that there was a direct relationship. From Christopher Tugendhat, *The Multinationals* (New York: Random House, 1972), p. 25.

13. "The Pitfalls of Global Restructuring," *Dun's Business Month,* June 1988, p. 41.

14. Warner-Lambert, *Annual Report,* 1990, p. 25.

15. "International Performance Outshines Domestic Results," *Business International,* September 29, 1986, p. 305.

16. "U.S. Corporations with the Biggest Foreign Revenues," *Forbes,* July 22, 1991, pp. 286–88.

17. "U.S. Concerns Seek Inspiration for Products from Overseas," *The Wall Street Journal,* January 3, 1984, p. 15.

18. "A Hard Row for Auto Parts Makers," *Fortune,* March 7, 1983, p. 110.

19. "Why Japan Keeps on Winning," *Fortune,* July 15, 1991, pp. 78–85.

20. "Mitsubishi Bank to Open Office," *The Columbus Dispatch,* March 20, 1987, p. 12.

21. "Kodak Will Open Its First Plant in Japan," *Modesto Bee,* October 18, 1985, p. B5.

22. "Zenith to Shift TV Assembly Work out of U.S. Plant," *The Wall Street Journal,* October 31, 1991, p. A13.

23. "Tendencias Recientes de la Localización en la Industria Maquiladora," *Comercio Exterior* (Mexico, D.F.: Banco Nacional de Comercio Exterior, September 1991), pp. 863–65.

24. "The In-Bond Industry," *Review of the Economic Situation of Mexico* (Mexico, D.F.: Banco Nacional de Mexico, December 1990), p. 595.

25. "Who Made Your Underwear?" *Forbes,* July 25, 1988, pp. 56–58.

26. "Where Tigers Breed," *The Economist,* November 1991, p. 9.

27. "Export Processing Zones and Trade Policy," *Finance & Development,* June 1988, pp. 34–36.

28. "Why the Kings of Crude Want to Be Pump Boys," *Business Week,* March 21, 1988, pp. 110–12.

29. It is not only the producers of metals and petroleum products that import a large part of the raw materials they use. Such diverse firms as A&P, Anderson Clayton, and Unilever also maintain large foreign operations to ensure a constant supply of coffee (A&P), cotton and coffee (Anderson Clayton), and vegetable oils (Unilever).

30. "Japan's Foreign Direct Investment," *Japan Report* (New York: Japan Information Service, April 16, 1977), p. 2.

31. *Handy Facts on U.S.–Japan Economic Relations* (Tokyo: JETRO, 1991), p. 28.

32. "Sprechen Sie High Tech?" *Forbes,* April 17, 1989, pp. 172–74.

33. "The Selling of America," *Fortune,* May 23, 1988, pp. 54–64.

34. "As Recession Bites, Many Multinationals Get Lift from Abroad," *The Wall Street Journal,* July 23, 1980, p. 1.

35. "Taking the Sting out of the Plunging Dollar," *Business Week,* December 7, 1987, pp. 72–73.

36. "U.S. Companies See 1992 as Opportunity," *San Jose Mercury News,* March 26, 1989, p. 1.

37. "The Selling of America," p. 61.

38. "Japanese Firms Hunt Big Foreign Game," *The Wall Street Journal,* November 10, 1988, p. A20.

39. "U.S. Business Enterprises Acquired or Established by Foreign Direct Investors in 1990," *Survey of Current Business,* May 1991, p. 30.

40. "Will Two Minuses Equal a Plus for Autolatina?" *International Management,* June 1987, p. 4.

41. "Coca-Cola Nestlé Taps Senior Management, Selects Headquarters," *The Wall Street Journal,* June 19, 1991, p. A7.

42. "Merck Has an Ache in Japan," *Fortune,* March 18, 1985, pp. 42–48; and "Merck to Buy 51 Percent of Japanese Firm," *The Wall Street Journal,* August 4, 1983, p. 6.

43. "Van Heusen–Polgat JV First to Take Advantage of U.S.–Israel FTA," *Business International,* August 18, 1986, p. 262.

44. One of the writers, who was employed by the Mexican affiliate of an American company, which held 33 percent equity in the affiliate, was asked by the Mexican secretary of commerce why the Mexican plant was not exporting to Guatemala. The reason, which he could not disclose, was that the company served the Guatemalan market from wholly owned plants in the United States and thus kept all the profits. A hurried call to Akron gave him permission to do some exporting to Guatemala to appease the Mexican government, but he was asked "not to try too hard."

45. Telephone conversation with Pfizer executive, April 6, 1989.

46. "New Profits from Patents," *Fortune,* April 25, 1988, pp. 185–90.

47. "U.S. International Transactions," *Survey of Current Business,* June 1991, Table 1, pp. 44–45.

48. "Two Makers of Microchips Broaden Ties," *The Wall Street Journal,* November 21, 1991, p. B4.

49. "Toshiba-Westinghouse JV Tunes In U.S. Tube Market," *Business International,* February 17, 1986.

50. "Stake in TV-Tube Venture Is Sold to Japan's Toshiba," *The Wall Street Journal,* November 1, 1988, p. A27.

51. "Making Global Alliances Work," *Fortune,* December 17, 1990, pp. 121–26.

52. "Is U.S. Business Giving Away Its Technology—Again?" *Fortune,* September 11, 1989, p. 10.

53. For a good analysis of the factors that have influenced U.S. foreign investment, read R. Peter DeWitt's "Factors Influencing U.S. Investment Abroad," *CSU, Los Angeles Business Forum,* Summer 1986, pp. 12–19.

Chapter 3

Economic Theories on International Trade, Development, and Investment

Protectionist barriers are to economics what steroids are to athletes—a temporary fix and a long-term disaster.

Robert Allen, chairman, AT&T

What one does oneself is fair trade and what the other fellow does is unfair.

Sir Ray Denman, EC ambassador to the United States

LEARNING OBJECTIVES

In this chapter, you will study:

1. Some of the theories that attempt to explain why certain goods are traded internationally.

2. The arguments for imposing trade restrictions.

3. The two basic kinds of restrictions: tariff and nontariff trade barriers.

4. The weaknesses of GNP/capita as an economic indicator.

5. The common characteristics of developing nations.

6. The new definition of economic development, which includes more than economic growth.

7. Why some governments are changing from an import substitution strategy of development to one of export promotion and the implications of this change for businesspeople.

8. Some of the theories of foreign direct investment.

KEY WORDS AND CONCEPTS

- Mercantilism
- Absolute advantage
- Comparative advantage
- Factor endowment
- Exchange rate
- Devalue a currency
- International product life cycle (IPLC)
- Dumping
- Countervailing duties
- Tariffs
- Ad valorem, specific, and compound duties
- Variable levy
- Nontariff barriers (NTBs)
- Quotas
- Voluntary export restraints (VERs)
- Orderly marketing arrangements
- Countertrade
- Developed, developing
- Newly industrializing countries (NICs)
- Nonmarket economy
- Underground economy
- Purchasing power parity
- Third World
- Human-needs approach
- Import substitution
- Monopolistic advantage theory
- Cross investment
- Internalization theory
- Eclectic theory of international production

BUSINESS INCIDENT

A Practical Application of the Law of Comparative Advantage . . .

After the Marxist government in Chile was overthrown in 1973, the Chicago Boys (a group of conservative Chilean economists educated at the University of Chicago) began decreasing import duties, which averaged about 94 percent, to force local manufacturers to lower their prices and become competitive in the export market. As Chile's economy improved, Chileans began to experience the benefits of lower duties. Shoppers could buy Heinz™ ketchup and Schlitz™ beer in the supermarkets and then wheel them in German shopping baskets to their Italian cars. Chilean-made products were cheaper also—suits that had cost $100 were selling for $80.

The disadvantage of this action was that a number of local firms either went out of business or contracted their operations. For example, when import duties on appliances were reduced from 100 percent to 32 percent, one of the principal local manufacturers suffered a 75 percent loss in sales. "We're going to lose a large part of our appliance industry," conceded Alvaro Bardon, a 37-year-old Chicago Boy, then head of the Central Bank of Chile, "and also our electronics industry and our automobile assembly plants." Mr. Bardon is hardly disappointed however. "Those are products we should be importing," he says. "We have other things based on our own farm products, our timberlands, our fisheries, and our mineral resources that we should be making because they give us a natural advantage over other countries."

In effect, this Chilean economist was admitting, as were policymakers and academicians worldwide, that the country's trade policy of *import substitution* (manufacturing goods locally to reduce their importation) was not helping to reduce its financial problems and attain higher economic growth rates. Import substitution had lost much of its former respect, and many governments were instituting a policy of *export promotion.* Government leaders

BUSINESS INCIDENT (concluded)

were noting the successes of the newly industrializing countries.

Any businessperson in Chile who knew anything about economic theory could have predicted what was about to happen. To increase exports, the economists were establishing policies to assist the industrial sectors, which had, as Bardon stated, a natural advantage; that is, because of a plentiful supply of the production factors, producers could compete pricewise in international markets. But, for this natural advantage to be effective, the exporters needed a more stable economy in which to operate. The economists responded with the traditional solutions: reduce public expenditure, lower the horrendous inflation rate of 131 percent (the annual rate between 1971 and 1980), and remove the protection from imports that many local manufacturers had enjoyed. A lower inflation rate enables exporters to quote reasonably stable prices and helps keep their costs down. Reducing public expenditure aids in reducing inflation and should reduce government bureaucracy, often the cause of considerable additional expense to business. Reducing protection from imports can force local manufacturers to lower their costs, which will contribute to lower inflation, provide a local source of competitively priced inputs to exporters, and, as happened in Chile, actually turn some of these manufacturers into exporters themselves.

How successful were these measures? Exports certainly increased—from 14 percent of the gross domestic product (GDP) in 1965 to 38 percent in 1989.

Much of this growth is in agricultural exports to the United States. Because of opposite seasons, Chile has a natural advantage in this market. Remember the anguish in 1989 among Chilean producers when just two grapes sent to the United States were found to contain cyanide? That single act of terrorism (a political force) might have drastically affected Chile's economic forces by wiping out a multimillion-dollar market for the country's agricultural exports. Increased attention to agriculture also resulted in a huge decrease in Chile's agricultural imports. Grain imports dropped from 1.7 million tons in 1974 to only 0.18 million tons in 1989. Imagine the savings in foreign currency from this decrease. Removing price controls, reducing public spending, and increasing competition for local manufacturers reduced the annual inflation rate from 131 percent to 20 percent.

The investing public's confidence in the effectiveness of Chile's economic policies is shown by the price in the New York secondary market of Chile's external debt paper. Offer prices have increased from 60 percent of face value in 1989 to 89 percent in 1991. **This is the highest percentage of all Latin American countries.** Colombia, with 76 percent, is second highest.

Source: Various tables in *World Development Report 1991* (Washington, D.C.: World Bank, 1991); "Economic Panorama of Latin America 1991," *Notas sobre la economia y el desarrollo* (Santiago, Chile: CEPAL, October 1991), p. 6; "Trade Policy Reform," *World Development Report 1987*, pp. 95–112; and "Capitalist Catch," *The Wall Street Journal*, December 12, 1977, p. 1.

The Business Incident illustrates a practical application of the keystone of international trade theory—the law of comparative advantage. Note, too, that the education of the head of Chile's central bank is typical of government policymakers and advisors worldwide. When they have a particularly strong influence in government affairs, they are frequently dubbed with such names as the "Chicago Boys" in Chile, "tecnicos" in Mexico, or "Berkeley Mafia" (economists educated at the University of California–Berkeley) in Indonesia. In fact, the people currently running Mexico are probably the most economically literate group to ever lead a country. The saying is that cabinet ministers who do not have doctorates in economics from the best American universities, as do President Salinas and others in the government, show up at meetings with young aides who do.[1]

What is the significance for international businesspeople? For one thing, since they frequently will be dealing with government officials trained in economics, they must be prepared to speak their language. When presenting plans requiring governmental approval, businesspeople must take care that the plans are economically sound, for they are almost certain to be studied by economists and will often need to be approved by them. Marketers proposing large projects to government planners must be aware that the key determinant now is economic efficiency rather than mere financial soundness.[2] Moreover, as you have seen in the case of Chile, knowledge of economic concepts, especially in the areas of (1) international trade, (2) economic development, and (3) foreign direct investment, frequently will provide insights as to future government action.

INTERNATIONAL TRADE THEORY

Why do nations trade? This question and the equally important proposition of predicting the direction, composition, and volume of goods traded are what international trade theory attempts to address. Interestingly, as is the case with numerous economic writings, the first formulation of international trade theory was politically motivated. Adam Smith, incensed by government intervention and control over both domestic and foreign trade, published *An Inquiry into the Nature and Causes of the Wealth of Nations* (1776) in which he tried to destroy the mercantilist philosophy.

▫ Mercantilism

mercantilism an economic philosophy based on the belief that a nation's wealth depends on accumulated treasure, usually gold. To increase wealth, government policies should promote exports and discourage imports

Mercantilism, the economic philosophy Smith attacked, held that it was essential to a nation's welfare to accumulate a stock of precious metals. These were, in the mercantilists' view, the only source of wealth. Because England had no mines, the mercantilists looked to international trade to supply gold and silver. The government established economic policies that promoted exports and stifled imports, resulting in a trade surplus to be settled in precious metals. Import duties and quotas reduced imports while government subsidies to exporters increased exports. These acts created a trade surplus.

Although the mercantilist era ended in the late 1700s, its arguments live on. A "favorable" trade balance still means that a nation exports more goods and services than it imports. In balance-of-payment accounting, an export that brings dollars to this country is called *positive,* but imports that cause dollar outflow are labeled *negative.*

An example of modern-day mercantilism, called *economic nationalism,* by some, was the new industrial policy based on heavy state intervention that the socialists were creating for France. They nationalized key industries and banks so as to use the power of the state as both (1) stockholder and financier and (2) customer and marketer to revitalize the nation's industrial base. With nearly one third of France's productive capacity and 70 percent of its high-tech electronic capabilities in the hands of the government, its power was approaching the level of state intervention in the 17th century. Some writers were calling this *high-tech mercantilism.* In 1986, after five years of little growth and high unemployment, the government reversed its policy when Jacques Chirac, a conservative, won the election for premier against President Mitterand's Socialist candidate. Chirac proceeded to denationalize

$23 billion worth of government holdings in banking, insurance, and industry.

In the United States, there is a growing opinion that Japan is the present-day "Fortress of Mercantilism." American businesspeople are concerned that its trade barriers to their imports are the result of Japanese insularity, traditional preoccupation with self-sufficiency, and an "us against them" mentality. The U.S. Secretary of Commerce recently stated, "They tell us they have to protect their markets because of their culture. They haven't joined the world yet." Comments from the Japanese seem to confirm what some Americans are saying. "The public is not in favor of perfect markets," says a Japanese bank manager. "We would like to preserve the substance of our culture. If we move to free trade, we may lose Japanese virtue in the process."[3]

▫ Theory of Absolute Advantage

Adam Smith claimed that market forces, not government controls, should determine the direction, volume, and composition of international trade. He argued that under free, unregulated trade, each nation should specialize in producing those goods it could produce most efficiently (had an absolute advantage, either natural or acquired). Some of these would be exported to pay for the imports of goods that could be produced more efficiently elsewhere. Smith showed by his example of **absolute advantage** that both nations would gain from trade.

absolute advantage the capability of one nation to produce more of a good with the same amount of input than another country

An example.   Suppose that for each unit of input, the following quantities of rice and automobiles can be produced in the United States and Japan:

| | Output per Unit of Input | |
Commodity	United States	Japan
Tons of rice	3	1
Automobiles	2	4

In the United States, three tons of rice can be produced per unit of input as can two automobiles. Therefore, in the United States, three tons of rice should have the same price as two automobiles. In Japan, however, only one ton of rice can be produced with the unit of output needed to produce four automobiles; therefore, one ton of rice should be as costly as four automobiles. The United States has an absolute advantage in rice production (3 to 1), while Japan's absolute advantage is in automobile manufacturing (4 to 2). Will anyone anywhere give the Japanese automaker more than one ton of rice for his four automobiles? According to the example, all American rice producers should because they can get only two automobiles for three tons of rice at home. Similarly, Japanese automakers, once they learn that they can obtain more than one ton of rice for every four automobiles in the United States, will be eager to trade Japanese autos for American rice.

Gains from trade.   Suppose the American rice growers and the Japanese automakers realize they are more efficient in these products and decide to specialize. The United States shifts all of its units of input to rice, and Japan makes only automobiles. Japan has an exportable surplus of four automobiles, and the United States has a surplus of three tons of rice.

Suppose each nation makes a straight swap of its surplus three tons of rice for four automobiles. The rice grower receives one and one third automobile for each ton of rice, which is more than the two thirds of an automobile received from domestic automakers. The Japanese automakers gained also because they now receive three fourths of a ton of rice per car through trade instead of one fourth of a ton of rice from Japanese growers. Both have gained through specialization. Each now has the following quantities:

Commodity	United States	Japan
Tons of rice	3	3
Automobiles	4	4

Terms of trade.   Although the rate of one ton of rice per three fourths of an automobile in our example was the result of each nation swapping its surplus, the rate of exchange could have been anything between the limits of the U.S. local exchange rate of three tons of rice for two autos to the Japanese internal rate of one ton of rice for four autos. Clearly, both nations have gained by trading. But what if one country has an absolute advantage in the production of *both* rice and automobiles? Will there still be a basis for trade?

◻ Theory of Comparative Advantage

Ricardo demonstrated in 1817 that even though a nation held an absolute advantage in the production of both goods, trade could still take place between two countries with advantages for each as long as the less efficient nation was not *equally* less efficient in the production of both goods.[4] Let us slightly change our first example so that now the United States has an absolute advantage in producing *both* rice and automobiles. Note, that compared to the United States, Japan is less inefficient in automaking than in producing rice. Therefore, it has a relative advantage (or **comparative advantage,** according to Ricardo) in producing automobiles.

comparative advantage a nation having absolute disadvantages in the production of two goods with respect to another nation has a comparative or relative advantage in the production of the good in which its absolute disadvantage is less

	Output per Unit of Input	
Commodity	United States	Japan
Tons of rice	6	3
Automobiles	5	4

In the absence of trade, one ton of rice would be exchanged in the United States for five sixths of an automobile; in Japan, the exchange rate would be one ton of rice for one and one third automobiles. If American rice growers can obtain more than five sixths of an automobile somewhere for a ton of rice (the local rate of exchange), it would pay them to trade. Obviously, they could do better by trading with Japanese automakers, who must pay one and one third automobiles for one ton of Japanese rice.

Gains from trade.   Suppose the United States and Japan again specialize in rice (U.S.) and automobiles (Japan). The American exportable surplus is now six tons of rice gained from shifting its inputs to rice production, and Japan has a surplus of four automobiles to export. However, a straight swap of six tons of rice for four automobiles would result in worse terms for the rice growers than they can get domestically. But, remember that a trade is beneficial to both sides if each can get more by trading with each other than by trading at home.

Locally, the American rice growers get five sixths of an automobile for a ton of rice, but the Japanese automakers have to give one and one third automobiles for a ton of Japanese rice. They split the difference at one ton of rice for one automobile. After the trade, each has the following:

Commodity	United States	Japan
Tons of rice	8	4
Automobiles	4	4

Note that this trade left the United States with some surplus rice and one less automobile than it had before the trade. Japan has more rice and the same number of automobiles. However, the U.S. rice growers should be able to trade the two-ton rice surplus for two automobiles elsewhere. The final result will be:

Commodity	United States	Japan
Tons of rice	6	4
Automobiles	6	4

Production possibility frontiers.   We can also illustrate the gains from trade graphically using production possibility frontiers. Figure 3–1 graphs the Japanese and U.S. production possibility frontiers using constant costs for simplicity. These curves, in the absence of trade, also illustrate the possible combinations of goods for consumption. Before trade, the United States might be producing and consuming six tons of rice and five automobiles (point A), while Japan is producing and consuming three tons of rice and four automobiles (point A).

With each nation specializing in the production of the goods in which it has a comparative advantage and trading its surplus with the other, both nations are able to consume at point B. The shaded areas under each curve indicate the gains from trade.

The simple concept of comparative advantage is the basis for international trade.

Notice that in our examples we mentioned a unit of input. This is a more modern version of the examples of Ricardo and Smith, who used only labor input. They did so because at that time only labor was considered important in calculating production costs.[5] Also, no consideration was given to the possibility of producing the same goods with different combinations of factors. Furthermore, no explanation was given as to why production costs differed. Not until 1933 did Ohlin, a Swedish economist building on work begun by the economist Heckscher, develop the theory of **factor endowment**.[6]

factor endowment
Heckscher-Ohlin theory that countries export products requiring large amounts of their abundant production factors and import products requiring large amounts of their scarce production factors

□ **FIGURE 3–1**   **Production and Consumption Possibility Frontiers before and after Trade**

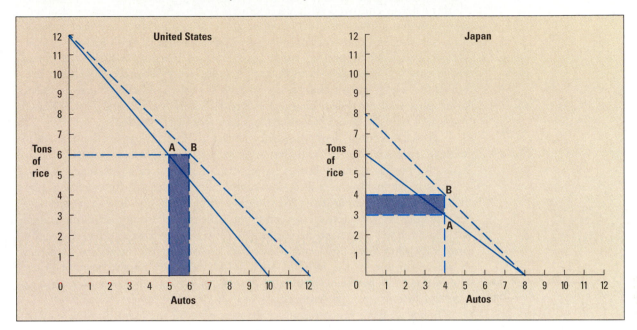

□ Heckscher-Ohlin Theory of Factor Endowment

The Heckscher-Ohlin theory states that international and interregional differences in production costs occur because of differences in the supply of production factors. Those goods that require a large amount of the abundant—thus less costly—factor will have lower production costs, enabling them to be sold for less in international markets. For example, China, relatively well endowed with labor compared to the Netherlands, ought to concentrate on producing labor-intensive goods; the Netherlands, with relatively more capital than labor, should specialize in capital-intensive products. When these countries trade, each will obtain the goods that require large amounts of the production factor in relatively short supply at a lower price, and both will benefit from the transaction.

How useful is this theory for explaining present-day trading patterns? Countries with relatively large amounts of land (such as Australia) do export land-intensive products (such as grain and cattle), whereas Hong Kong exports labor-intensive goods.[7] There are exceptions, however, due in part to the assumptions made by Ohlin. One assumption was that the prices of the factors depend only on the factor endowment. We know this is untrue. Factor prices are not set in a perfect market. Legislated minimum wages and benefits force the cost of labor to rise to a point greater than the value of the product that many workers can produce. Investment tax credits reduce the cost of capital below market cost, and so forth. The result is factor prices that do not fully reflect their supply.

Ohlin also assumed that a given technology is universally available, but this is not so. There is always a lag between the introduction of a new production method and its worldwide application. As a result, superior technology often permits a nation to produce goods at a cost lower than that of a country better endowed with the required factor. A closely related assumption was that a given product is either labor or capital intensive. Yet anyone who has watched construction methods in less developed nations knows that wet concrete can be poured either by a gang of laborers with buckets or a crane and its operator. Transportation costs were ignored, but there are goods for which freight charges are so high that the landed cost (export sales price plus transportation charges) is greater than local costs. In this case, there will be little trade. Why not say there will be no trade?

It is because of a demand-side construct that is always difficult to deal with in economic theory and that we have so far neglected—*differences in taste*. As businesspeople, however, we cannot neglect this difference, which enables trade to flow in a direction completely contrary to that predicted by the theory of comparative advantage—from high- to low-cost nations. France sells us wine, cosmetics, clothing, and even Perrier™ drinking water, all of which are produced here and generally sold at lower prices. Germany and Italy send Porsches™ and Maseratis™ to one of the largest automobile producers in the world. We buy these goods not only on the basis of price, the implied independent variable in the theory we have been examining, but also because of taste preferences.

Finally, we have presented these theories without the mention of money. It could have been introduced earlier, but it really would have added nothing to the explanation. Money can, however, change the direction of trade, as we shall see in the next section.

◻ Introducing Money

Suppose the total cost of land, labor, and capital to produce either the daily output of rice or automobiles in the example on absolute advantage is $10,000 in the United States or 2.5 million yen in Japan. The cost per unit is as follows:

	Price per Unit	
Commodity	**United States**	**Japan**
Tons of rice	$\frac{\$10,000}{3} = \$3,330$/ton	$\frac{2.5 \text{ million yen}}{1} = 2.5$ million yen/ton
Automobiles	$\frac{\$10,000}{2} = \$5,000$/auto	$\frac{2.5 \text{ million yen}}{4} = 0.625$ million yen/auto

For the traders to know if it is more advantageous to buy locally or to import, they need to know the prices in their own currencies. To convert from foreign to domestic currency, they must have the *exchange rate*.

exchange rate the price of one currency stated in terms of another currency

Exchange rate. The **exchange rate** is the price of one currency stated in terms of the other. If the prevailing rate is $1 = 250 yen, then 1 yen must be worth 0.004 dollar.* Using the exchange rate of $1 = 250 yen, the prices in the preceding example appear to the U.S. trader as follows:

---

* If $1 = 250 yen, to find the value of 1 yen in dollars, divide both sides of the equation by $\frac{250 \text{ yen}}{\text{dollar}}$. Then 1 yen $= \frac{2}{250} = \$0.004$.

Commodity	Price per Unit (Dollars)	
	United States	Japan
Tons of rice	$3,330	$10,000
Automobiles	5,000	2,500

The American rice producers can earn $6,670 more by exporting rice to Japan than they can by selling locally; but can the Japanese automakers gain by exporting to the United States? To find out, they must convert the American prices to Japanese yen.

Commodity	Price per Unit (Yen)	
	United States	Japan
Ton of rice	0.83 million yen	2.5 million yen
Automobiles	1.25 million yen	0.625 million yen

It is apparent that the Japanese automakers will export cars to the United States because a greater profit, 0.625 million yen, can be earned. The American automobile manufacturers, however, will need some very strong sales arguments to sell in the United States if they are to overcome the $2,500 price differential. Ricardo *did not consider* this possibility; in his time, products were considered homogeneous and therefore were sold primarily on the basis of price.

Influence of exchange rate.   Rice to Japan and cars to the United States will be the direction of trade as long as the exchange rate remains in a range around $1 = 250 yen. But if the dollar strengthens to $1 = 750 yen, the American rice will cost as much in yen as the Japanese rice, and importation will cease. On the other hand, should the dollar weaken to $1 = 125 yen, then a Japanese car will cost $5,000 to American traders, and they will have little reason to import. Incidentally, when the dollar did reach 125 yen in 1988, Japanese automakers were forced to accept less yen on their sales to the United States in order for their dollar prices to remain competitive with American car prices.

Another way a nation can avoid losing markets and regain competitiveness in world markets is to **devalue** its currency (lower its price in terms of other currencies). Notice that this leaves the domestic prices unchanged.

devalue a currency lower its price in terms of other currencies

> Mexico, which depends on American tourists for a large part of its foreign exchange earnings, was faced with losing this business because inflation had driven peso prices so high that at the rate of 12.5 pesos = $1, dollar prices to the Americans were excessive. Mexican officials had three alternatives: (1) deflate to drive peso prices down (time consuming and painful to the Mexicans); (2) lower prices by government edict (bureaucratic difficulties as with any system of price controls); or (3) devalue the peso. Overnight the rate was decreased to 25 pesos = $1, and without disturbing the peso prices, the prices in dollars were halved. Suddenly, trips to Mexico were a bargain for Americans.

The international trade theory we have been discussing was the only explanation of trade available to us until the 1960s, when a new concept—the international product life cycle—was formulated.[8]

Bargains in Mexico after devaluation

Philip and Karen Smith/Tony Stone Worldwide

◻ **International Product Life Cycle (IPLC)**

This approach, related to the product life cycle, concerns the role of innovation in trade patterns. The concept can be applied to new product introduction by firms in any of the industrialized nations, but because more new products have been successfully introduced on a commercial scale in the United States, let us examine the **IPLC** as it applies to this country. The four stages through which a new product is said to pass are illustrated in Figure 3–2 and described as follows.

1. *U.S. exports.* Because the United States possesses the largest population of high-income consumers in the world, competition for their patronage is intense. Manufacturers are therefore forced to search constantly for better ways to satisfy their customers' needs. To provide new products, companies maintain large research and development laboratories, which must be in constant contact with suppliers of the materials they need for product development. The fact that their suppliers are also in this country facilitates the contact.[9] In the early stages of the product life cycle, the design and the production methods are changing. By being close to the market, management can react quickly to customer feedback. These factors combine to make the United States a leader in new product introduction. For a while, American firms will be the only manufacturers of the product; overseas customers, as they learn

international product life cycle (IPLC) a theory explaining why a product that begins as a nation's export eventually becomes its import

□ **FIGURE 3-2**
International Product
Life Cycle

Source: Adapted from R. Vernon, "International Investment and International Trade in the Product Life Cycle," *Quarterly Journal of Economics,* May 1966, pp. 190–207.

of the product, will therefore have to buy from American firms. The export market develops.

2. *Foreign production begins.* Overseas consumers, especially those in developed nations, have similar needs and the capability to purchase the product. Export volume grows and becomes large enough to support local production. If the innovator is a multinational firm, it will be sending its subsidiaries new product information with complete details on how to produce it. Where there are no affiliates, foreign businesspeople, as they learn of the product, will obtain licenses for its production. Foreign production will begin. The American firm will still be exporting to those markets where there is no production, but its export growth will diminish.

3. *Foreign competition in export markets.* Later, as early foreign manufacturers gain experience in marketing and production, their costs will fall. Saturation of their local markets will cause them to look for buyers elsewhere. They may even be able to undersell the American producers if they enjoy an advantage in labor or raw material costs. In this stage, foreign firms are competing in export markets, and as a result, American export sales will continue to decline.

4. *Import competition in the United States.* If domestic and export sales enable foreign producers to attain the economies of scale enjoyed by the American firm, they may reach a point where they can compete in quality and undersell American firms in the American market. From that point on, the U.S. market will be served by imports only. Black-and-white television sets are an example of such a product.

The authors of the IPLC concept also claim that this cycle may be repeated as the less developed countries with still lower labor costs obtain the technology and thus acquire a cost advantage over the more industrialized nations.

Although little research has been done to substantiate the IPLC concept, the World Bank study mentioned previously seems to provide a plausible reason for these changes in production locations.

> With countries progressing on the comparative advantage scale, their exports can supplement the exports of countries that graduate to a higher level. . . . A case in point is Japan, whose comparative advantage has shifted towards highly capital-intensive exports. In turn, developing countries with a relatively high human capital endowment, such as Korea and Taiwan, can take Japan's place in exporting relatively human capital-intensive products, and countries with a relatively high physical capital endowment, such as Brazil and Mexico, can take Japan's place in exporting relatively physical capital-intensive products. Finally, countries at lower levels of development can supplant the middle-level countries in exporting unskilled labor-intensive commodities.[10]

□ Summary of International Trade Theory

In summary, we can say that international trade occurs primarily because of relative price differences among nations. These differences stem from differences in production costs, which are the result of differences in the endowment of the factors of production and the level of efficiency at which they are utilized. However, taste differences, a demand variable, can reverse the direction of trade predicted by the theory.

International trade theory clearly shows that nations will attain a higher level of living by specializing in goods for which they possess a comparative advantage and importing those for which they have a comparative disadvantage. Generally, trade restrictions that stop this free flow of goods will be harmful to a nation's welfare. If this is true, why is every nation in the world surrounded by trade restrictions?

TRADE RESTRICTIONS

This apparent contradiction occurs because both national and international procedures for making decisions about import restrictions are particularly sensitive to the interest groups who will be hurt by the international competition. These groups consist of a small, easily identified body of people—as contrasted to the huge, widespread number of consumers who gain from free trade. In any political debate over a proposed import restriction, the protectionist group will be united in exerting pressure on government officials, whereas pro-trade consumers rarely mount an organized effort. For example, steel companies and steelworker unions have protested vehemently to Congress and government officials about lower-priced imported steel, yet consumer organizations have said nothing. In other words, if you are employed by a chemical manufacturer, you probably are not going to fight for unrestricted steel imports even though you may believe they contribute to a lower price for your automobile.

In the next section, note the importance of special interest groups.

◻ Arguments for Trade Restrictions and Their Rebuttal

One argument for trade restrictions involves national defense.

National defense.   Certain industries need protection from imports because they are vital to the national defense and must be kept operating even though they are at a comparative disadvantage with respect to foreign competitors. If competition from foreign firms drives these companies out of business and leaves this country dependent on imports, those imports may not be available in wartime.

One problem with this argument is that the armed forces require hundreds of products ranging from pantyhose to bombs.

> **In 1984, the U.S. shoe industry, after failing to obtain relief from imports with arguments about loss of jobs, requested Congress to impose restrictions based on the fact that growing reliance on imported footwear is "jeopardizing the national security of the United States." In the event of war, shoemakers claim that there would be insufficient manufacturing capacity in this country.**
>
> **A Defense Department spokesman said he knew of no plan to investigate the prospects of a wartime shoe crisis. Furthermore, federal law already requires the armed forces to buy U.S.-made footwear exclusively.[11]**

Critics of this argument claim it would be far more efficient to pay a subsidy to a number of firms to maintain sufficient capacity for wartime use only. The output of these companies could be varied according to the calculated defense needs. Moreover, a subsidy would clearly indicate the cost to the nation of maintaining these companies in the name of national security. Currently, most American steamship companies receive government subsidies to compensate for their higher operating costs. In this way, we have a merchant marine ready in case of hostility, and we know what this state of readiness costs us.

Protect infant industry.   Advocates for the protection of an infant industry claim that in the long run, the industry does have a comparative advantage but needs protection from imports until the labor force is trained, production techniques are mastered, and the firm achieves economies of scale. When these objectives are achieved, import protection will no longer be necessary. Without the protection, they argue, the firm will not be able to survive because lower-cost imports from more mature foreign competitors will underprice it in its local market.

The protection is meant to be temporary; but realistically, a firm will rarely admit it has matured and no longer needs this assistance. Protected from foreign competition by high import duties, the company's managers have little reason to improve efficiency or product quality.

International businesspeople will find that the infant-industry argument is readily accepted by the governments of most developing nations. The first firm in an industry new to the country generally gets protection with no date stipulated for its removal. However, some of the larger developing nations, such as Brazil and Mexico, have been reducing their protection to force these companies to lower their prices and become more competitive in world markets.

Protect domestic jobs from cheap foreign labor.   The protectionists who use this argument will compare lower foreign hourly wage rates to those paid here and conclude that exporters from these countries can flood the United

States with low-priced goods and put America out of work. The first fallacy of this argument is that wage costs are neither all of the production costs nor all of the labor costs. In many LDCs, the legislated fringe benefits are a much higher percentage of the direct wages than they are in this country. Furthermore, the productivity per worker is frequently so much greater in the developed countries because of more capital per worker, superior management, and advanced technology that the labor cost is lower even though wages are higher.

The second fallacy results from failure to consider the costs of the other factors of production. Where wage rates are low, the capital costs are usually high, and thus production costs may actually be higher in a low-wage nation. Ironically, one of the arguments for protection used by manufacturers in developing nations is that they cannot compete against the low-cost, highly productive firms in the industrialized countries. Those who might be persuaded by this argument to stop imports to save domestic jobs should remember that American exports create jobs—every $1 billion in exports creates 25,000 new jobs. If we stop a country's imports, its government may retaliate with greater import duties on our exports. The result could be a net loss of jobs rather than the gain that was anticipated.

Scientific tariff or fair competition.   Supporters of this argument say they believe in fair competition. They simply want an import duty that will bring the cost of the imported goods up to the cost of the domestically produced article. This will eliminate any "unfair" advantage that a foreign competitor might have because of superior technology, lower raw material costs, lower taxes, or lower labor costs. It is not their intent to ban exports; they wish only to equalize the process for "fair" competition. If this were law, no doubt the rate of duty would be set to protect the least efficient American producer, thereby enabling the more efficient domestic manufacturers to earn large profits. The efficient foreign producers would be penalized, and, of course, their comparative advantage would be nullified.

Retaliation.   Representatives of an industry whose exports have had import restrictions placed on them by another country may request their government to retaliate with similar restrictions. An example of how retaliation begins is the ban by the European Community (EC) on imports of hormone-treated beef from the United States on January 1, 1989. Because the use of hormones is considered a health hazard in the EC, it closed the market to $100 million worth of beef (12 percent of total U.S. meat exports). American beef producers complained that no scientific evidence supports the claim, and the United States promptly retaliated by putting import duties on about $100 million worth of EC products, including boneless beef and pork, fruit juices, wine coolers, tomatoes, French cheese, and instant coffee. The EC then threatened to ban U.S. imports of honey, canned corn, walnuts, and dried fruit worth $140 million. In reply, the United States announced that it would follow the EC ban with a ban of all European meat. If that had happened, about $500 million in U.S.–EC trade would have been affected. A joint EC–U.S. task force has been meeting to try to find a solution to end a situation that could escalate into a trade war.[12] U.S. cattle producers are particularly suspicious of the ban because they know that the Europeans routinely use dangerous drugs in the $384 million of pork and beef annually exported to the United States.[13]

Dumping.   Another cause for retaliation is **dumping,** or selling a product abroad for less than (1) the cost of production, (2) the price in the home market, or (3) the price to third countries.

A foreign manufacturer may take this action because it wishes to sell excess production without disrupting prices in its domestic market, or it may have lowered the export price to force all domestic producers in the importing nation out of business. The exporter expects to raise prices in the market once that objective is accomplished. This is *predatory dumping.*

In the United States, when a manufacturer believes a foreign producer is dumping a product, it can ask the Office of Investigation in the Department of Commerce to make a preliminary investigation. If Commerce finds that products have been dumped, the case goes to the International Trade Commission* to determine if the imports are injuring U.S. producers. If the Commission finds that they are, the U.S. Customs is authorized to levy antidumping duties.

Most governments retaliate when dumping injures local industry. The EC, for example, levied dumping duties ranging from 23 to 43 percent on Japanese computer printers when investigators found that they were priced 20 percent lower in the EC than in Japan.[14] In fact, antidumping suits have become a favorite means for manufacturers in the EC and the United States to protect themselves against Japanese and Korean imports. However, even when an industry wins its case, there is no guarantee that the offending import will be kept out of the market.

> In 1989, Ingersoll-Rand, the largest American bearing manufacturer, convinced the U.S. International Trade Commission (ITC) that Japan, Germany, and seven other nations were selling bearings in the United States for one third of the price they were selling them for in their home markets. The ITC agreed and levied import duties as high as 213 percent. Cheap foreign bearings continued to pour in because although the bearing companies reduced shipments from their home plants, they increased them from their plants in countries that had not been involved in the antidumping case, such as Austria, Turkey, and Spain. Not only are foreign firms shipping bearings from countries on which antidumping duties have not been levied, but they are also avoiding duties by transshipping through a third country to the United States. Hong Kong, for example, does not have a bearing factory, but increased its bearing exports by 255 percent to $2 million.[15]

Export subsidies.   To encourage exports, governments will often offer export subsidies such as reduced transportation rates on government carriers, preferential exchange rates to exporters when they import capital equipment, and low-cost loans to foreign buyers. Such actions may prompt competitors in the importing nation to request their governments to impose **countervailing duties** equal to the amount of the subsidy.[16]

Other arguments.   The arguments we have examined are probably the most often quoted. Others that are sometimes given are the use of protection from

---

*   The International Trade Commission is a government agency that provides technical assistance and advice to the president and Congress on matters of international trade and tariffs.

imports to (1) permit diversification of the domestic economy or (2) improve the balance of trade. You should have gathered from this discussion that protection from imports generally serves the narrow interests of a special group at the expense of many. While their application can sometimes buy time for the protected industry to modernize and become more competitive in the world market, a real danger exists that a nation's trading partners will retaliate with restrictions causing injury to industries that have received no protection. Let's examine these restrictions.

◻ Kinds of Restrictions

Import restrictions are commonly classified as *tariff* (import duties) and *nontariff* barriers.

tariffs taxes on imported goods for the purpose of raising their price to reduce competition for local producers or stimulate their local production

Tariff barriers. **Tariffs,** or import duties, are taxes levied on imported goods primarily for the purpose of raising their selling price in the importing nation's market to reduce competition for domestic producers. A few smaller nations also use them to raise revenue on both imports and exports. Export of commodities such as coffee and copper are commonly taxed in the developing nations.

Ad valorem, specific, and compound duties. Import duties are either *ad valorem, specific,* or a combination of the two called *compound.* An **ad valorem duty** is stated as a percentage of the invoice value. For example, the U.S. Tariff Schedule states that flavoring extracts and fruit flavors not containing alcohol are subject to a 6 percent ad valorem duty. Therefore, when a shipment of flavoring extract invoiced at $10,000 arrives in the United States, the importer is required to pay $600 to U.S. Customs before taking possession of the goods. A **specific duty** is a fixed sum of money charged for a physical unit. If you were to import dynamite in cartridges or sticks suitable for blasting, you would have to pay $.37 per pound irrespective of the invoice value. When the flavoring extracts and fruit flavor just mentioned contain over 50 percent alcohol by weight, they are charged $.12 per pound plus 3 percent ad valorem. On a $10,000 shipment weighing 5,000 pounds, you would have to pay a **compound duty** of $900 ($.12 × 5,000 pounds + 0.03 × $10,000 = $600 + $300). Note that a specific duty, unless changed frequently in an inflationary period, soon loses its importance, whereas the amount collected from an ad valorem duty increases as the invoice price rises. Sometimes, however, an exporter may charge prices so much lower than domestic prices that the ad valorem duty fails to close the gap. Some governments set *official prices* or use *variable levies* to correct this deficiency.

ad valorem duty an import duty levied as a percentage of the invoice value of imported goods

specific duty a fixed sum levied on a physical unit of an imported good

compound duty a combination of specific and ad valorem duties

Official prices. These prices are included in the customs tariff of some nations and are the basis for ad valorem duty calculations whenever the actual invoice price is lower. The official price guarantees that a certain minimum import duty will be paid irrespective of the actual invoice price. It thwarts a fairly common arrangement that numerous importers living in high-duty nations have with their foreign suppliers whereby a false low invoice is issued to reduce the amount of duty to be paid. The importer sends the difference between the false invoice price and the true price separately.

variable levy an import duty set at the difference between world market prices and local government-supported prices

Variable levy. One form of **variable levy,** which guarantees that the market price of the import will be the same as that of domestically produced goods, is used by the European Community for imported grains. Calculated daily, the duty level is set at the difference between world market prices and the support price for domestic producers.

Lower duty for more local input.   Import duties are set by many nations in such a way as to encourage local input. For example, the finished product ready for sale to the consumer may have a 70 percent ad valorem duty. However, if the product is imported in bulk so that it must be packaged in the importing nation, the duty level may be at 30 percent. To encourage some local production, the government may charge only 10 percent duty on the semifinished inputs. These situations can provide opportunities for foreign manufacturers of low-technology products, such as paint and toilet articles, to get behind a high tariff wall with very modest investments.

nontariff barriers (NTBs) all forms of discrimination against imports other than import duties

Nontariff barriers.   Nontariff barriers (NTBs) are the name given to all forms of discrimination against imports other than the import duties we have been examining. As nations have reduced duties, the nontariff barriers, which are either quantitative or nonquantitative, have assumed greater importance. To illustrate that this trend has been occurring for some time, an English study found that while 40.3 percent of all world trade was under some kind of control in 1973, by 1979 it had risen to 45.7 percent.[17]

A more recent study of 16 Organization for Economic Cooperation and Development (OECD) nations compared trade coverage ratios of nontariff barriers for 1981 and 1986. To identify changes in the use, not the intensity, of specific nontariff barriers, the researchers applied the 1981 and 1986 nontariff barriers to a constant 1981 trade base. Note the increases in Table 3−1.

quotas numerical limits placed on specific classes of imports

Quantitative.   Quotas, a quantitative barrier, are numerical limits for a specific kind of good that a country will permit to be imported without restriction during a specified period. If the quota is *absolute*, once the specified amount has been imported, further importation for the rest of the period (usually a year) is prohibited.

> Kmart ordered a million dollars in wool sweaters from China. Before they arrived in this country, the quota was filled for the year, and Kmart had to wait until the following year to bring them in. By that time, they were out of fashion and had to be deeply discounted. The company expected to recover only 60 cents on a dollar.

Some goods are subject to *tariff quotas*, which permit a stipulated amount to enter the country duty free or at a low rate, but when that quantity is reached, a much higher duty is charged for subsequent importations. This process is repeated annually.

Quotas are generally *global;* that is, a total amount is fixed without regard to source. They may also be *allocated*, in which case the government of the importing nation assigns quantities to specific countries. For example, the United States allocates quotas for specific tonnages of sugar to 25 nations. Because of their nature, allocated quotas are sometimes called *discriminatory* quotas.

voluntary export restraints (VERs) export quotas imposed by the exporting nation

More recently, because of the general agreement among nations against imposing quotas unilaterally, governments have negotiated **voluntary export restraints** (**VERs**) with other countries. Although a VER is a generic term for

☐ **TABLE 3-1**
Nontariff Trade Coverage Ratios for 16 Industrialized Nations*

Importer	Trade Coverage Ratio†		
	1981	1986	Percentage Increase
Belgium-Luxembourg	12.6%	14.3%	13.5%
Denmark	6.7	7.9	17.9
Germany	11.8	15.4	30.5
France	15.7	18.6	26.8
Greece	16.2	20.1	24.1
Great Britain	11.2	12.8	14.3
Ireland	8.2	9.7	18.3
Italy	17.2	18.2	5.8
Netherlands	19.9	21.4	7.5
Switzerland	19.5	19.6	0.5
Finland	7.9	8.0	1.3
Japan	24.4	24.3	−0.4
Norway	15.2	14.2	−6.6
New Zealand	46.4	32.4	−30.2
United States	11.4	17.3	51.8
All above	15.1	17.7	17.2

*Nontariff measures include variable import levies, quotas, and nonautomatic import authorizations including restrictive import licensing requirements, quantitative voluntary export restraints, and trade restraints under the Multifiber Arrangement.

†The share of total imports (by value) subject to hard-core nontariff measures. In computing this index, the researchers applied 1981 and 1986 nontariff measures to a constant 1981 trade base. Petroleum products and European Community intratrade were excluded.

Source: "An Introduction to Nontariff Barriers to Trade," *Federal Reserve Bank of St. Louis Review,* January–February 1989, pp. 32–46.

all bilaterally agreed measures to restrict exports, it has a stricter legal definition in the United States—"an action unilaterally taken to restrict the volume or number of items to be exported during a given period and administered by the exporting country. It is 'voluntary' in the sense that the country has a formal right to eliminate or modify it."[18] It is also voluntary in that the exporting nation may prefer its consequences to any trade barriers the importing nation might impose.

To avoid formal restrictions on automobile imports by the United States, the Japanese government limits its exports to 1.65 million units. Interestingly, although fewer Japanese cars were imported into this country after the quotas were imposed, sales revenues went up because the Japanese automakers began to export more expensive models.[19]

orderly marketing arrangements formal agreements between exporting and importing countries that stipulate the import or export quotas each nation will have for a good

Orderly marketing arrangements. **Orderly marketing arrangements** are VERs consisting of formal agreements between governments to restrict international competition and preserve some of the national market for local producers. They differ from unilaterally imposed quotas and other trade barriers in that they result from negotiations between exporting and importing countries. Usually, they stipulate the size of import or export quotas that each nation will have for a particular good. Agreements that involve industry participation are often called *voluntary restraint arrangements.*

"To all department heads: While barter agreements are not opposed per se, caution must — I repeat, must — be observed."

Rotarian, September 1985.

The largest and oldest such arrangement is the Multifiber Arrangement (MFA), which began in 1973 and has subsequently been renewed every four years. The pact includes 54 exporting and importing nations. It regulates about 80 percent of the world's textile and clothing exports to the industrialized nations.

In 1986, Japanese computer chip manufacturers slashed prices on a common chip, the DRAM, because of high inventories. The two American producers appealed to the government for help, and an accord was made that fixed minimum prices and established voluntary import quotas. While the American chip manufacturers increased their profits, the makers of products containing the chips and the consumers who buy those products lost. The Brookings Institution, a famous "think tank," estimates that the DRAM's price rose from $2.50 in 1986 to $10 in 1988 and, as a result, added more than $100 to the price of a $500 personal computer. The arrangement helped American firms, but it benefited Japanese chip makers much more. Instead of having to cut their prices to compete, they were able to put their monopoly profits into research on higher-technology products where Americans still lead. "What we did was pretty stupid," said a trade analyst at the Institute for International Economics.[20]

A new five-year semiconductor accord signed in 1991 included a number of joint industry activities to help achieve a 20 percent market share in Japan for foreign chip makers by the end of 1992. According to the American method of calculating market share (captive sales to Japanese subsidiaries are not included), the U.S. market share of the Japanese market is now about 13 percent.[21]

WORLDVIEW
Our Taxing Tariff Code—Let Them Eat Lobster!

In 1790, the U.S. tariff code consisted of a single sheet of rates posted at custom houses; now, it occupies two hefty volumes with 8,753 different rates. While the average tariff now is only about 5 percent, hundreds of tariffs are still in the Smoot-Hawley league—with some as high as 67 percent.

Why the blizzard of discriminations against and among products? A cynic might say the tariff code is devoted to encouraging the poor to raise their standards of living:

- Mink furs are duty free. With the money a mother saves on her mink, maybe she can afford a polyester sweater—which carries a 34.6 percent tariff—for her baby.

- Lobster is duty free. With the savings, struggling parents may be able to afford infant food preparations, which carry a 17.2 percent tariff.

- Orange juice's tariff is 36 percent. But Perrier's is only 0.4 cent per liter. (If the Customs Service reclassifies Perrier as benzene, then it can enter duty free.)

- Fresh broccoli carries a 25 percent tariff. But, happily, truffles are duty free.

- Footwear valued at not more than $3 a pair with rubber or plastic outer soles and uppers is tariffed at 48 percent. If valued at more than $12, the tariff is only 20 percent.

Congress also uses the tariff code to deny equal rights to the malnourished. Vitamin B12, which is no longer produced in the United States, is hit with a 16.2 percent tariff, while vitamin B1 carries a 3.1 percent tariff. Vitamin C carries a 3.1 percent tariff—while Vitamin E is hit with a 7.9 percent levy.

Some tariffs were raised early last year, when the United States changed its tariff classification system to harmonize with widely used international tariff categories. In 1988, the rate on imported jams ranged from zero to 8.5 percent; now, the rate varies from 3 percent on currant jam, to 10 percent (plus 15.4 cents a kilogram) on cherry jam, to 20 percent on peach jam, to 35 percent on apricot jam. This is one more telling bit of evidence that the apricot jam cartel controls Washington.

The U.S. Trade Representative has submitted a plan to offer tariff reductions during the current Uruguay Round of negotiations under the General Agreement on Tariffs and Trade. The Trade Policy Staff Committee, a group of staffers from various federal agencies, held hearings on tariff reform in November—and some of the pleadings from protected industries were especially insightful:

- A producer of pimentos, tariffed at 9.5 percent, commented, "The present tariff on pimentos is not an impediment to imports and any reduction in the tariff would have an adverse—even a disastrous—effect on the domestic industry."

- Indiana Glass Company complained that glasses from Mexican companies were selling at Kmart for $1.99 a

---

countertrade a transaction in which goods are exchanged entirely or partially for goods

Countertrade.   Another barrier to free trade is **countertrade**. This is essentially a transaction in which goods are exchanged for goods. The simplest form of countertrade, barter, dates from ancient times, but in recent years various other kinds of countertrade have been used in East–West trade. Because of shortages of foreign exchange and a lack of markets for their products, many noncommunist nations have also been engaging in countertrade. Iraq obtained warships from Italy in exchange for crude oil, for example. Another example was the purchase by Spain of Colombian coffee in exchange for Spanish buses. Countertrade is a barrier to free trade because the sellers are forced to take goods that they would not otherwise buy, and in doing so, they close off another market from free and open competition. It is estimated that this type of transaction now accounts for about 25 percent of all world set—while Indiana Glass's sets were selling at Kmart for $3.99. As the company's brief noted, "There is absolutely no difference in quality" between the Mexican product and Indiana Glass's product. Indiana Glass concluded that "this evidence of [foreign] price advantage under current tariffs compels at least the maintenance, if not increase, of tariffs [currently up to 38 percent] on [such] glasses."

- Bobby McKown of the Florida Citrus League declared: "Many of our foreign competitors receive important government assistance. U.S. producers receive none." Mr. McKown must have been carried away by his dedication to high tariffs. The Agriculture Department has showered more than $30 million on American citrus companies and organizations in recent years to bankroll their foreign brand-name ads.

- The Committee to Preserve American Color TV gave a presentation on why the United States should retain its 15 percent duty on color picture tubes. The person who testified was Joseph Donahue, a senior vice president of Thomson Consumer Electronics, a subsidiary of Thomson S.A., the French corporation that recently bought GE's TV production facilities.

Why does the United States have 8,753 tariff rates? Partly because of the bargaining strategy followed by the United States for the past half century. As Washington trade lawyer Noel Hemmendinger

notes, there's been a constant subdividing of tariff categories to provide special rates for specific products from nations that were offering to reduce the tariff rate on some specific American export.

In the current GATT round, many nations favored working for an agreement to cut all existing tariffs across-the-board by 33 percent. But the United States preferred that nations haggle out mutually acceptable tariff-rate cuts on a product-by-product, rate-by-rate basis.

Our tariff code is part of our fossilized industrial policy—perpetuating handouts for the biggest political contributors to previous generations of congressmen. The lethargy of our democratic system allows high tariffs to remain long after the original beneficiaries have turned to dust.

Tariffs are either a bailout to perpetuate uncompetitive American industries, or a license for efficient American industries to gouge their customers. It makes no sense for the government to "improve" a level playing field by randomly inserting hundreds of bumps, boulders and brick walls. Regardless of what tariffs another country may have, it is not in America's national interest for the Customs Service to selectively blockade our own ports.

Source: James Bovard, *The Wall Street Journal*, March 28, 1990, p. A14.

trade. We shall examine countertrade in greater depth in later chapters and see that it also facilitates trade.

Nonquantitative nontariff barriers. Many international trade specialists claim that the nonquantitative nontariff barriers are the most significant nontariff barriers. Governments have tended to establish nontariff barriers to obtain the protection formerly afforded by import duties. A study of the nontariff nonquantitative barriers revealed over 800 distinct forms, which may be classified under three major headings: (1) direct government participation in trade, (2) customs and other administrative procedures, and (3) standards.

1. *Direct government participation in trade.* The most common direct government participation is the *export subsidy,* one form of which is a cash

payment to the exporter. It is considered an unfair trade practice because it enables exporters to sell at lower prices than they could otherwise and still earn a profit. The European Community, for example, extends subsidies of $196 per metric ton of broilers and $93.76 per metric ton of wheat in order to reduce inventories resulting from high domestic support prices. Importing nations frequently retaliate by levying countervailing duties in the amount of the subsidy. Other kinds of export subsidies include inexpensive credit offered to the exporter's foreign customer by government-owned export banks (most major exporting nations have one; the Export-Import Bank in the United States is an example), lower income taxes on profits earned on exports, and special low freight charges when exports are shipped on domestically owned ship and air lines.

2. *Customs and other administrative procedures.* These cover a large variety of government policies and procedures that either discriminate against imports or favor exports. For example, in France, the time of the year when delays occur in processing the import documentation necessary to import sweaters happens to coincide with the buying season. Italy permits textiles to be imported through only 10 specified ports. The Japanese customs authority changed the classification of a processed food product that an American firm had been importing at a 16 percent duty rate to a category with a rate of 35 percent. U.S. Customs ruled in 1989 that it would treat imported sport utility vehicles, such as the Suzuki Samurai, as trucks subject to a 25 percent duty instead of the 2.5 percent that they had been charged. While this raises the price of these vehicles in the United States, it permits Suzuki to use its quota under Japan's voluntary export restraint to import more automobiles in their place.[22]

As the exportation of services has increased, governments have found ways to discriminate against them. Data processing has been especially singled out. In Japan, the company that holds a monopoly on international telephone lines refused to lease lines to American companies that wished to connect Japanese clients to data bases in the United States. Brazil requires governmental approval to use international telephone circuits for computers; naturally, foreign companies rarely obtain access to these circuits. In Europe, a number of governments are searching for ways to tax incoming information flows. A major problem, of course, is how to put a commercial value on them. Other examples of discrimination are the Canadian government's giving tax deductions to local businesses who advertise on Canadian TV—but not when they use American stations across the border—or West Germany's allowing only German agencies to hire models to appear in TV advertising.

A case of discrimination was stopped when the European Court of Justice ruled that the principles of the common market are compromised if consumers are denied the right to receive advertisements published across the border even when they are against the local law. A Belgian supermarket on the border with Luxembourg distributed leaflets advertising a special promotional offer. This upset Luxembourg shopkeepers because the leaflet gave both the old and the new, lower prices. Price comparisons are permitted in Belgium but are banned in Luxembourg. By arguing that the ban restricts imports into Luxembourg, Belgium convinced the Court to hear the case. The Court held that consumers are not protected, as Luxembourg argued, by denying them access to information. It noted that the right to information is a key element in the EC's consumer policy and that price comparisons are allowed in every EC country except Luxembourg and Germany.[23]

3. *Standards.* Both governmental and private standards to protect the health and safety of a nation's citizens certainly are desirable, but for years exporting firms have been plagued by many that are complex and discriminatory. France, for example, prohibits the advertising of bourbon, alleging that grain spirits are injurious to health; but of course, spirits made from grapes are exempt from the ban. Australia, like most countries, requires imported livestock to be quarantined but has no quarantine facilities.

Even beer is not free of regulations. Germany has a 16th-century law requiring German beer to be made only of hops, malt, yeast, and water. Beer containing other ingredients such as corn or rice, which is common in other countries, could not cross the border. The law is still in effect in Germany, but it has been struck down by the European Community on behalf of a French brewery that wanted to enter the German market. Although the law no longer affects beer exports to Germany, the French minister of trade has another problem. She claims to have read in German newspapers that drinking French beer can make a person impotent. The beer issue, however, is only 1 of more than 800 protectionist measures that the EC is studying.[24]

Denmark uses a packaging rule to protect its soft-drink industry from foreign competition. All beverages must be sold in returnable bottles. This deters French mineral water producers, because it is too costly to ship the returned bottles back to France for refilling. The European Court of Justice recently ordered Belgium to stop requiring margarine to be packaged as cubes. This rule had been effective in stopping importation from EC countries whose producers used round or rectangular packaging. Japan ruled some imported canned goods unacceptable under its agricultural standards because the figures for the day, month, and year of canning were spaced too far apart on the labels.

"Uniqueness" is another ground that Japan has used to shut out foreign imports. The skin of the Japanese is different, so foreign cosmetics companies must test their products in Japan before selling there. Imports of American tangerines have been limited because the stomachs of the Japanese are small and thus have room only for the local tangerines. Probably the strangest claim that has been advanced is that the snow of Japan is different, and therefore its ski equipment should also be different. A private industry group drafted a new set of standards for ski equipment, including one that increased the thickness of the ski under the binding. It argued that wetter snow and narrower slopes made these standards necessary. Only manufacturers meeting them would be able to use the mark SG, which stands for safety goods. Foreign manufacturers, which have 50 percent of the $400 million Japanese market, argued that the standards set by the International Organization for Standardization were adequate and the Japanese standards were unnecessary. Only after considerable pressure were the standards canceled.

Denmark, Finland, Norway, and Sweden each apply separate standards for electrical equipment and require individual testing in the country prior to certifying imports. Imagine the plight of the American manufacturer that must make up special products for each of these countries in order to comply with its special standards. The cost of compliance may price the company out

☐ **TABLE 3–2**
Annual Costs to American Consumer for Import Protection

Product Group	Consumer Losses ($ millions)	Producer Gains ($ millions)	Cost per American Job Saved
1. Textiles and apparel	$27,000	$22,000	$ 42,000
2. Petroleum	6,900	4,800	160,000
3. Carbon steel*	6,800	3,800	750,000
4. Automobiles	5,800	2,600	105,000
5. Dairy products	5,500	5,000	220,000
6. Maritime industries	3,000	2,000	270,000
7. Benzenoid chemicals†	2,650	2,250	1,000,000
8. Meat	1,800	1,600	160,000
9. Sugar	930	550	60,000
10. Nonrubber footwear	700	250	55,000

*Used in car bodies.

†Used in insecticides, detergents, and motor fuels.

Source: C. C. Coughlin, K. Alec Chrystal, and Geoffrey E. Wood, "Protectionist Trade Policies: A Survey of Theory, Evidence, and Rationale," *Federal Reserve Bank of St. Louis Review,* January–February 1988, pp. 12–29.

of the market. This could be and frequently is the reason why such standards were set up in the first place.

These few examples will give the reader an idea of the complexity involved in trying to eliminate nontariff barriers. Some progress is being made, but it is slow. Meanwhile, the international businessperson should look for such barriers before attempting to conduct business in a foreign country.

☐ Costs of Barriers to Trade

You read previously that the computer chip voluntary trade restraint accord has proven costly to the final consumer, and you might have been amazed at how costly it was. But this is a small part of what trade restraints cost you. Economists of the Institute for International Economics studied 31 product groups for which trade volume exceeds $100 million annually. They estimated that import protection costs the American consumers *more than $100 million annually* in 25 of the 31 groups. Table 3–2 is a summary of their findings for the 10 product groups most affected. This is why your jeans cost what they do. Protectionism makes sugar, a commodity for which the United States has no comparative advantage, cost you 50 percent more than the world market price. The United States has lost valuable wetlands in the Florida Everglades to sugar growers. One single family controls most of the Florida sugar industry, and annually American consumers make involuntary contributions of over $50 million to that family.[25] Note, too, how much it costs to save one American job! Studies done in other countries show similar results.[26]

ECONOMIC DEVELOPMENT

When businesspeople move from domestic to international business, they encounter markets with far greater differences in levels of economic development than those in which they have been working. It is important to understand this because a nation's level of economic development affects *all aspects*

□ **TABLE 3–3**
Categories of Nations Based on Level of Economic Development

Category	Member Nations	Characteristics
Developed	United States, Western Europe, Japan, Australia, New Zealand, and Canada	Most industrially advanced and technically developed nations
Newly industrializing countries (NICs)	Mexico, Brazil, South Korea, Taiwan, Singapore, and Hong Kong	Fast-growing middle-income economies; possess a heavy concentration of foreign investment and export sizable quantities of manufactured goods, including high-tech products
Developing	Remaining noncommunist countries	Lower-income nations; less technically developed
Nonmarket economies	Remaining communist nations	

of business—marketing, production, and finance. Although nations vary greatly with respect to economic development levels, we commonly group them into the categories of developed, newly industrializing, developing, less developed, or least developed.

□ Categories Based on Levels of Economic Development

developed a classification for all industrialized nations, which are more technically developed

Developed is the name given to industrialized nations of Western Europe, Japan, Australia, New Zealand, Canada, and the United States. A comparatively new category, **newly industrializing countries** (**NICs**), includes Brazil, Mexico, and the four Asian tigers—South Korea, Taiwan, Hong Kong, and Singapore. These countries (1) have what the World Bank considers to be middle-income economies, (2) possess a heavy concentration of foreign investment, and (3) export large quantities of manufactured goods, including high-tech products. See Table 3–3.

newly industrializing countries (NICs) the middle-income economies of Brazil, Mexico, South Korea, Taiwan, Hong Kong, and Singapore

There is a strong possibility that there will soon be a fifth tiger, Thailand, which unlike the other four, has considerable natural resources. And there may be a new pack of felines in Latin America: the four jaguars, Chile, Venezuela, Colombia, and one that is already an NIC, Mexico. The shift in domestic policies of these four nations points to the creation of market-guided, export-oriented open economic systems.

developing a classification for the world's lower-income nations, which are less technically developed

Developing, less developed (LDCs), and least developed are names used to categorize the rest of the world except the communist nations, which are usually placed in a separate **nonmarket economy** classification.

Intergovernmental agencies such as the UN and the World Bank tend to employ low-, middle-, and high-income designations rather than developed and less developed. However, since the latter are commonly used in industry as a kind of shorthand to describe the characteristics of two distinct groups of nations, we shall also use them in this text. Note that GNP/capita is the basis for both methods of classification.

nonmarket economy the World Bank's designation for a communist nation

□ GNP/Capita as an Indicator

We mentioned in Chapter 2 that although GNP/capita is widely used to compare countries with respect to the well-being of their citizens and for market or investment potential, businesspeople must use it with caution. What does

☐ **FIGURE 3–3   Underground Economies**

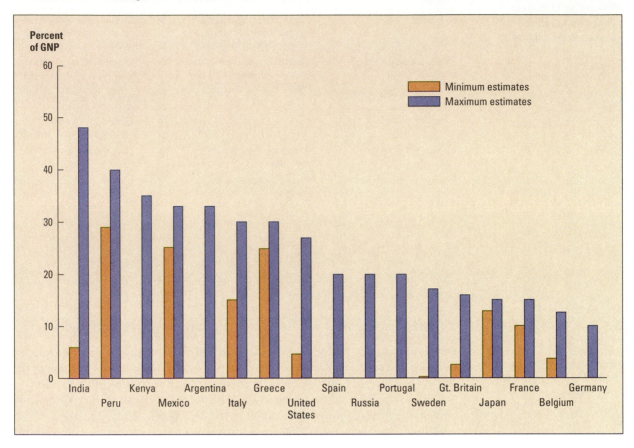

this value signify? Is a country with an $800 GNP/capita a better market for a firm's products than one whose GNP/capita is only $750? To assume this gives excessive credence to its accuracy. For example, to arrive at the GNP, government economists must impute monetary values to various goods and services not sold in the marketplace, such as food grown for personal consumption. Moreover, many goods and services are bartered in both low-income nations (because people have little cash) and high-income countries (because they wish to reduce reported income and thus pay less income tax). Transactions of this type are said to be part of the *underground economy*.

Underground economy.   Much has been written about the part of the national income that is not measured by official statistics because it is either underreported or unreported. Included in this **underground** (black, parallel, submerged, shadow) **economy** are undeclared legal production, production of illegal goods and services, and concealed income in kind (barter).

Figure 3–3 shows estimates of such economies. The estimates vary widely because of different methodologies used to compile them; also, people who have undeclared income are not going to admit it and be liable to prosecution

underground economy the part of a nation's income that, because of unreporting or underreporting, is not measured by official statistics for tax evasion. But there are many humorous incidents that people tell about others.

> **In Bonn, a gardener completes a large landscaping job and when asked for a bill replies, "If you want one, it will be DM1,500 plus 14 percent tax. If you don't need one, just pay me DM1,400 cash." In Greece, when a patient tries to pay with a check, the physician is reluctant to accept one or to give a receipt, and when he opens his desk drawer, it is crammed with cash. A visitor to an Italian company was talking to the chief executive when his secretary announced the unexpected arrival of a tax inspector. He told her to stall the inspector and then called the company's financial director. A few minutes later, the visitor looked out the window and saw the financial director running across the field with an armload of ledgers.[27]**

In addition to reducing the total taxes paid to government, the underground economy is responsible for all kinds of distortions of economic data. In Italy, for example, there was no record that a single pair of gloves was produced in Naples, yet it is now known that Naples is one of Italy's biggest glovemaking centers—the unreported output is produced by small groups of workers in kitchens and garages. The official government statistical agency estimates that the GDP is at least 15 percent greater than the official figure. The Italians are proud to say that, because of their underground economy, their per capita income has now overtaken that of the British. The *black work* in France is believed to be the reason why 50 percent of all the cement produced vanishes into thin air as far as official records are concerned. Mexico's underground economy involved 23 percent of the work force in 1990, up from 13 percent in 1986. The value of enterprises working without records and paying no taxes accounted for 10 percent of Mexico's GNP in 1990.[28]

Currency conversion.   Another problem with GNP estimates is that to compare them, values of GNP components expressed in the local currency must be converted into a common currency—conventionally the dollar—by using the prevailing exchange rate. If the relative values of the two currencies accurately reflect consumer purchasing power, this conversion would be acceptable, but often they do not. World Bank economists do make some adjustments of the official exchange rates but recognize that "their use to convert national currency values to the U.S. dollar does not attempt to measure the relative *domestic* purchasing powers of currencies."[29]

To overcome this deficiency, the United Nations International Comparison Program (ICP) has developed a method of comparing real GDP* based on **purchasing power parity** rather than on the international demand for currency (exchange rates). These comparisons result in GDP/capita that are considerably higher than those regularly given for LDCs and lower for most developed nations; that is, there are smaller GDP/capita differences between developed and developing nations than what are normally published (see Table 3–4). With the United States having changed in December 1991 to GDP from GNP to measure economic activity, only Japan and Germany still use GNP.

purchasing power parity
the exchange rate of two currencies expressed as a ratio equals the ratio of prices of goods in the two countries

---

* GDP, unlike GNP, excludes factor income from abroad.

◻ **TABLE 3–4**
GDP/Capita Based on UN ICP for Selected Countries, 1989

Country	GDP/Capita in US$s Converted at World Bank Adjusted Exchange Rates	GDP/Capita in US$s Based on Purchasing Power Parity
Japan	$22,896	$15,710
United States	20,690	20,690
Finland	20,172	15,230
Sweden	19,591	15,670
Canada	18,648	19,230
Botswana	2,083	3,990
Sri Lanka	377	2,160
Pakistan	326	1,700
India	283	980
Ethiopia	109	330

Source: *World Development Report 1991,* Tables 1, 3, and 30, pp. 204, 208, and 262.

◻ More than GNP/Capita Is Required

Even if the problems we have examined did not exist, businesspeople still would not obtain a true picture of the relative strengths of markets by comparing GNP/capita alone. Remember that GNP/capita is a mean, which infers that every inhabitant receives an equal share of the national income. This is patently untrue, especially in the developing nations, where the national income is much less evenly divided than it is in the developed countries. Thus, businesspeople who conclude from a low GNP/capita that a nation is too poor to buy their products will certainly miss some lucrative markets.

The dissatisfaction with GNP/capita as an indicator of a nation's level of living (it is an index of production, not consumption) has led to various attempts to create indexes by combining variables such as the consumption of steel, concrete, newsprint, and electricity with the ownership of automobiles, telephones, TVs, and radios. In Chapter 14 on market analysis, we shall examine an index to compare market size that *Business International* has constructed by combining population and GDP with the consumption and production of certain key commodities. Although GNP/capita is an imperfect yardstick for comparing the purchasing power and market size of nations, it does serve as a rough indicator of whether a country is in the developed or developing category. This is valuable because it gives a set of common characteristics that provide some insight to the approximately 140 nations belonging to the **Third World*** of developing nations.

Third World the developing nations

◻ Characteristics of Developing Nations

Although there is great diversity among the many developing nations, most share the following common characteristics:

1. GNP/capita of less than $2,000.
2. Unequal distribution of income, with a very small middle class.

* First World refers to industrial nations, Second World to the communist bloc, Third World to developing nations, and Fourth World to the bottom 30 nations of the Third World.

3. *Technological dualism*—a mix of firms employing the latest technology and companies using very primitive methods.

4. *Regional dualism*—high productivity and incomes in some regions and little economic development in others.

5. A preponderance (80 to 85 percent) of the population earning its living in a relatively unproductive agricultural sector.

6. Disguised unemployment or underemployment—two people doing a job that one person can do.

7. High population growth (2.5 to 4 percent annually).

8. High rate of illiteracy and insufficient educational facilities.

9. Widespread malnutrition and a wide range of health problems.

10. Political instability.

11. High dependence on a few products for export, generally agricultural products or minerals.

12. Inhospitable topography, such as deserts, mountains, and tropical forests.

13. Low saving rates and inadequate banking facilities.

You can see from these characteristics that a tremendous gap exists between the levels of living of Third World inhabitants and those of industrialized nations. Although economists have studied and theorized about the various aspects of economic development for over two centuries, their preoccupation with the poor nations of the world really began only after World War II.[30]

◻ A Human-Needs Approach to Economic Development

Until the 1970s, economists generally considered economic growth synonymous with economic development. A nation was considered to be developing economically if its real output per capita as measured by GNP/capita was increasing over time. However, the realization that economic growth does not necessarily imply development—because the benefits of this growth so often have occurred to only a few—has led to the widespread adoption of a new, more comprehensive definition of economic development.

human-needs approach defines economic development as the elimination of poverty and unemployment as well as an increase in income

The **human-needs approach** defines economic development as the reduction of poverty, unemployment, and inequality in the distribution of income. The definition of poverty also has been broadened. Instead of being defined in terms of income, as is common in developed countries, a reduction in poverty has come to mean less illiteracy, less malnutrition, less disease and early death, and a shift from agricultural to industrial production.[31]

Because of the increased emphasis on human welfare and the lack of a clear link between income growth and human progress, the United Nations Development Program has devised a Human Development Index (HDI) based on three essential elements of human life: (1) a long and healthy life, (2) the ability to acquire knowledge, and (3) access to resources needed for a decent standard of living.[32] These elements are measured by (1) life expectancy, (2) adult literacy, and (3) GDP/capita, adjusted for differences in purchasing power. In its first report, the program ranked Japan as the most developed with respect to social progress (HDI = 0.996); the United States ranked 19th

(HDI = 0.961), below most major industrial countries. The primary reason for this low ranking was the lower U.S. adult literacy rate.[33]

No accepted general theory.   The inclusion of noneconomic variables has made it impossible to formulate a widely accepted general theory of development. Instead of pursuing a general theory, development economists are concentrating on specific problem areas, such as population growth, income distribution, unemployment, transfer of technology, the role of government in the process, and investment in human versus physical capital.

Relevance for businesspeople.   What is the relevance of a lack of consensus among specialists about development theory? If a particular theory has fallen into disfavor among the experts, does this mean you can neglect it when dealing with government officials? That depends. It may be that those you are contacting still subscribe to it. In that case, you will want to emphasize the parts of your proposal that are germane to the theory, which is generally not too difficult because nearly every proposal will provide not only for investment in physical capital but also for training of employees, providing employment, and transferring technology. There will even be some redistribution of income through the creation of a middle class composed of managers and highly skilled technicians. As an example, let's look at how you might handle your proposal with respect to the investment in human capital theory.

Investment in human capital.   This recent development in theory recognizes that more than just capital accumulation is needed for growth. There must also be investment in the education of people so there will be managers to ensure that the capital is productive and skilled workers to operate and maintain the capital equipment.

If managers know that this theory has strong acceptance in the country where they have an operation or are seeking permission to establish one, they should emphasize this aspect of their investment. A multinational or global firm that does not have training programs for workers is rare, and nearly all send local managers to the home office to update their skills.

Import substitution versus export promotion.   Although developing nations have long considered the exporting of primary products (agricultural and raw materials) an important facet of their development strategy, they have not aggressively promoted the exporting of manufactured goods. Instead, they have concentrated on substituting domestically manufactured products for imports as a way to lessen their dependence on the developed countries.

Unfortunately, **import substitution** has not reduced their dependence on developed nations as much as it has changed the composition of imports from finished products to capital and semiprocessed inputs. Dependence on the developed nations has increased because the inability to obtain these imports due to, for example, a lack of foreign exchange now stops entire industries and throws thousands of people out of work. An example was the closing of automobile and agricultural machinery plants when the Turkish government could not obtain foreign exchange for importing the necessary intermediate products.

Another serious problem with the import substitution strategy stems from the protection to local industry that governments grant by levying high import duties on goods that are also made domestically. With this umbrella, local manufacturers are under no pressure to either lower their costs or im-

import substitution the local production of goods to replace imports prove their quality. Without such pressure, they rarely become competitive in world markets and thus cannot export. Furthermore, other domestic firms that must buy imports from these high-priced, protected industries cannot export either because their costs are excessive.

Problems such as these have caused numerous governments to change from a strategy of import substitution to one of promoting exports of manufactured goods. Spurring them on to this decision has been the rapid export growth of the newly industrializing nations, which we mentioned earlier. To force companies to become competitive in world markets, some governments are limiting the amount and duration of the protection.

This change in strategy affects the worldwide firm in a variety of ways. First, its local affiliate managers must be prepared for demands to export by government officials. They may even be handed an ultimatum, as were automobile manufacturers in Mexico: "If you need to import parts for your output, you must earn the foreign exchange to pay for them by exporting part of your production." A company asking for permission to set up a foreign manufacturing facility now will certainly be asked by government administrators about its plans for exporting. This is a new phenomenon to longtime managers accustomed to restricting an affiliate's sales to its internal market to save the export market for home country production. Second, managers can no longer count on having permanent protection from competing imports, as they once could. In some countries, they are likely to be told that after a certain date, they will lose their protection and will be expected to compete internationally. Last, in a situation where two firms are competing for permission to establish a plant, the deciding factor may be that one offers its multinational channels of distribution to the affiliate's exports.

The importance of keeping current.   These few examples illustrate (1) some of the concepts that underlie the strategies and policies of developing nations and (2) the relationship between the theories of international trade and development. Moreover, they show why experienced international businesspeople keep abreast of developments in both areas.

INTERNATIONAL INVESTMENT THEORIES

This third set of theories attempts to explain why international investment takes place. The contemporary theory has been expanded considerably from the classical theory, which postulated that differences in interest rates for investments of equal risk are the reason why international capital moves from one nation to another. For this to happen, there had to be perfect competition, but as Kindleberger, a noted economist, stated, "Under perfect competition, foreign direct investment would not occur, nor would it be likely to occur in a world wherein the conditions were even approximately competitive."[34]

monopolistic advantage theory foreign direct investment is made by firms in oligopolistic industries possessing technical and other advantages over indigenous firms

□ Contemporary Theories of Foreign Direct Investment

Monopolistic advantage theory.   The modern **monopolistic advantage theory** stems from Stephen Hymer's dissertation in the 1960s, in which he demonstrated that foreign direct investment occurred largely in oligopolistic industries rather than in industries operating under near-perfect competition.

This meant that the firms in these industries must possess advantages not available to local firms. Hymer reasoned that the advantages must be economies of scale, superior technology, or superior knowledge in marketing, management, or finance. Foreign direct investment took place because of these product and factor market imperfections.[35]

Product and factor market imperfections. Caves, a Harvard economist, expanded Hymer's work to show that superior knowledge permitted the investing firm to produce differentiated products that the consumers would prefer to similar locally made goods and thus would give the firm some control over the selling price and an advantage over indigenous firms. To support these contentions, he noted that companies investing overseas were in industries that typically engaged in heavy product research and marketing effort.[36]

International product life cycle (IPLC). We have already examined this theory to help explain international trade flows, but as we said, there is a close relationship between international trade and international investment. As you saw, the IPLC concept also explains that foreign direct investment is a natural stage in the life of a product. To avoid losing a market that it services by exporting, a company is forced to invest in overseas production facilities when other companies begin to offer similar products. This move overseas will be heightened during the third and fourth stages as the company that introduced the product strives to remain competitive, first in its export markets (stage 3) and later in its home market (stage 4), by locating in countries where the factors of production are less expensive. In-bond factories on the Mexican-American border are an example.

Other theories. Another theory was developed by Knickerbocker, who noted that when one firm, especially the leader in an oligopolistic industry, entered a market, other firms in the industry followed. The follow-the-leader theory is considered defensive because competitors are investing to avoid losing the markets served by exports when the initial investor begins local production. They may also fear that the initiator will achieve some advantage of risk diversification that they will not have unless they also enter the market.[37] In addition, there is always the suspicion that the competitor knows something that they do not and the feeling that it is better to be safe than sorry.

cross investment foreign direct investment by oligopolistic firms in each other's home country as a defense measure

Graham noted a tendency for **cross investment** by European and American firms in certain oligopolistic industries; that is, European firms tended to invest in the United States when American companies had gone to Europe. He postulated that such investments would permit the American subsidiaries of European firms to retaliate in the home market of U.S. companies if the European subsidiaries of these companies initiated some aggressive tactic, such as price cutting, in the European market.[38] Of course, as we noted in Chapter 2, there are a number of other reasons why investment in the United States by foreign multinationals takes place, such as *following the customer* (Japanese parts manufacturers following Japanese auto manufacturers), *seeking knowledge* (Japanese and European investment in the Silicon Valley), and *benefiting from the stability of the American government.*

internalization theory (an extension of the market imperfection theory) to obtain a higher return on its investment, a firm will transfer its superior knowledge to a foreign subsidiary rather than sell it in the open market

The **internalization theory** is an extension of the market imperfection theory. The firm has superior knowledge, but it may obtain a higher price for that knowledge by using it than by selling it in the open market. By investing in a foreign subsidiary rather than licensing, the company is able to send the knowledge across borders while maintaining it within the firm, where it presumably yields a better return on the investment made to produce it.[39]

Other theories relate to financial factors. Aliber believes the imperfections in the foreign exchange markets may be responsible for foreign investment. Companies in nations with overvalued currencies are attracted to investment where currencies are undervalued.[40] Although empirical tests are inconclusive, it does seem that a sizable number of U.S. takeovers by European globals and multinationals occurred during the late 1970s, when the dollar was relatively weak. One other financially based theory (portfolio theory) suggests that international operations allow for a diversification of risk and therefore tend to maximize the expected return on investment.[41]

Dunning's eclectic theory of international production.   This theory combines elements of some of the theories we have been discussing. Dunning maintains that if a firm is going to invest in production facilities overseas, it must have three kinds of advantages.

1. *Ownership-specific*—This is the extent that a firm has or can get tangible and intangible assets not available to other firms.
2. *Internalization*—It is in the firm's best interests to use its ownership-specific advantages (internalize) rather than license them to foreign owners (externalize).
3. *Location-specific*—The firm will profit by locating part of its production facilities overseas.

eclectic theory of international production
for a firm to invest overseas, it must have three kinds of advantages: ownership-specific, internalization, and location-specific

The **eclectic theory of international production** provides an explanation for the international firm's choice of its overseas production facilities. The firm must have both location and ownership advantages to invest in a foreign plant. It will invest where it is most profitable to internalize its monopolistic advantage.[42]

Note that there is one commonality to nearly all of these theories that is supported by empirical tests—the major part of direct foreign investment is made by large, research-intensive firms in oligopolistic industries. Note also that these theories offer reasons why companies find it *profitable* to invest overseas. However, as we stated in Chapter 2, all motives can be linked in some way to the desire to increase or protect not only profits, but also *sales* and *markets*.

SUMMARY

Why do nations trade? Mercantilist nations did so to build up storehouses of gold. Later, Adam Smith showed that a nation would export goods that it could produce with less labor than other nations. Ricardo proved that even though less efficient than other nations, a nation could still profit by exporting goods. All that was necessary was to hold a comparative advantage in the production of the goods.

The idea that a nation would tend to export products requiring a large amount of a relatively abundant factor was offered by Heckscher and Ohlin in their theory of factor endowment. Finally, the international product life cycle theory states that many products that are first produced in the United States or other developed countries are eventually manufactured in less developed countries and become imports to the very countries where their production began.

Although international trade theory argues for free, unrestricted trade for the benefit of everyone, restrictions on trade still exist because of the pressure of local interest groups. Such groups demand protection for defense industries and new firms, for example. In response to demands for protection, governments impose such restrictions on trade as import duties and quotas and other nontariff barriers.

A useful tool for international managers is an understanding of economic development theory. This will help them realize that in market analysis, a comparison of GNP/capita is not enough. They need to investigate the distribution of income and various indexes of consumption as well. Since many government officials are well versed in economic growth theory and are guided by it in their decision making, a knowledge of some of the most popular theories can be advantageous to managers. They must be aware, however, that today development includes not only economic growth but also political and social factors.

International investment theory attempts to explain why foreign direct investment takes place. Product and factor market imperfections provide firms, primarily in oligopolistic industries, with advantages not open to indigenous companies. The international product life cycle theory explains international investment as well as international trade. Some firms follow the industry leader, and the tendency of European firms to invest in the United States (and vice versa) seems to indicate that cross investment is done for defensive reasons. The internalization theory states that firms will seek to invest in foreign subsidiaries rather than license their superior knowledge to receive a better return on the investment used to develop that knowledge. There are also two financially based explanations of foreign direct investment. The first holds that foreign exchange market imperfections resulting in overvalued and undervalued currencies attract investors from nations with overvalued currencies to nations with undervalued currencies. The second is the portfolio theory, which postulates that foreign direct investment is made to diversify risk. Empirical tests indicate that most foreign direct investment is made by large, research-intensive firms in oligopolistic industries.

The eclectic theory of international production explains an international firm's choice of its overseas production facilities. The firm must have location and ownership advantages to invest in a foreign plant. It will invest where it is most profitable to internalize its monopolistic advantage.

QUESTIONS

1. *a.* Explain Adam Smith's theory of absolute advantage.
   b. How does Ricardo's theory of comparative advantage differ from the theory of absolute advantage?

2. What is the relationship between the Heckscher-Ohlin factor endowment theory and the theories in question 1?

3. Name some products that you believe have passed through the four stages of the international product life cycle.

4. It seems that free, unrestricted international trade in which each nation produces and exports products for which it has a comparative advantage will enable everyone to have a higher level of living. Why, then, does every country have import duty restrictions?

5. We certainly need defense industries, and we must protect them from import competition by placing restrictions on competitive imports. True or false? Is there an alternative to trade restrictions that might make more economic sense?

6. What is the "infant industry" argument? What is one problem with this argument?

7. "Workers are paid $20 an hour in the United States but only $4 in Taiwan. Of course we can't compete. We need to protect our jobs from cheap foreign labor." What are some possible problems with this statement?

8. There are two general classifications of import duties: tariff and nontariff barriers.
   a. Describe the various types of tariff barriers.
   b. What are some of the nontariff barriers?

9. Of what importance to marketers is a nation's level of economic development?

10. *a.* Although GNP/capita is commonly used to compare countries' market potentials, what are some of the problems associated with using this indicator?
    b. Is anything better than GNP/capita?

11. How does the present-day definition of economic development differ from the definition of economic growth?

12. What problems with the import substitution strategy have caused some governments to increase their emphasis on export promotion?

13. If countertrade permits nations that lack foreign exchange to trade, how can it be called a barrier to free trade?

14. What are the characteristics of most firms that invest overseas? What makes it possible for these firms to compete with local companies, according to the monopolistic advantage theory?

15. Describe two theories of foreign investment that are related to financial factors.

□ IS FREE TRADE GOOD FOR THE UNITED STATES?

Point

Counterpoint

Interview with Robert Lawrence
Senior Fellow, Brookings Institution

Interview with John Culbertson
Professor of Economics, University of Wisconsin

Q Mr. Lawrence, is free trade outdated?
A By no means. The basic principle—the so-called comparative advantage of nations—that motivated those advocating free trade under Adam Smith remains valid today. Nations gain by specializing through trade, both because producers gain from large-scale economies and consumers gain from being able to buy a broader range of goods.

OPEC countries have an advantage because of natural-resource endowments, such as oil. The United States has an advantage because of human endowments, its highly skilled and knowledgeable work force.

China has an advantage in unskilled labor, so it exports textiles. The Japanese and Europeans have an advantage in small cars, which we buy.

Q So free trade still benefits the United States by encouraging our economic growth and providing our consumers with a greater variety of goods at lower prices?
A Yes, encouraging not just economic growth but also improving our productivity.

Q But if other nations protect their industries, why shouldn't we do the same?
A Two wrongs don't make a right. Simply because other countries impose costs on their consumers doesn't mean we should do the same to ours.

Q Doesn't free trade endanger vital U.S. industries and forfeit millions of American jobs to foreigners?
A Our poor trade performance is not due to our free-trade policy. Rather, it reflects the strength of the dollar, which is related to the high interest rates caused by our record budget deficits.

It is preposterous to argue that protectionism by other countries has increased sufficiently to bring about the sharp drop in our trade balance over the past four years.

Q Professor Culbertson, is free trade still in the best interests of the United States?
A The administration's policy of permitting unlimited imports, rather misleadingly called "free trade," is ruinous to the country. It is causing us to lose desirable industries and jobs to other countries. We are losing steel, textiles, autos and even newer industries such as electronics and computers. So-called free trade is destroying America's industrial base and damaging our economic prospects.

Q Is there really very much free trade, as the term is generally understood, in the world today?
A As usually applied, free trade means all countries permit unlimited imports. But the United States is virtually the only country now doing that—to its great disadvantage.

Q But wouldn't protectionist legislation enacted now simply try to preserve industries that are dying?
A There's no reason to believe that steel, textiles and the other industries I've mentioned need to die. They will always be important to our economic well-being. We should not write them off and give away tens of millions of jobs.

Q Doesn't free trade lead to more-efficient worldwide production as countries specialize in what they do best?
A Those who advocate free trade do so in an imaginary world in which trade is balanced among countries and beneficial to all. We don't live in that kind of a world. The United States is suffering from a huge excess of imports.

Q What would you have us do as a country?
A We need to bring our trade back into balance by imposing restrictions on imports to approach equality with exports.

Point

Q Do you see any danger to our national security because of the decline of some of our basic industries?
A There is little evidence that our national security is being endangered. Take steel. The proportion of total steel output that goes for national defense is only 7 percent. Where free trade does make us vulnerable, we ought to subsidize domestic production through our national budget and not interfere with trade.

Q If we as a country turn to protectionism, how serious is the threat of foreign retaliation?
A Extremely great. Most of the bills in Congress would be counterproductive. They would close markets to our exports, not force our trading partners to open their markets.

Q What should we do instead?
A We should move toward liberalizing international trade. But unless we change our basic fiscal policies, any General Agreement on Tariffs and Trade round would be doomed. So we must do both: Get our own fiscal house in order and move toward a GATT round.

Counterpoint

Q Many experts say that if we go the protectionist route, that would bring slower economic growth, higher consumer prices and a lower standard of living for all Americans—
A Fallacious. They're referring to that imaginary case of idealized world trade. The real pattern of trade is damaging this country. The term "protectionism" is a propaganda tactic, a smear label, a pejorative. Nor is "free trade" really an issue of freedom. We should avoid such labels and try to design a sensible trade policy.

Q But doesn't free trade benefit American consumers?
A Only in the short run. The people who lose their jobs are damaged by unlimited imports. The effect of so-called free trade is to pull our wage level down by throwing American workers into competition with workers in low-wage countries. That is what lowers our standard of living.

Q Won't protectionist legislation set off a trade war and perhaps bring on another Great Depression?
A Most foreign countries already protect their industries. If we adopt a policy to bring our trade into balance, other countries won't retaliate. Bank failures, not trade policy, brought on the Great Depression of the 1930s.

Source: Copyright © 1985, U.S. News & World Report, Inc.

□ MINICASE 3–1

The Ricardo Case

Suppose that the output per man-day for wine and cloth in Portugal and England are the following:

Commodity	Output per Man-Day Portugal	England
Barrels of wine	2	1
Bolts of cloth	4	3

Suppose also that the total cost of land, labor, and capital to produce the daily output of either wine or cloth is 20 pounds in England or 1,600 escudos in Portugal and that the exchange rate is 1 pound = 50 escudos.

1. What are the prices for the English and Portuguese products in escudos?

2. What are they in English pounds?
3. What will be the direction of trade?
4. What are the upper and lower limits of the terms of trade?
5. The present exchange rate in this example is 1 pound = 50 escudos, but exchange rates do change.
   a. What will the exchange rate have to be to discourage Portuguese traders from importing English products?
   b. What will the exchange rate have to be to discourage English traders from importing Portuguese products?
6. What did you learn about comparative advantage from point 5?

☐ MINICASE 3–2

Tarus Manufacturing

John Baker, vice president of Tarus Manufacturing, called in Ed Anderson, the export manager, to discuss the sales results for the new adhesive that Tarus was exporting to its sales subsidiary in Colombia.

Baker:

Ed, How is Tarus Colombiana doing with the new adhesive we're sending them?

Anderson:

They're doing well. In the first six months, they've sold 6,000 quarts at 1,800 pesos or $3 a quart.

Baker:

Not bad for a small operation. If they keep it up, that cement is going to be a best-seller.

Anderson:

That's true, and our profit is good. Moreover, I've been studying Colombia's import tariff and I think I've found a way to improve our profit.

Baker:

Great. How are you going to do it? It has to be honest, Ed.

Anderson:

Well, you know that they have to pay a 40 percent ad valorem import duty on our $1.60 invoice price plus 60 pesos per quart specific duty. If, however, we send them the adhesive in 55 gallon drums, the import duty drops to 30 percent ad valorem plus a specific duty of 6,600 pesos per drum.

Baker:

Yes, but then they'll have to buy one-quart cans and labels and fill them in Colombia. This adds to their expense.

Anderson:

True, but because we won't have to fill the cans or charge them for cans and labels, we will save 20 cents per quart, which we'll pass on to them.

Baker:

How much will it cost to fill the cans locally?

Anderson:

They tell me the cans, labels, and labor to fill the cans will come to 180 pesos per can, and the only investment required is a shutoff valve, which they screw in the drumhead when the cans are filled.

Baker

I'm not sure I see the advantage, Ed. The cans, labels, and labor are more expensive in Ecuador than they are here. Where is the advantage?

Anderson

Let me show you, John.

Show Ed Anderson's calculations. Disregard any possible freight savings for shipping in bulk.

SUPPLEMENTARY READINGS

Human (Economic) Development

"Competition as a Tool of LDC Industrial Policy." *Finance & Development*, September 1989, pp. 27–29.

Hagen, Everett E. *The Economics of Development*. Homewood, Ill.: Richard D. Irwin, 1980.

Human Development Report 1990. New York: UNDP, 1990.

"The Challenge of Development." *World Development Report 1991*. Washington, D.C.: World Bank, 1991.

"The Human Condition." *The Economist*, May 26, 1990, pp. 80–81.

Todaro, Michael P. *Economic Development in the Third World*. New York: McGraw-Hill, 1981.

"UNDP's Human Development Index Places Japan 1st, United States 19th." *IMF Survey*, June 18, 1990, pp. 181–83.

International Investment Theories

Abdullah, Fuad A. *Financial Management for the Multinational Firm*. Englewood Cliffs, N.J.: Prentice-Hall, 1987.

Akaah, Ishmael P., and Attila Yaprak. "Identifying Target Segments for Foreign Direct Investment (FDI) Attraction: An Application of Conjoint Methodology." *International Marketing Review*, Autumn 1988, pp. 28–37.

Barrone, Robert N. "Risk and International Diversification: Another Look." *Financial Review*, Spring 1983, pp. 184–94.

Boddewyn, Jean J. "Foreign and Domestic Divestment and Investment Decisions: Like or Unlike?" *Journal of International Business Studies*, Winter 1983, pp. 23–35.

Caves, Richard. "International Corporations: The Industrial Economics of Foreign Investment." *Economica,* February 1971, pp. 5–6.

Davidson, Kenneth. "Strategic Investment Theories." *The Journal of Business Studies,* Summer 1985, pp. 16–28.

Hymer, Stephen. *The International Operations of International Firms: A Study in Direct Investment.* Cambridge, Mass.: MIT Press, 1976.

Madura, Jeff. *International Financial Management.* St. Paul, Minn.: West Publishing, 1986.

Rugman, Alan M. "Internalization Is Still a General Theory of Foreign Direct Investment: A Reappraisal of the Literature." *Review of World Economics,* September 1985, pp. 570–75.

International Trade

"Currency Depreciation and Imports." *Finance & Development,* June 1987, pp. 18–20.

Heckscher, Eli F. *Mercantilism.* Winchester, Mass.: Allen & Unwin, 1934.

"How to Solve the Trade Problem." *Newsweek,* January 12, 1987, p. 40.

"Jousting for Advantage." *The Economist,* September 22, 1990, pp. 5–39.

Ricardo, David. *The Principles of Political Economy and Taxation.* Homewood, Ill.: Richard D. Irwin, 1963.

Smith, Adam. "An Inquiry into the Nature and Causes of the Wealth of Nations." In *International Trade Theory: Hume to Ohlin,* ed. William R. Allen. New York: Random House, 1965.

The Extent of Nontariff Barriers to Industrial Countries' Imports. Washington, D.C.: World Bank, 1985.

Wells, Louis, Jr. "A Product Life Cycle for International Trade." *Journal of Marketing,* July 1968, pp. 1–6.

World Development Report 1988. Washington, D.C.: World Bank, 1988.

Protectionism

"An Introduction to Nontariff Barriers to Trade." *Federal Reserve Bank of St. Louis Review,* January–February 1989, pp. 32–46.

Bhagwati, Jagdish. *Protectionism.* Cambridge, Mass.: MIT Press, 1988.

"Cat and Mouse Game." *Forbes,* May 28, 1990, p. 48.

"Coping with the 'New Protectionism': How Companies Are Learning to Love It." *International Management,* September 1986, pp. 20–26.

Costs and Benefits of Protection. Paris: OECD, 1985.

"Despite Record Profits, Big Three Auto Firms Seek More Protection." *The Wall Street Journal,* January 24, 1989, p. 1.

Eliminating Barriers to International Trade. New York: The Conference Board, 1986.

"Fortress of Mercantilism Still Wary of Competitors." *Insight,* July 18, 1988, pp. 15–17.

Hufbauer, Gary Clyde, Dianne T. Berliner, and Kimberly Ann Elliott. *Trade Protection in the United States: 31 Case Studies.* London: Institute for International Economics, 1986.

"Is Japan Using the U.S. as a Back Door to Europe?" *Business Week,* November 14, 1988, p. 57.

"Protectionism and Economic Integration." *EFTA Bulletin,* April 1987, pp. 6–8.

"Protectionism Can't Protect Jobs." *Fortune,* May 11, 1987, pp. 121–28.

"Protectionist Trade Policies: A Survey of Theory, Evidence, and Rationale." *Federal Reserve Bank of St. Louis Review,* January 1988, pp. 12–29.

Report on United States Trade Barriers and Unfair Trade Practices 1990. New York: Commission of the European Communities, 1990.

"The Antidumping Dodge." *The Economist,* September 10, 1988, pp. 77–78.

"The Fanjuls of Palm Beach: The Family with a Sweet Tooth." *Forbes,* May 14, 1990, pp. 56–69.

"U.S. Trade-Remedy Laws: Do They Facilitate or Hinder Free Trade?" *Federal Reserve Bank of St. Louis Review,* July–August 1991, pp. 3–18.

Underground Economy

"Black Economies in Latin America." *The Economist,* November 12, 1988, pp. 78–79.

"Civil War and Migration Help Swell Central America's Pervasive Parallel Economy." *Business Latin America,* July 8, 1991, pp. 219–22.

De Soto, Hernando. *The Other Path.* New York: Harper & Row, 1989. An excellent book on the underground economy of Peru.

"Europe's Booming Black Economy." *International Management,* July–August 1987, pp. 24–30.

Houston, Joel F. "The Underground Economy: A Troubling Issue for Policymakers." *Business Review.* Philadelphia: Federal Reserve Bank of Philadelphia, September–October 1987, pp. 3–12.

"How to Make Poor Countries Rich." *Fortune,* January 16, 1989, pp. 101–06.

"Spain's Thriving Underground Economy Spurs Growth but Saps the State Treasury." *The Wall Street Journal,* September 22, 1988, p. 32.

Voluntary Export Restraints

Goto, Junichi. *A Formal Estimation of the Effect of the MFA on Clothing Exports from LDCs,* WPS 455. Washington, D.C.: World Bank, June 1990.

"Making Deals—Without Giving Away the Store." *Business Week,* June 17, 1991, p. 64.

"New U.S. Semiconductor Pact Irks Some Japanese Companies." *The Wall Street Journal*, June 6, 1991, p. A14.

"U.S. and Japan Agree to Extend Accord on Chips." *International Herald Tribune*, June 5, 1991, p. 11.

"Voluntary Export Restraints." *Finance & Development*, December 1987, pp. 2–5.

ENDNOTES

1. "The Rhythm of the Future," *The Economist*, December 14, 1991, p. 19.

2. Government administrators involved in project evaluation are increasingly applying socioeconomic rather than purely financial criteria. For example, social rates of discount and opportunity costs are considered rather than the pure costs of borrowing money. While marketing managers do not have to be development economists any more than they need to be specialists in marketing research, they should have a knowledge of the basic concepts.

3. "Fortress of Mercantilism," *Insight*, July 18, 1988, pp. 15–17.

4. David Ricardo, "The Principles of Political Economy and Taxation," in *International Trade Theory: Hume to Ohlin*, ed. William R. Allen (New York: Random House, 1965), pp. 62–67.

5. The idea that only hours of labor determine production costs is known as the *labor theory of value*. In fairness to Ricardo, we must admit that he included the cost of capital as "embodied labor" in his labor costs. Actually, as shown in the section "Introducing Money," the theory of comparative advantage can be explained by the cost of all factors of production.

6. Eli F. Heckscher, "The Effect of Foreign Trade on the Distribution of Income," *Economisk Tidskrift, XXI*, 1919, pp. 497–512; and Bertil Ohlin, *Interregional and International Trade* (Cambridge, Mass.: Harvard University Press, 1933).

7. The economist Bela Belassa, in his *Stages Approach to Comparative Advantage*, published by the World Bank in 1977, found in a study of 26 developed and developing countries that "the intercountry differences in the structure of exports are in a large part explained by differences in physical and human capital endowments."

8. Louis Wells, "A Product Life Cycle for International Trade," *Journal of Marketing*, July 1968, pp. 1–6.

9. Many new products come not from the manufacturer's laboratories but from its suppliers of machinery and raw materials. Du Pont, an important supplier to the rubber industry, maintains a large laboratory in Akron to give service to the laboratories of the tire manufacturers.

10. Belassa, *Stages Approach to Comparative Advantage*, pp. 26–27.

11. "Footwear Industry Tells Congress 'Shoe Gap' Threatens U.S. Defense," *The Wall Street Journal*, August 24, 1984, p. 21.

12. "Brie and Hormones," *The Economist*, January 7, 1989, pp. 21–22; and "No Solution in Sight," *The Modesto Bee*, March 23, 1989, p. B4.

13. "Double Your Standard," *Forbes*, March 6, 1989, p. 14.

14. "E. C. Imposes Antidumping Duties on Japanese Printers," *Europe*, October 1988, p. 42.

15. "The Antidumping Dodge," *The Economist*, September 10, 1988, p. 77; and "Cat and Mouse Game," *Forbes*, May 28, 1991, p. 48.

16. Countervailing duties on imported goods may be imposed under U.S. law when the production or export of such goods is subsidized by the government of the exporting country and when U.S. manufacturers of similar goods are injured as a result of the subsidy. The Department of Commerce is responsible for determining if an import is being illegally subsidized or dumped in the U.S. market. Before countervailing or antidumping duties may be imposed, it must also be shown that the U.S. industry has sustained or may sustain damages from these unfair practices. The International Trade Commission is responsible for the injury investigation and determination. See *International Letter*, September 10, 1982, published by the Federal Reserve Bank of Chicago.

17. Sheila A. B. Page, "The Increased Use of Trade Control by Industrial Countries," *Intereconomics* (London: National Institute of Economic and Social Research, 1980).

18. "Voluntary Export Restraints," *Finance & Development*, December 1987, p. 2.

19. "MITI Maintains Car Export Limits," *Automotive News*, June 4, 1991, p. 1.

20. "A Hidden Tax on All Our Houses," *U.S. News & World Report*, March 21, 1988, pp. 51–52.

21. "Washington, Tokyo Agree on Semiconductor Accord," *The Wall Street Journal*, June 5, 1991, p. A2; and "U.S. and Japan Agree to Extend Accord on Chips," *International Herald Tribune*, June 5, 1991, p. 11.

22. "U.S. Designates Suzuki Samurai as Truck Import," *The Wall Street Journal*, January 5, 1989, p. A4.

23. "EC Court Rules in Favor of Cross-Border Advertising," *Eurecom* (New York: European Community, May 1990), p. 2.

24. *Report on United States Trade Barriers and Unfair Trade Practices 1990* (New York: Commission of The European Communities, 1990).

25. "The Fanjuls of Palm Beach: The Family with a Sweet Tooth," *Forbes*, May 14, 1990, pp. 56–69.

26. The OECD published *Costs and Benefits of Protection,* which evaluates a wide range of studies on import restrictions of manufactured goods in OECD countries.

27. "Everybody's Doing It," *International Management,* July–August 1987, p. 27.

28. "Mexico's Underground Economy," *The Wall Street Journal,* October 9, 1991, p. A10.

29. "Technical Notes," *World Development Report, 1988,* p. 290.

30. Michael Todoro, *Economic Development in the Third World* (New York: Longman, 1981), p. 57.

31. Charles Kindleberger and Bruce Herrick, *Economic Development* (New York: McGraw-Hill, 1977), p. 1.

32. *Human Development Report 1990* (New York: UNDP, 1990), pp. 110–11.

33. "UNDP's Human Development Index Places Japan 1st, United States 19th," *IMF Survey,* June 18, 1990, p. 181.

34. Charles Kindleberger, *American Business Abroad* (New Haven: Yale University Press, 1969).

35. Stephen Hymer, *The International Operations of International Firms: A Study in Direct Investment* (Cambridge, Mass.: MIT Press, 1976).

36. Richard Caves, "International Corporations: The Industrial Economics of Foreign Investment," *Economica,* February 1971, pp. 5–6.

37. F. T. Knickerbocker, *Oligopolistic Reaction and Multinational Enterprise* (Boston: Harvard Business School, 1973).

38. E. M. Graham, "Transatlantic Investments by Multinational Firms: A Rivalistic Phenomenon," *Journal of Post-Keynesian Economics,* Fall 1978, pp. 82–99.

39. P. Buckley and M. Casson, *The Future of Multinational Enterprise* (New York: Macmillan, 1976).

40. R. Z. Aliber, "A Theory of Direct Investment," in *The International Corporation* (Cambridge, Mass.: MIT Press, 1970), pp. 17–34.

41. A. Rugman, *International Diversification and the Multinational Enterprise* (Lexington, Mass.: Lexington Books, 1979).

42. John H. Dunning, *International Production and the Multinational Enterprise* (London: George Allen & Unwin, 1981), pp. 109–10.

Section Two

The International Environment: Organizations and Monetary System

The world is becoming increasingly bureaucratized. National governments have grown as new agencies have been formed, and individuals and businesses must deal with bureaucracies for more and more permits, licenses, clearances, and so on.

This development has spread beyond national borders, and the same phenomenon has been occurring on an international scale. Individuals and businesses may not enjoy the delays and red tape involved in dealing with bureaucracies, but if they are to function successfully, they must learn to do so.

The truth is that dealing with international organizations has some positive features. Some of these organizations, such as the World Bank, the United Nations, the International Monetary Fund, and the Organization for Economic Cooperation and Development, are excellent sources of information for business executives and students. In addition, the World Bank, regional development banks, and private development companies are sources of billions of dollars and other currencies for financing government purchases from businesses.

A positive feature of the bureaucracies from the point of view of students and executives is that they are all sources of many good jobs. Not only do the national governments and international organizations hire thousands of people to be bureaucrats, but businesses must hire thousands more to deal with the bureaucrats.

As a result of huge foreign debt problems, which came to a head in the early 1980s, Poland and other eastern European countries, Argentina, Brazil, Mexico, and other Latin American countries, and countries elsewhere were unable to meet even interest, much less principal, payments on their debts. The International Monetary Fund was thrust into new prominence as a source of money and as an adviser and enforcer of how it would be spent. The Bank for International Settlements found itself in the unprecedented and unwanted position of making bridge loans.

In the late 1980s, the European Community and its 12 member-countries launched the extremely ambitious "Project 1992," the objective of which is to create a border-free market of some 320 million people by the end of 1992. At about the same time, the General Agreement on Tariffs and Trade began its Uruguay Round of negotiations aimed at nontariff barriers to trade plus restrictions on services, agriculture, and government procurement.

All of these reasons make international organizations an important subject for business executives and students. Therefore, we devote an entire chapter (Chapter 4) to these organizations.

The international monetary system is discussed in Chapter 5. This system is developing and changing constantly, and the international business student and executive must know where it is and where it has been. The past is important because some influential people and governments want to revive certain practices that are not presently in use.

Whenever you do business or travel internationally, you need different moneys, which are called currencies. Of course, you need U.S. dollars in the United States, but you must have pounds in Britain, francs in France, yen in Japan, and so forth.

Even if you don't travel or conduct any international business, it can be beneficial to know about the relative values of currencies. Currencies fluctuate in value constantly during one day, and over longer periods, their values can change significantly. On the forward, futures, or options markets, you can trade currencies for profit, just as you trade such commodities as wheat and silver. You would buy a currency if you thought its value was going up and sell it if you forecast a drop in its price. If you are in international business, you can use the same currency markets, or banks, to protect yourself against changes in currency values.

Also discussed in Chapter 5 are the gold standard, the gold exchange standard, nations' balances of payments, and fixed and floating currency exchange regimes.

Chapter 4

International Organizations

The United States gets back $3 in the form of sales by private firms for every $1 it contributes to the IDB.

> James Bass, economist,
> Inter-American Development
> Bank

The $64,000 question is whether or not there will be a Fortress Europe—where they'll be free traders internally and protectionist externally.

> Clayton Yeutter, White House
> chief domestic policy advisor

In several areas such as environment and external trade, the commission has too few staff to cope with the work load. Elsewhere, people have time to twiddle their thumbs. The personnel department . . . is grossly overstaffed. The directorate-general, laughingly called Information, has not got the communications skills to sell ice cream in a heat wave. The research establishments of the commission, parked in Italy, are known . . . as the holiday camp on Lake Maggiore. They have cost the European taxpayer a fortune and have produced little more than a suntan for those working there . . . .

> "A Fly on the Berlaymont Wall,"
> *The Economist,* June 1, 1991,
> p. 48

LEARNING OBJECTIVES

In this chapter, you will study:

1. The United Nations (UN), which is extremely active in the economic and social fields and is the source of much business for sellers of goods and services.

2. The new UN member-countries, which are almost all less developed countries (LDCs), are almost all poor, and comprise a majority of the UN membership.

3. World Bank loans, which provide borrowing countries with billions of dollars (and other currencies) and are used by these countries to buy goods and services from businesses in member-countries.

4. The International Finance Corporation (IFC), which is called the investment banker of the World Bank group because it encourages private investment in LDCs by LDC residents.

5. The International Development Association (IDA), which extends credits to the poorest countries.

6. The International Monetary Fund (IMF), whose size, powers, and activities have been expanding.

7. The General Agreement on Tariffs and Trade (GATT), which has had considerable success in reducing tariffs and quotas in international trade and in 1986 began a new (Uruguay) round of negotiations.

8. The Bank for International Settlements, which got unwanted publicity and activity as a result of the 1982 country debt crises.

9. The European Community (EC), which is the most extensive and successful regional economic grouping of nations. There is now a growing list of countries requesting EC membership.

10. The Organization of Petroleum Exporting Countries, (OPEC), which formed a cartel that was very effective for a time and may again become a powerful force.

11. The Organization for Economic Cooperation and Development (OECD), which is an excellent source for economic research and statistics.

KEY WORDS AND CONCEPTS

- Less developed countries (LDCs)
- Developed countries (DCs)
- Hard loans
- Soft loans
- Firm surveillance
- Debt default
- Debt rescheduling
- Managed trade
- Uruguay Round
- Tailored trade
- Marshall Plan

BUSINESS INCIDENTS

Michael Barth has learned that experts can be wrong. In the early 1980s, he helped organize a fund in the United States for investing in South Korean stocks. Wall Street experts said the fund would fail for want of investor interest.

Wall Street was wrong. Investors liked the potential of the South Korean economy and bought Korea Fund shares. It was listed on the New York Stock Exchange in 1984 and has since been one of the best-performing country investment funds.

Mr. Barth works for the International Finance Corporation (IFC) capital markets department. The Korea Fund has been followed by a $50 million emerging-markets growth fund, a $30 million Thailand Fund, and an $86 million Malaysia Fund. More are in the works.

Source: Cheah Cheng Hye, "IFC's Pioneering Investment Funds Funnel Capital to Asian Equity Markets," *Asian Wall Street Journal,* September 21, 1987, p. 28.

Indeed more country funds were in the works. Fifty new ones were created in 1990, and by the end of that year there were 150 such funds listed on the New York or London stock exchanges. They had net assets of $12 billion and offered investment opportunities in Asia, Eastern Europe, and Latin America.

Source: *The Economist,* June 1, 1991, p. 77.

Given the immense and growing numbers and importance of private and governmental international transactions, it is not surprising that a variety of international organizations have sprung up to facilitate, regulate, measure, or finance them. It behooves the business student—who is likely to be exposed to international opportunities and problems soon after graduation—to be aware of the existence and functions of a number of these organizations.

Some are worldwide organizations, and some are regional organizations with members from only one geographic area. Some are large, some small. Most are groupings of governments, but some are private.

The element common to all the organizations discussed in this chapter is that they all can be important to businesses. They may be sources of orders or sources of financing. They may be regulatory, or they may aim at standardization of weights and measurements. And, last but not least, they may be sources of jobs for you (see Figure 4–1).

THE UNITED NATIONS

Possibly the best-known worldwide organization is the United Nations (UN). Conceived and born amid the idealism and hopes that came with peace following World War II (1939–45), the UN has been a disappointment to many of its original supporters. Others foresaw more accurately what the UN's strengths and weaknesses would probably be.

> **During the early UN years, one international law scholar, Professor Edwin Borchard of Yale Law School, cautioned his classes, which contained a number of World War II veterans, not to be too sanguine about enduring peace resulting from the UN. He told them, in effect, to keep their powder dry, and indeed the education or early careers of many of them were interrupted by the Korean War. In fact, one side in that war fought in the name of the UN.**

Of course, there have been many other wars, declared and undeclared, between nations, colonies, provinces, tribes, and ethnic groups since the days of great expectation in the mid-1940s. These wars were waged despite the UN's peacekeeping efforts, and until recently many despaired of the UN as a keeper of the peace. However, during the late 1980s and into the 1990s, the UN was involved in negotiations and actions to cease or reduce armed conflicts. These resulted in the liberation of Kuwait from its Iraqi invaders, the Soviet withdrawal from Afghanistan, and the end of the Iran-Iraq fighting. It is, or recently was, at work in peace diplomacy, peacekeeping, or election monitoring in some of the world's worst trouble spots; in addition to those already named, they include Angola, Central America, Cypress, Haiti, Lebanon, Namibia, and the Western Sahara.[1]

In addition to its peacekeeping functions, the UN also conducts many activities potentially of great importance to businesspeople and students. It spends over $750 million annually for goods and services from businesses worldwide, and its agencies advise member-countries as they contract to buy goods and services in amounts that annually exceed $20 billion.

The UN is characterized by decentralization, which can be a source of frustration for the student or businessperson. To help businesses approach the UN, the Interagency Procurement Services Unit (IAPSU) was established

☐ **FIGURE 4–1   International Organization Job Opportunities**

International Fund for Agricultural Development (United Nations)
(Rome, Italy)
seeks

TECHNICAL ADVISER
(ENVIRONMENT)

RESPONSIBILITIES: Provide expertise on agriculture systems, natural resources management, land use planning and agro-ecosystem analysis in support of environmentally sustainable rural poverty alleviation, specifically, evaluate project interventions in terms of environmental considerations and provide technical support, develop environmental sustainability policies and procedures; assist in developing project pipeline and identify constraints affecting environmental sustainability and propose corrective action; develop and maintain data base on natural resource and environmental management aspects of rural/agricultural development; assist in staff training; liaise with external entities on natural resource management and environment issues; other related duties.

QUALIFICATIONS: Undergraduate degree in agricultural discipline, preferably agricultural economics, with interdisciplinary postgraduate degree in natural resource management 10-15 years experience in agricultural/rural development with at least seven years project experience in the developing world demonstrated work and/or research focus on ecological/environmental aspects of small-holder agricultural systems in tropical, sub-tropical and semi-arid areas. Familiarity with international development institutions and agricultural project financing. Full command of English and good working knowledge of Arabic, French or Spanish.

SALARY AND BENEFITS: IFAD as part of the United Nations common system offers competitive international salaries, benefits and allowances.

DURATION: Two year fixed-term.

DATE OF ENTRY ON DUTY: As soon as possible subject to funding arrangements.

Please send detailed résumé to:

Personnel Division, IFAD, Via del Serafico 107, 00142 Rome, Italy

Closing date for application: 7 August 1990.

Only shortlisted candidates will receive an acknowledgment.

United Nations Relief and Works Agency for Palestine Refugees in the Near East (UNRWA), an organization prociding education, health and relief services to a large refugee community in the Middle East, requires a

Chief, Supply Division

at its Headquarters in Vienna. Reporting to the Comptroller, he/she manages the Agency's central purchasing service for all commodities, total acquisitions amounting to US$60 million per annum. Oversees planning and co-ordination of inter-Field supply and transport movements. Is responsible for meeting Agency-wide transport requirements with a fleet of some 700 vehicles. Provides technical supervision of some 560 Field supply and transport staff and supervises some 10 professional level staff.

Annual net (tax free) remuneration at entry level US$76,000 (with dependants) and US$70,000 (single), plus fringe benefit package.

Detailed applications before 12 July 1990 to:

**Chief, Personnel Services Division (VN/12/90) (B)
UNRWA HQ Vienna, Vienna International Centre
PO Box 700, A-1400 Vienna/Austria
Tel: 21131 4310. Tlx: 135310 UNRWA A. Fax: 23 07 487**

International Fund for Agricultural Development (United Nations)
(Rome, Italy)

seeks

INTERNAL AUDITOR

RESPONSIBILITIES: The incumbent reports to the President and is responsible for the internal audit of IFAD's financial, operational and administrative control systems, specifically: propose an annual programme of work based on the need for auditing activities on a rotating basis, eg. cash, investments and investment income, administrative budget expenditures, loan and grant disbursements, loan income and repayments; coordinate annual programme of work with that of external auditors; develop audit programmes; participate in audits, plan and supervise work of internal audit staff; prepare audit reports, recommend improvements in internal controls, accounting and administrative procedures; monitor implementation of audit recommendations and propose action; conduct special studies and reviews; develop standards for the conduct of internal audit; perform other related duties as required.

QUALIFICATIONS: Recognised professional accounting qualification or University degree in a related field. Ten years experience in auditing, of which five should be at management level, preferably in a financial institution or an organisation of the UN system. Full command of English, knowledge of Arabic, French or Spanish would be an advantage.

SALARY & BENEFITS: IFAD as part of the United Nations common system offers competitive international salaries, benefits and allowances.

DURATION: 2 year fixed-term.

DATE OF ENTRY ON DUTY: as soon as possible subject to funding arrangements.

Please send detailed résumé to:

Personnel Division, IFAD, Via del Seratico 107, 00142 Rome, Italy.

Closing date for application: 7 August 1990.

Only shortlisted candidates will receive an acknowledgement.

Education Project Monitor

The Government of Sweden, the Government of the Netherlands and the World Bank, seek an experienced educational professional to serve as the monitor/evaluator of their five year, confinanced, General Education Project in Bangladesh. The objectives of this project are to increase equitable access to primary education as well as increase its quality.

The Project Moniotor will be responsible for analyzing data relative to project inputs, activities, and outcomes to provide a formative evaluation of the project's progress toward the achievement of its goals and objectives. The Project Monitor will be resident in Dhaka, Bangladesh. The minimum posting will be for two and one-half years.

Candidates should have an advanced degree in education; project management experience in developing countries (South Asia preferred); a demonstrated capacity to provide formative evaluations of project progress; and excellent interpersonal skills.

Applicants please submit curriculum vitae and cover letter before September 1, 1990 to: **The Search Committee, Room D 9015, The World Bank, 1818 H Street, N.W., Washington, D.C. 20433.**

The World Bank

Source: *The Economist*, June 30, 1990, p. 12.

□ UN Future

As we have stated, the UN's record in peacemaking and peacekeeping improved in the late 1980s and early 1990s. However, a number of people feel it needs a major overhaul.

One author says, "The UN is a legalistic absurdity, deeply flawed from birth. The accident of history that made the U.S.S.R. the West's glorious ally also made it a permanent member of the UN Security Council. . . . Furthermore, since the UN was the creation of the victorious allies, the emerging major democracies, Germany and Japan, were excluded from the role to which their economic power and military potential have long entitled them."[2]

Dealing in part with choosing the successor to UN Secretary General Perez de Cuellar, another article states, "African countries are persuaded that it is Africa's turn at a post that has previously been held by two Scandinavians, a Burmese, an Austrian, and now a Peruvian. The African assumption reveals the UN's fundamental flaw. Every senior post, every committee in the UN Secretariat has a government or a batch of governments to support it. Nepotism and national favoritism are rife."[3]

We named some UN specialized agencies. While saying some of them are doing good work, one article charges that too many "have become private worlds of cronyism, sloth, and incompetence."[4]

A minority of writers favor abolishing or at least ignoring the UN and turning instead to an organization of democracies that one author would name the Association of Free Nations.[5] Most believe such drastic changes would be impracticable and instead advocate more forceful efforts to improve the efficiency of the UN and its agencies.

THE WORLD BANK

The International Bank for Reconstruction and Development is usually referred to—in its own publications and elsewhere—as the World Bank. The World Bank Group consists of the Bank itself, the International Finance Corporation (IFC), and the International Development Association (IDA).

Applicable to the entire Group is the preference of most, if not all, governmental borrowers for multinational or international agency loans and assistance rather than bilateral loans or aid. Visions of imperialism, real or imagined, are less likely if the lender/donor is multinational or international.[6] The great majority of group loans or credits* are made to LDCs.

□ Importance to Business

There are a number of reasons why business should be aware of the World Bank Group's activities:

1. Many companies are suppliers to borrowers in group-financed projects, and these borrowers spend billions of dollars each year buying goods and services from businesses.

---

* In World Bank terminology, moneys lent by the bank are called *loans*, while those lent by the IDA are referred to as *credits*.

2. The development finance institutions (discussed below) in LDCs, which are partly financed and technically assisted by the group, are potential capital sources for businesses selling or working in LDCs.

3. The World Bank's center for arbitration may be able to resolve difficulties encountered by business in a foreign country.

4. Projects financed by the group tend to be mutually supportive (for example, general benefits resulting from improved infrastructure, and better economic resource inventories).

5. The information that the group gathers about a nation's or a project's finances, uses of funds, management abilities, and so forth tends to be more complete and accurate than the information likely to be available to a private, foreign business.

6. The Multilateral Investment Guarantee Agency (MIGA) was set up as a World Bank affiliate in 1988. Its insurance-type agreements will protect companies against expropriation, currency inconvertibility, wars, revolutions or civil disturbances, and other noncommercial risks to their new investments in LDCs that are signatories to the MIGA charter. MIGA has $780 million in subscribed capital and began writing agreements in 1990.

□ Hard Loans

hard loans made and repayable in hard, convertible currencies at market interest rates with normal market maturities

The World Bank makes **hard loans.** This means its loans are at prevailing market interest rates and are granted only to sound borrowers for periods not exceeding 25 years. The Bank must make relatively safe loans with high assurance of repayment because its own funds are acquired through the sale of securities offerings that must compete with government and private business offerings of all sorts. Investors would not buy World Bank securities at economical interest rates if they felt that the Bank's loans were insecure, because the Bank must repay the buyers of its securities out of proceeds and profits on its loans.

To date, there have been no defaults on loans made by the World Bank, and its bonds carry the highest quality rating available, that is, AAA. The World Bank has operated at a profit every year since 1947. That profit has been used to make additional loans and to furnish funds for the IDA, a part of the World Bank about which we shall talk shortly.

Although no World Bank loans have been officially declared to be in default, some countries have been unable to make payments when called for by the original loan terms. The Bank has rescheduled many of those loans, giving the debtor countries more time to repay them; however, it is quite possible that unless economic conditions improve for debtor LDCs, some World Bank loans will have to be recognized as in default.

□ Business Opportunities and Information Sources

The billions of dollars and other currencies lent by the World Bank create many opportunities for businesses to sell their products and services to the borrowers. International competitive bidding is a Bank requirement. However, although the Bank announces the signing of each loan, it does not invite bids or tenders from potential suppliers to the financed projects. Such invitations are the responsibility of the government or agency executing the project.

Thus, a company desiring to sell to a project must watch for the loan announcements and then contact appropriate officials in the borrowing country or at that country's embassy in its own country.[7]

Quite evidently, that procedure poses difficulties for firms, particularly smaller ones, which would like to sell their products or services to a Bank-financed project. In recognition of this, the UN began in 1978 to furnish procurement information. The UN Center for Economic and Social Information in Geneva publishes *Development Forum Business Edition,* a biweekly newspaper that gives details of all major business opportunities opened by World Bank loans. The newspaper publishes requirements for each project and instructions on how to bid for the business.

Among World Bank reports and publications that can be helpful to business and students are its *Annual Report, Statement of Loans* (quarterly), *Guidelines Relating to Procurement under World Bank Loans and IDA Credits, Uses of Consultants by the World Bank and Its Borrowers,* and *World Bank Atlas of Per Capita Product and Population.* Also available are reports of the World Bank's various General Survey Missions regarding certain countries or areas.

◻ International Finance Corporation (IFC)

The International Finance Corporation (IFC) is the World Bank Group's investment banker. Its sphere is exclusively private risk ventures in the LDCs. The purpose of the IFC is to further economic development by encouraging the growth of productive enterprise in member-countries, thus supplementing the activities of the World Bank.[8]

Joint ventures favored.   The IFC's policy is to favor joint ventures that have some local capital committed at the outset, or at least the probability of local capital involvement in the foreseeable future.[9] This is not to say that the IFC will not cooperate with capital sources outside the host country (the country in which the investment is being made), and there are many examples of such cooperation. Among the industries thus capitalized have been fertilizers, synthetic fibers, tourism, paper, and cotton fabric. The outside capital sources, if in related lines of business, are usually international companies (ICs). A few ICs that have cooperated with the IFC have been Phillips Petroleum, AKV Netherlands, ICI, Intercontinental Hotels, and Pechiney-Gobain.

Creation of local capital markets.   In return for its investment in a company, the IFC takes securities in the form of stock (equity ownership) or bonds (debt). One objective of the IFC is to sell its securities into a local capital market. To do that, it will help create and nurture such a market. For example, the IFC extended a $5 million credit line to a syndicate of private Brazilian investment banks to provide support for those banks' securities underwriting activities. The banks work with Fondo do Desenvolvimento do Mercado de Capitais, a revolving capital market development fund maintained by the Brazilian central bank. The objectives are (1) to induce the investment banks to assume a greater role in underwriting Brazilian securities in Brazil, (2) to improve the access of Brazilian companies to long-term domestic source capital, and (3) to encourage Brazilians to invest in sound domestic securities.

Liaison with development finance companies. The IFC is the liaison within the World Bank Group for the numerous development finance companies (DFCs)—sometimes called development banks, as in Ecuador—that have sprung up, primarily in the LDCs. These DFCs are in many ways local versions of the IFC. Each DFC seeks potentially profitable ventures within its country and assists with feasibility studies. If a venture proceeds, the DFC helps along the way with advice on plant, property, financing, management, or equipment. Finally, the DFC attempts to establish or enlarge a domestic capital market for securities of the venture.[10]

As you saw in this chapter's Business Incident, thanks to the IFC, investors from both poor and rich countries can now buy and sell securities (stocks and bonds) of companies operating in the developing countries through funds traded on the New York or London stock exchanges. In addition, stock markets are playing an increasing part in supplying and pricing fresh capital in emerging economies. During the 1980s, the combined capitalization of the 20 largest emerging markets grew sevenfold. By the start of 1991, turnover in these markets was nearly 40 times the 1980 figure. More telling, the average capitalization of these markets as a percentage of local GDP rose to 32 percent by 1990, compared to 6 percent in 1980.

The Third World's growing trend towards privatization will help its stock markets. As governments, especially in Latin America, trim back public sectors, they will deepen their markets with extra stock and open them to foreign capital and liquidity.[11]

The IFC published the *Emerging Stock Markets Factbook 1991*, which pulls together in one volume various series of data on the leading stock markets of the developing world. Copies are available from the World Bank Bookstore, 701 18th St. N.W., Washington, D.C. 20433, telephone (202) 473-2941.

Like the World Bank, the IFC is reluctant to admit default of a loan or failure of an investment and has rescheduled some loans. Unlike the World Bank, however, the IFC has written off a few investments that it judged could not be revived.

Figure 4–3 is an announcement of a project financed by the IFC together with private banks from various countries and the Export-Import Bank of the United States.

◻ International Development Association (IDA)

The IDA is the "soft" loan (or "credit," as an IDA loan is called) section of the World Bank. Although it shares the Bank's administrative staff and grants credits for projects covering the same sorts of projects in the LDCs as the Bank's loans, its **soft loans** differ from the "hard" loans of the bank in several important ways. They have up to 40-year maturities, compared to 15- and 25-year maturities of the Bank. The IDA may grant 10-year grace periods before repayment of principal or interest must begin, whereas the grace periods of the World Bank usually do not exceed 5 years. The IDA charges only three fourths of 1 percent as a service charge on disbursed loan balances plus one half of 1 percent on undisbursed balances. As is evident from these differences, borrowers from the IDA are the poorest of the poor LDCs, which need credit for development projects but cannot carry the burden on their

soft loans may be repayable in soft, nonconvertible currencies; carry low or no interest obligations; are frequently long term, up to 40 years; and may grant grace periods of up to 10 years during which no payments are required

☐ **FIGURE 4–3**
Announcement of an IFC Financing Together with Private Banks and the U.S. Export-Import Bank

This announcement appears as a matter of record only.

Mobil Producing Nigeria

U.S.$265,000,000
Project/Export Credit Facilities
for the
Oso Condensate Field Development Project

U.S.$170,000,000
Project Loan Facility

Funds Provided by

International Finance Corporation

and through IFC Participations by

Morgan Guaranty Trust Company	Union Bank of Switzerland
Banque Nationale de Paris	Crédit Lyonnais
ABN AMRO	Banque Française du Commerce Extérieur
Banque Indosuez	Banque Worms
The Long-Term Credit Bank of Japan, Ltd.	Morgan Grenfell & Co. Limited
New York Branch	
NMB Bank	Österreichische Länderbank
	Aktiengesellschaft

U.S.$95,000,000
Export Credit Facility

Guaranteed by

The Export-Import Bank of the United States

Funds Provided by

Morgan Guaranty Trust Company	Union Bank of Switzerland
Banque Nationale de Paris	Crédit Lyonnais
ABN AMRO	Banque Française du Commerce Extérieur
Banque Indosuez	Morgan Grenfell & Co. Limited
NMB Bank	Österreichische Länderbank
	Aktiengesellschaft

Documentation Agent	Administrative Agent
Morgan Guaranty Trust Company	**Union Bank of Switzerland**

April, 1991

Source: *The Economist,* May 11, 1991, p. 78.

economies or foreign exchange reserve positions that would result from normal commercial term loans. Determination of which countries qualify as poor enough for IDA credits is based on per capita incomes. The historic eligibility ceiling is $940, but scarcity of resources has long limited access to IDA funds to countries with per capita incomes less than $580. This is referred to as the "operational cutoff" for IDA eligibility. To the maximum extent possible, the credits are made in the currency of the borrowing member-country.

IDA capital sources.   Unlike the World Bank, the IDA cannot raise capital in competitive capital markets and depends instead on subscriptions donated by the DCs and some LDCs. Generally, the DC members make contributions in convertible currencies; the LDC members donate their own currencies.

IDA resources are renewed periodically by a process called "replenishment," whereby supporting nations donate money. In 1990, the Ninth Replenishment Agreement called for member donor contributions of SDR* 11.68 billion ($15.3 billion at the July 15, 1991, exchange rate) over the three-year period of the 1991–93 fiscal years.[12] Cofinancing from Switzerland (a nonmember) plus repayments of previous IDA grants would enable IDA to commit SDR 13.26 billion ($17.39 billion) over those three years, an increase of 15 percent over the Eighth Replenishment.[13]

□ Privatize the World Bank?

"The World Bank, designed to serve the nationalized industries and state sectors of developing nations, is being made obsolete by privatization in the Third World. . . . Opportunities for loans to finance state enterprise, the reason for being of the World Bank and of other multilateral development banks, will become scarcer if developing nation governments continue to sell state companies."

State companies already sold or leased and now owned or operated by private enterprises include telephones, airports, bridges, highways, tunnels, ports, railroads, water systems, and many other assets and operations. While the IFC efforts to aid private-sector companies have been generally successful, the Bank's efforts to direct its hard loans to private enterprise have created "a record of decades of botched lending."[14]

This is largely because the Bank's charter permits it to lend only to governments. To get around this, it has had to create lending intermediaries called development finance institutions (DFIs) run by local governments to relend World Bank funds to private borrowers. A Bank study found nearly 50 percent of those loans in arrears and said few DFIs have become financially viable.[15]

The United States has been particularly insistent on the Bank routing more funds to the private sector. In return for the Bank's agreement to study a charter amendment that would permit it to lend directly to private companies, eliminating DFIs, the United States supported an increase in IFC capitalization. The increase of $1 billion brings IFC capital to $2.3 billion.[16]

INTERNATIONAL MONETARY FUND (IMF)

Although the IMF deals solely with governments, its policies and actions have profound impact on business worldwide. Its influence may become even greater. Before explaining that statement, we should look briefly at the objectives and activities of the Fund and how they developed. Most of them continue to be important.

The IMF Articles of Agreement were adopted at the Bretton Woods Conference in 1944.[17] In general terms, the Fund's objectives were, and continue

* Special drawing rights are explained in Chapter 5.

to be, to foster (1) orderly foreign exchange arrangements, (2) convertible currencies, and (3) a shorter duration and lesser degree of balance-of-payments disequilibria. The premise of the Fund is that the common interest of all nations in a workable international monetary system far transcends conflicting national interests.[18] One of the Fund's original objectives, since abandoned, was the maintenance of fixed exchange rates among member-countries' currencies, with par value related to the U.S. dollar, which was valued at $35 per ounce of gold.

Each member-country has a quota equal to the amount it subscribes to the IMF. Votes at Fund meetings are weighted according to quota size, and the amount a member can draw is related to its quota.[19]

The IMF agreement was entered prior to the founding conference of the United Nations, and when the UN was formed, the Fund was brought into relationship with the UN by an agreement. This agreement preserved the Fund's independence, which was justified by the need for independent control of monetary management. This need results from the temptations of every government to overspend and cause inflation.[20]

◻ Changes in the IMF

The 1970s and 1980s saw some fundamental changes in the IMF's activities and roles. As stated above, the IMF abandoned the objective of maintaining the fixed exchange rate system. More accurately stated, the obligation of maintaining such a system remained in the Fund's Articles of Agreement, but the IMF was powerless to uphold it in the face of a situation in which all major currencies were floating* rather than fixed in value. In recognition of reality, the articles were amended to legalize the actual current practice, that is, floating exchange rates.

Greater power for the IMF?   The amended articles also included a new Article IV, which, among other things, empowers the IMF to "exercise **firm surveillance** over the exchange rate policies" of members. There are those who feel that this new surveillance power may permit the Fund to move toward the position in the world occupied by central banks nationally.[21] That, of course, would require the member-countries to surrender of a great deal of sovereignty, which many governments will stoutly resist.

The IMF fulfills its surveillance responsibilities in two principal ways. First, the board of governors regularly examines in depth each member's economic policies and performance and the interaction of those policies with economic developments in other countries. Second, the board holds regular discussions on the world economic outlook and periodic discussions on exchange rate developments in the major industrial countries.

The IMF contributes to policy coordination among the major industrial countries through its work on the economic indicators and the medium-term economic outlook. Those major industrial countries are sometimes referred to as the Group of Seven (Canada, France, Germany, Italy, Japan, the United Kingdom, and the United States), and the IMF managing director participates in the group's meetings. There are 148 other IMF member-countries, making a total of 155.

firm surveillance may permit the IMF to influence or even dictate fiscal and monetary policies of member-countries if the economically strong countries permit such intrusion

* Discussion of floating exchange rates as compared to fixed exchange rates will be found in Chapter 5.

"OK, I'm sorry we called you a dirty capitalist imperialist swine – now can we have the money?"

Reprinted from *The Wall Street Journal;* permission of Cartoon Features Syndicate.

debt default occurs when a debtor will not or cannot repay a loan when payment is due

debt rescheduling involves the debtor and creditor agreeing to permit a longer repayment period, lower interest rate, and/or forgiveness of some of the debt

World debt crisis and the IMF.   Over the years, countries have occasionally been unable or unwilling to pay their debts. When countries were unable to pay debts that came due (**debt default**), the debts were sometimes rescheduled to give them more time to pay (**debt rescheduling**). Debts of Peru, Zaire, and Turkey are among those that were rescheduled.

Usually due to government changes, countries sometimes refuse to pay the debts of previous governments; the new government repudiates the old debt. This occurred when communist governments assumed power in the former Soviet Union, the People's Republic of China, and Cuba.

Before 1981, such reschedulings and repudiations were relatively unusual. Suddenly that all changed. First Poland and other Soviet-bloc countries, then Mexico, followed by Brazil, Argentina, and other Latin American countries as well as countries in Africa and Asia found themselves short of money to repay their debts.

Financial and economic disaster?   Some observers foresaw massive debt repudiations, bank failures, world trade breakdown, and deep depressions with high unemployment. The debts of the non-OPEC developing countries totaled some $520 billion at the end of 1982, and the disaster scenario had all of them defaulting at once—perhaps after forming a "debt OPEC" to coordinate their debt repudiation.

Enter the IMF.   While Mexico was negotiating its emergency IMF loan in November 1982, it was preparing to inaugurate a new president in December. The outgoing president wanted no part of the austerity programs being insisted on by the IMF, and the incoming president had no official power until December. Jacques de Larosiere, the IMF's managing director, prodded both presidents into cooperation.

De Larosiere's problems did not end there. The some 1,400 large and small creditor banks of Mexico wanted no more to do with Mexico, so he called a creditors' meeting in New York, at which he bluntly warned them that unless they came up with $5 billion more for Mexico, the IMF would pull out. They would lose their entire loans if it did that. The creditors went along with the IMF plan.

Such aggressiveness by the IMF was a sharp departure from its previous low-key approach.[22] Add to that the large increases in the IMF lending resources provided by industrial member-countries between 1981 and 1986, and the Fund had become a major new world force.

Despite efforts of the IMF, private banks, and debtor and creditor countries and businesses, progress in solving the world debt problem has been slow and spotty. One development was that the United States became the world's biggest net debtor in 1986, with foreigners holding $107.4 billion more in American assets than U.S. investors held abroad. By the end of 1990, this amount had increased to $412.16 billion. Leaving the United States out of the picture, the 20 major debtor countries had external debt of $574.4 billion at the end of 1989 (see Table 4–1).

You will note some additional information available from Table 4–1. The countries' debit is shown by creditor types, that is, banks, other private creditors, and official, which includes governments and international agencies such as the IMF or World Bank. Debt is discussed further in Chapter 6.

Conditionality and cooperation with the World Bank.   Scarcity of trained personnel and lack of political will or strength are reasons why countries are unable or unwilling to take steps necessary to correct their economic problems. To assure better use of their funds, the IMF and the World Bank now cooperate with each other working with borrowing member-countries in what are called structural adjustment facilities (SAFs) or, if the problems are greater, enhanced structural adjustment facilities (ESAFs).

Funding by the IMF or Bank is conditional and linked to the member's progress in implementing policies geared to restoring balance-of-payments viability and sustainable economic growth. The borrowing member must file a policy framework paper that details annual programs it will undertake to reach the established goal. The Bank and IMF monitor the progress of the programs.

EUROPEAN BANK FOR RECONSTRUCTION AND DEVELOPMENT

This bank, known by its acronym EBRD, was created in 1990 to assist the countries of the ex-Soviet Union and its former Eastern European satellites. There were 42 founding member-countries, and its initial capitalization was $13 billion.

REGIONAL DEVELOPMENT BANKS

Regional development banks (DBs) are regional versions of the World Bank. There are three major ones: The African Development Bank, the Asian Development Bank, and the Inter-American Development Bank (IDB). Their function is to lend money in the less developed countries to build infrastructure,

□ **TABLE 4-1   The 20 Major Debtor Countries* (1989)**

	Bank Debt		Other Private Creditors		Official Debt		Total Debt
	$ Billions	Percent of Total	$ Billions	Percent of Total	$ Billions	Percent of Total	$ Billions
Venezuela	25.4	79.4	2.1	6.4	4.6	14.2	32.0
Mexico	69.8	69.7	1.9	1.9	28.5	28.5	100.3
Brazil	77.2	68.7	6.3	5.6	28.8	25.7	112.3
Bulgaria	6.6	66.3	1.0	10.4	2.3	23.2	10.0
Argentina	36.8	64.6	3.4	5.9	16.8	29.5	56.9
Ecuador	6.1	54.5	0.4	3.7	4.7	41.8	11.2
Chile	9.9	52.3	2.6	13.8	6.4	34.0	19.0
Costa Rica	2.1	45.4	0.4	8.8	2.2	45.8	4.7
Colombia	7.6	43.6	1.5	8.5	8.3	47.8	17.3
Philippines	11.8	39.9	2.1	7.0	15.8	53.2	29.6
Peru	8.0	39.2	2.2	10.8	10.2	50.0	20.4
Yugoslavia	6.6	37.3	0.8	4.7	10.2	58.0	17.6
Uruguay	2.4	32.2	3.9	52.9	1.1	14.8	7.3
Poland	8.8	21.7	1.5	3.8	30.1	74.4	40.4
Nigeria	6.8	21.2	4.2	13.1	21.1	65.7	32.1
Cote d'Ivorie	3.2	20.8	4.1	27.3	7.9	51.8	15.2
Morocco	3.6	17.5	0.1	0.3	17.0	82.1	20.7
Egypt	4.1	11.1	2.1	5.5	30.9	83.4	37.1
Jamaica	0.4	10.6	0.3	6.4	3.4	83.0	4.2
Bolivia	0.4	10.3	0.0	1.1	3.6	88.5	4.1

*Listed in descending order, according to percentage of debt accounted for by banks.

Source: *Barclays Economic Review,* August 1990, p. 34.

support agriculture and industry, and create jobs. The sources of their funds are several. All DBs get contributions from their member-countries, and all get money from developed countries that are permitted to be members even though they are not located in the geographic areas. DBs also raise money in the international capital markets, in the Eurocurrency market, and in the Eurobond market.

In 1987, the African DB's capital was tripled to $22 billion, while the African Development Fund replenishment was doubled to $3 billion. The Fund is analogous to the World Bank's IDA in lending to the poorest of the poor.

In addition to contributions from its 26 non-African member-countries, the Bank can raise money in the world's capital markets. To the surprise of many, it sports a triple-A credit rating.[23]

Although the majority of the African DB's loans have gone to governments, there is change in the wind. Due to the enormous problems engendered by public-sector mismanagement of finances and resources, the African DB and even some of the governments are moving to favor loans to private companies, including some privatized by those governments.[24] The Bank is also channeling more aid to two of Africa's most vital human resources, largely ignored in the past. They are rural women who produce more than two thirds of Africa's food and small-business entrepreneurs who keep many national economies afloat with their informal market trading. Figure 4−4 is

☐ **FIGURE 4-4**
Announcement of 1991
Bond Placement by the
African Development Bank

This announcement appears as a matter of record only.

AFRICAN DEVELOPMENT BANK

£100,000,000

11¼ per cent. Bonds due 2001

Issue price 99.63 per cent.

Baring Brothers &Co., Limited

IBJ International Limited	Barclays de Zoete Wedd Limited
Credit Suisse First Boston Limited	Deutsche Bank Capital Markets Limited
Goldman Sachs International Limited	Samuel Montagu & Co. Limited
J.P. Morgan Securities Ltd.	Nomura International
Salomon Brothers International Limited	Lehman Brothers International
UBS Phillips & Drew Securities Limited	S.G. Warburg Securities

BARINGS

July, 1991

Source: *Financial Times,* August 8, 1991, p. 13.

the announcement of a 1991 bond placement by the African DB. As you can observe, some very prominent international investment banks were involved.

At the Asian DB—the senior management of which is dominated by the Japanese—there is disagreement between Japan and the United States, the two largest shareholders. Washington wants to bring the Asian DB more in line with the World Bank, requiring borrowers to reform their economic policies before loans are granted, especially in countries where bloated government financial institutions are perpetuating inefficiency. While Tokyo pays lip service to this, it appears most interested in turning the Asian DB into a better channel for recycling its huge trade surplus and financing Japanese exports.[25]

In a move to direct more loans to private-sector borrowers, the Asian DB created a separate bank, the Asian Finance and Investment Corporation (AFIC), in August 1989. The AFIC is 30 percent owned by the Asian DB, the other shareholders being 25 commercial banks and securities companies. The AFIC is smaller than the Asian DB and therefore can act faster and consider much smaller projects.[26]

In 1989, the Inter-American DB's capital was increased to $51.5 billion, which allows it to lend as much as $22.5 billion through 1993. The increase followed a compromise that permits Bank directors from lending countries to delay loans for up to 12 months.[27]

The IDB also raises money in the world's capital markets. Bonds have been sold in the Eurobond market, Germany, Japan, the United States, and elsewhere.[28]

In 1986, the IDB was midwife to the birth of the Inter-American Investment Corporation as an affiliated organization. The corporation is to support the Latin American private sector with loans, investment, and technical and managerial assistance.

For our purposes, the importance of the regional development bank loans in less developed countries is that the LDC borrowers use much of the borrowed money to purchase goods and services from companies in other countries. The alert business management can earn some of that money.

BANK FOR INTERNATIONAL SETTLEMENTS (BIS)

The round tower of the BIS is the first landmark in Basle, Switzerland, for anyone leaving the main railway station and heading toward the city center. There is, however, no sign saying "BIS" because this is the most discreet financial institution in the world, the place where the central bankers of the major industrial countries meet 10 times a year to discuss the global financial system.

The BIS is such a convenient meeting place for central banker groups that one needs a program to sort them out. The BIS board of directors consists of the governors of several European central banks. A second group that meets in Basle consists of the central bank governors of the Group of 10—which has 11 members now that Switzerland has joined but is still called the Group of 10. The original 10 are Belgium, Britain, Canada, France, Holland, Italy, Japan, Sweden, Germany, and the United States. A third group is that of the European Community (Common Market) countries. Yet another group is the annual general meeting of the governors of the 29 central banks that are BIS shareholders.

In addition to providing a congenial and confidential meeting place for central bankers, the BIS provides secure, anonymous cover for shareholder countries as they transfer large amounts of currency or gold among themselves. When they do this through the BIS, the currency and gold traders may not be able to figure out the identity of the real buyers and sellers.

The world financial strains in 1982 that enhanced the IMF's role also caused some changes for the BIS. In 1982 and 1983, the BIS made loans to cash-strapped Hungary, Mexico, Argentina, Brazil, and Yugoslavia. These were called "bridge" loans because they were intended to bridge those debtor countries over a period until IMF, World Bank, government, and private bank loans could be mobilized. The first BIS bridge loans were made in 1931 to Spain, Hungary, Austria, Germany, and Yugoslavia to relieve the financial turmoil of the Great Depression. Even in those days, BIS understood how to adapt to pressing circumstances and to act quickly.

The BIS has four main functions. It serves as (1) a forum for international monetary cooperation, (2) a center for research, (3) a banker for central banks, and (4) an agent or trustee with regard to various international financial arrangements.

1. The forum function was touched on in the second and third paragraphs of this section.

2. Applied economic research finds an outlet in the series of economic papers published by the BIS. Probably the best known is the BIS *Annual Report,* published in June of each year.

3. Some 80 central banks from around the world have deposits with the BIS. In addition to placing surplus funds in the international markets, the BIS occasionally makes liquid resources available to central banks. The bridge loans referred to above and more traditional types of lending are other banking services the BIS provides.

4. As an agent and trustee, the BIS books and settles the balances that arise from currency exchange market interventions by European Community (EC)* central banks in observation of European Monetary System (EMS) rules. Officially, the BIS is agent for the European Monetary Co-operation Fund, which holds 20 percent of EC countries' gold and dollar reserves.

    The Bank also serves as agent for the private European Currency Unit (ECU)† clearing and settlement system. Large amounts of bonds and other securities and credits are denominated in ECUs, and the BIS-operated clearing and settlement system permits them to be efficiently bought and sold, transferred from seller to buyer, and paid at maturity.[29]

Since several East European countries broke out of the Soviet empire in 1989, a fifth function has been developed. A number of their central bankers now meet their Western counterparts at BIS headquarters to study free-market banking. Training courses have been established.[30]

GENERAL AGREEMENT ON TARIFFS AND TRADE (GATT)

◻ How GATT Was Conceived

Arising from the optimism among the Western allies following World War II was the ideal of an international organization that would function in the trade areas much as it was hoped the UN would function in the political and peacekeeping areas. A charter was drawn for an International Trade Organi-

---

*   The EC is introduced later in this chapter.
†   The EMS, European Monetary Co-operation Fund, and ECU are discussed in Chapter 5.

zation (ITO) at the Havana Conference in 1948. However, the ITO never came into existence because not enough governments ratified its charter.

At what were thought of as preliminaries to and preparations for an ITO, the American negotiators presented what they envisioned as a step toward an acceptable ITO treaty, which was to embody the numerous bilateral trade treaties into one multilateral treaty. They suggested, in the absence of any established international trade rules, that the commercial policy rules of the draft ITO charter be incorporated into a general agreement on tariffs and trade as an interim measure pending ITO ratification. The American suggestions were accepted, and so the General Agreement on Tariffs and Trade (GATT) was born in 1947.[31] Differently stated, the ITO was not ratified as a de jure organization, and GATT became a de facto international trade organization.[32]

Some observers felt GATT to be a "slender reed" on which to base world progress toward free international trade.[33] Nevertheless, it still exists and has been extremely successful in some areas of tariff reduction as well as in other fields.[34]

▫ GATT Successes

The 108 GATT members include all the OECD countries (Organization for Economic Cooperation and Development, covered later in this chapter), developing countries, and a few small communist countries. Together they account for almost 90 percent of world trade. Nine out of 10 disputes brought to GATT have been settled satisfactorily. Average tariffs in industrial countries have tumbled to around 5 percent from an average of 40 percent in 1947, and the volume of trade in manufactured goods has multiplied twentyfold.

▫ GATT Entirely Successful?

Despite these successes, the future of GATT is very much in question. Growing protectionism—usually by nontariff means—nurtured by the world's economic difficulties of the 1970s and 1980s has served to undermine GATT's credibility and threaten the open trading system it advocates.

managed trade special treatment of certain trade partners

Cars, steel, videos, semiconductors, and shoes have followed textiles and clothing into **managed trade.** In agriculture, where America, the European Community (EC, covered later in this chapter), and Japan are spending a total of some $70 billion a year on subsidies, GATT rules have had no effect. GATT has never covered services (nearly 30 percent of world trade), foreign investment, or intellectual properties (patents, copyrights, and so on).

The principle of equal treatment of all trade partners is much violated. The LDCs are permitted to protect their industries and discriminate among trade partners. The EC has abolished many of the tariffs on intra-EC trade, but tariffs are levied on goods from outside the community. In 1989, Canada and the United States formally began creation of a tariff-free trade area; goods from outside the area will be subject to tariff.

□ Will GATT Survive?

In 1986, GATT members met in Uruguay to begin the eighth round of negotiations aimed at reviving and strengthening the organization and broadening its scope. These negotiations are referred to as the **Uruguay Round** and are generally agreed to be a make-or-break affair for GATT.

It was hoped to bring under GATT's auspices new trade areas, including agriculture, services, intellectual properties, and managed trade. The timetable called for a four-year negotiation with final agreements in 1990. A midterm meeting was held in Montreal to measure progress in December 1988. There had been very little.

1990 came and went with no agreement. The planned wrap-up meetings were held in Geneva in December but ended in failure. It was generally conceded—at least outside Europe—that the main cause of the failure was the EC's refusal to compromise its high farm and agriculture export subsidies.[35] Strengthening GATT's survival possibilities was an EC decision in May 1992 to make major changes in its agriculture policy.

In the expectation that a new GATT agreement would be signed by December 1990, the U.S. Congress had agreed that if the agreement were submitted for treaty ratification by June 1, 1991, the Senate would vote yes or no, with no amendments permitted. This is referred to as "fast-track" authorization, which recognizes that if Congress were permitted to make amendments that must then be renegotiated with the other 107 GATT members, no agreement would be possible. Before June 1, 1991, Congress extended the fast-track provision for two years for the Uruguay GATT negotiators. The extension applies also to the agreement being negotiated that would add Mexico to the U.S.–Canada free trade area.

□ Is GATT Irrelevant?

So argues one school of thought, which holds that only the Anglo-American system is rooted in a free-and-fair trade approach. This school identifies five competing systems: Anglo-American, centrally planned, developing, mixed, and plan-driven. Countries identified with these systems are the United States (Anglo-American), the Soviet Union (centrally planned), Mexico (developing), France (mixed), and Japan (plan-driven).

Some economists and politicians believe the Anglo-American system is at a great disadvantage in playing by its free/fair trade rules against the other systems. **Tailored trade** is advocated, of which the U.S.–Canada trade agreement is an example. A *Harvard Business Review* article states, "American companies can't compete if foreign markets remain closed and the U.S. market remains open."[36]

ORGANIZATION OF PETROLEUM EXPORTING COUNTRIES (OPEC)

Realizing that if the oil-exporting countries were united they could bargain more effectively with the large oil companies, Iran and Venezuela joined the Arab Petroleum Congress at a Cairo meeting in 1959. Discussions and secret agreements at that meeting became the seeds for the Organization of Petroleum Exporting Countries (OPEC).[37]

◻ Oil Companies Should Have Listened

Early in 1960, the Venezuelan minister of mines and hydrocarbons and the Saudi oil minister wrote to the oil companies operating in Venezuela and the Middle East, requesting that they consult with the host governments before making any price changes. In August 1960, the oil companies reduced oil prices, and it is said that the host governments learned of it only when they read it in the newspapers. In any event, they had not been consulted. This made them angry and also increased their anxiety about the control and conservation of their natural resources. In that atmosphere, they called a meeting on September 14, 1960, in Baghdad.

Attending the meeting were representatives of Iran, Iraq, Kuwait, Saudi Arabia, and Venezuela. OPEC was formed, and the OPEC members took charge of pricing.

> This first headquarters of OPEC was in a relatively small apartment in Geneva. There was general skepticism as to the durability of the new organization and hesitancy on the part of some potential employees to take what they feared would be short-term jobs.
>
> Clearly, the skeptics have been proved wrong. OPEC's headquarters have been moved to Vienna, and its members, in addition to the founders named above, include Qatar, Libya, Indonesia, Abu Dhabi, Algeria, Ecuador, and Gabon.[38]

◻ Economic Muscle and Political Strength

OPEC soon began to test its strength, and the price of petroleum began to rise. At the end of 1973 and in early 1974, OPEC demonstrated its potentially devastating strength with the oil embargo by its Arab members against the Netherlands and the United States, accompanied by very large price increases to all customers. Its strength stemmed from the comparative cohesiveness of the members and from the fact that it controlled some 68 percent of the world's known petroleum reserves.[39] OPEC supplied some 84 percent of the European Community's oil needs and over 90 percent of Japan's.[40]

◻ Was OPEC Too Greedy?

Using its strength, OPEC drove up petroleum prices from about $3 a barrel in 1973 to close to $35 in 1980. Such a drastic increase in energy prices caused recession and unemployment in oil-importing countries, but it also sparked conservation measures, increased oil exploration in non-OPEC countries, and research for alternate energy sources.

Thanks to these initiatives, OPEC's market weakened, but its members refused to cut their production and thus an oversupply developed. OPEC had seized control of pricing in the mid-1970s, but by the early 1980s, the free markets were setting prices with major markets in Rotterdam, New York, and Chicago.[41] Prices fell to under $10 a barrel in 1986, recovered and traded between $12 and $19 until the Iraqi invasion of Kuwait in 1990, when the price spiked to about $34. When the market realized oil supplies would be adequate, the price dropped to around $17. The *IMF World Economic Outlook* forecast petroleum prices between $19 and $22 through 1993.[42]

Lower oil prices reversed conservation measures and greatly reduced both oil exploration and research into alternate forms of energy. There are those who worry that such trends may cause the world to become dependent on OPEC once again.

The accompanying cartoon of oil derricks topped with question marks symbolizes the many question marks surrounding the future of OPEC and OPEC's effects on the rest of the world.

THE EUROPEAN COMMUNITY (EC)

◻ Background

In the aftermath of the Second World War, Europe was in shambles as a result of the fighting and the devotion of all efforts and investments to the war. In order to assist Europeans back to their feet and to encourage strong, friendly governments, U.S. Secretary of State George C. Marshall recommended the United States give financial aid to and work with European countries in their reconstruction.

Marshall Plan named for American Secretary of State George C. Marshall, who suggested using U.S. capital and cooperation in Europe's reconstruction after WW II

Thus was born the **Marshall Plan,** which was immensely successful. It swung into action in 1948, and by the first quarter of 1950, European industrial production was already 138 percent ahead of the level reached in the last year of peace, 1938. Europeans achieved this success by working together, and they continued to do so. One milestone in this relationship was the Treaty of Rome. Signed in 1957, it created the European Community (EC), sometimes called the European Economic Community (EEC) or the European Common Market. The first six Common Market members were Belgium, the Federal Republic of Germany, France, Italy, Luxembourg, and the Netherlands. Chronologically, the

The EC Court of Justice building in Luxembourg

Raymond Reuter/SYGMA

next to sign the treaty were Denmark, Ireland, the United Kingdom, Greece, Portugal, and Spain, making a total of 12 member-nations.

EC objectives were to remove trade obstacles among members and to co-operate in many other ways. Brussels was established as headquarters, housing the EC Commission. The 17 commissioners are each responsible for a subject area somewhat similar to U.S. cabinet positions: labor, transportation, trade, and so forth.

The policy-setting body of the EC is the Council of Ministers. The foreign ministers of the 12 member-nations meet periodically to establish policy to be executed by the commissioners and the other Eurocrats, as the bureaucrats who work in Brussels are called.

The European Parliament (part of the EC) has its seat in Strasbourg and is popularly elected by voters in each member-country. It has broad but very blunt powers (e.g., it can fire all the commissioners but not fewer than all, and it can veto the entire EC budget but not a portion thereof). On one occasion, it did veto the budget—much to everyone's astonishment—and since then the commission and others have taken the parliament more seriously. Some feel if the parliament is given wider and more discreet powers, it could become the heart of an ultimate United States of Europe. The Single European Act of 1987 gave the European Parliament some power to amend legislation drafted by the commission.

The EC Court of Justice decides all cases arising under the Treaty of Rome, and its authority supersedes that of the member-countries' courts. Because the treaty covers many subjects and more and more cases are being decided by the Court of Justice, its influence is growing steadily.

From 1957 until the early 1970s, cooperation continued and measurable progress was made in eliminating tariff barriers among EC countries. Then

□ **TABLE 4-2   Comparisons and Forecasts**

		1983-87 Average	1989 Outturn	1990 Outturn	1991 Forecast	1992 Forecast
Growth (%)	United States	4.0	2.5	1.0	−0.1	3.0
Year averages	Japan	4.1	4.8	5.6	3.2	3.0
	Germany	2.2	3.9	4.5	2.7	2.1
	EC	2.5	3.5	2.9	1.4	2.2
	OECD	3.4	3.4	2.6	1.1	2.7
Inflation (%)	United States	3.4	4.8	5.4	4.2	3.2
Year averages	Japan	1.4	2.3	3.1	3.6	2.7
	Germany	1.6	2.8	2.7	3.5	3.5
	EC	5.2	4.9	5.1	4.5	3.8
	OECD	4.2	4.8	5.3	4.7	3.7
Current accounts ($ bn)	United States	−114	−110	−99	−20	−55
Yearly totals	Japan	56	57	36	35	35
	Germany	24	55	44	5	−10.0
Commodities	Oil ($/barrel)	23.7	18.0	23.5	19.0	19.0
Year averages	Non-oil (% change)	0.0	−8.0	−13.0	−5.0	6.0
Financial markets	U.S. interest rate (%)		8.4	7.9	6.0	7.5
End year	Japanese interest rate (%)		6.7	8.2	6.8	5.5
	German interest rate (%)		8.2	9.4	8.5	6.5
	Yen/dollar		144	134	145	160
	D.Mark/dollar		1.74	1.50	1.90	1.93

Source: "International Economy Summary Outlook," *Barclays Economic Review,* May 1991.

the Bretton Woods currency exchange regime collapsed;* the OPEC price increases hit; inflation, unemployment, and recession gripped the EC; and progress slowed considerably. The community languished for several years until it was jolted to life by Project 1992.

The EC joins most of the economic and industrial might of Western Europe and most of its population. The EC is the largest import and export market in the world. It is second only to the United States in the size of its gross domestic product, and it accounts for 20 percent of world trade, compared with 14 percent for the United States and 9 percent for Japan. Table 4-2 gives some comparisons between the EC, the United States, Japan, Germany, and the OECD[†] and makes some forecasts.

□ EC 1992

As indicated, the EC is a major world force. It has now embarked on Project 1992, which will likely make it an even more formidable force. The objectives are to eliminate all boundaries between the 12 member-countries so that people, capital, and goods can move freely and settle, work, and be used or sold anywhere from Greece in the east to Ireland in the west.

This offers great promise to European companies and possibly to companies from countries such as Japan and the United States, which are established in the EC. It also raises great fears outside the EC that as internal bar-

* The Bretton Woods system is discussed in Chapter 5.
† The Organization for Economic Cooperation and Development is dealt with later in this chapter.

riers are lowered, external ones may be raised, thus creating a Fortress Europe. Existing relationships between the EC and the outside world, particularly the United States, may perhaps mitigate Europe's protectionist urges.

EC–U.S.: A symbiotic web.   Well before 1992, the United States and the EC are of major importance to each other. For example, the 12-nation EC bloc buys over 25 percent of total U.S. exports—more than Canada and more than twice as much as Japan. In world trade, the EC is America's biggest customer; between 1986 and 1991, the United States went from a $26.4 billion deficit in its trade with the EC to a $16.1 billion surplus. On the investment front, over 40 percent of U.S. external investment is in the EC. These are America's most rewarding overseas investments.

The European money and capital markets have become major sources of U.S. corporate funds, rivaling U.S. domestic markets. Going the other direction, so many European companies raise money in U.S. markets that over $200 billion of transatlantic capital swaps each year have created a transatlantic financial network. Companies on both continents rely on this network for capital raising, risk diversification, debt management, import/export financing, and other purposes.[43]

Such symbiosis must be appreciated before we can intelligently forecast the impact of EC 1992 on America. Also, as the world's biggest traders, the EC and the United States share the major responsibilities for the future growth of free trade under the auspices of GATT. For a report on how unsatisfactorily they are meeting those responsibilities, see the discussion of GATT, earlier in this chapter.

Both the executive and legislative branches of the U.S. government and a number of state governments are taking steps to assist and provide information for American business as it strives to cope with and profit from EC 1992. Figure 4–5 shows key U.S. government contacts for EC 1992 information. Table 4–3 (pages 148 and 149) indicates state-level activities together with each state's exports to the EC.

In 1991, the American Chamber of Commerce in Belgium, EC Affairs Office, 50 Avenue des Arts, Bt 5, 1040 Brussels, published the *Business Guide to EC Initiatives.*

▢ Fortress Europe?

Although the EC's existing ties with the United States and other countries point away from isolationism, there are powerful forces of protectionism at work in the EC. Some say the big Japanese and American companies should not be beneficiaries of a 323-million-European market created by Europeans. Auto, textile, and other businesses are lobbying for protection, and the countries with weaker economies (such as Greece, Ireland, Portugal, and Spain) argue that their industries must be protected "temporarily."

Willy de Clercq, the EC commissioner for external trade, says nonmember countries must grant "reciprocal" rights to EC companies in their markets before the EC will permit their companies to operate in the EC market. There is as yet no clear definition of "reciprocal."

The best guess is there will be a Fortress Europe, but it will not be impregnable. Companies from nonmember countries that are established in the EC

ORGANIZATION FOR ECONOMIC COOPERATION AND DEVELOPMENT (OECD)

The members of the Organization for Economic Cooperation and Development (OECD) are the noncommunist DCs. The OECD originated in Europe, and most of its members are European. However, among its members now are Australia, Canada, Japan, New Zealand, Turkey, and the United States.

You should be familiar with the OECD because it produces and publishes extensive research and statistics on numerous international business and economic subjects. Also, it produced a declaration of guidelines of good business practices for firms operating in OECD countries.[51]

Material from and about the OECD may be obtained from OECD Publications and Information Center, 1750 Pennsylvania Avenue, N.W., Washington, D.C. 20006.

SUMMARY

The United Nations (UN) is probably the best known of the worldwide organizations. It is active in social and political matters. Its General Assembly, where each country has one vote, is dominated by the many less developed countries (LDCs). The UN's specialized agencies aid the LDCs in their fields such as agriculture, telecommunications, and so on.

The World Bank lends to LDCs for projects and has begun to insist that LDCs put their economic house in order as a condition to making loans. The International Finance Corporation (part of the World Bank) encourages private enterprise in LDCs.

The International Monetary Fund (IMF) helps countries with balance of payments deficits and has moved to the center of efforts to solve LDC debt problems. It is also working with the World Bank on LDC economic policies.

There are also regional development banks which make the same kinds of loans as the World Bank in their geographic regions. The regions are the Western Hemisphere, Africa, and Asia.

The European Bank for Reconstruction and Development was established in 1990.

The Bank for International Settlements (BIS) in Switzerland has become a sort of club for central bankers and national treasurers. It played a hand in helping LDC debtors.

The General Agreement on Tariffs and Trade (GATT) attempts to lower trade barriers. Its Uruguay Round of negotiations began in 1986.

The Organization of Petroleum Exporting Countries (OPEC) was for a time a successful cartel controlling the world's oil supply. There are those who fear it may regain control.

The European Community (EC) is a grouping of 12 Western European countries. They are engaged in Project 1992, whose aim is to abolish all barriers among them to the movement of people, money, and goods by the end of 1992. Besides the EC, there are many other but less ambitious groupings of nations.

The Organization for Economic Cooperation and Development (OECD) is an excellent source of research on many topics of value to business. The OECD has developed a code of conduct for firms operating internationally.

QUESTIONS

1. What are some reasons why businesspeople and business students should be aware of the more important international organizations?

2. What is the feature common to all or almost all new UN member-countries?

3. When the World Bank makes a loan, how can a business, which would like to sell products or services to the borrower, go about making sales?

4. a. Which part of the World Bank Group is referred to as its investment banker?
   b. Why?

5. How do IDA credits differ from World Bank loans?

6. The agreement between the IMF and the UN reserves considerable independence for the Fund. Why?

7. What new authority did the revised Article IV of the IMF Articles of Agreement give the Fund?

8. What changes have occurred at the IMF as a result of multinational debt repayment problems?

9. What are the aims of the Uruguay Round?

10. *a.* What group of nations brought about the creation of UNCTAD?
    b. Why?

11. What is the EC?

12. What is Project 1992?

13. Why do outsiders fear a Fortress Europe?

14. *a.* What happened to COMECON?
    b. What other organization would the ex-COMECON member-countries and other European states now like to join?

15. What is the importance of the OECD for business and students?

16. *a.* Stock and other securities markets are expanding in several LDCs. True or false?
    b. How are those markets likely to be affected by privatization of government-owned companies in the LDCs?

17. What are the purposes of the World Bank's Multilateral Investment Guarantee Agency?

□ MINICASE 4–1

Use of International Organizations—Setting Up a 100-Percent-Owned Subsidiary

You are an international business consultant in the United States. Your specialty is exporting to and investing, licensing, or franchising in LDCs.

One of your clients is a hotel company that wants to build, operate, and 100 percent own a hotel in Guatemala. Your client is willing to put up about half of the original capital but wants to be assured that its share of the profits can be converted to U.S. dollars and repatriated as dividends.

To what organizations discussed in Chapter 4 might you look for assistance in raising the rest of the needed capital? To what organizations might you look for information concerning a Guatemalan company's ability to convert profits into U.S. dollars and remit them to the United States?

□ MINICASE 4–2

Use of International Organizations—Establishing a Franchise Operation

Suppose this client wanted to put up little or none of the initial capital and wanted no ownership interest in the Guatemalan hotel. Your client will supply plans and knowledge for the design, construction, and furnishing of the hotel. It will publicize the hotel and sell rooms to tourists and conventions.

Your client will provide management and wants to be paid fees to compensate for its know-how, advertising, sales, and management.

Would you proceed any differently than in Minicase 4–1?

□ MINICASE 4–3

Sources of Information for an American Company Considering Doing Business in the EC

You are the owner of a small but growing electronics firm in New York. You have been reading about EC 1992 and wonder whether you should try exporting to that market or investing in it. What information sources for you are presented in this chapter?

SUPPLEMENTARY READINGS

Amuzegar, Jahangir. "Oil and a Changing OPEC." *Finance & Development,* September 1990, pp. 43–45.

Anjaria, S. J. "A New Round of Global Trade Negotiations." *Finance & Development,* June 1986, pp. 2–6.

Borpujari, Jitendra G., and Melhem F. Melhem. "Adjustment in Major Oil Exporting Countries." *Finance & Development,* September 1990, pp. 39–42.

Burki, Shahid Javed, and Norman Hicks. "International Development Association in Retrospect." *Finance & Development,* December 1982, pp. 22–25.

Childers, Erskine. *A World in Need of Leadership.* New York: Ford Foundation, November 1990.

Dunne, Nancy. "New GATT Round Opens This Month." *Europe,* September 1986, pp. 12–13.

"Evolution of the European Community." *Finance & Development,* September 1986, pp. 30–31.

Fliess, Barbara A. "Geneva Round to Uruguay Round." *Europe,* May 1990, pp. 13–14.

Hein, John. "What Will the GATT Beget?" *Across the Board,* September 1985, pp. 9–20.

"IFC Foreign Portfolio for Development: An IFC Initiative." *Finance & Development,* June 1986, p. 23.

"IMF's Structural Adjustment Facility." *Finance & Development,* June 1986, p. 39.

Johnson, Bryan T. "A U.S. Strategy for GATT." *The Heritage Foundation Backgrounder,* January 18, 1991.

Kelly, Margaret. "Fiscal Deficits and Fund-Supported Programs." *Finance & Development,* September 1983, pp. 37–39.

Keyes, Alan L. "The UN, a Wobbly House of Cards." *The Wall Street Journal,* August 30, 1990, p. A 8.

Lewis, Julian. "The Sheikhs of Wall Street." *Euromoney,* October 1990, pp. 16–22.

Lockhead, Carolyn. "Reports of the GATT's Death May Be Greatly Exaggerated." *Insight,* March 25, 1991, pp. 34–36.

Mehnert, Ralph J. "The ECU's Growing Role in Private Transactions." *Europe,* May 1986, pp. 31–34.

Morrison, Ann. "The Uruguay Round and the GATT: What They Are and What They Do." *Business America,* June 20, 1988, pp. 2–5.

Nakagama, Sam. "The Benefits of OPEC's Misery." *Euromoney,* December 1984, pp. 124–28.

"1992—Europe without Frontiers." *Europe,* April 1988, pp. 6–9.

"OECD Economic Outlook." *OECD Observer,* January 1986, pp. 27–33.

Ostry, Sylvia. "The Uruguay Round: An Unfinished Symphony." *Finance & Development,* June 1991, pp. 16–17.

Russell, Ruth B. *A History of the United Nations Charter.* Washington, D.C.: Brookings Institution, 1958.

Shihata, Ibrahim. "Increasing Private Capital Flows to LDCs." *Finance & Development,* December 1984, pp. 6–9.

"Take Advantage of the EC Market Now." *Business America,* August 1, 1988, pp. 1–6.

"Uruguay Round: Structure and Summary of Status of Negotiations." *IMF World Economic Outlook,* May 1991, pp. 116–119.

"World Bank: Soul Searching in Washington." *Euromoney,* December 1985, pp. 122–31.

ENDNOTES

1. "Renaissance on the East River," *The Economist,* December 15, 1990, pp. 43–44.

2. Brian Crozier, "Closing Time for the UN?" *National Review,* May 13, 1991, pp. 44–45.

3. "Thomas Pickering Excavates the United Nations," *The Economist,* March 2, 1991, p. 32.

4. "A Case for Emergency Treatment," *The Economist,* December 2, 1989, pp. 23–26.

5. Crozier, "Closing Time?" p. 45.

6. Alec Cairncross, *The International Bank for Reconstruction and Development,* Princeton University Essays in International Finance, no. 33 (March 1949), p. 27.

7. Maurice Wolf and Eiting Arnold, *Doing Business with the International Development Organizations in Washington, D.C.,* Tax Management, Inc., Bureau of National Affairs, 1982, pp. 20–88.

8. Article I of the Articles of Agreement of the International Finance Corporation (Washington, D.C., June 20, 1956), p. 3.

9. IFC General Policies (Washington, D.C.: IFC, 1970).

10. *Private Development Finance Companies* (Washington, D.C.: IFC, 1964).

11. "The Young Stock Markets," *The Economist,* June 1, 1991, p. 77.

12. Ernest Stern, "Mobilizing Resources for IDA: The Ninth Replenishment," *Finance & Development,* June 1990, pp. 20–23.

13. Ibid., p. 20.

14. Melanie Tammen, "Privatize the World Bank," *The Wall Street Journal,* May 17, 1991, p. A14.

15. Ibid.

16. Peter Truell, "U.S. Settles Dispute with World Bank," *The Wall Street Journal,* July 1, 1991, p. A16.

17. United Nations Monetary and Finance Conference, Bretton Woods, New Hampshire, July 1 to 22, 1944, Department of State Publication 287, Conference Series 55 (Washington, D.C.: Department of State, 1944).

18. A. Acheson et al., *Bretton Woods Revisited* (Toronto: University of Toronto Press, 1972).

19. Oscar L. Altman, "Quotas in the International Monetary Fund," *International Monetary Fund Staff Papers 5*, no. 2 (1956).

20. Leland M. Goodrich and Edward Hambro, *Charter of the United Nations: Commentary and Documents*, rev. ed. (Boston: World Peace Foundation, 1949), p. 349.

21. For a discussion of how surveillance is working, see G. G. Johnson, "Enhancing the Effectiveness of Surveillance," *Finance & Development*, December 1985, pp. 2–5.

22. Art Pine, "IMF Becomes Leader," *The Wall Street Journal*, January 11, 1983, p. 56.

23. Roger Thurow, "Third World Hope," *The Wall Street Journal*, May 16, 1989, p. 1.

24. Nicholas Woodsworth, "African Energy and Inertia," *Financial Times*, April 18, 1988, p. 5.

25. Richard Gourlay, "A Time for Critical Self-Study at the ADB," *Financial Times*, February 22, 1988, p. 3; and Cheah Cheng Hye, "ADB Goes Begging for Borrowers," *The Asian Wall Street Journal*, February 10, 1986, p. 5.

26. Cynthia Owens, "ADB Still Drawing Flack on Private-Sector Finance," *The Asian Wall Street Journal*, May 7, 1990, p. 24.

27. Peter Truell, "IADB Reaches Accord to Raise Capital Level," *The Wall Street Journal*, March 20, 1989, p. A 11.

28. *The IDB, Inter-American Development Bank*, January–February 1991, p. 16.

29. "The Bank for International Settlements: A Profile of an International Institution," CH 4002 Basle, June 1990, pp. 1–8.

30. Peter Marsh, "New East Meets Old West at Central Bankers' Bank," *Financial Times*, July 9, 1991, p. 2.

31. Richard N. Gardner, *Sterling-Dollar Diplomacy* (New York: Oxford University Press, 1956).

32. Gerard Curzon, *Multilateral Commercial Diplomacy* (New York: Praeger Publishers, 1965).

33. Gardner, *Sterling-Dollar Diplomacy*, pp. 379–80.

34. Bernard Norwood, "The Kennedy Round: A Try at Linear Trade Negotiations," *Journal of Law and Economics*, October 12, 1966, pp. 297–319; Ernest M. Preeg, *Traders and Diplomats* (Washington, D.C.: Brookings Institution, 1970); John W. Evans, *The Kennedy Round in American Trade Policy: The Twilight of GATT?* (Cambridge, Mass.: Harvard University Press, 1971); Sidney Golt, *The GATT Negotiations, 1973–1974 A Guide to the Issues* (London, Washington, and Ottawa: British–North America Committee, 1974); and B. Balassa and M. E. Dreinin, "Trade Liberalization under the Kennedy Round: The Static Effects," *Review of Economics and Statistics*, May 1967, pp. 125–37.

35. Bryan T. Johnson, "A U.S. Strategy for GATT," *The Heritage Foundation Backgrounder*, January 18, 1991, p. 2.

36. Pat Choate and Jayne Linger, "Tailored Trade: Dealing with the World as It Is," *Harvard Business Review*, January–February 1988, pp. 86–93. See also John B. Judis, "Time for an American Industrial Policy," *The Wall Street Journal*, February 14, 1991, p. A 13; and Kevin L. Kearns, "Behind Those Shrinking Trade Deficit Numbers," *The Wall Street Journal*, July 25, 1991, p. A15.

37. Perez Alfonze, "The Organization of Petroleum Exporting Countries," (Caracas) *Monthly Bulletin*, no. 2 (1966). See also John B. Judis, "Time for an American Industrial Policy," *The Wall Street Journal*, February 14, 1991, p. A13; and Kevin L. Kearns, "Behind Those Shrinking Trade Deficit Numbers," *The Wall Street Journal*, July 25, 1991, p. A15.

38. Wendell H. McCulloch, Jr., notes of interviews and conversations with OPEC employees and others in Geneva.

39. *International Petroleum Encyclopedia*, 1979, pp. 194–95, table 6.

40. Luis Vallenilla, *Oil: The Making of a New Economic Order* (New York: McGraw-Hill, 1975).

41. James Cook, "Comeuppance," *Forbes*, May 9, 1983, pp. 55–56.

42. "World Oil Situation: Recent Developments and Prospects," *IMF World Economic Outlook*, May 1991, pp. 77–85; and "Oil Price Assumptions and Economic Effects of Crisis in the Middle East," *IMF World Economic Outlook*, May 1991, pp. 21–25.

43. Wendell H. McCulloch, Jr., "United States of Europe 1992?" *Backgrounder*, no. 706, The Heritage Foundation, May 5, 1989, p. 2.

44. Martin Giles, "Business in Europe on the Defensive," *The Economist Survey*, June 8, 1991; and "A Relapse in Europe?" *The Wall Street Journal*, May 17, 1991, p. A 14.

45. McCulloch, "United States," p. 4.; and see Karen Elliott House, "Europtimism Dies," *The Wall Street Journal*, May 9, 1991, p. A14; Lucy Walker, "Rome Blots Its Market Copybook," *The European*, June 2, 1991, p. 4; "Laws unto Themselves," *The Economist*, June 22, 1991, p. 76; and Mark M. Nelson, "EC Summit Indicates Coming Months Will Be Both Divisive and Unpredictable," *The Wall Street Journal*, July 1, 1991, p. A10.

46. *EFTA Bulletin*, 3–4/91, pp. 1–32.

47. Anthony Robinson and Leyla Boulton, "High Hopes Give Way to Empty Shelves," *Financial Times*, April 9, 1991, p. 4; "COMECON Life after Death," *The Economist*, April 20, 1991, pp. 51–52; Richard D. Holman, "COMECON Problems Linger," *The Wall Street Journal*, July 1, 1991, p. A10; and Leyla Boulton, "COMECON's Divorce Bogged Down in Property Squabble," *Financial Times*, July 23, 1991, p. 2.

48. Wendell H. McCulloch, Jr., and Donald A. Ball, "Canada–United States Free Trade Agreement: Add Mexico?" *Proceedings of the International Trade and Finance Association Annual Meeting*, May 30–June 2, 1991, Volume I, pp. 1–14.

49. Leslie Crawford, "Chile makes U.S. free trade pact a top priority," *Financial Times*, April 16, 1991, p. 3.

50. "South American Common Market," *Review of the Economic Situation of Mexico*, Banamex, June 1991, pp. 259–63; "The Caracas Act," *Venezuelan News and Views*, June 1991, p. 9; "U.S. Signs Trade Pact with Four Latin Nations," *The Wall Street Journal*, June 21, 1991, p. B9.

51. OECD, International Investment and Multinational Enterprises, adopted June 21, 1976, OECD Doc. 21 (76)4/I (1976).

the United States increases its net reserve indebtedness with a balance-of-payments (BOP) deficit. The United States can increase its liquidity only at the expense of other countries; a U.S. BOP surplus would drain US$ reserves from other countries. Thus, under the present system, the reserves of other countries can increase only if the largest debtor nation in the world—the United States—goes further into debt.

It has been suggested that the five nations with the largest economies should agree to settle their accounts with one another in gold, not US$s.[4] If a gold standard were established, what should be the price of gold? Lewis Lehrman advocates $500 an ounce, based on production costs. Arthur Laffer picks a price in the $200 range, based on the increase in the consumer price level since gold was $35 an ounce. A third school of thought, identified with Robert Mundell, suggests pegging the price where it happens to be on the day that the five nations agree to institute a gold standard.[5]

◻ Present-Day Uses of Gold

In addition to its use in jewelry, gold has some industrial uses. It is an excellent conductor of heat and is used as protective insulation in the space programs.

In India, gold is a very popular dowry at weddings; at a typical wedding, about $500 worth is given. It also serves as a currency in the pervasive black market in India.[6] The Indian government also has uses for gold. In 1991, it shipped 45 tons to Switzerland and London. This Swiss shipment was to secure a $200 million loan from a Swiss bank. The Indian gold in London would permit India to borrow from the Bank of England and serves to "shore up the confidence of the international community."[7]

A new gold standard–type use has been suggested by Federal Reserve governor Wayne Angell and several economists. Speaking first about the Soviet Union and then the Russian Republic, they argue that the ruble—or whatever the currency is called—should be backed by gold.

To protect Russia against changes in the price of gold—if the price rises, there would be inflation; if it declines, there would be deflation—they advocate gold-backed U.S. dollars, convertible into the ruble and vice-versa. The United States would be cooperating with Russia to establish a stable international currency backed by gold.

A major objective is to bring about price stability and attract foreign investment in Russia. The political objective is to avoid economic chaos, which could cause social upheaval and the overthrow of the democratically elected government. For further discussion of this, see the supplementary reading by Judy Shelton.

BRETTON WOODS AND THE GOLD EXCHANGE STANDARD

During World War II, the countries of the world were much too involved with the hostilities to consider the gold standard or any other monetary system. However, many officials realized some system must be established to operate when peace returned. Actually, consideration of it did not await the firing of the last shot. Before that, in 1944, representatives of the major Allied

Bretton Woods a New Hampshire town where treasury and central bank representatives met near the end of World War II. They established the IMF, the World Bank, and the gold exchange standard

powers, with the United States and Britain assuming the dominant roles, met at **Bretton Woods,** New Hampshire, to plan for the future.

There was general consensus that (1) stable exchange rates were desirable, but experience might dictate adjustments; (2) floating* or fluctuating exchange rates had proved unsatisfactory, though the reasons for this opinion were little discussed; and (3) the government controls of trade, exchange, production, and so forth that had developed from 1931 through World War II were wasteful, discriminatory, and detrimental to expansion of world trade and investment. Despite the third consensus, the conferees recognized that some conditions—for example, reconstruction from war damage or development of less developed countries (LDCs)—would require government controls.

To achieve its goals, the Bretton Woods Conference established the International Monetary Fund (IMF). Article I of the IMF Articles of Agreement set forth its purposes, which reflected the consensus referred to above.[8] The IMF Articles of Agreement entered into force in December 1945.

central reserve assets are nations' savings accounts in which are held dollars and other hard currencies, gold, and SDRs

The IMF agreement was the basis for the international monetary system from 1945 until 1971. It is doubtful, however, that the future role assumed by, or thrust upon, the US$—which became the major **central reserve asset**—was fully foreseen.[9]

The US$ was agreed to be the only currency directly convertible into gold for official monetary purposes. An ounce of gold was agreed to be worth US$35, and other currencies were assigned so-called par values in relationship to the US$. For example, the British pound's par value was US$2.40, the French franc's was US$0.18, and the German mark's was US$0.2732.[10]

It was recognized that each member-country would be subject to different pressures at different times. The pressures could be caused by political or economic events or trends and could render the par values (currency exchange rates) established at Bretton Woods unrealistic. A major force that affects currency exchange rates is the balance of payments (BOP) of the member-countries.

□ Balance of Payments

market measures to end a BOP deficit include deflation of the economy and devaluation of the currency

One task assumed by the IMF was assistance to member-countries having difficulty keeping their balance of payments (BOP) out of deficit.[†] A country's BOP is a very important indicator for business management of what may happen to the country's economy, including what the government may cause to happen. If the BOP is in deficit, inflation is often the cause, and the company must adjust its pricing, inventory, accounting, and other practices to inflationary conditions. The government may take measures to deal with inflation and the deficit. These may be so-called **market measures** (such as deflating the economy or devaluing the currency) or **nonmarket measures** (such as currency controls, tariffs, or quotas).

nonmarket measures to end a BOP deficit include tariffs, quotas, and currency exchange controls

Even if a company does not consider itself international, it will be affected by inflation and by the government's methods of combating inflation and a

---

* A currency is said to float freely when the governments do nothing to affect its value in the world currency markets. Other varieties of floating are discussed later in this chapter.

† A deficit occurs when the residents of a country are paying nonresidents more than they are earning or otherwise getting from nonresidents. The opposite is a surplus.

BOP deficit. All of those methods have the common goals of causing the country's residents to buy fewer foreign goods and services and to sell more to foreigners.

Debits and credits in international transactions.   International debit transactions involve payments by domestic residents to foreign residents, and international credit transactions are the opposite. Taking America as the domestic economy, a list of debit transactions would include:

1. Dividend, interest, and debt repayment services on foreign-owned capital in America.
2. Merchandise imports.
3. Purchases by Americans traveling abroad.
4. Transportation services bought by Americans on foreign carriers.
5. Foreign investment by Americans.
6. Gifts by Americans to foreign residents.
7. Imports of gold.

The opposite would be examples of credit transactions. For example, dividend, interest, and debt repayment services on American-owned capital abroad are credits on the American ledger.

Double-entry accounting.   While writers use debit and credit transaction language, each international transaction is an exchange of assets with a debit and credit side. Thus, the BOP is presented as a double-entry accounting statement in which total credits and debits are always equal. The statement of a country's BOP is divided into several accounts (see Table 5–1).

Current account.   Three subaccounts are included in the current account: (A) goods or merchandise, (B) services, and (C) unilateral transfers. A and B are sometimes treated together, and they include the real (as opposed to the financial) international transactions—exports and imports.

A. The goods or merchandise account deals with "visibles," such as autos, grain, machinery, or equipment, that can be seen and felt as they are exported or imported. The net balance on merchandise transactions is referred to as the country's trade balance.

B. The services account deals with "invisibles" that are exchanged or bought internationally. Examples include (1) dividends or interest on foreign investments, (2) royalties on patents or trademarks held abroad, (3) travel, (4) insurance, (5) banking, and (6) transportation.

C. Unilateral transfers are transactions with no quid pro quo; some of these transfers are made by private persons or institutions and some by governments. Some private unilateral transfers are for charitable, educational, or missionary purposes; others are gifts from migrant workers to their families in their home countries and bequests or the transfer of capital by people migrating from one country to another. The largest government unilateral transfers are aid—which may be in money or kind—from developed countries to developing countries. Pension payments to nonresidents and tax receipts from nonresidents are two other government-related unilateral transfers.

Capital account.   The capital account records the net changes in a nation's international financial assets and liabilities over the BOP period, which is usually one year. A capital inflow—a credit entry—occurs when a resident

TABLE 5–1
Balance-of-Payments Accounts

	Debits	Credits
1. Current account		
A. Merchandise imports and exports		
B. Services		
Net goods and services balance		
C. Unilateral transfers		
To abroad		
From abroad		
Net current account balance		
2. Capital account		
A. Direct investment		
To abroad		
From abroad		
B. Portfolio investment		
To abroad		
From abroad		
C. Short-term capital		
To abroad		
From abroad		
Net capital account balance		
3. Official reserves account		
A. Gold export or import (net)		
B. Increase or decrease in foreign exchange (net)		
C. Increase or decrease in liabilities to foreign central banks (net)		
Net official reserves		
4. Net statistical discrepancy		

sells stock, bonds, or other financial assets to nonresidents. Money flows in to the resident, while at the same time the resident's long-term international liabilities are increased, because dividends (profit) may be paid on the stock, rent will be paid on other assets, and interest must be paid on the bonds. And at maturity the bonds' face amounts must be repaid.

Subaccounts under the capital account are (A) direct investment, (B) portfolio investment, and (C) international movements of short-term capital.

A. Direct investments are investments in enterprises or properties located in one country that are "effectively controlled" by residents of another country. Effective control is assumed for BOP purposes (1) when residents of one country own 50 percent or more of the voting stock of a company in another country or (2) when one resident or an organized group of residents of one country own 25 percent or more of the voting stock of a company in another country.

B. Portfolio investments include all long-term—more than one year—investments that do not give the investors effective control over the object of the investment. Such transactions typically involve the purchase of stocks or bonds of foreign issuers for investment—not control—purposes, and they also include long-term commercial credits to finance trade.

C. Short-term capital flows involve changes in international assets and liabilities with an original maturity of one year or less. Some of the fastest-growing types of short-term flows are for currency exchange rate and interest rate hedging in the forward, futures, option, and swap markets. (These subjects are dealt with in Chapter 18, Financial Management.) Among the more traditional types of short-term capital flow are payments and receipts for international finance and trade, short-term borrowings from foreign banks, exchanges of foreign notes or coins, and purchases of foreign commercial paper or foreign government bills or notes.

The volatility, private nature, and wide varieties of short-term capital flows make them the most difficult BOP items to measure—and therefore the least reliable. The wide fluctuations of currency exchange rates and interest rates during the 1980s and into the 90s have caused the surge in hedging activities mentioned above, with attendant surges in short-term capital movements.

Official reserves account.   The official reserves account deals with gold imports and exports, increases or decreases of foreign exchange (foreign currencies) held by the government, and decreases or increases in liabilities to foreign central banks.

Total BOP credits and debits must be equal because of the double-entry accounting system used to report the BOP. Because some BOP figures are inaccurate and incomplete (this is notably true of the short-term capital flows item), the statistical discrepancy item is plugged in to bring total credits and debits into accounting balance.

□ Balance-of-Payment Equilibrium and Disequilibrium

While the BOP is always in accounting balance, the odds are astronomical that it would be so without the statistical discrepancy item. There would be a surplus or a deficit in almost every case, but the BOP would nevertheless be considered in equilibrium if over a three- to five-year period the surpluses more or less canceled out the deficits.

Temporary and fundamental BOP deficits.   In IMF terminology, the deficit years for a country in equilibrium are referred to as temporary if they are corrected by the country's monetary and fiscal policies and perhaps by short-term IMF loans and advice.

The fundamental BOP deficit is too severe to be repaired by any **monetary policies** or **fiscal policies** that the country can apply; there are economic, social, and political limits to how much a country can deflate its economy, which causes unemployment, or devalue its currency, which causes higher prices for imports.

In these cases, the IMF rules permitted the countries' currencies to be devalued from the par values per US$ set at Bretton Woods; the amount of the devaluation was agreed by the country and the IMF. Although many par value changes occurred between 1946 and 1971, none led to international financial crises of the kind that followed the devaluations of 1931. This was due at least in part to the performance of the IMF; it was able to maintain generally stable exchange rates, and when changes became necessary, it was able to prevent the competitive devaluations that proved so futile and destructive in the 1930s.

The devaluations of the 1946–71 period were in terms of the US$, so its relative value went up in terms of the devalued currencies. This caused the prices of American goods and services to go up in terms of other currencies, because after devaluation, more units of those currencies were required to buy US$s. This, in turn, was one cause of an American BOP deficit that began in 1958.

monetary policies regulate the amount of growth or contraction of a nation's monetary stock

fiscal policies regulate a government's money receipts through taxes and its expenditure

◻ American BOP Deficit

From the end of World War II until about 1958, there was a shortage of US$s for the development of world trade and investment. Even during that era, many dollars flowed abroad due to government aid, private investment, and tourism. Around 1958, the United States began to run a series of BOP deficits, the flow of dollars became a flood, and the US$ shortage ended. The United States could have tried market methods (deflate the economy or devalue the US$) to slow or reverse the deficit, but it did not, and its trading partner countries did not urge it to do so.

Why market methods were not attempted.   Vivid recollections of the hunger and hardships of the 1930s depression caused U.S. leaders to see deflation as the greater danger, and until the late 1960s the U.S. government did not perceive inflation as a possible cause of another depression. The US$ had been enshrined at Bretton Woods as the key currency in the gold exchange standard and had become, along with gold, the central reserve asset of most countries. Those countries were understandably reluctant to see a reduction in the value of part of their reserves, and U.S. authorities seemed to feel that this nation's prestige would be tarnished by a devaluation of the US$.[11]

Moreover, foreign competitors of U.S. exports derived a price advantage from the overvaluation of the US$. As pointed out above, almost all of the 1946–71 currency value changes were devaluations in terms of the US$. Thus, foreign goods and services became relatively less expensive for holders of US$s; but at the same time, U.S. exports were becoming relatively more expensive for holders of other currencies, who bought fewer of those more expensive goods and services. The foreign competitors of U.S. firms did not want to lose that advantage, and their governments discouraged any U.S. inclination to devalue the US$.

Raising the US$ price of gold would amount to a dollar devaluation in terms of other currencies unless they also devalued. It was generally recognized that the US$ was overvalued and that, if permitted to float, its value would fall vis-à-vis the currencies of most industrialized countries.

The United States had thousands of troops stationed in Europe and Asia and could have saved billions of dollars in expenditures abroad by bringing them home. But the host countries—for example, Germany, Japan, South Korea, and South Vietnam—brought strong pressures on the U.S. government not to reduce its forces, and the United States felt obliged to maintain them.

central bank of a country manages the monetary policy

gold exchange standard cast the U.S. dollar as the central currency at $35 per ounce of gold, at which price the U.S. agreed to buy or sell gold from or to other central banks

◻ Gold Exchange Standard

As the United States failed to even try market methods to end its BOP deficit, and other rather halfhearted attempts had little success, dollars piled up in foreign hands, including those of government **central banks.** At this point, beginning in 1958, the "exchange" part of the **gold exchange standard** began to function.

Gold for dollars.   The exchange feature agreed on at Bretton Woods required the United States to deliver an ounce of gold to any central bank of an IMF member-country that presented US$35 to the U.S. Treasury. As dollars accumulated in foreign hands in amounts greater than were needed for trade and investment, the central banks began turning them in to the U.S. Treasury for gold.

□ **FIGURE 5–1**

Accumulation of US$s in Non–U.S.-Resident Hands and Loss of U.S. Gold

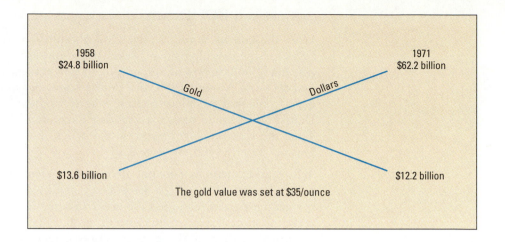

Gold and dollars go abroad.   From 1958 through 1971, the United States ran up a cumulative deficit of $56 billion. The deficit was financed partly by use of the U.S. gold reserves, which shrank from $24.8 billion to $12.2 billion,[12] and partly by incurring liabilities to foreign central banks. During this period, those liabilities increased from $13.6 billion to $62.2 billion.[13] This is illustrated by Figure 5–1.

The foreign central banks were willing to accept so many dollars primarily because those dollars were treated as a central reserve asset; they provided liquidity growth to support growing world trade and finance. But in the late 1960s and into 1971, the central banks became increasingly nervous at the volume of US$ accumulation. A number of them turned in excess dollars for gold, but by the mid-1960s, the banks held more dollars than there was gold left in the U.S. Treasury. By 1971, the Treasury held only 22 cents' worth of gold for each US$ held by those banks.[14]

As indicated, another reason foreigners accepted so many US$ was that these dollars provided liquidity to support world trade and investment, which grew rapidly in the post–World War II era. Of course, this meant liquidity growth depended on U.S. BOP deficits, but such deficits could not continue indefinitely without deterioration of confidence in the strength of the U.S. economy and of the US$. Here is illustrated the inherent contradiction of the gold exchange standard. Foreigners needed and wanted growing numbers of dollars for many purposes but became nervous when the amounts of dollars they held exceeded the amount of gold held by the United States at the established price of $35 per ounce of gold.[15]

AUGUST 15, 1971, AND THE NEXT TWO YEARS

As noted above, by 1971, many more dollars were in the hands of foreign central banks than the gold held by the U.S. Treasury could cover. The event said to have triggered the drastic decisions made at Camp David* on the weekend beginning Friday, August 13, 1971, was a request by the British

---

* Camp David is a relatively isolated retreat in the Maryland mountains that U.S. presidents frequently use to escape the pressures of Washington.

government that the United States cover US$3 billion of its reserve against loss.[16] President Nixon, with Treasury Secretary John Connally, Treasury Undersecretary Paul Volcker, and others, made the decisions that the president announced on Sunday night (the 15th). Those decisions shook the international monetary system to its roots.[17]

The president announced that the United States would no longer exchange gold for the paper dollars held by foreign central banks. He was said to have "closed the gold window."

The shock caused currency exchange markets to remain closed for several days, and when they reopened, they began playing a new game for which few rules existed. Currencies were floating, and the stated US$ value of 35 dollars per ounce of gold was now meaningless because the United States would no longer exchange any of its gold for dollars. The gold exchange standard was ended.

The president also imposed and announced a 10 percent surcharge on imports from all industrial countries except Canada. He demanded those countries lower their obstacles to imports from the United States in return for canceling the surcharges. Agreement on trade obstacles was reached in December 1971 along with new currency exchange rates that devalued the US$. The agreement was called the Smithsonian Accord because the final negotiations and signing ceremonies were held at the Smithsonian Institution in Washington, D.C. The new rates could not be maintained, and by 1973, currencies were floating.

◻ Politicians versus Speculators

Two attempts were made to agree on durable, new sets of fixed exchange rates, one in December 1971 and the other in February 1973. Both times, however, banks, businesses, and individuals (collectively referred to as speculators by unhappy politicians) felt that the central banks had pegged the rates incorrectly, and the speculators proved correct each time. Of course, the speculators' prophecies could be said to have been self-fulfilling in that they put billions of units of the major currencies into the currencies they felt to be strong—for example, the deutsche mark (DM), the Dutch guilder, and the Swiss franc—thereby making them even stronger. The speculators profited, and one writer commented, "It wasn't a holdup. It was more like an invited robbery."[18]

floating currency exchange rates values are not set by governments but by markets, although governments intervene frequently

In March 1973, the major currencies began to float in the foreign exchange markets, and the system of **floating currency exchange rates** still prevails.[19] However, Western Europe has moved back toward a fixed system, the European Monetary System, which is discussed later in this chapter.

1973 TO THE PRESENT

The two kinds of currency floats are referred to by various commentators as free or managed or as clean or dirty. The free (clean) float is one of the world's closest approaches to perfect competition, because there is no government intervention and because billions of the product (units of money) are being traded by thousands of buyers and sellers. Buyers and sellers may change sides on short notice as information, rumors, or moods change or as their clients' needs differ. In the managed (dirty) float, governments intervene in the currency markets as they perceive their national interests to be served. Nations may explain their interventions in the currency market in terms of "smoothing market irregularities" or "assuring orderly markets."[20]

Beginning in September 1985, governments' reasons for intervening in currency markets have been expressed more forthrightly. The US$ soared in value from 1981 to its peak in February 1985, gaining some 80 percent against a trade-weighted basket of other major currencies. Although there were many other reasons for the huge growth of the American trade deficit, the powerful US$ was probably the biggest single reason.[21]

The unprecedented U.S. trade deficit, which was $134 billion in 1985 and reached $170 billion at its peak in 1987, greatly concerned the United States and its trading partners. To seek a solution, the finance ministers of the Group of Five (Britain, France, Germany, Japan, and the United States) met at the Plaza Hotel in New York in September 1985. Although the US$ exchange rate had begun to move down in March, they decided it was still too high and agreed in the so-called Plaza Accord to cooperate in bringing its rate lower. The Plaza meeting was the first of several—including one in Paris at the Louvre in February 1987—whose objective was to set the US$ at the "right" exchange rate, particularly in terms of the Japanese yen and the German deutsche mark (the currencies of the other two major world economies). And so, since 1985, the governments of the Group of Five have been intervening in currency markets in order to maintain their currencies' exchange rates at the "right" levels or within "target zones."

The Group of Five grew to be the Group of Seven (G7) as Canada and Italy joined the meetings and deliberations. Economic policy coordination as practiced by the G7 has emerged as a key factor influencing the foreign exchange markets. There is little doubt that the central banks have become progressively more adept in their efforts to influence currency movements. The G7 heads of state meet each year, and between those summits there are frequent private discussions among G7 finance ministers and central bankers on economic policy issues.[22]

This is one of the important uses of the Bank for International Settlements. Its low-key facilities in Basle permit private, confidential meetings and discussions.

◻ Currency Areas

The U.S. dollar, Canadian dollar, Japanese yen (Y), Swiss franc, and several other currencies are floating in value against one another and against the European Currency Unit (ECU), a grouping of Western European currencies. Most currencies of developing countries (LDCs) are pegged (fixed) in value to one of the major currencies or to currency baskets such as the ECU, special drawing rights (SDRs), or some specially chosen currency mix or basket (see Figure 5–2).

Current developments may make the growth of currency areas, trading blocs, and currency blocs more likely. The most important of those developments are the EC 1992 project, the alleged attempts by Japan to use the Asian Development Bank to stimulate Japanese goods and services sales throughout Asia, and the U.S.–Canada Free Trade Agreement. In 1991, negotiations began to add Mexico to this agreement, and there is meaningful movement to expand it into a Western Hemisphere agreement.

□ **FIGURE 5–2**
Pegged LDC Currencies

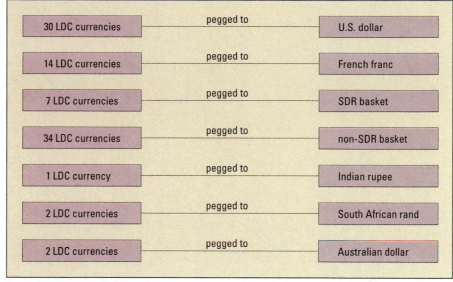

30 LDC currencies	pegged to	U.S. dollar
14 LDC currencies	pegged to	French franc
7 LDC currencies	pegged to	SDR basket
34 LDC currencies	pegged to	non-SDR basket
1 LDC currency	pegged to	Indian rupee
2 LDC currencies	pegged to	South African rand
2 LDC currencies	pegged to	Australian dollar

Source: *IMF Survey*, July 2, 1990, p. 253.

□ Snake

In Europe during the mid-1970s, a currency grouping called the snake was created. The snake comprised several European currencies, led by the German deutsche mark. There was an agreed central exchange rate, but currencies' values could fluctuate up or down to a ceiling or floor exchange rate shown by the solid lines.

The snake was so called because of how it appeared in a graph showing the member currencies floating against nonmember currencies, such as the yen or the Canadian or U.S. dollar.

The reptile's health was damaged by the departure of several currencies, including the pound sterling, the Italian lira, and the Swedish krona, and by the in-and-out relationship of the French franc.[23] The system's inflexibility, the major reason those currencies were removed, explains the snake's ultimate demise. Each member-country was responsible for keeping its currency's value within the agreed relationship to the other members' currencies, but each country had different inflation rates, fiscal and monetary policies, and BOP balances. Thus market pressures pushed currency exchange rates out of the agreed ranges, and the countries lacked the political will or resources to restore the agreed exchange rate. Then, the currency automatically fell out of the system.

The snake was the forerunner of the European Monetary System (EMS), discussed later in this chapter.

□ Experience with Floating

Such immense amounts of major currencies were being bought and sold each trading day that governments' efforts to keep their currencies at fixed exchange rates failed. The central banks stopped trying to peg the major currencies' exchange rates in 1973. OPEC hiked the price of petroleum over 400 percent early in 1974, and there were fears that the banking and monetary

WORLDVIEW
On the Hamburger Standard

Depressing though it may be to gourmets, the "Big Mac" hamburger sold by McDonald's could well oust the basket of currencies as an international monetary standard. After all, it is sold in 41 countries, with only the most trivial changes of recipe. That ought to say something about comparative prices. Think of the hamburger as a medium-rare guide to whether currencies are trading at the right exchange rates.

Big Mac watchers will rely on the theory of purchasing power parity (PPP) for currencies. This argues that an exchange rate between two currencies is in equilibrium (i.e., at PPP) when it equates the prices of a basket of goods and services in both countries—or, in this case, the rate of exchange that leaves hamburgers costing the same in each country. Comparing actual exchange rates with PPP is one indication of whether a currency is under- or overvalued.

The Economist's correspondents around the world have been gorging themselves in a bid to test Mac-PPPs. In Washington, a Big Mac costs $1.60; in Tokyo, our *Makudonarudo* correspondent had to fork out Y370 ($2.40). Dividing the yen price by the dollar price yields a Mac-PPP of $1 = Y231; but on September 1, the dollar's actual exchange rate stood at Y154. The same method gives a Mac-PPP against the deutsche mark of DM2.66, compared with a current rate of DM2.02. Conclusion: on Mac-PPP grounds, the dollar looks undervalued against the yen and the deutsche mark.

Sterling is different. The Mac-PPP for the pound is $1.45 (69p to the dollar), within a whisker of the actual rate of around $1.49. But the pound's Mac-PPP against the deutsche mark is DM3.86, suggesting that sterling is undervalued at DM3.02. British industrialists, who squeal about the pound's current "strength," will now like hamburgers even less.

The Australian dollar appears to have been heavily oversold; it is 34 percent below its Mac-PPP rate against the American dollar. Meanwhile, the Irish pound

Don Smetzer/Tony Stone Worldwide

seems to be spot on. However, our correspondent in Ireland has uncovered an opportunity for arbitrage. This month, a Big Mac can be enjoyed in Dublin for just 20 tokens from milk cartons.

The hamburger standard provides the United States with strong evidence for its contention that Asian NICs (newly industrializing countries) ought to upvalue their currencies; they are more or less tied to the dollar, so their exchange rates have barely budged during the past 18 months. A hamburger costs 64 percent more in Washington than in Hong Kong—i.e., on Mac-PPP grounds the dollar is 64 percent overvalued against the Hong Kong dollar. It is also 23 percent too high against the Singapore dollar.

Caveat Hamburger

The hamburger standard has its limitations. Using purchasing power parities to forecast movements in exchange rates can produce misleading results. For instance, price differences between countries can be distorted by taxes, transport costs, property costs, or such things as the famously high retail markups in Japan and West Germany.

A more serious objection is that a PPP simply indicates where exchange rates should be in the long run if price levels were the only difference between countries. In fact, there are many other differences. So even though PPPs are handy for converting living standards (GDP per person) into a common currency, they are not necessarily the best way to judge the exchange rate needed to bring the current account of the balance of payments into "equilibrium." Confused? Some economics can be hard to digest.

Source: © 1989 The Economist Newspaper Ltd.

Big MacCurrencies: Hamburger Prices around the World

Country	Hamburger Prices in Local Currency*	Implied Purchasing Power Parity of the Dollar†	Actual Exchange Rate Sept. 1	Percent over (+) or under (−) Valuation of the Dollar
Australia	A$1.75	1.09	1.64	+50
Belgium	BFr90	56	42	−25
Brazil	Cz$2.5	7.80	13.80	+78
Britain	£1.10	0.69	0.67	−3
Canada	C$1.89	1.18	1.39	+18
France	FFr16.4	10.30	6.65	−35
Hong Kong	HK$6.60	4.75	7.80	+64
Ireland	IR£1.18	0.74	0.74	−1
Japan	Y370	231	154	−33
Holland	F14.35	2.72	2.28	−16
Singapore	S$2.80	1.75	2.15	+23
Spain	Ptas260	163	133	−18
Sweden	SKR16.5	10.30	6.87	−33
United States	$1.60	—	—	—
West Germany	DM4.25	2.66	2.02	−24

*Prices may vary slightly between branches.
†Foreign price divided by dollar price.
Source: McDonald's.

WORLDVIEW
Big MacCurrencies

It is time for our annual update of *The Economist's* Big Mac index, a rough-and-ready guide to whether a currency is under- or over-valued. It was launched five years ago in the hope of making economic theory more digestible.

The index is based on the theory of purchasing-power parity (PPP), which argues that in the long run the exchange rate between two currencies should equate the prices of an identical basket of goods and services in the respective countries. Our "basket" is McDonald's Big Mac hamburger, made locally to a rigorous standard in more than 50 countries. Its local prices are less likely to be distorted by international transport and distribution costs than if we used, say, the price of *The Economist* in different countries.

So once again our correspondents have been gorging themselves on Big Macs. In four American cities they paid, on average, $2.25. In Tokyo the Big Mac costs Y380, equivalent to $2.81. This implies that the dollar is 20 percent undervalued against the yen: it should, on our Big Mac PPP basis, buy Y169 (the yen price divided by the dollar price) not the Y135 prevailing when we made our survey. Similarly, it is 13 percent undervalued against the D-mark; it should be worth DM1.91.

Indeed, on Big Mac PPP grounds the dollar looks undervalued against most currencies, so its recent rally could have further to run. The exceptions are the Australian, Canadian, Hong Kong, and Singapore dollars, the Hungarian forint, and the Yugoslav dinar, which all look too low in dollar terms.

The cheapest place for a Big Mac (i.e., the one with the currency most undervalued against the dollar) is Hong Kong. The most expensive is in Pushkin Square, where Muscovites pay the equivalent of $5.75 at the commercial exchange rate, implying that the dollar is 61 percent undervalued against the rouble.

One of the biggest Big Mac PPP changes since last year has been in the pound. Its PPP has slipped from $1.56 to $1.35; and, more important, from DM3.07 to DM2.58. The reason is that the price of a Big Mac in London has gone through the roof. It is up by 19 percent—more than twice as fast as retail prices generally—over the past year, while in Germany it has not changed. Other, more solemn, estimates of the pound's PPP vary between DM2.50 and DM3.20. But if London's Big Macflation is a pointer to the future, the Treasury is going to get severe heartburn defending the DM2.95 central rate at which sterling entered Europe's exchange-rate mechanism.

Source: *The Economist,* April 13, 1991, p. 78.

systems would not be able to handle the resulting changes in the amounts and directions of currency flows.[24]

Fears not realized.   However, despite occasional flare-ups and occasional sharp changes in the relative values of currencies, the system did not collapse. Indeed, the volatility of exchange rate movements diminished after a period of uncertainty with the new system, in 1973–74. Uncertainty was heightened by the sudden, drastic increase of oil prices by OPEC. In those days, it could be difficult and costly to engage in a foreign exchange transaction. By 1977, the cost of undertaking foreign exchange transactions was about the same as it had been under the Bretton Woods system.[25]

Big MacCurrencies

Country	Price in Local Currency*	Implied PPP of the Dollar†	Actual Exchange Rate, April 9	Percent over (+) or under (−) Valuation of the Dollar
Australia	A$2.45	1.09	1.27	+17
Belgium	BFr100	44.44	34.50	−22
Britain	£1.67	0.74	0.56	−24
Canada	C$2.35	1.04	1.15	+11
Denmark	DKr26.75	11.89	6.42	−46
France	FFf18.00	8.00	5.65	−29
Germany	DM4.30	1.91	1.67	−13
Holland	F15.25	2.33	1.88	−19
Hong Kong	HK$8.90	3.96	7.79	+97
Hungary	Forint115	51.11	75.12	+47
Ireland	I£1.40	0.62	0.62	—
Italy	Lire3600	1600	1239	−23
Japan	Y380	169	135	−20
Singapore	S$2.80	1.24	1.77	+43
S. Korea	Won2100	933	721	−23
Soviet Union	Rouble10	4.44	1.74**	−61
Spain	Ptas350	155	103	−34
Sweden	SKr26	11.56	6.04	−48
United States‡	$2.25	—	—	—
Yugoslavia	Dinar32	14.22	15.12	+6

*Prices may vary locally.
**Commercial rate.
†Purchasing-power parity in local currency: local price divided by dollar price.
‡New York, Chicago, San Francisco, and Atlanta.
Sources: McDonald's; *The Economist* correspondents

The system has still not collapsed, even though the value of the US$ fluctuated widely between 1977 and 1992. Beginning in June 1977, the US$ fell in value about 28 percent against the Swiss franc, 20 percent against the Japanese yen, and some 15 percent against the deutsche mark within a year. Many laid the blame for the dollar's weakness on inflationary American fiscal and monetary policies, particularly the latter.

In 1979, the American Federal Reserve System (Fed) slowed the rate of monetary growth, and the US$ began to move up in value. The new administration that took office in 1981 continued the anti-inflationary policies instituted by Fed chairman Paul A. Volcker in 1979, and indeed inflation did fall. As it fell, the value of the US$ rose, and by the beginning of 1985, it had

☐ **FIGURE 5–3   The Dollar's Summer Rally Didn't Last**

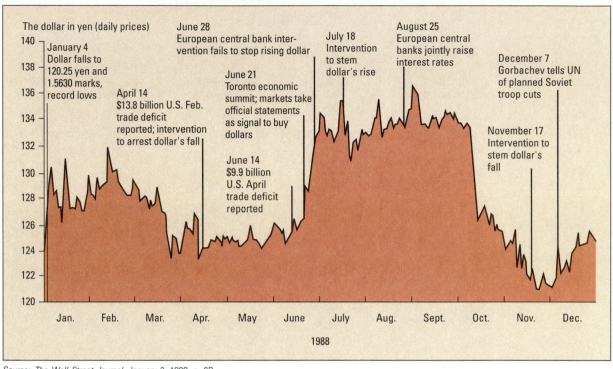

Source: *The Wall Street Journal*, January 3, 1989, p. 6R.

risen about 80 percent against a trade-weighted basket of other major currencies.

Then, beginning in March 1985, the dollar exchange rate reversed its climb, and by 1988, it had dropped about 40 percent. For an illustration of the US$'s volatility in relation to the yen during 1988, see Figure 5–3. This figure also indicates some of the major causes of the dollar's frequent rises and falls.

Figure 5–4 brings the US$'s exchange rate in terms of the currencies of the other G7 member-countries into 1991. It also introduces another—and very important—cause for currency value fluctuations: relative interest rate differentials. Note that the US$ value tends to be lower as the interest rate differential is wider.

The advocates of floating argued that it would end BOP disequilibria because the value of each currency would float up or down to a point where supply equaled demand. It has not worked that way, partly because of governments' reluctance to permit extreme changes in the value of their currencies. Governments have intervened in the currency markets to moderate or prevent value changes. The American BOP deficit set new records in 1985, 1986, and 1987 before turning down in 1988.

Forecasting float direction.   Such large changes in short time periods prompted efforts by everyone affected to forecast currency value changes. Such changes have many causes, including political events and expectations and government economic policies. A major cause is present and forecast rel-

□ **FIGURE 5–4   Bilateral Exchange Rates and Short-Term Interest Differentials vis-à-vis the U.S. Dollar, January 1985 to March 1991***

*Interest differentials shown are U.S. minus domestic three-month interest rates, in percent a year. Exchange rates are drawn on logarithmic scales. Monthly averages of daily data are plotted.

Source: *IMF World Economic Outlook,* May 1991, p. 92.

ative inflation from country to country. One means of measuring relative inflation is purchasing power parity (PPP), the theory of which is that an exchange rate between the currencies of two countries is in equilibrium when it equates the prices of a basket of goods and services in both countries.

One product sold worldwide that is—or is supposed to be—the same everywhere is McDonald's Big Mac hamburger. *The Economist* did a PPP study in 1989 using Big Mac as the basket in 15 countries. The report of that study is in the above Worldview.

The Economist annually updates its hamburger standard. The Worldview entitled "Big MacCurrencies" appeared in the April 13, 1991, issue on page 78. Compare the two Big MacCurrency tables and note the changes in two years.

◻ Money Markets, Foreign Exchange

money markets are places where monies can be bought, sold, or borrowed

The daily volume of foreign exchange trading in the world's three leading **money markets** has grown at a rapid pace. London is in the lead, handling some $187 billion; New York comes second, with some $129 billion; and Tokyo is a close third, with some $115 billion. The survey that generated those figures was conducted in 1989 by the Bank for International Settlements, which estimated a global net daily turnover of $640 billion. That BIS survey—the last official study of trading volume—found significant activity at 11 other trading centers, with the most active being Switzerland at $57 billion, Singapore at $55 billion, and Hong Kong at $49 billion.

The US$ is the most traded currency. The US$-deutsche mark market is the busiest, closely followed by that of the US$-yen. Third, fourth, and fifth are US$-sterling, US$-Swiss franc, and mark-yen.[26]

Although the US$ is the most traded currency, it need not be a part of every transaction. As indicated, the mark-yen market is big, and other major currencies are traded without going through the US$. Therefore, they are quoted in terms of each other, referred to as cross-rates of exchange.

London has a pivotal role in world currency trading. Because the London market shares trading hours with markets in Asia and the Middle East during its morning session and with the New York market during its afternoon session, it has more transaction opportunities than do the New York or Tokyo markets.

However, the Tokyo market is growing steadily, and its trading volume may have surpassed that of New York in 1990, although there has been no official study since the one in 1989 by the BIS. The Tokyo market is probably now larger than the New York market because while the United States has become a debtor nation, Japan has become the largest creditor country. At the same time, Japanese banks have become the world's biggest; thus more and more of the world's financial activity is centered in, or at least affected by, Tokyo markets.

The growth of foreign exchange trading in recent years has greatly outpaced world trade even though trade has also expanded. This has been due to the near explosions in international investment and in hedge and swap transactions. Hedges and swaps are explained in Chapter 18.

London, New York, and Tokyo have the biggest currency markets but by no means the only ones. Other important markets are in Los Angeles and San

Francisco, Hong Kong, Singapore, Bahrain, Frankfurt, Zurich, and Paris. Trades can be made 24 hours a day at one or more of these markets.

Billions of US$s are traded around the world in the various currency markets. Smaller—but still large—amounts of the other currencies of major market countries are also traded outside the borders of the issuing countries, and all of these currencies are used as countries' national reserve assets as well as in trade, investments, hedges, and swaps.

Beginning in the 1960s, there was a growing feeling that national currencies or gold should be replaced as central reserve assets. In 1970, the IMF established special drawing rights for that purpose.

□ SDRs in the Future

special drawing rights (SDRs) were established by the IMF as units of value to replace the dollar as a reserve asset

Special drawing rights (SDRs) may be a step toward a truly international currency. The US$ has been the closest thing to such a currency since gold in the pre—World War I gold standard system, but the US$ must also serve as a national currency, and the roles sometimes conflict.

SDRs, bookkeeping entries at the IMF, were created in 1970 by agreement of the IMF members, whose accounts are credited with certain amounts of SDRs from time to time. The objective was to make the SDR the principal reserve asset in the international monetary system.[27]

Value of the SDR.   The SDR's value is based on a basket of the following five currencies (the percentage of each currency is in parentheses): U.S. dollar (40), German mark (21), Japanese yen (17), British pound sterling (11), and the French franc (11). The weights broadly reflect the relative importance of the currencies in trade and payments, based on the value of the exports of goods and services by the member-countries issuing these currencies. In 1990, the percentages were changed to those indicated above; the previous percentages were US$ 42, mark 19, yen 15, and the pound and franc 12 each.

The value of the SDR in US$ terms is calculated daily by the Fund as the sum of the values in US$s based on market exchange rates of specified amounts of the currencies in the valuation basket.

An illustrative calculation of the SDR's value in terms of the US$ is shown in Table 5—2. Inasmuch as exchange rates fluctuate, so too does the SDR value from day to day.[28]

□ Uses of the SDR

The SDR's value remains more stable than that of any single currency, and that stability has made the SDR increasingly attractive as a unit for denominating international transactions. Future payment under a contract, for example, may be agreed to be made in a national currency at its rate in terms of the SDR on the payment date, and some Swiss and British banks will now accept accounts denominated in SDRs.

Holders of SDRs.   SDRs are held by the IMF, its 156 members,* and 16 official institutions, which typically are regional development or banking institutions prescribed by the IMF. All holders can buy and sell SDRs both spot and forward and receive or use SDRs in loans, pledges,

* As of October 31, 1991.

□ **TABLE 5–2**
SDR Valuation on August 6, 1990

Currency	(1) Currency Amount	(2) Exchange Rate on August 6	(3) US$ Equivalent
Deutsche mark	0.5270	1.57620	0.334348
French franc	1.0200	5.28800	0.192890
Japanese yen	33.4000	149.82000	0.222934
Pound sterling	0.0893	1.87220	0.167187
U.S. dollar	0.4520	1.00000	0.452000
SDR 1 =			1.369359

Column 1: The currency components of the SDR basket.
Column 2: Exchange rates in terms of currency units per U.S. dollar except for the pound sterling, which is expressed in U.S. dollars per pound.
Column 3: The U.S. dollar equivalents of the currency amounts in Column 1 at the exchange rates in Column 2—that is, Column 1 divided by Column 2.
Source: IMF Treasurer's Department.

swaps, grants, or settlement of financial obligations. Holders receive interest at a rate determined weekly by reference to the weighted-average interest rate on short-term obligations in the money markets of the five countries with currencies in the SDR valuation basket.

SDRs as central reserve assets.   A major purpose envisioned for SDRs was to replace currencies and gold as central reserve assets of nations. That has not happened. After the first allocation of 9 billion SDRs to members in 1972, they constituted 6.1 percent of the central reserves, while foreign exchange made up 65.3 percent and gold 24.5 percent at $35 per ounce. There was a second SDR allocation in 1979 of 13 billion, but total reserves went up faster, so that by 1983, SDRs constituted only 3.4 percent of the central reserves. Currencies had increased to 78.7 percent, and gold had fallen to 8.2 percent, but that was on the basis of valuing gold at $35 per ounce. In the gold markets, the price of gold had soared to over $800 in 1980, and gold traded between $300 and $465 per ounce from then into 1992.

The most recent SDR allocation to the 141 IMF member-countries at that time was on January 1, 1981, in the amount of SDR 4.1 billion. As of the end of 1990, the Fund had allocated a total of SDR 21.4 billion in six allocations, but SDR holdings by member-countries amounted to only 4 percent of their total nongold reserves.

Such lack of enthusiasm for SDRs as central reserve assets may have several explanations. Dollars and other hard currencies are more flexible and have more uses, usually yield higher interest returns, and can officially be credited and debited by anyone—in contrast to the limited numbers with official access to SDRs.

□ **European Monetary System (EMS)**

European Monetary System (EMS) is a grouping of most Western European nations cooperating to maintain their currencies at fixed exchange rates

As evidenced by the snake, the European countries prefer a fixed currency exchange rate regime to a floating one. Due to inflexibility and weaknesses, the snake expired in the mid-1970s. Nothing daunted, a larger group of European countries banded together in 1979 and created the **European Monetary System (EMS)**, which is a large step back toward fixed currency exchange rates. It is an enlarged and improved version of the snake.

WORLDVIEW
Central Reserve/National Currency Conflict

The US$ has been the most used central reserve asset in the world since the end of World War II. Somewhat analogous to a savings account, the dollars were available when needed to finance trade or investments or to intervene in currency markets. Held in the form of U.S. Treasury bonds, the US$s earn interest, and the more held in the savings/central reserve account, the better. But the countries don't want their central reserve asset US$s to lose value, and there lies a contradiction: at some point, greater numbers of US$s (or any other product) in supply cause them to lose value—supply and demand.

At the same time, the US$ is the national currency of the United States of America, whose government must deal with inflation, recession, interest rates, unemployment, and other national, internal problems. The U.S. government uses fiscal and monetary policies to meet those problems—higher or lower taxes, decisions as to how to spend available revenue, growth or contraction of the money supply, and rate of its growth or contraction.

It would be only accidental if the national interests of the United States in dealing with its internal problems coincided with the interests of the multitude of countries holding US$s in their central reserve asset accounts. The United States may be slowing money supply growth and raising taxes to combat U.S. inflation while the world needs more liquidity, in the form of US$s, to finance growth, trade, or investment. Or, the United States may be stimulating its economy by faster money supply growth and lower taxes at a time when so many US$s are already outstanding that their value is dropping—not a happy state of affairs for countries holding US$s.

It was a quirk of history that thrust the US$ into this conflicting role. It was the hope of the IMF that a non-national asset, the SDR, would rescue the US$ and the world from the conflict.

The EMS member-countries agreed to maintain their currency values within an agreed range in relation to one another. An important feature, not available to the old snake, is the European Monetary Cooperation Fund (EMCF). It is composed of dollars, gold, and member-country currencies, and it is used to support the efforts of member-countries to keep their currency values within the agreed relationship to the other currencies. The EMCF has the equivalent of about $32 billion with which to work.

Another difference between the EMS and its ancestor, the snake, is that the exchange rates of the EMS are flexible. If one currency proves weaker than another and the governments cannot or will not take steps to correct the situation, the EMS exchange rates can be changed. There have been several rate rearrangements since 1979. If a snake member-country could not keep its currency up to the agreed strength, it dropped out and ceased to be a member.

Two of the EMS fathers, former French president Valery Giscard d'Estaing and former West German chancellor Helmut Schmidt, think it's time their child was allowed to grow up. They are pushing hard for the never-implemented second stage of their plan, the economic and monetary union of Europe. This union would be accomplished through a European Central Bank and free use of the European Currency Unit (see the next section) by banks, companies, and consumers in all 12 EC countries.

□ **FIGURE 5–5   Current Composition of the ECU Currency Weightings**

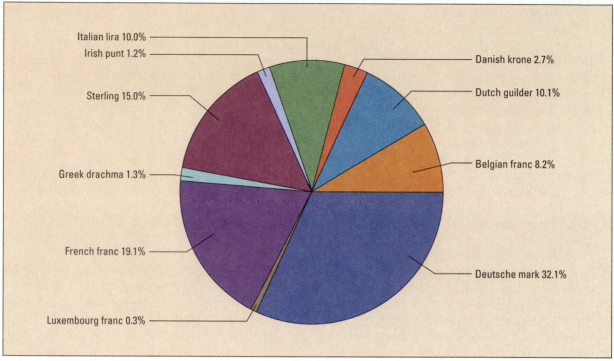

The ECU is a "basket currency" composed of a cocktail of the currencies of 10 European Community member-states, mixed in proportion to the relative strength of each country's economy.

Source: "Bulletin," *Swiss Banking Magazine*, November 1989.

Despite opposition from the German central bank (the Bundesbank) and the British government, the two men are optimistic the European Bank will be created. Mr. Schmidt says, "All the talk about European union will be rubbish if we don't do anything. We must create a European Central Bank because we must have a currency with which you could as easily buy a dress or a train ticket in Paris or Madrid."[29]

The EC took large steps toward those goals at a summit meeting in Maastricht, The Netherlands, during December 1991. There, the 12 members signed a commitment to proceed toward economic and monetary union (EMU) involving a single currency governed by a European Central Bank by 1999. For a clean, concise explanation of the results of the Maastricht meeting, see the supplementary reading by Bruce Barnard, "Making Sense of Maastricht."

□ **European Currency Unit (ECU)**

European Currency Unit (ECU) is a value established by the EMS for intra-EMS bookkeeping

The **European Currency Unit (ECU)** was established as the EMS bookkeeping currency. Its value is determined by reference to a basket of European currencies. The weights of each currency in the ECU are shown in Figure 5–5. The weights changed in 1989 when Portugal and Spain joined the EMS. The Portuguese escudo was accorded a 1 percent weight while the Spanish peseta was given 5 percent. The 6 percent loss was shared among the other currencies.[30]

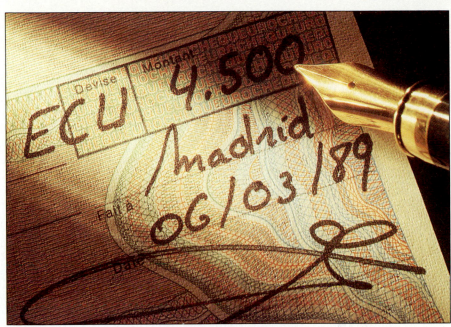

A Spanish letter of credit denominated in ECUs.

Courtesy of European Community Delegation, Washington D.C.

The international market for ECU-denominated bonds increased dramatically in liquidity and issuance during 1990 and 1991. All sorts of borrowers entered the market: international agencies such as the World Bank, numerous national governments, municipalities, and public and private companies. In the first six months of 1991, more bonds were denominated in ECUs than any currency except the US$.[31] Uses of ECUs have surpassed those of special drawing rights (SDRs), which were discussed earlier in this chapter. Figure 5–6 is an announcement of an ECU Eurobond placement.

One reason the ECU has become more popular than the SDR is that neither the US$ nor the yen is included in the currency basket that determines its value. The exchange rates of the US$ and the yen have fluctuated much more widely than have those of the European currencies in the ECU basket. Both the US$ and the yen are in the SDR basket, so the SDR's value has been less stable than that of the ECU.

Another reason the ECU's use has surpassed that of the SDR is active sponsorship of the ECU by European governments, banks, and businesses; the SDR has received no such support. The ECU is being used for various purposes, and support and supplementary networks have been put in place. Bank accounts can be denominated in ECUs, and ECU traveler's checks are available. Between units of some international companies, debits and credits are denominated in ECUs as they buy, sell, or borrow from one another.

Countries outside the European Community have begun to utilize ECUs (e.g., the Soviet Union, Cameroon, Romania, Sweden, and New Zealand), and American companies have recently issued bonds denominated in ECUs. ECU futures and options contracts are available at markets in Amsterdam, Chicago, and Philadelphia. And, last but not least, an association of banks together with the European Investment Bank (a unit of the European Community) has begun a multilateral, electronic clearing system for ECU transac-

□ **FIGURE 5–6**
ECU Denominated
Euro-Notes

This announcement appears as a matter of record only. These Securities have not been registered under the United States Securities Act of 1933 and may not, as part of the distribution, be offered, sold or delivered, directly or indirectly, in the United States or to United States persons.

New Issue / April, 1986

ECU 100,000,000

Phibro-Salomon Inc

$8\frac{1}{2}$% Series A Note Due February 24, 1996
and 100,000 Warrants to Purchase
ECU 100,000,000 $8\frac{1}{2}$% Series B
Notes Due February 24, 1996

Salomon Brothers International Limited

Banque Nationale de Paris   Banque Bruxelles Lambert S.A.

Banque Générale du Luxembourg S.A.   Banque Indosuez

Banque Internationale a Luxembourg S.A.   Bayerische Hypotheken-und Wechsel-Bank
                                                                     Aktiengesellschaft
Commerzbank Aktiengesellschaft   Crédit Agricole   Crédit Commercial de France

Crédit Lyonnais   Daiwa Europe Limited   Deutsche Bank Capital Markets Limited

Fuji International Finance Limited   Generale Bank   Goldman Sachs International Corp.

Kredietbank International Group   Morgan Guaranty Ltd.

Morgan Stanley International   Nippon Credit International (HK) Ltd.

Nippon European Bank S.A./LTCB Group   Nomura International Limited

Orion Royal Bank Limited   Shearson Lehman Brothers International

Swiss Bank Corporation International Limited   The Taiyo Kobe Bank (Luxembourg) S.A.

Takugin International Bank (Europe) S.A.   S.G. Warburg & Co. Ltd.

Source: © 1989 The Economist Newspaper Ltd.

tions. It will be administered by the Bank for International Settlements, which will perform functions for the ECU similar to the U.S. Federal Reserve's clearing of dollar transactions.

In addition, the ECU is now the third biggest reserve currency behind the US$ and the deutsche mark. At the end of 1990, the US$ share of countries' foreign exchange reserves was 51 percent, the DM 19 percent, the ECU 17 percent, and the yen 9 percent.[32] Some influential Europeans forecast and advocate still another ECU use: the role as EC's central currency.[33]

However, as a medium of exchange, the ECU has been slower to catch on; business and the public have shown a lack of enthusiasm for its use. The EC Commission has tried to promote it for years with little success even in its own financial operations. Hotels, restaurants, and shops in Luxembourg tried displaying prices in ECUs during 1990, but customer response was lukewarm to cool.[34]

SUMMARY

Although debate continues about the relative merits of fixed exchange rates compared to the floating (mostly dirty) ones that have been in effect since 1973, many feel that the shocks and strains suffered by the international monetary system since 1971 would have made fixed rates impossible. The inherent contradiction of the gold exchange standard led to the collapse of the fixed, or par, rates established at Bretton Woods. Then the shocks of the OPEC petroleum price increases, the strains of the BOP gyrations of such countries as the United Kingdom and Italy, and the U.S. deficits combined with the German and Japanese surpluses would have made impossible the sustained maintenance of fixed exchange rates during the mid- and late 1970s and the 1980s.

So we find ourselves at the present situation of currency areas, US$, £, Ff, or SDR, with the LDCs pegged to a major currency and those currencies in a managed float. But even with the float, persistent BOP imbalances have not been avoided, and the world is seeking methods to bring about better balance among the important economies. In theory, floating currencies should achieve balance, but they have not. The gold standard is in the past, and the gold exchange standard fell of its own weight.

As matters stand, coordination must be on a nation-by-nation basis, and the policies called for in the world's best interests may be extremely unpopular politically within a country. For example, restraint of monetary base growth may be called for, but fears of depression and unemployment may deter national leaders from implementing such a policy.

Developments mentioned in this chapter may hold some promise of making desirable coordination possible. The G7 finance ministers and central bankers are meeting more frequently and are cooperating more effectively in coordinating fiscal and monetary policies and to some extent limiting currency fluctuations.

IMF members hoped that they could control the growth of world liquidity through greater use of SDRs rather than have it depend on the existence and size of the U.S. BOP deficit. As matters have worked out, the US$ is still the major component of nations' central reserve assets, and the ECU has become the third most held asset after the DM.

Countries measure their BOP on an annual basis; the BOP measures the flows of money from residents of a country to nonresidents, and vice versa. It is in surplus if more money is coming in than is going out; the opposite is a deficit. The BOP contains a current account, a capital account, and an official reserves account, and it is balanced by the statistical discrepancy account.

Another attempt at coordination, and at fixed currency exchange rates, is the European Monetary System (EMS), inaugurated in 1979. Its members include most of Europe's most important economic powers, and it has a fund of gold, U.S. dollars, and European currencies with which to achieve its goals.

The EMS created a unit of value called the European Currency Unit (ECU), the use of which as a denomination for bonds issued by European and other organizations has surpassed that of the SDR. There are bank accounts and traveler's checks in ECUs, and some international companies use ECUs for settlement of accounts between company units. The original purpose of the ECU was that it be used for settlement of accounts among EMS members, just as the SDR is used for settlement of accounts among IMF members.

Finally, what about gold? Pulling in one direction have been economists and government officials who want to demonetize gold and substitute for it special drawing rights (SDRs) and national currencies. They point out that SDRs can be controlled in number by the IMF in response to world need for liquidity, while the quantity, not to mention the price, of gold cannot be so controlled. There are other arguments against gold, such as the sources of most newly mined ore—Russia and South Africa.

Other economists and officials pull in the other direction. They favor keeping gold as a part of reserve assets, which is what most nations and the EMS do. It is too soon to write it out of the international monetary system.

QUESTIONS

1. What was Rueff's argument for the gold standard?
2. *a.* Describe the international monetary system devised at Bretton Woods.
   b. What were its strengths?
   c. Discuss the inherent contradiction of the gold exchange standard.
3. How does "dirty" float differ from "clean"?
4. What sorts of currency areas have developed in the post-1973 international monetary system?
5. What institutions make up most of the world's current money markets?

6. *a.* What is a special drawing right?
   b. Discuss its current and potential uses.

7. Why would fixed exchange rates have been difficult to maintain from 1973 to the present?

8. Why might the EMS be able to achieve fixed currency exchange rates among its member-countries?

9. Why should business managers be aware and wary of the BOP of the country in which their business operates?

10. What is the ECU? Why is it used more than the SDR?

11. Explain the central reserve/national currency conflict.

12. What was the Maastricht summit, and what was accomplished there?

□ MINICASE 5–1

Payment Terms for an International Contract

You are the financial executive of an American construction company. Your company is about to contract for a multiphase project in Italy. Progress payments will be made, but most of the money will not be due until near the end of the project, eight or nine years in the future.

Your company wants to be paid in US$s. The Italian customer wants to make payments in Italian lira (Il). You fear devaluation of the Il in terms of the US$ over the term of the contract.

Draft a contract payment clause to be used as a compromise. Use an IMF or EMS developed value discussed in this chapter.

□ MINICASE 5–2

SDR Exchange Risk

The Bowling Green National Bank has made loans denominated in SDRs to several of its MNE customers. It has built up a portfolio to the amount of SDR 8 million. Management decides to hedge by selling in the forward market the currencies that make up the SDR basket. How much of each currency must be hedged?

"May I have my allowance in Deutsche Marks, Dad?"

Reprinted from *The Wall Street Journal;* permission Cartoon Features Syndicate.

SUPPLEMENTARY READINGS

Auerbach, Robert D. *Money, Banking and Financial Markets.* 2nd ed. New York: Macmillan, 1985.

Bareau, Paul Louis Jean. *The Disorder in World Money: From Bretton Woods to SDRs.* London: Institute of Economic Affairs for the Wincott Foundation, 1981.

Barnard, Bruce. "Making Sense of Maastricht." *Europe,* January–February 1992, pp. 14–15.

Bergel, Clive. "ECU Plays Growing International Role." *Europe,* January–February 1986, pp. 28–29.

Bernholz, Peter. "The Introduction of Inflation-Free Monetary Constitutions (Gold Standard)." *Economic and Financial Prospects,* April–May 1986, pp. 1–5.

Boschen, John F. "Should We Reduce the Role of Banks in the Monetary Policy Process?" (Federal Reserve Bank of Kansas City) *Economic Review,* February 1988.

Coffey, Peter. *The European Monetary System: Past, Present and Future.* Boston: Martinus Nijhoff, 1984.

"Common Currency for Europe in 1992 Looks Good on Paper." *Business Month,* October 1988, p. 26.

Dixon, Joly. "Monetary Reform and the ECU." *Europe,* May 1986, pp. 18–20.

Eiteman, David K., and Arthur I. Stonehill. *Multinational Business Finance.* Reading, Mass.: Addison-Wesley Publishing, 1982, chaps. 2 and 3.

Fekete, Janos. "Do We Need a Monetary System?" *USA Today,* January 1988, pp. 18–21.

Hood, William C. "International Money, Credit and the SDR." *Finance & Development,* September 1983, pp. 6–9.

Humpage, Owen F. "Central Bank Intervention: Recent Literature, Continuing Controversy." (Federal Reserve Bank of Cleveland) *Economic Review,* 2nd quarter 1991, pp. 12–26.

International Financial Markets. Lombard Odier and Cie., monthly publication.

Jager, Henk, and Eelke de Jong. "The Private ECU's Potential Impact on Global and European Exchange Rate Stability."

(Banca Nazionale del Lavoro) *Quarterly Review,* March 1988, pp. 33–60.

Kvasnicka, Joseph G. "Why the U.S. Is Trying to Reduce the Dollar's Value." (Federal Reserve Bank of Chicago) *International Letter,* September 1985.

Ludlow, Peter. *The Making of the European Monetary System.* Boston: Butterworth Scientific, 1982.

"Recent Developments in the Private ECU Market." *Bank for International Settlements, 61st Annual Report,* March 31, 1991, pp. 146–48.

Safire, William. *Before the Fall.* New York: Belmont City Books, 1975.

Sarcinelli, Mario. "The EMS and the International Monetary System: Toward Greater Stability." (Banca Nazionale del Lavoro) *Quarterly Review,* March 1986, pp. 57–84.

Shelton, Judy. "Only Gold Can Save the Soviets." *The Wall Street Journal,* February 27, 1990, p. A24.

Solomon, Robert. *The International Monetary System, 1945–1981.* 2nd ed. New York: Harper & Row, 1981.

Summer, Michael T., and George Zis. *European Monetary Union: Progress and Prospects.* New York: St. Martin's Press, 1982.

Thanassoulas, Constantine. "A Balance of Payments Mystery—The Case of the Growing Discrepancy." *Barclays Review,* August 1985, pp. 59–62.

Tyler, Bob. "ECU Heads for the Top Three." *Supplement to Euromoney,* May 1991, pp. 37–41.

Wanniski, Jude. *The Way the World Works: How Economies Fail and Succeed.* New York: Basic Books, 1978.

Williamson, John. *The Lending Policies of the International Monetary Fund.* Washington, D.C.: Institute for International Economics, 1982.

Zehnder, H. R. "The ECU as an Investment Currency." *Bulletin, Swiss Banking Magazine,* November 1989, pp. 37–38.

ENDNOTES

1. Charles N. Henning, William Pigott, and Robert Haney Scott, *International Financial Management* (New York: McGraw-Hill, 1978), p. 149.

2. Albert C. Whitaker, *Foreign Exchange,* 2nd ed. (New York: Appleton-Century-Crofts, 1933), p. 157.

3. Jacques Rueff, *The Wall Street Journal,* June 5, 6, and 9, 1969.

4. John Mueller, "The Reserve Currency Curse," *The Wall Street Journal,* September 4, 1986, p. 26.

5. "Sell Some Gold," editorial, *The Wall Street Journal,* September 4, 1986, p. 26.

6. "Taking In the Biscuits," *The Economist,* May 11, 1991, p. 79.

7. K. K. Sharma and R. C. Murthy, "India Sends 25 Tonnes of Gold to London," *Financial Times,* July 9, 1991, p. 3.

8. *Articles of Agreement, International Monetary Fund* (Washington, D.C.: IMF, 1944), Article I.

9. Robert Z. Aliber, *The Future of the Dollar as an International Currency* (New York: Praeger Publishers, 1966).

10. For a discussion of how the pars were set, see Henning et al., *International Financial Management,* pp. 108, 218.

11. Theodore Sorenson, *Kennedy* (New York: Harper & Row, 1965), p. 408. See also *Maintaining the Strength of the United States Dollar in a Strong Free World Economy* (Washington, D.C.: U.S. Treasury Department, January

1968), p. xi; and *Economic Report of the President,* January 1964, p. 139.

12. *Federal Reserve Bulletin,* September 1969 and January 1974.

13. Ibid., December 1971 and January 1974.

14. Ibid., January 1974, p. A75.

15. This was perceived by the French economist Jacques Rueff, who also forecast the results; see endnote 3.

16. William Safire, *Before the Fall* (New York: Belmont City Books, 1975), p. 514. The size of the British request has been questioned; see Charles Coombs, *The Arena of International Finance* (New York: John Wiley & Sons, 1976), p. 218, where Coombs says that the Bank of England request was for cover of only US $750 million.

17. Wilson E. Schmidt, "The Night We Floated," International Institute for Economic Research, Original Paper 9, October 1977.

18. Ibid., p. 7.

19. For detailed accounts of the international monetary system during the 1971–73 period, see Coombs, *Arena of International Finance,* chap. 12; and Robert Solomon, *The International Monetary System* (New York: Harper & Row, 1977), chaps. 12–15.

20. For discussions of the varieties and methods of clean or dirty floats plus comparisons of float versus peg, see, for example, Weir M. Brown, *World Afloat: National Policies Ruling the Waves,* Essays in International Finance, no. 116 (Princeton, N.J.: International Finance Section, Department of Economics, Princeton University, May 1976); Harry G. Johnson, *Further Essays in Monetary Economics* (Winchester, Mass.: Allen & Unwin, 1972); Anthony M. Lanyi, *The Case for Floating Exchange Reconsidered,* Essays in International Finance, no. 72 (February 1976); Raymond F. Mikesell and Henry M. Goldstein, *Rules for a Floating Regime,* Essays in International Finance, no. 109 (March 1975); and "Economics Brief: To Fix to Float," *The Economist,* January 9, 1988, pp. 66–67.

21. Wendell H. McCulloch, Jr., "American Exports: Why Have They Lagged?" A Study for the Subcommittee on Trade, Productivity, and Economic Growth of the Joint Economic Committee, Congress of the United States, May 14, 1985.

22. Peter Norman, "Adjusting to a New Climate," *Financial Times,* April 29, 1991, section IV, p. I.

23. Stanley W. Black, *Floating Exchange Rates and National Economic Policy* (New Haven: Yale University Press, 1977), pp. 23–26, 49–50, 129–30, 149–50, 154–56, and 173–74.

24. Charles N. Stabler, "Banks and Their Foreign Loans," *The Wall Street Journal,* January 29, 1976, p. 16.

25. Geoffrey Bell, "The International Financial System and Capital Shortages," in *The World Capital Shortage,* ed. Alan Heslop (Indianapolis: Bobbs-Merrill, 1977), pp. 35–57.

26. Jim McCallum, "Big Three Battle It Out," *Financial Times,* April 29, 1991, section III, p. IV.

27. Peter Kenen, "Techniques of Central International Reserves." Paper presented at the J. Marcus Flemming Memorial Conference, International Monetary Fund, November 12, 1976.

28. *IMF Survey,* August, 1990, pp. 6–7.

29. Philip Revzin, "Fathers of Europe's Monetary System Push Creation of a Joint Central Bank," *The Wall Street Journal,* February 23, 1988, p. 20.

30. "The Definition of the ECU," *Economic and Financial Prospects Supplement,* Swiss Bank Corporation, February/March 1989, pp. 2–3.

31. "A Fistful of ECUs," *The Economist,* July 13, 1991, p. 83.

32. Ibid.

33. Giscard d'Estaing, "The ECU and the European Monetary System," *Bulletin, Swiss Banking Magazine,* November 1989, pp. 11–13.

34. Lucy Kellaway, "ECU Still Faces Crises of Confidence despite Its Higher Profile," *Financial Times,* January 28, 1991, p. 6.

Section Three

Foreign Environment

In Chapter 1, we stated that many of the business practices followed in the home country can be transferred intact and applied in other countries. However, we also mentioned that because of the differences in environmental forces, some ways of doing business must either be adapted to meet local conditions or changed completely.

In Section Three, we shall examine these forces to see how they differ from those that home country businesspeople are accustomed to encountering in this country. Only by such an investigation can we discover whether (1) we can transfer the business practice as is, (2) we must adapt it to local conditions, or (3) we cannot use it at all.

Having examined the international monetary system in Section Two, we begin Section Three with a discussion of the uncontrollable financial forces (Chapter 6) with which international companies must contend. Some of these forces are foreign currency exchange risks, balance of payments, taxation, tariffs, monetary and fiscal policies, inflation, and national accounting rules.

In Chapter 7, we consider the economic forces. Managements must know how the scarce resources of land, labor, and capital are being allocated to the production and distribution of goods and services and the manner in which they are consumed. We explore important economic and socioeconomic dimensions of the economy.

Next we look at the physical forces—location, topography, and climate (Chapter 8). We offer examples to illustrate their influence on both the controllable and uncontrollable forces. The constantly changing situation in natural resources is emphasized not only because of their importance to firms that consume them but also because the income from new discoveries frequently creates new markets. The "Contamination of Resources" section focuses on the Bhopal and Rhine disasters and the Exxon oil spill and their consequences for international companies.

Chapter 9 discusses the significance of the sociocultural forces for international businesspeople. It points out that the wide variety of attitudes and values among cultures affects managers of all the business functions. Although executives normally do not have time to become thoroughly immersed in a nation's culture, they should be familiar with at least those aspects that affect their business relationships.

In Chapter 10, we investigate the political forces that are a powerful factor in the success or failure of a foreign venture. Some of these are nationalism, terrorism, unstable governments, international organizations, government-owned businesses, and various ideological forces.

Legal forces, the subject of Chapter 11, reflect a nation's political climate. Managements of international firms must be familiar with the host country's laws because those laws set the constraints within which the managers must operate. In this chapter, we discuss laws concerning taxation, antitrust, imports, price and wage controls, labor, currency, and industrial property.

The composition, skills, attitudes, and union activities of an area's labor pool must be investigated because these labor forces affect productivity and, ultimately, the firm's profitability. Chapter 12 discusses these forces.

In Chapter 13, we examine competition at the macro level among the United States, European Community, Japan, and the Asian newly industrializing nations. Then we look at competition at the industry level (specifically, the steel industry), followed by a discussion of competitive analysis. The last major topic in this chapter is the distributive forces.

Chapter 6

Financial Forces

We're getting used to volatility; we're getting good at coping with it now.

> Citicorp foreign exchange currency trader

Traders aren't paranoid—there really are people after them.

> Virick Martin, currency trader, Merrill Lynch Capital Markets

Countries don't go bust.

> Walter Wriston, chairman, Citibank

Do the wrong thing. That's the best advice anyone could possibly offer an ambitious young person eager to get ahead in banking.

> Alan Abelson, *Barron's*

LEARNING OBJECTIVES

In this chapter, you will study:

1. How to read and understand foreign exchange quotations.

2. The difference between spot and forward rates.

3. Some causes of exchange rate changes.

4. Government intervention in currency exchange markets.

5. How to recognize a currency exchange risk.

6. Government currency controls.

7. Some effects of inflation on business.

8. Monetary and fiscal policies that cause or combat inflation.

9. Why business must watch BOP developments, international monetary reserves, exchange rate forecasts, and comparative inflation rates.

10. The LDC debt crisis and some possible solutions to it.

11. The fact that the United States has the largest net negative international investment position in the world.

KEY WORDS AND CONCEPTS

- Sovereign debt
- Net negative international investment position
- Vehicle currency
- Intervention currency
- Safe haven
- Cross-rates
- Spot rate
- Forward rate
- Trading at a discount
- Trading at a premium
- Currency exchange controls
- Export incentives

BUSINESS INCIDENT

In 1984, after the U.S. dollar (US$) had increased in value against the Japanese yen (¥) in an almost uninterrupted rise since 1981, many "experts," including currency traders, thought that the US$ had peaked. Expecting the dollar's value to fall, the chief trader of Fuji Bank's New York money-dealing operation arranged to sell (short) large amounts of dollars for future delivery, betting that he would earn a huge profit when he purchased the lower-cost dollars for many fewer ¥ on the delivery date.

He lost the bet. Instead of going down, the US$ continued to go up, and he lost $48 million for Fuji over a four-month period.

sovereign debt the debt of a government or government agency

net negative international investment position the U.S. Commerce Department's description of what is commonly called the U.S. international debt

The "uncontrollable" financial forces on which we shall touch include foreign currency exchange risks, national balances of payment, taxation, tariffs, national monetary and fiscal policies, inflation, and national business accounting rules. *Uncontrollable* means that these forces originate outside the business enterprise. It does not mean that the financial management of companies is helpless to minimize their disadvantages; those disadvantages may even be turned to the company's advantage.

We shall have a look at what causes exchange rates to change and at how governments sometimes intervene in foreign exchange markets. We shall emphasize the importance for management to remain aware of BOP developments, exchange rate forecasts, inflation forecasts, government fiscal and monetary policies, and other financial forces. And at the end of the chapter, we look at the **sovereign debt** crises of developing countries, such as Brazil and Mexico. And not to be outdone, the United States has run up the biggest **net negative international investment position** in the world.

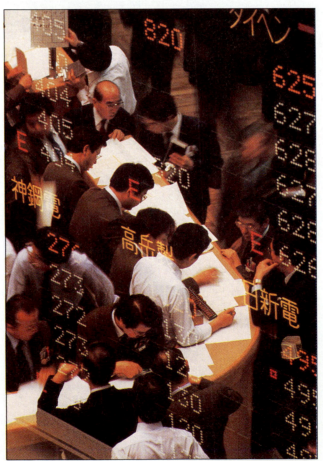

Another uncontrollable financial force, the rollercoaster Tokyo Stock Exchange.

Andy Caulfield/The Image Bank

FLUCTUATING CURRENCY VALUES

An attempt is being made to bind together the values of most of the major European currencies in the European Monetary System (EMS). Although EMS members have made several currency value realignments since its inception in 1979, there has been less value fluctuation than was experienced before EMS and less fluctuation than has occurred in the currencies of the major non-EMS countries. The currencies of the other leading trading countries float and fluctuate in value relative to each other and to the EMS. Those countries include Australia, Canada, Japan, and the United States.

The company financial manager must understand how to protect against losses or optimize gains from such fluctuations. Another level of currency exchange risk is encountered when a nation suspends or limits convertibility of its currency, and the manager must try to foresee and minimize or avoid losses resulting from large holdings of inconvertible and otherwise limitedly useful currencies.

When you have a currency that you want to convert into another currency, the first thing you might do is look for the value of the currency you have in terms of the one you want. You can find international currency exchange quotations in business publications such as *The Wall Street Journal* or the *Financial Times* and in the business section of most major newspapers.

FOREIGN EXCHANGE QUOTATIONS

The foreign exchange quotations—the price of one currency expressed in terms of another—can be confusing until you have examined how they are reported. In the world's currency exchange markets, the U.S. dollar (US$) is the common unit being exchanged for other currencies. Even if a holder of Japanese yen (¥) wants British pounds (£), the trade, particularly if it involves a large amount, usually will be to buy US$s with the ¥ and then to buy £s with the US$s. The reasons for this procedure are historical and practical.

Historically, the international monetary system established at Bretton Woods just before the end of World War II set the value of the US$ in terms of gold at $35 per ounce. The values of all the other major currencies were then stated in terms of the US$; for example, the yen was worth 0.28 of a U.S. penny, the French franc (Ff) was worth 18 cents, the German mark (DM) was worth 27 cents, and the £ was worth $2.40. In other words, the US$ was established as the keystone currency at the center of the world's monetary system.

The practical reasons for the continuing central position of the US$ are the several functions it has come to perform in the world. It is the main central reserve asset of many countries. It is the most used **vehicle currency** and **intervention currency.**

Liberia and Panama use the US$ as their official currency, and Israel uses it as a parallel currency to its shekel. One of the authors did some consulting and research in parts of South America during 1990; in most countries, and particularly in Argentina, the US$ was preferred to local currencies and even

vehicle currency a currency used as a vehicle for international trade or investment

intervention currency a currency used by a country to intervene in the foreign currency exchange markets (e.g., using some of its U.S. dollar reserve to buy—and thus strengthen—its own currency) to other equally hard, convertible currencies. It has been the preferred medium of exchange and store of value also in Poland, the former Soviet Union, and many other countries.

Among the reasons why the US$ is in great demand worldwide are its so-called **safe haven** aspect and its universal acceptance. Even if U.S. interest rates and investment opportunities were less attractive, there would still be a feeling that money is safe in American securities or property. Inflation has been brought to a low level, and the country is seen as less likely than others to be invaded or to elect a socialist government. It is seen as a safe haven.

As to universal acceptance, if you have traveled internationally with US$s, you have found them welcome everywhere. A dramatic example was the scene in the film *The Killing Fields,* which is based on a true story, in which the Cambodian doctor/prisoner was asked by the Vietnamese officer for whom he worked to take the officer's young son and try to escape with the boy to Thailand. The officer gave the doctor a small emergency kit whose contents included a roll of American $20 bills.

Although the US$ remains the most used currency, the currencies of the other noncommunist, industrial countries are also important in world transactions and growing more so. This is particularly true of the West German deutsche mark (DM) and the Japanese yen (¥). And, although most large currency exchanges go through the US$ (see the ¥–British pound [£] example above), it is also possible to directly trade yen for pounds. The exchange rates for trading directly between non-US$ currencies are called **cross-rates**. See Figure 6–1 for the cross-rate quotes on August 7, 1991.

> **safe haven** in reference to the U.S. dollar, a political concept based on the belief that the U.S. is less likely than most countries to elect a socialist or communist government or to be subjected to a military coup or revolution

> **cross-rates** currency exchange rates directly between non-US$ currencies; usually determined by comparing the US$ exchange rates of the other currencies

□ Exchange Rates

Figure 6–2 (page 196) shows that the price for one German deutsche mark is .5845. This means that one DM costs US$ 0.5845. For a less expensive currency, look at the Japanese yen, quoted at .007350; each yen costs that fraction of a dollar. Two currencies that cost more than US$1 on August 7, 1991, were the Bahrain dinar at $2.6525 and the British pound at $1.7125.

□ DM1.7110 = US$1.00

There is more to be learned from reading the exchange rates quotes. Using Figure 6–2, you will see the figure .5857 to the right of the "Germany (mark)" .5845 quote. Now look at the tops of the columns in which those numbers appear, and you will find the abbreviations, "Wed." and "Tues." As you probably have surmised, the .5845 quote is the price at the close of trading on Wednesday, August 7, 1991, while .5857 was the quote at the close of the previous trading day. Those two prices tell you the US$ strengthened a little vis-à-vis the German mark during Wednesday's trading; one DM cost US$.5845 at Wednesday's close, while it had cost fractionally more, US$.5857, at Tuesday's close.

There is another way of expressing the value relationships between currencies. Look again at the "Germany (mark)" line in Figure 6–2, and move to the right of the number about which we spoke. There you find another "Wed." and another "Tues." column; the quote in the "Wed." column is 1.7110, while it is 1.7075 under "Tues." These quotes inform us how many German marks it took to buy one US$ at the close of trading on each of those

□ **FIGURE 6-1   Key Currency Cross-Rates (Late New York Trading August 7, 1991)**

	Dollar	Pound	SFranc	Guilder	Yen	Lira	DMark	FFranc	CdnDlr
Canada	1.1470	1.9648	.76543	.59482	.00844	.00090	.67068	.19715	—
France	5.8180	9.966	3.8825	3.0172	.04281	.00455	3.4019	—	5.0724
Germany	1.7102	2.9296	1.1413	.88690	.01258	.00134	—	.29395	1.4910
Italy	1280.0	2192.6	854.19	663.80	9.419	—	748.45	220.01	1116.0
Japan	135.90	232.80	90.691	70.477	—	.10617	79.464	23.359	118.48
Netherlands	1.9283	3.3032	1.2868	—	.01419	.00151	1.1275	.33144	1.6812
Switzerland	1.4985	2.5669	—	.77711	.01103	.00117	.87621	.25756	1.3065
U.K.	.58377	—	.38957	.30274	.00430	.00046	.34135	.10034	.50895
U.S.	—	1.7130	.66733	.51859	.00736	.00078	.58473	.17188	.87184

Source: *The Wall Street Journal*, August 8, 1991, p. C12.

days, and they are the mirror images of the two quotes to the left. Observe that about one more German pfennig was needed to buy one US$ after Wednesday's trading than was needed after Tuesday's trading; in other words, the DM had weakened a little vis-à-vis the US$.

Spot rates.   The **spot rate** is the exchange rate between two currencies for their immediate trade for delivery within two days. The rate on the same line as the name of the country is the spot rate. You will note in Figure 6–2 that the spot rate for German marks was .5845.

Forward rates.   The **forward rate** is the cost today for a commitment by one party to deliver to or take from another party an agreed amount of a currency at a fixed, future date. The commitment is a forward contract, and for frequently traded currencies such contracts are usually available on a 30-, 60-, 90-, or 180-day basis. You may be able to negotiate with banks for different time periods or for contracts in other currencies.

Refer to the "Germany (mark) 30-day forward" quotation in Figure 6–2, and you will see that it is .5828. Compare that with the spot rate of .5845, and you can see that it would cost less in US$s to buy DMs for delivery in 30 days than for delivery today. Looking at the 90- and 180-day quotes, you can see that the discount grows larger. This means that traders in the forward markets believe the German mark will weaken in US$ terms for at least six months. The DM is said to be **trading at a discount** in the forward market. If the forward DM quotations were higher than spot, they would be said to be **trading at a premium.**

□ **So Many Yen, So Few Pounds**

Look again at Figure 6–2, and you will see that it took about 136 yen to buy 1 US$, whereas less than 1 pound was enough for a dollar. Glancing up and down the column, you find that an Indonesian rupiah holder would need 1,955 rupiahs for US$1 and that a different number is required by holders of each of the other currencies quoted. It might seem that the fewer units of a currency required to buy a dollar, the harder or "better" that currency is compared to the others, but that is not necessarily correct.

As we have seen, the currencies of the world's major countries were set in value relative to the US$ at the end of World War II. Those exchange rates

spot rate the exchange rate between two currencies for delivery within two business days

forward rate the exchange rate between two currencies for delivery in the future, commonly 30, 60, 90, or 180 days

trading at a discount when a currency's forward rate quotes are weaker than spot

trading at a premium when a currency's forward rate quotes are stronger than spot

☐ FIGURE 6-2   Exchange Rates (Wednesday, August 7, 1991)

The New York foreign exchange selling rates below apply to trading among banks in amounts of $1 million and more, as quoted at 3 P.M. Eastern time by Bankers Trust Co. and other sources. Retail transactions provide fewer units of foreign currency per dollar.

Country (currency)	US$ Equivalent		Currency per US$		Country (currency)	US$ Equivalent		Currency per US$	
	Wed.	Tues.	Wed.	Tues.		Wed.	Tues.	Wed.	Tues.
Argentina (austral)	.0001008	.0001008	9922.60	9922.60	Jordan (dinar)	1.4620	1.4620	.6840	.6840
Australia (dollar)	.7837	.7830	1.2760	1.2771	Kuwait (dinar)	z	z	z	z
Austria (schilling)	.08313	.08319	12.03	12.02	Lebanon (bound)	.001119	.001119	894.00	894.00
Bahrain (dinar)	2.6525	2.6525	.3770	.3770	Malaysia (ringgit)	.3613	.3604	2.7675	2.7745
Belgium (franc)	.02837	.02842	35.25	35.19	Malta (lira)	3.0170	3.0170	.3315	.3315
Brazil (cruzeiro)	.00281	.00292	355.30	342.90	Mexico (peso)				
Britain (pound)	1.7125	1.7155	.5839	.5829	Floating rate	.0003292	.0003292	3038.01	3038.01
30-day forward	1.7049	1.7080	.5865	.5855	Netherlands (guilder)	.5185	.5195	1.9285	1.9250
90-day forward	1.6900	1.6943	.5917	.5902	New Zealand (dollar)	.5745	.5750	1.7406	1.7391
180-day forward	1.6730	1.6766	.5977	.5964	Norway (krone)	.1498	.1499	6.6775	6.6732
Canada (dollar)	.8718	.8709	1.1470	1.1483	Pakistan (rupee)	.0408	.0408	24.50	24.50
30-day forward	.8695	.8687	1.1501	1.1512	Peru (new sol)	1.2821	1.3016	.78	.77
90-day forward	.8656	.8648	1.1553	1.1563	Philippines (peso)	.03724	.03724	26.85	26.85
180-day forward	.8598	.8594	1.1630	1.1636	Portugal (escudo)	.006819	.006832	146.65	146.36
Chile (peso)	.002863	.002953	349.24	338.62	Saudi Arabia (riyal)	.26663	.26663	3.7505	3.7505
China (renminbi)	.187017	.187017	5.3471	5.3471	Singapore (dollar)	.5794	.5804	1.7260	1.7230
Colombia (peso)	.001786	.001832	560.00	546.00	South Africa (rand)				
Denmark (krone)	.1511	.1511	6.6177	6.6168	Commercial rate	.3505	.3512	2.8533	2.8470
Ecuador (sucre)					Financial rate	.3103	.3103	3.2230	3.2230
Floating rate	.000966	.000966	1035.00	1035.00	South Korea (won)	.0013738	.0013738	727.90	727.90
Finland (markka)	.24245	.24294	4.1245	4.1163	Spain (peseta)	.009350	.009355	106.95	106.90
France (franc)	.17190	.17213	5.8175	5.8095	Sweden (krona)	.1610	.1612	6.2116	6.2043
30-day forward	.17134	.17157	5.8365	5.8285	Switzerland (franc)	.6673	.6705	1.4985	1.4915
90-day forward	.17020	.17050	5.8756	5.8650	30-day forward	.6660	.6693	1.5015	1.4942
180-day forward	.16873	.16903	5.9265	5.9162	90-day forward	.6636	.6669	1.5070	1.4994
Germany (mark)	.5845	.5857	1.7110	1.7075	180-day forward	.6605	.6659	1.5141	1.5017
30-day forward	.5828	.5839	1.7160	1.7125	Taiwan (dollar)	.037397	.037789	26.74	26.46
90-day forward	.5790	.5806	1.7270	1.7225	Thailand (baht)	.03893	.03893	25.69	25.69
180-day forward	.5743	.5757	1.7414	1.7369	Turkey (lira)	.0002274	.0002284	4398.00	4378.02
Greece (drachma)	.005295	.005306	188.85	188.45	United Arab (dirham)	.2723	.2723	3.6725	3.6725
Hong Kong (dollar)	.12884	.12884	7.7615	7.7615	Uruguay (new peso)				
India (rupee)	.03890	.03890	25.71	25.71	Financial	.000484	.000484	2066.00	2066.00
Indonesia (rupiah)	.0005115	.0005115	1955.03	1955.03	Venezuela (bolivar)				
Ireland (punt)	1.5615	1.5650	.6404	.6390	Floating rate	.01684	.01706	59.40	58.61
Israel (shekel)	.4283	.4326	2.3350	2.3118	SDR*	1.34578	1.34708	.74306	.74235
Italy (lira)	.0007806	.0007822	1281.00	1278.51	ECU†	1.19620	1.19808	—	—
Japan (yen)	.007350	.007383	136.05	135.45					
30-day forward	.007339	.007373	136.25	135.63					
90-day forward	.007319	.007355	136.63	135.97					
180-day forward	.007304	.007342	136.91	136.21					

*Special Drawing Rights (SDR) are based on exchange rates for the U.S., German, British, French, and Japanese currencies. Source: International Monetary Fund.
†European Currency Unit (ECU) is based on a basket of community currencies. Source: European Community Commission.
zNot quoted.
Source: The Wall Street Journal, August 8, 1991, p. C12.

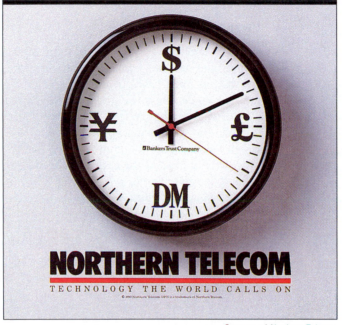

Courtesy of Northern Telecom

A global communications network makes every time zone in the world more accessible.

were the rates in the markets at that time; they were historical accidents. Since then, and particularly since 1973, the relative values of currencies, their convertibility, their hardness or softness, have been set by the supply and demand volumes of the foreign exchange markets. Those volumes are influenced by the policies of the various governments—their monetary and fiscal policies, their trade policies, and so on. Thus, the number of units of a currency per US$ on any given day does not indicate the relative strength of that currency. Many other factors must be examined to determine that.

The cost of a forward contract is the premium or discount compared to the spot rate. Whether there is a premium or a discount and its size depend on the expectations of the world financial community, businesses, individuals, and governments about what the future will bring. These expectations factor in such considerations as supply and demand forecasts for the two currencies, relative inflation in the two countries, relative productivity and unit labor cost changes, expected election results or other political developments, and expected government fiscal, monetary, and currency exchange market actions.

Bid and asked prices.   When travelers or businesses contact a bank or an exchange agency to buy or sell a currency, they find a bid price and an asked price. The bid is the lower. The quotation for the French franc may be .16

bid and .17 asked. If the customer has francs to sell, the bank or agency is bidding—offering—16 cents (U.S. pennies) for each franc. If the customer wants to buy francs, the bank or agency is asking 17 cents, a higher price. The difference provides a margin—profit—for the bank or agency.

Commercial and financial rates.   In Figure 6–2, you will note two spot reports for South Africa. They give commercial and financial rates. The commercial rate is for import/export transactions, and the financial rate is for all other transactions.

◻ Fluctuating Exchange Rates Create Risk

When your activities involve more than one country, you must deal with more than one currency. For example, an American company exporting to France will, in most cases, want to receive US$s. If credit is involved, payment is not made when the goods are delivered, and one of the parties will have a currency exchange risk. If the French importer agrees to pay French francs, then the American exporter bears a risk that the value of the French franc will fall and thus the French francs will buy fewer US$s when received than they would have at the earlier goods delivery date. On the other hand, if the French importer agrees to pay in US$ at a future time, then the importer bears that risk. (See Figure 6–3.)

The company financial manager is not without weapons for dealing with this type of risk. These are presented in Chapter 18. A greater potential hazard for the company is that a country in which the company has assets may institute exchange controls.

CURRENCY EXCHANGE CONTROLS

currency exchange controls government controls that limit the legal uses of a currency in international transactions

Currency exchange controls limit or prohibit the legal use of a currency in international transactions. Typically, the value of the currency is arbitrarily fixed at a rate higher than its value in the free market, and it is decreed that all purchases or sales of other currencies be made through a government agency. A black market inevitably springs up, but it is of little use to the finance manager, who usually wants to avoid breaking the laws of a country in which the company is operating. In addition, the black market is rarely able to accommodate transactions of the size involved in a multinational business.

Thus, the company, along with all other holders of the controlled or blocked currency, must pay more than the free market rate if permission to buy foreign currency is granted by the government. If permission is not granted or if the cost of foreign currency is uneconomically high, the blocked currency can be used only within the country. This usually presents problems of finding suitable products to buy or investments to make within the country.

People will go to remarkable extremes to get blocked money out of exchange-controlled countries. A few years ago, in the west of France, an employee of a company operating in France strapped on a big money belt packed with large-denomination French franc bank notes. He then put on hang glider wings and glided into Switzerland, where he bought Swiss francs and deposited them in a Swiss bank account.

□ **FIGURE 6–3**
Currency Exchange Risk

February 1	Goods delivery date exchange rate	August 1	Payment date exchange rate
Suppose:	US$1 = Ff6		US$1 = Ff6

Whichever party bore the currency exchange risk, neither gained nor lost.

Suppose:	US$1 = Ff6		US$1 = Ff7

Whichever party bore the currency exchange risk lost. It now requires Ff7 to buy the US$1, which could have been bought for Ff6 at the time the goods were delivered.

Suppose:	US$1 = Ff6		US$1 = Ff5

Whichever party bore the currency exchange risk gained. It now requires only Ff5 to buy the US$1, which would have cost Ff6 at the time the goods were delivered.

In New Delhi, the local manager of a major international airline gave a case of Scotch to a government official. Shortly thereafter, the agency for which that official worked granted the airline permission to use blocked rupees to buy almost US$20 million and transfer them to the airline's home country.

Those were extreme methods of converting blocked currencies to convertible currencies; the methods were, of course, also illegal. The great majority of finance managers do not resort to such methods, but they can take legal steps to protect the firm from the adverse effects of currency exchange controls. Those steps are considered in Chapter 18.

Table 6–1 shows the currency exchange control laws and regulations of several countries.* You can see that the controls differ greatly from country to country and even within a country, depending on the type of transaction. As a generality, only the relatively rich industrialized countries have few or no currency exchange controls. They are a minority of the world's countries, and thus the great majority of the countries do impose exchange controls. The international businessperson must carefully study those laws and regulations both before and while doing business in any country. Even the industrialized countries may have some restrictions.

BALANCE OF PAYMENTS

Balance of payments (BOP) was discussed in some detail in Chapter 5, but we would be remiss not to mention it as a major financial force. The state of a nation's BOP will tell observant management much of value. If the BOP is slipping into deficit, the government is probably considering one or more market or nonmarket measures to correct or suppress that deficit. Management should be alert for either currency devaluation or restrictive monetary or fiscal policies to induce deflation. Another possibility is that currency or trade controls may be coming. With foresight, the firm's management can adjust to the changing government policies or at least soften their impact.

* The information in Table 6–1 comes from *Business International Money Report*, July 26, 1990, pp. 210–15. Many more countries are covered in that publication; we have presented only a few to give you an idea of the types of controls and how countries differ. As of 1992, *Business International Money Report* had not updated the table, but for the countries named in this book, there had been no changes, so the information is still accurate.

☐ **TABLE 6–1** **Comparative Table of Worldwide Exchange Controls**

Country (currency)	Regulatory Environment	Borrowing from Abroad	Incoming Direct Investment	Incoming Portfolio Investment
Argentina (austral, A)	Two FX* tiers since October; official rate for trade and foreign loans; free market rate for other transactions.	Terms must be fixed in advance, with minimum of 1 year.	Amounts under $5 million and equity injections under 30% of firm's capital freely permitted.	Freely permitted for listed shares of amounts under $2 million.
Chile (peso, $)	Ongoing liberalization; official FX rate set by Banco Central used for most transactions.	Registration and approval of loan required.	Investments over $5 million or in certain sectors require approval.	Freely permitted.
China (renminbi, RmB)	Severe FX shortage; new foreign exchange centers offer minimal volume and high premiums.	A few local entities may borrow abroad, subject to restrictions.	Time-consuming approval process; minimum foreign equity, 25%.	No markets exist.
Egypt (pound, £E)	All transactions are at the free market rate, except basic commodity imports, traditional exports (e.g., cotton), and oil company transactions. These are at a rate of E0.7:US$1.	Permitted for new projects if within approved financing plan and for ongoing projects if they generate FX to service the debt.	Approval required; freely given in sectors needing foreign expertise or capital.	Approval required; foreign ownership limited in banking, insurance; priority given to export-oriented and import-substitution projects.
France (franc, F)	In the process of eliminating remaining controls.	Freely permitted.	Freely permitted, but advance notification required so authorities can check source of funds.	Regulations gradually being relaxed.
Germany (deutsche mark, DM)	Extremely liberal	Freely permitted.	No approval needed; stringent antitrust laws should be considered.	Freely permitted.
Hong Kong (dollar, $)	All controls abolished in December 1972.	Freely permitted.	Freely permitted; local business- registration procedures must be followed.	Freely permitted.
India (rupee, Rs)	Strict controls; managed FX rate; parallel market exists, at 15–20% premium.	Approval required; borrowing usually limited to capital investments.	Approval required; maximum foreign equity; 40% in most cases.	Limited to authorized mutual funds.
Japan (yen, ¥)	Liberalization continuing; controls persist in certain areas (e.g., netting).	Freely permitted; must be reported to Ministry of Finance.	3 months' prior notice required.	Notification usually required.
Nigeria (naira, N)	Highly controlled; two different exchange rates—interbank rate and FEM‡ rate. FEM rate determined at fortnightly auctions.	Subject to Finance Ministry approval.	Approval needed from Finance Ministry and Ministry of Internal Affairs; limits on foreign equity vary, 100% ownership not allowed.	Finance Ministry approval required.
Saudi Arabia (riyal, Sr)	No restrictions are placed on the inward or outward movement of funds.	Freely permitted.	Freely permitted	Freely permitted.
Switzerland (franc, SwF)	Controls usually avoided, but government has applied restrictions in the past.	Freely permitted.	Freely permitted, except for a few public services.	Freely permitted for registered shares.
United Kingdom (pound sterling, £)	All controls have been removed.	Freely permitted.	Freely permitted, although takeovers scrutinized by Department of Trade.	Freely permitted.
United States (dollar, $)	Virtually no controls.	Freely permitted.	Freely permitted in most sectors; some states have their own restrictions.	Freely permitted in most sectors.

*FX = Foreign exchange; †CB = National central bank; ‡FEM = Foreign Exchange Market.

Source: *Business International Money Report,* July 26, 1990. This table includes only a partial listing. For a more comprehensive list of countries and restrictions, see the *Business International Money Report.*

Remittance of Dividends and Profits	Remittance of Interest and Principal	Remittance of Royalties and Fees	Repatriation of Capital	Documentation for Remittances
Freely permitted at free market rate; heavy taxes on excess over 12% of capital base.	Freely permitted at commercial rate for approved loans.	Freely permitted at free market rate; fees must reflect market value.	Fully remittable 3 years after initial investment at free rate.	Authorization forms must be filed with the CB.†
Freely permitted.	Freely permitted for registered loans.	Freely permitted for approved contracts.	Freely permitted for full amount after 3 years.	Requests must be filed with the CB.
FX income and expense must be balanced before remitting.	FX income and expense must be balanced before remitting.	Limited to 4% and 10-year period; low FX priority for fees.	Freely permitted, but FX shortage makes conversion difficult.	Onerous and complex requirements.
Approval required; 20% reserve required; firms without FX to cover remittance must apply to banks for FX allocation.	Freely permitted if the project generates sufficient FX to cover payment; if not, approval required.	Freely permitted if the project generates FX for payment; if not, approval required.	Allowed after 5 years, to be remitted in 5 equal annual payments; exceptions sometimes made.	Accountant's certificate of source of funds and proof of tax payment required.
No restrictions if minimum capital and reserve requirements met.	No restrictions on bonds or loans; prepayment requires approval.	No restrictions, but the CB requires the account number.	Freely permitted, if repatriated within 3 months of liquidation.	Notification needed; local bank must run transaction.
Freely permitted.	Freely permitted.	Freely permitted.	Freely permitted.	Notification required for statistical purposes.
Freely permitted.	Freely permitted.	Freely permitted.	Freely permitted.	No official requirements.
Approval required; no ceiling on amount.	Freely permitted for approved loans.	Approval required; generally restricted to 4% of sales.	Approval required; amounts may be limited.	Onerous; FX must be obtained from authorized banks.
Freely permitted.	Freely permitted for approved loans.	Freely permitted for approved contracts; tax authorities monitor rate changes.	Freely permitted.	Handled by FX banks; mainly for reporting purposes.
Finance Ministry approval required; frequent delays. No ceilings if paid out of current-year after-tax profits.	Finance Ministry approval required.	Finance Ministry approval required; royalties limited to 1% of sales, fees to 2% of pretax profits.	Finance Ministry approval required, followed by authorized FX dealer's approval.	Onerous and complex requirements; transfers via authorized dealers only.
Freely permitted.	Freely permitted.	Freely permitted.	Freely permitted.	No official requirements.
No restrictions, except for reserve requirements.	Freely permitted.	Freely permitted.	Freely permitted.	Only that needed for ordinary bank transactions.
Freely permitted.	Freely permitted.	Freely permitted.	Freely permitted.	No official requirements.
Freely permitted.	Freely permitted.	Freely permitted.	Freely permitted.	Foreign bank transaction records must be kept for 5 years.

export incentives tax breaks, lower-cost financing, foreign aid, or other advantages that governments give to encourage businesses to export and foreign customers to buy goods and services

On the export side, the company may start shopping for **export incentives**—government incentives to make its exports easier or more profitable. Lower-cost capital may be available if the company can demonstrate that exports will be boosted.

One of the most common export incentives is the financing of exports by a government agency that offers foreign buyers lower interest rates than they could get from other money sources. Sometimes the agency's loans are accompanied by an aid grant, which need not be repaid.

Countries that levy value-added taxes (see Chapter 11) are permitted by GATT rules to rebate them to exporters. This makes the exports less expensive and thus more competitive.

When firms are engaged in tough competition for major export contracts, their home governments may intervene to assist. Often, the potential customer is a government agency, and the intervention may be contact with the customer's decision makers by their counterparts in the home government.

TARIFFS OR DUTIES

The words *tariffs* and *duties* are used interchangeably. These can be high or low, and it is of great importance to business to minimize them. They are discussed in the "Trade Restrictions" section of Chapter 3 and as one of the legal forces in Chapter 10, but they can certainly be classified as financial forces and therefore should be mentioned in this chapter.

The European Community (EC) and the other groupings of nations that we discussed in Chapter 4 have lowered or abolished tariffs on trade among member-countries. EC Project 1992 is an attempt to strip away all barriers to people, services, goods, and capital between the 12 member-countries. Such developments add new dimensions to the decision-making processes of companies located outside the groupings. For example, would the expenses and legal and personnel problems involved in establishing operations within a grouping be justified by tariff savings?

TAXATION

Inasmuch as most international business is conducted by corporations, we are concerned with tariffs paid by and taxes levied on corporations. The point may be made that corporations don't pay taxes; they only collect them. In the end, people pay taxes.[1] The taxes may be collected from customers in higher prices, from employees in lower wages, from stockholders in lower dividends or capital gains, or from suppliers in smaller orders. However, even though corporations act as tax collectors rather than bearing the ultimate burden, it is very much in their best interest to minimize taxes. If a corporation can achieve a lower tax burden than its competitors, it can lower prices to its customers or make higher profits with which to pay higher wages and dividends. The price of its stock tends to rise, and it can be a better customer for the components and raw materials it buys from others.

All of this is true for all corporations, but the multinational has more taxes—more countries—to consider, and therefore more risks. It also has more opportunities to save taxes.

☐ **FIGURE 6-4   Tax Revenues as a Percent of GDP**

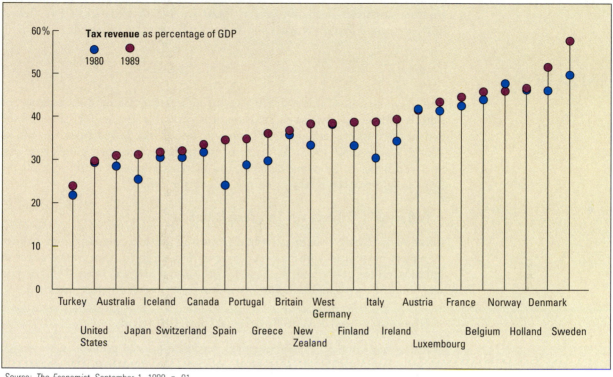

Source: *The Economist,* September 1, 1990, p. 91.

☐ Taxes as a Percent of GDP*

Figure 6-4 illustrates the almost universal increase in tax revenue as a percent of GDP. This ratio is a widely used indicator of a country's tax burden. On that basis, Sweden was easily the world's most heavily taxed nation, but all except two increased their ratios during the 1980s. The two exceptions were Austria and Norway, although, as you can see, their percentages are still near the top of the list.

☐ Different Taxes in Different Countries

In almost every country, the income tax is the biggest revenue earner for governments. Then there are sales or value-added taxes on goods or services, capital gains taxes, property taxes, and social security. A company must study carefully the tax laws of each country in which it operates. This subject is dealt with further in Chapter 11, and in Chapter 18 we shall see how financial managers can sometimes use different tax regimes and other measures to lower their taxes legally.

---

* The GDP (gross domestic product) of a country is the gross national product minus net property invisible payments, such as dividends, interest, and royalty, paid to and received from other countries.

The amount of taxes paid is affected by inflation. At one time, some thought that inflation was a problem limited to the LDCs and that the industrialized countries need not worry about it. Recent experience has shown how erroneous that view was, and so we shall examine inflation.

INFLATION

The phenomenon of increasing prices for almost everything over a period of time is familiar. Contagious inflation was probably the major cause of the end of the unprecedented world economic boom that lasted from the end of World War II until 1973. As prices of internationally traded goods rose due to a combination of rising demand and increased money supplies in all the DCs, inflation fever spread from one DC to the others.[2]

◻ Inflation's Effects on Interest Rates

Inflation is clearly a financial force from outside the company that finance managers must deal with as best they can. For an indication of the effect of inflation on the cost of money raised by the company, see Table 6–2. As you see, countries with higher inflation tend to have higher interest rates.

◻ Monetary and Fiscal Policies Affect Inflation

Nations may conduct their monetary policies and fiscal policies in ways that cause inflation or cut it. *Monetary policy* is the control of the amount of money in circulation, whether it is growing and, if so, at what pace. *Fiscal policies* address the collecting and spending of money by governments. What kinds of taxes at what rates? On what and in what amounts does the government spend money?

Successful policies have two common denominators: (1) they remove artificial economic controls, such as wage and price controls, and (2) they apply fiscal and monetary restraint. The restraint includes lower taxes and slower growth in the nation's money supply.[3]

As Table 6–2 illustrates, Japan, Germany, and the United States have had relatively good records in keeping inflation down in recent years. At the other extreme, many believe the infamous hyperinflation of the German mark in 1923 is the world's record. It is not. That dubious distinction belongs to the Hungarian pengo; inflation in Hungary in 1946 was a thousand times worse than the earlier German inflation. In 1939, 1 US$ bought 3.38 Hungarian pengos; in July 1946, the same dollar was worth 500,000,000,000,000,000,000 (500 million trillion) pengos. Never before or since has so much official money been worth so little.

Most Latin American countries have inflation troubles, although not as drastic as the Hungarian example. Two of the worst cases are Peru, where the 1990 inflation rate was almost 8,000 percent,[4] and Brazil, where Brazilians over age 30 have seen their money's face value divided by a billion since they started spending it.[5] In 1990, inflation was running at 1,783 percent.[6]

Two Latin American countries have taken the tough fiscal and monetary steps needed to reduce inflation dramatically. In Bolivia, inflation ran at around 20,000 percent in 1985 but was cut to 11 percent in 1987 and 1988.[7]

□ **TABLE 6–2**
1986 Inflation and Interest Rates

	Inflation Rates	Short-Term Interest Rates				
		1988	1989	1990	1991	1992*
Canada (C$)	5.0%	9.7%	12.2%	13.1%	11.6%	10.5%
France (Ff)	3.6	7.9	9.4	10.3	10.4	9.9
Germany (DM)	2.8	4.3	7.1	8.5	9.0	8.8
Japan (¥)	2.3	4.5	5.4	7.8	8.2	7.9
United Kingdom (£)	7.8	10.3	13.9	14.8	14.0	13.4
United States (US$)	4.8	6.7	8.1	7.5	7.8	8.2

*Projected.
Source: *OECD Economic Outlook,* December 1991.

Chile succeeded in bringing its inflation rate from some 1,000 percent to 10 percent in 1987.[8] In 1990, Bolivian inflation figures came in at 18 percent, a far cry from the Brazilian rate of 1,783 percent; and although it had climbed from 1987, the Chilean inflation rate for 1990 was back up to only 27.3 percent.[9]

□ ## Importance of Inflation to Business

Even within a single country, inflation is of concern to management. Should it raise capital at all and, if so, should this be done through equity or debt? High inflation rates encourage borrowing because the loan will be repaid with cheaper money. But high inflation rates bring high interest rates (see Table 6–2) or may discourage lending. Potential lenders may fear that even with high interest rates, the amount repaid plus interest will be worth less than the amount lent. Instead of lending, the money holder may buy something that is expected to increase in value.

Lenders have begun to use variable interest rates, which rise or fall with inflation, to shift the risk to the borrower. Of course, that risk requires the borrower to be much more careful about borrowing. The original rate and any future changes are based on a reference interest rate, such as the U.S. prime rate or the London Interbank Offer Rate (LIBOR).

High inflation rates make capital expenditure planning more difficult. Management may allocate $1 million for a plant and be forced to pay much more to complete construction.

Inflation and the multinational.   All of this also applies to international business, with the complication that inflation rates differ in different countries. For this reason, management of a multinational must try to forecast the rates for each of the countries in which the company is active. The comparative inflation rates will affect the comparative currency values as the currencies of high-inflation countries weaken vis-à-vis the currencies of the countries whose inflation rates are lower. Management will try to minimize holdings of the weaker currencies.

Higher inflation rates cause the prices of the goods and services produced or offered by a country to rise, and thus the goods and services become less competitive. The company's affiliate in that country finds it more difficult to sell its products in export, as do all other producers there. Such conditions

Coping with treble-digit inflation

Reprinted with special permission from *International Management,* October 1981.

tend to cause balance-of-payments (BOP) deficits, and management must be alert to changes in government policy to correct the deficit. Such changes could include more restrictive fiscal or monetary policies, currency controls, export incentives, and import obstacles.

Relative inflation rates affect where the multinational raises and invests capital. Interest rates tend to be higher where inflation is higher, and high inflation discourages new investment for all of the reasons we have seen.

Nominal and real interest rates.   Another important consideration for business, whether borrowing or lending, is the real rate of interest, and the inflation rate is one element in its computation. The nominal interest rate is the rate charged by the lender or the rate that a bond issue carries. From the nominal rate is subtracted the inflation rate, and the result is the real rate. When a lender charges, for example, 10 percent interest on a one-year loan and the inflation rate is 5 percent, the real rate of return for the lender is 5 percent, because the money is worth 5 percent less when it is repaid than it was worth when it was lent.

When money is lent for longer periods of time (5, 10, or 20 years), the lenders and borrowers must forecast—guess—what inflation will do over those longer periods. The longer the time, the more difficult the forecast; but the point here is that it is not only today's inflation rate that matters; it is also the lenders' and borrowers' forecasts that govern interest rates on loans or even whether loans will be made.

□ The Misery Index

The term *misery index* had its origin in American politics during the 1980 presidential campaign, when both inflation and unemployment were high. A simple total of a country's unemployment and inflation rates, it is a sort of indicator of economic success; the higher the total score, the worse the mis-

☐ **FIGURE 6–5**
Misery Index

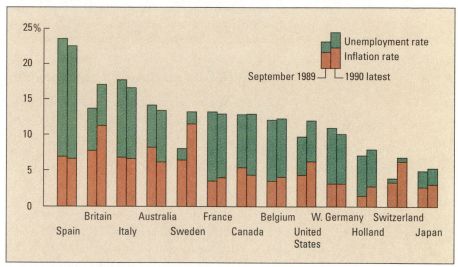

Source: *The Economist,* November 10, 1990, p. 123.

ery. Figure 6–5 is a comparison of the misery levels of various countries. It also indicates for each whether misery had increased or diminished from September 1989 to the end of 1990.

ACCOUNTING PRACTICES

Accounting practices vary widely from country to country and are financial forces with which multinational management must deal. Management must be prepared to use host country practices for subsidiaries operating in those countries. These results must then be translated into home country practices in order to be understood by home country investors, creditors, and government regulators. Accounting practices are financial forces, which is why we include the topic here. In Chapter 18, we shall examine some of management's solutions.

COUNTRIES WENT BUST

During the 1970s' lending binge by banks to developing countries (LDCs), the chairman of a major bank was quoted as saying, "Countries don't go bust." He was proved wrong, and a new and ominous financial force is now acting on international business. Contrary to many expectations, a number of developing countries found themselves unable to pay even the interest, much less the principal, on their debts. The sovereign debt crisis for Poland occurred in 1981; for Mexico, Brazil, Argentina, and others, it occurred in 1982 and thereafter.

We examined this matter in Chapter 4 from the point of view of the International Monetary Fund (IMF) and the Bank for International Settlements (BIS) because the IMF has been thrust into, and has taken the lead role in, trying to resolve these crises as they continue to arise, and the BIS has made bridge loans while the IMF was preparing to act.

Because these crises are so important and constitute a present and growing force on international business, we shall discuss some of the background in this chapter. Also, we can suggest some possible solutions.

◻ Causes of Increasing LDC Indebtedness

The immediate causes of the growing debts were the jumps in oil prices (crude oil represents an average of 16 percent of the merchandise imports of the nonoil LDCs). In 1973–74, oil prices quadrupled; they then doubled in 1979–80, and that increase from a higher base represented an even larger increase in absolute terms than the 1973–74 rise.

Those oil price increases made the already severe inflation that much worse, and the combination brought on a worldwide recession. The resulting drop in prices of primary nonoil commodities, which account for 45 percent of LDC (excluding Mexico and OPEC LDCs) exports, was a serious blow to LDCs' economies and abilities to pay their heavy debts. Mexico and the OPEC LDCs were hurt by the drops in oil prices beginning in 1981 as well as by uneconomic uses of the oil revenue and borrowed moneys they received during the 1970s and in the early 1980s.

Then, after the 1979–80 oil price jump, interest rates increased. That increase affected all new loans and the many existing loans that carried variable rather than fixed interest rates. Every 1 percent increase in US$ interest rates costs the LDCs some $2.5 billion per year more in interest payments.

On top of all that, the US$ began to strengthen in value in the foreign exchange markets during 1980. It continued up into 1985 and gained over 80 percent on a trade-weighted basis by March 1985. LDCs borrow mainly in dollars but export in many currencies, so the rise in the value of the US$ created new burdens; they had to earn that much more in deutsche marks, yen, francs, and so on to pay the US$ debts.

The US$ peaked in value in terms of the yen and West European currencies in February 1985. At that time, it began to move down in terms of those currencies, and by January 1988, it had fallen some 45 percent against the yen and the deutsche mark and 30 percent against the British pound. However, the US$ weakened little or even continued to gain in exchange for currencies of Canada, Asian newly industrializing countries (NICs), and Mexico and other Latin American countries, all of which are important trading partners of the United States. From 1988 into the 1990s, the US$ ceased to weaken in terms of the currencies of the other G7 countries and fluctuated within a relatively narrow range in trades involving them and those of the newly industrializing countries. The Latin American countries' currencies continued to weaken in US$ terms.

◻ Debt Problem Solutions

The IMF, the BIS, national central banks, and commercial banks have been scrambling for solutions.

Short-term solutions.   The short-term answers have been rescheduling of debts that the debtor country was unable to pay as they came due. But renegotiations are becoming more and more difficult. The BIS, the commercial banks, and the central banks are reluctant to come up with more money, and the IMF's resources are finite.

The debtor countries are balking at the stringent austerity programs being insisted on by the IMF. The LDCs' economic growth has halted as they must use new money they receive from exports or loans to repay debt rather than for productive investments. Social unrest, including rioting, has broken out in several countries, notably Venezuela, Argentina, and Brazil.

The debtor countries are in desperate straits, but the industrialized countries are also being damaged. As the debtor countries use money to repay debts, they do not buy goods and services from the developed countries. As a result, the developed countries have lost billions of dollars of export business and thousands of jobs.

The LDC debtor countries can reduce their debts only by exporting more than they import and thus running BOP surpluses. Some of the LDC debtor countries have been able to run BOP surpluses and make debt payments. However, these surpluses have been achieved as much by cutting imports as by expanding exports, and that has slowed or stopped economic development in the debtor countries and also hurt exports from countries that had been suppliers before the imports were curtailed.

Most of the LDC debtor countries have needed more money from private banks and international agencies and have been lent more. This has caused the debt burdens of these countries to increase at the same time that their economic development has been retarded, a process that cannot be sustained.

All is not lost.   The debt renegotiations accompanied by stringent austerity were part of the first phase of the world's efforts to solve the debt problems. This phase led to declines in living standards and curtailed economic growth and exports.

The second phase saw a growing awareness that short-term adjustment policies would not do the job alone. The problem for the LDCs was not the outstanding debt per se but the economic policies they followed and the cultural and attitudinal barriers they faced.

Recognizing this, the Baker Plan (named for then U.S. secretary of the treasury James Baker) called for market-oriented strategies to encourage growth and bring inflation under control. Measures were needed to rebuild confidence in and lure flight capital and new investment back to debtor countries.[10]

The Baker Plan was followed by the Brady Plan, which built on its predecessor and made debt relief conditional on the debtor country's pursuit of an IMF-approved economic adjustment program. The plan called on private banks for more money backed by funds from the IMF, the World Bank, and developed country governments.

Brady debt relief is provided through three mechanisms: (1) the exchange of old debt for new at a discount, (2) the exchange of old debt for new at a lower interest rate, and (3) the buying back of debt from creditor banks at a discount.[11]

Growing LDC debt market.   The third mechanism has resulted in debtor countries buying their own debt and retiring it. The creditor banks have also sold LDC debt to other banks and investors, resulting in a large LDC debt market.[12]

WORLDVIEW
Third World Debt that Is Almost Always Paid in Full

You think it would be utter folly to lend money to a Third World nation? So, how about a Third World vegetable stand?

U.S. development organizations are finding that some of the world's poorest entrepreneurs repay their debts at rates approaching 100 percent. To encourage grass-roots private business in Latin America, Asia, and Africa, these organizations are expanding programs that already lend thousands of these struggling entrepreneurs amounts ranging from $50 to several hundred dollars.

Tiny Third World businesses commonly repay these "microloans" faithfully because they crave the security of a favorable credit rating. This rescues them from the clutches of loan sharks—microloans typically charge the prevailing commercial loan rate—and lets them borrow again in hard times. The money helps them start or expand their businesses—selling vegetables, sewing, repairing shoes, making furniture, and the like—and boosts their local economies.

Their repayment performance shines when compared with that of many sovereign nations. It also looks good compared with a default rate of 17 percent by U.S. recipients of federally guaranteed student loans.

Though microlending has been around for years, it is now booming. With the decline of communism, U.S. development groups believe they are exporting free-market economics to tiny businesses that can fuel growth in the developing world.

"Micro-enterprise lending is the hottest thing in development since the Green Revolution. Everybody does it," says Accion International spokeswoman Gabriela Romanow. The Green Revolution sent farm output surging in many poor nations.

Ms. Romanow cites the case of Aaron Aguilar, an unemployed factory worker in Monterrey, Mexico, who borrowed $100 to buy clay and glazes for making figurines with his wife in their backyard. In six years, the couple took out and repaid five loans and built their business to 18 full-time employees.

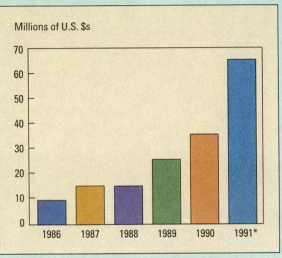

*Projection.

Source: Accion International.

Microlending at One Development Agency, Accion International

Sometimes borrowers have to struggle against setbacks that might seem comical in the prosperous West. One group of women in Cameroon received $100 from Trickle Up to start a rabbit-breeding business, but the rabbit ate her offspring, recalls Mildred Leet, cofounder of the U.S. agency. Undaunted, the women switched to chickens and made enough money selling eggs to branch out into tomatoes and tailoring, ultimately opening two shops, Ms. Leet says.

Some Third World commercial banks are taking note of poor entrepreneurs' repayment rates. Accion persuaded family-owned Multi Credit Bank of Panama City, Panama, to start making microloans two months ago. Isaac Btesh, a director and son of the founder, says the bank has lent $80,000 to 100 people so far on 60-day, rotating lines of credit—with a 100 percent repayment rate. "When we got in touch with Accion, we were incredulous," Mr. Btesh says. "We couldn't believe their figures. But everything they said is true."

Poverty lending has such promise that Multi Credit plans to make it the bank's number one activity, ahead of trade financing, consumer loans, and merchant loans, the official adds.

Average Loan: $303

Accion, a Cambridge, Massachusetts–based nonprofit international development group and a leader in the U.S. microloan movement, says it plans to increase its microlending this year to $66.5 million from $37.8 million in 1990 and $9.8 million five years ago. It says it plans to add 64,000 new clients, up from 40,000 last year and 9,000 five years ago. Its average loan is $303.

Accion's Ms. Romanow says the group, which serves Latin America, plans to expand the lending to a total of between $500 million and $1 billion over the next five years. The payback rate is 98 percent.

CARE, New York, perhaps the world's largest private international development group, says small economic activity development—primarily microlending—is its fastest-growing portfolio. "There's energy and creativity out there, people bootstrapping who aren't waiting for the next handout," says Larry Frankel of CARE.

Trickle Up, which makes thousands of $100 loans annually, says its budget rose to $1 million this year from $800,000 in 1989 after doubling almost every year throughout the 1980s. Trickle Up makes $100 loans in two installments of $50 each to small groups of individuals. "We feel private enterprise is the way to help the poor," says Mrs. Leet, who founded Trickle Up with her husband in 1979. The group started a program in China in 1989 and moved into Laos, Vietnam, and Namibia last year.

Betsy Campbell, economic development manager of Westport, Connecticut–based Save the Children, says her group underwent a shift in the 1980s "from being primarily a charitable organization" to being one oriented towards helping profit-making activities. She says microlending to individuals in 20 nations is rising sharply, with more than $3 million in circulation at the moment. Repayment rates in most nations exceed 90 percent. "These people value access to credit so highly that default isn't really a problem," she says.

Some Third World banks, notably in Asia, have been making microloans for years. Grameen Rural Bank of Bangladesh is considered a pioneer. However, most such banks were set up with state support specifically to target the poor.

Some Detractors

Not every charity group in the United States has joined the microloan bandwagon. The Christian Children's Fund of Richmond, Virginia, sticks to relief efforts and to person-to-person sponsorships, in which a U.S. donor makes regular payments to an impoverished Third World child, for example, while Africare House in Washington, D.C., focuses on helping cooperatives improve food production and health care.

Nor is the booming field of microlending without its detractors—or its controversies. David Munro, an official with Techno-Serve of Norwalk, Connecticut, says he prefers to work on a larger scale and "I also don't see [microlending] as passing on much in the way of skills."

And officials at the U.S. Agency for International Development (AID), which finances a big chunk of many private groups' overseas operations, say they support the principle of expanding poverty lending but oppose congressional efforts to mandate minimum levels. AID has more than doubled its micro-enterprise budget, which includes microlending, training, and other activities, to an estimated $114 million this year from $58 million in 1988.

Source: Brent Bowers, *The Wall Street Journal*, June 7, 1991, p. B 2.

Other positive developments, and a laggard.   In 1991, the Paris Club, which is a group of Western creditor governments, forgave half of Poland's debt. That is a reduction of some $17.5 billion. Also in 1991, the United States forgave the Egyptian debt as an expression of thanks for Egypt's support in the war against Iraq. And in 1991, Chile floated a $320 million Eurobond issue that was fully subscribed by 20 European, Japanese, and North American banks. This was the first time since the Latin American debt crisis began in 1982 that a country from that region has obtained credit not arising from the crisis.[13]

The laggard country is Brazil. The Third World's biggest debtor, Brazil owes $123 billion, and until March 1991 it had made no payment on the $8 billion in interest owed to private bank creditors since July 1989. The March interest payment was $480 million and came after urging by the Inter-American DB, which was under pressure from the United States. There was no payment of principal.

Few creditors believe that Brazil is yet serious about changing its economic ways. When President Fernando Cullor de Mello was elected in 1990, he promised to began privatizations within three months; none was in sight by the end of 1991. Banks were withdrawing short-term trade credit, starving Brazilian exporters and importers.

As one article put it, "Brazil's continued sloth is a pity, because some other countries are fast becoming more creditworthy as they make progress against the twin Latin American bogeys of soaring budget deficits and hyperinflation. Leading the pack are Chile and Mexico."[14]

Longer-term solutions.   A number of cures have been suggested. We shall list a few.

1. Borrowing countries will have to pursue policies ensuring that new money they obtain is used for economic growth rather than for consumption, capital flight, or overambitious government schemes or armaments.

2. Borrowers should build up reserves in good years to enable them to withstand the fluctuations in commodity export prices that are inevitable even if no more oil price shocks occur.

3. The developed countries must strive for their own economic growth and open their markets to LDC exports even though that means competition with some DC industries.

4. The IMF and other creditors must not try to enforce too stringent austerity measures on debtors. Social unrest and trade contraction must be avoided or at least minimized.

5. The IMF, the World Bank, and other agencies that aid LDCs must be assured of sufficient funding so that they can take long-term views.

6. Parts of the huge LDC external debts must be changed in form to types of equity. These could be ownership interests in projects being developed or shares of export earnings. Other parts of the debts should be lengthened in maturity, with interest rate ceilings applied.

7. The LDCs must relax their restrictions on foreign investments and on repatriation of profits from existing investments. They must encourage new money from foreign private sources—nonbank sources—because the banks are now overcommitted with LDC loans and are not likely prospects for new, economic growth money.

WORLDVIEW
Do the Wrong Thing, Young Bankers

Do the wrong thing. That's the best advice anyone could possibly offer an ambitious young person eager to get ahead in banking.

We hasten to reassure you: We're not scoffing at one of the world's oldest professions. Quite the contrary. We have the highest regard for bankers, to whom each and every one of us mortals is indebted for all sorts of ingenious innovations, from legalized usury (otherwise known as the interest charges on credit card balances) to spendthrift thrifts.

But the evidence is incontrovertible: If you're ambitious and seek success in banking, do the wrong thing.

Nor do you have to take our word for it. Rather, we refer you to the stock market, and even its severest critics concede that the stock market is real smart. So what does the stock market say about the way to get ahead in banking?—why, of course, do the wrong thing.

Last week, for example, a number of banks, including Manny Hanny, Chase, and J.P. Morgan, were forced to admit they'd been real dumb lending money to countries that never had a prayer of paying it back. And to show their remorse, these banks confessed in public that the loans were bummers and, by way of penance, vowed to write the loans down. This act of contrition so impressed normally cynical Wall Street professionals that, after dabbing at their eyes with their hankies, they bid up the stocks of the guilty banks in a gesture of understanding and sympathy.

This isn't the first time, either, that owning up to mistakes has induced supportive action on the part of hard-boiled investors. A similar episode in which errant lenders keened over their wayward past behavior evoked very positive emotions in the breasts of money managers and also resulted in an appreciation of the banks' share prices.

All of which we find enormously affecting, but it also reinforces the conclusion that if you're a banker, it pays to make a mistake. For, if Manny Hanny, Chase, et al. hadn't erred to begin with, they'd never get the chance to say they're sorry, take their medicine, and boost the value of their stock. The moral is clear: If you want to get ahead in banking, do the wrong thing.

That isn't, we're well aware, exactly a freshly minted truism. Remember Walter Wriston? Mr. Wriston, when he exercised sovereignty over Citicorp, was an ardent advocate of the LDC loan (LDC stands for "let depositors cry"). He didn't invent LDC loans, but neither did Henry Ford invent the automobile. Mr. Wriston was the Henry Ford of the LDC, and he reached the apogee of banking.

Now, we suppose that if you are a young person eager to make your mark in banking, you may fear that you're too late, that by the time you've risen sufficiently in status to benefit from the banks' mistakes, the LDC loans will have been written down to zero. Not to worry. For even as we write, banks are preparing against that day by vigorously laying in a store of new mistakes called LBO loans. After all, LDC loans may have made last week's headlines, but let's not forget REITs and energy loans, which also set new standards for sourness. In other words, bankers are farsighted people, and, with an eye toward enhancing shareholder value, they always rise to the challenge of finding a new set of potential deadbeats to lend to.

Source: Alan Abelson. "Up and Down Wall Street." *Barron's*, September 25, 1989, pp. 1 and 53.

---

8. Blame for the debt crises belongs to several parties. The LDCs borrowed more than they could productively invest, and much of the borrowed money was wasted at home or corruptly sent abroad for the personal accounts of political leaders. The lending banks were encouraged to lend by the governments of their countries because the governments were thus relieved to that extent of foreign aid demands by the LDCs. But the banks must also bear a share of the blame; they made limited inquiries regarding the uses of the borrowed money or the soundness of the projects in which the money would be invested. They failed to get collateral to secure the loans, and one reason they

were so casual was that the loans were almost always to governments or guaranteed by governments. One leading banker said, "Countries don't go bust"; he and his colleagues were proved wrong.

As a contribution to the solution of the debt crises, the banks should establish schedules to write down the loans on their books over a period of several years. Some banks have already begun to sell off portions of these loans at discounts, and a market now exists for the discounted loans.

◻ The Biggest "Debtor"? The United States

After 70 years as the world's leading creditor, the United States was indebted to foreigners to the tune of over $412 billion at the end of 1990. Although that was down from the $440 billion at the end of 1989, it is deeply troubling for some, and unless the "debt" growth stops or reverses, there *will* be adverse effects for America. Before looking at some of those effects, we should define the "debt," see how it differs from the LDC debts, and put its growth into perspective with the growth rates of the other G7 countries.

U.S. debt defined.   Conceptually, the U.S. foreign debt—what the Department of Commerce calls net negative international investment position—is the difference between the value of overseas assets owned by Americans and the value of United States assets owned by foreigners. These assets consist of commercial bank deposits, foreign exchange holdings, corporate securities, real estate, physical plant, and other direct investments. The popular press calls the difference "debt," but the Commerce phrase, "net negative investment position," is more accurate. One reason is the differences between LDC and U.S. debt.

Differences between U.S. and LDC debt.   First, over $300 billion of the U.S. foreign-owned assets are obligations of the U.S. Treasury or U.S. corporations that are traded daily in world financial markets. Their worth, unlike the face value of an LDC debt, is subject to constant change.

Second, U.S. foreign assets are often measured at book value, which results in an estimated undervaluation of up to $200 billion. Book value would be cost when bought, which may have been years ago, less depreciation. Inflation alone would result in prices much higher than book if the assets were sold today.

Third, U.S. assets abroad reportedly earn more in interest and dividend per dollar of investment than foreign holdings earn in America. Foreign-owned assets in the United States earned an estimated $67 billion in 1989, while the smaller U.S. balances abroad yielded $88 billion.

Fourth, although current U.S. net liabilities are immense in absolute terms, they are relatively small in terms of other economic indicators. Total U.S. debt in 1989 amounted to 6 percent of U.S. GNP—as compared to over 40 percent for Brazil, upward of 50 percent for Mexico, and over 60 percent for Venezuela. The annual service cost of the U.S. debt is less than 1 percent of U.S. exports of goods and services. The corresponding cost for the three developing countries mentioned above averages more than 32 percent. As pointed out previously, Mexico, in particular, and Venezuela are bringing their debt loads down.

Fifth, the most distinctive characteristic of the U.S. foreign debt is its denomination in US$s. In theory, at least, this implies that the United States could discharge its foreign obligations at any time by printing the needed number of US$s. The LDCs, whose debt is not denominated in their own currencies, do not have that power.

G7 debt growth.   During the 1973–87 period, the national debt growth rates of all G7 countries except the United Kingdom were faster than that of the United States. A legitimate complaint about using the 1973–87 period is that the American debt growth accelerated during the 1980s, when it more than doubled. But, even in the 1980–89 period, the debt growth rates of Canada, France, and Italy were faster than that of the United States; they were slower in Germany, Japan, and the United Kingdom. Thus the U.S. rate is about the same as the average for the other G7 countries.[15]

Adverse effects on America.   Having made the distinctions and comparisons, it cannot be denied that continuing growth of the U.S. net negative investment position will damage America. Financially, the interest cost of foreign debts is a drag on the balance of payments. Foreign creditors and suppliers may become reluctant to accept US$s. An increasing volume of world trade denominated in other currencies would cause losses for American companies and banks.

Politically, pressures could build up for protectionism, exchange controls, or restrictions on capital flows. A large debtor country could not remain a major reserve currency economic power for long, and America's power to affect world events would erode.

In sum, while the U.S. net foreign obligations may not create for the U.S. economy or policies the same problems that LDC debts present LDCs, these obligations are very real dangers for the American world position. It has been suggested that increasing the very low current rate of U.S. national savings would be an important step toward a solution. The U.S. savings rate is by far the lowest among the G7 countries.[16]

Even though America is the world's biggest debtor, the OECD estimates it will earn a surplus of $13 billion on its foreign investments in 1991 (down from $16.2 billion in 1985). One possible explanation for this paradox is that America's investment abroad is older than foreigners' investments in the United States, which might mean that American investments in factories, say, earn a higher rate of return than new ones saddled with start-up costs.[17]

SUMMARY

The international company's financial management must be aware of many financial forces that originate outside the company. Some of them, such as inflation, taxation, and fiscal and monetary policies of government, affect domestic as well as international business. But even for such forces, the concerns of the domestic manager are of a different magnitude than the concerns of the international manager because the domestic manager has to cope with only one country, whereas the international manager has to cope with two or more countries. The same may be said of accounting principles, which differ widely from country to country.

Fluctuating currency exchange rates, currency controls, and attendant risks are almost uniquely international problems. So are quotas and tariffs.

The balance of payments affects both domestic and international companies. It is, of course, related to inflation, taxation, fiscal and monetary policies, and such other factors as the competitiveness of a country's goods and services in the world markets.

The international debt crises have added new financial forces with which managers must cope. Many debtor countries must struggle to pay debts and thus have less money to pay for imports of goods or services.

Within the terms of the Brady Plan and with help from the IMF, several Latin American countries are restoring economic growth, lowering debt, and making progress against the twin Latin American bogeys of soaring budget deficits and hyperinflation. Chile and Mexico are leaders in this process, while Brazil lags behind.

The United States is now the world's biggest debtor, and although the U.S. and the LDC debt situations differ greatly and the growth of the U.S. debt is about average for the G7 countries, the U.S. debt will harm America if its growth is not reversed.

As suggested in the introduction, the financial manager is not without means for protecting and advancing the company. Those means are subjects of Chapter 18.

QUESTIONS

1. In an American financial paper, you see the quotation: "Norway (krone) . . . 1478." What does that mean?
2. On the same day, you see the quotation: "Norway (krone) . . . 6.7635." What does that mean?
3. In the world's currency-trading markets, why is the US$ the central currency through which most major trades go?
4. What is the difference between spot and forward currency markets?
5. What does it mean when a currency is said to be trading at a premium to the US$ in the forward market? Why would this happen?
6. If you agree to pay a certain amount of foreign currency to someone in six months, which of you bears the currency fluctuation risk? Explain.
7. What are currency controls? Why are they imposed?
8. What is the importance of the state of the BOP to private companies?
9. What are some ways in which inflation affects business decisions?
10. Have countries ever succeeded in stopping inflation? How?
11. What two other numbers must you know to compute real interest rates?
12. What is the LDC debt market, and why did it develop?
13. To surmount the current debt crises, what are some things that must be done by (a) the LDCs, (b) the developed, creditor countries, and (c) the creditor banks?
14. What are some of the differences between the American and the LDCs' foreign debt situations?
15. Might the huge U.S. debt have adverse consequences for America? Explain.

◻ MINICASE 6–1

Borrowing Money at the Lowest Interest Rates

You are the chief financial officer of an international company that borrows frequently to meet operating and other capital needs. In 1988 and 1989, where could you have found the lowest interest rates? Was there any change in 1990 and 1991? What is the projection for 1992?

◻ MINICASE 6–2

Management Faces a BOP Deficit

You are the chief executive officer of a multinational's subsidiary in a developing host country. The sub has been in business for about eight years, making electric motors for the host country's domestic market with mediocre financial results. Before you left the home country a month ago, you were told to make the sub profitable or consider closing it.

After a month in the host country, you have discovered that it is running a worsening BOP deficit and that the government officials are very concerned about the situation. They are considering various measures to stanch or reverse the deficit flow.

What measures might be adopted? Can you think of some ways your company might profit from them, or at least minimize damage?

SUPPLEMENTARY READINGS

"Bank Debt Restructurings and Secondary Market Developments." *IMF International Capital Markets,* May 1991, pp. 74–83.

Bartlett, Bruce. "Supply Side Sparkplug." *Policy Review,* Summer 1986, pp. 42–47.

Bingham, T. R. G. "Financial Innovation and Monetary Policy." *OECD Observer,* January 1985, pp. 24–26.

Carbaugh, Robert J. *International Economics.* 2nd ed. Belmont, Calif.: Wadsworth Publishing, 1985.

Crespo-Velasco, Jorge. "Swamping Bolivia in a Sea of Negatives." *The Wall Street Journal,* July 31, 1991, p. A 13.

Davidson, Paul. *International Money and the Real World.* New York: John Wiley & Sons, 1982.

DeSaint-Phalle, Thibaut. *Trade, Inflation and the Dollar.* New York: Oxford University Press, 1981.

Emele, Bruno. "The Global Purchasing Power, Effects of Oil Price Changes." *Economic and Financial Prospects,* August–September 1986, pp. 1–4.

Ethier, Wilfred J. *Modern International Economics.* 2nd ed. New York: W. W. Norton, 1988.

Fidler, Stephen. "Last Rites in Sight for Debt Crisis." *Financial Times,* April 10, 1991, p. 5.

Friedman, Milton, ed. *Studies in the Quantity Theory of Money.* Chicago: University of Chicago Press, 1956.

Gajdeczka, Przemyslaw, and Mark Stone. "The Secondary Market for Developing Country Loans." *Finance & Development,* December 1990, pp. 22–25.

Harvey, Jack L. "Expected Growth in the Industrial Countries Revised Upward." (Federal Reserve Bank of Chicago) *International Letter,* June 1986.

Humphrey, Thomas N. *The Monetary Approach to the Balance of Payments, Exchange Rates and World Inflation.* New York: Praeger Publishers, 1982.

Kleitz, Anthony. "Tariff Preferences for the Developing Countries." *OECD Observer,* March 1983, pp. 38–41.

Krugman, Paul R., and Maurice Obstfeld. *International Economics.* Glenview, Ill.: Scott, Foresman, 1988.

Kvasnicka, Joseph G. "Restrictions on Imports: An Answer to U.S. Trade Problems?" (Federal Reserve Bank of Chicago) *International Letter,* April 1985.

Mayer, Martin. *The Fate of the Dollar.* New York: Times Books, 1980.

Michalski, Wolfgang; Henry Ergas; and Barrie Stevens. "Cost and Benefits of Protection." *OECD Observer,* May 1985, pp. 18–23.

Newman, Nigel. "Fiscal Expansion." *Barclays Review,* November 1985, pp. 69–80.

Ogi, Adolph. "World Free Trade in Danger." *Bulletin, Credit Suisse Magazine,* September 1985, pp. 14–16.

Owens, Jeffrey. "Tax Reform: Some European Ideas." *Europe,* September 1986, pp. 18–20.

Salemi, Michael K. "The Efficiency of Forward Exchange Markets." *Economic and Financial Prospects,* August–September 1986, pp. 5–6.

Salvatore, Dominick. *International Economics.* 5th ed. New York: McGraw-Hill, 1984.

Tax News International. Various issues, published by Ernst & Young.

"The Latin Market Comes to Life." *The Economist,* June 8, 1991, pp. 77–80.

Todd, Jonathan. "Battle Threatens over Tax on Multinationals." *Europe,* November–December 1983, pp. 22–23.

Winder, Robert. "Be Big and Bright." *Euromoney,* May 1986, pp. 184–202.

"World Tax News." Quarterly Newsletter, KPMG International Tax Centre. Strawinskylaan 957, 1077 XX Amsterdam, The Netherlands.

ENDNOTES

1. Discussed by Robert Z. Aliber, *The International Money Game,* 2nd ed. (New York: Basic Books, 1976), pp. 189–90.

2. Samuel I. Katz, " 'Managed Floating' as an Interim International Exchange Rate Regime, 1973–1975," *New York University Bulletin,* 1975–3 (New York: Center for the Study of Financial Institutions, New York University, 1975), pp. 13–14.

3. Vermont Royster, "Thinking Things Over, 'A Thrice-Told Tale,' " *The Wall Street Journal,* May 10, 1978, p. 18.

4. "Peru," *Abecor Country Report,* distributed by Barclays, June 1991.

5. "First, Divide by a Thousand," *The Economist,* January 21, 1989, p. 39.

6. "Brazil," *Abecor Country Report,* distributed by Barclays, December 1990.

7. "Bolivia Doing It by the Book," *The Economist,* May 28, 1988, pp. 74–75.

8. "Key Facts, Chile," *Financial Times,* September 28, 1988, section IV, p. 2.

9. Thomas Kamm, "Bolivia, Having Stabilized Economy, Searches for Ways to Promote Growth," *The Wall Street Journal,* June 18, 1991, p. A16; and "Chile," *Abecor Country Report,* distributed by Barclays, April 1991.

10. Georg Junge and Max Schieler, "The Real Choices Facing the Debtor Countries," *Economic and Financial Prospects,* April–May 1990, pp. 1–5.

11. "Life under Brady," *Barclays Economic Review,* August 1990, pp. 30–35.

12. Stephen Fidler, "A Market Transformed," *Financial Times,* April 5, 1991, p. 28.

13. Stephen Fidler, "Brady Plan for Reducing Debt Makes Good Progress," *Financial Times,* September 13, 1990, p. 16; Peter Truell, "Paris Club Pact to Forgive Half of Polish Debt," *The Wall Street Journal,* March 15, 1991, p. A3; Leslie Crawford, "The Happy Passing of a Debt Negotiator," *Financial Times,* March 22, 1991, p. 3.

14. "Latin American Debt Catching Up," *The Economist,* April 13, 1991, pp. 77–78.

15. Mack Ott, "Growth Rates of National Debt in the G7, 1973–1987," (Federal Reserve Bank of St. Louis), *International Economic Conditions,* October 1988 p. 1, and October 1990, p. 2.

16. Jahangir Amuzegar, "The U.S. External Debt in Perspective," *Finance & Development,* June 1988, pp. 18–19.

17. "Overseas Investments," *The Economist,* August 10, 1991, p. 90.

Chapter 7

Economic and Socioeconomic Forces

Profound thoughts about economic forecasting:

Forecasting is difficult, especially about the future.

Victor Borge

Randell's Law of Economic Indicators:

Increased productivity occurs when the number of unemployed not working is greater than the number of employed not working.

Warren Randell

LEARNING OBJECTIVES

In this chapter, you will study:

1. The purpose of economic analyses.

2. The importance of monitoring interest and inflation rates in the firm's markets.

3. The economic and socioeconomic dimensions of the economy.

4. The importance of income distribution studies.

5. How a nation's consumption patterns change over time.

6. What factors cause changes in unit labor costs expressed in dollars.

7. The significance for businesspeople of the large foreign debts of some nations.

8. The reasons for the worldwide downward trend in birthrates and its implication for businesspeople.

9. Why declining birthrates are causing concern for the European and Japanese governments.

10. About national economic plans and their usefulness for businesspeople.

KEY WORDS AND CONCEPTS

- GDP (gross domestic product)
- Income distribution
- Discretionary income
- Unit labor costs
- Vertically integrated
- Population density
- Population distribution
- Rural-to-urban shift
- Promotional mix
- National economic plans
- Indicative plan

BUSINESS INCIDENT

The Good Statistics Guide

The slightest rumor to the effect that the U.S. trade deficit is about to be revised upward can cause a sharp drop on Wall Street. In most countries, bond prices will rise or sink according to the latest inflation report. Each new change in the official statistics on economic performance brings a reaction in financial markets. And yet, how good are the figures? Are the statistics of all nations equally good (poor)? According to a study conducted by *The Economist,* there are differences among nations, and the differences are probably not what you might expect.

The Economist asked a panel of statisticians from various countries to rank the government statistical agencies in 10 large countries according to the perceived reliability of their published figures (see table below). The magazine also looked at the amount each country had revised its quarterly GDP figures for 1987–89. Admittedly, revisions alone are not a good gauge of statistical accuracy. If a nation does not revise its figures or waits a year until it has all the detailed information, it would have no revisions but its statistics would be poor. The study also ranked the statistical agencies on their average speed of publication of GDP, industrial production, consumer prices, and trade data.

BUSINESS INCIDENT (concluded)

Country	Statisticians' Ranking	Revisions* (percentages)	Timeliness†
Canada	1	1.0%	10
Australia	2	1.7	8
Sweden	3	2.4	5
Netherlands	4	1.6	9
France	5	1.3	6
Germany	6	3.0	1
United States	7	1.1	4
Japan	8	2.7	7
United Kingdom	9	1.7	1
Italy	10	1.7	1

*Mean absolute deviation between initial estimate of GDP/GNP growth and final figure.

†Average speed of publication of GNP/GDP, industrial production, consumer prices, and trade data—1 is fastest and 10 is slowest

All the statisticians agreed that Canada's statistics were the best based on coverage and reliability of the statistics, methodology used, and the integrity and objectivity of the agency. Canada had the smallest revisions but was also the tardiest, which may explain the small revisions. Note that the United States and France also had small revisions, but that Japan and Germany revised their original figures by as much as 3 percent.

The first four countries have the advantage of centralized systems, in which the statistics are collected by a single agency, whereas the other, lower-ranked nations have decentralized systems with statisticians in various government agencies subject to greater political pressure.

Source: "The Good Statistics Guide, "*The Economist,* September 7, 1991, p. 88.

Among the most significant uncontrollable forces for businesses are the economic forces. How the scarce resources of land, labor, and capital are being allocated to the production and distribution of goods and services and the manner in which they are consumed are of paramount importance to managers. To keep abreast of the latest developments and also to plan for the future, firms for many years have been assessing and forecasting the economic conditions at the local, state, and national levels.

Even though the data published by governments and international organizations, such as the World Bank and the IMF, are not as timely or as accurate as business economists would like, these are what they have and they must work with them. However, economists do not work solely with government-published data. Private economic consulting specialists—such as Data Resources, Inc., Chase Econometric Associates, Business International, the Economist Intelligence Unit, and Wharton Economic Forecasting Associates—provide economic forecasts (some do industry forecasts as well) to which many multinationals subscribe. Other sources are various industry associations, which generally provide industry-specific forecasts to their members.

In addition, economists and marketers use certain economic indicators that they have found to predict trends in their industry. Pitney Bowes' Data Documents division, for example, uses changes in the growth of the U.S. GNP to predict the sales of its business forms because its sales have for years generally lagged changes in GNP growth by six months.[1] We shall discuss the use of market indicators in Chapter 14, Market Assessment and Analysis.

The purpose of economic analyses is, first, to appraise the overall outlook of the economy and then to assess the impact of economic changes on the firm. To appreciate the extent to which a change in just one factor of the

☐ **FIGURE 7–1   Impact of Economic Forecast on Firm's Functional Areas**

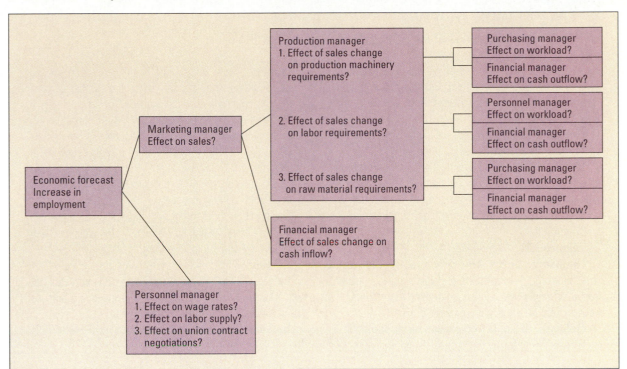

economy can affect all the major functional areas of the firm, let us examine Figure 7–1.

A forecast of an increase in employment would cause most marketing managers to revise upward their sales forecasts, which, in turn, would require production managers to augment production. This might be accomplished by adding another work shift, but if the plant is already operating 24 hours a day, new machinery will be needed. Either situation will require additional workers and raw materials, which will result in an extra workload for the personnel and purchasing managers. Should both the raw materials and labor markets be tight, the firm will probably have to pay prices and wage rates that are higher than normal. The financial manager may then have to negotiate with the banks for a loan to enable the firm to handle the greater cash outflow until additional revenue is received from increased sales.

Note that all of this occurs because of a change in only *one factor*. Actually, of course, many economic factors are involved, and their relationships are complex. By means of an economic analysis, an attempt is made to isolate and assess the impact of those factors believed to affect the firm's operations.

INTERNATIONAL ECONOMIC ANALYSES

When the firm enters overseas markets, economic analyses become more complex because now managers must operate in two new environments: foreign and international. In the foreign environment, not only are there many economies instead of one, but they are also highly divergent. Because of these

WORLDVIEW
Compiling EC Data: The Blind Leading the Blind

Indifference, inertia, and inefficiency among member governments are the biggest obstacles to compiling meaningful EC-wide data. Here's how EC statisticians rate the 12:

Greece: "Too centralized. Athens has statistics only up to 1986, and only for basic industry."

Britain: "One of the worst. Their numbers are outdated and nearly always incomplete. The prevailing attitude in Britain is that statistics are the prerogative of government; if business wants them, let business collect them itself."

Luxembourg: "Very good."

Germany: "Worse than Britain, despite its reputation for orderly recordkeeping. Everything is decentralized. Each time we request something from Bonn, they have to rely on state governments to get it."

Holland: "Good, but no service-sector statistics."

Spain: "Fine for recent industry stats, but nothing on services—except hotels and transportation."

France: "Slow but generally delivers what we request. But then, they should: there are 40,000 employees in the country's statistical office."

Portugal: "Extremely understaffed. If the Commission doesn't pay for Portugal's upcoming agricultural survey—the country's first—then it won't get done. Figures for small business are based on the national business register, which is outdated. Many of the firms on the books no longer exist."

Denmark: "Everything we need including service statistics. They have a survey on almost every company—a statistician's dream."

Belgium: "Too many classification problems."

Italy: "We've had no headache at all with the Italians. They've simply not responded. They're too busy revising their GNP calculations each year."

Ireland: "Very bad. We offered to go there to help. They told us not to bother."

Source: *International Management,* May 1988, p. 46.

---

differences, policies designed for the economic conditions in one market may be totally unsuitable for the economic conditions in another market. For example, headquarters may have a policy requiring its subsidiaries to maintain the lowest inventories possible, and the chief financial officer may decree that they make only foreign currency–denominated loans because of more favorable interest rates. For nations whose annual inflation rates are low (0 to 15 percent), these policies usually work well. But what about countries such as Nicaragua—with a 1990 inflation rate of 7,479 *percent*—or Peru—with 5,699 percent? The last thing headquarters wants is for the subsidiaries in these countries to have cash or foreign currency–denominated loans, so the policy for markets with high inflation rates will be just the reverse of what it is for countries with low inflation rates. Table 7–1 illustrates that the chief financial officer has more than just Nicaragua and Peru to be concerned about.

Besides monitoring the foreign environments, economists must also keep abreast of the actions taken by components of the international environment, such as regional groupings (EC, EFTA) and international organizations (UN, IMF, World Bank). American firms are very attentive to the EC's progress in reaching its Europe 1992 goals and to the impact this will have on EC–U.S. trade relations. They are also following closely the UN's progress in developing world pollution standards, health standards, and so forth. Any of these actions can seriously affect the firm.[2]

□ **TABLE 7–1**
Annual Rates of Inflation for Selected Developing Countries*

Country	1990	1989
Nicaragua	7,479%	5,854%
Peru	5,699	3,121
Brazil	2,830	1,234
Argentina	1,449	3,072
Uruguay	101	73
Sierra Leone	90	46
Turkey	55	64
Uganda	55	90
Ecuador	53	76
Dominican Republic	50	43

*Inflation rates are based on GDP deflator.
Source: World Bank, *Trends in Developing Economies, 1991.*

International economic analyses should provide economic data on both actual and prospective markets. Also, as part of the competitive forces assessment, many companies monitor the economic conditions of nations where their major competitors are located, because changing conditions may strengthen or weaken their competitors' ability to compete in world markets.

Because of the importance of economic information to the control and planning functions at headquarters, the collection of data and the preparation of reports must be the responsibility of the home office. However, foreign-based personnel (subsidiaries and field representatives) will be expected to contribute heavily to studies concerning their markets. Data from areas where the firm has no local representation can usually be somewhat less detailed and are generally available in publications from national and international agencies.[3] The reports from central or international banks are especially good sources for economic information on single countries. A listing of these and other useful publications can be found in Appendix A at the end of this book.[4] Other possible sources are the American chambers of commerce located in most of the world's capitals, the commercial officers in U.S. embassies, the United Nations, the World Bank, the International Monetary Fund, and the Organization for Economic Cooperation and Development.

□ Dimensions of the Economy

To estimate market potentials as well as to provide input to the other functional areas of the firm, managers require data on the size and the rates of change of a number of economic and socioeconomic factors. For an area to be a potential market, it must have sufficient people with the means to buy a firm's products. Socioeconomic data provide information on the number of people, and the economic factors tell us if they have purchasing power.

Economic dimensions.   Among the more important economic dimensions are GNP, distribution of income, personal consumption expenditures, personal ownership of goods, private investment, unit labor costs, exchange rates, inflation rates, and interest rates.

□ FIGURE 7–2
Five-Year Real Projected Growth in GDP (Cumulative percentage change 1991–1995)*

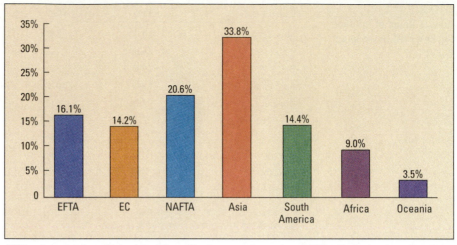

*EFTA—European Free Trade Association; EC—European Community; NAFTA—North American Free Trade Agreement. Figure 7–2 serves only as an example.

GNP.   Gross national product, the total of all final goods and services produced, and gross domestic product (GNP less net foreign factor incomes) are the values used to measure an economy's size. GNPs range from $5.2 trillion for the United States to $43 million for São Tomé and Príncipe (in the Gulf of Guinea off the coast of Gabon). What is the significance of GNP for the international businessperson? Is India, with a GNP of $287 billion, a more attractive market than Denmark, with $105 billion?

Imagine the reaction of managers who receive a report containing Figure 7–2, which shows a high *real* growth rate of **GDP** (**gross domestic product**) projected for Asia, at an annual rate of 6 percent. They will want to examine the data for individual countries in the area and compare growths with their subsidiaries' growths. The data might indicate that some markets where they have no operations need to be investigated. Of course, this is only the initial step. To compare the purchasing power of nations, managers also need to know among how many people this increase in GNP or GDP is divided.

GNP/capita.   The not altogether satisfactory method of employing GNP/capita to compare purchasing power reveals that Denmark is far ahead of India, with $20,510 versus $350. In other words, although India's pie is 2.7 times as big as Denmark's, there are 162 times as many people to eat it.

What can we learn from GNP/capita? As we saw in Chapter 3, we can generally assume that the higher its value, the more advanced the economy. Generally, however, the rate of growth is more important to marketers because a high growth rate indicates a fast-growing market—for which they are always searching. Frequently, given the choice between investing in a nation with a higher GNP/capita but a low growth rate and a nation in which the conditions are reversed, management will choose the latter.

Although differences in GNP/capita do tell us something about the relative wealth of a nation's inhabitants, the information is somewhat misleading because few of them have the equal share indicated by what is an arithmetic mean. This first crude estimate of purchasing power must be refined by incorporating data on how the national income is actually distributed.

GDP (gross domestic product) the total value of all goods and services produced domestically, not including (unlike GNP) net factor income from abroad

Country	Lowest 20 Percent	20–40 Percent	40–60 Percent	60–80 Percent	Highest 20 Percent	Highest 10 Percent
Australia (85)	4.4%	11.1%	17.5%	24.8%	42.2%	25.8%
Bangladesh (85–86)*	10.0	13.7	17.2	21.9	37.2	23.2
Belgium (78–79)	7.9	13.7	18.6	23.8	36.0	21.5
Botswana (85–86)	2.5	6.5	11.8	20.2	59.0	42.8
Brazil (83)	2.4	5.7	10.7	18.6	62.6	46.2
Canada (87)	5.7	11.8	17.7	24.6	40.2	24.1
Colombia (88)‡	4.0	8.7	13.5	20.8	53.0	37.1
Costa Rica (86)‡	3.3	8.3	13.2	20.7	54.5	38.8
Denmark (81)	5.4	12.0	18.4	25.6	38.6	22.3
Finland (81)	6.3	12.1	18.4	25.5	37.6	21.7
France (79)	6.3	12.1	17.2	23.5	40.8	25.5
West Germany (84)	6.8	12.7	17.8	24.1	38.7	23.4
Ghana (87–88)*	6.5	10.9	15.7	22.3	44.6	29.1
Guatemala (79–81)	5.5	8.6	12.2	18.7	55.0	40.8
Hong Kong (80)	5.4	10.8	15.2	21.6	47.0	31.3
Hungary (83)‡	10.9	15.3	18.7	22.8	32.4	18.7
India (83)*	8.1	12.3	16.3	22.0	41.4	26.7
Indonesia (87)*	8.8	12.4	16.0	21.5	41.3	26.5
Israel (79)	6.0	12.1	17.8	24.5	39.6	23.5
Italy (86)	6.8	12.0	16.7	23.5	41.0	25.3
Ivory Coast (86–87)*	5.0	8.0	13.1	21.3	52.7	36.3
Jamaica (88)*	5.4	9.9	14.4	21.2	49.2	33.4
Japan (79)	8.7	13.2	17.5	23.1	37.5	22.4
Malaysia (87)‡	4.6	9.3	13.9	21.2	51.2	34.8
Mauritius (80–81)	4.0	7.5	11.0	17.0	60.5	46.7
Morocco (84–85)†	9.8	13.0	16.4	21.4	39.4	25.4
Netherlands (83)	6.9	13.2	17.9	23.7	38.3	23.0
New Zealand (81–82)	5.1	10.8	16.2	23.2	44.7	28.7
Norway (82)	6.0	12.9	18.3	24.6	38.2	22.8
Pakistan (84–85)†	7.8	11.2	15.0	20.6	45.6	31.3
Peru (85–86)*	4.4	8.5	13.7	21.5	51.9	35.8
Philippines (85)†	5.5	9.7	14.8	22.0	48.0	32.1
Poland (87)‡	9.7	14.2	18.0	22.9	35.2	21.0
Singapore (82–83)	5.1	9.9	14.6	21.4	48.9	33.5
Spain (80–81)	6.9	12.5	17.3	23.2	40.0	24.5
Sri Lanka (85–86)‡	4.8	8.5	12.1	18.4	56.1	43.0
Sweden (81)	8.0	13.2	17.4	24.5	36.9	20.8
Switzerland (82)	5.2	11.7	16.4	22.1	44.6	29.8
United Kingdom (79)	5.8	11.5	18.2	25.0	39.5	23.3
United States (85)	4.7	11.0	17.4	25.0	41.9	25.0
Venezuela (87)‡	4.7	9.2	14.0	21.5	50.6	34.2
Yugoslavia (87)‡	6.1	11.0	16.5	23.7	42.8	26.6

Note: Numbers in parentheses indicate year of study.

*Data refer to per capita expenditure.

†Data refer to household expenditures.

‡Data refer to per capita income.

Source: *World Development Report, 1991* (Washington, D.C.: World Bank, 1991), Table 30, pp. 262–63.

income distribution
a measure of how a nation's income is apportioned among its people, commonly reported as the percentage of income received by population quintiles

Income distribution. Data on **income distribution** are gathered by the World Bank from a number of sources and published yearly in the *World Development Report.* Note that data in Table 7–2 (page 227) refer to the distribution of the total income of the entire household rather than the *per capita* income except where noted. This distinction is important to market analysts because households with low per capita income are frequently large households with a high *total* income while households with a lower total income are often smaller households with higher per capita income. Unfortunately, only a few countries gather data on the distribution of per capita income.

Despite the difficulties associated with income distribution studies, such as inconsistent measuring practices and wide variations in the representativeness of samples, the data provide some useful insights for businesspeople:

1. They confirm the belief that, generally, income is more evenly distributed in the advanced nations, although there are important variations among *both* developed and developing nations.
2. From comparisons over time (not shown), it appears that income redistribution proceeds very slowly, so that older data are still useful.
3. These same comparisons indicate that income inequality increases in the early stages of development, with a reversal of this tendency in the later stages. This is true for developed, developing, and socialist nations. The fact that the middle quintiles are growing at the expense of the top and bottom 20 percent signifies an increase in middle-income families, which are especially significant to marketers.

Contingent on the type of product and the total population, either situation (relatively even or uneven income distribution) may represent a viable market segment. For example, although Costa Rica's total GNP is $4.9 billion, the fact that just 20 percent of the population receives over 50 percent of that income (10 percent gets 39 percent) indicates that there is a sizable group of people who are potential customers for low-volume, high-priced luxury products. On the other hand, the market is rather small (2.7 million population) for low-priced goods requiring a high sales volume.

This simple calculation based on GNP, total population, and income distribution may be all that is required to indicate that a particular country is not a good market; however, if the results look promising, the analyst will proceed to gather data on personal consumption.

discretionary income the amount of income left after paying taxes and making essential purchases

Personal consumption. One area of interest to marketers is the manner in which consumers allocate their disposable income (after-tax personal income) between purchases of essential and nonessential goods. Manufacturers of a certain class of essentials—household durables, for instance—will want to know the amounts spent in that category, whereas producers of nonessentials will be interested in the magnitude of **discretionary income** (disposable income less essential purchases), for this is the money available to be spent on their products. Fortunately, disposable incomes and the amounts spent on essential purchases are available from the *UN Statistical Yearbook,* and discretionary income may be obtained by subtracting the total of these items from disposable income. More detailed expenditure patterns can frequently be found in economic publications. Table 7–3, which reproduces data found in *Business International,* is an example.

□ TABLE 7–3
Consumption Patterns for Selected Countries, 1989 (1979)

Country	Private Consumption Expenditures/ Capita(US$)	Percentage of Private Consumption Expenditures		
		Food and Beverages	Clothing	Household Durables
Switzerland	$15,263 ($8,532)	26.2% (28.3%)	4.4% (5.0%)	5.3% (6.0%)
United States	13,869 (6,214)	13.6 (16.3)	7.3 (6.8)	6.2 (7.2)
Japan	12,961 (4,694)	19.9 (25.5)	5.8 (7.1)	6.0 (6.2)
Canada	12,269 (4,984)	15.7 (20.8)	6.3 (7.6)	13.6 (8.4)
Sweden	11,647 (5,579)	21.3 (26.5)	7.8 (7.0)	6.1 (6.1)
Denmark	10,916 (6,106)	23.5 (27.5)	5.9 (5.6)	6.8 (7.9)
Norway	10,827 (5,081)	25.4 (27.9)	10.8 (8.9)	7.3 (8.7)
Germany	10,394 (5,767)	21.2 (26.5)	8.4 (9.5)	9.2 (11.4)
France	10,175 (5,470)	19.8 (23.1)	6.4 (7.0)	8.2 (9.7)
Belgium	9,899 (6,093)	20.2 (25.4)	6.6 (6.7)	10.3 (14.5)
Australia	9,726 (5,547)	21.2 (27.9)	6.4 (9.0)	7.8 (8.6)
Italy	9,338 (2,908)	25.3 (32.8)	9.4 (8.6)	8.9 (6.2)
United Kingdom	9,301 (3,278)	17.4 (24.4)	7.2 (7.8)	6.7 (7.2)
Netherlands	8,948 (5,547)	19.1 (22.2)	7.2 (8.7)	8.1 (9.8)
Greece	3,739 (2,227)	37.6 (41.1)	7.2 (11.3)	7.7 (10.2)
South Korea	2,657 (1,328)	37.8 (54.5)	5.1 (9.3)	6.1 (45.1)
Venezuela	1,460 (1,570)	45.5 (39.3)	4.3 (6.3)	5.2 (8.8)
Jamaica	970 (797)	42.1 (45.3)	5.3 (n.a.)	6.3 (n.a.)
Sri Lanka	327 (125)	43.1 (65.8)	10.6 (7.4)	4.4 (4.4)
India	220 (125)	53.5 (58.2)	13.1 (8.7)	4.9 (3.7)

Note: n.a. = Not available.

Source: "Indicators of Market Size for 117 Countries," *Business International,* 1991; and "Indicators of Market Size for 131 Countries," *Business International,* 1980.

Note how the consumption patterns have changed in just 10 years. With the exception of Venezuela, consumers in all the countries shown have decreased the percentage spent on food as their total consumption expenditures have increased. As you would expect, a significantly higher percentage goes for food in the poorer nations, and less is spent on consumer durables. Interestingly, the clothing percentages do not vary much among nations—although would you expect the percentage spent on clothing in Italy to be nearly 50 percent more than in France?

Don't underestimate the importance of the small percentage differences among nations. Marketers do not—each percentage point is worth a large sum of money. To appreciate its value, try multiplying the total per capita consumption expenditure times 0.01 times the population. If U.S. consumers had spent 1 percent more on clothing in 1989, for example, this would have amounted to $13,869 × 0.01 × 248.8 million, or $34.5 billion greater sales for the clothing industry. For more detailed information on consumption expenditures, see *World Development Indicators* published by the World Bank, the UN's *Monthly Bulletin of Statistics,* the IMF's *International Financial Statistics,* the UN's *Yearbook of National Accounts Statistics,* and Eurostat's annual *Basic Statistics of the Community* for the EC.

"Here's a leading economic indication—my wallet is empty!"

Reprinted from *The Wall Street Journal;* permission Cartoon Features Syndicate.

Other indicators that add to our knowledge of personal consumption are those concerned with the ownership of goods. In addition, the per capita values for the consumption and production of strategic materials, such as steel and energy, serve as measures of a nation's affluence and level of development. As Table 7–4 illustrates, the more industrialized nations have considerably higher values for these indicators than do the developing nations. See the following Worldview for one expert's opinion as to the most significant indicator.

Private investment.   The amount of private investment (the part of national income allocated to increasing a nation's productive capacity) is another factor that contributes to the analysis of market size and growth. New investment brings about increases in GNP and the level of employment, which are signals to the analyst of a growing market. A history of continual investment growth signifies, furthermore, that a propitious investment climate exists; that is, there are numerous profitable investment opportunities, and the government enjoys the confidence of the business community.

Table 7–5 on page 232 shows the impact of the worldwide recession on the growth of investment. In the table from which Table 7–5 was excerpted, 72 of the 91 countries for which complete data are available suffered a smaller increase during the 1980–89 period, compared with the 1965–80 period. The industrialized nations fared considerably better than the rest of the world, with the rates of growth for the United Kingdom and the United States showing sizable increases over the previous period.

All nations reduced the growth rate of government spending except the United States, India, and some of the developing nations of Africa. Interestingly, of the industrial nations, only the United States, the United Kingdom, and Finland experienced increases in the growth rates of private consumption. You can also see the impact of the austerity measures that Mexico has

☐ **TABLE 7–4   Per Capita Ownership or Consumption of Key Goods and Materials for Selected Countries**

Country	1989 Private Consumption Expenditure ($/capita)	1989 Passenger Cars/000 Population	1989 Telephones/ 000 Population*	1990 TV Sets/ 000 Population	1989 Steel Consumed (kilos/ capita)	1988 Percentage of U.S. Energy Consumption (capita)	1989 Personal Computers/ 000 Population	1989 Electricity (1,000 KWH/ capita)
Europe								
France	$10,175	401	612	599	313	37%	77	7.2
Germany	10,394	471	673	609	609	56	99	7.1
Italy	9,338	409	534	450	487	36	48	3.7
Sweden	11,647	410	872	441	455	49	94	16.4
Switzerland	15,263	413	910	415	380	38	109	7.8
United Kingdom	9,301	373	516	461	304	49	105	5.4
Middle East								
Egypt	891	8	27	81	88	7	n.a.	0.7
Israel	5,987	164	507	261	261	28	n.a.	4.3
Kuwait	5,268	284	177	390	25	81	n.a.	9.8
Syria	1,049	24	46	60	11	11	n.a.	0.7
Africa								
Ghana	268	4	5	12	n.a.	1	n.a.	0.3
Kenya	205	5	14	7	8	1	n.a.	0.1
Mauritius	1,359	33	72	124	n.a.	4	n.a.	0.6
South Africa	1,476	90	138	100	100	28	n.a.	4.5
Asia								
India	220	2	5	25	25	3	<1	0.3
Japan	12,961	250	541	557	761	39	57	6.5
Pakistan	277	4	7	19	17	3	n.a.	0.3
Philippines	539	6	16	102	36	3	n.a.	0.4
South America								
Bolivia	501	10	27	74	6	3	n.a.	0.3
Brazil	1,746	65	95	190	85	8	2	1.5
Colombia	830	21	80	107	43	8	n.a.	1.2
Eastern Europe								
Romania	1,460	13	n.a.	173	527	47	n.a.	3.3
Hungary	1,358	172	171	411	271	38	5	2.8
Poland	1,609	119	128	263	358	47	3	3.8
Yugoslavia	1,520	130	192	276	193	25	3	3.5
North America								
Canada	12,269	450	768	599	530	105	153	19.5
Mexico	1,545	64	111	146	86	16	4	1.2
United States	13,869	565	506	864	411	100	204	11.2

n.a. = Not available.

*Telephone access lines.

Source: "Indicators of Market Size for 117 Countries," *Business International,* 1991.

□ **TABLE 7–5**
Average Annual Growth Rate of Consumption and Investment for Selected Countries (Percent)

Country	Public Consumption*		Private Consumption		Gross Domestic Investment†	
	1965–80	1980–89	1965–80	1980–89	1965–80	1980–89
Low-income countries						
Nigeria	13.9%	−2.6%	6.9%	−4.8%	14.7%	−12.9%
Burundi	7.3	5.4	7.5	2.4	9.0	9.3
India	4.7	8.2	2.6	5.6	4.5	4.5
Central African Republic	−1.1	−2.5	4.9	2.1	−5.4	5.7
Lower-middle-income countries						
Philippines	7.7	1.4	4.9	3.1	8.5	7.8
Senegal	2.9	1.6	1.7	2.9	3.9	3.9
Chile	4.0	−0.2	0.9	1.1	0.5	2.7
Mexico	8.5	2.1	5.9	0.7	8.5	−5.0
Upper-middle-income countries						
Korea	7.7	5.7	8.0	7.8	15.9	11.6
South Africa	5.3	3.7	3.8	2.2	4.1	−4.5
Brazil	6.8	7.1	8.7	2.4	11.3	0.7
Greece	6.6	2.8	5.1	2.9	5.3	−1.7
Industrial market economies						
United Kingdom	2.3	1.0	2.8	3.4	1.3	6.9
Japan	5.2	2.6	6.3	3.2	6.9	5.7
United States	0.8	3.3	3.3	3.7	2.8	4.7
Germany	3.5	1.5	3.8	1.5	1.7	1.9

*Includes all levels of government and defense spending.
†Includes changes in inventory levels.
Source: Adapted from *World Development Report, 1991* (Washington, D.C.: World Bank, 1991), pp. 218–19.

had to take to service its huge foreign debt. In this environment of high inflation and reduced spending, investors were unwilling to invest in plants and inventories.

Unit labor costs.   One factor that contributes to a favorable investment opportunity is the ability to obtain **unit labor costs** (total direct labor costs/units produced) lower than those currently available to the firm. Foreign trends in these costs are closely monitored because each country experiences a different rate of increase.

Countries with slower-rising unit labor costs attract management's attention for two reasons. First, they are investment prospects for companies striving to lower production costs, as discussed in Chapter 2; second, they may become sources of new competition in world markets if other firms in the same industry are already located there.

Changes in wage rates may also cause the multinational firm that obtains products or components from a number of subsidiaries to change its sources of supply.

unit labor costs total direct labor costs divided by units produced

WORLDVIEW
If You Want to Get Ahead, Get a Telephone

What is the best gauge for measuring a country's level of development? Is it (1) per capita income, (2) state of the construction industry, (3) density of pollution, or (4) number of telephones? If you selected number four you are right, according to the International Telecommunications Union (ITU). In a recent report, the ITU observed that the total number of telephones installed in a country can often provide a better barometer of economic development than even per capita income.

The corollary is that nations with widespread and efficient telephone systems also have highly developed economies and large disposable incomes. Conversely, countries with poor telephone service are often plagued with underdeveloped economies and low-income levels.

In using the number-of-telephones principle to assess a country's fortunes, it is interesting to look at the United States. Recent statistics show that there are 95 telephones for every 100 households; and Beverly Hills, California, and Washington, D.C., have more telephones than people.

In contrast, Asian Development Bank (ADB) data show that in Asian countries, the telephone density per 100 population is only 2 compared to 5.5 in Latin America and 0.8 in Africa. In Bangladesh and Nepal, there is less than one (0.1) telephone per 100 persons.

Most developing countries thus have a nagging communications problem. For example, an ADB report points out that in Pakistan the telephone density is 0.5 per 100 population. But in rural areas, the situation is even worse, with as little as one telephone per 1,000 people. In fact, out of Pakistan's 45,000 villages, only about 1,900 have access to telephone services. One reason for this is that less than 15,000 villages have electricity.

Moreover, the demand for telephone service continues unabated in Pakistan, where people sometimes have to wait 10 years to obtain a telephone. The quality of service also leaves much to be desired. A sample survey revealed that only 25 percent of local and 15 percent of international call attempts were successful.

Poor telecommunications services take their developmental toll. According to Yoshiro Takano, a telecommunications specialist of the ADB, there is evidence of significant losses in efficiency incurred in agriculture, transportation, commerce, banking, government, tourism, and other sectors due to the lack or inadequacy of telecommunications services. Telecommunications also contribute to the quality of life by facilitating communication with kin and friends as well as access to emergency services.

Source: Truman Becker, "If You Want to Get Ahead, Get a Telephone," *UN Development Forum*, November–December 1986, p. 7.

Zenith, the American TV and computer manufacturer, moved the production of its monochrome computer monitors from Taiwan to Mexico in 1992 because of the lower Mexican wage rates.

What are the reasons for the relative changes in labor costs? Three factors are responsible: (1) compensation, (2) productivity, and (3) exchange rates. Hourly compensation tends to vary more widely than wages because of the appreciable differences in the size of fringe benefits. Unit labor costs will not rise in unison with compensation rates if the gains in productivity outstrip the increases in hourly compensation. In fact, if productivity increases fast enough, the unit costs of labor will decrease even though the firm is required to pay more to the workers.

Table 7–6 illustrates the rapidity with which labor compensation costs change. In 1975, five nations had higher average hourly rates when expressed in dollars than did the United States. This number had increased to seven by 1980, but then dropped to zero in 1982 (not shown). The United States had the highest hourly rate until 1986, when it was surpassed by Switzerland,

□ **TABLE 7-6   Labor Compensation Rates, 1975–1987***

Country	Average Hourly Rate Including Fringe Benefits (US$)				Relative Index (US = 100)		Average Annual Exchange Rates (units local currency to $1)	
	1990	1989	1980	1975	1990	1989	1990	1989
Germany	$23.38	$19.01	$12.33	$6.35	157	132	1.6157	1.8800
Switzerland	22.68	18.32	11.04	6.24	152	127	1.3892	1.6359
Sweden	21.78	18.30	12.51	6.78	146	127	5.9188	6.4469
Norway	20.21	17.01	11.68	6.60	135	118	6.2597	6.9045
Denmark	18.85	15.32	10.95	7.18	126	106	6.1890	7.3100
Netherlands	18.74	15.45	12.06	6.60	126	107	1.8207	2.1207
Belgium	18.55	15.11	13.15	6.07	124	105	33.4180	39.4040
Italy	18.41	15.28	8.00	4.65	123	106	1,198.1000	1,372.1000
Austria	17.57	14.13	8.56	4.70	118	98	11.3700	13.2310
Japan	15.96	15.79	5.61	3.05	107	110	144.7900	137.9600
France	15.83	12.79	9.12	4.33	106	89	5.4354	6.3723
United Kingdom	15.26	12.84	7.38	3.01	102	89	0.5603	0.6117
United States	14.92	14.41	9.80	6.33	100	100	—	—
Spain	13.51	10.70	5.96	2.55	91	74	101.9300	118.3800
Ireland	12.62	10.37	5.88	3.27	85	72	0.6030	0.4249
Greece	6.47	5.56	3.73	1.40	43	39	158.5100	162.4200
Portugal	4.41	3.44	2.06	1.58	30	24	142.5500	152.4600

*Dollar conversions are at average annual exchange rates.

Source: *Business Europe,* January 28, 1983, p. 26; and *Business International,* August 12, 1991, p. 270.

West Germany, and Norway. Note that in 1990, the dollar bought fewer units of all currencies, and, as you would expect, the average labor cost expressed in dollars increased in all countries. However, the dollar cost did not increase at the same rate as the exchange rate did. Why? Because an increase expressed in dollars may be due to one or both of the following: (1) a real increase in labor costs and (2) an appreciation of the local currency with respect to the dollar.

For example, the German average hourly rate in dollars rose from $19.01 in 1989 to $23.38 in 1990, a large rise of 23 percent. But did that increase result from real wage gains, or did it occur because the conversion to dollars in 1990 was made with more expensive German marks? To find out:

1. Convert the 1989 hourly rate to marks: $19.01 × 1.8684 = 35.52 marks.
2. Convert the 1990 hourly rate to marks: $23.28 × 1.6073 = 37.42 marks.
3. Percentage increase in marks = 5.3 percent (real wage gains).
4. Therefore, 77.0 percent [(23 − 5.3)/23] of the apparent increase in the hourly cost was due to a more expensive currency in terms of the dollar.[5]

If you wish to prepare a table of average wage costs for countries not included in Table 7–6, you will find a method for doing this in endnote 5 of this chapter.

□ **TABLE 7–7**
The Latin American Debt Problem

Country	Total External Debt, 1991 ($ billion)	Change in Debt since 1986 (percent)	Annual Interest Payments as a Percentage of Export Revenue		Total External Debt as a Percentage of GNP	
			1986	1991	1980	1989
Brazil	$122.8	+10.5%	42.4%	23.7%	31.2%	33.8%
Mexico	100.9	+0.4	38.3	23.0	30.3	54.9
Argentina	61.0	+18.6	50.9	35.0	48.4	84.8
Venezuela	33.0	−0.3	34.2	15.9	42.1	61.0
Peru	18.5	+27.8	31.7	34.8	51.0	88.9

Source: *Trends in Developing Economies, 1991,* World Bank; *World Development Report, 1991,* World Bank.

Other economic dimensions.   We have mentioned only a few of the many economic indicators that economists study, and you learned about the importance to businesspeople of interest rates, balances of payments, and inflation rates in Chapter 6, Financial Forces. Which of the economic measures the analyst chooses to study will depend on the industry and on the purpose of the study. Executives of an automobile manufacturer, for example, will want the economist's opinion as to where interest rates are headed and what is the rate of growth of a nation's GNP. GNP, as you saw earlier, is important to other producers of industrial products, such as Pitney Bowes.

The large international debts of a number of Latin American nations are causing multiple problems not only for their governments but also for multinational firms. Just look at the situation of the five countries that are listed in Table 7–7.

Is this a problem for international bankers only, or should it concern multinational managements as well? Is it significant to global and multinational firms with subsidiaries in these countries that a high percentage of the countries' export earnings must go to service their foreign debts? If it is, then management will expect periodic reports on this situation from the economist. Let's examine the ramifications for an international firm of these large foreign debts.

If a large part of the foreign exchange the nation earns cannot be used to import components used in local products, then either local industries must begin their manufacture or the companies that import them must stop production. Either alternative can cause the multinational to lose sales if it has been selling to its subsidiary the parts made in one of its home country plants, a common occurrence because the home plant is usually more **vertically integrated** than its subsidiaries. A scarcity of foreign exchange can also make it difficult for the subsidiary to import raw materials and spare parts for its production equipment. If headquarters wants its affiliate to continue production, it may have to lend the foreign exchange and wait for repayment. Campbell Soup, Sears, Revlon, and Gerber closed their operations in Brazil because of this problem.[6] Other multinationals have resorted to barter or have begun to export their subsidiaries' products even though these actions have reduced exports or even local sales of their domestic plants.

Governments may impose price controls (which make it difficult for a subsidiary to earn a profit), cut government spending (which reduces company sales), and impose wage controls (which limit consumer purchasing power). The economic turmoil that follows can turn into a political crisis, such as

vertically integrated
describes a firm that produces inputs for its subsequent manufacturing processes

occurred in Venezuela when rioting and looting resulted after the president tried to impose similar austerity measures.[7]

One aspect of debt reduction that has been of interest to some multinationals has been debt/equity swaps, which we discussed in Chapter 6. They have bought foreign debt for as little as 60 cents on a dollar and have used it to buy up local companies that the government has privatized. When Chile sold a government-owned insurance company, telephone system, and its national electricity grid, it permitted foreigners to pay with foreign debt they had purchased. Grupo Visa, a Mexican conglomerate, reduced its foreign debt from $1.7 billion to $400 million by giving foreign creditors a 40 percent share in the company.[8]

Scarcity of foreign exchange can affect even those firms that merely export to nations with high foreign debt because the governments will surely impose import restrictions. When Latin American debt increased rapidly from 1981 to 1983, that region's share of U.S. exports dropped by one third. To protect these export markets, firms had to extend long-term credit. From this you can see that managements will expect to receive information on the status of the foreign debt in nations where it is high in addition to the other economic data we have been examining.

Socioeconomic dimensions.   A complete definition of market potential must also include detailed information about the population's physical attributes as measured by the socioeconomic dimensions. Just as we began with GNP in the study of purchasing power, we shall begin this section with an analysis of the total population.

Total population.   Total population, the most general indicator of potential market size, is the first characteristic of the population that the analysts will examine. They readily discover that there are immense differences in population sizes, which range from a billion inhabitants in China to less than 1 million each for 34 countries. The fact that many developed nations have less than 10 million inhabitants makes it apparent that population size alone is a poor indicator of economic strength and market potential. Switzerland, for example, with only 6.6 million people, is far more important economically than Bangladesh, with 110 million. Clearly, more information is needed; only for a few low-priced, mass-consumed products, such as soft drinks, cigarettes, and soap, does population size alone provide a basis for estimating consumption.

For products not in this category, large populations and populations that are increasing rapidly may not signify an immediate enlargement of the market; but if incomes grow over time, eventually at least a part of the population will become customers. Insight into the rapidity with which this is occurring may be obtained by comparing population and GNP growth rates (see Table 2–11, pp. 52–53). Where GNP increases faster than the population, there is probably an expanding market, whereas the converse situation not only indicates possible market contraction but may even point out a country as a potential area of political unrest. This possibility is strengthened if an analysis of the educational system discloses an accruement of technical and university graduates. These groups expect to be employed as and receive the wages of professionals, and when sufficient new jobs are not being created to absorb them, the government can be in serious trouble. Various developing

Rioting and looting greeted the attempts of Venezuela's new president, Carlos Andrés Pérez, to impose the austerity and price increases demanded by foreign creditors.

AP/Wide World Photos

nations already face this difficulty: Egypt and India are two notable examples.[9]

Age distribution. Because few products are purchased by everyone, marketers must identify the segments of the population that are more apt to buy their goods. For some firms, age is a salient determinant of market size; but unfortunately, the distribution of age groups within populations varies widely. Generally, because of higher birth and fertility rates, the developing countries have a more youthful population than the industrial countries. Figure 7–3 illustrates the tremendous difference in age distribution between developed and developing countries, which is the result of much higher birthrates in the developing nations. According to the World Bank, past and estimated average annual population percentage increases for nations grouped according to income are the following:

	1965–80	1980–89	1989–2000
Low-income economies	2.3%	2.0%	1.9%
Middle-income economies	2.3	2.1	1.9
High-income economies	0.9	0.7	0.6

Source: *World Development Report, 1991* (Washington, D.C.: World Bank, 1991), pp 254–55.

This situation is far from static, however, as decreasing birthrates are becoming a worldwide phenomenon. Of the 120 nations for which the United Nations provided information, only 11 experienced increases in their crude (born live) birthrates per thousand population over the 1965–89 period. Three were middle-income nations, and eight were low-income nations.[10]

☐ **FIGURE 7–3   Population by Age and Sex—1975 and 2000 (Millions)**

Source: Based on U.S. Bureau of Census projections.

The population of developing countries, which now account for about 75 percent of the world's population, will rise to 80 percent by the year 2000. Figure 7–4 shows you that of the 11 nations predicted to have over 100 million inhabitants by the year 2000, only 3 are industrialized; the rest are developing countries.

What does this signify for businesspeople? In the developed nations, there will be a decrease in the demand for products used in schools and for products bought by and for children, a smaller market for furniture and clothing, but an increased demand for medical care and related products, tourism, and financial services. Firms confronted by a decreasing demand for their products will have to look for sales increases in the developing economies, where the age distribution is reversed. The high growth rates in the developing nations will provide markets for transportation systems, higher-yield food grains, fertilizers, agricultural tools, appliances, and so forth.

☐ **FIGURE 7–4   Population Growth of Countries with over 100 Million Inhabitants in the Year 2000**

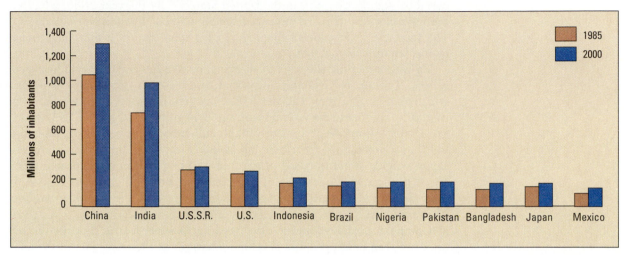

Whirlpool, concerned about the decline in the number of householders aged 25 or less in the United States while noting the opportunities in overseas markets, acquired 53 percent of the Dutch electronics giant Philips' domestic appliance business in 1988. The acquisition enabled Whirlpool to become the world's largest major home appliance company with manufacturing facilities in 11 countries and a distribution network covering 45 countries. In August 1991, Whirlpool bought the remaining 47 percent of the business from Philips.[11]

Many forces are responsible for reductions in birthrates. Governments are supporting family planning programs, to be sure, but there is ample evidence that improved levels in health and education along with an enhanced status for women, a more even distribution of income, and a greater degree of urbanization are all acting to reduce the traditional family size. In Colombia, for example, 46 percent of the women with seven years or more of schooling use contraceptives, as compared with 14 percent of those who have not attended school. In Mexico, the percentages were 72 percent compared to 31 percent.[12]

While this is welcomed by governments in developing nations, the declining birthrate is causing concern in the governments of the industrialized countries. In Europe, for example, EC governments and businesses are concerned that for over a decade European birthrates in every major European nation have been below the "replacement number" of 2.1 children per woman. An increasing number of young Europeans are not getting married, and those that do are marrying later and having fewer children. By the year 2000, today's unemployment rate of 8 percent will be replaced by a shortage of workers. European governments will have to provide medical care and pensions for the 25 percent of their population that will be over 60 years old, and there will be fewer working taxpayers.[13]

Japan's situation seems to be even more serious. Its fertility rate is only 1.57 children per woman, and its elderly population is growing at six times the American rate.[14] The labor shortage has inflated wages to the point where the average manufacturing pay in Japan is nearly $12 an hour compared to slightly over $10 in the United States.[15] By the year 2000, what had been the world's youngest industrial society will become the world's oldest.[16] The Japanese Federation of Employers calls this "the most difficult problem facing Japanese companies."

To counteract the shortage of workers, companies are investing heavily in robots. Toyota, for example, expects to increase its output by 30 percent with robots rather than add the 3,000 workers that otherwise would be required.[17] The mandatory retirement age is also higher than the 55 it was in the 1970s. About 70 percent of Japan's full-time employees work for a firm that has a mandatory retirement age of 60 or more. [18] Important changes in Japan's rigid, seniority-based promotion and pay system are expected to occur. To attract younger employees, Japanese firms will have to reduce the large difference between the wages of the newly hired and the older workers. They will also have to promote younger employees faster.

Company presidents in the developed nations are fearful that the discrepancy between developed and developing nations in the aging rate of the labor force will put their companies at a competitive disadvantage. Morale among younger workers in the developed countries may fall because the slowing of turnover in the higher-paying jobs requiring years of experience will keep them from advancing in their careers.

Also, the hospitalization costs for firms in the developed countries will be higher than those for firms in the LDCs and NICs because of a greater proportion of older workers. Similarly, pension costs are increasing because more employees live to full retirement age and then live longer after retirement. For example, the worker-to-retiree ratio, now 2.2 to 1 in Germany and 4.4 to 1 in Japan, is expected to fall to 1.1 to 1 and 1.6 to 1, respectively, by the year 2030. However, the demographic outlook for Great Britain is more optimistic because its dependency ratio will go from 3.3 to 1 to 2.1 to 1 in 2030. In the United States, the ratio, now 4.6 to 1, will reach only 2.4 to 1.[19] Due to relatively lower pension costs for American firms, economists are predicting that U.S. competitiveness in world markets will be enhanced.[20]

---

population density a measure of the number of inhabitants per area unit (inhabitants per square kilometer or square mile)

---

population distribution a measure of how the inhabitants are distributed over a nation's area

---

rural-to-urban shift the movement of a nation's population from the rural areas to cities

---

Population density and distribution. Other aspects of population that concern management are **population density** and **population distribution.** Densely populated countries tend to make product distribution and communications simpler and less costly than they are where population density is low; thus you might expect Pakistan, with 138 inhabitants per square kilometer, to be an easier market to serve than Canada (2.6 inhabitants/square kilometer) or Brazil (17.3 inhabitants/square kilometer).[21] The expectation, though, is another of those based on an arithmetic mean. We must know how these populations are distributed.

One needs only to compare the urban percentages of total population to learn that Canada and Brazil possess population concentrations that facilitate the marketing process. While only 32 percent of Pakistan's population is urban, the percentages for Brazil and Canada are 74 and 77 percent, respectively. The physical forces, as we shall see in Chapter 8, contribute heavily to the formation of these concentrations.[22]

An important phenomenon that is changing the population distribution is the **rural-to-urban shift,** which is occurring everywhere, especially in developing countries, as people move to cities in search of higher wages and more

□ Population Density

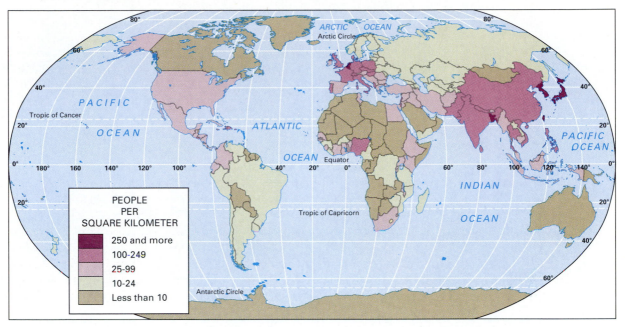

PEOPLE
PER
SQUARE KILOMETER

- 250 and more
- 100-249
- 25-99
- 10-24
- Less than 10

□ **TABLE 7–8**
The Most Populous Cities in the Year 2000 (Millions)

1975		2000	
1. New York–Northeastern New Jersey	19.8	1. Mexico City	31.0
2. Tokyo–Yokohama	17.7	2. São Paulo	25.8
3. Mexico City	11.9	3. Tokyo–Yokohama	24.2
4. Shanghai	11.6	4. New York–Northeastern New Jersey	22.8
5. Los Angeles–Long Beach	10.8	5. Shanghai	22.7
6. São Paulo	10.7	6. Beijing	19.9
7. London	10.4	7. Rio de Janeiro	19.0
8. Greater Bombay	9.3	8. Greater Bombay	17.1
9. Rhine–Ruhr	9.3	9. Calcutta	16.7
10. Paris	9.2	10. Djakarta	16.6

Note: Six of the largest urban centers will be in Asia, and none will be in Europe.

conveniences. This shift is significant to marketers because city dwellers, being less self-sufficient than persons living in rural areas, must enter the market economy. City governments also become customers for equipment that will expand municipal services to handle the population influx. Table 7–8 contains some good sales prospects. Note also in Figure 7–5 that most fast-growing cities that will be megacities by the year 2000 are in developing nations.

An indicator of the extent of this movement is the change in the percentages of urban population. As Table 7–9 indicates, the greatest urban shifts are occurring in the low- and middle-income countries. In no country anywhere is there a net flow in the other direction.

☐ **FIGURE 7–5   25 Mega Cities, 1970–2000 (Millions)**

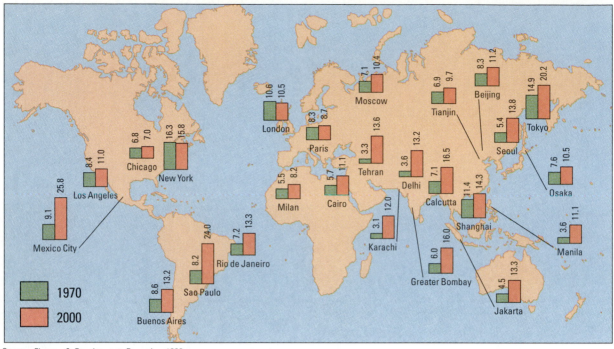

Source: *Finance & Development,* December 1989.

☐ **TABLE 7–9**
Rural-to-Urban Shift

	Percentages of Population in Urban Areas		
	1965	**1989**	**Percentage Increase**
Low-income countries	17%	36%	111%
Middle-income countries	42	58	38
High-income countries	71	77	8

Source: *World Development Report, 1988* (Washington, D.C.: World Bank, 1988), pp. 282–83; and *World Development Report, 1991,* pp. 264–65.

Other socioeconomic dimensions.   Other socioeconomic dimensions can provide useful information to management. The increase in the number of working women, for example, is highly significant to marketers because it may result in larger family incomes, a greater market for convenience goods, and a need to alter the **promotional mix.** Personnel managers are interested in this increase because it results in a larger labor supply. It also signifies that changes may be required in production processes, employee facilities, and personnel management policies.

Data on the country's divorce rate, when available, will alert the marketer to the formation of single-parent families and single-person households, whose product needs and buying habits differ in many respects from those of a two-parent family (see Figure 7–6). In many countries, important ethnic groups require special consideration by both marketing and personnel managers.

promotional mix a blend of the promotional methods a firm uses to sell its products

□ **FIGURE 7–6**
Changing Divorce Rates in Selected Countries

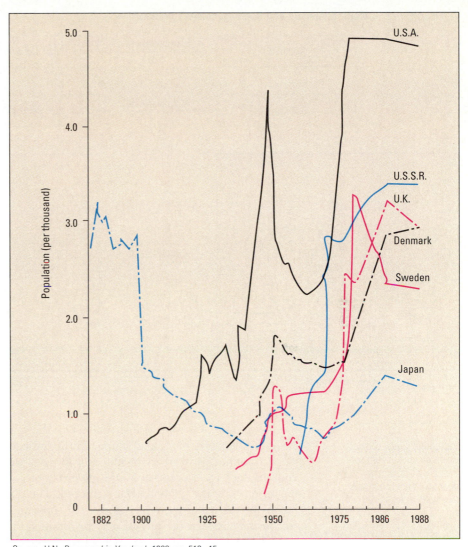

Source: U.N. *Demographic Yearbook 1989,* pp. 513–15.

Canada, for example, has eight radio stations in five cities broadcasting 100 percent of the time to specific ethnic groups such as Italian, Ukrainian, German, Greek, and Chinese because more than 9 million of the country's 25 million people speak languages other than English and French. In addition, 8 television stations and 60 radio stations include some ethnic programs in their broadcast schedules.[23]

Major economic and socioeconomic variables.   Figure 7–7 compares the three major economic and socioeconomic variables.

□ **National Economic Plans**

national economic plans
plans prepared by governments stating their economic goals and means for reaching them, usually for periods of up to five years

One other source of economic data that may prove useful to the firm, especially for its marketers, is the **national economic plans** that many countries publish. These range from the annual and five-year plans (in reality, budgets)

◻ **FIGURE 7–7   Major Economic and Socioeconomic Variables**

Economic forces   **Socioeconomic forces**

---

indicative plan forecast made by government with industry collaboration of the direction the economy is expected to take

used as production control instruments by the remaining communist nations, such as Cuba, Vietnam, and China, to the **indicative plans** of some free market economies. Instead of production targets, the five-year indicative plans contain the basic targets set by the government and some general policy statements on how the goals will be achieved. The government then attempts by means of the usual monetary and fiscal tools to create favorable conditions for business so that the targets may be attained. This favoritism may be manifested in many ways, among which are special tax concessions to investors and foreign exchange allocations (when foreign exchange is controlled) to purchase imported capital equipment and raw materials.

Information about national development plans and budgets is regularly reported in such publications as *Business International* and *Business America*. Commercial attachés in American embassies and the overseas American chambers of commerce are additional sources of information.

In the *Highlights of Ninth Medium-Term Economic Development Plan for Taiwan (1986–1989)*, for example, the government states that one policy is to "enhance energy efficiency." Then the strategy, called *supporting measure*, is to "develop mass transit systems, promote the production of oil-saving transport equipment, and establish efficiency standards for oil-consuming vehicles." What business opportunities are there in this strategy? It looks as though producers of subway systems, electric trolleys, and electric buses may have a chance to make some sales, but automobile manufacturers should find a way to provide input to the body responsible for the new standards, which could cause some expensive design changes.[24]

□ Industry Dimensions

Every firm is concerned about the general economic news because of its impact on consumer purchases, prices of raw materials, and investment decisions, but certain factors are more significant than others to a given industry or to a specific functional area of the firm. The size and growth trend of the automobile industry is of paramount importance to a tire manufacturer, for example, but is of no interest to an appliance manufacturer. Nor would the quantity of machine operators graduated by technical schools be useful to financial officers, although these data are of vital interest to human resources managers of manufacturing plants. Managers want data not only about the firm's industry but also about industries that supply and purchase from the company. Minicase 7–1 at the end of this chapter illustrates the use of both macroeconomic and industry-specific data.

Industry studies are generally made by the firm's economists or its trade association, but they can also be purchased from independent research organizations, such as Fantus (New York) and The Economist Intelligence Unit (London). Government agencies, chambers of commerce, and trade publications such as *Advertising Age* publish them as well. Many international banks publish free newsletters containing useful economic data.

SUMMARY

To keep abreast of the latest economic developments and also to plan for the future, firms regularly assess and forecast economic conditions at the local, state, and national levels. When they enter international operations, the economic analysis increases in complexity because managers are operating in two new environments: foreign and international. There are more economies to study, and these economies are frequently highly divergent.

The various functional areas of the firm require data on the size and rates of change of a number of economic and socioeconomic factors. Among the more important economic dimensions are GNP, GNP/capita, distribution of income, personal consumption expenditures, private investment, unit labor costs, and financial data, such as exchange rates, inflation rates, interest rates, and the amount of a nation's foreign debt. The principal socioeconomic dimensions are total population, rates of growth, age distribution, population density, and population distribution.

Considerable information is available from publications put out by international agencies, governments, and banks and from business publications. National economic plans, for which no American counterpart exists, provide an insight as to government expectations. In the communist countries, national plans are often the equivalent of market studies.

Many developed and developing nations use indicative plans to set out their goals and provide some general policy statements as to how they will be achieved.

QUESTIONS

1. Management learns from the economic analysis of Country A that wage rates are expected to increase by 10 percent next year. Which functional areas of the firm will be concerned? Why are they concerned?

2. Check the *World Development Report* in the library to learn which country in each income group (low-, medium-, and high-income economies) is the leader in the rate of GNP/capita growth over the last 15 to 20 years. In each case, is the rate of increase greater than the population growth? What can you deduce from that?

3. What common problem does the use of GNP/capita and population density values present?

4. Choose three poor nations from Table 7–2 that appear to be good candidates for high-priced luxury goods even though their GNP/capita as shown in Table 2–11 are low. What is the approximate size of the population segment with the highest income? How can you use this information?

5. If the clothing industry association to which your firm's Swiss subsidiary belongs could mount a successful promotional program to cause the Swiss to increase their clothing expenditures by 1 percent annually, what would be the total increase in sales for the clothing industry?

6. In 1990, Switzerland had the second-highest average hourly compensation rate.
   a. What was the percentage increase in dollars?
   b. What was the percentage increase in the labor cost stated in Swiss francs?
   c. What percentage of the change when stated in dollars was due to changes in the franc–dollar exchange rate?

7. The staff economist has given to the chief financial officer a report on the foreign debt situation of Venezuela, as shown in Table 7–7. What concerns might the chief financial officer have?

8. Declining birthrates appear to be a worldwide phenomenon.
   a. Why are they falling?
   b. What does this signify for businesspeople?

9. Of what use to businesspeople are the five-year plans of the communist bloc or the indicative plans of other countries?

10. What would be the concerns of the chief financial officer if he or she were to receive the information on annual inflation rates from Table 7–1?

11. What problems is the reduction in birthrates causing for European governments?

12. Choose a country and a product, and estimate the market potential of the product based on the economic and socioeconomic dimensions. What other environmental forces should you investigate?

□ MINICASE 7–1

International Drug Corporation

International Drug Corporation (IDC) is a multinational firm specializing in the production of ethical pharmaceuticals; that is, those available to the public from a pharmacist only on prescription. These products are characterized by a high degree of research effort and, because of the limited protection offered by patents, have a relatively short product life. IDC does make some over-the-counter products, but these are only about 20 percent of total company sales.

The vice president for the South American division needs to make a forecast for ethical drug sales, which he will use as a basis for setting quotas for the six countries that have manufacturing facilities in his division. These products produce about 75 percent of the total sales in each country. At present, IDC's market share and sales by category of drug (pediatric or geriatric and general) in each country are as follows:

	Market Share (percent)	Pediatric (0–14 years)	Geriatric and General (15 years and over)
Argentina	30%	32%	68%
Brazil	24	38	62
Chile	55	32	68
Paraguay	65	41	59
Peru	45	42	58
Uruguay	38	27	73

Total health care has grown faster than world population and world income since 1970. A conservative average of the total amount per capita spent on health care, both private and public, for pharmaceuticals in South America is 20 percent. This is considerably lower than in the United States and Europe; but in government clinics, medicine is generally offered without charge or at a substantial discount from the price charged in pharmacies. According to IDC's subsidiaries, the patients at the clinics probably pay, on average, 40 percent of the drugs' listed prices when those given at no charge are included. Obviously, the private drugstores that get only 40 percent off list (60 percent of the list price is their cost) cannot compete. IPC, however, still earns a 12 percent profit based on its selling prices when it sells to the governments at list less 50 percent because of the low marketing costs on such large volumes, as compared to an average of 20 percent of its selling prices on sales to private pharmacies.

Here are the data that the staff economist has just given to the vice president. Help him do his forecast. If you have to make any assumptions, please make a note of them. If marketing costs for government sales average 6 percent of IDC's selling price, while they average 11.7 percent of the selling price to private pharmacies, should the vice president try to change the present government–private pharmacy sales ratio that now prevails in any of the six markets? Should he have any other concerns based on these data?

	GNP (billions of dollars)			GNP/Capita			Foreign Debt (billions of dollars)			Percent Change from Previous Year		
	1982	1986	1989	1982	1986	1989	1983	1986	1989	1983	1986	1989
Argentina	54.7	73.1	$ 67.8	$1,880	$2,380	$2,160	$45.1	$ 51.4	$ 64.7	12.8%	4.5%	+9.8%
Brazil	262.9	249.8	375.1	2,070	1,810	2,540	98.2	111.0	111.3	10.8	4.2	−2.4
Chile	25.6	16.6	22.9	2,220	1,350	1,770	18.0	20.7	18.2	7.6	4.7	−7.1
Paraguay	5.8	3.6	4.3	1,740	950	1,030	1.5	1.9	2.5	24.4	8.1	0
Peru	25.0	21.4	23.0	1,380	1,080	1,090	12.4	14.5	19.9	14.0	2.3	−7.0
Uruguay	10.1	5.8	8.1	3,410	1,910	2,620	4.6	5.2	3.8	22.0	4.6	0

	Total Debt Service as Percentage of Export Receipts			Total Government Expenditures as Percentage of GNP			Percentage of Government Expenditures on Health Care		
	1983	1986	1989	1981	1986	1989	1982	1983	1989
Argentina	58.4%	50.9%	36.1%	15%	12%	15.5	1.1%	1.4%	2.0%
Brazil	43.5	41.4	31.3	n.a.	9†	30.6	7.8	7.3	6.1
Chile	38.9	37.9	27.5	13	13	32.5	6.8	6.0	5.9
Paraguay	14.3	18.5	11.9	7	7	8.9	3.7	3.7	3.0
Peru	29.8	26.2	6.8	13	11	11.6	5.3‡	6.2‡	5.5
Uruguay	24.8	24.7	29.4	13	14	25.8	3.3	6.5	4.5

	Population per Physician*			Annual Inflation Rate			Population (millions)			Population Distribution 1989	
	1977	1980	1984	1983	1986	1989	1982	1983	1989	0–14 Years	15 Years and Over
Argentina	530	430	370	444%	82%	3,072%	28.4	29.6	31.9	30%	70%
Brazil	1,700	1,200	1,080	179	58	1,234	126.8	129.7	147.3	36	64
Chile	1,930	1,930	1,230	24	17	14	11.5	11.7	13.0	31	69
Paraguay	2,190	1,310	1,460	14	24	31	3.1	3.2	4.2	41	59
Peru	1,530	1,390	1,040	125	63	3,121	17.4	17.9	21.2	38	62
Uruguay	540	510	510	52	76	73	2.9	3.0	3.1	26	74

n.a. = Not available.
*Latest estimate available from World Health Organization.
†1985.
‡1981.
Sources: Various *World Development Reports* and Banco Nacional de Comercio Exterior, *Comercio exterior,* February and March 1989 issues.

◻ MINICASE 7–2

Taiwan's Economic Development Plan, 1986–1989

Following are excerpts from Taiwan's Ninth Economic Development Plan that pertain to industry. The policies, priorities, and supporting measures that the government intends to take are listed. What business opportunities do there seem to be for local and foreign firms? What problems for foreign multinationals may occur in the future?

II INDUSTRY

An annual growth target of 6.1 percent has been set for the industrial sector during the plan period. Among subsectors, mining is targeted to grow 1.0 percent, manufacturing 6.3 percent, construction 5.7 percent, and public utilities 5.8 percent.

1. Basic Policies

1. Continue to intensify the development of strategic and important exporting industries and improve the industrial structure.
2. Speed up the development of technology-intensive industries and promote the export of capital goods and technology.
3. Continue to improve the domestic investment climate, promote the liberalization of investment, and encourage investment by domestic and foreign investors.
4. Facilitate coordinated development of private and public enterprises and technological exchanges between them.
5. Expand international cooperation in resource development and ensure a stable long-term supply of basic industrial materials.
6. According to the principles of international division of labor and comparative advantage, avoid any overexpansion of energy-intensive intermediate industries.
7. Assist existing labor-intensive industries to modernize machinery and equipment, to raise labor productivity and product quality, and to enhance their competitive position in international markets.

2. Development Priorities

(1) Strategic industries

A. Machinery industry—Accelerate the transfer of technology and automation of production, plan for the standardization of parts and components, establish production and marketing order, and promote the exports of package plants.

B. Transportation equipment industry—Implement the "Automobile Industry Development Program" and the "Guidelines for the Financing of China Shipbuilding Corp.," formulate a "Motorcycle Industry Development Program" to enhance export competitiveness, and development of allied industries.

C. Electrical machinery industry—Strengthen research and development in new technology, promote computerized management, push forward with the manufacture of supplies and development of the heavy electrical machinery industry, encourage rationalization and standardization of production, and lower the degree of import dependency.

D. Electronics and information industries—
   a. Speed up the development of digital electronic products and technologies for Very Large Scale Integrated Circuits (VLSI) and computers, recruit and cultivate manpower as needed, and set up market, technology, and parts-and-components

	Private Consumption Expenditures (billions of dollars)			Private Consumption Expenditures as Percentage of GNP			Annual Percentage of Private Consumption Spent on Medical Care
	1982	1986	1989	1982	1986	1989	1980–88
Argentina	$38.7	$53.7	$43.7	70.7%	73.5%	64.5%	4%
Brazil	201.3	157.2	257.4	76.6	59.8	68.6	6
Chile	18.6	11.6	17.1	72.7	69.9	74.7	5
Paraguay	4.6	3.1	3.4	79.3	86.1	79.1	2
Peru	15.4	18.0	17.8	61.6	84.1	77.4	4
Uruguay	7.3	3.9	6.1	72.3	67.2	75.3	6

information centers, and a marketing service network.

b. Vigorously develop microcomputers, digital electronic switching systems, and opto-electronic communications facilities; consolidate communications technology and machinery manufacturing to develop integrated products; study and develop an "Integrated Services Digital Network (ISDN)" to provide a combination of telephone, telegram, data, facsimile, TV, video telephone, and electronic mail services.

(2) Other industries

A. Continue to encourage the modernization of equipment and facilities and the merger of manufacturers, and promote the automation and specialization of industrial production and the system of core-satellite plans with a view to improving production efficiency and product quality.

B. Encourage Chinese nationals and foreigners to invest in the manufacture of high value-added and high-technology industrial products, research and develop new products, and establish domestic manufacturers' own trademarks and marketing networks to lay a solid foundation for sustained industrial growth.

C. Devote greater efforts to controlling industrial pollution to protect public health and the ecological environment.

3. Supporting Measures

(1) Fiscal measures

A. Modernize tax and customs administration, make timely adjustments in the structure of taxes and import tariffs, expand the list of duty-free, basic raw materials, and promote the rationalization of industrial operations.

B. Implement the value-added tax and amend tax legislation to avoid double taxation.

C. Amend legislation relating to the income tax, land-value-increment tax, and other relevant taxes to spur the recovery of the building industry.

D. Continue to offer tax credit to industry as an incentive for investment.

E. Liberalize raw materials imports to eliminate abuses of the tariff-rebate system and reduce tariff-rebate costs.

(2) Financial measures

A. Strengthen the roles of the Development Fund and all specialized banks in investment and financing

and ease restrictions on bank financing of building and home construction.

B. Continue the promotion of international banking and the timely adjustment of the central bank rediscount rate and deposit-and-loan rates of the banking industry to accelerate the liberalization of interest rates.

C. Gradually relax restrictions on export-import foreign exchange collections and payments and ease foreign exchange control.

(3) Foreign trade

A. Expand the role of the Export-Import Bank of China in export financing and the provision of export and exchange rate fluctuation insurance.

B. Streamline customs-clearance formalities and promote modernization of the customs reporting system.

(4) Assistance to small and medium enterprises

A. Strengthen the role of the Medium Business Bank of Taiwan as a specialized bank and provide more medium- and long-term development credits to small- and medium-size enterprises.

B. Promote the modernization and automation of production and encourage the merger of small and medium business enterprises.

C. Assist small and medium enterprises in setting up a sound accounting system and provide them with commercial information to improve their operations and management.

(5) Assistance to industry

A. Promote software technology of the information industry and upgrade the calibre of information software professionals.

B. Promote the development of industrial products with growth potential and cooperation with internationally recognized certification institutions, and establish a favorable international image for domestic brands.

C. Enforce "Good Manufacturing Practices (GMP)" and set up "Building and Equipment Standards for Food Processing Plants."

(6) Pollution prevention and control

A. Provide credit assistance and tax and other incentives to encourage the purchase of pollution control equipment.

B. Tighten pollution control measures at existing plants and step up inspections at newly built plants.

C. Encourage pollution-producing plants to move to industrial estates where common pollution control measures may be taken, and promote the establishment of effective pollution detection and monitoring systems.

D. Tighten the controls of poisonous chemicals and noise in mining areas.

(7) Technology

A. Step up international technological cooperation and transfer of key technologies, and encourage technological innovations and product development.

B. Promote the transfer and development of new technology to raise energy efficiency and prevent pollution.

C. Develop a basic ability to conduct research and development in materials science and technology, and establish an industrial technology information system.

(8) Promotion of investment

A. Adopt the "negative list" approach and ease restrictions on investment to encourage the flow of capital into industry.

B. Continue to improve investment services, simplify administrative procedures, offer incentives to private investment, and promote the liberalization and rationalization of investment.

C. Relax restrictions on overseas investment by domestic concerns.

D. Amend the Labor Standards Law to take into account the interests of both labor and management.

III SERVICES

The service sector is targeted to grow 7.5 percent a year on average during the plan period, with transportation and communications targeted to grow 10.9 percent annually, commerce 7.5 percent, financing and insurance 10.0 percent, and other services 6.0 percent.

I. Basic Policies

1. Strengthen laws and regulations governing the service sector to improve commercial discipline and safeguard the interests of the entire economy and society.

2. Introduce modern managerial know-how and techniques to raise the productivity of the service sector.

3. Proceed gradually with financial and trade liberalization.

4. Upgrade the capacity and quality of the service sector, with a view to meeting the increasing needs of both agricultural and industrial producers and consumers.

2. Supporting Measures

1. Amend existing laws and regulations to strengthen commercial and financial administrative machinery, streamline regulatory and supervisory systems, create an environment for fair competition, and set up codes for conduct of business.

2. Improve the operation and management of the transportation and communications industries and promote the integrated development of various types of transport.

3. Promote a more rational rate structure for the transportation and communications industries and establish comprehensive transportation and communications services networks.

4. Strengthen modern business education, promote the concept of marketing-oriented business management, create marketing profits, and raise the productivity of commerce.

5. Ease restrictions on foreign investment in financing, insurance, and leasing operations; gradually liberalize import and export controls and bank interest rates; and promote the internationalization of the service sector.

6. Strengthen the protection of intellectual property rights, maintain discipline in trade, and establish a favorable international image for Taiwan's exports.

7. Develop an intelligent software industry and promote the sound development of professional services and family and personal services, such as health and medical care, sanitation, security, tourism, and entertainment.

VI. EXTERNAL SECTOR

In order to cope with changes in international economic conditions and to achieve an average annual economic growth target of 6.5 percent during the plan period, the following growth targets for goods-and-services imports and exports have been set:

- Goods-and-services exports are targeted to grow at a real annual rate of 7.3 percent (goods exports 7.0 percent, services exports 11.1 percent). Goods-and-services exports at 1985 prices will reach US$43.40 billion in 1989, up from US$32.76 billion in 1985. (Goods exports will climb to US$40.12 billion from US$30.61 billion.)

- Goods-and-services imports are targeted to grow at a real rate of 10.1 percent annually on average (goods imports 10.4 percent, services imports 8.5 percent). Goods-and-services imports at 1985 prices will approach US$36.96 billion in 1989, up from US$25.19 billion in 1985. (Goods imports will rise from US$20.10 billion to US$29.90 billion.)

I BASIC POLICIES

1. Actively promote trade liberalization, speed up the upgrading of industries, and enhance the competitiveness of exports.

2. Improve the environment for trade development, strengthen the capability of developing foreign trade, work for greater diversification of foreign markets, and promote balanced development of trade.

3. Strengthen trade discipline and establish a favorable international image for Taiwan's exports.

4. Raise administrative efficiency in trade and strengthen the role of trade administration.

II DEVELOPMENT PRIORITIES AND SUPPORTING MEASURES

1. Actively Promote Trade Liberalization

1. Continue to lower import tariffs and liberalize import control.

2. Reestablish a regulatory system for imports and exports with a "negative list."

3. Streamline procedures for customs clearance and reporting system.

4. Cut down the number of trade goods subject to inspection and establish an "Inspectors Licensing System."

2. Improve the Composition of Foreign Trade

1. Promote the development of strategic and technology-intensive industries, introduce key technologies, and push the export of new products.

2. Expand the exports of package plants.

3. Improve the domestic environment for investment and relax restrictions on investment overseas.

3. Take Steps to Counteract Protectionism

1. Promote trade ties with other nations, on the basis of equality and reciprocity.

2. Set up a specialized agency responsible for coordinating international trade negotiations.

3. Establish trade order and improve the international image of Taiwan-made products.

4. Set up a worldwide trade information network and assist local traders in developing counter- and triangular-trade relations.

4. Promote Financial Liberalization and Internationalization

1. Relax foreign exchange controls and permit business concerns to retain part of their foreign exchange proceeds.

2. Promote the internationalization of banking operations.

3. Set up a set of clear guidelines for Central Bank intervention in foreign exchange markets.

Source: Council for Economic Planning and Development, *Highlights of Ninth Medium-Term Economic Development Plan for Taiwan, Republic of China (1986–1989)*, January 1986.

SUPPLEMENTARY READINGS

Economics

"And Now, the Home-Brewed Forecast." *Fortune*, January 20, 1986, pp. 53–54.

"Grossly Deceptive Product." *The Economist*, March 10, 1990, p. 71.

"Indicators of Market Size for 117 Countries." *Business International*, June 1988.

"In a Maze of Numbers." *The Economist*, August 20, 1988, pp. 61–62.

"Norway Leaps Ahead in Labor Costs League." *Business Europe*, May 30, 1988, pp. 1–2.

OECD Economic Outlook. Paris: OECD, June 1991.

"Pick a Number, Any Number." *International Management*, May 1988, pp. 45–46.

"The Hamburger Standard." *The Economist*, April 15, 1989, p. 86.

"Weaker Dollar Boosts Costs of Production in Europe." *Business International*, August 12, 1991, pp. 269–76.

Foreign Debt

"A Latin Debt Plan That Might Work." *Fortune*, April 29, 1989, pp. 205–12.

"Balance preliminar de la economia de America Latina y el Caribe 1991." *Notas sobre la economia y el desarrollo.* Santiago de Chile: CEPAL, December 1991.

"Can Third World Debtors Climb out of the Hole?" *U.S. News & World Report,* January 20, 1986, p. 12–15.

"Deals That Are Making a Dent in Third World Debt." *Business Week,* October 3, 1988, pp. 111–14.

"Issues in the Measurement of External Debt." *Finance & Development,* March 1990, pp. 14–16.

Kim, Chongyoul. "Multinational Banks and the Third World's Debt: Are They in the Same Boat?" *Issues in International Business,* Summer–Fall 1985, pp. 13–20.

"Latin America's New Currency." *The Economist,* October 29, 1988, pp. 87–88.

"LDC Debt Conversions—A Survey." *Prospects.* Basel: Swiss Bank Corporation, February–March 1989, pp. 1–5.

"Suddenly the Money Goes Home to Peru." *The Economist,* June 22, 1991, p. 33.

"The Real Choices Facing the Debtor Countries." *Prospects.* Basel: Swiss Bank Corporation, April–May 1990, pp. 1–5.

Inflation

"Brazil Back at the Brink." *The Economist,* January 7, 1989, pp. 18–19.

"Fear of Social Unrest Grows in Argentina as Economy Crumbles Ahead of Vote." *The Wall Street Journal,* April 29, 1989, p. A4.

"The Case for Hyperinflation." *The Economist,* May 13, 1989, p. 73.

National Plans

Peters, Tom. "A Case for Chaos." *U.S. News & World Report,* April 14, 1986, p. 54.

"Planning in a Market Economy." *Economic Review.* Taipei: Bank of China, January 1988, pp. 8–17.

Review of the Netherlands Economy. Amsterdam: Bank Mees & Hope NV, March–April 1988.

"The Six-Year National Development Plan for Taiwan, Republic of China (1991–1996)." *Economic Review.* Taipai: The International Commercial Bank of China, May–June 1991, pp. 10–23.

Socioeconomic

"An Aging Society Also Means Slower Growth in the Labor Force." *Japan Report,* January 1990, p. 4

"Deutschland, Deutschland, älter alle." *The Economist,* January 7, 1989, pp. 39–40.

"Further Evidence Japan's Society Is Aging." *Japan Reports,* November 1989, p. 6.

"Imported Youth." *The Economist,* December 3, 1988, p. 75.

"Population Policy: Country Experience." *Finance & Development,* September 1984, pp. 18–20.

"Squeezing In the Next Five Billion." *The Economist,* January 20, 1990, pp. 19–22.

"The Coming World Labor Shortage." *Fortune,* April 9, 1990, pp. 70–77.

"The Silvering of Japan." *The Economist,* October 7, 1989, pp. 81–82.

"White Goods' Makers Seek to Counter the Baby Bust." *The Wall Street Journal,* May 9, 1989, p. A23.

ENDNOTES

1. "And Now, the Home-Brewed Forecast," *Fortune,* January 20, 1986, pp. 53–54.

2. Many of these factors, of course, also affect the domestic firm, but the multinational firm is generally more vulnerable and usually must act more quickly.

3. If management for some reason is interested in a country as a possible site for investment, the same detailed information will be required as is required for an area where the firm is already involved.

4. An excellent bibliography, *International Bibliography, Information, Documentation (IBID),* is published quarterly by UNIPUB. It includes abstracts of publications and studies containing economic and demographic data.

5. You can make your own table for 34 countries by first getting the average hourly earnings in national currency from the U.S. Department of Labor, Bureau of Statistics, *Handbook of Labor Statistics.* However, the data in this publication lag considerably, so you then go to the latest issue of *International Financial Statistics,* published monthly by the IMF. Here, for each country listed in the *Handbook,* you can find a very recent index of average hourly costs. Multiplying a ratio of the IMF's index values by the latest value in national currency in the *Handbook,* you can derive more recent values in local currency. Then you go back to the IMF publication and select the average exchange rates for the years you are comparing and convert national currencies to dollars. You will find differ-

ences between *Business Europe's* figures and the results you obtain by this method. We're not sure why, but obviously *Business Europe* either used different exchange rates or obtained different values expressed in national currency (probably the exchange rates). This illustrates the problem in expressing any national statistic in dollars.

6. "How the Debt Crisis Is Battering Multinationals," *Businessweek,* July 25, 1983, p. 52.

7. "A Latin Debt Plan That Might Work," *Fortune,* April 29, 1989, p. 205.

8. "Latin America's New Currency," *The Economist,* October 29, 1988, p. 87.

9. Developed nations are not immune, either. France, the Netherlands, and Belgium have faced this problem.

10. *World Development Report, 1991* (Washington, D.C.: World Bank, 1991), pp. 256–57.

11. "Whirlpool Jumps into the Global Market," *The European,* November 1–3, 1991, p. 25; "Planning for Global Expansion at Whirlpool," *Business International,* April 15, 1991; and "Whirlpool Is Gathering a Global Momentum," *The New York Times,* April 23, 1989, p. 10.

12. "Population Policy: Country Experience," *Finance & Development,* September 1984, pp. 18–19.

13. "The Coming World Labor Shortage," *Fortune,* April 1990, pp. 72–74.

14. "The Dwindling Japanese," *The Economist,* January 26, 1991, p. 36.

15. "Motherhood and the Future of Japan," *U.S. News & World Report,* December 24, 1990, p. 57.

16. "The Silvering of Japan," *The Economist,* October, 7, 1989, p. 81.

17. "The Coming World Labor Shortage," p. 72.

18. "An Aging Society Also Means Slower Growth in the Labor Force," *Japan Report* (New York: Japanese Consulate General, January 1990), p. 4.

19. "Pensions after 2000," *The Economist,* May 19, 1984, pp. 59–62; and "The Case for More Immigrants," *U.S. News & World Report,* February 13, 1989, p. 29.

20. "The Economies of the 1990s," *Fortune,* February 2, 1987, p. 24.

21. *World Development Report, 1991,* pp. 204–5.

22. Ibid., pp. 264–65.

23. "Airing the Ethnic Message," *Canada Reports,* Fall 1987, p. 11.

24. Council for Economic Planning and Development, *Highlights of Ninth Medium-Term Economic Development Plan for Taiwan, Republic of China (1986–1989),* January 1986, pp. 41–42.

Chapter 8

Physical Forces

If you do this . . .

Look at a map of the world, as large a map as possible. At first sight, it seems to be a maze of lines, colors, and unfamiliar names. Go on looking and studying until the mere mention of a town, country, or river enables it to be picked out immediately on the map. Those who are concerned with overseas marketing must, as a basis, know their export geography as well as the streets around their home.

Henry Deschampneufs, *Selling Overseas* (London: Business Publications, 1960), p. 46.

You won't be told this . . .

Middle East consultant, piqued by his clients' ignorance of the region, begins his briefings by saying, "Iraq isn't the past tense of Iran."

The Wall Street Journal, July 5, 1985, p. 32.

LEARNING OBJECTIVES

In this chapter, you will study:

1. The importance of a country's location in political and trade relationships.

2. How surface features contribute to economic, cultural, political, and social differences among nations and among regions of a single country.

3. The importance of inland waterways and outlets to the sea.

4. How climate exerts a broad influence on business.

5. Why managers must monitor changes in the discovery and use of mineral resources and energy sources.

6. Why managers must be alert to changes in a nation's infrastructure.

7. The impact of industrial disasters, such as the Bhopal accident, the Alaska oil spill, and the Rhine River spill, on global and multinational firms.

KEY WORDS AND CONCEPTS

- Topography
- Canadian Shield
- Rhine waterway
- Climate
- Natural resources
- Shale
- Polymetallic deposits

BUSINESS INCIDENT

Watches, lace, carvings, chocolate, cheese, precision machinery, pharmaceuticals—what do they have in common? All are produced in Switzerland, all have a high value per kilo, the Swiss versions are known for their quality, and the physical forces are primarily responsible for their being produced in Switzerland.

To appreciate why this is so, review the following about the physical forces in Switzerland:

1. Switzerland is mostly mountainous; there is little level land.
2. Switzerland is close to the heavily populated lowlands of Western Europe.
3. Transportation across the mountains to these markets is relatively expensive.
4. Switzerland has practically no mineral resources.

One way to overcome the lack of local sources of raw materials and high transportation costs is to import small amounts of raw materials, add high value to them, and export a lightweight finished product. The Swiss have done precisely this with the manufacture of watches. They import small volumes of high-quality Swedish steel costing 40 cents per ounce that they then convert to watch movements selling for $60 per ounce. Because of their light weight, the cost of transporting these movements to market is minimal. Precision machinery and pharmaceuticals are other products that minimize the need for importing bulky raw materials. For all of these products, emphasis is placed on the value added by manufacturing, which is based on skill, care, and tradition.

Although the Swiss slopes do not support much agriculture, they are adequate for raising cattle and goats. Production of milk is no problem, but getting it to its major markets outside Switzerland is. Fluid milk is bulky in relation to its value and expensive to transport. The dairymen do to the milk what the watchmakers do to the

BUSINESS INCIDENT (concluded)

steel—convert it to a concentrated, high-value product: cheese. Because Swiss cheesemakers have no advantage over their counterparts in the lowland dairying areas nearer to the important markets, they have to compete on the basis of high quality and reputation, which they have carefully promoted.

The plentiful supply of milk is responsible for another product: milk chocolate. The Swiss import the raw chocolate and convert the milk into another high-value-per-kilo product. Certainly the Swiss manufacturer pays higher transportation costs to bring sugar and chocolate in and ship the finished product out than does Hershey in Pennsylvania. Again, their product must be perceived to be

superior so that it will bring a higher price to offset the greater costs.

What about the lace and carvings? The physical forces are responsible for these also. The heavy snowfall and cold temperatures of the Swiss winter leave the dairymen and their wives with little to do. About the only work necessary is feeding the animals with stored hay. To help pass the time and earn some money, Swiss women make lace and embroidery while the men carve figures and cuckoo clocks.

Source: Adapted from Rhoads Murphey, *The Scope of Geography*, 2nd ed. (Skokie, Ill.: Rand McNally, 1973), pp. 65–67.

The Business Incident illustrates what one writer meant when he wrote that "the physical character of a nation is perhaps the principal and broadest determinant of both the society found there and the means by which that society undertakes to supply its needs."[1]

Strictly speaking, the physical elements are not forces because, except for natural disasters (such as earthquakes, floods, and hurricanes), they are passive. However, there are similarities between them and the uncontrollable forces we describe in this section: their effects are not constant, and although they have a profound impact on the way people organize their activities, the physical forces are only one set of the many factors that influence humanity. In fact, cultural, political, and economic factors may be more important than the physical factors in determining land use and the nature of the economy. How else can you explain the great differences between southeast China and the U.S. Southeast? Their physical environments are very similar, but they support different people with wide divergencies in their cultures and land use.

Probably the most important reason for considering the physical elements as uncontrollable forces is that they have many aspects of the foreign environmental forces we discussed in Chapter 1. Also, as we shall illustrate, managers must adjust their strategies to compensate for differences among markets of the physical forces just as they do for the other uncontrollable forces.

Although the scope of geography is extremely broad, it is possible to select some elements that are particularly significant for the businessperson: (1) location, (2) topography, (3) climate, and (4) natural resources.

LOCATION

Where a country is located, who its neighbors are, and what its capital and major cities are should be part of the general knowledge of all international businesspeople. Location is important because it is a factor in explaining a number of a nation's political and trade relationships, many of which directly affect a company's operations.

◻ Political Relationships

At the height of the cold war, the location of Austria enabled that country to be a political bridge between the noncommunist nations of the West and the communist nations of the East. It is bounded on the west by Germany, Italy, and Switzerland and on the east by Czechoslovakia, Hungary, and Yugoslavia. In addition Austria's political neutrality made it a popular location for the offices of international firms servicing Eastern European operations.

Now with the political and economic changes that have been occurring in both Western and Eastern Europe, Austria wants to take advantage of its location to (1) strengthen its political role and (2) become the principal financial intermediary between the two regions. Already, the planned merger between the nation's third- and fourth-largest banks has been announced, and further mergers are expected. Politically, Austria is working to strengthen commercial ties with the former communist nations on its borders, Hungary and Czechoslovakia, while also trying to move from its current membership in EFTA to become a full EC member for which it applied in 1990. The EC, however, will not consider further expansion until 1993.[2]

Finland is another country whose location has shaped its political relationships. For years, Finland, which shared a 780-mile common border with the Soviet Union, thrived on a balancing act it did between that country and Western Europe. It was the only nation in the world that was at the same time a member of the Soviet trading bloc, COMECON, and the European Free Trade Association. However, with the Soviet collapse came the loss of an important market. In 1985, the Soviets bought 21.5 percent of Finland's exports, but in 1991, the amount was about 5 percent. This and the Finnish recession are causing businesspeople to want their country to join the European Community. The government plans to apply for membership by 1993.[3]

◻ Trade Relationships

Geographical proximity is often the major reason for trade between nations. As you saw in Chapter 2, the largest and the fourth-largest trading partners of the United States—Canada and Mexico—lie on its borders. Deliveries are faster, freight costs are lower, and it is less expensive for sellers to service their clients. This is also one of the reasons why so many American firms have plants on the Mexican side of the common border. Geographic proximity has always been a major factor in the formation of trading groups, such as the EC, EFTA, and now the agreement for the U.S.–Canada Free Trade Association, which was formed in 1989. Discussions between Canada, Mexico, and the United States are under way with the goal of bringing Mexico into what would then be known as the North American Free Trade Agreement.[4]

Nearness to the market is also why Japan's sales to the Association of Southeast Asian Nations (ASEAN), the Southeast Asian trade group, are 40 percent higher than U.S. sales and 75 percent greater than sales of the European Community, a still more distant supplier.[5] Because it is closer to Japan,

China has been able to take over part of the sales of soybeans and wheat formerly supplied by the United States.

Did you ever stop to think where the fresh grapes and raspberries that you eat in the dead of winter come from? Probably not, until cyanide poison was found in two grapes imported from Chile in 1989. Interestingly, Chile's sales of $700 million annually are possible for just the opposite reason that we have been discussing—its U.S. market is geographically distant.

TOPOGRAPHY

topography the surface features of a region

Surface features such as mountains, plains, deserts, and bodies of water contribute to differences in economies, cultures, politics, and social structures, both among nations and among regions of a single country. Physical distribution is aided by some features but hindered by others. Differences in **topography** may require products to be altered. For example, the effects of altitude on food products begin to be seen at heights above 3,000 feet (producers of cake mixes must change their baking instructions); and internal combustion engines begin to noticeably lose power at 5,000 feet, which may require the manufacturer of gasoline-powered machinery to use larger engines.

Let us examine some of the principal surface features to give you an idea of what the businessperson should look for.

□ Mountains and Plains

Mountains are barriers that tend to separate and impede exchange and interaction, whereas level areas (plains and plateaus) facilitate them. The extent to which mountains serve as barriers depends on their height, breadth, length, ruggedness of terrain, and whether there are any transecting valleys.

An example of such a barrier is the Himalaya Mountains. Travel across them is so difficult that transportation between India and China has been by air or sea rather than overland. The contrast between the cultures of the Indo-Malayan people living to the south of the mountains and the Chinese living to the north is evidence of the Himalayas' effectiveness as a barrier. In similar fashion, the Alps, Carpathians, Balkans, and Pyrenees have long separated the Mediterranean cultures from those of northern Europe.

Mountains divide markets. A greater problem for the businessperson is posed by those nations that are divided by mountain ranges into smaller regional markets, each with its own distinctive industries, climate, culture, dialect, and sometimes even language. Such is the case of Spain, where there are five separate regions. The cultural differences of two of them, Catalonia and the Basque country, are so great that they have separate languages, not dialects, and each has a sizable group that wishes to secede from Spain to form a separate nation. Although the Basques and the Catalans can speak Spanish, when they are among themselves they use their own languages, which are completely unintelligible to other Spaniards in both commerce and the home. This creates the same kind of problems found wherever there are language differences: Spanish-speaking managers do not attain the empathy with their local employees that they do in other parts of Spain, and sales representatives who speak the local language are more effective.[6] Moreover, the language

□ **FIGURE 8–1   The Cantons and Major Language Areas of Switzerland**

differences increase promotional costs if, to be more effective, Spanish companies choose to prepare their material in Basque, Catalan, and Spanish.

Political unrest is prevalent among the Basques on the northern Spanish–French border and, to a lesser extent, among the Catalans on the southern Spanish–French border. Like the IRA in Northern Ireland, separatist terrorists from both groups frequently attack and kill government officials and the police. All three groups are said to receive training and financial support from Gadhafi in Libya.[7]

In 1979, a majority of Basque voters chose greater autonomy, but not total separation, from Spain, and for a while, the killings stopped. However, in 1989, a terrorist group known as the ETA renewed its terrorism.

Switzerland is another country that is separated into distinctive cultural regions by mountains. In a country one half the size of Maine, four different languages and 35 different dialects are spoken—Italian, French, German, and Romansh (see Figure 8–1). To the consternation of the advertising manager attempting to reach all regions of the country, each of the three major language groups has its own radio and television network, and the fourth, Romansh (Latin), is also used by the German stations.

Source: Reproduced by permission of the World Bank.

☐ **FIGURE 8–2**
Map of Colombia

Three ranges of the Andes divide Colombia from north to south into four separate markets, each with its own culture and dialect (see Figure 8–2). Depending on the product, this could require the creation of four distinctive promotional mixes.

Moreover, not only are the cultures different, but so are the climates. Because of its location near the equator, Colombia has no seasons but does experience a variety of climates due to the great differences in altitude. These range from hot and humid at sea level (mean average temperature of 82 degrees in Baranquilla) to cold and dry in the 10,000-foot-high snow-capped mountains (57 degrees in Bogota). Imagine the production and inventory problems that such differences occasion for the manufacturer that must supply a distinct product and package for each zone.[8]

Because these climatic conditions are not peculiar to Colombia, market analysts should examine topographical maps to see which tropical countries possess this combination of lowlands and mountains. If the firm's products will not function properly in such climatic extremes, either they must be redesigned or the company must bypass this market.

Population concentration.   Mountains also create concentrations of population either because the climate is more pleasant at higher altitudes or because they are barriers to population movement. For example, nearly 80 percent of Colombia's population is located in the western highlands (only one third of the nation's area) because the climate there is moderate. Eighty percent of Brazil's 140 million people inhabit a 300-mile-wide coastal strip separated from the remainder of the country by a mountain range. Except in the tropics, the population density generally decreases as the elevation increases. If you were to place a population map over a topographic map, the blank areas on the population map would generally coincide with the areas of higher elevation. For example, 90 percent of Switzerland's population is located in a narrow belt at the base of the Alps. The reason for this is that dense population requires commerce, manufacturing, and agriculture, which all depend on the good transportation and ease of communication afforded by the plains.

◻ Deserts and Tropical Forests

Deserts and tropical forests, like mountains, separate markets, increase the cost of transportation, and create concentrations of population.

Deserts.   Over one third of the earth's surface consists of arid and semiarid regions located either on the coasts where the winds blow away from the land or in the interior where mountains or long distances cause the winds to lose their moisture before reaching these regions. Every continent has them, and every west coast between 20 and 30 degrees north or south of the equator is dry. Since people, plants, and animals must have water to exist, the climatic and vegetational deserts are also the human deserts. Only where there is a major source of water, as in Egypt, is there a concentration of population.

Nowhere is the relationship between water supply and population concentration better illustrated than in Australia, a continent the size of the continental United States but with only 16 million inhabitants. Its surrounding coastline is humid and fertile, whereas the huge center of the country is mainly a desert closely resembling the Sahara (see Figure 8–3).

Because of its geography, the population has tended to concentrate (1) along the coastal areas in and around the state capitals, which are also major seaports, and (2) in the southeastern fifth of the nation, where more than one half of the population lives. This gives Australia one of the highest percentages of urban population in the world. The 86 percent of the total population

☐ **FIGURE 8–3   Map of Australia**

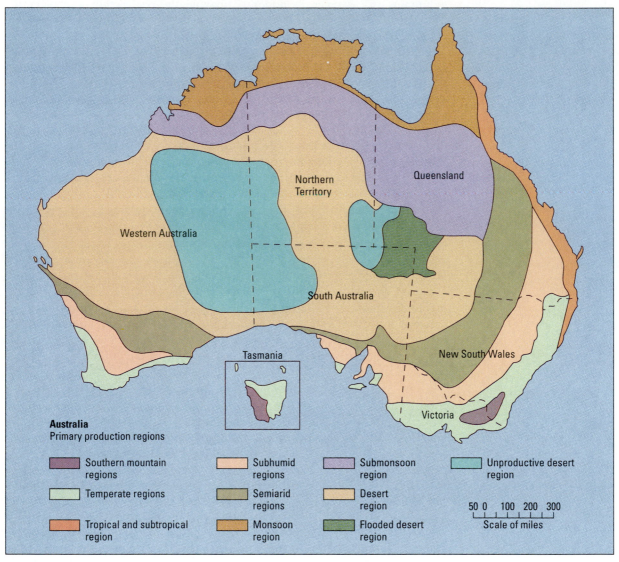

Australia
Primary production regions

Southern mountain regions	Subhumid regions	Submonsoon region	Unproductive desert region
Temperate regions	Semiarid regions	Desert region	
Tropical and subtropical region	Monsoon region	Flooded desert region	

50 0   100 200 300
Scale of miles

Courtesy Australian Information Service.

living in cities is surpassed only by Belgium (97 percent), Kuwait (95 percent), Israel (91 percent), the United Kingdom (89 percent), the Netherlands (89 percent), and Denmark (87 percent).[9]

The distances between these cities and the fact that they are seaports make coastal shipping preferred over road and rail transportation.[10] However, these long distances between major markets result in transportation accounting for as much as 30 percent of the final cost of the product, as compared with the more usual 10 percent in the United States and Europe.

The population distribution also has a profound impact on Australia's media. First of all, there are only three upper-socioeconomic-group newspapers and a few magazines that can be considered national media. All other media are concentrated in capital city areas. This requires advertisers to buy space or time on a state-by-state or city-by-city basis. Although most capital city areas have three commercial TV channels, there is little networking.

Even though 70 percent of the country is arid or semiarid, some areas in the northern rim receive up to 100 inches of rainfall annually, much like the monsoon areas of India. Thus the firm entering the Australian market faces the same extreme differences of temperature and humidity encountered in Colombia.

Were it not for the uniform topography of Australia, the temperature differences would be even greater, as they are in countries with large, hot desert areas and irregular surfaces. Iran is such a nation. In the summer, temperatures may reach 130°F, whereas winter temperatures in high altitudes may drop to −18°F. From December to March, it is possible to ski just an hour-and-a-half's drive from Teheran, the capital. Like Australia, Iran's population distribution is heavily influenced by climate and topography. More than 70 percent of the country—consisting mostly of mountains and deserts—is uninhabited, and one half of the population lives in urban areas.

Tropical rain forests. Vegetation can be an effective barrier to economic development and human settlement, especially when it is combined with harsh climate and poor soil. This occurs in the world's tropical rain forests located in the Amazon basin, Southeast Asia, and the Congo. Except in parts of West Africa and Java, they are thinly populated and little developed economically. For example, the greatest rain forest of them all—in the Brazilian Amazon—has been called one of the world's greatest deserts because of its low population density. Although it covers more than 1 million square miles (one fourth of the U.S. land area) and occupies one half of Brazil, it is inhabited by just 4 percent of the country's population. Only true deserts have a population density lower than the Amazon's one person per square mile.

Canadian Shield a massive area of bedrock covering one half of Canada's land mass

Canadian Shield. Although the **Canadian Shield** is neither a desert nor a tropical forest, this massive area of bedrock covering one half of Canada's land mass has most of their characteristics—forbidding topography, poor soil, and harsh climate. The Shield is swept by polar air, which permits a frost-free growing season of only four months. During that time, residents are molested by swarms of black flies and mosquitoes. Like deserts and tropical forests, its population density is very low: only 10 percent of Canada's population inhabits the region.

Relevance for businesspeople. Managers know that in more densely populated nations, it costs less to market their products (population centers are closer, and communication systems are better), more people are available for employment, and so forth. Therefore, when they compare population densities such as Canada's 2.6 inhabitants per square kilometer, Australia's 2.2, and Brazil's 17.3 with the Netherlands' 400 or Japan's 327, they may draw the wrong conclusions. However, if they are aware that the population in each of the first three countries is highly concentrated in a relatively small area for the reasons we have been examining, then a very different situation prevails. Notice in the next section how bodies of water also are responsible for concentrations of population.

H. Armstrong Roberts

Although located deep inland, Basel, Switzerland, is a major port for ocean freight.

◻ Bodies of Water

This surface feature, unlike mountains, deserts, and tropical forests, attracts people and facilitates transportation. A world population map clearly shows that nearly all bodies of water have attracted more people than have the surrounding areas. Those densely populated regions that do not coincide with rivers or lakes are generally close to the sea. You would note from the map that populations cluster around the Amazon, the Congo, the Mississippi, the St. Lawrence, and the Great Lakes. In Europe, the plain of the Po (Italy) and the Rhine are easily recognizable. So are rivers that cross deserts, such as the Nile, the Indus (Pakistan), the Tigris-Euphrates (Iraq), and the Amu Darya in Russian Central Asia, although these are more important for the irrigation water and fertile soil they bring than for transportation.[11]

However, bodies of water that are significant because of their ability to provide inexpensive access to markets in the interior of various nations are the inland waterways.

Inland waterways.   Before the construction of railways, water transport was the only economically practical carrier for bulk goods moving over long distances. Water transport has increased even after the building of railroads, although its importance relative to railroads has diminished everywhere with one exception—the Rhine waterway, the world's most important inland waterway system.

Rhine waterway a system of rivers and canals, the main transportation artery of Europe

Rhine waterway.   The **Rhine waterway,** the main transportation artery of Europe, carries a greater volume of goods than the combined railways that run parallel to it. As an illustration of the Rhine's significance, one half of Switzerland's exports and nearly three fourths of its imports pass through

□ **FIGURE 8–4**
Europe's Major Inland Waterways

Source: Waterways map provided by the European Conference of Ministers of Transport, 1989.

Basel, the Swiss inland port. This cargo is carried on the country's own 31-vessel oceangoing fleet via the Rhine waterway to Rotterdam, 500 miles to the north (see Figure 8–4).

For years, shipments have moved between the Netherlands, Belgium, Germany, France, Austria, and Switzerland by means of the Rhine and its connecting waterways; but the new Rhine–Main–Danube canal gives access to the Atlantic Ocean, 13 countries, and the Black Sea. From there, shipments can continue to Moscow over the interconnected system of the Volga and Don rivers. While it is unlikely that many ships will undertake the entire 30-

day voyage from Rotterdam to the Black Sea (3,500 kilometers), the completed waterway will stimulate shipping over shorter East–West routes, such as Nuremburg to Budapest or Vienna to Rotterdam.[12] See the Worldview on page 269 for additional information on the new waterway.

Other waterways.   In every continent except Australia, which has no inland waterways, extensive use is made of water transportation. In South America, the Amazon and its tributaries offer some 57,000 kilometers of navigable waterways during the flood season. Oceangoing vessels can reach Manaus, Brazil (1,600 kilometers upstream), and smaller river steamers can go all the way to Iquitos, Peru (3,600 kilometers from the Atlantic).

Based on economic value, the most important South American river system is the Paraná. Ocean freighters travel from the Rio de la Plata near Buenos Aires to Santa Fe, Argentina (240 kilometers upstream), and riverboats bring cargo 1,360 kilometers to Asunción, the capital of the landlocked nation of Paraguay.

The five nations of the River Plate Basin have announced they will finance development of the Paraná–Paraguay Waterway that will connect parts of Argentina, Brazil, Paraguay, and Uruguay—members of Mercosur (the Southern Cone common market)—and Bolivia. The waterway is expected to spur the industrialization of Paraguay, the northeastern provinces of Argentina, and two underdeveloped Brazilian states as well as provide a new outlet to the sea for Bolivia.[13]

In Asia, the major waterways are the Yangtze (China), the Ganges (India), and the Indus (Pakistan). Rivers are especially important in China because water is the least expensive, and often only, means of moving industrial raw materials to the manufacturing centers. Oceangoing vessels can travel up the Yangtze as far as Wuhan, 1,000 kilometers from the sea. This river and its tributaries form the densest waterway system in the world, with over 30,000 kilometers usable by steamships, launches, or junks.

Although the United States possesses extensive rail and highway systems, it also depends heavily on two waterways. One, the Great Lakes–St. Lawrence, enables ocean freighters to travel 3,700 kilometers inland, thus transforming lake ports into ocean ports. The other waterway, the Mississippi, connects the Great Lakes to the Gulf of Mexico and is especially important for carrying bulky commodities, such as wheat, cotton, coal, timber, and iron ore.

Outlets to the sea.   Historically, navigable waterways with connections to the ocean have permitted the low-cost transportation of goods and people from a country's coast to its interior and even now are the only means of access from the coasts of numerous developing nations.

This has been a particularly troublesome problem for Africa, in which 14 of the world's 20 landlocked developing countries are located. Almost one third of all sub-Saharan countries are landlocked, and some are more than 1,000 kilometers from the sea by the shortest land route. The implications for these poor nations are obvious: they must construct costly, long truck routes and extensive feeder networks for relatively low volumes of traffic. Furthermore, governments in countries with coastlines through which the imports and exports of the landlocked nations must pass are in a position to exert considerable political influence. Small wonder that struggles for outlets to the sea still exist and are an important factor in the political as well as economic forces.

One outstanding example is the century-long struggle by Bolivia to regain from Chile an outlet to the Pacific Ocean. These countries have held discussions for decades, but they have not reached a workable agreement. Until Bolivia has its own coastline, it must use Arica, the free port in northern Chile, and inland waterways. The lack of a satisfactory solution continues to be a source of tension between the two governments.[14]

Farther south, two of the giants of South America, Brazil and Argentina, have been using Paraguay's need for an outlet to the Atlantic to further their ambitions to be the leader of South America. For years, Paraguay's only connection to the ocean was through the port of Buenos Aires. Brazil, observing that Paraguay was experiencing difficulty with the Argentine government over the right to use that nation's waterways, erected the Friendship Bridge on the Paraguay–Brazil border and completely paved a highway linking Paraguay with the Brazilian port of Paranagua. To further facilitate the movement of Paraguayan goods, the port was declared a free zone only for Paraguay. This has led to numerous cooperative ventures between the two countries, and it appears that Paraguay is now solidly in Brazil's area of influence. Important to international businesspeople is the knowledge that closer political ties bring closer economic ties, which alter traditional trading patterns. That certainly has been the case in this instance.[15]

CLIMATE

climate meteorological conditions, including temperature, precipitation, and wind, that prevail in a region

Climate (temperature and precipitation) is probably the most important element of the physical forces because it, more than any other factor, sets the limits on what people can do both physically and economically. Where the climate is harsh, there are few human settlements, but where it is permissive, generally there are great clusters of population. However, climate is not deterministic—it allows certain developments to occur, but it does not cause them. Nonclimatic factors, such as mineral deposits, accessibility to an area, economic and political organizations, cultural tradition, availability of capital, and the growth of technology, are more important than climate in the development of trade and manufacturing.[16]

Similar climates occur in similar latitudes and continental positions, and the more water-dominated an area, the more moderate its climate. Thus, the northwest United States and northwest Europe, which are at similar latitudes and are both influenced by the sea, have mild, moist climates. Southeast Australia, New Zealand, and part of South Africa are at the same latitude and are close to the sea. They too have mild, moist climates. At the other extreme, Kansas and Central Asia, which are both far from the sea and at the same latitude, are dry and have cold winters and hot summers.

◻ Climate and Development

For centuries, writers have used climatic differences to explain differences in human and economic development. They have suggested that the greatest economic and intellectual development has occurred in the temperate climates of northern Europe and the United States because the less temperate climates limit human energy and mental powers.[17] The map in Figure 8–5 seems to support this thesis. However, marketers must not be taken in by this

□ **FIGURE 8–5   Impact of Climate on Economic Development**

Source: Andrew M. Kamarack, *The Tropics and Economic Development* (Baltimore: Johns Hopkins University Press, 1976), pp. 6–7. Copyright © 1976 by the International Bank for Reconstruction and Development/The World Bank.

ethnocentric reasoning, which fails to explain the difference in the level of technology employed in the 1600s by the inhabitants of northeastern North America and the inhabitants of northern Europe. Clearly there were other factors involved, such as the Industrial Revolution, population size, and location.

This is not to say that climate has not had some influence on economic development. Studies by the World Bank have shown that many of the factors responsible for the underdeveloped state of most tropical nations are present because of the tropical climate. Continuous heat and the lack of winter temperatures to constrain the reproduction and growth of weeds, insects, viruses, birds, and parasites result in destroyed crops, dead cattle, and people infected with debilitating diseases.[18]

As grim as this may sound, there is hope. The World Bank points out that techniques are becoming available to control pests and parasites. Once this is accomplished, the very characteristics that are now detrimental to tropical Africa will give it sizable advantages over the temperate zones in agriculture. The resulting income would create a market in tropical Africa that could easily surpass that of the Middle East at the time oil prices were at their highest.

□ Climatic Implications for Businesspeople

The differences in climatic conditions among a firm's markets can have a significant impact on its product mix. For example, internal combustion engines designed for temperate climates generally require extra cooling capacity and special lubrication to withstand the higher temperatures of the tropics. Goods that deteriorate in high humidity require special, more expensive packaging,

WORLDVIEW
Rhine–Main–Danube Canal

To many Europeans, the Rhine–Main–Danube canal is the greatest engineering feat ever, greater even than the unfinished tunnel under the English channel. Completed in 1992, this canal links Europe's two great rivers, the Rhine and the Danube, enabling ships to travel 4,400 kilometers across the heart of Europe between Rotterdam and Romania's Black Sea ports. One engineering accomplishment is a lock on the canal that can lift oceangoing ships 600 feet so they can cross a range of mountains which lies between the Rhine's main tributary, the Main River, and the Danube.

Countries as far away as Turkey and the new republics of Georgia and Ukraine want the Danube to be their highway to Europe. When plans were first drawn up for the canal, planners estimated that it would move 4 million tons of cargo annually, but since the fall of the communist governments of Eastern Europe, estimates have been raised to 10 million tons per year. The neglected infrastructure of countries such as Hungary, Bulgaria, and Romania is hindering the development of new markets for their products. Roads and railways will take a decade or more to build, but the opening of the canal connecting the Rhine to the Danube has permitted these countries to send their goods immediately to the rich markets of northern Europe.

The economic benefits are substantial. "Roll-on, roll-off" ports in river cities such as Passau and Strasbourg will enable inland ports to operate the same way ocean container ports operate. A large barge can carry 60 truck trailers for about 30 percent of the cost of hauling the freight by rail and only 15 percent of what motor carriers charge.

Source: "Artery That Will Restore Lifeblood of a Continent," *The European*, November 22–24, 1991, p. 13.

---

machinery operating in dusty conditions needs special dust protection, and so forth.

When climatic extremes exist in a single market and the product is temperature- or humidity-sensitive, the company may have to produce and stock two distinct versions to satisfy the entire market. Severe winters, such as those in Canada, or the heavy monsoon rains that fall in northern Australia and India can impede distribution. This may require the firm to carry extraordinarily large inventories in its major markets to compensate for delays in delivery from the factory. All of these conditions, of course, have an adverse effect on profitability.

NATURAL RESOURCES

natural resources anything supplied by nature on which people depend

What are **natural resources?** There is no commonly accepted definition among the professionals who work with them. One well-known economic geographer, Professor Joseph H. Butler, states, "To meet their economic needs—including the basic ecological requirements of water, food, clothing, and shelter—people undertake the production of goods and services by extracting *natural resources* from the environment." He adds that all three sectors of the natural environment provide raw materials: the solid portion of the earth, the water portion, and the atmosphere.[19] For our purposes, we can define natural resources as anything supplied by nature on which people depend.

Until fairly recently, business managers' and government officials' main concern about natural resources has been the supply of exhaustible minerals and mineral fuels, certainly an immediate and pressing problem. During the Arab–Israeli war in 1973, we saw how Arab exporters of petroleum used an oil embargo on some nations and the threat of an embargo on other nations to obtain political support from Western Europe. The realization by oil-importing nations that not only their industries but also their national defense depended on a substance other nations could use as a political force initiated a worldwide campaign to conserve minerals and mineral fuels and to search for new energy sources.

◻ Alternative Energy Sources

Oil sands and shale. One potential energy source is the tar sands of Athabasca, Canada, which contain bitumen, a tarlike crude. Instead of being pumped from wells, bitumen is strip-mined and sent to a separation plant, where it is converted into a higher-quality synthetic crude oil. Although this crude is more costly to produce than conventional crude, after OPEC quadrupled its prices in 1974, a Sun Oil plant at Athabasca, which began production in 1967, suddenly became profitable.

The subsequent decline in world prices made the future of synthetic oil production uncertain, but the lack of discoveries of conventional crude to replace Canada's depleting reserves motivated the Canadian government to offer new tax incentives to bitumen producers. As a result, the Sun Oil plant now produces 49,000 barrels of synthetic crude daily and a Canadian Exxon plant's daily output is at 39,000 barrels.[20] These are two examples of a number of oil and gas companies that are processing bitumin. In 1990, 29 percent of all crude produced in Canada was heavy grade, and this figure is expected to rise to 39 percent by 2010. The oil companies are turning to the plentiful heavy oil as they see production of light crude dropping in their major oil fields.[21]

The United States has an equal amount of oil that is known to be recoverable from **shale** in Colorado, Utah, and Wyoming. However, the recovery process is also expensive, which makes the end product unable to compete with today's prices of conventional crude. In addition, there are environmental problems connected with the disposition of huge quantities of waste shale. So far, Union Oil is the only company to have built a recovery plant, with a daily production of 6,000 barrels.[22] The total U.S. shale oil reserves are estimated to be 600 billion barrels—more than all of OPEC's total proven reserves.

Crude from coal. A promising source of synthetic oil and gas is coal gasification. South Africa, concerned about being shut off from crude oil imports for political reasons, has built three Sasol plants; these supply a large portion of its oil and gas needs from low-grade coal, which is in plentiful supply. A coal gasification plant built in North Dakota with South Africa's help will produce enough gas to heat a quarter of a million homes. At present, a consortium operates a 1,000-ton-per-day plant in California.[23]

New finds. Spurred by the high oil prices of the 1970s, which required oil-importing nations to divert huge sums of foreign exchange to pay for their oil imports, many governments opened their countries to oil exploration by for-

shale a fissile rock (capable of being split) composed of laminated layers of claylike, fine-grained sediment

☐ **FIGURE 8-6   Energy Sources in Major Industrial Countries**

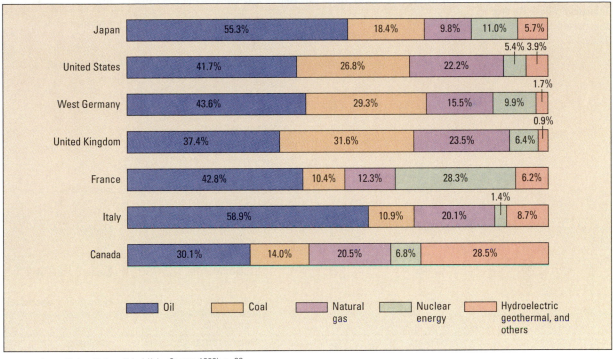

Source: *Japan Update* (Tokyo: Keizai Koho Center, 1990), p. 26.

eign firms. In just a few years, new oil finds were made in the Middle East, Africa, Asia, and Latin America. Nations that are either approaching self-sufficiency in oil or have even begun to export it include Egypt, Syria, Oman, Tunisia, Malaysia, Zaire, Angola, Congo, Benin, Cameroon, India, Australia, Argentina, Peru, Brazil, and Colombia.[24]

Renewable sources of energy.   There are at least seven renewable sources of energy: hydroelectric, solar, wind, geothermal, waves, tides, and OTEC (ocean thermal energy conversion), which can be used where there is a sufficient temperature difference between the warm surface water and deeper cold water. None is universal, but all seem to have an application under appropriate conditions. Of the seven, only hydroelectric power has had extensive application—nearly 4 percent of the total energy consumed in the United States is hydroelectric. Solar panels successfully provide heating for both industrial and home installations, and the photovoltaic cell, such as is used in solar calculators, is providing electric power. Figure 8–6 shows the sources of energy for some major industrial countries.

As the cost of producing the photovoltaic cell is reduced and its generating capacity is increased, it will find more applications, including transportation. British Solar, a subsidiary of British Petroleum, claims to be one of the world's leading suppliers of photovoltaic power systems, and Mobil Oil says that it makes the world's largest and most powerful solar panels in addition to doing research on photovoltaic cells.[25] The wind generation of electricity has gained popularity in parts of Europe but has not yet become economically viable in the United States. The other methods mentioned for generating energy are still in the pilot-plant stage.

□ **TABLE 8–1**

Major World Sources of Industrial Minerals that the United States Must Import

Mineral	Percentage of Consumption Imported	Distribution of Reserves (percent of world total)	Use
Aluminum	97%	Guinea (27), Australia (21), Brazil (11), Jamaica (9), India (5)	Aluminum products
Chromium	75	South Africa (78), U.S.S.R. (12), Zimbabwe (2), Finland (2), Philippines (1)	Stainless steel
Cobalt	86	Zaire (38), Cuba (29), Zambia (10), New Caledonia (6), Indonesia (5)	Aerospace alloys
Columbium	100	Brazil (79), U.S.S.R. (17), Canada (3), Nigeria (2), Zaire (1)	Aerospace alloys
Manganese	100	South Africa (41), U.S.S.R. (36), Gabon (11), Australia (8), Brazil (2)	Electronics
Nickel	74	Cuba (34), Canada (14), U.S.S.R. (13), Indonesia (7), South Africa (5)	Stainless steel
Platinum	88	South Africa (79), U.S.S.R. (20)	Catalytic converters
Silver	57	U.S.S.R. (16), Canada (15), Mexico (14), U.S. (12), Australia (10)	Photography, electronics
Tantalum	92	Thailand (27), U.S.S.R. (17), Australia (17), Nigeria (12)	Electronics
Titanium	n.a.	Brazil (20), South Africa (14), India (12), Norway (14), Australia (9)	Aerospace alloys
Vanadium	96	U.S.S.R. (60), South Africa (20), China (14), U.S. (4)	Aerospace alloys
Zinc	69	Canada (15), U.S. (13), Australia (11), South Africa (6), U.S.S.R. (6)	Metal plating

Note: n.a. = Not available, but some U.S. production.
Source: *World Almanac, 1986* (New York: Newspaper Enterprise Association), p. 121; 1989, p. 179; and 1991, p. 686.

□ Nonfuel Minerals

Although much of the world's attention has centered on the discovery of new energy sources, Table 8–1 shows that there are also other mineral resources about which governments and industry are apprehensive. Nearly all of the world's chrome, manganese, platinum, and vanadium are produced by South Africa and the former Soviet Union. Chrome and manganese are indispensable for hardening steel; platinum is a vital catalytic agent in the oil-refining process and is used in automotive catalytic converters; and vanadium is an ingredient in a steel alloy for metal-cutting tools. The United States depends on South Africa to supply 79 percent of its platinum, 78 percent of its chromium, 41 percent of its manganese, and 20 percent of its vanadium. Although South Africa never threatened to stop the export of these strategic metals, government and industry leaders are well aware that if the South African source had been lost, the major industrial societies in the West would have been heavily dependent on their communist enemies for their supply, in both wartime and peacetime.

**TABLE 8–2
Average Metal Content
(Percent)**

	Copper	Cobalt	Nickel	Manganese
North Pacific	1.16%	0.23%	1.28%	24.6%
North Atlantic	0.15	0.34	0.30	14.2
South Atlantic	0.15	0.31	0.48	18.0
Indian Ocean	0.19	0.28	0.50	14.7
Continental reserves				
Minimum	0.50	0.07	0.40	40.0
Maximum	0.50	0.10	1.00	50.0

Source: "In Search of Metals on the Seabed," *Kredietbank Weekly Bulletin* (Brussels), June 13, 1980, p. 1.

Bleak situation? The situation appears bleak, but remember that we are discussing known reserves. Do other sources exist? Consider this. Only relatively small areas, mostly in the traditional mining countries, have been adequately explored. For example, it is estimated that only 5 percent of the potential mineral-containing areas in Mexico and only 10 percent of those in Bolivia have been studied extensively.

Furthermore, a relatively new technology, satellite mapping, has enabled geologists to locate new sources. They now know that Brazil, for example, possesses extensive deposits of chrome, nickel, copper, lead, zinc, and manganese.

Seabed mining—an untapped source. The existence of metal deposits on the ocean floor was discovered in 1876, when a British explorer found a number of small, metal-containing nodules. Little attention was paid to them until the 1960s, when tests showed that these nodules were present in practically every sea and in some lakes, such as Lake Michigan. However, the nodules richest in metallic content are nearly all located on the ocean floor, at depths of from three to five miles. Although geologists are not sure how they are formed, they do know where they are most numerous and what their metallic content is. Analysis shows that all of the nodules contain some 30 metals but have an extremely high copper, nickel, manganese, and cobalt content. This last metal, all of which is now imported in the United States, is especially important, as it is widely used in military and vital civilian technologies. For example, 900 pounds of cobalt are needed to produce just one engine for the F16 fighter plane. Table 8–2 compares the metal content of seabed sources with that of land sources.

Metal deposits are also found in the crust of chimneylike structures up to 100 feet in height that were formed when hot water rushed up from active volcano vents in the sea floor. The **polymetallic deposits** contain significant quantities of cobalt, manganese, nickel, and other metals.

Since 1974, 140 nations have been negotiating an agreement to put seabed mining under the control of the International Seabed Authority, a UN affiliate. In July 1982, the United States announced that it would not sign the Law of the Sea Convention because it objected to the seabed mining provisions. Instead, President Reagan proclaimed a U.S. Exclusive Economic Zone, which extends the jurisdiction of the United States to include all mineral resources within 200 nautical miles of the U.S. coast and the coast of U.S. island territories. Six international consortia, which include American compa-

polymetallic deposits those that contain a number of metals nies, have already spent millions of dollars perfecting technologies to mine the seabed nodules. However, the combination of low mineral prices and the uncertainty of mining rights have kept the firms from proceeding on a commercial scale.

□ Changes Make Monitoring Necessary

Mineral resources.   You saw how crude oil prices spurred the discovery of oil by non-OPEC members as they sought to lessen their dependence on imported oil. New land-based sources of strategic nonfuel minerals have also been discovered, and we have learned that the seabeds contain vast amounts of these minerals in the form of nodules and seafloor crusts.

Concomitantly, important discoveries are being made that could lessen our need for these minerals. For example, in 1984 the U.S. Air Force in conjunction with Pratt and Whitney announced the development of two new *cobalt-free* superalloys for possible application in a new generation of fighter jet engines.

Probably the most fascinating discovery of all is a solar-powered technique to produce hydrogen from *water*. Instead of using gasoline for fuel, aircraft and automobiles might use hydrogen. In the 1950s, Lockheed flew a B-57 bomber that had one engine converted to burn hydrogen, and in 1988, a similarly converted Russian plane completed a test flight.[26] Hydrogen can also be used in conventional gasoline engines. South African engineering students have already built and driven an automobile that does so.[27]

What is the significance to businesspeople of these new discoveries? Obviously, sellers of commodities and products that are being threatened by the discoveries must monitor them and prepare for new competition. More important, all firms supplying goods and services to nations that depend on the traditional minerals for foreign exchange to pay for those goods and services must be aware of developments that can destroy old markets and create new ones. Imagine the loss of purchasing power in the Middle Eastern countries if lower-cost hydrogen available from water takes the place of gasoline! We have already seen cutbacks in the purchases of these countries because of lower crude oil prices, but what if petroleum were needed only by the petrochemical industry and not for transportation?

Other changing physical forces.   Mineral resources are not the only physical forces that change. Modifications of infrastructure, most of which are of great significance to businesspeople, are being made constantly. For example, new settlements and new industries are attracted to areas in which dams have been built to control flooding and to provide power and irrigation water. New highways and new railways reduce delivery times to present markets and thus enable firms to cut their distribution costs by reducing their inventories. For example, improved highways now permit regularly scheduled overland delivery service from London to cities as far east as Moscow. One Russian trucking firm now makes the London–Moscow run in just eight days, a trip that formerly took months by sea.

However, when the Brazilian government sought a World Bank loan to construct a paved highway to connect the mineral-rich but economically stagnant state of Acre to the rest of Brazil, American environmentalist groups complained, and the loan was postponed. Their concern was that the road

The Trans-Andean Highway

Courtesy of Inter-American Development Bank

would destroy the Amazon tropical forest, which they say converts carbon dioxide to oxygen and absorbs heat, thus reducing the greenhouse effect. Nevertheless, Brazil's foreign minister said, "Brazil isn't going to become the ecological reserve for the rest of the world. Our biggest commitment is with economic development."[28] Despite its cost, one of Latin America's major infrastructural achievements, the Trans-Andean Highway, has greatly increased trade and tourism between Argentina and Chile.

New infrastructure is responsible for economic development in developed nations also. The Channel Tunnel, which will connect England and Calais, France, by 1993, is already attracting heavy investment. Calais, for example, expects its population to double to 200,000, many of whom will be British citizens attracted by cheaper housing and the ability to live in France and commute daily to work in Great Britain. Distribution costs will be significantly lower because the trip by train from London to Paris will take less than three hours instead of the present seven hours.[29]

Another timesaver is the new Seto Ohashi Bridge in Japan, which links the island of Shikoku with the central island of Honshu. What was formerly a two-hour ferry ride is now a 10-minute drive. The sharp reduction in travel time is having a profound impact on agriculture. Faster delivery times for produce are calculated to result in a $30 million increase in farmers' income.[30]

☐ Contamination of Resources

Historically, nations have paid relatively little attention to the contamination and destruction of the world's natural resources. Entire forests have been destroyed by people wanting to get firewood or to clear land and by contaminated air and water. Pollution control of air and water was considered a luxury that governments, anxious to attract new industry and to keep the industry they had, could ill afford to impose. As the secretary of mines and energy

Exxon vowed it would pick up all the oil and leave the area as it was before the accident. After spending $2.2 billion on the Valdez cleanup, Exxon has cleaned most of the beaches that were soiled by the spill. A company spokesman promises, "We are ready to go back in next summer and do whatever is necessary." As a safeguard against future spills, Alyeska, the consortium that operates the trans-Alaskan pipeline, now has equipment that would have mopped up the entire Valdez spill in 10 hours.[35]

Eco-terrorism in the Gulf war.   An ecological disaster far worse than the Valdez oil spill was caused by the Iraqi army before its retreat from Kuwait. A total of 732 oil wells were either sabotaged by the army or were set fire during combat. Moreover, 75 million barrels of oil spilled out over the desert forming lakes, which birds mistakenly took for real ones, flying to their deaths.[36] Iraqi troops also let oil escape from Kuwait's Sea Island terminal, creating a spill 27 times larger than the Valdez disaster.[37] Unfortunately, despite the great polluted areas in Kuwait and Saudi Arabia, neither nation has shown much interest in cleaning up anything other than the oil fields.[38] Iraq was not the only loser in the Gulf War. The region's plants and animals and the quality of its air and water may be a long time in recovering.[39]

Consequences for multinationals.   Antipollution activism, already a potent force in Europe and North America, is spreading to other parts of the world. Local citizen groups have increased their impact on government policies and have worked to delay the projects of multinationals in newly industrializing countries, such as Brazil, India, Malaysia, Mexico, and Thailand. The notion of economic growth at any cost is being challenged, and many nations, developing as well as developed, are now requiring environmental impact assessments before approving new industrial plants. Multinational producers of hazardous materials are finding that these changes are resulting in higher costs and are making the locating of overseas plants more difficult.[40]

Multinationals in hazardous industries will resist the minority positions in joint ventures mandated by numerous governments when such positions cause them to lose control to the local majority on questions of equipment, plant safety, and environmental controls. Warren Anderson, chairman of Union Carbide at the time of the Bhopal disaster, voiced the concern of many multinational managements when he said, "India sued us on the novel theory that any multinational engaged in hazardous operations is totally liable for any mishap, regardless of what share it may own. Is the insistence by Third World countries on local content in goods manufactured for local markets always realistic? It was, for example, at India's insistence that Carbide started making, instead of just mixing, agricultural chemicals in the Bhopal plant."[41]

SUMMARY

The importance of a good knowledge of geography has perhaps not been given the emphasis it deserves. Because of the changes that have occurred, what was learned in grammar school geography will not suffice today. Businesspeople should be familiar with the locations of countries, their significant landforms, and their climates. These elements of the physical forces exert a powerful influence on the environmental forces. Mountain ranges, deserts, and tropical forests act as barriers to the movements of people, goods, and ideas, whereas bodies of water facilitate such movements.

Businesspeople must not be misled into believing that because the major industrialized nations are located in temperate climates, it follows that natives of the tropics are inherently inferior. Parasitic diseases and poor nutrition are responsible for their lower productivity.

Eco-terrorism, such as that committed by the Iraqi army, can have disastrous environmental, social, and economic impacts.

P. J. Griffiths/Magnum Photos, Inc.

Because of the rapid depletion of the known sources of natural resources, firms dependent on them for production have been forced to search for new supplies in previously unexplored regions. New discoveries are important to all firms, however, because they frequently create new markets. If substitutes are found that will decrease the need for a natural resource, a number of currently strong markets may diminish in importance.

Industrial accidents like the Bhopal disaster and the Rhine River spill have caused both the industrialized and the developing nations to be more concerned about the protection of national resources. The concept of growth at any cost is giving way to environmental considerations. Many nations, for example, now require environmental impact assessments before approving new industrial plants.

Managements of international firms are reassessing the desirability of taking minority positions in joint ventures when they cannot control choice of equipment, plant safety, and maintenance. Eco-terrorism committed on a grand scale by the Iraqi army has gravely endangered the Persian Gulf ecosystem for a long time to come.

QUESTIONS

1. Go to the chalkboard and draw a map of the European Community. How many countries can you locate? Do you know their capitals?

2. Of the 25 nations listed by the United Nations as the least developed among the developed nations, 14 are landlocked. Is this a coincidence, or is the lack of a seacoast a contributing factor to their slower development?

3. Analyze the potential of oil shale and oil sands as future energy sources. What problems are involved in using these natural resources?

4. Assume you are a member of your company's long-range planning committee. You have heard that experiments have been successful in separating hydrogen from water and that the hydrogen is then combined with carbon to form hydrocarbons. It is said that the product may cost 20 percent less than crude oil obtained from wells. Discuss with your colleagues how this development may affect your marketing plans in the Middle East and in the oil-poor developing countries.

5. a. Why do you suppose the blank areas on a population map generally coincide with the areas of higher elevation on a topographic map?

   b. Why are the tropics an exception to this rule?

6. The director of personnel in your firm's home office tells you, the plant manager home on leave from the Indonesian subsidiary, "The only reason we have an infirmary in our American plants is to take care of workers injured on the job. Why do you want to staff our infirmary in Indonesia with nutritionists and experts in parasitic diseases?" How would you answer that?

7. Your firm is planning to enter the markets in northern South America with electric motors. The vice president of marketing, who has had no experience in selling to this region, announces, "Our inventory requirements will be simple. Since the climate is moist and humid in these countries, we'll have to supply the higher-priced models that we market along the U.S. Gulf Coast, and we can forget about the less expensive motors we sell up North. Fortunately, our competitors will have to do the same thing because of the climate, so we won't have to worry much about price competition." You are the export manager. What is your reaction?

8. Explain how the physical forces of a country influence its sociocultural forces.

9. International businesspeople, unless they are in the business of refining minerals or petroleum, have no need to concern themselves with world developments in natural resources. True or false? Explain.

10. There are many critics of the U.S. policy of friendship with South Africa. Do you believe the physical forces influence our policy? (Hint: Analyze Table 8–1, and check South Africa's location at the tip of Africa on a world map.)

11. What will be the consequences for multinational firms of such disasters as the Rhine spill, Bhopal accident, and the Alaskan oil spill?

◻ MINICASE 8–1

Brazil Balks at International Pressure to Save the Amazon

"This is the greatest international pressure Brazil has experienced in its history." The secretary-general of Brazil's Foreign Ministry was referring to the growing pressure from industrialized nations to protect its environment. The American outcry over the destruction of the Amazon rain forest has especially outraged the Brazilians for several reasons.

Brazil considers the Amazon rain forest, which is about half the size of the United States, as hinterland to be developed just as the United States moved westward as it developed. Moreover, Brazil interprets U.S. complaints to be patronizing. Most Americans see Brazil as a developing nation heavily in debt instead of the image the Brazilians have of themselves—the eighth-largest industrial power, which exports aircraft, tanks, rocket launchers, and automobiles. The Minister of Justice said Brazil would not accept any international monitoring of its protection of the Amazon. Such monitoring would be all right for small nations such as Costa Rica, the official implied, but not for a country almost as large as the United States.

Brazilians believe this pressure amounts to unjustified foreign meddling by industrialized nations to keep their economic supremacy at the expense of the developing world. In the words of former President Sarney, "By what right does the United States, which spews out more pollutants than any other nation, lecture poor countries like Brazil on their responsibilities to mankind?" A former government employee who helped build a highway through part of the Amazon asks, "How would Americans feel if years ago we had told them they could not build a road from New York to California because it would destroy their forests?"

Because Brazil has become an important soybean producer thanks to Japanese financing, the Brazilians expected the Japanese to finance a highway through the Amazon to Peru so that Brazilian soybeans could be delivered by a shorter shipping route to Japan. The lengthy route used now adds $10 per ton to the shipping costs relative to the cost of shipping American soybeans. Environmentalists, fearing that cutting the rain forests would further damage the world's ozone layer and destroy wildlife, sought help from President Bush. He requested the Japanese not to fund the highway and they acquiesced.

The Amazon does not have to disappear. There has been a dramatic reduction in the country's birthrate that should reduce future pressure to clear the forests. The government can remove the subsidies and incentives for clearing land and stop some of the wasteful projects it is planning, such as the hydroelectric dams. For example, a dam completed in 1987 flooded a huge area at great cost to produce little power. It killed trees, poisoned fish, and became the breeding ground for billions of malarial mosquitoes.

Although the politicians will not admit it, there are Brazilians who believe the rest of the world has a legitimate interest in what happens to the Amazon. Philip Fearnside of Brazil's National Institute for Research in the Amazon says that unless things change, the forest will disappear, and this will be more than a South American disaster. If the forests vanish, more than 1 million species of plant and animal life will disappear. The destruction of the Amazon caused by the "slash and burn" method of opening up

farmland could have dramatic effects on global weather patterns, such as the warming trend resulting from the greenhouse effect. Thomas Lovejoy of the Smithsonian Institute states, "The Amazon is a library for life sciences, the world's greatest pharmaceutical laboratory, and a flywheel of climate. It's a matter of global destiny."

What may save the Amazon is the growing recognition that the forests are more valuable when left standing. A botanist of the New York Botanical Garden recently published a three-year study showing that the market value of the exotic produce and the wild rubber that can be harvested from the jungle would, over time, be worth twice the income from cattle ranching or lumbering.

What, if anything, can the industrialized nations do to persuade Brazil to save the Amazon?

Source: "Jungle Road to Tokyo," *Forbes,* May 29, 1989, p. 96; "Playing with Fire," *Time,* September 18, 1989, pp. 76–85; "Brazil Balks at International Pressure to Save Environment in Industrializing," *The Wall Street Journal,* p. A7; "U.S. Complaints on Amazon Destruction Spur Brazil's Resentment and Defiance," *The Wall Street Journal,* February 2, 1989, p. A6; and "A Back Door into the Amazon," *The Economist,* February 11, 1989, pp. 38–39.

□ MINICASE 8–2

Bhopal Fallout

Harry Johnson, CEO of International Chemical, called a meeting of the newly formed crisis management committee, which consists of the vice president of manufacturing; the vice president–legal; the vice president of health, safety, and environment; the chief financial officer; and the public relations officer. Johnson had formed the committee after Union Carbide's Bhopal disaster to examine International Chemical's contingency plans. Because the two companies have similar international organizations and produce similarly toxic products, he asked the members to review the information they had on the Bhopal disaster and make recommendations as to what each person's area would do should their company have a similar accident. Johnson also asked the vice president of health, safety, and environment to begin the meeting by giving the committee a synopsis of the series of events that occurred during the first days after the disaster.

He begins, "As you know, on the night of December 2, a series of runaway chemical reactions heated the interior of a partially buried tank holding 10,000 gallons of methyl isocyanate (MIC) used in the manufacture of Sevin and

other pesticides. An escape valve opened, which released a lethal cloud over Bhopal. No one knows how it happened, but Union Carbide investigators say that, by accident or through sabotage, a large quantity of water had been poured into the tank, which then reacted with the MIC to produce heat and open the valve. A refrigeration unit that could have kept the tank temperature at a manageable level had broken down five months previously and had not been repaired. A temperature alarm that would have alerted workers was not properly set. Last of all, a scrubber designed to neutralize toxic vapors was not turned on until the reaction was out of control.

"Union Carbide headquarters in Connecticut first heard of the accident at 3 A.M. on December 3, when employees from Union Carbide in Bhopal called Lutz (chairman of UC Eastern, the division responsible for Asian operations) at his home. By 6 A.M., Lutz, Oldfield (president of the agricultural products division, which markets the insecticides produced at Bhopal), Browning (director of health, safety, and environment), and Van Den Ameele (manager of press relations) met at headquarters. Although they were skeptical about the accuracy of the growing estimate of the numbers of dead and injured, they agreed that a swift response was needed and that top management would need to make some decisions. By midmorning, they called UC's president and went to a hastily called meeting of the senior management committee. When Carbide board chairman Warren Anderson, in bed with a bad cold, was informed by telephone of the problem, he organized a crisis committee of legal, finance, and public affairs people.

"Within 12 hours, the committee dispatched a medical and technical team to arrange relief for the victims, to investigate the incident, and to assist with the safe disposal of the remaining MIC supplies at the plant. They held a press conference even though they did not have all the answers for the press. The next day, as the death toll continued to mount, Anderson took the company jet to Bhopal. On arrival, he was arrested, held briefly, and then sent to New Delhi, the capital. There, Indian officials told him to leave for his own good. His offer of $1 million in aid and the use of the company guest house to shelter orphans of the victims was refused.

"Because Carbide managers did not know what had caused the leak, they stopped production of MIC in the United States and converted all of their stocks of MIC worldwide into pesticides. The crisis caused the price of Carbide stock to fall, so the team began to stress the company's financial soundness in press releases and briefings.

To bolster employee morale, the UC president made a videotape for Carbide employees worldwide in which he assured them of the company's ability to handle any likely damage settlement. By the way, even though Carbide provided the specifications for the Indian plant, it was designed and built in India at the insistence of the Indian government, which has a 20 percent interest in the Indian company. Carbide has 50.9 percent, but it has been essentially an Indian operation. The other investors are Indian."

"Thanks for the rundown," says Johnson. "I don't need to tell you that managements of multinational producers all over the world are studying Union Carbide's situation very closely. I read that one executive said this accident could rewrite the whole book on how to operate in foreign countries and how one covers one's risks overseas. Who wants to start the discussion on (1) what we need to do now to avoid both an accident and risk to the company if there should be one and (2) what should our plan be in case—and I hope it never happens—we should have a similar accident?"

Source: Information on Bhopal disaster from "Union Carbide: Coping with Catastrophe," *Fortune,* January 7, 1985, pp. 50–53; "Anderson Reflects on Managing Bhopal," *Industry Week,* October 13, 1986, p. 21; "For Multinationals It Will Never Be the Same," *Businessweek,* December 24, 1984, p. 57; and "Bhopal Report," *C&EN,* February 11, 1985, pp. 14–52.

SUPPLEMENTARY READINGS

Climate, Location, and Topography

"A New Wave of Basque Terrorism." *U.S. News & World Report,* April 24, 1989, p. 45.

"Austria Scrambles to Become Key Player in Central Europe." *Business International,* June 10, 1991, p. 191.

"Between Two Worlds." *The Economist,* October 12, 1991, p. 77.

Butler, Joseph H. *Economic Geography.* New York: John Wiley & Sons, 1980.

"Doing Something about the Weather." *World Monitor,* December 1988, pp. 28–37.

"EC, EFTA to Prepare for 1992." *Europe,* November 1988, p. 39.

"Finland Breaks Away." *The European,* October 4–6, 1991.

Kamarck, Andrew M. *The Tropics and Economic Development.* Washington, D.C.: World Bank, 1976.

Murphey, Rhoads. *The Scope of Geography.* 2nd ed. Skokie, Ill.: Rand McNally, 1973.

"North America into the Year 2000." *Business International,* October 3, 1988, pp. 301–12.

"Perestrikeout." *Financial World,* November 29, 1988, pp. 20–21.

Price, L. W. *Mountains and Men.* Berkeley: University of California Press, 1981.

"The Inconsistent Climate." *Geographical Magazine,* February 1989, pp. 26–29.

"The Rhythm of the Future." *The Economist,* December 14, 1991, pp. 19–21.

"U.S., EC Compete for Markets in ASEAN Countries." *Europe,* November/December 1985, pp. 24–25.

Natural Resources

"A Back Door into the Amazon." *The Economist,* February 11, 1989, pp. 38–39.

"A Bumpy Ride for Oil." *U.S. News & World Report,* August 5, 1991, pp. 26–30.

"Alaskan Oil Spill." *Management Review,* April 1990, pp. 13–18.

"CS Resources Puts All Bets on Heavy Oil." *The Wall Street Journal,* November 4, 1991, p. A7.

"How Shale-Oil Fever Burned Colorado." *Business Week,* April 9, 1990, p. 12.

"Jungle Road to Tokyo." *Forbes,* May 29, 1989, p. 96.

"Metal Factories of the Deep." *Natural History,* January 1988, pp. 52–56.

"Ocean Mining: Boom or Bust?" *Technology Review,* April 1984, pp. 55–56.

"Playing with Fire." *Time,* September 18, 1989, pp. 76–85.

"Polymetal Sulphides: More Riches from the Sea?" *DESI Facts 82/2.* New York: United Nations, March 1982.

"Sea Law: Highlights." *UN Chronicle* 19, no. 6 (June 1982), pp. 5–6.

"The Jigsaw Environment." *U.S. News & World Report,* December 26, 1989, pp. 92–93.

"The Mines of Apartheid." *Newsweek,* August 11, 1986, p. 30.

"U.S., Europe Eye Aerospace Planes." *Europe,* November–December 1985, pp. 22–23.

"Using Red Ink to Keep Tropical Forests Green." *U.S. News & World Report,* March 6, 1989, p. 48.

"U.S. Needs S. A. Minerals." *S. A. Digest,* February 13, 1987, pp. 5–7.

Pollution

"And Toxic Flows the Rhine." *World Health,* March 1987, pp. 24–26.

Bhargava, Ashok, and Suresh Desai. "Multinationals and Developing Countries: Impact of the Bhopal Disaster." *Issues in International Business,* Winter 1988, pp. 28–34.

"Bhopal Report." *C&EN,* February 1985, pp. 14–52.

"Bhopal Ruling to Affect Multinationals." *Business Insurance,* October 5, 1987, pp. 55–56.

"Changing Environmental Rules and Regulations at a Glance." *Business International,* September 12, 1988, pp. 280–81.

"How Green Is Your Company?" *International Management,* January 1989, pp. 24–27.

"India's High Court Upholds Settlement Paid by Carbide in Bhopal Gas Leak." *The Wall Street Journal,* October 4, 1991, p. B12.

"It's Time to Drill Alaska's Refuge." *Fortune,* January 28, 1991, pp. 32–39.

"Legacy of War." *The Wall Street Journal,* October 15, 1991, p. A1.

"Military Victory, Ecological Defeat." *World Watch,* July–August 1991, pp. 27–33.

"Smothering the Waters." *Newsweek,* April 10, 1989, pp. 54–57.

"The Blotch on the Rhine." *Newsweek,* November 24, 1986, pp. 58–60.

"The Dead Sea in the Making." *Time,* February 11, 1991, p. 40–41.

"Union Carbide: Coping with Disaster." *Fortune,* January 7, 1985, pp. 50–52.

Transportation

"Artery That Will Restore Lifeblood of a Continent." *The European,* November 22–24, 1991, p. 13.

"At the End of the Tunnel." *American Way,* May 15, 1991, pp. 24–30.

"Bracing for the 'Gold Rush.'" *International Management,* December 1988, pp. 32–34.

"Europe's Great Waterway." *Standard Chartered Review,* February 1986, pp. 2–7.

"Full Throttle toward a New Era." *Fortune,* November 20, 1989, pp. 131–35.

"How the Channel Link Could Change Europe." *International Management,* January 1986, pp. 30–34.

"Moving the Third World." *OECD Observer,* June 6, 1988, pp. 9–10.

"Seto Ohashi Bridge." *Japan Update,* Winter 1989, pp. 10–11.

"The Honshu–Shikoku Bridge Is Redrawing the Industrial Map." *Japan Update,* Autumn 1987, pp. 1–2.

"Waterway to Aid Southern Cone." *Business Latin America,* September 10, 1990, p. 287.

ENDNOTES

1. Robert Bartels, ed., *Comparative Marketing: Wholesaling in 15 Countries* (Homewood, Ill.: Richard D. Irwin, 1963), p. 4.
2. "Austria Scrambles to Become a Key Player in Central Europe," *Business International,* June 10, 1991, p. 191.
3. "Between Two Worlds," *The Economist,* October 12, 1991, p. 77; and "Finland Breaks Away," *The European,* October 4–6, 1991, p. 4.
4. "The Rhythm of the Future," *The Economist,* December 14, 1991, pp. 19–20.
5. "U.S., EC Compete for Markets in ASEAN Countries," *Europe,* November–December 1985, p. 24.
6. When a sales engineer from Madrid and one of the writers went to Barcelona, the Detroit of Spain, on a business trip, we were accompanied on our visits to customers by our salesman from Barcelona. Our meetings with customers always followed the same pattern. The Barcelona salesman would begin the meeting by telling the customer we were from Madrid and did not speak Catalan, the local language. The meeting would proceed in Spanish until

either the customer or our local salesman, in searching for a word in Spanish, would use the more familiar (to him) word in Catalan. This would trigger the other to begin speaking in Catalan (completely unintelligible to anyone speaking only Spanish), and the sales engineer and the writer would be completely in the dark as to what was being discussed. After a moment, the local salesman and the customer would realize what they were doing and apologize. The discussions in Spanish would be resumed, and then the switch to Catalan would be repeated. If our local salesman had not been present to smooth over these lapses and provide the necessary empathy with the customer, these meetings would have been disastrous.

7. "Trinidad Fiasco Spotlights Libya's Terror Network," *The Wall Street Journal,* August 3, 1990, p. A11; and "A New Wave of Basque Terrorism," *U.S. News & World Report,* April 24, 1989, p. 45.

8. A product with adequate cooling and lubrication for the temperate zone would function well in Bogota but might be woefully deficient in Barranquilla.

9. *World Development Report, 1991* (Washington, D.C.: World Bank, 1991), Table 31, "Urbanization," p. 265.

10. Australia has no north–south railway mainly because there is little population and economic activity in the center of the country to support one. There is an east–west coastal system in the more populous southern region that was completed partly because the federal government feared the western states might secede from the Australian union. The system, however, has the same problems as those of other large developing nations, such as India and Brazil. There are three different gauges along its length, with a few disconnected feeder lines going inland from the ports to mining and farm districts. Goods in transit between Sydney and Perth take 14 days when, because of the distance, they should take 5. Some unification has been done, but it is not complete. Goods and passengers still must be transferred at some state borders.

11. Rhoads Murphey, *The Scope of Geography,* 2nd ed. (Skokie, Ill.: Rand McNally, 1973), pp. 188–89.

12. "Europe's Great Waterway," *Standard Chartered Review,* February 1986, pp. 2–7.

13. "Waterway to Aid Southern Cone," *Business Latin America,* September 10, 1990, p. 287.

14. Until 1866, Bolivia possessed a 160-mile coastline, but a treaty with Chile that year reduced it by 60 miles. As a result of a war in 1879 primarily between Bolivia and Chile, although Peru also intervened, Bolivia lost its coastline to Chile. Peru also lost 160 miles of coastline but, in 1929, was able to regain 35 miles. Bolivia has been holding discussions with Chile ever since in an effort to obtain its outlet to the sea. In 1975, Chile proposed ceding a narrow strip to Bolivia but demanded what Bolivia considered excessive compensation. Peru offered an alternative solution in 1976 by which all three countries would share in the sovereignty of a port in northern Chile. Rumors were strong that there might be an armed confrontation between Peru and Chile. This crisis passed without a serious incident, and it looked as though Bolivia and Chile

might reach an agreement based on a new Bolivian proposal made in 1987. However, the Chilean government rejected it.

This dispute affects business transactions between the two countries. One of the writers, representing a Chilean subsidiary of an American multinational, called on a large government-owned mine in Bolivia to sell Chilean-made products. The purchasing agent asked how anyone could expect her, a Bolivian, to buy goods made in Chile. She appreciated the fact that the parent company was American, but as she said, "The products are still made in Chile."

15. One author claimed that Brazil has constructed highways, railroads, and bridges to connect its borders with those of its neighbors for the purpose of bringing them under Brazil's political and economic influence. See "Brasil: Potencia Emergente," *Vision,* August 1976, pp. 8–10.

16. Murphey, *Scope of Geography,* p. 115.

17. Ibid., p. 119.

18. Andrew M. Karmack, *The Tropics and Economic Development* (Washington, D.C.: World Bank, 1976), p. 5.

19. Joseph H. Butler, *Economic Geography* (New York: John Wiley & Sons, 1980), p. 108.

20. *Exxon Corporation's 1990 Annual Report,* p. 58.

21. "CS Resources Puts All Bets on Heavy Oil," *The Wall Street Journal,* November 4, 1991, p. A7.

22. "How Shale-Oil Fever Burned Colorado," *Business Week,* April 9, 1990, p. 12.

23. *1985 Annual Report* (Washington, D.C.: U.S. Synthetic Fuels Corp.).

24. "Discovery in Colombia Points Up Big Change in World Oil Picture," *The Wall Street Journal,* May 13, 1985, p. 1.

25. *Mobil Annual Report, 1990,* p. 20; and *BP Annual Report, 1989,* p. 27.

26. "An Airplane Fuel That's Lighter than Air," *Business Week,* May 9, 1988, p. 107.

27. The engine output is altered by varying the amount of hydrogen, not the air, as in a conventional carburetor. From "Students Develop Unique Gas Car," *S. A. Digest,* April 27, 1984, p. 10. Mitsubishi, working with the Japanese government, is also trying to develop a hydrogen-powered car. Mercedes has already shown its hydrogen-powered prototype to the public.

28. "Brazil Balks at International Pressure," *The Wall Street Journal,* February 13, 1989, p. A7B.

29. "At the End of the Tunnel," *American Way,* May 16, 1991, pp. 24–30; and "Full Throttle toward a New Era," *Fortune,* November 20, 1989, pp. 131–35.

30. "Seto Ohashi Bridge," *Japan Update,* Winter 1989, pp. 10–11.

31. "India's High Court Upholds Settlement Paid by Carbide in Bhopal Gas Leak," *The Wall Street Journal,* October 4, 1991, p. B12.

32. "Union Carbide, India Reach $470 Million Settlement," *The Wall Street Journal,* February 15, 1989, p. A3.

33. "The Blotch on the Rhine," *Newsweek,* November 24, 1986, pp. 58–60; and "Suddenly, a Deathwatch on the Rhine," *Business Week,* November 24, 1986, p. 52.

34. "Beyond the Spill on the Rhine," *World Press Review,* January 1987, p. 50.

35. "It's Time to Drill Alaska's Refuge," *Fortune,* January 28, 1991, pp. 38–39.

36. "Lakes of Spilled Oil Plunge Kuwait into Ever-Deeper Mess," *The Wall Street Journal,* August 12, 1991, p. A8.

37. "Dead Sea in the Making," *Time,* February 11, 1991, p. 40.

38. "Legacy of War," *The Wall Street Journal,* October 15, 1991, p. A1.

39. "Military Victory, Ecological Defeat," *World Watch,* July–August 1991, p. 27.

40. "What's in Store for MNCs as Concern for Environment Breeds Tougher Regulation," *Business International,* August 1987, pp. 250–54.

41. "Anderson Reflects on Managing Bhopal," *Industry Week,* October 13, 1986, p. 21.

Chapter 9

Sociocultural Forces

You can't understand a country's economy without also understanding its family structures, religions, and values.

M. L. Baba, professor of
anthropology and consultant to
General Motors

KEY WORDS AND CONCEPTS

- Culture
- Ethnocentricity
- Aesthetics
- Demonstration effect
- Protestant work ethic
- Confucian work ethic
- Asian religions
- Caste system
- Material culture
- Technological dualism
- Appropriate technology
- Boomerang effect
- Brain drain
- Reverse brain drain
- Lingua franca
- Unspoken language
- Bribes
- Extortion
- Extended family
- Associations

BUSINESS INCIDENT

Five Rules of Thumb for Doing Business in Another Culture

"Know your customer" is just as important anywhere in the world as it is at home, whether aiming to sell computers in Abidjan or soft drinks in Kuala Lumpur or hotel construction in Caracas. Foreign people are not inscrutable. Each culture has its logic, and within the logic of the culture are real, sensible reasons for the way foreigners do things. If the salesperson can figure out the fundamental pattern of the culture, he/she will be less frustrated and more effective interacting with foreign clients and colleagues.

1. The first rule of thumb is *be prepared.* Whether traveling abroad or selling from home, no one should approach a foreign market without doing his or her home-work. A mentor is most desirable, complemented with endless reading which covers social and business etiquette, history and folklore, current affairs (including current relations between your two countries), the culture's values, geography, sources of pride (artists, musicians, novelists, sports, great achievements of the culture), religion, political structure, and practical matters such as currency, transportation, time zones, and hours of business. Mimi Murphy, an exporter who trades primarily in Indonesia, says, "Whenever I travel, the first thing I do in any town is read the newspaper, front to back. Then when I meet my customer, I can talk about the sports, or whatever the news of the day is. He knows that I am interested in the things he is interested in, and he will want to do business with me."

2. The second rule, for most Americans, is *slow down.* Americans are clock-watchers. Time is money. In many countries, we are seen to be in a rush, in other words, unfriendly, arrogant, and untrustworthy. Almost everywhere, we must learn to wait patiently.

3. The third rule: In many countries, American-style crisp business relationships will get the sales representative nowhere. Product quality, pricing, and clear contracts

BUSINESS INCIDENT (concluded)

are not as important as the personal *relationship and trust* that is developed carefully and sincerely over time. The marketer must be established as simpatico, worthy of the business, and dependable *in the long run.*

4. Fourth: *Language* is extremely important. Obviously, copy must be translated by a professional who speaks both languages fluently, with a vocabulary sensitive to nuance and connotation in each culture, as well as talent with idiom and imagery in each culture. An interpreter is often critical and may be helpful even where one of the parties speaks the other's language.

5. The fifth rule is to *respect the culture.* Manners are important. The traveling sales representative is a guest in the country and must respect the hosts' rules. As a Saudi Arabian official states in one of the *Going International* films, "Americans in foreign countries have a tendency to treat the natives as foreigners and they forget that actually it is *they* who are the foreigners themselves!"

Source: U.S. Department of Commerce, *Business America,* June 25, 1984, p. 7.

The Business Incident emphasizes some of the differences among business cultures that businesspeople should be aware of when they leave their home country to work in other cultures. Of course, even without leaving the country, we all find it necessary to increase our cultural knowledge as we mature, take business courses in a college or university, and then obtain employment. You may not consciously appreciate that you have acquired knowledge about three dimensions of our culture: general, business, and corporate. Yet, when you analyze what you have learned, you realize that each succeeding dimension going from general to corporate is increasingly specific and constrained by the one preceding it.[1]

For instance, you learn early in life about the spirit of fair play and what is acceptable conduct, but in college, you learn more specifically about the conduct that businesses expect from their employees. When you go to work, you learn about the values and norms governing acceptable behavior in that company. If you change jobs, you probably shall find a different emphasis in another firm.

At Procter & Gamble, you would soon learn that new managers are judged on their ability to increase sales volume and profits; but at J. C. Penney, the dominant cultural values are customer satisfaction and employee satisfaction. However, don't use the term *employees*—at Penney's, they're *associates.* Part of your cultural training is learning the corporate language.[2]

After the extensive international bribery scandals of the 1970s (discussed in this chapter and in Chapter 10), companies operating worldwide were quick to formulate and publish codes of conduct for their employees. These codes became basic parts of each company's culture.

Figure 9–1 shows the table of contents from *Worldwide Code of Ethics* published by PPG Industries, an international manufacturer ($6 billion sales) of glass, coatings, and chemicals. A copy goes to all associates (employees) everywhere in the world. Note how comprehensive it is. The following excerpt from the chairman's letter emphasizes the seriousness of the firm's expectation of employee adherence to the stated principles:

☐ **FIGURE 9–1**
Worldwide Code of Ethics **Table of Contents**

TABLE OF CONTENTS

This booklet represents an attempt to organize the various ethical beliefs which have guided PPG's conduct and policy formulation over the years. It is not a comprehensive document. Many of the company's ethical beliefs are imbedded in practice and custom rather than in official policy. Nevertheless, the guidelines offered here apply to all our associates, no matter where they are located. As an integral part of PPG's organization, you are responsible for familiarizing yourself with the contents of this Code, for observing its requirements, and for reporting any violations which come to your attention. Failure to do so not only harms PPG, it may damage your own career prospects as well.[3]

WHAT IS CULTURE?

culture sum total of beliefs, rules, techniques, institutions, and artifacts that characterize human populations

Although there are almost as many definitions of culture as there are anthropologists, most anthropologists view **culture** as the *sum total of the beliefs, rules, techniques, institutions, and artifacts that characterize human populations*.[4] In other words, culture consists of the learned patterns of behavior common to members of a given society—the unique lifestyle of a particular group of people.[5] Most anthropologists also agree that

1. Culture is *learned*, not innate.
2. The various aspects of culture are *interrelated*.
3. Culture is *shared*.
4. Culture *defines the boundaries* of different groups.[6]

Because society is composed of people and their culture, it is virtually impossible to speak of one without relating to the other. Anthropologists often use the terms interchangeably or combine them into one word—*sociocultural*.[7] This is the term we shall use, because the variables in which businesspeople are interested are both social and cultural.

SIGNIFICANCE OF CULTURE FOR INTERNATIONAL BUSINESS

When people work in societies and cultures that differ from their own, the problems they encounter in dealing with a single set of cultures are multiplied by the number of cultural sets they find in each of their foreign markets.

All too often, unfortunately, people who are familiar with only one cultural pattern may believe they have an awareness of cultural differences elsewhere, when in reality they do not. Unless they have had occasion to make comparisons with other cultures, they are probably not even aware of the important features of their own. They are probably also oblivious to the fact that each society considers its culture superior to all others (**ethnocentricity**) and that their attempts to introduce the "German way" or the "American way" may be met with stubborn resistance.

ethnocentricity belief in the superiority of one's own ethnic group

How do international businesspeople learn to live with other cultures? The first step is a realization that there are cultures different from their own. Then they must go on to learn the characteristics of those cultures so that they may adapt to them. E. T. Hall, a famous anthropologist, claims this can be accomplished in only two ways: (1) spend a lifetime in a country or (2) undergo an extensive, highly sophisticated training program that covers the main characteristics of culture, including the language. The program he mentions is more than an area orientation in which participants are briefed on a country's customs. What Hall refers to is a study of what culture is and what it does and the acquisition of some knowledge of the various ways in which human behavior has been institutionalized.[8]

☐ Culture Impacts All Business Functions

Marketing.   In marketing, for example, the wide variation in attitudes and values prevents many firms from using the same marketing mix in all markets.

> In Japan, Procter & Gamble (P&G) used an advertisement for Camay soap in which a man meeting a woman for the first time compared her skin to that of a fine porcelain doll. Although the ad had worked well in South America and Europe, it insulted the Japanese. "For a Japanese man to say something like that to a Japanese woman means he's either unsophisticated or rude," said an advertising man who worked on the account. Interestingly, P&G used the ad despite the warning from the advertising agency.
>
> P&G also erred because it lacked knowledge of the business culture. The company introduced Cheer detergent by discounting its price, but this lowered the soap's reputation. Said a competitor, "Unlike in Europe and the United States, once you discount your product here, it's hard to raise the price again." Wholesalers were alienated because they made less money due to lower margins. Moreover, apparently P&G didn't realize that Japanese housewives do not have a family car to carry groceries, so they shop in the neighborhood mom-and-pop stores close to home. These small retailers, who sell 30 percent of all the detergent sold in Japan, have limited shelf space and thus do not like to carry discounted products because of the lower profit earned. P&G is estimated to have lost a quarter of a billion dollars since entering the Japanese market. As a bitter Japanese ex-P&G employee put it, "They didn't listen to anybody." Evidently P&G has learned from its costly mistakes: its latest detergent is formulated for Japanese washing habits—short cycles, cold water, and small machines.[9]

Unlike P&G, Walt Disney seems to have an ideal global product. According to the *Tokyo Disneyland Guidebook,* the theme park in Tokyo is the same as those in California and Florida. Euro Disneyland is also similar, although, because of the French insistence on protecting their language and culture, Mickey and Donald have developed French accents and the Sleeping Beauty castle is called *Le Château de la Belle au Bois Dormant.* However, a hot dog will still be called a hot dog.[10]

Human resource management.   The national culture is also a key determinant for the evaluation of managers. In the United States, results are generally the criteria for the selection and promotion of executives; but in Great Britain, an American general manager complained that people were promoted because of the school they attended and their family background but not for their accomplishments. School ties are important in France, too. IBM would hire an Italian who fits within the IBM way of doing things, but Olivetti, whose corporate culture is informal and nonstructured with little discipline, looks for strong personalities and not "too good grades."[11] You can get Olivetti's address from the nearest AT&T office.

Production and finance.   Personnel problems can result from differences in attitudes toward authority, another sociocultural variable. Latin Americans

Walt Disney Productions is a successful example of a company that takes into account the culture of its target market.

Craig Davis/SYGMA

have traditionally regarded the manager as the *patron* (master), an authoritarian figure responsible for their welfare. When American managers accustomed to a participative leadership style are transferred to Latin America, they must become more authoritarian, or their employees will consider them weak and incompetent and they will encounter serious difficulties in having their orders carried out.

> **A production manager who had been sent to Peru from the United States was convinced that he could motivate the workers to higher productivity by instituting a more democratic decision-making style. He brought in trainers from the home office to teach the supervisors how to solicit suggestions and feedback from the workers.**
>
> **Shortly after the new management style was introduced, the workers began quitting their jobs. When asked why, they replied that the new production manager and his supervisors apparently didn't know what to do and were therefore asking the workers for advice. Obviously, the company wouldn't last long with that kind of management, and they wanted to quit before the collapse, because then everyone would be hunting for a job at the same time.**

Production managers have found that attitudes toward change can seriously influence the acceptance of new production methods; even treasurers come to realize the strength of the sociocultural forces when, armed with excellent balance sheets, they approach local banks, only to find that the banks attach far more importance to who they are than to how strong their companies are.[12] These are just a few examples to show that sociocultural differences do affect all of the business functions. As we examine the components of the sociocultural forces, we shall mention others.

SOCIOCULTURAL COMPONENTS

From the foregoing, it should be apparent that to be successful in their relationships with people in other countries, international businesspeople must be students of culture. They must have factual knowledge, which is relatively easy to obtain, but they must also become sensitive to cultural differences, and this is more difficult. Hall, as we saw, recommended spending a lifetime in a country or, in lieu of this, undergoing an extensive program to study what the culture is and what it does. But most newcomers to international business do not even have the opportunity for area orientation. They can, however, take the important first step of realizing that there are other cultures. In this short chapter, we cannot do more than point out some of the important sociocultural differences as they concern businesspeople, in the hope that the readers will become more aware of the need to be culturally sensitive—to know that there are cultural differences for which they must be on the lookout. Remember that the more you know about another's culture, the better will be your predictions of that person's behavior.

The concept of culture is so broad that even the ethnologists (cultural anthropologists) have to break it down into topics to facilitate its study. A listing of such topics will give us a better understanding of what culture is and may also serve as a guide to the international manager when he or she is analyzing a particular problem from the sociocultural viewpoint.

As you can imagine, experts vary considerably as to the components of culture, but the following list is representative of their thinking:

1. Aesthetics.
2. Attitudes and beliefs.
3. Religion.
4. Material culture.
5. Education.
6. Language.
7. Societal organization.
8. Legal characteristics.
9. Political structures.[13]

We shall examine the first seven components in this chapter and leave the legal characteristics and political structures for later chapters.

□ Aesthetics

aesthetics a culture's sense of beauty and good taste

Aesthetics pertains to a culture's sense of beauty and good taste and is expressed in its art, drama, music, folklore, and dances.

Art.   Of particular interest to international businesspeople are the formal aspects of art, color, and form, because of the symbolic meanings they convey. Colors, especially, can be deceptive because they mean different things to different cultures. The color of mourning is black in the United States, white in the Far East, purple in Brazil, and yellow in Mexico. Because green is a propitious color in Islam, any ad or package featuring green is looked at favorably in the Islamic world. However, it is repugnant in parts of Asia, where it connotes the illness and death of the jungle. While in the United States mints are packaged in blue or green paper, in Africa the wrapper is red. These examples illustrate that marketers must be careful to check if colors have any special meanings before using them for products, packages, or advertisements.

Be careful of symbols, too. Seven signifies good luck in the United States but just the opposite in Singapore, Ghana, and Kenya. In Japan, the number 4 is unlucky. In general, the marketer should avoid using a nation's flag or any symbols connected with religion.

> Saudi religious leaders were enraged when a Taiwanese firm sold "blasphemous" shoes in their country. How could they walk on the sacred name, Allah, which was molded into the sole?[14]

It is also important to learn whether there are local aesthetic preferences for form that could affect the design of the product, the package, or even the building in which the firm is located. The American style of steel and glass in the midst of oriental architecture will be a constant reminder to the local population of the outsider's presence.

Music and folklore.   Musical commercials are generally popular worldwide, but the marketer must know what kind of music each market prefers, because tastes vary. Thus, the commercial that used a ballad in the United States might be better received to the tune of a bolero in Mexico or a samba in Brazil. However, if the advertiser is looking to the youth market with a product patently American, then American music will help reinforce its image.

Those who wish to steep themselves in a culture find it useful to study its folklore, which can disclose much about a society's way of life. Although this is usually more than the foreign businessperson has time for, the incorrect use of folklore can sometimes cost the firm a share of the market. For example, associating a product with the cowboy would not obtain the same results in Chile or Argentina as it does in the United States, because in these countries the cowboy is a far less romantic figure—it's just a job. In another instance, a U.S. company may be paying handsome royalties to use American cartoon characters in its promotion, only to find they are considerably less important in foreign markets. In Mexico, songs of the "Singing Cricket" are known to all youngsters and their mothers, and a commercial tie-in with that character would be as advantageous to the firm as its use of Peanuts or Mickey Mouse. In many areas, especially where nationalistic feeling is strong, local firms have been able to compete successfully with foreign affiliates by making use of indigenous folklore in the form of slogans and proverbs. As Herskovits states, tales of folklore are valuable in maintaining a sense of group unity.[15] Knowing them is an indication that one belongs to the group, which recognizes that the outsider is unfamiliar with its folklore.

□ Attitudes and Beliefs

Every culture has a set of attitudes and beliefs that influence nearly all aspects of human behavior and help bring order to a society and its individuals. The more managers can learn about certain key attitudes, the better prepared they will be to understand why people behave as they do, especially when their reactions differ from those that the managers have learned to expect in dealing with their own people.

Among the wide variety of subjects covered by attitudes and beliefs, some are of prime importance to the businessperson. These include attitudes toward time, toward achievement and work, and toward change.

Attitudes toward time.   This cultural characteristic probably presents more adaptation problems for Americans overseas than any other. Time is important in the United States, and much emphasis is placed on it. If we must wait past the appointed hour to see an individual, we feel insulted. This person is not giving our meeting the importance it deserves. Yet the wait could mean just the opposite elsewhere. Latin American or Middle Eastern executives may be taking care of the minor details of their business so that they can attend their important visitor without interruption.

> **An American who has worked in the Middle East for 20 years explains the Middle Eastern concept of time this way: "A lot of the misunderstandings between Middle Easterners and foreigners are due to their different concepts of time and space. At worst, there is no concept at all of time in the Middle East. At best, there is a sort of open-ended concept." The head of Egypt's Industrial Design Center, an Egyptian, states, "The simple wristwatch is, in some respects, much too sophisticated an instrument for the Middle East. One of the first things a foreigner should learn in Egypt is to ignore the second hand. The minute hand can also be an obstacle if he expects Egyptians to be as conscious as he of time ticking away."[16]**

Probably even more critical than short-term patience is long-term patience. American preoccupation with monthly profit and loss statements is a formidable barrier to the establishment of successful business relationships with Asian and Middle Eastern executives, especially during the development of joint ventures and other business relationships that have good potential in the long run—precisely the factors in which these people are most interested.[17]

Americans, be prompt.   Few cultures give the same importance to time that Americans and Europeans do. If any appointment is made with a group of Germans to see them at 12 noon, we can be sure they will be there; but to get the same response from a Brazilian, we must say noon English hour. If not, the Brazilian may show up anytime between noon and 2 o'clock. Compare this with Japan, where a description of an apartment in the rental contract includes the time in minutes required to walk to the nearest train station![18]

Should Americans follow the local custom or be prompt? It depends. In Spain, a general rule is to never be punctual. If you are, you will be considered early.[19] However, in the Middle East, the American penchant for punctuality is well known, and lateness from Americans is considered impolite. The Arabian executives, nonetheless, will usually not arrive at the appointed hour; why should they change their lifetime habits just for a stranger?[20]

Mañana.   Probably one of the most vexing problems for the newcomer to Latin America is the *mañana* attitude. Ask the maintenance man when the machine will be ready, and he responds *mañana*. The American assumes this means "tomorrow," the literal translation, but the maintenance man means "some time in the near future," and if he is reprimanded for not having the machine ready the next day, he is angry and bewildered. He reasons that everyone knows *mañana* means "in the next few days."

This example illustrates that the ability to speak the local language is only half the task of communicating. A manager of an American subsidiary in Saudi Arabia says, "You can be talking the same language with someone, but are you talking on the same wavelength?" He states that he has met few Japanese or Koreans fluent in Arabic, yet they are able to understand and adapt to local conditions much better than Westerners can because they seem to be more sensitive to the Middle Easterner's mentality.[21]

Directness and drive.   The American pride in directness and drive is interpreted by many foreigners as being brash and rude. Although we believe it expedient to get to the point in a discussion, this attitude often irritates others. Time-honored formalities are a vital part of doing business and help to establish amicable relations, considered by people in many countries to be a necessary prerequisite to business discussions.[22] Any attempt to move the negotiations along by ignoring some of the accepted courtesies invites disaster.

Deadlines.   Our emphasis on speed and deadlines is often used against us in business dealings abroad. In Far Eastern countries such as Japan, the American may be asked how long he or she plans to stay at the first meeting. Then negotiations are purposely not finalized until a few hours before the American's departure, when the Japanese know they can wring extra concessions from the foreigner because of his or her haste to finish and return home on schedule.

> **Three Americans, none of whom had ever been to Japan, went to sell tractors to Japanese buyers. They thought the discussions had gone well and prepared to wrap up the deal. However, there was no reaction from the Japanese. The silence became disquieting, and so the Americans lowered the price. Because there was still no reaction, they again lowered the price. This went on until their price was far lower than they had planned. What they didn't know was that the Japanese had become silent not to indicate rejection of the proposition, but merely to think it over, a customary Japanese negotiating practice.[23]**

Attitudes toward achievement and work.   There is a saying in Mexico, "Americans live to work, but we work to live." This is an example of the extreme contrasts among cultural attitudes toward work. Where work is considered necessary to obtain the essentials for survival, once these have been obtained, people may stop working. They do not make the accomplishment of a task an end in itself. This attitude is in sharp contrast to the belief in many industrial societies that work is a moral, and even a religious, virtue.

To the consternation of the production manager with a huge back order, the promise of overtime often fails to keep the workers on the job. In fact, raising employees' salaries frequently results in their working less (economists call this effect the backward-bending labor supply curve).

It is important, however, to note that an additional change has occurred repeatedly in many developing countries as more consumer goods have be-

demonstration effect result of having seen others with desirable goods

come available. The **demonstration effect** (seeing others with these goods) and improvements in infrastructure (roads to bring the products to them and electric power to operate them) cause workers to realize they can have greater prestige and pleasure by owning more goods. Thus, their attitude toward work changes, not because of any alteration of their moral or religious values, but because they now want what only money can buy.

> A Mexican distributor came to one of the writers to complain that a number of his salesmen were producing well for the first week or two of the month but were then slacking off. Investigation showed that the commissions plus salary earned during the periods of high production were about the same each time. It was apparent that the salesmen had earned what they required to live so that they could loaf the rest of the month. By instituting contests and informing the salesmen's wives about the prizes to be won, considerable improvement was obtained.

In the industrialized nations, the opposite trend is being observed. A feeling of prosperity is causing a tendency toward longer vacations (a month in Europe), shorter workweeks, and a greater emphasis on leisure activities. The same is true of Japan. In 1987, the Japanese workweek was pared from 48 to 46 hours, and it will drop to 40 hours by 1993.[24]

Religion and achievement.   Researchers have found differences among cultures with respect to achievement motivation, and attempts have been made to explain these differences on the basis of religion, as we will see in the next section. Although religion is not the only explanatory variable, and may not be the principal explanatory variable, the correlation between the predominant religion and a nation's per capita income is too high to disregard the influence of religion on past economic growth.[25]

Prestigious jobs.   Another aspect of the attitude toward work is the prestige associated with certain kinds of employment. In this country, some types of work are considered more prestigious than others, but there is nowhere near the disdain for physical labor here that there is in many developing countries. The result is an overabundance of attorneys and economists and a lack of toolmakers and welders even when the wages are higher for the latter. The distinction between blue-collar workers and office employees is especially great, as typified by the use of two words in Spanish for the worker—*obrero* (one who labors) signifies a blue-collar worker, whereas *empleado* (employee) signifies an office worker.[26]

Source of recruits.   The lesson to be learned from this discussion is that there are generally sharper differences in the attitudes toward work and achievement among other cultures than American managers find in their own culture. When these managers go abroad, their problem is to recruit subordinates with a need to progress, whatever the underlying motive. Many firms have been successful in locating such persons among relatively well-educated members of the lower social class who view work as a route to the prestige and social acceptance that have been denied them because of their birth.

Attitudes toward change.   The American firm, accustomed to the rapid acceptance by Americans of something new, is frequently surprised to find that new does not carry that kind of magic in markets where something tried and

"The Protestant work ethic isn't cutting
it, so we're switching to Shinto."

Reprinted from *The Wall Street Journal;* permission of Cartoon Features Syndicate.

proven is preferred to the unknown. Europeans are fond of reminding Americans that they are a young nation lacking traditions. The near reverence for traditional methods makes it more difficult for the production manager to install a new process, for the marketer to introduce a new product, or for the treasurer to change the accounting system.

The new idea.   Yet, undeniably, international firms are agents of change, and their personnel must be able to counter resistance to it. The new idea will be more readily acceptable the closer it can be related to the traditional one while at the same time being made to show its relative advantage. In other words, the more consistent a new idea is with a society's attitudes and experiences, the more quickly it will be adopted.

Economic motivation.   In these times of rising expectations, economic motives can be a strong influence for accepting change. Thus, if factory workers can be shown that their income will increase with the new machine or housewives can be convinced that the new frozen food will enable them to work and still provide satisfactory meals for their families, they can be persuaded by the gain in their economic welfare to accept ideas that they might otherwise oppose.

▢ Religion

Religion, an important component of culture, is responsible for many of the attitudes and beliefs affecting human behavior. A knowledge of the basic tenets of some of the more popular religions will contribute to a better understanding of why people's attitudes vary so greatly from country to country.

Protestant work ethic
Christian duty to glorify God by hard work and the practice of thrift

Confucian work ethic same as Protestant work ethic

Work ethics.   We have already mentioned the marked differences in the attitudes toward work and achievement. Europeans and Americans generally view work as a moral virtue and look unfavorably on the idle. This view stems in part from the **Protestant work ethic** as expressed by Luther and Calvin, who believed it was the duty of Christians to glorify God by hard work and the practice of thrift.

In Asian countries where Confucianism is strong, this same attitude toward work is called the **Confucian work ethic,** and in Japan, it's called the Shinto work ethic after the principal religion of that nation.[27] Interestingly,

Courtesy of Paul Chesley: Photographers/Aspen

Generational differences show up in this unposed photo at Kawasaki Steel. Older workers grind away while younger ones share a laugh.

because of other factors—such as a growing feeling of prosperity and a shift to a five-day workweek (with two days off, workers develop new interests)—Japanese employers are finding that the younger workers no longer have the same dedication to their jobs that their predecessors had. Workers rarely show up early to warm the oil in their machines before their shifts start, and some management trainees are actually taking all of their 15 days' vacation time. A representative of the Employers Association states, "Our universities are leisure centers." A recent college graduate claims, "Students ski in the winter and play tennis in the summer. What the companies sometimes find out is that they like skiing better than working."[28]

Asian religions the primary ones are Hinduism, Buddhism, Jainism, and Sikhism (India); Confucianism and Taoism (China); and Shintoism (Japan)

Asian religions.   People from the Western world will encounter some very different notions about God, Man, and Reality in **Asian religions.** In the Judeo-Christian tradition, this world is real and significant because it was created by God. Human beings are likewise significant; so is time, because it began with God's creation and will end when His will has been fulfilled. Each human being has only one lifetime to heed God's word and achieve everlasting life.

In Asian religions, especially in the religions of India, the ideas of reality are different. There is a notion that this world is an illusion because nothing is permanent. Time is cyclical, so all living things, including humans, are in a constant process of birth, death, and reincarnation. The goal of salvation is to escape from the cycle and move into a state of eternal bliss *(nirvana)*. The notion of *karma* (moral retribution) holds that evil committed in one lifetime will be punished in the next. Thus, *karma* is a powerful impetus to do good so as to achieve a higher spiritual status in the next life. Asians who hold these views cannot imagine that they have not had past lives when they may have been plants, animals, or human beings. Of the seven best-known religions that originated in Asia, four came from India (Hinduism, Buddhism,

□ Major Religions of the World

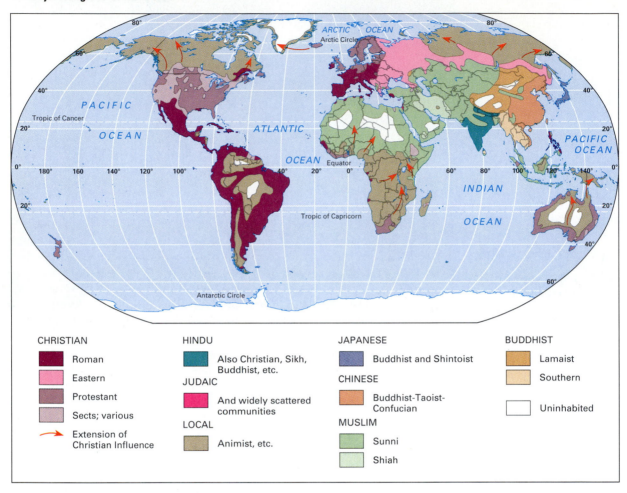

CHRISTIAN
- Roman
- Eastern
- Protestant
- Sects; various
- → Extension of Christian Influence

HINDU
- Also Christian, Sikh, Buddhist, etc.

JUDAIC
- And widely scattered communities

LOCAL
- Animist, etc.

JAPANESE
- Buddhist and Shintoist

CHINESE
- Buddhist-Taoist-Confucian

MUSLIM
- Sunni
- Shiah

BUDDHIST
- Lamaist
- Southern

- Uninhabited

Jainism, and Sikhism), two from China (Confucianism and Taoism), and one from Japan (Shintoism).[29]

Hinduism. This is a conglomeration of religions, without a single founder or a central authority, that is practiced by more than 80 percent of India's population. Although there is great diversity among regions and social classes, Hinduism has certain characteristic features. Most Hindus believe that everything in the world is subject to an eternal process of death and rebirth *(samsura)* and that individual souls *(atmans)* migrate from one body to another. They believe one can be liberated from the *samsura* cycle and achieve that state of eternal bliss *(nirvana)* by (1) yoga (purification of mind and body), (2) devout worship of the gods, or (3) good works and obedience to the laws and customs *(dharmas)* of one's caste.

caste system an aspect of Hinduism by which the entire society is divided into four groups (plus the outcasts) and each is assigned a certain class of work

A knowledge of the **caste system** is important to managers because the castes are the basis of the social division of labor. The highest caste, the Brahmins or priesthood, is followed by the warriors (politicians, landowners), the merchants, the peasants, and the untouchables. An individual's position in a caste is inherited, as is that person's job within the caste, and movement to a higher caste can be made only in subsequent lives. If the gods choose to punish a person, his or her next life will be at a lower caste level. Although the government of India has officially outlawed discrimination based on the caste system, and in fact has worked to improve the situation of those in the lower castes, such discrimination still exists. The manager who places a member of a lower caste in charge of a group of people from a higher one does so at a considerable risk of employee dissatisfaction.

Buddhism.   This religion began in India as a reform movement of Hinduism. At the age of 29, Prince Gautama rejected his wife, son, and wealth and set out to solve the mysteries of misery, old age, and death. After six years of experimenting with yoga, which brought no enlightenment, he suddenly understood how to break the laws of *karma* and the endless cycle of rebirth *(samsura).* Gautama emerged as the Buddha (the Enlightened One).

He renounced the austere self-discipline of the Hindus as well as the extremes of self-indulgence, both of which depended on a craving that locked people into the endless cycle of rebirth. Gautama taught that by extinguishing desire, his followers could attain enlightenment and escape the cycle of existence into *nirvana.* By opening his teaching to everyone, he opposed the caste system.

Because Buddhist monks are involved in politics in the areas where their religion is prevalent and because they are a mobilizing force for political and social action, managers working in these areas need to be aware of what these religious leaders are doing. Even American public opinion was influenced by pictures of Buddhist monks who had set themselves on fire to protest American participation in the Vietnam War.

The Buddhist teaching that if the followers of Buddha have no desires, they will not suffer is also important, because if they have no desires, Buddhists and Hindus have little motive for achievement and for the acquisition of material goods.

Jainism.   This religion was founded by Mahavira, a contemporary of Buddha. The Jain doctrine teaches that there is no creator, no god, and no absolute principle. Through right faith, correct conduct, and right knowledge of the soul, Jains can purify themselves, become free of *samsura,* and achieve *nirvana.* Although relatively few in number, Jains are influential leaders in commerce and scholarship. Their greatest impact on Indian culture is manifested in the widespread acceptance of their nonviolence doctrine, which prohibits animal slaughter, war, and even violent thoughts.

Sikhism.   This is the religion of an Indian ethnic group, a military brotherhood,* and a political movement that was founded by Nanek, who sought a bridge between Hinduism and Islam. Sikhs believe there is a single god, but they also accept the Hindu concepts of *samsura, karma,* and spiritual liberation. The Sikh's holiest temple was partly destroyed by Indian troops who suppressed their movement for self-government. More than 80 percent of all Sikhs live in the Indian state of Punjab, which they hope to make an autonomous state.

Confucianism.   The name of Confucius is inseparable from Chinese culture and civilization, which were already well developed when he set out to master ancient traditions and transform them into a rational system capable of

---

* Baptism into the Sikh brotherhood requires all members to take Singh as a second name.

guiding his people's personal and social behavior. Confucianism may be considered a religion inasmuch as Confucius built a philosophy on the notion that all reality is subject to an eternal mandate from heaven; however, he refused to speculate on the existence of Chinese folk deities and was agnostic on the question of life after death. Essentially, Confucianism is a humanism that elaborates the moral ideals governing human relations.

Confucius taught that each person bears within himself the principle of unselfish love for others, *jen*, the cultivation of which is its own reward. A second principle, *li*, prescribes a gentle decorum in all actions and accounts for the Chinese emphasis on politeness, deference to elders, and ritual courtesies such as bowing.

Taoism.   This is a mystical philosophy founded by Lao-tzu, a contemporary of Confucius. Taoism, which means "philosophy of the way," holds that each of us mirrors the same forces, the male and the female energies (yin and yang) that govern the cosmos. The aim of Taoist meditation and rituals is to free the self from distractions and become empty so as to allow the cosmic forces to act. There should be a unity of the person with nature, so that good acts become spontaneous.

Fung shui.   This ancient custom, with roots in Taoism and nature worship, is based on a simple concept. If buildings, furniture, roads, and other manmade objects are placed in harmony with nature, they can bring good fortune. If not, they will cause a disaster. Although the Chinese government discourages *fung shui* in China, Chinese people around the world practice it, and foreigners living in cities such as Hong Kong and Singapore frequently find *fung shui* can impact their lives.[30]

> Shortly after arriving in Hong Kong, a Citibank vice president moved to a new office building. To please his staff, he called a *fung shui* man to analyze the omens of the office. The man examined the office with a compasslike instrument and then gave the vice president the bad news. He would be harmed seriously unless he installed an aquarium with six black fish and put his desk in an inconvenient spot near his office door. The executive ignored the warnings and within days developed a back problem, caused—he thought—by stretching exercises. A physician found two discs had slipped and said the vice president would be paralyzed for life if he didn't spend two weeks in traction. While he was in the hospital, his secretary installed the fish tank and rearranged the furniture. Today, he sits by the door, near the fish. He says his health is better than ever, and he is frightened of *fung shui*.[31]

Shintoism.   This is the indigenous religion of Japan. It has no founder or bible. Shinto legends define the founding of the Japanese empire as a cosmic act, and the emperor was believed to have divine status. As a part of the World War II settlement, the emperor was forced to renounce such a claim. Shintoism has no elaborate theology or even an organized weekly worship. Its followers come to the thousands of Shinto shrines when they feel moved to do so.

Islam.   About 850 million followers make this youngest universal faith the second largest after Christianity (which has 1.4 billion adherents). Islam means "to submit" in Arabic; and Muslim, meaning "submitting," is the present participle of the same verb. This faith accepts as God's eternal word the Koran, a collection of Allah's (God's) revelations to Muhammad, the founder of Islam. Unlike the founders of the other major religions, the prophet Muhammad was not only the spokesman of Allah but also the founder of what became a vast temporal and ecclesiastical empire; in other words, he was a head of state as well as a prophet of God. In Muslim nations, there is no separation of church and state.

The basic spiritual duties of all Muslims consist of the five pillars of faith: (1) accepting the confession of faith ("There is no God but God, and Muhammad is the Messenger of God"); (2) making the five daily prayers while facing Mecca (Muhammad's birthplace, where he was inspired to preach God's word in the year A.D. 610); (3) giving charity; (4) fasting during the daylight hours of Ramadan, a 29- or 30-day month in Islam's lunar calendar; and (5) making a pilgrimage to Mecca at least once in their lifetime. Some Muslims claim there is a sixth duty, *jihad,* which refers to the various forms of striving for the faith, such as the inner struggle for purification. However, this term is often translated as "the holy war."

The split that occurred between the Sunnis and the Shiites over the succession to Muhammad's authority is as important as the division that took place in Christendom with the Reformation. Muhammad's survivors decided that his successors (called *caliphs*) should be elected by members of the Islamic community, and they were—four times. But after the fourth successor, Ali (Muhammad's cousin), was murdered, the caliphate passed to the monarchical house of Ummaya. Ali's son, Hussayn, claimed the caliphate was his, as Muhammad's heir, and he started a rebellion to confirm his claim. Hussayn was killed in a battle by a Sunni caliph.

This split the Muslim world between the Sunnis (followers of the Prophet's Path) and the Shiites (Party of Ali). After their defeat, the Shiites, feeling that they had been wronged, became dissenters within the Arab empire who were given to violence against authority. Although the Shiites and the Sunnis agree on the fundamentals of Islam, they differ in other respects. The Sunnis are an austere sect that is less authoritarian and more pragmatic than the Shiites. In their view, as long as Muslims accept Allah, they are free to interpret their religion as they like. The Shiites, on the other hand, insist that those claiming to be Muslim must put themselves under the authority of a holy man *(ayatollah).* This has created a clergy that wields enormous temporal and spiritual power. It was the Iranian Shia clergy who brought down the shah of Iran.[32]

Salman Rushdie. Another example of the Shiite's political power occurred in early 1989, when a book, *The Satanic Verses,* precipitated what some Islamic experts regard as the most incendiary literary fight in Islamic history. Although Salman Rushdie, the author, denied that his novel was antireligious, nearly all Muslims considered it blasphemous. On February 14, Ayatollah Khomeini, Iran's spiritual ruler, announced that the author must die for the sin of insulting Islam and promised martyrdom for anyone who killed him. Another cleric announced that a bounty of $2.6 million had been offered. The following day, the bounty was doubled.[33]

Critics claim that the ayatollah had noticed a sharp decline in revolutionary fervor among his followers and used the book as a tool to mobilize his constituency. Marvin Zonis, a political scientist at the University of Chicago, said, "It's a way to make domestic capital out of foreign adventure." But

Georges Sabagh, director of UCLA's Near East Studies Center, stated, "If the man is struck by a thunderbolt, all the better."[34] Later, Iran's president remarked that Rushdie's death threat might be withdrawn if he would apologize to Muslims and to Khomeini. A day later, Rushdie apologized, but the death threat has never been withdrawn. In a clandestine visit to the United States in December 1991, Rushdie pleaded not to be forgotten.[35]

Sunni–Shia conflict. Businesspeople doing business with Muslim countries should understand the Sunni–Shia conflict, because much of what occurs in these countries is the result of it. Although most Muslim countries are Sunni governed, many of them, such as Kuwait, the emirates, Bahrain, and other small states in the Gulf, have substantial Shia populations. Furthermore, small Shia minorities can cause trouble for the government. For example, Saudi Arabia's Shia population is very small—only 250,000—and is concentrated in the eastern oil fields. Iran's Shia government continually broadcasts appeals to the Saudi Shiites to overthrow the regime. In Iraq, 52 percent of the population is Shiite, and, as you can imagine, this division has given rise to violent clashes between religious dissidents and the government's all-Sunni army. Syria, on the other hand, is predominantly Sunni, but its government is controlled by secular pro-Soviet Baathist socialists who belong to a Shia sect (Alawi).[36]

Even where the Sunni–Shia conflict is not a problem, two of the five pillars of faith can be bothersome to Western managers. The dawn-to-dusk fasting during the month of Ramadan causes workers' output to drop sharply, and the requirement to pray five times daily also affects output, because when they hear the call to prayer, Muslim workers stop whatever they are doing to pray where they are.

> **An American manager in Pakistan for the purpose of getting a new factory into production came to the plant the first day, saw that production had started as it should, and went into his office to do some work. Suddenly, all of the machinery stopped. He rushed out, expecting to find a power failure. Instead, he found workers on their prayer rugs. The manager returned to his office and lowered his production estimates.**

Animism. In a number of African and Latin American countries, animism, a kind of spirit worship that includes magic and witchcraft, is a major religion. It is often combined with Catholicism to present a strange mixture of mysticism, taboos, and fatalism. Animists believe their dead relatives are ever present and will be pleased if the living act in the same way as their ancestors. The resultant strong tendency to perpetuate traditions makes it extremely difficult for marketers and production managers to initiate changes. To be accepted, these changes must relate to the animists' beliefs. The foreign manager must also be cognizant of the proper religious protocols in situations such as factory and store dedications. If the evil spirits are not properly exorcised, they will remain to cause all sorts of problems, such as worker injuries, machinery breakdowns, and defective products.

> **Evil spirits wreaked havoc in an American-owned semiconductor factory in Kuala Lumpur, Malaysia. The plant consists of an enormous room filled with hundreds of women looking into microscopes and television monitors.**

☐ **TABLE 9–1   Estimated Religious Population of the World (In thousands)**

Religionists	Africa	Asia	Europe	Latin America	North America	Oceania	U.S.S.R.	World	Percent
Christians	310,600	252,800	411,300	419,078	235,500	22,000	107,500	1,758,778	33.3%
Roman Catholics	116,670	118,900	261,080	390,050	95,600	7,980	5,500	995,780	18.8
Protestants	82,900	78,380	73,500	16,600	94,900	7,310	9,700	363,290	6.9
Orthodox	27,100	3,516	35,950	1,696	5,920	560	92,200	166,942	3.2
Anglicans	25,500	680	32,760	1,250	7,230	5,560	0	72,980	1.4
Other Christians	58,430	51,324	8,010	9,482	31,850	590	100	159,786	3.0
Muslims	264,132	612,768	12,500	1,300	5,600	100	38,600	935,000	17.7
Nonreligious	1,800	686,600	52,100	16,500	22,100	3,200	83,700	866,000	16.4
Hindus	1,400	700,448	700	850	1,250	350	2	705,000	13.3
Buddhists	20	301,215	270	520	550	25	400	303,000	5.7
Atheists	300	155,280	17,500	3,100	1,300	520	55,000	233,000	4.4
Chinese folk religionists	12	179,717	60	70	120	20	1	180,000	3.4
New religionists	20	136,009	50	510	1,400	10	1	138,000	2.6
Tribal religionists	67,006	24,000	1	900	40	65	0	92,012	1.7
Jews	25	17,578	230	8	250	9	1	18,100	0.3
Sikhs	320	5,375	1,460	1,050	6,900	95	2,200	17,400	0.3
Shamanists	1	9,845	2	1	1	1	250	10,100	0.2
Confucians	1	5,766	2	2	26	1	2	5,800	0.1
Baha'is	1,420	2,578	90	770	360	75	7	5,300	0.1
Jains	50	3,576	15	4	4	1	0	3,650	0.1
Shintoists	2	3,097	1	1	1	1	0	3,100	0.1
Other religionists	410	11,825	1	3,433	478	4	327	17,938	0.3
World population	647,518	3,106,479	497,743	448,098	275,880	26,478	287,991	5,292,178	100.0

Note: Totals not exact due to rounding.
Source: *World Almanac 1992,* p. 725.

One afternoon, a girl claimed she saw an ugly woman in her microscope. The operator was pulled screaming to the first-aid room. The manager admitted that was a mistake: "Before I knew it, we had girls all over being held down by supervisors. It was like a battlefield."

The factory was evacuated, but when the night crew arrived, the spirit returned. "Word had gone out that evil spirits were loose in the factory because of a dance we had the previous weekend. At night, it was worse. All we could do was hold them down, carry them out to the buses, and send them home."

The next morning, a licensed healer was brought in. His recommendation—sacrifice a goat. That afternoon, a goat was killed and its blood was sprinkled on the factory floor. It was cooked in the cafeteria and eaten by the workers.

"Next morning, we started up, and everything was fine."[37]

Table 9–1 lists the religious populations of the world.

The importance of religion to management.   You have seen that religions have a pervasive influence on business. How effective can offers to pay time and a half for overtime and bonuses based on productivity be in a company whose workers are mainly Buddhists or Hindus? Strict adherents to these religions attempt to rid themselves of desires, and thus they have little need for an income beyond that which permits them to attain the basic necessities of life. When their incomes begin to rise, they have a tendency to reduce their efforts so that personal incomes remain unchanged.

Religious holidays and rituals can affect employee performance and work scheduling. When members of different religious groups work together, there may even be strife, division, and instability within the work force. Managers must respect the religious beliefs of others and adapt business practices to the religious constraints present in other cultures. Of course, to be able to do this, they must first know what those beliefs and constraints are.

◻ Material Culture

material culture all manmade objects; concerned with *how* people make things (technology) and *who* makes *what* and *why* (economics)

Material culture refers to all manmade objects and is concerned with *how* people make things (technology) and *who* makes *what* and *why* (economics).

Technology.   The technology of a society is the mix of the usable knowledge that the society applies and directs toward the attainment of cultural and economic objectives; it exists in some form in every cultural organization.[38] It is significant in the efforts of developing nations to improve their level of living and a vital factor in the competitive strategies of multinational firms.

Technological superiority is the goal of most companies, of course, but it is especially important to international companies because:

1. It enables a firm to be competitive or even attain leadership in world markets.

   At one time, Procter & Gamble and Unilever were competing worldwide for the laundry detergent market, but then P&G introduced Tide, a synthetic detergent with superior cleaning power. Its sales took off and left Unilever far behind. Finally, Unilever introduced its own synthetic detergent, but P&G had stolen the lead.[39]

2. It can be sold (licensing or management contract), or it can be embodied in the company's products.

3. It can give a firm confidence to enter a foreign market even when other companies are already established there.

4. It can enable the firm to obtain better-than-usual conditions for a foreign market investment because the host government wants the technology that only the firm has (for example, permission for a wholly owned subsidiary in a country where the government normally insists on joint ventures with a local majority).

   IBM, confident of its superior technology, insisted on and obtained permission from the Mexican government to set up a wholly owned subsidiary when other computer manufacturers were forced to accept local partners.

5. It can enable a company with only a minority equity position to control a joint venture and preserve it as a captive market for semiprocessed inputs that it—but not the joint venture—produces.

6. It can change the international division of labor. Firms that had moved production overseas where labor was cheaper have now

returned to their home countries because automation has drastically reduced the direct labor content of their products.

7. It is causing major firms to form competitive alliances in which each partner shares the high costs of research and development.

Cultural aspects of technology.   Technology includes not only the application of science to production, but also skill in marketing, finance, and management. Its cultural aspects concern governments because their people may not be ready to accept the cultural changes a new technology may bring.[40] Some say the shah of Iran's overthrow resulted in part from his trying to introduce new technology at a too rapid rate.

Technology's cultural aspects are certainly important to international managers, because new production methods and new products often require people to change their beliefs and ways of living. The self-employed farmer frequently finds the discipline required to become a factory worker excessively demanding. If workers have been accustomed to the production conditions of cottage industries in which each individual performs all of the production operations, they find it difficult to adjust to the monotony of tightening a single bolt. The "throw away instead of repair" philosophy behind the design of so many new products necessitates a change in the use habits of people who have been accustomed to repairing something to keep it operating until it is thoroughly worn out. *Generally, the greater the difference between the old and new method or product, the more difficult it is for the firm to institute a change.*

High GNP—High level of technology.   The differences in levels of technology among nations are used as a basis for judging whether nations are developed or developing. Generally, a nation with a higher GNP per capita utilizes a higher level of technology than one whose per capita income is smaller. Because of technological dualism, however, analysts must be wary of assuming that just because the general technological level is low, the particular industry they are examining is employing a simple technology.

technological dualism
the side-by-side presence of technologically advanced and technologically primitive production systems

Technological dualism.   **Technological dualism** is a prominent feature of many LDCs. In the same country, one sector may be technologically advanced, with high productivity, while the production techniques of another sector may be old and labor intensive. This condition may be the result of the host government's insistence that foreign investors import only the most modern machinery rather than used-but-serviceable equipment that would be less costly and could create more employment.

Sometimes the preferences are reversed. The host government, beset by high unemployment, may argue for labor-intensive processes, while the foreign firm prefers automated production, both because it is the kind the home office is most familiar with and because its use lessens the need for skilled labor, which is usually in short supply. To understand which policy the host government is following, management must study its laws and regulations and talk with host country officials.

appropriate technology
the technology (advanced, intermediate, or primitive) that most closely fits the society using it

Appropriate technology.   Rather than choosing between labor-intensive and capital-intensive processes, many experts in economic development are recommending **appropriate technology,** which can be labor intensive, intermediate, or capital intensive. The idea is to choose the technology that most closely fits the society using it. For example, in Africa, bricks are usually made in large-city factories using modern technology or locally in hand-poured, individual molds. In Botswana, an American group, AT International, designed an inexpensive small press with which four people can produce 1,500 bricks a day.[41] This is an intermediate technology that is also an appropriate technology.

In India, a small manufacturer, Patel, has taken three fourths of the detergent market from Lever, the giant multinational, by using labor-intensive technology. Lever's Surf™ brand dominated the market until Patel, realizing that a high-quality, high-priced product was not appropriate for a poor country, set up a chain of shops in which people mixed the ingredients by hand. This primitive method is tailored to Indian conditions and now enables the company to outsell Lever on the basis of price. Its annual sales exceed $250 million.[42]

Technology transfer's impact on politics.   The transfer of technology is also an important part of international politics. For over 40 years, the United States and its allies have tried to keep sensitive technology from getting into the hands of the Soviet bloc. A body called the Coordinating Committee on Multilateral Export Controls (COCOM), comprising Australia, Japan, and all the NATO members except Iceland, administers a common set of export controls.

Since the breakup of the Soviet Union, COCOM members have relaxed restrictions on the exports of high-tech equipment to the Eastern bloc, but they continue to maintain strict controls on items that were found to be critical to the security of the United States and its allies in the Persian Gulf War. These include night-vision devices and fiber-optic communications systems. The allied coalition had difficulty in disrupting the fiber-optic links that Iraq used for military communication. A new feature of the 1991 agreement allows individual nations to continue to control goods and technologies dropped from the COCOM list that could contribute to the development of nuclear, chemical, and biological weapons.[43]

boomerang effect when technology sold to companies in another nation is used to produce goods to compete with those of the seller of the technology

Boomerang effect.   Besides national security, another reason firms fear to sell their technology abroad is the **boomerang effect.** For example, Japanese firms have become less willing to sell their technology to NICs, such as Korea. They fear that by giving Korea their technology today, they make Korea a tougher competitor tomorrow. As a result, Korea is turning more to the United States for technical assistance. This suggests why Korean–American ties of all kinds are strengthening. As an official from the Korean Ministry of Science and Technology said on a visit to the United States, "If America and Korea join together, we can overcome Japan."[44] Interestingly, fear of the boomerang effect has caused some American firms to restrict the sale of their technology to the Japanese.

Government controls.   The influence of technology is very great because the level of technology used affects the size of the foreign investment, the quality and number of workers employed, and even what a particular country can produce.[45] For these reasons, plus what many LDC governments consider abuses in the sale of technology by the multinationals, many LDCs have enacted strong laws controlling the purchase of technical assistance. Some have laws that limit the amount of royalties paid and prohibit many of the restrictions regularly used by the multinationals, such as those that oblige licensees to purchase raw materials from the licensor, prohibit licensees from exporting, and require licensees to transfer to licensors any improvements they have made in the technology. This worldwide trend among developing nations toward a severe limitation on the after-sale control an international firm has over its own technology has caused many firms not only to cut back on licensing but also to reduce new foreign investments.[46]

The LDCs' reaction.   Because of complaints from developing nations that technology from the industrialized countries was excessively capital-intensive as well as expensive, the United Nations Industrial Development Organization (UNIDO) established an Industrial and Technological Bank (INTIB) in 1977 to facilitate the exchange of technologies that are simpler, less expensive, or more appropriate than those obtainable from developed nations. In addition, a Technological Information Exchange System was created to permit the exchange of information concerning the terms and conditions of the technology contracts approved by government technology regulatory agencies. Another INTIB activity is a Joint Patents Program with the World Intellectual Property Organization. Valuable information is obtained from patent documents, cataloged, and made available to firms in developing nations.

Apparently, the activities of INTIB will reduce the profitability in sales of technology by international firms. Because all governments will have access to the terms of licensing contracts, charging one client more than another for the same technology will be difficult. The inclusion of technology as part of a package deal will be less lucrative because information furnished by INTIB will improve the ability of an LDC regulatory body to separate the cost of know-how from that of hardware and engineering. Finally, some technology that firms in LDCs would have heretofore had to purchase from multinationals will be available free of charge.

Economics.   The decision the global or multinational headquarters makes as to the kind of technology to be used by a subsidiary will, within any constraints imposed by the host government, depend on various measurements of the material culture. Economic yardsticks such as power generated per capita and number of high school graduates can uncover possible problems in the distribution and promotion of the product, help determine market size, and provide information on the availability of such resources as raw materials, skilled and unskilled labor, capital equipment, economic infrastructure (communications, financial system), and management talent. You studied these in Chapter 7.

□ Education

Although education in its widest sense can be thought of as any part of the learning process that equips an individual to take his or her place in the adult society, nearly everyone in the Euramerican culture equates education with formal schooling.

Education yardsticks.   The firm contemplating foreign investment has no indicators of the educational level of a country's inhabitants except the usual yardsticks of formal education: literacy rate, kinds of schools, quantity of schools and their enrollments, and possibly the amount per capita spent on education. Such data underestimate the size of the vocationally trained group in the many developing countries where people learn a trade through apprenticeships starting at a very early age (12 to 13 years). Like other international statistics, the published literacy rate must be suspect. The literacy census often consists of asking respondents whether they can read and write, and the signing of their names is taken as proof of their literacy. Nonetheless, these data do provide some assistance. Marketers are interested in the literacy rate because it helps them decide what type of media to employ and at what level they should prepare advertisements, labels, point-of-purchase displays, and owner's manuals. The personnel manager will use the literacy rate as a guide in estimating what kinds of people will be available for staffing the operation.

As with most kinds of data, the trends in education should be studied. It is important to realize that the general level of education is rising throughout the world. Table 9–2 illustrates the extent of this increase.

Note that in a little over 20 years, the percentage has tripled in the low-income nations, increased by 12 times in the high-income oil-exporting countries, and doubled in the industrial nations. The implication for international businesspeople is that they must prepare to meet the needs of more sophisticated and better-educated consumers. They also can expect a better-educated work force.

While these data are indicative of the general level of education, unfortunately they tell us nothing about the quality of education, nor do they indicate how well the supply of graduates meets the demand.

Educational mix.   Until the 1970s, management education in Europe lagged far behind what was available in the United States. There was a feeling that managers were born, not made, and that they could be trained only on the job. Thus, there was little demand for formal business education.

However, a combination of factors has caused a proliferation of European business schools patterned on the American model:

1. Increased competition in the European Community, resulting in a demand for better-trained managers.
2. The return to Europe of American business school graduates.
3. The establishment of American-type schools with American faculty and frequently with the assistance of American universities.

This trend has been much slower in developing countries, where, historically, higher education has emphasized the study of the humanities, law, and medicine. Engineering has not been popular because, with the exception of architecture and civil engineering, there have been few engineering job opportunities in these preindustrial societies. Business education has been less popular than other fields because a business career lacked prestige.

In Chile, one of the writers was given an engineer to train as a V-belt technician. When he began using engineering terms, he noticed that the engineer could not comprehend him, and so he asked the man what kind of engineer he was. To his surprise, the answer was *commercial engineer.* In a land of professional titles,

TABLE 9–2
Percentage of Adults, Ages 20 to 24, in Post–High School Education

Economies	1965	1988
Low income	1%	3%
Lower-middle income	7	17
Upper-middle income	6	16
High income oil-exporting	1	12
Industrial market	21	40

Source: *World Development Report, 1991* (New York: World Development Bank, 1991), pp. 260–61.

apparently the government thought this was the best way to give professional recognition to business graduates. In Latin America, a person is commonly addressed by his professional title—*Ingeniero* Garcia (engineer) or *Licenciado* Lopez (economist or attorney). A similar practice is followed in Germany and in most central European countries.

As developing nations industrialize, there is a greater competition in the marketplace and the job opportunities for engineers and business school graduates increase. Not only do the multinationals recruit such personnel, but the local firms do too when they find that the new competition forces them to improve the efficiency of their operations.

Brain drain. Most developing nations are convinced that economic development is impossible without the development of human resources, and for the last two decades especially, governments have probably overinvested in higher education in relation to the demand for students. The result has been rising unemployment among the educated, which has led to a **brain drain**—the emigration of professionals to the industrialized nations. A study done by UNCTAD estimated that about 500,000 professionals had left Third World countries since World War II. However, the incidence of brain drain varied enormously because most come from a limited number of countries in Asia, such as India, Pakistan, Egypt, and Korea.[47]

The International Labor Organization estimates that each emigrant signifies a loss of $20,000 to that country; on that basis, the cost of the brain drain to the developing nations would be over $6 billion.[48]

Brain drain facts:

1. Each year, 6,000 Taiwanese come to study in the United States, but only 20 percent return home.
2. There are 8,000 Israeli engineers in the United States, which Israel says has created a severe bottleneck in its own development of sophisticated industry.
3. About one half of the 1,000 students who graduate annually from the 27 Philippine medical schools go abroad.
4. The United States alone has 4,000 Greek research scientists, compared with just 5,000 living in Greece. There are also 1,200 Greek business professors working in the United States, but there is no university M.B.A. program in Greece and there is an acute shortage of skilled managers.
5. In U.S. graduate schools of engineering, half of the assistant professors under age 35 are foreign.

brain drain the emigration of highly educated professionals to another country

6. At IBM's research headquarters, 27 percent of the researchers are foreign.[49]

7. Israel is absorbing some 2,000 scientists who have emigrated from the former Soviet Union, and there may be as many as 10,000 more wishing to emigrate.[50] Israel now has the highest concentration of scientists in the world—30 for every 10,000 citizens versus 25 for the United States.[51]

8. Governments of industrialized nations fear that unemployed Soviet scientists will work for countries such as Iraq, Syria, and Libya on the development of nuclear, biological, and chemical weapons. To prevent this, other nations besides Israel are offering them employment. The South Koreans, for example, agreed in 1992 to hire 110 scientists to work at their research institutes.[52]

The prime minister of Jamaica made an interesting observation. During the 1977–80 period, over 8,000 top professionals, 50 percent of the country's most highly trained citizens, emigrated, primarily to the United States. He estimated that the education of these people cost his nation $168.5 million. During that same period, U.S. aid to Jamaica totaled only $116.3 million.[53]

Developing countries are now demanding that the industrial nations pay compensation for the loss of revenue due to the outflow of skilled people. In rebuttal, a U.S. State Department economist told a UN conference that "the proposal tends to ignore the fact that people are people. They aren't commodities, and they aren't traded."[54] Obviously, he knew nothing about professional baseball.

Government authorities are deeply concerned about the loss of skills and have come to realize that there must be faster new job creation, not only to stop the costly loss but also to avoid serious political repercussions. To provide more jobs, they are adopting developmental plans that encourage labor-intensive exports and discourage the introduction of labor-saving processes. The pressure of the unemployed educated is also forcing officials in many areas to soften the terms for foreign investment.

reverse brain drain
the return of highly educated professionals to their home countries

Reverse brain drain. A "**reverse brain drain**" is preoccupying American educators and businesspeople. After suffering a severe brain drain for over 30 years, Korea and Taiwan are luring home those Korean and Taiwanese engineers and scientists with American doctorates and 10 or more years' experience in American high-tech firms. More money and the opportunity to start businesses in these industrializing countries are the attractions.[55] The returnees are having a visible effect on their countries' competitiveness. A vice president at TRW, which employs many scientists and engineers, calls the reverse brain drain "the largest technology transfer program in the history of the world."[56]

The director of the Commission on Professionals in Science and Technology said, "We've been counting on foreign graduates to stay here and fill our needs because we haven't been filling our own needs for a long time. There's nobody to replace them." According to the Council on Competitiveness, between 1,300 and 1,800 jobs for engineering professors are unfilled, and the shortage is expected to grow as many American professors are approaching retirement age.[57]

□ **FIGURE 9-2**
Nations Whose Adult Literacy Rate Is Less than 20 Percent

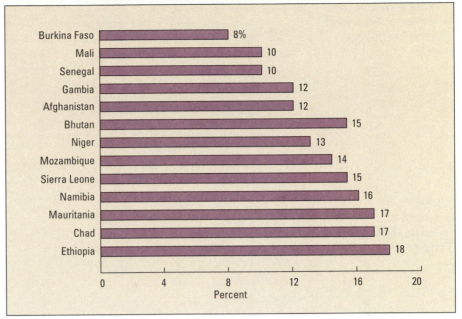

Source: *World Almanac 1992,* pp. 647–737.

Adult literacy.   Many governments are also questioning the wisdom of spending funds to highly educate a few and are now giving priority to primary educators as a means of achieving universal *literacy*. The success of these programs is evidenced by the reduction of world adult illiteracy from 42 percent in 1960 to 31 percent in 1980.

However, the latest data show that the literacy rate was still below the world average in at least 70 nations. Only Norway claimed 100% adult literacy, and in Saudi Arabia and Togo, only the male literacy rate was mentioned. Figure 9–2 lists the nations with literacy rates of less than 20 percent.

Inasmuch as the results of an adult literacy program are immediate, whereas it takes 10 to 20 years for the primary school generation to be productive, more attention is being given to adult education, an important trend for international managements to note. For example, in only four years, Brazil was able to reduce the illiteracy rate for adult Brazilians by one third, and the cost, allowing for dropouts, was only $11 per student. The program's annual budget was $26 million, which is less than New York City spends just to repair and maintain its school buildings.

Women's education.   Another important trend is the fall in the illiteracy rate for women. The literacy differences between older and younger female age groups is striking. In Africa, which has the world's highest illiteracy rate, the percentage of women who could read and write grew from 18 percent to 27 percent between 1970 and 1980 and was expected to rise to 40 percent by 1990.

Nearly every government now has a goal, if not an actual policy, of providing free and compulsory education for both genders. Notice in Table 9–3 the improvement from 1965 to 1988.

Many more women are enrolling in universities worldwide. As you can see

□ **TABLE 9–3**
Percentage of School-Age Population in Primary Schools

Economies	Total		Female	
	1965	1988	1965	1988
Low income	49%	75%	37%	68%
Lower-middle income	89	103*	81	101
Upper-middle income	98	104	94	103
Oil exporters	50	87	37	81
OECD members	104	103	106	103

*Percentages may exceed 100 percent because some pupils are younger or older than the country's standard primary school age.
Source: *World Development Report, 1991* (New York: World Bank, 1991), pp. 260–61.

□ **TABLE 9–4**
Percentage of University-Age Women Enrolled in Universities

	1960	1990
World	39%	54%
Developed nations	65	79
Developing nations	29	48
Africa	14	38
North America	82	93
Arab states	16	50
Asia	33	48
Oceania	65	75

Source: *UNESCO Statistical Yearbook 1990* (New York), pp. 2–30, 2–31.

in Table 9–4, the percentage of women of university age attending universities in Africa and the Arab states has tripled in just 25 years.

These statistics are significant to businesspeople because in almost every country, educated women have fewer, healthier, and better-educated children than do uneducated women. They achieve higher labor force participation rates and higher earnings. Undoubtedly, this is leading to an increased role for women in the family's decision making, which will require marketers to redo their promotional programs to take advantage of this consequential trend.

□ Language

Probably the most apparent cultural distinction that the newcomer to international business perceives is in the means of communication. Differences in the spoken language are readily discernible, and after a short period in the new culture it becomes apparent that there are variations in the unspoken language (manners and customs) as well.

Spoken language.   Language is the key to culture, and without it, people find themselves locked out of all but a culture's perimeter. At the same time, in learning a language, people can't understand the nuances, double meanings of words, and slang unless they also learn the other aspects of the culture. Fortunately, the learning of both goes hand in hand; a certain feel for a people and their attitudes naturally develops with a growing mastery of their language.

Courtesy of European Community

Evidence of the language division in Belgium. Where to go? North or South?

Languages delineate cultures.   Spoken languages demarcate cultures, just as physical barriers do. In fact, nothing equals the spoken language for distinguishing one culture from another. If two languages are spoken in a country, there will be two separate cultures (Belgium); if four languages are spoken, there will be four cultures (Switzerland); and so forth.[58]

A poll taken of the German-speaking and French-speaking cultures in Switzerland illustrates how deeply opinions on crucial issues diverge even in a small country.[59] For example, 83.3 percent of the German Swiss regard environmental protection as one of Switzerland's five major problems, compared to 45.1 percent of the French Swiss. Note in Figure 9–3 how each culture rates the importance of various domestic issues.

What is occurring in Canada because of the sharp divisions between the English- and French-speaking regions is ample evidence of the force of languages in delineating cultures. The differences among the Basques, Catalans, and Spaniards and the differences between the French and Flemish of Belgium are other notable examples of the sharp cultural and often political differences between language groups. However, it does *not* follow from this generalization that cultures are the same wherever the same language is spoken. As a result of Spain's colonization, Spanish is the principal language of 21 Latin American nations, but no one should believe that Chile and Mexico are culturally similar. Moreover, generally because of cultural differences, many words in both the written and spoken languages of these countries are completely different. Even within a country, words vary from one region to another, also due in part to cultural differences.

Foreign language.   Where many spoken languages exist in a single country (India and many African nations), one foreign language usually serves as the principal vehicle for communication across cultures. Nations that were

☐ **FIGURE 9–3   Differences in What's Worrying the Swiss (Percent)***

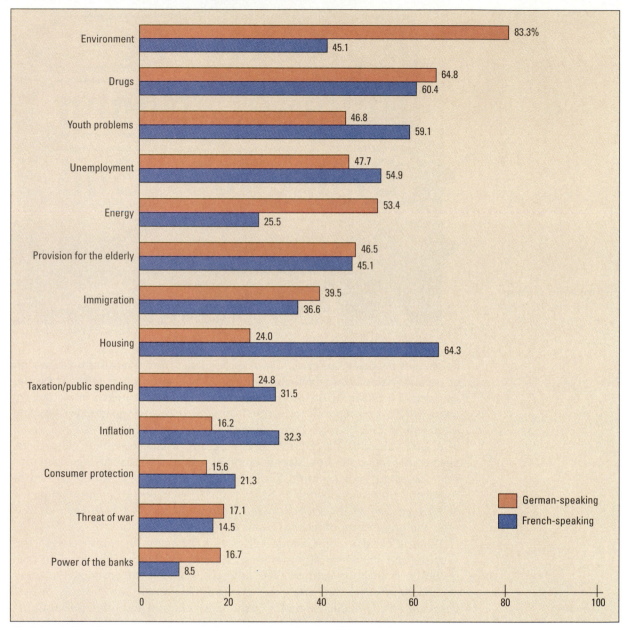

*Carried out by Isopublic on a representative sample of respondents from all sections of the population between May 4 and July 8, 1988.
Source: "What's Worrying the Swiss?" *Bulletin* (Zurich: Crédit Suisse, April 1988), p. 4.

lingua franca a foreign language used to communicate among a nation's diverse cultures that have diverse languages

formerly colonies generally use the language of their ex-rulers; thus French is the **lingua franca,** or "link" language, of the former French and Belgian colonies in Africa, English in India, and Portuguese in Angola.[60] Although they serve as a national language, these foreign substitutes are not the first language of anyone and, consequently, are less effective than the native tongues for reaching mass markets or for day-to-day conversations between managers

Dutch-speaking

Brussels

French-speaking

Belgium divided

Courtesy of European Community

and workers. Even in countries with only one principal language, such as Germany and France, there are problems of communication because of the large numbers of Greeks, Turks, Spaniards, and others who were recruited to ease labor shortages. A German supervisor may have workers from three or four countries and be unable to speak directly with any of them. To ameliorate this situation, managements try to separate the work force according to origin; that is, all Turks are placed in the paint shop, all Greeks on the assembly line, and so on, but the preferred solution is to teach managers the language of their workers. Invariably, such training has resulted in an increase in production, fewer product defects, and higher worker morale.

> General Tire—Chile sponsored a reverse language training program in which every employee could take free English courses given on the premises after work. Not only managers but also supervisors and even workers attended classes. The program was an excellent morale builder.

English, the link language of business.   When a Swedish businessperson talks with a Japanese businessperson, the conversation generally will be in English. The use of English as a business *lingua franca* is spreading in Europe so rapidly that it is replacing French and German as the most widely spoken language among Europeans. Satellite television is credited for bringing it to millions of homes where English was previously not spoken. Already 10 million homes receive English news broadcasts from the Super Channel in England, and this number is expected to rise to 45 million homes by 1996. In Norway, for example, learning English is compulsory; but even where it is not, young Europeans choose to study it as their second language. English is now spoken by 42 percent of the 15-to-25-year olds. This is double the number of people who have learned French and over four times as many who know German.[61] A number of European multinationals—such as Philips, the Dutch electronics manufacturer ($26 billion annual sales), and SKF, the Swedish producer of ball bearings ($3 billion annual sales)—have adopted English as their house language. Similarly, some major Japanese firms have adopted English as their official language. Matsushita Electric, for example,

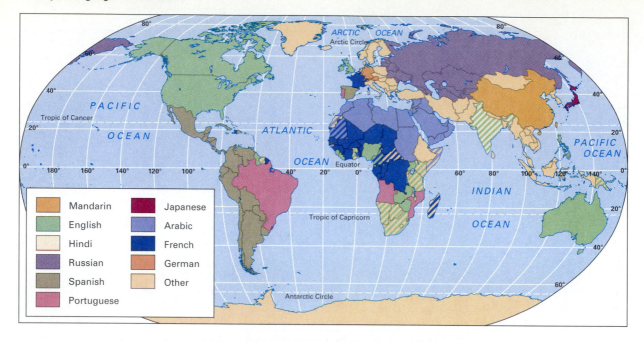

Major Languages of the World

Legend:
- Mandarin
- English
- Hindi
- Russian
- Spanish
- Portuguese
- Japanese
- Arabic
- French
- German
- Other

has warned its employees that by 1993, all international in-house conferences will be conducted in English.[62]

Must speak the local language. Even though more and more businesspeople are speaking English, when they buy, they insist on doing business in their own language. The seller who speaks it has a competitive edge. Moreover, knowing the language of the area indicates respect for its culture and the area's people.

In many countries, it is a social blunder to begin a business conversation by talking business. Most foreigners expect to establish a social relationship first, and the casual, exploratory conversation that precedes business talks may take from 15 minutes to several meetings, depending on the importance of the meetings. Obviously, people can establish a better rapport in a one-on-one conversation than through an interpreter. Look at the trouble this person would have avoided if he had spoken Spanish.

> **A German engineer, in Colombia to work on a pipeline, arrived at a hotel in the interior, where he tried to explain to the desk clerk that he had a suitcase full of cash that he wanted the hotel to keep. Because he knew no Spanish, he was having difficulty making himself understood. During the conversation, the desk clerk opened the suitcase in front of everyone in the lobby. A week later, the engineer was kidnapped by a guerrilla group and held for a month.[63]**

Translation. The ability to speak the language well does not eliminate the need for translators. The smallest of markets requires technical manuals, catalogs, and good advertising ideas, and a lack of local talent to do the work does not mean that the organization must do without these valuable sales aids. The solution, even when the parent firm does not insist on international standardization, is to obtain this material from headquarters and have it translated if the costs are not prohibitive and suitable reproduction facilities are available locally. If the catalog or manual cannot be reproduced locally, the translation can be made and sent to the home office for reproduction. The

WORLDVIEW
Devolve and Rule

Belgian Prime Minister Martens's government fell for the eighth time, and the events that led to the collapse and those after were straight from Hooterville. First, two arms makers in French-speaking Wallonia were given permission to sell weapons to the Middle East. The Flemish (Dutch-speaking) ministers walked out in protest and the government collapsed. Martens formed another government and the arms sale went ahead. The French-speaking parties in the new government crowed so loudly about this that the Flemish parties decided to renege on an agreement that was going to allow the proceeds from the sale of television licenses (each TV owner must buy a license) to help pay the wages of French-speaking teachers. French-speaking ministers retaliated by threatening to block contracts for new telephone exchanges that would primarily benefit Flemish firms. The Belgian telecommunications minister (Flemish) signed the contracts anyway, for the Flemish companies, that is. He refused to sign contracts for the Walloon (French-speaking) firms.

Political party leaders began treating each other like rival tribal chiefs. The head of the Flemish Christian Democrats refused to be in the same TV studio as the head of the French Socialists and gave interviews to the French-speaking press only in Flemish. Just a week after forming the ninth government, Prime Minister Martens, a Flemish Christian Democrat, resigned again, but the Belgian king refused to accept it. Instead, he called for general elections, after which the next parliament will turn into a constituent assembly for more constitutional reform. This has become the Belgian way to resolve disputes. In each reform, more powers are devolved to the regions.

The regions of Flanders (Dutch), Wallonia (French), and Brussels (bilingual) were set up under one of the reforms and now have power over public works, environment, employment, health, and transport. Authorities representing the three language groups—German, Flemish, and French—are responsible for culture and education. Even more will be returned to the regions in the next parliament. Foreign trade, overseas aid, and farming are slated to be returned.

Social security may be troublesome. The Flemish do not want to subsidize the poorer Wallonia and do want to give responsibility for social security to the regions. The Prime Minister is against the idea as he fears it could lead to the breakup of Belgium. Containing communal conflict by devolvement may have reached its limit.

Source: "Devolve and Rule," *The Economist,* October 12, 1991, pp. 50–53.

---

home office already has the artwork, so the only additional cost is setting the type for the translations. Remember, though, that a French or Spanish translation will be up to 25 percent longer.

Allowing headquarters to translate can be extremely risky because words from the same language frequently vary in meaning from one country to another or even from one region to another, as was mentioned earlier. A famous example that illustrated how only a single word incorrectly translated can ruin an otherwise good translation occurred in Mexico. The American headquarters of a deodorant manufacturer sent a Spanish translation of the manufacturer's international theme, "If you use our deodorant, you won't be embarrassed in public." Unfortunately, the translator used the word *embarazada* for embarrassed, which in Mexican Spanish means pregnant. Imagine the time that the Mexican subsidiary had with that one.[64]

Use two translations.   To avoid translation errors, the experienced marketer will prefer what are really two translations. The first will be made by a bilingual native, whose work will then be translated back to a bilingual foreigner to see how it compares with the original. This work should preferably be done in the market where the material is to be used. No method is foolproof, but the double-translation approach is the safest way devised so far.

Some problems with translations:

1. "Hydraulic ram" was translated from English to Italian as "wet sheep."
2. A sign in a Moscow hotel—"The passenger must get free the room before two o'clocks of the day they are abandoning in other case, as the passenger fracture the day and must the administration pay for full."
3. A hotel sign in Czechoslovakia—"Take one of our horse-driven city tours. We guarantee no miscarriages."
4. Sign in an Italian shop—"Dresses for streetwalking."
5. Probably the best translation was found on an elevator door of a Romanian hotel—"The lift is being fixed for the next few days. During that time, we regret that you will be unbearable."

Technical words.   The usual run of translators have a problem with technical terms that do not exist in a language and with common words that have a special meaning for a certain industry. Portuguese, for example, is rich in fishing and marine terms, a reflection of Portugal's material culture; but unlike English, it is exceedingly limited with respect to technical terms for the newer industries. The only solution is to employ the English word or fabricate a new word in Portuguese. Unless translators have a special knowledge of the industry, they will go to the dictionary for a literal translation that frequently makes no sense or is erroneous.

Resolving such problems by using English words may not be a satisfactory solution even if the public understands them, especially in France or Spain, which have national academies to keep the language "pure." The French have gone so far as to ban by law over 300 anglicisms, and have even fined a fast-food chain $300 for advertising hamburger instead of *steak haché.*

Although the French government has admitted defeat in its efforts to get rid of the old standbys, such as *le weekend, le parking,* and *le jogging,* it has drawn the line on the scientific use of such American computer terms as *le hardware,* and *le data bank.* The French Computer Terminology Commission has been asked to create French substitutes.[65]

At first thought this may seem to be another bureaucratic boondoggle akin to studying the love life of a gnat; but on further reflection, one comprehends that these countries have good economic reasons for keeping their languages pure as part of their global campaign to teach it to foreigners. Those learning French are not only potential tourists but also become more empathetic toward anything French. The Argentine engineer who reads French and not English will turn to French technical manuals and catalogs before specifying the supplier for the new power plant he is designing. However, if he constantly finds English technical terms in the French text, which forces him to go to his Spanish—English dictionary, he may decide to learn English and read American manuals and catalogs.

In Japan, the reverse situation exists, probably because for decades the country coveted foreign products while it struggled to overtake the more advanced West. Even now, most Japanese cars sold in the domestic market have

"First, le coca cola. Now peanut butter. Who will save La Belle Langue Française?"

Pearson, *Knickerbocker News,* Albany, New York.

almost nothing but English on them. A Nissan official explains that English is thought to be more attractive to the eye. Perhaps this is why people quench their thirst with a best-selling soft drink called "Pocari Sweat" and order from menus announcing "sand witches" and "miss Gorilla" (mixed grill). They also puff away on a cigarette called Hope.[66]

No unpleasantness.   One last aspect of the spoken language worthy of mention is the reluctance in many areas to say anything disagreeable to the listener. The politeness of the Japanese and their consideration for others make *no* a little-used word even when there are disagreements. The American executive, pleased that her Japanese counterpart is nodding and saying yes to all of her proposals, may be shaken later to learn that all the time the listener was saying yes (I hear you) and not yes (I agree). Western managers who ask their Brazilian assistants whether something can be done may receive the answer *meio difícil* (somewhat difficult). If managers take this answer literally, they will probably tell the assistants to do it anyway. The assistants will then elaborate on the difficulties until, hopefully, it will finally dawn on the executives that what they ask is impossible, but the Brazilians just don't want to give them the bad news.

unspoken language
nonverbal communication, such as gestures and body language

Unspoken language.   Nonverbal communication, or the **unspoken language,** can often tell businesspeople something that the spoken language does not—if they understand it. Unfortunately, the differences in customs among cultures may cause misinterpretations of the communication.

Gestures.   Although gestures are a common form of cross-cultural communication, the language of gestures varies from one region to another. For instance, Americans and most Europeans understand the thumbs-up gesture to

Politeness at a Japanese department store

mean "all right," but in southern Italy and Greece, it transmits the message for which we reserve the middle finger. Making a circle with the thumb and the forefinger is friendly in the United States, but it means "you're worth zero" in France and Belgium and is a vulgar sexual invitation in Greece and Turkey.[67] The best advice for the foreign traveler is to leave gestures at home.

Closed doors.   Americans know that one of the perquisites of an important executive is a large office with a door that can be closed. Normally, the door is open as a signal that the occupant is ready to receive others, but when it is closed, something of importance is going on. Contrary to the American open-door policy, Germans regularly keep their doors closed. Hall says that the closed door does not mean that the person behind it wants no visitors but only that he or she considers open doors sloppy and disorderly.[68]

Office size.   Although office size is an indicator of a person's importance, it means different things to different cultures. In the United States, the higher the executive, the larger and more secluded the office; but in the Arab world, the president may be in what for us is a small, crowded office. In Japan, the top floor of a department store is reserved for the "bargain basement" (bargain penthouse?) and not for top management. The French prefer to locate important department heads in the center of activities, with their assistants located outward on radii from this center. To be safe, never gauge people's importance by the size and location of their offices.

Conversational distance.   Anthropologists report that conversational distances are smaller in the Middle East and Latin America, though our personal experience in Latin America has not shown this to be the case.[69] Whether this generality is true or false, we must remember that generalities are like arithmetic means; perhaps more people do than do not act in a certain way in a culture, but the businessperson will be dealing with just a few nationals at a time. Luck may have it that he or she will meet exceptions to the stereotype.

The language of gift giving.   Gift giving is an important aspect of every businessperson's life both here and overseas. Entertainment outside office hours and the exchange of gifts are part of the process of getting better acquainted. However, the etiquette or language of gift giving varies among cultures, just as the spoken language does, and although foreigners will usually be forgiven for not knowing the language, certainly they and their gifts will be better received if they follow local customs.

Acceptable gifts.   In Japan, for example, one never gives an unwrapped gift or visits a Japanese home empty-handed. A gift is presented with the comment that it is only a trifle, which implies that the humble social position of the giver does not permit giving a gift in keeping with the high status of the recipient. He in turn will not open the gift in front of the giver because he knows better than to embarrass him by exposing the trifle in the giver's presence.

The Japanese use gift giving to convey one's thoughtfulness and consideration for the receiver, who over time builds up trust and confidence in the giver. Japanese never give four of anything or an item with four in the name because the word sounds like the one for death. White and yellow flowers are not good choices for gifts because in many areas they connote death. In Germany, red roses to a woman indicate strong feelings for her, and if you give cutlery, always ask for a coin in payment so that the gift will not cut your friendship. Cutlery is a friendship cutter for the Russians and French also. Traditions vary greatly throughout the world, but generally safe gifts everywhere are chocolates, red roses, and a good Scotch whiskey (not in the Arab world, however—instead, bring a good book or something useful for the office).[70]

Gifts or bribes?   The questionable payments scandals (called bribery scandals by the press) exposed the practice of giving very expensive gifts and money to well-placed government officials in return for special favors, large orders, and protection. Some payments were **bribes;** that is, payments were made to induce the payee to do something for the payer that is illegal. But others were **extortion** made to keep the payee from harming the payer in some way. Still others were tips to induce government officials to do their jobs.[71]

bribes gifts or payments to induce the receiver to do something illegal for the giver

extortions payments to keep the receiver from causing harm to the payer

All three are payments for services, and usually they are combinations of two or possibly all three types. To distinguish among them, look at this example. If you tip the headwaiter to get a good table, that is a bribe; but if you tip him because you know that without it, he'll put you near the kitchen, that's extortion. If you tip him for good service after eating, that is a tip. Part of the problem of adhering to American laws is the difficulty in making this distinction.[72]

Although the media exposure about questionable payments is fairly recent, for a long time it has been common knowledge in the international business community that gifts or money payments are necessary to obtain favorable action from government officials, whether to obtain a large order, avoid having a plant shut down, or receive faster service from customs agents. Their pervasiveness worldwide is illustrated by the variety of names for bribes— *mordida* (bite in Latin America), *dash* (West Africa), *pot de vin* (jug of wine——France), *la bustarella* (envelope left on Italian bureaucrat's desk), or *grease*

(United States). Even the Soviets were not exempt according to a *Business International* study of multinational managers, who declared that representatives of the Russian state trading organization permitted gifts to be deposited in their Swiss bank accounts.

According to Radio Moscow, one man who was arrested for taking bribes had in his possession 12 cars, 47 tape recorders and color TVs, 79 suits, and 149 pairs of shoes. Another had 735,000 rubles ($970,000 in cash), 450 gold coins, and 398 gold watches.[73]

Questionable payments.   These come in all forms and sizes, from the petty "expediting" payments that have been necessary to get poorly paid government officials to do their normal duties to huge sums to win large orders.

> One of the writers was able to reduce by one half the average age of receivables from a major governmental customer by the payment of $4 a month to a clerk whose sole job was to arrange suppliers' invoices according to their dates, so that the oldest were on top and would be paid first. His company's invoices were placed on top regardless of their date and were paid promptly.

Included by the Securities and Exchange Commission (SEC) as questionable payments are contributions to foreign political parties and the payment of agents' commissions, even when these actions are not illegal in the country where they are made.[74] The United States, in effect, is requiring American firms to operate elsewhere according to this country's laws, which frequently places these firms at a competitive disadvantage.* Many managements have responded by issuing strict orders not to make any questionable payments, legal or illegal, and some have been surprised to find that their business has not fallen off as they expected. Their action has been reinforced by a number of governments that have either passed stricter laws or begun to enforce those they already have. Given the combination of low salaries of foreign officials and the intense competition for business, one should not be too sanguine about the prospects for completely eliminating this practice.

▢ Societal Organization

Every society has a structure or an organization that is the patterned arrangement of relationships defining and regulating the manner by which its members interface with one another. Anthropologists generally study this important aspect of culture by breaking down its parts into two classes of institutions—those based on *kinship* and those based on the *free association* of individuals.

Kinship.   The family is the basic unit of institutions based on kinship. Unlike the American family, which is generally composed of the parents and their children, families in many nations—especially in the developing ones—are extended to include all relatives by blood and by marriage.

extended family includes blood relatives and relatives by marriage

Extended family.   For the foreign firm, the **extended family** is a source of employees and business connections. The trust that people place in their relatives, however distant, may motivate them to buy from a supplier owned by

---

*   Especially the Foreign Corrupt Practices Act discussed in Chapter 11.

their cousin's cousin, even though the price is higher. Local personnel managers are prone to fill the best jobs with family members, regardless of their qualifications.

Member's responsibility.   Although the extended family is large, each member's feeling of responsibility to it is strong. An individual's initiative to work is discouraged when he or she may be asked to share personal earnings with unemployed extended family members, no matter what the kinship is. Responsibility to the family is frequently a cause of high absenteeism in developing countries where the worker is called home to help with the harvest. Managements have spent large sums to provide comfortable housing for workers and their immediate families, only to find them living in crowded conditions when members of the extended family have moved in.

Pedro Diaz Marin.   In Latin America, where the extended family form is common, individuals use the maternal surname (Marin) as well as the paternal (Diaz) to indicate both branches of the family. It is a common sight to find two businesspeople or a businessperson and a government official, when meeting for the first time, exploring each other's family tree to see whether they have common relatives. If they find any kinship at all, the meeting goes much more smoothly—after all, they're relatives. Incidentally, the name appearing first in Korea is the paternal surname.

Associations.   Social units not based on kinship, known as **associations** by the anthropologists, may be formed by age, gender, or common interest.[75]

associations social units based on age, gender, or common interest, not on kinship

Age.   Manufacturers of consumer goods are well aware of the importance of segmenting a market by age groups, which often cut across cultures. This fact has enabled marketers to succeed in selling such products as clothing and records to the youth market in both developed and developing nations. However, international marketers may go too far if they assume young people everywhere exert the same buying influence on their parents as they do here. Kellogg's attempt to sell cereals in Great Britain through children was not successful because English mothers are less influenced by their children with respect to product choice than are American mothers. The senior citizen segment is an important separate group in the United States, where older people live apart from their children; but where the extended family concept is prevalent, older people continue to live with and exert a powerful influence on younger members of the family.

Gender.   Generally, the less developed the country, the less equal are the genders with respect to job opportunities and education. Even today, the Chinese offer congratulations only on the birth of a son; the birth of a daughter draws condolences.[76]

As nations industrialize, more women enter the job market and thus assume greater importance in the economy. This trend is receiving further impetus as the women's movement for equality of the sexes spreads to the traditionally male-dominated societies of less developed countries. Among the industrialized nations, the United States has the greatest percentage of women in upper management. Although women in Germany, Great Britain, Denmark, and France make up 40 percent of the work force, only 4 percent are in executive positions.[77] According to a United Nations report, women do two thirds of the world's work, receive a tenth of its income, and own a hundredth of its property.[78]

A word of caution, however, must be given to those who, noting the apparently sequestered life of women in some areas, conclude that they have little voice in what the family buys or how it acts. Despite the outward appearance of male domination, women exert a far more powerful influence behind closed doors than the unknowing outsider might suspect.

Common interest.   The common interest groups are composed of people who are joined together by a common bond, which can be political, occupational, recreational, or religious. Even before entering a country, management should identify such groups and assess their political and economic power. As we will see in later chapters, consumer organizations have forced firms to change their product, promotion, and prices, and investments have been supported or opposed by labor unions, which are often a powerful political force.

Class mobility.   In most countries, the ease of moving from one social class to another lies on a continuum from the rigid caste system of India to the relatively flexible social structure of the United States. Less developed countries tend to be located nearer the position of India, whereas the industrial nations are closer to the U.S. position. As industrialization progresses, barriers to mobility become weaker. Management must assess mobility between classes because interclass rigidity, especially when it is accompanied by low social status for business, can make it extremely difficult for the firm to obtain good management personnel locally.

SUMMARY

Culture, the sum total of the beliefs, rules, techniques, institutions, and artifacts that characterize the human population, is of interest to anyone who does business in other countries because of its pervasive influence on all the functions of the firm. To be successful in their relationships overseas, international businesspeople must be students of culture. They must not only obtain factual knowledge, they must also become culturally sensitive. Because society is composed of people and their cultures, we have followed the practice of many anthropologists in calling the variables *sociocultural*. Although the experts differ considerably as to the relevant components of culture, the following list is representative of their thinking: (1) aesthetics, (2) attitudes and beliefs, (3) religion, (4) material culture, (5) education, (6) language, (7) societal organization, (8) legal characteristics, and (9) political structures.

Aesthetics is concerned with a culture's sense of beauty and good taste and is expressed in the arts, drama, music, folklore, and dances. Examples have been given to illustrate their importance in business. Attitudes and beliefs, especially those concerned with time, achievement, work, and change, can be radically different from those to which the businessperson is accustomed. Being aware of the differences can often de-

cide the outcome of a business venture. A knowledge of the basic tenets of other religions will contribute to a better understanding of their followers' attitudes.

Material culture, especially technology, is of great importance to managements contemplating overseas investments. Foreign governments are becoming increasingly involved in the sale and control of technical assistance. The educational level will not only determine the kinds of people available to staff foreign operations but will also exert an important influence on the affiliate's marketing mix.

Language is the key to culture and must be learned if a person is to understand the people of a culture. Generally, there will be as many cultures in a country as there are languages. Students of culture should learn both the spoken and unspoken language. A knowledge of how a society is organized is useful because the societal organization defines and regulates the manner in which its members interface with one another. The extended family and the responsibility of each member to it are especially significant.

The nine cultural components mentioned in this chapter will serve as a helpful checklist to managers who must make cultural assessments.

QUESTIONS

1. How do attitudes toward time, attitudes toward change, and attitudes toward achievement and work affect the various functional areas of international business (personnel, marketing, and so forth)?

2. Why are international firms called agents of change? Give some examples.

3. John Adams, with 20 years' experience as a general foreman in an American firm, is sent as production superintendent to the company's newest plant in Cali, Colombia. He was chosen because of his outstanding success in handling workers. Adams uses the participative leadership style. Can you foresee his having any problems in this new job?

4. The governments of developing nations should impose restrictions forcing U.S.-trained engineers and scientists to return home after graduation. Agree or disagree? What is the basis of your opinion?

5. How can the international firm get people to accept a new idea?

6. Is there a relationship between religion and the attitude toward achievement?

7. What is the relationship between religion and business in the Middle East?

8. Discuss the various ways a nation's educational level impacts a firm's marketing effort.

9. What is probably the most foolproof way to avoid translation errors?

10. Gift giving in other countries seems very involved. How can traveling business executives keep track of all the rules?

11. The competition is giving bribes—shouldn't we? Discuss.

12. What is the significance of the extended family for the international manager?

□ MINICASE 9–1

Be Attuned to Business Etiquette

The proverb, "When in Rome, do as the Romans do," applies to the business representative as well as the tourist. Being attuned to a country's business etiquette can make or break a sale, particularly in countries where 1,000-year-old traditions can dictate the rules for proper behavior. Some of the considerations anyone interested in being a successful marketer should be aware of include:

Local customer, etiquette, and protocol. (An exporter's behavior in a foreign country can reflect favorably or unfavorably on the exporter, the company, and even the sales potential for the product.)

Body language and facial expressions. (Often, actions do speak louder than words.)

Expressions of appreciation. (Giving and receiving gifts can be a touchy subject in many countries. Doing it badly may be worse than not doing it at all.)

Choices of words. (Knowing when and if to use slang, tell a joke, or just keep silent is important.)

The following informal test will help exporters rate their business etiquette. See how many of the following you can answer correctly. (Answers follow the last question.)

1. You are in a business meeting in an Arabian Gulf country. You are offered a small cup of bitter cardamom coffee. After your cup has been refilled several times, you decide you would rather not have any more. How do you decline the next cup offered to you?
   a. Place your palm over the top of the cup when the coffee pot is passed.
   b. Turn your empty cup upside down on the table.
   c. Hold the cup and twist your wrist from side to side.

2. In which of the following countries are you expected to be punctual for business meetings?
   a. Peru.
   b. Hong Kong.
   c. Japan.
   d. China.
   e. Morocco.

3. Gift giving is prevalent in Japanese society. A business acquaintance presents you with a small wrapped package. Do you:
   a. Open the present immediately and thank the giver?
   b. Thank the giver and open the present later?
   c. Suggest that the giver open the present for you?

4. In which of the following countries is tipping considered an insult?
   a. Great Britain.
   b. Iceland.
   c. Canada.

5. What is the normal workweek in Saudi Arabia?
   a. Monday through Friday.
   b. Friday through Tuesday.
   c. Saturday through Wednesday.

6. You are in a business meeting in Seoul. Your Korean business associate hands you his calling card, which states his name in the traditional Korean order: Park Chul Su. How do you address him?
   a. Mr. Park.
   b. Mr. Chul.
   c. Mr. Su.

7. In general, which of the following would be good topics of conversation in Latin American countries?
   a. Sports.
   b. Religion.
   c. Local politics.
   d. The weather.
   e. Travel.

8. In many countries, visitors often are entertained in the homes of clients. Taking flowers as a gift to the hostess is usually a safe way to express thanks for the hospitality. However, both the type and color of the flower can have amorous, negative, or even ominous implications. Match the country where presenting them would be a social *faux pas*.
   a. Brazil.   1. Red roses.
   b. France.   2. Purple flowers.
   c. Switzerland.   3. Chrysanthemums.

9. In Middle Eastern countries, which hand does one use to accept or pass food?
   a. Right hand.
   b. Left hand.
   c. Either hand.

10. Body language is just as important as the spoken word in many countries. For example, in most countries, the thumbs-up sign means "OK." But in which of the following countries is the sign considered a rude gesture?
    a. Germany.
    b. Italy.
    c. Australia.

Answers: 1—*c.* It is also appropriate to leave the cup full. 2—*a, b, c, d,* and *e.* Even in countries where local custom does not stress promptness, overseas visitors should be prompt. 3—*b.* 4—*b.* 5—*c.* 6—*a.* The traditional Korean pattern is surname, followed by two given names. 7—*a, d,* and *e.* 8—*a* and 2. Purple flowers are a sign of death in Brazil, as are chrysanthemums in France (*b* and 3). In Switzerland (*c* and 1), as well as in many other north European countries, red roses suggest romantic intentions. 9—*a.* Using the left hand would be a social gaffe. 10—*b.*

How's Your Business Etiquette?

8–10 Congratulations—you have obviously done your homework when it comes to doing business overseas.

5–7   While you have some sensitivity to the nuances of other cultures, you still might make some social errors that could cost you sales abroad.

1–4   Look out—you could be headed for trouble if you leave home without consulting the experts.

Where to Turn for Help

Whether you struck out completely in the business etiquette department or just want to polish your skills, there are several sources you can turn to for help.

Books. While two years ago business etiquette information may have been difficult to locate, most good bookstores today carry a variety of resource materials to help the traveling business representative.

Workshops and seminars. Many private business organizations and universities sponsor training sessions for the exporter interested in unraveling the mysteries of doing business abroad.

State marketing specialists. In some states, your first contact should be your state agriculture department, where international specialists there can pass on their expertise or put you in touch with someone who can.

Source: *Foreign Agriculture,* U.S. Department of Agriculture, February 1987, pp. 18–19.

□ MINICASE 9–2

Is It a Bribe?

Nick Brown, the sales manager of the Johnson Rubber subsidiary in El Pais, has been selling about a half-million dollars a year in industrial rubber products (rotary drilling hose, oil suction and discharge hose) to the government-owned oil monopoly. He faces stiff competition from the local subsidiary of another multinational rubber manufacturer, which is trying to increase its share of the business. The principal reason for his success is his personal friendship with Captain Corona, the buyer. Brown has never bought anything for Corona except an occasional lunch and a reasonably priced ($50) Christmas gift.

One day in December, he received a call from Captain Corona, who said that just as he was leaving the house, his wife complained that she needed a new refrigerator. Corona was calling Brown because he knew that the marketing manager of a refrigerator manufacturer was Brown's close friend and he wondered whether Brown could arrange for a discount through his friend. Brown told Captain Corona that he would call his friend to see whether the friend could get Corona the discount.

After the call, Brown began thinking about his conver-sation with Corona. The man was responsible for his receiving a half-million dollars in orders every year. This was three times the business his competitor was obtaining, even though the product quality and prices were similar. Every year, he gave the captain a Christmas present worth about $50. The refrigerator would cost $250. Never had the captain asked him for anything. Johnson Rubber had no rules regarding restricting the value of gifts, but employees were expected to exercise good judgment. Could this be the beginning of a series of requests for expensive gifts, or was Captain Corona only interested in getting the best price possible?

What would you do if you were Nick Brown?

◻ MINICASE 9–3

Evans Machinery–France

Evans Machinery–France is the French subsidiary of Evans Machinery, headquartered in Chicago. The firm specializes in the production of highly sophisticated materials-handling equipment, most of which must be specially designed for the job. There are few competitors in France or in any other part of the European Community.

Business has been excellent, though recently the company lost two sizable orders to a French competitor. One customer was the government-owned automobile factory, Renault, and the other was a French-owned textile factory. Both customers had made various purchases from Evans Machinery in the past.

Frank Bowen, the subsidiary's managing director, sat in his office reviewing the two lost sales. He knew that the French competitor did not have Evans's technical capability, and he was confident that the competitor's price could not have been significantly lower. Bowen walked to the window overlooking the front of the building. He was proud of that plant. The lawn was well kept. There was a flagpole with the American flag flying, just as in Chicago. Bowen was thinking that he had a good chance for the executive vice president's job that was coming up soon back at headquarters if Evans Machinery–France continued to do as well as it had done for the last three years under his management. The loss of two sizable orders wouldn't help his record, though. What was the reason? An idea came to him. He called his friend Henri in Renault's technical department. Bowen liked Henri, who had been educated in the United States and spoke English like an American. He explained to Henri that he was concerned about having lost Renault's order. Did Henri know why this had happened? After a pause, Henri said, "Frank, my friend, the boom years in France are over, and the government is concerned. The order was earmarked for a French company."

What can Frank Bowen do to stop this loss of orders?

SUPPLEMENTARY READINGS

Brain Drain

"A Reverse Brain Drain That's Pumping up East Asian Economies." *International Management*, April 1986, pp. 22–23.

"Brain Drain." *The Wall Street Journal*, October 21, 1983, p. 1.

"Brain Drain in Reverse." *Forbes*, April 17, 1989, pp. 114–15.

"Brain Drain Slows Mexico's Development." *The Wall Street Journal*, May 5, 1989, p. A10.

"China Chicken Feed." *The Economist*, November 26, 1988, p. 36.

"China Weighs Shifts in Overseas Studies: Brain Drain Feared." *The Chronicle of Higher Education*, May 11, 1988, p. A1.

"Costly Export." *The Wall Street Journal*, April 18, 1989, p. A1.

"Let Open Doors Swing Both Ways." *The Wall Street Journal*, June 15, 1988, p. 22.

"Soviet Brain Drain May Overwhelm Israel." *New Scientist,* March 3, 1990, p. 23.

"The Brains Keep Draining In." *Business Week,* June 15, 1990, p. 160.

"Train 'em Here, Keep 'em Here." *Forbes,* May 27, 1991, pp. 110–16.

Culture in Business

Axtell, Roger E., ed. *Do's and Taboos around the World.* 2nd ed. New York: John Wiley & Sons, 1990.

"Blunders Abroad." *Nation's Business,* March 1989, pp. 54–55.

"Capitalist Chic." *The Wall Street Journal,* June 10, 1988, p. A1.

Copeland, Lennie, and Lewis Griggs. *Going International.* New York: Random House, 1985.

"Enjoy, Enjoy." *Forbes,* December 12, 1988, pp. 144–50.

Harris, Philip R., and Robert T. Moran. *Managing Cultural Differences,* 3rd ed. Houston: Gulf Publishing Company, 1991.

Hofstede, Geert. "National Cultures Revisted." *Asia Pacific Journal of Management,* September 1984, pp. 22–29.

"In Japan, It's 'Learn the Hard Way.'" *Advertising Age,* August 20, 1987, p. 144.

"Japan's Leaders Urge Businesses to Shift Their Focus to Improve Quality of Life." *The Wall Street Journal,* January 28, 1992, p. A9.

Kim, W. Chan, and R. A. Mauborgne. "Cross-Cultural Strategies." *The Journal of Business Strategy,* Spring 1987, pp. 28–35.

Knotts, Rose. "Cross-Cultural Management: Transformations and Adaptations." *Business Horizons,* January–February 1989, pp. 29–33.

Lee, James A. "Cultural Analysis in Overseas Operations." *Harvard Business Review,* March–April 1966, pp. 106–14.

"Monsieur Mickey." *Time,* March 21, 1991, pp. 48–49.

"Regulations Direct Ad Traffic Differently around the World." *Advertising World,* April–May 1988, pp. 39–40.

Terpstra, Vern, and Kenneth David. *The Cultural Environment of International Business,* 3rd ed. Cincinnati: South-Western Publishing Co., 1990.

"Tradition." *The Wall Street Journal,* September 15, 1986, p. 20.

Education

"A People Problem." *The Economist,* November 26, 1988, pp. 49–50.

"Chinese M.B.A. Holders Find a Degree Earned in the West Doesn't Go Far at Home." *The Wall Street Journal,* June 2, 1988, p. 8.

"Degrees of Confusion." *International Management,* January 1988, pp. 34–38.

The European Community and Education. Brussels: Commission of the European Community, 1985.

Gifts

Axtell, Roger E., ed. *Do's and Taboos around the World.* 2nd ed. New York: John Wiley & Sons, 1990.

Fadiman, Jeffrey A. "A Traveler's Guide to Gifts and Bribes." *Harvard Business Review,* July–August 1986, pp. 122–36.

"How to Succeed in Business by Polishing Your Manners." *U.S. News & World Report,* October 25, 1985, p. 45.

Reeder, John A. "When West Meets East: Cultural Aspects of Doing Business in Asia." *Business Horizons,* January–February 1987, pp. 69–74.

"Venturing through China's 'Open Door.'" *Business Marketing,* February 1988, pp. 63–66.

Language

"A Linguistic Problem." *Europe,* September 1986, pp. 3–4.

"Computers Threaten Another Tradition: The Glory of France." *The Wall Street Journal,* October 10, 1985, p. 1.

"English: The Common Language of Europeans?" *International Management,* February 1988, pp. 59–61.

"English Out to Conquer the World." *U.S. News & World Report,* February 18, 1985, pp. 49–52.

"The International Language of Gestures." *Psychology Journal,* May 1984, pp. 64–67.

"Why Speaking English Is No Longer Enough." *International Management,* November 1986, pp. 39–42.

Religion

"Asia Conjures Wind and Water to Boost Business." *International Management,* July–August 1987, pp. 57–60.

"Central Asia: The Rise of the Moslems." *U.S. News & World Report,* April 3, 1989, pp. 48–49.

"Free Speech Is Life Itself." *Time,* December 23, 1991, pp. 50–51.

"Hunted by an Angry Faith." *Time,* February 27, 1989, pp. 28–33.

"Islam for Beginners." *The Economist,* March 18, 1989, pp. 95–96.

"Islamic Fundamentalism: Friend or Foe?" *Business International,* December 20, 1985, pp. 401–2.

"Islam: Seeking the Future in the Past." *U.S. News & World Report,* July 6, 1987, pp. 33–41.

"Some Chinese Simply Won't Make a Move without Fung Shui." *The Wall Street Journal,* December 19, 1983, p. 1.

"Star of Islam." *The Economist,* December 14, 1991, pp. 3–18.

"Religions of Asia." *Modern Maturity,* December 1984–January 1985, pp. 72–78.

"Rising Islamic Fervor Challenges the West, Every Moslem Ruler." *The Wall Street Journal,* August 7, 1987, p. 1.

Technology

"A Maverick Man and His Steam Machine." *Far Eastern Economic Review,* June 9, 1988, p. 85.

"COCOM Eases Restrictions on Export of High-Tech Equipment to Eastern Bloc." *Aviation Week & Space Technology*, June 10, 1991, p. 73.

Fatemi, Khosrow. "Multinational Corporations, Developing Countries, and Transfer of Technology: A Cultural Perspective." *Issues in International Business*, Summer–Fall 1985, pp. 1–6.

"Global Reach." *The Wall Street Journal*, April 29, 1985, p. 1.

"How to Sell Soap in India." *The Economist*, September 10, 1988, p. 82.

"Inside the Chocolate Box." *The Economist*, September 7, 1991, p. 70.

"Reaching Out." *The Wall Street Journal*, January 7, 1986, p. 1.

Reddy, Allan C., and C. P. Rao. "Technology Transfer from Developed to Developing Countries: Needs, Problems, and Suggestions." *Issues in International Business*, Summer–Fall 1985, pp. 7–12.

"Secrets Police." *The Wall Street Journal*, November 15, 1987, p. 1.

"Staying Ahead in High Tech." *U.S. News & World Report*, April 1, 1991, p. 53.

"They Didn't Listen to Anybody." *Forbes*, December 15, 1986, pp. 168–69.

"Where Technology Is the Appropriate Word." *The Economist*, April 18, 1987, pp. 83–84.

Women

"Equality of the Sexes Threatens Cultural Ecology." *Liberal Star*, October 10, 1988, pp. 6–7.

"Europe's Women Unite to Throw Off Their Chains." *International Management*, July–August 1987, pp. 42–49.

"How the Other Half Works." *The Economist*, June 30, 1990, pp. 21–24.

"Japan's Secret Economic Weapon: Exploited Women." *Business Week*, March 4, 1985, pp. 54–55.

"Look Whose Sun Is Rising Now: Career Women." *Business Week*, August 25, 1986, p. 50.

"More and More Women at Work." *Deutsche Bank Bulletin*, December 1986, pp. 9–12.

"The Old Sexism in the New China." *U.S. News & World Report*, April 24, 1989, pp. 36–38.

"The Triumphant Spirit of Nairobi." *Time*, August 5, 1985, pp. 38–40.

"Women Managers and Turkey's Sexist Society." *The Wall Street Journal*, May 15, 1985, p. 38.

"Women's Movement in Corporate Japan Isn't Moving Very Fast." *The Wall Street Journal*, June 16, 1991, p. A1.

ENDNOTES

1. P. Harris and R. Moran, *Managing Cultural Differences,* 3rd ed. (Houston: Gulf Publishing, 1991), p. 13.

2. Richard L. Daft, *Management* (Hinsdale, Ill: Dryden Press, 1988), p. 492.

3. *Worldwide Code of Ethics* (Pittsburgh: PPG Industries, September 1991), p. 2.

4. I. Brady and B. Isaac, *A Reader in Cultural Change,* vol. 1 (Cambridge, Mass.: Schenkman Publishing, 1975), p. x.

5. V. Barnouw, *An Introduction to Anthropology* (Homewood, Ill.: Dorsey Press, 1975), p. 5.

6. E. T. Hall, *Beyond Culture* (Garden City, N.Y.: Doubleday, 1977), p. 16.

7. G. Foster, *Traditional Societies and Technological Change* (New York: Harper & Row, 1973), p. 11; and Vern Terpstra and K. David, *The Cultural Environment of International Business* (Cincinnati: South-Western Publishing, 1985), p. 7.

8. Hall, *Beyond Culture,* p. 54.

9. "In Japan, It's 'Learn the Hard Way,' " *Advertising Age,* August 20, 1987, p. 144; and "They Didn't Listen to Anybody," *Forbes,* December 15, 1986, pp. 168–69.

10. "Monsieur Mickey," *Time,* March 25, 1991, p. 48.

11. "National versus Corporate Culture: Implications for Human Resource Management," *Human Resource Management,* Summer 1988, pp. 232–45.

12. One of the writers installed in a Spanish factory new production equipment that was to replace old but still serviceable machinery. Before leaving for a week's work in Madrid, he tested the equipment, trained some workers to use it, and advised the supervisor that it was ready. On his return, he was surprised to find that the new equipment was not being utilized. The supervisor explained that the old machinery was working well and he didn't want to "disrupt production." Actually, the new equipment was easier to use and would greatly increase output. Realizing that drastic action was called for, the writer grabbed a sledgehammer and made a token effort to destroy the old equipment. Only then did the supervisor get the message. Admittedly, the action was unorthodox, but it did bring immediate results. Not wanting to replace a still serviceable object with a new object, even when the new object is superior, is a quite common attitude in many countries.

13. This classification depends in part on M. J. Herskovits, *Man and His Works* (New York: Alfred A. Knopf, 1952), p. 634. It was embellished by anthropologists at the University of South Alabama.

14. L. Copeland and Lewis Griggs, *Going International* (New York: Random House, 1985), pp. 63–64.

15. Herskovits, *Man and His Works,* p. 414.

16. "The Middle East Mirage," *International Management,* April 1979, p. 21.

17. John A. Reeder, "When West Meets East: Cultural Aspects of Doing Business with Asia," *Business Horizons,* January–February 1987, pp. 18–22.

18. "Tokyo Pedestrians Run on Time," *The Wall Street Journal,* November 19, 1983, p. 2.

19. "European Etiquette," *European Community,* May 1975, p. 17.

20. "Bridging That Other Gulf," *Vision,* May 1975, p. 50.

21. "Middle East Mirage," p. 23.

22. Rose Knotts, "Cross-Cultural Management: Transformations and Adaptions," *Business Horizons,* January–February 1989, p. 30.

23. "Blunders Abroad," *Nation's Business,* March 1989, p. 54.

24. "Free, Young, and Japanese," *The Economist,* December 21, 1991–January 3, 1992; and "Enjoy, Enjoy," *Forbes,* December 12, 1988, p. 144.

25. Benjamin Higgins, *Economic Development* (New York: W. W. Norton, 1968), pp. 241–44.

26. It is difficult to adequately translate the connotations of the two words. No one proudly says he is an *obrero* even if he earns more than the *empleado* who is a file clerk.

27. "What Is Culture's Role in Economic Policy?" *The Wall Street Journal,* December 22, 1986, p. 1.

28. "How the Japanese Are Changing," *Fortune,* Pacific Rim, 1990, pp. 15–22; and "Cracks in the Japanese Work Ethic," *Fortune,* May 14, 1984, pp. 162–68.

29. Kenneth L. Woodward, "Religions in Asia," *Modern Maturity,* December 1984–January 1985, pp. 72–74.

30. "Asia Conjures Wind and Water to Boost Business," *International Management,* July–August 1987, pp. 57–60.

31. "Some Chinese Simply Won't Make a Move without Fung Shui," *The Wall Street Journal,* December 19, 1983, p. 1.

32. Woodward, "Religions in Asia," pp. 75–78; and "Islam: Seeking the Future in the Past," *U.S. World News & World Report,* July 6, 1987, pp. 33–36.

33. "Hunted by an Angry Faith," *Time,* February 27, 1989, pp. 28–33; and "Islam's Arrow of Death," *The Economist,* March 11, 1989, p. 41.

34. "Hunted by an Angry Faith," p. 32.

35. "Free Speech Is Life Itself," *Time,* December 23, 1991, p. 50.

36. "Sunnis? Shiites? What's That Got to Do with the Price of Oil?" *Forbes,* April 12, 1982, pp. 88–92; and "Mosque and State," *The Wall Street Journal,* August 7, 1987, p. 1.

37. "Malaysian Malady: When the Spirit Hits, a Scapegoat Suffers," *The Wall Street Journal,* March 3, 1980, p. 1.

38. Daniel D. Roman and Joseph F. Puett, Jr., *International Business and Technological Innovation* (New York: North-Holland, 1983), p. xxi.

39. "Sensing Your Way up the 'S-Curve,'" *International Management,* October 1986, p. 72.

40. Khosrow Fatemi, "Multinational Corporations, Developing Countries, and Transfer of Technology: A Cultural Perspective," *Issues in International Business,* Summer–Fall 1985, p. 1.

41. "Where Technology Is the Appropriate Word," *The Economist,* April 18, 1987, p. 83.

42. "How to Sell Soap in India," *The Economist,* September 1988, p. 82.

43. "COCOM Eases Restrictions on Export of High-Tech Equipment to Eastern Bloc," *Aviation Week & Space Technology,* June 10, 1991, p. 73.

44. "Weak in Technology, South Korea Seeks Help from Overseas," *The Wall Street Journal,* January 7, 1986, p. 1.

45. Exports and foreign exchange earnings can be affected if the product cannot compete in the world market because of excessive manufacturing costs, inferior quality, or an obsolete design.

46. The reason is that multinationals will generally make licensing agreements even with wholly owned foreign subsidiaries to establish a legal basis for requiring royalty payments and service fees.

47. "Let Open Doors Swing Both Ways," *The Wall Street Journal,* June 15, 1988, p. 22.

48. "Migracion de profesionales," *Comercio exterior* (Mexico City: Banco Nacional de Comercio Exterior, May 1978), p. 581.

49. "Costly Export," *The Wall Street Journal,* April 18, 1989, p. A1.

50. "Soviet Brain Drain May Overwhelm Israel," *New Scientist,* March 3, 1990, p. 23.

51. "The Brains Keep Draining In," *Business Week,* June 15, 1990, p. 160.

52. "South Korea to Recruit 110 Top Scientists during 1992," *The McAllen Monitor,* February 8, 1992, p. 10A.

53. "Costly Brain Drain," *Development Forum* (Geneva: United Nations, March 1982), p. 12.

54. "Developing Nations Demand Compensation for Loss of Skilled People to Industrial Nations," *The Wall Street Journal,* September 3, 1982, p. 30.

55. "Train 'em Here, Keep 'em Here," *Forbes,* May 27, 1991, p. 110; and "Costly Export," p. A1.

56. "Costly Export," p. A1.

57. Ibid., p. A20.

58. Africa has an unparalleled mixture of cultures and languages. Kenya, for example, has 22 distinct languages, and Nigeria has 125.

59. "What's Worrying the Swiss?" *Bulletin* (Zurich: Crédit Suisse, April 1988), pp. 4–5.

60. To avoid using English as the link language in India, Hindi was declared the official language. As late as 1986, Tamil-speaking students from the south were rioting against the imposition of Hindi, which was spoken by 30 percent of the population, mainly in the north. The students wanted English to be the link language. From *Los Angeles Times,* December 11, 1986, part I, p. 5.

61. "Europe's Youth Vote for English," *The European,* November 15–17, 1991, p. 2; and "English: The Common

Language of Europeans?" *International Management,* February 1988, pp. 59–61.

62. "When It Comes to Doing Business with Japan, English Is Emerging as the Language of Choice," *Journal of Commerce,* September 3, 1991, p. 3A.

63. "Why Speaking English Is No Longer Enough," *International Management,* November 1986, p. 42.

64. This mistake was caught before it was published locally, but an incident happened to one of the writers, newly arrived in Brazil, that did go all over the country. The ad manager, a Brazilian, brought him a campaign emphasizing that car owners should maintain 24 pounds per square inch in their tires to get maximum wear. To really get the point across, life-size figures of a tire company salesman were made up, with the name of the company and a large "24" printed across his chest. Care was taken to get these figures out to the dealers, who were to set them up on a "D day." The writer, sitting in his São Paulo office, proud of the unusually good coordination of the campaign, began receiving calls from competitors asking what type of people worked in his company. Over the laughter came the message—24 in Brazilian Portuguese means homosexual!

65. "Computers Threaten Another Tradition: The Glory of France," *The Wall Street Journal,* October 10, 1985, p. 1.

66. "In Japan, They Demand English—Even If It's Bad," *Modesto Bee,* July 10, 1983, p. E–6.

67. "The International Language of Gestures," *Psychology Today,* May 1984, p. 64–67.

68. E. T. Hall, *The Hidden Dimension* (Garden City, N.Y.: Doubleday, 1969), pp. 134–35.

69. One of the writers, who lived in Latin America for 15 years, was surprised to read this statement in *The Silent Language in Overseas Business* by E. T. Hall. His Mexican wife, who had lived on both sides of the border, absolutely refuted it, so when he went to Ecuador recently as a consultant, he was careful to observe conversational distances. In no instance did he note any appreciable difference.

70. Roger E. Axtell, ed., *Do's and Taboos around the World,* 2nd ed. (New York: John Wiley & Sons, 1990), pp. 113–47.

71. Neil H. Jacoby, Peter Nehemkis, and Richard Eells, *Bribery and Extortion in World Business* (New York: Macmillan, 1977), pp. 174–75.

72. "Bribes versus Gifts: Soviet Interpretation Unclear," *Business Eastern Europe,* February 10, 1986, p. 45; and "Ethical Codes in Industry: Dealing with the FCPA and with Ambiguity," (Lubin School of Business) *Letter,* February–March 1988, pp. 10–12.

73. "On the Take," *Parade Magazine,* March 1977, p. 8.

74. Interestingly, the Foreign Corrupt Practices Act of 1977 permits *grease* to be paid when its sole purpose is to expedite nondiscretionary official actions.

75. Herskovits, *Man and His Works,* p. 303.

76. "The Old Sexism in the New China," *U.S. News & World Report,* April 24, 1989, p. 37.

77. "Europe's Women Unite to Throw Off Their Chains," *International Management,* July–August 1987, pp. 42–49.

78. "Sexes' Equality a Myth," *U.S. News & World Report,* July 8, 1985, p. 40.

Chapter 10
Political Forces

Politics have no relation to morals.

Niccoló Machiavelli

Man's capacity for justice makes democracy possible, but man's inclination to injustice makes democracy necessary.

Reinhold Niebuhr, American theologian

You cannot hope to heal our economy without private property. It is like trying to treat an elephant with an aspirin.

Stanislav Shatalin, Soviet economist

Eastern Europeans today talk about capitalism much the same way that American teenagers talk about sex: with growing anticipation, excitement, and a tone of bravado that's not quite endearing.

Michael Schrage, *The Wall Street Journal,* March 28, 1991, p. D1

LEARNING OBJECTIVES

In this chapter, you will study:

1. The ideological forces that affect business, and how they affect it.

2. The importance of government-owned business even in countries that refer to themselves as capitalist.

3. Nationalism as a powerful emotional force with political repercussions on business.

4. The necessity for adequate government protection of business and its personnel from terrorism and invasion.

5. How government instability and sudden changes in government policy affect business.

6. The effects on business of traditional hostilities between peoples and nations.

7. The political power of international organizations.

8. Labor as a political force.

9. International companies' abilities to influence political decisions.

KEY WORDS AND CONCEPTS

- Communism
- Expropriation
- Confiscation
- Capitalism
- Socialism
- Conservative
- Right wing
- Liberal
- Left wing
- Privatization
- Nationalism
- Terrorism
- Stability
- Instability
- Traditional hostilities
- Country risk assessment (CRA)

BUSINESS INCIDENT

Governments sometimes take over privately owned businesses, expropriate them, and pay the previous owners some compensation. But frequently it goes the other direction, and governments sell businesses to private buyers.

In 1982, the British government sold National Freight Corporation (NFC), Britain's largest freight handler, to its 12,000 workers. They paid the equivalent of $1.50 per share, and by August 1983, the shares were valued at about $5.10.

The worker-owners say they now turn off unnecessary lights and take better care of trucks and other equipment than they did before. Sales and profits rose, in part because of the boost in workers' drive and motivation.

This story has a happy ending. In 1988, NFC's profits were almost $105 million on turnover of over $2 billion, up from profits of about $20 million and turnover of some $838 million five years earlier. Also in that year, the NFC employee-owners voted to list the company shares of stock on the London stock exchange, which made instant millionaires of many of those owners—who are trying to have their cake and eat it too. They will attempt to maintain control of NFC against purchasers of new shares on the stock exchange by allowing employee-shareholders to have double voting powers in the event of a takeover bid.

Source: John Marcom, Jr., *The Wall Street Journal,* August 30, 1983, p. 30; and Kevin Brown, *Financial Times,* February 22, 1988, p. 6.

◻ **1991 Map of Freedom**

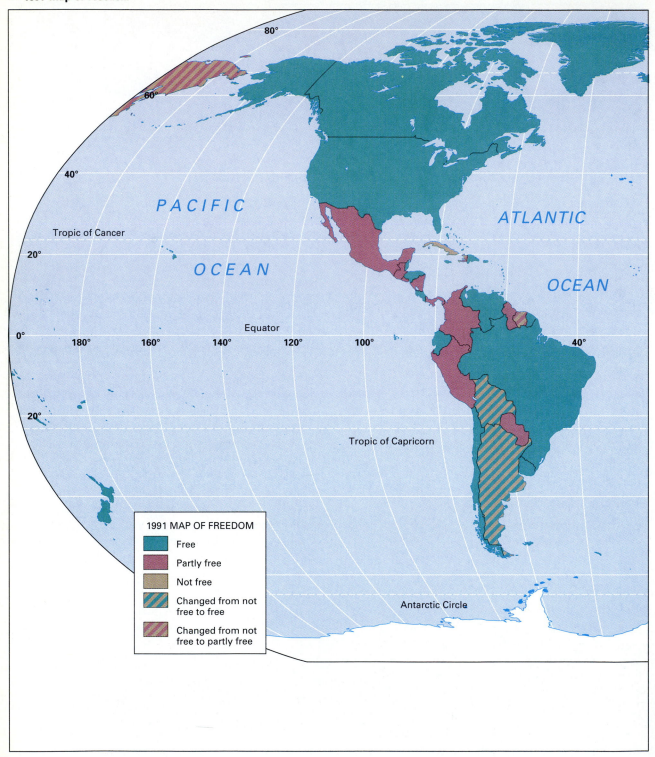

1991 MAP OF FREEDOM

- Free
- Partly free
- Not free
- Changed from not free to free
- Changed from not free to partly free

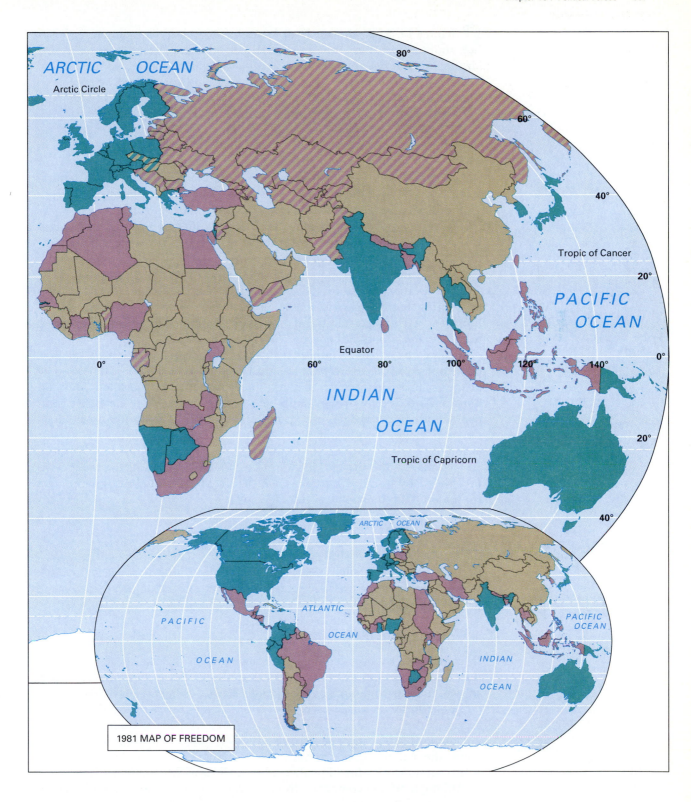

1981 MAP OF FREEDOM

hapter 11 deals with the legal forces affecting international business. Of course, laws and their interpretation and enforcement reflect political ideologies and outlooks as well as government stability and continuity. Therefore, this chapter is intended as background for and a companion to Chapter 11.

In a number of ways, the political climate of the country in which a business operates is as important as the country's topography, its natural resources, and its meteorological climate. Indeed, we shall see examples in which a hospitable, stable government can encourage business investment and growth despite geographic or weather obstacles and scarcity of natural resources. The opposite is equally true. Some areas of the world that are relatively blessed with natural resources and with not too difficult topography and weather have been very little developed because of government instability. Occasionally, a country's government is hostile to investment in its territory by foreign companies even though they might provide capital, technology, and training for development of the country's resources and people.

Many of the political forces with which business must cope have ideological sources, but there are a large number of other sources. These include nationalism, terrorism, traditional hostilities, unstable governments, international organizations, and government-owned business.

It should be pointed out that the international company (IC) itself can be a political force. Some firms have budgets or sales larger than the GNP of some of the countries with which they negotiate. Although budgets and GNPs do not translate directly or necessarily into power, it should be clear that companies with bigger budgets and countries with bigger GNPs possess more assets and facilities with which to negotiate. Refer to Table 1–1 for some examples.

This chapter will provide an indication of the types of risks to private business posed by political forces. As we shall see, some of the risks can stem from more than one political force.

IDEOLOGICAL FORCES

Such names as communism, socialism, capitalism, liberal, conservative, left wing, and right wing are used to describe governments, political parties, and people. These names indicate ideological beliefs.

◻ Communism

In communist countries, the government owns all the major factors of production. With minor exceptions, all production in these countries is by state-owned factories and farms. Labor unions are government controlled.

Communism as conceived by Karl Marx was a theory of social change directed to the ideal of a classless society. As developed by Lenin and others, communism advocates the seizure of power by a conspiratorial political party, the maintenance of power by stern suppression of internal opposition, and commitment to the ultimate goal of a worldwide communist state.

Although private companies from noncommunist countries usually cannot own plants in a communist country, they can do business with it. We shall discuss how this is done in Chapter 17. But before we get there, we should

communism Marx's theory of a classless society, developed by his successors into control of society by the Communist party and the attempted worldwide spread of communism point out that recent developments in the People's Republic of China, the former Soviet Union, and Eastern Europe are opening opportunities for foreign investment.

Communist government takeover of a previously noncommunist country. This business risk is not dealt with in Chapter 17. Given one of communism's basic tenets—state ownership of all the productive factors—the government will take over private business. This occurred in Russia after the 1917 Bolshevik Revolution, and it has been repeated after each communist takeover of a country.

Compensation for expropriated property.   To date, none of the new communist governments has compensated the foreign former owners directly. A few of the owners have gotten some reimbursement indirectly out of assets of the communist government seized abroad after the communist government confiscated foreign private property within its country. For example, the U.S. government seized assets of the Soviet Union in the United States after American property in the U.S.S.R. was confiscated. American firms or individuals whose property had been confiscated in the U.S.S.R. could file claims with a U.S. government agency, and if they could substantiate their loss, a percentage of it was paid.

Expropriation and confiscation.   The rules of traditional international law recognize a country's right to expropriate the property of foreigners within its jurisdiction. But those rules require the country to compensate the foreign owners, and *in the absence of compensation,* **expropriation** *becomes* **confiscation.**[1]

expropriation government seizure of the property within its borders owned by foreigners, followed by prompt, adequate, and effective compensation paid to the former owners

confiscation government seizure of the property within its borders owned by foreigners without payment to them

Communism collapses.   We have insufficient space here to detail the reasons for communism's failure as an economic and social system. We shall present a couple of basic reasons and a few anecdotes that illustrate the results. See the endnotes and suggested readings for more.

The U.S.S.R. concentrated its best scientists, engineers, managers, and raw materials in production for the military; it neglected production of consumer goods. Gross production was the goal, and managers would go to ridiculous extremes to be able to report the production figures set by government central planners.

Since Soviet central planning allowed only one condom factory and birth control pills were very expensive under the communist regime, they were rarely available except to the privileged. As a result, abortion was by far the country's most common form of birth control. All these abortions were then counted as part of doctors' gross production and therefore swelled the reported national income.

Factories under construction got a certificate putting them into commission on the scheduled completion date even though they were almost never actually completed on schedule. Because of the certificate, the factory had to report production coming from it even though it had not yet produced anything.

The first deputy chairman of the U.S.S.R. Committee for National Control, with the splendidly appropriate name of A. Shitof, reported that at least half the enterprises lied to exaggerate their output. Some enterprises used other deceptions. For instance, a factory reaching only 50 percent of its targeted output could have made a small change in its next shipped machine and doubled the price, say from \$10,000 to \$20,000—presto, doubled output.[2]

◻ Capitalism

capitalism an economic system in which the means of production and distribution are for the most part privately owned and operated for private profit

The capitalist, free enterprise ideal is that all the factors of production should be privately owned. Under ideal **capitalism,** government would be restricted to those functions that the private sector cannot perform—national defense; police, fire, and other public services; and government-to-government international relations. No such government exists.

Reality in so-called capitalist countries is quite complex. The governments of such countries typically regulate privately owned businesses quite closely, and frequently these governments own businesses.

Regulations and red tape.   All businesses are subject to countless government laws, regulations, and red tape in their activities in the United States and all other capitalist countries. Special government approval is required to practice the professions, such as law or medicine. Tailored sets of laws and regulations govern banking, insurance, transportation, and utilities. States and local governments require business licenses and impose use restrictions on buildings and areas.

Complying with all the laws and regulations and coping with the red tape require expertise, time, and of course, expense. A business found in noncompliance may incur fines or even the imprisonment of its management.

◻ Socialism

socialism public, collective ownership of the basic means of production and distribution, operating for use rather than for profit

Socialism advocates government ownership or control of the basic means of production, distribution, and exchange. Profit is not an aim.

In practice, so-called socialist governments have frequently performed in ways not consistent with the doctrine. One of the most startling examples of this is Singapore, which professes to be a socialist state but in reality is aggressively capitalistic.[3]

European socialism.   In Europe, socialist parties have been in power in several countries, including Great Britain, France, Spain, Greece, and Germany. In Britain, the Labour party—as the socialists there call their political party—has nationalized some basic industries, such as steel, ship-building, coal mining, and the railroads, but has not gone much further in that direction. A vocal left wing of the Labour party advocates nationalizing all major British business, banks, and insurance companies.

Social Democrats is the name the Germans use for their socialist political party. During the several years that this party was in power before it lost to the Christian Democrats in 1982, it nationalized nothing and, in action and word, seemed more capitalist than socialist. The socialist governments of France and Spain have embarked on programs to privatize government-owned businesses; such programs do not conform to pure socialist doctrine.

LDC socialism.   The less developed countries (LDCs) often profess and practice some degree of socialism. The government typically owns and controls most of the factors of production. Among the characteristics of an LDC are shortages of capital, technology, and skilled management and labor. Aid from DCs or from international organizations usually comes to (and, it is hoped, through) the LDC government. Many of the educated citizens tend to be in or connected with the LDC government. It follows that the government would own or control major factories and farms.

Unless the LDC government is communist, it will make occasional exceptions and permit capital investment. This happens when the LDC perceives advantages that would not be possible without the private capital. The advantages could be more jobs for its people, new technology, skilled managers or technicians, and export opportunities.

Risks for businesses dealing with socialist countries.   As you can see, there is an extremely wide range of practice among the countries that profess socialism. At the extreme illustrated by Singapore, one must be careful to comply with all the applicable laws and regulations, as in any capitalist country. At the other extreme, such as an LDC, where most or all of the major production factors are government owned, one must do business much as it is done in a communist country.

◻ Conservative or Liberal

We should not leave the subject of ideology without mention of these words as they have come to be used in the mid- and late 20th century. Politically, in the United States, the word **conservative** connotes a person, group, or party that wishes to minimize government activity and to maximize the activities of private businesses and individuals. Conservative is used to mean something similar to **right wing,** but in the United States and the United Kingdom, the latter is more extreme. For instance, the Conservative party, one of the major political parties in the United Kingdom, is said to have a right-wing minority.

There is at least one exception to the generalization that conservatives wish to minimize government activities: the antiabortion movement calling for governmental control of abortion decisions. Although not all antiabortionists are conservative, the press presents their position as such.

Politically, in the United States in the 20th century, the word **liberal** has come to mean the opposite of what it meant in the 19th century. It has come to connote a person, group, or party that urges greater government participation in the economy and regulation or ownership of business. Liberal and **left wing** are similar, but the latter generally indicates more extreme positions closer to socialism or communism.

Unique to the United States.   This usage has not spread outside the United States.

> A conversation one of the authors had with an Italian lawyer at lunch in Rome turned to politics. The Italian identified himself as a liberal, and the author understood it in the American meaning. As the conversation proceeded, the author learned that he had been wrong. The lawyer meant it in the Italian sense; he was a member of the Liberal party, a political party near the right end of the Italian political spectrum.

There are other Liberal parties in Europe. They are not liberal in the American sense.

With the recent developments in the former U.S.S.R. and Eastern Europe, a still different use of the word *conservative* has emerged. There, the conser-

---

conservative a person who wishes to minimize government activities and maximize private ownership and business

right wing a more extreme conservative

liberal in the 20th-century United States, a person who urges greater government involvement in most aspects of human activities

left wing a more extreme liberal

WORLDVIEW
Right and Left—What Do These Terms Mean?

After the French Revolution, an assembly was chosen, and it settled down to face the problems of reform. The radicals sat on the president's left and the conservatives on his right. This disposition provided thereafter—in other countries as well as France—a useful addition to the terminology of politics.

A former member of the British Parliament made some interesting points on this subject. He found the Far Left similar to the Far Right. The terms "Right" and "Left" are losing their purchase. Under conventions established earlier in our century, people on the Far Right are seen as "Fascists" and people on the Far Left as "Communists," so that on the Left–Right axis, the two are supposed to be opposites, or at least at opposite extremes as far away from each other as it is possible to get. But a majority of observers seem to agree that the kinds of society they establish when they get into power have fundamental features of a striking nature in common—and are a good deal more like each other than either of them is like Liberal Democracy, which is supposed to separate them in the middle, halfway between them.

Source: *Forbes,* May 23, 1983, p. 20.

vative wants continuing, heavy, and deep governmental involvement in business and society. The conservative typically is found in the old-line Communist party, the armed forces, and the KGB (secret police). The people and organizations opposed to the conservatives are called *radicals* who favor market economies and political democracies.

We do not want to overemphasize the importance of the labels *conservative, liberal, right wing,* and *left wing.* For one thing, individuals and organizations may change over time or may change as they perceive shifts in the moods of voters. Some feel that these labels are too simplistic or even naive and that reality is more complex. Nevertheless, we wanted to bring them to your attention because they are much used in media and other discussions of international events and because different political forces flow from, for example, a right-wing government than from a left-wing one.

GOVERNMENT OWNERSHIP OF BUSINESS

One might reasonably assume that government ownership of the factors of production is found only in communist or socialist countries, but that assumption is not correct. Large segments of business are owned by the governments of numerous countries that do not consider themselves either communist or socialist. From country to country, there are wide differences in the industries that are government owned and in the extent of government ownership.

□ Why Firms Are Nationalized

There are a number of reasons, sometimes overlapping, why governments put their hands on firms. Some of them are (1) to extract more money from the firms—the government suspects that the firms are concealing profits; (2) an extension of the first reason—the government believes it could run the firms more efficiently and make more money; (3) ideological—when left-wing governments are elected, they sometimes nationalize industries, as has occurred in Britain, France, and Canada; (4) to catch votes as politicians save jobs by putting dying industries on life-support systems, which can be disconnected after the election; (5) because the government has pumped money into a firm or an industry, and control usually follows money; and (6) happenstance, as with the nationalization after World War II of German-owned firms in Europe.

All governments are in business to some degree, but outside the communist nations or LDCs, none is so far into business as Italy or France.

Italy.   The Italian government-owned Institute for Industrial Reconstruction (IRI) has been called an "industrial octopus."[4] In 1978, IRI was a leader in one category: it lost more money—$970 million—than any other company. (The number two loser was another state-owned company, British Steel, which lost $798 million.) The Italian government owns companies in many industries, including salt, tobacco, matches, mining, railways, airlines, auto manufacturing, steel, telephone, power plants, banking, restaurants, chocolate and ice cream production, radio and television stations, and refineries. IRI continues to grow, and by 1991 it controlled 477 companies employing 416,000 people.

In the mid-1980s, IRI brought in some new management that turned enough of its companies around so that it reported a profit in 1990. Even so, its shipbuilding and airline businesses are still showing hefty losses.[5]

Having named British Steel as a loser, that story should be brought up to date: by 1991, it had become the world's most profitable integrated steel company and had been privatized. Privatization is discussed later in this chapter.

United States.   Historically, the United States has been opposed to nationalizing industries, but it took a large step in that direction when it set up the Consolidated Rail Corporation (Conrail) in 1976. Conrail took over six bankrupt railroads in the northeastern United States. Ten years later, the U.S. government was taking steps to sell Conrail; one proposal was to sell it to a private rail company, but this evoked opposition from Conrail's managers and employees as well as from competing railroads. Instead, its stock was sold publicly to private buyers who included many Conrail workers and managers. Since then, the United States has done little more to privatize government-owned businesses or operations.

France.   The French government has been in business for centuries. When Louis XIV began building the magnificent Versailles Palace, the plans included thousands of mirrors and crystal chandeliers. The Venetians were the dominant glassmakers of the world at that time, and Louis's finance minister, Colbert, did not like the thought of paying them for all of those mirrors and chandeliers. Colbert set up the company now known as Saint-Gobain, and Louis insisted on owning the company himself, rather than allowing idle nobles and courtiers to own it. Louis feared that if they owned the company, they would become rich and powerful and possible rivals to his rule.

Likewise, socialists did not nationalize the Renault automobile company. Charles de Gaulle's post–World War II government did so to avenge its founder's collaboration with the occupying Germans. Renault has drawn money from the French government for investments and has made occasional profits in the years since.

France's state-owned businesses account for about one third of the nation's GNP. State-owned manufacturers and banks employ about a million people.

In France, as in Britain and Italy, some government-owned companies have been brought into profitability. A notable example is Usinor Sacilor. As late as 1986, the French company had the reputation of being one of "Europe's most intractable industrial and political nightmares." Then, in that year a professional manager with no political links was put in charge. He was able to make heavy industrial investment in modern, efficient equipment and to improve employee efficiency through training and better job flexibility. In 1988, Usinor Sacilor produced its first profit in 14 years; in 1989, it paid its first dividend in 16 years.[6]

In 1991, the French government relaxed its prohibition against sale of government-owned company shares. The decision permits domestic or foreign investors to take minority stakes up to 49.9 percent in state companies. Usinor Sacilor and a number of other companies and banks are negotiating for new capital and partners.[7]

◻ Unfair Competition?

Where government-owned companies compete with privately owned companies, the private companies sometimes complain that the government companies have unfair advantages. Some of the complaints are (1) government-owned companies can cut prices unfairly because they do not have to make profits; (2) they get cheaper financing; (3) they get government contracts; (4) they get export assistance; and (5) they can hold down wages with government assistance.[8]

Another huge advantage state-owned companies have over privately owned business comes in the form of direct subsidies, payments by the government to their companies. They total some 100 billion ECUs per year.[9] Italy is the leader here also (see Figure 10–1).

The EC Commission is trying to discourage such subsidy payments. In 1991, it began requiring annual financial reports from state-controlled companies as part of a crackdown on the subsidies that can distort competition.[10]

◻ Government–Private Collaboration Difficult

The objectives of private firms and those of government agencies and operations usually differ. Figure 10–2 (page 346) illustrates some of the differences.

PRIVATIZATION

Privatization of government-owned and -operated companies and services continued through the 1980s; and by 1991, the selling of state assets—from airlines to telephone companies—had captivated politicians everywhere, even in socialist Spain and communist China. Given the American devotion to private enterprise, it is odd but accurate to report that the United States is lagging behind other countries in selling its assets.

□ FIGURE 10–1
Europe's Gravy Train:
State Aid to EC Industry
(Annual average,
1981–1986)

Source: *The Economist,* November 18, 1989, p. 85.

privatization the transfer of public-sector assets to the private sector, the transfer of management of state activities through contracts and leases, and the contracting out of activities previously conducted by the state

Countries involved in the **privatization** movement include Canada, the United States, Mexico, Chile, Brazil, Britain, France, Spain, Italy, Holland, Germany, Turkey, Thailand, Singapore, Japan, the Philippines, Malaysia, Pakistan, and Argentina. Britain, under Margaret Thatcher, was the acknowledged leader of the movement. During her 11 years as prime minister, Thatcher decreased state-owned companies from 10 percent of GNP to 3.9 percent. She sold over 30 companies, raising some $65 billion.[11]

□ Privatization in Eastern Europe and the Former U.S.S.R.

Moving at various speeds and using different strategies, the countries of Eastern Europe and the former U.S.S.R. are shifting from totally state-owned and planned economies toward market economies. The magnitude of this privatization movement is of an entirely different order than that of any country not previously centrally planned. We shall name a few of the differences, but you should refer to sources listed in our endnotes and supplementary readings to understand the complexities and difficulties involved.

One difference is that in these countries almost all companies and activities have been government-owned and -operated for many years, while Western Europe and Latin America have a history of private business. The following percentages illustrate the prevalence of state-sector production in Eastern Europe and the former U.S.S.R.[12]

Countries	Percentages of State-Sector Production
Czechoslovakia	97 %
East Germany (prior to reunification)	96.5
U.S.S.R. (prior to its dissolution)	96
Poland	81.7
Hungary	65.2

☐ **FIGURE 10–2   Planners and Business Investors—Why Can't They Collaborate?**

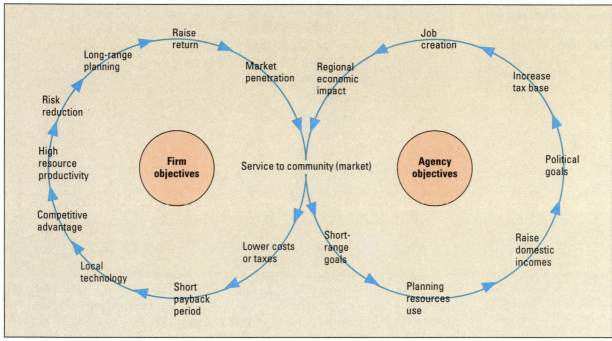

Source: Robert P. Vichas and Kimon Consias, "Public Planners and Business Investors—Why Can't They Collaborate?" *Long Range Planning*, no. 3 (Pergamon Press, Ltd., 1981), p. 83.

As a result of the state-sector's dominance, very few managers have any idea how to run a company without being told by a government central planner. Knowledge of such things as market prices, capital markets, convertible currencies, or profit and loss are almost completely foreign to the people who "manage" in the centrally planned economies.

Nevertheless, the states of the ex–U.S.S.R. and Eastern European countries are groping toward market economies. Once again, we recommend you supplement this text with outside reading, as there is inadequate space for us to detail their efforts.

PRIVATE SECTOR MORE EFFICIENT THAN STATE?

Proof beyond all doubt may be impossible to obtain. Academics nonetheless try. One study found that it cost the New York Department of Sanitation $40 (of which $32 was for labor) to deal with a ton of rubbish. It cost private collectors only $17 (of which $10 was for labor).

Research in Australia found the private airline, Ansett, considerably more productive than the public sector's Trans Australian Airline. In interviews, a large majority of managers moving from the public to the private system say that privatization has improved their performance. They cite the demoralizing effects of political interference and bureaucratic delay when their companies were government owned. Pierre Suard, chairman of Alcatel Alsthom, which was privatized in 1987, makes no secret of his opinion: "Privatization gave the firm a big advantage: freedom from government meddling. When the majority of your shares belong to the government, then sooner or later you have to incorporate into your policy some targets of government policy." The company's profits have more than doubled since privatization.[13]

▫ Other Forms of Privatization

Privatization does not always involve ownership transfer from government to private entities. For example, activities previously conducted by the state may be contracted out, as Indonesia has contracted a Swiss firm to run its customs administration and Thailand has private companies operating some of the passenger lines on its state-owned railroad.

Governments may lease state-owned plants to private entities, as Togo has done, or they may combine a joint venture with a management contract with a private group to run a previously government-owned business. Rwanda did this with its match factory.[14]

NATIONALISM

nationalism a devotion to one's own nation, its political and economic interests or aspirations, and its social and cultural traditions

Nationalism has been called the "secular religion of our time." In most of the older countries, loyalty to one's country and pride in it were based on such shared common features as race, language, religion, or ideology. Many of the newer countries, notably in Africa, have accidental boundaries resulting from their colonial past, and within these countries, there are several tribes and languages. This has resulted in civil wars, as in Nigeria and Angola, but it has not prevented these new countries from developing instant and fierce nationalism.

Nationalism is an emotion that can cloud or even prevent rational dealings with foreigners. The ills of a society can be blamed on foreign companies, which is what the chief of the joint staffs of the Peruvian military did when the military forces took charge in Peru.

Some of the effects of nationalism on ICs are (1) requirements for minimum local ownership or local product assembly or manufacture; (2) reservation of certain industries for local companies; (3) preference of local suppliers for government contracts; (4) limitations on the number and types of foreign employees; (5) protectionism, using tariffs, quotas, or other devices; (6) seeking a "French solution"* instead of a foreign takeover of a local firm;[15] and (7) in the most extreme cases, expropriation or confiscation.

GOVERNMENT PROTECTION

A historical function of government, whatever its ideology, has been the protection of the economic activities—farming, mining, manufacturing, and so forth—within its geographic area of control. These must be protected from attacks and destruction or robbery by terrorists, bandits, revolutionaries, and

* The French solution is to make every effort to find a French company rather than a foreign one to take over the French firm.

WORLDVIEW
British Gas Privatized

The following statement was issued by British Gas. It shows the sort of profitable expansion a privatized company can realize. We've been helping to provide Britain with gas to meet its energy needs for many years now. And very successfully too. But success can't last unless you build on it. Which is why we've developed opportunities abroad.

In one sense, we've been fortunate. The increased concern over environmental issues has helped people to see the advantage of gas over other fossil fuels.

But think. How many companies could have capitalised on this development the way British Gas has?

Even a very quick summary of our major projects shows the scale of our growth worldwide. Our Exploration and Production business, for example, has invested over £1billion in acquisitions over the past four years. Their entrepreneurial spirit has established British Gas across five continents.

Our Global Gas business has made a major investment in Consumers' Gas of Toronto, Canada. Which means there is now a British gas company with customers on both sides of the Atlantic. Us.

The changes in East/West relations also gave British Gas enormous opportunities. In the U.S.S.R., for example, we've agreed in principle to take a stake in the development of a major oil and gas field. And in what was formerly the German Democratic Republic, we now have a stake in two large gas distribution companies. Then there's the Gulf of Suez. Our oil discovery there is one of the largest in the area for more than a decade.

Does all this activity mean we are neglecting Britain? Not in the slightest. If we were, we wouldn't have signed up 270,000 new customers last year, or added half a million central heating systems to homes throughout the country. We wouldn't be selling gas to generate electricity. Also we wouldn't have succeeded in keeping gas prices amongst the lowest in Europe.

And with the world and its leaders coming closer together recently, there has never been a better time for British Gas to become a superpower in world energy.

The world is turning to British Gas.

Source: Advertisement for British Gas, 1991.

foreign invaders. A war was required to free Kuwait and its oil wealth from Iraq.

☐ Iraq Grabs for Economic-Political Power

In 1990, the Iraqi armed forces moved massively into Kuwait, quickly overwhelming the defenders of that much smaller country. Although Kuwait is small, it is oil rich. If Iraq held Kuwait, the combined petroleum reserves of the two countries would make Iraq a major player in petroleum politics.

An even greater prize was lying next door: Saudi Arabia, with the world's largest proved petroleum reserves. With armed forces no match for those of Iraq, Saudi Arabia might even have followed Iraqi orders without an invasion. That would have made Iraq the world's mightiest petroleum power and permitted it to influence strongly the policies and actions of Europe, Japan, North America, and most of the rest of the world.

Led by the United States and sanctioned by the UN, an international coalition mobilized and transported armed forces to the Middle East. A short war in early 1991 forced Iraqi forces out of Kuwait, although they set fire to hundreds of Kuwaiti oil wells as they retreated.

Ancient and modern war vehicles in Desert Storm.

▫ Terrorism

Since the 1970s, the world has been plagued by various groups that have hijacked airplanes, shot and kidnapped people, and bombed people and objects. A common denominator of these **terrorist** groups has been hatred of the social, economic, and political orders they find in the world. Another characteristic is their confusion as to what sort of order they would substitute if they had the chance.

During the 1970s and 1980s, Italy was particularly hard hit by terrorist violence directed against businesses and politicians. Between 1975 and 1982, terrorist groups almost shattered Italy's faith in its ability to govern itself without resorting to a communist or fascist-style police state. However, the democratic Italian government struck back successfully by creating a special, 25,000-strong antiterrorist squad. Once caught, terrorists were tried, convicted, and sentenced to prison by the Italian courts.

Coinciding with those events, the attraction of terrorist groups for educated young Italians lessened. And with their charisma fading, the groups had many penitents and defectors.

As educated, idealistic young Italians—their original source of recruits—became disenchanted, terrorist leaders turned to more conventional crime. They began cooperating with the Mafia, which is now growing and more feared by Italian authorities. The Bank of Italy has given warning that the Mafia threatens to contaminate Italy's financial system.[16]

Terrorism worldwide.   Italy is by no means alone as a victim of terrorism. The names of some of the groups reflect their geographic scope. A few of the better known gangs are the Irish Republican Army (IRA), the Palestine Liberation Organization (PLO), the Basque separatist movement (ETA), the Japanese Red Army, and the German Red Army Faction.

terrorism unlawful acts of violence committed for a wide variety of reasons, including to overthrow a government, gain release of imprisoned colleagues, exact revenge for real or imagined wrongs, or punish nonbelievers of the terrorists' religion

All of them and others had sanctuaries in the former East Germany, other former East European Soviet satellites, and the Soviet Union itself. The East German secret police, the Stasi, and the Soviet secret police, the KGB, provided financing, training, and protection to the terrorist groups.[17]

Government-sponsored terrorism; acts of war. In addition to the Soviet Union and its European satellites, other countries financed, trained, and protected terrorists. They included Iran, Iraq, Libya, and Syria. In 1986, a British court convicted a Palestinian of trying to smuggle explosives (concealed in the baggage of his pregnant girlfriend) aboard an El Al Israel 747 aircraft. The flight from London to Tel Aviv would have been blown up over Austria. It was developed at the trial that the material for the explosives had been brought into London in Syrian diplomatic pouches aboard the Syrian government airline; the Syrian ambassador had sanctioned or even directed the operation. In international law, government action to damage or kill in another country is an act of war.

Kidnapping for ransom. Kidnapping is another weapon used by terrorists. The victims are held for ransom, frequently very large amounts, which provides an important source of funds for the terrorists. Italian industry is not alone in being subjected to terrorism and kidnapping for ransom. For example, it is said that industry in Argentina has paid ransom of several hundred million dollars for the release of kidnapped business executives.[18]

By 1986, Colombia and Peru had become the most dangerous places for American executives, and a long stay by a high-ranking American executive in either country is risky. Brief visits are usually fairly safe because kidnappings take a while to plan, so top executives from the United States practice what is called commando management. They arrive in Bogota or Lima as secretly as possible, meet for a few days with local employees, and fly off before kidnappers learn of their presence.[19]

Countermeasures by industry. Insurance to cover ransom payments, antiterrorist schools, and companies to handle negotiations with kidnappers have come into being.

As kidnapping and extortion directed against businesses and governments have become common fund-raising and political techniques for terrorists, insurance against such acts has grown into a multimillion-dollar business. The world's largest kidnapping and extortion underwriting firm is located in London. The firm, Cassidy and Davis, underwrites for Lloyd's of London and says that it covers some 9,000 companies. Cassidy and Davis does not sit back and wait for claims to be filed. It runs antiterrorism training courses for executives, with subjects ranging from defensive driving techniques—escape tactics and battering through blockades—to crisis management. Country-by-country risk analyses are instantly available on international computer hookups.

Cassidy and Davis works closely with Control Risk, Ltd., a London-based security service company. Control Risk works behind the scenes to advise companies or families in negotiations with kidnappers.

Cassidy and Davis encourages its clients to use Control Risk services. The premiums for the insurance underwritten by Cassidy and Davis range from some $3,000 a year for $1.5 million of coverage in low-risk England to $60,000 a year for the same coverage in high-risk Peru.[20]

Wreckage of terrorist-bombed Pan Am flight 103 in the Scottish village of Lockerbie.

D. Hudson/SYGMA

Figures 10−3 and 10−4 are checklists for executives traveling to and in countries where they are at risk of being kidnapped. Figure 10−3 indicates what should be done before leaving the home country; Figure 10−4 is about what to do once in the host country.

Terrorism changes.   On the positive side, terrorists have lost their havens, finance sources, and training bases in East Europe and the Soviet Union. There is better cooperation between antiterrorist officials in governments of Europe, Japan, and North America. New American laws give the United States powers to hunt down terrorists anywhere in the world. Since 1985, the United States has convicted more than 460 people on domestic terrorism charges and more than 60 on international charges.[21]

But there are negatives. A different kind of terrorism is breaking out in the post−Soviet empire period. This is ethnoterrorism, as various European racial groups fight to establish their own nations and for land for their people. The Croats, Serbs, and Slovenians of Yugoslavia are killing each other as are various racial groups in the splintered Soviet Union.

Germany has emerged as the weak link in the Western countries' antiterrorist chain. It has never had decisive success against the Red Army Faction, which continues its series of spectacular murders, including the 1989 killing of the Deutsche Bank head, Alfred Herrhausen.

The German mishandling of the investigation of the Pan Am Lockerbie bombing is emblematic of German security shortcomings. At one point, 16 terrorists were rounded up, but 14 were released almost immediately, enraging antiterrorist agents around the world.[22]

The Western world thought it had seen the end of activities of the infamous Stasi, the East German secret police. However, evidence is appearing that it has simply gone underground and is now being funded by leaders of the old East German communist regime. They are said to have spent their last months in power disguising and moving assets in order to reemerge as a financially potent and internationally organized force. After they denounced

□ **FIGURE 10–3**
Before Leaving

- Your personal and legal affairs should be in order.

- Except on a need-to-know basis, tell no one of your travel plans. This is not hysterical paranoia, it's good discipline. A business executive on a fishing boat out of Miami, who discusses an upcoming business trip to Central America in the presence of Cuban deckhands, may find that future stay in Central America considerably longer than was planned.

- Sanitize all documents and business identity. All company logos and identification should be removed from briefcases and luggage. A last name, or fictitious name you've created, is sufficient identification on these items. If you use business cards, acronyms such as CIA for certified internal auditor should be eliminated. Whatever documents you need to conduct your business can be mailed or wired ahead so that they are waiting for you. If the trip comes up very suddenly or there are no company offices to receive the documents, carry them in your luggage. Never carry any business identification or documents on your person. In addition to a passport with visas, a jewelry bracelet or pendant type ID with name, social security number, and blood type would be the ideal and only identification the traveler would need while in transit.

- Check with your company, and other companies to find someone who has conducted business in the country you are going to. Contact that person and ask questions about cultural mores and the political climate in that country. Then look in an encyclopedia or go to the library and read all you can on the subject.

- If your company doesn't already have an individual designated to coordinate and monitor foreign trips, contact the appropriate management and see that someone knows the where, when, and how of your trip. Your family should be given that person's name and phone numbers.

- The company should have an established code for use by all its personnel who are engaged in foreign business. If not, a simple code system should be devised so that communication can be made under extraordinary circumstances (like on a video made by terrorists who have kidnapped you). The code should be provided to the company and your family.

- Have your company acquire a telephone directory for the State Department from the Government Printing Office. It can be used to contact the appropriate departmental sections for pretrip inquiries (operational intelligence). And, in the unfortunate event of a company employee kidnapping, it would be an absolute necessity in crisis management.

Source: *The Internal Auditor*, October 1986, p. 25.

Detlev Rohwedder, the director of Treuhandanstalt,* he was murdered, an act for which Stasi members are suspected.[23]

GOVERNMENT STABILITY

stability a government can be said to be stable if it maintains itself in power and when its fiscal, monetary, and political policies are predictable and not subject to sudden, radical changes

Government **stability** can be approached from two directions. One can speak of either a government's simple ability to maintain itself in power or the stability or permanence of a government's policies. It is safe to generalize that business (indeed almost all agricultural, commercial, and financial activities) prospers most when there is a stable government with permanent—or at most, gradually changing—policies.

□ Stability and Instability: Examples and Results

Instability in Lebanon. Here is a classic example of the impact of a change from order to chaos—from stability to **instability**—on the business and finance of a prosperous country. Until 1974, Lebanon prospered as the trading, banking, international company regional headquarters, business services

instability an unstable government is the opposite of a stable one. It cannot maintain itself in power or makes sudden, unpredictable, and/or radical policy changes

* The Treuhandanstalt is the organization in charge of privatizing companies and properties owned by the government of the previous East Germany.

□ **FIGURE 10–4**
After Arriving

- First, slow down. Leave yourself time to think and evaluate. You're not in America. The rush and rat-race pace of hyperactivity typical of American business people will only get you in trouble here.

- Take nothing for granted. Locate where elevators and stairways are so you can find them, even in the dark.

- Learn your rooms. Locate windows and doors and check to see if they are locked or if they can be locked. If you are not satisfied with your room, either change rooms or change hotels. Remember, if you change hotels, let the company and your family know.

- Do not conduct any business in your room or over the phone. The reasons are obvious.

- Whenever possible, you schedule business meetings and the locations. If this is not possible, check with your contacts and determine whether the location of scheduled meetings is safe. Remember, it's not the people you're conducting business with that present the threat (unless you're a major corporate executive and that fact is well known in advance); the danger is in becoming an object of surveillance.

- You are most vulnerable when you're moving, particularly if that movement is predictable. Vary times and methods of movement. Whether you're using a company-provided car and driver or taxis, use different entrances and exits when you enter and leave the hotel. If you are using company or rented transportation, change cars whenever the mood strikes you. Always follow your instincts.

- Always be aware of your surroundings and alert for surveillance. If terrorists are following you and they realize you recognize that fact, you've just made yourself a higher risk for them to consider. Terrorists will not just be lurking in the streets waiting for someone they can attack. They will spend many hours and much effort to observe potential targets. Then, they will select the target that's going to cost them the least. Being alert makes you a more difficult target and raises the possibility, from the terrorist's point of view, that you have or will notify the authorities.

- Avoid being photographed.

- Do not respond to telephone inquiries or apparent spontaneous interest by people you meet to know more about you, however innocent or sincere either may seem. Handle it diplomatically.

- Avoid night movements, but if you must, never walk. Not walking anywhere, anytime, is the best rule; but if it can't be avoided, be particularly sensitive to surveillance and try to stay in crowded areas.

- Read newspapers and stay in touch with your in-country contacts on a daily basis to stay informed on political climate indicators.

- Try to fit in with the native people as much as possible regarding dress and manners. This not only ingratiates you with the locals but also makes you more difficult to see.

Source: *The Internal Auditor,* October 1986, p. 27.

(that is, accounting, legal, and financial services), transportation, and tourist center of the Middle East. The country achieved this prosperity with virtually no natural resources; its land is mostly arid desert or mountains. Its prosperity was the work of an industrious people given political stability.

Then civil war broke out in Lebanon. The details of that civil war are beyond the scope of this book, but its reasons included ideological and religious differences. The results were catastrophic.

Homes, offices, banks, stores, transportation, communications, and hospitals were destroyed. The people fled the country or fought and survived as best they could. Almost all of the previous commercial activities ended.

Stability in Bolivia?   In 152 years of independence from Spain, Bolivia had 187 governments. Then, in 1972, a government seized power and by 1976 had established the durability record for any Bolivian government in the 20th century. The economic results were startling and encouraging.

Bolivia's GNP grew by 7.3 percent in 1975 and 7 percent in 1976, and its inflation rate was about 12 percent. At the same time, such neighbors as Argentina, Chile, and Peru were experiencing varying types of political unrest, were growing more slowly or not at all, and were suffering much higher rates of inflation.

Hector Ormachea, the Bolivian government official in charge of negotiating development loans abroad, spoke of "projects, not politics." And projects resulted—more than 300 by 1977. They ranged from roads into areas previously accessible only by air, to oil exploration, mining ventures, and agricultural and industrial development.

Unused wealth. Bolivia is potentially a rich country. Its resources include tin, zinc, antimony, copper, gold, tungsten, and bismuth, and it is more than self-sufficient in oil despite very little recent exploration or drilling.

The country's resources have scarcely been touched, at least in part because of Bolivia's previous political instability. Past governments had been quick to nationalize foreign mines. Given the mid-1970s stability, European, Japanese, and U.S. firms negotiated to explore for and extract the resources.[24]

Renewed foreign confidence. Another sign of renewed foreign confidence in Bolivia was given in 1977. Underwriters led by the Arab Finance Corporation and Merrill Lynch International handled the sale in Europe of Bolivian debt securities. Although the amount was a relatively small $15 million, it was the first offering to foreign investors in about 50 years. Until Bolivia had achieved political stability, it would have been fruitless to try to borrow money abroad; no one would have lent it.[25]

Perils of Pauline. By 1979, there was further political turmoil in Bolivia; between then and 1985, there were 12 Bolivian governments—most of them military. Inflation soared to about 25,000 percent in 1985, and in that year over half of Bolivia's export earnings—some $600 million—came from sales of cocaine; less than $500 million came from sales of minerals, oil, gas, and agricultural products. While the few cocaine traffickers got rich, the great bulk of the Bolivian population—growing at 2.6 percent a year—sank more deeply into poverty. Domestic investment declined and production collapsed.

Miracle of La Paz? * In 1985, a new Bolivian president, Victor Paz Estenssero, was democratically elected. Estenssero immediately froze salaries in the state sector (which accounted for roughly 40 percent of the economy), removed price controls, stopped subsidies, slashed many import tariffs, floated the peso, and liberalized labor laws to allow easy firing and hiring. He told state enterprises to cover their costs or close, put new taxes on cars and houses, and offered a back tax amnesty.

Inflation plunged to near zero, foreign development aid is being restored, local investments have been starting up, and an attack has begun on the big drug traffickers. Both the World Bank and the International Monetary Fund have provided millions to finance Bolivia's agricultural and industrial recovery and to compensate it for the collapse of international tin prices (tin was once Bolivia's main export).[26]

Nevertheless, Bolivia's growth was slow at about 2.6 percent per year until 1991, when it sped up to 4 percent, and its inflation at 15 percent was the lowest in South America. Bolivia's commercial debt was paid off at the end of 1991, and the currency—the boliviano—was freely convertible into the US$.

---

* La Paz is the capital of Bolivia.

*Arabs (Palestinian intifada)
burn an Israeli flag.*

A. Tannenbaum/SYGMA

Confidence was growing, bringing savings out from under mattresses or from Miami and into Bolivian banks. With new mining and investment laws in place, mining exploration is starting after three decades of stagnation, although both economic growth and democracy are fragile due to continuing poverty and corruption.[27]

TRADITIONAL HOSTILITIES

traditional hostilities
long-standing enmities
between tribes, races,
religions, ideologies, or
countries

One need mention only a few of the **traditional hostilities** to illustrate their powerful impact on business and trade.

☐ Arab Countries—Israel

Israel is surrounded on three sides by Arab countries, but until the peace efforts initiated by the Egyptian Anwar Sadat, the Arab countries would not trade or have other peaceful dealings with it. Indeed, some Arab countries still boycott companies that trade with Israel, and because some of the Arab countries are extremely rich OPEC members, the boycott can be financially painful.*

☐ Vietnam—Cambodia

The people of these two countries have been hostile to each other for centuries. After American involvement in Vietnam ended, the Vietnamese army invaded Cambodia. Vietnamese forces left the country in September 1989, leaving behind a puppet Cambodian government they had supported. The

---

* See Chapter 11 for a discussion of U.S. law dealing with this boycott.

Vietnamese do not want the brutal Khmer Rouge faction to resume control of the country, but the Khmer Rouge are supported by China and are well armed. The Vietnamese may return. In 1992, the UN was trying to support a coalition government, but Cambodia has been closed to outside business or investment for many years.

◻ Tamils and Sinhalese in Sri Lanka

The Tamils form a substantial minority of the Sri Lankan population. An armed group calling itself the Tamil Tigers has been fighting a bloody series of battles with the Sri Lankan army and has committed terrorist murders and bombings of the Sinhalese population.

The Tamils want a separate state, and a large Tamil population in India has given them support. The late Indian president, Rajiv Ghandi, sent troops to Sri Lanka in an attempt to suppress the Tamil uprising. They failed, and the troops were withdrawn, but Ghandi gained Tamil hatred for his attempt. His murder—by a bomb hidden in a flower arrangement offered him by a woman when he was campaigning for election in the Indian Tamil state in 1991—was blamed on the Tigers or their allies.

◻ Croats, Bosnians, and Serbs in Yugoslavia

This historical enmity was mentioned above, and they are killing each other despite EC efforts at peacemaking. The Croats want to form an independent state of Croatia, and the Serbs, with cooperation of the Yugoslav army, are trying to capture and keep areas of what would be part of Croatia. They are doing the same things in Bosnia.

◻ South Africa

We should emphasize that the examples given above are, unfortunately, only a few of many racially based hostilities around the world. We presented another in the last edition of this book: the black-white strife of South African apartheid. Since that was written, South Africa has repealed many of the laws that created apartheid, released imprisoned black leaders, and permitted exiles back into the country.

There is hope in the world that apartheid may be dead and that a democratic South Africa will emerge. As a result of those hopes, many of the investment, lending, and trading curbs placed on businesses, banks, and traders doing business with South Africa have been lifted. Europe, Japan, and North America all enforced such curbs.

INTERNATIONAL ORGANIZATIONS

As discussed above, nationalism is a powerful political force that has grown greatly during the mid- and late 20th century. There are also international political forces with which business must contend. Here we shall cover briefly the political impact of some of the international organizations introduced in Chapter 4.

◻ United Nations (UN)

The UN is highly politicized. The member-countries vote as blocs formed because of ideology or perceived similar objectives. There are the communist and noncommunist groupings and the developed countries versus the less developed countries. It remains to be seen how the changes in the former U.S.S.R. and Eastern Europe will affect these blocs.

United Nations personnel advise UN members on such matters as tax, monetary, and fiscal policies. The UN is active in the harmonization of laws affecting international trade. It had a hand in drafting an international commercial arbitration convention. It has drafted a code of conduct for multinational business. Any of the political ideologies we have discussed can be reflected in the content and spirit of tax, trade, and arbitration laws; conduct codes; and fiscal or monetary policies.

UNCTAD is credited with having influenced the IMF to ease its restrictions on loans to LDCs. This is important to banks lending to and suppliers selling to LDCs.

Virtually all of the specialized UN agencies are now actively advising LDCs about what to buy for their agriculture, industry, airlines, health programs, weather stations, and so forth. These are huge markets for business.

◻ World Bank Group

One or another member of the World Bank Group finances large parts of the purchases made by LDCs. Although the Bank's charter bans political activity by its officers and employees, it is reported that its president was involved in campaign-planning strategy for one of the U.S. presidential candidates in 1980.[28]

◻ IMF, GATT, and OPEC

The IMF can have great influence on the fiscal and monetary policies of the nations that it assists, and, as reported in Chapter 4, many believe its power is growing.

Although GATT has in general striven to lower barriers to trade, it has condoned their erection by LDCs in some cases. Import barriers are, of course, an important political force affecting multinational business operations.

The political power of OPEC was discussed in Chapter 4. We mention it here again to remind you that petroleum is now as much a political force as it is a commodity.

◻ EC

Slowly but surely, the member-nations of the EC are surrendering parts of their sovereign powers to the Brussels headquarters. Mention of only a few areas will illustrate the extent of the EC's influence on business. Among other things, the EC is working to harmonize laws dealing with taxes, patents, labor conditions, competition, insurance, banking, and capital markets.

Harmonization of differing national laws is one matter, but the EC has now gone a step beyond that—to lawmaking. This is occurring in such fields as company law, antitrust, and consumer and environmental protection.[29]

Now the EC is embarked on Project 1992, which is continuing past 1992. The objective of some Europeans is to create a political—as well as an economic—power to rival America and Japan.

▫ Organization for Economic Cooperation and Development (OECD)

This 24-member organization of industrialized countries has issued "Guidelines for Multinational Enterprises." One writer states that rather than being a stifling set of legal do's and don'ts, the guidelines create a voluntary set of principles upon which to build sound international economic relations.[30] Nevertheless, these ostensibly voluntary guidelines can have a significant impact.

> **When Badger, Raytheon's subsidiary in Belgium, closed shop, it did not have enough money to meet its labor termination obligations. The Belgian government and labor unions used the pressure of the OECD "voluntary" guidelines to require Raytheon to pay Badger's obligations.[31]**

LABOR

Workers and labor unions are the subject of Chapter 12, but we would be remiss if we did not mention them in connection with the political forces bearing on business. The European labor unions are ideologically oriented, usually toward the left. The American unions are said to be more pragmatic, but in practice they are extremely active politically. They supply large amounts of money and political workers to support the political candidates they favor.

In Europe, the United States, and, increasingly, in Japan, labor makes its political force felt not only at the polls but also in the legislatures. The unions lobby for or against laws as these are perceived to be for or against the interests of labor.

INTERNATIONAL COMPANIES (ICs)

International business is not merely a passive victim of political forces. It can be a powerful force in the world political arena.[32]

▫ Forty Percent of World's Top Economic Units Are Firms, Not Nations

An IC negotiating with a country may be bigger than the country. According to rankings in 1989, General Motors' sales of $127 billion made it the 20th largest economic unit. Its sales were larger than the $109.7 billion GNP of Finland. Ford's sales of $96.9 billion made it the 23rd largest economic unit, surpassing Norway. Of course, the GNP of the great majority of other countries is even smaller.[33]

Such financial size carries power. However, an IC's power need not rest solely on size. It can come from the possession of scarce capital, technology, and management, plus the capability to deploy those resources around the world. An IC may have the processing, productive, distributive, and marketing abilities necessary for the successful exploitation of raw materials or for the manufacture, distribution, and marketing of certain products. Those abilities are frequently not available in LDCs. Recognition of the desirability of IC investments is growing.[34]

COUNTRY RISK ASSESSMENT (CRA)

country risk assessment (CRA) a bank or business having an asset in or payable from a foreign country, or considering a loan or an investment there, evaluates that country's economic situation and policies and its politics to determine how much risk exists of losing the asset or not being paid

It is arbitrary to place this subject in a chapter on political forces because **country risk assessment (CRA)** involves many risks other than political risks. It is probably important enough to warrant a separate chapter, but one of our objectives is to avoid an overlong book. We shall introduce our readers to CRA here; there is a growing literature about it, and those who are interested can find much material.[35]

Although it is arbitrary to put CRA in this chapter, it is not unreasonable since the political events of recent years have caused firms to concentrate much more on the practice. Firms that had already done CRA updated and strengthened the function, and many other companies began CRA.

▫ Types of Country Risks

Country risks are increasingly political in nature. There are wars, revolutions, and coups. Less dramatic, but nevertheless important for businesses, are government changes by election of a socialist or nationalist government, which may be hostile to private business and particularly to foreign-owned business.

The risks may be economic or financial. There may be persistent balance-of-payments deficits or high inflation rates. Repayment of loans may be questionable.

Labor conditions may cause investors to pause. Labor productivity may be low, or labor unions may be militant.

Laws may be changed about such subjects as taxes, currency convertibility, tariffs, quotas, or labor permits. The chances for a fair trial in local courts must be assessed.

Terrorism may be present. If it is, can the company protect its personnel and property?

▫ Information Content for CRA

The types of information a firm will need to judge country risks will vary according to the nature of its business and the length of time required for the investment, loan, or other involvement to yield a satisfactory return.

Nature of business. Consider, for example, the needs of a hotel company compared with those of heavy-equipment manufacturers or manufacturers of personal hygiene products or mining companies. Banks have their own sets of problems and information needs. Sometimes there are variations between firms in the same industry or on a project-to-project basis. The nationality—home country—of the company may be a factor; does the host country bear a particular animus, or friendly attitude, toward the home country?

Length of time required. Export financing usually involves the shortest period of risk exposure. Typically, payments are made within 180 days—usually less—and exporters can get insurance or bank protection.

Bank loans can be short, medium, or long term. However, when the business includes host country assembly, mixing, manufacture, or extraction (oil or minerals), long-term commitments are necessary.

With long-term investment or loan commitments, there are inherent problems with risk analysis that cannot be resolved. Most such investment opportunities require 5, 10, or more years to pay off. But the utility of risk analyses of social, political, and economic factors decreases precipitously over longer time spans.

▫ Who Does Country Risk Assessing?

General or specific analyses, macro or micro analyses, and political, social, and economic analyses have been conducted—perhaps under different names—for years. The Conference Board located bits and pieces of CRA being performed in various company departments—for example, the international division and public affairs, finance, legal, economics, planning, and product-producing departments. Sometimes the efforts were duplicative, and the people in one department were unaware that others in the company were similarly involved.

Efforts are now being made to concentrate CRA and to maximize its effectiveness for the company. These efforts include guidelines about the participation of top management.

Another source of country risk analysis is the outside consulting and publishing firm. As CRA has mushroomed in perceived importance, a number of such firms have been formed or have expanded.

Instead of or in addition to the outside consultants, a number of firms have buttressed their internal risk analysis staffs by hiring such experts as international business or political science professors or retired State Department, CIA, or military people.

▫ CRA Procedures

The Economist Intelligence Unit breaks its assessments down into three categories. First, there is medium-term lending risk, covering such factors as external debt and trends in the current account. Second is political and policy risk, including factors such as the consistency of government policy and the quality of economic management. Third is short-term trade risk, including foreign exchange reserves.[36]

The *International Country Risk Guide (ICRG)*, put out by a U.S. division of International Business Communications Ltd. of London, takes a somewhat different approach. It offers individual ratings for political, financial, and economic risk, plus a composite rating. The political variable includes factors such as government corruption and how economic expectations diverge from reality. The financial rating looks at such things as the likelihood of losses from exchange controls and loan defaults. Economic ratings take into account such factors as inflation and debt service costs.[37] Table 10–1 shows the *ICRG* rating of 129 countries.

▫ Lessons of the International Debt Crisis

There are at least five lessons that CRA analysts should have learned. First, many developing countries are vulnerable to external shocks. One thing that has become apparent is the importance of a country's export and import structure in weathering an external economic shock. For example, the newly industrialized countries of Asia with their diversified export structures have been in a much better position to deal with the collapse of commodity prices and the erection of protectionist barriers than have been other countries with a comparable level of development but lopsided export structures (such as Indonesia and Mexico).

Second, the development of the debt crisis has shown clearly that the economic policies of debtor countries have a decisive impact on default risk. The countries that have become most deeply mired in the crisis are the ones that adopted expansionary fiscal and monetary policies. The results were inflation, current account deficits, loss of international competitiveness, and capital flight. Such has been the fate of the Philippines and the high-debt countries of Latin America.

By contrast, those countries that allowed the altered world market prices and demand conditions to take effect on their economies and adapted their economic policies to accommodate changed conditions have fared much better. Restrictive fiscal and monetary policies damped inflation, while occasional devaluations of their currencies kept trade balances under control. South Korea withstood the debt crisis through skillful economic policies.

Third, sustained economic growth is a major requirement for high-debt countries to service their debt and reduce its burden. Austerity alone cannot be a solution—economically, politically, or socially.

Fourth, the social and potential political costs of overindebtedness combined with austerity are proving high. In Latin America, real imports fell by about 30 percent, and real per capita income by some 7 percent, between 1981 and 1985. Social and political tensions have risen sharply and threaten the survival of several democratically elected governments. That, in turn, greatly increases the danger of a debt moratorium.

The fifth lesson from the debt crisis for CRA analysts is the global ripple effect of seemingly independent risks or economic shocks. For example, the oil price collapse at the beginning of 1986 jacked up oil-exporting countries' default risk while lessening that risk for oil importers, thus affecting international interest and exchange rates and triggering a whole series of fiscal and monetary policy responses.

The 1987 stock market crash caused worldwide economic reverberations. Other events that would have global effects if they were to occur include sustained changes in world interest rates, recession in major market countries, creation of debtor-country cartels, or the banking system's loss of confidence in an entire region.

In 1990, Crédit Suisse created a new subsidiary, Crédit Suisse Financial Products, to help its clients assess CRA. The new company suggests and offers a broad range of financial derivatives and swaps* tailored to meet the clients' needs.[38]

---

* Currency and interest rate swaps are discussed in Chapter 18.

□ **TABLE 10–1   A Global Rating by ICRG**

Country	Political Risk	Financial Risk	Economic Risk	Composite Risk	Country	Political Risk	Financial Risk	Economic Risk	Composite Risk
1. Switzerland	93.0	50.0	39.5	91.5	34. Oman	65.0	34.0	42.0	70.5
2. Luxembourg	93.0	49.0	36.0	89.0	35. Chile	67.0	42.0	30.0	69.5
3. Norway	87.0	47.0	42.0	88.0	36. Czechoslovakia	73.0	36.0	30.0	69.5
4. Austria	88.0	47.0	39.5	87.5	37. Costa Rica	71.0	35.0	32.0	69.0
5. Germany	83.0	50.0	88.5	86.0	38. Indonesia	57.0	44.0	35.5	68.5
6. Netherlands	85.0	46.0	40.5	86.0	39. Uruguay	66.0	39.0	32.0	68.5
7. Brunel	81.0	48.0	41.5	85.5	40. Thailand	55.0	42.0	37.0	68.0
8. Japan	80.0	50.0	39.0	84.5	41. Colombia	60.0	41.0	34.0	67.5
9. Singapore	79.0	48.0	39.5	83.5	42. Hong Kong	58.0	42.0	35.0	67.5
10. U.S.	78.0	49.0	39.5	83.5	43. Paraguay	59.0	39.0	34.5	66.5
11. Canada	81.0	48.0	37.0	83.0	44. Qatar	56.0	33.0	42.0	65.5
12. Belgium	82.0	45.0	36.5	82.0	45. Gabon	57.0	33.0	39.0	64.5
13. Denmark	88.0	41.0	37.0	82.0	46. Mongolia	65.0	36.0	28.0	64.5
14. Sweden	81.0	47.0	35.0	81.5	47. Greece	65.0	33.0	29.5	64.0
15. Taiwan	71.0	49.0	43.0	81.5	48. Jamaica	66.0	37.0	24.0	63.5
16. United Kingdom	76.0	50.0	36.0	81.0	49. Saudi Arabia	60.0	31.0	35.5	63.5
17. Finland	85.0	44.0	32.0	80.5	50. Israel	55.0	33.0	34.5	63.0
18. France	79.0	46.0	34.5	80.0	51. Trinidad/Tobago	59.0	35.0	31.5	63.0
19. Ireland	80.0	42.0	37.5	80.0	52. U.A.E.	53.0	33.0	39.5	63.0
20. New Zealand	78.0	46.0	35.0	79.5	53. Bahrain	54.0	30.0	40.5	62.5
21. Australia	76.0	45.0	37.0	79.0	54. Brazil	67.0	34.0	23.0	62.0
22. Iceland	82.0	42.0	33.5	79.5	55. Hungary	68.0	32.0	24.0	62.0
23. Malaysia	71.0	45.0	88.5	77.5	56. Gambia	53.0	33.0	35.5	61.0
24. Italy	72.0	47.0	35.0	77.0	57. Poland	62.0	29.0	31.0	62.0
25. Venezuela	75.0	40.0	36.0	75.5	58. China	58.0	24.0	88.0	60.0
26. Portugal	69.0	42.0	38.5	75.0	59. South Africa	56.0	30.0	32.5	59.5
27. South Korea	63.0	47.0	36.5	73.5	60. Bolivia	52.0	34.0	32.0	59.0
28. Botswana	70.0	34.0	42.0	73.0	61. Cote d'Ivoire	66.0	29.0	23.0	59.0
29. Cyprus	69.0	39.0	88.0	73.0	62. Algeria	54.0	30.0	32.5	58.5
30. Bahamas	66.0	39.0	36.5	71.0	63. Argentina	63.0	30.0	23.0	58.0
31. Spain	65.0	42.0	35.0	71.0	64. Senegal	53.0	29.0	33.5	58.0
32. Malta	64.0	34.0	43.0	70.5	65. Bulgaria	61.0	28.0	25.5	57.5
33. Mexico	71.0	41.0	28.5	70.5	66. Ecuador	58.0	29.0	26.0	56.5

Source: *The Wall Street Journal,* September 20, 1991, p. R4.

SUMMARY

Ideologies are defined in dictionaries and textbooks. Countries and political parties use names with ideological meanings to describe themselves, but you must view these names cautiously because the political and economic actions of countries and parties may not be what you would expect from their names.

Until recently that was not true for the communist countries, whose political and economic actions fol-

lowed true to form, including ownership or control of all important factors of production. Some changes are now taking place in communist countries, such as possibilities for private ownership or operation of farms and businesses and for foreign private companies to own or joint venture businesses. These changes began in the People's Republic of China and spread to the ex–Soviet Union and most of the former Soviet satellite

□ **TABLE 10–1 (concluded)**

Country	Political Risk	Financial Risk	Economic Risk	Composite Risk	Country	Political Risk	Financial Risk	Economic Risk	Composite Risk
67. Egypt	54.0	30.0	29.0	56.5	99. Peru	45.0	28.0	21.5	47.5
68. Libya	52.0	27.0	34.0	56.5	100. Sri Lanka	36.0	26.0	32.5	47.5
69. Nigeria	49.0	29.0	35.0	56.5	101. Suriname	44.0	23.0	28.0	47.5
70. Syria	53.0	23.0	36.0	56.0	102. Philippines	41.0	22.0	29.5	46.0
71. Iran	56.0	28.0	26.5	55.5	103. Yugoslavia	45.0	24.0	23.5	46.5
72. Morocco	52.0	38.0	30.5	55.5	104. Kuwait	38.0	24.0	23.5	46.5
73. U.S.S.R.	53.0	36.0	21.5	55.5	105. New Caledonia	44.0	13.0	34.5	46.0
74. Ghana	53.0	30.0	27.0	55.0	106. North Korea	59.0	15.0	16.0	45.0
75. Namibia	47.0	24.0	38.0	54.5	107. Mali	40.0	19.0	30.5	45.0
76. Panama	47.0	28.0	34.0	54.5	108. Zambia	45.0	19.0	25.5	45.0
77. Tunisia	54.0	23.0	32.0	54.5	109. Nicaragua	44.0	27.0	17.0	44.0
78. Cameroon	47.0	27.0	34.0	54.0	110. Pakistan	34.0	22.0	32.0	44.0
79. Papua	54.0	26.0	28.0	54.0	111. Vietnam	50.0	18.0	20.0	44.0
80. Dominican Rep.	53.0	23.0	30.5	53.5	112. El Salvador	37.0	18.0	32.0	43.5
81. Congo	52.0	20.0	33.5	53.0	113. India	34.0	25.0	27.0	43.0
82. Tanzania	56.0	27.0	23.0	53.0	114. Mozambique	44.0	26.0	15.5	43.0
83. Angola	45.0	19.0	41.0	52.5	115. Yemen	49.0	23.0	12.0	41.0
84. Honduras	49.0	28.0	28.0	52.5	116. Cuba	54.0	16.0	12.0	41.0
85. Albania	55.0	33.0	16.0	52.0	117. Bangladesh	33.0	18.0	29.0	40.0
86. Malawi	51.0	28.0	25.0	52.0	118. Lebanon	32.0	11.0	35.0	39.0
87. Madagascar	57.0	20.0	26.0	51.5	119. Sierra Leone	37.0	20.0	20.5	39.0
88. Togo	41.0	26.0	35.0	51.0	120. Guinea-Bissau	46.0	19.0	21.0	38.5
89. Guyana	51.0	29.0	20.5	50.5	121. Zaire	30.0	18.0	20.0	34.0
90. Burkina Faso	41.0	23.0	36.0	50.0	122. Haiti	28.0	12.0	26.5	33.5
91. Kenya	48.0	26.0	26.0	50.0	123. Ethiopia	22.0	16.0	25.0	31.5
92. Zimbabwe	51.0	25.0	23.5	50.0	124. Uganda	36.0	21.0	5.0	31.0
93. Romania	55.0	29.0	15.0	49.5	125. Burma	27.0	9.0	22.5	28.5
94. Turkey	52.0	19.0	27.5	49.5	126. Iraq	19.0	4.0	25.5	24.5
95. Niger	45.0	24.0	29.0	49.0	127. Sudan	15.0	10.0	22.5	24.0
96. Guinea	48.0	21.0	28.0	48.5	128. Somalia	22.0	12.0	5.0	19.5
97. Guatemala	41.0	24.0	30.5	48.0	129. Liberia	10.0	8.0	12.0	15.0
98. Jordan	45.0	20.0	30.5	48.0					

countries. This topic will be discussed in Chapter 17.

The problem in capitalist countries is to abide by the many laws and regulations that affect business. In addition, several governments of capitalist countries own companies that operate both domestically and internationally, sometimes in competition with privately owned companies. As in the case of Great Britain, countries sometimes denationalize or privatize government-owned companies by selling them to private investors who are, in some instances, the company's employees.

Nationalism is an emotional force with political effects. If foreign companies wish to operate in a country, they must deal with nationalism, and there are quite a few ways to do so.

Some governments are unable, to a greater or lesser degree, to protect business and its managers from terrorism or other forms of attack. Countermeasures being taken against terrorism promise to reduce its frequency and success. Terrorism seems to be becoming less idealistic and more brutal as it turns to collaboration with the Mafia and other criminal groups.

Another new development in the terrorist tale is the increasing evidence that nations are training and financing terrorists and directing terrorist attacks in other countries. Evidence has implicated Syria, the former Soviet Union, Iran, and Libya. In international law, such state activities are acts of war.

Gradual changes of government policies toward business are expected by business and can be coped with. However, sudden changes of such government policies or sudden changes of government are unsettling or alarming to business. When confronted by such changes, it tends to go away or stay away.

Traditional hostilities between world groups cause problems for business. One of these groups may boycott a company if it deals with the other. The UN or other groups of nations may embargo trade with some country or other group.

International organizations such as the UN and the EC are becoming more politicized and are gaining more political powers. Their influence on international business is growing.

Labor is a major political force. Even where it does not control important political parties, it can dispose of large amounts of money and personnel to affect elections and influence governments.

ICs have political power. Some ICs have more resources than the nations with which they deal. In addition, ICs can use technology, distribution, management, capital sources, and other strengths in their negotiations with host countries.

Increasing world unrest, which stems from many causes, has made systematic country risk assessment necessary for banks and businesses operating internationally. They can seek help for such assessments from a number of internal and external sources. CRA must now be more global and should not be limited to one country alone; this is one of the lessons CRA analysts should have learned from the debt crisis.

QUESTIONS

1. *a.* What is ideology?
   b. Why is it important to international business?
2. *a.* What is the capitalist, free enterprise ideal?
   b. What is the actual situation in capitalist countries?
3. How and why do socialist LDCs and privately owned ICs cooperate to their mutual profit?
4. What are some reasons why "capitalist" governments nationalize private businesses?
5. *a.* What is nationalism?
   b. What are some effects it can have on foreign business?
6. What impact can terrorism have on business?
7. Why does business fear sudden changes in government policies?
8. How can traditional hostilities affect business?
9. Give some examples of international organization activities that affect business.
10. Why do labor organizations have political power?
11. How can ICs use their strengths to influence government policies?
12. What is country risk assessment as practiced by ICs? Why is it a growing project?
13. Is country risk assessment an exact science? Explain.
14. *a.* In terms of exposure to political risk (for example, expropriation), which of the following businesses would you consider the most and least vulnerable?

banks	cosmetics manufacturers
mines	manufacturers of personal
oil fields	hygiene products
oil refineries	hotels
heavy-equipment	automobile
manufacturers	manufacturers

   b. Are the most vulnerable businesses high profile or low profile? What are some ways to change the profile of a company in a foreign country?
15. Discuss the lessons CRA analysts should have learned from the world debt crisis.

□ MINICASE 10–1

Company Privatization

You are the chief executive officer of a company that the government has just denationalized by selling the company's stock to the company's employees. In the past, any major decision about company policy required approval by a government agency, which was time consuming. Wages and salaries had been established by reference to civil service "equivalents," and incentive payments were unheard of. Maintenance of the plant and equipment was lax, breakdowns were frequent and expensive, and utility expenses were high.

You want the newly privatized company to be a success. Suggest some programs that you would institute to improve its chances of success.

SUPPLEMENTARY READINGS

Aitken, Thomas. "Assessing the Political Environment: An Emerging Function in International Companies." New York: Conference Board, 1980.

Ball, Donald A., and Wendell H. McCulloch, Jr. "Country Risk Analysis: Fad or Business Investment?" *Collegiate Forum,* Spring 1982, p. 12.

Burns, Jimmy. "Terrorism Moves In on Business." *Financial Times,* December 13, 1990, p. 31.

"Capitalism in Triumph, in Flux." *The Economist,* May 5, 1990, pp. 14–15.

"Creating the Invisible Hand." *The Economist,* May 11, 1991, pp. 63–65.

Crozier, Brian. "The Collapse of Communism." *National Review,* August 5, 1988, pp. 28–29.

Ford, Robert. "The Cost of Subsidizing Industry." *The OECD Observer,* October–November 1990, pp. 4–7.

"From Marx to the Market." *The Economist,* May 11, 1991, pp. 11–12.

Grunwald, Henry Anatole. "New Challenges to Capitalism." *Fortune,* May 7, 1990, pp. 138–44.

Haner, F. T., and J. S. Ewing. *Country Risk Assessment: Theory and Worldwide Practice.* New York: Praeger Special Studies, 1985.

Israel, Arturo. "The Changing Role of the State in Development." *Finance & Development,* June 1991, pp. 41–43.

Lodge, George. "Roles and Relationships of Business and Government." *Business in the Contemporary World,* Winter 1989, pp. 4–6.

Marchant, Garry. "For Sale." *International Herald Tribune,* May 28, 1991, p. 9.

Mazwai, Thami. "Now We Know What Doesn't Work." *Los Angeles Times,* December 20, 1989, p. B7.

Parry, Thomas G. *The Multinational Enterprise: International Investment and Host-Country Impacts.* Greenwich, Conn.: JAI Press, 1980.

Pattison, John C. "The Management of Regulatory Risk in Banking: An International Perspective." *Sistemi Finanziari,* December 1991, pp. 20–53.

Peel, Quentin. "Unlikely Slayer of the Great Communist Dragon." *Financial Times,* March 25, 1990, p. 7.

Pirie, Madsen. *Dismantling the State: The Theory and Practice of Privatization.* Dallas: National Center for Policy Analysis, 1985.

"Poles to Share in Massive Privatization of State Industry." *The Wall Street Journal,* June 28, 1991, p. A9.

Raddock, David M. *Assessing Corporate Political Risk: A Guide for International Businessmen.* Totowa, N.J.: Rownan and Littlefield, 1986.

Rogers, Jerry, ed. *Global Risk Assessments: Issues, Concepts, and Applications.* Riverside, Calif.: Global Risk Assessments, Book 1, 1983; Book 2, 1986; Book 3, 1988.

Rudolph, Barbara. "A Global Fire Sale." *Time,* April 22, 1991, pp. 58–60.

Sachs, J. D. "The Current Account and the Macroeconomic Adjustment in the 1970s." Washington, D.C.: Brookings Papers on Economic Activity, no. 1, 1981.

———. "External Debt and Macroeconomic Performance in Latin America and East Asia." Washington, D.C.: Brookings Papers on Economic Activity, no. 2, 1985.

Schrage, Michael. "Eastern Europeans Focus on a Capital Idea." *The Wall Street Journal,* March 28, 1991, p. D1.

Sorman, Guy. "Hayek's Testament." *International Management,* October 1988, pp. 53–55.

Streeten, Paul. *Development Perspectives.* New York: St. Martin's Press, 1981.

Thompson, Alice. "A Front Seat on the Front Line." *Financial Times,* May 26, 1990, p. VII.

Vernon, Raymond, ed. *The Promise of Privatization.* New York: Council on Foreign Relations, 1988.

"Why Half-Reformed Communism Isn't Working." *The Economist,* May 28, 1988, pp. 63–68.

Wilkins, Keith. "A Minimanual on Surviving Business Trips." *The Internal Auditor,* October 1986, pp. 23–27.

"Wounded Pride: Why Communism Fell." *The Economist,* May 25, 1991, pp. 98–99.

ENDNOTES

1. Ian Brownlie, *Principles of Public International Law* (Oxford, England: Oxford University Press, 1966), pp. 435–36.

2. "Why Planned Economies Fail," *The Economist,* June 25, 1988, p. 67.

3. Jack Lowenstein, "Ready to Join the Big League?" *Euromoney,* October 1990, 66–73.

4. Murray Seeger, "Italy Takes Prize for Its Corporate Octopus," *Los Angeles Times,* November 1, 1979, part 1, p. 12.

5. "Europe's Dirigiste Dinosaurs," *The Economist,* November 17, 1990, pp. 83–84.

6. William Dawkins, "How the Nightmare Faded," *Financial Times,* October 24, 1990, p. 11.

7. William Dawkins, "France's Restive State Sector Senses Freedom," *Financial Times,* April 11, 1991, p. 3.

8. Charles C. Tillinghast, Jr., "Competing against State-Owned Companies," paper presented at the Academy of International Business Annual Meeting, 1979.

9. "Loaded Down with Lolly," *The Economist,* November 18, 1989, p. 85.

10. Richard L. Holman, "EC Widens Business Control," *The Wall Street Journal,* July 25, 1991, p. A10.

11. "Thatcher's Sales," *Business Week,* December 10, 1990, p. 26.

12. Lindley H. Clark, Jr., "Privatizing: It May Be Best to Think Small," *The Wall Street Journal,* July 23, 1991, p. A14.

13. "Power Play," *The Economist,* August 3, 1991, pp. 65–66.

14. Mary Shirley, "The Experience with Privatization," *Finance & Development,* September 1988, p. 34–35.

15. Felix Kessler, "France's Erratic Policies on Investment by Foreigners Confuse Many U.S. Firms," *The Wall Street Journal,* April 7, 1980, p. 24.

16. "Italy's Ever-Growing Monster," *The Economist,* July 27, 1991, pp. 43–44.

17. Henrik Bering-Jensen, "The Dirty Secrets of State Terror," *Insight,* August 6, 1990, pp. 34–35; and Jonas Bernstein, "When in Need, Terrorist Groups Turned Eastward," *Insight,* January 21, 1991, pp. 18–21.

18. David G. Hubbard, "Lilliput Revisited: A Data-Based Critique of Corporate Captivity in Connection with Kidnapping and Terrorist Threat," in *The International Essays for Business Decision Makers,* vol. 4, ed. Mark B. Winchester (Dallas: Center for International Business, 1979), pp. 19–31.

19. Brian O'Reilly, "Business Copes with Terrorism," *Fortune,* January 6, 1986, pp. 47–55.

20. Peter Almond with Bill Whalen, "Insurance against Terrorists an Emerging Growth Industry," *Insight,* March 17, 1986, pp. 52–54.

21. Robin Wright, "U.S. Hoping to Turn Corner in Terrorism War," *Los Angeles Times,* August 18, 1991, pp. A1 and 10–11.

22. "Germany's Latest Victim," *The Wall Street Journal,* April 4, 1991, p. A14.

23. Holman Jenkins, Jr., "East's Stolen Loot Haunts Germany," *Insight,* September 2, 1991, pp. 20–21.

24. Everett G. Martin, "Playing It Cool in Bolivia," *The Wall Street Journal,* June 3, 1976, p. 14.

25. *The Wall Street Journal,* April 11, 1977, p. 12.

26. *The Economist,* May 24, 1987, p. 76; and Eric Morgenhaler, "Clamping Down," *The Wall Street Journal,* August 13, 1986, p. 1.

27. Jorge Crespo Velasco, "Swamping Bolivia in a Sea of Negatives," *The Wall Street Journal,* July 31, 1991, p. A13; "Bolivia the Forgotten," *The Economist,* August 17, 1991, p. 40; and John Barham, "Poverty Gnaws at Patience with Democracy," *Financial Times,* April 16, 1992, p. 5.

28. Shirley Hobbs Scheibla, "McNamara's Band Sour," *Barron's,* December 3, 1979, pp. 9, 26, and 27.

29. Barbara Linehan, "The European Community, Its Legislation and Where to Find It," *The California International Practitioner* 2, no. 2, 1990–91, pp. 22–28.

30. Lee L. Morgan, "Opportunities for Mutual Action by Government and Business Leaders in 1977," in *Contemporary Perspectives in International Business,* ed. Harold W. Berkman and Ivan R. Vernon (Skokie, Ill.: Rand McNally, 1979), p. 284.

31. William J. Barton, "International Government Relations: A Required Management Function for International Business," in *The International Essays for Business Decision Makers,* vol. 3, ed. Mark B. Winchester (New York: AMACOM, 1978), pp. 218–19.

32. For a good discussion of the powers that an MNE can use, see Stefan H. Robock and Kenneth Simmonds, *International Business and Multinational Enterprises* (Homewood, Ill.: Richard D. Irwin, 1989), chap. 15.

33. See Table 1–1.

34. "Come Back Multinationals," *The Economist,* November 26, 1988, p. 73.

35. For several good discussions of various aspects of CRA, see Jerry Rogers, ed., *Global Risk Assessments: Issues, Concepts, and Applications,* book 2 (Riverside, Calif.: Global Risk Assessments, 1986); also see the supplementary readings dealing with CRA.

36. Monua Janah, "Rating Risk in the Hot Countries," *The Wall Street Journal,* September 20, 1991, p. R4.

37. Ibid.

38. Josef Ackermann, "New Dimensions in Risk Management," *Crédit Suisse Bulletin,* IV 90, pp. 30–31.

Chapter 11

Legal Forces

After 35 years, I have finished a comprehensive study of European comparative law. In Germany, under the law, everything is prohibited, except that which is permitted. In France, under the law, everything is permitted, except that which is prohibited. In the Soviet Union, under the law, everything is prohibited, including that which is permitted. And in Italy, under the law, everything is permitted, especially that which is prohibited.

Newton Minow, former chairman of the U.S. Federal Communications Commission, in a speech to the Association of American Law Schools

The incidence of tax evasion in Italy is truly phenomenal, reflecting a culture which still regards the state as an occupying power and its defrauding as almost a social duty.

John Wyles, *Financial Times*

The U.S. corporate income tax is one of the more damaging things we do to ourselves. It is something we have blundered into as a result of years of pursuing the politically expedient, rather than what is known to be sound policy.

Bill Modahl, IRET Policy Bulletin

LEARNING OBJECTIVES

In this chapter, you will study:

1. The complexity—due to their many sources (e.g., national laws, treaties, international organizations, private international law)—of the legal forces that may confront you.

2. Taxes, which frequently have purposes other than the raising of revenue.

3. U.S. antitrust laws and their enforcement.

4. Industrial espionage, which in some countries is a crime punished by fines or imprisonment.

5. Contract devices, and institutions that assist in interpreting or arbitrating international contracts.

6. The need to examine the law of each country where you do business to ensure protection of your intellectual properties such as patents, trademarks, trade names, copyrights, and trade secrets.

7. Why tariffs, quotas, and other trade obstacles of each country into which you wish to import a product are important.

8. The possibility that your property in a foreign country may be seized by the government or that you may be forced to give up control of it.

9. The risk of monetary damages or imprisonment if your company manufactures/sells a faulty or dangerous product, or if an employee fails to observe host country law or falls afoul of corrupt officials.

10. The need to comply with wage and price controls and with currency exchange controls.

11. The numerous difficulties and burdens placed by U.S. laws and practices on American ICs, which no other industrialized country imposes on its ICs.

KEY WORDS AND CONCEPTS

- Nonrevenue tax purposes
- Foreign tax credit
- Tax treaties
- Antitrust laws
- Restrictive trade practice laws
- Extraterritorial applications of laws
- Domestication
- Product liability
- Price and wage controls
- Arbitration
- Industrial espionage
- National tax jurisdiction
- Territorial tax jurisdiction
- Questionable or dubious payments

BUSINESS INCIDENT

Kenny International Corporation is a stamp-distributing company owned by two New Yorkers, Finbar B. Kenny and his wife, Marianne. Kenny had the exclusive rights to distribute the stamps of the Cook Islands. Most of the stamps are sold to collectors, and such sales totaled $1.5 million in 1978. Domestic sales, for actual postage, were only about $20,000 in 1978. Kenny split the $1.5 million with the Cook Islands.

In March 1978, there was a general election in the Cook Islands. According to the U.S. Justice Department, in an effort to protect its valuable franchise, Kenny agreed to help reelect the then premier, Sir Albert Henry, and his political party. To that end, Kenny used $337,000 out of the Cook Island account to charter jet passenger planes. The planes flew some 450 Cook Islanders in from New Zealand, and their votes provided the margin of victory that secured Sir Albert's reelection. In July 1978, however, the Cook Islands High Court disallowed those votes as "tainted by bribery" and threw Sir Albert out of office.

Kenny pleaded guilty to breaking Cook Island law and repaid the $337,000. But American law? It was also broken, said the U.S. Justice Department, and the Kennys pleaded guilty in a U.S. federal district court in Washington. Their company was fined $50,000.

The U.S. law that was broken was the Foreign Corrupt Practices Act of 1977. The Kenny case was the first criminal action brought under it.

Source: *The Wall Street Journal,* August 3, 1979, p. 29. Reprinted with permission. © Dow Jones & Company, Inc., 1979. All rights reserved.

Any attempt to teach a course on "The Legal Forces That Affect International Business" would be overwhelmed or bogged down by the immensity and variety of those forces. International business is affected by many thousands of laws and regulations on hundreds of subjects that have been issued by states, nations, and international organizations.

Nevertheless, this text, which is an introduction to international business, would be incomplete if it did not inform students or businesspersons that many legal forces do affect international business and if it did not give them an idea of what some of the most important are. We shall examine first several national legal forces, with brief comments; we'll then discuss some international legal forces.

Although many U.S. laws and regulations affect the activities of international firms, there has been no successful effort to coordinate them. Some of them are at cross-purposes, and some diminish the competitiveness of American business as it attempts to compete with foreign companies. We shall close this chapter with a brief examination of some of these laws and regulations. The business incident about Kenny International's legal difficulties illustrates the application of one such law.

We shall now proceed to deal with specific legal forces. (They are not presented in any particular order.) Some of them, such as taxation, concern every business and businessperson, whereas others, such as antitrust, involve fewer firms.

SOME SPECIFIC NATIONAL LEGAL FORCES

□ Taxation

nonrevenue tax purposes include redistributing income, discouraging consumption of some product, such as tobacco or alcohol, or encouraging purchase of domestic rather than imported products

Purposes.   The primary purpose of certain taxes is not necessarily to raise revenue for the government. That fact may surprise the reader who has not had occasion to study taxation. Some of the many **nonrevenue tax purposes** are to redistribute income, to discourage consumption of such products as alcohol or tobacco, to encourage consumption of domestic rather than imported goods, to discourage investment abroad, to achieve equality of the tax amounts paid by taxpayers earning comparable amounts, and to grant reciprocity to resident foreigners under a tax treaty.

Even this short list of purposes (there are many more) suggests the economic and political pressures brought to bear on government officials who are responsible for tax legislation and collection. Powerful groups in every country push for tax policies that favor their interests. These groups and interests differ from country to country and frequently conflict, which accounts, in part, for the complexity of the tax practices that affect multinationals.

National differences of approach.   Among the many nations of the world, there are numerous differences in tax systems.

Tax levels.   For one thing, tax levels range from relatively high (up to 100 percent in some instances) in some West European countries to zero in tax havens.* Some countries have capital gains taxes,† and some do not. Those

---

*   A tax haven is a country in which income of defined types incurs no tax liability.
†   Capital gain is realized when as asset is sold for an amount greater than its cost.

☐ **TABLE 11–1**
Capital Gains Tax Rates in Industrial Countries

Country	Period to Qualify for Long-Term Treatment	Maximum Long-Term Rate	Maximum Short-Term Rate
United States	None	33%	33%
United Kingdom	None	40	40
Sweden	One year	18	45
Canada	None	19.33	19.33
France	None	16	16
Germany	Six months	Exempt	56
Belgium		Exempt	Exempt
Italy		Exempt	Exempt
Japan	None	5	5
Netherlands		Exempt	Exempt
Hong Kong		Exempt	Exempt
Singapore		Exempt	Exempt
South Korea		Exempt	Exempt
Republic of China		Exempt	Exempt

Source: *Financial Times*, October 2, 1989, p. 3.

that have them tax capital gains at different levels. Incidentally, the United States levies one of the highest long-term capital gains taxes. Capital gains tax rates of the world's major industrial nations are as shown in Table 11–1.

The comparisons given above are not exact since levels of exemption vary for small gains and treatment of gains differ because of inflation. For instance, the 40 percent U.K. rate is misleading because gains there are inflation-proofed, that is, not taxed if they are caused by inflation.

Tax types. There are different types of taxes. We have just introduced one, the capital gains tax. Although the United States levies a relatively high capital gains tax, it relies for most of its revenue on the income tax. As indicated by the name, this tax is levied on the income of individuals and businesses. A generality, subject to exceptions, is that the higher the income, the higher the income tax. In the 1970s and 1980s, much discontent developed among Americans over the impact of the income and other taxes. Possibly as a result of that, there has been growing support for a *value-added tax (VAT)* in the U.S. Congress and Treasury.

Suggestions are that the U.S. VAT be similar to the VATs in effect in all European Community countries, for which the VAT is a main source of revenue. A simplified example of how the VAT works on a loaf of bread can be seen in Table 11–2. We shall assume a VAT of 10 percent. The wheat farmer sells to the miller for 30 cents the part of the wheat that eventually becomes the loaf. So far, the farmer has added 30 cents of value by planting, growing, and harvesting the wheat. The farmer sets aside 3 cents (10 percent of 30 cents) to pay VAT. The miller makes loaves of bread out of the wheat and sells them to the wholesaler for 50 cents each. Thus, the miller has added 20 cents of value (50 cents − 30 cents) and must pay a VAT of 2 cents (10 percent of 20 cents). The wholesaler now advertises and distributes the loaves, selling them to retailers at 70 cents. The wholesaler has added 20 cents of value and owes 2 cents VAT. Finally, the retailer adds 40 cents by its display,

☐ TABLE 11-2
Value-Added Tax on a Loaf
of Bread

Stage of Production	Selling Price	Value Added	VAT at 10 Percent	Cumulative VAT
Farmer	30¢	30¢	3¢	3¢
Miller	50¢	20¢	2¢	5¢
Wholesaler	70¢	20¢	2¢	7¢
Retailer	$1.10	40¢	4¢	11¢

advertising, and sales efforts and owes 4 cents of VAT. The loaf of bread is sold for $1.10 retail and has borne a cumulative VAT of 11 cents, 10 percent of $1.10.

The VAT has proponents and opponents.[1] You can read the endnotes and other material for details, but in general they are as follows: The proponents say the VAT is relatively simple and can be raised or lowered easily to balance desired income with the burden. The opponents argue that it is a consumption-type tax that bears most heavily on the poor.

Another argument of VAT proponents in the United States is that the present situation, in which the major European countries rely heavily on the value-added tax, is unfair to the United States because of GATT* regulations. GATT permits the rebate of VAT when a product is exported from a country but does not permit the rebate of income taxes. The rebates permit lower-priced, more competitive goods, and VAT proponents want the United States to inaugurate the VAT and lower income taxes to take advantage of those GATT rules.

While the VAT may be introduced in the United States, another form of tax on ICs has been held unconstitutional: the unitary tax. Twelve states levied the tax, not on the money an IC earns directly from operations within the given state but on a percentage of the company's overall income, calculated on the percentage of its sales, property, and payroll within the state.[2]

By 1990, threats by foreign-based ICs had induced all but four of the states to repeal their unitary tax laws. In December of that year, a California appeals court held that state's unitary tax law unconstitutional.[3]

Complexity of tax laws and regulations.   From country to country, the complexity of tax systems differs. Many consider that of the United States to be the most complex; the Internal Revenue Code runs over 5,000 pages, and official interpretations add more than 10,000 to that number. In addition to the code and Treasury interpretations, there are many thousands of pages of judicial rulings.

Who obeys the law?   Compliance with tax laws and their enforcement vary widely. Some countries, such as Germany and the United States, are strict. Others, such as Italy and Spain, are relatively lax. The Italian practice allows the taxpayer to declare a very low taxable income amount to which the government counters with a very high amount. They then negotiate to a compromise figure.[4]

> One of the authors remembers the shock and horror that greeted his suggestion to Italian tax advisors that a new Italian subsidiary of an American IC declare its

* See Chapter 4 for discussion of the General Agreement on Tariffs and Trade.

true income to the Italian authorities. As the advisors forcefully pointed out, no one would believe us.

Other differences.   There are many other differences, too numerous even to list here, but a few are tax incentives to invest in certain areas, exemptions, costs, depreciation allowances, **foreign tax credits,** timing, and double corporate taxation—that is, taxation of the profits of a corporation and then of dividends paid to its stockholders.

Tax conventions (treaties).   Because of the innumerable differences among the nations' tax practices, many of them have signed **tax treaties** with each other. Typically, a tax treaty defines such terms as income, source, residency, and what constitutes taxable activities in each country. It also reduces taxation by each country of income going to residents who are nationals of the other and deals with taxation by each country of nationals of the other living or working in the country. All of these treaties contain provisions for the exchange of information between the tax authorities of the two countries.

Taxpayers' rights and obligations.   Rights and obligations also differ from country to country. Table 11–3 illustrates some of the differences among OECD countries' laws and practices.

▫ Antitrust and Restrictive Trade Practices Legislation

In the tax area, it is the taxpayers (we are dealing with international business taxpayers) against the tax collectors (the governments). In antitrust, it is business versus government and, occasionally, government versus government.

U.S. laws and attitudes are different.   The U.S. **antitrust laws** are stricter and more vigorously enforced than those of any other country. However, other countries, as well as the EC, are becoming more active in the antitrust field. In the EC, these laws are referred to as **restrictive trade practices laws.**

The West German antitrust laws are the toughest after those of the United States, and, during 1986, the German Federal Cartel Office was tightening its grip—literally, in some cases. Wolfgang Kartte, president of the Cartel Office, tells the story of a raid his investigators made on the office of a heating equipment supplier. One of the supplier's managers stuffed a memo in his mouth and tried to swallow it, but a quick-thinking investigator grabbed the man by the throat and forced him to spit out the memo. Half-chewed but still legible, it provided valuable evidence of illegal price-fixing.

In 1991, the European Court of Justice gave a major boost to EC efforts to inject competition into economic sectors still largely dominated by powerful state monopolies. The Court confirmed that the EC Commission can force EC member-governments to dismantle state monopolies that block progress toward an open, community-wide market by the end of 1992.[5]

Article 85 of the Treaty of Rome outlaws any agreement or action to rig markets or distort competition. Under the authority of that article, the Commission fined the Dutch chemicals group, Akzo, ECU 7.5 million in 1991.[6] Later in 1991, empowered by Article 86, which bans abuse of dominant positions, the Commission imposed a record ECU 75 million fine on Tetra Pak, a Swiss-based liquid packaging group, for eliminating competitors in the European market.[7]

foreign tax credit
U.S. citizens who reside and pay income taxes in another country can credit those taxes against U.S. income tax

tax treaties treaties between countries that bind the governments to share information about taxpayers and to cooperate in tax law enforcement

antitrust laws American laws to prevent price-fixing, market sharing, and business monopolies

restrictive trade practices laws the European phrase for what are called antitrust laws in the United States

☐ **TABLE 11-3   A Survey of Selected Legal Provisions in OECD Countries***

	Taxpayers' Charter	Ombudsman	Taxpayers' Identification Number†	Powers of Entry into Dwelling‡	Self-Assessment Systems	Use of Tax Amnesties
Australia	No	Yes	T	Yes	No	Yes
Austria	No	Yes	T	Yes	No	Yes
Belgium	No	No	T	5 A.M. to 9 P.M.	No	Yes
Canada	Yes	No	T	Yes	Yes	No
Denmark	No	Yes	G	Yes	No	No
Finland	No	Yes	T	If penal crime suspected	No	Yes
France	Yes	Yes	T	Yes	No	Yes
Germany	No	No	T	If fraud suspected	No	No
Greece	No	No	T	5 A.M. to 9 P.M.	No	Yes
Ireland	Yes	No	T	Yes	No	Yes
Italy	No	Yes	T	Yes	Yes	Yes
Japan	No	No	None	Yes	Yes	No
Netherlands	No	Yes	T	Yes	No	Yes
New Zealand	Yes	Yes	T	Yes	No	Yes
Norway	No	Yes	G	Yes	No	No
Portugal	No	Yes	T	Yes	No	Yes
Spain	No	Yes	T	Yes	Yes	Yes
Sweden	No	Yes	G	Yes	No	Yes
Switzerland	No	No	None (Fed)	Yes	No	Yes
Turkey	No	Yes	T	Yes	No	No
United Kingdom	Yes	Yes	T	Yes	No	No
United States	Yes	Yes	S	Yes	Yes	No

*Iceland and Luxembourg did not participate in the exercise.

†G = General number used for all transactions with government; S = social security number; T = tax file number.

‡A warrant is normally required and in many countries the taxpayer must be present.

Source: Reprinted from *The OECD Observer,* October–November 1990.

Also in 1991, the Commission for the first time used its authority under a 1990 law to veto a major business transaction. Using its expanded power, it blocked the acquisition of Boeing's de Haviland subsidiary by a French–Italian consortium, Avions de Transport Regional (ATR). The Commission said the acquisition would have given ATR an unfair advantage that would allow it to crowd out competition.

A number of important differences in antitrust laws, regulations, and practices exist between the United States, other nations, and the EC. One difference is the effort of the United States to apply its laws extraterritorially (outside the United States). We deal with that later in this chapter. Another difference is the per se concept of the U.S. law.

Under the U.S. laws, certain activities, such as price-fixing, are said to be illegal per se. This means that they are illegal even though no injury or damage results from them.

The Treaty of Rome articles dealing with restrictive trade practices do not contain the per se illegality concept of U.S. antitrust law. For example, a cartel that allows consumers a fair share of the benefits is legally acceptable in the EC. Also, the treaty is not violated by market dominance—only by misuse of that dominance to damage competitors or consumers.

The EC versus Hoffman-La Roche.   The EC Court of Justice upheld the Commission's decision that the giant Swiss drug company Hoffman-La Roche was guilty of abusing its dominant position. Hoffman was fined DM732,000.

There was at least one bizarre element in the Hoffman case. Stanley Adams, a British subject, was an employee at the company's head office in Basel, Switzerland. He took some confidential documents about Hoffman's pricing and marketing practices and made them available to the EC antitrust regulators, who were already investigating the company. The company and the Swiss government reacted furiously, and when Adams, who was in Italy when the loss of the documents was discovered, returned to Switzerland, he was arrested and convicted under Swiss laws against industrial espionage. He was sent to prison, and his wife committed suicide on being told that he would be there at least 20 years. Finally, the EC bailed him out of the Swiss prison and he left the country.

Although Adams had his freedom, his troubles were not over. He was unable to get credit or employment, and he lost a farm he tried to operate in Italy. He then moved to England and sued the EC Commission for £500,000 damages for revealing his identity to Hoffman and for not warning him of the dangers he faced if he returned to Switzerland. In 1985, Adams won his case in the European Court of Justice.[8]

The Swiss government versus the EC.   The Hoffman-La Roche case caused government-versus-government friction. The EC complained to the Swiss that Adams should not be prosecuted under Swiss law, because all he had done was cooperate with the EC Commission's efforts to enforce the law. The Swiss prosecuted and convicted him, notwithstanding the EC's complaints, because he had violated Swiss law in Switzerland.

The U.S. government versus other governments.   More common examples of government-versus-government conflict occur when the U.S. government attempts to enforce its antitrust laws outside the U.S. borders. This is referred to as **extraterritorial application of laws.** In 1979, a grand jury in Washington, D.C., indicted three foreign-owned ocean-shipping groups on charges of fixing prices without getting approval from the U.S. Federal Maritime Commission. The other governments, European and Japanese, protested bitterly, arguing (1) that shipping is international by definition, so the United States has no right to act unilaterally and (2) that the alleged offenses were both legal and ethical practices outside the United States.[9]

Sir Freddie Laker's airline, a low-price transatlantic service, ceased operations on February 5, 1982. Shortly thereafter, its liquidators commenced a private antitrust suit in an American court, alleging that some other airlines had conspired to put Laker out of business. They asked over $1 billion in damages, and two other British airlines were among the defendants.

The private suits irked the British government, but what disturbed it most was the U.S. Justice Department's move in spring 1983 to begin a criminal grand jury investigation of essentially the same allegations. It was another example of the U.S. government's efforts to apply its law extraterritorially.

extraterritorial application of law   when a country attempts to apply its laws to foreigners or nonresidents and to acts and activities that took place outside its borders

Other governments versus the U.S. government.   In 1977, the United States tried to force seven executives of the British company Rio Tinto-Zinc to testify in connection with an antitrust action in the United States. In that instance, Britain's highest court, the House of Lords, turned down the U.S. demands on the grounds that they infringed on British jurisdiction and sovereignty and that the United States was trying to investigate the activities of companies not subject to U.S. jurisdiction.[10]

A number of countries have passed statutes to prevent persons within their territories from cooperating with the United States and have established criminal sanctions for those who comply with U.S. law in violation of those statutes. Among these countries are Australia, Canada, Britain, the Netherlands, and Germany. Thus, persons or companies can find themselves in the position of being forced to break the law of either the United States or of a country with this type of statute.

In January 1991, Sir Leon Brittan, the EC Commission's vice president of competition policy, met with U.S. Attorney General Dick Thornburgh in Washington, D.C., to begin coordinating U.S. and European antitrust policy. Brittan's goal is some variety of formal agreement that will prevent Europe and the United States from colliding over mergers involving both.[11]

However, a change of U.S. policy in 1992 may cause collisions. The new policy is to enforce antitrust laws against foreign companies suspected of colluding to hurt U.S. exporters. Prior to the policy change, the Justice Department challenged anticompetitive activity by foreign companies only if direct harm to U.S. consumers resulted from the activity. Some 15 countries, including Canada, Japan, and some in Europe, urged the United States to be cautious in implementing the new policy.[12]

□ Tariffs, Quotas, and Other Trade Obstacles

Although we introduced these subjects in Chapter 3, they are legal forces. For that reason, we mention them again here.

Every country has laws on one or more of these subjects. The purposes of tariffs are to raise revenue for the government and to protect domestic producers. Tariffs are either ad valorem, which means they are a percentage of the value of the imports, or they are specific. The specific tariff is based on the weight or number of items imported. Quotas, which limit the number or amount of imports, are for protection.

There are many other forms of protection or obstacles to trade in national laws. Some are health or packaging requirements. Others deal with language, such as the mandatory use of French on labels and in advertising, manuals, warranties, and so forth for goods sold in France.

The following list is a sampling of U.S. export products, export destinations, and the trade barriers encountered at the destinations.

Product	Destination	Barrier
Carbon steel	EC	Imports limited to 8 percent of market
Pesticides	Canada	Residue standards bar some U.S. chemicals
Machine tools	Japan	Government subsidizes domestic industry
Machine tools	Argentina	Money from sales must remain in Argentina for months
Paperboard	Japan	Specifications require smoother board than is produced in the United States

□ **TABLE 11–4**
The Cost of Protectionism

Georgetown University Professor Gary Hufbauer researched the costs of special protection legislation in a 1986 book published by the Institute for International Economics. Some of his results are shown in the following table. Where an asterisk follows a date of enactment, it means that the current program replaced some previous form of protection. The price increase column represents Hufbauer's estimate of the percentage boost in U.S. prices caused by protection. The consumer cost is that increase applied to total U.S. consumption of the products protected. VRA is Voluntary Restraint Agreement.

Industry	Type of Restraint	Dates From	Price Increase	Annual Consumer Cost ($ millions)
Maritime	Restricted	1789	60.0%	$ 3,000
Book publishing	Quota	1891	12.0	500
Glassware	Tariff	1922	4.5	200
Rubber footwear	Tariff	1930	21.0	230
Ceramic articles	Tariff	1930	7.0	95
Ceramic tiles	Tariff	1930	17.3	116
Orange juice	Tariff	1930	35.0	525
Canned tuna	Tariff	1951	10.0	91
Textiles, apparel	Tariff, quota	1982*	22.0	27,000
Steel	VRA	1982*	12.0	6,800
Specialty steel	VRA	1986*	15.0	520
Automobiles	VRA	1981	4.4	5,800
Semiconductors	VRA	1986	15.0	3,000
Machine tools	VRA	1986	10.0	500
Softwood lumber	Tariff	1986	20.0	1,000
Sugar	Quota	1982*	30.0	930
Dairy products	Restricted	1953	40.0	5,500
Peanuts	Restricted	1953	28.0	170
Meat	Restricted	1965	7.0	1,800
Fish	Quota, restricted	1977	10.0	560

Source: *Barron's*, June 27, 1988, p. 70.

In other countries, U.S. exports may encounter weak patent or trademark protection, very high tariffs, zero quotas, quarantine periods, or a variety of other obstacles.

Of course, the United States imposes barriers against the import of a number of products. It sometimes uses tariffs, sometimes quotas, and often a more modern form of quota called by some "voluntary" restraints agreements (VRAs) and by others "voluntary" export restraints (VERs). "Voluntary" is in quotes because these barriers are imposed by the U.S. government on the exporting countries. The inevitable result is higher costs to American consumers as exporters send only the higher-priced, top of their lines and importers charge more for scarcer products.[13] Table 11–4 shows one researcher's estimate of the price increase percentage and annual additional cost to consumers.

One justification for protectionism is that it saves domestic jobs. One estimate of the cost to the American consumer to save one job in the U.S. car industry was $250,000.[14]

It should be understood that the United States is not the only country that imposes VRAs and VERs on its trading partners. Far from it; Japan, Canada, the EC countries, and many others require countries exporting to them to "voluntarily" limit the number or value of goods exported.

In 1982, the French came up with a novel protectionist device. Japanese videotape recorders were one of the French imports causing a large balance-of-payments deficit with Japan. The recorders normally entered France through the major port of Le Havre, which had a large detachment of customs officers to process imports. Then the French government issued a decree requiring all of the recorders to enter France through Poitiers, which had a tiny customs post. The result was long delays that reduced the number of recorders entering France. Japan then "voluntarily" agreed to limit the number of recorders it exported to France.

▫ Expropriation or Confiscation

Governments may pass laws under which they expropriate or confiscate foreign-owned property. OPEC members have seized foreign-owned assets within their borders, particularly natural resource assets.

▫ Domestication

domestication a host government takes—by law or persuasion—a share of ownership (usually less than 100 percent but more than 50 percent) of a foreign-owned company operating in the host country

Domestication is a less drastic takeover of foreign assets. Here the host government uses various forms of pressure to "persuade" foreign owners to sell some significant percentage, usually enough to enable the host government or local shareholders to gain control of the foreign-owned company.[15] A number of countries, including the Andean Pact nations, Brazil, India, Mexico, and Nigeria, have enacted laws or enforced policies to require or encourage foreign-owned companies to sell part ownership to the host government or to local shareholders. This is referred to as "Mexicanization" if it occurs in Mexico, "Brazilianization" if it occurs in Brazil, and so forth.

Although the Andean Pact nations, Brazil, and Mexico are involved to some extent in domestication, they and other nations in Latin America are busily negotiating and signing free trade agreements, as pointed out elsewhere in this book. Those agreements will encourage and protect both investments and trade, very much diminishing the likelihood of domestication in the Western Hemisphere.

▫ Product Liability, Civil and Criminal*

Manufacturers' liability for faulty or dangerous products was a boom growth area for the American legal profession in the 1960s and 70s. Liability insurance premiums have soared, and there are concerns that smaller, weaker manufacturing companies cannot survive.

product liability holding a company and its officers and directors liable and possibly subject to fines or imprisonment when their product causes death, injury, or damage

Now that boom has spread to Europe, where the EC Commission and the Council of Europe are pushing new **product liability** laws that would standardize and toughen existing ones.[16]

Another development in Europe is causing what the president of one U.S.-controlled company in France called a "fear psychosis." This development is criminal liability of management for workers' death or injuries. In France,

---

* Civil liability calls for payment of money damages. Criminal liability results in fines or imprisonment.

"Excuse me, sir... Want to sue a multinational?"

© 1987, Cartoonists & Writers Syndicate.

managers have been found guilty of involuntary homicide* and criminal responsibility after accidents caused workers' deaths.

In Britain, a 1976 Health and Safety Act gave inspectors the right to haul accused managers into courts that have the power to impose prison terms.

Pressures that could result in stiffer product safety standards are coming from numerous directions. One of them is the UN Economic and Social Council; another is the International Organization of Consumers Unions.[17]

The European Parliament and many other groups have expressed concern that too sweeping government involvement in product safety and too heavy liability burdens on industry will stifle product innovation and hit small producers, which would be less able to either afford higher insurance premiums or pass on higher self-insurance costs. The British government has also expressed that view.

The British dissented from a July 1985 EC Council of Ministers directive to the effect that plaintiffs could seek redress for damages without having to prove negligence on the part of the manufacturers. The British position is that manufacturers should not be liable for product defects that—given the state of scientific and technological knowledge—could not have been detected when the product was made. This is called a "state-of-the-art" or "development risks" defense. In 1988, a new German law agreed with the British position that companies should have the development risks defense, but the same law extended

---

* This means causing the death of some person or persons, and it is a crime even though it was "involuntary"—that is, unintentional.

THE WALL STREET JOURNAL

"He's in jail. May I take a message?"

Reprinted from *The Wall Street Journal;* permission of Cartoon Features Syndicate.

companies' responsibility by permitting them to be liable for damages from faulty products without plaintiffs having to prove negligence.[18]

Nevertheless, the costs of liability insurance have risen and the availability of liability insurance has shrunk in all European countries. Product liability laws varied among EC countries in 1987, but an EC directive required all countries to introduce new legislation by July 1988. One important difference between European and American law in this field is that punitive damages,* which have played a large part in high U.S. awards, are not permitted in EC countries. Another difference is that European lawyers cannot take cases on a contingency fee basis;† American lawyers commonly do so.[19]

In a survey of more than 500 chief executives by the Conference Board, more than one fifth believe strict American product liability laws have caused their companies to lose business to foreign competitors.[20] But, as foreign firms buy or build U.S. plants, they are being hit by the same liability and insurance problems long faced by American companies.[21]

◻ Price and Wage Controls

Although some countries call their price and wage control laws "voluntary," the governments can pressure companies or labor unions that raise prices or demand wage increases above established percentages. The U.S. government, for example, has withheld government business from companies that violate its guidelines. This has resulted in union lawsuits challenging the legality of such punishment by the government because wage increases exceeded "voluntary" guidelines.

Communist countries, of course, just set prices and wages. There are no significant free markets and no effective labor unions that are not government agencies. Most noncommunist countries also have some price and wage control laws. As inflation spreads and grows in the world, **price and wage controls** can be expected to become more widespread and more restrictive.

price and wage controls
prohibitions or limits on upward movements of prices or wages that are imposed by governments to combat inflation when the government has been unable or unwilling to slow or halt it by fiscal or monetary measures

* Punitive damages are in addition to the actual damages proven and are awarded to punish the manufacturer of a faulty product.
† Contingency fees are lawyers' fees paid only if the plaintiff's case is won or is settled by agreement of the defendant to make a payment.

◻ Labor Laws

Virtually every country has laws governing working conditions and wages for its labor force. Even though hourly wages may be low in a country, the employers must beware, because fringe benefits can greatly increase labor costs. Fringe benefits can include profit sharing, health or dental benefits, retirement funds, and more. Some labor laws make the firing of a worker almost impossible or at least very expensive. This subject is considered more extensively in Chapter 12.

◻ Currency Exchange Controls

Almost every country has currency exchange controls—laws dealing with the purchase and sale of foreign currencies. Most countries, including the LDCs and the communist countries, have too little hard foreign currency.* There is the rare case, such as Switzerland, that sometimes feels it has too much.

Exchange control generalities. The law of each country must be examined, but some generalizations can be made. In those countries where hard foreign currency is scarce, a government agency allocates it. Typically, an importer of productive capital equipment gets priority over an importer of luxury goods.

People entering such a country must declare how much currency of any kind they are bringing in. On departure, they must declare how much they are taking out. One side of the intent is to discourage bringing in the national currency that the traveler may have brought abroad at a better exchange rate than the traveler can get inside the country. The other side is to encourage the bringing in of hard foreign currency.

Switzerland—a special case. Switzerland is a special case because its government has imposed controls to keep foreign currencies out rather than in. Switzerland enjoyed relatively low inflation during the 1970s and into the 1990s, and its Swiss franc has remained one of the hardest of the hard currencies. As a result, people from all over the world have wanted to get their money into Switzerland, and the Swiss have felt the need to defend against being inundated by too much currency, which would escalate their inflation. They have used several devices to discourage the inflow of foreign money. Among these devices are low interest rates and even a negative interest rate on some kinds of deposits. Limitations have been placed on the sale to foreigners of bonds denominated in Swiss francs.

◻ Miscellaneous Laws

Individuals working abroad must be alert to avoid falling afoul of local laws and of corrupt police, army, or government officials. Some examples may serve to make the point.

A Plessey employee, a British subject, is serving a life sentence in Libya for "jeopardizing the revolution by giving information to a foreign company." In the summer of 1986, two Australians were executed in Malaysia for possession of 15 grams or more of hard drugs. Saudi Arabia and other Muslim countries strictly enforce sanctions against importing or drinking alcohol or wearing revealing clothing. Foreigners in Japan who walk out of their homes

---

* A hard currency is readily exchangeable for any other currency in the world.

without their alien registration cards can be arrested, as was one man caught without his card while he was carrying out the garbage. In Thailand, you can be jailed for mutilating paper money or for damaging coins that bear the picture or image of the royal prince, as was one foreigner who stopped a rolling coin with his foot. Neither *Playboy* nor *Penthouse* can be brought into Singapore.

Travelers and vacationers can also run afoul of unexpected laws in different countries. In the People's Republic of China, unmarried couples—foreigners included—face a possible 10 days in jail if they stay overnight in the same room. In Greece, travelers who exceed their credit card limits may be sentenced to prison for as long as 12 years.

A Philadelphia law firm, International Legal Defense Counsel (ILDC), has made a reputation dealing with countries where American embassies and consulates are of little legal help and where prison conditions are so squalid that survival is the first concern. One of their cases involved a Virginia photographer named Conan Owen. He was duped into transporting a package of cocaine from Columbia to Spain, where he was arrested and slapped with a stiff prison sentence.

The U.S. attorney general personally interceded on Owen's behalf with no success, and Owen languished in prison for nearly two years. Then ILDC sprang him by use of a bilateral prisoner transfer treaty that permits American inmates in foreign jails to do their time in a facility back home. Once in the United States, Owen was quickly freed.

Among ILDC publications that give travelers legal advice are *The Hassle of Your Life: A Handbook for Families of Americans Jailed Abroad* and *Know the Law: A Handbook for Hispanics Imprisoned in the United States.*[22]

INTERNATIONAL FORCES

▢ Business Contracts

When contracting parties are residents of a single country, the laws of that country govern contract performance and any disputes that arise between the parties. That country's courts have jurisdiction over the parties, and the court's judgments are enforced in accordance with the country's procedures. When residents of two or more countries contract, those relatively easy solutions to disputes are not available.

United Nations solutions.   When contract disputes arise between parties from two or more countries, which country's law is applicable? Many countries, including the United States, have ratified the UN Convention on Contracts for the International Sale of Goods (CISG) to solve such problems.

The CISG established uniform legal rules to govern the formation of international sales contracts and the rights and obligations of the buyer and seller. The CISG applies automatically to all contracts for the sale of goods between traders from different countries that have ratified the CISG. This automatic application will take place unless the parties to the contract expressly exclude—opt out of—the CISG.[23]

European Community solutions.   The law applicable to contracts between EC residents is determined by the Rome Convention, which came into effect in 1991. It established two principles. First, if the parties agree at the outset which country's law should apply, then that choice will be upheld. Second, if no such choice is made, the law of the country most closely connected with the contract will apply. A set of rules has been established to make this work in practice.[24]

Private solutions, arbitration.   Many parties either cannot or do not wish to accept UN or EC solutions. Instead of going to court in any country, they opt for **arbitration.** At least 30 organizations now administer international arbitrations, the best known of which is the International Court of Arbitration of the International Chamber of Commerce in Paris. More than 350 disputes were filed with that body during 1990, and the number is expected to increase 15 to 20 percent annually over the next several years.[25] People and businesses may prefer arbitration for several reasons. They may be suspicious of foreign courts, but regardless of that, arbitration is always faster than law courts, where cases are usually backlogged and procedures are formal. Arbitration procedures are informal. They can also be confidential, avoiding the perhaps unwelcome publicity accompanying an open court case.

Although London, New York, and Paris are traditional arbitration centers, Hong Kong is growing as one. This follows from the explosive growth of business and trade in the Pacific Rim countries and a 1991 cooperation agreement between the Hong Kong International Arbitration Center and its counterpart in the People's Republic of China.[26]

Enforcement of foreign arbitration awards.   Enforcement can pose problems. One solution is the UN Convention on the Recognition and Enforcement of Foreign Arbitral Awards. The United States and most UN member-countries of industrial importance have ratified this convention. It binds ratifying countries to compel arbitration when the parties have so agreed in their contract and to enforce resulting awards.

In instances where the contract in dispute involves investment in a country from abroad, another arbitration tribunal is available. This is the International Center for Settlement of Investment Disputes, sponsored by the World Bank. Investors were encouraged in 1986 when Indonesia proved willing to abide by a decision of the center even though an adverse opinion could have cost the country several million dollars.

Other organizations are working toward a worldwide business law. The Incoterms of the International Chamber of Commerce and its Uniform Rules and Practice on Documentary Credits now enjoy almost universal acceptance. The UN Commission on International Trade Law and the International Institute for the Unification of Private Law are doing much useful work. The Hague-Vishy Rules on Bills of Lading sponsored by the International Law Association have been adopted by a number of countries.[27]

Despite legal uncertainties, trade grows.   It is to the credit of international business that, with the exception of the recession years between 1980 and 1983, world trade has grown each year. That is evidence that despite legal uncertainties, most international contracts are performed fairly satisfactorily.

---

arbitration parties to disputes agree not to sue each other in a court but rather to appoint—or have appointed by a neutral person—an arbitrator to hear both sides and make a decision by which both parties agree to be bound

World trade volume grew 3 percent in 1991, a slower pace than the previous year's 5 percent but faster than the 1 percent growth in the overall global economy.[28]

Of the big industrial countries, the United States posted the fastest export growth between 1985 and the first quarter of 1991, surging by 91 percent, thanks mainly to the 40 percent fall in the US$'s trade weighted exchange rate over that period. French exports grew the second fastest at 31 percent. On the other side, Germany's import growth was fastest at 65 percent, with Japan second at 63 percent.[29]

▫ Patents, Trademarks, Trade Names, Copyrights, and Trade Secrets

A patent is a government grant to the inventor of a product or process of the exclusive right of manufacturing, exploiting, using, and selling the invention or process. Trademarks and trade names are designs and names, often officially registered, by which merchants or manufacturers designate and differentiate their products. Copyrights are exclusive legal rights of authors, composers, playwrights, artists, and publishers to publish and dispose of their works. Trade secrets are any information that a business wishes to hold confidential.

Trade secrets can be of great value, but each country deals with and protects them in its own fashion. The duration of protection differs, as do the products that may or may not be protected. Some countries permit the production process to be protected but not the product. Therefore, international business must study and comply with the laws of each country where it might want to manufacture, create, or sell a product.

Patents.   In the field of patents, some degree of standardization is provided by the International Convention for the Protection of Industrial Property, sometimes referred to as the Paris Union. Some 90 countries, including the major industrial nations, have adhered to this convention.

Most Latin American nations and the United States are members of the Inter-American Convention. The protection it provides is similar to that afforded by the Paris Union.

A major step toward the harmonization of patent treatment is the European Patent Organization (EPO). Members are the EC countries plus Austria, Sweden, and Switzerland. Through EPO, an applicant for a patent need file only one application in English, French, or German to be granted patent protection in all member-countries. Prior to EPO, an applicant had to file in each country in the language of that country. This is still necessary in every country that is not a member of EPO.

Early hopes that the EPO would facilitate patent granting and protection were disappointed for two reasons: (1) the patent courts of individual nations retain the right to defy EPO guidelines; (2) the acceleration of technology has flooded national courts and the EPO in a sea of new patent applications. They doubled from 600,000 in 1965 to 1.2 million in 1986. In some cases, the EPO needs up to seven years to process a patent application, time enough for today's leading-edge gadget to become yesterday's obsolete box.[30]

At the UN, representatives of the developing nations have been mounting attacks on the exclusivity and length of patent protection. They want to

Want to buy a phoney "Rolex"? Only $5.

© Billy L. Mason/U.S. Customs Service

shorten the protection periods from the current 15 to 20 years down to 5 years or even 30 months. The companies in the industrialized countries, which are responsible for the new technology eligible for patents, are resisting the changes. They point out that the only incentives they have to spend the huge amounts required to develop the technology are periods of patent protection long enough to recoup their costs and make profits.

Trademarks.   Trademark protection varies from country to country, as does its duration, which may last from 10 to 20 years. Such protection is covered by the Madrid Agreement of 1891 for most of the world, though there is also the General American Convention for Trademark and Commercial Protection for the Western Hemisphere. In addition, protection may be provided on a bilateral basis in friendship, commerce, and navigation treaties.

An important step in harmonizing the rules on trademarks was taken in 1988 when regulations for a European Community trademark were drafted. A single European Trademark Office will be responsible for the recognition and protection of proprietary marks in all EC countries—including trademarks belonging to companies based in non-EC member-countries.

Trade names.   Trade names are protected in all countries adhering to the Industrial Property Convention, which was mentioned above in connection with patents. Goods bearing illegal trademarks or trade names or false statements on their origin are subject to seizure at importation into these countries.

Copyrights.   Copyrights get protection under the Berne Convention of 1886, which is adhered to by 55 countries, and the Universal Copyright Convention of 1954, which has been adopted by some 50 countries. The United States did not ratify the Berne Convention until 1988, by which time it was driven to do so by the need for greater protection against pirating of computer software.

Trade secrets.   Trade secrets are protected by laws in most nations. Employers everywhere use employee secrecy agreements, which in some countries are rigorously enforced.*

industrial espionage the effort of one company to steal another company's trade secrets by, for example, attempting to bribe an employee, eavesdropping electronically on internal communications, or hacking into the target company's computer data

Industrial espionage.   Industrial espionage among companies that develop and use high technology is not unusual, but 1983 saw the end of an extraordinary example of corporate warfare between two of the world's mightiest and most technologically advanced corporations. Hitachi tried to obtain trade secrets of IBM, and in June 1982, two Hitachi employees were arrested by the FBI. IBM and the FBI had cooperated in what *Fortune* called a "superbly executed sting." In February 1983, Hitachi and two of its employees pleaded guilty to an indictment of conspiring to transport stolen IBM property from the United States to Japan.

Costly intellectual property rip-offs.   Patents, trademarks, trade names, copyrights, and trade secrets are collectively referred to as intellectual property, and the U.S. International Trade Commission says unauthorized use abroad of American-owned intellectual property costs the United States more than $61 billion a year. That is the amount of lost exports, domestic sales, and royalties. But total extended losses are actually much higher since the $61 billion does not reflect related losses such as increased unemployment that stems from intellectual property piracy.[31]

U.S. industry and the government are trying to combat this. Among other means, several companies have gathered evidence of pirating in countries that have laws against such activities but whose police are unwilling or unable to actively enforce them. On being presented with evidence of illegal practices, they have no excuse not to do their duty.

The government is using bilateral aid and trade pressures to push other countries—including Japan, Taiwan, South Korea, Thailand, and Indonesia—to pass and enforce intellectual property protection laws.

The U.S. government is also trying to have GATT's Uruguay Round deal effectively with intellectual property piracy. It is having some success, but strong opposition is being led by Brazil and India.[32]

INTERNATIONAL STANDARDIZING FORCES

Several international standardizing forces have already been discussed. In the tax area, there are tax conventions (treaties) among nations. Each country tries to make each such treaty as nearly as possible like the others, so that patterns and common provisions may be found among them.

In antitrust, the EC member-countries operate under Articles 85 and 86 of the Treaty of Rome. In an unusual bilateral move, West Germany and the United States signed an executive agreement on antitrust cooperation. This was the first attempt by national governments to cooperate on antitrust matters concerning firms operating in both countries.

---

* Remember the unfortunate Mr. Adams, who was imprisoned by the Swiss for giving Hoffman-La Roche secrets to the EC, and the even more unfortunate Mrs. Adams, who committed suicide after being told that her husband would be in prison 20 years.

In the field of commercial contract arbitration, we mentioned the UN Convention. If the disputed contract involves investment from one country into another, it can be submitted for arbitration by the International Center for Settlement of Investment Disputes at the World Bank, and, in 1988, the UN Convention on the International Sale of Goods came into effect.

Several international patent and other agreements were pointed out. Chapter 4 covered a number of UN-related organizations and other worldwide associations. Each of them has some harmonizing or standardizing effect. The same can be said of the regional international groupings and organizations dealt with in Chapter 4.

Two standardizing organizations that American industry will ignore at its peril are the International Organization for Standardization (IOS) and the International Electrotechnical Commission (IEC). The IEC promotes standardization of measurement, materials, and equipment in almost every sphere of electrotechnology. The IOS recommends standards in other fields of technology. Most government and private procurement around the world demands products that meet IEC or IOS specifications, and therein lies the danger for American companies. All IEC and IOS measurements are in the metric system, which has not been adopted in the United States, thereby imposing an additional burden on American firms trying to export American-made products.

U.S. LAWS THAT AFFECT THE INTERNATIONAL BUSINESS OF U.S. FIRMS

Although every law relating to business arguably has some effect on international activities, some laws warrant special notice. We will look briefly at U.S. antitrust and taxation laws, the Foreign Corrupt Practices Act, and the antiboycott act.

◻ Antitrust

Earlier in this chapter, we mentioned the hostility aroused among foreign governments by the aggressive enforcement abroad of U.S. antitrust laws.

The laws impede U.S. exports.   The U.S. antitrust rules preventing American companies from teaming up to bid on major products abroad impede U.S. exports. For example, General Electric and Westinghouse had to compete against each other for pieces of the $450 million Brazilian Itaipu Dam generator and turbine contracts. The contracts went to a huge European group led by Siemens of Germany and Brown Boveri of Switzerland. The European governments actively supported their companies. The U.S. government, however, would not let GE and Westinghouse cooperate and did nothing to support their efforts.[33]

Such restrictions on cooperation abroad were cited as the worst obstacle to exports caused by the U.S. antitrust regulations and enforcement procedures in a study by the National Association of Manufacturers (NAM). About 70 percent of the over 100 companies that responded to the NAM questionnaire said U.S. antitrust laws and practices caused a decline in their international competitiveness.

Export trading companies (ETCs).   In October 1982, the Export Trading Company Act of 1982 was signed into law by President Reagan. The centerpiece of the ETC Act is its limitation of the applicability of antitrust law to foreign trade. There are many ambiguities in the act, but it does make some important changes in antitrust law.

Companies wishing to establish ETCs apply to the U.S. government for a certificate of antitrust immunity. The certificate safeguards the ETC from government prosecution—assuming the ETC performs as indicated in the certificate of application—but does not immunize the ETC against private party antitrust suits. However, any damages awarded in such suits are limited to actual damages rather than the treble damages awarded in other such private actions.*

The ETC Act also permits American banks to own shares of ETCs. Some of the larger banks are moving aggressively into the ETC field, offering financing and even countertrade† services to ETC shareholders. Smaller banks are feeling competitive pressures to get involved in ETCs for fear that larger banks will take their export company customers.[34]

Despite passage of the ETC Act, there is strong feeling both in and out of government that the antitrust laws constitute severe burdens on the ability of American companies to compete at home or abroad with foreign competitors. The late Malcolm Baldrige, secretary of commerce in the Reagan administration, made several points. The U.S. antitrust laws were largely written in the early 1900s, and they followed the economic theory of that time: "Big is bad; small is good." That theory was proper when other countries could not compete with America, and U.S. companies did not need to export to grow. But now, more than 80 years later, U.S. goods face severe competition, and the range and variety of that competition are increasing. The world economy has changed, trade patterns have changed, but the antitrust laws have not.

Baldrige and others would like Congress to repeal Section 7 of the Clayton Act, which prohibits mergers and acquisitions that *may* reduce competition or *tend* to create a monopoly. Baldrige made this comment on the italicized words: "No one can live in an environment where the antitrust enforcers try to read your mind and then can arrest you for their idea of what you might be thinking."[35]

□ Taxation

As we have remarked, the U.S. tax system is considered by many to be the world's most complicated. That in itself makes doing business more complicated and, therefore, more expensive for a U.S. company than for companies based elsewhere. There is, however, one tax incentive for exports worthy of mention.

Export incentive.   In 1971, the U.S. Congress amended the Internal Revenue Code (IRC) to permit the Domestic International Sales Corporation (DISC) as an encouragement for American companies to export. This gave a tax break to companies that manufactured in the United States with American labor and exported the product.

---

* The possibility of treble damages against British Airways is one of the worries of the U.K. government because of the private antitrust action being brought against BA and other airlines by the Laker Airways liquidator.

† *Countertrade* is a generic term for the many methods of trading when the customer does not have enough hard currency to buy what it wants from other countries. This subject is discussed in Chapter 17.

It worked. The U.S. Treasury estimated that in the fiscal year ended June 30, 1976, DISC operations boosted U.S. exports to an amount some $2.9 billion higher than they would have been without DISCs.[36] In spite of that and in the face of continuing and growing U.S. BOP deficits, the Carter administration recommended abolishing the DISC. U.S. labor unions favor its abolition on the basis that it favors big business, even though exports mean jobs. Congress did not abolish the DISC, but it did cut back the tax benefit originally provided.

The Tax Reform Act of 1984 largely replaced the DISC with the new Foreign Sales Corporation (FSC). From the point of view of exporters, a major advantage of the FSC over the DISC is that the tax exemption is permanent—there is no recapture of the benefit in future years if dividends are paid or if the FSC no longer satisfies qualification requirements. Another break given exporters by the 1984 law is permanent forgiveness of taxes deferred under DISC provisions.

national tax jurisdiction
a tax system for expatriate citizens of a country whereby the country taxes them on the basis of nationality, even though they live and work abroad

territorial tax jurisdiction
expatriate citizens who neither live nor work in the country—and therefore receive none of the services for which taxes pay—are exempt from the country's taxes

Taxing Americans who work abroad. Observing a so-called **national tax jurisdiction,** rather than a **territorial tax jurisdiction,** the United States is almost alone among countries in taxing its people according to nationality rather than on the basis of where they live and work. As a result, Americans living or working in another country must pay taxes there and to the United States. In addition to higher tax payments, this requires the time and expense of completing two sets of complicated tax returns. In 1981, the sections of the IRC dealing with this subject were again amended. Although the burden of completing two tax returns was not lifted, the new law gave relief, starting in 1982, in the amount of American taxes to be paid by exempting the first $85,000 of earned income.* In 1986, this exemption was lowered to $70,000.

When American taxes are anti-American. Suppose an American multinational wants to open a new factory, store, warehouse, or office building in the United States. That would create new jobs for Americans, along with all the benefits that flow from new jobs.

But when the company's executives look at the new U.S. tax law, they hesitate because of the section dealing with allocation of interest expense. When an American company with subsidiaries in many countries borrows money to finance a U.S. business, the interest is treated as if it were paid in part to finance foreign operations. That results in a partial loss of the tax deduction and, thus, higher after-tax interest cost.

Foreign companies—including foreign-based multinationals—have no such requirement and can deduct 100 percent of interest on borrowings to finance a U.S. operation. Therefore, they have lower after-tax interest costs and, to that extent, can be more competitive in the United States than many U.S. companies.[37]

There is much more to be said about how America's tax system burdens the competitiveness of U.S. business throughout the world. We lack space in this book for a comprehensive discussion but refer you to the endnotes and supplementary readings for more on the subject.

---

* Earned income includes salaries, bonuses, and commissions. Interest, dividend, and royalty income is called unearned income.

☐ Foreign Corrupt Practices Act (FCPA)

questionable or dubious payments bribes paid to government officials by companies seeking purchase contracts from those governments

During the 1970s, revelations of **questionable or dubious payments** by American companies to foreign officials rocked governments in the Netherlands and Japan. Congress considered corporate bribery "bad business" and "unnecessary," and President Carter found it "ethically repugnant." As a result, the Foreign Corrupt Practices Act (FCPA) was passed and signed.

Uncertainties. There were a number of uncertainties about terms used in the FCPA. An interesting one involves *grease*. According to the FCPA's drafters, the act does not outlaw grease, or facilitating payments made solely to expedite nondiscretionary official actions. Such actions as customs clearance or telephone calls have been cited. There is no clear distinction between supposedly legal grease payments and illegal bribes. To confuse matters further, U.S. Justice Department officials have suggested that they may prosecute some grease payments anyway under earlier antibribery laws that were written to get at corruption in the United States.[38]

Other doubts raised by the FCPA concerned the accounting standards it requires for compliance. That matter is connected to questions about how far management must go to learn whether any employees, subsidiaries, or agents may have violated the act; even if management were unaware of an illegal payment, it could be in violation if it "had reason to know" that some portion of a payment abroad might be used as a bribe.[39]

Other countries' reactions to bribes.* Attitudes of business and government officials in Europe toward the FCPA range from amusement to incredulity, and no other government has taken a position similar to that represented by the FCPA—quite the opposite.[40] German tax collectors, for example, permit resident companies to deduct foreign bribes, which are called *sounderpesen,* or special expenses. In Britain, corrupt payments, even to British government officials, qualify for tax deductions. Even the government-owned British Leyland (BL) was found to have been paying bribes overseas to obtain orders for its Range Rovers.

> One comical aspect of the BL story was that its factories were unable to produce enough Rover vehicles to meet the very large demand for them in the export market. The bribes for new orders were being paid at a time when BL already had more orders than it could fill.

Another interesting, and possibly embarrassing, facet of the BL story is that it was published in British newspapers only two weeks after the British prime minister had promised to eliminate "irregular practices and improper conduct" in international business. The promise was made to President Carter, who wanted other countries to cooperate with the United States in stopping such practices and conduct.

Just how pervasive these practices are was disclosed by Lloyd N. Cutler, a Washington attorney who did a study of the subject for the Northrop Corpo-

---

* Other words with similar connotations are *dash, squeeze, mordida, cumshaw,* and *baksheesh.* Bribes and questionable payments were mentioned in connection with sociocultural forces in Chapter 9.

ration. Cutler was quoted as saying, "Almost all European and Japanese export sales of the type that generate corrupt payments are arranged with government export financing or other government support."[41] So far, no other industrialized nation has a law resembling the FCPA, and an anticommercial bribery treaty proposed by the United States is languishing in an inactive committee of the United Nations.

In 1985, Dancare Corporation, a Danish company, got in trouble because of $730,000 in bribes it had paid to get a contract in Saudi Arabia. The trouble was not that it had paid the bribes, but that the bribes were not clearly indicated as such in the company's tax records. The Danish tax chief now advises Danish firms to book illicit payments openly under "bribes." Whether the bribes are in the form of cash, sexual favors, or luxury goods doesn't matter, as long as their value is noted on the tax records. Receipts are desirable but not essential.[42]

Bribes paid in Denmark are illegal; bribes paid abroad to secure export business are both legal and tax-deductible expenses. In the contest for the Saudi Arabian business, the Dancare Corporation bid was more than $730,000 above potential American competitors. Of course, they would have been in violation of the FCPA if they paid a bribe to get the contract and certainly would have been unable to deduct the payment from American taxes.

Is America losing?   Is the FCPA causing American exporters to lose business? Yes, answer a number of companies, several of which are in the construction business. The United States, which in 1976 ranked first in the overseas construction market, dropped to fifth in 1987, falling behind Japan, Korea, West Germany, and Italy.

A White House task force on export disincentives studied the FCPA, among other disincentives. Its estimate of exports lost to American business as a result of the FCPA is $1 billion per year.[43]

The view that the FCPA is causing American companies to lose export business is not unanimous. In 1976, the Securities and Exchange Commission (SEC) forecast that cessation of the payment of foreign bribes would not seriously affect the ability of American business to compete in world markets.[44]

The consensus now is that America's unilateral approach to payoffs is very costly in terms of export business lost to foreign competitors. They can pay to get it.

Billions lost overseas.   There are estimates of losses in the billions of dollars. Critics have cited the ambiguities in the FCPA as one of the possible causes of U.S. business foregoing legitimate overseas opportunities. It cannot operate comfortably in an environment in which management is unsure of the FCPA's interpretation and application.

In response to the negative feedback about the FCPA's effect, the General Accounting Office completed a survey in 1981. It randomly selected 250 companies from *Fortune*'s list of the 1,000 largest industrial firms. About one third of the respondents stated they had lost overseas business as a result of the FCPA. Over 60 percent were of the opinion that, all other things being equal, U.S. multinationals could not profitably compete against foreign companies that could legally bribe to make sales.[45]

□ Antiboycott Law

As a part of the hostility and wars between the Arab countries and Israel, several of the Arab countries boycott foreign companies that do business with Israel. They will not buy from such companies. Inasmuch as several Arab countries are extremely rich oil producers, they are very large potential markets from which sellers do not like to be excluded. In 1977, however, the United States passed an act forbidding American companies to comply with any Arab boycott law or regulation.

Contrast American and British attitudes.   As in the case of the FCPA, few other countries have any such antiboycott law. A British House of Lords select committee studying similar legislation for Britain found 2.7 billion reasons to bury it in 1978. During 1977, British exports to Arab markets totaled £2.7 billion.[46]

Other attitudes.   In the aftermath of the Iraq-Kuwait war, some other countries seemed to come around to the U.S. view. Belgium, Canada, France, Germany, Luxembourg, and the Netherlands now forbid their companies to comply with the boycott.

Action under the antiboycott law.   Some complained that the antiboycott law was laxly enforced in the early years of its existence; fines ran around $500 to $600 for each violation. Then, in 1982, the Department of Commerce, which enforces the law, became more aggressive; more companies were charged with boycott-related offenses, and the fines imposed were in larger amounts.[47] The largest so far is a $995,000 fine levied against Safeway Stores. As the Department of Commerce continued to tighten enforcement, it collected $1.4 million in fines in 1984, up from $520,000 the previous year; in 1988 it levied fines of $3.9 million.[48]

The regulations that implement the antiboycott legislation forbid response to any Arab question or questionnaire that deals with Israel. As a condition of bidding on a contract with an Arab country, your company may be asked whether any components to be supplied under the proposed contract will be sourced in Israel. Even though your company has no Israeli suppliers and no intentions of using any, it would be in violation of the antiboycott law and regulations to so inform the Arab country.

Are export contracts being lost?   Is the antiboycott law causing American exporters to lose business? Yes, according to Chase Manhattan Bank, especially in the relatively hard-line Arab countries, such as Iraq, Libya, and Syria. Even in other Arab countries friendlier to the United States, the law causes difficulties and burdens not faced or borne by most non-American competitors.[49] Commenting on the law and the government's tough enforcement of it, Philip Hinson, Middle East affairs director of the U.S. Chamber of Commerce, says, "They've had a randomly harmful effect on U.S. exports."

Another complaint by American companies about the law is the cost of compliance. Joseph Komalick, editor of the *Boycott Law Bulletin,* says that some U.S. multinationals have as many as 20 lawyers check the legality of Middle East contracts to make sure they don't violate the law.[50]

One argument against the boycott legislation is that it hurts American business but does no harm to the Arab countries. They can buy whatever they want—or adequate substitutes—from Europe or Japan.[51]

Post Iraq–Kuwait war relaxation?   Arab actions are mixed. Kuwait, which had been one of the boycott's most zealous enforcers, redefined its boycott's targets to include only companies with significant investment in Israel; selling to Israel will no longer be enough to put a company on the blacklist.[52]

Pepsi-Cola, for years the cola of choice in the Arab world, is now on sale at Pepsico-owned Pizza Huts in Israel. Toyota, Nissan, and Mazda are in both markets. In 1991, the Arab League removed Coca-Cola and three other U.S. companies from its blacklist.

However, even as the League was removing four companies from the list, it was adding 110 new names. True, 104 of the 110 had the same owner, British publishing baron Robert Maxwell, but the other 6 are major Western companies, including a large British chemicals company, Courtaulds.[53]

The most Western and Israeli officials can hope for in the near future is the type of relaxation announced by Kuwait. The bans on direct trade between Israel and Arab states are likely to remain in place.[54]

◻ 1988 Trade Law

Frustrated by years of presidential unwillingness to identify countries that maintain "unfair" trade policies, Congress passed new trade legislation that it thought would force the administration to take a hard line against U.S. trade partners. Harold B. Malmgren, a former Democratic trade official, calls the law a "Frankenstein monster" that will only tie U.S. trade policy in knots, divert attention from GATT and other international trade talks, and make policymaking more difficult.

Bush administration officials fear that the only exports created by the 1988 law will be red tape. It requires voluminous reports to Congress from the administration on short deadlines, plus time-consuming testimony to congressional committees by administration officials—notably by Carla A. Hills, the U.S. trade representative. One trade official said, "These days we're spending more time negotiating with Congress than with other countries."[55]

◻ Some Laws and Agencies Aid U.S. Exports and Investment

We do not mean to give the impression that all U.S. laws and government agencies pose obstacles to the international business of U.S. companies. The U.S. Department of Commerce actively encourages exports by American companies. U.S. embassies and consular offices can be helpful with information and introductions for Americans who wish to export to or invest in foreign countries. The FSC provides some tax incentives for U.S. exporters.

COMMON LAW OR CIVIL LAW?

Historically, there has been a clear distinction between common law, which developed in England and spread to the English colonies, and civil law, which originated on the continent of Europe. Courts made common law as they decided individual cases; civil law was made by kings, princes, or legislatures issuing decrees or passing bills.

As time has passed, legislatures and government agencies in the United States have made more and more laws and regulations. The courts, in turn, have interpreted these laws and regulations as parties have argued about what they mean.

WORLDVIEW
European Parliament, U.S. Congress Compared

Photri

Chad Ehlers/International Stock Photography Ltd.

European Parliament

Legislative roles. Advisory, and may amend commission proposals before their consideration by the council. Approves budget.

Relation to executive. Reacts to specific commission proposals, but provides public forum for EC issues. Can remove entire commission but not replace it. Can force some changes in budget. Questions commissioners in plenary.

Election, chambers, sessions. Elected for five-year term by direct vote, but under national electoral laws. Single chamber meets one week in plenary, two weeks in committee, and one week in political groups each month.

Jurisdictions. Community laws, regulations, and budget (in part), which cover areas defined by the Treaty of Rome creating the EC. Defense excluded.

U.S. Congress

Legislative roles. Exclusive authority to introduce legislation. Two houses consider, amend, and move draft laws to the other for final vote: bills passed proceed to president for action.

Relation to executive. Legislative coresponsibility. Consents to treaties and appointments (Senate). Has own investigative and budget arms to check on executive. Committees both authorize and allot funds and oversee expenditure. Questions executive officials in committee.

Election, chambers, sessions. Two chambers: House elected for two years by equal population districts; Senate elected for six years by states; generally equal roles in legislation. House and Senate together set a calendar of sessions, which average 180–200 days a year.

Jurisdictions. Entire federal structure, which under the Constitution extends to almost every aspect of country except local and state taxing, police, and education functions.

European Parliament

Staffs. Entrance exam into civil service for secretarial; free hire for political groups. Very small personal staff.

Committee structure. *Substantive* (12): Political Affairs; Agriculture; Economics & Monetary; Energy, Research & Technology; External Economic Relations; Social Affairs & Unemployment; Regional Policy & Planning; Transport; Environment, Public Health, & Consumer Protection; Youth, Culture, Education, Information, & Sport; Development & Cooperation. *Budgetary:* Budget; Budgetary Control. *Institutional:* Rules of Procedure & Petitions; Verification of Credentials; Institutional Affairs.

Leadership. President and 12 vice presidents represent national and party balance in plenary vote; they form Bureau for general direction of Parliament. Seven political group chairmen are added to form Enlarged Bureau, which handles most important matters involving political management. Five *questors* serve as ombudsmen for many administrative matters. *Rapporteurs*, selected by committee members, draft and defend reports. Committee chairmen function as leaders and coordinators of their committees.

Role of parties. Committee assignments, chairmenships, and interparliamentary delegations determined by relative size of each of seven political groups. Discipline varies depending on ideological breadth of groups, but generally is much greater than in U.S. Congress. Group chairmen elected for one half of five-year term of Parliament but may be reelected. Parties tried to run Community-wide electoral campaigns in first direct election in 1979, with varying success. Most members elected on party-list system, which requires them to keep active role in national parties.

U.S. Congress

Staffs. Generally meritocratic entrance to committee staff. Political appointment for some housekeeping jobs. Large personal staffs.

Committee structure. *Substantive* (17) (House used as example, but Senate is similar): Agriculture; Armed Services; Banking, Finance, & Urban Affairs; Education & Labor; Energy & Commerce; Foreign Affairs; Intelligence; Interior & Insular Affairs; Judiciary; Merchant Marine & Fisheries; Post Office & Civil Service; Public Works & Transportation; Science & Technology; Small Business; Veterans; Ways & Means. *Budgetary:* Appropriations; Budget. *Institutional:* Administration; Rules; Standards of Conduct. *Investigative:* Government Operations.

Leadership. *House:* Speaker elected by majority party and speaks for it, but his function, partly, is to represent House in broad nonpartisan way; majority and minority parties each name leader and whip. These five form leadership for the management of 435-member House. *Senate:* Vice president is constitutionally presiding officer, but this is largely a ceremonial function; majority and minority leaders, and their whips, manage 100-member Senate on collegial basis. *Both:* Committee chairmen and (in last decade) subcommittee chairmen play major role in writing legislation and managing it on floor.

Role of parties. Only two major parties. Decisions taken by each house on organization generally follow party votes. Substantive issues bring more diversity, although speaker and president can have effects in organizing party positions. National parties weak and have little effect on Congress, which runs own campaign committees, by party, in each house. No effective means of disciplining errant members. Committee assignments and chairmanships depend on party caucus votes. Seniority plays presumptive role in these votes.

That is the sort of procedure one finds in Europe, but vast differences in practices have developed that have less to do with the traditional common–civil law approaches than with historical government–citizen (or subject) relationships and attitudes.

◻ European Practice

Europe has a history of thousands of years of tyranny, which recently has been covered with a veneer of democracy. People have greater reason to fear their governments in Europe than in the United States, and government service has more prestige. Before a new law is presented to the legislature (which, unlike legislatures in the United States, is always controlled by the same political party that controls the executive branch), consensus is achieved among most of the people, businesses, and government agencies that will be affected.

In contrast to American practices, European legislation is rarely amended, and regulations are rarely revised. Courts are not as often asked to give their interpretations, and if they are, the decisions are rarely appealed. Once a consensus has been reached, it is considered very bad form to open the subject again, and those who do may find themselves left out of the consultations the next time around.

◻ American Practice

In contrast to European custom, Americans have a weaker tradition of obeying their governments and have had very little fear of them. Americans are much more likely than Europeans to challenge laws in the courts, in the streets, or by disobedience. Legislation in America is a product of an ongoing adversarial proceeding, not of consensus; law is written by one independent branch of government for implementation by a second and for interpretation by yet a third. Different political parties or people with conflicting philosophies frequently control the three different branches of government.

Laws and regulations are constantly being amended or revised by the legislatures and the agencies. Courts interpret laws in ways that are sometimes surprising, and courts may strike laws down as being unconstitutional.

In the United States, the legislative body is now called Congress, and it convened as representatives of the several English colonies even before the United States become a country. In Europe, the legislative body of the European Community is called the European Parliament. It was brought into being by the Treaty of Rome, which was signed in 1957. The Worldview contains an interesting comparison of those two legislatures. Bear in mind that the European Parliament is gradually gaining power and can be expected to be a growing force in the EC.

SUMMARY

We have seen that taxes can have many purposes, and raising revenue for the government is only one of them. Other purposes are the encouragement of activities deemed desirable by the government and the discouragement of others. Taxes are used to redistribute income, to protect certain industries, and to accomplish many other goals.

Taxes differ greatly from country to country. Some countries have high taxes, others low or no taxes. Most countries have some sort of income tax, but many rely more on the value-added tax (VAT). Enforcement of tax laws is strict in the United States and some other countries but relatively lax elsewhere.

The United States has the most comprehensive antitrust laws, and it tries to apply and enforce them extraterritorially. Other countries resent what they perceive as intrusion into their sovereignty as the United States attempts to bring their citizens and companies under U.S. law for acts performed outside the United States. Other countries and the European Community have antitrust-type laws, which are frequently called restrictive trade practices laws, but none of them is as vigorously enforced as are the U.S. antitrust laws.

Nations try to protect or favor their own businesses by putting obstacles in the way of imports. The obstacles can be tariffs, quotas, packaging requirements, health requirements, or any of hundreds of other requirements that foreign goods must satisfy before they are permitted into the country.

Nations sometimes seize foreign-owned property. If they don't take 100 percent of the property, they may "domesticate" it by taking enough—for example, 51 percent ownership—to control it.

Executives of companies in Europe are discovering that their companies—and even they personally—can be liable to workers or to the public if one of their products causes injury or death. The liability can be civil or criminal.

Price and wage control laws are found in most countries. As inflation continues, these laws can be expected to be expanded.

Labor laws exist everywhere and must be studied. They can greatly increase labor costs above the hourly wage paid to employees.

Although money (currency) flows relatively freely among the industrialized countries, they are the minority. Almost all LDCs and communist countries have currency control laws, and some of them enforce these laws very harshly.

Contracts between parties in different countries can cause problems that are not present when the parties to contracts are citizens of only one country, in situations where one of the parties fails to perform satisfactorily. However, many solutions have been found, such as agreements in the contracts as to applicable law or language or as to arbitrating differences before a named body, such as the International Chamber of Commerce.

Intellectual property, such as patents, is protected by a number of multinational conventions (treaties) and by bilateral treaties. The protection of trade secrets took a step forward in 1980, when the United States got the first criminal conviction under an industrial espionage law. Other countries enforce similar laws.

There is a growing complaint by American business that U.S. laws and their enforcement by the government are lessening the competitiveness of U.S. companies as compared to foreign companies. Cited are the antitrust and tax laws, the Foreign Corrupt Practices Act, and the antiboycott law.

QUESTIONS

1. What are some purposes of taxes other than to raise revenues?

2. Why do some people feel that a VAT should replace some or all of the U.S. income tax?

3. What is a national tax system?

4. What objections have other countries to extraterritorial application by the United States of its antitrust laws?

5. When an American traveling abroad falls afoul of the criminal laws of a foreign country, are the U.S. embassy or the U.S. consulates likely to be of much help? Where else can the traveler look for aid?

6. What are some advantages that arbitrating contract disputes may have as compared to using the courts?

7. Are tariffs the only type of obstacle to international trade? If not, name some others.

8. Can product liability be criminal? If so, in what sorts of situations?

9. Why do most countries impose currency exchange controls?

10. How might the ETC Act limit U.S. antitrust activity abroad?

11. *a.* Does the Foreign Corrupt Practices Act forbid all bribes? Explain.

    b. Does the antiboycott law permit U.S. exporters to Arab countries to certify that the products are not of Israeli origin if that is true?

    c. Are attitudes and practices of Arab countries and the Arab League concerning the Israeli boycott changing? If so, to what extent?

12. *a.* Comparing the United States with Western Europe, what are the differences in practices as to making, amending, and interpreting laws?

    b. What are the reasons for those differences?

◻ MINICASE 11–1

American Law

Your company manufactures specialty motors in the United States. Business in the United States has been slack, and you have embarked on an export drive using facilities of the Department of Commerce as well as a private export sales agency.

You know that Saudi Arabia is an excellent potential market for your motors as it rapidly expands factories, ports, hospitals, and many other facilities. Therefore, you are delighted when your sales agency phones you one day to inform you that your motors are perfect for a new Saudi refinery for which procurement is beginning. The agent has the Saudi invitation to bid for the contract and is sending it by express to you today.

The invitation is received the next day. The agent was

right. Your motors precisely match the specifications, you know the competition, and you feel confident that you can win this big, market-entry order.

Accompanying the invitation is a questionnaire for new bidders for Saudi business. The questions are about your company—how long in business, the identity of its customers and suppliers, its financial strength, and the identity of its officers, directors, and major shareholders. The company is well established and has many satisfied customers and dependable suppliers, all in the United States. There is no single, dominant stockholder, and all of the directors and officers are experienced, reputable Americans.

Should the above facts alert you to any possible American law problems?

◻ MINICASE 11–2

Italian Law

A California-based company is expanding very well and has just made its first export sale. All of its sales and procurement contracts up to now have contained a clause providing that if any disputes should arise under the contract, they would be settled under California law and that any litigation would be in California courts.

The new foreign customer, which is Italian, objects to these all-California solutions. It says it is buying and pay-

ing for your products, so Italian law and courts should govern and handle any disputes.

You are the CEO of the California company, and you very much want this order. You are pleased with the service your law firm has given, but you know it has no international experience. What sorts of solutions would you suggest that your lawyers research as possible compromises between your usual all-Californian clause and the customer's wish to go all-Italian?

SUPPLEMENTARY READINGS

Aaron, Henry J., ed. *The Value-Added Tax: Lessons from Europe*. Washington, D.C.: Brookings Institution, 1981.

"Annual National Trade Estimate Report." Washington, D.C.: *U.S. Trade Representative's Office*.

Bailey, Jeff. "Birth of a Haven." *The Wall Street Journal*, September 22, 1989, p. R32.

Burton, Thomas M. "Baxter Fails to Quell Questions on Its Role in the Israeli Boycott." *The Wall Street Journal*, April 25, 1991, pp. A1 and 10.

Campbell, Dennis, ed. *Legal Aspects of Doing Business in Asia and the Pacific*. Cambridge, Mass.: Kluwer Law and Taxation Publishers.

Cowell, Frank A. *Cheating the Government: The Economics of Evasion*. Cambridge, Mass.: MIT Press, 1990.

Crosswick, Stanley A. "U.S. Protectionism as Seen from Europe." *Europe*, January–February 1986, pp. 8–10.

Dahlberg, Jacquelin L. "U.S. Taxation of Foreign Investment." *Beyond EC 1992: Implications for the Pacific Rim*, April 4, 1991.

de Jantscher, Milka Casanegra. "Tax Havens Explained." In *Contemporary Perspectives in International Business*, ed. Harold W. Berkman and Ivan R. Vernon. Skokie, Ill.: Rand McNally, 1979, pp. 83–92.

Ernst & Young, ed. *Tax News International*. London: Quarterly.

————. *Tax Reform around the World*. London: 1988.

"Foreign Patent Protection for Exporters." *Business American*, August 27, 1979, pp. 3–14.

Greanias, George C. *The FCPA: Anatomy of a Statute.* Lexington, Mass.: Lexington Books, 1982.

Kochan, Nick. "Cleaning Up by Cleaning Up." *Euromoney,* April 1991, pp. 73–77.

KPMG "World Tax News," a quarterly newsletter.

Lauterpacht, E. *Aspects of the Administration of International Justice.* Cambridge, England: Grotius Publications, Ltd.

Lewis, P. "Taxing Americans Abroad: New U.S. Tax Law May Affect Business in Europe." In *Contemporary Perspectives in International Business,* ed. Harold W. Berkman and Ivan R. Vernon. Skokie, Ill.: Rand McNally, 1979, pp. 77–82.

Meijboom, Alfred P., and Corien Prinz. *The Law of Information Technology in Europe.* Cambridge, Mass.: Kluwer Law and Taxation Publishers.

Minor, Michael. "Changes in Developing Country Regimes for Foreign Direct Investment." *South Carolina Essays in International Business,* no. 8, September 1990.

Modahl, Bill. "Competitiveness and the U.S. Taxation of Corporate Income." *IRET Policy Bulletin,* June 28, 1991.

Owens, Jeffrey. "Taxpayers' Rights and Obligations." *The OECD Observer,* October–November 1990, pp. 17–20.

Pletka, Danielle. "Boycott Squeezes U.S. Firms, Israel." *Insight,* September 19, 1988, p. 44.

"Report on United States Trade Barriers and Unfair Practices 1991." *Commission of the European Communities.*

Robock, Stefan H., and Kenneth Simmonds. *International Business and Multinational Enterprises.* Homewood, Ill.: Richard D. Irwin, 1989, chaps. 8 and 12.

Schmitthoff, Clive M., and Chia-Jui Cheng, ed. *Select Essays on International Trade Law.* London: Martinus, Nijhoff, Graham & Trotman, 1988.

Schuyler, Michael. "The IRS's Unlegislated Tax on Foreign-Source Income." *IRET Byline,* June 2, 1991.

The International Lawyer. American Bar Association, Section of International Law, quarterly.

ENDNOTES

1. Dan Throop Smith, "Value-Added Tax: The Case For," *Harvard Business Review,* November–December 1970, pp. 77–85; and Stanley S. Surrey, "Value-Added Tax: The Case Against," *Harvard Business Review,* November–December 1970, pp. 86–94.

2. Kenneth Jost, "Tough Questions in a Taxing Case," *California Law Journal,* October 1989, pp. 28 and 34.

3. Jane Applegate, "Foreign Companies Hail Court Ruling on Unitary Tax," *Los Angeles Times,* December 5, 1990, pp. D1 and 13; and "U.S. Court Limits Multinationals' Ability to Defy State Taxes," *Bangkok Post,* January 12, 1990, p. 21.

4. Chris Endean, "Italians Urged to Shop Tax-Dodging Friends," *The European,* June 2, 1991, p. 4.

5. Richard L. Holman, "EC Antitrust Efforts Boosted," *The Wall Street Journal,* March 20, 1991, p. A17; and "EC Court Reinforces Commission's Antitrust Clout," *Eurecom,* April 1991, p. 1.

6. Andrew Hill, "Predatory Pricing Judgment Confirmed," *Financial Times,* July 5, 1991, p. 2.

7. Andrew Hill, "Tetra Pak: Swiss Precision in Seeing Off Its Competitors," *Financial Times,* July 21, 1991, p. 2; and Martin Du Bois and Brian Coleman, "EC Blocks Sale of a Boeing Unit to French–Italian Joint Venture," *The Wall Street Journal,* October 3, 1991, p. A14.

8. Raymond Hughes, law courts correspondent, "Partial Victory for Adams in Commission Case," *Financial Times of London,* July 12, 1985, p. 2.

9. *The Economist,* June 9, 1979, pp. 91–92.

10. *The Economist,* December 10, 1977, pp. 77–78.

11. Joel Haveman, "EC Getting Close to a Joint Antitrust Policy," *Los Angeles Times,* February 12, 1991, p. H3.

12. Joe Davidson, "U.S. Decides to Enforce Antitrust Laws against Collusion by Foreign Concerns," *The Wall Street Journal,* April 6, 1992, p. C10.

13. Thomas G. Donlan, "Not So Free Trade: U.S. Preaches What It Doesn't Always Practice," *Barron's,* June 27, 1988, pp. 70–71.

14. "The American Car Industry's Own Goal," *The Economist,* February 6, 1988, p. 69. For a good discussion of protectionism, see Robert Z. Lawrence and Robert E. Litan, "Why Protectionism Doesn't Pay," *Harvard Business Review,* May–June 1987, pp. 60–67.

15. "Brazil: Even Components Must Be Brazilianized," *Business Week,* January 24, 1977, p. 34.

16. *The Economist,* July 30, 1977, pp. 64–65.

17. *Business International,* April 22, 1983, pp. 123–24.

18. "New Law Extends Company Responsibility," *Business Europe,* May 2, 1988, p. 7.

19. Michael Skapinker, "Why the Product Liability Plague Is No Longer Just a U.S. Malady," *International Management,* July 1986, pp. 27–34.

20. Carolyn Lochhead, "Strict Liability Causing Firms to Give up on Promising Ideas," *The Washington Times,* August 22, 1988, p. B5.

21. Steven P. Galante, "American Insurance Crisis Begins to Hurt European Firms with Operations Here," *The Wall Street Journal,* December 29, 1985, p. 12; and Patrick Cockburn, "The Tricky Waters of U.S. Liability Insurance," *Financial Times,* March 29, 1990, p. 21.

22. Tom Dunkel, "Saving Hapless Americans Abroad," *Insight,* March 26, 1990, pp. 47–49.

23. Mark A. Goldstein, "The UN Sales Convention," *Business America,* November 21, 1988, pp. 12–13.

24. Lucy Kellaway, "EC Legal Convention on Contracts Approved," *Financial Times,* January 30, 1991, p. 7.

25. "Firms Specify Arbitration for International Fights," *The Wall Street Journal,* July 29, 1991, p. B1.

26. Michael Moser, "A Good Place to Make Peace," *Euromoney,* July 1991, special supplement, pp. 50–54.

27. A. H. Herman, "Growth in International Trade Law," *Financial Times,* March 30, 1989, p. 10.

28. "World Trade Growth Sputters," *The Wall Street Journal,* March 18, 1992, p. A10.

29. "Trade," *The Economist,* August 31, 1991, p. 84.

30. Richard Evans, "The Mouse that Got Away," *International Management,* June 1990, pp. 46–49.

31. Alan W. Lepp, "Intellectual Property Rights Regimes in Southeast Asia," *Journal of Southeast Asia Business,* Fall 1990, pp. 28–40.

32. Eduardo Lachica, "Trade Thievery," *The Wall Street Journal,* March 16, 1989, pp. AL and 10.

33. *Business Week,* April 10, 1978, p. 60.

34. "Trading Company Act—I: A Look at What It Does in Antitrust Area," *Business International,* November 12, 1982, pp. 361–63; "Trading Company Act—II: Opening for Bankers Is Wide but Complex," *Business International,* November 26, 1982, pp. 379 and 382; "Trading Company Act—III: Allowable Scope of Action Poses Real Dilemmas for ETCs," *Business International,* December 17, 1982, pp. 401–3; "Trading Company Act—IV: Conflicting Interests and Goals Key Concerns of Banks, MNCs," *Business International,* December 31, 1982, pp. 409–11. For a look at perceived flaws in the ETC Act, see "Export Trading Companies: Current Legislation, Regulation, and Commercial Bank Involvement," *Columbia Journal of World Business,* Winter 1981, pp. 42–47; and "Drawback Seen in Liberal Export Trading Company Regs from FRB," *Peat, Marwick Executive Newsletter,* June 16, 1983, p. 4.

35. Malcolm Baldrige, "Rx for Export Woes: Antitrust Relief," *The Wall Street Journal,* October 15, 1985, p. 32. See also, Thomas M. Jorde and David J. Teece, "To Keep U.S. in the Chips, Modify the Antitrust Laws," *Los Angeles Times,* July 24, 1989, part II, p. 5.

36. *The Wall Street Journal,* April 14, 1978, p. 14.

37. "When We Wear the Black Hats," *The Wall Street Journal,* March 22, 1990, p. A16.

38. John S. Estey and David W. Marston, "Pitfalls (and Loopholes) in the Foreign Bribery Law," *Fortune,* October 9, 1978, pp. 182–88.

39. Barbara Crutchfield George, "The U.S. Foreign Corrupt Practices Act: The Price Business Is Paying for the Unilateral Criminalization of Bribery," *International Journal of Management,* September 1987, pp. 391–402; and "Some Guidelines on Dealing with Graft," *Business International,* February 25, 1983, p. 62.

40. Wendell H. McCulloch, Jr., interviews conducted in Europe during July and August 1979.

41. Jerry Landauer, "Proposed Treaty against Business Bribes Gets Poor Reception Overseas, U.S. Finds," *The Wall Street Journal,* March 28, 1977, p. 26.

42. *The Wall Street Journal,* October 31, 1985, p. 32.

43. *International Herald Tribune,* August 3, 1979, p. 11.

44. Report of the Securities and Exchange Commission on Questionable and Illegal Corporate Payments and Practices, May 1976.

45. George, "The U.S. Foreign Corrupt Practices Act," p. 400.

46. *The Economist,* September 2, 1978, p. 101.

47. Laurie McGinley, "Boycott Law Enforcement Is Toughened," *The Wall Street Journal,* December 9, 1982, p. 33.

48. Victor Mallet, "Dodging the Arab Blacklist," *Financial Times,* July 27, 1989, p. 15.

49. *The Wall Street Journal,* April 3, 1978, p. 6.

50. Eduardo Lochia, "U.S. Law Successfully Blocks Arab Bid to Keep American, Israeli Firms Apart," *The Wall Street Journal,* July 14, 1984, p. 28.

51. David Ignatius, "Catch 22: Trading with Iraq," *The Wall Street Journal,* March 25, 1982, p. 22.

52. "A Boycott Backs Off," *The Wall Street Journal,* May 31, 1991, p. A10.

53. "Things Go Better for Coca-Cola in the Arab World," *Financial Times,* May 7, 1991, p. 3.

54. Kim Murphy, "Cracks in a 45-Year Boycott," *Los Angeles Times,* May 22, 1991, pp. A1 and 14–15.

55. Art Pino, "New Trade Law Has the Makings of a Monster," *Los Angeles Times,* March 26, 1989, pp. 1 and 1G.

Chapter 12
Labor Forces

Moves of unions to join a board of directors offer little to American unions. We do not want to blur in any way the distinctions between the respective roles of management and labor in the plant. If unions were to become a partner in management, they would be most likely the junior partner in success and the senior partner in failure.

> Thomas R. Donahue, executive
> assistant to the president,
> AFL–CIO

To stay competitive, U.S. manufacturers must redesign their products to be assembled by robots that act like machines, not humans.

> Technology Review

LEARNING OBJECTIVES

In this chapter, you will study:

1. Forces beyond management control that affect the availability of labor.

2. Political or economic repression, which causes people to flee. As many leave as can get out, regardless of age, skills, gender, or state of health.

3. Why refugees are a source of labor yet a burden for the countries to which they flee.

4. Guest workers, who go to countries to fill specific jobs for which they have the requisite skills.

5. The composition of a nation's labor force, which affects productivity.

6. Other forces that affect productivity.

7. Why a foreign employer's failure to take into account the social status, gender, race, traditional society, or minorities attitudes of the host country can be costly.

8. How labor union strengths and philosophies differ mightily from area to area.

9. Why labor is getting a voice in management in important parts of the industrial world.

KEY WORDS AND CONCEPTS

- Labor quality
- Labor quantity
- Labor mobility
- Labor force composition
- Labor productivity
- Unit labor cost
- Traditional society
- Minorities
- Labor market
- Labor unions
- Codetermination

BUSINESS INCIDENT

"Responsibility follows power" is a law of politics. If it is disregarded—as it was by the union members on the board of Volkswagen, who delayed the company's plan to build a plant in the United States because it would have meant "exporting German workers' jobs"—the result is serious damage. In VW's case, the share of the American automobile market fell from 8 percent in 1969 to less than 1 percent now. As a result, the survival of the whole operation is threatened, including the jobs of many German workers.

The threat reported in *The Wall Street Journal* article was real. By 1987, the last VW had rolled off the production line of the Pennsylvania plant in which the company had invested millions of dollars.

Source: *The Wall Street Journal,* September 22, 1982, p. 28, and February 8, 1989, p. A4.

T he quality, quantity, and composition of the available labor force are considerations of great importance to an employer. This is particularly true if the employer is required to be efficient, competitive, and profitable. As we have indicated, there are government-owned plants whose objectives are to provide employment or essential services, and in these plants profitability and competitiveness are secondary.

Labor quality refers to the attitudes, education, and skills of available employees. **Labor quantity** refers to whether there are enough available employees with the skills and so forth required to meet your business needs. Circumstances can arise in which there are too many available workers, and this can be good or bad for the business.

If there are more qualified people than you can economically employ, your bargaining position as an employer is strengthened; you can choose the best at relatively low wages. On the other hand, high unemployment can cause and precede social and political unrest, which is usually not conducive to profitable business.

Many of the labor conditions in an area are determined by the social, cultural, religious, attitudinal, class distinction, and other forces we have already discussed. Other determinants of labor conditions are political and legal forces, and here we shall enlarge somewhat on those that were introduced in Chapters 10 and 11. A number of steps that management can take to avoid or minimize labor problems or maximize labor strengths are presented in Chapters 20 and 22, which deal with personnel and staffing.

Here we shall look at such subjects as labor availability, the reasons for its availability or scarcity, the types of labor likely to be available or scarce under different circumstances, productivity, and employer–employee relationships. These relationships are affected by employee organizations, such as labor unions. One cannot generalize about unions because they differ so greatly from country to country or even within one country.

Management of private business in capitalist societies has been thought of as representing the shareholders/owners and bondholders/lenders who put up the money that enabled the business to start and run. The shareholders and bondholders could call the tunes. Some new and different music is now being heard by management in several countries where labor is getting seats on the boards of directors. Management has been reluctant to see that happen, and one reason for that reluctance is illustrated in the business incident.

labor quality the skills, education, and attitudes of available employees

labor quantity whether there are enough available employees with the skills required to meet an employer's business needs

LABOR MOBILITY

Classical economists assumed the immobility of labor, one of the factors of production. Undoubtedly, labor is imperfectly mobile; leaving aside political and economic obstacles, more complications are involved in moving people than in moving capital or most goods.

But however imperfect it may be, **labor mobility** does exist. At least 60 million people left Europe to work and live overseas between 1850 and 1970. Between the end of World War II and the mid-1970s, some 30 million workers from southern Europe and North Africa flowed into eight northern European countries where they were needed due to the economic boom enjoyed by most of the world during those years. This movement is slowing or even

labor mobility people do move from country to country or area to area to get jobs reversing now.[1] These "guest workers" are discussed further later in this chapter.

Another huge worker migration began during the 1970s as the sparsely populated Arab OPEC countries needed labor not only in their oil fields but also for the burgeoning construction projects and services being sought by the newly very rich host countries. Countries supplying most of these workers were Egypt, Algeria, Morocco, Pakistan, and India.

There are probably 11 million Mexicans at work in the United States (most illegally), and the number is growing. In addition, there are many Cubans, Haitians, Central Americans, Southeast Asians, and others in the U.S. work force. The causes of these migrations were and are combinations of problems, economic or political, at their sources and perceived opportunities at their destinations.

□ Refugees: Political and Economic

Throughout history, there have been flights of people from oppression. During the decades of the 1960s and 70s, millions fled from East to West Germany, from the People's Republic of China to Hong Kong and elsewhere, from North to South Vietnam and then as "boat people" from Vietnam to wherever they could land and hope to be accepted. In 1980, the flight of people from Cuba resumed. These were and are political refugees. Those going from Mexico to the United States and from southern Europe to northern Europe go for primarily economic reasons: better jobs and pay.

Population pressures.   The most important pressure creating both political and economic refugees is the booming population growth taking place primarily in the poor LDCs. Some 95 percent of the projected increase in the world's population from 5 billion in 1989 to over 6 billion by the year 2000 will be in those areas.[2]

Women bear most of the burdens of the multiple baby boom, as is graphically illustrated by the photograph of a pregnant woman carrying her still-infant last child in a back sling. The closely spaced pregnancies plus the resulting constant child-care responsibilities are resulting in a growing number of female illiterates and the deterioration of female health.

These are human tragedies first and foremost. In terms of labor force efficiency and productivity, the women and children victims of these developments will be negative forces.

25 million migrants.   Around the world, there are estimated to be at least 25 million people who have migrated to another country. Several million Afghan refugees in Pakistan and Iran are awaiting reestablishment of peace in their country now that the Soviet army has left. Colombians move into the Venezuelan oil country, though that migration slowed as oil prices slid during the late 1980s. The drop in oil prices made Nigeria a less attractive destination, and the strong Ivory Coast economy has made it the new magnet country in central Africa. More than 200,000 men trek into South Africa each year from black African states to work that country's mines. Oil-producing and industrializing Malaysia is estimated to have more than a million illegal aliens, most of whom are from overcrowded Indonesia. Because most

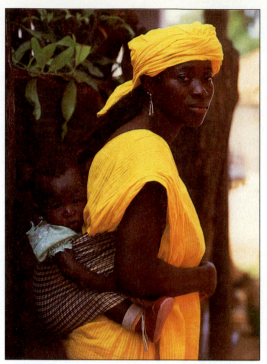

The burdens of women in poor countries: working while pregnant and carrying her still-infant last child on her back.

Hillarie Kavanagh/Tony Stone Worldwide

Argentineans are urbanites, much fertile land is not being farmed, and that draws immigrants from Chile, Bolivia, Paraguay, and Uruguay.

The ex-Soviet empire.   As the previous Soviet satellite countries of Eastern Europe and the parts of the disintegrating Soviet Union struggle to change from centrally planned to market economies, unemployment and discontent are dangerously high. Their people can see and read about the wealth of Western Europe.

The Iron Curtain was erected to keep those people from fleeing to the non-communist West. Now that the Curtain has collapsed, watchtowers and armed guards have made a jarring reappearance—this time on the Western side of the border. The Western European countries are trying to control and regulate a tide of migrants from Albania, Bulgaria, Hungary, Romania, and, it is feared, the ex-Soviet Union. An Austrian army major, Peter Logar, who helps coordinate the border patrol, says, "There are 40 million Russians living below the poverty level, and they're hungry."[3]

Refugees welcome?   Refugees are not welcome in most countries. As indicated in the previous section, Western Europe is living in dread of a flood from the East. The few countries willing to accept some refugees will take only limited numbers. Their reasons differ. Countries near Vietnam and Cambodia, from which refugees flow, are poor and have difficulty feeding their own people. Most of the richer countries, such as Japan and the countries of Western Europe, are not racially diverse and are reluctant to bring in large numbers of alien races. European countries with guest workers (see below) are experiencing some race relations problems. Even in such a relatively rich and racially diverse country as the United States, which is accepting—or

☐ International Immigration

☐ International Emigration

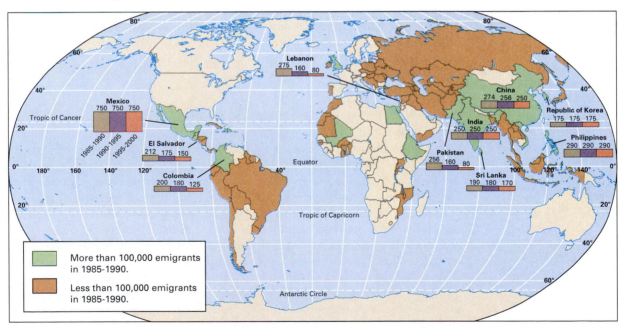

getting—millions of refugees, there are difficulties. One of them is finding work for all of the new people; another is educating their children.

Packing up.   When oil prices were high, the Middle East's fastest-growing export was labor. For such countries as Egypt, Jordan, Pakistan, and North and South Yemen, workers' remittances were bigger than total merchandise exports. As tumbling oil prices pushed the area's oil producers into recession, the expatriates who flocked to jobs there in the 1970s and early 1980s were packing their bags and going home. The home countries will sorely miss the income; and their already large unemployment rolls will swell.[4]

Once the Iraqis had been driven out of Kuwait, the Kuwaitis turned in fury on the Palestinian residents of Kuwait, accusing them of collaborating with the Iraqis. Of course, Palestinian reputations in that regard were not helped by the Palestinian Liberation Organization's open support for Saddam Hussein and Iraq. Kuwaitis are reported to have tortured and killed many Palestinians; they expelled many more from the country. These Palestinians, who in most cases had no other home than Kuwait, now add to the world's horde of refugees.

LABOR SHORTAGES AND GUEST WORKERS

Countries that receive many refugees or have high birthrates may have too many people for the available jobs, but there are also countries that have too few people. France, Germany, the Scandinavian countries, and Switzerland fall into the latter category. Those countries have low birth rates and to them have come the so-called guest workers, who are in the country legally to perform certain types of jobs, usually in service, factory, or construction work.

In 1991, there were 4.3 million immigrants in France who did not qualify for French nationality, including 3.4 million Arabs and 206,000 people from black Africa. West Germany had 4.6 million foreigners, of whom 1.7 million are Turks. England, Switzerland, and the Scandinavian countries also had large numbers of foreign workers and their families. Most of the guest workers are from southern Europe, North Africa, and Turkey.

□ Guest Worker Problems

Economic.   The guest workers provide the labor host countries need, which is desirable as long as the economies are growing. But when the economies slow, as they did during the mid-1970s, 1980s, and 1990s, fewer workers are needed and problems appear. Unemployment increases among the native workers, who then want the jobs held by guest workers. It is conveniently forgotten that the guest workers took jobs that the natives would not do when times were good. To appease their citizens, some countries refused to renew the guest workers' permits. In other countries, where the work was seasonal, the guest workers were deported at the end of the season instead of being permitted to stay and take other work. The French, for example, paid surplus foreign workers 10,000 francs (about $1,500) as a "go home" bonus; and Germany offered "repatriation assistance"—equivalent to about $4,000, plus a lesser amount per child—for certain unemployed foreign workers to leave.

Racial.   The introduction of large numbers of foreigners into host countries caused some racial frictions even while the economies were healthy. In France, for instance, French workers often refuse to share low-cost housing projects with outsiders, especially Arabs and Africans.

By 1991, the racial content of the anti–guest worker arguments in France had become loud and clear.

During 1991, both authors attended conferences and conducted other research in France. The conferences were in Marseille. One author flew to Paris, the other to Nice; they then proceeded to Marseille, which has a high percentage of immigrant guest workers. People advised both authors not to go to dangerous Marseille, but if they were foolhardy enough to travel there, to be very careful. The warnings left no doubt that the dangers were due to the large numbers of Arabs and blacks in Marseille. In any event, the authors and their families had a delightful stay in Marseille, with none of them experiencing any difficulties.

But the point is that the French feelings against the immigrants has escalated and is based largely on race. French leaders of the left, right, and center are speaking out against more immigration. One leader denounced the "smell and the noise" of France's "scrounging" immigrant population. Carrying the immigrant debate still further, Edith Cresson, who became prime minister in 1991, spoke of how to organize the mass expulsion of immigrants.[5]

The Swiss complain about "overforeignization," and a proposal to drastically cut the number of foreigners was only narrowly defeated in a national referendum.

In Germany, there is concern about the foreigners—workers and their families—who show no signs of wanting to leave. The worst relations are with the Turks, who form the largest alien group.

The alien workers and their families are frequently crowded into older, substandard housing. They have created slum neighborhoods in the midst of wealthy Western Europe, and with higher birthrates they are growing in numbers more rapidly than the natives, whose birthrates are among the world's lowest.

France and Germany are not alone in their foreign labor problems. We have mentioned the problems oil-rich Arab countries faced as oil prices declined and Kuwait's treatment of its Palestinian workers after the Iraqis were driven out. The Worldview, "The Door Creaks Open," is a look at the situation in Japan.

Another country that is making a 180-degree turn in its attitude toward immigration is Italy. Traditional tolerance made Italy a haven for untold thousands of illegal immigrants, many of them from poor, black African states. More recently, Albanians and Yugoslavs have swelled their ranks.

Now sentiment toward immigrants has soured sharply as their numbers have increased and the economy has slowed. Violent racial incidents have become more commonplace. In 1991, Italy appointed a new immigration minister, Margherita Boniver. Her tasks are to keep racism under control while enforcing immigration limits on a country-by-country quota basis.[6]

□ New Guest Workers?

Rent a Russian.   The Russian republic is sending an army of up to 6 million migrant workers to fill a gap in Western Europe's labor market. The guest workers are being offered two-year contracts, at the end of which they will be obligated to go home. Despite unemployment in the West, there are shortages of skilled workers in key areas, and the overall work force is shrinking as birthrates decline.

Russian authorities envision three advantages for Russia in these arrangements. First, the returning workers will bring savings in hard currency; second, they will bring new skills learned in the West; and third, the returnees

WORLDVIEW
The Door Creaks Open

Japan's obsession with racial purity has always made foreign workers unwelcome, but a labour shortage and global business pressure are forcing a gradual change.

Thousands of dark, ramshackle buildings crowd the lowlands near Tokyo's Arakawa River. The odourous sprawl is a cluster of small factories typical of those that once formed the backbone of Japan's industrial economy. Few Japanese are willing to work in these unpleasant and smelly tanning and metalworking plants, but destitute foreigners—many of them illegal itinerant workers—are eager to oblige. The cheap labour of young South and Southeast Asians is helping to keep many of these small-scale industries afloat.

Japan has become the salvation for young unemployed men and women from other Asian countries, willing to work for lower-than-average wages despite hardship and the risk of being caught and deported. The growing flood of illegal foreign labourers embarrasses the government. Mindful of the "guest worker" situation in Europe, Japanese officials say they want to avoid developing what could become a permanent "underclass" of unskilled foreign labourers. At the same time, Japan is anxious to attract highly educated foreign professionals, in part to demonstrate progress in "internationalizing" its closed society.

But the growing presence of illegal workers, mostly from the Philippines, Bangladesh, and Pakistan, has provoked a hot debate in Japan over whether Asians from developing countries, lured by the yen's strength, should be allowed to fill jobs Japanese apparently do not want.

In the absence of adequate controls, foreign manual labourers like "Shak," a young sturdy man from Bangladesh, keep coming. The Justice Ministry reports that 11,307 foreigners were arrested and deported for working illegally in Japan in 1987; almost twice as many as in 1986. Officials admit the vast majority are not caught, and that as many as 50,000 foreigners are employed in factories, at construction sites and ports, and in the bars and massage parlours of Japan's ubiquitous "entertainment" industry.

Shak's work in a metal parts factory along the Arakawa River is unpleasant, but he says it pays about 20

times what he would make at home. These workers are welcome in Japan's "second economy," a world of day labour and temporary work in small factories that contrasts sharply with Japan's conventional image of clean, modern efficiency.

Government and industry leaders oppose allowing foreign labourers to work legally in Japan on the grounds that their presence will lower average wages and working conditions, says Eri Aoki, head of the Labour Ministry's employment policy section.

Most business leaders agree. A delegation of the Japan Chamber of Commerce and Industry recently visited Sweden, West Germany, France, and Italy to investigate the situation of foreign workers in Europe. They had hoped to gain some insight into how Japan could deal with migrant labour, but found mostly "cases of failure," says JCCI Chairman Rokuro Ishikawa.

"Many social problems could arise as Japan becomes wealthy and more workers come here from developing countries to do the dirty work," Ishikawa says.

Pointing to social problems faced by migrant workers and their dependents in Germany and other European countries, Aoki says foreign workers could deprive Japanese citizens of jobs during times of economic hardship and eventually overburden the social welfare system.

"It's natural for unemployed, poor labourers to leave their homes when there are higher-paying jobs overseas. That's how the labour market works," Aoki says. "But it's absolutely unacceptable to have an underclass of foreigners in the least desirable, most dangerous jobs. Tens of thousands of people are working illegally, and we feel it's a serious problem."

In Japan, where uniformity is a deeply ingrained value, workers from less affluent countries are viewed as potential troublemakers. Officials cite an alarming rise in the number of non-Japanese apprehended for theft. Illegal foreign workers, of course, evade Japan's strict residential registration system, which keeps track of household members and where they work. The system is one reason Japan's crime rate is so low. "We saw there was a very undesirable gap between the Turkish migrant workers and Germans, who have very different cultures and lifestyles," says Munechika Goh, who headed the JCCI study mission to Europe. "And due to language problems, even if they wanted to have the same labour conditions, it's impossible."

Most illegal workers travel to Japan with tourist visas, often on false passports, find jobs and stay. The lack of a visa requirement for citizens of Bangladesh and Pakistan makes it particularly easy for "sightseers," who are allowed to stay legally in Japan for 90 to 180 days, to come with the purpose of finding work.

No one knows exactly how many firms have hired illegal workers, but a construction boom and the powerful recovery from last year's economic slump have generated a huge demand for workers. Companies unable to find skilled Japanese labourers are hiring and training foreigners to fill the jobs.

A few industrial leaders have spoken out in favour of hiring foreign workers. Nobuo Ishibashi, chairman of the Japan Prefabricated Construction Suppliers and Manufacturers Association, says he plans to campaign to persuade the government to permit employment of foreign labourers. "We are now suffering from a severe shortage of workers for assembly and paint jobs," Ishibashi told a local newspaper.

Just as European contractors did in the 1970s, Japan's smaller manufacturers have begun to depend on cheap foreign labour to cut rising costs associated with the yen's appreciation, says labour economist Eiko Shinotsuka of Ochanomizu University in Tokyo.

The experiences of clandestine workers in Japan parallel those of illegal migrants in other countries. Fearing detection, most refuse to be identified by their real names. Like "Shak," they share cramped (2.5 square metre) rooms with three or four other illegal workers.

A recent Labour Ministry survey of 43 companies employing 154 foreign labourers showed that on average they earn less than half the wages of their Japanese co-workers. Firms save even more on labour costs because clandestine workers do not receive the insurance or other benefits usually demanded by Japanese employees.

Those non-Japanese labourers work an average 60 to 70 hours a week as boiler inspectors, tanners, in small factories, and in the fast-food industry. Sometimes recruited overseas, they often find themselves entangled with Japan's underworld, says Father Joseph Wellens, a Catholic priest who assists Filipinos staying illegally in Japan. The involvement of Japanese gangs in hiring day labourers puts illegal workers at the mercy of gang members. It also inhibits enforcement of laws against hiring foreign workers because police find it convenient to look the other way.

The law only prohibits migrant labourers from working in Japan. It does not prohibit employers from hiring them. So clandestine workers in Japan have no legal rights. They cannot force employers to pay fair wages or appeal to the police for protection. "The government and police view these people as lawbreakers, so it doesn't matter to them if the employers refuse to pay their wages or make them work under dangerous conditions," says Yaeko Takeoka, a lawyer active in Japan's human rights movement.

The situation is particularly dangerous for young women employed in Japan's hostess bars, nightclubs, and massage parlours. "These young women come to Japan expecting to work as waitresses and hotel clerks. But once they are here, their passports are taken away and the girls are sometimes forced to work as prostitutes in order to pay the fees demanded by the brokers who brought them to Japan," Takeoka says.

"The government and police have not yet recognized that the people bringing these people to Japan and hiring them are breaking the law by depriving them of basic human rights," she says. But officials agree that the ban on foreign manual labour cannot be enforced unless employers face severe punishment for hiring illegally.

Japan historically has relied heavily on foreign workers to fill labour shortages, but it is far from a melting pot. Thousands of Koreans and Chinese were forcibly recruited during World War II to work in factories and mines. Most of the 656,000 people of Korean and Chinese ancestry are virtually indistinguishable from their Japanese neighbours. But they are still considered "resident aliens" and must carry alien registration cards.

Today, Tokyo is going all out to attract more non-Japanese with special expertise to Japan. Proposals now under consideration would allow a broader range of

(continued)

foreigners, including those with managerial skills, doctors, nurses, guides, language teachers, engineers, and foreigners who graduate from Japanese universities, to work legally in Japan.

The push comes from trading partners and from major Japanese corporations that are actively recruiting foreign professionals for their growing international operations. NEC Corp., Hitachi Lt., Matsushita Electric Industrial Co., Nippon Telegraph and Telephone Corp., (NTT) and Kobe Steel are particularly active in the hiring of non-Japanese.

Japanese companies with international operations that once hired non-Japanese just for their foreign language ability are increasingly turning to foreign professionals for their understanding of overseas markets, their business ties, and experience. "People are no longer being hired just for their English ability. They have to at least speak Japanese and have experience and professional connections," says Charlotte Takahashi-Kennedy, director of Oak Associates, a company that recruits foreigners for placement in 150 Japanese firms.

Takuya Maruiwa, a board director at computer maker Fujitsu Ltd., says his company recently employed 10 foreigners from the United States, Britain, Taiwan, and South Korea and plans to hire more engineers, managers, and researchers.

"We are hiring foreign specialists because we need to suit our products to overseas markets and need employees who understand how things like satellite communication systems work overseas," Maruiwa says.

A shortage of qualified scientists and engineers to keep Japan's high-tech boom rolling is another factor prompting Japanese firms to hire foreign specialists. Ricoh Co., a copier and office machines firm, has hired 17 Irish engineering graduates and plans to employ 12 more. The foreign scientists work in Ricoh's computer technology development labs.

Cross-cultural employment presents a challenge both to the foreigners working in an unfamiliar environment and to firms integrating individualistic non-Japanese into an organization where promotion and authority depend on demonstrated commitment to the company.

"I've had emergency phone calls from foreigners who have worked in Japanese companies for three to five years who have a tremendous sense of isolation," says Kennedy-Takahashi. But she views the experience, however difficult, as very valuable.

"I think young foreigners can really benefit from the discipline of a Japanese company," she says. "When counseling people, I tell them 'Think of what you'll learn. The isolation and culture shock will make you a stronger professional.' "

Gary Tsuchida, 33, an American who has worked for Kobe Steel for seven years, says he enjoys the sense of responsibility his job provides, although "every day is not a bed of roses."

Kobe has found that its 25 foreign employees play an important role in acquainting Japanese employees to the ways of foreigners. "Aside from the benefit of raising their linguistic abilities, having foreigners working in the company lets Japanese know how they behave," Tsuchida says. "That way, when they go overseas, they make fewer mistakes."

However, even companies anxious to recruit more foreigners are generally not interested in altering practices to accommodate their non-Japanese employees. "We have no plans to change our business style to something like in the United States," says Fujitsu's Maruiwa. "This is Japan, and our management style is suited to Japanese society," he says.

Due to the limits imposed by cultural and linguistic differences, foreigners will probably remain in the margins of Japanese companies, as in the society as a whole. They are needed to do jobs that Japanese workers cannot or will not take but are usually not fully integrated into the corporate structure.

Source: Elaine Kurtenbach, "The Door Creaks Open," *International Management,* September 1988, pp. 49, 52–53.

will have experienced free markets and can lead in the establishment and operation of markets in Russia.

More guest worker problems?   Although this program is similar to the programs we discussed previously, there are two differences. First, at the end of the two-year contract period, the workers are to go home—and two years may not be enough time for them to settle and have children. Second, while Russia wants its workers back, that is not the case with Turkey and the North and Central African countries, the sources of most of the present guest workers.[7]

COMPOSITION OF THE LABOR FORCE

◻ Political or Economic Refugees

When people flow into a country as refugees, the resulting growth of the labor force includes whatever ages, genders, and skills are able to get in. They are not coming for specific jobs; they are fleeing oppression or poverty. At the outset, they cause problems for the host country, which must try to feed, clothe, educate, and find work for the newcomers.

Some, for various reasons, remain burdens on the host country or on international refugee relief agencies. So it has been for many of the Palestinians who fled from Israel. This is not to suggest that the Palestinians are less intelligent or industrious than other groups. Their problems and difficulties have been tremendously increased by the wars and political upheavals in the Middle East.

Others find more peaceful surroundings, adapt relatively quickly, and become upwardly mobile in their new society. This holds true for many of the Cuban refugees in the United States. Many believe the rehabilitation and growth of downtown Miami owes much to the Cubans' influence and work.[8]

Quite different is the type of worker involved in the movement from southern to northern Europe. Specific types of workers and skills were needed there, and only persons who fit the needs were given work permits. They often did not or could not bring their families. They tended to be immediate benefits rather than burdens to the host economy.

The status of the Mexicans in the United States falls between that of the guest worker and that of the political refugee. For one thing, the great majority of guest workers are legally in the host country; the opposite is true for the Mexicans in the United States. For the most part, the Mexicans are economic, not political, refugees, but they bring their families when possible, thus creating more social burdens than do guest workers. Although the Mexicans usually come to work, they do not necessarily come prepared for specific jobs that are available in the host country.

◻ Labor Force Composition and Comparative Productivity

labor force composition
the mix of people available to work, their age, skill, gender, race, and religion

Another change in **labor force composition** in the United States began in the mid-1970s. The percentage of adult women in the American labor force increased by some 10 percent during the decade of the 1970s. By 1988, 62 percent of all American women aged 18 to 64 worked at least part time. In that

Illegal immigrants wade across the river into the United States.

J. P. Laffont/SYGMA

year, 52 percent of all women over the age of 16 were in the labor force, up from 43 percent in 1970 and less than 34 percent in 1950.[9] It is forecast that women will compose 12 million of the 19 million new entrants to the U.S. labor force during the 1990s, rising from 45 percent of the total in 1990 to 47 percent.[10]

The size of the U.S. labor force increased by 30.2 million workers between 1974 and 1991, a gain of over 32 percent. A unique feature of U.S. labor force growth—female and male—is that many of the new workers are political or economic refugees who speak little, if any, English in addition to being unskilled. This growth and heterogeneity of the American labor force made an increase of **labor productivity** difficult but not impossible.

By 1991, a productivity increase for America seemed to be a silver lining of the country's recession. Due to global competition, U.S. firms cut costs early in the recession instead of later as they had done in previous recessions. The result was a 0.1 percent productivity rise in the first six months of the 1989–91 recession as compared to an average 1.2 percent fall in the same period of the past four recessions. Then, for the first three quarters of 1990, productivity increased by 4 percent—four times the typical gain in efficiency at that stage of the cycle.

Another good sign was that productivity in America's inefficient service industries was rising at a 1.2 percent rate compared with a typical decline of 1.5 percent in past recessions. Productivity is the key to U.S. competitiveness well beyond the recovery.[11]

Comparative **unit labor cost** figures do not present as optimistic a picture. Unit labor cost is the cost in labor to produce one unit of output. Figure 12–1 shows U.S. unit labor costs rising faster than in other industrial countries. It also indicates average earnings.

Levels (as opposed to growth rates) of productivity are hard to compare because they first have to be converted into a common unit of account using

labor productivity measures how many acceptable units of a product are produced by a worker during a given time and the cost per unit

unit labor cost the cost in labor to produce one unit of output

☐ **FIGURE 12–1   Industrial Countries: Average Earnings and Unit Labor Costs* (Percent change)**

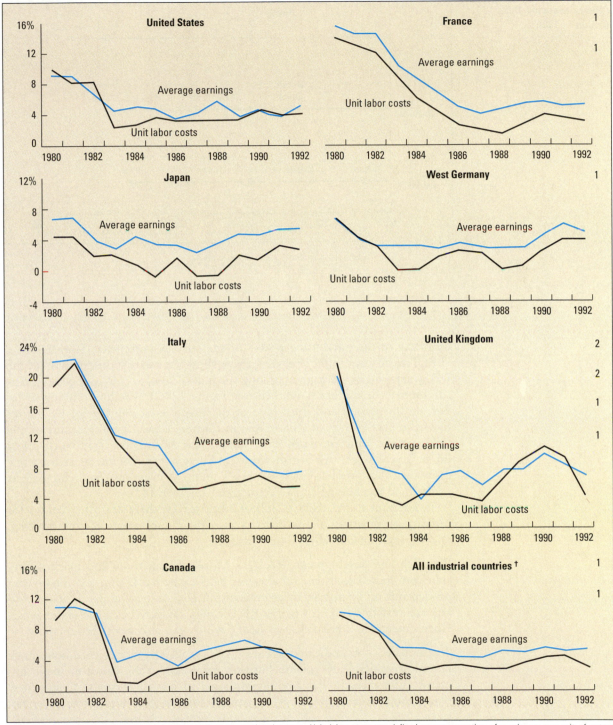

*Average earnings are defined as total compensation per employed person. Unit labor costs are defined as compensation of employees per unit of output. Shaded areas indicate staff projections.

†Composites are based on 1988–90 GDP/GNP weights.

Source: International Monetary Fund, "World Economic Outlook," May 1991.

□ FIGURE 12–2
Relative Productivity (Whole economy 1986, Britain = 100)

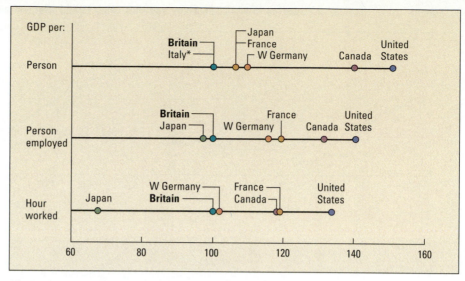

*Figures for Italy incomplete due to uncertain size of hidden economy.
Source: *The Economist,* April 29, 1989, p. 6.

estimates of the purchasing power of the various currencies. Statistics in a U.K. Treasury economic progress report show the relative productivity of the U.S. worker to be the highest among the industrial countries, per person, person employed, and hours worked (see Figure 12–2). The low ranking of Japan on the second and third bars of the Figure is accounted for by the remarkable inefficiency of its workers in farming and distribution and by the fact that the Japanese work more hours than the others. They work 2,129 hours a year while the British work 1,511. It is the opinion of at least one economist that productivity levels in all countries eventually will converge as capital and technology spread throughout the world.[12]

In addition to the relative skill of labor forces, there are other causes for rapidity or slowness of productivity growth. These causes are interlocking, and we shall look briefly at some of them.

Research and development (R&D).   More efficient tools and machines result from more extensive and effective R&D. The R&D that a company can do depends on its management policies but also on how many after-tax dollars are available and on whether R&D can be deducted as a pre-tax expense. Governments do a great deal of R&D, which can also boost productivity.[13]

Tax policies.   As indicated, a nation's tax policies can influence how much money is available to private business for R&D. They can also make immense differences in the amount available to private business to buy new plant, tools, and machines. They can do this through higher or lower tax rates.

Policies on depreciation are also important. Present U.S. tax policy permits depreciation only of the historic cost of plant, tools, and machines. With inflation, however, the replacement cost will be higher than the historic cost. If business could depreciate the current or replacement cost, the result would be lower taxes and more money left to the company for R&D, reinvestment, or other uses. See Chapter 6 for more on this.

Savings rates.   If people save a large percentage of their income (as opposed to spending it on current consumption), there is a larger pool of money available with which to buy company stocks or lend to business. People save for such reasons as creating a nest egg against hard times and because they have confidence in their currencies. A number of countries give tax breaks to interest or dividends earned on savings, and some countries have involuntary savings plans. Most OECD countries have savings rates higher than those of the United States and have higher economic and productivity growth rates.

The savings rates for the G7 countries in descending order from the biggest savers to the smallest are given below.[14]

Countries	Percentages of National Income
Japan	20.9%
Germany	11.6
Italy	11.0
Canada	9.9
France	8.9
United Kingdom	5.5
United States	4.0

The pessimist—realist?   Dr. Paul W. McCracken, an eminent economist who is now professor emeritus, University of Michigan, says the United States must improve its productivity performance. He says that if the trends of the 1980s continue through the 1990s for the Big Seven of the industrial world, Japan's per capita output will exceed that of the United States by nearly 40 percent. Real incomes in France and Germany will also be well above those here; Italy and Britain would still be lower than the United States but would be closing the gap.

Dr. McCracken says the Bush administration and Congress must severely restrain the stampede to launch new programs and sweeten old ones. Most economies of the industrial world delivered stronger gains in productivity than the United States during the 1980s, and the United States must learn how they did it.

An economy's rate of productivity gain is closely related to the amount of capital in place per worker, and the reduced rate of improvement in U.S. productivity parallels a comparable slowdown in the rate of increase in U.S. capital stock per worker.

The cost of capital confronting U.S. companies is higher than it is for their international competitors, and more U.S. capital has been devoted to objectives not included in output (for example, cleaner air and water and other social objectives).

Dr. McCracken also points out that the American education system has been sending employers less well-educated workers than is the case in some other countries. He calls on national, state, and local governments and business to cooperate in solving these problems.[15]

A walk on the brighter side.   The United States came out of World War II with undamaged factories and a hoard of technology developed during the war. As a result, its productivity level was four to five times higher than the ravaged European and Japanese economies. A major American policy goal was the reconstruction of Europe and Japan. Reconstruction was successful, and the gap was narrowed. By the mid-60s, European and Japanese growth slowed, and in the late 70s, the German growth rate for manufacturing fell behind the American rate. It is still falling, and the Japanese rate since 1980 has been virtually identical to that of America. As of 1992, the American worker's productivity is 30 percent higher than the Japanese overall rate and 28 percent higher in manufacturing. For more on this, see the supplementary reading "The Truth about the American Worker" by Myron Magnet.

SOCIAL STATUS, GENDER, RACE, TRADITIONAL SOCIETY, OR MINORITIES: CONSIDERATIONS IN EMPLOYMENT POLICIES

□ Social Status

There are societies in which a person's social status is established by the caste or social group into which the person is born. India presents an extreme example of the caste system, and intercaste battles that cause fatalities and home burnings still occur between upper-caste Hindus and the untouchables, whom Mahatma Gandhi called *harijans,* the children of God.[16] Obviously, a would-be employer must tread carefully when both upper-caste Hindus and harijans are in the employee pool.

Some say that the class system in Great Britain is eroding, but people there are still classified by the accents they acquire at home and school. When Margaret Thatcher was elected prime minister, commentators saw fit to point out that she was "only" the daughter of a small-store owner even though her accent was "upper class," apparently acquired at Oxford University. Although class differences do not cause riots in Britain, as caste differences do in India, a foreign employer should, nevertheless, be conscious of the possibilities for friction arising from those differences.

In Japan, there remains an odd caste holdover from the 17th century, when the feudal Togugawa regime imposed a rigid social pecking order on the country. The warrior-administrator samurai were at the top. Below them were farmers and artisans, then merchants, and at the very bottom, those with occupations considered dirty and distasteful, such as slaughterers, butchers, and tanners.

As in India, where discrimination against untouchables is illegal, all natives of Japan are legally equal. However, the descendants of the lowest Japanese class remain trapped in their ghettos, working in small family firms that produce knitted garments, bamboo wares, fur and leather goods, shoes, and sandals. They call themselves *burakumin* (ghetto people) and claim they number about 3 million people living in some 6,000 ghettos. Their average income is far below that of other Japanese.

□ Gender

Degrees of women's liberation and of women's acceptability in the work force range from fairly advanced in the United States and Western Europe to virtually nil in many countries. Even where women have made some strides out of their traditional roles, their progress is not necessarily secure, as witness the women's marches in Iran when the Islamic government that succeeded the shah ordered women back to their traditional dress and roles.

The employer must consider the sexist attitudes of the host society. In a country such as the United States, which has seen large strides in the status and acceptability of women in business and the professions, the hiring and promotion of women can be a business advantage. It can also be a legal advantage, because it complies with "affirmative action" laws and regulations of the U.S. and state governments. These laws encourage the hiring and promotion of women and minorities. But there are many countries in which customs, attitudes, or religion are hostile to women in the professions or business.

> Think like a man, act like a lady, work like a dog.
> That is the formula for the success of a woman working in the man's world of Japanese business.*

One of the quotations at the beginning of Chapter 22 indicates the scarcity of females in Japanese management. Women make up only 6.7 percent of the executive roster of the country, far below the American or Swedish rates. Tradition, a burden for women executives in most countries, is one reason.

A second reason is after-hours drinking sessions, which are common in many countries but more prevalent in Japan. Much of Japanese consensus decision making is accomplished during such sessions. Female managers tend to consider these a waste of time and to be somewhat uncomfortable at the freewheeling exchanges among the men as inhibitions fall away. The drinking is often very heavy, and drunkenness is not a disgrace; overimbibers are delivered carefully home.

The discomfort goes both ways. One computer salesman, talking about after-hours drinking sessions with his female section chief, complained, "I don't know what to talk about with her. She's not married, so I must avoid any remarks with sexual connotations. With a man, I could have a drink and talk about anything."

Other countries hinder women.   Japan is not the only country where women are encountering problems in making or retaining progress. We spoke of the setback for women in Iran, and women have been having troubles in other Moslem countries also.

One step forward in Pakistan has been accompanied by several steps backward. The forward step was a decision by the federal court that women could serve as judges. Two of the backward steps are banning women from taking part in public sporting events and changing the law of evidence to make the

---

* "Japan's Women Executives Finding Progress Painful," *Asian Wall Street Journal,* December 13, 1982, p. 11.

The strike—labor's weapon of last legal resort.

Les Stone/SYGMA

with wages and working conditions frequently legislated. Many Latin American governments are very active in employer–employee relationships, frequently because the unions are weak and the union leaders are inexperienced or uneducated.

There has been so much discussion and writing about Japanese labor and labor policies that we should comment at least briefly about them. Already mentioned have been the growing productivity of Japanese labor and the low number of days lost to strikes.

The better productivity is probably the result of greater savings being invested in capital equipment and may be due in part to the loyalty of labor to the employer. Some say that traditional loyalty to the family or the emperor has been transferred to the employer. The practice of lifetime employment by much of Japan's larger industry would reinforce the loyalty and reduce the tendency to strike.

In 1989, Japan's two labor federations united. The 4.5-million-member General Council of Trade Unions of Japan, which was known as Sohyo and represented mostly public-sector employees, saw its power eroded by rising prosperity, declining unionization, and increased use of part-timers. Therefore, Sohyo was merged into the 5.4-million-member Japanese Private Sector Trade Union Confederation, called Rengo.

The merger isn't expected to have much impact on the usually cooperative relations between companies and their employees. If anything, relations could be even more cordial, because the socialist-inclined Sohyo was more likely to have been confrontational than was Rengo.[23]

In West Germany and France, the influences of law and government administrative actions are more extensive and evident. Negotiations are conducted on national or at least regional levels, and in France, government representatives take part.

Membership trends.   The average share of trade union membership among total employees across 18 OECD member-countries fell from 35 percent in 1980 to 28 percent in 1988. In some countries, including the United Kingdom, Australia, and Italy, the falls in membership during the 1980s merely reversed gains made during the 1970s.

In the United States and France, by contrast, trade unions have been losing members for two consecutive decades. Since 1970, union coverage in France has fallen by 10.3 percent—to the lowest level of any OECD country—and by 13.6 percent in the United States.

In the United States, evidence suggests that unions are weaker precisely because they have been so effective at raising their members' wages. This has given employers a strong incentive to oppose unions.[24]

◻ Multinational Labor Activities

The internationalization of business has been under way for many years, and multinational companies have expanded rapidly since the 1950s. National unions have begun to perceive opportunities of companies to escape the organizing reach of unions by the relatively simple step of transferring to or commencing production in another country. The companies' opportunities are seen as dangers to the unions.

To combat those dangers, national unions have begun to (1) collect and disseminate information about companies, (2) consult with unions in other countries, (3) coordinate with those unions' policies and tactics in dealing with some specific companies, and (4) encourage international companies' codes of conduct. Such multinational labor activity is likely to increase, although unions are divided by ideological differences and are frequently strongly nationalistic. Vastly more effort and money have been spent on lobbying for protection of national industries than on cooperating with unions in other countries.

Some developments that occurred in 1980 demonstrate, however, that cooperation is possible. The Geneva-based International Union of Food and Allied Workers Association coordinated a boycott of Coca-Cola in Sweden, Spain, Mexico, and Finland. The cause of the boycott was alleged "antilabor practices" by the Coca-Cola franchise holder in Guatemala.

The International Metalworkers Federation asked West European governments to use their economic power against International Telephone & Telegraph Corporation (ITT) because it wanted changes in ITT's "personnel and social policies."

The first important arena in which successful multinational unionism may develop is the European Community (EC). The 12 EC member-countries are steadily eliminating or harmonizing their tariffs, taxes, monetary systems, laws, and much more. The resulting atmosphere will be more hospitable for the cooperation of national unions.

Also working in this area is the European Trade Union Confederation (ETUC), an umbrella organization of 15 pan-European industry committees representing 39 national union federations. One ETUC official is not very optimistic about the strength of the EC's social action program for labor; he says it will be at best a "rubber sword."

However, some ETUC member-unions are doing very well on their own, cooperating across borders in pursuit of a common goal. For four months, the Federation of European Metalworkers (FEM) supported a strike against British Aerospace (BAe) demanding a shorter workweek. BAe is part of the European Airbus consortium, supplying wings for the planes. The strike cost the consortium an estimated $200 million.

Settlement of the strike won a 37-hour workweek for the members of Amalgamated Engineering, a British union. Demonstrating cross-border union cooperation during the strike, the German engineering union, IG Metall, made financial donations to the British strikers. FEM's aim is for a standard work week for its six million members in 16 European countries.[25]

The American union federation, the AFL–CIO, cooperates with LDC labor in three organizations: the African-American Labor Center; the American Institute for Free Labor Development for Latin America; and the Asian-American Free Labor Institute.

However, in one highly competitive field—automobiles—the internationalization of the industry is emphasizing differences rather than cooperation among national unions. The managements of car companies have long since stopped being as alarmed by threats of international action as they were when the unions first made them. Natural nationalism is made worse in some countries by multiunion industries, and when political differences are added, unions frequently find themselves competing rather than cooperating with one another.[26]

▫ Codetermination

Europe, particularly Germany, is in the vanguard of another labor development, which, at first sight, horrified many business managers and owners. Laws were adopted that required employees to be given seats on the employer boards of directors.

It began in Germany.   Worker participation in management, frequently called **codetermination,** began in the German coal and steel industries in 1951. The law gave worker and shareholder representatives each 50 percent of the directorships. A neutral board member selected by both sides breaks any deadlocks, but that vote has rarely been needed, as labor and shareholder representatives usually resolve their differences.

The 50–50 system was extended to all large German industry by a 1976 law that was challenged in court by German employers but upheld by the West German high court in March 1979.[27]

It has spread.   Other European countries and Japan either have or are seriously discussing codetermination-type legislation or practices. In the United States, neither business nor labor showed much enthusiasm for codetermination until the late 1970s. However, things are changing in the United States, where the terms *industrial democracy* and *worker participation* are sometimes used.

Developments in the United States.   During the late 1970s and into the 1980s, the concept of industrial democracy spread in America. Both Chrysler Corporation and American Motors have had United Automobile Workers (UAW) officers as members of their boards of directors. Workers at General Motors get together in "quality circles" to help make decisions about their

---

codetermination
participation by workers in a company's management

jobs and production quality. The Communications Workers of America signed a contract in August 1980 with American Telephone & Telegraph that included worker participation concepts. New Labor contracts in the steel, rubber, oil, paper, glass, aerospace, food processing, and electrical products industries contain similar concepts. In addition, hundreds of large and small nonunion employers have adopted their own versions of industrial democracy; among these are IBM and Texas Instruments.[28]

Not everyone in the United States is pleased with worker participation (see the first quotation at the beginning of this chapter). When Douglas Fraser, the UAW president, was elected to Chrysler's board in 1980, there were fears in labor and management that the conflicts between the two jobs were too great.

In his efforts to sell a new Chrysler contract to the UAW rank and file, Fraser reversed the typical charge of labor leaders—that management is bargaining in bad faith when it claims that it cannot afford fatter wage and benefit offers. Fraser took just the opposite tack and chided the Chrysler chairman for painting too rosy a picture of Chrysler's finances. He even said that Chrysler's reported profits were based in part on financial "manipulations."

As a result, neither the UAW nor Chrysler management was happy with Fraser. Some union members felt he had not squeezed the company hard enough; management feared his talk of financial weakness and manipulation would hurt the company's reputation with its bankers and the investment community.[29]

Despite misgivings by both the UAW and Chrysler, Fraser was replaced on the carmaker's board by his successor as UAW president, Owen F. Bieber. Even though Bieber kept a lower profile than had Fraser, his board seat was one of five eliminated by Chrysler in 1991.

Joseph Blasi, who studies labor issues at Rutgers University, sums up American business and labor attitudes toward codetermination as follows: "American management seems to be very lukewarm about the idea, and American unions seem to be totally uninterested except when they own big portions of the company. So there is no one asking for it."[30]

◻ Workers of the World

Some comparisons are interesting as to how long workers work and how much they are paid in cities around the world.

Hours they work. The average Japanese worker still clocks 47 hours a week, compared with the Dutch worker's 34 hours. Such differences are partly explained by the importance of part-time employment, which is highest in countries that appear to have the laziest workers. One quarter of Holland's work force is part-time, more than twice the share in Japan. Also, most Dutch workers take five weeks of paid vacation; the Japanese are entitled to 15 days, and many still take only half that. Average hours worked fell in most OECD countries in the 1980s. The exceptions were Japan, where hours

□ **FIGURE 12–3** **Average Weekly Hours Worked (Full- and part-time employees)**

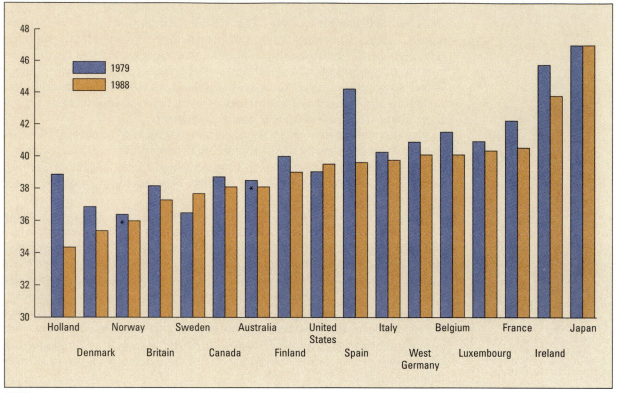

*1980.
Source: *The Economist,* July 21, 1990, p. 101.

□ **FIGURE 12–4** **Average Hourly Wages ($US)**

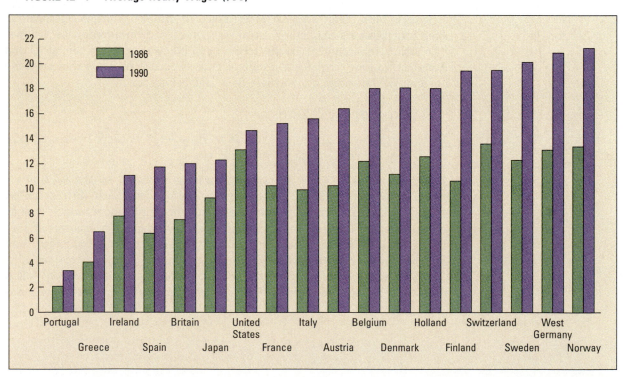

worked remained unchanged, and Sweden and America, where workers seem to have become more industrious (see Figure 12–3).

Money they earn.   For statistics on average hourly wages, see Figure 12–4. In 1986, the average hourly wage paid to American workers made them look rich. In dollar terms, only West German, Swiss, and Norwegian workers were paid more. By 1990, thanks mainly to the dollar's weakness, America is well down in the wages ranking. Its workers receive $14.74, far behind Norway's $21.59.

SUMMARY

Before investing in a country or an area, a company's management will examine the potential employee pool—its composition, skills, and attitudes. These are elements over which management has no control before it invests and which may change for reasons beyond its control after investments have been made. It is the purpose of this chapter to bring at least some of these elements to your attention.

Management may find itself dealing with a labor force that consists of local citizens or foreigners. If the workers are foreign to the host country, they may be guest workers who are legally in the country to perform certain tasks that the natives do not want to do. Foreign workers may also be refugees, legally or illegally in the host country, who came primarily to escape something and not primarily to perform specific work.

Foreign workers sometimes cause problems. When the economy slows, the local citizens want the jobs held by them. Even in prosperity, there are racial conflicts between foreign workers and the natives.

The composition of the labor force affects labor productivity, and when the labor force grows rapidly due to an influx of unskilled workers, productivity suffers.

Another influence on productivity is the capital equipment available to the labor force. The amount of capital equipment is affected by (1) research and development and (2) savings rates, both of which can be encouraged or discouraged by tax policies.

Management moving into a different country should also consider, as they affect employment policies, the local attitudes toward social status, gender, race, religion, and minorities. Management would have to perform differently in a traditional society than in a more-developed, industrialized country.

A company management weighing investment in a country should study the labor unions and the strike records. Labor laws and government intervention in employer–employee relationships should be examined.

Labor unions have begun to be active internationally and to coordinate studies and labor action. Such coordination has been growing in Europe, and it was in Europe—first in Germany—that codetermination began. Some sort of worker participation in management can now be found in several European countries, Japan, and the United States.

QUESTIONS

1. *a.* How could an excess of qualified employees be beneficial for an employer?
   b. How could it be detrimental?

2. Classical economists assumed the labor factor of production to be immobile. Is this assumption correct in the modern world?

3. What are some differences between labor that moves as do the European guest workers and labor that moves as do political or economic refugees?

4. What is the effect on productivity of the influx into the work force of inexperienced, unskilled workers?

5. How could a caste system affect employment decisions?

6. What effects do the levels of a country's savings have on its relative competitiveness?

7. In several Southeast Asian and South Pacific countries, the Chinese minority is prominent in banking, finance, and business. What are the dangers for a foreign employer staffing the local company primarily with such a minority?

8. What is a major difference between European and American unions?

9. What are the prospects for effective multinational union collaboration? Discuss.

10. *a.* What is codetermination?
    b. Has codetermination worked well? Discuss.

11. What are some arguments against codetermination?

12. In Soviet law, women are equal with men. How does Soviet life reflect Soviet law in this respect?

◻ MINICASE 12–1

Codetermination—Deutsche Stevens*

"Have you been following the problems that Opel has been having because of Mitbestimmung (codetermination)?"† Mat Burns, the president of Deutsche Stevens, a wholly owned subsidiary of Houston-based Stevens Industries, was talking to his management committee. "The worker representatives on the board of directors have become very militant. They are bringing up a lot of issues in board meetings that ought to be settled by labor negotiations."

"What kinds of issues, Mat?" asked Ned Webster, vice president for production.

Burns:

Things like the right to name the new personnel director, improve retirement benefits, and even plant ventilation. This militancy is also being felt in the legitimate issues that the board ought to discuss. It used to be that management presented the worker representatives with investment decisions after they were made, but now, I'm told, they want to review them one at a time very carefully. They say it is as important to use funds to improve working conditions as it is to spend them for increased production capacity and product development.

Jim Perrin, vice president for personnel:

Mat, do you know the cause of this increased militancy?

Burns:

I've been told there are a number of causes. One is the rapid growth of the work force. Since 1975, it has grown from 33,000 to 43,000 employees. The newest workers are younger and, of course, do not have the loyalty to Opel that the old-time employees have.

Perrin:

Do you think that's the only reason?

Burns:

No, I've been told there are others. The plant is running at full capacity and is crowded and uncomfortable. Part of the plant dates from the 1930s. The head of the works council claims that the workers are under pressure to produce every second, as he puts it, and that conditions are very severe.‡

Webster:

Sounds bad, Mat, but we don't have these problems; not yet, anyway.

Burns:

That's true, but remember, we have less than 2,000 employees, so only a third of our board of directors consists of workers' representatives. However, as you know, we are getting close to that figure. Marketing wants to add a whole new product line, and this will require us to add at least 400 new employees, which will put us over the 2,000 level. That means we shall have an equal representation of labor and management on the board. In the event of a tie, I can still cast the deciding vote for management. However, every time I have to do that, the labor representatives are going to feel frustrated, and it's going to show up on the production line.

Ludwig Schmidt, company attorney:

Mat, maybe there's another way to do it.

Burns:

How's that, Ludwig?

Schmidt:

Well, ITT's subsidiary, Standard Elektrik Lorenz, has changed two of its companies to limited partnerships, which makes them exempt from the law. Other companies are spinning off operations into separate companies so that no one company has more than 2,000 employees. They still must have one-third worker representation on the board, as we do now, but that's better than a 50–50 split.¶

Burns:

That seems like a good idea, Ludwig—the forming of another company, I mean. Will you get together with Don here [Don Jones, vice president for marketing] and see if we should form a new company? You'll want to be in on these discussions, too, Ned. Also, Ned, I wish you and Jim would review our working conditions to see if we have any potential problem areas similar to Opel's. Parts of our plant are rather old, and we have been pushing the workers pretty hard to get the production out, haven't we?

---

* "West Germany, the Worker Dissidents in Opel's Boardroom," *Business Week*, July 23, 1979, p. 79.

† Opel is General Motors' German subsidiary.

‡ The works council is a body composed of employees elected by all the employees of the plant. It monitors the carrying out of labor agreements and is involved in grievance proceedings.

¶ "Companies in Germany Confront Codetermination Practice," *Business Europe*, January 20, 1978, p. 22.

1. What would you suggest if you were either the attorney or the marketing manager? Are there any problems involved if a separate company is formed to handle the new product line?

2. What should the vice president for production and the vice president for personnel consider?

3. Do any large American companies have worker representatives on their boards of directors?

□ MINICASE 12–2

Racism

Your company, an American IC, has decided to expand aggressively in Asia. It plans to source much of its raw material and subcontracting there and manufacture and market throughout Asia, from Japan in the north through New Zealand in the south.

You were appointed to organize and direct this major new effort, and one question was where to locate the regional headquarters for the Asian Division. After considerable study, you selected the island nation of Luau.

Luau's advantages are several. It is about equidistant between New Zealand and Japan. It was a British colony, so the main language is English. It has a relatively efficient telephone and telegraph system and good air service to all the major Asian destinations in which you are interested and to the United States.

Not least important, the Luau government is delighted to have your company locate and invest there. It has made very attractive tax concessions to the company and to its personnel who will move there.

The company moves in, leases one large building, and puts out invitations to bid on the construction of a larger building, which will be its permanent headquarters. Now, as you begin to work much more with the private banking and businesspeople of Luau and less with government officials, you begin to be more aware of a Luau characteristic about which you had not thought much previously. Almost all of the middle- and upper-management personnel in the business and finance sector are of Chinese extraction. The native population of Luau, which is the great majority, is a Micronesian race.

On inquiring why the Chinese are dominant in banking and business while the Micronesians stay with farming, fishing, government, and manual labor, you are told that this is the way it developed historically. The Chinese enjoy and are good at banking and business, while the native Luauans do not like those activities and have stayed with their traditional pastimes. The two groups buy and sell from and to each other, but there are almost no social relations and very little business or professional overlap between the groups. Occasionally, some of the Micronesians study abroad, and some work abroad for periods; when they return, they frequently go to work in a bank or business or take a government position.

You must staff your headquarters with middle- and lower-management people and with clerical help. You find that the only applicants for the jobs are Chinese, and you select the best available. They are quite satisfactory, and the operation gets off to a good start.

Then, as the months pass, you notice a gradual change of attitude toward you and the company among the government officials and among the people in general. They have become less friendly, more evasive, and less cooperative. You ask your Chinese staff about it, but they have noticed nothing unusual.

What could be happening? Why might the Chinese staff not notice it? What might you do to improve government and public relations?

SUPPLEMENTARY READINGS

Aggarwal, R., and I. Khera. "Exporting Labor: The Impact of Expatriate Workers on the Home Country." *International Migration* 25, no. 4 (1987), pp. 415–24.

Arnold, Fred. "Revised Estimates and Projections of International Migration: 1980–2000." Planning and Research working paper no. 275. The World Bank and World Population Projections, June 1991.

Baile, Stephanie. "Women and Health in Developing Countries." *The OECD Observer*, December 1989–January 1990, pp. 18–20.

Bain, Trevor. "German Codetermination and Employment Adjustments in the Steel and Auto Industries." *Columbia Journal of World Business,* Summer 1983, pp. 40–47.

Bairstow, Frances. "The Trend toward Centralized Bargaining—A Patchwork Quilt of International Diversity." *Columbia Journal of World Business,* Spring 1985, pp. 75–83.

Benelli, Giuseppe, Claudio Loderer, and Thomas Lys. "Labor Participation in Corporate Policymaking Decisions: West Germany's Experience with Codetermination." *Journal of Business,* October 1987, pp. 553–75.

Blum, Alfred, ed. *International Handbook of Industrial Relations: Contemporary Developments and Research.* Westport, Conn.: Greenwood Press, 1981.

Brooke, Michael Z. *International Management.* London: Hutchinson, 1986.

Enderwick, Peter. *Multinational Business and Labor.* New York: St. Martin's Press, 1985.

Furobotn, Erik G. "Codetermination and the Modern Theory of the Firm: A Property-Rights Analysis." *Journal of Business,* April 1988, pp. 165–181.

Herz, Barbara. "Bringing Women into the Economic Mainstream." *Finance & Development,* December 1989, pp. 22–25.

Kao, Charles. *Brain Drain.* Hong Kong: Mei Ya China International Specie Bank, 1980.

Liebhaberg, Bruno. *Industrial Relations and Multinational Corporations in Europe.* New York: Praeger Publishers, 1981.

Lindert, Peter. *International Economics.* Homewood, Ill.: Richard D. Irwin, 1986.

Magnet, Myron. "The Truth about the American Worker." *Fortune,* May 4, 1992, pp. 48–65.

Scholl, Wolfgang. "Codetermination and the Ability of Firms to Act in the Federal Republic of Germany." *International Studies of Management and Organization,* Summer 1987, pp. 27–37.

Thim, Alfred L. "How Far Should German Codetermination Go?" *Challenge,* July 1981, p. 13.

Wahren, Carl. "The Imperative of Population Control." *The OECD Observer,* December 1990–January 1991, pp. 34–37.

ENDNOTES

1. Barry Newman, "Unwelcome Guests," *The Wall Street Journal,* May 9, 1983, pp. 1, 22.

2. Carl Wahren, "The Impact of Population Growth," *OECD Observer,* December 1988–January 1989, pp. 8–11.

3. Tim Carrington, "Central Europe Borders Tighten as Emigres Flood in from East," *The Wall Street Journal,* February 8, 1991, p. A10; and Richard Gwyn, "Fortress Europe on Horizon: Tidal Wave," *The Toronto Star,* October 14, 1990, p. H1.

4. Lara Marlowe, "Guest Workers Say Their Farewells to Saudi Arabia," *Financial Times,* September 25, 1990, p. 2.

5. Margareta Pagano, "Problems Go Skin Deep," *The European,* September 13–15, 1991, p. 19; and George Graham, "Newcomers Hit by Left, Right, Centre," *Financial Times,* August 8, 1991, p. 11.

6. Haig Simonian, "Charged with a Gentle Closing of the Door," *Financial Times,* May 1, 1991, p. 2; and "A Different Sort of Docksider," *The Economist,* August 17, 1991, p. 42.

7. Chris White, "Wanted: Jobs in the West for Six Million Soviets," *The European,* September 20–26, 1991, p. 1.

8. Anthony Ramirez, "Making It," *The Wall Street Journal,* May 20, 1980, pp. 1 and 27.

9. *Equal Employment Opportunity for Women: U.S. Policies* (Washington, D.C.: Women's Bureau, U.S. Department of Labor, 1982), Table 2.

10. James Flanigan, "The Power of the Changing Work Force," *The Wall Street Journal,* May 13, 1990, p. D1.

11. "Productivity Pick-up," *The Economist,* May 25, 1991, p. 72.

12. William J. Baumol, "A Modest Decline Isn't All That Bad," *The New York Times,* February 15, 1987, p. 14.

13. Paul W. McCracken, "Congress and the Budget Beanstalk," *The Wall Street Journal,* February 29, 1980, p. 22.

14. "National Saving in Major Industrial Countries," *Bank for International Settlements 61st Annual Report,* June 10, 1991, p. 34.

15. Paul W. McCracken, "Lick the American Disease before It's an Epidemic," *The Wall Street Journal,* January 16, 1989, p. A8.

16. *Los Angeles Times,* February 27, 1980, part 1, p. 2; see also "The Cost of Caste," *The Economist,* February 16, 1980, pp. 46–47.

17. Julia Voznesenskaya, *The Women's Decameron* (New York: Atlantic Monthly Press, 1986); also see Maska Hamilton, "Soviet Super-Moms Want Changes," *Los Angeles Times,* March 6, 1989, part 1, pp. 10–11.

18. "Rebuilding the Top Table," *The Economist,* December 15, 1990, p. 44; Krystyna Labelska, "Polish Women Still Wait in Line—For Their Rights," *Los Angeles Times,* May 26, 1991, p. M1; and "An Unfinished Chinese Revolution," *The Economist,* March 16, 1991, p. 34.

19. Gerard O'Dwyer, "The Fair Sex Gets the Fairest Deal in Scandinavia," *The European,* June 2, 1991, p. 3.

20. Daniel Wattenberg, "Internationalism Turns Ugly with Attacks on Africans," *Insight,* January 30, 1989, pp. 28–30.

21. See the discussion of employee attitudes and motivation in Sincha Ronen, *Comparative and Multinational Management* (New York: John Wiley & Sons, 1986), chap. 5.

22. Everett M. Kassalow, *Trade Unions and Industrial Relations: An International Comparison* (New York: Random House, 1969).

23. Masayoshi Kanabayashi, "Union Union," *The Wall Street Journal*, March 14, 1989, p. A1.

24. Edward Balls, "Trends in Trade Union Membership in the 1980s," *Financial Times*, August 5, 1991, p. 4.

25. Noemi Trevino, "The Struggle for European Unions," *International Management*, December 1990, pp. 70–75.

26. *The Economist*, March 15, 1986, pp. 69–70.

27. *The Wall Street Journal*, March 12, 1979, p. 18.

28. Harry Bernstein, "Democracy Moves into Workplace," *Los Angeles Times*, October 23, 1980, part 1, pp. 1 and 14–15.

29. "Doug Fraser's Conflicts," *The Wall Street Journal*, September 22, 1982, p. 28.

30. Jesus Sanchez and Donald Wontat, "Chrysler to Drop Union President's Spot on Its Board," *Los Angeles Times*, March 14, 1991, p. D1.

Chapter 13

Competitive and Distributive Forces

If there is a single great fact of our era, it is the emergence of the first truly international marketplace and the struggle between the leading trading nations and blocs: the United States, Western Europe, Japan, Singapore–Taiwan–Hong Kong– Korea, Mexico–Brazil, and, potentially, China.

> Paraphrased from H. Lewis and D. Allison, *The Real War: The Coming Battle for the New Global Economy and Why We Are in Danger of Losing*

LEARNING OBJECTIVES

In this chapter, you will study:

1. Why international competition has increased among the United States, Japan, the EC, and the newly industrializing nations in Asia.

2. The responsibilities of government, management, labor, and consumers in returning the United States to international competitiveness.

3. The changes in the EC that are the basis of Europe 1992.

4. The magnitude of product counterfeiting.

5. Competitor analysis.

6. The sources of competitive information.

7. The channel members available to those who export indirectly or directly or manufacture overseas.

8. Structural trends in wholesaling and retailing.

9. Parallel importing.

10. The factors influencing channel selection.

11. The bases on which management compares channel alternatives.

KEY WORDS AND CONCEPTS

- National (macro) competitiveness
- Hit list (super 301)
- Keiretsu
- Industrial targeting
- European Economic Area
- Lomé Convention
- Generalized System of Preferences (GSP)
- Hollowing out
- Counterfeiting
- Reverse engineering
- Industrial espionage
- Competitor analysis
- Competitor intelligence system (CIS)
- Benchmarking
- Sogo shosha
- Export trading company (ETC)
- Cooperative exporters
- Manufacturers' agents
- Distributors
- Trading companies
- Parallel importers
- Gray market
- Hypermarkets
- Superstores

BUSINESS INCIDENT

THIS IS WAR! At least it is according to William Peacock, former assistant secretary of the U.S. Army and a colonel in the Marine Corps Reserve. He says that although society sets up rules to prevent unfair practices, and the objective is not to destroy your competitors, business and war have much in common. Executives should apply the nine principles of war (MOOSEMUSS) that have always brought victorious military campaigns:

1. *Mass*—concentrate your strength at the enemy's weak point.
2. *Objective*—you must be clear as to what you want to accomplish.
3. *Offense*—few competitions are won by passivity.
4. *Simplicity*—make your own strategy simple and clear for your employees.
5. *Economy of force*—the fewest resources possible to keep the operation functioning.
6. *Maneuver or strategy used*—frontal, flanking, or rear assault.
7. *Unity of command*—clear assignments of responsibility.
8. *Surprise*—timing of battle.
9. *Security*—keep your strategy secret.

It is apparent that many chief executives, a number of whom have military training, are following these concepts. Companies go to great lengths to keep their plans secret: IBM, for example, has a sign posted in its offices that shows two people at a lunch table and a warning, "Be careful in casual conversation. Keep security in mind." And, like the military, many have installed intelligence systems. Motorola, seeking a full-scale intelligence effort, hired a former CIA agent to organize its program. Its intelligence efforts paid off.

The company's top managers, in a meeting with the corporate intelligence people and European managers, raised the question, "Are you concerned about Japanese semiconductor makers?" One European manager said,

BUSINESS INCIDENT (concluded)

"We see the Japanese—they have operations in Europe. But they're not aggressive." This prompted the intelligence staff to wonder why the Japanese weren't as aggressive with semiconductors as they were with VCRs and TVs. Motorola sent one of its intelligence staff, fluent in Japanese, to Tokyo. By visiting the U.S. embassy and various government offices, he learned that Japanese electronic manufacturers did plan within the next two years to double their capital investment in Europe for semiconductor plants, not for more VCR and TV plants.

With this information, Motorola changed its strategy and began to work more closely with European manufacturers and customers and to compete vigorously with the Japanese for more partnerships in Europe. As a result, the company increased its market share even though the Japanese had begun their European assault.

Source: William Peacock, *Corporate Combat* (Berkeley, Calif.: Berkeley Publishing, 1987), pp. 1–12; P. Kotler and G. Armstrong, *Principles of Marketing,* 4th ed. (Englewood Cliffs, N.J.: Prentice-Hall, 1989), p. 93; "Competitive Intelligence Efforts on the Rise," *Marketing Communications,* January 20, 1987, p. 5; and "Corporate Spies Snoop to Conquer," *Fortune,* November 7, 1988, p. 76.

For a number of reasons, many of which were discussed in Chapter 2, world competition has intensified, and four nations and distinguishable groups of nations whose firms are in worldwide competition with each other have emerged: (1) the United States, (2) the European Community, (3) Japan, and (4) the newly industrializing countries (NICs), especially South Korea, Taiwan, Hong Kong, and Singapore (see the quotation at the beginning of this chapter).

Some writers talk of three areas by combining Japan and the Asian NICs. It is true that Japan has invested heavily in these nations and thus is well represented in the region. However, it is overly simplistic to talk of Japan and the Asian NICs as one trading bloc. In fact, an analysis of two groups in the Pacific as we shall make is not completely adequate. For example, there are very strong flows of trade among the Asian NICs as well as between the NICs and Association of South East Asian Nations (ASEAN) nations. The exports from Asian NICs to other Asian NICs and ASEAN nations are greater than their exports to Japan. In addition, their firms are important investors in ASEAN nations.

Moreover, there is no longer a division of labor only between Japan and the Asian NICs or Japan and the ASEAN countries. It has developed among the Asian NICs themselves and between the ASEAN nations and Asian NICs.

The company that manufactures shoes for Nike, L.A. Gear, and others is an Indonesian conglomerate trained by South Koreans who used to produce the shoes in Korea. When rising wages forced them to move from Korea, they made a deal to provide training and production machinery from their Korean factory.

By paying wages of $0.15 per hour to the Indonesian production workers, Nike can obtain the shoes that it sells in the United States for $75 to $150 per pair for just $5.60 per pair. Furthermore, by purchasing the shoes under contract, Nike has no capital investment. The only firms manufacturing athletic shoes in the United States are Saucony, Vans, and New Balance.[1]

Let us now examine the competition among the United States, the European Community, Japan, and the Asian NICs, first at the macro level (national competitiveness) and then at the micro (industry) level.

COMPETITION AT THE MACRO LEVEL (NATIONAL COMPETITIVENESS)

In the 1980s, there was great concern in the United States and Europe over the ability of these nations to compete in world markets. More recently, the strong yen has caused the same uneasiness in Japan. Nations, of course, do not compete against each other; their companies do. However, because most economic and social conditions, as well as political actions, affect the ability of all of a nation's firms to compete in world markets, it is convenient to speak of **national (macro) competitiveness.**

national (macro) competitiveness ability of a nation's producers to compete successfully in world markets and with imports in their own domestic markets

□ United States

Although the lag in national competitiveness did not become apparent until the 1980s, it began in the 1970s. During that time, imports were getting a bigger share of the market, but they were offset by a growing share of the export market achieved with a dollar whose value was dropping relative to other major currencies at an average annual rate of 2.5 percent. However, when the dollar's value rose at the beginning of the 1980s, American unit labor costs mounted, causing imports to increase and U.S. exports to decrease; not until 1985—when the dollar's value again declined—did labor costs begin to fall and American exports become more price competitive.[2]

During these years, American firms first experienced growing competition in this country from European and Japanese firms that were buying U.S. firms because the cheap dollar made them inexpensive in those countries' currencies. Moreover, the size of the market, the availability of raw materials, the developed capital markets, and the political stability combined to attract massive foreign investment, which created new competitors and strengthened old ones.

As the value of the dollar rose and U.S. firms experienced difficulty competing in both the U.S. and overseas markets, protectionist sentiment grew in this country, which provided additional impetus for foreign investors to set up U.S.-based operations. Of course, when the dollar again fell in the late 1980s, foreign firms that were still supplying this market with exports found it difficult to compete pricewise with domestic products, and thus they too established production in the United States. Those that did not lost either sales or profits if they cut prices to remain competitive. Japanese exporters of high-technology items, including automobiles, electronics, and computers, lost over 40 percent of their profits as they tried to meet U.S. prices in face of a yen that rose from 260 per dollar to 123 in just two years.[3]

Although the overvalued dollar was one of the principal reasons for the decrease in American competitiveness, it was not the only one. A number of nonprice factors, such as quality, delivery time, after-sales service, reliability of supply, and trade barriers to U.S. exports, were also responsible. It was obvious that to increase American exports, corrective measures had to be taken by government, management, and labor.

Government.   Government officials have for some time been pressuring other governments to lower their trade barriers and stimulate their economies to increase demand for American exports. As a result of American insistence, Germany lowered its discount rate, and Japan adopted several fiscal and monetary measures to encourage consumption. The U.S. government is also using the threat of retaliation more effectively. This caused Japan to stop dumping semiconductors into third markets and to open up its telecommunications market to American firms. The threat of retaliation has worked even better in Taiwan and Korea because they are more dependent on the American market than is Japan. Both have eliminated some trade barriers and have enacted laws to protect American patents, which is important because of the illegal copying of U.S. goods.

Hit list. The U.S. trade representative, acting under Section 301 of the 1988 Trade Act, nicknamed "super 301," may place nations on an unfair trading partner **hit list** for specific reasons. The law requires the government to negotiate with these countries on specific points and, if they are not resolved, to impose trade sanctions. In 1989, for example, Japan was designated specifically for resisting imports of satellites, supercomputers, and forest products; Brazil for requiring import licenses to protect local industry (90 percent of applications for importing capital goods are refused); and India for its barriers to foreign investment and foreign insurance companies. These cases were settled through negotiation. Japan agreed to buy American satellites, supercomputers, and more forest products but less timber, for instance. The threat of being placed on the hit list caused South Korea and Taiwan to make various concessions that the United States had requested.[4]

An example of ongoing negotiations are the discussions between Japan and the United States on the Structural Impediments Initiative, the effort begun in 1989 to deal with the root causes of the huge Japanese trade surplus with the United States. U.S. trade officials claim that the **keiretsu** system contributes to the huge trade imbalance between the United States and Japan.[5] A keiretsu is a group of large firms financially connected that tend to do business among themselves rather than with others.

Keiretsu. There are various forms of *keiretsu,* but two of the most important from the U.S. standpoint are (1) the vertically integrated production group as found in all the major Japanese automakers and (2) the horizontal group that is the present-day version of the pre-war *zaibatsu.* Although these family-owned conglomerates were broken up by the Allies after World War II, they continue to operate in much the same way because the Japanese government has never enforced the antimonopoly laws. This kind of keiretsu has a large bank at its core, and member-companies own minority interests in each other. Mitsui, Mitsubishi, Sumitomo, and Marubeni are examples.[6]

U.S. trade representative Carla Hills argues that keiretsu groups construct informal barriers to the sale of foreign goods in Japan. A keiretsu such as Toyota can assemble an automobile from parts supplied only by keiretsu members, for example. This makes it nearly impossible for potential suppliers outside the keiretsu to obtain business from Toyota. Many fear that Japanese firms are using the keiretsu system in the United States. The U.S. Federal Trade Commission is investigating whether Japanese automakers in the United States discriminate against U.S. firms for the benefit of keiretsu members who have set up American plants.[7]

Other efforts of the government to improve U.S. competitiveness include (1) stricter enforcement of dumping laws, (2) focusing on improvement of the nation's educational system, and (3) working to complete deregulation of industry (as an example from the trucking industry, a Dallas retailer pays *less*

---

hit list (super 301) Section 301 of the U.S. 1988 Trade Act, which requires U.S. trade representative to prepare a list of countries that systematically restrict access of American products to their markets

---

keiretsu a group of financially connected Japanese firms that tend to do business among themselves transportation costs to import a pair of jeans from Taiwan than it does to bring them in from Texas manufacturers in El Paso).

Complaints against the United States.   The United States has come under attack from its trading partners for ignoring GATT rules while insisting that GATT's dispute procedure be strengthened. In 1988, a GATT panel agreed with a complaint from the EC that Section 337 of the 1988 Trade Act discriminates against non-American patent holders. At four subsequent GATT meetings, American representatives have blocked adoption of the report.[8] A number of governments also complain about U.S. restrictions of the imports of automobiles, textiles, and steel. The Commission of the European Community publishes an annual report on the United States, *Trade Barriers and Unfair Trade Practices*.

Government must do more.   Critics, nonetheless, point out that more must be done. Some economists believe the most significant action the government can take to reduce the trade deficit is to lower the federal budget deficit, thereby decreasing the amount of savings consumed by the government.[9] But others claim a trade deficit was created because the U.S. demand for imports when its economy was strong was greater than the volume of American exports that the less robust foreign economies could buy.

The Competitiveness Policy Council, a panel created by Congress as part of the Trade Act of 1988, says the government must reform its policies concerning taxes, technology, education, trade, and health care. The council recommends the administration issue competitiveness impact statements for each bill it submits to Congress. The Trade Act mandated the competitiveness statements for a six-year trial period, but both the administration and Congress have ignored the requirement. The panel also recommends that American intelligence agenices be authorized to collect information on foreign competitors.[10]

Another measure suggested is to eliminate the double taxation of company profits. If shareholders' dividends aren't taxed, proponents say, more will be invested in America's industries. They want capital gains taxes brought back for the same reason. Some say the United States must have a national economic plan, but others compare this country's economic preference with that of countries having plans and say the less government involvement, the better. Legal experts recommend changes in U.S. antitrust laws to permit firms to finance, construct, and operate expensive high-tech production facilities jointly without fear of an antitrust suit. Such arrangements are becoming commonplace in Europe and Japan.

Research consortia are permitted in the United States, however, and in fact, the government is encouraging their formation. More than 100 research consortia have been formed by U.S. firms to foster development of products ranging from computers to light bulbs.[11]

Industrial targeting.   The government can also do more to support American companies that face competition from targeted industries. **Industrial targeting,** the practice of government assisting selected industries to grow by a variety of means, is becoming common in Europe and Japan. France, for example, modernized its railroad construction industry by modernizing its rail system. Equipment contracts were given only to French suppliers. By building a strong home base first, French suppliers were ready for the export market.

industrial targeting
government practice of assisting selected industries to grow

Increasingly, the U.S. mass transit market is being dominated by the French and the Japanese, both of whose governments support target industries. Another industry targeted by European nations is the manufacture of aircraft built around the Airbus, which is estimated to have received $6 billion in subsidies since the 1970s. A Boeing official states that the "Airbus was allowed to start a program without a sufficient order base and at production rates that would force a U.S. manufacturer to shut down."[12]

Accusations that Japan had targeted its aviation industry for world status arose when General Dynamics announced a plan to produce jointly with Mitsubishi Industries a U.S. fighter plane, the FSX, an improved version of the F-16. Instead of buying the F-16 from General Dynamics, as opponents of the arrangement argued it should, the Japanese government wanted joint Japanese-American development of the new plane. It guaranteed that the U.S. partner would get 40 percent of the aircraft's production as well as 40 percent of its research and development. Mitsubishi will also provide advanced radar and electronic warfare systems not currently available in the United States. Furthermore, it will not gain access to the F-16's computer software, which controls the plane's flight and weapons systems. General Dynamics expects to earn $480 million from the new plane's development and $2 billion from production of the 130 fighter planes.[13] There were arguments against the project from both sides. Japanese industry did not want the arrangement because Mitsubishi, the Japanese prime contractor of the plane, said it had the capability to design and build an airplane without foreign assistance.[14] Some representatives from Congress and industry objected that the United States was giving away its technology.

As you can see, the role of the government in improving the competitive position of American industry is significant; however, there is much that management, labor, and the consumers can do.

Management.   Company presidents must make product quality and increased productivity their top priorities. They must also prepare long-range strategic plans and be willing to invest long-term instead of expecting an immediate return, and they must be more aggressive against foreign competition.

It appears that there has been a marked change in how American executives assess the blame for the U.S. decline in competitiveness. A poll of Fortune 500 CEOs showed that nearly all believed it was their fault.[15] When asked what were the most important steps U.S. industry can take to improve its world competitiveness, 30 percent responded, "Improve quality"; 29 percent answered, "Improve productivity"; and 21 percent replied, "Increase R&D and modernize plants." One executive commented, "We make too many excuses rather than tailor our products to serve foreign markets."

However, look at some of the successful foreign products in Japan—Listerine™ mouthwash, Coca-Cola, McDonald's hamburgers, Kodak™ color film—and you will readily see that, aside from the packaging, they are essentially the same as in the United States, although many Japanese believe the local version is different. Given the number of books that tell the Japanese how special they are, logically they believe they should have distinct products. Japanese officials have again and again used the idea of Japanese uniqueness as an argument against imported goods. For example, a top poli-

WORLDVIEW
Industrial Targeting of Cutting Edge Technology

A major industrial nation entirely dependent on imported petroleum is offered high-tech metals that could save the country 25 million barrels of petroleum annually. Allied-Signal, based in New Jersey, developed amorphous metals that when used in transformer cores, permit the transformers to run much cooler, wasting only a third of the electricity that iron cores waste. Did Japanese utilities rush out to import this new electricity-saving metal? Although Japanese engineers wanted to buy it, Japanese officials told them to wait for American patents to expire so they could use homemade versions instead.

It was the latest chapter in a very familiar story. Instead of relying on a foreign supplier for a high-tech product, the Japanese government and a group of companies obstruct imports while they rush to clone the invention in Japan. Allied-Signal spent $100 million and 15 years developing the metal alloy used in transformer cores and in the heads of tape recorders and VCRs. The firm applied for a patent, but the Japanese government manipulated the patent process so that it took 11 years to obtain it. Meanwhile, the government organized and financed a group of 34 Japanese companies to develop a product to compete with the amorphous alloys and discouraged any purchase from Allied-Signal.

Look at some similar examples. In 1985, Monsanto was kept from entering the Japanese silicone wafer market until Japanese producers could catch up. The company sold its wafer division because it said it was not permitted to enter the Japanese market. Motorola was blocked when it tried to market its palm-size Micro TAC cellular telephone in Japan. It finally won its bureaucratic fight, but now Matsushita has even a smaller phone that it was able to design and produce during the time Motorola was trying to get governmental permission to sell its phone.

Finally, because American trade officials threatened to impose "super 301" sanctions on Japanese exports to the United States if the government continued to obstruct the sale of amorphous metals in Japan by Allied-Signal, the Japanese agreed to buy 32,000 amorphous metal transformers by 1993—less than ½ percent of the Japanese market. Who'll supply the rest? Allied-Signal? No way—they will be supplied in due time by Japanese companies. As *The Economist* stated, "To suspicious occidentals, fortress Japan is still a place where industry officials spill blood rather than surrender an inch to business intruders from abroad."

Source: "Japan's Latest End Run around Free Trade," *Business Week,* October 1, 1990, p. 32; "Low Tricks in High Tech," *The Economist,* September 29, 1990, p. 78; and "Allied-Signal Charges Japan Seeks to Bar U.S. Companies from a Lucrative Market," *The Wall Street Journal,* February 20, 1990, p. B1.

---

tician argued that Japanese cannot eat American beef because their intestines are longer than American intestines.[16] Another claimed that Japanese could not eat American tangerines because their intestines are too small. American cosmetics manufacturers had to have their products tested in Japan; U.S. tests were not valid because Japanese skin is different.

Marketing myths.   As we pointed out in the previous section, the American and the Japanese versions are the same for many products. Obviously, it is a marketing myth to claim that foreign products must always be adapted to local tastes. It is also a myth that Japanese cannot consume many imported products because they are very different people.

This myth is like another that has been told for many years. As the story goes, Chevrolet couldn't sell Novas in _____ (the storyteller picks a Spanish-speaking country) because Nova means *no va* (doesn't go) in Spanish. What the person doesn't realize is that the two are pronounced differently— Nova has the accent over the first syllable, whereas the accent for *no va* falls

Pemex gasoline doesn't go.

Donald Ball

on the *va*. Therefore, to someone speaking Spanish, the words are pronounced very differently and have very different meanings. You may be surprised to learn that Pemex, the government-owned oil monopoly that is the exclusive refiner and retailer of gasoline in Mexico, named its regular gasoline *Nova*.[17]

Labor.   Labor must also take the long-term view, and unions have done so in recent years. There has been a marked increase in their willingness to work with management instead of maintaining the traditional adversarial role. An example is the looser work rules. Workers can be transferred to another workstation when needed and can perform a simple maintenance job instead of calling a maintenance worker to do it while they wait and do nothing. Managers' efforts to share profits and to involve workers in decision making by means of quality circles and shop floor meetings have contributed to this change in attitude.

Consumers.   The U.S. consumer plays a very important part in American industry's drive to improve its competitiveness. Although American automobiles often cost less than comparable foreign models, American buyers seem to ignore the price advantage. As a result, the market share of General Motors, Ford, and Chrysler in the United States has declined to less than 70 percent.

It has been exceedingly frustrating to Chrysler dealers, for example, to see American buyers prefer the Mitsubishi Eclipse™ to the Plymouth Laser™ when they are identical sports coupes built by Diamondstar Motors, a Chrysler-Mitsubishi joint venture. A *Popular Mechanics* survey found that many Americans say they'd rather buy American rather than Japanese if the cars are similar. Yet, in a case where the cars are *identical,* not just similar, the Japanese outsells the American car. A dealer who owns both a Mitsubishi and a Chrysler dealership in the same city said, "People perceive the Japanese car to be better quality. It's a lot easier to sell an Eclipse than a Laser.[18] Foreign car buyers apparently don't realize that all U.S. automakers have gotten the message on quality. One Olds dealer says, "Our quality is good now. We've laid off mechanics because the warranty business is not there. But a few years ago, customers were lined up to get in for repairs."[19]

But it isn't only the American automakers that have the problem of convincing American consumers to buy their products. How about this example of schizophrenia? A secretary in Chicago said, "I resent foreigners coming in and taking over our country." But she recently bought a Mitsubishi color television and video recorder.[20] Meanwhile, Matsushita exports U.S.-made TV sets to Japan.

For the most part, Japanese manufacturers don't have this problem. Japanese consumers, unlike Americans, seem to have a bias against foreign goods. Look at the results of a poll conducted by a Tokyo research organization for *Fortune* magazine.[21]

1. Do you consider Japanese products superior to American products?
   Yes   71%
   No   11
   No opinion   18

2. Do you consider Japanese products superior to European products?
   Yes   72%
   No   11
   No opinion   17

3. Would you buy   Yes   No   No opinion

Would you buy	Yes	No	No opinion
an American car?	8%	86%	6%
a European car?	16	77	7
an imported TV?	3	91	6

Evidently, as Figure 13–1 illustrates, the bias against American goods does not extend to locally made products from American affiliates.

United States regaining competitiveness. The 1991 trade data show that many American firms have regained competitiveness. The trade deficit has gone from a record $146 billion in 1987 to just $7 billion in 1991. This includes a surplus in services of $49.5 billion and a surplus of $10 billion in net investment income, not quite enough to overcome the merchandise trade deficit of $66.8 billion.[22]

Three factors have combined to cause this great change in competitiveness:

1. The dollar's value with respect to other currencies has fallen by a third since 1985.

2. American productivity has risen strongly since 1982.

3. American wages have risen only an average of 3 percent between 1982 and 1990, compared to 10.5 percent in Japan and 9.7 percent in Germany.

The fastest growing markets for American exports are Europe, the Asian NICs, and most recently, Latin America. In 1991, the U.S. trade balance with Europe was $16 billion compared with a $23 billion deficit in 1985. The United States had its first trade surplus in 10 years with Germany, where American car imports doubled in a year.[23] Still U.S. exports amount to only 7

◻ **FIGURE 13–2   The European Economic Area (EC and EFTA) Takes In Some 380 Million Consumers**

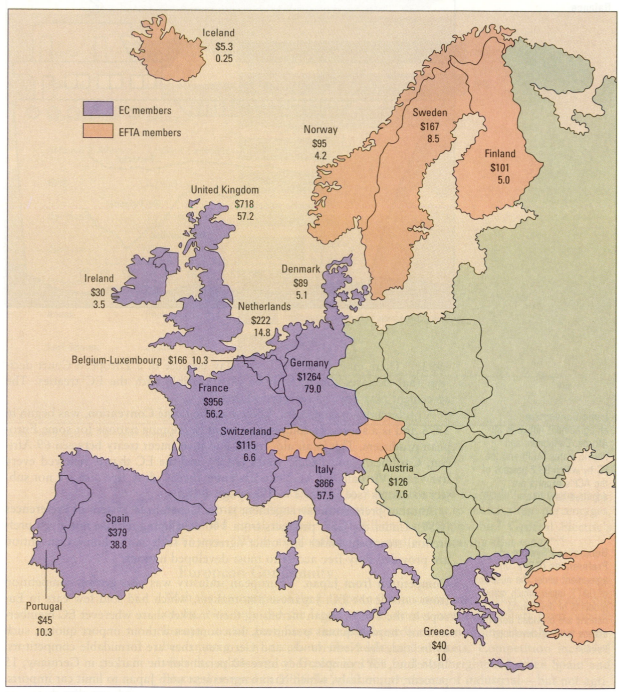

Iceland
$5.3
0.25

EC members
EFTA members

Norway
$95
4.2

Sweden
$167
8.5

Finland
$101
5.0

United Kingdom
$718
57.2

Denmark
$89
5.1

Ireland
$30
3.5

Netherlands
$222
14.8

Belgium-Luxembourg $166 10.3

Germany
$1264
79.0

France
$956
56.2

Switzerland
$115
6.6

Italy
$866
57.5

Austria
$126
7.6

Spain
$379
38.8

Portugal
$45
10.3

Greece
$40
10

Note: $00 is GDP in billion dollars.
          00.0 is population in millions.

Source: Data from *World Development Report, 1991* (New York: World Bank, 1991), pp. 205 and 209.

☐ FIGURE 13–3   Countries Linked to the EC in the Lomé Convention Trade-and-Aid Treaty

As you know, many Japanese firms have established production facilities in the United States because of the threat of protectionism, and now they have begun to produce in the EC for the same reason. Three Japanese car manufacturers, Nissan, Toyota, and Honda, have already set up factories in Great Britain, which by the mid-1990s should have a combined capacity of 500,000 cars a year.[31]

Not only automobiles.   Automobiles are only one facet of the Japanese onslaught in Europe. As in the United States, Japanese imports have nearly eliminated the European motorcycle industry. Japanese cameras and watches are market leaders, and every small color TV tube used in Europe is made by Japanese electronic companies with local production facilities.

Since 1982, Japanese exports to Europe have doubled—from $17 billion to over $40 billion. European firms have reacted by initiating a wave of dumping complaints to force the European Community to raise antidumping duties, but even more worrisome to Japanese exporters is the threat to include an "antiscrewdriver" provision in EC import regulations. European and also American officials complain that Japanese companies are avoiding dumping penalties by importing products in pieces involved at lower prices and assembling them with no more capital equipment than a screwdriver. Requiring higher local content would halt this practice, but it would also accelerate local investment by Japanese parts manufacturers, thus reducing the benefits that European firms could expect to receive from this provision. In fact, the EC's rules state that any car must have a minimum of 80 percent European content to be treated as European-made and therefore exempt from import quotas. What about automobiles made in the United States by Japanese companies? Fiat chairman Agnelli replies, "American car exports are welcome in Europe—provided they are American products, not Japanese cars made in the United States." In other words, U.S.-made Japanese cars will have to increase their American content from the present 55 percent average to be considered American exports in Europe.[32] The Mazda in 1992 was the first Japanese vehicle to be classified as a U.S. car under the federal fuel-economy rules. The new 626 assembled in Michigan has 75 percent U.S. content, which is the minimum for being an American car under the Corporate Average Fuel Economy Law.[33]

Competition from the United States.   European firms face competition from American exports like they do from Japan, but, unlike Japan, U.S. companies have had European-based manufacturing facilities for a long time. European-produced GM and Ford cars compete in the automobile market; brands such as Heinz, Kodak, and Coca-Cola are household names (the English "hoover" their rugs instead of vacuuming them); and computer manufacturers IBM and Digital Equipment dominate the market. Probably because of the long-term political and cultural ties plus the fact that European multinationals have been free to invest in the United States with minimum hindrance, American companies have generally been well accepted in Europe. The occasional EC–U.S. "chicken," "pasta," and "citrus" wars have not had a serious impact on the European subsidiaries of American globals and multinationals.

Yet, European governments are working to defend certain national companies from American competition. They have helped Airbus in its battle against Boeing and have funded the Joint European Submicron Silicon (JESSI), a semi-conductor consortium, to help European companies compete against American and Japanese chipmakers. IBM, which makes 35 percent of its chips in Europe, wants to join, but JESSI is resisting because Sematech—a U.S. consortium composed of 13 firms such as Texas Instruments, IBM, Motorola, Intel, and AT&T—refuses to admit foreigners.[34] However, and most important of all for American firms, the European Community is preparing for Europe 1992.

Europe 1992.   Three changes that have taken place are the basis of Europe 1992:

1. Europeans have come to realize that they cannot compete with the United States and Japan as long as EC markets are fragmented.

2. EC nations have agreed to trust each other sufficiently to reach a decision by majority vote rather than by unanimity, as was previously required.

3. They have recognized that the 12 member-nations could only become a single market by harmonizing safety, health, and other standards.[35]

One of the few generalizations that can be made about post–Europe 1992 is that competition is going to be much greater and that it will come from (1)

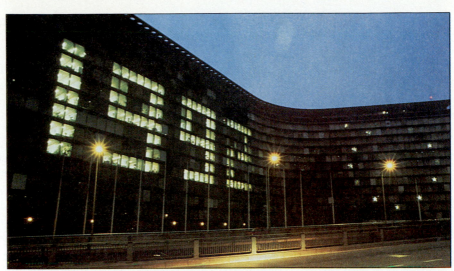

Signs announcing Europe 1992 are located throughout many cities.

Courtesy of European Community Delegation, Washington, D.C.

European firms made stronger by mergers, alliances, and acquisitions and (2) American and Japanese firms that are rushing to become established within the EC. Despite EC assurances to the contrary, many believe "fortress Europe" is a realistic threat because the whole object of Europe 1992 is to make the EC a true economic superpower. As a representative of British International Computers put it, "We shall buy from European sources whenever we can. We want to create a third force, like the United States and Japan, and frankly, we're going to use the same methods they've used for years."[36]

A counselor at the EC Delegation offices in Tokyo made a statement that troubles many Japanese firms: "We may well have to create a Community regime for very specific sectors which are still sensitive, where we cannot afford, in a period of high unemployment, to see an industry go under to the kind of laser beam torrential exports which we have suffered, only too painfully, in the past." This is something the Japanese understand, because they have protected various industries from foreign competition until they became world competitors. Fortunately for U.S. and Canadian firms, the U.S.–Canada Free Trade Agreement will give these nations more strength in dealing with the new EC.[37]

Competition from the Asian newly industrializing countries.   Much as Japanese firms have done, the Asian NICs have increased their exports—especially of electronics, textiles, and shoes—to Europe in the face of increasing U.S. pressure to lower their trade surpluses with the United States. The EC is Taiwan's second largest export destination. Only the United States is larger. However, the International Commercial Bank of China expects that Europe will become Taiwan's top trading partner.[38] Korea also has expanded the European share of its total exports at an annual rate of 23 percent since 1983. In 1987, for example, Korean firms sold 1.7 million microwave ovens, more than were produced in all of the EC. Hong Kong and Singapore have also made large gains in their EC exports. Low labor costs and favorable exchange rates have enabled manufacturers from all these countries to sell at prices at which European producers cannot compete. The European Commission found that Korean shoe manufacturers were underselling French firms by 70 percent. It put antidumping duties of almost 30 percent on VCRs made by Samsung, Daewoo, and Goldstar. Because the EC is fighting their predatory pricing, Korean firms are following the Japanese example of setting up plants inside the EC.[39]

▫ Japan

Thirty-eight percent of the textile manufacturers have shut down, and textile employment has halved. Cheap imports and a strong currency make it impossible for them to compete. They're accusing developing nations of dumping. And it is not only textiles—electrical appliances and cameras are also suffering. Walk into any mass marketer like Kmart and you no longer see foreign-made products with national brand names. Now those foreign manufacturers are putting their own brands on them.

Trying to remain competitive, national manufacturers are cutting prices (and their profits) and cutting costs by laying off workers and moving many operations overseas, where labor costs are lower. They've closed production facilities and slashed salaries and overtime pay. Unemployment is record high, and so are business failures. There are complaints that key industries are **hollowing out,** that is, closing their local production facilities and becoming marketing organizations for other, mostly foreign, producers. Complaints are being heard that the nation is becoming a service economy.[40]

hollowing out firms closing their production facilities and becoming marketing organizations for other, mostly foreign, producers

Japan is facing increased competition, too.   Is this the United States? No, this is Japan. In 1988, its industry faced increasing competition in foreign markets as well as at home. Much of it was caused by a strong yen, whose value doubled with respect to the dollar in only three years! In addition, pressure from Japan's trading partners to relax the legal and administrative barriers to imports and foreign investment has been a contributing factor. Japanese response has been tariff reductions, changes in the law that permit wholly owned subsidiaries, and a general streamlining of government administrative procedures.

These activities have resulted in a stepped-up involvement of foreign firms in the Japanese economy. In computers, for example, six American companies compete with Japanese producers for a share of the world's second-largest market. IBM once held first place, but because it has moved too slowly to introduce new products, it slipped to third place (15.7 percent market share) behind Fujitsu (23.1 percent) and NEC (18.6 percent). IBM continues to hold 30 percent of the Japanese mainframe market, however.[41] Worldwide, IBM's revenue in 1990 was $67 billion (see Table 13–1).

Another area of business in which American international firms have achieved significant market penetration is the restaurant industry. Fast-food chains, such as McDonald's, Kentucky Fried Chicken, and Denny's, have been so successful in what is described as a $34 billion market that they have appreciably altered Japanese dining habits. Multinationals such as PepsiCo, Exxon, Nestlé, and Coca-Cola have shown that the Japanese market is penetrable when time and money are spent first to investigate the market and then to make a long-term commitment to develop it. U.S. companies are rep-

☐ **TABLE 13–1**
Ranking of Top Ten
Computer Manufacturers
by 1990 Sales

World Rank	Company	Revenue ($ billions)
1	IBM (Am.)	$67,090
2	Digital (Am.)	13,072
3	Fujitsu (Jap.)	12,362
4	NEC (Jap.)	12,350
5	Hitachi (Jap.)	9,591
6	Unisys (Am.)	9,302
7	Hewlett-Packard (Am.)	9,300
8	Siemens-Nixdorf (Ger.)	7,735
9	Olivetti (Ital.)	6,415
10	Groupe Bull (Fr.)	6,350

Source: "The Datamation 100," *Datamation,* June 15, 1991, p. 11.

resented in over 85 percent of Japan's 126 industrial sectors, and 12 American companies hold the top market position in their fields.[42]

Japan has quality problems too. Following a government disclosure in 1990 that a Pioneer™ TV may have caused Japan's first major high-rise apartment fire, Japanese TV makers recalled dozens of models that smoked or caused fires. The maker of Epson™ laptop computers recalled 100,000 because they smoked. Meanwhile, various car and motorcycle manufacturers recalled several models of their products. Even Toyota's expensive Lexus™ was recalled in the United States because of brake-light and cruise-control problems. Why are Japanese producers having so many quality problems?

Experts say that because Japanese manufacturers must keep cutting costs to be competitive, they are including new components and materials with insufficient testing. Imported parts from other Asian countries may be the problem; or as some say, the fault lies with the erosion of the work ethic. A Chicago quality consultant says, "I've met people who have said, 'I've stopped buying Japanese electronic components . . . because the quality seems to have suffered.'" A managing director at a Japanese communications firm says, "Japanese quality is going downhill. In the past, Japanese factory workers who handled finished products wore gloves to keep the final packaging clean. Nobody bothers with that now, so you've got fingerprints all over everything."[43]

Expensive yen causes export problems. As you saw in the beginning of this section, Japanese manufacturers are finding their greatest challenge in the export market. The appreciation of the yen from 260 per dollar in 1985 to 123 per dollar in 1988 caused exporters' profits to decrease by more than 60 percent. Since then, the Japanese yen has depreciated by only 6 percent; thus prices in yen are still high compared to those in dollars.

The newly industrializing countries whose currencies have risen less against the dollar than has the yen are making serious inroads into Japanese export markets, especially the United States. South Korea has greatly increased both its U.S. and Japanese market share of television sets, steel, and VCRs.

□ **TABLE 13-2**
Average Annual Increases in Merchandise Exports for Selected Countries, 1965-1989 (Dollars in billions)

	Average Annual Growth Rate		
	1980-89	1965-80	Value in 1989
Turkey	11.4%	5.5%	$ 11.6
South Korea	13.8	27.2	62.3
Taiwan	14.9	19.0	66.0
China	11.7	5.5	52.5
Hong Kong	6.2	9.1	28.7
Thailand	12.8	8.6	20.1
Malaysia	9.8	4.6	25.1
Mexico	3.7	7.7	23.0
Canada	6.0	5.4	114.1
Singapore	8.1	4.7	44.6
Japan	4.6	11.4	275.0
Brazil	5.6	9.3	34.4
Germany	4.4	7.2	340.6
United States	2.3	6.4	347.0
EC (12)	5.9	2.1	1,125.9

Source: *World Development Report, 1991* (Washington, D.C.: World Bank, 1991), Table 14, pp. 230-31.

In response to this competition, Japanese firms have tried to maintain export market share by passing through to the buyers only part of the yen's appreciation against the dollar. As we would expect, this has caused a marked deterioration in the profit on sales to the United States.

Japanese firms are trying to avoid direct competition from the NICs by bringing to market sophisticated new products that justify higher prices, such as luxury automobiles and large-screen TVs. They also are building plants where labor costs are lower, and they are increasing their production facilities in the United States and Europe in order to build and invoice in the local currency rather than in yen.

□ Developing Nations

Not only have the Asian NICs greatly increased their merchandise exports, but certain developing nations have done so as well, as Table 13-2 illustrates.

Although the export growth of the Asian NICs should be no surprise, you might not have been aware that nations such as Turkey, Brazil, Thailand, Mexico, and China had made such sizable gains. You can also see from Table 13-2 why the rest of the world is following the development of Europe 1992, already the world's largest trading bloc. Thailand's export growth rate shows why this country is predicted to become another NIC shortly.

Counterfeiting.   A special kind of competition confronted by ICs in developing and developed nations is **counterfeiting.** The use of manufacturers' names on products that are copies of the genuine products is estimated to cost the legitimate owners over $70 billion annually and is especially prevalent in countries such as Korea, Hong Kong, Thailand, and Indonesia. Until recently, Taiwan was one of the major sources of counterfeit products; shoppers

counterfeiting illegal use of a well-known manufacturer's brand name on copies of the firm's merchandise

Cheseborough-Pond's   COUNTERFEIT

Fake hair tonic is just one of numerous counterfeit items flooding the world market.

Courtesy of Cheseborough-Pond's

couldn't tell Oranges and Pineapples from Apples. But after four years and more than 100 lawsuits against the product pirates, Apple has stopped the illegal copying of its computers.

Although Apple used a former narcotics agent and attorneys to locate and prosecute counterfeiters and their dealers, the company gives the Taiwanese government much of the credit for its success, as does General Motors, who says Taiwan's police have closed shops making fake GM parts.[44] A new law levies a $3,750 fine or a sentence of up to five years in jail for violators.

Counterfeit products can be dangerous.   Is your Polo shirt or Gucci handbag real? Easy-to-copy products with high markups, such as luxury goods (Gucci, Vuitton, and Cartier) have long been counterfeited, but products now routinely copied include pesticides, fertilizers, drugs, toys, car and airplane parts, and electronic items. Besides causing legitimate manufacturers to lose sales, these fakes sometimes bring tragedy to users when, as is frequent, they fail to perform as well as the original. Farmers in Zaire and Kenya bought what they thought was Chevron's top-quality pesticide, which turned out to be a fake made of chalk. The two countries lost two thirds of their cash crops for that year. Bell Helicopter found counterfeit parts in 600 helicopters sold to civilians and the military; it said some of them may have caused crashes. In Mexico, officials confiscated 15,000 counterfeit burn remedies because many contained sawdust or dirt and caused raging infections. Nigerian pharmacists estimate that over a quarter of the 4,000 different medicines in that market are fake. In Europe, hospitals and pharmacies dispensed millions of counterfeit doses of a cardiac medicine, some at only half the labeled strength.[45]

Combating imitations.   Levi Strauss has probably gone further than most firms to rid the market of imitations. The company has a corporate security organization with an annual million-dollar budget to stop this unfair competition. Levi Strauss was also instrumental in forming the International Anticounterfeiting Coalition (IAC), which now has 60 member-firms from 11 countries. Member-firms exchange information on problems they are encountering in certain markets and how they are handling them. The coalition lobbies in the United States and other countries to increase the penalties for commercial counterfeiting. Because of these efforts, U.S. Customs is now empowered to seize and destroy counterfeit goods when they are discovered at a point of entry.

In addition to the IAC, other industry groups are working to stop product counterfeiting. One is the Intellectual Property Committee comprising 13 of the largest U.S. patentholders, such as IBM, General Electric, and Pfizer (the pharmaceutical industry is one of the biggest victims of international piracy). Another group, the International Intellectual Property Alliance, represents 1,600 firms in the software, motion picture, computer, and book and music publishing industries. A third, Business Software Alliance, claims that illegal copies in such countries as Brazil, Taiwan, Mexico, India, and Korea cost its members $4.1 billion in lost sales annually.[46] Industry pressure was a significant factor in motivating the U.S. government to negotiate a worldwide agreement to protect intellectual property rights at the ongoing GATT meeting in Uruguay.

Industrial espionage.   Usually, a counterfeiter can copy a patent design by **reverse engineering** (taking the finished article apart), but when that is not feasible, the copier may obtain blueprints or process information by means of **industrial espionage.**

For years, companies have been acquiring information about each other by hiring competitors' employees, talking to competitors' customers, and so forth. More recently, however, intensified competition has motivated firms to become more sophisticated in this endeavor, even to the point of committing illegal acts. Mitsubishi, for example, was indicted on charges of stealing industrial secrets from Celanese, and Hitachi pleaded guilty to conspiring to transport stolen IBM technical documents to Japan.

The Soviet Union had a massive program to steal technology from American firms, especially those in the aircraft and computer industries. West Germans employed by Russia successfully moved semiconductor equipment from Silicon Valley through Western Europe to the U.S.S.R. Only 16 months after Boeing had flown its first short takeoff and landing plane (STOL), the Russians flew an exact copy with all of Boeing's breakthroughs in aerodynamic design.[47] Industrial espionage by foreign companies and governments is estimated to cost American industry $20 billion annually.

reverse engineering dismantling a competitor's product to learn everything possible about it

industrial espionage spying on a competitor to learn its trade and production secrets

COMPETITION AT THE INDUSTRY LEVEL

In looking at competition at the macro or national level, we examined factors affecting business generally; we will now look at competition at the micro or industry level. Interestingly, when studying the histories of certain industries, such as steel, electronics, industrial equipment, and electronics—all industries in which the United States is not the major player—you will find a similar set of circumstances.

▫ Steel Industry

After World War II, the U.S. steel industry possessed technological superiority over its international competitors. By 1955, the United States supplied 40 percent of the world's steel needs and imported only 1 percent of its domestic consumption. Thirty years later, however, the U.S. steel industry accounted for just 11 percent of the world's production, and over 25 percent of U.S. consumption was imported.[48] What caused this change?

Reasons for the decline in U.S. competitiveness.   First, many producers misjudged their demand prospects. Because the demand for steel is a derived demand (that is, sales depend on the demand for products using steel), managements failed to appreciate that the major growth industries, such as telecommunications, energy, aerospace, computers, and electronics, unlike the leading industries prior to 1950, were not intensive users of steel. They also failed to foresee the impact that the large increases in energy prices would have on the automotive industry, one of their largest customers. Lighter-weight and more corrosion-resistant materials, such as aluminum, plastics, and fiberglass, took a large share of their market. The amount of steel required to produce $1 of GDP in the United States fell by 4 percent annually from 1973 to 1984.

Second, during the 1970s and 80s, the developing nations more than doubled their steel output, which not only resulted in a loss of export markets for steelmakers in the United States and other industrialized nations but also gave them more competition in their home markets. Tables 13–3 and 13–4 illustrate what occurred.[49]

A third reason for the decline in U.S. competitiveness is past bad management. Look at some of its manifestations: (1) bad labor relations, (2) low productivity growth, (3) overgenerous wage settlements that were paid for by price increases, and (4) slow adoption of new technology. For example, a major technological innovation during the 1970s was the continuous-casting process, which reduces wastage of molten steel, lowers energy used, and produces more uniform quality. By 1984, only 40 percent of the U.S. steelmaking capacity used continuous casting, compared with 89 percent in Japan and 65 percent in the EC.[50]

Other problems have been burdensome environmental and other governmental regulation and, at times, unfavorable exchange rates.

Japan's steel industry.   In answer to the strong yen in the mid-1980s, Japan's five major steel companies drastically cut their work forces and restructured themselves to be among the most efficient producers in the world. They bought into American steel producers to have a share of the Japanese automobile "transplants" market in the United States. They also invested heavily in automation and in making higher-margin products such as stainless and coated steels. However, their most serious competition, just as in the United States, is coming from minimills, small mills with lower production costs that make the lower grades of steel (construction) from scrap steel in electric furnaces instead of the enormous and expensive blast furnaces.

Interestingly, they tried the same strategy of diversification that some American steel companies followed, but with disastrous results. All have

□ **TABLE 13–3**
World Production of Raw Steel (Percentage share)

	United States	EC	Japan	Other Industrial Countries	LDCs	Communist Nations
1950	47%	26%	3%	4%	2%	19%
1960	26	28	6	5	3	31
1970	20	23	16	6	5	30
1980	14	18	16	7	10	36
1985	11	17	15	6	12	38

□ **TABLE 13–4**
Share of U.S. Imports (Percent of apparent U.S. supply)

	Total	Japan	EC	LDCs	Other*
1955	1.2%	0.1%	0.8%	—	0.3%
1965	10.4	4.4	4.9	0.2%	0.9
1975	13.5	6.6	4.6	0.6	1.7
1985	25.2	6.2	7.2	5.3	6.0

*Includes industrial countries other than Japan and the EC, plus communist countries.
Source: "The Decline of the U.S. Steel Industry," *Finance & Development,* December 1987, p. 31.

started manufacturing semiconductors or semiconductor production equipment. Their combined losses in 1990 were $1.5 billion. Another problem has been the loss of profitable sales of stainless steel. South Korea, whose huge Pusan steel company has begun producing stainless steel, now is an exporter. For years, the country imported large quantities from Japan. Taiwan's steel plant has doubled its stainless steel capacity, therefore closing another export market for Japanese suppliers.[51]

Recipe for survival.   To survive, steel producers in the industrialized nations know they must restructure their operations. In the United States, the industry has reduced production capacity by 27 percent, reduced employment by half, and invested $11 billion to make it the world's most productive. Bethlehem Steel is an example: it has slashed jobs, closed old mills, and invested billions of dollars in upgrading those mills that remain. Management has formed teams of hourly and salaried employees who get customer input so they can solve quality problems. With pay incentives tied to profits, workers now monitor production lines to prevent errors instead of waiting to reject bad steel after it is made. These changes have reduced the percentage of steel rejected by Ford from 8 percent to 0.8 percent. Bethlehem's CEO says, "We will not be satisfied until it's zero."

European steelmakers are expanding their activities in the United States because they are realizing that exporting steel is not good enough for the U.S. car and appliance makers—some of the largest steel consumers in the world. These manufacturers want steel suppliers close by to make just-in-time deliveries and collaborate on product development. France's Usinor Sacilor, the world's second-largest steelmaker after Japan's Nippon Steel, has been in this country for 50 years selling their steel from France, but now it has purchased several midsized specialty steelmakers that sell to the auto industry. Italy's Ilva, Europe's third-largest steelmaker, is studying the American market because, as its chairman says, "The U.S. is one of the best markets for steel. We have to be in all major markets because competition is global."[52]

Minimills—the new competitors. Despite the great progress the large American steelmakers have made in lowering costs and increasing productivity, they still face the minimills that do not make steel from iron ore, thus requiring huge blast furnaces, but use the less expensive electric furnaces to melt down scrap steel.

While the minimills made only construction steel, the large integrated mills did not try to compete because the big money was in the high-quality sheet steel supplied to automakers and appliance manufacturers. But now Nucor, an innovative minimill, is producing a high-quality sheet steel directly from molten metal instead of first casting the hot steel into slabs and then rolling them into sheet steel as the large mills do. Nucor's new mill produces sheet steel of such high quality that it intends to sell it for auto bodies. Says Nucor's general manager, "We're Big Steel's worst nightmare, and we're not going away."[53] While "Big Steel" boasts that it can produce steel in just under three hours, the Nucor minimill regularly rolls out a ton of steel in 54 minutes.

Japanese steel executives who boasted that their more modern plants would bury Bethlehem are impressed that Bethlehem makes steel in only 2.8 hours, a record their plants have not yet matched. Said one executive to a Japanese newspaper after he had visited Bethlehem: "We have to be more humble."[54] There is no record of any Japanese comment on Nucor's production time.

ANALYSIS OF THE COMPETITIVE FORCES

"The biggest single problem in international planning is the lack of efficient and good competitive information.[55] This is the conclusion of *Business International's* study of 90 worldwide companies. The study also found that many companies have no organized approach to global competitive assessment; whatever is done is diffused among the various parts of the company. The Conference Board found, however, that more companies are establishing systematic methods for tracking competitive activity, and, according to a recent Fortune 500 survey, 82 percent of the executives questioned considered a competitor analysis program to be very important.[56]

□ Is Competitor Assessment New?

Sales and marketing managers have always needed information about their competitors' products, prices, channels of distribution, and promotional strategies to plan their own marketing strategies. Sales repesentatives are expected to submit information on competitors' activities in their territories as part of their regular reports to headquarters. It also has been common practice to talk to competitors' customers and distributors, test competitors' products, and stop at competitors' exhibits at trade shows. Larger firms maintain company libraries whose librarians regularly scan publications and report their findings to the functional area they believe would have an interest in the information.

One of the writers was working at Goodyear when a librarian reported reading about a patent application for vulcanizing hose that Dunlop, a competitor, had filed in South Africa. The process, although new, had already been patented elsewhere. She reasoned correctly that this new application in South Africa indicated Dunlop was preparing to use the process, which would enable it to produce a better-quality product at a lower price in its South African plant.

Inasmuch as the Goodyear–South Africa facility had nothing to equal it, the process would give Dunlop a strong competitive advantage. Headquarters immediately notified the South African affiliate, which hurredly modernized its vulzanization process. By the time Dunlop installed its new process, the local Goodyear plant was ready. Thanks to an alert librarian, Dunlop failed to gain the competitive advantage it had expected.

Inasmuch as gathering information about the competition has been going on for so long, what is different about present-day **competitor analysis?** Essentially, the difference lies in top management's recognition that (1) increased competition has created a need for a broader and more in-depth knowledge of competitors' activities and (2) the firm should have a **competitor intelligence system** (CIS) for gathering, analyzing, and disseminating information to everyone in the firm who needs it. Moreover, many firms hire consultants or firms specializing in competitor analysis to provide information, and others send employees to seminars to learn how to do it themselves. Some even employ former CIA agents or investigators to handle data gathering and analysis (recall Motorola in the Business Incident).

◻ Sources of Information

There are five sources of information about the strengths, weaknesses, and threats of a firm's competitors: (1) within the firm, (2) published material, (3) customers, (4) competitors' employees, and (5) direct observation or analyzing physical evidence of their activities.[57] These sources are all used in the United States and other industrialized countries, but they can be especially helpful in developing nations, which usually have a paucity of published information.

Within the firm.   As we mentioned previously, a firm's sales representatives are the best source of this kind of information. Librarians, when firms have them, can also provide input to the CIS. Another source is the technical and R&D people, who, while attending professional meetings or reading their professional journals, frequently learn of developments before they are general knowledge. Incidentally, government intelligence agencies from all countries subscribe to and analyze other nations' technical journals.

Published material.   We mentioned technical journals, but other types of published material can also provide valuable information. Business data bases provide information from SEC reports, annual reports, patent information, balance sheets, and so forth. England's Economist Intelligence Unit and the U.S.'s Predicast publish useful industry reports; and under the Freedom of Information Act, American firms and their foreign competitors can get information about companies from public documents. Aerial photographs of competitors' facilities are often available from the EPA or the U.S. Geological Survey if the company is near a waterway or has done an environmental impact study. The photos may reveal an expansion or the layout of the competitor's production facilities. Be careful not to take unauthorized aerial photographs—this is trespassing and is illegal.

Customers.   Companies frequently tell their customers in advance about new products to keep them from buying elsewhere, but often the customer passes this information on to competitors. For example, Gillette told a Canadian distributor when it planned to sell its new disposable razor in the United States. The distributor called BIC, who hurried its development and was able to begin selling its own razor shortly after Gillette did.[58]

A company's purchasing agent can ask its suppliers how much they are producing or what they are planning to produce in the way of new products. Because buyers know how much their company buys, any added capacity or new products may be for the firm's competitors. They can also allege that they are considering giving a supplier new business if the sales representative can prove the firm has the capacity to handle it. Salespeople often are so eager for the new business that they divulge their firm's total capacity and the competitor's purchases to prove they can handle the order.

Competitors' employees.   Competitors' employees, actual or past, can provide information. Experienced human relations people pay special attention to job applicants, especially recent graduates, who reveal they have worked as interns or in summer jobs with competitors. They sometimes reveal proprietary information unknowingly. Companies also hire people away from competitors, and unscrupulous ones even advertise and hold interviews for jobs they don't have to get information from competitors' employees.

Direct observation or analyzing physical evidence.   Companies sometimes have their technical people join a competitor's plant tour to get details of the production processes. A crayon company sent employees to tour a competitor's plants under assumed names. Posing as potential customers, they easily gained access and obtained valuable information about the competitor's processes; admittedly, this was unethical, although standing outside a plant to count employees and learn the number of shifts a competitor is working is not considered unethical.

We have already mentioned the common practice of reverse engineering, which is an example of analyzing physical evidence, but intelligence analysts even buy competitors' garbage. It is illegal to enter a competitor's premises to collect it, but it is permissible to obtain refuse from a trash hauler once the material has left the competitor's premises. Another interesting analysis was done by a Japanese company that sent employees to measure the thickness of rust on train tracks leaving an American competitor's plant. They used the results to calculate the plant's output.[59]

Governments have often used their espionage networks to spy on American firms. For example, an FBI–CIA team learned that French spies had infiltrated the European offices of IBM, Texas Instruments, and other electronics firms and passed information to Groupe Bull, the French government–owned computer firm. The spies were fired.[60] An NBC report, "Expose," also quoted U.S. intelligence specialists who said that American businesspeople should not fly Air France because of possible bugged seats and French government spies posing as passengers and flight personnel. On the same program, a man said that after being named the French intelligence chief in 1981, he organized an espionage network to help acquire foreign companies' secrets for French businesses.[61]

You have noticed that we have pointed out when an act is legal or illegal and we have also commented on whether, in our opinion, it was ethical.

Certainly, businesspeople have a responsibility to use all ethical means to gather information about their competitors. The Japanese owe much of their rapid progress in high technology to their ability to gather information. Mitsubishi occupies two floors of a New York office building in which dozens of people screen technical journals and contact companies for brochures and other materials. Mitsubishi and other large Japanese firms do their own microfilming, which they send to their Tokyo headquarters for analysis.[62]

Benchmarking.   This is an increasingly popular way for firms to measure themselves against world leaders. Whereas competitor analysis will help the firm spot differences between its performance in the market and that of its competitors, it does not provide a deep understanding of the processes that cause these differences.

Benchmarking involves several stages:

1. Management examines the firm for the aspects of the business that need improving.
2. It then looks for companies that are world leaders in performing similar processes.
3. The firm's representatives visit those companies, talk with managers and workers, and determine how they perform so well. Because the people who are going to use the newly acquired knowledge are line personnel, they, not staff people, should make these visits.

The problem, of course, is whom to use as a benchmark. Some firms have been successful in choosing companies in their own industries, but often the ideal benchmark is in a completely different industry. A computer manufacturer that wanted to improve its distribution system found a benchmark in a large retailer.[63] Xerox's investigation of leading Japanese manufacturers in a variety of industries has led to some basic changes in its relations with suppliers and how it develops products.[64]

Although sometimes a visit to another firm will provide an idea that can be used without change, generally some adaptation will be needed. The basic purpose of benchmarking is to make managers and workers less parochial by exposing them to different ways of doing things so as to encourage creativity.

benchmarking a technique for measuring a firm's performance against the performance of others who may be in the same or a completely different industry

DISTRIBUTIVE FORCES

The channels of distribution—systems of agencies through which a product and its title pass from the producer to the user—are both controllable and uncontrollable variables. We shall discuss the uncontrollable aspects in this section where we examine all the uncontrollable forces and then return to them in Chapter 15 when we consider them as controllable variables in the marketing mix.

How can the channels of distribution be both controllable and uncontrollable forces? They are controllable to the extent that the channel captains are free to choose from the available channels those that will enable them to reach their target markets, perform the functions they require at a reasonable cost, and permit them the amount of control they desire.* If the established channels are considered inadequate, they may assemble different networks.

* The *channel captain* is the dominant and controlling member of a channel of distribution.

Coca-Cola, dissatisfied with the complex Japanese system of distributing through layers of wholesalers, created its own system in which 17 bottlers sell directly to over 1 million retailers. The dramatic reduction in distributive costs coupled with the fact that each bottler was well versed in its own market enabled Coca-Cola to obtain 60 percent of the Japanese market. Note, however, that although a new system was created, new agencies were not.

The distributive *structure,* the agencies themselves, is generally beyond the marketer's control, so it must use those that are available. Yet new agencies are occasionally created when the established institutions do not fulfill the channel captain's requirements.

UK automaker Austin Rover, long established in Germany, had lost 60 percent of its dealers because of a low-quality image. Although its new models had achieved European-wide success, its German dealers managed to sell only 0.15 percent of the market. Searching for a novel approach, Austin Rover concluded a deal with Massa, Germany's largest retailer and owner of 27 hypermarkets (huge combination supermarkets/discount stores), under which Massa was to build showrooms and service departments at each of its store sites. The enormous advertising power obtained through Massa's newspapers, delivered to 5.5 million households, coupled with Massa's reputation for quality enabled the chain to sell 800 cars the first month. Rover expects Massa to sell more cars than all of its 200 traditional dealers.[65]

INTERNATIONAL CHANNEL OF DISTRIBUTION MEMBERS

The selection of channel of distribution members to link the producer with the foreign user will depend first of all on the method of entry into the market. In Chapter 2, you learned that to do business overseas, a firm must either export to a foreign country or manufacture in it. If the decision is to export, the firm may do so *directly* or *indirectly*. Figure 13−4 shows that management has considerable latitude in forming the channels.

▫ Indirect Exporting

For indirect exporting, a number of U.S.-based exporters (A) sell for the manufacturer, (B) buy for their overseas customers, (C) buy and sell for their own account, or (D) purchase on behalf of foreign middlemen or users. Although each type of exporter usually operates in the following manner, any given company may actually perform one or more of these functions.

A. Exporters that sell for the manufacturer.
   1. *Manufacturers' export agents* act as the international representatives for various noncompeting domestic manufacturers. They usually direct promotion, consummate sales, invoice, ship, and handle the financing. They are commonly paid a commission for carrying out these functions in the name of the manufacturer.
   2. *Export management companies* (EMCs), formerly known as combination export managers (CEMs), act as the export department for several noncompeting manufacturers. They will also transact business in the name of the manufacturer and handle the routine details of shipping and promotion. When the EMC works on a commission basis, the manufacturer invoices the customer directly and carries any financing required by the foreign

☐ **FIGURE 13–4   International Channels of Distribution**

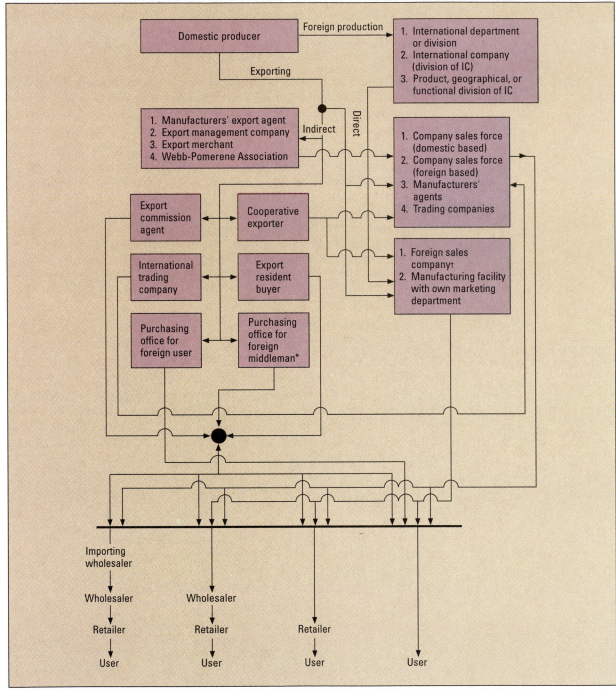

*There should be no direct connection between this category and the user. For simplification, a separate line to eliminate the user is not shown.

†Can be wholly owned or a joint venture. The foreign sales company may sell imports as well as local production from licensee, contract manufacturer, or joint venture.

‡Can be wholly owned, joint venture, or a licensee.

Colonel Sanders in Japan (a joint venture with Mitsubishi Corporation, a sogo shosha)

Courtesy of R. J. Reynolds

buyer. However, most EMCs work on a buy-and-sell arrangement under which they pay the manufacturer, resell the product abroad, and invoice the customer directly. Depending on the arrangement, the EMC may act in the name of the firm it represents or in its own name.

3. *International trading companies* are similar to EMCs in that they also act as agents for some companies and as merchant wholesalers for others. This, however, is only part of their activities. They frequently export as well as import, own their own transportation facilities, and provide financing. W. R. Grace was at one time a major trading company that operated on the Pacific coast of South America. It owned sugar mills, large import houses, various manufacturing plants, a steamship company, and an airline. Although there have been a number of European and American international trading companies in operation for centuries, certainly the most diversified and the largest are the Japanese **sogo shosha** (general trading companies).

a. *Sogo shosha.* The general trading companies were originally established by the *zaibatsu*— centralized, family-dominated economic groups, such as Mitsui, Mitsubishi, and

sogo shosha the largest of the Japanese general trading companies

Sumitomo—to be the heart of their commercial operations. The head of Mitsui, for example, established a general trading company, Mitsui Bussan, at the same time (1870s) that he created the Mitsui Bank. Both institutions served as the nucleus for the rest of the Mitsui empire. The general trading companies obtained export markets, raw materials, and technical assistance for other companies of the zaibatsu and also imported goods for resale. Included in the zaibatsu in addition to banks and general trading companies were transportation, insurance, and real estate companies and various manufacturing firms. In 1933, 6.2 percent of Japan's social overhead capital belonged to four major zaibatsu—Mitsui, Mitsubishi, Yasuda, and Sumitomo. Although the zaibatsu were forced to dissolve after World War II, the companies that had been their major components survived.

The largest general trading company is Mitsui & Co. This sogo shosha has $150 billion in sales and employs 12,000 persons throughout the world. It also has equity investments in more than 620 companies in Japan and 320 overseas.[66]

Although Mitsui & Co. is huge, it is only one company in the Mitsui Group (formerly the Mitsui zaibatsu), which consists of several hundred companies whose activities range from steelmaking and shipbuilding to banking and insurance, from paper to electronics, and from petroleum to warehousing, tourism, and nuclear energy. The Mitsui Group is not a legal entity but exists as an informal organization of major enterprises that have related interests and related financial structures. They cooperate in promoting the economic interests of group members. To ensure cooperation, the top executives of the 68 major components of the former Mitsui zaibatsu meet for a weekly luncheon.[67] Interestingly, the American subsidiaries of Mitsubishi and Mitsui together account for 10 percent of *all* U.S. exports.

b. *Korean general trading companies.* Many general trading companies are owned by the huge Korean diversified conglomerates called *chaebol,* which are similar in scope to the Japanese sogo shosha. They are responsible for a major part of Korea's exports and are also the principal importers of key resources.

c. *Export trading company.* In 1982, the Reagan administration, impressed by the success of the Japanese, Taiwanese, and Korean general trading companies, worked closely with Congress to obtain the passage of the Export Trading Company Act. The measure provides the mechanism for creating a new indirect export channel, the **export trading company** (ETC). For the first time in U.S. history, businesses were permitted to join together to export goods and services or offer export-facilitating services without fear violating antitrust legislation. Bank holding companies may also participate in ETCs. This not only increases the ability of trading companies to finance export transactions but also gives them access to the banks' extensive international information systems. Furthermore, because ETCs can import as well as export, they can engage in countertrade by selling their customers' products in other markets.[68]

export trading company (ETC) a firm established principally to export domestic goods and services and to assist unrelated companies to export their products

Any potential exporter may apply to the Department of Commerce for a *certificate of review,* a legal document that provides immunity from state and federal antitrust prosecution and significant protection from certain private antitrust lawsuits. The certificate allows firms and associations to engage in joint price setting and joint bidding and gives them the freedom to divide up export markets among companies and jointly own warranty, service, and training centers in various overseas markets. Note that the benefits of the ETC Act are available to *all exporters,* not just export trading companies.[69]

The Commerce Department has issued over 100 certificates covering 4,400 companies. Most companies that have received certificates are export intermediaries for two or more firms from the same industry, although now the majority of the certificates are being issued to groups of companies. For example, the National Tooling and Machining Association, a national trade association with 3,150 members, received a certificate in 1988. The American Film Marketing Association (67 members) is another example.

B. Exporters that buy for their overseas customers.
   Export commission agents represent overseas purchasers, such as import firms and large industrial users. They are paid a commission by the purchaser for acting as resident buyers in industrialized nations.

C. Exporters that buy and sell for their own account.
   1. *Export merchants* purchase products directly from the manufacturer and then sell, invoice, and ship them in their own names so that foreign customers have no direct dealing with the manufacturer, as they do in the case of the export agent. If export merchants have an exclusive right to sell the manufacturer's products in an overseas territory, they are generally called *export distributors.* Some EMCs may actually be export distributors for a number of their clients.

   2. Sometimes called piggyback or mother hen exporters, **cooperative exporters** are established international manufacturers that sell the products of other companies in foreign markets along with their own. Carriers (exporters) may purchase and resell in their own name, or they may work on a commission basis. Carriers, like EMCs, serve as the export departments for the firms they represent. Large companies, such as General Electric and Borg-Warner, have been acting as piggyback exporters for years. A single carrier usually represents between 10 and 20 suppliers, though there is one large manufacturer of industrial machinery that has more than 1,000!

   3. *Webb-Pomerene Associations* are organizations of competing firms that have joined together for the sole purpose of export trade. The Export Trade Act of 1918 provides for the formulation of such groups and generally exempts them from antitrust laws. They are permitted to buy from the members and sell abroad, set export prices, or simply direct the promotional activities that are destined for overseas markets. At this time, there are only 30 associations, of which those in phosphate rock, wood pulp, movies, and sulfur are the most active. The Webb-Pomerene Associations failed to

cooperative exporters
established international manufacturers who export other manufacturers' goods as well as their own

become an important export channel because (1) the antitrust exemption was very vague and (2) the exporting of services was not included. The intent of the Export Trading Act is to remedy these deficiencies.

D. Exporters that purchase for foreign users and middlemen.
   1. Large foreign users, such as mining, petroleum, and international construction companies, buy for their own use overseas. The purchasing departments of all the worldwide companies are continually buying for their foreign affiliates, and both foreign governments and foreign firms maintain purchasing offices in industrialized countries.
   2. *Export resident buyers* perform essentially the same functions as export commission agents. However, they are generally more closely associated with a foreign firm. They may be appointed as the official buying representatives and paid a retainer, or they may even be employees. This is in contrast to the export commission agent, who usually represents a number of overseas buyers and works on a transaction-by-transaction basis.

□ Direct Exporting

If the firm chooses to do its own exporting, it has four basic types of overseas middlemen from which to choose: (A) manufacturers' agents, (B) distributors, (C) retailers, and (D) trading companies. These may be serviced by sales personnel who either travel to the market or are based in it. If the sales volume is sufficient, a foreign sales company may be established to take the place of the wholesale importer. The manufacturing affiliates of most worldwide companies also import from home country plants or from other subsidiaries products that they themselves do not produce.

A. *Manufacturers' agents* are residents of the country or region in which they are conducting business for the firm. They represent various noncompeting foreign suppliers, and they take orders in these firms' names. **Manufacturers' agents** usually work on a commission basis, pay their own expenses, and do not assume any financial responsibility. They often stock the products of some of their suppliers, thus combining the functions of agent and wholesale distributor.

manufacturers' agents independent sales representatives of various noncompeting suppliers

B. *Distributors* or wholesale importers are independent merchants that buy for their own account. They import and stock for resale. **Distributors** are usually specialists in a particular field, such as farm equipment or pharmaceuticals. They may be given exclusive representation and, in return, agree not to handle competing brands. Distributors may buy through manufacturers' agents when the exporter employs them, or they may send their orders directly to the exporting firm. Instead of manufacturers' agents, exporters may employ their own salespeople to cover the territory and to assist the distributors. For years, worldwide companies such as Caterpillar, Goodyear, and Goodrich have utilized field representatives in export territories.

distributors independent importers that buy for their own account for resale

C. *Retailers,* especially of consumer products requiring little after-sales servicing, are frequently direct importers. Contact on behalf of the exporter is maintained either by a manufacturers' agent or by the exporter's sales representative based in the territory or traveling from the home office.

D. *Trading companies* are relatively unknown in the United States but are extremely important importers in other parts of the world. In a number of African nations, **trading companies** are not only the principal importers of goods ranging from consumer products to capital equipment, but they also export such raw materials as ore, palm oil, and coffee. In addition, they operate department stores, grocery stores, and agencies for automobiles and farm machinery. Although many trading companies are large, they are in no way comparable in either size or diversification (products and functions performed) to the sogo shosha.

> **trading companies** firms that develop international trade and serve as intermediaries between foreign buyers and domestic sellers and vice versa

Trading companies in Brazil, Korea, Taiwan, and Malaysia are a recent development. They are of little use to exporters to these countries, inasmuch as their primary function is to promote their own country's exports. On the other hand, the English *importer/factor,* which performs some of the functions of a trading company, is of value to exporters. It will, on behalf of foreign manufacturers, warehouse goods, price them for the local market, deliver anywhere in the country, and factor (buy the seller's accounts receivable). The exporter must still develop the sales, however.

Another form of trading company is owned by the state. State trading companies handle all exports and imports in China, Vietnam, and Cuba; and in noncommunist nations where an industry is a government monopoly, such as petroleum in Mexico, exporters or their agents must deal with these government-owned entities.

▫ Foreign Production

When the firm is selling products produced in the local market, whether they are manufactured by a wholly owned subsidiary, a joint venture, or a contract manufacturer, management is concerned only with the local channels of distribution. Generally, the same types of middlemen are available as in the home country, although the established channels and their manner of operating may differ appreciably from that to which management is accustomed. Differences between the foreign and domestic environmental forces are responsible.

Wholesale institutions.   In other developed nations, as in the United States, the marketer will be able to select wholesalers that take title to the goods (merchant wholesalers, rack jobbers, drop shippers, cash-and-carry wholesalers, truck jobbers) and those that do not (agents, brokers). However, just as in the United States, as retailers have become larger, they have sought to bypass wholesalers to purchase directly from local manufacturers and foreign suppliers. Direct imports accounted for 10 percent of 1988 sales at Daiei, Japan's largest store chain, and they are rising 30 percent annually.[70] They accounted for an even higher percentage—16 percent—for Japan's 1,600 largest department stores and supermarkets, who either import directly or buy from an importer. In contrast, few foreign products are stocked by small retailers (four clerks or less), who compose 75 percent of the Japanese retailers

□ **TABLE 13–5   Wholesaling and Retailing in Selected Countries**

Country	Number of Wholesalers	Employees per Wholesaler	Population per Wholesaler	Number of Retailers	Employees per Retailer	Population per Retailer	Ratio of Retailers to Wholesalers
United States (1985)	416,000	12.0	557	1,410,000	11.4	170	3.4
Austria (1985)	13,019	11.6	590	36,039	6.2	211	2.8
Brazil (1980)	46,000	9.6	2,630	885,600	2.2	143	19.3
Chile (1983)	561	28.3	20,600	1,125	21.2	10,300	2.0
El Salvador (1983)	396	16.9	131,300	1,416	8.5	3,672	3.6
Finland (1983)	5,400	14.5	888	35,800	5.1	134	6.6
France (1984)	79,700	4.0	689	608,600	1.9	90	7.6
Greece (1983)	24,400	2.0	406	164,400	1.8	60	6.7
Hungary (1982)	17,500	11.4	611	55,400	6.0	193	3.2
Italy (1983)	113,600	4.6	500	1,266,000	n.a.	45	11.1
Japan (1985)	413,000	9.7	292	1,629,000	3.9	74	3.9
Korea (1982)	45,568	3.8	862	542,458	1.7	72	11.9
Norway (1984)	16,429	6.3	250	34,784	3.6	118	2.1
Philippines (1981)	20,642	7.6	2,403	280,000	2.5	173	13.6
Portugal (1981)	6,600	21.0	1,506	14,800	8.2	672	2.2
Spain (1982)	35,700	9.1	1,061	371,800	3.3	102	10.4
Sweden (1984)	31,960	6.2	260	83,640	3.6	99	2.6
Swaziland (1984)	67	16.5	11,220	656	6.9	1146	9.8
United Kingdom (1984)	70,600	12.4	718	337,700	6.5	167	4.3

Source: *Statistical Yearbook,* 1986 (New York: United Nations, 1988), pp. 656–70.

and are supplied by the usual chain of primary to secondary to tertiary wholesalers. To remain competitive under these conditions, wholesalers have specialized and become smaller.

Diversity of wholesaling structures.   The diversity of the wholesaling structures among nations may be seen in Table 13–5. Generally, you will find that the structure varies with the stage of economic development. In the less developed countries that depend on imports to supply the market, the importing wholesalers are large and few in number, and the channels are long. Historically, many of the importers were trading companies formed by international companies to import the machinery and supplies required by their local operation and to export raw materials for use in the home country plants. To obtain distributor prices, they were required by their suppliers to sell to other customers as well. Some of these operations became extremely diversified, owning automobile and industrial machinery agencies, grocery stores, and department stores. They literally could and did supply a complete city and an industry with all of its requirements.

As colonies became nations, the new governments began applying pressure to convert these trading companies to local ownership. Furthermore, these countries were industrializing, which meant more goods were being produced locally and fewer goods were being imported. Many of the local manufacturers were able to take control of the channels from the import jobber. To obtain more extensive market coverage, they canceled the importing wholesaler's exclusivity and gave their product lines to new wholesalers, many of which were formed by ex-employees of the importer. As economic development continued, markets broadened, permitting greater specialization by more and smaller wholesalers. The small sample in Table 13–5 hints at this cycle. Compare the few large wholesalers in Chile, El Salvador, and Swaziland (employees per wholesaler and population per wholesaler) with the smaller and more numerous wholesalers in the United States and Austria. By comparing the Japanese and American ratios of population to wholesalers and noting that the number of wholesalers are the same in both countries, you can understand foreigners' complaints about the complexity of Japan's distribution system. Note the similarity among the population-per-wholesaler ratios of the United States, Austria, the United Kingdom, Italy, and France, although the employee-per-wholesaler ratios indicate that French and Italian wholesalers are much smaller.

Japan's multilayered system. Characterized as a formidable trade barrier by foreign firms attempting to enter the market, the maze of wholesalers and retailers employed to reach the Japanese consumer has been severely criticized for its inefficiency. Figure 13–5 illustrates that channels for automobiles are certainly complex; but even simple products like soap may move through a "sales agent" (primary wholesaler) named by the manufacturer to sell to the rest of the wholesalers, two or three wholesalers, and a retailer in going from the manufacturer to the final consumer. Note the presence of the parallel importer.

Parallel importers and gray market goods. **Parallel importers** are either wholesalers that import products independently of the authorized (by the manufacturer) importer or that buy products for export and then sell them in the domestic market. Four transactions are possible:

parallel importers
wholesalers that import products independently of manufacturer-authorized importers or buy goods for export and divert them to the domestic market

1. Importer buys from an overseas dealer in the home country. This occurs when authorized dealers charge more for the import than do home country dealers. When the strong dollar lowered the dollar price of Mercedes automobiles and the American authorized dealers did not lower their prices, a parallel importer could make money by selling a Mercedes 500 SEL with American pollution-control equipment for $8,000 less than the authorized dealer would. French Opium perfume was sold at a profit for $75 an ounce, compared to the $165 price that retailers buying from the authorized importer were asking.[71]

2. Unauthorized dealer imports from the foreign subsidiary and competes in the home country against locally made products. Caterpillar dealers of U.S.-made excavators and loaders were competing against unauthorized dealers selling the same products made in Scotland, Belgium, and Japan for 15 percent less.[72] Again, this occurred when the dollar was strong. Honda and other Japanese manufacturers are legitimately *reverse exporting*—exporting American-made products to Japan.

3. Unauthorized importer buys products overseas from the home office and competes with the local subsidiary. Most ICs can price lower for the export market than for the domestic market because they have

☐ **FIGURE 13–5   Passenger Car Distribution Channels in Japan**

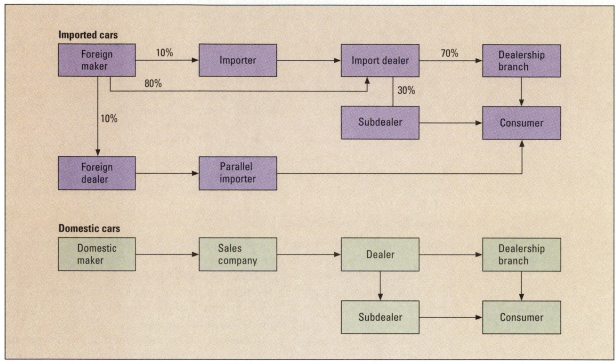

Note: A parallel importer acts independently of the foreign manufacturer and its authorized importer by obtaining the product from another source. It is a competitor of the authorized importer.

less promotional expense. The subsidiary's price can be higher than that of the home country because of production volume, higher distribution costs, and so forth.

4. Goods are bought for export but are sold on the domestic market instead. This can occur when a manufacturer's export prices are lower than its domestic prices. Quality King Distributors in New York annually sells millions of dollars' worth of Pampers,™ Tylenol,™ and Johnson & Johnson™ toothbrushes to dealers at prices 30 percent lower than domestic wholesalers can. The firm buys such products from exporters who sell to it rather than export them. A number of Japanese exports actually make a round trip from Japan to New York and back again. Unauthorized Japanese dealers can buy a Sony Walkman in New York for $90 and retail it in Tokyo for $165, the price that Japanese retailers normally ask.[73]

gray market the sale of goods that are either legal-but-unauthorized imports bearing domestic manufacturers' trade names, or exports that have been diverted to the domestic market

Although American manufacturers have gone to court trying to stop these **gray market** operations, they have had little success. U.S. gray market sales are estimated to total $10 billion annually.[74]

Retail institutions.   The variation in size and number is even greater for retailers than for wholesalers. In Table 13–5 compare Chile, Austria, Japan, and France, for example. Generally, *the less developed the country, the more numerous, the more specialized, and the smaller the retailers.* France, Japan,

☐ **FIGURE 13–6**
Food Distribution Methods at Various Levels of Development

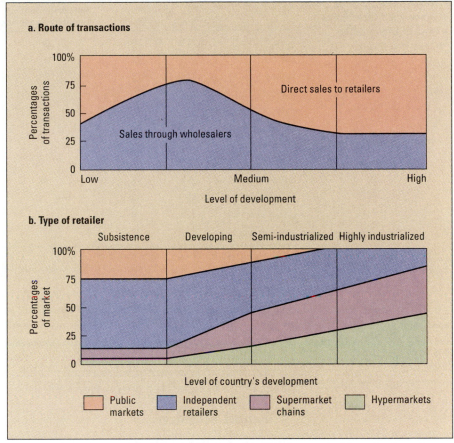

Source: L. Solis and A. Montemayor, "Modernización commercial y desarollo economico," *Comercio y Desarroll,* November–December 1977, p. 7.

and Italy are exceptions because the situation of many small retailers has been maintained by stringent laws that have kept the expansion of supermarkets and mass merchandisers at a much lower rate than that of similarly developed countries. Obviously, Chile's ambulatory peddlers, common in all LDCs, are not included in its retailer count, even though from the manufacturers' standpoint, these retailers can be responsible for considerable sales volume. In Africa, the market "mammy" who walks the street selling to passersby from a pan on the top of her head is a major outlet for small-unit goods, such as soap, cigarettes, and candy. Although the system seems primitive and ineffective to a Westerner, the market mammy is a powerful force, and associations of these women act as banks, back wholesalers, and even influence politicians.

When retailing methods in the developed and developing nations are compared, the following generalizations are notable: *in going up the scale from LDCs to developed countries, one encounters more mass merchandising; more self-service, large-sized retail units; and a trend toward retailer concentration* (see Figure 13–6).

Typical of this trend is the emergence of the European **hypermarket**—a huge combination supermarket/discount house with five or six acres of floor

hypermarkets
huge combination supermarkets/discount stores where soft and hard goods are sold

☐ **TABLE 13–6**
European Food Distribution by Type of Organization (Percent of market)

	Co-ops	Chains	Retailer-Controlled Voluntary Associations	Independents	Other*
Austria	15%	44%	36%	—	5%
Belgium	—	48	30	18%	5
Finland	31	3	63	—	3
France	3	30	25	—	42
Italy	13	10	22	55	—
Netherlands	1	50	24	—	25
Norway	23	23	—	—	54
Portugal	1	10	—	86	3
Sweden	21	8	44	—	27
Switzerland	40	12	—	—	48
United Kingdom	12	58	—	—	30
West Germany	11	24	59	—	6

*Other refers to specialty shops and department stores.

Source: *European Marketing Data & Statistics, 1991* (London: Euromonitor, 1991), p. 297.

superstores name given to hypermarkets in Japan, some parts of Europe, and the United States

space where both soft goods and hard goods are sold. A similar type of outlet in Japan, the **superstore,** is a recent phenomenon that now accounts for over 10 percent of all retail sales. In Scandinavia and Switzerland, there is also a marked trend toward retailer concentration, but it is occurring for the most part through retailer-controlled voluntary chains and consumer cooperatives rather than through company-owned chains (see Tables 13–6 and 13–7).

☐ Channel Selection

Direct or indirect marketing.   The first decision that management must make is whether to use middlemen, because it frequently has the option of marketing directly to the final user. Sales to original equipment manufacturers (OEMs)* and governments are, for the most part, made directly, as are the sales of high-priced industrial products like turbines and locomotives, because the firm is dealing with the relatively few customers and transactions but with large dollar value. Even in these cases, export sales may be consummated by local agents if (1) management believes this is politically expedient or (2) the country's laws demand it.

Other types of industrial products and consumer goods are marketed indirectly. The channel members are selected on the basis of their market coverage, their cost, and their susceptibility to company control. They must also, of course, perform the functions required by management.

Factors influencing channel selection.   The factors that influence the selection of market channels may be classified as the characteristics of the market, the product, the company, and the middlemen.

Market characteristics.   Inasmuch as the reason for using channels is to enable the manufacturer to reach its target markets, the obvious place to start in channel selection is at those markets. Which of the available alternatives

---

*   Original equipment manufacturers buy components that are incorporated into the products they produce (for example, spark plugs to an automobile manufacturer).

□ **TABLE 13-7**
European Hypermarkets and Superstores (Quantity)

	1980	1983	1989
Austria	51	53	60
Belgium	79	82	91
Denmark	29	38	45
Finland	27	30	50
France	421	515	708
Greece	—	2	6
Ireland	—	—	35*
Italy	14	20	22
Luxembourg	3	4	5
Netherlands	37	35	34
Norway	67	73	80
Portugal	—	—	21*
Spain	34	58	75
Sweden	65	73	75
Switzerland	81	82	85
United Kingdom	201	287	416
West Germany	813	880	998

*Estimated.

Source: *European Marketing Data & Statistics, 1991* (London: Euromonitor, 1991), p. 298.

offer the most adequate coverage? Because of the variance in the target markets, the firm will most likely require multiple channels. Large retailers, governments, and OEMs may be handled by the company sales force or manufacturers' agents, whereas smaller retailers are supplied through wholesalers.

Product characteristics.   A low-cost product sold in small quantities per transaction generally requires long channels, but if the goods are perishable, short channels are preferable. If the product is highly technical, it may be impossible to obtain knowledgeable middlemen, and the manufacturer will be forced either to sell directly through company-owned distributors or to train independent middlemen. Caterpillar has enjoyed tremendous success in choosing this second alternative.

Company characteristics.   A firm that has adequate financial and managerial resources is in a much better position to employ its own sales force or agents than one that is lacking in these areas. A financially weak company must use middlemen that take title to and pay for the goods. If management is inexperienced in selling to certain markets, it must employ middlemen who have that experience.

Middlemen's characteristics.   Most industrial equipment, large household appliances, and automobiles require considerable after-sales servicing, and much of the firm's success in marketing depends on it. If the firm is not prepared to provide this service, it cannot use agents. The same is true for warehousing and promotion to the final user. If the firm is unable to perform these functions or perceives a cost advantage in not performing them, then it must select middlemen that will service, warehouse, and promote its products.

It may be that no channel members are available to reach the firm's target markets and perform the desired functions. If there are none, management must decide to (1) desist from entering the market, (2) select other target markets, or (3) create a new channel. For example, if a frozen-food processor, after studying the available channels, finds that wholesale and retailer cold-storage facilities are nonexistent, it can either abandon the market or persuade middlemen to acquire the facilities. In a number of overseas markets, firms have purchased the equipment and either rented, leased, or sold it on easy terms to distributors and retailers.

> **An Italian cheese producer in Brazil not only supplied cold-storage equipment but also established gathering facilities for the dairy farmers. The company provides veterinarians and dairy experts to teach the dairy farmers how to maintain their herds and increase output. Nestlé has similar programs throughout its LDC markets.**

Legal requirements. Because the legal requirements for terminating middlemen vary from country to country, the time to think about how to terminate an agreement is before it is made. Although most countries have no special laws penalizing or precluding the termination of an agreement between the manufacturer and middlemen, some do. In Venezuela, for example, unjustly discharged agents may be entitled to the same severance benefits as discharged employees. In other countries, laws specify high termination compensation related to an agent's longevity, past earnings, goodwill, or "investment" in the product line. Countries with laws making it difficult to terminate agreements include Belgium, Costa Rica, the Netherlands, Norway, and Sweden. Evidently, before preparing a contract, management must consult local attorneys or local correspondents of international law firms.[75]

□ Information Sources

Various sources will provide information about channels of distribution. The U.S. Department of Commerce, banks, credit agencies, and American chambers of commerce in foreign cities are all good. If the names of other companies whose products are being handled by prospective channel members are known, these companies should be contacted. We will discuss the information sources at greater length in the chapter on exporting (Chapter 16).

SUMMARY

World competition has intensified, and there are four nations and groups of nations whose firms are in worldwide competition with each other—the United States, Japan, the EC, and the NICs. Nations do not compete with each other—their firms do; but most economic and social conditions, as well as political actions, affect the ability of all of a nation's firms to compete. Using the term *national competitiveness* is a convenience.

As the dollar's value rose, American companies experienced difficulty competing in world markets, but the dollar's high value was only one of the reasons. Various nonprice factors were also responsible. The government, industry, labor, and consumers can contribute to the return of American competitiveness. Industry in the European Community has problems similar to those of the United States. By 1992, competition among European firms and from companies of other nations will be greater. Japan is beginning to face the same competitive problems that the United States and Europe have been facing. Counterfeiting and industrial espionage are also competitive problems. Although competitor assessment is not new, its use is increasing, and companies are establishing competitor intelligence systems.

Channels of distribution are both controllable and uncontrollable variables. To assist a firm to export indirectly or directly or to distribute in a foreign market, various kinds of channel members are available. The wholesaling and retailing structures vary among nations. An unauthorized wholesaler, the parallel importer, costs authorized importers billions of dollars in lost sales annually.

When selecting channels of distribution, management must consider the characteristics of the market, the product, the company, and the intermediaries available.

QUESTIONS

1. If firms, not nations, compete worldwide, how can we speak of national competitiveness?

2. How can the U.S. government help American industry increase its competitiveness? What can industry and labor do? Do consumers have a role to play?

3. What similarities do you see in the sequence of events concerning the export performances of the United States and Japan? Can they occur in the Asian NICs?

4. What changes that took place in the EC are bringing about Europe 1992?

5. Do American firms have anything to fear from Europe 1992? How about Japanese firms?

6. Define *counterfeiting* in the sense used in the text. Why is counterfeiting a problem for legitimate trademark owners? For consumers? How can the legitimate owners protect themselves?

7. Did the American steel industry lose competitiveness due to special problems that other industries have not had? If so, what were these problems?

8. Is competitor assessment new? Compare present-day competitor analysis with what used to be done.

9. What are some sources of information for firms to know more about their competitors? What are some of the ethical issues involved in using these sources?

10. Name and discuss the four basic types of U.S.-based exporters available to firms that prefer to export directly.

11. What can you learn from Table 13–5, Wholesaling and Retailing in Selected Countries?

12. How do you define *parallel importers*? What is the gray market?

13. Discuss the five factors affecting the selection of marketing intermediaries.

14. What are the sogo shosha? How do they differ from their American counterpart?

□ MINICASE 13–1

Aikens-Malaysia and the Parallel Importer

Jim Hutton, managing director of Aikens-Malaysia, is discussing the latest competitive threat with Irene Olson, the marketing manager.

Hutton:

So you say that product from the home plant in Cleveland is being imported and sold here in competition with our locally made product?

Olson:

That's right, Jim. There's a parallel importer that buys in the United States and ships the product here. I wonder how he can compete pricewise when he has to pay those transportation costs. In fact, he and his wholesalers are making more than our wholesalers because they sell to the public at a higher price. My wholesalers tell me that the Malaysians will pay more for the imported product. There isn't any difference in quality, is there, Jim?

Hutton:

No. On the contrary, we're following Cleveland specs to the letter. The people here can get the same high-quality product made locally, and they're supporting a local industry that hires 500 Malaysian workers. As to the costs, remember, Irene, that our production costs are higher here. Our plant is newer and is being depreciated rather heavily. Furthermore, our production runs are much smaller, and that also makes our costs higher. We just don't have the economies of scale that Cleveland has. The lower wages here just can't compensate for this big difference. There's another angle, though. What about the import duties on the Cleveland product?

Olson:

They're rather low, although they're higher than the duties on the raw materials we import.

Hutton:

But the difference in duties is not high enough to compensate for our higher production costs, right?

Olson:

That's about it, Jim. There's also another aspect to consider.

Hutton:

What's that?

Olson:

As you know, the Malaysian ringgit fluctuates with respect to the dollar. My wholesalers tell me that the importer watches the fluctuation closely, and when the ringgit is low, he places a large order. At times, he can gain as much as a 20 percent advantage. Jim, do we take advantage of these currency fluctuations when we buy imported raw materials?

Hutton:

We try to, but since we have to order them months in advance, we're not able to respond very quickly to changes in the currency values.

Olson:

You know, Jim, the importer has another advantage. He gets a free ride from our advertising. We do all the promoting, and he reaps the benefits. He doesn't need to advertise.

Hutton:

Irene, I've just thought of something. How does this guy get our American product in the first place?

Olson:

I understand that he just places orders with our export department in Cleveland.

Hutton:

Don't these people know what the final destination is?

Olson:

Sure they do. He has to tell them when he places the order. By U.S. law, the destination has to be on the U.S. invoice. Cleveland knows he is not an American distributor. In fact, he gets an extra 10 percent because he does buy for export. Cleveland figures that exports should not have to pay any part of the domestic marketing costs.

Hutton:

This is a tough one, Irene. I have an idea. Didn't we and not Cleveland register our trademark here in Malaysia?

Olson:

Yes, Aikens-Malaysia is the owner of the trademark.

Hutton:

It seems to me, Irene, that there are a number of things we can do to reduce and possibly eliminate competition from this parallel importer. Will you draw up a plan for us?

Assume you are Irene Olson. Draw up a plan for Jim Hutton.

◻ MINICASE 13–2

America-Bashing—To Buy or Not to Buy American?

President Bush and a group of company CEOs went to Tokyo in January 1992 to explore, with the Japanese, ways to reduce the trade imbalance and increase Japan's imports of American cars. Three days of negotiations, in which the CEOs of the three American automobile manufacturers took part, produced few concrete agreements, although the Japanese did agree to buy an additional 19,000 automobiles, the equivalent of about four-days worth of Japanese shipments to the United States. Another agreement to buy more American auto parts was somewhat dubious. As one executive said, "I think you're going to see an awful lot of those parts being produced by Japanese companies in the United States."

Another factor that hardened the U.S.–Japanese relationship was a series of offending remarks made by prominent Japanese. In September 1986, Prime Minister Nakasone said that Japan has a high intelligence level, while on the average, the U.S. level is lower because of a considerable number of blacks, Puerto Ricans, and Mexicans. A book written in 1989 by Morita, the chairman of Sony, and Ishahara, a member of the Japanese parliament, was characterized by *U.S. News & World Report* as a "crash course in Japanese-style America-bashing." For example, Ishahara wrote that Japan can bring the United States to its knees by denying its technology to America: "If, for example, Japan sold computer chips to the Soviet Union and

Union and stopped selling them to the United States, this would upset the entire military balance."

After the book, there was a lull in public utterances of this type until just after President Bush and his group returned from Japan. Then the speaker of the lower house of the Japanese parliament called American workers lazy and illiterate. Just as the foreign minister apologized for those remarks, Ishihara announced that American managers are inferior, which he thought was due to cultural differences. Only a week later, Japanese Prime Minister Miyazawa said American workers lack drive and a strong work ethic in a parliamentary discussion of the declining U.S. economy. There were some Japanese supporters of American workers—precisely those left out on a limb by those remarks. For example, the president of Toyota U.S.A. spoke out in favor of American workers on whom he depends for output in his factory.

Anger over this series of Japanese remarks and the massive trade deficit with Japan led to a ground swell of support for American products, especially American automobiles. Companies began offering their employees bonuses to buy American cars. Monsanto, for example, offers each of its 12,000 employees $1,000 for buying or leasing an American car. However, this brought up the question, what is an American car or American anything? If a foreign-owned subsidiary located in the United States produces it, is it American? What about the product an American firm assembles in Mexico or Canada?

One company handles it this way. *First, buy from an American firm,* even if it assembles the product in Mexico or Singapore so as to be able to compete with foreign exports. Here are the reasons:

1. Being American, the firm will keep its profits in the United States; they will not be repatriated to some foreign country.

2. An American-owned company will give preference to American-made parts. We have all seen the high per-centage of parts used in Japanese auto transplants that are manufactured in the United States by Japanese-owned parts manufacturers. They also purchase capital equipment from Japanese companies.

3. The top management is American, and the decisions it takes will generally benefit the United States, not another country.

4. You live in the United States, you work in the United States, so buy in the United States from American companies.

5. If there is more than one American company, buy from the one whose products are clearly marked as made in the United States.

There are people who do not agree with the idea of "Buy American." They say that the principles of free trade and freedom of choice are more important and that we should not let the heated rhetoric lead us to greater protectionism. On the other hand, one person said, "We Americans have it within our power to correct the trade deficit with Japan. If each one of us buys Ford, General Motors, or Chrysler, there will be no more deficit."

1. Should we give preference to buying American products? Is it in our interest to do so?

2. Does it make sense to distinguish between American-owned and foreign-owned companies in the United States? If it is made in the U.S.A., it's American. It does not make any difference where the owners live. Do you agree?

Source: "Executives Divided on Bush Trade Trip," *The Wall Street Journal,* January 13, 1992, p. B1; "America-Bashing, Japanese Style," *U.S. News & World Report,* October 16, 1989, p. 45; "U.S.-Bashing by Japanese Turns Upward," *McAllen Monitor,* January 26, 1992, p. 1A; and "Anti-Japan Sentiments Called Counterproductive," *San Antonio Light,* January 24, 1992, p. F1.

SUPPLEMENTARY READINGS

Competition and the Europeans

"Airbus's Lease Terms on Delta Jet Order May Inflame U.S.–Europe Trade Tension." *The Wall Street Journal,* March 12, 1992, p. A3.

"EC, EFTA Create a Larger Common Market." New York: European Community, November 1991, p. 1.

"EEC and Japan." *The Economist,* February 18, 1989, p. 52.

"Europe Goes Wild for Yankee PCs." *Fortune,* June 5, 1989, pp. 257–60.

Europe without Frontiers—Completing the Internal Market. Luxembourg: European Communities, 1987.

"Europeans Start to Play a Little Rough." *Business Week,* February 9, 1987, p. 47.

"Fortress Europe." *International Management,* December 1988, pp. 24–30.

"Gianni Agnelli's Days in the Sun." *Forbes,* November 14, 1988, pp. 130–36.

"How the Member-States Are Preparing for 1992." *Business International,* June 27, 1988, pp. 200–02.

"1992: A Tremendous Challenge for EFTA." *EFTA Bulletin,* 1/89, pp. 6–15.

"1992: The Bad News." *International Management,* September 1988, pp. 22–26.

"Scrambling for 1992." *Business Management,* February 1989, pp. 49–59.

"The Coming Superpower." *Traffic Management,* April 1989, pp. 97A–102A.

"The Rise and Rise of European Takeovers." *International Management,* November 1988, pp. 24–28.

"Unequal Partnership." *The Banker,* January 1990, pp. 40–41.

"U.S. Business Should Prepare Now for EC 1992." *Business America,* October 24, 1988, pp. 12–16.

Competition and the Japanese

"Advantage Mitsubishi." *Forbes,* March 18, 1991, pp. 100–04.

"Ideal State." *The Wall Street Journal,* August 19, 1988, p. A1.

"Inside the Charmed Circle." *The Economist,* January 5, 1991, p. 54.

"International Perspective: Trading with Japan: Why the U.S. Loses." *Business Economics,* January 1992, pp. 25–29.

"Japan and Europe: What Next?" *International Management,* December 1988, pp. 35–52.

"Japan's Latest End Run around Free Trade." *Business Week,* October 1, 1990, p. 32.

"Japan's Latest Trade War Is with Its Own Customers." *Business Month,* December 1988, p. 21.

"Low Tricks in High Tech." *The Economist,* September 29, 1990, p. 78.

"Now Japan is Getting Jumpy about Quality." *Business Week,* March 5, 1990, pp. 40-41.

"The Japanese Talk about Themselves." *Fortune,* Pacific Rim, 1990, pp. 17–22.

"Trade Liberation." *Japan Update,* Spring 1989, pp. 3–7.

"Trade Switch." *The Wall Street Journal,* July 20, 1988, p. A1.

Competition and the United States

"A Humbler IBM Switches Its Marketing Strategies to Win Back Japanese Buyers." *The Asian Wall Street Journal,* April 11, 1988, p. 14.

"America's Competitive Revival." *Fortune,* January 4, 1988, pp. 44–52.

"Can America Compete?" *The Economist,* January 18, 1992, pp. 65–66.

"Can Consortiums Defeat Japan?" *Fortune,* June 5, 1989, pp. 245–54.

"CEOs Grid for Global Battle." *Fortune,* April 24, 1989, pp. 65–66.

"Competitiveness: Getting It Back." *Fortune,* April 27, 1987, pp. 217–23.

Dertouzos, Michael L., Richard K. Lester, and Robert M. Solow. *Made in America.* Cambridge, Mass.: MIT Press, 1989.

"Designation of Japan as Unfair Trader Holds Promise but Much Risk." *The Wall Street Journal,* May 26, 1989, p. A1.

"Europe, Too, Is Edgy about Imports—from America." *Business Week,* January 27, 1992, pp. 48–49.

"Global Competition." *Industry Week,* October 7, 1991, pp. 45–50.

"Going for the Lion's Share." *Business Week,* July 18, 1988, pp. 70–72.

"Habit Dies Hard." *Forbes,* May 29, 1989, pp. 264–66.

"How American Industry Stacks Up." *Fortune,* March 9, 1992, pp. 30–46.

"Made in the USA." *Business Week,* February 29, 1988, pp. 60–66.

"Panelists Compete to Pinpoint Faults in Competitiveness." *The Wall Street Journal,* March 5, 1992, p. A6.

"The U.S. Gets Back in Fighting Shape." *Fortune,* April 24, 1989, pp. 42–48.

"The Toughest Companies in America." *U.S. News & World Report,* October 1991, pp. 65–74.

"Upstart Economic Think Tank Irks Bush Administration with Tough U.S.-First Agenda." *Business International,* June 24, 1991, p. 211.

"U.S. Exporters That Aren't American." *Business Week,* February 29, 1988, pp. 70–71.

Whitehill, Arthur M. "America's Trade Deficit: The Human Problems." *Business Horizons,* January–February 1988, pp. 18–23.

"Why Made-in-America Is Back in Style." *Business Week,* November 7, 1988, pp. 116–20.

Competitor Analysis

"Competing with Tomorrow." *The Economist,* May 12, 1990, pp. 65–66.

Competitive Intelligence. New York: The Conference Board, 1988.

"Corporate Spies Snoop to Conquer." *Fortune,* November 7, 1988, pp. 68–76.

"First Find Your Bench." *The Economist,* May 11, 1991, p. 72.

"George Smiley Joins the Firm." *Newsweek,* May 2, 1988, pp. 46–47.

Peacock, William E. *Corporate Combat.* Berkeley, Calif.: Berkeley Publishing, 1987.

"Tackling the Technobandit." *U.S. News & World Report,* February 1, 1988, p. 36.

"These Guys Aren't Spooks, They're 'Competitive Analysts.'" *Business Week,* October 14, 1991, p. 97.

"The New Face of Japanese Espionage." *Forbes,* November 12, 1990, p. 96.

"What Motorola Learns from Japan." *Fortune,* April 24, 1989, pp. 157–68.

Counterfeiting

"A Really Nasty Business." *Newsweek,* November 5, 1990, pp. 36–43.

"Asia's Export Upstarts Face High Winds from Washington." *Business Week,* November 7, 1988, pp. 52–53.

"Busting the Software Pirates." *Business Week,* June 17, 1985, p. 56.

"Companies Are Knocking Off the Knock-off Outfits." *Business Week,* September 26, 1988, pp. 86–87.

"How Copycats Steal Billions." *Fortune,* April 22, 1991, pp. 157–64.

"The Counterfeit Trade." *Business Week,* December 16, 1985, pp. 64–72.

"The Hidden Threat to Air Safety." *Fortune,* April 13, 1987, pp. 81–84.

"The High Cost of Bolts." *Forbes,* June 13, 1988, pp. 56–57.

"Tips on How to Spot Counterfeit Goods." *U.S. News & World Report,* February 10, 1986, p. 52.

Distributive Forces

"A Land of Papa-Mama Shops." *U.S. News & World Report,* April 24, 1989, pp. 47–48.

Anderson, Erin, and Anne T. Coughlan. "International Market Entry and Expansion via Independent or Integrated Channels of Distribution." *Journal of Marketing,* January 1987, pp. 71–82.

"Cheaper Shopping in Japan." *The Economist,* January 28, 1989, p. 15.

"Consumer/Drug MNC Offers Thailand Distribution Tips." *Business Asia,* February 6, 1989, pp. 44–45.

"Corporate Strategies: Differences in American and Japanese Approaches." *Pacific Northwest Executive,* July 1988, pp. 23–25.

"Drug on the Market." *The Economist,* December 1988, p. 70.

"Foreign Business in Japan." *The Economist,* November 12, 1988, pp. 76–77.

"How Amstrad Successfully Set up a Distribution Channel in Spain." *BI/Ideas in Action,* March 14, 1988, pp. 4–6.

"How to Avoid Pitfalls with LA Distributor and Agent Agreements." *Business Latin America,* June 13, 1988, pp. 187–91.

"Japan's Next Retail Revolution." *The Economist,* December 21, 1991–January 3, 1992.

"Setting Up Shop across Europe." *International Management,* June 1991, pp. 29–32.

"The Hungry Frenchman's Recipe for Europe." *International Management,* April 1988, pp. 20–27.

"They Have Names Too." *The Economist,* December 24, 1988, pp. 98–99.

"Tough on the Streets." *The Economist,* February 24, 1990, p. 69.

"Using Overseas Trade Fairs to Locate Agents and Distributors." *Business America,* July 18, 1988, pp. 3–4.

"What the Worst Laws Say." *Business International,* July 12, 1988, p. 218.

Export Trading Companies

"Commerce Certificate Gives Antitrust Protection for Export Ventures of 3,150 Tooling and Machining Firms." *Business America,* November 7, 1988, p. 14.

"Export Trading Companies." *Business America,* October 12, 1987, pp. 2–9.

Howard, Donald G. "Export Management Companies?" *International Marketing Review,* Winter 1988, pp. 4–10.

Lenberg, Robert A., and Thomas H. Becker. "A New International Marketing Era for U.S. Small & Medium-Size Business?" Paper presented at the Western Marketing Educators' Conference, April 21–23, 1983.

"The Export Trading Company Act Is Alive, Healthy, and Promoting U.S. Exports." *Business America,* February 16, 1987, pp. 19–21.

"Yarn Producers Boost Foreign Sales with an Export Trading Company." *Business America,* February 13, 1989, p. 15.

Zurawicki, Leon. "Brazilian Trading Companies." *Issues in International Business,* Winter–Spring 1986, pp. 25–30.

Parallel Importing

"Gray Market Update: Destined to Get Darker before Getting Better?" *Business International,* June 2, 1986, pp. 171–74.

"Now, Japan Is Feeling the Heat from the Gray Market." *Business Week,* March 14, 1988, pp. 50–51.

"Owners of U.S. Trademarks Fight Treasury Department over 'Gray Market' Imports." *Business International,* April 12, 1985, pp. 113–114.

"See the Nice, Gray Cat." *Forbes,* May 6, 1985, p. 31.

"The Opening of Japan." *The Economist,* December 17, 1988, pp. 69–70.

"There's Nothing Black-and-White about the Gray Market." *Business Week,* November 7, 1988, pp. 172–80.

"The $7 Billion Gray Market: Where It Stops, Nobody Knows." *Business Week,* April 15, 1985, pp. 86–87.

Steel Industry

Ballance, Robert H. *International Industry and Business.* London: Allen & Unwin, 1987.

"Bessie's Blessings." *Forbes,* Januray 8, 1990, pp. 40–42.

"Faded Glory." *Forbes,* March 16, 1992, pp. 40–42.

"Forging the New Bethlehem." *Business Week,* June 5, 1989, pp. 108–9.

"The Big Threat to Big Steel's Future." *Fortune,* July 15, 1991, pp. 106–08.

"The Decline of the U.S. Steel Industry." *Finance & Development,* December 1987, pp. 30–33.

"Value Is Its Own Reward." *The Economist,* April 28, 1990, p. 79.

ENDNOTES

1. "Indonesian Workers Manufacture Nikes on a Shoestring," *San Antonio Light,* January 26, 1992, p. E2.
2. "Competitiveness: Getting It Back," *Fortune,* April 27, 1987, pp. 217–23.
3. "Waiting for the Yen to Stop Pummeling Profits," *Business Week,* June 1, 1987, pp. 58–59.
4. Priority watch list—Brazil, India, South Korea, Taiwan (all for other practices), Mexico, China, Saudi Arabia, Thailand. From "Singled Out," *The Wall Street Journal,* May 26, 1989, p. A1.
5. "Japan: All in the Family," *Newsweek,* June 10, 1991, p. 38.
6. "Inside the Charmed Circle," *The Economist,* January 5, 1991, p. 54.
7. "Japan: All in the Family," pp. 38–39.
8. "Bashing America," *The Economist,* May 20, 1989, pp. 79–80.
9. "Dollar Signs," *The Wall Street Journal,* January 26, 1987, p. 1.
10. "Panelists Compete to Pinpoint Faults in Competitiveness," *The Wall Street Journal,* March 5, 1992, p. A6.
11. "Love Thy Competitor as Thyself," *U.S. News & World Report,* June 5, 1989, p. 12.
12. "America's Hidden Problem," *Business Week,* August 29, 1983, pp. 50–54.
13. "The FSX—Done Deal at Last," *The Economist,* May 20, 1989, pp. 32–33.
14. "FSX—a View from Japan," *Overseas Business,* Premier 1990, p. 52.
15. "CEOs Gird for Global Battle," *Fortune,* April 29, 1989, pp. 65–66.
16. "Myth and Marketing in Japan," *The Wall Street Journal,* April 6, 1989, p. B2.
17. Most native Spanish-speaking people connect *nova* with the star or with *nuevo* (new), which is probably what General Motors had in mind.
18. "Advantage, Mitsubishi," *Forbes,* March 18, 1991, p. 100.
19. "Habit Dies Hard," *Forbes,* May 29, 1989, pp. 264–66.
20. "Why Americans Aren't Likely to Start Buying American," *Business Week,* November 27, 1987, p. 34.
21. "The Japanese Talk about Themselves," *Fortune,* Pacific Rim 1990, p. 17.
22. "The World's Most Competitive Economy," *Forbes,* March 30, 1992, p. 84.
23. "Europe, Too, Is Edgy about Imports—from America," *Business Week,* January 27, 1992, p. 48.
24. "The World's Most Competitive Economy," p. 85.
25. "EC, EFTA Create a Larger Common Market," *Eurocom,* November 1991, p. 1.
26. "The EC and EFTA," *The Economist,* December 21, 1991–January 3, 1992, p. 11.
27. "Unequal Partnership," *The Banker,* January 1990, p. 40.
28. "Now Japan's Autos Push into Europe," *Fortune,* January 29, 1990, p. 96.
29. "Car Wars," *Europe,* September 1987, p. 26.
30. "America's New King of Europe's Roads," *The Economist,* March 9, 1991, p. 63.
31. "The Nasty Pileup in Europe's Auto Industry," *Business Week,* September 17, 1990, p. 48.
32. "Gianni Agnelli's Days in the Sun," *Forbes,* November 14, 1988, pp. 130–40.
33. "Mazda Sedan Will Be First Japanese Vehicle Classified as U.S. Car," *The Wall Street Journal,* February 7, 1992, p. A7.
34. "LSI Logic Pulls Out of U.S. Semiconductor Consortium," *Financial Times,* January 8, 1992, p. 28.
35. "U.S. Business Should Prepare Now for EC 1992," *Business America,* October 24, 1988, pp. 12–16.
36. "United Front," *The Wall Street Journal,* December 29, 1988, p. A1.
37. "North America's New Trade Punch," *Fortune,* May 22, 1989, pp. 123–127.
38. *Monthly Economic Survey* (Tapei: The International Commercial Bank of China, May 1991), p. 2.
39. "Dragons against the Fortress," *International Management,* October 1988, pp. 59–63.
40. "Japanese Managers Alarmed in Land of Rising Yen," *International Management,* December 1986, pp. 58–64; "Trade Switch," *The Wall Street Journal,* July 20, 1988, p. A1; and "The Rampaging Yen Is Leaving a Trail of Misery," *Business Week,* February 16, 1987, p. 46.
41. "Computer Wars in Japan," *International Herald Tribune,* June 4, 1991, p. 1.
42. Vernon R. Alden, "Who Says You Can't Crack Japanese Markets?" *Harvard Business Review,* January–February 1987, p. 52.
43. "Now Japan Is Getting Jumpy about Quality," *Business Week,* March 5, 1990, p. 40.

44. "Trade Thievery," *The Wall Street Journal,* March 16, 1989, p. A1.

45. "A Really Nasty Business," *Business Week,* November 5, 1990, pp. 36–43.

46. "Computing Manufacturers Combat Third World Pirates," *Personal Computing,* November 1988, p. 40.

47. "Cutting Russia's Harvest of U.S. Technology," *Fortune,* May 30, 1983, p. 103.

48. "The Decline of the U.S. Steel Industry," *Finance & Industry,* December 1987, pp. 30–33.

49. Robert H. Ballance, *International Industry and Business* (London: Allen & Unwin, 1987), p. 215.

50. "Decline of the U.S. Steel Industry," p. 32.

51. "Fool's Paradise," *The Economist,* February 3, 1990, p. 81.

52. "European Steelmakers," *The Wall Street Journal,* July 8, 1991, p. A8; and "Forging the New Bethlehem," *Business Week,* June 5, 1989, pp. 108–10.

53. "The Big Threat to Big Steel's Future," *Fortune,* July 15, 1991, p. 107.

54. "Virtue Is Its Own Reward," *The Economist,* April 28, 1990, p. 79.

55. *Business International* proposal describing multiclient study on the practice and application of assessing competitors internationally.

56. "CI Systems Take Root at US Firms—but Slowly," *Business International,* November 18, 1991, p. 389; and "George Smiley Joins the Firm," *Newsweek,* May 2, 1988, pp. 46–47.

57. Adapted from "How to Snoop on Your Competitors," *Fortune,* May 14, 1984, pp. 28–33.

58. Ibid., p. 31.

59. "George Smiley Joins the Firm," *Newsweek,* May 2, 1988, pp. 46–47.

60. "Trade Secrets: Next Frontier for U.S. Spies," *USA Today,* June 4, 1990, p. 4.

61. "Airline Denies Business Spying," *The Wall Street Journal,* September 16, 1991, p. A14.

62. "The New Face of Japanese Espionage," *Fortune,* November 12, 1990, p. 96; and "The Business Intelligence Beehive," *Business Week,* December 14, 1981, p. 52.

63. "First Find Your Bench," *The Economist,* May 11, 1991, p. 72.

64. "A Backstage View of World-Class Performers," *The Wall Street Journal,* August 26, 1991, p. A10.

65. "Austin Rover Links with Retailer to Break Open German Market," *Business Europe,* January 18, 1985, pp. 17–18.

66. *Mitsui Trade News* (Tokyo: Mitsui & Co., March/April 1988), p. 2.

67. Actually, major companies within the zaibatsu were split up and made independent organizations. The present Mitsui sogo shosha, Mitsui & Co., was started in 1947. See *Mitsui Group,* rev. ed. (Tokyo: Mainichi Newspapers, 1982), pp. 30–31.

68. *The Export Trading Company Act of 1982* (Washington, D.C.: Chamber of Commerce of the United States of America, January 1983).

69. "The Exports Trading Company Act Is Alive, Healthy, and Promoting U.S. Exports," *Business America,* February 16, 1987, p. 19.

70. "A Land of Papa-Mama Shops," *U.S. News & World Report,* April 24, 1989, p. 48.

71. "The Assuault on the Right to Buy Cheap Imports," *Fortune,* January 7, 1985, p. 89.

72. "See the Nice, Gray Cat," *Forbes,* May 6, 1985, p. 31.

73. "Now, Japan Is Feeling the Heat from the Gray Market," *Business Week,* March 14, 1988, p. 50.

74. "A Red-Letter Date for Gray Marketers," *Business Week,* June 13, 1988, p. 30.

75. "What the Worst Laws Say," *Business International,* July 12, 1985, p. 218.

Section Four

How Management Deals with Environmental Forces

Section One introduced you to international business, trade, investment, and economic development. Section Two presented the framework of international organizations and the monetary system within which international business functions. Section Three discussed a number of the forces affecting international business with which its management must cope.

Section Four will give you a number of the management responses and solutions to problems caused or magnified by the foreign and international environments. The reader should bear in mind that this book is intended to be only an introduction to international business. The student or businessperson who wishes to delve more deeply into specific areas should look to textbooks specializing in those areas. Fortunately, some business and law schools are offering more internationally oriented courses.

Chapters 14 and 15 deal with assessing and analyzing markets and with international marketing as it differs from domestic marketing. Chapter 16, on export practices and procedures, logically follows international marketing. Chapter 17 covers developments flowing from the momentous changes in the former Soviet Union, Eastern Europe, and elsewhere as countries struggle to move from centrally planned to market economies.

Chapters 18 through 22 present management solutions to or methods of dealing with the environmental forces discussed in Section Three. Chapter 18 covers financial management, while Chapter 19 deals with production systems. Chapter 20 presents material on labor relations' policies as they relate to nonexecutive, technical, or sales employees. Chapters 21 and 22 are intended to cap the solutions and methods material dealing with planning, organization, political risks, control, and executive personnel policies. The final chapter, Chapter 23, presents our thoughts on what the future holds for international business.

Chapter 14

Market Assessment and Analysis

The worst enemy of good research is the client who appears with a standard sampling technique and questionnaire and tells us to administer it across four or five countries. In some countries, high consumption of alcohol is seen as a macho attribute; but in others, where driving after only one drink can land you in jail, it is not surprising that people underclaim consumption.

Dawn Mitchell, managing
director of RSL/Burke, English
advertising research firm

LEARNING OBJECTIVES

In this chapter, you will study:

1. Environmental analysis and a modified version, market screening, used for market assessment and analysis.

2. Market indicators and market factors.

3. Statistical techniques for estimating market demand and grouping similar markets.

4. The value to businesspeople of trade missions and trade fairs.

5. Some of the problems market researchers encounter in foreign markets.

6. The purpose of an international management information system (IMIS).

7. Sources of information for the screening process.

KEY WORDS AND CONCEPTS

- Market screening
- Environmental scanning
- Market indicators
- Market factors
- Estimation by analogy
- Regression analysis
- Trend analysis
- Cluster analysis
- Trade mission
- Trade fair
- International management information system (IMIS)

BUSINESS INCIDENT

Entrepreneur Peter Johns, a veteran of 30 years in international marketing, had the idea of distributing mail-order catalogs for upscale U.S. firms in Mexico. He felt that because of the improvement in the Mexican economy, the rich would want to buy foreign-made luxury goods. He also knew that the well-to-do Mexicans regularly make trips to the United States to load up on things they cannot get in their country. In fact, there is an axiom: the richer they are, the farther inland they go in the United States; for example, the poorer ones to McAllen, the richer ones to Dallas, and so forth. However, when Johns went to confirm his beliefs with hard data, the market veteran found none to his liking. Government data were of no help.

The other alternative was personal observation, so Johns visited the affluent neighborhoods and shopping areas to see for himself. The satellite dishes, imported sports cars, and women carrying Vuitton purses, along with other information he gathered, led him to the conclusion that his target market was about 300,000 families. To him, there was no doubt that there is a sense of consumer deprivation in the Mexico City luxury market.

Johns formed a company to distribute the catalogs of 20 American firms, Choices Unlimited, in which Mexican investors owned 60 percent. But now he had a second problem. He needed mailing lists, but he couldn't find what he needed in Mexico. This time Johns went to the Mexican investors of his own company. They gave him memberships of the city's exclusive golf clubs. He also obtained directories of the parents of the students at some of the exclusive private schools. The information he

BUSINESS INCIDENT (concluded)

gathered enabled him to make a flashy debut at a fancy members-only night club. After a fashion show followed by heavy food and drink, 800 people each put down $28 in pesos to become charter members. They'll get catalogs, promotional discounts, and more fashion-show invitations. Choices Unlimited has pledged to make deliveries from the United States in 15 days and has hired Federal Express to do it. Mexican Customs has also promised to give its packages fast service.

The entrepreneur is optimistic that the expected signing of the North American Trade Agreement between Canada, United States, and Mexico will give his business a big boost because it would eliminate or greatly reduce Mexico's import duty of 15 percent on clothing and 20 percent on luxury goods. By then, Johns expects to have customer base of 7,500 families spending an average of $600 annually. This means he should then have another product to sell—his customer list.

Source: "Grass-Roots Marketing Yields Clients in Mexico City," *The Wall Street Journal,* October 24, 1991, p. B2.

The Business Incident illustrates the difficulties that experienced marketers from industrialized nations have when they do market assessment and analysis in developing nations, even in one as advanced as Mexico. It also shows that experienced international marketers like Johns will not be stopped by lack of data but will use whatever methods are available to get what they need. Often these methods are quite ingenious. Note how Johns compiled his mailing list at no cost when he could not find what he needed. Later in this chapter, we shall look at other problems marketers have in doing research, especially in the developing nations.

The market research Johns did is the first step of the market screening process, determining the basic need potential. We shall describe this process fully in the next section. **Market screening** is a modified version of environmental scanning in which the firm identifies markets by using the environmental forces to eliminate the less desirable markets. **Environmental scanning**, from which market screening is derived, is a procedure in which a firm scans the world for changes in the environmental forces that might affect it.

market screening a version of environmental scanning in which the firm identifies desirable markets by using the environmental forces to eliminate the less desirable markets

For some time, environmental scanning has been used by management during the planning process to provide information about world threats and opportunities. Various studies have indicated that firms that scan outperform those that do not. In a related study by the Conference Board in 1988, 71 percent of the respondents expected to increase their monitoring efforts. As you can imagine, the greater global competition from Europe 92, Japan, and the Asian NICs, which we examined in Chapter 13, is the motivating factor for this increase.[1]

environmental scanning a procedure in which a firm scans the world for changes in the environmental forces that might affect it

Market screening assists two different kinds of firms. One is selling exclusively in the domestic market but believes it might increase sales by expanding into overseas markets. The other is already a multinational but wants to be certain that changing conditions are not creating markets about which its management is unaware. In both situations, managers require an ordered, relatively fast method of analyzing and assessing the nearly 200 countries to pinpoint the most suitable prospects.

MARKET SCREENING

Market screening is a method of market analysis and assessment that permits management to identify a small number of desirable markets by eliminating those judged to be less attractive. This is accomplished by subjecting the countries to a series of screenings based on the environmental forces examined in Section Three. Although these forces may be placed in any order, the arrangement suggested in Figure 14–1 is designed to progress from the least to the most difficult analysis based on the accessibility and subjectivity of the data. In this way, the least number of candidates is left for the final, most difficult screening.[2]

▫ Initial Screening

Basic need potential.   An initial screening based on the basic need potential is a logical first step, because if the need is lacking, no reasonable expenditure of effort and money will enable the firm to market its goods or services. For example, the basic need potential of certain goods is dependent on various physical forces, such as climate, topography, or natural resources. If the firm produces air conditioners, the analyst will look for countries with warm climates. Manufacturers of large farm tractors would not consider Switzerland a likely prospect, because of its mountainous terrain, and only countries known to possess gold deposits would be potential customers for gold-dredging equipment.

Generally, producers of specialized industrial materials or equipment experience little difficulty in assessing their basic need potential. The builder of cement kilns, for example, can obtain the names and addresses of cement plants worldwide merely by contacting the Portland Cement Association in Chicago. A list of firms in an industry, often on a worldwide basis, is available either from the industry association or from specialized trade journals.

This is certainly straightforward, but what about the less specialized products of more widespread consumption?

Foreign trade and investment.   If the nature of the good or service is such that a definite basic need potential cannot be readily established, an analyst can learn if other American competitors are already exporting its products and if so, where. Two U.S. Department of Commerce foreign trade publications, *FT925* and *FT447*, are available in most public and university libraries and Department of Commerce district offices. You saw a page from the *FT925* in Minicase 2–2. The advantage of using the *FT447*, which is only for exports, is that it publishes both the dollar value and the amount of physical units of the exports. This enables the analyst to calculate the average unit value for the product being examined. Minicase 14–1 shows part of a page from the *FT447 (see page 502).*

Analysts can obtain from the nearest Department of Commerce field office numerous studies prepared by U.S. embassies to help their search for markets. *Annual Worldwide Industry Reviews* and *International Market Research Reports* indicate major markets for many products. The *Country Market Surveys* indicate products for which there is a good market in a given country. We shall discuss these publications in greater detail in Chapter 16.

□ FIGURE 14–1
Selection of Foreign
Markets

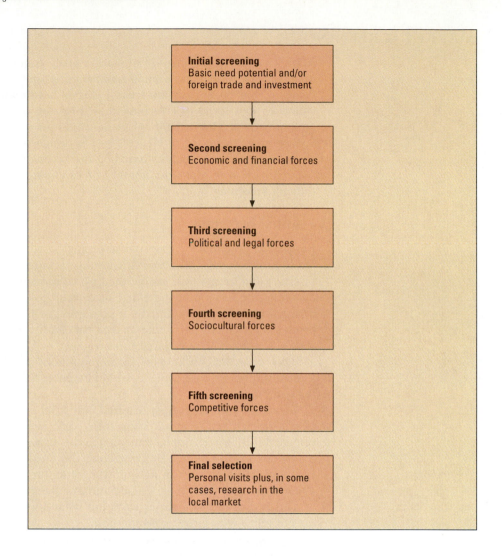

Other countries publish similar data. For example, the data office of the European Community, Eurostat, publishes an annual, *External Trade*. Additional information is available from *The Economist, Business International*, and other business publications listed in the appendix to this chapter. Many trade associations also publish export data.

Imports don't completely measure market potential.   Even for the situation where a basic need is clearly indicated, most experienced researchers will still investigate the trade flows to have an idea of the magnitude of present sales.

Management is aware, of course, that imports alone are rarely a measure of the full market potential. Myriad reasons are responsible, among which are lack of foreign exchange, high prices (duties and markups), and political pressures.

Moreover, import data indicate only that a country has been buying certain products from abroad and are no guarantee that it will continue to do so. Managements know that a competitor may decide to produce locally, which in many markets will cause imports to cease. Change in a country's political structure may stop imports also, as we saw in the case of Iran, where orders worth billions of dollars were suddenly canceled. Nevertheless, when there is no local production, import data do enable the firm to know how much is currently being purchased and provide management with an estimate, though conservative, of the immediate market potential at the going price. If local production is being considered and calculations show that goods produced in the country could be sold at a lower price, even without knowing the price elasticity of demand, the firm can reasonably expect to sell more than the quantity being imported.

Companies wanting to know about the amounts and geographic areas of U.S. foreign investment can obtain information at the industry level from certain issues of the *Survey of Current Business,* which also publishes similar information about foreign investors in the United States.

◻ Second Screening—Financial and Economic Forces

After the initial screening, the analyst will have a much smaller list of prospects. This list may be further reduced by a second screening based on the financial and economic forces. Trends in the rates of inflation, exchange, and interest are among the major financial points of concern. The analyst should consider other financial factors such as credit availability, paying habits of customers, and rates of return on similar investments. It should be noted that this screening is not a complete financial analysis. This will come later if the market analysis and assessment disclose that a country has sufficient potential for capital investment.

Economic data may be employed in a number of ways, but two measures of market demand based on them are especially useful. These are *market indicators* and *market factors.* Other methods for estimating demand that depend on economic data are *regression analysis, trend analysis,* and *cluster analysis.*

market indicators economic data used to measure relative market strengths of countries or geographic areas

Market indicators.   **Market indicators** are economic data that serve as yardsticks for measuring the relative market strengths of various geographic areas. A well-known American example is the Buying Power Index published in the annual "Survey of Buying Power" by *Sales & Marketing Management.* The purpose of this index is to enable marketers to compare the relative buying power of countries and cities in the United States.

A somewhat similar index on a worldwide scale is published by *Business International.* This index employs 40 indicators for 117 nations. The indicators include population, GDP, various categories of private consumption expenditures, and the production or consumption of steel, cement, electricity, and energy. These indicators are weighted and combined to form composite indexes of (1) market size, (2) market intensity, and (3) market growth.

1. *Market size* shows the relative size of each market as a percentage of the total world market. The percentages for each market are obtained by averaging data on population (given double weight), urban population, private consumption expenditures, steel consumption, cement and electricity production, and ownership of telephones, cars, and television sets.

2. *Market intensity* measures "the richness of the market" or the degree of concentrated purchasing power as compared to the world intensity of 1.00. The intensity for each market is calculated by averaging per capita consumption of energy, ownership of passenger cars, and telephone access lines. Double weight is given to overall private consumption expenditures. The proportion of urban population is also included and double-weighted because in many developing countries, much of the rural population does not actually participate in the money economy.

3. *Market growth* is an average of the percentage growth of the following indicators over the past five years: population; steel consumption; electricity production; ownership of cars, trucks, buses, and television sets; private consumption expenditure; and real GNP.

An analysis of these three indexes will show the international sales manager which major regions and major markets were the fastest growing, what their growth rates were, and which have the highest degree of concentrated purchasing power. Table 14–1 presents these indexes, which show that from 1978 to 1989, the EC, Middle East, Asia, Latin America, and Africa increased their market size measured as a percentage of world market. However, of these areas, the market intensity indexes of Asia and Africa are below the world average. Of the 12 major markets, 8 of them failed to increase their market size, but all increased their "richness." The percentage of five-year growth ranged from 8.32 percent for the U.S.S.R. to 168.20 percent for communist China.

By comparing the values of the indexes with the sales results of the company's subsidiaries, management can quickly judge their performance. Other uses of the indexes are to set sales targets and to serve as a basis for allocating the promotional budget. Although Euromonitor does not calculate indexes, it does publish two annuals, *European Marketing Data & Statistics* and *International Data & Statistics,* which provide valuable data, some of which you saw in Chapter 13.

market factors economic data that correlate highly with market demand for a product

Market factors.   **Market factors** are similar to market indicators, except they tend to correlate highly with the market demand for a given product. If the analyst of a foreign market has no factor for that market, he or she can usually use one from the domestic market to get a reasonable approximation. Moreover, an analyst who works for a multinational firm may be able to obtain market factors developed by comparable subsidiaries. To be able to transfer these relationships to the country under study, the analyst must assume that the underlying conditions affecting demands are similar in that market.

estimation by analogy using a market factor that is successful in one market to estimate demand in a similar market

The transfer process, **estimation by analogy,** works like this: If car registration × 1.6 is used to estimate annual tire purchases in the United States, the forecaster who has no market factor for the country under study can use the same 1.6 for that market. The constant in the country under study may be somewhat different (it usually is); but with this approach, the estimates will be in the right ballpark. Many such factors exist, and generally research personnel, either in the domestic operation or in foreign subsidiaries, are familiar with them.

□ **TABLE 14–1**
World Market Intensity Index, 1978 versus 1989

	Market Size (percent of world market)		Market Intensity (world = 1.00)		Five-Year Market Growth (percent)
	1978	**1989**	**1978**	**1989**	**1989**
Major regions					
Western Europe	25.49	22.81	2.71	7.56	9.15
EC	18.01	19.64	3.09	8.37	18.20
EFTA	2.76	2.24	2.95	9.90	12.39
Eastern Europe	20.64	11.55	2.19	2.59	9.38
Middle East	1.52	2.59	0.52	1.77	10.75
Africa	1.70	2.77	0.18	0.47	12.39
Asia	17.84	29.68	0.30	0.85	26.80
Oceania	1.24	1.21	3.29	3.11	8.50
North America	25.53	22.41	4.77	11.85	13.00
Latin America	6.03	6.98	0.74	1.77	16.00
LAIA*	5.51	6.25	0.79	1.85	15.00
World (total or average)	100.00	100.00	1.00	1.00	
Major markets					
United States	23.30	20.34	4.82	11.85	13.00
U.S.S.R.	14.32	7.95	2.14	2.58	8.32
Japan	9.14	9.23	3.31	10.43	15.90
Germany	4.92	4.62	3.55	10.33	9.41
United Kingdom	3.47	3.36	2.75	8.33	27.05
France	3.67	3.58	3.10	9.03	21.23
Italy	3.94	3.61	3.09	8.77	12.87
Brazil	2.24	2.66	0.82	2.05	14.00
Canada	2.23	2.06	4.25	11.07	10.00
Spain	2.30	1.88	2.64	6.44	38.69
China	3.84	9.79	0.16	0.56	168.20
India	1.33	5.07	0.08	0.32	45.00

*LAIA = Latin American Integration Association.

Source: Reprinted from "Indicators of Market Size for 117 Countries," July 1991, with the permission of the publisher, Business International Corporation, New York.

regression analysis statistical technique utilizing a linear model to establish relationships between independent variables and the dependent variable

trend analysis statistical technique by which successive observations of a variable at regular time intervals are analyzed to establish regular patterns that are used for establishing future values

Regression analysis. In **regression analysis,** instead of one economic variable (such as car registration), the domestic division may be utilizing several in a linear regression model of the form $MP = a + bx_1 + \ldots zx_n$, where MP = market potential and the xs are independent economic variables, such as GNP, number of telephones, or births. Again, the analyst has the choice of employing the same model or, when sufficient historical data are obtainable locally, constructing a new one by means of regression analysis.[3]

Trend analysis. When the historic growth rates of either the pertinent economic variables or imports are known, future growth can be forecast by means of **trend analysis.** A time series may be constructed, or the arithmetic mean of past growth rates may be applied to historical data. Caution is advised when using this second method because if the average annual growth rate is applied mechanically, in just a few years the dependent variable may reach an incredible size. For example, a 5 percent growth rate compounded annually will result in a doubling of the original value in only 15 years.

Inasmuch as trend analysis is based on the assumption that past conditions affecting the dependent variable will remain constant, the analyst will generally modify the outcome to take into account any changes that can be foreseen. Often there are obvious constraints that will limit upward growth, one of which is the near certainty that competitors will enter the market if large increases in demand continue for very long.

Cluster analysis and other multivariate techniques.   As multinationals extend their presence to more markets, managers in all functional areas are searching for ways to group countries and geographic regions by common characteristics to simplify their control. **Cluster analysis,** for which various computer programs are available, divides objects (market areas, individuals, customers, and other variables) into groups so that the variables within each group are similar. Marketers, for example, use cluster analysis to identify a group of markets where a single promotional approach can be employed; attorneys can use it to group nations according to similarities in certain types of laws; and so forth. Multidimensional scaling, factor analysis, and conjoint analysis are other techniques for examining differences and similarities among markets.[4]

> **cluster analysis** statistical technique that divides objects into groups so that the objects within each group are similar

Periodic updating.   If the estimates are altered appreciably in the periodic updatings that all long-term forecasts undergo, management may change the extent of the firm's involvement to be in line with the new estimates. Fortunately, the alternative forms of participation in a market permit the firm to become progressively more involved, with corresponding increases in investment. Most companies can enter a market in stages, perhaps in this sequence: exporting, establishment of a foreign sales company, local assembly, and, finally, manufacturing. Even when the decision is whether to produce overseas, management may plan to assemble a combination of imported and domestically produced parts initially and then progressively to manufacture more components locally as demand rises. Automobile manufacturers have begun a number of foreign operations employing this strategy.

◻ Third Screening—Political and Legal Forces

The elements of the political and legal forces that can eliminate a nation from further consideration are numerous.

Entry barriers.   Import restrictions can be positive or negative, depending on whether management is considering exporting (can the firm's products enter the country?) or setting up a foreign plant (will competitive imports be kept out?). If one of management's objectives is 100 percent ownership, will the nation's laws permit it, or is some local participation required? Will the government accept a minority local ownership, or must a minimum of 51 percent of the subsidiary be in the hands of nationals? Are there laws that reserve certain industries for either the government or its citizens?[5] Depending on management's preferences, any one of these conditions may be sufficient cause for eliminating a nation from further consideration. For example, in the business incident study, foreign equity restriction was ranked second in the respondents' concerns. Only repatriation of profits was greater.[6]

Profit remittance barriers.   When there are no objectionable requisites for entry, a nation may still be excluded if there are what management believes to be undue restrictions on the repatriation of earnings. Limits linked to the amount of foreign investment or other criteria may be set, or the nation may have a history of inability to provide foreign exchange for profit remittances.

> Decision 24 of the Andean Group has for years limited remittances to 14 percent of the foreign investment and automatic reinvestment of profits to 5 percent.
> Now these restraints have been loosened to 20 and 70 percent, respectively, in an effort to make foreign investment more attractive.

Other factors.   Another factor of serious import is the stability of the government, which is more important than its form. Business can adapt to form and thrive as long as the conditions are stable. Instability creates uncertainty, and this complicates planning. An often heard complaint of businesspeople is that "they've changed the rules again."

Other concerns of management are tax laws, safety standards, price controls, and the many other factors we examined in the chapters on the political and legal forces. No matter how large a nation's potential market is, if its legal and political constraints are unacceptable to management, that nation must be eliminated from further consideration.

Some excellent sources of this kind of information may be found in *Financing Foreign Operations,* published by Business International; *Overseas Business Reports,* obtainable from the U.S. Department of Commerce; the *Ernst & Young International Series;* and *Digest of Commercial Laws of the World,* published by Oceana.

◻ Fourth Screening—Sociocultural Forces

A screening of the remaining candidates on the basis of sociocultural factors is arduous because these "facts" are highly subjective. The analyst, unless he or she is a specialist in the country, must rely on the opinions of others. It is possible to hire consultants, but they are expensive. U.S. Department of Commerce specialists can provide some assistance, and professional organizations and universities frequently hold seminars to explain the sociocultural aspects of doing business in a particular area or country. Reading *Overseas Business Reports* (U.S. Department of Commerce), international business publications *(Business International* and *The Economist),* and specialized books will augment the analyst's sociocultural knowledge. The use of a checklist of the principal sociocultural components as explained in Chapter 9 will serve as a reminder of the many factors the analyst must consider in this screening.

After the fourth screening, the analyst should have a list of countries for which an industry demand appears to exist. However, what management really wants to know is which of these countries seem to be the best prospects for the *firm's* products. A fifth screening based on the competitive forces will help to provide this information.

◻ Fifth Screening—Competitive Forces

In this screening, the analyst examines markets on the basis of such elements of the competitive forces as:

1. The number, size, and financial strength of the competitors.
2. Their market shares.
3. Their apparent marketing strategies.
4. The apparent effectiveness of their promotional programs.
5. The quality levels of their product lines.
6. The source of their products—imported or locally produced.
7. Their pricing policies.
8. The levels of their after-sales service.
9. Their distribution channels.
10. Their coverage of the market. (Could market segmentation produce niches that are currently poorly attended?)

Countries in which management believes strong competitors make a profitable operation difficult to attain are eliminated unless management (1) is following a strategy of being present wherever its global competitors are or (2) believes entering a competitor's home market will distract the competitor's attention from its home market, a reason for foreign investment we discussed in Chapter 3 (cross investment).

◻ Final Selection of New Markets

An executive of the firm should visit those countries that still appear to be good prospects. Before leaving, this person will review the data from the various screenings along with any new information that the researcher can supply. Based on this review and on experience in making similar domestic decisions, the executive will prepare a list of points on which information must be obtained on arrival. Management will want the facts uncovered by the desk study (the five screenings) to be corroborated and will expect a firsthand report on the market, which will include information on competitive activity and appraisal of the suitability of the firm's present marketing mix and the availability of ancillary facilities (warehousing, service agencies, media, credit, and so forth).

Field trip.   The field trip should not be hurried; as much time should be allotted to this part of the study as would be spent on a similar domestic field trip. Often time can be saved if the executive can join a government-sponsored trade mission or visit a trade fair, because such events attract the kinds of people this person will want to interview.

trade mission a group of businesspeople and/or government officials (state or federal) that visits a market in search of business opportunities

Government-sponsored trade missions and trade fairs.   An important mission of foreign diplomatic ministries, such as the U.S. Department of State and the government department representing industry (the Department of Commerce in the United States), is to promote a nation's foreign trade. This is why commercial officers stationed in U.S. embassies report to both State and Commerce. One of the many means of assisting American firms is to sponsor a **trade mission.**

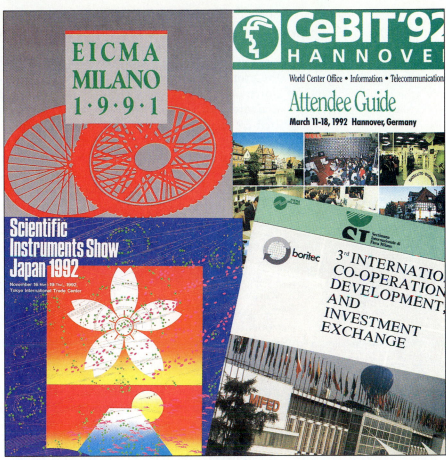

Prominent international trade fairs

Courtesy of Italian Trade Commission, Japanese Chamber of Commerce of Chicago, German American Chamber of Commerce of Chicago

When U.S. Department of Commerce trade specialists perceive an overseas market opportunity for an industry, they will organize a trade mission. The purpose is to send a group of executives from firms in the industry to a country or group of countries to learn firsthand about the market, meet important customers face to face, and make contacts with people interested in representing their products. Because of discounted air fares, hotels, and so forth, the cost to the firm is less than what it would pay if it went on its own. Moreover, the impact of a group visit is greater than it is for an individual. Before the mission's arrival, consular or embassy officials will have publicized the visit and will have made contact with local companies they believe are interested. Most governments organize trade missions.

Probably every nation in the world holds a **trade fair** periodically. Usually, each nation has a specifically marked area where its exhibitors have their own booths staffed by company representatives. Although trade fairs are open to the general public, at certain hours (generally mornings), entrance is limited to businesspeople interested in doing business with the exhibitors.

trade fair a large exhibition, generally held at the same place and same time periodically, at which companies maintain booths to promote the sale of their products

Sometimes local research is required. For many situations, the executive's report will be the final input to the information on which the decision is based. However, occasionally the proposed human and financial resource commitments are so great that management will insist on gathering data in the proposed market rather than depending solely on the desk and field reports.[7] This would undoubtedly be the position of a consumer products manufacturer that envisions entering a large competitive market of an industrialized country. It might also be the recommendation of the executive making the field trip if he or she discovered that market conditions were substantially different from those to which the firm was accustomed. Often, in face-to-face interviews, information is revealed that would never be written. In these situations, research in the local market will not only supply information on market definition and projection but will also assist in the formulation of an effective marketing mix.

Research in the local market. When the firm's research personnel have had no experience in the country, management should hire a local research group to do the work unless there is a subsidiary in a neighboring country from which a research team may be borrowed. Generally, home country research techniques may be used, though they may need to be adapted to local conditions. It is imperative, therefore, that the person in charge of the project have experience either in that country or in one that is culturally similar and preferably in the same geographic area.

Just as at home, the researchers will first try to obtain secondary data, but they frequently find that, except in developed nations, they either cannot find what they need or what they encounter is suspect. Fortunately, international agencies, such as the United Nations and the IMF, regularly hold seminars to train government officials in data collection, so that the recency and quality of secondary data in some countries are improving.

If secondary data are unavailable, the researchers must collect primary data, and here they face other complications caused by *cultural problems* and *technical difficulties.*

Cultural problems. If the researchers are from one culture and are working in another, they may encounter some cultural problems. When they are not proficient in the local language or dialect, the research instrument or the respondents' answers must be translated. As we learned in the chapter on sociocultural forces, a number of languages may be spoken in a country, and even in countries where only one language is used, the meaning of some words changes from one region to another.

Cultural problems continue to plague the researchers as they try to collect data. The low level of literacy in many developing nations makes the use of mail questionnaires virtually impossible. If a housewife is interviewed in a country where the husband makes the buying decisions, the data obtained from her are worthless. Respondents sometimes refuse to answer questions because of their general distrust of strangers. In other instances, however, the custom of politeness toward everyone will cause respondents to give answers calculated to please the interviewer.

Often there is a practical reason for not wanting to be interviewed. In some countries, income taxes are based on the apparent worth of individuals as measured by their tangible assets. In such countries, when asked if there is a stereo or TV in the household, the respondent may suspect the interviewer of being a tax assessor and refuse to answer. To overcome this problem, experienced researchers often hire college students as interviewers because their manner of speech and dress correctly identify them for what they are.

Technical difficulties.   As if the cultural problems were not enough, the researcher may also encounter technical difficulties. First, up-to-date maps are often unavailable. Streets chosen to be sampled may have three or four different names along their length, and the houses may not be numbered. Telephone surveys can be a formidable undertaking, because in many countries, only the wealthy have telephones and the telephone directories are frequently out of date. In such countries as Brazil and Mexico, researchers often have problems in using their own phones because overloaded circuits make it next to impossible to get a line.[8] Mail surveys can be troublesome too, as mail deliveries within a city may take weeks or are sometimes not even made.

> **The postal service in Italy has been so slow (two weeks for a letter to go from Rome to Milan) that Italian firms have used private couriers to go to Switzerland to dispatch their foreign mail.**

Mail questionnaires are not well received in Chile, where the recipient is required to pay the postman for each letter delivered. The response to a mail survey is often low by American standards in countries where the respondent must go to the post office to mail a letter—for example, Brazil. To increase returns, firms often offer such premiums as lottery tickets or product samples to persons who complete a mail questionnaire.

In some developing nations, the researcher may have to obtain governmental permission to conduct an interview and, in some cases, submit the questionnaire for prior approval. Some countries prohibit certain kinds of questions. For example, you cannot ask Egyptians about the ownership of consumer durables, and in Saudi Arabia, you are not permitted to ask questions about nationality.[9]

Research as practiced.   The existence of hindrances to marketing research does not mean it is not carried out in foreign markets. As you might surmise from the discussion of the availability of secondary data, marketing research is highly developed in industrialized nations, where markets are large and incorrect decisions are costly. Problems like those we have mentioned are prevalent in the developing nations, but they are well known to those who live there. It does not take long for the newcomer to become aware of them either, because longtime residents are quick to point them out.

There is a tendency in these nations to do less research and use simpler techniques, because often a firm is in a seller's market, which means everything produced can be sold with a minimum marketing effort. Bigger headaches, such as a constant lack of foreign exchange for importing raw materials or the necessity of operating in an economy suffering from hyperinflation, require top management to concentrate its efforts in areas other than marketing. Competition is generally less intense because there are fewer competitors and their managements are grappling with the same problems, which keep them from devoting more time to the marketing function. Although the situation is changing, the most common technique still seems to be a combination of trend analysis and the querying of knowledgeable persons (salespeople, channel members, and customers), whose findings are then adjusted on the basis of the subjective considerations of the researchers.[10]

WORLDVIEW
Monitoring Competition: Do You Know What's Happening in the Outside World?

Change is the only certainty in tomorrow's world. Only companies and executives who can adapt to change are likely to survive in the new technological age.
How well do you monitor the outside world? Answering these questions will help you to find out.

1. **Would you form a quality circle to**
   a. Select employees for senior management jobs? ☐
   b. Encourage employees to generate ideas for improvements? ☐
   c. Assist you in determining long-range strategies? ☐

2. **What is the "Boston effect"?**
   a. A personality test that measures resistance to stress. ☐
   b. A method of categorizing products and services. ☐
   c. A statistical technique used in inventory control. ☐

3. **How would you use "positive reinforcement"?**
   a. Allocating more resources to high-growth activities. ☐
   b. Improving the organization's public image. ☐
   c. Recognizing good performance by individuals or groups. ☐

4. **What is "synectics"?**
   a. A creative problem-solving technique. ☐
   b. A branch of laser technology used in glass manufacture. ☐
   c. A method of forecasting retail sales. ☐

5. **Who wrote the best-selling book *Quality Is Free?***
   a. Peter Drucker. ☐
   b. Philip Crosby. ☐
   c. Yukio Mishima. ☐

6. **Which computer is likely to have had the highest sales growth during the 1980s?**
   a. General-purpose computers. ☐
   b. Minicomputers. ☐
   c. Desktop computers. ☐

7. **Which computer language would you be most likely to learn in order to program your personal computer?**
   a. PL/1. ☐
   b. Basic. ☐
   c. Fortran. ☐

8. **What is the no. 1 objective of most large Japanese companies?**
   a. High market share. ☐
   b. Maximum profit. ☐
   c. Excellent employee relations. ☐

9. **The book *The Third Wave* describes the kind of society that will result from the influence of new technologies. Who wrote it?**
   a. Herman Kahn. ☐
   b. Alvin Toffler. ☐
   c. E. F. Schumacher. ☐

RECAPITULATION OF THE SCREENING PROCESS

Although the screening process we have described may appear time consuming, it does assure management that the principal factors have not been overlooked. Because most market-entry decisions can be implemented in stages, the firm can usually make adjustments in time to avoid significant losses when conditions change or if additional information indicates the initial decision was incorrect.

Where do you find this information? You may believe data are difficult to find, but the list in the appendix at the end of this chapter will show you

10. How would you use "transactional analysis"?
  a. Forecasting potential bad debts. ☐
  b. Improving communication and personal relationships. ☐
  c. Identifying companies as possible acquisition prospects. ☐

11. Which of the following types of work is likely to provide the greatest opportunities for the use of industrial robots?
  a. Assembly work. ☐
  b. Handling soft goods, e.g., the garment and shoe industries. ☐
  c. Packaging and package distribution. ☐

12. What is the most important capability which the more advanced robots of the future will need?
  a. Improved sense of vision. ☐
  b. Better tactile sensing. ☐
  c. Greater mobility. ☐

13. Who was the famous writer who devised "the three laws of robotics"?
  a. Kurt Vonnegut. ☐
  b. Erich von Daniken. ☐
  c. Isaac Asimov. ☐

14. What is "Scimitar"?
  a. A systematic approach to new-product development. ☐
  b. A computerized production system. ☐
  c. A linear programming technique used by Japanese companies for controlling suppliers. ☐

15. What do you plan to do to fill any gaps in your knowledge revealed by this test?
  a. I'll hire a top-flight consultant for advice. ☐
  b. Nothing—I'll wait until I'm sure I know what I need. ☐
  c. As a first step I'll read some books on each subject. ☐

Rate yourself by checking your score below.

How you rate in adapting to change
(5 marks for each correct answer)

1. (b)	**6.** (c)	**11.** (a)
2. (b)	**7.** (b)	**12.** (a)
3. (c)	**8.** (a)	**13.** (c)
4. (a)	**9.** (b)	**14.** (a)
5. (b)	**10.** (b)	**15.** (c)

60–75 *You actively manage your own development. For you, change is welcome and exciting.*
40–55 *You have a positive attitude to change but could push yourself a little harder to keep up with new developments.*
20–35 *You are in danger of becoming out of date. Act now and set yourself some really challenging goals.*
0–15 *You have a great deal of catching-up to do.*

Source: *International Management,* March 1984, pp. 29–30.

there are many sources. The difficulty lies in converting all of these data into information that managers can utilize. For this, the firm needs an international management information system.

INTERNATIONAL MANAGEMENT INFORMATION SYSTEM (IMIS)

The **international management information system (IMIS)** is an organized, continuous process of gathering, storing, processing, and disseminating information for the purpose of making business decisions. The system's size and complexity can range from a simple filing cabinet in a small firm to a system

international management information system (IMIS)
organized process of gathering, storing, processing, and disseminating information to managers to assist them in making business decisions

employing computers to process and store data, as is found in large firms. The means are less important than the end, which is to enable marketing and other managers to use all the sources of information at their disposal. These are:

1. *Internal sources*—market analyses, special research reports, and data from company sales, production, financial, and accounting records as reported by foreign subsidiaries, sales representatives, customers, and channel of distribution members.

2. *External sources*—reports from governments, trade associations, banks, consultants, customers, and data bases.

Both types of sources can provide data concerning the changes and trends in the uncontrollable environmental variables as well as feedback on the performance of the firm's controllable variables. There is a trend now toward decision support systems, which permit managers to make inquiries and receive specific answers not only from the firm's data base, but from external, on-line data bases as well.

SUMMARY

A complete market analysis and assessment as described in this chapter would be made by a firm that either is contemplating entering the foreign market for the first time or is already a multinational but wants to monitor world markets systematically to avoid overlooking marketing opportunities and threats. Many of the data requirements for a foreign decision are the same as those required for a similar domestic decision, though it is likely that additional information about some of the international and foreign environmental forces will be needed.

Essentially, the screening process consists of examining the various forces in succession and eliminating countries at each step. The sequence of screening based on (1) basic need potential, (2) financial and economic forces, (3) political and legal forces, (4) sociocultural forces, (5) competitive forces, and (6) personal visits is ordered so as to have a successively smaller number of prospects to consider at each of the succeedingly more difficult and expensive stages.

When the proposed commitment of the financial and human resources is large, managements may be reluctant to make a decision based solely on the desk study and will require that research be undertaken in the market. If the researchers cannot obtain satisfactory secondary data, they will need to collect primary data.

Cultural problems, such as a low level of literacy and distrust of strangers, complicate the data-gathering process, as do technical difficulties, such as a lack of maps, telephone directories, and adequate mail service. These hindrances to marketing research do not prevent the work from being done. There is a tendency in many markets, however, to do less research and use simpler techniques.

To provide continuing information on changes in the uncontrollable variables as well as feedback on the performance of the firm's controllable variables, many companies have set up an international management information system to gather, store, and use information in an organized manner.

QUESTIONS

1. Select a country and a product that you believe your firm can market there. Prepare a study based on the information obtained from the first four screenings for your firm's executive committee, which will decide whether to proceed with your recommendations.

2. What is the basis for the order of screenings presented in the text?

3. If import data for a country are unobtainable, what readily available data might serve as a substitute?

4. Do a country's imports completely measure the market potential for a product? Why or why not?

5. What are some barriers related to the political and legal forces that may eliminate a country from further consideration?

6. What is the reason for making personal visits to markets that survive the first five screenings?

7. Why should a firm's management consider going on a trade mission or exhibiting in a trade fair?

8. What are the two principal kinds of complications that researchers face when they collect primary data in a foreign market?

9. Is there any connection between Europe 1992 and an increase in the use of clustering analysis and similar statistical techniques?

10. What is an international management information system? What is the minimum recommended computer size?

◻ MINICASE 14–1

The Doan Rubber Company

The Doan Rubber Company is a small manufacturer of top-quality vulcanized rubber surgical and medical gloves. Annual sales are about $800,000. Tom Doan, the president and founder of the company, has heard accounts of the success with exporting that other small firms have had and wonders if his company might also increase sales by selling overseas. Doan is concerned though, because his products are "low tech" compared to those most of the small firms he knows are exporting. Moreover, he has seen imported gloves in his market, so perhaps no one exports rubber surgical and medical gloves from the United States. Perhaps the higher price Doan must charge for his higher-quality gloves will keep him out of the export market.

To satisfy his curiosity, he calls a friend who is a professor of international business at the university and tells him he wants to do some preliminary market research. Specifically, he wants to know:

1. Are vulcanized rubber surgical and medical gloves exported from the United States?

2. What is the average wholesale price? Can Doan Rubber compete?

3. If there are exports, is the export market broad or are exports sold in just a few foreign markets?

4. What are the top five export markets? The exports to each one are what percentage of the total export market? What is the average wholesale price per dozen that these markets pay for American gloves?

5. If price is an indicator of quality, is there any market that seems to be buying high-quality gloves?

His friend tells him to meet him at the government documents section of the library. When Doan arrives, the professor already has the *FT477* annual open to page G-31, U.S. Exports, Section 7, which covers articles of plastic and rubber. The illustration on page 502 is from that page.

◻ MINICASE 14–2

Benton Products (Revised)

Benton Products is a multinational firm producing kitchen appliances (washers, dryers, electric ranges, refrigerators, and dishwashers). They have wholly owned production facilities in the United States, Canada, Japan, five EC countries, Brazil, and Mexico. The complete product line is manufactured only in the United States and Brazil. Although no single plant in the EC produces all the company's products, the five taken together do produce the complete product line. Joint ventures are manufacturing some products in India and Indonesia; and in South Korea and Australia, certain products are obtained from contract manufacturers who supply them with the Benton brand name. Benton markets in South Korea and Australia through wholly owned sales companies.

Bill Easton, vice president of marketing, has just finished reading an article on *Business International's* market indexes and is wondering if they could be useful in analyzing Benton's sales. Easton calls in Lianne Ball, head of marketing research, and asks her to study the article, which contains the indexes for 33 major countries, and give him her recommendations. Later that day, she gives him the following note:

To Bill Easton

From the desk of L. Ball

Bill, I gave the article a "quick read" as you requested, and it has possibilities. I converted the market size in

Table 1. SCHEDULE B COMMODITY BY COUNTRY—DOMESTIC MERCHANDISE—Con.

[IN THOUSANDS OF DOLLARS. SEE DESCRIPTION OF STATISTICS FOR INFORMATION ON COVERAGE, VALUATION, SECURITY RESTRICTIONS, SAMPLING PROCEDURES, SOURCES OF ERROR IN THE DATA, OTH CTY (OTHER COUNTRIES), AND OTHER DEFINITIONS AND FEATURES OF THE EXPORT STATISTICS.]

COUNTRY OF DESTINATION	NET QUANTITY	VALUE	COUNTRY OF DESTINATION	NET QUANTITY	VALUE	COUNTRY OF DESTINATION	NET QUANTITY	VALUE
4013900000 INNER TUBES OF RUBBER NESOI NO—Con.			**4014905000 HYGENIC ARTICLE EXC NURSING NIPPLES NESOI X — Con.**			**4015900000 ARTICLE OF APPAREL EXC GLOVE VULCANIZE RUB NESOI X — Con.**		
JAMAICA	7 132	113	ITALY	–	415	JAPAN	–	1 871
DOM REP	7 737	122	PAKISTN	–	310	AUSTRAL	–	103
TRINID	9 653	59	MALAYSA	–	160	OTH CTY	–	664
COLOMB	17 515	270	SINGARP	–	60	TOTAL	–	9 395
VENEZ	13 339	209	CHINA T	–	156			
ECUADOR	5 172	95	JAPAN	–	57	**4016100000 OTHER ARTICLE OF VULCANIZED RUB OF CELLULAR RUB X**		
BOLIVIA	3 736	50	AUSTRAL	–	181			
CHILE	6 251	95	ZMBABWE	–	59			
ARGENT	3 187	53	OTH CTY	–	473	CANADA	–	2 309
SWEDEN	13 104	175	TOTAL	–	4 463	MEXICO	–	1 037
						PERU	–	70
U KING	36 573	906	**4015110000 SURGICAL & MED GLOVE VULCANIZE RUBBER NESOI DPR**			SWEDEN	–	128
BELGIUM	10 666	287				U KING	–	1 583
FRANCE	7 572	156				NETHLDS	–	97
FR GERM	2 410	51	CANADA	921 020	2 106	BELGIUM	–	573
ITALY	1 770	93	MEXICO	36 833 022	50 512	FRANCE	–	388
S ARAB	42 683	633	GUATMAL	110 154	289	FR GERM	–	176
MALAYSA	7 903	132	PANAMA	105 529	222	SINGARP	–	90
SINGARP	7 519	81	BAHAMAS	22 166	57			
KOR REP	4 369	61	JAMAICA	66 307	253	HG KONG	–	54
CHINA T	3 688	81	HAITI	22 771	53	CHINA T	–	307
			DOM REP	30 871	102	JAPAN	–	323
JAPAN	61 895	928	TRINID	39 651	106	TNZANIA	–	193
AUSTRAL	95 148	846	VENEZ	606 407	1 130	OTH CTY	–	495
LIBERIA	4 794	83				TOTAL	–	7 823
OTH CTY	37 186	670	ECUADOR	76 211	216			
TOTAL	754 430	9 966	CHILE	30 693	57	**4016910000 FLOOR COVERING & MAT VULCANIZE RUB EXC HARD RUB X**		
			BRAZIL	115 991	270			
4014100000 SHEATH CONTRACEPTIVE OF VULCANIZE RUB EXC HD RUB X			U KING	117 302	299			
			IRELAND	26 575	128	CANADA	–	16 369
			NETHLDS	228 646	744	MEXICO	–	1 325
CANADA	–	892	FRANCE	63 930	349	SALVADR	–	84
MEXICO	–	1 595	FR GERM	239 590	500	ICELAND	–	76
GUATMAL	–	253	SWITZLD	145 879	262	SWEDEN	–	205
SALVADR	–	214	SPAIN	137 783	214	U KING	–	474
C RICA	–	251				NETHLDS	–	80
JAMAICA	–	504	ITALY	466 898	1 218	BELGIUM	–	152
HAITI	–	130	GREECE	107 793	65	FRANCE	–	131
DOM REP	–	66	ISRAEL	71 007	179	FR GERM	–	276
TRINID	–	157	S ARAB	242 042	645			
COLOMB	–	363	QATAR	10 220	64	ITALY	–	476
			SINGARP	11 776	50	S ARAB	–	187
ECUADOR	–	122	PHIL R	11 411	54	SINGARP	–	81
PERU	–	658	CHINA M	27 059	69	CHINA M	–	50
CHILE	–	650	KOR REP	23 092	59	HG KONG	–	122
BRAZIL	–	176	CHINA T	224 544	308	CHINA T	–	339
URUGUAY	–	83	JAPAN	791 026	3 057	JAPAN	–	13 847
FINLAND	–	424	AUSTRAL	21 065	54	AUSTRAL	–	657
DENMARK	–	124	OTH CTY	289 884	782	EGYPT	–	68
U KING	–	319	TOTAL	42 238 315	64 471	OTH CTY	–	468
FR GERM	–	111				TOTAL	–	35 468
SPAIN	–	321	**4015190000 GLOVES EXCEPT SURGICAL AND MEDICAL GLOVES NESOI DPR**					
						4016920000 ERASERS OF VULCANIZED RUBBER EXC HARD RUBBER X		
ITALY	–	1 507						
GREECE	–	106	CANADA	96 324	1 282			
TURKEY	–	1 413	MEXICO	463 378	4 948			
S ARAB	–	89	DOM REP	17 888	145	CANADA	–	509
INDIA	–	569	VENEZ	41 425	162	MEXICO	–	258
PAKISTN	–	5 530	CHILE	10 478	244	SALVADR	–	134
BNGLDSH	–	9 685	BRAZIL	4 522	51	U KING	–	367
THAILND	–	426	SWEDEN	23 108	750	FR GERM	–	258
KOR REP	–	63	NORWAY	11 991	364	PHIL R	–	76
HG KONG	–	103	DENMARK	2 967	73	KOR REP	–	58
			U KING	53 152	1 209	HG KONG	–	51
AUSTRAL	–	631				OTH CTY	–	273
IN ZEAL	–	80	IRELAND	3 530	55	TOTAL	–	1 984
MOROC	–	235	BELGIUM	20 988	316			
TUNISIA	–	55	FRANCE	12 572	264			
EGYPT	–	2 747	FR GERM	28 452	502	**4016930000 GASKET WASHERS & OTHER SEALS OF VULCANIZED RUB X**		
SENEGAL	–	98	ISRAEL	4 587	74			
GHANA	–	89	MALAYSA	6 174	87			
NIGER	–	54	PHIL R	2 922	57	CANADA	–	35 525
ZAIRE	–	132	CHINA T	6 551	97	MEXICO	–	23 170
UGANDA	–	130	JAPAN	11 308	242	GUATMAL	–	95
			AUSTRAL	38 524	742	SALVADR	–	66
KENYA	–	941	REP SAF	3 742	59	C RICA	–	269
THZANIA	–	112	OTH CTY	46 829	543	PANAMA	–	75
BOTSWAN	–	61	TOTAL	911 412	12 266	JAMAICA	–	130
OTH CTY	–	449				DOM REP	–	85
TOTAL	–	32 719	**4015900000 ARTICLE OF APPAREL EXC GLOVE VULCANIZE RUB NESOI X**			TRINID	–	102
4014901000 NURSING NIPPLES OF VULCANIZE RUB EXC HARD RUB GRS						N ANTIL	–	158
			CANADA	–	1 777			
			MEXICO	–	2 056	COLOMB	–	349
CANADA	41 473	453	BERMUDA	–	174	VENEZ	–	581
KOR REP	5 429	57	N ANTIL	–	100	SURINAM	–	137
JAPAN	11 111	109	VENEZ	–	55	ECUADOR	–	223
OTH CTY	31 056	317	U KING	–	213	PERU	–	102
TOTAL	89 069	937	NETHLDS	–	65	CHILE	–	354
			FRANCE	–	338	BRAZIL	–	789
4014905000 HYGENIC ARTICLE EXC NURSING NIPPLES NESOI X			FR GERM	–	274	PARAGUA	–	56
			AUSTRIA	–	62	ARGENT	–	210
						SWEDEN	–	640
CANADA	–	245	SWITZLD	–	67			
MEXICO	–	704	POLAND	–	57	FINLAND	–	134
CHILE	–	189	SPAIN	–	103	DENMARK	–	103
U KING	–	912	PORTUGAL	–	75	U KING	–	5 575
IRELAND	–	127	ITALY	–	890	IRELAND	–	268
FRANCE	–	144	GREECE	–	82	NETHLDS	–	702
FR GERM	–	215	MALAYSA	–	147	BELGIUM	–	1 568
SWITZLD	–	55	HG KONG	–	222	LUXMBRG	–	63
						FRANCE	–	1 798

percentages for each BI country that is also a country where Benton operates to a Benton world market size. Note that the BI percentages add up to 56 percent so I had to convert them to 100 percent. For example, Ja-

pan's value of 7.16 percent becomes in the Benton world (7.16 × 100)/56 = 12.8 percent.

See the following tables. If you agree, I can do a detailed analysis after I finish the rush job I'm on now.

Business International's Market Indicators for Benton Countries

Country	BI Market Size (percent)	Benton World Market Size (percent)	Actual Percentage of Total Benton Sales (percent)	Market Intensity Index	Five-Year Market Growth (percent)
United States	19.12%	34.14%	36.1%	3.9	8.84%
Japan	7.16	12.79	11.7	2.7	12.27
India	5.22	9.32	7.8	0.1	40.90
Germany	3.95	7.05	8.3	2.8	5.26
France	3.49	6.23	6.6	2.7	9.16
United Kingdom	2.96	5.29	5.5	2.5	6.61
Italy	2.96	5.29	6.0	2.3	7.09
Brazil	2.30	4.11	3.3	0.8	24.32
Canada	2.09	3.73	3.9	3.7	9.76
Spain	1.63	2.91	2.7	1.7	6.61
Mexico	1.54	2.75	2.3	0.7	10.18
South Korea	1.26	2.25	2.0	1.2	41.59
Indonesia	1.25	2.23	1.8	0.1	31.13
Australia	1.07	1.91	2.0	2.9	11.79
Total	56.00%	100.00%	100.0%		

Benton Products Sales by Country

Country	1990 Sales ($ millions)	Five-Year Market Growth (percent)
United States	$299	9.1%
Japan	97	13.1
India	65	22.8
Germany	69	8.4
France	55	11.1
United Kingdom	46	6.7
Italy	50	6.8
Brazil	27	18.1
Canada	32	9.6
Spain	22	7.8
Mexico	19	10.7
South Korea	17	29.3
Indonesia	15	32.1
Australia	17	11.5
Total	$830.0	

Easton looks her note over and decides to call in Jim Allen, marketing manager for international sales.

Easton:

Good morning, Jim. Do you know anything about the market indexes that *Business International* publishes?

Allen:

I've heard of them, but I haven't used them. They try to do for the world what the Buying Power Index of *Sales & Marketing Management* does for the United States.

Easton:

Something like that. You know, I'm wondering if the sales of our foreign subsidiaries are keeping up with the growth in their markets. I notice that many countries' GNPs are growing, levels of living are rising—it seems to me that more people are becoming able to buy our products.

Allen:

Yes, Bill, sales are rising everywhere. Look at these sales in India—a 23 percent growth over the past five years; Korea, 29 percent; Indonesia, 32 percent; Brazil, 18 percent. You don't see that kind of increase in this country, do you? I tell you, Bill, everything's just fine. Our people are really on the ball.

Easton:

Don't be so sure. I made a calculation off the top of my head for India with the index Lianne calculated, and I'm not so certain as you seem to be. Look at the following table:

(1) Benton-India Sales	(2) Benton World Market Size (percent)	(3) Sales Should Be	(4) India Sales Total Sales	(5) Column (4) Column (2)
$65 million	9.3%	$77.2 million	$65 m/$830 m = 7.80%	0.839

Allen:

How did you calculate what India's sales should be in column (3)?

Easton:

I multiplied the Benton World market size percentage by the total company sales of $830 million.

Allen:

What does column (5) indicate?

Easton:

I was trying to come up with a single number to measure how each market is doing compared to what it should do based on Lianne's index; in other words, despite India's remarkable sales increase, its sales are still not what they should be according to the index. According to *Business International,* they should be doing considerably more.

Allen:

This may have possibilities. Let me work with it. By the way, do you know how *BI* arrives at this market size index?

Easton:

Yes, here are their calculations in the article.

$$\text{Size (\%)} = \frac{2(\text{POP}) + \text{POPU} + \text{PCE} + \text{KWH} + \text{STL} + \text{CEM} + \text{TEL} + \text{CAR} + \text{TV}}{2(\text{POPR}) + \text{POPUR} + \text{PCER} + \text{KWHR} + \text{STLR} + \text{CEMR} + \text{TELR} + \text{CARR} + \text{TVR}} \times 100$$

where:

POP	=	Total population
POPU	=	Urban population
PCE	=	Private final consumption in U.S. dollars
KWH	=	Electricity production
STL	=	Apparent crude steel consumption
CEM	=	Cement production
TEL	=	Telephones in use
CAR	=	Passenger cars in use
TV	=	Television sets in use

A variable ending in R stands for regional or world total.

Allen:

Well, these aren't the market factors we use. We look at housing starts, size of households, marriages, population, and private consumer expenditures. In some countries, we can even get data on expenditures for household appliances.

Easton:

Do you combine them in any way?

Allen:

Yes, we use a regression equation that includes these variables.

Easton:

So, if each market's sales increase is in the line with

the increases in these variables, you feel that we're doing a decent job in that market?

Allen:

At least this indicates we're holding our own, and, of course, we're always trying to increase market share. Another calculation we make is sales dollars per household in each market. We divide our sales in Germany, for example, by the number of households in Germany. We do that for each market and compare them. I learned that from our domestic manager.

Easton:

Yes, I know about that one. Tell you what, Jim. Why don't you take Lianne's index and the rest of the *BI* data and make some comparisons. Look at the "richness" index—they call it Market Intensity Index—and compare their market growth rates with ours. Let's look over your calculations together when you're ready.

Allen:

Give me a couple of days, Jim.

Make your calculations and point out which subsidiaries are doing well and which should be able to improve.

SUPPLEMENTARY READINGS

"A European Researcher's View of European Business Marketing." *Business Marketing,* April 1984, pp. 72–76.

"Attitude Research Assesses Global Market Potential." *Marketing News,* August 1, 1988, p. 10.

Day, Ellen; Richard J. Fox; and Sandra M. Huszagh. "Segmenting the Global Market for Industrial Goods: Issues and Implications." *International Marketing Review,* Autumn 1988, pp. 14–27.

"Do-It-Yourself Marketing Research." *Management Review,* May 1991, pp. 34–37.

Douglas, Susan P., and C. Samuel Craig. *International Marketing Research.* Englewood Cliffs, N.J.: Prentice-Hall, 1983.

"Euronet." *Europe,* July–August 1982, p. 7.

"Eyeing the Consumer." *The Economist,* April 22, 1989, pp. 63–66.

"First Worldwide Survey of Leading Researchers." *Advertising Age,* July 18, 1983, p. 3.

"From Market Research to Business Research." *McKinsey Quarterly,* Autumn 1984, pp. 50–62.

"Grass-Roots Marketing Yields Clients in Mexico City." *The Wall Street Journal,* October 24, 1991, p. B2.

Johansson, Johny K., and Ikujiro Nonaka. "Market Research the Japanese Way." *Harvard Business Review,* May–June 1987, pp. 16–18.

"Making IMIS Work for You." *Business Marketing,* October 1987, pp. 71–73.

Malhotra, Naresh K. "A Methodology for Measuring Consumer Preferences in Developing Countries." *International Marketing Review,* Autumn 1988, pp. 52–65.

"Marketing Research Wins Fans in India." *Advertising Age,* January 26, 1987, p. 57.

Ofir, Chezy, and Donald R. Lehman. "Measuring Images of Foreign Products." *Columbia Journal of World Business,* Summer 1986, pp. 105–08.

"Overcoming the Obstacles to International Research." *Marketing News,* August 29, 1988, p. 12.

"Probing Japanese Buyers' Minds." *Business Marketing,* November 1987, pp. 85–90.

"The Importance of Market Research." *Japan Update,* Autumn 1988, pp. 12–15.

"Third World Research Is Difficult, but It's Possible." *Marketing News,* August 26, 1987, pp. 50–51.

"Why Re-Invent the Wheel?" *Business America,* February 15, 1988, pp. 8–9.

ENDNOTES

1. J. F. Preble, P. A. Rau, and A. Reichel, "The Environmental Scanning Practices of U.S. Multinationals in the Late 1980s," *Management International Reports,* April 1988, pp. 4–13; and *Competitive Intelligence* (New York: The Conference Board, 1988), p. 7. Sixty-eight percent of the respondents said monitoring competitors' activities is important, but only 9 percent believed they have an effective system now.

2. Richard D. Robinson recommends a similar methodology, which he calls filtering, in *International Business Management,* 2nd ed. (Hinsdale, Ill.: Dryden Press, 1978), pp. 52–55. Also see F. T. Haner, *Multinational Management* (Columbus, Ohio: Charles E. Merrill Publishing, 1973),

pp. 20–25; and R. W. Walvoord, "Export Market Research," *American Export Bulletin,* May 1980, pp. 82–91. Robin Peterson, "Screening Is First Step in Evaluating Foreign Market," *Marketing News,* June 1990, p. 13, captures the idea we are describing.

3. Regression analysis is a statistical technique employing the least squares criterion to determine the relationship between the dependent variable and one or more independent variables. In the text, MP is the dependent variable, and x_1 through x_n are the independent variables. The analyst wants to solve for the constants a through z. For an in-depth explanation of regression analysis, see any statistics text.

4. Susan P. Douglas and C. Samuel Craig, *International Marketing Research* (Englewood Cliffs, N.J.: Prentice-Hall, 1983), pp. 259–73.

5. Commonly, public utilities, mineral extraction, banking, and communications are reserved either for the government or its citizens. Many of the LDCs tend to limit foreign participation to 49 percent generally and even less in certain industries.

6. Preble et al., "Environmental Scanning Practices," p. 12.

7. Secondary data and some primary data will be gathered on the field trip, but the visitor rarely has the time or the ability to conduct a complete research study.

8. While in São Paulo, one of the writers wanted to call Santos (an hour's drive away). The assistant to his secretary, whose principal job was to dial for an outside line, had tried to place the call all morning. Finally, at noon, he drove to Santos, completed his business, and returned to find the assistant still dialing.

9. "Third World Research Is Difficult, but It's Possible," *Marketing News,* August 26, 1987, p. 51.

10. "Market Research Wins Fans in India," *Advertising Age,* January 26, 1987, p. 57; and "Third World Research Is Difficult, but It's Possible," *Marketing News,* August 26, 1987, pp. 50–51.

APPENDIX

Sources of Information Used in Screening

I–II. First and second screening (basic need potential, economic and financial forces).
  A. GATT *Yearbook*.
  B. IMF *Direction of Trade* and other publications.
  C. OECD *Economic Outlook* and other publications.
  D. United Nations.
    1. Statistical Yearbook.
    2. *Demographic Yearbook*.
    3. Contact UN for catalog of publications.
  E. Eurostat publishes much data on EC trade. Ask EC office in New York City.
  F. World Bank—*World Development Report* (annual)—also available on computer disk. Ask for catalog of publications.
  G. Asian Development Bank—*Annual Report* and newsletter.
  H. InterAmerican Development Bank—*Annual Report* and newsletter.
  I. Small Business Administration—*Export Information System Data Reports*.
  J. U.S. Department of Commerce.
    1. *FT477, FT925*, and other foreign trade reports.
    2. *Foreign Trade Highlights*.
    3. *Annual Worldwide Industry Reviews*.
    4. *International Data Base* from Center for International Research, Department of Commerce.
    5. *Country Trade Statistics* and many others. See *A Basic Guide to Exporting* ($8.50 from the Government Printing Office) for a complete list or request information from nearest Department of Commerce field office. Additional Commerce publications are listed in Chapter 16.
  K. *Business International* "Indicators of Market Size for 117 Countries" (annual).
  L. Monitor, London, England.
    1. *Europe Marketing Data & Statistics* (annual).
    2. *International Marketing Data & Statistics* (annual).
  M. Commercial officers of foreign embassies in Washington, D.C.
  N. Trade associations.
  O. Banks with international departments.
  P. Chambers of commerce, such as the German–American Chamber of Commerce in New York City or the Mexican–American Chamber of Commerce in Mexico City.
  Q. Data bases such as Reuters' Textline, Dun & Bradstreet's Datastream International, Predicasts in Cleveland, Ohio, and The Economist Intelligence Unit in London, England.
  R. Many state governments have trade offices with country and market specialists and good libraries.
  S. Write to commercial officers in American embassies.

Chapter 15

Marketing Internationally

We will market world brands that share global technology and common positioning, but with appropriate regional testing of product aesthetics and form, packaging materials, and market execution to best satisfy local customer demands for quality and value.

Edwin L. Artzt, chairman and CEO, Procter & Gamble Company

LEARNING OBJECTIVES

In this chapter, you will study:

1. Why sometimes there are differences between marketing domestically and internationally.

2. Why multinational managers wish to standardize the marketing mix.

3. Why it is often impossible to standardize the marketing mix worldwide.

4. The importance of distinguishing among the total product, the physical product, and the brand name.

5. Why consumer products generally require greater modification than industrial products and services.

6. The importance of the environmental forces on the marketing mix.

7. The product strategies that can be formed from three product alternatives and three kinds of promotional messages.

8. "Glocal" advertising strategies.

9. The intricacies of transfer pricing.

KEY WORDS AND CONCEPTS

- Total product
- Promotion
- Advertising
- Programmed-management approach
- Sales promotion
- Public relations
- Foreign national pricing
- Transfer price

BUSINESS INCIDENT

Procter & Gamble, an evolving global corporation . . .

There have been some false starts and even some failures, but now Procter & Gamble's global marketing efforts are starting to bring results. The company, ranked number 41 in *Fortune*'s "The World's Largest Corporations" and 15 in its "Largest U.S. Industrial Corporations," obtained $9.6 billion (40 percent of its total sales) from its non-U.S. operations.

This is all the more notable inasmuch as P&G faces more pressures in most foreign markets than it does in the United States. Many foreign countries have price controls, and there are more competitors in Europe because of the ease of shipping products across borders. For example, in France, P&G competes against Swedish, Danish, and Italian firms in many of its product categories. Commercial TV time, the most efficient way to introduce new products quickly, is limited, and in many countries, such as Belgium, Germany, Italy, and Japan, the use of premiums and gifts for promotion is either banned or severely restricted.

In the 1940s, P&G's strategy was to export its core products to build demand and then establish local sales companies or production facilities. Whether the products were exported or produced locally, they were marketed similarly everywhere. Although those products were not launched with global distribution in mind, new products are. According to Edwin Artzt, P&G's chairman, "If P&G were introducing Pampers today, it would plan to get the product into world markets in five years or less." It took the company 15 years to get them into 70 countries. Now the company tries to introduce products on a worldwide scale early in their development, not after they are established in one market, which gives competitors time to react in all other markets.

Sometimes P&G approaches foreign markets more as a regional market than as a global one; many of its products are changed to suit the local markets, for example.

BUSINESS INCIDENT (concluded)

Camay's™ smell, Crest's™ flavor, and Head & Shoulders'™ formula vary from one region to another, as does the company's marketing strategy. "The idea of moving quickly by taking a piece of technology and implementing it to fit the habits of local markets has taken hold and is leading our operation," says Artzt. "[But] there is a reluctance to fix something that isn't broke—i.e., alter a product or a marketing strategy that is successful in one market just because it doesn't fit the global pattern."

For many years, P&G had a philosophy of employing overseas the same policies and procedures that had been successful in the United States, but this practice sometimes gave the company problems. The company rolled out Vizir, based on Liquid Tide,™ in Europe in the 1980s. What the marketers failed to realize was the European washing machines were not equipped to accept liquid detergents. When Vizir was added to a powder dispenser, 20 percent was lost in the bottom of the washer. P&G developed a plastic dispenser that fit into powder dispensers and offered it free to consumers. One small problem—European washing machines are bolted to the wall. "When we called these women and said we wanted to mail you a liquid dispenser free, just tell us the washer model number, they said, 'I don't know, the washer is bolted to the wall and I can't see it,'" explained Artzt. The company finally solved the problem by inventing a reusable ball that sits on top of the clothes and dispenses the liquid. Vizir is now the third-largest-selling detergent in France and has been relaunched in other European countries. Artzt claims, "I think this will go down in history as one of the great all-time rescue jobs."

On the other hand, P&G recycled an ad campaign previously used in the United States when it relaunched Orange Crush in Peru. The TV spot showed a small boy who promises to save his soccer-playing brother's Orange Crush but then succumbs to temptation and drinks it himself. It is credited with playing an important part in a 60 percent sales increase.

To avoid a repetition of the washing machine problem, P&G's present strategy is to make global plans, then re-plan for each region and execute the plan locally. It uses autonomous "core teams" composed of representatives of each country in a region to plan a testing program or a development program for new products and product improvement. They recommend products and marketing strategies for the core products (product lines)—soap, toothpaste, diapers, and shampoo. P&G core teams are working on the smell and concentration levels of fabric softeners for different parts of the world, for example.

Even the core team concept is evolving; a new one for disposables and beverages has been organized globally rather than regionally, as the first four teams were.

Source: "P&G's Artzt on Ads: Crucial Investment," *Advertising Age,* October 28, 1991, p. 1; "Stodgy No More," *The Wall Street Journal,* March 5, 1991, p. A1; and "P&G Rushes On Global Diaper Rollout," *Advertising Age,* November 24, 1991, p. 6.

The Business Incident illustrates how P&G has changed its marketing strategy from using the same policies and procedures overseas that have first been successful in the United States to making global plans, adjusting them for regions, and then adapting them to satisfy local customer demands. Whether a policy or technique is first designed for global use and then adapted for local market differences or, as in the case of the Orange Crush advertisement, the idea comes first from the home country and then is used overseas, marketers must know where to look for possible differences between marketing domestically and marketing internationally. Sometimes, the differences are great, but at other times, there are no differences.

Certainly there are some strong commonalities. Isn't it true that marketers everywhere must (1) know their markets, (2) develop products or services to satisfy customers' needs, (3) price the products or services so that they are readily acceptable in the market, (4) make them available to the buyers, and (5) inform potential customers and persuade them to buy?

ADDED COMPLEXITIES OF INTERNATIONAL MARKETING

Although the basic functions of domestic and international marketing are the same, the international markets served often differ widely because of the great variations in the uncontrollable environmental forces that we examined in Section Three. Moreover, even the forces we think of as controllable vary among wide limits: distribution channels to which the marketer is accustomed are unavailable, certain aspects of the product may be different, the promotional mixes are often dissimilar, and distinct cost structures may require different prices to be set.

The international marketing manager's task is complex. He or she frequently must plan and control a variety of marketing strategies rather than one and then coordinate and integrate those strategies into a single marketing program. Even the marketing managers of global firms such as P&G who utilize a single, worldwide strategy must know enough about the uncontrollable variables to be able to make changes in its implementation when necessary.

Both global and multinational marketing managers, like their domestic counterparts, must develop marketing strategies by assessing the firm's potential foreign markets and analyzing the many alternative marketing mixes. Their aim is to select target markets that the firm can serve at a profit and to formulate combinations of tactics for product, price, promotion, and distribution channels that will best serve those markets. In the previous chapter, we examined the market assessment and selection process; in this chapter, we shall study the formulation of the marketing mix.

THE MARKETING MIX (WHAT AND HOW TO SELL)

As we indicated above, the marketing mix consists of a set of strategy decisions made in the areas of product, promotion, pricing, and distribution for the purpose of satisfying the customers in a target market. The number of variables included in these four areas is extremely large, making possible hundreds of combinations. Often the domestic operation has already established a successful marketing mix, and the temptation to follow the same procedures overseas is strong. Yet, as we have seen, important differences between the domestic and foreign environments may make a wholesale transfer of the mix impossible. The question that the international marketing manager must resolve is, "Can we standardize worldwide, must we make some changes, or must we formulate a completely different marketing mix?"

□ Standardization, Adaptation, or Completely Different?

Management would prefer global standardization of the marketing mix—that is, it would prefer to employ the same marketing mix in all of the firm's operations because standardization can produce significant cost savings. If the same product that is sold in the domestic market can be exported, there can be longer production runs that lower manufacturing costs. Even when the standard product is manufactured overseas, production costs will be less because the extra research and design expense of either adapting domestic products or designing new ones for foreign sales will be avoided. Just the task of keeping many sets of specifications current requires additional, highly paid personnel in the home office.[1] For the many products, both consumer and industrial, that require spare parts for after-sales servicing, standardization greatly simplifies logistics and acquisition.

If advertising campaigns, promotional materials (catalogs, point-of-purchase displays), and sales training programs can be standardized, the expensive creative work and artwork need be done only once. Standardized pricing strategies for multinational firms that source markets from several different plants avoid the embarrassment of having an important customer receive two distinct quotations for the same product. Although economies of scale are not as readily attainable for standardizing channels of distribution as for the other elements of the marketing mix, there is some gain in efficiency when the international marketing manager can use the same strategy in all markets. In summary, the benefits from standardization of the marketing mix are (1) lower costs, (2) easier control and coordination from headquarters, and (3) reduction of the time consumed in preparing the marketing plan.

In spite of the advantages of standardization, many firms find it necessary to either modify the present mix or develop a new one. The extent of the changes depends on the type of product (consumer or industrial), the environmental forces, and the degree of market penetration desired by management.

◻ Product Strategies

The product is the central focus of the marketing mix. If it fails to satisfy the needs of consumers, no amount of promotion, price cutting, or distribution will persuade them to buy. The housewife will not repurchase a detergent if the clothes do not come out as clean as the TV commercials say they will. She will not be deceived by advertisements announcing friendly service when her experience demonstrates otherwise.

In formulating product strategies, the international marketing manager must remember that the product is more than a physical object. The **total product,** which is what the customer buys, also includes the package, the brand name, accessories, after-sales service, warranty, and instructions for use. The fact that the total product is purchased often makes it less expensive and easier for the international company to adapt the present product or even create a new one without altering its physical characteristics. Different package sizes and promotional messages, for example, can create a new total product for a distinct market. The relative ease of creating a new total product without changing the manufacturing process is an important reason why there is more physical product standardization internationally than one might expect.

Total and physical product.   Much of the confusion in the ongoing discussion about whether a global firm can have global products results from the discussants not clarifying whether they are referring to the total product, the physical product, or the brand name. For example, Coca-Cola is always offered as an example of a global product and it is true that the total product and the brand are global. However, the physical product is multinational; its sweetness varies according to local tastes, even in the United States.

Consider two products that Cadbury-Schweppes, the British-based food and soft drink multinational, produces—tonic water and chocolate. The tonic water is a global product physically, but, as a total product, it is multi-

> **total product** what the customer buys, including the physical product, brand name, after-sales service, warranty, instructions for use, company image, and package

national because people buy it for different reasons. The French drink it straight, and the English mix it with alcohol. Chocolate is neither a global physical product nor a global total product; it is eaten as a snack in some places, put in sandwiches in some places, and eaten as a dessert in others. Because of strong local preferences, it also varies greatly in taste.[2] So does Nestlé instant coffee, which is produced in 200 different blends globally, all of which are sold under the brand name Nescafe™, another example of brand name globalization.[3]

Type of product.   One important factor that influences the amount of change to be made in a product is its classification as a consumer or industrial product or service. Generally, consumer products require greater adaptation than industrial products to meet the demands of the world market. If the consumer products are high style or the result of a fad, they are especially likely to require changes. We can think of these product types as being on a continuum ranging from insensitive to the foreign environment to highly sensitive, as shown in Figure 15–1.

Industrial products.   As one would gather from Figure 15–1, many highly technical industrial products can be sold unchanged worldwide. Transistors, for example, are used wherever radios are manufactured. Timken advertises that its bearings are interchangeable no matter where produced (see Figure 15–2 on page 517).

If product changes are required, they may be only cosmetic, such as converting gauges to read in the metric system by pasting a new face on a dial or printing instruction plates in another language. Relatively simple adaptations, such as lengthening pedals or changing seat positions, are frequently sufficient to compensate for the physical differences of foreign operators.

Somewhat more drastic modifications in the physical product may be necessary because of two problems that are especially prevalent in the developing countries—a tendency to *overload equipment* and to *slight maintenance.* These problems are comprehensible to anyone familiar with the cultural and economic forces in the foreign environment. Unlike American children, who grow up owning automobiles and working with tools, the mechanics and operators in many foreign countries rarely have such experience until they enter a training program, which is often on the job.[4]

A bulldozer operator learns that if he pulls a lever and steps on a pedal, his machine will push whatever is in front of it. It is not uncommon to see a bulldozer pushing on some immovable object until the engine fails or a part breaks from the overload. The extraordinary noise coming from the engine makes no impression on the operator. Despite the careful instructions con-

WORLDVIEW
On Global Marketing

"The globalization of markets is at hand. With that, the multinational commercial world nears its end and so does the multinational corporation. Different cultural preferences, national tastes and standards, and business institutions are vestiges of the past." So says Theodore Levitt, a Harvard business professor. The world has been homogenized, and the smart firms sell standardized products using standardized promotion methods. Levitt cites such examples as Coca-Cola, Pepsi-Cola, Mc-Donald's, and Revlon.

But Coca-Cola's own advertising director replies, "What looks good as a generalization sometimes doesn't follow. The world is certainly becoming more globalized, but the global village is certainly not here, nor will it ever be." Coke's marketing manager noted that "Diet Coke clearly in many ways isn't appropriate for some undeveloped worlds." PepsiCo lets its overseas offices choose and reedit commercials it makes in the United States and makes local soft drinks like Shani, a currant-and-blackberry soda popular in the Mideast during Ramadan, the Moslem holy month. McDonald's, another company cited by Levitt, says it isn't an advocate of global marketing; it sells beer in Germany, wine in France, pot pie in Australia, and noodles in the Philippines. "We rely on the people native to the country to develop marketing programs," says the marketing vice president. Interestingly, McDonald's retains 74 different ad agencies in the United States to customize its promotion for local markets. Campbell Soup split the country into 22 different regions, each with different marketing strategies.

Is global marketing a nice fad, as a member of Booz, Allen & Hamilton, a well-known consulting firm, says it is? Is it a new idea? No, to both questions. Timken has made the same product and promoted it the same way for decades; its ad in this chapter is more than 15 years old. Thirty years ago, Goodyear's Hi-Miler truck tire was being produced in Akron and its overseas plants and sold under translated names such as *Tragaleguas* (league-eater) for Spanish-speaking markets.

What is new is that companies are first studying their global markets and then, where possible, making a single product for all of them instead of making the product for the domestic market and adapting it to foreign markets. They search for global themes and adapt the promotion of them to fit the local markets. Products that are not culturally sensitive, such as nearly all industrial products and most consumer durables, clothing, and toilet articles, lend themselves to a single, worldwide theme and message; food products require much more adaptation to the local culture. For example, Colgate-Palmolive's Oral Care promotional program (for toothpaste) was successful worldwide.

To sum up, the success of global marketing depends on the kind of product and knowing when product and/or promotional adaptations are necessary.

Source: Theodore Levitt, "The Globalization of Markets," *Harvard Business Review,* May–June 1983, pp. 92 and 96; and "Ad Fad," *The Wall Street Journal,* May 12, 1988, pp. 1 and 17.

cerning cleanliness that ball bearing manufacturers include in the package, one can find a mechanic removing the protective oiled paper to leave the bearing exposed to dust and grime before using it (he probably can't read). A very low-paid, uneducated man may be given the responsibility of lubricating equipment worth millions of dollars. He may overgrease or miss half of the fittings, and the equipment is destroyed.

To overcome these difficulties, such manufacturers as Caterpillar and Allis-Chalmers have established very thorough training programs wherever their products are sold. Many manufacturers have prepared simple instructions with plenty of pictures to get their message across to persons with limited reading ability. The other alternative is to modify the equipment, perhaps using a simpler bearing system that requires little maintenance. The machine

Courtesy The Timken Company

may make more noise and be less efficient, but it runs longer with less maintenance.

Where the technology of even an adapted product is too advanced for their customers, manufacturers may market an entirely different product to accomplish the same purpose. A firm that produces electric cash registers in the United States, for example, may be able to earn good profits by marketing a hand-operated model in areas where electricity is unavailable. Products considered obsolete in advanced countries are frequently what the developing countries need.[5] Also, foreign subsidiaries sometimes find market opportunities for product lines not manufactured by the parent company.

> Marketing managers in General Tire's affiliates saw the profit possibilities in selling fan and industrial V-belts in their markets. Although General Tire—USA did not produce them, management obtained the technology for their subsidiaries through licensing agreements with Gates Rubber, a renowned maker of V-belts, so that this totally new product was manufactured in a number of foreign plants.

Occasionally, adaptations are necessary to meet local legal requirements, such as those that govern noise, safety, or exhaust emissions. To avoid changing the product, some manufacturers design it to meet the most stringent laws even though it will be overdesigned for the rest of the markets. A number of foreign car manufacturers, for example, produce a model for the entire U.S. market that meets the California emission requirements (the most demanding in the United States).

In some instances, governments have passed very strict laws to protect a local manufacturer from imports. When this occurs, the company may prefer to design the product to the next most stringent laws and stay out of the first market. Of course, this is what the government had in mind when it passed the laws. However, a word of caution for the company in this situation—test the local manufacturer's product before giving up on the market. On occasion, the local product also has failed to meet the specifications. When confronted with this evidence, the government has had to change the laws.

Consumer products.   Although consumer products generally require greater modification to meet local market requirements than do industrial products, some of them can be sold unchanged to certain market segments. Consumer products of this kind include a number of luxury items, such as large automobiles, sporting equipment, and perfumes. This is because every country in the world contains a market segment that is more similar to the same segment in other countries with respect to economic status, buyer behavior, tastes, and preferences than it is to the rest of the segments in the same country. This market segment includes the "jet-set," foreign-educated and well-traveled citizens, and expatriates. Many products and services foreign to local tastes and preferences have been successfully introduced by first being marketed to this group. Gradually, members of other market segments have purchased these products and services until consumption has become widespread.

> Before McDonald's and other American fast-food franchisors went abroad, a common complaint among U.S. expatriates was that they couldn't get a good hamburger. A Brazilian returned from college in the United States and opened a drive-in similar to Dairy Queen in Rio de Janeiro. The first customers were Americans and members of the international set, but before long, word spread and Brazilians became customers. Thirty years ago, there was only one A&W root beer stand and one Dairy Queen in Mexico City. American expatriates and tourists were the principal customers. Today, many of the American fast-food franchisors are in such cities as Mexico City, Guadalajara, and Monterrey. When you arrive in Acapulco, the signs of Ponderosa, Kentucky Fried Chicken, and so forth make you think you never left home.

In introducing new products, especially when the goal is immediate market penetration, the marketer must be aware that *generally, as you go down the economic and social strata in each country, you tend to find greater dissimilarities among countries with respect to social and cultural values.* It follows from this that in general, the deeper the immediate market penetration desired, the greater must be the product modification. This does not necessarily mean the physical product must be changed. Perhaps a modification of one of the other elements of the total product is sufficient—a different size or color of the package, a change in the brand name, or a new positioning if the product is consumed differently.

> Mars faced a drop in Bahrain's imports of candy when it was ready to launch M&Ms™. Fortunately, its marketing research discovered that Bahrainis consider the peanut to be a health food, so Mars repositioned its peanut M&Ms. The company was able to turn the hot Gulf climate to its advantage by emphasizing

its traditional slogan, "M&Ms melt in your mouth, not in your hand." As you will see later in this chapter, Mars followed promotional strategy number 2: same product—different message, although part of the message (slogan) remained the same.[6]

Detergent manufacturers were able to achieve deeper market penetration by offering consumers with limited purchasing power the small packages that we find only in American laundromats. In humid climates, cookies and crackers are packed in metal boxes to preserve both the package and the product.

Services.   The marketing of services, sometimes called *intangibles,* is similar to the marketing of industrial products in that these products are generally easier to market globally than consumer products are. Consultant McKinsey & Bain's professional staff of 1,750 people offer worldwide the same kinds of expertise in business strategy that they sell to American clients. It is true that laws and customs sometimes force providers to alter their products. There are some markets that Manpower cannot operate in, for example, because in these countries, private employment agencies are against the law. Accounting laws vary substantially between nations, but Big Eight accounting firms operate globally. Ernst & Young, for instance, has 400 offices in 80 countries, and over half of its 32,000 employees work overseas. There are worldwide subscribers to Nexis, Mead Corporation's data base, one aspect of the fast-growing international computer and data processing industry. Service Master, American Express, and Visa are other examples of successful firms in global markets. The physical product may vary slightly because of the local environmental forces, but the total product remains the same.

Foreign environmental forces.   In Section Three, we examined the foreign environmental forces rather extensively, so here we will limit our discussion to a few concrete examples of how some of these forces affect product offerings.

Sociocultural forces.   Dissimilar cultural patterns generally necessitate changes in food and other consumer goods. The worldwide variation in the mundane chore of clothes washing certainly has caused problems for Procter & Gamble, as you read in the Business Incident, but it is also troublesome for appliance makers. The French want to load their washing machines from the top, and the British want front loading; the Germans insist on high-speed machines that remove most of the moisture in the spin-dry process, but the Italians prefer slower spin speeds because they let the warm sun do the drying. Hence, Whirlpool must produce a variety of models. And this is on' the EC![7] The company must make still other models for other parts world.

Although some multinational firms, such as Kodak and Camp' been extremely successful in employing the same brand name, la' ors worldwide, other firms are sometimes surprised to learn the to other names, labels, or colors because of cultural differen ages are taboo in the Far East because they remind the pub and illnesses of the jungle, but gold appears frequently o America because Latin Americans view it as a symbol o In the Netherlands, blue is considered warm and fe consider it masculine and cold.

WORLDVIEW
There Still Is No European Consumer

Although casual observation seems to indicate that there is a convergence in shopping habits among Europeans, new comprehensive research reveals that national shopping and buying habits vary greatly.

A survey of 7,000 citizens of six EC countries—the United Kingdom, France, Germany, Italy, the Netherlands, and Spain—was conducted by a London-based research center. The results, published in *Frontiers: Planning for Customer Change in Europe,* show that in Italy, both rich and poor believe in paying high prices to get the best quality, whereas in Germany, even the rich shop for a bargain. Three quarters of the Spaniards believe the most expensive wine is the finest, compared to only 5 percent of the French.

Only 30 percent of the British 25- to 44-year-olds know what they want to buy in a supermarket, compared to 47 percent of the same age group in the Netherlands. Still the East Germans beat them—only 18 percent know what they want, but they are still recovering from the trauma of going to the store for decades without knowing what they would find. In comparison, 40 percent of the methodical West Germans have their shopping lists ready.

Even bread has national differences. The wide selection of German branded breads signifies that the Germans are spending more for special types, whereas the English regard bread as a commodity. Also types of bread that are common in one market are considered luxuries in other markets. French sophisticates form lines to buy sliced white bread, a common purchase in Great Britain, in the same way the English are buying French croissants.

Differences in consumer patterns are likely to be more cultural than economic and may be more pronounced within countries than between them. When considering such products as stereos and automobiles, London yuppies may have more in common with young, rich Parisians than with their own older countrymen. There are still some striking differences, however. While 60 percent of the British own a VCR, only 40 percent of the Germans do, and just 19 percent of the Italians. Unlike Americans, who prefer imported cars, the majority of the Italians would rather buy an Italian car even when it is clearly inferior to the same-priced foreign car. The Germans show above-average support for their domestic car industry also.

However, not all age groups are so different. According to a study by McCann-Erickson, the ad agency, European teenagers are a more homogeneous group now than ever. They are also more practical, materialistic, and hedonistic than their predecessors. As a result of being brought up in the market-led economies of the 1980s, they have become "expert consumers."

Source: "The New European Consumer," *Eurobusiness,* July 1989, pp. 10–11; and "Revealed: How Shopping Habits Still Split Europe," *The European,* September 27–29, 1991, p. 17.

Procter & Gamble found out that a gold package has value in Europe too after it launched its Crest Tarter Control Formula in the United Kingdom in a silver box, which was followed two months later by Colgate's equivalent in a gold box. Sheepish P&G officials, agreeing that Colgate's choice of gold was better than their silver, explained that silver was required because that was how the product was packaged in the United States.[8]

Even if the colors can remain the same, instructions on labels, of course, must be translated into the language of the market. Firms selling in areas where two or more languages are spoken, such as Canada or Switzerland, may need to use multilingual labels. Where instructions are not required, as in the case of some consumer or industrial products whose use is well known, there is an advantage to printing the label in the language of the country best known for the product. French labels on perfumes and English labels on industrial goods help to strengthen the product's image.

A Mexican firm in which one of the writers had an interest copied an American brand of penetrating oil that was the best-selling import, even to the blue color. It put a label in English on the can. Then, to comply with the law, a gummed sticker saying *Envasado in Mexico* (Can filled in Mexico) was placed over part of the label. The Mexican product, unlike most locally made industrial products, had excellent acceptance from the start.

A perfectly good brand name may have to be scrapped because of its unfavorable connotations in another language. An American product failed to make it in Sweden because its name translated to "enema." In Latin America, a product had to be taken off the market when the manufacturer found that the name meant "jackass oil." Of course, this problem occurs in both directions, as a Finnish brewery found when it was about to introduce "Koff" beer and "Siff" soft drinks to this country. Incidentally, an economic constraint to the international standardization of brand names is the refusal of some firms to let a subsidiary put their brand on a locally made product if it fails to meet their quality standards because of the inability to import the necessary raw materials or because the required production equipment is unavailable.

An important difference in the social forces to which American marketers are not accustomed is the housewife's preference in other nations, both developed and developing, for making daily visits to the small neighborhood specialty shops and the large, open markets where she can socialize while shopping. More frequent buying permits smaller packages, which is especially important to the shopper when she has no automobile in which to carry purchases. However, this custom is changing in Europe, where a growing sophistication of consumption patterns is demanding the kinds of assortments that only a large store can offer. Shopping frequency is also slowing as the European housewife, especially if employed, is finding that she does not have as much free time as she previously had. As we mentioned in Chapter 13, the solution to her problem has been the huge combination supermarket–discount house (e.g., *hypermarché* in France) with ample parking and generally located in the suburbs. One can easily draw a parallel in this situation to that which began in the 1940s in the United States. The same conditions of rising incomes, a growing middle class, and an increasing number of working wives have combined to put a premium on the shopper's time, and just as occurred in the United States, supermarkets, mass merchandising, and catalog selling have moved in to fill this need.

Legal forces.   Legal forces can be a formidable constraint in the design of product strategies because if the firm fails to adhere to a country's laws governing the product, it will be unable to do business in that country. Laws concerning pollution, consumer protection, and operator safety are being enacted rapidly in many parts of the world and are severely affecting the marketer's freedom to standardize the product mix internationally. For example, American machinery manufacturers exporting to Sweden have found their operator safety requirements to be even stricter than those required by OSHA, so that if they wish to market in Sweden, they must produce a special model. Similarly, the stricter American emission-control laws force producers of foreign automobiles to make significant model changes to sell in the United States.

Laws prohibiting certain classes of imports are extremely common in developing nations, as potential exporters learn when they research the world for markets. We know that products considered luxuries, as well as products already being manufactured, are among the first to be excluded from importation, but such laws also affect local production. As we saw in the previous section, prohibition of essential raw material imports can require a subsidiary to manufacture a product substantially different from what the parent company produces.

Foods and pharmaceuticals are especially influenced by laws concerning purity and labeling. Food products sold in Canada, whether imported or produced locally, are subject to strict rules that require both English and French on the labels as well as metric and inch-pound units. The law even dictates the space permitted between the number and the unit—16 oz. is correct, but 16oz. is not. The Venezuelan government, in an effort to protect the consumer from being overcharged for pharmaceuticals, has decreed that the manufacturer or the importer must affix to the package the maximum retail price at which the product can be sold.[9] Because of the Saudi Arabians' preoccupation with avoiding food containing pork, the label of any product containing animal fat or meat that is sold in Saudi Arabia must state the kind of animal used or must state that no swine products were used.

Legal forces may also prevent a worldwide firm from employing its brand name in all of its overseas markets. Managements accustomed to the American law, which establishes the right to a brand name by priority in use, are surprised to learn that in code law countries, a brand belongs to the person registering it first. Thus, the marketer may go into foreign markets expecting to use the company's long-established brand name only to find that someone else owns it. The name may have been registered by someone who is employing it legitimately for his own products, or it may have been pirated—that is, registered by someone who hopes to profit by selling the name back to the originating firm.

Both reasons stopped Ford from marketing its automobiles under established names in Mexico and Germany. In the case of Mexico, the reason was brand piracy. Ford refused to pay the high price the registrant wanted for the name, so for years the Falcon was known as the Ford 200. The use of the name Mustang by a bicycle manufacturer in Germany was legitimate. The firm was producing under that name when Ford entered the market.

To avoid Ford's predicament, the firm must register its brand names in every country where it wants to use them or where it might use them at a future date. And this must be done rapidly. The Paris Convention grants a firm that has registered a name in one country only six months' priority in registering it elsewhere. Unilever, the English-Dutch manufacturer of personal care products, has over 100,000 trademarks registered throughout the world, most of which are not in use but are kept in reserve.

Economic forces.   The great disparity among the world markets with respect to income is an important obstacle to worldwide product standardization. Many products from the industrialized countries are simply too expensive for consumers in the developing countries, so if the firm wishes to achieve market penetration, it must either simplify the product or produce a different, less costly one.

When Gillette discovered that only 8 percent of Mexican men used shaving cream (the rest use soapy water), it introduced a plastic tube of shaving cream at half the price of its aerosol can. Now more than twice that percentage use the less expensive package, and Gillette is selling the tube in other parts of Latin America. Because many Latin American customers can't afford to buy American-sized packages, the company sells packages of single razor blades and half-ounce packages of Silkience™ shampoo. Use of the plastic squeeze bottle, "the poor man's aerosol," is common where incomes are low.[10]

Similarly, Hoover saw an opportunity to sell a simple washing machine to Mexicans who could not afford the high-priced American-type machine. Although Hoover had no American model to simplify, it was able to copy its inexpensive English washer, which became an overnight success.

Economic forces affect product standardization in still another way. Poor economies signify poor infrastructure—bad roads, lack of sufficient electric power, and so on. Driving conditions in Mexico required Goodrich to design a tire for cut and bruise resistance rather than for high speed, as in the United States. The tire was so successful that residents in U.S. border towns preferred it to the U.S. product even though its price was higher.

The lack of a constant supply of electricity, another characteristic of many poorer countries, has compelled refrigerator manufacturers to supply a gasoline-driven product and office equipment firms to manufacture hand-operated machines. As one would expect, this condition has also provided the producers of small diesel standby generators with a ready market. Any users requiring a steady source of power, such as hospitals and theaters, are potential customers.

Market size influences the product mix, and, in the poorer countries, the populations are not only frequently smaller but also contain a large number of people who have no means to purchase anything but the bare necessities of life, thereby making the already small market even smaller. This means that normally the foreign subsidiary cannot afford to produce as complete a product mix as does the parent. Most automobile manufacturers assemble only the least expensive line and broaden the local product mix by importing, when permitted, the luxury cars. All international firms practice this marketing technique whenever possible because a captive foreign sales organization is available to promote the sales of the home organization's exports and because the revenue derived helps pay the subsidiary's overhead. Philips, the Dutch electrical products giant, owns a light-bulb plant in Chile that supplements its revenue by importing various small domestic appliances from its parent. Some foreign manufacturing subsidiaries carry this practice one step further by selling imports from other firms when these products are suited to their present distribution channels and marketing expertise.

Physical forces.   Elements of the physical forces, such as climate and terrain, also mitigate against international product standardization. Where the heat is intense, gasoline-driven machinery and automobiles must be fitted with larger radiators for extra cooling capacity. Gasoline must have a higher flash point to prevent vapor locks and stalling. As we noted in the chapter on the physical forces, insects proliferate when the winters are not cold enough to kill them. The problems this causes the agricultural industry are obvious, but even some consumer products are affected. In Brazil, the combination of intense heat and wooden floors forced the floor wax manufacturers to add a flea killer to their formulations.[11]

The heat and high humidity in many parts of the tropics require electrical equipment to be built with extraheavy insulation. Consumer goods that are affected by moisture must be specially packaged to resist its penetration. Thus, one finds pills wrapped individually in foil and baked goods packaged in tin boxes to prevent their degradation by moisture.

High altitudes frequently require product alteration. Food manufacturers have found that they must change their cooking instructions for people who live at high altitudes because at such altitudes it takes much longer to cook and bake. The thinner atmosphere requires producers of cake mixes to include less yeast. Gasoline and diesel motors generate less power at high altitudes, so the manufacturer must often supply a larger engine.

Mountainous terrain implies high-cost highways, so in the poorer countries, roads of the quality we know are nonexistent. Trucks traveling poorer-quality roads need tires with thicker treads and heavy-duty suspensions. Because of the rough ride, packaging must be stronger than that used in the United States. From these examples, we can appreciate that even though an unchanged product may be culturally and economically acceptable in a market, the effect of the physical forces alone may be strong enough to require some product modification.

Boeing's 737 has become the best-selling commercial jet in history partly because its engineers redesigned it for Third World aviation after its initial sales to developed nations dropped off. The runways in developing countries were too short for the original design and, being made of less expensive asphalt rather than concrete, were also too soft. By redesigning the wings to allow shorter takeoffs and landings and by selling 1 or 2 at a time instead of batches of 20 or 30, which airlines in the developed nations order, Boeing built a reputation with developing countries' airlines, which, as they grew, began to buy Boeing's larger planes.[12]

Due to space limitations, it is impossible to examine the influence of every environmental force on foreign product strategies. We believe sufficient practical examples have been offered so that these, together with the information contained in the chapters on these forces, will give the reader an idea of their pervasiveness not only in the formulation of the product strategies but also in the design of the entire marketing mix. In fact, as we will show at the end of this chapter, a useful guide in the marketing mix preparation is a matrix in which the marketing mix variables are tabulated against the environmental forces.

▫ Promotional Strategies

promotion all forms of communication between a firm and its publics

Promotion, one of the basic elements of the marketing mix, is communication that secures understanding between a firm and its publics to bring about a favorable buying action and achieve a long-lasting confidence in the firm and the product or service it provides. Note that this definition employs the plural, publics, because the seller's promotional efforts must be directed to more than just the ultimate consumers and the channel of distribution members. Far too often, the other publics have been ignored by business not only in the United States but in other markets as well. Managements have awakened to the fact that the old advice of always maintaining a low profile in a foreign country is not necessarily the best course of action. Many companies have changed this strategy and are now making the general public and governments aware of their public-service activities.

Because promotion both influences and is influenced by the other marketing mix variables, it is possible to formulate nine distinct strategies by combining the three alternatives of (1) marketing the same physical product everywhere, (2) adapting the physical product for foreign markets, and (3) designing a different physical product with *(a)* the same, *(b)* adapted, or *(c)* different messages.[13] Let us examine the six strategies most commonly used.

1. *Same product—same message.* When marketers find that target markets vary little with respect to product use and consumer attitudes, they can offer the same product and use the same promotional appeals in all markets. Avon, Maidenform, and A.T. Cross follow this strategy.

2. *Same product—different message.* The same product may satisfy a different need or be used differently elsewhere. This means the product may be left unchanged, but a different message is required. Honda's campaign, "You meet the nicest people on a Honda," appeals to Americans who use their motorcycles as a pleasure vehicle; but in Brazil, Honda stresses economy as it tries to make its product a means of basic transportation.

3. *Product adaptation—same message.* In cases where the product serves the same function but must be adapted to different conditions, the same message is employed with a changed product. In Japan, Lever Brothers puts Lux soap in fancy boxes because much of it is sold for gifts.

4. *Product adaptation—message adaptation.* In some cases, both the product and the promotional message must be modified for foreign markets. In Latin America, Tang™ is especially sweetened, pre-mixed, and ready to drink in pouches. Unlike Americans, Latin Americans do not drink it for breakfast. There it is promoted as a drink for mealtime and for throughout the day, but not for breakfast.

5. *Different product—same message.* As we pointed out in our discussion of the economic forces' influence on product strategies, the potential customers in many markets cannot afford the product as manufactured in the firm's home country. The product may also be too technologically advanced to gain widespread acceptance. To overcome these obstacles, companies have frequently produced a very distinct product for these markets. The previously mentioned low-cost plastic squeeze bottle and inexpensive manually operated washing machines are two examples. The promotional message, however, can be very similar to what is used in the developed countries if the product performs the same functions.

6. *Different product for the same use—different message.* Frequently, the different product requires a different message as well. Welding torches rather than automatic welding machines would be sold on the basis of low acquisition cost rather than high output per labor-hour. LDC governments faced with high unemployment would be persuaded by a message emphasizing the job-creating possibilities of labor-intensive processes rather than the labor saving of highly automated machinery.

The tools for communicating these messages—the promotional mix—are advertising, personal selling, sales promotion, public relations, and publicity. No one of these tools is inherently superior to the others, though circumstances in a given situation may dictate that one of them should be emphasized more than the others. Just as in the determination of the product strategies, the composition of the promotional mix will depend on the type of product, the environmental forces, and the amount of market penetration desired.

advertising paid, nonpersonal presentation of ideas, goods, or services by an identified sponsor

Advertising.   Of all the promotional mix elements, **advertising** is the one with the greatest similarities worldwide. This is because most advertising everywhere is based on American practices. U.S. ad agencies have greatly aided the global propagation of American techniques as they have followed their domestic customers overseas. Today the major American agencies are all global, with wholly owned subsidiaries, joint ventures, and working agreements with local agencies. In the latest annual worldwide ranking by income of the top 50 advertising agencies, 20 agencies are American, 14 are Japanese, 5 are French, and 5 are British. Table 15–1 lists the 15 largest agencies.

There is an increasing use of *global brands* by international firms, fueled in part by Europe 1992. Many firms first moved from national to pan-European brands in preparation for a barrier-free Europe.[14] This required regional promotional campaigns to tell the same story about the regional brand in all of the region's markets. Pan-European cable and satellite TV made this possible. However, a regional or global campaign is appropriate only where the same product specification is sold to the same target consumers for the same end use and where the firm's competitors are offering a similar mix of advantages and disadvantages with a similar market maturity.[15]

A number of U.S. international advertisers who meet these qualifications, such as Gillette, P&G, Kelloggs, Levi Strauss, IBM, Quaker, and Seven-Up, are sponsors on Sky Channel, the British-owned satellite TV that reaches across Europe.[16] The first firm to be a regional TV advertiser, Coca-Cola, has sponsored its Coca-Cola Eurochart, a pop music program since 1983. It was not until 1992, however, that Coca-Cola made its first global media buy. For 24 hours on January 24, CNN and CNN International ran a 30- or 60-second spot once an hour around the world featuring Coke's Olympic-based commercials. CNN and Coca-Cola announced that this was the first time an advertising message had appeared simultaneously around the world.[17]

Economies of scale have also prompted firms to stress the standardization of advertising procedures. Coca-Cola, for example, estimates that it saves more than $8 million annually in the cost of thinking up new imagery by repeating the same theme everywhere. Texas Instruments, which used to have four different creative approaches in Scandinavia (one for each country), now runs similar ads in all four countries at a savings of $30,000 a commercial.

The global advertising agencies obviously argue for international standardization because their presence in various world markets gives them a sales advantage over the local agency. This approach often appeals as well to top managements, which want their firms to present a single, unified image and logo in all markets.

Even when the advertising campaigns are standardized worldwide, international advertisers have generally preferred national media to reach mass audi-

☐ **TABLE 15–1   World's Top 15 Advertising Organizations (Ranked by gross income in $ millions)**

Organization, Headquarters	Gross Income		Percent Change
	1990	1989	
1. WPP Group, London	$2,715.0	$2,404.0	12.9%
2. Saatchi & Saatchi, London	1,729.3	1,575.8	9.7
3. Interpublic Group, New York	1,664.0	1,493.7	11.4
4. Omnicom Group, New York	1,335.5	1,177.9	13.4
5. Dentsu, Tokyo	1,254.8	1,262.7	0.6
6. Young & Rubicam, New York	1,073.6	925.6	16.0
7. Eurocom Group, Paris	748.5	472.3	58.5
8. Hakuhodo Inc., Tokyo	586.3	585.5	0.1
9. Grey Advertising, New York	583.3	489.9	19.1
10. Foote, Cone & Belding, Chicago	536.2	506.5	5.9
11. D'Arcy Masius Benton & Bowles, New York	532.5	471.5	12.9
12. Leo Burnett Co., Chicago	531.8	483.8	9.9
13. Publicis-FCB Communications, Paris	430.0	358.8	19.9
14. Roux Seguela Cayzac & Goudard, Issy les Moulineaux, France	346.2	224.4	54.3
15. BDDP Worldwide, Boulogne, France	236.0	151.3	56.0

Source: "World's Top 50 Advertising Organizations," *Advertising Age,* January 6, 1992, p. S6.

ences. One exception to this generalization, however, is the situation in which the advertisements are shown on a TV station that is also viewed in neighboring countries or are placed in internationally distributed publications such as *Reader's Digest, Time, The Wall Street Journal, Business Week*, and *Fortune.*

This may change, however, as global media packages become available. In 1992, Ford Motor Company signed a contract worth $10 million with Hachette, a French global media concern, that involved placing ads in 84 magazines around the world, 16 of which are American, including *Car & Driver, Road & Track, Woman's Day,* and *Popular Photography.* Hachette has made international ad deals in Europe with L'Oreal and Benetton, but Ford is the first to use Hachette to reach a general worldwide audience.[18]

When weighing global standardization against local campaign preparation, the international advertising manager must be prepared to hear arguments against standardization from personnel in the foreign subsidiaries. "Our market is unique," they will argue, "and so we can't use what the home office sends us." The manager's task is to weigh the pros and cons of standardization, taking into consideration the cost of lower morale that it might bring and then choosing the approach that will produce the greatest sales at the least cost. When making this decision, he or she needs to realize that certain factors may at times be decisive, such as the type of product, media availability, and the foreign environmental forces.

Type of product.   Buyers of industrial goods and luxury products usually act on the same motives the world over; thus these products lend themselves to the standardized approach. This enables manufacturers of capital goods, such as NCR and Westinghouse, to prepare international campaigns that

☐ **FIGURE 15–3   All Roads Lead to Visa in Many Languages**

Courtesy of Visa International

require very little modification in the various markets. Certain consumer goods markets are similar too, as we saw in the previous section. However, another set of characteristics also permits firms to use the same appeals and sales arguments worldwide: when the product is low priced, is consumed in the same way, and is bought for the same reasons. Examples of such products are gasoline, soft drinks, detergents, cosmetics, and airline services. Firms such as Exxon (Esso overseas), Coca-Cola, Avon, and Levi Strauss have for years used the international approach successfully. Generally, the only changes they have made are a translation into the local language and the use of indigenous models. Figure 15–3 illustrates how a successful Visa campaign looked in several languages.

Availability of media.   Even when the message is standardized, advertisers will find that they cannot always use the same media mix from country to country because the media are not equally available in all markets. Historically, radio and TV have been highly government regulated, and many stations did not accept advertising. This, until recently, was the case in most EC and EFTA nations. However, the advent of Sky Channel and Super Channel (satellite TV broadcasters from England that transmit to local cable TV networks) and of other local cable networks with their own programming made it impossible for governments to keep out commercial television.

The competition from American programs, which all of these systems buy, forced the English, French, and most other European governments to relax their ban on commercial television. They simply did not have the money or the production capacity to compete with American firms (the three major TV networks, the motion picture industry) and Japanese producers. Disney, for example, sells TV shows for profit and also uses them to promote its Euro-Disneyland theme park near Paris. Likewise, American professional sports leagues send their teams to play exhibition games in Europe not only to earn money, but also to promote the sales of broadcast rights to regular games they play in the United States. In 1989, British, French, and Italian networks relayed the Super Bowl game to national audiences.[19] Now the World Football League started by the National Football League has teams in major European cities.

At present, 70 percent of European programming consists of fictional series from the United States, about 15 percent in advertising, some American and Japanese animated series, and a minimum amount of European production and national news programs.[20] But this situation is about to change. At the end of 1991, member-nations of the European Community adopted its broadcasting directive designed to create a single European market for television, although both American and European broadcasters continue to criticize it.

The main issue in contention is a requirement for European broadcasters to reserve a majority of broadcasting time (excluding sports, game shows, news, and advertising) for European programs "by all practical means and wherever possible." American broadcasters see a possibility of losing the $700 million they make supplying European TV with American programs. In fact, the United States is threatening to take its case to GATT, alleging protectionism on the part of the EC. Meanwhile, the Europeans complain that the "wherever possible" clause offers no protection at all.[21]

There are some restrictions on advertising. The EC broadcast directive bans tobacco advertising, but it is already banned in Western Europe. There are guidelines for alcohol advertising, but these are comparable to what the industry already follows under self-regulation.

The advertising directive is generally less restrictive on broadcasters than the local rules on programming and advertising they have been following. For example, Germany bans advertising on Sundays and public holidays. In Great Britain, the agency that regulates commercial TV limits the nation's commercial channels to 14 percent non-EC programming between 6 P.M. and midnight. This, of course, puts them well within the EC quota.[22]

Pan-European media availability is enabling companies to take a regional approach to promotion. Gillette used to market a razor under different brand names—Desechable ("throw-away") in Spain, Radi & Getta in Italy, and Blue II in England—but changed to a uniform Blue II across Europe. It then ran a uniform spot dubbed in 10 languages on a Europeanwide network that invited shavers "to step into the blue."[23] Coca-Cola has no name problem and is using Sky Channel to reach the youth market in all Europe with a clone of "American Bandstand." That Sky Channel's programming is in English is no handicap, because it is precisely the younger population that has the largest percentage of people who already speak English or who want to learn.

Africa is marked by a scarcity of all media. Only 163 radio stations serve an area twice the size of the United States, and although there are 84 TV stations in all, one third of them are located in just two countries (Nigeria—18 and Ivory Coast—10). Ten countries have no TV. Even these numbers are misleading, because in many countries the stations are government owned and noncommercial. Although there are 168 daily newspapers in the 51 African countries, 86 of them are located in only 6 countries. Nine countries have no daily paper, and 13 have only one.[24] In this seller's market, an advertiser may find that the newspaper has accepted too many ads for the available space. Some newspapers' solution is a raffle to decide which ads will be published!

In Latin America and the Middle East, the opposite situation exists: there are too many newspapers and magazines. The problem in those regions is choosing the right ones for the firm's target market. In which of the 900 newspapers in Brazil or the 400 in Turkey should the ad be placed? Circulation figures are greatly exaggerated, and the advertisers must also be careful of the publication's political position to avoid associating their firms with the "wrong side"—the one contrary to what the majority of their potential customers believe in.

These problems and the high illiteracy rate in some nations have forced advertisers to go to other media to reach their markets. Cinema advertising is heavily used in many parts of the world, as are billboards. In the Middle East, where media options are limited, videotape ads are rapidly becoming an integral part of the media mix. Advertisers penetrate this lucrative market by buying spots on popular video tapes. Three or four breaks with six or seven spots each are created at the beginning, middle, and end of the film. Three quarters of the households in the United Arab Emirates, Saudi Arabia, and Kuwait have videocassette recorders, and in the first three months after release, a well-received video tape can draw an audience of 1 million viewers in Saudi Arabia alone.[25] In a number of less developed countries, automobiles equipped with loudspeakers circulate through the cities announcing products, and street signs are furnished by advertisers that hang their messages on them. Homeowners can get a free coat of paint by permitting advertisers to put ads on their walls. Where mail delivery is reliable, direct mail is a powerful medium, as are trade fairs. Probably one of the most ingenious campaigns ever was that of a tea company that gave away thousands of printed prayers with a tea commercial on the other side to pilgrims bound for Mecca. Table 15–2 and its footnotes illustrate how the constraints we have discussed affect the distribution of advertising expenditures.

The point is that media of some kind are available in every country, and the local managers and ad agencies are familiar with the advantages of each kind. Media selection is extremely difficult for international advertising managers who try to standardize their media mix from the home office. We have mentioned only some of the problems, but from these the reader can appreciate that the variation in media availability is a strong reason for leaving this part of the advertising program to the local organization.

Foreign environmental forces.   Like variations in media availability, the foreign environmental forces act as deterrents to the international standardization of advertising, and, as you would expect, among the most influential of these forces are the *sociocultural* forces, which we examined in Chapter 9.

A basic cultural decision for the marketer is whether to position the product as foreign or local, and which way to go seems to depend on the country, the product type, and the target market. In Germany, for example, consumers are not at all impressed by the carmaker that announces it has American know-how. "After all," reason the Germans, "if so many Americans prefer BMWs and Mercedes over U.S. cars, why shouldn't we?" At the same time, such purely American products as bourbon, fast-food restaurants, and blue jeans have made tremendous inroads in Germany and the rest of Europe.

☐ **TABLE 15–2   Advertising Expenditures in Selected Countries, 1989**

Rank	Country	Total Expenditures ($ millions)	Percent of Total					Advertising Expenditures as Percentage of GNP
			Print	Cinema	Radio	TV	Direct Advertising	
1	United States	$123,930	40.6%	n.a.	6.7%	21.7%	17.7%	2.4%
2	Japan	35,760	33.7	n.a.	4.1	29.7	9.5	1.3
3	United Kingdom	13,631	57.8	0.4%	1.9	27.5	9.1	1.6
4	Germany	12,030	71.7	0.9	3.6	10.0	11.1	1.0
5	France	8,669	37.4	0.7	5.7	20.8	25.6	0.9
6	Spain	7,265	39.8	0.6	8.4	22.7	14.7	2.0
7	Canada	7,013	38.2	n.a.	9.0	20.3	22.4	1.4
8	Italy*	4,574	42.8	n.a.	1.6	51.5	n.a.	0.5
9	Australia	3,983	49.9	1.3	8.5	33.4	n.a.	1.6
10	Netherlands	3,740	45.3	0.2	1.2	6.3	28.7	1.6
12	Brazil	2,735	25.1	n.a.	1.7	35.3	n.a.	0.7
13	South Korea	2,294	45.2	n.a.	4.1	34.2	n.a.	1.2
20	India	780	71.2	0.8	3.0	21.0	n.a.	0.3
32	Malaysia	253	44.1	0.1	1.3	42.7	0.1	0.7
49	Kenya	19	51.0	4.2	17.7	10.9	1.0	0.2

*As an illustration of how commercial TV availability affects promotional expenditures, in 1981, when freedom of TV advertising in Italy was just beginning, only 15.2 percent of total advertising expenditures was spent on TV. With no commercial TV and radio, Sweden and Norway use print (96 and 97 percent), outdoor transit, and cinema.

n.a. = Data not available.

Source: *World Advertising Expenditures,* Starch, INRA, Hooper & LAA 1991, pp. 34–35.

Similarly in Japan and other countries in the Far East, American identity of consumer products enhances their image. The young and the status conscious prefer the casual American look in clothing and seek the American label that identifies the wearer as belonging to the "in group." The influence of the American-style fast-food restaurants on Japanese youth was emphasized in a survey taken by the Japanese Ministry of Agriculture, which found that more than 50 percent of the country's teenagers would rather eat occidental foods than the traditional dishes. These restaurants are now grossing over $2 billion, with U.S.-based ventures such as McDonald's (already the second-largest Japanese restaurant business), Dairy Queen, Mister Donut, and Kentucky Fried Chicken accounting for over 50 percent of that amount.[26] The experience of the suppliers to the youth market already indicates that this too is essentially an international market segment, much like the market for luxury goods. This means marketers can formulate global advertising campaigns for these consumers that will require little more than a translation into the local language. Before making the decision concerning local versus foreign identity, however, management should check with local personnel on a country-by-country basis.

Inasmuch as communication, the reason for advertising, is impossible if the language is not understood, translations must be made into the language of the consumers. Unfortunately for the advertiser, almost every language varies from one country to another. The same word may be perfectly apt in one country while signifying something completely different or even vulgar in

Courtesy of Japan National Tourist Organization

McDonald's—Japan's second-largest restaurant chain

another, as was illustrated in Chapter 9. To avoid translation errors, the experienced advertising manager will use (1) a double translation and (2) plenty of illustrations with short copy.

Because a nation's laws generally reflect public opinion, closely allied to the cultural forces are the legal forces, which exert an extremely pervasive influence on advertising. We have seen how laws affect media availability, but they also restrict the kinds of products that can be advertised and even the copy employed in the advertisements.

Goodyear found that it could not use its multinational campaign claiming the nylon tire cord was stronger than steel in Germany, because doing so would violate a law against comparing products. Coca-Cola thought Malaysia also had such a ban. Consequently, when Pepsi-Cola mounted a half-million-dollar taste test campaign on TV, Coke's ad agency protested. However, Pepsi had followed the rules in not naming the competitor's products. It merely showed side-by-side taste tests of two different products in unmarked bottles. The government body that regulated advertising had no objection to the taste tests, and the commercials resumed.

Until 1986, many products were banned from French TV: jewelry, margarine (to protect milk producers), airlines (to protect Air France), publications, films, concerts, records, retailers, and alcoholic drinks. But many changes occurred when La 5, France's first all-commercial network, began operation in 1986. First, the programs are livelier, and even more important for advertisers, commercial breaks during programs are permitted. Also, companies can advertise such products as books, wine, beer, and margarine, all of which are banned from government-owned stations. However, the ban still exists for child models in ads and for the use of non-French words when there is a

French equivalent. Announcers cannot get friendly with the audience either—they must always use the formal *vous*.[27]

France is stereotyped as being very anti-American. However, a consumer survey taken of France—as well as the United Kingdom, Spain, Germany, Italy, and the Netherlands—found it to be one of the most pro-American markets from the consumers' viewpoint. Of the 1,034 French consumers surveyed, 40 percent considered American products to be fashionable, 38 percent believed they're innovative, and 15 percent said they were of high quality. When asked what nationality they preferred for a new company in their area, five of the six countries surveyed chose a U.S. company after a local firm. Only the Spanish chose the Japanese as a second choice after the local company.[28]

Advertisers in the Islamic nations have had to be resourceful to avoid censorship. The use of women's photos in advertisements is forbidden unless the models are clearly Western—preferably blondes or redheads. "Erotic" sound effects are not permitted: a TV soft-drink commercial with a girl licking her lips to show she liked the taste was declared "obscene." In Pakistan, the government decreed that women models could advertise only women's products on TV. They cannot advertise cars or men's cologne, for example. Imagine Ford trying to sell its Mercury with a slinky male posed seductively behind the wheel, or how about an all-male Old Spice commercial?[29]

Just as in the United States, there is a strong tendency for governments elsewhere to control advertising even more as government leaders, urged on by consumer groups, enact stricter laws. In Sweden, consumer ombudsmen (government officials) can require companies to provide total disclosure in advertising. If they wish, these ombudsmen can force a manufacturer of cameras to state not only the cost of the camera but also what the film and processing will cost the buyer. Products that do not live up to their claims can be forced off the market. Mexico's law on consumer protection gives major emphasis to advertising. Dealers as well as suppliers are obligated to make good any guarantees or offers announced to the public and must even obtain governmental approval before announcing a sale or a special offer.

In some governments, a strong bias against advertising in general or against certain media is reflected in advertising taxes. The result of variations in the taxation of advertising media is to limit the advertisers' choice among media and to cause them employ more of the other promotional mix elements than they might normally use. All national governments in Europe except Switzerland apply a value-added tax to advertising, though France, Ireland, the Netherlands, Norway, the United Kingdom, and West Germany exempt foreign-based companies that place advertising from the home country. Some of these countries also place additional taxes on advertising. Greece is notorious for extra taxes that are really punitive—47 percent on TV, 20 percent on newspapers and radio, and 16 percent on magazines. Advertisers using billboards pay as much as 50 percent extra when municipal taxes are included. It is important to know whether local taxes are levied, because they can be very discriminatory. Outdoor advertising is subject to an additional local tax in Italy, as is outdoor and cinema advertising in Portugal. Furthermore, in many countries such taxes vary among municipalities.[30] One of Europe 1992's objectives is to standardize all value-added taxes.

Globalization versus localization.   With so many obstacles to international standardization, what should be the approach of the international advertising manager? The opinion of some experts seems to be that good ideas and good promotions can cross international borders. Robert Trebus, an ad agency executive, believes that far too often businesspeople ask how the product can be sold in Germany without first asking how the firm did it successfully in Sweden. Trebus stated back in the 1970s that "rarely will a campaign be a success in Sweden without having registered a like success in Greece." He believes too many managers are convinced that to be successful in different markets, they must approach each market differently.[31] This school of thought looks for similarities across segments and countries so as to capitalize on them by providing promotional themes with worldwide appeal, the strategy now followed by global corporations.

A second school of thought believes that even though human nature is the same everywhere, it is also true that a Spaniard will remain a Spaniard and a Belgian a Belgian. Thus, it is preferable to develop separate appeals to take advantage of the differences among customers in different cultures and countries.

The results of a study made by *International Advertiser* confirms our previous discussion. It showed that the primary result (50 percent of the respondents) of global standardization was cost reduction in planning and control. International brand and corporate image was second (38 percent), and simplification of coordination and control was third (31 percent). The primary reasons against standardization were insufficient consideration of local peculiarities (53 percent), the heterogeneous media scene (25 percent), and differences in the stage of the product life cycle (19 percent). The survey indicated that the extent of actual standardization of advertising decisions was generally higher than the judgment on the possibility of standardization. This means that the reasons in favor of standardization influence the basic objective of the international firm more than do the obvious differences among nations.[32]

Neither purely global nor purely local.   You probably have already gathered from the previous discussion that for most firms neither the global nor the purely local campaign is the best way to handle international advertising. In fact, the president of a large international ad agency states, "About 15 percent of the multinational companies have global approaches, meaning campaigns will be roughly the same everywhere. Another 15 percent have strictly local approaches. But these two groups are rapidly disappearing into a group we call 'glocal,' meaning advertisers that have developed a common strategy for large regions."[33]

Gillette's panregional approach.   Gillette has its advertising organized in the following regional and cultural clusters: pan–Latin America, pan–Middle East, pan-Africa, and pan-Atlantic. The international advertising manager says the arrangement is based on the belief that the company can identify the same needs and buying motives among consumers in regions or countries linked by culture, consumers' habits, and level of market development for their products. Gillette might use the same European-style advertising for Australia and South Africa; but in Asia, it would link developing economies such as the Philippines, Indonesia, Thailand, and Malaysia. It will market the Asian tigers, Singapore, Hong Kong, and Taiwan, together, but handle Japan, China, and India separately.

Gillette, which sells 800 products in 200 countries, is trying to approximate a global marketing strategy with its panregional strategy, while allowing for regional and national differences. A vice president of Gillette's ad agency who is also the firm's associate media director explains Gillette's approach this way: "Our strategy is to develop the best media plans for each country, but then look for pangeographic opportunities to enhance the coverage."[34]

Programmed-management approach.   Another middle-ground advertising strategy is what some call the **programmed-management approach,** in which the home office and the foreign subsidiaries agree on marketing objectives, after which each puts together a tentative advertising campaign. This is submitted to the home office for review and suggestions. The campaign is then market tested locally, and the results are submitted to the home office, which reviews them and offers comments. The subsidiary then submits a complete campaign to the home office for review. When the home office is satisfied, the budget is approved and the subsidiary begins implementing the campaign. The result may be a highly standardized campaign for all markets or one that has been individualized to the extent necessary to cope with local market conditions. The programmed-management approach gives the home office a chance to standardize those parts of the campaign that may be standardized but still permits flexibility in responding to different marketing conditions.[35]

programmed-management approach a middle-ground advertising strategy between globally standardized and entirely local programs

> Instead of having 43 different versions of ads running worldwide, as in the past, Playtex asked its ad agency, Grey, a huge multinational with affiliates in 33 major cities overseas, to develop a global campaign for TV that would work in every market. Grey's main office in New York prepared the boards (a series of still pictures with suggested dialogue depicting the commercial) and sent them to its overseas affiliates with instructions to look for things that would not work in their markets. The agency also showed Playtex foreign managers videotapes of potential models. Dozens were rejected until they all agreed on three that were deemed to have universal appeal.
>
> Although the cross-your-heart message was the same everywhere, there were some local differences that had to be taken into account. One was the brassiere style. The French like lacy bras, whereas Germans and Americans prefer the plainer types. Also, European and American TV permit live models, whereas South African TV does not. To accommodate these differences, shots were made both ways then spliced into the ads for each market. To comply with Australian law, the Australian ads had to be shot locally.
>
> Names for the bras had to be found for different languages because WOW (without wires) could not be translated literally. Traumbugel (dream wire) was used in Germany, Alas (wings) in Spain, and Armagique (contraction for structure and magic) was chosen for France. Interestingly, even the packaging is different. Bras are put on hangers in the UK and the United States but are packaged in boxes elsewhere.
>
> Global advertising permitted Playtex to present one unified message in all markets and also to save money. Grey claims it was able to produce the WOW ad for a dozen countries at a cost of only $250,000. The average cost of producing a single U.S. ad is $100,000.

Personal selling.   Along with advertising, personal selling constitutes a principal component of the promotional mix. The importance of this promotional tool as compared to advertising depends to a great extent on the relative costs, the funds available, media availability, and the type of product sold.

Just as in the United States, manufacturers of industrial products rely more on personal selling than advertising to communicate with their overseas markets. However, producers of consumer products may also emphasize personal selling overseas, especially in the developing countries, because salespeople in these countries will often work for less compensation than would be demanded in the home country. A newcomer to marketing must be careful, nonetheless, to consider all of the expenses in maintaining a salesperson, as expense items like automobiles and their maintenance (rough treatment on bad roads) frequently may be three or four times the U.S. cost. Fringe benefits are commonly stipulated by law, and these too often comprise a higher percentage of the base wage in other countries.

Marketing managers will also give greater emphasis to personal selling where commercial TV and radio are unavailable or where the market is too small to support expensive TV advertising campaigns.

International standardization.   By and large, the organization of the overseas sales force, sales presentation, and training methods are very similar to those employed in the home country.

> Avon follows the same plan of person-to-person selling in Venezuela or the Far East as it does in this country and is extremely successful with it. When Avon entered Mexico, many of the local experts predicted that its plan would fail. The Mexican middle-class housewife would be out of the home shopping and playing bridge. The wall around the house would keep the Avon lady from reaching the front door, and when she rang the bell, the maid, as she did with all peddlers, would not let her in. Other American firms had used this approach and had failed for these reasons. However, Avon made small but important changes. For one thing, it mounted a massive advertising campaign to educate the Mexicans as to what they could expect from the visits before sending its salespeople out. Although the advertisements were the same as those in the United States, the advertising campaign was more extensive because the Mexican housewife had to be taught a new concept. This was not the common door-to-door salesperson whom she knew but a professional trained to help her look beautiful. Avon recruited educated middle-class women as representatives and trained them well. They were encouraged to visit their friends, much as Tupperware representatives do. What was essentially an American plan, with slight changes for cultural differences, made Avon's entry into the Mexican market an unqualified success. Avon still follows this strategy.
>
> When it first entered China a few years ago, it made an exception and sold only through foreign-currency stores while management learned about the market and built up a customer base. In 1990, Avon entered into a joint venture with the Guangzhou cosmetics factory. The firm owns 60 percent of the JV for which it paid $1 million. For the start-up, Avon will establish two distribution and training locations. By the end of the first year, the company expects to have a minimum of 3,000 representatives just in the Guangzhou area.[36]

Other firms also follow their home country approach. Missionary salespeople from pharmaceutical manufacturers, such as Pfizer and Upjohn, intro-

Avon ladies are everywhere.

Courtesy of Avon

duce their products to physicians, just as they do in the United States. Sales engineers from General Electric and Westinghouse supply their customers with the same kind of information required in this country. Salespeople calling on channel members perform the same tasks of informing middlemen, setting up point-of-purchase displays, and fighting for shelf space as do their American counterparts.

Because of the high costs of a sales call, many firms are using telemarketing and direct mail to qualify prospects and make appointments for the sales representatives. As you can imagine, European subsidiaries of American firms, such as Ford, Digital Equipment, and IBM, having learned the advantages of telemarketing from their American parents, are using the technique to increase sales. Barbie™ doll sends her French fans messages in special ink that they can read only under special lights in toy stores where the dolls are sold.

Now, European companies are also using telemarketing. Peugeot, the French car manufacturer, regularly sends personalized letters to its customers all over Europe, telling them when they need service calls, where to get the best deal on tires, and how to buy special-offer accessories. Its marketing

□ **FIGURE 15–4   Cost of a Sales Call**

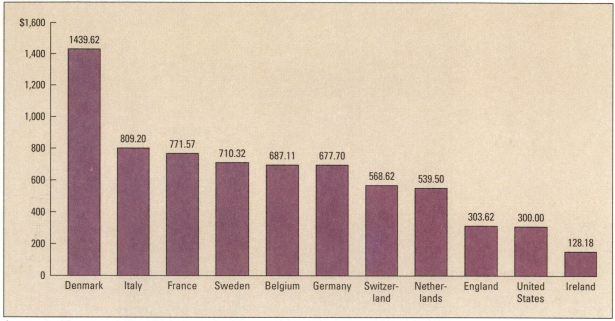

Average cost of European call is $640.13.
Source: *International Management,* May 1988, p. 15.

manager says, "It's a far more scientific way of getting to people likely to want our products than straightforward advertising."

> Direct mail and telemarketing are only beginning in Japan. There are no bulk postal rates, and 800 numbers did not become available until 1986. Dentsu, the Japanese ad agency, has formed a telemarketing joint venture with the American firm of Young & Rubicam and is already selling computers successfully by mail. In the opinion of a director of a London ad agency, "The Japanese have discovered it now, and once they start to use it effectively, it will be a frightening experience."[37]

Computerized prospecting, or using computers to analyze customer call patterns to plan customer visits, is another American sales tool adopted by Europeans to reduce the cost of a sales call. Obviously, it's needed. According to the latest McGraw-Hill survey, the average cost of making a European sales call is $640 (see Figure 15–4) and it takes six calls before a sale is made.[38]

Recruitment.   Recruiting salespeople in foreign countries is at times more difficult than recruiting them in the home country because sales managers frequently have to cope with the stigma attached to selling that exists in some areas (cultural forces). To help overcome this obstacle, salespeople are given titles that are essentially translations of American titles designed for the same purpose (territory or zone manager).

Another instance of the influence of cultural forces on recruiting is the need to hire salespeople who are culturally acceptable to customers and channel members. This can be difficult and costly in an already small market that is further subdivided into several distinct cultures with different customs and even languages, as we saw in the chapter on physical forces. If a cultural pocket will support a salesperson at all, the experienced sales manager will make every effort to recruit a person indigenous to the region.

American firms are aided in recruitment by their reputation for having excellent training programs. These generally come from the home office and are adapted, if necessary, to local conditions. When the product is highly technical, the new employees are often sent to the home office for training. Of course, the opportunity to take such a trip is also an effective recruiting tool.

sales promotion selling aids, including displays, premiums, contests, and gifts

Sales promotion.   **Sales promotion** provides the selling aids for the marketing function and includes such activities as the preparation of point-of-purchase displays, contest, premiums, trade show exhibits, cents-off offers, and coupons. If no separate department exists for these activities, either the advertising or the sales department will perform them.

The international standardization of the sales promotion function is not difficult, because experience has shown that what is successful in the United States generally proves effective overseas. Couponing is a good example. Although the United States is the world's leader in couponing, several European markets and Canada are experiencing a rapid growth. A 1991 study reported that the consumers in the United Kingdom and Belgium are the most active EC coupon users. In 1990, an average of 17 coupons per household were redeemed in the United Kingdom and 18 per household in Belgium, compared to 77 in the United States and 26 in Canada. In Italy and Spain, only 3 coupons per household were redeemed. Although the number of coupons redeemed was much lower elsewhere, the growth in their use was much higher. In the United Kingdom, for example, there was a 21 percent increase in redemption from 1989 to 1990—the largest increase in the world.[39]

When marketers are considering transferring sales promotion techniques to other markets, they must consider some cultural and legal constraints.

Legal constraints.   Laws concerning sales promotions tend to be more restrictive in other countries than they are in the United States or Great Britain. The Belgian, German, and Scandinavian governments are rather negative toward premiums, for example, because they believe premiums detract consumers from considering just the merits of the product. "Two-for-one" offers are prohibited in Sweden and Norway, and, although free samples are permitted everywhere, some governments limit their size. Mexico requires special offers and cents-off deals to be approved by a government agency before they can be used. Although these legal restrictions are bothersome, they have not stopped the use of sales promotions.

Sociocultural and economic constraints.   The cultural and economic constraints are more consequential than the legal constraints and do make some sales promotions difficult to use. If a premium is to fulfill the objective of being a sales aid for the product, it must be meaningful to the purchaser. A gadget to be used in the kitchen will be valued by the American housewife but will not be particularly attractive to a Latin American housewife if she has two maids to do the housework. Firms that attach premiums to the outside of packages in the less developed countries usually do this just once. Less than a week after the packages are on the shelf, the detached premiums are already being sold in the streets. Putting the prize inside the package is also no guarantee that it will be there when the purchaser takes the package home.

While living in Mexico, one of the writers bought a product for the plastic toy it contained. When he opened the package at home, there was no toy for the children. Examining the package closely, he found that a small slot had been made in the top. Where labor costs and store revenues are low, the income from the sales of these premiums is extra profit for the retailer.

Contests, raffles, and games, however, have been extremely successful in countries where people love to play the odds. If Latin Americans or the Irish will buy a lottery ticket week after week, hoping to win the grand prize playing against the odds of 500,000 to 1, why shouldn't they participate in a contest that costs them nothing to enter? Point-of-purchase displays are well accepted by retailers, though many establishments are so small that there is simply no place to put all of the displays that are offered to them. Sales promotion is generally not as sophisticated overseas as it is in the United States, and our experience indicates that even American subsidiaries do not make sufficient use of the ideas coming from headquarters. The marketing manager who prepares a well-planned program after studying the constraints of the local markets can expect excellent results from the time and money invested.

public relations various methods of communicating with the firm's publics to secure a favorable impression

Public relations.   **Public relations** is the firm's communications and relationships with its various publics, including the governments where it operates, or, as one writer has put it, "Public relations is the marketing of the firm." Although American internationals have had organized public relations programs for many years in the United States, they have paid much less attention to this important function elsewhere.

Ironically, it is on the whole not true that they have neglected public-service activities through their foreign subsidiaries—only that they have failed to inform their publics of what they are doing. Exxon has for years sponsored the study of foreign art students in the United States, and the ITT International Fellowship Program, started in 1973, has already enabled more than 750 students from 54 countries to pursue advanced degrees in the United States and abroad.

Overseas subsidiaries of American firms support public-service activities locally. In Japan, Coca-Cola spends $5 million annually on good works such as programs for children and the handicapped. IBM Japan puts 1 percent of its profits into good works. In 1990, young ballerinas and basic-research scientists were among those receiving $14 million. Eastman Kodak sponsors soccer, and Du Pont, golf.[40]

The rising wave of nationalism and antimultinational feeling in many countries has made it imperative for companies with international operations to improve their communications to their nonbusiness publics with more effective public relations programs.

An example of a successful public relations program was the one launched by Nestlé in response to an attack by the International Baby Food Action Network (IBFAN). This consumers' organization accused the company of persuading mothers in LDCs to bottle-feed their babies with formula rather then breast-feed. The IBFAN and various church groups that advocated breast-feeding charged that contaminated water in the formula was contributing to infant mortality. This was the same water, of course, that had always been mixed with homemade baby food. Although 17 firms sold infant formula, Nestlé was singled out for attack, according to the boycott director, "Because it has the largest market share."[41]

The company responded to the attack by implementing the 1981 World Health Organization's code on the marketing of breast-milk substitutes. It also created a semi-independent review panel to examine its marketing practices and its adherence to the code. This unprecedented action slowed the attack of its critics, who finally called the boycott off. However, five years later, another group, Action for Corporate Accountability, began to boycott the company for the same reasons. Although Nestlé claims it complies fully with the World Health Organization's code, it did hire the publication relations unit of Ogilvy & Mather's ad agency to help it respond to this latest attack.[42]

Other consumer activist groups that appear to be in a position to inflict significant public relations damage on international firms are the (1) Pesticide Action Network, (2) Health Action International for pharmaceuticals, and (3) World Council of Churches, which is concerned with such issues as the nature of Third World poverty and Western support for "racist, authoritarian" regimes.

One of the firms' most vexing problems is how to deal with such critics. Some try to defuse criticism before it becomes a full-scale attack by holding regularly scheduled meetings at which topics of interest are debated. Others prefer to meet with critics privately, though they might find themselves caught in a never-ending relationship in which the critics continually escalate their demands. This is especially true of single-issue groups, whose existence depends on the continuance of the issue.

A successful strategy employed by some firms has been to address the issue without dealing directly with the critics. Instead, they work with international or governmental agencies. Another alternative is to do nothing. If the criticism receives no publicity, it may die from lack of interest. However, bad handling of a situation can have serious repercussions for a firm. Union Carbide's bungling of the Bhopal accident is an example. An example of a firm that uses public relations effectively is IBM. Its strong lobbying effort convinced EC commissioners that the highly regulated state-owned telephone and postal organizations are responsible for costly, inefficient phone systems. Partly because of IBM's efforts, one of the EC's main objectives for Europe 1992 is to standardize and liberalize telecommunications.[43]

□ Pricing Strategies

Pricing, the third element of the marketing mix, is an important and complex consideration in formulating the marketing strategy. Pricing decisions affect other corporate functions, directly determine the firm's gross revenue, and are a major determinant of profits.

Pricing, a controllable variable.   Most marketers, especially Americans, are aware that effective price setting consists of more than mechanically adding a standard markup to a cost. To obtain the maximum benefits from pricing, management must regard it in the same manner as it does other controllable variables; that is, pricing is one of the marketing mix elements that can be varied to achieve the marketing objectives of the firm.

 For instance, if the marketer wishes to position a product as a high-quality item, setting a relatively high price will reinforce promotion that emphasizes quality. However, combining a recognizably low price with a promotional emphasis on quality could result in an incongruous pairing that would adversely affect its credibility with the consumer—the low price might be interpreted as the correct price for an inferior product. Pricing can also be a determinant in the choice of middlemen, because if the firm requires a wholesaler to take title, stock, promote, and deliver the merchandise, it must give the wholesaler a much larger trade discount than would be demanded by a broker, whose services are much more limited.

These examples illustrate one of the reasons for the complexity of price setting—the interaction of pricing with the other elements of the marketing mix. In addition, two other sets of forces influence this variable: (1) interaction between marketing and the other functional areas of the firm and (2) environmental forces.

Interaction between marketing and the other functional areas.   To illustrate this point, look at the following:

1. The finance people want prices that are both profitable and conducive to a steady cash flow.
2. Production supervisors want prices that create large sales volumes, which permit long production runs.
3. The legal department worries about possible antitrust violations when different prices are set according to type of customer.
4. The tax people are concerned with the effects of prices on tax loads.
5. The domestic sales manager wants export prices to be high enough to avoid having to compete with company products that are purchased for export and then diverted to the domestic market (one aspect of parallel importing).

The marketer must address all of these concerns and also consider the impact of the legal and other environmental forces that we examined in Section Three. Table 15–4 at the end of this chapter examines this aspect of pricing in greater detail.

International standardization.   Companies that pursue a policy of unifying corporate pricing procedures worldwide know that pricing is acted on by the same forces that militate against the international standardization of the other marketing mix components. Pricing for the overseas markets is more complex because managements must be concerned with two kinds of pricing: (1) **foreign national pricing**, which is domestic pricing in another country, and (2) international pricing for exports.

foreign national pricing
local pricing in another
country

Foreign national pricing.   Many foreign governments in their fight against inflation have instituted price controls, and the range of the products affected varies immensely from country to country. Some governments attempt to fix prices on just about everything, while others are concerned only with essential goods. Unfortunately, no agreement exists on what is essential, so in one market the prices of gasoline, food products, tires, and even wearing apparel may be controlled, while in another market only the prices of staple foods may be fixed. In nations with laws on unfair competition, the minimum sales price may be controlled rather than the maximum. The German law is so comprehensive that under certain conditions, even premiums and cents-off coupons may be prohibited because they are considered to violate the minimum price requirements. The international marketer must be watchful of a recent tendency of many nations, especially EC members, to open up their markets to price competition by weakening and even abolishing retail price maintenance laws.

Prices can vary because of appreciable cost differentials on opposite sides of a border. One government may levy higher import duties on imported raw materials or may subsidize public utilities, while another may not. Differences in labor legislation will cause labor costs to vary. Competition among local suppliers may be intense in one market, permitting the affiliate to buy inputs at better prices than those paid by an affiliate in another market, which must purchase raw materials from a single supplier, possibly a government monopoly.

Competition on the selling side is also diverse. Frequently, an affiliate in one market will face heavy local competition and be severely limited in the price it can charge, while in a neighboring market, a lack of competitors will allow another affiliate to charge a much higher price. As regional economic groupings reduce trade barriers among members, such opportunities are becoming fewer because firms must then meet regional as well as local competition.

Because the firm, for a number of reasons, does not introduce a new product simultaneously in all markets, the same product will not be in the same stage of the product life cycle everywhere. In markets where it is in the introductory stage, there is an opportunity to charge a high "skimming" price or a low "penetration" price, depending on such factors as market objectives, patent protection, price elasticity of demand, and competition. As the product reaches the maturity or decline stage, the price may be lowered, if doing so permits a satisfactory return. Because life cycles vary among markets, prices too will be different.

International pricing.   International pricing involves the setting of prices for goods produced in one country and sold in another. The pricing of exports to unrelated customers falls in this category and will be treated separately in the chapter on exporting. A special kind of exporting, *intracorporate sales,* is exceedingly common among worldwide companies as they attempt to rationalize production by requiring subsidiaries to specialize in the manufacture of some products while importing others. Their imports may consist of components that are assembled into the end product, such as engines made in one country that are mounted in car bodies built in another, or they may be finished products imported to complement the product mix of an affiliate. No matter what the end use is, problems exist in setting an intracorporate price (**transfer price**).

Because it is possible for the firm as a whole to gain while both the buying and selling subsidiaries "lose" (receive prices that are lower than would be obtained through an outside transaction), the tendency is for transfer prices to be set at headquarters. The reason for this apparent anomaly is that the company obtains a profit from *both* the seller and the buyer.

The selling affiliate would like to charge other subsidiaries the same price that it charges all customers, but, when combined with transportation costs and import duties, such a price may make it impossible for the importing subsidiary to compete in its market. If headquarters dictates that a lower-than-market transfer price be charged, the seller will be unhappy because its profit-and-loss statement suffers. This can be a very real headache to personnel

transfer price intracorporate price, or the price of a good or service sold by one affiliate to another, the home office to an affiliate, or vice versa whose promotion bonuses depend on the bottom line. In Chapter 22, we will see how home office management deals with this problem.

Both foreign governments and the U.S. government are also interested in profits and the part transfer prices play in their realization, because of the influence of profits on the amount of taxes paid. American and foreign tax agents have become very much aware that because of differences in tax structures, a firm can obtain meaningful profits by ordering a subsidiary in a country with high corporate taxes to sell at cost to a subsidiary in a country where corporate taxes are lower. The profit is earned where less income tax is paid, and the company clearly gains. Figure 15–5 shows how firms can hide profits with transfer pricing.

Transfer prices may also be employed to circumvent currency restrictions. When a country is suffering from a lack of foreign exchange, it may impose controls that totally prohibit, or at least place a low limit on, the amount of profit that can be repatriated. Suppose Country A, lacking dollars, places severe controls on all dollar transactions. There is trade with Country B, which does have dollars or another convertible currency. The home office could order its subsidiary in A to buy from the B affiliate at a price well over cost, which would transfer A's profit to B. Once in B, the profits could be sent home. The same strategy could be followed in any situation where it appeared necessary to either reduce A's profits or take them out of the country, such as:

1. Imminent currency devaluation.
2. Government pressure to reduce prices because of excessive profits.
3. Labor's clamor for higher wages based on high profits earned.

The manipulation of transfer prices for the reduction of income taxes and import duties or the avoidance of exchange controls has caused many governments to insist on arm's-length prices—the prices charged to unrelated customers. Under Section 482 of the Internal Revenue Code, U.S. tax authorities are empowered to reconstruct an intracorporate transfer price and tax the calculated profits whenever there is reason to suspect that low prices were set for tax evasion. Customs authorities in a number of European countries have increased the invoice price of imports by as much as 125 percent, forcing the importing subsidiary to pay a much higher than normal duty.

Despite the advantages of price manipulation, a recent study found that many large American companies most often used the market price as the transfer price.[44] One imposing reason is government intervention, especially under Section 482 of the tax code; in addition, it is much easier to monitor and evaluate foreign managers' performance when the market price is the transfer price.

□ Distribution Strategies

The development of distribution strategies is a difficult task in the home country, but it is even more so internationally, where marketing managers must concern themselves with two functions rather than one: (1) getting the products *to* foreign markets (exporting) and (2) distributing the products *within* each market (foreign distribution). In this section, we will examine foreign distribution only, leaving the export channels for the next chapter.

□ **FIGURE 15–5**
Hiding Profits with
Transfer Pricing

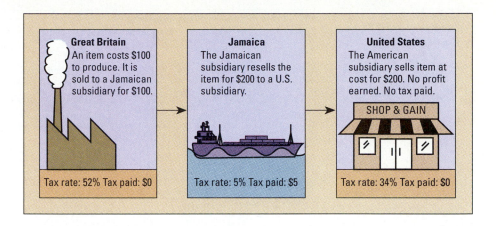

Great Britain
An item costs $100 to produce. It is sold to a Jamaican subsidiary for $100.

Tax rate: 52% Tax paid: $0

Jamaica
The Jamaican subsidiary resells the item for $200 to a U.S. subsidiary.

Tax rate: 5% Tax paid: $5

United States
The American subsidiary sells item at cost for $200. No profit earned. No tax paid.

SHOP & GAIN

Tax rate: 34% Tax paid: $0

Interdependence of distribution decisions.   When making decisions on distribution, care must be taken to analyze their interdependence with the other marketing mix variables. For example, if the product requires considerable after-sales servicing, the firm will want to sell through dealers that have the facilities, personnel, and capital to purchase equipment and spare parts and to train servicepeople. This will necessitate using a merchant wholesaler, which will demand a larger trade discount than would an agent, because an agent does not perform these functions. Channel decisions are critical because they are *long-term* decisions; once established, they are far less easy to change then those made for price, product, and promotion.

International standardization.   Although management would prefer to standardize distribution patterns internationally, there are two fundamental constraints on its doing so: (1) the variation in the availability of channel members among the firm's markets and (2) the inconsistency of the influence of the environmental forces. Because of these constraints, international managers have found it best to establish a basic but flexible overall policy. The subsidiaries then implement this policy and design channel strategies to meet local conditions.

Availability of channel members.   As a starting point in their channel design, local managers have the successful distribution system used in the domestic operation. Headquarters' support for a policy of employing the same channels worldwide will be especially strong when the entire marketing mix has been built around a particular channel type, such as direct sales force or franchised operators. Avon, Encyclopaedia Britannica, and McDonald's are examples of firms that consider their distribution systems inviolate, so locally there is little latitude in planning channel strategies. However, companies utilizing the more common types of middlemen are usually more inclined to grant the local organization greater freedom in channel member selection.

Although a general rule for any firm entering a foreign market is to adapt to the available channels rather than create new ones, a number of companies have successfully avoided the traditional channels because of their appalling inefficiencies. Coca-Cola did this in Japan, as we mentioned in Chapter 13.

Experienced marketers know they cannot get their products to the consumer by the same retail channel in every country, and even in Europe the

□ **TABLE 15–3**
Percentage of Total Sales by Type of Outlet

Shoes	Percent of Total Sales	Toys	Percent of Total Sales
Germany		**Germany**	
Organized independents (buying groups)	35%	Organized independent toy stores (buying groups)	37%
Major shoe chains	29	Department stores	27
Mail	7	Hypermarkets	15
Department stores	6	Mail	8
Hypermarkets	6	Independent toy stores	4
Discount stores	6	Other retailers	9
Independent shoe stores	4		100%
Other retailers	7		
	100%		
France		**France**	
Independent shoe stores	56%	Hypermarkets/supermarkets	36%
Direct sales	14	Toy stores	22
Clothing stores	2	Department and variety stores	14
Department stores	2	Mail	8
Variety stores	1	Other retailers	20
Other retailers	25		100%
	100%		

Source: *Retail International* (London: Euromonitor, 1988), pp. 162, 171, 480, and 489.

differences are substantial. What is the best way to sell toys in France? A sure outlet is the hypermarket, which sells 36 percent of all toys purchased in France. In Germany, however, the hypermarket accounts for only 15 percent of toy sales (see Table 15–3). The most important kind of outlet for toys in Germany is independent retailers, which are organized into buying groups. Table 15–3 also indicates the differences in the way shoes are sold in these two neighboring countries.

Foreign environmental forces.   Environmental differences among markets add to the difficulty in standardizing distribution channels. Changes caused by the cultural forces generally occur over time, but those caused by the legal forces can be radical and quick and can dramatically slow trends responding to cultural demands.

To illustrate, hypermarkets, which are changing distribution patterns in Europe and particularly in France, a nation of small shopkeepers, numbered only 11 in that country in 1972. The combination of lower prices and one-stop shopping caught on with the French consumer, and 51 hypermarkets were opened in 1973. Manufacturers that saw a quick end to small shopkeepers failed to appreciate their political power. The Royer Law, passed in 1973, gave local urban commissions, often dominated by small merchants, the power to refuse construction permits for supermarkets and hypermarkets. After the law took effect, only 40 percent of the large-store applications were approved.

Although the trend toward more giant stores has not been stopped by the law (there were about 1,000 French hypermarkets in 1991), it has certainly been slowed. The president of Carrefour, France's largest hypermarket chain, says, "It is becoming increasingly hard to find a site where we can get a building permit. Opposition of small shopkeepers is the only thing keeping us from growing more rapidly."

Japan's Large Scale Retailers Law, very similar to the French law, had also slowed the opening of large retailers. However, because of pressure from Carla Hills, U.S. trade representative, and the trade talks called the Structural Impediments Initiative (SII), the Japanese Ministry of International Trade and Industry suddenly found it could reduce the period that small retailers could block the opening of new stores in their neighborhoods from an incredible *10 years* to a maximum of 18 months. This was a breakthrough that foreign retailers needed.[45]

The first large U.S.-owned discount store to take advantage of the U.S. SII aimed at prying open new markets for American firms in Japan was Toys "R" Us. After three years of haggling with Japanese bureaucracy, local vested interests, and heavy, often hostile press coverage, the company opened its first store 40 miles north of Tokyo. It opened a second store in January 1992 and expects to have 100 stores within a decade. Although it has signed agreements with 50 toy manufacturers to sell their products directly, cutting out the layers of distribution that make prices so high in Japan, many other manufacturers are afraid to upset their old distributers and retailers. The company estimates that half of its annual sales will be from toys made outside Japan.[46]

Another restriction of distribution has been tried in the EC. Manufacturers have attempted to prevent distributors from selling across national borders, but the Commission has prohibited them from doing so by invoking EC antitrust laws. Exclusive distributorships have been permitted, but every time the manufacturer has included a clause prohibiting the distributor from exporting to another EC country, the clause has been stricken from the contract. In effect, the firm that has two factories in the EC with different costs, and thus distinct prices, is practically powerless to prevent products from the lower-cost affiliate from competing with higher-cost products from the other affiliate.

Economic differences also make international standardization difficult, although marketers can adapt to economic changes. In 1960, very little frozen food was sold in France because of the consumer's preference for fresh food. However, tight economic conditions forced many housewives to seek employment, and with less time to spend preparing meals, they turned to frozen food. An added attraction of frozen food items was that their prices did not rise as fast as those of fresh foods. The result has been sales increases of 10 percent or more a year since 1973.

In Japan, high prices have also forced women to find jobs, and they no longer have time to shop and prepare the traditional Japanese foods. They fill their needs by purchasing more convenience foods advertised on TV with home delivery or by going to the more than 50 chains of convenience stores. The largest, 7-Eleven, has over 3,200 licensees, most of whom are former small shopkeepers. Its point-of-sale computer network is eliminating the need for small-scale wholesalers, whose number is already declining all over Japan.[47] Worldwide, marketers are seeing cultural barriers fall as economic conditions force housewives to obtain employment to supplement household income. The premium that outside employment places on their time is leading

☐ **TABLE 15-4   Environmental Constraints to International Standardization of Marketing Mix**

Factors Limiting Standardization	Product	Price	Distribution	Personal Selling	Promotion
1. Physical forces	1. Climatic conditions—special packaging, extra insulation, mildew protection, extra cooling capacity, special lubricants, dust protection, special instructions 2. Difficult terrain—stronger parts, larger engines, engines, stronger packing	1. Special product requirements add to costs 2. Difficult terrain—extra transportation costs, higher sales expense (car maintenance, longer travel time, more per diem expense)	1. Difficult terrain—less customer mobility, requiring more outlets, each with more stock 2. Varying climatic conditions—more stock needed when distinct products required for different climates	1. Buyers widely dispersed or concentrated—impacts on territory and sales force size 2. Difficult terrain—high travel expense, longer travel time, fewer daily sales calls 3. Separate cultures created by physical barriers—salespeople from each culture may be needed	1. Cultural pockets created by barriers—separate ads for languages, dialects, words, customs 2. Different climates—distinct advertising themes
2. Sociocultural forces	1. Consumer attitudes toward product 2. Colors of product and package—varying significance 3. Languages—labels, instructions 4. Religion—consumption patterns 5. Attitudes toward time—differences in acceptance of timesaving products 6. Attitudes toward change—acceptance of new products 7. Educational levels—ability to comprehend instructions, ability to use product 8. Tastes and customs—product use and consumption 9. Different buying habits—package size 10. Who is decision maker? 11. Rural–urban population mix	1. Cultural objections to product—lower prices to penetrate market 2. Lower educational level, lower income—lower prices for mass market 3. Attitudes toward bargaining—impacts list prices 4. Customers' attitude toward price	1. More and perhaps specialized outlets to market to various subcultures 2. Buyers accustomed to bargaining—requires small retailers 3. Attitudes toward change—varying acceptance of new kinds of outlets 4. Different buying habits—different types of outlets	1. Separate cultures—separate salespeople 2. Varying attitudes toward work, time, achievement, and wealth among cultures—difficult to motivate and control sales force 3. Different buying behavior—different kinds of sales forces 4. Cultural stigma attached to selling?	1. Language, different or same but with words having different connotations—advertisements, labels, instructions 2. Literacy, low—simple labels, instructions, ads with plenty of graphics 3. Symbolism—responses differ 4. Colors—significances differ 5. Attitudes toward advertising 6. Buying influence—gender, committee, family 7. Cultural pockets—different promotions 8. Religion—taboos and restrictions vary 9. Attitudes toward foreign products and firms

◻ **TABLE 15–4**   **(continued)**

Factors Limiting Standardization	Product	Price	Distribution	Personal Selling	Promotion
3. Legal-political forces	1. Some products prohibited 2. Certain features required or prohibited 3. Label and packaging requirements 4. Varying product standards 5. Varying patent, copyright, and trademark laws 6. Varying import duties 7. Varying import restriction 8. Local production required of all or part of product 9. Requirements to use local inputs that are different from home country inputs 10. Cultural stigma attached to brand name or artwork?	1. Varying retail price maintenance laws 2. Government-controlled prices or markups 3. Anti-trust laws 4. Import duties 5. Tax laws 6. Transfer pricing controls	1. Some kinds of channel members outlawed 2. Markups government-controlled 3. Retail price maintenance 4. Turnover taxes 5. Only government-owned channels permitted for some products 6. Restrictions on channel members—number, lines handled, licenses for each line 7. Laws on canceling contracts of channel members	1. Laws governing discharge of salespeople 2. Laws requiring compensation on discharging salespeople 3. Laws requiring profit sharing, overtime, working conditions 4. Restrictions on channel members	1. Use of languages 2. Legal limits to expenditures 3. Taxes on advertising 4. Prohibition of promotion for some products 5. Special legal requirements for some products (cigarettes, pharmaceuticals) 6. Media availability 7. Trademark laws 8. Taxes that discriminate against some kinds of promotion 9. Controls on language or claims used in ads for some products
4. Economic forces	1. Purchasing power—package size, product sophistication, quality level 2. Wages—varying requirements for labor-saving products 3. Condition of infrastructure—heavier products, hand instead of power-operated 4. Market size—varying width of product mix	1. Different prices 2. Price elasticity of demand	1. Availability of outlets 2. Size of inventory 3. Size of outlets 4. Dispersion of outlets 5. Extent of self-service 6. Types of outlets 7. Length of channels	1. Sales force expense 2. Availability of employees in labor market	1. Media availability 2. Funds available 3. Emphasis on saving time 4. Experience with products 5. TV, radio ownership 6. Print media readership 7. Quality of media 8. Excessive costs to reach certain market segments
5. Competitive forces	1. Rate of new product introduction 2. Rate of product improvement	1. Competitors' prices 2. Number of competitors	1. Competitors' control of channel members 2. Competitors' margins to channel members	1. Competitors' sales force-number and ability 2. Competitors' emphasis on personal selling in promotional mix	1. Competitors' promotional expenditures 2. Competitors' promotional mix

(Continued)

□ **TABLE 15–4**   **(Concluded)**

Factors Limiting Standardization	Product	Price	Distribution	Personal Selling	Promotion
	3. Quality levels 4. Package size 5. Strength in market	3. Importance of price in competitors' marketing mix	3. Competitors' choice of channel members	3. Competitors' rates and methods of compensation	3. Competitors' choice of media
6. Distributive forces	1. Product servicing requirements 2. Package size 3. Branding—dealers' brands	1. Margins required by channel members 2. Special payments required—stocking, promotional	1. Availability of channel members 2. Number of company distribution centers 3. Market coverage by channel members 4. Demands of channel members	1. Size of sales force 2. Kind and quality of sales force	1. Kinds of promotion 2. Amounts of promotion

them to prefer one-stop shopping, labor-saving devices. and convenience foods. The result is an upheaval in the way goods are distributed, but American marketers that have U.S. experience as a guide are in a position to make inroads on their foreign competitors, for which this is a new phenomenon.

Can retailing be globalized? Retailers like France's Carrefour, with stores in France, Spain, Brazil, Argentina and the United States, think it can. So do Safeway supermarkets, Gucci, Cartier, Benetton, and Toys "R" Us, which has made aggressive penetration in Canada, Europe, Hong Kong, and Singapore. Kaufhof, the German retailing giant, has 100 shoe stores located in Austria, France, Switzerland, and Germany and is also the leading mail-order shoe retailer in Europe. As Peter Drucker said in 1987, "To maintain a leadership position in any one developed country, a business—whether large or small—increasingly has to attain and hold leadership positions in all developed markets worldwide."[48]

□ **Foreign Environmental Forces and Marketing Mix Matrix**

The matrix[49] shown in Table 15–4 summarizes many of the constraints on the internationalization of the marketing mix that have been discussed in this chapter and in Section Three. Table 15–4 will serve as a reminder of the many factors that marketing managers should consider when they are contemplating the standardization of one or more marketing mix elements.

SUMMARY

Whether a policy or a technique is designed for global use or is first used in the home market and then used overseas, marketers must know where to look for possible differences between marketing domestically and marketing internationally. Sometimes there are great differences; sometimes there are none. Although the basic functions of marketing are the same for all markets, international markets can differ greatly because of the

variations in the uncontrollable environmental forces. The marketing manager must decide if the marketing program can be standardized worldwide, if some changes must be made, or if a completely different marketing mix must be prepared.

Much of the confusion about whether a global firm can have global products is because the discussants do not differentiate between the physical and total products. A total product is easier than a physical product to standardize. Industrial products and services generally can be marketed globally with less change than can consumer products. As you go down the economic and social strata in a country, you tend to find greater dissimilarities among countries' social and cultural values.

Six commonly used promotional strategies can be formulated by combining the three alternatives of marketing the same product everywhere, adapting it, or designing a new product with the same, adapted, or different message.

Advertising is the promotional mix element with the greatest global similarities. The advertiser is constrained in standardizing the advertising campaign by type of product, media availability, and the environmental forces. The programmed-management approach assists in the standardization. Many companies standardize the personal-selling function. Telemarketing and computerized prospecting are helping to reduce sales call costs. Legal constraints and the other environmental forces often require the manager to adapt the global promotion program to local conditions.

Marketers must be concerned with foreign national, export, and transfer pricing. The availability of channel members and the variability of the environmental forces are responsible for deviations from a global distribution policy.

QUESTIONS

1. "Consumers are not standardized globally; therefore, with global brands, you either get lowest common denominator advertising or you get advertising that's right somewhere, but wrong elsewhere." This is an actual statement of a CEO of an international advertising agency. What's your opinion?

2. What future do you see for global advertising?

3. Are there any advantages to standardizing the marketing mix worldwide?

4. On what does the extent of changes in the marketing mix among markets depend?

5. What are the two sets of conditions mentioned in the text that favor regional or global promotional campaigns?

6. What is the basis for Gillette's taking its panregional approach?

7. What is a generality about similarities of social and cultural values in a country?

8. Why is food retailing changing in Europe and Japan?

9. Why must a marketer consider the economic forces when formulating a product strategy? Give some examples.

10. Discuss the six distinct strategies that can be formulated by combining the three alternatives of selling the same product everywhere, adapting it to foreign markets, or designing a completely different product with the same, adapted, or different message.

11. Why might the advertising manager in the global corporation's home office not be able to standardize the firm's advertising campaigns?

12. Which product classes are the easiest to standardize globally?

13. Personal sales calls are expensive. Why would a company use personal selling instead of TV and print media?

14. What are firms doing to improve the effectiveness of their sales forces? Have these techniques arrived in the United States from Japan yet?

15. At least sales promotion techniques can be standardized. True or false?

16. How should firms deal with critics' attacks?

17. If manipulation of transfer pricing is so advantageous, why do so many companies use the market price as the transfer price?

18. Compare the amount of tax paid in the transactions showed in Figure 15–5 with a straight sale by the British subsidiary for $100 to the U.S. subsidiary, which then sells the item for $200.

19. Can manufacturers in the EC prevent their distributors from selling across national borders?

□ MINICASE 15–1

U.S. Pharmaceutical of Korea*

U.S. Pharmaceutical of Korea (USPK) was formed in 1969. Its one manufacturing plant is located just outside Seoul, the capital. Although the company distributes its products throughout South Korea, 40 percent of its total sales of $5 million were made in the capital last year.

There are no governmental restrictions on whom the company can sell to. The only requirement is that the wholesaler, retailer, or end user have a business license and a taxation number. Of the 400 wholesalers in the country, 130 are customers of USPK, accounting for 46 percent of the company's total sales. The company also sells directly to 2,100 of the country's 10,000 retailers; these account for 45 percent of total sales. The remaining sales are made directly to high-volume end users, such as hospitals and clinics.

Tom Sloane, marketing manager of USPK, would prefer to make about 90 percent of the company's sales directly to retailers and the remaining 10 percent directly to high-volume users. He believes, however, that this strategy is not possible because there are so many small retailers. Not only is the sales volume per retailer small, but there is also a risk involved in extending them credit. USPK tends to deal directly with large urban retailers and leaves most of the nonurban retailers to the wholesalers.

However, the use of wholesalers bothers Sloane for two reasons: (1) he has to give them larger discounts than he gives retailers that buy directly from the firm and (2) because of the intense competition (300 pharmaceutical manufacturers in Korea), his wholesalers frequently demand larger discounts as the price for remaining loyal to USPK.

This intense competition affects another aspect of USPK's operations—collecting receivables. USPK has

*Based on an actual situation in Korea.

found that many wholesalers collect quickly from retailers but delay paying it. Instead, they invest in ventures that offer high short-term returns. For example, lending to individuals can bring them interest rates of up to 3 percent a month. The company's receivables, meanwhile, range from 75 to 130 days. Wholesalers are also the cause of another problem. Many are understaffed and have to rely on "drug peddlers" for sales. The drug peddler (there are perhaps 4,000 just in Seoul) make most of their money either by cutting the wholesalers' margins (selling at lower than recommended prices) or by bartering USPK's products for other pharmaceuticals. They do this by finding retail outlets where products are sold for less than the printed price. They exchange USPK's products at a discount for other drugs, which they sell to other retail outlets at a profit. As a result, USPK's products end up on retailers' shelves at prices lower than those that the company and its reputable wholesalers are selling them for.

The pharmaceutical industry has made some progress in persuading wholesalers and retailers to adhere to company price lists, but nonadherence is still a serious problem. One issue that manufacturers have not been able to resolve as yet is the manner in which demands from hospitals and physicians for gifts should be handled.

Sloane believes the industry can do much to solve these problems, although intense competition has thus far kept the pharmaceutical manufacturers from joining together to map out a solution.

1. What should Tom Sloane and U.S. Pharmaceutical of Korea do to improve collections from wholesalers?
2. How would you handle the distribution problem?
3. Can anything be done through firms in the industry to improve the situation?
4. How would you handle the demands for gifts?

□ MINICASE 15–2

An Ethical Situation*

The Swiss pharmaceutical global corporation Hoffman-La Roche has made a major breakthrough in the relief of a serious disabling disease that affects 3 percent of the

*This is an actual situation.

world's population. Their new product, Tigason, is the first product that effectively controls severe cases of psoriasis and dyskeratoses, skin disorders that cause severe flaking of the skin. Sufferers from this disease frequently retreat from society because of fear of rejection, thus losing their families and jobs. Tigason does not cure the disease, but it causes the symptoms to disappear.

There is one potential problem. Because of the risk of damage to unborn babies, women should not take the drug for one year before conception or during pregnancy. Hoffman-La Roche is well aware of the potential for harm to the company if the product is misused. It has seen the problems of another Swiss firm, Nestlé. After much discussion, the company has decided the product is too important to keep off the market. It is, after all, the product that gives the greatest relief to sufferers.

The marketing department is asked to formulate a strategy for disseminating product information and controlling Tigason's use.

As marketing manager, what do you recommend?

◻ MINICASE 15–3

Black & Decker's Brand Transfer Strategy

The largest market segment of Black & Decker's business, consumer power tools, was saturated. Nearly every household had an electric drill. Although the company had a 50 percent market share worldwide in power tools, new competitors such as Japan's Makita Electric Works were beginning to take market share, especially in professional power tools. The president of Black & Decker, Laurence Farley, who assumed his position in 1982, stated, "We had recognized for some time that our core business faced limited growth. With our worldwide franchise, my vision is that we should be a broad-based marketer." Farley believed that the Black & Decker brand was strong enough to support not only tools and appliances, but almost any household gadget.

Although the company had developed a successful line of cordless appliances such as the Dustbuster™ vacuum, Spotliter, and the Scrub Brusher, it had difficulty in getting shelf space in retailers' appliance sections. That experience persuaded the company that it could not start its own brand of small appliances. In 1983, Black & Decker decided to buy an existing appliance line that would be strong enough to command its own shelf space. One of the members of the board of directors suggested that Farley try General Electric.

General Electric had at least 50 percent of the market in irons, toaster ovens, and portable mixers, but after-tax profits were only 4 percent of sales. This was not good enough for GE's CEO, and he concluded that small appliances could not meet GE's standards for success. To improve profitability, GE needed lower production costs, which Black & Decker could provide with its more efficient factories. In partial payment for its small appliance operation, GE received 3 million shares, or 6 percent, of Black & Decker stock, making it the company's largest shareholder. Black & Decker received about 100 household appliances and 7 manufacturing facilities. GE sales of small appliances in 1983 amounted to $470 million, 40 percent of Black & Decker's total sales of $1.17 billion, making this the largest brand transfer in history.

GE's top management in small appliances also moved to Black & Decker. They did not like the way GE sold small appliances. Innovations were limited and products made by all competitors were similar. The result was that everyone sold on the basis of price. Black & Decker will market brands harder and there will be innovations. The company will have subbrands; that is, groups of products with separate identities but still carrying the Black & Decker logo.

Under the terms of the acquisition agreement, Black & Decker has three years to eliminate the GE name from the product line.

1. Establish a brand transfer strategy for Black & Decker.

2. Before the acquisition of GE's small appliances, individual Black & Decker companies acted autonomously. Managers had complete control over their operations because top management assumed they knew their countries. Would you prepare a different brand transfer strategy for Black & Decker's overseas markets?

Source: "How Black & Decker Forged a Winning Brand Transfer Strategy," *Business International*, July 20, 1987, pp. 225–27; and "Black & Decker's Gamble on Globalization," *Fortune*, May 14, 1984, pp. 40–48.

SUPPLEMENTARY READINGS

Advertising

"Agencies Brace for New Europe." *Advertising Age,* June 5, 1989, p. 42.

"Centralized International Advertising." *International Advertiser,* September 1986, pp. 35–36.

"Comparative Advertising." *The Economist,* May 18, 1991, pp. 79–80.

"EC Pleases TV Advertisers." *Advertising Age,* October 16, 1989, p. 56.

"Europe's Priorities." *The Economist,* December 20, 1986, pp. 16–18.

"Fulfilling an Eastern Fantasy." *Advertising Age,* May 8, 1989, p. 40.

"How to Do Multinational Advertising Internationally." *Advertising World,* June 1985, pp. 6–30.

"No Women, No Alcohol; Learn Saudi Taboos before Placing Ads." *International Advertiser,* February 1986, pp. 11–12.

"No. 1 Dentsu Hits Lofty $1.2 Billion in Gross Income." *Advertising Age,* March 29, 1989, pp. 1–70.

"P&G's Artzt on Ads: Crucial Investment." *Advertising Age,* October 28, 1991, p. 1.

"Poll Favors U.S. Products." *Advertising Age,* September 23, 1991, p. 16.

"Similarity of Cultures Simplifies Advertising to the Pan-Arab World." *International Advertiser,* February 1986, pp. 6–10.

"Solving the Cost Crunch in Foreign Advertising." *Business Marketing,* January 1985, pp. 62–64.

"Tube Wars." *Business Month,* December 1988, pp. 61–62.

"World Brands." *Advertising Age,* February 9, 1992, pp. 25–35.

Global versus Multinational

"A Global Comeback." *Advertising Age,* August 20, 1987, pp. 142–214.

"At Procter & Gamble, Change under Artzt Isn't Just Cosmetic." *The Wall Street Journal,* March 5, 1991, p. A1.

"Creative Ad Ventures." *World,* January–February 1986, pp. 8–20.

"Differences, Confusion Slow Global Marketing Bandwagon." *Marketing News,* January 16, 1987, p. 1.

"Global Advertising: Multinational versus International Pros and Cons." *International Advertiser,* February 1986, pp. 34–37.

"Global Competitors: Some Criteria for Success." *Business Horizons,* January–February 1988, pp. 34–41.

"Global Marketing Campaign with a Local Touch." *Business International,* July 4, 1988, pp. 205–10.

"Global versus Local Advertising." *Management Review,* June 1986, pp. 27–31.

"How Countries Compare in Their Efforts to Think Internationally." *International Management,* November 1986, pp. 24–31.

Keegan, Warren. "Global Competition: Strategic Alternatives." Paper for Lubin Graduate School of Business, Pace University, January 1989.

Levitt, Theodore. "The Globalization of Markets." *The McKinsey Quarterly,* Summer 1984, pp. 2–20.

"Marketing Can Be Global, but Ads Must Remain Cultural." *Marketing News,* July 31, 1987, p. 24.

"Penmanship with a Flourish." *Forbes,* April 3, 1989, pp. 152–54.

Quelch, John A., and Edward J. Hoff. "Customizing Global Marketing." *Harvard Business Review,* May–June 1986, pp. 59–68.

Personal Selling

"Cut Bureaucracy with Shared Salesmen." *Business Europe,* June 21, 1985, pp. 193–97.

"Direct Marketing Wins High-Value Sales." *Business Europe,* April 26, 1985, pp. 132–33.

"Electrolux Brings Direct Sales Techniques to Asia's Front Door." *Business Asia,* November 1, 1985, pp. 349–52.

"Getting Maximum Results from Computerized Prospecting." *Business International Ideas in Action,* August 4, 1986, pp. 2–4.

"How Rank Xerox Profits from In-House Telephone Sales." *Business Europe,* February 15, 1985, pp. 49–50.

"Meeting the Competition: Burroughs Taps New Channel for Sales to Tough Markets." *Business International,* July 26, 1985, pp. 233–34.

"Organizing for Sales Force Effectiveness." *Business International Ideas in Action,* June 8, 1987, pp. 2–6.

"Why Direct Selling Is Now a Crucial Tool for Big Business." *International Management,* March 1986, pp. 38–46.

Pricing

Adelberg, Arthur. "Resolving Conflicts in Intracompany Transfer Pricing." *Accountancy,* November 1986, pp. 86–89.

"Avon's Close-In Pricing: Four Steps toward Implementing the Strategy." *Business International Money Report,* February 10, 1986, pp. 42–43.

"Close-In Pricing System Protects Avon's Margins in Hyperinflationary Nations." *Business International Money Report,* February 3, 1986, pp. 33–34.

"Do You Want to Avoid a Government Review of Your Transfer Pricing?" *Business International Money Report,* May 2, 1988, pp. 147–51.

"Firms Use EEC Law to Fight Price Controls." *Business Europe*, September 7, 1987, pp. 1–4.

"How Transfer Pricing Can Support Business Strategies." *Business International Money Report*, March 7, 1988, pp. 82–88.

"MNCs Face Tighter Net over Transfer Pricing Rules." *Business International*, October 31, 1988, pp. 337–38.

Samiee, Saeed. "Pricing in Marketing Strategies of U.S.- and Foreign-Based Companies." *Journal of Business Research*, 1987:15:1730.

"Seven Ways to Get an Edge in the Pricing Tug of War." *Business Latin America*, September 12, 1988, p. 284.

Product

"America's International Winners." *Fortune*, April 14, 1986, pp. 34–46.

"Europewide Plans Arise at Sara Lee." *Advertising Age*, June 5, 1989, p. 50.

Hill, John S., and Richard R. Still. "Adapting Products to LDC Tastes." *Harvard Business Review*, March–April 1984, pp. 92–101.

"How to Be a Global Manager." *Fortune*, March 14, 1988, pp. 52–58.

"How to Check the Quality of Customer Service and Raise the Standard." *International Management*, February 1987, pp. 34–35.

"More Companies Shop Abroad for New-Product Ideas." *The Wall Street Journal*, March 14, 1990, p. B1.

"Picking Pithy Names Is Getting Trickier as Trade Applications Proliferate." *The Wall Street Journal*, January 14, 1992, p. B1.

"Southern Europe Heats up for '92." *Advertising Age*, June 5, 1989, p. 6.

"The Name's the Game." *The Economist*, December 24, 1988, p. 100.

"The Year of the Brand." *The Economist*, December 24, 1988, pp. 95–96.

Public Relations

"IBM Lobbies for Freer European Market." *The Wall Street Journal*, April 20, 1988, p. 18.

"Making Company Disasters Less Disastrous." *The Economist*, January 31, 1987, pp. 55–56.

"MNC Image-Building Comes of Age as a Working Tool." *Business International*, January 13, 1986, p. 13.

Muskie, Edmund S., and Daniel J. Greenwood III. "The Nestlé Infant Formula Audit Commission as a Model." *Journal of Business Strategy*, Spring 1988, pp. 19–23.

"Nestlé Rejects Militant PR Plan to Combat Renewal of Boycott." *The Wall Street Journal*, April 25, 1989, p. B6.

"The Gall in Mother's Milk." *The Journal of Advertising* 1, 1982, pp. 1–10.

"Trend-Setting Companies Elevate PR to the Level of Strategic Weapon." *International Management*, June 1985, pp. 50–55.

Retailing

"Avon's Marketing Approach Wins Big in Latin America." *Business Latin America*, June 17, 1991, pp. 193–99.

"Cable TV Shopping Service Now a Reality in Europe." *Business International Ideas in Action*, May 11, 1987, p. 11.

"Cherchez la Store." *Forbes*, January 9, 1989, pp. 311–14.

"Europe's Hypermarkets Making Waves Here." *Advertising Age*, May 4, 1987, pp. S18–19.

"Fishing Only Where the Fish Swim." *Business Europe*, April 26, 1991, pp. 2–3.

"Guess Who's Selling Barbies in Japan Now?" *Business Week*, December 9, 1991, pp. 72–76.

"Japan's Next Retail Revolution." *The Economist*, December 21, 1991–January 3, 1992, pp. 79–80.

Kacker, Madhav. "Coming to Terms with Global Retailing." *International Marketing Review*, Spring 1986, pp. 7–19.

"Retailers Fly into Hyperspace." *Fortune*, October 24, 1988, pp. 150–52.

"Retailing in Japan." *The Economist*, January 4, 1992, p. 62.

"The New Japan Goes Shopping." *The Economist*, August 13, 1988, pp. 55–56.

"U.S., European Retailers Are Becoming More Transnational." *Europe*, January–February 1989, pp. 20–54.

Sales Promotion

Boddewyn, J. J. *Premiums, Gifts, Competitions, and Other Sales Promotions*. New York: International Advertising Association, 1988.

Foxman, Ellen R., Patriya S. Tansuhaj, and John K. Wong. "Evaluating Cross-National Sales Promotion Strategy: An Audit Approach." *International Marketing Review*, Winter 1988, pp. 7–15.

"How Companies Profit from Promotions in Italy." *Business Europe*, June 26, 1985, pp. 201–2.

"How Sumitomo Is Making Dunlop's Tires Profitable." *Business Europe*, June 7, 1985, pp. 177–78.

Service Marketing

"As World Shrinks, Nielsen Expands." *Advertising Age*, June 5, 1989, p. 52.

"At Your Service." *The Rotarian*, May 1989, pp. 20–25.

"Creativity with Discipline." *Forbes*, March 6, 1989, pp. 41–42.

"Services: U.S., EC Prepare for Talks." *Europe*, January–February 1986, pp. 16–18.

"The Bright Future of Service Exports." *Fortune*, June 8, 1987, pp. 32–38.

"The Ever-Bigger Boom in Consulting." *Fortune*, April 24, 1989, pp. 113–34.

Television

"Europe's Audiovisual Challenge." *Europe*, April 1989, pp. 28–30.

"Europe's Priorities." *The Economist*, December 20, 1986, pp. 16–18.

"How Companies Are Advertising on Pan-European Television." *Business International Ideas in Action*, June 9, 1986, pp. 13–18.

"Murdoch's Sky Channel Beams Strong Signal across Europe." *International Management*, March 1985, pp. 48–50.

"Profile of Sky-Watchers." *International Advertiser*, June 1986, pp. 22–23.

"Satellite Success." *Europe*, May 1989, p. 5.

"Satellite TV Becomes a Credible Advertising Medium." *Business International Ideas in Action*, April 14, 1986, pp. 2–9.

"The Appeal of China TV." *International Advertiser*, June 1986, pp. 37–41.

"TV Moguls Air Angry Views on Single Market." *The European*, October 11–13, 1991, p. 18.

"Uncertain Future Plagues Marketers Planning for 1992." *Advertising Age*, June 5, 1989, pp. 1–42.

"U.S.-Style TV Turns on Europe." *Fortune*, April 13, 1987, pp. 96–98.

ENDNOTES

1. R&D is still highly concentrated in the home country, although some internationals have had overseas research facilities for years and, recently, global firms have been locating R&D centers in foreign markets. When R&D is still highly concentrated in the home county, the important product changes have to be made there. Foreign and domestic personnel compete for R&D time. Also, a product specification is rarely frozen (look at the minor changes in automobiles in a single model year). Notifying all of the production facilities worldwide about these modifications is difficult enough, but it is much more complex when the product is not internationally standardized.

2. "Multinational, Not Global," *The Economist*, December 24, 1988, p. 99.

3. "Nestlé Shows How to Gobble Markets," *Fortune*, January 16, 1989, p. 75.

4. One of the writers went to pick up his car in a garage and asked the mechanic whether he had test-driven it after finishing his work. Much to his surprise, the mechanic answered that he had not—he didn't know how to drive!

5. When it was an American company, General Tire used to do a good business in the United States selling tires for antique cars. The company imported the tires from its foreign subsidiaries, where the special sizes were in regular production because the old cars were still on the road in those countries.

6. "Consumer Nondurables," *Business International*, June 16, 1986, p. 190.

7. "Whirlpool Is Gathering a Global Momentum," *The New York Times*, April 23, 1989, p. F10.

8. "A Global Comeback," *Advertising Age*, August 20, 1987, p. 146.

9. Other LDCs follow this practice also. The pharmaceuticals mentioned are those sold in the United States with a prescription. To our knowledge, there is no country other than the United States where prescription drugs are counted or weighed and then packaged and labeled by the pharmacist. Elsewhere, the manufacturers, many of which are American subsidiaries, package the prescription drugs in small packages containing dosages that are commonly prescribed by the physician. The patient takes a prescription written by the physician in the language of the country (no Latin) and hands it to the pharmacist. He or she reaches up on the shelf and gives the customer a package. The pharmacist does not count, does not fill a plastic vial, and does not type labels. Incidentally, each package carries an insert that describes the common dosage, symptoms of overdose, and precautions to take when using the drug. Interestingly, the American Medical Association and owners of pharmacies have striven to block the idea of inserts in the United States. Their reason: the American public, unlike people in other countries, is not well enough educated to understand the insert.

10. "Gillette Keys Sales to Third World Tastes," *The Wall Street Journal*, January 23, 1986, p. 36.

11. We believe but cannot prove that sales of flea powder per capita should be high there. All the Americans we knew used to douse their legs liberally with it before going to the movies. If not, they would be eaten alive.

12. "How to Be a Global Manager," *Fortune*, March 14, 1988, pp. 52–53.

13. Warren J. Keegan, "Multinational Product Planning: Strategic Alternatives," *Journal of Marketing*, January 1969, pp. 58–62, combines these alternatives to formulate five product strategies.

14. "World Brands," *Advertising Age*, February 9, 1992, p. 25.

15. "Advertising the European Way," *Europe*, November 1989, p. 32.

16. "A Profile of Sky-Watchers," *International Advertiser*, June 1986, p. 22.

17. "New GE, Coke Deals Boost CNN," *Advertising Age*, January 22, 1992, p. 4.

18. "Hachette Signs Ford in Global Media Deal," *Advertising Age*, February 10, 1992, p. 3.

19. "Le Défi Disney," *Forbes*, February 20, 1989, pp. 39–40.

20. "Europe's Audiovisual Challenge," *Europe*, April 1989, pp. 28–30.

21. "TV Moguls Air Angry Views on Single Market," *The European*, October 11–13, 1991, p. 18.

22. "EC Pleases TV Advertisers," *Advertising Age,* October 16, 1989, p. 56.

23. "U.S.-Style TV Turns on Europe," *U.S. News & World Report,* May 25, 1987, p. 97.

24. Data from *Africa South of the Sahara* and *The Middle East and North Africa* (London: Europe Publications, 1988).

25. "Videotapes Are Common throughout Middle East," *International Advertiser,* February 1986, p. 31.

26. Various annual reports.

27. "More Freedom on French TV," *International Advertiser,* June 1986, p. 12.

28. "Poll: Europe Favors U.S. Products," *Advertising Age,* September 23, 1991, p. 16.

29. "Women, Advertising, and Islam," *Chicago Tribune,* August 4, 1982, sect. 3, p. 2; and "No Women, No Alcohol: Learning Saudi Taboos before Placing Ads," *International Advertiser,* February 1986, pp. 11–12.

30. From various articles in *Advertising World* and *Business International.*

31. Robert S. Trebus, "Can a Good Ad Campaign Cross Borders?" *Advertising World,* Spring 1978, pp. 6–8.

32. "Global Advertising: Multinational versus International Pros and Cons," *International Advertiser,* February 1986, pp. 34–37.

33. "World Brands," *Advertising Age,* February 2, 1992, p. 33.

34. "Gillette's Panregional Approach," *Business International,* February 20, 1989, p. 51.

35. D. Peebles, J. Ryans, and I. Vernon, "Coordinating International Advertising," *Journal of Marketing,* January 1978, pp. 28–34; and "Centralized International Advertising," *International Advertiser,* September 1986, pp. 35–36.

36. Avon news release, November 14, 1990.

37. "Why Direct Selling Is Now a Crucial Tool for Big Business," *International Management,* March 1988, pp. 38–46.

38. "Fishing Only Where the Fish Swim," *Business Europe,* April 26, 1991, p. 3.

39. "Global Coupon Use Up; U.K., Belgium Tops in Europe," *Marketing News,* August 5, 1991, p. 5.

40. "U.S. Philanthropy in Japan," *Fortune,* March 11, 1991, p. 13.

41. "A Boycott over Infant Formula," *Business Week,* April 23, 1979, pp. 137–38; and "New Attack on Nestlé," *Advertising Age,* October 17, 1983, pp. 28–29.

42. "Nestlé Rejects Militant PR Plan to Combat Renewal of Boycott," *The Wall Street Journal,* April 25, 1989, p. B6.

43. "IBM Lobbies for Freer European Market," *The Wall Street Journal,* April 20, 1988, p. 18.

44. Arthur Adelberg, "Resolving Conflicts in Intracompany Pricing," *Accountancy,* November 1986, pp. 86–89.

45. "Guess Who's Selling Barbies in Japan Now?" *Business Week,* December 9, 1991, p. 72.

46. "Toy Joy," *The Economist,* January 4, 1992, p. 62.

47. "The New Japan Goes Shopping," *The Economist,* August 13, 1988, pp. 55–56.

48. "U.S., European Retailers Are Becoming More Transnational," *Europe,* January–February 1989, pp. 20–54.

49. The idea for this matrix came to one of the writers when he was working on the first edition of this book. It is a kind of checklist to help those working on the standardization of an element of the marketing mix to remember the impact of the uncontrollable forces. He wishes he had such a tool when he was an international marketing manager.

Chapter 16

Export and Import Practices and Procedures

At no other time in U.S. history has international commerce been as important to our domestic growth as it is today. . . . America has been the world's market. Now it is time for the world to be our market.

President Bush

LEARNING OBJECTIVES

In this chapter, you will study:

1. Why large and small companies export.

2. The three problem areas of exporting.

3. The main elements of the export sales assistance program of the U.S. Department of Commerce.

4. The meaning of the various terms of sale.

5. The kinds of payment terms that are offered.

6. The kinds of export documents that are required.

7. Activities of a foreign freight forwarder.

8. Some sources of export financing.

9. Export documentation.

10. The important innovations in materials handling in sea and air transport.

11. Why it may be more advantageous to use air freight rather than ocean freight.

12. How to identify import sources.

13. The activities of a customhouse broker.

KEY WORDS AND CONCEPTS

- Terms of sale
- Letter of credit (L/C)
- Confirm
- Irrevocable
- Air waybill
- Pro forma invoice
- Export, sight, and time drafts
- Banker's acceptance
- Factoring
- Forfaiting
- Eximbank
- Overseas Private Investment Corporation (OPIC)
- Foreign Sales Corporation (FSC)
- Free trade zone
- Foreign trade zone (FTZ)
- Foreign freight forwarders
- General Export License
- Validated Export License
- Coordinating Committee on Multilateral Export Controls (COCOM)
- Export bill of lading (B/L)
- Collection documents
- Customhouse brokers
- Bonded warehouse

BUSINESS INCIDENT

Global corporations export . . .

Du Pont, the sixth largest U.S. exporter, has been able to remain a competitor in the tough chemical export market because it began to pay serious attention to exports back in 1978, when the dollar's value fell sharply. "We recognized that our business was changing from national to regional or global, so you didn't have a lot of options," says P. J. Roessel, Du Pont's director of international planning. "If you didn't participate in those foreign markets, your competitors would gradually get stronger and come and eat your lunch in the U.S."

Du Pont's marketing strategy is to promote the sale of U.S. exports by its overseas manufacturing subsidiaries. "We have plotted back for 25 years and have found that as we have invested and built abroad, exports have gone up in complete tandem," says Roessel. "Such subsidiaries are able to 'pull' products from the parent company to achieve real market synergy." A Japanese Du Pont subsidiary, for example, makes engineering plastics for autos and has developed markets for polyester and acetyl products made by Du Pont in the United States.

So do small companies . . .

Can a four-employee Tennessee manufacturer successfully sell its products in Japan?

Quality Control Instruments (QCI) of Oak Ridge, Tennessee, not only can—it is selling there: Japan is the largest of its 26 foreign-country markets. The company, which started six years ago in a one-room warehouse, makes products for the metal-plating and metallurgy industries that have a wide variety of applications, such as molds for Barbie dolls and instruments for the aircraft and electronic industries. It now exports one third of its production.

The Japanese business started with a QCI advertisement in a trade journal, spotted by executives of Nippon Steel. Three Nippon executives arranged to meet Roger

BUSINESS INCIDENT (concluded)

Derby, QCI president, at a trade show in Philadelphia in 1986. The meeting, which lasted three hours, led to regular orders, currently running on the scale of $5,000 a month. Derby says he likes doing business with the Japanese because they pay promptly and keep placing more orders.

Derby, confident that his products can compete technologically overseas, says the company now needs to emphasize marketing. It has sales agents in Japan, Hong Kong, South Korea, Singapore, the Philippines, and Taiwan and is looking for more. The company is exploring the Chinese market; to get ready, Derby is studying conversational Chinese.

Exporting caused QCI to develop a new product: a battery charger used for batteries in its products. Foreign battery chargers, made for different voltages overseas, do not work on batteries that QCI puts in its instruments without adjustments. For the convenience of its foreign customers, QCI makes it a practice to enclose battery chargers with shipments of its products. However, the company had trouble finding American-made battery chargers it considered reasonably priced and well made. So it developed its own battery charger. Now, QCI anticipates a new market for its charger: other U.S. instrument manufacturers that also want to send battery chargers with their overseas shipments for customers' convenience.

QCI uses U.S. Department of Commerce export services through the Nashville District Office of the International Trade Administration. The company participated in Matchmaker 85 in the United Kingdom, the Korea Trade Promotion Corporation (KORTA) U.S. Products Show in Seoul in 1987, and Analytical 87 in Mexico City.

Source: "Smoother Sailing Overseas," *Business Week,* April 18, 1986, p. 289; "50 Leading U.S. Exporters," *Fortune,* July 18, 1988, p. 71; and "Exporting Pays Off," *Business America,* September 26, 1988, p. 18.

D u Pont is typical of the large firms that do considerable exporting even though they possess foreign production facilities. Of the 20 largest U.S. exporters listed in Table 16–1, only the aircraft manufacturers have no overseas plants.

WHY EXPORT?

We already have examined in Chapter 2 some reasons why companies go overseas, but we did not distinguish among them. Now let us look at some specific reasons for exporting.

▫ Large Firms

No firm can produce every product in every market. Many of these firms, like Du Pont, supply numerous foreign markets by exporting to them because no firm, no matter how large it is, can afford to manufacture in every country where its goods are sold. Markets that are too small to support local production are supplied by exports from either the home country or a foreign affiliate. In markets of sufficient size to justify the manufacturing of some, but not all, of the product mix, it is rather common to supplement the sales of local production with imports. Thus, an automobile plant in a developing nation will produce the least expensive cars and, laws permitting, import the luxury models. A notable exception to this generality was Iran, where, because of the wealth generated from high crude oil prices, General Motors began its assembly operations with the Cadillac. Also, home country plants, which usu-

☐ **TABLE 16-1**
The 20 Largest U.S. Exporters

Company	Products	Exports ($ millions)	Total Sales ($ millions)	Exports as Percent of Sales
Boeing	Aircraft	$16,093	$ 27,595	58.3%
General Motors	Autos, locomotives	10,315	126,017	8.2
General Electric	Aircraft engines, locomotives	7,128	58,414	12.2
Ford	Autos and parts	7,098	98,275	7.2
IBM	Information systems	6,195	69,018	9.0
Chrysler	Autos and parts	5,004	30,868	16.2
Du Pont	Chemicals, fibers, plastics	4,352	39,839	10.9
United Technologies	Aircraft engines, helicopters	3,606	21,783	16.6
McDonnell Douglas	Aircraft, missiles	3,538	16,351	21.6
Caterpillar	Construction equipment	3,435	11,540	29.8
Eastman Kodak	Photographic equipment	2,957	19,075	15.5
Philip Morris	Tobacco, food	2,928	44,323	6.6
Hewlett-Packard	Computers	2,816	13,233	21.3
Motorola	Semiconductors, radio equipment	2,801	10,855	25.7
Unisys	Computers	2,204	10,111	21.8
Occidental Petroleum	Agricultural products, coal	2,077	21,947	9.5
Digital Equipment	Computers	1,920	13,084	14.7
Allied Signal	Aircraft, chemicals	1,838	12,396	14.8
General Dynamics	Tanks, aircraft, missiles	1,624	10,182	15.9
Weyerhaeuser	Wood, pulp, lumber	1,560	9,024	17.3

Source: "America's 50 Biggest Exporters," *Fortune*, special edition, Spring–Summer 1991, pp. 58–59.

ally are more vertically integrated than overseas plants (discussed in Chapter 2), export semifinished products that are inputs for the less integrated subsidiaries.

Until regional economic groups were formed, many firms had no interest in exporting to some markets that (1) were rather small and (2) had local competitors. But after the creation of the EC, EFTA, ASEAN, and others, managements realized that by setting up a plant in one member-nation, they could then market their products throughout the region.

The free movement of goods within the EC and similar groups has enabled companies to obtain greater economies of scale by dividing the production of components among their subsidiaries rather than requiring each foreign plant to produce all parts of the finished product. For example, Ford's engine plant in England supplies engines to its German plant, which in turn supplies various components to Ford's English plant. Each subsidiary must export and import so that assembly plants in both countries can produce an automobile.

Host government may require it.   Increasingly, LDC governments are stipulating that the local affiliate must export. Some have gone so far as to insist that sufficient foreign exchange be earned by the affiliate to cover the cost of all its imports. For this reason, Ford located a radio plant in Brazil that exports to Ford assembly plants in Europe.[1] The new Mexican law on foreign investments stipulates that for investors to have 100 percent ownership of a

WORLDVIEW
The 12 Most Common Mistakes and Pitfalls Awaiting New Exporters

The following may be considered the 12 most common mistakes and pitfalls made by new exporters.

1. Failure to obtain qualified export counseling and to develop a master international marketing plan before starting an export business. To be successful, a firm must first clearly define goals, objectives, and the problems encountered. Second, it must develop a definitive plan to accomplish an objective despite the problems involved. Unless the firm is fortunate enough to possess a staff with considerable export expertise, it may not be able to take this crucial first step without qualified outside guidance.

2. Insufficient commitment by top management to overcome the initial difficulties and financial requirements of exporting. It may take more time and effort to establish a firm in a foreign market than in domestic ones. Although the early delays and costs involved in exporting may seem difficult to justify when compared to established domestic trade, the exporter should take a long-range view of this process and carefully monitor international marketing efforts through these early difficulties. If a good foundation is laid for export business, the benefits derived should eventually outweigh the investment.

3. Insufficient care in selecting overseas distributors. The selection of each foreign distributor is crucial. The complications involved in overseas communications and transportation require international distributors to act with greater independence than their domestic counterparts. Also, since a new exporter's history, trademarks, and reputation are usually unknown in the foreign market, foreign customers may buy on the strength of a distributor's reputation. A firm should therefore conduct a personal evaluation of the personnel handling its account, the distributor's facilities, and the management methods employed.

4. Chasing orders from around the world instead of establishing a basis for profitable operations and orderly growth. If exporters expect distributors to actively promote their accounts, the distributors must be trained and assisted and their performance must be continually monitored. This requires a company marketing executive permanently located in the distributor's geographical region. New exporters should concentrate their efforts in one or two geographical areas until there is sufficient business to support a company representative. Then, while this initial core area is expanded, the exporter can move into the next selected geographical area.

5. Neglecting export business when the U.S. market booms. Too many companies turn to exporting when business falls off in the United States. When domestic business starts to boom again, they neglect their export trade or relegate it to a secondary place. Such neglect can seriously harm the business and motivation of their overseas representatives, strangle the U.S. company's own export trade, and leave the firm

Mexican company, they must at least balance their foreign exchange earnings and expenditures for the first three years of operation. Note that the exports do not have to relate to the firm's products; Nissan Mexicana exports coffee, honey, and horsemeat. This is also true in one form of countertrade, which you will study in the next chapter.

Export to remain competitive in home market.   One other reason why more foreign affiliates have engaged in exporting is that many companies need their exports to remain competitive in their home markets. Various firms either import labor-intensive components produced in their foreign affiliates or export without recourse when domestic business falls off once more. Even if domestic business remains strong, the company may eventually realize that it has only succeeded in shutting off a valuable source of additional profits.

6. Failure to treat international distributors on an equal basis with domestic counterparts. Often, companies carry out institutional advertising campaigns, special discount offers, sales incentive programs, special credit term programs, warranty offers, etc., in the U.S. market but fail to make similar assistance available to their international distributors. This is a mistake that can destroy the vitality of overseas marketing efforts.

7. Assuming that a given market technique and product will automatically be successful in all countries. What works in one market may not work in others. Each market has to be treated separately to ensure maximum success.

8. Unwillingness to modify products to meet regulations or cultural preferences of other countries. Local safety and security codes, as well as import restrictions, cannot be ignored by foreign distributors. If necessary modifications are not made at the factory, the distributor must do them—usually at greater cost and, perhaps, not as well. It should also be noted that the resulting smaller profit margin makes the account less attractive.

9. Failure to print service, sale, and warranty messages in locally understood languages. Although a distributor's top management may speak English, it is unlikely that all sales personnel (let alone service personnel) have this capability. Without a clear understanding of sales messages or service instructions, these persons may be less effective in performing their functions.

10. Failure to consider use of an export management company. If a firm decides it cannot afford its own export department (or has tried one unsuccessfully), it should consider the possibility of appointing an appropriate export management company (EMC).

11. Failure to consider licensing or joint venture agreements. Import restrictions in some countries, insufficient personnel/financial resources, or a too limited product line cause many companies to dismiss international marketing as unfeasible. Yet, many products that can compete on a national basis in the United States can be successfully marketed in most markets of the world. A licensing or joint venture arrangement may be the simple, profitable answer to any reservations. In general, all that is needed for success is flexibility in using the proper combination of marketing techniques.

12. Failure to provide readily available servicing for the product. A product without the necessary service support can acquire a bad reputation in a short period, potentially preventing further sales.

Source: *Business America*, December 7, 1987, pp. 14–15.

the components for assembly in countries where labor is less expensive. The final product is then imported for sale in the home country. The Mexican-American in-bond plants discussed in Chapter 2 are based on this concept.

Test the market first with exports.   This is a fairly common strategy employed by firms that want to test a market for product acceptance before going to the expense of establishing local production. A trial with exports also enables them to test marketing strategies and make adjustments with less risk. If either the product or the strategy fails, the company can withdraw without having a costly production facility to sell at a loss.

□ Smaller Firms

Like the large firms, no smaller firm can afford to ignore the international marketplace. Increasingly, all companies must penetrate new markets overseas to sustain their growth; they can no longer depend on their competitive home markets for it. Smaller companies can gain significant sales by establishing overseas market niches.[2]

As you read in the Business Incident, a four-employee operation with superior products began exporting because it was asked to, and now it exports one third of its production. This *accidental exporting* is fairly common—foreign buyers see an advertisement in an American trade journal, as the Japanese did, or, in searching for a source of supply for something unavailable locally, they come across a company name in the *Thomas Register*. This publication, which lists American suppliers for hundreds of products, is used in the United States by purchasing agents. Every American consulate, overseas library of the American Information Service, and local chamber of commerce (French-American, German-American, etc.) has a copy, which anyone can use.

Another reason for accidental exporting is the unfavorable trade balances the United States has with such nations as Japan and Taiwan. Their governments have organized buying missions, which come to this country to see what they can buy. Amazingly, their requests for quotations have sometimes been turned down because "exporting is too much trouble."[3]

> Pressure to reduce trade surpluses creates export opportunities in other countries as well. One of the writers was working for General Tire–Chile when a Chilean government official asked him if his company made anything that could be sold to Bolivia. That government had promised to buy Chilean products for its tin mines to help reduce the trade imbalance, and the official was asking someone to visit them. The writer went and, with difficulty, made some sales. See a related incident on that trip in endnote 14 of Chapter 8.

Not all companies wait for customers to come to them, of course, and many actively seek export business as a means of increasing their sales. Still, if exporting is a means to increase sales and profits, why did the United States export only 7.2 percent of its GNP in 1990, when exports of some nations amounted to up to half of their total output?[4] The U.S. Department of Commerce estimates that 20,000 firms in this country sell exportable products but avoid foreign markets. Why don't they export?

WHY DON'T THEY EXPORT?

The two major reasons U.S. firms give for not exporting are (1) preoccupation with the vast American market and (2) a reluctance to become involved in a new and unknown operation. When nonexporting firms are asked why they are not active in international markets, they generally mention the following as problem areas: (1) locating foreign markets, (2) payment and financing procedures, and (3) export procedures. Although considerable assistance is available from the federal and state departments of commerce, banks, the Small Business Administration, Small Business Development Centers (does your school have one?), private consultants (your international business professor may consult), and numerous other sources, some of which we mentioned in Chapter 14, too few managers are taking advantage of this assistance. Let us examine the three problem areas.

LOCATING FOREIGN MARKETS

The first step in locating foreign markets, whether for export or foreign manufacturing, is to determine whether a market exists for the firm's products. The initial screening step described in Chapter 14 indicated a procedure to follow that will pose no problem for the experienced market analyst who is well acquainted with the available sources of information and assistance. However, newcomers to exporting, especially the smaller firms, may still be at a loss as to how to begin; for them, there are a number of export assistance programs available, including the following:

1. Assistance from the International Trade Administration at the U.S. Department of Commerce district offices.
2. Assistance from the Office of International Trade of the Small Business Administration (SBA) offered at the SBA district offices. The Office of International Trade also works through:
   a. SCORE/ACE programs—experienced executives offer free one-on-one counseling to small firms.
   b. SBDC/SBI programs—Small Business Development Centers (SBDCs) in many universities and colleges give export counseling. Business students in Small Business Institutes (SBIs) provide in-depth, long-term counseling under faculty supervision.
3. International market and credit assistance through the Foreign Agricultural Service, U.S. Department of Agriculture, for potential exporters of agricultural products.
4. Every state has an office to promote its exports.[5]

Small manufacturing firms generally will go to the nearest district office of the U.S. Department of Commerce for export assistance. However, if the prospective exporter knows nothing about exporting, at least one member of the firm's management should first attend an export seminar offered either by the SBA or the SBDC of the local university.

□ Department of Commerce Export Assistance Program

Foreign market research.   After learning about the company and its products, the international trade specialist might advise the potential exporter to consult the National Trade Data Bank (NTDB), a service that selects the most recent trade promotions, "how to" publications, and international trade and economic data from 15 federal agencies and puts them on one CD-ROM that is updated monthly. The NTDB provides (1) a comprehensive guide for new exporters and (2) a source of specific product and regional information for experienced exporters searching for new markets. It also contains the Foreign Traders Index—a list of foreign importers, with descriptions of each and the products they wish to import.[6] From this list, the exporter can prepare a mailing list of those interested in its products and then make a bulk mailing. The NTDB is usually available in university SBDCs offering export assistance and in the government documents sections of university libraries. A business can also subscribe to the service for $360 annually.

The trade specialist might also suggest signing up for the Trade Opportunities Program, which provides subscribers with current sales leads from overseas firms wanting to buy or represent their products or services. Another possibility is advertising in *Commercial News USA*, a monthly magazine that promotes the products and services of American firms to over 100,000 overseas agents, distributors, and government officials.

Smaller number of potential markets.   When the research has identified a small number of potential markets, the firm may wish to use the Department of Commerce's Comparison Shopping Service. For $500 per market, the customer will receive a custom-tailored market research survey on a specific product of its choice. This service provides information on marketability, names of competitors, comparative prices, distribution channels, and names of potential sales representatives. Each study is conducted on-site by a U.S. commercial officer. For markets not included in the service, a Department of Commerce specialist may recommend such publications as *Country Market Surveys, Competitive Assessments,* and *Annual Worldwide Industry Reviews,* all of which are available on an industry basis.

There are still other helpful publications and services. *Foreign Economic Trends Reports* summarize the economic and commercial trends in a country and are a good source of information as to which American products are most in demand. A series of reports, *Overseas Business Reports (OBR),* provide basic background data on specific countries. Each *OBR* discusses separate topics on a single country, such as basic economic data, foreign trade regulations, market factors, and trade with the United States. The firm may subscribe to *Business America,* a biweekly magazine, whose "International Commerce" section contains announcements about (1) U.S. promotions abroad in which the firm can participate; (2) foreign concerns looking for licensors, joint venture partners, or distributorships; and (3) opportunities to make direct sales.

Direct or indirect exporting.   When it has been established that there is an existing or potential market for its goods, the firm must choose between exporting indirectly through U.S.-based exporters or exporting directly using its own staff. If it opts for indirect exporting as a way to test the market, the trade specialist can provide assistance in locating one of the types of exporters listed in Chapter 13. However, should the firm prefer to set up its own export operation, it must then obtain overseas distribution.

The exporter may, as we mentioned previously, try a broad-based mailing to solicit representatives or use the Department of Commerce Agent/Distributor Search service. Commercial officers of American embassies or consulates will, within 90 days, personally interview and identify up to six local prospects who have seen the company literature and expressed an interest in representation. The exporters may then obtain information covering their commercial activities and competence by asking the Department of Commerce to supply a *World Traders Data Report.* Credit reporting agencies, such as Dun & Bradstreet, FCIB (Finance, Credit, and International Business Association), and the exporter's bank, will also supply credit information.

The Foreign Agricultural Service of the U.S. Department of Agriculture offers similar services to potential exporters of agricultural products.

Show and sell.   The Department of Commerce also organizes trade events that are helpful in both locating foreign representatives and making sales.[7] There are four kinds:

1. *Trade fairs.* Commerce organizes exhibitions or American pavilions at international trade fairs, which are held regularly in major cities worldwide. At one time, the U.S. government owned 15 trade centers in which American industry periodically held exhibitions, but for budgetary reasons, these have been reduced to 4 (London, Mexico City, Seoul, and Tokyo).

2. *Matchmaker program and trade missions.* Commerce representatives accompany groups of American businesspeople overseas to meet with qualified agents, distributors, and customers. Prior to their arrival, overseas consular officials make appointments with qualified agents, distributors, and customers. The Department of Commerce also sponsors state- and industry-organized trade missions.

3. *Foreign buyer program.* The Commerce Department annually sponsors about 20 domestic trade shows, which bring foreign buyers and U.S. manufacturers together. American consular officers promote these trade shows in over 60 countries to attract foreign business representatives.

4. *Catalog and video shows.* American manufacturers can gain market visibility without going overseas by participating in a catalog and video show. They merely give their literature and promotional videos to Commerce, which displays it for select audiences in several foreign countries.

◻ Other Sources of Assistance

Other sources of assistance available to the exporter include the following:

World Trade Centers Association.   The World Trade Centers Association, another aid to marketing for the new exporter, was founded by the New York–New Jersey Port Authority, which has licensed over 60 centers worldwide. Through membership, exporters and importers have access to an online trading system called NETWORK. Exporters need only a computer and a modem to put offers to sell in an electronic data base, and importers anywhere can send messages to the exporters' mailboxes accepting advertised prices or initiating electronic negotiations. Access can be gained with a local telephone in 800 cities in 64 countries.

District export councils.   The Department of Commerce has 51 district export councils composed of volunteer business and trade experts who assist in workshops and also arrange for consultation between experienced and prospective exporters.

State governments.   All states have export development programs that offer assistance to exporters by providing sales leads, locating overseas representatives, and counseling. Twenty-two states also have export-financing programs, and more are setting them up.[8]

□ Export Marketing Plan

As soon as possible, an export marketing plan must be drawn up. The experienced firm will already have a plan in operation, but newcomers will usually need to wait until they have accumulated at least some of the information from the foreign market research.

Same as domestic marketing plan.   Essentially, the export marketing plan is the same as the domestic marketing plan. It should be specific about (1) the markets to be developed, (2) the marketing strategy for serving them, and (3) the tactics required to make the strategy operational. Sales forecasts and budgets, pricing policies, product characteristics, promotional plans, and details on the arrangements with foreign representatives are required. In other words, the export marketing plan will spell out what must be done and when, who should do it, and how much money will be spent.

Marketing mix.   Because the comments in Chapter 15 concerning the marketing mix are valid for exporters, there is no need for a detailed discussion here. Two aspects that do require some explanation, however, are *export pricing* and *sales agreements for foreign representatives*.

Pricing policies.   Pricing is a problem even for experienced exporters. Noncompetitive prices cause sales to be lost to foreign competitors, but incorrect pricing can also cause the exporter to lose money on a sale.

One new area of concern for many firms beginning to export is the necessity to quote **terms of sale** that differ from those normally used. For domestic sales, the company may be quoting FOB factory, which means all costs and risks from that point on are borne by the buyer. Foreign customers, however, may insist on one of the following terms of sale:

terms of sale conditions of a sale that stipulate the point where all costs and risks are borne by buyer

1. *FAS (free alongside ship), port of exit.* The seller pays all of the transportation and delivery expense up to the ship's side. The buyer is responsible for any loss or damage to the shipment from that point on.

2. *CIF (cost, insurance, freight), foreign port.* The seller quotes a price that includes the cost of the goods, insurance, and all transportation and miscellaneous charges to the named foreign port in the country of final destination. If the buyer requires an on-board bill of lading (the usual case), then it is responsible for any loss or damage to the goods after they are delivered on board the vessel.

3. *C&F (cost, freight), foreign port.* This is similar to CIF except the buyer purchases the insurance, either because it can obtain the insurance at a lower cost or because its government, to save foreign exchange, insists that it use a local insurance company.[9]

CIF and C&F terms of sale are more convenient for foreign buyers because, to establish their cost, they merely have to add the import duties, landing charges, and freight from the port of arrival to their warehouse.

However, these terms can present a problem for new exporters if they forget the miscellaneous costs—wharf storage and handling charges, freight forwarder's charges, and consular fees—incurred in making a CIF shipment and simply add freight, insurance, and export packing costs to the domestic selling price. The resulting price may be too low, but more often it will be too high, because the domestic marketing and general administrative costs included in the domestic selling price are frequently greater than the actual cost of making the export sale.

The preferred pricing method is the use of the *factory door cost* (production cost without domestic marketing and general administrative costs), to which are added the direct cost of making the export sale and a percentage of the general administrative overhead. This percentage can be derived from managers' estimates of the part of their total time spent on export matters. The minimum FOB price will be the sum of these costs plus the required profit. If research in a market has shown either that there is little competition or that competitive prices are higher, then, of course, the exporter is free to charge a high price in that market (price skim) or to set a low price to gain a larger percentage of the market (penetration pricing). The course of action taken will depend on the firm's sales objectives, just as it does in the domestic market.

Sales agreement.   The sales agreement should specify as simply as possible the duties of the representative and the firm. Most of what is contained in the contract for a domestic representative can be used in export also, but special attention must be given to two points: (1) designation of the responsibilities for patent and trademark registration and (2) designation of the country and state, if applicable, whose laws will govern a contractual dispute. To be absolutely safe, the firm should register all patents and trademarks. Policing them may be left to the local representative if management so chooses.

U.S. exporters would prefer to stipulate the laws of the United States and their home state, but many nations, especially those of Latin America, will not permit this (Calvo Doctrine). The Calvo Doctrine, promulgated by Calvo, an Argentine jurist, holds that trying cases locally under foreign laws should not be permitted because it gives the foreign company an advantage over local firms, which must be tried under local laws. If an American state can be designated, its laws may be followed even though the dispute is adjudicated in a foreign country. The presiding judge will have the pertinent parts of the law translated or will call on witnesses who are known experts in the area of law involved.

PAYMENT AND FINANCING PROCEDURES

The second major problem area concerns payment and financing procedures.

□ Export Payment Terms

Payment terms, as every marketer knows, are often a decisive factor in obtaining an order. As a sales official of an international grain exporter put it, "If you give credit to a guy who is broke, he'll pay any price for your product." This is somewhat exaggerated, but customers will often pay higher prices when terms are more lenient. This is especially significant in countries where capital is scarce and interest rates are high. The kinds of payment terms offered by exporters to foreign buyers are (1) cash in advance, (2) open account, (3) consignment, (4) letters of credit, and (5) documentary drafts.

Cash in advance.   When the credit standing of the buyer is not known or is uncertain, cash in advance is desirable. However, very few buyers will accept these terms, because part of their working capital is tied up until the merchandise has been received and sold. Furthermore, they have no guarantee that they will receive what they ordered. As a result, few customers will pay cash in advance unless the order is either small or for a product of special manufacture.

Open account.   When a sale is made on open account, the seller assumes all of the risk, and therefore these terms should be offered only to reliable customers in economically stable countries. The exporter's capital, of course, is tied up until payment has been received.

Consignment.   This follows the procedure well known in the United States by which goods are shipped to the buyer and payment is not made until they have been sold. All of the risk is assumed by the seller, and such terms should not be offered without making the same extensive investigation of the buyer and country that is recommended for open account terms. Multinationals frequently sell goods to their subsidiaries on this basis.

Letters of credit.   Only cash in advance offers more protection to the seller than an export **letter of credit** (L/C). This document is issued by the buyer's bank, which promises to pay the seller a specified amount when the bank has received certain documents stipulated in the letter of credit by a specified time.

Confirmed and irrevocable.   Generally, the seller will request that the letter of credit be **confirmed** and **irrevocable.** Irrevocable means that once the seller has accepted the credit, the customer cannot alter or cancel it without the seller's consent. Figure 16–1 is an example of an irrevocable letter of credit. If the letter of credit is *not* confirmed, the correspondent bank (Merchants National Bank of Mobile) has no obligation to pay the seller (Smith & Co.) when it receives the documents listed in the letter of credit. Only the issuing bank (Banco Americano in Bogota) is responsible. If the seller (Smith & Co.) wishes to be able to collect from an American bank, it will insist that the credit be confirmed by such a bank. This is generally done by the correspondent bank, as it was in Figure 16–1. In this case, when the Merchants National Bank of Mobile confirmed the credit, it undertook an obligation to pay Smith & Co. if all of the documents listed in the letter were presented on or before the stipulated date.

Note that nothing is mentioned about the goods themselves; the buyer has stipulated only that an **air waybill** issued by the carrier be presented as proof that shipment has been made. Even if bank officials knew that the plane had crashed after the takeoff, they would still have to pay Smith & Co. *Banks are concerned with documents, not merchandise.*

Prior to opening a letter of credit, a buyer frequently requests a **pro forma invoice.** This is the exporter's formal quotation containing a description of the merchandise, price, delivery time, proposed method of shipment, ports of exit and entry, and terms of sale. It is more than a quotation, however. Generally, the bank will use it when opening a letter of credit, and in countries requiring import licenses or permits to purchase foreign exchange, government officials will insist on receiving copies.

---

letter of credit (L/C) document issued by the buyer's bank in which the bank promises to pay the seller a specified amount under specified conditions

confirm guarantee by a bank generally in the seller's vicinity that it will honor the issuing bank's letter of credit

irrevocable a stipulation that a letter of credit cannot be canceled

air waybill a bill of lading issued by an air carrier

pro forma invoice exporter's formal quotation containing a description of the merchandise, price, delivery time, method of shipping, terms of sale, and points of exit and entry

□ **FIGURE 16–1**
Letter of Credit

Figure 16–1 Letter of Credit

Letter of credit transactions. Figure 16–2 illustrates the routes taken by the merchandise, letter of credit, and documents in a letter of credit transaction.

When a German buyer accepts the terms of sale that provide for a confirmed irrevocable letter of credit, it goes to its bank to arrange for opening the required letter. The buyer will furnish the bank with the information contained in the pro forma invoice, specify the documents that the exporter must present to obtain payment, and set the expiration date for the credit.

The German bank then instructs its correspondent bank in the United States to confirm the credit and inform the seller that it has been established. The seller prepares the merchandise for shipment and notifies the freight for-

□ **FIGURE 16–2**
Letter of Credit
Transaction

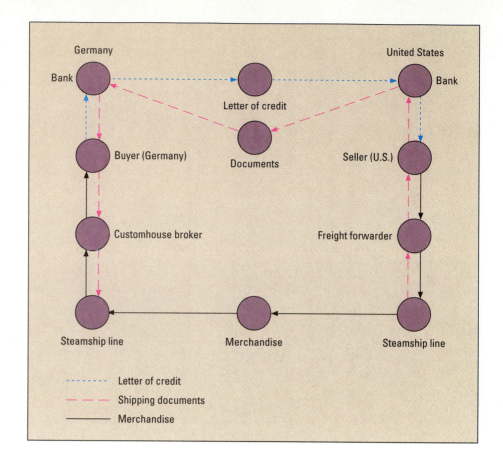

warder, which books space on a ship, prepares the export documents, and arranges to have the merchandise delivered to the port. The documents, together with a sight or time draft drawn by the seller, are presented to the U.S. bank, which pays the seller and forwards the documents for collection to the German bank.

To obtain the documents that give title to the shipment, the buyer in Germany must either pay the *sight draft* or accept a *time draft*. Having done so, the buyer receives the documents, which are then given to the customhouse broker. The customhouse broker acts as the buyer's agent in receiving the goods from the steamship line and clearing them through German customs.

Documentary drafts.   When the exporter believes the political and commercial risks are not sufficient to require a letter of credit, the exporter may agree to payment on a documentary draft basis, which is less costly to the buyer.

An **export draft,** shown in Figure 16–3, is an unconditional order drawn by the seller on the buyer instructing the buyer to pay the amount of the order on presentation (**sight draft**) or at an agreed future date (**time draft**). Generally, the seller will request its bank to send the draft and documents to a bank in the buyer's country, which will proceed with the collection as described in the letter of credit transaction.

Although documentary draft and letter of credit terms are similar, there is one important difference. A confirmed letter of credit guarantees payment to

export draft an unconditional order that is drawn by the seller on the buyer to pay the draft's amount on presentation (**sight draft**) or at an agreed future date (**time draft**) and that must be paid before the buyer receives shipping documents

◻ FIGURE 16–3   Sight Draft

the seller if the seller conforms to its requirements, but there is no such guarantee with documentary drafts. An unscrupulous buyer can refuse to pay the drafts when presented and then attempt to bargain with the seller for a lower price. The seller must then acquiesce, try to find another buyer, pay a large freight bill to bring back the goods, or abandon them. If the seller chooses the last alternative, customs will auction off the goods, and chances are the original buyer will be able to acquire them at a bargain price. The seller, of course, receives nothing.

Compensatory trade.   A form of payment that has become increasingly popular is compensatory trade—any transaction that involves asset transfers as a condition of purchase, including local content requirements, licensing, and other performance requirements as well as the traditional forms of countertrade, which are described in detail in Chapter 18. For example, the government of a nation importing railway cars might insist that they be assembled locally as a condition of the purchase, or a construction company building roads might be asked to put up some low-cost housing as part of the deal.

Barter-type arrangements, which are estimated to comprise 5 percent of world trade ($150 billion), are occurring because (1) Third World and communist nations lack convertible currency and (2) these nations wish to exploit the marketing networks in the industrialized nations. However, even Australia is demanding offsets (a portion of the work on a project or product to be performed in that country) or a counterpurchase (the seller agrees to purchase goods in Australia equivalent in value to a minimum of 30 percent of the cost of goods sold).

Compensatory trade has become so important that a number of international firms, such as General Motors and Volkswagen, have wholly owned subsidiaries to handle such transactions. Smaller firms can contract with independent barter-switch companies, which will do the work for them. Figure 16–4 illustrates a countertrade operation by means of which Chrysler automobiles were exchanged for Jamaican bauxite.

□ FIGURE 16–4   Jamaican Countertrade

Elwood H. Smith

Countertrade made simple: If you think it's tough selling cars and trucks in the United States, this is what Chrysler went through to sell several hundred vehicles to credit-starved Jamaica. The American and Canadian mining companies (far left), which dig Jamaica's bauxite and refine it into alumina, hand over some 50,000 tons of alumina to the government's Bauxite & Alumina Trading Co. The trading company, in turn, gives the alumina to Metallgesellschaft, a German metals company. MG sells the alumina to a refiner, which converts it to aluminum. The money MG gets for the alumina goes to the European American Bank, Chrysler's adviser. EAB sends part of the money back to the Bauxite & Alumina Trading Co., which pays the mining companies. The balance goes to finance a letter of credit made out to Chrysler, which then ships trucks to Jamaica. Title is taken by another government firm, the Jamaican Commodity Trading Co., which sells the vehicles to Motors Sales & Services Co., Chrysler's local distributor. The dealer sells them to the public. The part you don't see—and the parties want to keep hidden—is what makes the convoluted deal click. Jamaica probably is shaving price to unload bauxite, while Chrysler is absorbing extra costs to make the sale.

Source: "The Explosion of International Barter," *Fortune*, February 7, 1983, pp. 88–89.

□ Export Financing

Although exporters would prefer to sell on the almost riskless letter of credit terms, increased foreign competition and the universally tight money situation are forcing them to offer credit. To do so, they must be familiar with the available sources and kinds of export financing, both private and public.

Private source.   Commercial banks have always been a source of export financing through loans for working capital and the discounting of time drafts. A bank may discount an export time draft, pay the seller and keep it until maturity, or, if it is the bank on which the draft is drawn, "accept" it. By accepting a time draft, a bank assumes the responsibility for making payment at maturity of the draft. The accepting bank may or may not purchase (at a discount) the draft. If it does not, the exporter can sell a **banker's acceptance** readily in the open market. In recent years, new types of financing have been developed—factoring and forfaiting.

Factoring.   This financing technique permits the exporter to be more competitive by selling on open account rather than by means of the more costly letter of credit method. Long used in the United States, factoring is now being employed in international trade.

Factoring is essentially discounting *without* recourse because it is the sale of export accounts receivable to a third party, which assumes the credit risk. A factor may be a factoring house or a special department in a commercial bank.

banker's acceptance a time draft with maturity of less than 270 days that has been accepted by the bank on which the draft was drawn, thus becoming the accepting bank's obligation; may be bought and sold at a discount in the financial markets like other commercial paper

factoring discounting without recourse an account receivable

Under the export factoring arrangement, the seller passes its order to the factor for approval of the credit risk. Once the order has been approved, the exporter has complete protection against bad debts and political risk. The customer pays the factor, which, in effect, acts as the exporter's credit and collection department. The period of settlement generally does not exceed 180 days.

forfaiting purchasing without recourse an account receivable whose credit terms are longer than the 90 to 180 days usual in factoring; unlike factoring, political and transfer risks are borne by the forfaiter

Forfaiting.   **Forfaiting** denotes the purchase of obligations that arise from the sale of goods and services and fall due at some date beyond the 90 to 180 days that are customary for factoring. These receivables are usually in the form of trade drafts or promissory notes with maturities ranging from six months to five years.

Because it is sold without recourse, forfaited debt is nearly always accompanied by bank security in the form of a guarantee or aval. While the guarantee is a separate document, the aval is a promise to pay written directly in the document ("per aval" and the signature).

The forfaiter purchases the bill and discounts it for the entire credit period. Thus, the exporter, through forfaiting, has converted its credit-based sale into a cash transaction.

Although banks have traditionally concentrated on short-term financing, they have become involved in medium- and even long-term financing because numerous government and government-assisted organizations are offering export credit guarantees and insurance against commercial and political risks.

Eximbank principal federal government agency that aids American exporters by means of loans, guarantees, and insurance programs

Export-Import Bank, FCIA, and PEFCO.   The U.S. Export-Import Bank (**Eximbank**) is the principal government agency responsible for aiding the export of American goods and services through a variety of loan, guarantee, and insurance programs.[10] Generally, its programs are available to any American export firm regardless of size.

Direct and intermediary loans.   The Eximbank provides two types of loans: (1) direct loans to foreign buyers of American exports and (2) intermediary loans to responsible parties, such as a foreign government lending agency that relends to foreign buyers of capital goods and related services (for example, a maintenance contract for a jet passenger plane). Both programs cover up to 85 percent of the value of the exported goods and services, with repayment terms of one year or more.

Working capital guarantee.   This program helps small businesses obtain working capital to cover their export sales. It guarantees working capital loans extended by banks to eligible exporters with exportable inventory or export receivables as collateral.

Guarantees.   Eximbank's guarantee provides repayment protection for private-sector loans to buyers of U.S. capital equipment and related services. The guarantee is available alone or may be combined with an Eximbank direct or intermediary loan, a PEFCO (see below) loan, or a private loan.[11]

Export credit insurance.   An exporter may reduce its financing risks by purchasing export credit insurance from the Foreign Credit Insurance Association (FCIA), the Eximbank's agent. FCIA insurance may be obtained for export sales, leasing of equipment, and consignments in foreign markets. The coverage may be comprehensive or limited to political risk only.

Since its inception in 1934, the Eximbank has supported nearly $200 billion in U.S. exports. Every industrialized nation and many that are industrializing have similar banks. Another government agency, the Small Business Administration, operates loan guarantee and direct loan programs to assist small-business exporters.

PEFCO.   PEFCO (Private Export Funding Corporation), a corporation owned by 54 commercial banks, 7 large manufacturers, and an investment bank, was established to be a supplemental lender. PEFCO makes financing available only in cases where other private-sector lenders will not provide sufficient financing on competitive terms. Although PEFCO's loans are mostly medium term (average seven years), some are made for as long as 12 years. All of its loans must be covered by an unconditional guarantee of the Eximbank.

OTHER GOVERNMENT INCENTIVES

Other government incentives for trade, although not strictly a part of export financing, are certainly closely related to it. These are the Overseas Private Investment Corporation (OPIC), the Foreign Sales Corporation (FSC), and the foreign trade zone (FTZ).

◻ Overseas Private Investment Corporation (OPIC)

Overseas Private Investment Corporation (OPIC) government corporation that offers American investors in developing countries insurance against expropriation, currency inconvertibility, and damages from wars and revolutions

The **Overseas Private Investment Corporation (OPIC)** is a government corporation formed to stimulate private investment in developing countries. It offers investors insurance against expropriation, currency inconvertibility, and damages from wars or revolutions. OPIC also offers specialized insurance for American service contractors and exporters operating in foreign countries. Exports of capital equipment and semiprocessed raw materials generally follow these investments.

◻ Foreign Sales Corporation (FSC)

Foreign Sales Corporation (FSC) special corporate form authorized by the federal government that provides tax advantages for exporting firms

The **Foreign Sales Corporation (FSC)** was authorized by the Tax Reform Act of 1984. It replaces the Domestic International Sales Corporation (DISC), which U.S. trading partners complained violated the General Agreement on Tariffs and Trade.

Unlike its DISC predecessor, an FSC must be located either in a U.S. possession other than Puerto Rico or in a foreign country that has an information exchange agreement with the United States. The FSC's shareholders' and directors' meetings must be held outside the United States, and its principal bank account must be maintained outside the United States.

The portion of the FSC's income that is exempt from U.S. corporate taxation is 32 percent if the FSC buys from independent suppliers or uses the Section 482* arm's-length pricing rule with related suppliers.[12]

*   See Chapter 15 for details on Section 482.

◻ Foreign Trade Zones

For centuries, various forms of duty-free areas have existed in many parts of the world to facilitate trade by lessening the effect of customs restrictions. These customs-privileged areas may be free ports, transit zones, free perimeters, export processing zones, or free trade zones. In each instance, a specific and limited area is involved, into which imported goods may be brought without the payment of import duties. At present, there are nearly 350 such areas located in 72 countries. Of the five types, the free trade zone is the most common.

free trade zone an area designated by the government of a country for duty-free entry of any nonprohibited good

The **free trade zone** is an enclosed area considered to be outside the customs territory of the country in which it is located. Goods of foreign origin may be brought into the zone pending eventual transshipment, reexportation, or importation into the country. While the goods are in the zone, no import duties need to be paid.

The American version, called the **foreign trade zone** (**FTZ**), has been growing in popularity, and there are now more than 240 of these zones in operation.* Many are situated at seaports, but some are located at inland distribution points.

foreign trade zone (FTZ) American version of a free trade zone

Goods brought into the FTZ may be stored, inspected, repackaged, or combined with American components. Due to differences in the import tariff schedule, the finished product often pays less duty than what would be charged for the disassembled parts. Bicycles have been assembled in the Kansas City FTZ for that reason. Importers of machinery and automobiles improve their cash flow by storing spare parts in an FTZ, because duty is not paid until they are withdrawn.

Although the advantages of the FTZ to importers are well known, its benefits to exporters appear to have been overlooked. Foreign trade zones can provide accelerated export status for purposes of excise tax rebates and customs drawbacks. Manufacturers of such items as tires, trucks, and tobacco products are required to pay federal excise taxes when these items are produced, but the taxes are rebated if the items are exported. Firms including imported parts in their finished product must pay duty on the imports, but this duty is returned when the product is exported (customs drawback). The recovery of this money takes time, however, and meanwhile the exporter can have considerable capital tied up in excise taxes and import duties. Because a product is considered exported as soon as it enters an FTZ, the exporter can immediately apply for a rebate or a drawback while waiting to make an export sale. Although U.S. Customs has had the duty-drawback program in place for 200 years, many firms do not claim the money they're owed. As a result, each year a billion dollars in customs-duty refunds go unclaimed.[13]

If assembly or manufacturing is done in the FTZ using imported components, no duties need ever be paid when the finished product is exported. This is also the purpose of the previously mentioned export processing zones in which firms use cheap local labor for assembly. There are various such zones in China, for example.

---

* Includes subzones for individual plants.

EXPORT PROCEDURES

When nonexporters complain about the complexity of export procedures, they are generally referring to documentation. Instead of the two documents (the freight bill and the bill of lading) to which they are accustomed when shipping domestically, they are suddenly confronted by five to six times as many documents for a foreign shipment. According to an OECD study, the average overseas transaction needs 35 documents with a total of 360 copies. The study states that the "paper costs" of international trade come to between 1.4 percent and 5.7 percent of the value of the trade. "Exports move on a sea of documents" is a popular saying in the industry. Although the extra burden may be handled by the traffic department, many firms give all or at least part of the work to a foreign freight forwarder.

◻ Foreign Freight Forwarders

foreign freight forwarders
independent businesses that handle export shipments for compensation

Foreign freight forwarders act as agents for exporters. They prepare documents, book space with a carrier, and in general act as the firm's export traffic department. If asked, they will offer advice about markets, import and export regulations, the best mode of transport, and export packing, and they will supply cargo insurance. After shipment, they forward all documents to the importer or to the paying bank, according to the exporter's requirements.

◻ Export Documents

Correct documentation is vital to the success of any export shipment. For discussion purposes, we shall divide export documents into two categories: (1) shipping documents and (2) collection documents.

Shipping documents.   Shipping documents are prepared by exporters or their freight forwarders so that the shipment may pass through U.S. Customs, be loaded on the carrier, and sent to its destination. They include the domestic bill of lading, export packing list, export licenses, export bill of lading, and insurance certificate. Inasmuch as the first two documents are nearly the same as those used in domestic traffic, we shall limit our discussion to the export licenses, the insurance certificate, and the export bill of lading. Note, however, that a domestic bill of lading for goods to be exported must contain a statement by the seller that these goods will not be diverted to another destination. Export package marks and the latest allowable arrival date in the port of export should be noted. The export packing list differs from the domestic list in that it is much more detailed with respect to the weights and measurements of each package. The material in each package must be itemized.

General Export License
any export license covering export commodities for which a validated license is not required; no formal application required

Export licenses.   All exported goods with the exception of those going to U.S. possessions or Canada (with a few exceptions) require export licenses—either a *General License* or a *Validated Export License.*

Most products can be exported under the **General Export License,** for which no special authorization is necessary. The correct General License symbol, which is obtainable from the Department of Commerce district office, is merely written in the *Shipper's Export Declaration*. This document, which

Validated Export License
a required document issued
by the U.S. government
authorizing the export of
specified commodities

must be filed with U.S. Customs, indicates that there is an authorization to export and also provides the statistical information for The Bureau of Census. For strategic materials and all shipments to unfriendly countries, a **Validated Export License** is mandatory. This is a special authorization for a specific shipment and is issued only on formal application to the Department of Commerce's Office of Export Administration for scarce materials, strategic goods, and technology or to the Department of State for war materials.

Exporters selling strategic and high-tech products overseas must be aware that the Department of Commerce checks very thoroughly license applications for these products, as do all member-governments of the **Coordinating Committee on Multilateral Export Controls (COCOM),** a voluntary group comprising Australia, Japan, and all NATO countries except Iceland. COCOM nations administer a common set of export controls intended to prevent the transfer of critical goods and technologies, thus maintaining the gaps between the Western military systems and those based in the former Soviet Union. The United States has convinced COCOM members to maintain control over products such as night vision devices and fiber-optic communications systems that were vital in the Gulf War.[14] To enforce controls in this country, the Department of Commerce has an Office of Export Enforcement with armed agents in field offices located near high-tech production centers and in U.S. embassies in Vienna and Stockholm. Violators of diversion laws and export controls can be fined and imprisoned.

**Coordinating Committee on
Multilateral Export Controls
(COCOM)** voluntary group of
most NATO nations that
administers a common set of
export controls to prevent
transfer of sensitive goods to
Soviet-bloc nations

> **Two brothers, secret owners of a West German helicopter firm that was a former distributor of Hughes Helicopters, pleaded guilty in Los Angeles to illegally exporting over 100 U.S. helicopters to North Korea. One was given three years in jail, and the other, one year. Each was fined $40,000.[15]**

export bill of lading (B/L)
contract of carriage between
shipper and carrier: straight
bill of lading is
nonnegotiable; endorsed "to
order" bill gives holder claim
on merchandise

Export bill of lading.   The **export bill of lading** (B/L) serves a dual purpose. First, it is a contract for carriage between the shipper and the carrier; second, it is evidence of title to the merchandise. Bills of lading are generally called *air waybills* (air shipments) or *ocean bills of lading* (steamships).

Ocean bills of lading may be either "straight" or "to order," but air waybills are always "straight." A straight bill of lading is nonnegotiable, and only the person stipulated in it may obtain the merchandise on arrival. An order bill of lading, however, is negotiable. It can be endorsed like a check or left blank. In this case, the holder of the original bill of lading is the owner of the merchandise. Sight draft or letter of credit shipments require "to order" bills marked "Clean on Board" by the steamship company, which means there is no apparent damage to the shipment and it has actually been loaded onto the vessel.

Insurance certificate.   The insurance certificate is evidence that the shipment is insured against loss or damage while in transit. Unlike domestic carriers, oceangoing steamship companies assume no responsibility for the merchandise they carry unless the loss is caused by their negligence.

Marine insurance on an international transaction may be arranged by either the exporter or the importer, depending on the terms of sale. The laws of a country often require the importer to buy such insurance, thus protecting the local insurance industry and saving foreign exchange. If the exporter has sold on sight draft terms, it is at risk while the goods are in transit. In this case, the firm should buy contingent interest insurance to protect it in the event that the shipment is lost or damaged and it is unable to collect from the buyer. We believe that the exporter selling on C&F terms (the buyer purchases the insurance) should also buy contingent interest insurance to protect itself in case the buyer's insurance does not cover all risks. The premiums are low because damages are paid only on what is not covered by the buyer's policy.

Broadly speaking, there are three kinds of marine insurance policies: (1) basic named perils, (2) broad named perils, and (3) all risks.

1. *Basic named perils* includes perils of the sea, fires, jettisons, explosions, and hurricanes.
2. *Broad named perils* includes theft, pilferage, nondelivery, breakage, and leakage in addition to the basic perils. Both policies contain a clause that determines the extent to which losses caused by an insured peril will be paid. The purchaser of the insurance may request either *(a)* free of particular average (excluding partial loss) or *(b)* with particular average (covering partial loss). Obviously, the rates differ.
3. *All risks* covers all physical loss or damage from any external cause and is more expensive than the policies previously mentioned. War risks are covered under a separate contract.

For the sake of convenience, the occasional exporter will ask the forwarder to arrange for insurance, but when shipments begin on a regular basis, the shipper can economize by going directly to a marine insurance broker. The broker, acting as the shipper's agent, will draw up a contract to fit the shipper's needs by choosing appropriate clauses from among the hundreds that are available.

The premiums charged depend on a number of factors, among which are the goods insured, the destination, the age of the ship, whether the goods are stowed on deck or under deck, the volume of business (there are volume discounts), how the goods are packed, and the number of claims the shipper has filed. Brokers will sometimes admit that in the long run it is preferable not to file numerous small claims, even if justified, because the higher premiums charged for future shipments will be greater than the money recovered.

Because neither the policies nor the premiums are standard, it is highly recommended that the exporter obtain various quotations.

Collection documents.   The seller is required to provide the buyer with these documents to receive payment. For a letter of credit transaction, the **collection documents** must be submitted to a bank, but to collect against documentary drafts, anyone may be designated to act on the seller's behalf. A few exporters send their drafts overseas to a representative or bank for collection, but it is preferable to have a bank in the exporter's country forward them to its correspondent bank in the city of destination.

First of all, the collection costs are usually less, because the correspondent bank charges the exporter's bank less than it would charge the exporter. Second, because of the correspondent relationship between the banks, the foreign bank will generally exert a greater effort to collect the money on time. Should the exporter wish to change instructions to the foreign bank, the private cable codes and tests of banks permit new instructions to be authenticated and acted on quickly, whereas a cable from the exporter to a foreign

collection documents all documents submitted to the buyer for the purpose of receiving payment for a shipment bank would probably be ignored until it had been confirmed by a letter with a signature that could be checked for authenticity.

The documents required for collection vary among countries and among customers, but some of the most common are (1) commercial invoices, (2) consular invoices, (3) certificates of origin, and (4) inspection certificates.

Commercial invoices.   *Commercial invoices* for export orders are similar to domestic invoices but include additional information, such as the origin of the goods, export packing marks, and a clause stating that the goods will not be diverted to another country. Invoices for letter of credit sales will name the bank and the credit numbers. Some importing countries require the commercial invoice to be in their language and to be visaed by their local consul.

Consular invoices.   A few countries require both the commercial invoice and a special form called the *consular invoice*. These forms are purchased from the consul, prepared in the language of the country, and then visaed by the consul.

Certificates of origin.   Although the commercial invoice carries a statement regarding the origin of the merchandise, a number of foreign governments require a separate *certificate of origin*. This document is commonly issued by the local chamber of commerce and visaed by the consul.

Inspection certificates.   *Inspection certificates* are frequently required by buyers of grain, foodstuffs, and live animals. These are issued by the Department of Agriculture in the United States. Purchasers of machinery or products containing a specified combination of ingredients may insist that an American engineering firm or laboratory inspect and certify that the merchandise is exactly as ordered.

EXPORT SHIPMENTS

Most newcomers are so preoccupied with making a sale and handling the extra paperwork needed when exporting that they fail to be concerned about the physical movement of their goods. Yet, if they knew about the advances in material-handling techniques, they might not only save money but also reach markets they previously could not serve.

For example, do you want to reduce handling costs? Do you want to reduce pilferage, always a problem in both the port of exit and the port of entry?

> One of the writers, a crew member of a merchant ship docked in an American port to discharge cargo, was leaving the ship when he heard a tremendous thump. The stevedores who were unloading the ship were picking up a large crate with the ship's winch and dropping it on the ground to break it open. Obviously, they suspected that it contained valuable merchandise. Within a few hours of a ship's arrival to unload, you can see peddlers in the street offering merchandise that arrived on the ship. You can purchase bananas, for example, outside the dock area soon after their arrival.

One means of drastically reducing both theft and handling costs is to use containers.

Container ship

Courtesy of Lykes Brothers Steamship Company, Inc.

◻ Containers

Containers are large boxes—8 by 8 feet in cross-section by either 10, 20, or 40 feet in length—that the seller fills with the shipment in its own warehouse. Airlines also provide smaller containers with rounded cross-sections for a better fit in the fuselage. The containers are then sealed and opened only when the goods arrive at their final destination. Containers will be picked up by a tractor-trailer or a railroad for delivery to shipside, where they will be loaded aboard ship. From the port of entry, railroads or trucks will deliver them, often unopened even for customs inspection, to the buyer's warehouse. In most countries, customs officials will go to the warehouse to examine the shipment. This not only reduces handling time, but it also minimizes the risks of damage and theft because the buyer's own employees unload the containers. If the importer or exporter has a warehouse on a river too shallow for ocean vessels, it can save time and expense by loading containers on barges, which are towed to the harbor where a LASH vessel is anchored.

RO–RO vessel

Courtesy of Lykes Brothers Steamship Company, Inc.

□ LASH

LASH (lighter aboard ship) vessels give exporters and importers direct access to ocean freight service even though they are located on shallow inland waterways. Sixty-foot-long barges are towed to inland locations, loaded, and towed back to deep water where they are loaded aboard anchored LASH ships. Exporters who are not located in deep-water ports should check to see if this service is available. Not only will they decrease their risks, but they may gain from their competitors those customers facing the same problems because they too are located far from seaports. This is especially true in LDCs, where oceangoing vessels may wait in anchor a month or more for docking space. Not only do customers have to wait for the merchandise, but freight charges will be higher because the ship has a long, unproductive wait. All the expenses of operating the vessel, which can amount to thousands of dollars daily, are included in a demurrage charge added to the exporter's or importer's normal freight charge.

□ RO–RO

Another innovation in cargo handling is the RO–RO (roll on–roll off) ship, which permits loaded trailers and any equipment on wheels to be driven onto this specially designed vessel. RO–RO service has brought the benefits of containerization that we discussed to ports that have been unable to invest in the expensive lifting equipment required for containers. Innovative exporters might be able to combine their container shipments with other exporters' shipments of rolling stock. Of course, they must first know that RO–RO vessels exist.

□ Air Freight

Air freight has had a profound effect on international business because it permits shipments that once required 30 days to arrive in 1 day. Huge freight planes carry payloads of 200,000 pounds, most of which goes either in containers or on pallets. Airlines guarantee overnight delivery from New York to many European airports and claim that their planes can be completely loaded or unloaded within 45 minutes.

Many newcomers to exporting use ocean freight rather than air freight because ocean freight is so much cheaper. But if they compare the total costs of each mode, they frequently find that air freight is less costly. Total cost components that may be lower for air freight include the following:

1. *Insurance rates*—less chance of damage.
2. *Packing*—can go in domestic packaging instead of the heavier, more costly export packing, which the exporter may have to pay to have done by an outside firm.
3. *Customs duties*—when calculated on gross weights.
4. *Replacement costs for damaged goods*—less chance of damaging shipment. Mercedes ships many of its automobiles to the United States by air freight.
5. *Inventory costs*—rapid delivery by air freight often obviates the need for expensive warehouses.
6. *Increased customer satisfaction*—receives shipment sooner with less chance of damage or delays caused by replacing damaged product.

Table 16–2 illustrates how the total cost of air freight may be lower than ocean freight.

Even when the total costs based on these items are higher for air freight, it may still be advantageous to ship by air when factors other than the conventional expense, inventory, and capital are considered:

1. *Production and opportunity costs,* although somewhat more difficult to calculate, are properly a part of the total cost. Getting the product to the buyer more quickly results in faster payment, which speeds up the return on investment and improves cash flow. The firm's capital is released more quickly and can be invested in other profit-making ventures or can be used to repay borrowed capital, thus reducing interest payments. Production equipment may be assembled and sent by air so that it goes into production sooner without the transit and setup delays associated with ocean shipments, a strong sales argument.
2. *The firm may be air dependent;* that is, the exporter is in business only because of air freight. Suppliers of perishable food products to Europe, Japan, and the Middle East are in this category, as are suppliers of live animals (newly hatched poultry and prize bulls) and fresh flowers, a big, legal Colombian export. *Without air freight, these firms would be out of business.*
3. *The products may be air dependent* because the market itself is perishable. Consumer products with extremely short life cycles (high-fashion and fad items) are examples, but many industrial products also fit into this category. A computer, for example, is

□ **TABLE 16–2**
Sea–Air Total Cost Comparison (Shipment of spare parts)

	Ocean Freight (with warehousing)	Air Freight (no warehousing)
Warehouse administrative costs	$ 850	—
Warehouse rent	1,400	—
Inventory costs		
Taxes and insurance	630	$ 330
Inventory financing	240	160
Inventory obsolescence	1,500	0(minimal)
Seller's warehouse and handling costs	1,550	950
Transportation	350	2,000
Packaging and handling	250	100
Cargo insurance	60	30
Customs duties	110	107
Total	$ 6,940	$3,677

perishable to the extent that the time it loses between the final assembly and the installation at the customer's location is time in which it is not earning income (the leasing fee).

4. The sales argument that *spare parts and factory technical personnel are available within a few hours* is a strong one for the exporting firm that has to compete with overseas manufacturers.

IMPORTING

In one sense, importers are the reverse of exporters; they sell domestically and buy in foreign markets. However, many of their concerns are similar. As in the case of exporters, there are small firms whose only business is to import, and there are global corporations for which importing is just one of their functions.

How does the prospective importer identify import sources? In a number of ways:

1. If similar imported products are already in the market, go to a retailer that sells them and examine the product label to see where it is made. U.S. law requires the country of origin to be clearly marked on each product or on its container if product marking is not feasible (individual cigarettes, for example).

   Once you know where the product is produced, call the nearest consul or embassy of that country and request the names of manufacturers. One of the principal duties of all foreign government representatives is to promote exports. Some countries publish newsletters in which products are offered for export. Ask to be on their mailing lists. You can also call foreign chambers of commerce in your country (the German-American Chamber of Commerce in New York City is an example). The Japan External Trade Organization (JETRO), which provides information on Japanese exporters, has a number of offices in the United States and other countries. Foreign governments sponsor trade shows in many countries, as we mentioned

Two 10-foot "bungalows" and an outsized piece of cargo that is even longer than its pallet move to their loading positions on the main deck of Lufthansa's Boeing 747F

Courtesy of Lufthansa

in our discussion of how the U.S. Department of Commerce assists exporters. Visit these as well as industry shows in your home country. Once you have names and addresses of foreign manufacturers, you can write to them for quotations.

2. If the product is not being imported, you should contact all the sources listed in item 1. The only difference is that you will have to contact more countries. Banks may be another source of names.

3. Accidental importing also takes place. When you visit a foreign country, look for products that may have a market at home. Finding one could put you into a new business, one that makes foreign traveling tax deductible.

Let's look at some of the technical aspects of importing for which customhouse brokers can provide assistance.

□ Customhouse Brokers

customhouse brokers
independent businesses that handle import shipments for compensation

In every nation, there are **customhouse brokers** just as there are foreign freight forwarders; but instead of helping exporters to export (the function of foreign freight forwarders), they help importers to import. The functions of the two are very similar; in fact, a number of firms provide both services. In the United States, both are licensed: customhouse brokers are licensed by U.S. Customs after passing an extensive examination, and foreign freight forwarders are licensed by the U.S. Maritime Administration after passing an examination.

Principal activity.   Acting as the agent for the importer, customhouse brokers bring the imported goods through customs, which requires them to know well the many import regulations and the extensive Tariff Schedule mentioned in Chapter 2. If a customs official places the import in a category requiring higher import duties than the importer had planned on paying, the importing firm may not be able to compete pricewise and still make a profit. Generally, customs evaluators everywhere use units for products that carry specific duties and the invoice price as the basis for ad valorem duties. As we explained in Chapter 2, there are some exceptions.

The practice of U.S. Customs is to use the transaction price, which appears on the commercial invoice accompanying the shipment, plus any other charges not included in the transaction price. These may be royalty or license fees, packing, or any assists. *Assist* is the U.S. Customs term for any item that the buyer provides free or at reduced cost for use in the production or sale of merchandise for export to this country. Examples are molds and dies sent overseas to produce the product, a common practice of importers that want the goods produced using their design, and components and parts that the buyer provides for incorporation in the finished article.

American-made goods can be returned to this country duty free; if they have been improved in any way, however, the importers must pay import duties. Mexico's twin-plant concept would not exist if Congress had not passed a law exempting American firms from paying import duties on the American components in finished products that are assembled in Mexico and exported to the United States.

Other activities.   Customhouse brokers can also provide other services, such as arranging transportation for the goods after they have left Customs or even transportation for the goods from a foreign country if the exporter has not done so. Another important function is to know when imports are subject to import quotas and how much of the quota has been filled at the time of the import. No matter at which port the goods arrive, U.S. Customs, aided by a computer network to all American ports, knows immediately the quantity that has been imported. Merchandise subject to import quotas can be on the dock of an American port awaiting clearance through Customs; if the quota fills anywhere meanwhile, those goods cannot be imported for the rest of the fiscal year. The would-be importer must either (1) put them in a **bonded warehouse** or a foreign trade zone, where merchandise can be stored without paying duty and wait for the rest of the year, (2) abandon them, or (3) send them to another country. Importers of high-fashion clothing have lost millions of dollars because the quotas were filled and they could not sell the clothing until the following year—by then, it was out of fashion.

A prospective importer should follow these rules:

1. Disclose fully to the U.S. Customs Service all foreign and financial arrangements before passing the goods through Customs. The penalties for fraud are high.

2. Ask the advice of a customhouse broker *before* making the transaction. Frequently, a simple change in the product can result in much lower import duties. For example, if you are an importer of jeans, you will pay higher duties if the label is outside the back pocket instead of under the belt. If the words on the label are stylized, duties are more than if they are in simple block letters. Any clothing that is ornamented pays more duty. This is why one importer brings in plain sports shirts and sews on an animal figure after they are in the United States.

3. Calculate carefully the landed price in advance. If there is a doubt about the import category, the importer can ask Customs to

bonded warehouse
authorized by customs authorities for storage of goods on which payment of import duties is deferred until the goods are removed

determine the category in advance and to put it in writing—just as you can obtain advanced rulings from the Internal Revenue Service. At the time of importation, customs inspectors must respect this determination. Many customs procedures are like those of the IRS. Both have similar procedures for appealing their decisions, for example. This is no coincidence—both are under the secretary of the Treasury.

SUMMARY

Firms of all sizes export, including worldwide corporations that own overseas production facilities. You studied the reason why firms go overseas in Chapter 2, and, in this chapter, you saw some specific reasons why they export: completing product lines; exporting production inputs to affiliates; the host government requiring an affiliate to export; importing from their affiliates to be competitive in their home markets; or testing a new market or a new product first with exports.

Smaller firms, like the larger ones, export to increase sales. Some begin to export accidently, while others seek out foreign customers. Generally, companies choose not to export because of the perceived difficulties in (1) locating new markets, (2) payment and financing procedures, and (3) export procedures.

Market screening as described in Chapter 14 will enable the firm to locate foreign markets, and various Department of Commerce programs are also helpful. When preparing the export marketing mix, special attention must be given to export pricing and the preparation of sales agreements for overseas representatives.

The terms of payment offered in the export market are (1) cash in advance, (2) open account, (3) consignment, (4) letters of credit, and (5) documentary drafts. Although exporters would prefer to sell on letter of credit terms, the competitive situation in world markets forces them to offer credit. A number of sources and kinds of export financing, both private and public, are available. Government incentives to export trade include OPIC, Foreign Sales Corporations, and foreign trade zones.

Export procedures are considered a problem by newcomers because of the multiplicity of the documents required. Foreign freight forwarders are available to act as agents in the preparation of documents and in the booking of space on carriers. In addition to the documents required for domestic shipments, goods for export usually require export licenses and export bills of lading. Inasmuch as oceangoing steamship companies assume no responsibility for the merchandise they carry, the shipper must buy marine insurance. The documents required for collection vary among customers and destinations, but they commonly include (1) commercial invoices, (2) consular invoices, (3) certificates of origin, and (4) inspection certificates.

Innovations in transportation and materials handling, such as containerization, RO–RO, and LASH, are enabling exporters to reach new markets.

Importers sell domestically and buy overseas, the reverse of what exporters do. Like exporters, large and small firms import. Customhouse brokers are agents who help importers to import. They bring goods through Customs but also perform other duties, such as arranging for transportation after the goods have cleared Customs. They also know what products are subject to import quotas, a nation's import regulations, and its tariff schedule.

American importers should follow these rules: (1) disclose fully to U.S. Customs all foreign financial arrangements before passing goods through Customs, as penalties for fraud are high, (2) ask the customhouse broker for advice before making the transaction, and (3) calculate carefully the landed price in advance. Customs will examine a product and determine the import category in advance on request.

QUESTIONS

1. What are the major problem areas that nonexporting firms cite as reasons for not exporting?

2. What are the common terms of sale quoted by exporters? For each, explain to what point the seller must pay all transportation and delivery costs. Where does the responsibility for loss or damage pass to the buyer?

3. What two parts of a sales agreement with a foreign representative deserve special attention?

4. *a.* Explain the various export payment terms that are available.
   b. Which two offer the most protection to the seller?

5. What is the procedure for a letter of credit transaction?

6. What government and government-assisted organizations offer assistance in export financing?

7. The manager of the international department of the Modesto Bank learns on the way to work that the ship on which a local exporter shipped some goods has sunk. The manager has received all of the documents required in the letter of credit and is ready to pay the exporter for the shipment. In view of the news about the ship, the manager now knows that the foreign customer will never receive the goods. Should the manager pay the exporter, or should he withhold payment and notify the overseas customer?

8. What is a foreign trade zone? Check with a customhouse broker or a U.S. Customs official or do some research in the library to find out the advantages of a foreign trade zone over a bonded warehouse.

9. What are the purposes of an export bill of lading?

10. Air shipments can lower inventory costs in at least three ways. What are they?

11. An importer brings plain sports shirts to this country because the import duty is lower than it is for shirts with adornments. It then sews on a figure of a fox in this country. Should the importer do this operation in a foreign trade zone?

12. How would you find sources for a product that you want to import?

13. What does a customhouse broker do?

▢ MINICASE 16–1

State Manufacturing Export Sales Price

State Manufacturing Company, a producer of farm equipment, had just received an inquiry from a large distributor in Italy. The quantity on which the distributor wanted a price was sufficiently large that Jim Mason, the sales manager, felt he had to respond. He knew the inquiry was genuine, because he had called two of the companies that the distributor said he represented, and both had assured him that the Italian firm was a serious one. It paid its bills regularly with no problems. Both companies were selling the firm on open account terms.

Mason's problem was that he had never quoted on a sale for export before. His first impulse was to take the regular FOB factory price and add the cost of the extra-heavy export packing plus the inland freight cost to the nearest U.S. port. This price should enable the company to make money if he quoted the price FAS port of exit.

However, the terms of sale were bothering him. The traffic manager had called a foreign freight forwarder to learn about the frequency of sailings to Italy, and during the conversation she had suggested to the traffic manager that she might be able to help Mason. When Mason called her, he learned that because of competition, many firms like State Manufacturing were quoting CIF foreign port as a convenience to the importer. She asked him what payment terms he would quote, and he replied that his credit manager had suggested an irrevocable, confirmed letter of credit so as to be sure of receiving payment for the sale. He admitted that the distributor, however, had asked for payment against a 90-day time draft.

The foreign freight forwarder urged Mason to consider quoting CIF port of entry in Italy with payment as requested by the distributor to be more competitive. She informed him that he could get insurance to protect the company against commercial risk. To help him calculate a CIF price, she offered to give him the various charges if he would tell her the weight and value of his shipment FOB factory. He replied that the total price was $21,500 and that the gross weight, including the container, was 3,629 kilos.

Two hours later, she called to give him the following charges:

1. Containerization	$ 200.00
2. Inland freight less handling	798.00
3. Forwarding and documentation	90.00
4. Ocean freight	2,633.00
5. Commercial risk insurance	105.00
6. Marine insurance—total of items 1–5 × 1.1 = $27,858.60 at 60¢/$100*	167.15

*Total coverage of marine insurance is commonly calculated on the basis of the total price plus 10 percent.

During that time, Mason had been thinking about the competition. Could he lower the FOB price for an export sale? He looked at the cost figures. Sales expense amounted to 20 percent of the sales price. Couldn't this be deducted on a foreign order? Research and development amounted to

10 percent. Should this be charged? Advertising and promotional expense amounted to another 10 percent. What about that? Because this was an unsolicited inquiry, there was no selling expense for this sale except for his and the secretary's time. Mason felt that it wasn't worth calculating this time.

If you were Jim Mason, how would you calculate the CIF port of entry price?

◻ MINICASE 16–2

Morgan Guaranty Trust Company Letter of Credit

MORGAN GUARANTY TRUST COMPANY
OF NEW YORK
INTERNATIONAL BANKING DIVISION
23 WALL STREET, NEW YORK, N. Y. 10015   March 5, 19*

Smith Tool Co. Inc.
29 Bleecker Street
New York, N.Y. 10012

On all communications please refer to

NUMBER IC - 152647

Dear Sirs:

We are instructed to advise you of the establishment by
. Bank of South America, Puerto Cabello, Venezuela . . . .
of their IRREVOCABLE Credit No. 19845. . . . .
in your favor, for the account of John Doe, Puerto Cabello, Venezuela . . . .
for U. S. $3,000.00 (THREE THOUSAND U. S. DOLLARS) . . . .
available upon presentation to us of your drafts at sight on us, accompanied by:
Commercial Invoice in triplicate, describing the merchandise as indicated below

Consular Invoice in triplicate, all signed and stamped by the Consul of Venezuela

Negotiable Insurance Policy and/or Underwriter's Certificate, endorsed in blank, covering marine and war risks

Full set of straight ocean steamer Bills of Lading, showing consignment to the Bank of South America, Puerto Cabello, stamped by Venezuelan Consul and marked "Freight Prepaid",

evidencing shipment of UNA MAQUINA DE SELLAR LATAS, C.I.F. Puerto Cabello, from United States Port to Puerto Cabello, Venezuela

> Page 6
> Advice of irrevocable letter of credit issued by
> a foreign bank in favor of a U.S. exporter and
> confirmed by Morgan Guaranty, which is
> obliged to honor drafts drawn under credit.

Except as otherwise expressly stated herein, this credit is subject to the Uniform Customs and Practice for Documentary Credits (1974 revision), International Chamber of Commerce Publication No. 290.

The above bank engages with you that all drafts drawn under and in compliance with the terms of this advice will be duly honored if presented to our Commercial Credits Department, 15 Broad Street, New York, N. Y. 10015, on or before March 31, 19* on which date this credit expires.

We confirm the foregoing and undertake that all drafts drawn and presented in accordance with its terms will be duly honored.

Yours very truly,

Authorized Signature

Immediately upon receipt, please examine this instrument and if its terms are not clear to you or if you need any assistance in respect to your availment of it, we would welcome your communicating with us. Documents should be presented promptly and not later than 3 P.M.

1. Who issued the letter of credit?
2. Is it irrevocable?
3. Has it been confirmed?
4. If so, by whom?
5. Who is the buyer?
6. Who is the seller?
7. What kind of draft is to be presented?
8. What documents are required?
9. What are the terms of sale?
10. When does the letter of credit expire?
11. Where does the seller go for payment?
12. Who pays the freight?
13. Who pays the marine insurance?
14. Must the steamship company attest that the merchandise has been loaded on ship?
15. What is the reason for your answer to question 14?

☐ MINICASE 16–3

Eckerd Manufacturing

Eckerd Manufacturing Company is a Los Angeles firm that sells pool tables and accessories in the United States and in various world markets. To be competitive pricewise, the firm sources the components worldwide. For example, it imports slate for the tables from Sicily, rubber bumpers from Taiwan, pool balls from Africa, and wood from Brazil. The tables are assembled in the Los Angeles plant. About half of the company's sales are for export.

Shirley Thomas, Eckerd's president, is searching for ways to lower the costs of the tables. She does apply for drawbacks on the duty that the company pays for imported components that are incorporated into the exported tables. However, she has to wait for these Customs rebates, which amount to 90 percent of all duties paid. Interestingly, the import duty on a finished pool table is less than the sum of the duties on all the components.

Based on what you have learned from Chapter 16, what do you recommend?

SUPPLEMENTARY READINGS

Export Assistance

"ABCs of Exporting." *Business America*, special edition, 1991, pp. 2–27.

"District Export Councils." *Business America*, April 24, 1989, pp. 2–6.

Exporters' Guide to Federal Resources for Small Business. Rev. ed. Washington, D.C.: Interagency Task Force on Trade, 1988.

"Going Global, Here's How." *Business Week*, July 2, 1990, pp. 88–89.

"Small Business: Obstacles to Exporting." *Business America*, May 8, 1989, pp. 5–11.

Export Assistance, U.S. Department of Commerce

"Be Ready for 1992—Export to EUROPE NOW." *Business America*, August 1, 1988, pp. 14–16.

"Commerce Program Matches Foreign Buyers with Suppliers and Exhibitors at U.S. Shows." *Business America*, May 23, 1988, p. 20.

"Learning the Ropes." *INC*, August 1988, pp. 103–6.

"TOP Program Helps U.S. Firms Tap Foreign Markets." *Business America*, February 27, 1989, pp. 12–13.

William A. Delphos, ed. *The World Is Your Market*. Washington, D.C.: Braddock Communications, 1990.

Export Licensing and Control

"COCOM Eases Restrictions on Export of High-Tech Equipment to Eastern Bloc." *Aviation Week & Space Technology*, June 10, 1991, p. 73.

"Export Enforcement Secures America's Technology." *Business America*, February 29, 1988, pp. 22–24.

"Export Licensing from A to Z." *Business America*, February 29, 1988, pp. 12–15.

"ITA's Export Control Automated Support System Cuts Down Processing Time for Export Licenses." *Business America*, July 6, 1987, p. 6.

"The Electronic Age of Export Licensing." *Business America*, February 29, 1988, pp. 7–10.

"The New Bureau of Export Administration." *Business America*, February 29, 1988, pp. 3–6.

Exporting, General

A Basic Guide to Exporting. Washington, D.C.: U.S. Department of Commerce, 1986.

"A Step-by-Step Approach to Market Research." *Business America*, March 16, 1987, pp. 4–5.

Axinn, Catherine N. "Export Performance: Do Managerial Perceptions Make a Difference?" *International Marketing Review*, Summer 1988, pp. 61–71.

"Export Strategies." *Small Business Reports,* May 1989, pp. 20–27.

"Finding the International Niche: A 'How to' for American Small Business." *Business Horizons,* March–April 1991, pp. 13–17.

"Good Follow-Up Is Vital to Export Success." *Business America,* October 26, 1987, pp. 14–17.

"How to Prepare Your Product for Export." *Business America,* May 25, 1987, pp. 10–11.

"New Tariff Code Streamlines Global Trading System." *Business America,* November 23, 1987, pp. 2–5.

"The CEO's Role in a Successful Export Strategy." *Small Business Reports,* May 1989, pp. 28–32.

"The New Export Entrepreneurs." *Fortune,* June 6, 1988, pp. 89–102.

"The Revised Incoterms: Key Features." *International Trade Forum,* June 1990, pp. 8–30.

Importing

"Importing for Exporters." *Distribution,* October 1982, pp. 95–108.

Importing into the United States. Washington, D.C.: Department of the Treasury, 1986.

Payments and Financing

"A Guide to Eximbank Programs." *Business America,* November 5, 1990, pp. 10–13.

"Eximbank, TDP, and OPIC Are Active in South America." *Business America,* June 5, 1989, pp. 16–20.

"How to Take Advantage of Duty Drawback." *Traffic Management,* September 1990, pp. 59–62.

"Investigating International Payments Methods." *Business Age,* January–February 1989, pp. 26–29.

"Letting Go of the L/C Security Blanket." *Northeast International Business,* September 1988, p. 12.

"The New and Improved Eximbank." *Small Business Reports,* November 1988, pp. 30–33.

ENDNOTES

1. Telephone conversation on June 19, 1989, with Al Chambers, Ford International.

2. Bonnie Heineman Wolfe, "Finding the International Niche: A 'How to' for American Small Business," *Business Horizons,* March–April 1991, p. 13.

3. Wendell McCulloch, Jr., *American Exports: Why Have They Lagged?* (Washington, D.C.: Joint Economic Committee, Congress of the United States, May 14, 1985).

4. "U.S. Trade Facts," *Business America,* May 22, 1989, p. 12.

5. William A. Delphos, ed., *The World Is Your Market* (Washington, D.C.: Braddock Communications, 1990), pp. 107–21.

6. *National Trade Data Bank User's Guide* (Washington, D.C.: U.S. Department of Commerce, July 1991), p. 1.

7. "Export Services of Commerce's ITA," *Business America,* special edition, 1991, p. 9.

8. "States See Exports as a Tool for Local Business Expansion," *Business America,* February 27, 1989, pp. 7–11.

9. These and other terms have been codified in INCO-*TERMS,* 1990 by the International Chamber of Commerce, which has been adopted by the U.S. Chamber of Commerce, the National Council of American Exporters, and the National Foreign Trade Council. The point at which title and risk pass from the seller to the buyer is specified, as are the duties of each party.

10. "Other Federal Export Assistance," *Business America,* May 22, 1989, p. 18.

11. "A Guide to Eximbank Programs," *Business America,* November 5, 1990, pp. 11–12.

12. *A Basic Guide to Exporting* (Washington, D.C.: U.S. Department of Commerce, 1988), p. 56.

13. "How to Take Advantage of Duty Drawback," *Traffic Management,* September 1990, p. 59.

14. "COCOM Eases Restrictions on Export of High-Tech Equipment to Eastern Bloc," *Aviation Week & Space Technology,* June 10, 1991, p. 73.

15. "Export Enforcement Secures America's Technology," *Business America,* February 29, 1988, pp. 22–23.

Chapter 17

East–West Relations

Official Chinese news and peoples' daily lives move in different spheres that rarely intersect.

Laszlo LaDany, S.J.

Soviet bottom line is that few people know what one is.

The Wall Street Journal, February 5, 1989, headline for an article about a new business school in the Soviet Union

If wealthy former West Germany finds it more and more difficult to get the former German Democratic Republic (which was an economic front-runner among the East European countries) back on its feet, one can imagine the difficulty of achieving this goal with the rest of Eastern Europe—including the parts of what used to be the U.S.S.R. In 1991 alone, $100 billion was spent by Bonn on its new eastern states, and an estimated $65 billion will be needed annually until the year 2000. It is doubtful that much can be achieved with the $40 billion from the European Bank for Reconstruction and Development.

Europe 92, September 1991

LEARNING OBJECTIVES

In this chapter, you will study:

1. What countries are meant when you read or hear about "East–West relations."

2. The meaning of "centrally planned economy."

3. The meaning of "market economy."

4. About the demise of COMECON.

5. What the East should try to achieve, and how and why the West should help.

6. Why the People's Republic of China (PRC), with its huge population, has never become a large consumer market.

7. Why the United States and the PRC began to trade in the 1970s and recognized each other in 1979.

8. What the East wants most from the West.

9. Why the East cannot afford to pay for all its wants.

10. Some departures by the PRC from the usual practices of the East in its dealings with the West.

11. Tensions in the PRC between liberalizing economic activities and the rigid communist bureaucracy in Beijing.

12. Results of the fact that communism was in full control of the PRC for a much shorter time period than in the U.S.S.R.

13. How Western companies do business with the East.

14. How the East has paid and is trying to pay for imports from the West.

15. Common objections in the West to goods and services from the East.

16. Changes occurring in the East.

KEY WORDS AND CONCEPTS

- Centrally planned economy
- Market economies
- East–West trade
- Joint venture
- Countertrade
- Dumping

BUSINESS INCIDENT

Joint ventures (JVs) between Soviet agencies and Western companies are favored by the Soviet government. The first American company to sign a JV surprised some people. Trenton, New Jersey, is Moscow's U.S. sister city, and in 1987 the mayor of the Lenin district of Moscow visited Trenton. While there, he sampled the pizzas of Roma Food Enterprises and immediately invited Roma's president, Louis Piancone, to visit Moscow and discuss a JV.

When Mr. Piancone got to Moscow, he encountered skepticism about the ability of Roma, which had never done export business, to handle the logistics of operating successfully in the world's biggest nation. The turning point came when an interpreter asked Mr. Piancone whether he had seen the world's largest pizza on television a few days earlier. "See it? I made it," he responded. When the Soviet negotiators realized Roma was the creator of a 15-ton pizza, they stood up and saluted, and a JV agreement was signed in short order.

Now Roma's Pizza van cruises Moscow, selling about 6,000 slices a day. The company plans to open 25 Italian restaurants in the Soviet Union by 1993.

Source: Patricia A. Dreyfus, "Negotiating the Kremlin Maze," *Business Month,* November 1988, pp. 55–63.

"**E**ast is east and west is west and never the twain shall meet" was not accurate when Rudyard Kipling wrote it, and it is even less correct today. The former East European satellite countries of the Soviet Union and its three now independent Baltic states are moving toward the West as fast as they can. East and West Germany are no more, having united as Germany.

The Soviet Union has broken up, but most of its previous states may form a common economic market. The Soviets have ended or are ending economic and military aid to countries such as Cuba, Afghanistan, and Angola, which will turn to the West for aid or trade.

The so-far implacably communist North Korea has begun talking with capitalist South Korea, and Vietnam is now seeking investments from the West.

Politically, the great communist iceberg, the Peoples' Republic of China, has barely begun to melt, but economically, the thaw is fairly well advanced from strict communism, and that is continuing. How the resulting tensions and contradictions will be resolved remains to be seen.

As the Soviet Union dissolves and its power and influence over Eastern Europe and its states wane, historical ethnic hostilities are bubbling up. There has been fighting, death, and damage in many places, including Yugoslavia and Georgia, and it is feared there will be more. Aside from the human toll it takes, fighting will impede the peoples' abilities to produce, buy, and sell. And, of course, investment, not to mention tourism, which brought much income to several of the affected areas, will dry up. These are developments the international business manager must watch carefully.

Although momentous changes are taking place in the Eastern countries, it will be useful to identify them and thus distinguish them from the Western countries.

THE EAST COUNTRIES

East, as used in this chapter, included the centrally planned economies of the Union of Soviet Socialist Republics (U.S.S.R.), its East European satellites (Poland, East Germany, Czechoslovakia, Hungary, Romania, and Bulgaria), and its other satellites, such as Cuba, Ethiopia, South Yemen, and Vietnam. It also included Yugoslavia and the People's Republic of China (PRC), which occupies mainland China and is to be differentiated from the Republic of China, which occupies Taiwan.

centrally planned economies the government owns all the important factors of production and dictates how much of each product will be made

In the preceding paragraph, we spoke of **centrally planned economies.** In countries with such economies, the central, national government decides how much of what product will be made during each year or other planning period, such as a five-year plan. Historically in centrally planned economies, the governments have owned and controlled all major factors of production. They have also controlled labor, as the unions are essentially government agencies and workers must obtain government approval to move from one area or job to another.

THE WEST COUNTRIES

West, as used here, includes the industrial countries of Western Europe and North America plus Japan and such other countries as Australia and New Zealand. For practical purposes, the Western countries are members of the Organization for Economic Cooperation and Development (OECD).

market economies most factors of production are privately owned, and markets, prices, and profits determine how much of which products will be made

All the OECD countries have **market economies** to one degree or another; that is to say, market forces, although government regulated, are permitted to operate. The governments do not own or control all farms, factories, mines, and labor unions. Supply and demand are important forces in establishing market prices, and sooner or later, privately owned businesses must make profits to survive.

EAST–WEST ECONOMIC RELATIONS

Prior to World War I and again in the 1920s and 30s, many American companies played important roles in the economic development of the U.S.S.R. During World War II (WW II), hundreds of American suppliers provided billions of dollars' worth of goods and services to the U.S.S.R.[1]

East–West trade trade between the countries of the East and those of the West, as they have been identified above

Following WW II, the hostilities of the Cold War succeeded the WW II alliance, and **East–West trade** dropped sharply. Even though it revived considerably in the 1960s and 70s, it has still not achieved the percentages of pre-WW II 1938. Then, East–West trade accounted for 74 percent of the total trade of Eastern countries and for 9.5 percent of that of Western countries. In 1987, 49 years later, Eastern countries' trade with the West was only 30 percent of their total trade, and Western countries' trade with the East was less than 3 percent of their total trade.

In past editions of this book we presented historical and most current figures for trade between the OECD countries and the communist countries. There were three categories of communist countries. First there were the members of the Council for Mutual Economic Assistance, referred to in the West as COMECON. It consisted of the U.S.S.R. and its satellites, and we shall speak a bit about its demise in a moment. Second, there was East Germany, which no longer exists. The People's Republic of China (PRC), the third category, still exists in a very big way.

While COMECON was in existence, and could be expected to continue, it was useful to explain and draw conclusions from trends in historical trade figures. Now most of the former COMECON member-countries are struggling in their own fashions to convert to market economies and to change their trade and investment orientations to the West. The old continuity has been broken. New patterns are forming. We believe that examining how the former COMECON members are trying to change economically and politically will be more interesting and meaningful than discussing historical trade figures.

East Germany used to be a special trade case because of the different treatment given it by West Germany. They are now united as one Germany.

The PRC, with its huge population and growing economy, is extremely important. We shall deal with it separately. But first, let's look briefly at what happened to COMECON and see how some former members are trying to cope.

A resident of the former West Germany celebrates German reunification with a resident of the former East.

Thomas Hoepker/Magnum Photos, Inc.

COMECON

It may seem odd to devote space to a dead organization, but the life and death of COMECON may teach some lessons. Communism—in the form it assumed under Lenin, Stalin, and their successors—had complete political control over the COMECON member-countries. In addition to the Soviet Union, they were Bulgaria, Cuba, Czechoslovakia, East Germany, Hungary, Mongolia, Poland, Romania, and Vietnam. Yugoslavia had observer status and participated in many COMECON projects. Afghanistan, Angola, Ethiopia, Laos, Mozambique, and South Yemen tried to adapt the Soviet-style planned economy to their countries and took part on a lesser scale.

◻ Background and Flaw

The Council for Mutual Economic Assistance, which in practice proved to be neither mutual nor economic, was founded by Stalin in 1949 as the Soviet response to the U.S. Marshall Plan, which was rebuilding the economies of Western Europe. COMECON sought to integrate its members' economies through the pooling of capital and other resources and extensive specializa-

Breaking Up Is Hard To Do. Conversion to free-market economics sounds fine in theory. In practice, obstacles abound.

Paul Davies

tion. The economic aim was to achieve both economies of scale and improvement in quality. The political aim was to orient the member-countries toward the Soviet Union and away from the West.

At its peak in the 1950s, COMECON accounted for an estimated 30 percent of world industrial output. In theory, it should have created a dynamic, expanding market for its members, but its isolation from the world economy deprived it of the discipline of international competition and cost-based pricing. This hastened the collapse of the members' state-controlled economies and of COMECON itself.[2]

◻ Aftermath of Collapse

The newly liberated nations of Eastern and Central Europe, after four decades of Soviet domination, tried to turn abruptly to the West, but old trade habits die hard, and a zero-sum game with no winners developed. Trade among the former COMECON members during the first quarter of 1991 fell to just 10 percent of the volume of the corresponding 1990 period, causing shortages in all the economies.[3]

◻ Change More Slowly

COMECON locked its members into a rigid and technologically inhibiting relationship. They now realize that as much as they would like economic integration with the West, they still need each other, although the degree of need varies from country to country. Although Poland and Hungary are having some success exporting to the West, Bulgaria, Czechoslovakia, and Romania still depend heavily on the old COMECON area.

A new body called the Organization for International Economic Cooperation has been proposed as COMECON's replacement. But the Hungarians and Poles prefer the idea of a free trade area at least in their part of Europe.[4]

THE NEW EAST

In this section, we exclude the PRC from the East countries. The situation and developments in the PRC differ so much from those in the former COMECON countries that we deal with it separately later in this chapter.

◻ The Former Soviet Union: Current Developments

In the former Soviet Union, the command economy is dead, but the market is little to be seen. This prompts a disturbing question: Just how far can the economy fall? Industrial and agricultural output are down, and forecasts are gloomy. Hyperinflation is being pushed by round-the-clock running of two ruble printing presses and the two state mints pumping new but potentially useless currency into the economy.

The output of oil, which has been the country's main foreign exchange earner, is falling from 607 million tons in 1989 to an estimated 440 million tons in 1992. It is feared there may not be enough to export.[5]

In October 1991, Soviet officials projected a frightening widening of the nation's budget deficit. It will be about 14 percent of the Soviet equivalent of gross national product compared with 4.1 percent in 1990. More bad news was that the Soviet foreign debt totaled $65 billion. And, worse, inflation in the first eight months of 1991 was 100 percent.[6]

What to do?   Dr. James R. Wilburn, an economic advisor to officials of the Russian Federation, lists the country's needs.

- Overhaul the physical infrastructure, which is currently sadly deficient. This includes telecommunications, highways, and railroads. While it is nearly two and one half times as large as the United States, the Soviet Union has only about one fourth as many roads, and one fourth of those are unpaved and subject to disappearing when the spring thaw turns dirt tracks into unpassable quagmires. Entire trains disappear, sometimes to be found months later, their cargoes stolen.
- Overhaul the economic infrastructure. Create modern systems of banking, finance, distribution, and wholesale trade.
- Revamp the legal system. Clarify legal rights affecting private property ownership and basic business dealings.
- Make money meaningful. The ruble is discredited, but a convertible currency is necessary whether it is called a ruble or something else.

- Create capitalists. Give people the incentives and skills to produce more, better, and faster.
- Persuade the West to help. The West should provide know-how, technology, and investment.

Dr. Wilburn comments, "There's no painless way to make the transition from communism to free enterprise."[7]

The Harvard Plan.   Prior to the August 1991 coup attempt to overthrow Mikhail Gorbachev, he had rejected a plan for the Soviet Union put forward by a group of Harvard professors and Soviet economists. However, Boris Yeltsin embraced the plan, and he became much more powerful after the coup. The Harvard plan is similar to the one outlined above. One addition is that the Harvard plan would accord IMF and World Bank membership to the government(s) that succeed the Soviet Union.[8] In October 1991, the Soviet Union was granted associate IMF membership, but by 1992 there was no longer a Soviet Union, and Russia was granted the Soviet membership.

Joint ventures (JVs) and cooperatives.   In 1988 and 1989, JVs were so hot that foreigners in Moscow joked about the new form of Russian greeting— "Hello! my name is Ivan. Would you like to start a joint venture with me?" But the mood has changed. "In my opinion," says Gerald A. Manassov, a former official of the Soviet State Statistics Committee, "everyone is disappointed with joint ventures."

Probably the most famous JV is the McDonald's on Pushkin Square in Moscow. But it took 14 years to work out, and the Canadian partners finally decided that they could only solve the problem of undependable Soviet supplies by setting up their own farm and bakery. The Soviet magazine, *New Times,* told of a hapless JV that had to fight the bureaucracy for a year to get a rubber stamp needed for most official documents.[9]

Not all JV news is bad. The Soviet State Statistics Committee stated that although JVs are a tiny and embattled part of the economy, they are growing strongly.[10] A Hong Kong TV manufacturer has inaugurated a trilateral JV using a Russian factory and a Chinese distributor in the PRC. It has already received orders for 100,000 sets in the republic of Uzbekistan.[11]

The cooperative movement started in 1987 as the U.S.S.R. permitted private businesses to operate. They began in consumer services and expanded into light industry and other services.

Cooperatives were successful, and their owners began making good incomes, which aroused animosity and envy among nonowners and government officials. The government passed new laws forbidding cooperatives from engaging in many forms of business, putting price controls on products and services they were permitted to sell, and giving the 15 Soviet states unlimited rights to tax cooperatives. The new laws were condemned by Lev Nikferov, a specialist in the cooperative section of the Soviet Academy of Sciences. He warned that those laws could lead to the end of the cooperatives.[12] Now that the Soviet Union has dissolved, each of the independent states will deal with private business in its own fashion.

Small free markets.   A Russian widow asked for a death certificate after her husband's funeral, but authorities first demanded back his tobacco ration coupons. "Tobacco is for the living," officials in the Lipetsk region south of Moscow told the woman.

In 1991, a Soviet newspaper reported a lucrative black market trade in death certificates in a Siberian town because they give bereaved families the right to a suit to bury male relatives. Of course many survivors buried dead relatives in old suits, keeping the new ones for themselves.[13]

Buy shares of a Soviet company?   Kamaz, the country's largest truck manufacturer, in 1990 became the first big state-owned firm to turn itself into a joint stock company. In 1991, it became the first to take the next step by offering a second block of shares for sale to raise more cash. Stock trading is primitive in the ex-Soviet Union, so selling for a capital gain would not be easy. Kamaz is unlikely to pay much, if any, dividend. So, why would anyone buy its stock?

A block of 1,500 shares gives the shareholder the right to buy one Kamaz truck per year at the price fixed by the state, 32,000 rubles. So, most of the Kamaz shareholders are enterprises needing trucks, such as transport companies and collective farms. In addition, Kamaz trucks can be sold on the free market for up to 230,000 rubles.

Like its customers, Kamaz is now trying to cement ties with its own suppliers by taking a stake in them. It has already accomplished that with its drive shaft supplier and is planning to do so with others. Westerners call this *vertical integration,* but, in a crumbling command economy, it may be a way of replacing central planners in an effort to avoid chaos.[14]

▫ The Former Soviet Union: Looking Ahead

The choice is stark: some kind of Commonwealth of Independent States or a breakup, and there is the probability of civil wars. On the positive side, it was the power of the people that frustrated the August 1991 coup attempt. There were crowds, not mobs; protests, not looting; clarity of purpose, not confusion. The people have won the respect of the rulers who will now be wary of abusing their power.

One result has been that, under duress, Mikhail Gorbachev dissolved the Communist party. The party insisted on the loyalty of the bureaucracy, police, and armed services. It watched over all education. It published a newspaper called *Truth (Pravda),* which was full of lies. The party was not just a political poison; it dominated and deadened the whole economy too.

Who owns what land?   Fifteen republics have been caged inside the Soviet Union for most of the 20th century, and in different degrees they all long to get out. It could be a messy, even bloody, process.

The internal borders of the Soviet Union were changed 90 times between 1921 and 1991, and someone resented each change. Of the 23 borders between the republics, 20 are disputed. Boris Yeltsin, president of the huge Russian republic, talks of taking pieces of adjacent republics into Russia, which has raised his neighbors' fears of a new imperialism.

What people are where?   Not only land borders were moved; the Soviet schemers and planners also moved people—mostly Russians—around. Some 25 million Russians now live outside Russia. In Kazakhstan and Kirghizia, the natives barely make a majority; so when they start taunting the Soviet old guard, they will also be taunting—and perhaps attacking—their neighbors down the street. Thus, ethnic battles could arise within as well as between the republics.

The world has had a foretaste of that kind of civil war in Yugoslavia. A miniversion of the Soviet Union once held together by Marx and machine guns, Yugoslavia is now splitting apart as republics want out and tribe turns on tribe. Multiply the Yugoslav population by 12, the land area by 100; throw in 30,000 nuclear warheads and an equally tangled history. Welcome to the disintegrating Soviet Union, and stand by for big trouble.

In autarky, failure.   The breakaway republics will want the trappings of economic autonomy to complement their flags, parliaments, and ambassadors. But such trappings could trap them in an economic future with an alarming resemblance to Latin America's past. Political pride demanding economic "self-sufficiency" will lead to economic disaster.

Attempts at self-sufficiency will cut the republics off from many of their customers and suppliers because much of their trade has been with each other. Protection of their industries, separate national—probably nonconvertible—currencies, and currency exchange controls will reduce trade and standards of living, which are low already.

Moreover, foreign investors will not bring money, technology, and marketing skills to small, poor markets. Investment and joint venture interest in pieces of the former Soviet Union will be small.

Western assistance.   Stopping autarky is the greatest contribution Westerners can make to the republics' health. They should offer trade agreements to the republics so that farms and factories can sell to the rich markets of the West. Eastern access to those markets would in turn attract investment in the East by Western companies anxious to supply the markets from plants or farms using the well-educated, low-wage labor of the republics.

A loose, voluntary confederation of the republics as democracies with private property, market economies, a convertible currency, and free trade should be the goal. It would benefit not only the republics, but the world. That will be terribly difficult to accomplish, and for years there will be tensions, economic dislocation, and probably a lot more fighting in the disintegrating empire. It is to be hoped that help from the West may minimize the difficulties.[15]

◻ East Europe

The Worldview, "Pointing Way to Prosperity for East Europe Countries," presents an excellent overview of the East European situation and some country-to-country differences. Supplementing that, we discuss some difficulties and hopes for the region. Hong Kong, ever alert for export markets, is finding some there.

Realities chill investment climate.   The parting of the iron curtain was accompanied by euphoria of would-be Western investors as they thought of a 130-million-person market. A cold dose of reality followed close behind. Blaming everything from state bureaucracy, regional politics, and the recession in the West to radical environmentalists and demands for bribes from entrenched communists, countless Western investors have aborted, delayed, or scaled back their entry into Eastern Europe. By one estimate, 90 percent of

WORLDVIEW
Pointing Way to Prosperity for East Europe Countries

As we approach the second anniversary of the revolutions in Eastern Europe, it becomes clear that none of the countries has found an open road to prosperity. Their experience is mixed, but some general lessons can be learned.

First, no one knows how to plan the transformation of a command economy into a market economy. Thick plans that lay out a sequence of steps to be taken are worthless. The best course is to scrap the old system as quickly as possible. Delay doesn't make change easier; it helps the old guard to grab the best properties for themselves.

Second, inflation is a serious risk. The risk is realized if the governments maintain the many subsidies to consumers and state enterprises and finance them by printing money. When prices are freed from controls, subsidies must be ended; the government must be willing to let living standards drop, and enterprises must get rid of their excess labor to control costs. If enterprises match the increase in prices with increased wages, their costs will rise and they will demand more subsidies. If they get them, inflation is almost certain to soar.

Third, markets are uncommon and competition is unknown. Even when companies are sold, they face little or no internal competition. To get more competition quickly, Eastern European economies must let world exports enter. This forces a wrenching adjustment as local products are forced to compete with foreign products at home and abroad.

Fourth, property rights are essential for efficiency, competition, and a well-functioning market system, but property rights are badly defined in these countries. All of them have been slow to privatize large state enterprises, but several countries have sold off many of the retail stores and service businesses.

Fifth, statistics are unreliable, so they cannot be used to guide decisions. In Poland and probably elsewhere, the measurement of production reports what is happening in the state industries. Private production and the output of new enterprises is estimated at 20 percent of the total but is not recorded in official statistics. Reported declines in output overstate the drop in production and living standards. Markets are growing in many of these countries, but market transactions are not recorded.

Sixth, several Eastern European countries agreed to make restitution of the property claims of former owners. Adjudication of claims takes time and delays the sale and revitalization of factories, businesses, and housing. This, in turn, delays the recovery. Payment of compensation to prior owners, instead of restitution of property, allows the transformation to proceed.

Seventh, the breakdown of COMECON—the communists' block trading arrangement—and the collapse of the Soviet economy have been hard blows for Eastern Europe. These countries now demand hard-currency payment and must pay hard currency for oil from the Soviet

the Western businesspeople who investigate investments in Eastern Europe go home without opening their purses or wallets.[16]

Some specific disincentives were:

- A Polish steelmaker, offering itself for sale, claimed to be earning generous profits. But the deal fell through when the Western investors learned the company had been getting its iron ore "free" from the state.

- An equipment contract was not entered after a Polish bureaucrat grilled a California businessman seeking a license: "Are you a Jew? You look like a Jew to me."

- A big U.S. motel chain was scared out of Czechoslovakia by the demand of a communist bureaucrat for a "fee to facilitate" the investment. Such a payment would be illegal under American law.

Union. Trade has slowed as a result, causing large losses of output and employment.

Eighth, setting the wrong exchange magnifies the cost of adjustment. Germany and Poland are opposite examples. The prosperous West Germans "helped" their East German cousins by exchanging East German marks at an effective rate of 1.8 to 1. This gave the East Germans a big boost in purchasing power that many used to buy Western goods. But, after the exchange, costs of products in East Germany were far above costs in competing countries. Many factories became uncompetitive and were forced to close. Poland took the opposite course. The Poles stabilized the currency at an exchange rate that favored exports in the first year of readjustment. Their pains were severe but less than in eastern Germany, where unemployment rates may reach 40 percent to 50 percent by year's end.

Achievements and commitment to reform differ from country to country, but there are some common features.

Poland, Hungary, and Czechoslovakia have made the most dramatic changes. All have made major transformations to establish democratic political systems and market economies. Currencies are convertible. Western goods are available and prices are decontrolled. Each has developed its own way of privatizing state enterprises.

Romania, Bulgaria, Albania, and Yugoslavia have not freed themselves fully from communist rule, and they have not established stable, democratic political systems and other requisites for a market system. The evolution of these countries is uncertain. At best, they will drift downward.

The former East Germany is in a different position than the others. As part of Germany, it is able to export to members of the European Community. Once the union was complete, eastern Germany had established legal, accounting, financial, and tax systems and developed social benefits and transfers. Yet, despite these advantages, the transition has been one of the most difficult.

Why? There is no single answer. German law imposes high costs for social benefits and pollution control. Also important is the assistance eastern Germans get from western Germans. Eastern Germans know they don't have to make the hard choices that the Poles and Czechoslovaks have made, so they are slow to adjust, demand wage increases up to 60 percent, and collect transfers when they are unemployed.

There is a lesson there about aid to Eastern Europe. The West should help by opening markets, not by offering financial assistance and loans to central governments.

Reprinted by permission of Allan H. Meltzer, University Professor of Economics and Visiting Scholar, American Enterprise Institute.

- A New Hampshire resort developer proposed a major ski complex in Czechoslovakia's Tatras Mountains but was driven out by the environmentalist Greens party.[17]

Germany. Given their common language, currency, culture, and history—except for 45 years of communist rule in East Germany—one would think investors from the former West Germany would have smooth sailing into the East. It ain't necessarily so; those 45 years loom large. BASF, the German chemical giant, was one of the first investors in the former East Germany, buying a chemical company there. The litany of problems it experienced—some of which follow—won't encourage many other investors.

- BASF had difficulty purging from the staff former communist apparatchiks unwilling to cooperate with plant modernization.
- It had to rewire the old telephone network, which was bugged.

- When drawing up the eastern company's first real set of accounts, BASF found that some 20 percent of total costs went for the factory's outdoor heated swimming pool, a hospital, and an abattoir.
- The factory buses that carry employees to and from their residential neighborhoods leave before the end of the workday and, therefore, so do the employees.
- About 40 percent of the eastern firm's output went to Eastern Europe, mostly Russia, and another 40 percent went to East German customers. Those sales have fallen by three quarters. The Russians still place orders but cannot pay for them.

Nevertheless, BASF insists that eventually its eastern investment will pay off, and it is investing another DM500 million for further expansion. The majority of the eastern employees know that most of eastern Germany's chemical industry is being shut down, and they are willing to cooperate with BASF's radical reshaping of the plant. The eastern labor force is still relatively cheap, about half the cost of western equivalents. But BASF says it is unlikely ever to buy another east German chemical plant.[18]

Other investments in Eastern Europe.   One American firm that appears on the way to a successful Eastern European investment is Levi Strauss. Thanks in part to the eagerness and cooperation of the people and government of the Polish town of Plock (pronounced Pwotsk), the Levi's producer has been able to cut through red tape and other obstacles to set up production in the town.[19]

Some other U.S. companies invested in Eastern Europe are shown in Figure 17–1. The figure details the country, amount invested, and the type of project.

The EC and the East.   In a hopeful move, the EC slowly is opening trade doors to the East over a 10-year period starting in 1993. The Eastern countries would like it to be faster, but "sensitive" commodities such as coal, steel, farm goods, and textiles are involved, and they are jealously protected by various EC members.

A compromise in the farm goods area would see food bought by the EC from Eastern countries diverted as food aid to other Eastern countries. For example, meat would go to parts of the ex–Soviet Union and wheat to Albania.

Poland, Hungary, and Czechoslovakia are a step closer to EC membership. They became the EC's first associate members.[20]

Hong Kong sells to East Europe.   Hong Kong companies are making inroads into Eastern European markets. Poland is their biggest market, while Hungary, Czechoslovakia, and the Russian markets are also growing.

A Hong Kong pioneer in those markets is Styland Holdings, which sells clothes and electronics. In return for its goods, it gets canned foods and textiles that it sells in Western Europe. If Styland is unable to get salable Eastern European goods, it insists on payment in U.S. dollars.[21]

Pollution.   An immense problem for East Europe is pollution. As Soviet troops are pulling out of the occupied countries, they are leaving a legacy of pollution. One writer reports that "after 40 years, once victorious soldiers will be remembered for creating a trail of disaster."[22] Soviet soldiers were not

□ **FIGURE 17–1**
U.S. Companies in Eastern Europe

While American firms have been slower than those in other nations to invest in the rebuilding of Eastern Europe, the list of U.S. projects is growing. Here are examples of large-scale U.S. corporate investment in manufacturing and commerce in the region. Some dollar figures are estimates.

Company	Country	Amount (millions)	Type of Project
General Motors	Eastern Germany	$630	Car assembly
	Hungary	$200	Car assembly, engine production
Coca-Cola	Eastern Germany	$450	Soft drink plants, distribution network in 12 cities
	Hungary	$14	Bought control of two bottling plants
	Poland	$110	11 new bottling plants
General Electric	Hungary	$197	Bought 75% of lighting manufacturer Tungsram
Guardian Industries	Hungary	$120	Bought 80% of Hungarian Glass Works
Golub & Co. and A. Epstein & Sons	Poland	$100	Office complex
Ford	Hungary	$80	Fuel pump, ignition coil production
Sara Lee	Hungary	$50–60	Bought control of food firm Compack
Schwinn	Hungary	n.a.	Bought control of bike maker Csepel
U.S. West and Bell Atlantic	Czechoslovakia	$50	Cellular phones
Marriott	Poland	$20–40	Hotel
U.S. West	Hungary	$11	Cellular phones
United Technologies	Hungary	$10	Auto wiring harness production

Note: n.a. = not available.

Source: *Los Angeles Times,* July 9, 1991, p. A6.

the only polluters. The Eastern countries' industries polluted themselves, their neighbors, and nearby waterways. Figure 17–2 gives an indication of the extent and types of pollution.

THE PEOPLE'S REPUBLIC OF CHINA (PRC)

Often, images of trade with the PRC do not represent reality: The myth of the China market has persisted although consumer demand has never approached Western expectations. China, an agrarian nation, has always been desperately poor, surviving on a subsistence level except for a tiny wealthy elite. The Confucian class has now been replaced by the elitist Communist party. Although this remains true, change is under way. If the rapid economic growth of the PRC coastal provinces continues and spreads to the rest of the country, the old myth may become reality.

After the communist armies forced the nationalist forces off the mainland to Taiwan in 1949, American contacts with the mainland were almost nonexistent until 1970. By then the PRC leadership had apparently embarked on

□ **FIGURE 17–2   Polluted Eastern Europe**

The nations of Eastern Europe and the region's seas all have severe environmental problems. Some of the worst are listed below:

A   **North Sea:**
  • Heavy-metals pollution: mercury, cadmium, lead.
B   **Black Sea:**
  • 90% biologically dead from pollutants.
  • Beaches periodically closed because of bacterial pollution.
C   **Baltic Sea:**
  • Much of the sea floor lifeless due to nitrogen compounds and organic wastes.
  • Beaches periodically closed because of pollution.

D   **Poland:**
  • Little or no air polution control.
  • Half the cities and 35% of industry do not treat waste.
  • Children have five times the lead of Danish children.
  • Air pollution damage to 82% of forests.
E   **Eastern Germany:**
  • A third of rivers and 9,000 lakes biologically dead.
  • Air pollution damage to 57% of forests.
  • 15,000 unmonitored hazardous waste dumps.
F   **Czechoslovakia:**
  • Heavy air pollution.
  • 70% of rivers badly polluted; 50% of drinking water below national standards.
  • 30% of children have allergies.
G   **Hungary:**
  • 1 of every 17 deaths blamed on air pollution.
  • 44% of plants only do crude treatment of sewage.
  • 700 of the country's 3,000 urban wells contaminated.
  • 750 plant and 150 animal species declared endangered or rare.
H   **Romania:**
  • 80% of river water unpotable.
  • Improperly stored radioactive waste.
  • Massive over-logging of forests.
I   **Bulgaria:**
  • Some children have extremely high lead levels.
  • Erosion damage to 80% of agricultural land.
  • Air pollution damage to 78% of forests.
J   **Yugoslavia:**
  • Sava River watershed heavily polluted.
  • Adriatic Sea coastline polluted by sewage, toxics.
  • Air pollution from coal burning, leaded gasoline.
  • 17,500 acres of agricultural land lost annually to urban sprawl, soil erosion, acid rain.
K   **Albania:**
  • Air and rivers polluted.
  • 10% of land drained, destroying wetlands.
  • Tirana, the capital city, does not treat its sewage.

Source: *Los Angeles Times,* July 12, 1991, p. A17.

a fundamental reappraisal of policies that included a new perception of the military threat posed by the Soviet Union.

During the early 1970s, the United States was winding down its Vietnam involvement while observing the U.S.S.R.'s growing military might. Both the PRC and the United States perceived each other as counterweights against the U.S.S.R., and they began political and trade relations based on mutual political advantage. In the matter of trade, the success of the changed relationship can be seen by comparing the U.S.–PRC trade figure of 1971, which was $4.9 million, to that of 1990, when it surged to some $22 billion. Exports continued to rise in 1991 while imports were flat, and that combination led to U.S. complaints that its big trade deficit with the PRC was due in large part to Chinese obstacles to importation of U.S. goods and services.

Chinese trade barriers were only part of U.S. complaints. The PRC was also accused of exporting prison-made goods, falsely labeling them as made in nonprison factories. Another major U.S. complaint was PRC abuse of intellectual property rights such as patents and copyrights.[23]

The U.S. trade deficit with the PRC declined from 1983 through 1985, when it was only about $6 million. But from 1986 through 1990, the deficit exploded to over $10 billion, illustrated in Figure 17–3.

□ **FIGURE 17–3**
The U.S. Trade Deficit with China (US$ billions)

Source: U.S. Commerce Dept.

The United States is not alone in running a trade deficit with the PRC. As Figure 17–4 illustrates, from 1989 to 1990, the PRC's $5.6 billion trade deficit turned around, shooting up to an $8.5 billion surplus. The figure also shows current account numbers.

□ A Capitalist People's Republic of China?

Although the PRC bureaucratic maze is probably second to none, some developments are now under way that would have shocked Chairman Mao.* The PRC is admitting foreign, private ownership of production facilities within the country, flirting with corporate stock issues, and investing abroad.

Joint ventures (JVs).   In 1979, the PRC published a **joint venture** law, and companies came from America, Europe, Japan, and elsewhere to try the Chinese market. At first the influx was slow due to vagaries in the law, so the Chinese released an implementing act in 1983 to clarify the law, and more foreign firms moved in.

joint venture (as used in this chapter) a West firm operating in an East country in some form of cooperation with an agency of the East country government or with one of the new private organizations that are springing up

JV difficulties in the PRC.   Although some 666 joint ventures were in place by 1986, the difficulties for foreigners operating in the PRC caused some failures, losses, and low-profit or low-quality products. As a result, the first nine months of 1986 saw a 40 percent decline in foreign investments. This so concerned the government that it began giving seminars featuring successful joint ventures. The profitable foreign venturers told others how they had done it. Some of the keys are:

Insist on the right to hire and fire employees and to reward good workers with bonuses or otherwise.

Establish good training programs.

Choose the right location even if the costs are higher.

Obtain the support of local as well as Beijing authorities.

Be prepared to invest in infrastructure, such as power cables and water pipes.

* Mao Tse-tung was the absolute dictator of the PRC until his death in 1976.

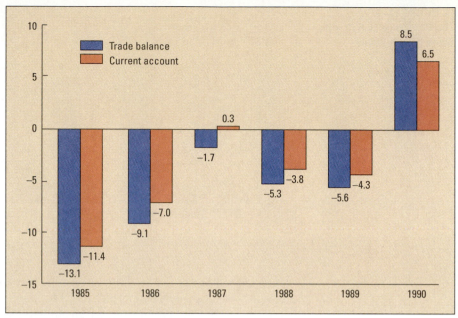

Source: U.S. Commerce Dept.

□ **FIGURE 17–4**
PRC Trade and Current Account (US$ billions)

Keep quality standards high.

Establish reliable foreign suppliers, because PRC sources may be unreliable.

The best technology isn't necessarily the most advanced; the technology should be easy to learn and maintain.[24]

Specific difficulties for the foreign firm in a PRC JV include getting out profits or interest in convertible currency, finding qualified employees, and, even more difficult, firing employees. Both types of problems can be ameliorated by making clear, detailed agreements with the Chinese JV partner before investing. It is extremely important for these agreements to be approved by the highest appropriate PRC government agency; the Chinese partner—or local bureaucrats—may have inflated notions of their own power and fail to consult their superiors.[25]

The PRC is given to sudden policy shifts and zigzags, which make business management very difficult. In October 1988, China abruptly adopted stiff measures to slow economic growth, including import restrictions and a credit squeeze. JVs that needed some foreign source components and those that needed operating capital from PRC banks—which is virtually all of them—suffered.[26]

These import restrictions and credit squeezes contributed to the huge 1991 balance-of-trade deficit that the United States was so upset about, as we discussed above. But in addition, the PRC has many ways of blocking imports, including a complex system of tariff and nontariff controls to restrict foreign companies' access to its domestic market.[27]

Corporate stock.   In 1983, the PRC authorized three enterprises to raise money by selling stock to private buyers. Many residents of the country, plus overseas Chinese and others, are potential buyers, but there are obstacles to the widespread, successful use of stock sales to raise capital for Chinese companies. Diehard communist cadres have to be convinced that stock issues are just a means of raising money and do not mean the PRC is giving up communism. Managers have to learn to report to a board of directors and be answerable to shareholders. The legal status of stock companies needs to be established in the PRC, and the mechanics of issuing and trading securities must be learned. Officials at the Bank of China's overseas branches and its 12 affiliates are probably ready to assist with the procedural problems.[28]

Until September 1986, there was no formal, legal method to trade the securities. Then, for the first time since the communists came to power in 1949, the government authorized the establishment of a stock and bond exchange, in Shanghai. Public interest and trading are growing, but there is opposition. A number of Communist party faithful complain that a stock exchange is capitalist. The banks complain that people withdraw their deposits to buy securities.[29]

It must be recognized that the PRC is engaged in a unique historic experiment. It is attempting to liberalize toward a free market economy with private ownership of securities and private operation of farms and factories, while maintaining rigid Communist party control of the government and large parts of industry. Tensions grew and finally snapped at Beijing's Tienanmen Square in June 1989.

Political backlashes.   The liberalization movement has been led by Deng Xiaoping, who was 85 years old in 1989, and many wondered whether his moderate, pragmatic policies would continue after his death or retirement. The American State Department felt there were enough like-minded leaders behind Deng to prevent reversal of his policies. However, others remember the "let a thousand flowers bloom" era under Mao Tse-tung. Mao encouraged playrights, poets, and writers to speak out without fear of government reprisal. Quite a number of people took him at his word, and there was an outpouring of works that could not have been published previously. Suddenly, Mao changed his mind and his policy. The people who had spoken out were imprisoned, sent to labor gangs, or otherwise punished.

During 1986, Chinese students from a dozen campuses began to march and demonstrate for political democracy, which is anathema to a communist government. After some hesitation, the government began to suppress the students, and the students returned to campus. One result was that the Communist party chief, Hu Yaobang, was forced to resign because of accusations that he encouraged the students' demands for democratization.

Hu's downfall began a six-month campaign against "bourgeois liberalism," and in March 1989, a reporter for the *Financial Times* stated, "The halcyon days of China's economic and political liberalism appear to be over." Xinhua, the official Chinese news agency, made an unusually strident attack on Western influence, stating, "The Chinese people suffered enough from foreign invasions. . . . The Chinese people have become masters of themselves. . . . Copying foreign political systems and experiences will not save China."[30]

Hu's death in April 1989 triggered an outpouring of student sympathy and renewed demands for political democracy. Despite government crackdown

Chinese troops beginning to
clear students out of
Tienanmen Square, June 3,
1989.

J. Langevin/SYGMA

threats, the student marches and calls for "democracy" spread from campus
to campus.[31]

As the students' demonstrations continued and grew while the government
refused to talk with their representatives and failed to use force to disperse
them, the students were joined by workers and others. Although demonstrations and marches occurred in many parts of the country, the ones that received the most attention were held in Tienanmen Square in the capital,
Beijing. The demonstrators, unarmed and peaceful, were requesting political
freedoms to accompany the new freedoms being applied to the economy. The
demonstrations and marches went on through May until the night of June 3,
1989.

Deng had encouraged economic liberalizations but would have no part of
political freedom for China. Zhao Ziyang, the party general secretary, was
the highest-ranking supporter of the students' goals and was ousted from
power in May. Then, supported by other hardliners such as Li Peng, Deng
ordered the "People's Liberation Army" to open fire and to use its tanks to
crush—sometimes literally—the demonstrations and the demonstrators.

The army moved in during the nights of June 3 and 4, and according to
observers—both Chinese and foreign—and the foreign press, thousands

were killed. This action was followed by months of arrests of people who had been involved, many of whom were summarily executed.

The Chinese government dismissed the Tienanmen massacre, saying that because the demonstrators had attacked and killed many of the soldiers, the square had to be cleared and the demonstrators dispersed. The government invited foreign businesspeople, most of whom had fled the country, to return and resume business as usual. Those people and their companies had to make decisions involving safety, ethics, and finance.

Ethically, do foreign companies want to do business with a government that ruthlessly butchers its own people? The fact is the PRC's civil rights record has been dreadful for years, yet foreign governments and firms have chosen to look the other way. Recently it seemed possible that civil rights might improve, particularly if Zhao took power when Deng retired or died. But, beginning on June 3, 1989, when the government's brutal suppression was televised for several days before the foreign media were evicted, the probability of a more humane PRC seemed far less likely.

With regard to financial considerations, because China is a huge potential market just beginning to open, a firm would not want to be beaten out by its competitors. Because change is constant in China, there is the possibility that Zhao or other like-thinkers could return to power, creating even greater business opportunities for foreign firms.

Post–Tienanmen PRC.   Before the end of 1990, U.S. companies were ending their unofficial moratorium on new investment in the PRC, encouraged to do so by the U.S. government in the person of the American ambassador to the PRC, James R. Lilley, whose argument was that U.S. companies now had more negotiating leverage with the Chinese, who are anxious to get foreign investment and are very flexible.[32] So during 1991, many American and other foreign companies were quietly scoring more successes in the PRC than at any time since economic reform began there in 1979. Some are manufacturing for export and for the PRC domestic market, while others are exporting to that market and watching their sales grow.

But most foreign companies are reluctant to talk about their PRC successes for fear of being "associated with the butchers of Beijing." They are afraid that even if the PRC keeps its most favored nation (MFN) status with the United States, the debate about MFN, including arguments about PRC civil rights violations, will bring political pressure and bad publicity to U.S. firms doing business there.[33]

In December 1990, a new stock exchange opened in Shanghai, but there were no senior PRC leaders at the opening ceremonies, raising questions about top-level support. After Mao's thousand flowers and Deng's Tienanmen Square, Chinese economic and political freedom seekers must always look over their shoulders.[34]

But then in March 1991, the PRC premier, Li Peng, called in officials for a briefing on the ABCs of stock markets. Officials of security markets are encouraged that the top leaders of the government and the party are taking an interest, and other cities including Canton and Shenyang are lobbying Beijing to allow them to open their own stock exchanges.[35]

Southern PRC has one of the world's boom economies. By 2000, its coastal provinces could be as rich as southern Europe—if politics lets the boom go on.

The economic reforms that Deng Xiaoping introduced in 1979 had two main themes. The first, applied throughout rural PRC (where four fifths of Chinese still live), was to restore the family farm and let the market set most farm prices. Rural incomes doubled in six years, creating two things still sorely lacking in the republics of the former Soviet Union: a constituency for reform and a solid base for further growth.

The second vital part of Deng's reforms, which also distinguished the PRC from other would-be reformers like the Soviets and India, was the "open door," a cautious welcome for foreign firms and somewhat free trade. The provinces along PRC's coast were set free first; fourteen cities were given the status of "coastal open cities" with freedoms and tax breaks for foreign trade and investment. Also created were five "special economic zones" (SEZs) with greater privileges still.

The results were explosive. Shenzhen, one of the SEZs, is an example. In 1979, Shenzhen had 100,000 inhabitants, mostly poor farmers and fishermen. Today there are more than 2 million people, glossy high rises, a limitless supply of prostitutes, traffic jams, and a GDP per capita close to $2,000 per year.[36]

Look out, Western Europe. The PRC will catch you unless ideology interrupts.

Two Chinas.   There are two Chinas. Not the old two Chinas of communist Beijing and nationalist Taipei, but the political fiction as concocted in Beijing and the life as lived by the Chinese people. When these two Chinas mix in any room, there are embarrassing, awkward silences.

After Tienanmen, the Communist party reverted to heavy ideological propaganda that had nothing to do with the reality of PRC life. As a result, an experienced Hong Kong businessman stated, "I think it is no longer possible for them to make a quiet transition away from communism."

The failure of the hard-liners' coup in the Soviet Union served to heighten the post-Tienanmen paranoia of PRC leaders. After all, the Soviet plotters had all been handpicked by President Gorbachev. Whom could you trust?

The PRC leaders launched a campaign to test the loyalty of senior cadres. When asked to describe the test, a party historian said, "They're being told to point at a deer and call it a horse."[37]

In closed crisis meetings held in late 1991, the PRC Communist party failed to agree about who should own the means of production. Party pragmatists argued that the inefficient state-owned factories should be made more responsive to the market while nonstate industry should be allowed to flourish. But party ideologues were in favor of pumping more funds into state factories and increasing state control over the thriving nonstate sector.[38]

The contrast between the success of the PRC's private-sector business and the failure of its state-owned firms is stark. But ideology dies hard, and the ideologues control the army and police—or at least they controlled enough of them in 1989 to crush the students and workers calling for democracy in Tienanmen Square.

One consideration that may influence the ideologues to moderate their stance is the PRC's successful foreign investment progress, as indicated by investments in private business outside the PRC.

Investments abroad.   Since 1979, the PRC has invested in over 700 joint ventures outside China. These ventures were at first in trading houses, department stores, and servicing agencies, but in 1983, the emphasis changed to focus on manufacturing companies. The PRC wants overseas stakes in iron ore, aluminum, paper pulp, fertilizer, and fisheries projects and also wants to acquire technology and management skills.

In 1988, China invested $150 million abroad and, by the end of the year, had direct investments in 79 countries. The host countries ranged from LDCs to the most developed and included Australia, Canada, Hong Kong, Malaysia, Mauritius, Pakistan, the United States, and Zambia.[39]

When the PRC invests abroad, it must observe the market economy practices, laws, and regulations of the host country just as must any investor. And while every country has its bureaucracy, the PRC is in a class by itself in that regard.

Don't forget the bureaucratic maze.   The red tape is unbelievably costly and time consuming. It takes at least two years to start a business. In Shanghai, over 60 "chops" are required to get government approval of a project (chops are authorization stamps from various government bureaus—they even have a bureau governing the giving of prizes at parties). The bureaucracy created such obstacles that the mayor of Shanghai set up a new office—called the "one chop shoppe"—in an attempt to consolidate the bureaucratic maze.

Bribery of government officials is essential to get anything done. Even after government approval, there is a two-year wait to get a telephone, after which only 30 percent of local calls and 20 percent of long-distance ones make it through.[40]

The picture of the three men was drawn to illustrate the bureaucracy at "work." Each bureaucrat is indicating "not me" and pointing to another.

The bureaucrats were too much for one poor Western businessman. He was French and had been negotiating with the Chinese over a problem for a year and a half. When he believed he had finally resolved the matter and was preparing to board his aircraft for home, the Chinese came to him at the airport, saying another organization had not agreed to the terms. Problems remained. This was too much. The Frenchman was subsequently found running naked around Tienanmen Square and was taken out of China in a straitjacket.[41]

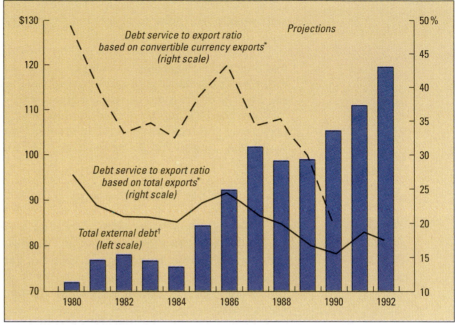

FIGURE 17–5
Eastern Europe Debt and Debt Service Ratios
(Excluding the U.S.S.R.; US$ billions)

*Based on debt service actually paid.
†Excludes liabilities to the Fund.
Source: *IMF World Economic Outlook,* May 1991, pp. 30–31.

EAST–WEST TRADE PROBLEMS

Getting paid for goods sold to the East is not easy. The Eastern nations' demand for Western goods and technology has been far greater than Western demand for Eastern exports. Therefore, the Eastern countries have not been able to pay for their imports with their exports.

The East Owes the West a Lot of Money

To finance East–West trade gaps, the countries of the late COMECON borrowed heavily from Western banks, institutions, and suppliers. The total external debt of Eastern Europe, excluding the Soviet Republics, amounted to $105 billion at the end of 1990, an increase of almost 7 percent over the previous year. By the end of 1992, the debt is projected to rise to $118 billion, and the debt service to export ratio is forecast to be 18.5 percent, up from 15 percent in 1990. This is illustrated in Figure 17–5.

By 1991, the former Soviet Union owed the West over $65 billion and faced a liquidity crisis on its hard-currency indebtedness. At the 1991 annual meeting of the IMF and World Bank in Bangkok, Hilmar Kopper, head of the board of managing directors of Deutsche Bank urged the G7 nations to make money available very quickly. He estimated $4 to 5 billion would be needed to avoid default or payment moratorium, which would be a serious blow to democratization in the Soviet states.[42]

The Eastern European countries and the states of the former U.S.S.R. are not the only communist or formerly communist nations with growing debts to the West. The PRC's external debt reached $50.2 billion in 1990, up from $46.9 billion the previous year. However, its debt as a percentage of exports

□ **FIGURE 17–6**
PRC Debt as Percentage of Exports (US$ billions)

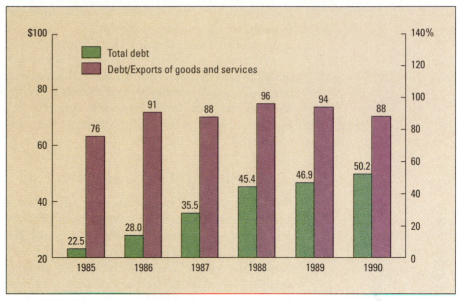

Source: *ABECOR Country Report,* March 1991.

declined to 88 percent in 1990, down from a high of 98 percent in 1988. This was due, of course, to growth in exports of PRC goods and services (see Figure 17–6).

The reasons for the East's trade deficits and resulting large debts are easily stated. The manufactured products of the East European countries are not of sufficient quality to compete in markets of the West against Western products. They do not export enough raw materials to pay for the imports they desire. In lower-technology or labor-intensive products in which their quality is competitive, they encounter protectionism due to pressure from labor unions in the Western countries. Nevertheless, as has been noted, in 1990, the PRC achieved a trade and current account surplus.

□ **Western Strategic Technology for the East?**

Because of long-standing East–West hostilities—the Warsaw Pact countries versus NATO; the cold war, or communism versus capitalism—the Western countries have limited the strategically useful technology they would sell to the East. To be sure, the countries have applied the limits with varying degrees of rigor—German and Japanese limits have probably been the leakiest, but there have been leaks from all Western countries. And successful Eastern espionage has stolen vast amounts of Western "secrets."

The Western agency charged with enforcing the limits is the Coordinating Committee on Multilateral Export Controls (CoCom), whose members are the NATO countries plus Japan and minus Iceland. Each member-country is responsible for enforcing the technology export limitations, and despite leaks and espionage, the consensus is that CoCom has prevented or at least delayed Eastern countries' receipt of militarily useful technology.

This situation is changing. CoCom restrictions on sales to China have been relaxed as its perceived strategic threat has abated. The Warsaw Pact has dissolved, and some CoCom members—notably the Germans—want more freedom to sell the East technology.[43]

In another major change, Third World countries such as Iran, Iraq, Libya, North Korea, and Syria replaced the Warsaw Pact countries on CoCom's worry list. After Desert Storm, UN investigators found that Iraq was close to developing nuclear weapons and rockets capable of delivering them as well as bacterial and poison gas weapons. Iraq, the other countries named above, and probably more received technology and hardware from CoCom member-countries.[44]

◻ Nevertheless, West Trades with East

So, as we see, the East has not been able to sell enough to the West to make the money to pay for what it wants to buy from the West. Nevertheless, there has been a large volume of trade between the West and the Soviet-dominated East, with the U.S. share shrinking after 1979. As the immense debts of the Soviet bloc to the West illustrate, a lot of that trade has been financed by credits from Western banks, suppliers, and governments. One method that the East favors to obtain goods and technology is **countertrade.** There are many varieties of countertrade, all of which involve the Western seller taking all or part of its payment in Eastern goods or services rather than in money. Still another device used by Western suppliers and Eastern customers is industrial cooperation between Western companies and Eastern factories through subcontracting, joint ventures, licensing, or other schemes to minimize the need for hard-currency payments East to West.

Both countertrade and industrial cooperation are important and growing means for maintaining trade between the industrial West and countries that are short of hard, convertible currency. Such countries include not only the East but also the many noncommunist developing countries, frequently called less developed countries or LDCs.

Another term used to identify those noncommunist LDCs is *Third World countries*. This means that in addition to the Third World there are two other "worlds" of countries, and those worlds are the East and the West.

Inasmuch as countertrade and industrial cooperation are as much applicable to West–LDC trade as they are to West–East trade, we shall deal with those subjects in more detail in Chapter 18. There we deal with finance, and both countertrade and industrial cooperation are used as substitutes for money.

In the West, resistance has developed to countertrade and industrial cooperation. Some of that resistance is directed particularly at the East, and so we shall discuss that here.

◻ Opposition to Countertrade and Industrial Cooperation

Resistance to Eastern goods is sometimes based on (1) the inferior quality of the goods and of Eastern technology, (2) damage to competing Western companies and their workers, or (3) damage to producers and their workers in friendly countries with which the West has trade agreements.

As to quality and technology, these may not be enduring problems. One need only remember the Japanese example. After World War II, Japanese

countertrade payment for imports at least in part with something other than money products were dismissed as inferior. Within 20 years, Japan was a world leader in technology and exports. Furthermore, it has been estimated that as many as 25 percent of all the scientists in the world are now employed in what was the U.S.S.R.[45] There are technical areas in which the ex-U.S.S.R. leads the United States, and there has been an increase of their patent registrations in the United States.[46]

Dumping.   Resistance to Eastern goods being imported into Western countries is sometimes based on damage to competing Western companies and their workers. Western companies and unions have begun to complain that Eastern products are being dumped in Western markets.

Dumping is selling in one export market at a price lower than prices charged in the domestic market or in third-country export markets. The sales prices may be lower than the production costs. *Predatory dumping* is dumping whose objective is to damage or destroy competitors in the country where the goods are dumped.

EC makers of steel, cars, chemicals, shoes, textiles, clothing, and electric motors are complaining loudly about unfair Eastern competition. Some of those EC producers, and related labor unions, are already getting protection from EC antidumping action, and others want more protection.[47]

In 1989, a dumping complaint was lodged against the Soviet Union for allegedly dumping the chemical, potassium permanganate, into the EC market. The complaint was on behalf of the Spanish company, Industrial Quimica de Nalon, which warned that its survival was threatened. It is the EC's only producer of this chemical.[48]

We mentioned above that the PRC exports products to the United States that are competitive with American products particularly sensitive to foreign competition. In addition to textiles, these include footwear, watches, electronics, and glass products.[49]

Attitude of American labor.   One American labor union official said building factories for Eastern-bloc countries (industrial cooperation) was fine if production was for their home markets. But he pointed out that if an Eastern factory exported its products to the West in payment for the factory, it would be difficult for noncommunist trade unionists—"who have the right to bargain collectively and to strike"—to compete with the controlled and subservient labor of the East.[50]

The union official was talking about the cost of the labor, one determinant of the price of goods produced. He was complaining that the East had an unfair cost advantage because it had the power to keep labor under its thumb.

Now that communism is fading in most of Eastern Europe and the Soviet republics, it remains to be seen whether free and strong labor unions will come into being. If they do, presumably the attitudes of Western labor leaders will change.

Competition with traditional suppliers and allies.   As to damage to suppliers and workers in friendly countries, it is clear that many Eastern exports will compete with products from other countries, particularly LDCs. The U.S. market has traditional suppliers and allies such as the Philippines, South Korea, Taiwan, Hong Kong, and Central and South American countries. The

dumping the selling abroad of products at prices lower than those charged in the producing country or in other national markets

EC countries have their ex-colonies in Africa and Asia, with which they maintain relatively close economic ties.

Some of these U.S. trading partners may exert behind-the-scenes pressures to protect their American markets. The countries mentioned above—the Philippines and so forth—all have embassies or representatives in the United States and friends in Congress and the executive branch. These can be expected to lobby for protection of their U.S. markets from the competition of Eastern countries.

□ PRC and Soviet Reforms Compared

Just as seemingly deep-seated forces are causing changes in the PRC, so also have changes in the former U.S.S.R. moved it away from the rigid, centralized, communist-state condition that characterized it for more than 70 years.

Differences. Start with agriculture. Soviet agriculture has never recovered from the dual blow of the Bolshevik Revolution and Joseph Stalin's war against the kulaks, as Russia's farmers were called. Stalin forced the creation of huge state farms and starved, murdered, or deported the kulaks. The communist Soviet Union was a predominantly urban economy, and the people who worked on the collectivized farms were nothing but hired hands with little interest in the output of the farms or the maintenance of their equipment. The tradition of an independent, self-employed farmer hardly survived, even as a folk memory, 60 years after eradication of the kulaks.

Thus Gorbachev's offer to lease land to the hired hands fell on uncomprehending and unenthusiastic ears. The farm workers were making low but living wages. Why give that up and take chances with their own plot of farmland?

By contrast, China at the end of the 1970s was still an overwhelmingly agrarian economy, and the experience of farm collectivization was only a decade-and-a-half old. It was already breaking down at the roots before Deng proclaimed reform from the top.

The results were startling as the Chinese farmers were given the freedom to grow and sell their own crops at market prices. Production soared, and many farmers became prosperous.

Not all Russian farmland was collectivized. Currently some 1.6 percent of its arable land is farmed by private farmers who can sell at market prices. That 1.6 percent of the land produces 30 percent of the food. About one third of the state farm crops never reach the consumer because of poor storage, poor transportation, poor roads, and poor refrigeration, but pests aplenty.

So, cooperation and participation by the people who must make it work are the major reasons the Chinese agricultural reforms were much more successful than those of the Soviet Union.

The same seems to have occurred with industrial reforms. As with agriculture, the reforms began sooner in the PRC than they did in the U.S.S.R. Probably more important, the communist system was not imposed in China until after the communists won their civil war in 1949. The system was put in place in the Soviet Union after the 1917 revolution. Many Chinese had experienced private business and farming and noncommunist governments; not so for the people of the U.S.S.R.

Lenin, a communist hero, comes off his pedestal.

Patricia Forester/ SYGMA

Intellectuals in the former U.S.S.R. are delighted at the prospects of reform. They want to be free to research, write, compose, publish, and travel. However, as Gorbachev has said, the reform will "bog down if we fail to rally the people to its cause." That is not proving easy.

Workers are willing to recognize that the number one problem is productivity, but the overwhelming majority tend to lay blame on almost anyone but themselves. Notably absent are references to the alcoholism, absenteeism, and general lethargy that continue to cripple production.

All this is scarcely surprising. Today's work force in what was the Soviet Union comes from a system that for generations treated the individual as little more than a meaningless cog in the wheel of production. The centralization of political and economic power has at best discouraged and at worst viciously punished individual innovation and initiative. Having endured decades of powerlessness and alienation from the basic decisions that affect their lives, the Soviet people seem numb.

□ Selling to the East Is Changing

Selling to the East has never been easy. The centrally planned economies those countries had made their institutions, trading techniques, and behavior quite different from those of the West.

In past editions of this book, we presented East countries' purchasing procedures in terms of Soviet practices, to which other East countries were similar. Those practices included 11 steps, from the decision that new equipment was needed to the point the foreign supplier was paid. It was a cumbersome, highly bureaucratic procedure, and suppliers grumbled about it.

Then, in 1986, Mikhail Gorbachev began making changes in the Soviet trade bureaucracies. Some of them lost their monopoly powers, and some individual enterprises were given the right to deal directly with foreigners. In

☐ **FIGURE 17–7**
East–West Broker

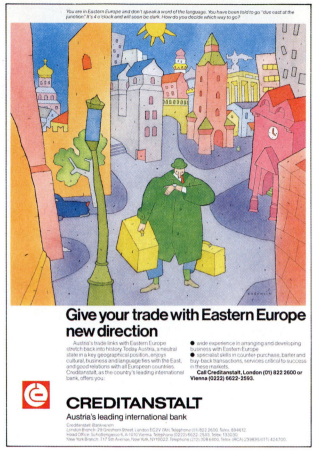

Courtesy of Creditanstalt

1988, the government abolished the all-powerful Ministry of Foreign Trade, a move heralded as the cornerstone of reform.

The results were confusion instead of simplification. The enterprise managers were not prepared for their new responsibilities, and, partly as a result, government ministries continued to impose binding instructions in the form of state orders covering up to (and sometimes more than) 100 percent of factories' output.[51]

The confusion was not only on the Soviets' side. Byzantine as it was, the pre-Gorbachev system of Soviet procurement had been learned by foreigners selling to the U.S.S.R., and the foreign suppliers had come to know the Soviet bureaucrats who ran the system. Now the suppliers have to learn a new system and deal with different people.

To bridge this confusion gap, a growing number of firms are offering to act as go-betweens. (See the advertisement for one such firm in Figure 17–7.) These are Western companies that have traded in the U.S.S.R., and there is at least one Soviet private consulting company, FAKT, offering its services. A German company, Varioline, and the accounting firm Ernst & Young linked up with a Soviet-Finnish company to get into the business. One rather unique entry in the field is Aldriedge & Miller, Inc., a company formed by two American women with long experience working in the U.S.S.R.[52]

□ How Western Companies Sell to the East

Selling to the East is usually extremely time consuming and complex. How do Western companies sell in the East? A minority of Western companies open and maintain representative offices in Moscow or some other city. Most Western companies utilize the services of companies that specialize in dealing with the East, such as Satra Corporation or Tower International, Inc. These companies have dealt in many sorts of products and services, including chrome, steel, grain, shoes, hotels, and soybean mills. Their clients have included such major firms as IBM, Borg-Warner, Caterpillar Tractor, and USX.

There are at least two other methods of selling to the East—trade fairs and personal visits.

Trade fairs.   Exhibits at fairs are important ways for Western companies to reach potential customers in both Eastern Europe and the People's Republic of China. Attendance at the Chinese fairs is by invitation, and if you are not invited, it is unlikely that you can sell your product to the PRC. However, when a new exhibition is planned, it may be advertised with invitations issued to qualified exhibitors. Figure 17–8 is an example of one of these. Note that the United Nations Industrial Development Organization is a cosponsor of this one.

Common sense should probably indicate what to do and what not to do when your company has a stand at a trade fair. However, there have apparently been some unfortunate departures from common sense, so two UN officials have drawn up a checklist for "Manning a Trade Fair Stand." It is reproduced as Figure 17–9 on page 625.

Personal visits.   Personal contacts are important, and when you are trying to sell products to Eastern customers, you should not rely too much on correspondence. Personal business visits to Moscow or other capitals, as appropriate, are almost always necessary if you hope to make sales. However, travel in China and Eastern Europe is expensive and not many sales are made, so a trip should not be made without some combination of the following conditions: (1) company personnel can meet key government officials; (2) the company is contemplating a long-term sales campaign or is at a crucial negotiating point near the end of a campaign; or (3) the volume and profitability of a potential sale warrants the trip.

The Chinese customer wants to scrutinize the Western executives personally and make assessments of their trustworthiness and goodwill. The Chinese want to feel they are dealing with a friend who will play fair and make possible a comfortable, long-term relationship.

> **Hugh P. Donaghue, vice president of Control Data Corporation, visited China carrying three large boxes stuffed with product brochures and other literature, which he expected to hand to his Chinese hosts at the first meeting. It didn't work that way. They first asked him about his philosophy of life and then about Control Data's business philosophy. For 10 days, they talked about all sorts of subjects except Control Data products. Finally, as Donaghue was about ready to**

□ **FIGURE 17–8**
Trade Fair Invitation

UNIDO UNITED NATIONS INDUSTRIAL DEVELOPMENT ORGANIZATION

in co-operation with

INSTITUTE OF SCIENTIFIC AND TECHNICAL
INFORMATION OF CHINA

and

TECHNOLOGY EXCHANGE, U.K.

invite you to

UNIDO TECHMART '91

Beijing, China, 2-6 December 1991

Venue: **Exhibition Hall
The Institute of Scientific and Technical Information of China
(ISTIC)
15 Fu Xing Lu, P.O. Box 3827
Beijing 100038
People's Republic of China
Tel: (01) 801 4020
Tlx: 20079 ISTIC CN
Fax: (01) 801 4025**

✂ -

From: _____
_____
_____
_____

To: **United Nations Industrial Development Organization (UNIDO)**
Industrial and Technological Information Bank (INTIB)
Vienna International Centre
P.O. Box 300
A-1400 Vienna
Austria (EUROPE)

Fax:	+(43) (222) 2307584 or 232156
Tel:	+(43) (222) 21131-3691 or 3693
Tlx:	135612 uno a

carry the three boxes home still full, the Chinese finally asked him what he had to sell. Control Data made sales and has been doing increased business with China.

As foreign companies have sold or tried to sell to the PRC over recent years, much experience has been acquired, and some checklists have been developed. One list is suggested by Ronald Wombolt, vice president and director of international operations of John Fluke Manufacturing Company, an American producer of electronic test and measurement instrumentation. Wombolt's checklist is:

**□ FIGURE 17–9
Manning a Trade Fair
Stand**

1. Company representatives should be knowledgeable about the company and its products, empowered to conduct business negotiations, and clear on its objectives in exhibiting.

2. Never ignore a visitor to your stand.

3. Approach visitors who seem interested in your display; do not wait for them to approach you.

4. Look interested. Do not sit about chatting with your colleagues. Do not position yourself so as to hide your products or to block access to them.

5. Start the conversation with a positive remark about your product or a question that will generate a discussion.

6. Identify as quickly as possible the visitor's business and specific interest and his importance as a prospect. Always keep your objective in mind.

7. Answer all questions as forthrightly and factually as possible.

8. Remember to sell your company as well as your products, and relate your remarks to the visitor's interests.

9. Use the conversation to elicit information about the market and reactions to your products.

10. Carry negotiations as far forward as you are empowered to, if you are convinced the visitor represents a solid prospect.

11. Use inquiry forms and supplementary notes to record details about the visitor's company, his interests, and follow-up action to be taken.

12. Allow time after the fair closes to continue important discussions.

13. Provide promised information as soon as possible.

14. Observe fair hours, and never leave your exhibit unattended.

15. Use slack periods to make contacts at other stands, provided your own is manned.

Source: Umphon Phanachet and Zhang Huixiang, *Guidebook on Trading with the People's Republic of China* (Trade Promotion Centre of ESCAP, 1982), p. 33.

Do not always offer your most favorable price up front. The Chinese want to bargain and negotiate.

Do not, without good cause, insist on selling on letter of credit terms. The Chinese are usually prompt payers.

Do not make any statement you can't back up, because the Chinese record everything you say in negotiating sessions.

Do not offer or accept any terms or conditions that you will not want in future transactions. Although the Chinese will constantly ask for something "this time only," it means every time.

Offer training in China and abroad.

Maintain a consistent pricing policy.

To follow the rules listed above, have the same group in your company deal with the Chinese over time, at least one of whom understands the language.[53]

Information about East–West business.   The U.S. Commercial Office in Moscow is available to U.S. companies wishing to do business there. Interested firms can contact the Trade Promotion Division, Bureau of East–West Trade, U.S. Department of Commerce, Washington, D.C. 20230, or the U.S. Commercial Office, U.S. Department of State–Moscow, Washington, D.C. 20520.

In recognition of the bureaucratic, linguistic, and cultural difficulties for Americans attempting to sell in the PRC market, the Chinese government set up its first U.S. trade promotion office in Los Angeles in 1986. It is called the China–U.S. Trading Corporation, and it is operated by the Foreign Enterprises Services Corporation (FESCO), a government agency.[54]

Self-help. In 1989 a Soviet Trade Directory became available. It contains addresses of industrial branches of Soviet enterprises and information on how to make direct contact with factory managers and engineers. Addresses from which it may be ordered in several countries can be seen in an ad for the directory shown in Figure 17–10.

Other help. International publishers such as *Euromoney* and the *Financial Times* sponsor conferences, workshops, and seminars to instruct Westerners how to invest in and trade with the East. Figure 17–11 advertises a conference concerning Czechoslovakia.

The UN Economic and Social Commission for Asia and the Pacific publishes a "Guidebook on Trading with the People's Republic of China." Copies can be obtained from the UN at United Nations Plaza, New York, N.Y., 10017, U.S.A.

Help is also available for people in the East who are looking to the West. In Chapter 4, we mentioned classes and seminars given by the Bank for International Settlements for Eastern European private and central bankers.

■ **FIGURE 17–11**
Financial Times
Czechoslovakia
Conference

FINANCIAL TIMES CONFERENCES

R I I A

FINANCE INVESTMENT & TRADE WITH CZECHOSLAVKIA

PRAGUE, 7 & 8 NOVEMBER 1991

This high-level conference brings together a distinguished panel of senior politicians and leading figures from Czechoslovakia and the international business community to review the political and economic developments, the policies for managing the transition to a market economy and the new opportunities opening up for investment and business. Speakers include:

Dr Vladimír Dlouhý
Minister of the Economy
Czech and Slovak Federal Republic

Dr Karel Dyba
Minister of Economy and Development
The Czech Republic

Mr Torsten Thiele
Principle Banker, Merchant Banking Department,
European Bank for Reconstruction and
Development

Dr Alex Pravda
Fellow
St Antony's College, Oxford

Ing Ladislav Novotný
President
SKODA Concern, Pizen Limited Company

Dr Romáš Ježek
Minister of the Control of National Property and
Its Privatisation
The Czech Republic

Ing Jaroslav Jurečka
Deputy Minister of Finance
Czech and Slovak Federal Republic

Dr Václav Klaus
Minister of Finance
Czech and Slovak Federal Republic

Prof Dr Ing Milan Buček
Deputy Minister for Economic Strategy
The Slovak Republic

Mr Josef Tošovský
Governor of the State Bank
Czech and Slovak Federal Republic

Mr William R Rhodes
Senior Executive – International
Citibank NA

Mr Pablo Benavides Salas
Directorate – General 1 (External Relations)
Commission of the European Communities

Ing Ivan Mikloš
Minister for Adminstration and Privatisation
of State Property
The Slovak Republic

Mr Frank R Bakos
Vice President, Power Generation
Westinghouse Electric Corporation

Financial Times Conferences and The Royal Institute of International Affairs
in association with
Institute of Economics of the Czechoslovak Academy of Sciences
International Finance Corporation

- -

FINANCE INVESTMENT & TRADE WITH CZECHOSLAVKIA

There is a limited amount of exhibition space available at the conference

☐ Please send me conference details
☐ Please send me exhibition details

Financial Times Conference Organisation
126 Jermyn Street, London SSW1Y 4UJ, UK
Tel: 071-925 2323. Tlx: 27347 FTCONF G
Fax: 071-925 2125

Name _____
Position _____ Dept _____
Company/Organisation _____
Address _____
_____
_____ Postcode _____
Tel _____ Tlx _____ Fax _____
Type of Business _____

HA

Source: *Financial Times,* September 3, 1991, p. 25

SUMMARY

The countries of the late COMECON and the PRC have huge populations, landmasses, and resources. In theory, they should be excellent trading partners for the OECD countries, but translation of theory to fact has proved most difficult.

There is trade, but much of it has been unnatural from the points of view of both sides. The East has been unable to earn enough money to pay for what it desires to buy from the West; therefore, the East wants the West to take payment in the form of Eastern goods and services.

But complaints have been made about many Eastern goods in Western markets. The complaints are based on the grounds that Eastern goods are of inferior quality or that they are unfairly competitive with Western or traditional suppliers or labor.

Now in the East, immense changes have occurred or are under way. Both the Soviet military alliance, the Warsaw Pact, and its economic grouping, COMECON, have been dissolved. The Soviet republics have declared independence and have been recognized by the major countries of the world.

Each of the Eastern European countries and the ex-Soviet republics is groping toward democracy, market economies, and new trading relationships. As the old Marx and machine gun enforced borders and central governments blur or are weakened, border and ethnic disputes have broken out. Some of them are bloody.

As the old bureaucracies that handled foreign trading for their communist masters break down, free markets are very slowly replacing central planning. Complicated as it was, foreign sellers had learned the system and knew the bureaucrats. Now the sellers must master—perhaps help create—new systems and deal with new people.

There is help available from numerous sources. There are trading companies and consultants. The U.S. government, the UN, and other agencies offer advice on how to trade with the East, and conferences, workshops, and directories are available. The PRC has established an agency in the U.S. to help American firms deal with PRC complications.

QUESTIONS

1. a. When East–West is spoken of, what countries are included in "East"?
   b. "West"?
2. What is a centrally planned economy?
3. What is a market economy?
4. Why has the PRC never become a large market for consumer goods?
5. a. What is a major probable reason that the PRC recognized the United States in 1979 and wanted to trade with the United States?
   b. What changes are occurring in the PRC's economic relations with foreigners?
6. What does the East want most from the West?
7. What are the major obstacles to the East getting what it wants?
8. How is the East getting—and trying to get means to pay for—imports from the West?
9. Why is the East having difficulties getting the West to accept its products?
10. What caused COMECON's demise?
11. a. What should Eastern countries do to achieve market economies with democracy?
    b. Should the West help them? Why?
    c. If yes, how?
12. Explain tensions in the PRC between its political and private economic sectors.
13. What are the results of the fact that communism was in power much longer in the U.S.S.R. than in the PRC?
14. How do Western companies do business in and with the East, and what sorts of assistance can they find?

□ **MINICASE 17–1**

Marketing in the People's Republic of China

You are the CEO of a company that manufactures machine tools in American factories. Sales were low in 1985 and 1986 but began to pick up in 1987. Even with the increased order volume, your plant operations are well below capacity, and even though your technology is well advanced, import competition is tough.

You are beginning to consider export possibilities, and your marketing vice president suggests the PRC. She shows you academic studies, Department of Commerce publications, and PRC trade fair literature that convince you that the PRC market is worth a try.

What steps should your marketing vice president take to gain acceptance of your product by the PRC and to get orders? What should you and she avoid?

□ **MINICASE 17–2**

Joint Venturing in Eastern Europe

You are the vice president for planning of an American manufacturer of machine tools. You report to the president, and he calls you to his office one day.

When you get there, he starts talking about how tough it is to get new business and about how well the company's European and Japanese competitors have been doing in the American market. He then points out that the company has never made a sale in Eastern Europe, and he asks you why that is.

You reply that business has been good enough in the United States and in the several Latin American markets where the company's products are sold, so no sales efforts have been made in Eastern Europe. You can anticipate the president's next words, and they are not long in coming.

"Latin America has gone to hell in a hand basket! They are spending all their money paying back the greedy banks that lent them too much money, and they're broke when it comes to buying our stuff. We need new markets! Get out of here and see how we can get into Eastern Europe."

What steps are you going to take to try to get into that market—or those markets? To whom should you talk? Where can you turn for information? Should you make a trip to the area? If so, when? If not, why not?

SUPPLEMENTARY READINGS

Bryson, Phillip J., and Manfred Melzer. *The End of the East German Economy*. New York: St. Martin's Press, 1991.

Collins, Susan M., and Dani Rodrik. "Economic Reform in Eastern Europe Will Benefit Western Europe and Hurt Developing Countries." *News Institute for International Economics*, May 21, 1991.

"Expectations Play a Key Role in Moving to Market Economies." *IMF Survey*, July 15, 1991, pp. 213–16.

Greene, Joshua E., and Peter Isard. "Currency Convertibility and the Transformation of Centrally Planned Economies." *Occasional Paper 81*. International Monetary Fund, June 1991.

Hanson, Philip. *Trade and Technology in Soviet–Western Relations*. New York: Columbia University Press, 1981.

Hogberg, Bengt, and Clas Wahlbin. "East–West Industrial Cooperations: The Swedish Case." *Journal of International Business Studies*, Spring–Summer 1984, pp. 72–83.

Hungarian Chamber of Commerce. "Ideas for Joint Ventures." Budapest: Foreign Investment Promotion Service, 1989/1.

Junge, Georg. "Macroeconomic Stabilization and the New Order in Eastern Europe." *Economic and Financial Prospects*, August–September 1991, pp. 5–6.

Kanet, Roger E., ed. *Soviet Foreign Policy and East–West Relations*. Elmsford, N.Y.: Pergamon Press, 1982.

Kemme, David M. *Economic Transition in Eastern Europe: Issues and Strategies*. New York: Institute for East–West Security Studies, 1991.

Manasian, David. "A Survey of Business in Eastern Europe." *The Economist*, September 21, 1991.

Marsh, Peter. "Joint Ventures in the Soviet Union: Marriage contracts." *Financial Times*, September 20, 1991, p. 12.

Nigh, Douglas, Peter Walters, and James A. Kuhlman. "U.S.–U.S.S.R. Joint Ventures: An Examination of the Early Entrants." *Columbia Journal of World Business*, Winter 1990, pp. 20–27.

Parker, John. "A Survey of the Soviet Union: Now What?" *The Economist*, October 20, 1990.

Robinson, Anthony, Sir William Ryrie, Neil McCartney, and Kevin Done. "Eastern Europe in Transition." *Financial Times,* February 4, 1991, pp. 1–6.

Sjoberg, Orjan, and Michael Wyzan. *Economic Change in the Balkan States.* New York: St. Martin's Press, 1991.

Starr, Robert, ed. "Practical Aspects of Trading with the U.S.S.R." Montreux, Switzerland: Worldwide Information, 1989.

———. "Joint Ventures in the U.S.S.R." Montreux, Switzerland: Worldwide Information, 1989.

"The Shattered Dream, China/1989, Special Report." *Los Angeles Times,* June 25, 1989, part IA.

Thompson, Robert. "Mao and Mammon: The Torment of the Dragon." *Financial Times,* October 26–27, 1991, p. I.

Williamson, John. "Successful Economic Opening of Eastern Europe Requires Competitive Exchange Rates and Early Engagement with European Community." *News Institute for International Economics,* May 21, 1991, pp. 2–6.

Woolcock, Stephen. *Western Policies on East–West Trade.* Boston: Routledge & Kegan Paul, 1982.

ENDNOTES

1. Anthony C. Sutton, *Western Technology and Soviet Economic Development,* vols. 1 and 2 (Stanford, Calif.: Hoover Institution Press, 1968 and 1971).

2. Michael Parks, "Soviet-Led Trading Bloc Will Be Scrapped," *Los Angeles Times,* January 6, 1991, p. A5.

3. Anthony Robinson and Leyla Boulton, "High Hopes Give Way to Empty Shelves," *Financial Times,* May 9, 1991, p. 17.

4. "COMECON, Life after Death," *The Economist,* April 20, 1991, pp. 51–52.

5. "Free Fall," *The Economist,* September 28, 1991, p. 73.

6. "Soviet Officials Project Widening National Deficit," *The Wall Street Journal,* October 7, 1991, p. A13.

7. Jonathon Peterson and James R. Wilburn, "Transforming an Economy," *Los Angeles Times,* September 10, 1991, p. H4.

8. Alan Murray, "Harvard, to the Dismay of U.S. Conservatives, May Replace Communism as Soviets' Planner," *The Wall Street Journal,* August 27, 1991, p. A14.

9. Carey Goldberg, "Joint Ventures Failing to Lift Soviet Economy," *Los Angeles Times,* May 26, 1991, pp. D1 and 16; and "Russian Roulette with Six Bullets," *The Economist,* January 12, 1991, pp. 64–65.

10. John Lloyd, "Joint Ventures Gleam amid Economic Gloom," *Financial Times,* September 27–28, 1991, p. 2.

11. "From China to U.S.S.R. with 100,000 TV Sets," *Hong Kong Trader,* September 1991, p. 3.

12. Quentin Peel, "Tax Threat to Soviet Cooperative Movement," *Financial Times,* April 27, 1989, p. 14.

13. "Free Markets, Soviet Style," *Fortune,* September 9, 1991, p. 188.

14. "Soviet Share Ownership: Command Capitalism," *The Economist,* September 28, 1991, pp. 75–76.

15. "Flight from the Kremlin," *The Economist,* August 31, 1991, pp. 13–14.

16. Donald Woutat, "East Europe's Realities Put Chill on Investment Climate," *Los Angeles Times,* July 9, 1991, pp. A1 and 6.

17. Ibid.

18. "Investing in Eastern Europe: The Money Pit," *The Economist,* June 22, 1991, pp. 74–75.

19. Charles T. Powers, "Levi Strauss Sews Up Enthusiastic Support for Factory in Polish City," *Los Angeles Times,* July 9, 1991, p. A6.

20. Lucy Walker, "EC Opens Trade Doors to the East," *The European,* October 4–6, 1991, p. 17.

21. Laurena Cahill, "Eastern Europe Brings Rewards," *Hong Kong Trader,* September 1991, p. 1.

22. Tony Paterson, "The Time Bomb They Left Behind," *The European,* October 11–13, 1991, p. 12.

23. Robert Thompson, "China's Row with the U.S. Reveals Discord in Beijing," *Financial Times,* October 4, 1991, p. 8.

24. Vigor Keung Fung, "China Flirts with a Basic Capitalist Tool: Stocks," *The Asian Wall Street Journal,* September 26, 1983, p. 14.

25. "Managing Money Matters in China Joint Ventures," *Business Asia,* June 13, 1988, pp. 194–96.

26. Julia Leung, "Foreign Companies in China Devising Plans to Weather Sudden Policy Shifts," *The Asian Wall Street Journal,* November 14, 1988, p. 22.

27. Lynne Curry, "Trading in China Is Not for the Light-Hearted," *Financial Times,* April 24, 1991, p. VI.

28. Vigor Keung Fung, "China Aims to Revive Foreign Interest," *The Asian Wall Street Journal,* December 8, 1986, p. 13; and "China, New Foreign Investment Incentives," *Standard Chartered Review,* November 1986, pp. 21–22.

29. Vigor Keung Fung, "Chinese Are Eager to Take the Plunge," *The Asian Wall Street Journal,* November 17, 1986, p. 22.

30. Peter Ellingsen, "China Shuts Door on Rapid Reform," *Financial Times,* March 20, 1989, p. 26.

31. Adi Ignatius, "Death of Ex-Party Chief Hu Is Viewed as Blow to China's Liberal Reformers," *The Wall Street Journal,* April 17, 1989, p. A7.

32. George White, "U.S. Firms Lift Taboo on Doing Business in Beijing," *Los Angeles Times,* December 1, 1990, pp. D1–2.

33. James McGregor, "Success Stories in China Stay Untold as U.S. Firms Strive for Low Profiles," *The Wall Street Journal,* November 7, 1991, p. A11.

34. John Elliott, "Share Dealing Returns to Shanghai," *Financial Times,* December 19, 1990, p. 6.

35. Julia Leung, "Chinese Officials Signal They Are Prepared to Revive Experiment in Wider Stock Trading," *The Wall Street Journal,* April 11, 1991, p. A10.

36. "The South China Miracle," *The Economist,* October 5, 1991, pp. 19–22.

37. James McGregor, "China's Conundrum," *The Wall Street Journal,* September 24, 1991, p. A1.

38. Robert Thompson, "What Price Ideology?" *Financial Times,* October 18, 1991, p. 22.

39. "No Order Too Small," *The Economist,* February 18, 1989, p. 34.

40. Mark Skousen, "Bureaucratic Nightmare," *Forecasts & Strategies,* April 1989, p. 7.

41. Curry, "Trading in China," p. VI.

42. Richard Rescigno interviews Hilmar Kopper, "The View from Deutsche Bank," *Barron's,* November 18, 1991, p. 8.

43. Peter Montagnon, "Key Questions Raised," *Financial Times,* December 13, 1989, p. 36.

44. Peter Montagnon, "Tighter Export Controls Likely for Third World," *Financial Times,* August 30, 1990, p. 3.

45. John W. Kiser III, "Technology Is Not a One-Way Street," *Foreign Policy,* Summer 1976, pp. 131–48.

46. Ibid.

47. *The Economist,* August 5, 1979, pp. 38–39.

48. William Dawkins, "Soviet Union Faces EC Probe on Chemical Pricing," *Financial Times,* August 1, 1989, p. 6.

49. Jay F. Henderson, Nicholas H. Ludlow, and Eugene A. Theroux, "China and the Trade Act of 1974," *U.S.-China Business Review,* January–February 1975.

50. Benjamin A. Sharman, in an interview reported in *Contemporary Perspectives in International Business,* ed. Harold W. Berkman and Ivan R. Vernon (Skokie, Ill.: Rand McNally, 1979), p. 142.

51. "Every Step Hurts," *The Economist,* January 14, 1988, pp. 44–45.

52. Peter Gumbel, "Soviet Trade Awaits the Next Revolution," *The Wall Street Journal,* February 21, 1989, p. A14.

53. Robert McCluskey, "The Bottom Line," *International Management,* July 1986, pp. 49–50.

54. Nancy Yoshihara, "China to Open Office to Aid U.S. Firms," *Los Angeles Times,* April 13, 1986, pt. 4, p. 4.

Chapter 18

Financial Management

Ten minutes is a long-term outlook.

> Foreign currency dealers,
> Manufacturers Hanover Trust
> Company

In countertrading, companies sometimes let themselves get stuck with products they don't know anything about. A computer guy called me to help get rid of 30,000 tons of oranges he'd taken in a deal. I told him to squeeze them into orange juice and freeze the concentrate, or he would wind up with oranges good for nothing but penicillin.

> Takis Argentinis, director,
> Countertrade Operations, General
> Electric Company

LEARNING OBJECTIVES

In this chapter, you will study:

1. How the currencies of the main trading nations change in value in terms of each other.

2. How currency value changes affect international business transactions and the reporting of profits, losses, assets, and liabilities.

3. The tremendous importance of financial management to an international company (IC).

4. How financial management can protect an international company from risks and create advantages as a result of currency value changes.

5. Financial management tools, including hedging, timing of payments, exposure netting, price adjustments, balance sheet neutralizing, and swaps.

6. Why the financial management of an international company encounters more problems and opportunities in raising capital than does the financial management of a domestic company.

7. Why international competition has forced exporters to customers in soft-currency countries to accept payment in forms other than money.

8. Why a foreign investor in a soft-currency country must sometimes accept dividends, interest, or repayment in forms other than money.

9. Why noncommunist less developed countries (LDCs) and soft-currency countries are usually more open about their economies than are communist countries.

10. Why noncommunist less developed countries are more likely to receive and accept financial and technological assistance from UN agencies and developed-country (DC) governments and companies.

11. International finance centers, which handle the entire intra-IC invoicing procedure for some ICs and may coordinate all international financial activities of the organization's parent and its affiliates.

KEY WORDS AND CONCEPTS

- Fluctuating exchange rates
- Transaction risks
- Hedging
- Leads
- Lags
- Exposure netting
- Translation risks
- Neutralizing the balance sheet
- Swaps
- Equity capital
- Debt capital
- Countertrade
- Industrial cooperation
- International finance centers

BUSINESS INCIDENT

David Edwards was born in Wichita Falls, Texas, but was intrigued by international business and finance. He worked his way up the ladder of Citibank's international operation, where he moved into a senior slot in Paris as head of *les cambistes,* as the fast-and-furious currency exchange traders are called. His boldness and quick mind equipped him well for this high-pressure operation, and he did very well for his employer and for himself. Occasionally, however, his Wichita Falls French got him in trouble. He tells of one occasion when Citibank's currency trader at the Bourse,* who was a Frenchman, phoned him and reported that the U.S. dollar bids were going down fast. Edwards shouted into the telephone, "Aw, shit!" and slammed down the receiver. A few seconds later, the trader called Edwards on another phone and reported proudly that he had bought a large block of U.S. dollars. "You did what?" Edwards yelled, to which the startled trader protested, "But you said, *'Achete.'* "† That evening, Edwards walked into his boss's office and said, "I've got a funny story to tell you, but it's going to cost you a quarter of a million dollars to hear it."

Bourse is the French word for stock and currency markets.
†*Achete* means "buy" in French.
Source: Roy Rowan, *Fortune,* January 10, 1983, p. 46.

I n Chapter 6, we spoke of some of the financial forces with which IC management is confronted and of the financial problems it must try to solve. In this chapter, we shall examine some of the tools and methods that financial management uses to solve those problems. The forces or problems that we identified were fluctuating currency exchange rates, currency exchange controls, tariffs, taxes, inflation, and accounting practices.

One problem faced by the financial management of an IC that can be turned into an opportunity is in what currency to raise capital. The company may need or be able to use two or more currencies. If so, its financial management can shop the many financial centers around the world to raise the currency it can use at the lowest cost.

A related problem results from payment for products sold internationally. If you are the seller, the buyer may pay you in your currency, which is the same as a domestic sale. But payment may be made in another currency. If it is a convertible currency, you can convert it to your currency, though there may be a currency exchange rate risk if payment is delayed—for example, if you extend credit to the buyer.

If the buyer has too little convertible currency, the seller may accept goods or services instead of money. Financial management must convert the goods or services to money, a growing phenomenon as international competition grows keener.

Elsewhere in the book, we deal with market assessment and analysis and with production planning. Early in their assessment, analysis, and planning, marketing and production management should bring in financial management to coordinate capital needs with capital availability.

The financial managers must examine the alternative ways of financing the marketing and production plans. How much capital of what sorts will be needed, and when? What are the best sources of this capital, and how long can the new operations be expected to need support before they are financially self-sufficient?

FLUCTUATING CURRENCY EXCHANGE RATES

fluctuating exchange rates currencies of different countries go up and down in value in terms of each other

Wherever the IC does business, the financial manager must consider **fluctuating exchange rates**—the fluctuating values of currencies in terms of each other. Also to be considered is the value of each of those currencies in terms of the currency of the IC's home or financial and tax-reporting country.

The fluctuations create currency value risks. These may be categorized as (1) transaction risks and (2) translation risks.

▢ Transaction Risks

transaction risks in import/export transactions, the party that must pay or receive a foreign currency in the future takes the risk that the currency value will change to its disadvantage

Transaction risks usually involve a receivable or a payable denominated in a foreign currency. These risks arise from transactions, such as a purchase from a foreign supplier or a sale to a foreign customer. There are several methods by which the financial manager can buy protection against these risks.[1] The company can engage in several types of **hedging,** in various ways, or if it is a buyer or a borrower, it may be able to accelerate or delay payments or provisions for payments. Within limits, price increases may be used.

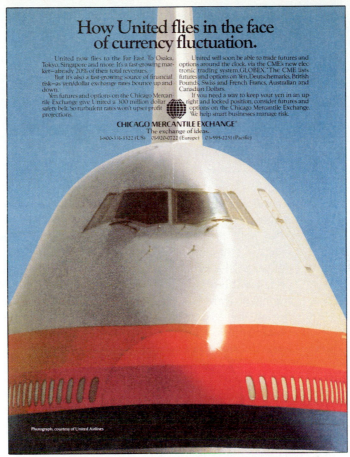

How United flies in the face of currency fluctuation.

United now flies to the Far East. To Osaka, Tokyo, Singapore and more. It's a fast-growing market—already 20% of their total revenues.

But it's also a fast-growing source of financial risk—as yen/dollar exchange rates bounce up and down.

Yen futures and options on the Chicago Mercantile Exchange give United a 300 million dollar safety belt. So turbulent rates won't upset profit projections.

United will soon be able to trade futures and options around the clock, via the CME's new electronic trading system, GLOBEX. The CME lists futures and options on Yen, Deutschemarks, British Pounds, Swiss and French Francs, Australian and Canadian Dollars.

If you need a way to keep your yen in an upright and locked position, consider futures and options on the Chicago Mercantile Exchange. We help smart businesses manage risk.

CHICAGO MERCANTILE EXCHANGE
The exchange of ideas.
1-800-331-3322 (US)   01-920-0722 (Europe)   03-595-2251 (Pacific)

Photograph, courtesy of United Airlines

Currency futures market

Courtesy of Chicago Mercantile Exchange

---

hedging trying to protect yourself against losses due to currency exchange rate fluctuations

Forward hedge. This is accomplished in the foreign exchange market and involves a contract. The IC contracts with another party to deliver to that other party at an agreed future date a fixed amount of one currency in return for a fixed amount of another currency. Contracts in the major trading country currencies are generally available for 30-, 60-, 90-, or 180-day deliveries. Longer-term contracts can sometimes be negotiated, as can contracts with other than 30-, 60-, 90-, or 180-day maturities.

5 Norwegian krone = 1 U.S. dollar. An example could work as follows. An American exporter sells $1 million of goods to a Norwegian importer. The rate of exchange on the date of sale is 5 Norwegian krone to 1 U.S. dollar (NK5 = US$1) and therefore involves NK5 million. The agreement is that the importer will pay the exporter NK5 million in 180 days.

The risk of any change in the US$–NK exchange rate is now on the American exporter. If the NK loses value, say, to NK7 = US$1, during the 180 days, the NK5 million will buy only US$714,285.71 when received. But the American exporter's expectation was to receive US$1 million, and the exchange rate change causes a loss of more than $285,000.

Traded Currency	Ticker Code
British pound	BP
Canadian dollar	CD
Deutsche mark	DM
Dutch guilder	DG
French franc	FF
Japanese yen	JY
Mexican peso	MP
Swiss franc	SF

The hedge involves a contract.   The U.S. exporter could use a forward hedge to protect against such a loss by contracting at the time of sale to sell NK5 million to be delivered to the buyer (the other party to the hedge contract) in 180 days in return for US$1 million, which the other party agrees to deliver to the exporter at the same time. The actual amount the exporter receives will be less than $1 million because the other party to the hedge contract will want compensation for the risk of a drop in the value of the NK during the 180 days. Assume the other party wants 1 percent and the exporter agrees. One percent would be $10,000, and the other party would deliver $990,000 in exchange for NK5 million.[2]

The $10,000 can be regarded as a sort of insurance premium that the exporter pays to be certain how much in US$s it will receive in 180 days. Of course, it must have made the business decision that $990,000 is an acceptable amount for the goods it is selling.

As with other prices in a free market society, there is no law or regulation that mandates 1 percent, or $10,000, as the cost for a $1 million hedge. In our example, the good financial manager for the exporter will shop around among banks and will find some prices lower than others. The NK is not traded on the International Monetary Market (IMM) at the Chicago Mercantile Exchange. If the currency of payment were one of the eight traded there, the financial manager should also get a quote for an IMM contract. The traded currencies are shown in Figure 18–1.

The IMM contract is a futures hedge.   If the financial manager uses IMM contracts, the hedge is with a futures, not a forward, contract. At the IMM, the traded currencies are treated as commodities (wheat, soybeans, sow bellies, and so forth) and traded as futures contracts. Futures contracts are traded by brokers, and the exporter must have a margin account with a broker. Futures contracts come in fixed amounts, such as BP25,000, and standardized delivery dates are used.

Currency options.   At the end of 1982, the Philadelphia Stock Exchange began dealing in options to buy or sell currencies. That offered another hedge opportunity, which has been expanded since then in at least two ways. First, other exchanges have begun dealing in currency options in, among other cities, London, Chicago, Amsterdam, and New York. Second, there now exists an over-the-counter currency option market involving banks, multinationals, and brokers. Figure 18–2 is an advertisement for foreign currency trading.

□ **FIGURE 18–2**
Foreign Currency Trading

Intra-IC hedge. A rapidly growing practice is for international companies to seek an internal hedge within their own network of parent, subsidiary, and affiliated companies. Suppose that in our NK–US$ case, the financial manager found that one of the IC companies owed about NK5 million, payable about the same time as the NK5 million was receivable under the export contract. The NK payable by one unit of the IC could then be hedged (netted) against the NK receivable carried by the other IC unit. Thus, two hedges are achieved at no outside cost, and the bank, option, or IMM fees are avoided.

A covered position.   Even though the exporter in the above forward hedge example does not have any NKs at the time it enters the hedge contract, it does have the Norwegian importer's obligation to pay the NK5 million, which can be delivered to the other party to the hedge contract. If you either have the funds (NK5 million) when you enter the hedge contract or they are due from another business transaction on or before the due date under your hedge contract (as here), you are in a "covered" position.[3]

An uncovered position.   A financial manager can also use the foreign exchange market to take advantage of an expected rise or fall in the relative value of currency. There will then be created an "uncovered" long or short position. For example, if the financial manager of an American company believes the NK will appreciate in value in the next few months, the procedure would be to go long on the NK at the spot rate, NK5 = US$1. This is a contract whereby the company buys, say, NK5 million for US$1 million, both currencies to be delivered at a future date. If the NK appreciates to NK4 = US$1, the financial manager was correct, and the NK5 million received by the company is worth $1,250,000. The company pays, as agreed, $1 million. If the financial manager believes the NK will depreciate in the next few months, the procedure would be to short NKs at the spot rate. An uncovered short position results when you sell the money or any other commodity without having it either on hand or due you under another business transaction.

Using the same rate (NK5 = US$1), and the same amount (NK5 million), the company agrees to deliver NK5 million at a future date in return for US$1 million. If, in fact, the NK depreciates to NK6 = US$1, the financial manager was again correct. The company can buy the NK5 million for approximately $830,000. The company will be paid, as agreed, $1 million.

Both of the above stories had happy endings for the company, but it exposed itself to risk. Short-term currency value movements are extremely uncertain in both direction and amount, and those company stories (and perhaps the financial manager) could have had sad endings if the currencies had moved in the other directions. People who study currency markets and deal in them daily tend to be modest in their forecasts of short-term movements.

We have interviewed and talked at length with foreign exchange market officers, bank traders, and bank economists in America, Asia, and Europe. Almost all of them expressed definite views, opinions, and forecasts about long-term currency value changes. Not one of them would hazard more than a guess about tomorrow's prices.

Credit or money market hedge.   As indicated by its name, the credit or money market hedge involves credit—borrowing money. The company desiring a hedge is the borrower. The credit or money market hedge may be illustrated by the same transaction used above to discuss the forward exchange market hedge.

The Norwegian importer will pay NK5 million to the American exporter for the goods in 180 days. With the money market hedge, the exporter will borrow NK5 million from an Oslo bank on the day of the sale to the Norwegian importer.* The exporter will immediately convert to US$s at the current NK5 = US$1 rate, giving the exporter the $1 million selling price, but it owes NK5 million to the Norwegian bank, due in 180 days. That will be repaid with the Norwegian importer's NK5 million payment.

The exporter has a variety of options for use of the $1 million. It can lend it, put it in certificates of deposit, use it in a swap (see below), or use it as internal operating capital. The financial manager will study all of the options to find which will be most beneficial.

Before the money market hedge is used, a comparison must be made of the interest rates in the exporter's and the importer's countries. If the interest on the exporter's borrowing in the importer's country is significantly higher than the amount the exporter can earn on the money in its country, the cost of this type of hedge may be too great.

Other comparisons and checks should be made before borrowing the NK from an Oslo bank. Even though the NK is not one of the most widely traded currencies, the financial manager should inquire of banks in major Eurocurrency centers (such as London, Paris, Zurich, and Frankfurt) to ascertain whether NKs could be borrowed at a lower interest cost. And in the case of NKs, other Scandinavian financial centers—Copenhagen, Helsinki, and Stockholm—should be checked for competitive bids.

Just as in the foreign exchange market hedge situation, an IC should check its company units to learn whether any of them have an NK balance that could be lent internally, that is, from the unit with the balance to the unit with the NK foreign exchange exposure. Thus, interest payments to banks outside the IC could be avoided.

Acceleration or delay of payment. If you are an importer in a country whose currency is expected to depreciate in terms of the currency of your foreign supplier, you are motivated to buy the necessary foreign currency as soon as you can. This assumes the importer must pay in the currency of the exporter, the opposite of our assumption in the hedging discussions.

Which way will the exchange rates go? If you have agreed to pay $1 million when the exchange rate was NK5 = US$1, your cost at that time would be NK5 million. If, before payment is due, the rate drops to NK6 = US$1, your cost will be NK6 million. You are tempted to pay early or, if possible, to make the currency exchange at once and use the foreign currency until the payment due date.

Of course, the opposite would be the case if you expect the NK to strengthen from the NK5 = US$1 rate at the time of the purchase contract. You are motivated to delay payment and to delay conversion from NKs to US$s. For example, if the rate goes to NK4 = US$1, the necessary $1 million will cost you only NK4 million. Payment accelerations or delays are frequently called **leads** or **lags.**

leads buying a foreign currency immediately to satisfy a future need because you believe it will strengthen vis-à-vis your own currency

lags waiting until the last moment to buy a foreign currency you will need in the future because you believe it will weaken vis-à-vis your own currency

---

* Actually, the amount borrowed will usually be less than NK5 million. It will be an amount that, plus interest for 180 days, will total NK5 million at the end of that period. Thus, the NK5 million payment from the importer will exactly repay the loan, with no odd amounts plus or minus.

Unrelated companies.   Although independent, unrelated companies use acceleration or delay on each other, one may be doing so at the expense of the other. Usually, however, the exporter is indifferent as to the method used by the importer to protect itself against currency risk as long as payment is received on time in the agreed currency. The IC, on the other hand, may be able to realize enterprise-wide benefit using payment leads and lags.

Within an IC.   For purposes of examining potential payment accelerations or delays between different country operations of one IC, we should differentiate two types of ICs. At one extreme is the IC that operates a coordinated, integrated worldwide business with the objective of the greatest profit for the total enterprise. At the other extreme is the independent operation of each part of the IC as its own separate profit center.

As pointed out above, international payment leads and lags between independent companies are usually of no concern to the exporter as long as it receives payment as agreed. The same would be true of IC units that operate autonomously. But an integrated, coordinated IC can benefit the enterprise as a whole by cooperating in payment leads or lags. The overall IC objective is to get its money out of weak currencies and into strong currencies as quickly as reasonably possible.

Thus, instead of incurring the hedging costs incurred by independent companies while awaiting the future day of payment, IC units can make payment immediately if trading out of a weak currency or delay payment until the payment date if trading out of a strong currency. If the profit of the unit paying immediately suffers from loss of interest on the money or shortage of operating capital (manager compensation and promotion frequently depend on profit), adjustment can be made to recognize that the IC gained as a result of the cooperation of that management's IC unit. We shall deal with management performance measurements and compensation packages in Chapter 22.

Effects of leads and lags on foreign exchange markets.   When an importer in a weak currency country buys from an exporter in a strong currency country with payment in the future, the usual practice is to convert or hedge immediately. And by selling the currency expected to go down in value and buying the one expected to go up in value, the importer helps realize those expectations; the prophecies are self-fulfilling.

The opposite is done when the importer in a country with a strong currency buys from a country with a weak currency. Now the importer will hold onto its perceived strong currency until the last moment and not buy the weak currency till then. Again, this strengthens the perceived strong currency and weakens the other.

Purposes of intra-IC payments.   Payments between IC affiliates or between them and the parent[4] are of the same kinds as any company makes. On the operations side, they may be for:

1. Services, such as management or consulting fees.
2. Rental or lease payments for land, buildings, or equipment.
3. Royalties under license agreements.
4. Receivables and payables for parts, components, or raw materials provided by one part of the IC to another.

On the capital side, they may be for:

1. Dividends out of an affiliate's profit on stock owned by the parent.
2. Interest or principal repayment of a loan from one part of an IC to another.
3. Investment of additional capital, usually by the parent in an affiliate.

Objectives of intra-IC payments.   Within the strictures of applicable laws and the minimum working capital requirements of the parent and affiliates, ICs can maximize their currency strengths and minimize their currency weaknesses.[5] Their objectives are to:

1. Keep as much money as is reasonably possible in countries with high interest rates. This is done to avoid borrowing at high rates, or perhaps to have capital to lend at those rates.
2. Keep as much money as is reasonably possible in countries where credit is difficult to obtain. If the IC unit in such a country needs capital, it may be able to generate it internally.
3. Maximize holdings of hard, strong currencies, which may appreciate in value in terms of soft, weak currencies. Minimize, as much as is reasonably possible, holdings of the latter. You may observe that this objective may conflict with the first objective because strong currencies are usually available at lower interest rates than are weak ones. Financial management must consider all of the conditions, needs, and expectations and make a balanced judgment.
4. Minimize holdings of currencies that either are subject to currency exchange controls or can be expected to be subject to them during the period in which the company will hold those currencies.

exposure netting taking open positions in two currencies that are expected to balance each other

Exposure netting.   **Exposure netting** is the acceptance of open positions* in two or more currencies that are considered to balance one another and therefore require no further internal or external hedging. Basically, there are two ways to accomplish this: (1) currency groups and (2) a combination of a strong currency and a weak currency.

Currency groups.   Some groups of currencies tend to move in close conjunction with one another even during floating rate periods.[6] For example, some LDC currencies are pegged to the currency of their most important DC trading partner; and among European DCs, the European Monetary System is an effort to coordinate movements of the participating governments' currencies vis-à-vis other currencies. In this situation, exposure netting could involve the simultaneous long and short of, say, the Belgian franc and the Dutch guilder; the financial manager would have a franc receivable and a guilder payable and would feel that they cover each other.[7]

A strong currency and a weak currency.   A second exposure netting possibility involves two payables (or two receivables), one in a currently strong currency, such as the deutsche mark, and the other in a weaker one, such as the Canadian dollar. The hope is that weakness in one will offset the strength of the other.[8] This is not to infer that the deutsche mark is always strong and

* An *open* position exists when you have greater assets than you have liabilities (or greater liabilities than you have assets) in one currency. A *closed*, or *covered*, position exists when your assets and liabilities in a currency are equal.

the Canadian dollar always weak. At any given time it could be just the opposite, or both strong, or both weak.

An advantage of exposure netting is that it avoids the costs of hedging. It is also more risky; the currencies may not behave as expected during the periods of the open receivables or payables.

Price adjustments.   Sales management often desires to make sales in a country whose currency is expected to be devalued. In such a situation, financial management finds that neither hedging nor exposure netting is possible or economic. Within the limitations of competition and the customer's budget, it may be possible to make price adjustments—to raise the selling price in the customer's currency. The hope is that the additional amount will compensate for the expected drop in value of the customer's currency.

Price adjustments within an IC group.   If an IC is of the coordinated, integrated type, there is much opportunity to adjust selling prices on intraenterprise transactions between the parent and/or affiliated companies. The selling prices are raised or lowered by billing rate adjustments in attempts to anticipate currency exchange rate changes, thereby maximizing gains and minimizing losses.

Government reactions to intraenterprise price adjustments.   Such intraenterprise pricing practices are often used for purposes of (1) realizing higher profits in countries with lower tax rates and harder currencies and (2) decreasing import duties. Tax and customs officials have become more knowledgeable about such practices and now have the power to disregard prices that they consider unreasonably low or high. They then levy taxes or tariffs on what they determine to be reasonable profits or prices. Therefore, such practices must be used carefully and with discretion; financial management should be able to substantiate its prices with convincing cost data. Some writers do not recommend aggressive use of transfer pricing* for foreign exchange management.[9]

The alternatives the financial manager for the American exporter should consider to reduce the risk of exchange losses are shown in Figure 18–3. We use the transaction discussed above, in which an American exporter sold $1 million of goods to a Norwegian importer. At the time of sale, the exchange rate was $1 = 5 Norwegian krone. The sales contract called for the Norwegian importer to pay the American exporter NK5 million in six months, which placed the currency exchange risk on the exporter.

▢ Only for Big Business?

Generally, only larger companies can afford the expertise and deal in big enough amounts to make currency risk hedging practical. However, in 1990 a new development brought some hedging possibilities within reach of medium and small businesses.

In January 1990, the U.S. Federal Reserve allowed American banks to hold foreign currency deposits in the United States. It is difficult or even im-

---

* Transfer pricing is a term that means the price when one unit of an IC buys from another. See discussion of transfer pricing in Chapter 15.

□ **FIGURE 18–3   Hedging Currency Risks**

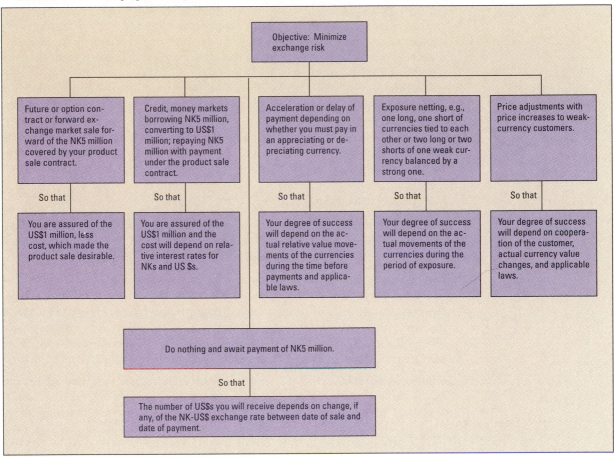

possible for a smaller firm to open a modest account at a foreign bank, but it is much less intimidating to deal with the firm's regular, local bank.

Now, to protect against a drop in the US$'s value, an importer from France can buy the number of French francs that will be needed to pay the French exporter. They can be held in its local account, earning interest until needed.

□ Translation Risks

We have just examined the risks that an international business incurs when it buys and sells between two or more countries and agrees to either make or receive a future payment in a foreign currency. The purchase or sale is a transaction, and the currency value change risk is called a transaction risk.

Financial statements of multinationals must be stated in one currency, just as are the statements of any domestic business. The IC may have businesses and assets in several currencies, such as German marks, French francs, and Japanese yen, but the financial statements would be meaningless for most people if all of those currencies were used. One must be chosen, and the values of the others must be translated to the chosen currency.

Sooner or later, companies with international operations will have assets, liabilities, revenues, and expenses in more than one currency. The financial statements of an American IC must translate assets and so forth from the currencies of their locations into US$s.

The **translation risks** can be illustrated by assuming an American opens a Canadian dollar (C$) bank account of C$1 million at a time when the exchange rate is C$1 = US$1. If, one year later, the exchange rate has changed to C$1.10 = US$1 and the bank balance is still C$1 million, the American IC still has its C$1 million. However, the company must report financially in US$s, and the Canadian bank account is now worth only about US$909,090.

translation risks the assets and liabilities/payables and receivables arising from investments abroad must be translated from the other currencies to your currency

□ *FASB 8* and *FASB 52*

Due to significant variations in the translation methods used by American firms, the Financial Accounting Standards Board (FASB) issued a ruling called *FASB 8* in 1975 to establish uniform translation standards.

Foreign exchange reserves. U.S. companies once established foreign exchange reserves for their foreign subsidiaries to compensate for financial disclosure requirements of foreign exchange gains and losses. However, *FASB 8* put an end to those reserves. Accountants distrusted foreign exchange reserves, feeling they could be juggled, added to, or depleted, not so much to hedge exposure as to hide or disguise management mistakes.

Some did not like *FASB 8*. Some argue that foreign currency gains and losses should not be translated and reported as required by *FASB 8* unless and until an actual gain or loss has been realized. They argue that unrealized gains or losses are only paper entries and that their translation and reporting distort actual business results. *FASB 8* requirements were relaxed in 1981 to lessen the effects of translation on company financial statements. *FASB 52* replaced *FASB 8*.

Realistic information. However, you should bear in mind that ongoing translating and reporting bring up to date the values in US$s of previously reported assets and so forth. Management must base important decisions, such as dividends, pricing, new investment, and asset location, on the consolidation of all such asset and earnings values. It is unrealistic for management to base key decisions on the assumption that exchange rates have not and will not change.

Previously used foreign exchange reserves gave management at least some cushion or leeway in making decisions, regardless of changing exchange rates. Now, unable to use those reserves but required to translate and consolidate, management is taking action to hedge its balance sheets against translation losses.

Management fears. Managers fear that shareholders and analysts will regard translated and reported foreign exchange losses as speculation, or worse, bad management. It is difficult to explain that reported losses are irrelevant or should be ignored. Even though reserves are not permitted under *FASB 52,* management is attempting to insulate financial statements from foreign exchange market fluctuations by other means.[10]

Some of the means for insulating financial statements from currency value fluctuations are the same as those discussed above in connection with transaction risks. Management can hedge, accelerate, or delay payment, net exposures, or adjust prices. There are other means that can be used against transaction risks, but these are more often used in translation situations. Management can neutralize the company's balance sheet through the use of swaps.

neutralizing the balance sheet having monetary assets in amounts approximately equal to monetary liabilities

Neutralizing the balance sheet.   **Neutralizing the balance sheet** means to endeavor to have monetary assets in a given currency approximate monetary liabilities in that currency. In that condition, a fall in the currency value of your assets will be matched by the fall in your payment obligations; thus, the translation risk is avoided.

However, before financial management neutralizes its balance sheet to avoid translation risk, it must look to the business needs of the parent and subsidiary companies. The ongoing business flow of and need for capital, the cost of capital from country to country, payrolls, payables and receivables, optimum location for new investment, and dozens of other business considerations must be factored in before an attempt is made to neutralize the balance sheets of all subsidiaries. In other words, maximizing the profit of the enterprise should be more important than avoiding translation risk where they conflict.

▫ Swaps

swaps trades of assets and liabilities in different currencies or interest rate structures to lessen risks or lower costs

Swaps may be used to protect against transaction risks, are more likely to be used against translation risks, but are most likely to be useful as companies raise or transfer capital. Therefore, we shall treat swaps separately and examine several types: (1) spot and forward market swaps, (2) parallel loans, and (3) bank swaps. Interest rate swaps are dealt with below in the "Capital Raising and Investing" section.

Spot and forward market swaps.   Suppose an American parent wants to lend Italian lira (Il) to its Italian subsidiary and to avoid currency exchange risk. The parent will buy Il in the spot market and lend them to the subsidiary. At the same time, the parent will short the same amount of Il (buying US$s for forward delivery) for the period of the loan. The short Il position is covered with the Il repaid by the subsidiary, and the parent receives the dollars. The cost will depend on the discount rate in the forward market as compared to the spot market rate.

Parallel loans.   Keeping the American parent and its Italian subsidiary of the previous example, let's add an Italian parent company and its American subsidiary. Assume each parent wants to lend to its subsidiary in the subsidiary's currency. This can be accomplished without using the foreign exchange market. The Italian parent lends the agreed amount in lira to the Italian subsidiary of the American parent. At the same time and the same loan maturity, the American parent lends the same amount (at the spot Il US$ rate) in US$s to the American subsidiary of the Italian parent. Figure 18–4 illustrates this.

As you see, each loan is made and repaid in one currency, thus avoiding foreign exchange risk. Each loan should have the right of offset, which means that if either subsidiary defaults on its repayment, the other subsidiary can withhold its repayment. This avoids the need for parent company guarantees.

□ **FIGURE 18–4**
Parallel Loans by Two Parent Companies (Each to the subsidiary of the other)

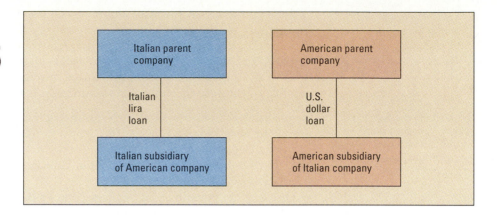

This sort of parallel loan swap can be adapted to many circumstances and can involve more than two countries or companies. If a subsidiary in a blocked currency country has a surplus of that currency in its local operation, perhaps the local subsidiary of another IC needs capital.[11] The other IC would like to provide that capital but would not like to convert more of its hard currency into a soft currency. The subsidiary of the first IC lends its surplus currency to the subsidiary of the second IC. The parent company of the second IC lends the parent company of the first IC an equivalent amount in some other currency that it can use. Figure 18–5 illustrates this.[12]

Interest may or may not be charged on swaps. That usually depends on whether interest rates in the two countries were at similar rates or were widely different. In the latter situation, the borrower getting the higher-cost currency might pay an equivalently higher interest on repayment.

You may have observed that we have not mentioned banks in our discussion of swaps. These company-to-company loans are competition for commercial banks, but some banks will facilitate negotiations or act as a broker between clients in arranging swaps. Investment banks and other money brokers sometimes facilitate or even instigate swaps as a service to clients.

Bank swaps.   Historically, swaps of this kind have been between banks (commercial or central) of two or more countries for the purpose of acquiring temporarily needed foreign exchange; but in recent years, companies have entered the field. A typical use of a bank swap is to finance expansion of an IC subsidiary in an LDC whose currency is soft and nonconvertible or blocked.

The mechanics are simple. Assume a Swiss IC wishes to expand a subsidiary's plant in Indonesia and, in doing so, to minimize foreign exchange risks and to avoid exchanging any more hard Swiss francs (Sfs) for soft Indonesian rupiahs (Irs).

The Swiss parent company may deal either with a commercial bank in Indonesia or with the Indonesian central bank. In either event, the Swiss IC deposits Sfs in a Swiss bank to the credit of the Indonesian bank. In turn, the Indonesian bank lends Irs to the Indonesian subsidiary. At an agreed future date, the Indonesian bank repays the Sfs and the subsidiary repays the Irs.

You may have observed that in this example the Indonesian rupiahs are lent and repaid in Indonesia and the Swiss francs are lent and repaid in Swit-

□ **FIGURE 18–5**
Parallel Swap (Where a soft currency is involved)

zerland, which eliminates the need to use the foreign exchange markets. Thus, exchange market costs are avoided while both parties obtain a foreign currency for which they have a use.

We have spoken of swaps as methods to lessen translation risks and raise capital. There are also more common ways to raise capital.

CAPITAL RAISING AND INVESTING

When a company wishes to raise capital, financial management must make a number of decisions. To cut the costs of capital, financial managers are increasingly exploring the uses of interest rate swaps and currency swaps. As these are relatively new and growing in popularity, we shall treat them separately.

□ Decisions

1. The currency in which the capital will be raised.
2. Long-term estimate of the strength or weakness of that currency.
3. Whether part or all of the capital should be raised by the sale of **equity** instead of **debt**.[13]

equity capital capital raised by selling common stock representing ownership of the company

4. Whether the money should be borrowed from (a) a commercial bank by an ordinary loan; (b) a bank as part of a swap, discussed above; (c) another company as part of a swap or otherwise; (d) another part of the IC; or (e) a public offering in one of the world's capital markets, for example, in the New York or Eurobond markets.

debt capital capital raised by selling bonds representing debt of the company

5. If the decision is made to use one of the world's capital markets, management must then decide in which of those markets it can achieve its objectives at lowest cost. The IC can shop among the national markets in such diverse centers as New York, London, Paris, Zurich, Bahrain, Singapore, Tokyo, and the Cayman Islands. Or it can try the international, or Eurobond, Eurocurrency-type, markets in the above-named centers and elsewhere.[14]

6. How much money the company needs and for how long. For instance, if the company is moving into a new market or product,

there will probably be a period during product introduction, plant construction, or whatever when the new venture will need more capital than it can generate.

7. Whether other sources of money are available. For example, if the company is forming or expanding a joint venture operation, the joint venturer may be a good source of money. Or if the move is into a country or area that wants the IC's technology or management or the jobs that will be created, the government may be a source of low-cost funds. Under such circumstances, the company may also be able to negotiate tax reductions or holidays.*

To optimize the decision results, the company needs up-to-date, accurate information. It should also have good, ongoing relationships with international bank officers and with financial management at other firms.

We have been dealing with external sources of capital, that is, sources outside the company's operations. Of course, a successful company generates its own capital internally, but that subject is not included here.

◻ Interest Rate Swaps

London interbank offering rate

Interest rate swaps are a product of the advent and evolution of currency swaps, which were intended as an arbitrage between currency markets. Interest rate swaps are themselves a form of arbitrage but are between the fixed-rate and the floating-rate interest markets. An interest rate swap, in its most basic form, is nothing more than an exchange by two parties of interest rate flows on borrowings made in these two markets—fixed for floating and floating for fixed. The result: each party obtains the type of liability it prefers and at a more attractive rate.

Bank-intermediated "plain vanilla" swaps. In a typical plain vanilla swap, a BBB-rated U.S. corporation is paired with an AAA-rated foreign bank. The BBB corporation wants to borrow at fixed rates but is discouraged from doing so by the high rates attached to its low rating. The company can borrow in the floating-rate market, however. The AAA foreign bank wants to borrow at floating rates, as its assets are tied to LIBOR. The bank normally pays LIBOR to obtain lendable funds. It is able to borrow at fixed rates, which are better than those the corporation could get.

When the swap is planned, the bank borrows at fixed rates in the Euro-bond market, and the BBB corporation borrows at floating rates. With this done, the two then swap rates on their respective loans. The corporation entices the bank into doing this by discounting the floating rate to the bank by LIBOR minus 0.25 percent. In return, the bank gives the BBB corporation a fixed rate that is better than the one the corporation could acquire on its own. A hypothetical numerical example is shown below.

Assume the BBB firm can borrow fixed-rate at 12.5 percent.

1. AAA bank issues 11 percent fixed-rate debt.
2. BBB firm taps floating-rate market at LIBOR plus 0.5 percent.

---

* A tax holiday is a period after an investment is made during which the government agrees not to tax the company's operations, profits, or executives.

"We need two hundred million bucks by Friday—any ideas?"

Reprinted from *The Wall Street Journal;* permission Cartoon Features Syndicate.

3. BBB firm swaps floating-rate to bank at LIBOR minus 0.25 percent.
4. AAA bank swaps 11 percent fixed-rate to BBB firm.

Net result: the BBB firm saves 150 basis points and passes 75 of them on to the AAA bank; the bank saves 25 basis points on the normal floating rate.

There are nine basic advantages to interest rate swaps. First, swaps give the corporation the flexibility to transform floating-rate debt to fixed-rate, and vice versa. Second, there are potential rate savings, as illustrated previously. Third, swaps may be based on outstanding debt and may thus avoid increasing liabilities. Fourth, swaps provide alternative sources of financing. Fifth, swaps are private transactions. Sixth, there are no SEC reporting or registration requirements, as yet. Seventh, the swap contract is simple and straightforward. Eighth, rating agencies, such as Moody's and S&P, take a neutral to positive position on corporate swaps. Ninth, tax treatment on swaps is uncomplicated, as there are no withholding taxes levied on interest payments to overseas swap partners, and the interest expense of the fixed-rate payer is treated as though it were on a fixed-rate obligation.

The only drawback to swaps is the risk that one swap partner may fail to make the agreed payments to the other swap partner.

The impact of swaps on financial management practices is predicted to be great. It is foreseeable that corporations will use swaps to match assets to liabilities and to protect investments in capital assets, such as plant and equipment, from floating-rate interest fluctuations. Financial institutions also see swaps as a way to match receivables (loans made) to liabilities (investors' deposits). For example, to match a fixed-rate loan, the financial institution would sell a floating-rate CD and then swap it for a fixed-rate liability.

Many corporations and financial institutions have engaged in swaps. The Greyhound Corporation, for example, was involved in $80 million of swaps with Bank of America (three times) and Goldman Sachs (once). Transamerica, ITT Financial, Great Western Financial Corporation, and Consumer Power Company have also been involved in swaps.

□ Currency Swaps

Companies use the currency swap markets when they need to raise money in a currency issued by a country in which they are not well known and must therefore pay a higher interest rate than would be available to a local or better-known borrower. For example, a medium-size American company may have need of Swiss francs (Sfs), but even though it is a sound credit risk, it may be relatively unknown in Switzerland.

If it can find, or if a bank or broker can pair it with, a Swiss company that wants US$s, the swap would work as follows. The American company would borrow US$s in the United States, where it is well known and can get a low interest rate; the Swiss company would borrow SFs in Switzerland for the same reason. They would then swap the currencies and service each other's loans; that is, the Swiss company would repay the US$ loan, while the American company would repay the Sf loan.

SALES WITHOUT MONEY

A number of countries desire goods and products for which they do not have the convertible currency to pay. That has not prevented efforts by many suppliers to sell to them anyway. Such countries are usually communist and/or less developed, and there are differences in dealings with a communist as compared to a noncommunist customer, although applicable to both are variations on the two main nonmoney trade themes—countertrade and industrial cooperation.

□ Communist Customers Are Different

As indicated above, there are some differences between the communist and noncommunist countries in terms of nonmoney trade. The differences can be important.

The noncommunist countries tend to be more open with their production, trade, employment, education, fiscal, and monetary statistics. Such statistics are not notably reliable in LDCs, but the noncommunist ones are more likely to let in and take advice from World Bank, International Monetary Fund, or national aid experts. The statistics are improving.

The noncommunist countries are more likely to get financial aid and technology from UN agencies.[15] They are also more likely to get aid and technology from the Western developed countries, which have the most to give.

It is well to remind ourselves at this point that many former communist and socialist countries are now endeavoring to become democracies and to develop market economies. They are trying to move closer to the West and get IMF and World Bank aid and advice. But their degrees of success are extremely varied, and some are not trying at all. Thus, vast differences remain.

Those differences noted, it is still necessary to utilize the barter, countertrade, compensation, coproduction, and switch devices to sell to the nonoil LDCs and the communist (LDC/C) countries.[16]

Pepsi-Cola truck in Moscow

Courtesy of PepsiCo, Inc. © 1985

◻ Countertrade

countertrade international trade in which at least part of the payment is in some form other than hard, convertible currency

Countertrade usually involves two or more contracts, one for the purchase of DC products or services and one or more for the purchase of LDC/C products or services. A Mitsui study speaks of six varieties of countertrade.[17] They are called (1) counterpurchase, (2) compensation, (3) barter, (4) switch, (5) offset, and (6) clearing account arrangements. All involve to a greater or lesser degree the substitution of LDC/C goods, products, or services for scarce DC money. They may be relatively simple, involving only two countries or companies, or quite complex, calling for a number of countries, companies, currencies, and contracts.

Counterpurchase.   In counterpurchase situations, the goods supplied by the LDC/C are not produced by or out of the goods or products imported from the DC. An example of counterpurchase is PepsiCo's arrangement with the former U.S.S.R., to which PepsiCo sells the concentrate for the drink, which is then bottled and sold in that country. In exchange, PepsiCo has exclusive rights to export Soviet vodka for sale in the West. In 1990, the two parties renewed and expanded the agreement, increasing the amounts of Pepsi-Cola and vodka to be sold and adding a new element. PepsiCo committed itself to buying at least 10 Soviet-built freighters and tankers. PepsiCo intends to lease them on the world market through a Norwegian partner.[18]

Compensation.   Such transactions call for payment by the LDC/C in products produced by DC equipment. The products made in the LDC/C by the DC equipment are shipped to the DC in payment for the equipment. Dresser Industries has a compensation agreement with Poland for tractors. Poland is paying with tractors and other machines that Dresser then markets.

Barter.   Barter is an ancient form of commerce and the simplest sort of countertrade. The LDC/C sends products to the DC that are equal in value to the products delivered by the DC to the LDC/C.

Switch.   Frequently, the goods delivered by the LDC/C are not easily usable or salable. Then a third party is brought in to dispose of them. This process is called *switch trading*.

Offset.   The offset form occurs when the importing nation requires a portion of the materials, components, or subassemblies of a product to be procured in the local (importer's) market. The exporter may set up or cooperate in setting up a parts manufacturing and assembly facility in the importing country.

Clearing account arrangements.   These are used to facilitate the exchange of products over a specified time period. When the period ends, any balance outstanding must be cleared by the purchase of additional goods or settled by a cash payment. The bank or broker acts as an intermediary to facilitate settlement of the clearing accounts by finding markets for counterpurchased goods or by converting goods or cash payments into products desired by the country with a surplus.

How important is countertrade?   Frequently, countertrade agreements and their executions are not reported publicly. Indeed, the parties often prefer privacy and confidentiality for competitive reasons and to not set precedents for future deals. Therefore, estimates of the extent of countertrade vary widely. The U.S. Commerce Department estimates that between 20 and 30 percent of world trade is now subject to some form of countertrade and that the proportion could reach 50 percent in 15 years.

Major U.S. firms report transactions involving some form of countertrade. *Business Week* and General Electric each independently estimate the volume at 30 percent of world trade. By far the lowest estimate, 8 percent, was made by the General Agreement on Tariffs and Trade.

Regardless of which estimate is nearest the truth, the value of countertrade is very large. Apply any of the estimates to the over $3.53 trillion volume of world trade and the result is big.[19]

U.S. government's positions on countertrade.   We say "positions" because different agencies contradict each other, and Congress contradicts itself. The Treasury Department is flatly opposed to countertrade, the Commerce Department helps companies engage in it, and the Export-Import Bank has no policy for dealing with it. In Congress, legislation has been introduced both to curtail countertrading and to encourage countertrading of U.S. surplus agricultural commodities.[20]

Other governments' positions on countertrade.   The governments of most LDCs either encourage or require countertrade, but so also do such industrialized countries as Australia and New Zealand. No country forbids countertrade. For information about the attitudes and laws of individual countries on the subject, see *Business International* listings, such as the one in its July 14, 1986, issue, pages 220–21, which lists the positions of Asian and Pacific countries on countertrade.

Twin problems.   The age-old twin problems with goods coming from the LDC/C side of countertrade transactions are product quality and delivery reliability. In general, there are two ways the DC side is coping with those problems.

One solution is inspection of the goods before they leave the LDC/C plant by a reliable, third-party organization. Two such organizations are the Paris-based Bureau Veritas and the Societé Generale de Surveillance, whose main office is in Geneva.

Roger Gyarmaty of Veritas says, "We go back to the production process to see if the goods are being made to specifications. We see to it that delivery times and terms are being met. And we check the packaging and loading to be sure the goods are not damaged at those points. Companies can save up to two or three times the cost of our services just through fewer headaches when they receive the goods."[21]

A second solution is growing in popularity. The Eastern European banking structure is developing, and the DC countertrade party is increasingly getting a guarantee of quality and delivery from a bank in the LDC/C country. When such a guarantee has been given, the bank takes a stern interest in the product's production line to avoid having to come up with precious foreign exchange in the event of quality or delivery that is not in accordance with the contract.[22]

New directions.   Not all countertrade is between DCs and LDC/Cs. There is trade of Angolan coffee for Russian equipment, and developing countries frequently have agreements encouraging trade with each other, such as those between Argentina and Brazil and among the ASEAN member-countries.

Alan Linger, Lloyds Bank countertrade manager, believes such business could become triangular by including DCs. For example, DC goods would be exported to an Eastern European country, products of which would go to an LDC, which would then complete the triangle by shipping its commodities to the DC.[23]

◻ Industrial Cooperation

industrial cooperation
long-term relationships between DC companies and LDC/C plants in which some or all production is done in the LDC/C plant

Industrial cooperation, which is favored by the LDC/C, requires long-term relationships, with part or all of the production being done in the LDC/C. Part of the resulting products is sold in the DCs or the Third World.

One writer, Ronald E. Hayt, speaks of five different industrial cooperation methods.[24]

1. *Joint venture.* Two or more companies or state agencies combine assets to form a new and distinct economic entity, and they share management, profits, and losses.

2. *Coproduction and specialization.* The factory in the LDC/C produces certain agreed components of a product, while a company in the DC produces the other components. The product is then assembled at both locations for their respective markets.

3. *Subcontracting.* The LDC/C factory manufactures a product according to specifications of the DC company and delivers the product to the DC company, which then markets it.

4. *Licensing.* The LDC/C and DC parties enter into a license agreement whereby the LDC/C enterprise uses DC technology to manufacture a

product. The DC company is paid a license royalty fee in money or in product. The latter method is preferred by the LDC/C.

5. *Turnkey plants.* The DC party is responsible for building the entire plant, starting it, training LDC/C personnel, and turning over the keys to the LDC/C party. Of course, the LDC/C wants to pay in products of the new plant.

Two threads run through countertrade and industrial cooperation. The first is that the LDC/C does not have enough hard, convertible currency to buy what it wants from the DC. That leads to the second, which is the effort of the LDC/C to substitute goods for currency.

INTERNATIONAL FINANCE CENTER

A number of new developments are forcing international companies to pay more attention to financial management. International financial management has become more and more different than domestic financial management, and in several such companies, the finance operation has become a profit center and is no longer merely a service. Some of the new developments are (1) floating exchange rates, whose fluctuations are sometimes volatile; (2) *FASB 52,* which requires translation of assets, liabilities, payables, and receivables from foreign currencies to the company's currency; (3) growth in the number of capital and foreign exchange markets where an IC can shop for lower interest costs and better currency rates; (4) different and changing inflation rates from country to country; (5) advances in electronic cash management systems; and (6) realization by financial managers that through innovative management of temporarily idle cash balances of the IC units, they can increase the yields and the enterprise's profit. The ICs have established **international finance centers.**

international finance
centers handle most or all
international financial
transactions for all units of
an IC

◻ Volatile, Floating Currency Exchange Rates

An international finance center can take advantage of volatile, floating currency exchange rates to make money for the IC in several ways. It would be aware of which currencies are most susceptible to sudden weakness, avoid borrowing in undervalued currencies, and maximize short-term assets in strong currencies.[25] This is currency exposure management.

◻ *FASB 52*

This rule introduced the concept of the "functional currency"—that is, the dominant currency of the economic environment of each IC affiliate. If the functional currency is the local currency (for example, French francs for the French affiliate), *FASB 52* allows translations to flow to the equity section of the parent company's balance sheet, which is less visible and more desirable than putting them in the profit and loss statement, as was required by *FASB 8.* Nevertheless, it is better to minimize dramatic changes in equity, and the international finance center simplifies this in three ways.

1. *Intraenterprise trading.* Financial dealings of this kind are funneled through the center. It can net out open positions for each of the affiliates.

2. *Borrowing*. The center quickly spots exposed assets and receivables that cannot be netted. It can borrow or lend in the appropriate currency to cover those positions.

3. *Hedging*. Other positions that do not net out can be hedged, which the center can do quickly and efficiently.[26]

□ Capital and Exchange Markets

Like any company, an IC needs to raise capital from time to time. Unlike most domestic companies, it needs to exchange currencies. Given the proliferation of capital and exchange markets, the international finance center should advise and direct the parent and affiliates where to raise and exchange money at the lowest costs.

□ Inflation Rates

Inflation goes up and inflation goes down, and while it's going up in one country, it's going down in another. The international finance center should be aware of all those trends and advise and direct the IC system how to protect assets and profits from monetary erosion and other economic and political risks.

□ Electronic Cash Management

Currency exposure management is being simplified. New technology is permitting the creation of worldwide networks that enable firms to transfer funds electronically. The international finance center should evaluate and use the best of those developing systems. Some of them are Electronic Funds Transfer Network, Society for Worldwide Interbank Financial Telecommunications, Clearing House Automated Payment System, and Clearing House Interbank Payments Transfer.[27]

□ Other Uses of the International Finance Center

Mentioned above are only a few of the possible functions of an international finance center. Here are some others:

1. *Handle internal and external invoicing*. The center can make complex decisions about financing international trade among the IC units and between them and outside suppliers and customers. All data on imports and exports can be channeled through the center, which can determine which currencies will be used and how the trades will be financed.[28]

2. *Help weak currency affiliate*. An affiliate with a weak currency could have difficulty obtaining needed imports. By placing itself in the trade chain, the center can arrange the financing needed by such an affiliate.

3. *Strengthen affiliate evaluation and reporting systems*. The center is in a unique position to understand and interpret the performance of affiliates in countries around the world. Inherent differences are exacerbated by volatile exchange rates, different inflation rates, varying tax laws and accounting rules, transfer price policies, and a host of environmental factors. IC decisions about transfer pricing, choosing one subsidiary over another to compete for a

Another sort of Toyota convertible

Courtesy of Toyota Motor Sales, U.S.A., Inc.

contract, or adding capital to one subsidiary rather than another, also complicate performance evaluations, with which the international finance center can assist.

▫ A Racy Convertible from Toyota

Although Toyota, Japan's biggest automaker, was flush with cash during 1986, in that year it floated the biggest convertible yen bond that had ever been seen in Japan. In one go, it raised ¥200 billion (about $1.23 billion), twice as much as any other Japanese company had ever raised in this way. Why?

As the bluest of Japanese blue chips, Toyota commanded the finest of fine terms, and those convertibles carried a coupon of only 1.7 percent. The normal interest for other companies was around 2.5 percent.

Toyota reinvested the ¥200 billion in financial instruments on better terms than it paid and thus made more than it could have made from building and selling automobiles. In Japan, this practice is called *Zaiteku*, or "financial engineering," and numerous companies have been doing it.

For the 10 biggest earners from *Zaiteku*, it accounted for at least a third of their pre-tax profits in the first half of 1986. For Nissan, *Zaiteku* made the difference between a profit and a loss. But not all *Zaiteku* practitioners were as skilled as Nissan—some lost money at it.[29]

SUMMARY

The importance of financial management has so increased in the last few years that some ICs have made financial management a profit center. Financial management is no longer just a service. Foreign currency exchange gains or losses on payables, receivables, assets, and liabilities can substantially alter profit and loss statements and balance sheets.

The chapter examined transaction and translation risks and the means used by multinational company managers to deal with these risks, such as hedges, acceleration or delay of payment, exposure netting, price adjustments, and swaps. It spoke of how *FASB 8* dealt with translation risks and of how *FASB 8* was replaced by *FASB 52.*

The chapter also dealt briefly with the raising and investing of capital and the decisions that financial management must make in connection with those activities. Other types of decisions are called for if a company wishes to do business with a customer that has little or no convertible currency. This involves some form of countertrade or industrial cooperation.

Relatively new and of growing importance are international finance centers. These represent an extension of the increasing recognition of financial management as a potential profit center.

Both interest rate and currency swaps are becoming more and more popular. They are used to cover open positions and to lower interest costs when raising capital.

The objectives of this chapter have been not to identify all the problems of financial management nor all the tools and practices used to solve them, but to introduce you to the subject, to make you aware that international business presents more financial problems than does purely domestic business, and to assure you that most of these problems can be overcome. In fact, not only can they be overcome, but in some instances they can be turned to the company's advantage.

Some of the big Japanese companies have such good credit ratings that they can borrow money at lower interest rates than are available to most Japanese companies. They are therefore able to borrow money and to lend the borrowed money at a profit. The Japanese call this process *Zaiteku*, which translates as "financial engineering."

QUESTIONS

1. Why is an exporter that is to be paid in six months in a foreign currency worried about fluctuating foreign exchange rates?

2. Are there ways that this exporter can protect itself? If so, what are they?

3. How does the credit or money market hedge work?

4. Why is acceleration or delay of payments more useful to an IC than to smaller, separate companies?

5. How would you accomplish exposure netting with currencies of two countries that tend to go up and down together in value?

6. Why is the price adjustment device more useful to an IC than to smaller, separate companies?

7. Some argue that translation gains or losses are not important so long as they have not been realized and are only accounting entries. What is the other side of that argument?

8. Is the parallel loan a sort of swap? How does it work?

9. What advantage does an IC have over a single-country operation in raising capital?

10. How and why would a seller make a sale to a buyer that has no money the seller can use?

11. DC partners in countertrade contracts have had problems with quality and timely delivery of goods from the LDC/C partners. How are they trying to deal with those problems?

□ MINICASE 18–1

Dealing with the Transaction Risk Caused by Fluctuations of Relative Currency Values

You are the finance manager of an American multinational. Your company has sold US$1 million of its product to a French importer. The rate of exchange on the day of sale is US$1 = Ff5, so on that day the 1 million U.S. dollars equals 5 million French francs.

The contract calls for the French importer to pay your company Ff5 million six months from the date of sale. Therefore, your company bears the transaction risk of a change in the currency exchange rates between the US$ and the Ff.

Assume your company has no need for French francs and will want U.S. dollars no later than the payment date. Assume further that you do not wish to carry the transaction risk. Give two methods by which you might protect your company from that risk.

◻ MINICASE 18–2

Countertrade

An American company and a Soviet foreign trade organization (FTO) have reached agreement on all the technical aspects of the product that the company wants to sell and the Soviet Union wants to buy. All export license problems have been cleared, but one obstacle remains. The Soviet Union is not willing to pay in a hard, convertible currency.

The product includes late technology, but it has some relatively simple components. The company has not sold previously to the East or to any customer for which U.S. dollar availability was a difficulty.

The company turns to you, an international business consultant with extensive experience in dealing with communist and Third World customers. What inquiries will you advise your client to make? What steps would you advise the client to take in efforts to consummate the sale and get the U.S. dollars it needs?

◻ MINICASE 18–3

Countertrade

In your countertrade experience, you have encountered two serious problems. Sometimes the quality of the goods supplied by the LDC/C partner is not up to specifications. On other occasions, the LDC/C partner was late in making deliveries or delivered only part of the goods promised.

What are two methods you might try to avoid those problems in future contracts?

◻ MINICASE 18–4

CFO Decisions when the Company Has a Temporary Surplus of Funds

You are the chief financial officer (CFO) of an IC. The parent company has a temporary surplus of funds. You do not foresee an operating need for the money, $5 million, for about six months.

What are some possible uses for that money by the parent? What uses are possible within the IC system? What considerations will govern your decision as to how best to utilize the money?

◻ MINICASE 18–5

Using a Temporary Fund Surplus to Make Some Profit in Currency Forward Markets

Assume your decision in Minicase 18–4 was to use the $5 million to buy one or more open contracts in the currency forward markets. The first contract was long in British pounds at 1.5138 for 30 days with your $5 million.

How many pounds and pence is your company long?

In 30 days when you cover the contract, the price is 1.5347. Did you make or lose money for your company? How much? (For purposes of these minicases, ignore commissions.)

◻ MINICASE 18–6

Short the French Franc

Use the same facts as in Minicase 18–5. Your decision is to invest the $5 million in a contract shorting the French franc at 8.0475 for 30 days. How many francs and cents are you short? In this instance, you cover at the end of the 30-day contract at 7.8992. Did you make or lose money for your company? How much?

SUPPLEMENTARY READINGS

Argy, Victor E. *Exchange Rate Management in Theory and Practice*. Princeton, N.J.: International Finance Section, Department of Economics, Princeton University, 1982.

Babbel, David F. "Determining the Optimum Strategy for Hedging Currency Exposure." *Journal of International Business Studies*, Spring–Summer 1983, pp. 133–39.

Batra, Raveendra N., Shabtai Domenfeld, and Josef Hadar. "Hedging Behavior by Multinational Firms." *Journal of International Business Studies*, Winter 1982, pp. 59–70.

"Big Is Beautiful in Countertrade." *Euromoney*, January 1985, pp. 144–48.

Blin, J.M., Stuart I. Greenbaum, and Donald P. Jacobs. *Flexible Exchange Rates and International Business*. Washington, D.C.: British-North American Committee, 1981.

"Caribbean Financial Centres and Bermuda." *Abecor Country Report*, February 1991.

Countertrade. Antwerp: Kredietbank, September 18, 1987.

East–West Trade: Recent Developments in Countertrade. Paris: Organization for Economic Cooperation and Development, 1981.

Fitzgerald, Bruce. "Countertrade Reconsidered." *Finance & Development*, June 1987, pp. 46–49.

Foreign Currency Translation. Stamford, Conn.: Financial Accounting Standards Board, 1981.

Gernon, Helen. "The Effect of Translation on Multinational Corporations' Internal Performance Evaluations." *Journal of International Business Studies*, Spring–Summer 1983, pp. 103–12.

Herring, Richard J., ed. *Managing Foreign Exchange Risk: Essays Commissioned in Honor of the Centenary of the Wharton School, University of Pennsylvania*. New York: Cambridge University Press, 1983.

Höberg, Bengt, and Clas Wahlbin. "East–West Industrial Cooperation: The Swedish Case." *Journal of International Business Studies*, Spring–Summer 1984, pp. 63–80.

"Japan/China." *Countertrade Outlook* IV, no. 10, March 10, 1986, p. 3.

Kenyon, Alfred. *Currency Risk Management*. New York: John Wiley & Sons, 1981.

Kettell, Brian. *The Finance of International Business*. Westport, Conn.: Quorum Books, 1981.

Kyung, Mo Huh. "Countertrade: Trade without Cash?" *Finance & Development*, December 1983, pp. 14–16.

Lake, D. "The Sogo Shosha Show the Way to Trade." *Trade Finance*, no. 60, April 1988, pp. 23–31.

Miramon, Jacques. "Countertrade: An Illusory Solution." *OECD Observer*, May 1985, pp. 24–29.

Mirus, Rolf, and Bernard Yeung. "Economic Incentives for Countertrade." *Journal of International Business Studies*, Fall 1986, pp. 27–40.

Mitsui's Countertrade Services. *Mitsui Trade News*, March–April 1987.

Neumann, Edward. "Dow Chemical: Profitable Finance in Latin America." *Business Latin America*, November 19, 1990, pp. 365–67.

Palia, A.P. "Worldwide Network of Countertrade Services." *Industrial Marketing Management*, February 1990, pp. 67–76.

Rodriquez, Rita M. *Foreign Exchange Management in U.S. Multinationals*. Lexington, Mass.: Lexington Books, 1980.

Sakamoto, H. "Current Status and Evaluation of Countertrade." *Mitsui Trade News*, March–April 1987, p. 4.

Sanchez, Jesus. "Cola Works Where Currency Can't in Global Barter System." *Los Angeles Times*, April 10, 1990, p. A18.

Sulong, W. "Japanese in Malay Palm Oil Venture." *Financial Times*, March 3, 1988, p. 6.

"Technology Bypassing Banks." *The Economist*, December 16, 1989, p. 79.

Vinson, Joseph D. "Financial Planning for the Multinational Corporation with Multiple Goals." *Journal of International Business Studies*, Winter 1982, pp. 43–58.

Warren, Geoffrey. "Latest in Currency Hedging Methods." *Euromoney*, May 1987, pp. 245–64.

Zonana, Victor. "Boom in Swaps Is Welcome to Some but Worries Others." *Los Angeles Times*, June 21, 1992, pp. D1 and 2.

ENDNOTES

1. There is almost always some cost for protection, and an important management function is to compare the magnitude of the risk with the cost of protection against it.

2. If you were dealing in a currency more actively traded than the krone, such as the British, Canadian, French, Japanese, Swiss, or West German currency, you would use the 180-day futures quotation for that currency.

3. Covered positions are also referred to as "square" or "perfect" positions.

4. In every IC, there is one central company at the top of the organization. That company is called the parent company. The other companies are referred to as affiliated or subsidiary companies.

5. The power of ICs to control the timing and currencies of payment and of asset accumulation has not been ignored by governments. In furtherance of their tax and exchange control policies, most countries have legal limits on acceleration, delays, and intra-IC netting.

6. Currencies may be fixed in value in terms of each other by international agreement; if there are no such agreements, they are said to float.

7. The Netherlands and Belgium are both members of the European Monetary System.

8. Andreas R. Prindl, *Foreign Exchange Risk* (New York: John Wiley & Sons, 1976), p. 61.

9. Ibid., p. 65.

10. "Why a Reserve Is Cheaper," *Euromoney*, February 1979, p. 56.

11. A blocked currency situation arises either because there is no satisfactory market for the currency or because of a country's laws.

12. In such circumstances, the equivalent amount is subject to some negotiation, because a blocked, nonconvertible currency does not have a free market spot or other exchange rate, which would be used when dealing with two convertible currencies.

13. When equity securities (stock) are issued, part of the ownership is being sold. No money is being borrowed that must be repaid, as is the case when debt securities (bonds) are issued.

14. The international, or Euro-type, capital market has been created by national currencies being traded, borrowed, and lent outside their countries of origin. Thus, U.S. dollars outside the United States are Eurodollars, and West German deutsche marks outside Germany are Euromarks.

15. See Chapter 4.

16. Nonoil LDCs are LDCs that are net petroleum importers.

17. *Mitsui Trade News,* March–April 1987, pp. 1–4.

18. John-Thor Dahlburg, "PepsiCo to Swap Cola for Soviet Vodka and Ships," *Los Angeles Times,* April 10, 1990, pp. A1 and 18.

19. Richard L. Holman, "World Trade Volume Grows," *The Wall Street Journal*, March 26, 1991, p. A18; and "World Trade Growth Sputters," *The Wall Street Journal*, March 18, 1992, p. A10.

20. Stephen S. Cohen and John Zysman, "Countertrade Deals Are Running out of Control," *Los Angeles Times,* March 23, 1986, part 4, pp. 3 and 7.

21. "Countertrade: Avoiding Problems with Suppliers," *Business Eastern Europe,* May 16, 1988, p. 155.

22. Alan Spence, "East–West Countertrade Entering New Era of Complexity," *Financial Times,* December 13, 1988, p. 38.

23. Ibid.

24. Ronald E. Hayt, "East–West Trade Growth Potential for the 1980s," *Columbia Journal of World Business,* Spring 1978, p. 63.

25. "Defending against a Strong Dollar," *Business International,* July 16, 1982, p. 226.

26. Christopher Power, "RJR's Foreign Coup," *Forbes,* September 12, 1983, p. 226.

27. "Fine-Tuning Financial Management," *Business International,* January 14, 1983, p. 10.

28. For an account of one reinvoicing center, see "An Invoice Center That Juggles Currencies," *Business Week,* November 27, 1978, p. 128. For a more complete account of international finance centers and in-house banks, see "A Special Report: Global Finance and Investing," *The Asian Wall Street Journal,* October 6, 1986, p. 10.

29. *The Economist,* December 13, 1986, p. 84.

Chapter 19

Production Systems

There is a significant difference between the American and European philosophy of production and the Japanese philosophy of production. The Americans think stock is a necessary evil for smooth-running production, but the Japanese believe stock is an absolute evil.

Shigeo Shingo, dean of Japanese productivity and quality consultants

LEARNING OBJECTIVES

In this chapter, you will study:

1. Japanese efforts to improve quality and lower costs.

2. Problems with just-in-time (JIT).

3. Synchronous production.

4. American and European efforts to improve quality and lower costs.

5. Why multinational firms wish to standardize production processes and procedures on a worldwide basis.

6. The impediments to worldwide standardization of production processes and procedures.

7. The four principal factors involved in the efficient operation of the production system—plant location, plant layout, materials handling, and the human element.

8. The two general classes of activities, productive and supportive, that must be performed in all production systems.

9. Some of the reasons why a given production system may not perform as expected.

10. The principal supportive activities—purchasing, maintenance, and the technical function.

KEY WORDS AND CONCEPTS

- Just-in-time
- Total quality control (TQC)
- Quality circles (quality control circles)
- Taylor's scientific management system
- Preventive (planned) maintenance
- Synchronous production
- Bottleneck
- Manufacturing rationalization
- Backward vertical integration
- Intermediate technology
- Appropriate technology
- Export processing zones

BUSINESS INCIDENT

Allen-Bradley and Computer Integrated Manufacturing

Daily, the Milwaukee plant of Allen-Bradley produces between 1,000 and 4,000 controllers for electric motors. It prices them competitively, guarantees they will work, and promises they will be ready to deliver the day after the order is in. The company does this with only six people attending 26 machines, which use 180 components in producing up to 1,000 variations of contactors and relays. A mainframe computer receives the customer's order and downloads manufacturing instructions to microcomputers that guide the production machinery. Products go through 3,500 checks during the process, and, when a product fails, it's rejected and the system automatically builds a new one so that the order is complete at the end of the day. Production lot sizes can be as small as *one*.

The plant was built to lower production costs because European manufacturers were taking some of Allen-Bradley's domestic market, although the company's president says it was also part of his plan to build international sales. How successful was the plan? Not only does the company compete pricewise in the United States with French and German manufacturers, but its overseas sales now make up 25 percent of its total sales. Ten years ago, overseas sales were only 3 percent. Based on its U.S. experience, the company has since installed two similar production lines in its English plant.

Source: "Allen-Bradley Tries to Fight Competition by Tooling Up," *Datamation*, March 15, 1988, pp. 33–36; "Manufacturing's New Window of Opportunity," *The Wall Street Journal*, April 29, 1988, p. 29; and telephone conversation with Janet Gottfredeen, March 13, 1992.

The quotation at the beginning of the chapter states what had been a long-standing difference between the production philosophies of Japan and those of other industrialized nations. There are a number of reasons for this difference.

Immediately after World War II, General Douglas MacArthur, the supreme commander of the Allied powers in Japan, wanted reliable radios so the Japanese could hear the broadcasts of the occupation forces' order and propaganda programs. However, the Japanese radio vacuum tubes had a 90 percent failure rate. Because the local manufacturers could not give him the reliable radios he wanted, MacArthur sent for two American engineers, who prepared a two-month seminar on mass production as a system in which quality inspection is expensive and wasteful. They taught that statistics can be used to analyze what the system is doing and to get it under control to produce quality products. MacArthur ordered senior executives of the major Japanese firms to attend.

The final phase of the training was a course in the statistical control of quality. Because the man the engineers wanted to teach the course was not available, they turned to W. Edwards Deming, a statistician who had taught thousands of American industrial engineers how to use statistics in manufacturing during the war. In less than five years after the ending of World War II, which destroyed Japan's production capability, Americans were teaching statistical quality control to Japan's engineers and the importance of quality to Japan's senior industrialists.[1] In appreciation of Deming's assistance, for 40 years Japan has awarded the prestigious Deming Prize annually to companies that meet a standard based on an evaluation process.[2] Florida Light & Power was a winner in 1989.

What did Japan have to do to compete internationally? Japanese manufacturers realized that because of the limited size of the country's economy, they would have to export to grow. They were also aware that, because of the country's lack of natural resources, they would have to earn foreign exchange from exports to pay for the importation of petroleum, coal, and raw materials.

To be competitive in world markets, Japanese companies would have to provide high-quality products at low prices. But "Made in Japan" meant poor quality and shoddy manufacture to the rest of the world. For example, Toyota's first export, the Toyopet, was a disaster, and the company withdrew from the U.S. market. In the 1950s, the Japanese brought in various American experts, such as Juran, Feigenbaum, Deming, and others, who were largely ignored by American manufacturers. There are too many reasons for the Americans' attitudes to describe here, but essentially American firms were very successful at that time concentrating on producing quantity. They were selling everything they could make.[3]

JAPANESE EFFORTS TO LOWER COSTS AND IMPROVE QUALITY

◻ Lower Costs

In examining the components of their costs, Japanese managers realized what all firms know: inventory costs are a major factor. Getting rid of inventory lowers labor cost by 40 percent, for example.[4] To operate without inventory, however, certain requirements would have to be met:

Toyopet—the first Japanese car to be exported

Courtesy of Toyota Motor Sales, U.S.A., Inc.

just-in-time a balanced system in which there is little or no delay time and idle in-process and finished goods inventory

1. Components, whether purchased from outside suppliers or made in the same plant, had to be defect free, or else the production line would be shut down while the workers in all successive operations waited for usable inputs.

2. Parts and components had to be delivered to each point in the production process at the time they were needed; hence the name **just-in-time.**

3. Customers everywhere want delivery when they make the purchase, so sellers maintain inventories of finished products. Sales often are made because one firm can supply the product from stock but a competitor cannot. How long do you want to wait for delivery of your car after you buy it?

To eliminate inventories of finished goods and still respond quickly to customers' orders required manufacturers to set up flexible production units, which necessitated rapid setup times. Toyota, for example, learned to change a punch press die in 12 minutes; the same operation required three to six hours at General Motors.

4. It was also necessary to reduce process time. One way is to lower the time to transport work in progress from one operation to the next. American and European preoccupation with economic order lots resulted in their grouping machines by function (all drill presses together, punch presses together, etc.), but transporting the machines' output to the next functional area takes time and costs money. Japanese firms grouped machines according to the workflow of a single product (an American invention—a separate production line for each product), which virtually eliminated transport cost. Also, because parts were arriving immediately from one operation to the next, when the output of the preceding operation was defective, that operation could be stopped until the cause was rectified. Moreover, this too lowered production costs because fewer defective parts were produced.

5. Flexible manufacturing enables product changes to be made rapidly, but each change in the production line still costs money. So, the manufacturers simplified product lines and designed the products to use as many of the same parts as possible. This also contributed to the company suppliers' acceptance of the just-in-time concept because they received fewer but larger orders, which permitted longer, less costly (fewer production changeovers) production runs.

6. For just-in-time to be successful, manufacturers had to have the cooperation of their suppliers. They could not follow the common American practice of having numerous vendors, which buyers often play against one another to get the best price. Japanese firms used fewer vendors and sought to establish close relationships with them, including calling them in during the design of the product.

7. To lower costs, improve quality, and lower production times, Japanese managements required product designers, production managers, purchasing people, and marketers to work as a team. They realized that something better than the American and European "bucket brigade" was needed. That term stems from an analogy between the ancient method of putting out fires and the process by which an idea becomes a product in many firms.

> The research laboratory gets an idea. It passes the idea to the engineering department, which converts it to a design with all parts specified. Manufacturing gets the specifications from engineering and figures out how to make the product. Responsibility for selling it is "dumped" on marketing.

8. Getting these people together enabled suppliers to suggest using the lower-cost standard parts they regularly produce, manufacturing to indicate when a design change could simplify the production process, and marketing to contribute the customer's viewpoint, *all before the first product was produced.*[5]

□ Improve Quality

To improve quality, Japanese managers had to use a different human relations approach than the one common in the United States and Europe (more about this in the next chapter). Everyone—from top management to worker—had to be committed to quality. Getting worker involvement was not especially difficult, thanks to the Japanese practice of lifetime employment and the social benefits that Japanese companies offer their employees.

The idea for **total quality control** (**TQC**)—quality control in all functions of the firm—originated, like many of the ideas that the Japanese adopted, with an American. Armand Feigenbaum first wrote about total quality control in 1951, and he suggested assigning quality control specialists to all functional areas of the firm. The Japanese interpreted the idea to mean that every functional area should think about quality control without the need for inspectors, an important difference.[6]

A Japanese quality expert, Ishikawa, extended the TQC concept to include **quality circles** (**quality control circles**). Look at how the president of Komatsu, Caterpillar's Japanese competitor, describes the use of quality circles in his company.

total quality control (TQC) a system that integrates the development, maintenance, and improvement of quality among all functional areas of the firm

quality circles (quality control circles) small work groups that meet periodically to discuss ways to improve their functional areas and the quality of the product

The objective of the quality circle is to take part of the responsibility for the quality goal of each section. "Quality circle members are aware of the extent to which their achievement of their objectives will contribute to the results of their department, and also to the business of the company as a whole."

A small group of employees, led by a foreman who has previously received quality control education, independently undertakes quality control activities. The circle's activities are divided among subdivisions of the circle led by a person junior to the foreman. Here is an example to illustrate that quality circles are used in all functional areas, not just in manufacturing.

One day, telephone operators received complaints from outside callers regarding delays in answering telephones, so they surveyed company employees, who confirmed that the complaint was valid. They then studied the average time they were taking to answer a call and found that it was 7.4 seconds. They called the telephone company, who informed them that its standard was three seconds. The quality circle then discussed how to reach the three-second standard.[7]

Problems with Implementing the Japanese Just-In-Time System

Many American manufacturers rushed to Japan to study the just-in-time (JIT) "miracle" and mistakenly copied parts of it without realizing that it was a *total system* covering management of materials, people, and relations with suppliers. Another difficulty was the difference in attitudes (a cultural force) between Japanese and Western managers. American managers and unions still valued highly the specialization of worker functions based on **Taylor's scientific management system.** This system contradicts the principles of quality circles: (1) participative decision making and (2) problem-solving capabilities of workers. Americans, pressured for quick results, were disappointed when quality circles didn't offer immediate solutions for improvement. The practice of not guaranteeing long-term employment also made it more difficult to attain the company loyalty for JIT.[8]

Problems with JIT

American production experts also realized that there were problems with JIT itself:

1. JIT is restricted to operations that produce the same parts repeatedly because it is a *balanced* system; that is, all operations are designed to produce the same quantity of parts. Yet, as Westinghouse saw when visiting Mitsubishi, repetitive operations may appear only in parts of the manufacturing process. It is far less useful for job shops (firms, or departments within larger firms, that specialize in producing small numbers of custom-designed products).*

2. Because JIT is a balanced system, if one operation stops, the entire production line stops—there is no inventory to keep succeeding operations working.

3. Achieving a balanced system is difficult because production capacities differ among the various classes of machines. It might require five

---

Taylor's scientific management system
a system based on scientific measurements that prescribes a division of work whereby planning is done by managers and plan execution is left to supervisors and workers

---

*Job shop also refers to a production system in which departments are organized around specific operations (grinding, drilling, etc.).

lathes to keep one punch press busy, for example, and it takes dozens of tire-building machines to use the output of just one calender, a huge machine (similar in size to a newspaper printing press) that rubberizes the fabric used in making tires. This problem is less severe for large production units, of course.

4. JIT makes no allowances for contingencies, so every piece must be defect free when it is received, and delivery promises must be kept. **Preventive (planned) maintenance** is crucial. A sudden machine breakdown will stop the entire production process.

5. JIT is a slow process to put into effect because it is the result of trial and error (it is evolutionary).[9]

preventive (planned) maintenance maintenance done according to plan, not when machines break down

□ Synchronous Production

The problem with JIT, especially the long time required for its installation in a production system, caused some American firms to realize that something else was needed if they were to regain market share lost to the Japanese. Some turned to **synchronous production,** also called synchronized manufacturing or optimized production technology. It is a production system whose output is set at the output of the operation (**bottleneck**) that is working at full capacity.[10] Software was available that took into account such constraints as limited facilities, personnel, and machines when developing production schedules. This made installation much faster because production schedules and simulation could be done on a computer instead of having to arrive at solutions by trial and error, as is necessary with JIT.[11]

synchronous production an entire manufacturing process with unbalanced operations that emphasizes total system performance

bottleneck operation in a production system whose output sets the limit for the entire system's output

Instead of attempting to achieve a balanced system like JIT, in which the capacities of all operations are equal, synchronous production aims to balance the *product flow* through the system, which leaves output levels of the various operations *unbalanced*.[12] For example, with the bottleneck operation producing at full capacity, perhaps only 60 percent capacity is needed at another operation. Because there is no reason for this operation to produce over 60 percent of its capacity, it is stopped at that point; anything more would be unwanted inventory. Inasmuch as work is assigned to each operation rather than to the entire system, as in JIT, there is no need for more work in process than that which is actually being worked on. Inventory may also be placed near the bottleneck to avoid any shutdown in this crucial operation, and sometimes, unlike JIT, there may even be a quality control inspector to check the bottleneck operation's input.

Notice that management's attention is focused on the bottleneck rather than on the other operations, because a production increase at the bottleneck means an increase for the entire production system; an increase in a nonbottleneck operation only adds to that machine's idle time.

Note another important difference between JIT and synchronous production: a defective part or component at any point of the production process can shut down a JIT system. But because a synchronous production system has excess capacity in all operations except at the bottleneck, any defective part produced before the bottleneck can be remade, and thus the entire system is not stopped.

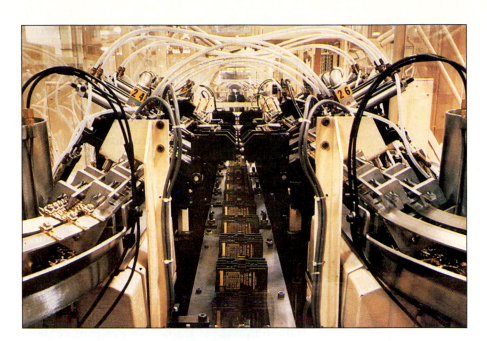

The world–class contactor assembly line at Allen-Bradley.

Incidentally, the deemphasis of the full utilization of resources is requiring a change in the use of some historical cost accounting measurements. Inventory is valued at the cost of the materials it contains; value added is ignored, for example.

AMERICAN AND EUROPEAN EFFORTS TO IMPROVE QUALITY AND LOWER COSTS

We all know how the Japanese efforts to improve product quality while reducing cost have changed world opinion about their products. There are exceptions, however, as the Worldview on p. 673 illustrates.

Many companies, such as Allen-Bradley in the Business Incident, have successfully put into place the JIT system or have highly synchronized their manufacturing systems. Moreover, they have taken advantage of the capabilities of computers and robots to further improve productivity and quality. You recognize, of course, that neither robots nor computers are essential for the implementation of most of the concepts we have described.

□ Western Firms that Are Succeeding

General Motors, General Electric, Ford, IBM, Motorola—the list is long of American firms that have a synchronous production and total quality control (TQC) system. Corning, the glass manufacturer, has changed the way it designs and makes products to better compete with its Japanese and European competitors. It analyzed the 235 operations in its manufacturing process, eliminated 115 of them, and reduced production time from four weeks to three days. The company reduced the worker job classifications to two, so

OUR FUNDAMENTAL OBJECTIVE
(Everyone's Overriding Responsibility)

Total Customer Satisfaction

(M) **MOTOROLA INC.**

KEY BELIEFS—*how we will always act*
- Constant Respect for People
- Uncompromising Integrity

KEY GOALS—*what we must accomplish*
- Increased Global Market Share
- Best in Class
  —*People*
  —*Marketing*
  —*Technology*
  —*Product*
  —*Manufacturing*
  —*Service*
- Superior Financial Results

KEY INITIATIVES—*how we will do it*
- Six Sigma Quality
- Total Cycle Time Reduction
- Product and Manufacturing Leadership
- Profit Improvement
- Participative Management Within, and Cooperation Between Organizations

Courtesy of Motorola

REASONS FOR WORLDWIDE STANDARDIZATION OF PRODUCTION SYSTEMS AND FACILITIES

The advantages of synchronous production and TQC are compelling reasons why numerous global and multinational corporations are installing them worldwide. Certainly, customers everywhere want quality products at low prices. In large markets, such as the EC and Japan, some American firms are copying home country production systems (for example, Allen-Bradley in Scotland). Tecktronix, a leading American producer of oscilloscopes, introduced in its English plant a system similar to the one in its home plant.[21] Ford's German plant has installed a pilot just-in-time program, which will be adopted in its other European plants.[22] In addition to those just mentioned, there are other important, although perhaps less obvious, advantages to worldwide standardization.

◻ Organization and Staffing

Simpler and less costly when standardized.   The standardization of production processes and procedures simplifies the production organization at headquarters because their replication enables the work to be accomplished with a smaller staff of support personnel. Fewer labor-hours in plant design are involved because each new plant is essentially a scaled-up or scaled-down version of an existing one. The permanent group of experts that worldwide companies maintain to give technical assistance to overseas plants can be smaller. Extra technicians who are accustomed to working with the same machinery can be borrowed from the domestic operation as needed.

Worldwide uniformity in production methods also increases headquarters' effectiveness in keeping the production specifications current. Every firm has hundreds of specifications, and these are constantly being changed because of

WORLDVIEW
"Made in Japan" Could Mean Made for Mischief

Tokyo—If you think "Made in Japan" means the world's best, come over to my house for a piece of toast.

If you're lucky, just the upper half will be black. More likely, your toast won't pop up until the smoke alarm screams. Or it won't stay down. Four years of breakfasts haven't produced a quality-controlled piece of toast from my Toshiba toaster.

Sure, everyone has evil-tempered-toaster stories. But Japanese goods aren't supposed to behave badly. Japan has a trade surplus because its products are flawless and Americans make junk, right?

Hogwash. Japan still churns out its share of schlock, and I'd swear it has all landed in my house.

Take my Japanese computer. With fine-tuned reliability, the NEC desktop machine I'm using right now inserts uncalled-for letters into my text. I type "w-o-r" and get "w-o-j-r." "Wojrse" still is a bug lurking in the laptop machine that I bring home from "wojrk." Every few months, the bug sneaks into the memory, devouring articles, letters, memos, everything. The bug is hungriest around deadline time.

Other Japanese junk abounds in the house's every corner. In my closet hang shirts whose buttons popped off on first wearing. The telephone picks up radio baseball broadcasts.

Our Japanese-made stereo is an assemblage of lemons. The Akai tape deck eats the Maxell tapes. The Kenwood compact disk player is persnickety about its music; it adores Mozart, but skips and stutters over Billie Holiday disks. And now that its warranty has run out, the machine flatly rejects Dire Straits, producing a sort of munching noise instead.

The Kenwood people say they can fix the machine—for nearly as much money as the price of a new one. Experience makes me wonder. Nikon specialists have "fixed" my Nikon camera three times, but it still doesn't work right.

Japanese junk has even caused minor tragedies in our home. His first day in Japan, my six-year-old nephew spent his hard-earned allowance on one of those tin toy helicopters that twirls its little plastic blades when you scuff its wheels along the floor. After 15 minutes of normal kid use, the propellers went limp, fatally crippled by some internal injury.

The dead chopper rests in pieces deep in toy box. Try explaining Japanese design superiority to my nephew.

Another demise was the ice cream maker my wife bought for my birthday. A "marvel" of Japanese engineering, it was designed so that salty ice water trickled into the motor. The electric coils turned into a hunk of rust that had to be overhauled on the kitchen table every time we dragged the thing out. It now rusts away in a landfill somewhere.

Then there's the house itself. Owned by an executive on transfer, it has the features of a typical, new Japanese upper-middle-class home: kitschy light fixtures made of fake-brass-colored tin, walls as thin as cardboard, and aluminum window frames that belong on a trailer home.

In fairness, I admit to having my share of Japanese wonders—like the vintage Sony Trinitron I picked out of the neighbor's trash heap four years ago. It still works perfectly, as do a score of other electronic gizmos around the house.

But I think I've found a solution to the other junk. I now buy Korean shirts, am switching to an IBM-compatible computer, and am eyeing a Swedish Hasselblad camera. We hand-crank ice cream in an American freezer we bought at a yard sale.

As for the toaster, a colleague has explained the problem to me. "The Japanese simply haven't gotten down the learning curve on toasters yet," he tells me.

In the meantime, I'm sending for my parents' old chrome General Electric toaster—the one that's worked since they got it as a wedding present in 1953.

Source: Stephen Kreider Yoder, " 'Made in Japan' Could Mean Made for Mischief," *The Wall Street Journal,* September 21, 1987, p. 24.

new raw materials or manufacturing procedures. If all plants, domestic and foreign, possess the same equipment, notice of a change can be given with one indiscriminate mailing; there is no need for highly paid engineers to check each affiliate's list of equipment to see which ones are affected. Companies whose production processes are not unified have found that maintaining a current separate set of specifications for each of 15 or 20 affiliates is both more costly (larger staff) and more error prone.

Logistics of supply.   Management has become increasingly aware that greater profits may be obtained by organizing all of its companies' production facilities into one logistical supply system that includes all of the activities required to move raw materials, parts, and finished inventory from vendors, between enterprise facilities, and to customers. The standardization of processes and machinery provides a reasonable guarantee that parts manufactured in the firm's various plants will be interchangeable. This assurance of interchangeability enables management to divide the production of components among a number of subsidiaries to achieve greater economies of scale and to take advantage of the lower production costs in some countries.

manufacturing rationalization division of production among a number of production units, thus enabling each to produce only a limited number of components for all of a firm's assembly plants

Rationalization.   **Manufacturing rationalization,** as this production strategy is called, involves a change from manufacturing by a subsidiary only for its own national market to producing a limited number of components for use by all subsidiaries. The Ford Escort™ car, for example, is sourced from a number of Ford factories. Figure 19–1 illustrates that the global car receives components from 15 nations.

SKF, a major bearing manufacturer with headquarters in Sweden, was able to reduce the types of ball bearings produced in five major overseas subsidiaries years ago from 50,000 to 20,000. Of the 20,000 remaining types, 7,000 have been rationalized among the five plants, and the other 13,000 are produced solely by one or another subsidiary for its local customers.[23]

These examples illustrate that for production rationalization to be possible, the product mix must first by rationalized; that is, the firm must elect to produce products that are identical worldwide or regionwide. Once this has been done, each subsidiary can be assigned to produce certain components for other foreign plants, thus attaining a higher volume with a lower production cost than would be possible if it manufactured the complete product for its national market only. Obviously, this strategy is not viable when consumers' tastes and preferences differ markedly among markets. For less differentiated products, however, manufacturing rationalization permits economies of scale in production and engineering that would otherwise be impossible. Nissan Motors has been able to employ the most modern methods, including CAM,* in its Mexican motor plant because of the high input it obtains through exports (80 percent of the total) to Tennessee, Japan, and Latin America. And Ford, as you read in Chapter 16, supplies engines for all Ford-Europe from one plant in England.[24]

---

* CAM—computer-assisted manufacturing—generally includes automated materials handling and programmable robots.

☐ **FIGURE 19–1**
Global Manufacturing: The Component Network for the Ford Escort in Europe

United Kingdom
Carburetor, rocker arm, clutch, ignition, exhaust, oil pump, distributor, cylinder bolt, cylinder head, flywheel ring gear, heater, speedometer, battery, rear wheel spindle, intake manifold, fuel tank, switches, lamps, front disc steering wheel, steering column, glass, weatherstrips, locks, mirrors, starter, alternator

France
Cylinder head, master cylinder, brakes, underbody coating, weatherstrips, clutch release bearings, seat pads and frames, transmission cases, clutch cases, tires, suspension bushes, ventilation units, heater, hose clamps, sealers, hardware

Canada
Glass, radio

United States
EGR valves, hydraulic tappet, glass

Italy
Carburetor, lamps, defroster grills

Sweden
Hose clamps, cylinder bolt, exhaust down pipes, pressings, hardware

Netherlands
Tires, paints, hardware

Belgium
Tires, tubes, seat pads, brakes, trim

Spain
Wiring harness, radiator and heater hoses, fork clutch release, air filter, battery, mirrors

Switzerland
Underbody coating, speedometer gears

Federal Republic of Germany
Locks, pistons, exhaust, ignition, switches, front disc, distributor, weatherstrips, rocker arm, speedometer, fuel tank, cylinder bolt, cylinder head gasket, front wheel knuckles, rear wheel spindle, transmission cases, clutch cases, clutch, steering column, battery, glass, mirrors, starter, alternator

Norway
Exhaust flanges, tires

Denmark
Fan belt

Austria
Tires, radiator and heater hoses

Japan
Starter, alternator, cone and roller bearings, windscreen washer pump

Note: Final assembly takes place in Halewood (United Kingdom) and Saarlouis (Federal Republic of Germany).
Source: Based on information from Ford representative, June 19, 1989.

Purchasing.   When foreign subsidiaries are unable to purchase raw materials and machinery locally, they generally look for assistance from the purchasing department at headquarters. Because unified processes require the same materials everywhere, buyers can handle foreign requirements by simply increasing their regular orders to their usual suppliers and passing on the volume discounts to the subsidiaries. However, when special materials are required, purchasing agents must search out new vendors and place smaller orders, often at higher prices.

□ Control

All the advantages of the worldwide standardization of production cited thus far also pertain to the other functions of management. Three aspects of control—quality, production, and maintenance—merit additional discussion, however.

Quality control.   When production equipment is similar, home office control of quality in foreign affiliates is less difficult because management can expect all plants to adhere to the same standard. The home office can compare the periodic reports that all affiliates submit and quickly spot deviations from the norm that require remedial action, such as a large number of product rejects. Separate standards for each plant because of equipment differences are unnecessary.

Production and maintenance control.   A single standard also lessens the task of maintenance and production control. The same machinery should produce at the same rate of output and have the same frequency of maintenance no matter where it is located. In practice, there will be deviations because of the human and physical factors (dust, humidity, temperature), but at least similar machinery permits the home office to establish standards by which to determine the effectiveness of local managements. Furthermore, the maintenance experience of other production units as to the frequency of overhauls and the stock of spare parts needed will help plants avoid costly, unforeseen stoppages from sudden breakdowns.

□ Planning

When a new plant can be built that is a duplicate of others already functioning, the planning and design will be both simpler and quicker because it is essentially a repetition of work already done:

1. Design engineers need only copy the drawings and lists of materials that they have in their files.
2. Vendors will be requested to furnish equipment that they have supplied previously.
3. The technical department can send the current manufacturing specifications without alteration.
4. Labor trainers experienced in the operation of the machinery can be sent to the new location without undergoing special training on new equipment.
5. Reasonably accurate forecasts of plant erection time and output can be made based on the experience with existing facilities.

In other words, the duplication of existing plants greatly reduces the engineering time required in planning and designing the new facilities and eliminates many of the start-up difficulties inherent in any new operation. To be sure, a newly designed plant causes problems when it is erected domestically, but those problems are greater when the plant is located in a different environment at a great distance from headquarters. Just how important the savings from plant duplication are was emphasized in a study of the chemical and refining industries that indicated the cost of technology transfer was lowered by 34 and 19 percent for the second and third start-ups.[25]

Since the case for international standardization of production is so strong, why do differences among plants in the same company persist?

IMPEDIMENTS TO WORLDWIDE STANDARDIZATION OF PRODUCTION FACILITIES

Generally, it is easier for international corporations to standardize the concepts of total quality control and synchronous production in their overseas affiliates than it is to standardize the actual production facilities. Units of a multiplant operation differ with respect to size, machinery, and procedures because of the intervention of the foreign environmental forces, especially the economic, cultural, and political forces.

◻ Environmental Forces

Economic forces.   The most important element of the economic forces that impedes production standardization is the wide range of market sizes, which we examined in Chapter 14.[26] To cope with the great variety of production requirements, the designer generally has the option of selecting either a *capital-intensive process* incorporating automated, high-output machinery or a *labor-intensive process* employing more people and semimanual general-purpose equipment with lower productive capacity. The automated machinery is severely limited in flexibility (variety of products and range of sizes), but once set up, it will turn out in a few days what may be a year's supply for some markets.[27] For many processes, this problem may be resolved by installing one machine of the type used by the hundreds in the larger home plant. However, sometimes this option is not available; some processes use only one or two large machines, even in production facilities with large output—as we mentioned in the discussion of standardized manufacturing. Until recently, when the option was not available, plant designers had to choose between the high-output specialized machinery and the lower-output general-purpose machines mentioned earlier.

However, a third alternative has become available, though its high cost and high technological content have limited its application to manufacturers in industrialized nations. *Computerized integrated manufacturing (CIM)* systems enable a machine to make one part as easily as another in random order on an instruction from a bar code reader of the kind used in supermarkets. This reduces to one the economic batch quantity—the minimum number of a part that can be made economically by a factory. There is a limit, nevertheless, to the variety of shapes, sizes, and materials that can be accommodated.

Another economic factor that influences the designer's selection of processes is the *cost of production*. Automation tends to increase the productivity per worker because it requires less labor and results in higher output per machine. But, if the desired output requires the machines to be operated only a fraction of the time, the high capital costs of automated equipment may result in excessive production costs even though labor costs are low. In situations where production costs favor semimanual equipment, the designer may be compelled to install high-capacity machines instead because of a lack of floor space. Generally, the space occupied by a few high-capacity machines is less than that required for the greater number of semimanual machines to produce the same output. On the other hand, because the correct type and quality of process materials are indispensable for specialized machinery, the engineers could not recommend this equipment if such materials are unobtainable either locally or through importation. Occasionally, management will bypass this obstacle by **backward vertical integration;** that is, manufacturing capacity to produce essential inputs will be included in the plant design even though it would be preferable from an economic standpoint to purchase these materials from outside vendors. For example, a textile factory might include a facility for producing nylon fibers.

backward vertical integration establishing facilities to manufacture inputs used in the production of a firm's final products

The economic forces we have described are fundamental considerations in plant design, yet elements of the cultural and political forces may be sufficiently significant to override decisions based on purely economic reasoning.

Cultural forces. When a factory is to be built in an industrialized nation where there is a sizable market and high labor costs, capital-intensive processes will undoubtedly be employed. However, such processes may also be employed in developing countries, which commonly lack skilled workers despite their abundant supply of labor. This situation favors the use of specialized machines because, although a few highly skilled persons are needed for maintenance and setup, the job of *attending* these machines (starting, feeding stock) can be performed by unskilled workers after a short training period. In contrast, general-purpose machinery requires many more skilled operators.[28]

These operators could be trained in technical schools, but the low prestige of such employment, a cultural characteristic, affects both the demand for and the supply of vocational education. Students do not demand it, and the traditional elitist attitude of the educational administrators in many developing nations causes resources to be directed to professional education instead of to the trades where they are needed.

Firms that attempt to reduce their requirements for skilled workers by installing automatic machinery, are, of course, left vulnerable to another cultural characteristic of the less developed countries—absenteeism. If the setup and maintenance crews fail to report to work, the entire production line may be shut down. Some managers resolve this difficulty by training a few extra people as backups. Having extra personnel is viewed as production insurance necessary to keep the plant in operation. This extra expense may be far less than the expense of handling the greater number of labor-management problems resulting from larger work force in a nonautomated factory of similar capacity.

These economic and cultural variables, important as they are, are not the only considerations of management; the requirements of the host government must be met if the proposed plant is to become a reality.

Political forces. When planning a new production facility in a developing country, management is frequently confronted by an intriguing paradox. Although the country desperately needs new job creation, which favors labor-intensive processes, government officials often insist on the most modern equipment. Local pride may be the cause, or it may be that these officials, wishing to see the new firm export, believe only a factory with advanced technology can compete in world markets. They not only may be reluctant to take chances on "inferior" or untried alternatives, they may also feel that low-productivity technology will keep the country dependent on the industrialized countries. In some developing countries, this fear has been formalized by laws prohibiting the importation of used machinery.

□ Some Design Solutions

Hybrid design.   More often than not, the resultant plant design will be a hybrid of capital-intensive processes when they are considered essential to ensure product quality and labor-intensive methods. As an example, machine welding rather than hand welding may be required, while the painting, packaging, and materials handling are performed with semimanual equipment.

Intermediate technology.   In recent years, the press of a growing population and the rise in capital costs have forced governments of developing nations to search for something less than highly automated processes. They are becoming convinced that there should be something midway between the capital- and labor-intensive processes that will create more jobs, require less capital, but still produce the desired product quality. Governments are urging investors to consider an **intermediate technology,** which, unfortunately, is not readily available in the industrialized nations. This means that the ICs cannot transfer the technology with which they are familiar but must develop new and different manufacturing methods. It is also possible that the savings in reduced capital costs of the intermediate technology may be nullified by higher start-up costs and the greater expense of its transfer.

intermediate technology
production methods between capital- and labor-intensive methods

□ Appropriate Technology

One global corporation, Philips in the Netherlands, has worked systematically to match a country's markets with its resources and ability to produce certain components to obtain an optimal technological mix. A pilot plant devises commercially viable production patterns based on the factors that enable foreign subsidiaries to manufacture small volumes with processes less automated than those of the home plant.

Rather than search for an intermediate technology, the emphasis of Philips and others is on employing the **appropriate technology,** which can range from the most advanced to the most primitive, depending on the economic, sociocultural, and political variables. For some products, the superiority in productivity and product quality of the modern process is so marked that it makes the labor-intensive method totally inappropriate. Compare resource mapping by satellites with geologists on horseback, for example. Yet in the case of sugar refining, it was found in India that for the same amount of capital, either a large plant capable of producing 12,000 tons of sugar annually with 900 employees or 47 small plants with an output of 30,000 tons employing 10,000 workers could be built.[29]

appropriate technology
production methods—intermediate, capital-, or labor-intensive (or a mixture)—considered most suitable for an area according to its cultural, political, and economic situation

Table 19–1 compares appropriate technology and capital-intensive technology with respect to cost, number of workers, and cost per job for various industries. Note that the differences are significant.

Does this mean that the government of a developing nation should urge a company to adopt a less capital-intensive process? It depends. It is possible that the cost per unit produced will be higher with this process. In this case, government administration must choose between (1) the use of the less

☐ **TABLE 19–1**
Comparison of Appropriate Technology (AT) and Capital-Intensive Technology (CIT)

Industry	Annual Output of Plant	Ratios		
		Cost, AT Plant/Cost, CIT Plant	No. Workers, AT Plant/No. Workers, CIT Plant	Cost per Job, AT Plant/Cost per Job, CIT Plant
Brick making	16 million bricks	.2	3.2	.1
Cotton spinning	2,000 tons	.3	2.5	.1
Sugar processing	50,000 tons	.6	4.8	.1
Cotton weaving	40 million square yards	.5	2.1	.2
Corn milling	36,000 tons	.4	1.5	.3
Shoes	300,000 pairs	.5	1.4	.4
Leather processing	600,000 hides	.7	1.7	.6
Beer brewing	200,000 hectoliters	.6	0.9	.7
Fertilizer	528,000 tons of urea	.9	1.0	.9

Source: Calculated from Tables 2 and 3, Howard Pack, *Macroeconomic Implications of Factor Substitution in Industrial Processes*, World Bank Staff Working Paper No. 377 (March 1980).

capital-intensive technology to save scarce capital and create more jobs and (2) the more capital-intensive processes that will provide a less expensive product for its citizens. The choice obviously depends on government priorities.

These examples help substantiate a growing belief that there is no universally appropriate technology. In fact, proponents of this concept state that what may be suitable for the cultural, political, and economic situation in one region is not necessarily applicable even in another area of the same country. The concept's effect on attempts to standardize production facilities worldwide is obvious.

THE LOCAL PRODUCTION SYSTEM

☐ Basis for Organization

Except for plants in large industrialized nations, the local production organization is commonly a scaled-down version of that found in the parent company. If at home the firm is organized by product companies or divisions (tires, industrial products, chemicals), the subsidiary will be divided into product departments. Manufacturing firms that use process organizations (departmentalized according to production processes) in the domestic operation will set up a similar structure in their foreign affiliates. In a paper-box factory, separate departments will cut the logs, produce the paper, and assemble the boxes. The only noticeable difference between the foreign and domestic operations is that in the foreign plant, all of these processes are more likely to be at one location because of the smaller size of each department.

☐ Horizontal and Vertical Integration

The local production organization is rarely integrated either vertically or horizontally to the extent the parent is. Some vertical integration is traditional, as in the case of the paper-box factory, and some will occur if it is necessary to assure a supply of raw materials. In this situation, the subsidiary might be more vertically integrated than the parent, which depends on outside sources for much of its inputs. However, the additional investment is a deterrent to vertical integration, as are the extra profits gained by supplying inputs to these captive customers from the home plants. In some countries, vertical integration is prohibited by law for certain industries. Mexico, for example, has not allowed automobile manufacturers to own parts suppliers. But in Mexico, Brazil, and numerous other nations, a percentage of local content in the finished product is required by law. When the subsidiary cannot meet the requirement by local outside sourcing, it may be forced to produce components that its parent does not.

Horizontal integration is much less prevalent in the foreign subsidiaries, although restaurant chains, banks, food-processing plants, and other industries characterized by small production units will, of course, integrate horizontally in the manner of the domestic company. Overseas affiliates themselves become conglomerates when the parent acquires a multinational. The many mergers and acquisitions of the late 1980s have turned various affiliates into conglomerates.

> **European ITT affiliates found themselves in hotels (Sheraton), car rental (Avis), and electrical connectors (Cannon Electric) when these multinationals were bought by the parent. The affiliates themselves have acquired insurance companies, schools, and manufacturers of auto parts, cosmetics, and food products. When considered as a separate company, ITT Europe ranks 25th in sales among European firms.**

◻ Design of the Production System

A *production system* is essentially a functionally related group of activities for creating value. Although the production system as described below is basically one for producing tangible goods, nearly everything that is said applies equally to the production of services. Factors involved in the efficient operation of a production system include:

1. Plant location.
2. Plant layout.
3. Materials handling.
4. Human element.

Plant location.   Plant location is significant because of its effect on both production and distribution costs, which are frequently in conflict. The gain in government incentives and in the lower land and labor costs obtained by locating away from major cities may be offset by the increased expense of warehousing and transportation to serve these markets. Management will, after ascertaining that adequate labor, raw materials, water, and power are available, seek the least-cost location, or the one for which the sum of production and transfer costs is minimized. Management's first choice may then be modified by market requirements, the influence of competitors' locations, employee preference (climate, recreational facilities), and conditions imposed by the local authorities.

Governments that are anxious to limit the congestion of large urban areas may either prohibit firms from locating in the major cities or offer them important financial inducement to locate elsewhere.

Businesses that establish plants in the Mezzogiorno (southern Italy) can obtain soft loans, tax exemptions, and outright grants of up to 40 percent of the fixed investment. Nearly all of the European nations and some nations in Latin America offer similar advantages. For example, since 1989, a foreign firm that wants a wholly owned subsidiary in Mexico must locate outside Mexico City, Monterrey, and Guadalajara, which, in the government's opinion, are already overcrowded.

Firms that have come to a country to take advantage of low labor costs and export their production have a limited selection of plant locations. They must locate in **export processing zones,** such as Mexico's in-bond manufacturing zones, most of which are on the Mexican–American border. Similar zones exist in South Korea, Taiwan, Singapore, and some 50 other nations.[30]

export processing zones specific and limited areas into which imported components may be brought for further processing. The finished product must be reexported to avoid payment of import duties

Plant layout.   Modern practice dictates that the arrangement of machinery, personnel, and service facilities should be made prior to the erection of the building. In this way, the building is accommodated to the layout that is judged most capable of obtaining a smoothly functioning production system.

The designer must attempt to obtain the maximum utility from costly building space while providing room for the future expansion of each department. Space can become critical very quickly if forecasts, especially for new products, prove to have been unduly pessimistic. Managements of plants located in developing countries may attempt to stint on space for employees' facilities, reasoning that the workers' standard of living in these countries is lower and that they will accept less just to have employment. Often, however, foreign labor laws are more demanding than those of the home country.

Materials handling.   Considerable savings in production costs can be achieved by a careful planning of materials handling, which, as you have seen, is a major consideration in synchronous production. Production managers have often failed to appreciate that inefficient handling of materials may cause excessive inventories of partly finished parts to accumulate at some workstations, while at others, expensive machinery was idle for lack of work (bottleneck). This concerned marketers too, because poor materials handling can result in late deliveries and damaged goods, which, in turn, lead to order cancelation and a loss of customers. Therefore, marketers must also be included in the total quality control approach that we discussed earlier in this chapter.

Human element.   The effectiveness of the production system depends on people, who are, in turn, affected by the system. Productivity suffers when there is extreme heat or cold, excessive noise, or faulty illumination. Colors also influence human behavior—pale colors are restful and unobtrusive, whereas bright colors attract attention. Plant designers take advantage of this fact by painting the walls of the working areas pale blue and green but marking exits with a bright yellow and painting safety equipment red. This practice is accepted nearly everywhere, although, as we indicated in the sociocultural chapter, color connotations vary among cultures.

For reasons of safety and ease of operation, controls of imported machinery must frequently be altered to accommodate the smaller worker. Extra lifting devices, unnecessary in the home country, may be required. Where illiteracy is a problem, safety signs must include pictures. For example, a picture of a burning cigarette with a red line through it may substitute for a "No Smoking" sign. Plants in multilingual nations and plants that employ large numbers of foreign workers will require warnings in more than one language.

Because of the prohibitive cost of automobiles in many developing nations, employees ride bicycles to work, so bicycle stands must be provided in the parking lots. Special dietary kitchens are necessary when workers from more than one culture work together. These and other special conditions caused by environmental differences must be reckoned with in the design of the production system.

◻ Operation of the Production System

Once the production system has been put into operation, two general classes of activities—*productive activities* and *supportive activities*—must be performed.

Productive activities.   After the initial trial period, during which the workers become familiar with the production processes, management will expect the system to produce at a rate sufficient to satisfy market demand. It is the function of the line organization—from production manager to first-level supervisor—to work with labor, raw materials, and machinery to produce on time the required amount of product with the desired quality at the budgeted cost.

Obstacles to meeting production standards.   Management must be prepared to deal with any obstacle to meeting the production standards. Among these obstacles are (1) low output, (2) inferior quality, and (3) excessive manufacturing costs.

Low output.   Any number of factors may be responsible for the system's failure to meet the design standards for output.

1. Raw materials suppliers may fail to meet delivery dates or may furnish material out of specification. This is a common occurrence in the sellers' markets of developing countries, but it is also occasionally a problem in the industrialized countries. The purchasing department must attempt to educate the vendor as to the importance of delivery dates and specifications, although the effectiveness of this strategy is limited when, as is often the case in developing nations, there is only one supplier. Increasing the price paid and sending technicians to assist the vendor generally improve this situation.

> **When the automobile plants in Mexico were required to incorporate locally made parts into the product, they not only provided their own technical assistance to vendors but also arranged for licensing agreements from U.S. suppliers and even guaranteed bank loans enabling the vendors to buy production machinery. This tremendous assistance program, literally dumped in the laps of small local manufacturers, was a leading factor in creating the Mexican parts industry.**

2. Poor coordination of production scheduling slows the delivery of finished products when, for example, completely assembled automobiles wait for bumpers. Scheduling personnel may require additional training or closer supervision. Often, scheduling personnel—or any production workers, for that matter—are unaware of the importance of their jobs because they have not been shown "the big picture." Firms that teach employees why they do what they do, as well as how, find that this pays off in creating a better attitude, which results in higher productivity. This has become crucial as firms

strive for participative management, which is essential to synchronous production.

Remember from Chapter 9 the experience of the American manager who tried to introduce participative management in Peru? The cultural forces of attitude toward authority and great difference between the educational levels, common in many countries, establishes a gulf between managers and workers. In fact, this is one of the reasons why Japanese affiliates have had trouble introducing their production methods in the United States, where distances between managers and workers are much smaller than they are in most developing nations. Getting the participative management necessary for JIT and synchronous production will necessitate workers making sizable cultural changes, which, in our opinion, will require many years to attain.

Another cultural problem is the desire to please everyone and the aversion to long-range planning. You have seen the importance of planning for the success of JIT, and you also learned that firm production schedules at least a month long are requisite. The desire to please everyone prevalent in some cultures tends to cause neglect of the schedule while production stops to attend the latest request from a customer. Moreover, because the markets are smaller in developing countries than in industrialized nations, product variations will have to be pared even more, and production systems will have to be even more flexible, if possible.

3. *Absenteeism,* always a problem for production managers everywhere in meeting production standards, has become even more significant in a bottleneck operation of a synchronous production system. Imagine the problems that occur when an entire department is idled because workers are at home helping the extended family with the harvest. When poor transportation systems make getting to work difficult, companies frequently provide transportation. To counteract absences due to illness and injury, they subsidize workers' lunches—prepared by trained nutritionists—and provide special shoes and protective clothing. Of course, management has the problem of educating workers not to remove the restraining apparel that they have never used before.

Low morale conducive to high absenteeism will result if foreign managers trying to introduce the participative management necessary for synchronous production fail to assume the role of *patron* that most workers in developing countries expect. When employees have personal problems, they presume that the boss, not the personnel office, will find a solution. Personal debts, marital problems, and difficulties with the police are all part of manager-employee relations.

All too often, expatriate managers accept high absenteeism and low productivity as the norm instead of attempting to correct them. Yet those who apply all of the corrective means used at home, making adjustments for the foreign enviroment when necessary, do achieve notable success. One corrective measure, the discharge of unsatisfactory workers, is frequently impossible to apply because of legal constraints; but a consistent, energetic program of employee training, good union and labor relations, and the use of such morale builders as employee recognition, company reunions, sponsorship of team sports, and even suggestion boxes with rewards can be as successful in a foreign location as in the domestic operation.

Inferior product quality.   Good quality is relative. What passes for good quality in the industrialized nations may actually be poor quality where a lack of maintenance and operating skills requires looser bearing fits and strong but more unwieldy parts. If the product or service satisfies the purpose for which it is purchased, then the buyer considers it to be of good quality.

> **In World War II, the American military found that the Japanese submachine gun, poorly finished except at the working surfaces, was as effective a weapon as the American Thompson, which was finely finished all over. A gun collector would consider the American weapon to be of higher quality, but was it of higher quality from the Japanese standpoint?**

Production quality standards are not set arbitrarily. It is the responsibility of the marketers, after studying their target market, to choose the price-quality combination they believe is most apt to satisfy that market. On the basis of this information, the quality standards for incoming materials, in-process items, and finished products should be established.

When the headquarters of global corporations insist that all foreign subsidiaries maintain the high-quality standards of the domestic plants, a number of problems can occur. Production may have to accept inputs of poorer quality when there is no alternative source of supply and then rework them. As we have pointed out, quality tolerances are especially tight for automated machinery. Finished-product standards set by a home office concerned about maintaining its global reputation can cause a product to be too costly for the local market. Many globals resolve this problem by permitting the subsidiary to manufacture products of lower quality under different brand names. If they wish the local plant to be a part of a worldwide logistic system, they may require a special quality to be produced for export. In some areas, "export quality" still denotes a superior product. Quality control, by the way, is not left exclusively in the hands of the subsidiary. Nearly all worldwide corporations require their foreign plants to submit samples of the finished product for testing on a regular basis.

Excessive manufacturing costs.   Any manufacturing cost that exceeds the budgeted cost is excessive and naturally is of concern to the marketing and financial manager as well as to production personnel. Low output for any of the reasons we have discussed may be the cause, but the fault may also lie with the assumptions underlying the budget. Overoptimistic sales forecasts, the failure of suppliers to meet delivery dates, the failure of the government to issue import permits for essential raw materials in time, and unforeseen water or power failure are a few of the reasons why output may be lower than expected.

Managements have always tried to limit inventories of raw materials, spare parts for plant machinery, and finished products, and those managements with synchronous production systems have a goal of almost complete elimination. But when there is an uncertainty of supply, as in most developing nations, stocks of these items can quickly get out of control. Production tends to overstock inputs to avoid the expense of changing production schedules when a given raw material has been exhausted. Maintenance personnel lay in an excessive stock of spare parts because they worry about not having something when they need it. Marketers, fearful of the frequent delays in production, overreact by building up finished goods inventories to avoid lost sales. When sales decrease, production may continue to produce finished products rather than lay off workers, because the labor laws in many countries, unlike American labor laws, make employee layoffs both difficult and costly. In countries where skilled workers are in short supply, management does not dare to lay them off even if the law permits, because these people will obtain employment elsewhere. The only alternative in the short run is to keep the factory running.

Finance, the one headquarters department that would ordinarily act to limit inventory building, will not move aggressively to stop this practice in countries afflicted with hyperinflation. It knows that under this condition, sizable profits can be made by being short in cash and long in inventory.

Supportive activities.   Every production system requires staff units to provide the *supportive activities* essential to its operation. Two of these, quality control and inventory control, were examined in the previous section. Let us look now at the purchasing, maintenance, and technical functions.

Purchasing.   Production depends on the purchasing department to procure the raw materials, component parts, supplies, and machinery it requires to produce the finished product. The inability to obtain these materials when needed can result in costly shutdowns and lost sales. If the buyers agree to prices higher than what competitors are paying, the firm must either sell the finished product at higher prices or price competitively and earn less profit. The quality of the finished product may suffer if the quality of the purchased materials is inadequate.

Even in the industrialized countries before JIT was introduced, purchasing agents rarely could satisfy all of their companies' needs by waiting for the suppliers' representatives to come to them. They had to seek out and develop suppliers by visiting their plants and arranging for their companies' production and technical personnel to discuss materiel problems with the vendors' counterparts. In the developing countries, where many suppliers do not retain a sales force because they can sell everything they produce, supplier development assumes greater importance. The ability to locate vendors can easily compensate for a lack of other skills that management would require of a buyer at home.

When the firm depends heavily on imported materials, the prime criterion for hiring will be the purchasing agents' knowledge of import procedures and their connections with key government officials. The purchasing agents must constantly monitor government actions that can affect the availability of foreign exchange. They will often buy as much as possible of regularly consumed materials because they know they can always sell the excess to others, possibly at a profit. Interestingly, a study has found that the use of locally available raw materials varies according to the company's ownership. Those owned by parents from other developing nations imported 39 percent of their raw materials, locally owned plants imported 65 percent, and factories owned by multinationals or globals imported 76 percent.[31]

Whether to fill the critical position of purchasing agent with a local citizen or with someone from the home office is often the subject of considerable debate at headquarters. A native has the advantage of being better acquainted with the local supply sources and government officials, but he or she might suffer from such cultural disadvantages as a tendency to favor members of the extended family or to accept as a normal business practice the giving (scarce supply) or receiving (plentiful supply) of bribes. The employee from the home office, on the other hand, will be experienced in company purchasing procedures and should be free of these cultural disadvantages. Managers are not so naive as to believe that belonging to a certain culture guarantees an individual will or will not engage in unethical activities. However, the tendency to commit these acts may be greater when there are no cultural constraints.

Maintenance.   A second function supporting production is the maintenance of buildings and equipment. The aim of the maintenance department is to prevent the occurrence of unscheduled work stoppages caused by equipment failures. Because of difficulty in obtaining imported spare parts and machinery, the machine shops of many maintenance departments actually manufacture these items.

> **General Tire – Spain began building tire molds for its own use but became so proficient that it was soon selling them to other affiliates. General Motors subsidiaries are regularly supplied with tools and dies made by GM in Mexico.**

It is common practice in the industrialized countries to establish preventive maintenance programs in which machinery is shut down according to plan and worn parts are replaced. Such programs are especially important for a synchronous production system, as you know. The production department with advance notice of a shutdown can schedule around the machine, or, by working the machine overtime, inventories can be built up temporarily, permitting the production process to continue during its overhaul.

This concept is not widely accepted in developing countries, where firms seem to take a fatalistic attitude toward equipment: "If it breaks down, we'll repair it." Furthermore, in a seller's market, maintenance personnel are pressured by production and marketing managers to keep machinery running. This short-term view allows no time for scheduled shutdowns. The subsidiaries that do practice preventive maintenance with overhaul periods based on headquarters standards frequently find these standards inadequate because of local operating conditions (humidity, dust, and temperature) and the manner in which the operators handle the machinery. When the amount of spare parts ordered with the machinery is based on domestic experience, it is often insufficient.

In one sense, proper maintenance is more critical than 100 percent attendance of workers. The absence of one worker from a group of six usually will not halt production, but if a key machine suddenly breaks down, the entire plant can be idled.

Technical function.   The function of the technical department is to provide production with manufacturing specifications. Usually, technical personnel are also responsible for checking the quality of inputs and the finished product. The task of the technical department in a foreign subsidiary is not simply one of maintaining a file of specifications sent by the home office, because difficulty in obtaining the same kinds of raw materials as those used by the home plants may require substitutions that necessitate the complete rewriting of specifications.

> When a synthetic rubber plant was established in Mexico to produce some kinds of synthetic rubber, the government banned imports of all synthetic rubbers. Technical departments worked day and night to produce specifications that enabled the tire companies to substitute the few types available locally for the many kinds formerly imported.

The affiliate's technical manager is a key figure in the maintenance of product quality and thus is extremely influential in selecting sources of supply. Global and multinational companies go to great lengths in persuading host governments and joint venture partners of the need to place one of their people in this position. In this way, they are certain to keep the affiliate as a captive customer purchasing all of the inputs that the more highly integrated parent manufactures.

SUMMARY

Immediately after World War II, General MacArthur, supreme commander of the Allied forces in Japan, brought over two engineers to train Japanese senior executives about the importance of quality because he wanted to have reliable radios produced. The engineers brought W. Edwards Deming, a statistician, to teach statistical quality control.

Japanese manufacturers realized that because of the limited size of Japan's economy and its lack of natural resources, they would have to export to grow. To do so, they would have to be competitive with other nations in both cost and quality. This meant improving their quality and lowering their costs. To achieve these goals, they created a production system based primarily on American production concepts. This system, now called just-in-time, required coordinated management of materials, people, and suppliers. JIT's goal was to eliminate inventories, reduce process and setup times, and use participative management to ensure worker input and loyalty to the firm. Total quality control (TQC) in all functional areas was necessary. Quality circles were an important component of TQC.

There were some problems with JIT. And American production experts, aided by computer software, developed synchronous production, whose goal is *unbalanced* production scheduling rather than the balanced scheduling of JIT; attention is focused on the bottleneck of the production system, and scheduling for the entire system is controlled by the output of the bottleneck operation.

In 1988, the U.S. government awarded the first Baldrige awards to Motorola and the Westinghouse Commercial Nuclear Fuel Division for producing products as good as anywhere in the world and for continuing to improve their quality.

Although many of the production processes and procedures employed by the parent can be transferred overseas, some must be altered or discarded because of environmental differences. Central managements prefer worldwide standardization because unified methods simplify the execution of the management functions and are usually less costly.

Governments of developing nations, preoccupied with high unemployment and rising capital costs, are urging investors to consider an *intermediate technology* rather than the highly automated processes of the industrialized nations. The multinationals' response, in some instances, has been to search for an *appropriate technology*, which matches a country's market with its resources. Under this concept, the production processes used may vary from the most advanced to the most primitive, depending on the influence of the economic, sociocultural, and political variables.

A production system is essentially a functionally related group of activities for creating value. Factors included in the system's operations are (1) plant location, (2) plant layout, (3) materials handling, and (4) the human element. After the system is operable, two general classes of activities, productive and supportive, must be performed. Among the important supportive activities are purchasing, maintenance, and the technical function. The primary aim of both types of activities is to ensure that the system produces on time the required amount of product of the desired quality at the budgeted cost.

QUESTIONS

1. What are the trade-offs for a firm that uses a just-in-time production system?

2. What advantages does synchronous production have over JIT?

3. What does quality in a pickup truck mean to you? To a farmer in Africa?

4. What difficulties do you see for global firms when they implement synchronous production in their plants located in developing countries? Are there any advantages that are more valuable to them than to plants in industrialized nations?

5. What is the connection between manufacturers' insistence on receiving components with zero defects from outside suppliers and JIT?

6. What are the advantages to a worldwide firm of global standardization of its production facilities?

7. Discuss the influence of the uncontrollable environmental forces in global standardization of a firm's production facilities.

8. Why are plant location and materials handling important factors in the design of a production system?

9. Why might production costs be excessive?

10. Who should be in charge of the purchasing function of an overseas affiliate, a local person or someone from the home office? Why?

11. What is the importance of preventive maintenance? Why might it be difficult to establish a preventive program in an overseas plant?

12. What is the connection between quality circles and participative management?

□ MINICASE 19–1

Site Selection: Johnson Machine Tool Manufacturing (Europa)

A site selection committee was named by the president of a small company, Johnson Machine Tool Manufacturing (annual sales—$21 million), to recommend the location of Johnson's first plant in Europa. A subcommittee consisting of the managers of finance, marketing, and production has just returned from a two-week visit. Its members are in agreement that two locations in Europa are preferable to all others:

1. Carlsburg, the capital and largest city (2,300,000 population).

2. Andein (180,000 population).

Carlsburg, also a manufacturing center for the country, is located almost equidistant from the borders. Andein, on the other hand, occupies the southeastern corner of the nation, almost 350 kilometers away. There are some light manufacturing plants in Andein.

To reduce the time required to gather the information needed to choose a plant site, the subcommittee divided the work as follows:

1. Marketing manager:
   a. Confirmed desk study concerning the marketing analysis.
   b. Checked on the availability of freight carriers, especially carriers of motor freight, and on freight rates.
   c. Investigated the availability and rent of warehouse space in Carlsburg.

2. Production manager:
   a. Obtained information concerning wages and the cost of fringe benefits for various skill levels in Carlsburg and Andein. Checked both markets for labor supply.
   b. Obtained cost estimates for plant construction in Carlsburg and Andein.
   c. Visited the utility companies to learn about the supply and rates in both cities.
   d. Checked the availability and cost of housing in both cities.
   e. Inquired about cultural and recreational activities and schools in both cities.

3. Finance manager:
   a. Inquired about taxes in both cities—property, state, income, and payroll taxes.
   b. Visited the national development office to confirm the amount and kinds of assistance to be obtained from the national government for establishing a manufacturing plant in Europa.
   c. Obtained prices on tracts of land in Carlsburg and Andein.

The results of the investigation are as follows:

1. Monthly rent of warehouse and office space in Carlsburg—$1,500. This is necessary if the plant is set up in Andein. Warehousing and offices will be at the plant site if the company locates at Carlsburg.

2. Annual transportation costs for incoming raw materials and component parts should average $160,000 if the plant is located in Carlsburg and $270,000 if it is established in Andein. Transportation costs for finished goods will be $270,000 for the Carlsburg location and $390,000 if the plant is set up in Andein. Service is adequate to both locations.

3. Labor costs are somewhat higher in the capital. With fringe benefits included, the cost should be $1,100,000 for Carlsburg and $970,000 for Andein. The supply of labor is adequate at both locations.

4. Annual depreciation of building and equipment will amount to $160,000 in Carlsburg and $100,000 in Andein. It is planned to use straight-line depreciation over a 10-year period.

5. To include differences in land costs, the treasurer has recommended that 10 percent of the value of the land purchase be included under the heading of Implied Interest. This amounts annually to $90,000 for Carlsburg and $50,000 for Andein.

6. Power and heat are expected to cost $76,000 annually in both Carlsburg and Andein because the same power company supplies both areas. The power supply is adequate at both locations.

7. Water will cost $15,000 annually in Carlsburg and $12,000 in Andein. The supply is adequate in both cities.

8. Insurance is slightly higher in Andein—$39,000 annually versus $36,000 for Carlsburg.

9. Property values are lower in Andein, as are the tax rates. Property taxes are expected to be $27,000 in Carlsburg and $14,000 in Andein.

10. State income taxes are also lower in Andein—$14,000 versus $27,000 in Carlsburg.

11. Although the payroll tax is a federal tax with the same rate in all parts of the country, Andein's lower wage rates cause its payroll to be lower than that of Carlsburg. Payroll taxes are $15,400 in Carlsburg and $13,600 in Andein.

12. The federal government is urging companies to locate away from the capital and offers a 10-year exemption equal to 50 percent of federal income taxes to those that do. The financial manager estimates that by the second year, the subsidiary would have taxable earnings of approximately $750,000. The tax rate is 40 percent.

13. There are state parks within an hour's drive from each city. Carlsburg has an opera company, a symphony orchestra, and various golf courses and tennis courts. The major university of the nation is located in Carlsburg. There is also an English-speaking school with grades K through 12.

14. Andein is near two lakes and a forest. Fishing and hunting are permitted. A regional university is in the city. Although there is no English-speaking school for grades K through 12 in Andein, the U.S. Army base 15 miles away does have such a school for army dependents, some of whom live in Andein. There is a daily bus service from Andein to the school on the base, and American children who are not army dependents are permitted to attend if they pay an $80 monthly tuition.

In light of these results:

1. Which city do you recommend as a plant site?

2. Show all of your calculations.

3. In addition to costs, what other factors are you considering?

☐ MINICASE 19–2

Maquinas para el Hogar Penwick

Maquinas para el Hogar Penwick is a manufacturing subsidiary of Penwick Home Appliances in Boston. It is located in El Pais, a nation with 25 million inhabitants whose GNP/capita is $1,480. The country's annual inflation rate is about 30 percent, but the local company makes a good profit, in part because it keeps large stocks of components and raw materials purchased as much as 12 months before they are needed for production. The finished products are sold at prices set as if the raw materials and components had been purchased recently; hence the high profits. Penwick's competitors use the same strategy.

Penwick–El Pais has three competitors, none of which produces as complete a product mix or as many variations in each of the product lines of refrigerators, kitchen stoves and washing machines as does the local Penwick plant. José Garcia, the local marketing manager, is proud of the fact that Penwick–El Pais makes as many kinds of products and variations of products as the much larger home plant, and he has told the managing director of the local company that it is the wide product mix that maintains Penwick–El Pais's number-one position in sales. It is true that Manuel Cardenas, the local production manager, and Garcia frequently have heated discussions, because Cardenas wants to make fewer product variations. Garcia accuses him of wanting to make black stoves like Henry Ford made black cars, but Cardenas claims he could double his production if he could make fewer kinds of products and less variations. Cardenas knows the value of long production runs and tries to get them. Garcia retorts that if Cardenas would pay attention to what he wants instead of making what Cardenas wants to make, he could sell more.

This is a sore spot with Cardenas, because he tries hard to produce a new product according to Garcia's written request. If Garcia's memo says he wants a new size refrigerator in three colors to be available with or without beverage coolers or ice cube makers, these are the models that Cardenas asks the product design department to design and make production specifications for. True, Garcia at one time or other has asked to attend meetings with Cardenas and his staff, but Cardenas considers this a waste of time. After all, he doesn't waste the design department's time by asking to attend their meetings; why should a salesperson attend his meetings? He has enough

problems with the high prices for parts that the purchasing department gives him. When he complains, they tell him that everything he orders is special manufacture for the vendors. That's their problem; this is what the design department specifies, and this is what he has to use to build the product.

Cardenas has more pressing problems. Headquarters has adopted a new production system, synchronous production, and now wants him to do the same. In fact, he had to send his assistant manager to Boston for a month's training. Now she and the design manager, who also went, are back, and they brought one of the home office experts with them. They're all going to have a long meeting with him this afternoon. Cardenas has read about synchronous production in technical journals, and it does seem to have some advantages. But all of them have been in highly industrialized nations, and there are a lot of cultural and economic differences between El Pais and those countries.

You might role-play this case. Imagine you are one of the group of three that has come from Boston. Even though you know the local plant has orders to convert to synchronous production, you still have to win over the local personnel.

1. What will you say?
2. Can you think of any advantages that might be even more important for the local plant than they are for the larger home plant?
3. What problems do you foresee in putting synchronous production in place?

SUPPLEMENTARY READINGS

JIT and Synchronous Production

"Allen-Bradley Tries to Fight Competition by Tooling Up." *Datamation*, March 15, 1988, pp. 33–34.

"Applying Business Methods and Techniques." *Business*, October–December 1990, pp. 36–38.

Chase, Richard B., and Nicholas J. Aquilano. *Production and Operations Management*, 6th ed. Homewood, Ill.: Richard D. Irwin, 1992.

"Factories That Turn Nuts into Bolts." *U.S. News & World Report*, July 14, 1986, pp. 44–45.

"How Hewlett-Packard Combines Just-in-Time with Quality Control." *Business International*, April 18, 1988, pp. 113–15.

"Installing Successful Factories in Developing Countries." *The International Executive*, September–October 1990, pp. 29–32.

" 'Just-in-Time' Inventories Putting Australian Firms on More Competitive Footing." *Business Asia*, November 9, 1987, p. 360.

"Manufacturing's New Window of Opportunity." *The Wall Street Journal*, April 19, 1988, p. 29.

Schonberger, Richard J., and Edward M. Knod, Jr. *Operations Management*, 3rd ed. Plano, Tex.: Business Publications, 1988.

Shingo, Shigeo. *Non-Stock Production: The Shingo System for Continuous Improvement*. Cambridge, Mass.: Productivity Press, 1988.

"Smart Factories: America's Turn?" *Business Week*, May 8, 1988, pp. 142–48.

"The Price Is Right." *Management Today*, September 1990, pp. 92–94.

"Time Running Out for Just-in-Time." *Journal of Commerce,* October 25, 1990, p. 1.

"Understanding the Elements of JIT." *Purchasing,* April 4, 1991, pp. 52–53.

"Why U.S. Companies Are Embracing JIT." *Traffic Management,* November 1990, pp. 30–39.

Manufacturing Rationalization

"A BI Checklist: Points to Consider in Rationalization Plans." *Business International,* January 29, 1982, pp. 35–37.

"Cutting Production Costs: Seven Ways to Check when Auditing Operations." *Business International,* February 1, 1988, p. 30.

"Rationalization Planning Is Becoming a Must for International Companies." *Business International,* December 19, 1980, pp. 401–2.

New Accounting for Synchronous Production

Chase, Richard B., and Nicholas J. Aquilano. *Production and Operations Management,* 6th ed. Homewood, Ill.: Richard D. Irwin, 1992, pp. 796 and 911–13.

"Costing the Factory of the Future." *The Economist,* March 3, 1990, pp. 61–62.

"How Costs Lead Firms Astray." *Management Today,* June 1990, pp. 114–17.

"How the New Math of Productivity Adds Up." *Business Week,* June 6, 1988, pp. 103–12.

"Japan's Smart Secret Weapon." *Fortune,* August 12, 1991, pp. 72–75.

McNair, Carol. "Timely Information for High Tech." *New Accountant,* November 1988, pp. 4–9.

Quality and Quality Circles

"Aerospace Suppliers Adopting TQM to Remain Competitive." *Aviation Week & Space Technology,* July 16, 1990, pp. 70–71.

"Armand Feigenbaum: Making Quality a Way of Life." *International Management,* January 1984, pp. 16–18.

Deming, W. Edwards. *Out of the Crisis.* Cambridge, Mass.: MIT Press, 1986.

"French Quality Circles Multiply." *International Management,* December 1986, pp. 30–32.

"Future Perfect." *The Economist,* January 4, 1992, p. 28.

"How AVCO's Quality System Boosts Profits Worldwide." *Business International,* January 18, 1988, pp. 9–11.

Ishikawa, Kaoru. *Guide to Quality Control,* 2nd ed. Tokyo: Asian Productivity Organization, 1982.

"Marketers Discover What 'Quality' Really Means." *Business Marketing,* April 1987, pp. 58–72.

"Motivation Systems for Small-Group Quality Control Activities." *The Japan Economic Journal,* June 28, 1983, pp. 33–35.

"Stalking Six Stigma." *Business Month,* January 1990, pp. 42–46.

"What American Makes Best." *Fortune,* March 28, 1988, pp. 40–53.

ENDNOTES

1. Lloyd Dobyns and Clare Crawford-Mason, *Quality or Else* (Boston, Mass.: Houghton Mifflin, 1991), pp. 10–17.

2. Richard B. Chase and Nicholas J. Aquilano, *Production & Operations Management,* 6th ed. (Homewood, Ill.: Richard D. Irwin, 1992), p. 229.

3. *Quality or Else,* p. 18.

4. Shigeo Shingo, *Non-Stock Production: The Shingo System for Continuous Improvement* (Cambridge, Mass.: Productivity Press, 1988). p. 36.

5. "Innovation," *Business Week,* Special Issue, June 1989, p. 107.

6. Richard J. Schonberger and Edward M. Knod, Jr., *Operations Management,* 3rd ed. (Plano, Tex.: Business Publications, 1988), p. 544; and Shingo, *Non-Stock Production,* p. 320.

7. "Motivation Systems for Small-Group Quality Control Activities," *The Japan Economic Journal,* June 28, 1983, pp. 33–35.

8. Franklin Strier, "Quality Circles in the United States: Fad or Fixture?" *Business Forum,* Summer 1984, pp. 19–23.

9. Richard B. Chase and Nicholas J. Aquilano, *Production and Operations Management* (Homewood, Ill.: Richard D. Irwin, 1989), pp. 736–68.

10. "Installing Successful Factories in Developing Countries," *International Executive,* September–October 1990, p. 29.

11. *Production & Operations Management,* 6th ed., p. 908.

12. Ibid., p. 913.

13. "A Select Few Poised to Lead Business in the 90s," *The Wall Street Journal,* Centennial Edition, June 23, 1989, p. A3.

14. Ibid., p. A22.

15. "How AVCO's Quality System Boosts Profits Worldwide," *Business International,* January 18, 1988, pp. 9–11.

16. "The Export of a Japanese Idea," *The Economist,* April 25, 1987, p. 68.

17. "French Quality Circles Multiply," *International Management,* December 1986, p. 31.

18. " 'Just-in-Time' Inventories Putting Australian Firms on More Competitive Footing," *Business Asia,* November 9, 1987, p. 360.

19. "How to Win the Baldrige Award," *Fortune,* April 23, 1990, pp. 101–16.

20. *Production & Operations Management,* pp. 229 and 237.

21. "Export of a Japanese Idea," p. 68.

22. "Ford Tests Just-in-Time Parts Delivery at German Plant," *Automotive News,* October 17, 1988, p. 40.

23. Yves L. Doz, "Managing Manufacturing Rationalization within Multinational Companies," *Columbia Journal of World Business,* Fall 1978, pp. 82–93.

24. Conversation with Ford International representative, June 19, 1989; and "Gearing Up to Export Three Million Engines to Auto Plants Abroad," *R&D Mexico,* February 1982, pp. 20–23.

25. D. J. Teece, "Technology Transfer by Multinational Firms," *Economic Journal,* June 1977, pp. 242–61.

26. A number of studies confirmed by personal experience have shown that the foremost criterion for plant design is the output desired. Once this is known, the engineering department of a multiplant operation will check to see whether a factory already built has a capacity similar to the output specified. If so, this facility will serve as a design standard for the new plant, though modifications may be made to eliminate problems encountered in the original design. Many large multiplant firms actually have standard designs for large, medium, and small production outputs.

27. A highly automated machine might make only one or two sizes or types of a product, whereas a general-purpose machine may be capable of producing not only all sizes of a product but other products as well. Its output, however, may be as little as 1 percent of that of a specialized machine.

28. The skill level required of general-purpose machine operators is much higher than that required of operators attending automated machinery, but it is lower than that needed to set up and maintain this equipment.

29. This does not mean that unit production costs are lower in the small plants, and certainly the coordination of their activities will be formidable. The example does illustrate the extreme range of possibilities when capital costs are a primary consideration. From Colin Norman, *Soft Technology, Hard Choice* (Washington, D.C.: Worldwatch Institute, June 1978), p. 14.

30. *Transnational Corporations in World Development* (New York: United Nations, 1988), p. 170.

31. Louis T. Wells, *Technology and Third World Countries,* ILO Working Paper, Geneva, 1982.

Chapter 20

Labor Relations Policies and Management

You can get an assembly robot today for $20,000. Compared to a person, that's cheap. A robot also shows up every day. It doesn't have to have a raise. You've got it for life. It releases the manufacturer of geographical limitations on the availability of labor.

Vincent M. Altamuro, robotics
consultant

LEARNING OBJECTIVES

In this chapter, you will study:

1. The importance of thoroughly analyzing the available labor force before a company makes an investment requiring workers in a foreign country.

2. Employee recruitment and selection methods, which may vary depending on whether the host country is in a developed or a developing state.

3. The necessity and methods of training new employees and upgrading training for existing employees.

4. Some precautions managers from industrialized countries should observe when recruiting, selecting, and training employees in nonindustrialized countries.

5. Changes in American compensation and incentive practices.

6. Japanese labor management practices.

7. Labor unions, which may be parts of an industry's disciplinary system and which negotiate all sorts of other matters, such as wages and working conditions, with employers.

8. Laws that mandate working conditions and other labor matters, such as severance pay when workers are fired.

9. Codetermination, which puts worker representatives on company boards of directors.

10. Quality circles and why they might or might not work.

11. Robotics and CADCAM.

12. How faster, cheaper computers together with robotics are creating the factories of the future.

13. The importance for an IC of coordinating labor relations among the parent, subsidiary, and affiliated companies.

14. Some labor relations differences between LDCs and industrialized countries.

KEY WORDS AND CONCEPTS

- Fringe benefits
- Skilled labor
- Unskilled labor
- Employee facilities
- In-house training programs
- On-the-job training
- Apprenticeship programs
- Off-premises training
- Incentive pay plans
- Quality circles
- Robotics
- CADCAM
- Collective bargaining
- Codetermination

BUSINESS INCIDENT

How do you make an American worker as enthusiastic, loyal, and hardworking as a Japanese? A few years ago, the fashionable answer was to copy Japanese ways, such as quality circles and suggestion boxes. Monsanto seems to have found better ways, as illustrated in its Luling, Louisiana, agricultural chemicals plant.

It is making employees feel "ownership" for their company by allowing them to use their brains as well as their hands. Monsanto's main organizational change has been to do away with most of its foremen, supervisors, and quality inspectors and instead to have plant workers oversee themselves. To assist them, it now gives the workers financial information about their part of the operation, which had previously been kept secret.

Another step was to encourage them to form teams and look for measurable improvements, big or small. The 30-year-old Luling plant leaks. Instead of calling for expensive outside repair people, the workers formed a team and plugged the leaks, saving Monsanto some $155,000 a year.

A further successful change was to put workers in touch with distributors and customers so they know where the product goes and how it is used. One result was that a Luling team redesigned the packaging when they saw what was really needed. Also, quality control improved markedly based on feedback from vendors and customers. Complaints were halved in 1988.

Source: "No Blues on the Mississippi," *The Economist,* January 7, 1989, p. 56.

I n Chapter 12, we saw some of the labor forces that international business management faces from country to country. Are there enough bodies present? Do the persons in the bodies possess the skills your operation needs? Even if there are sufficient bodies and skills, will they work for your operation? If there are insufficient bodies, skills, or willingness to work, can you find and train other labor?

In this chapter, we shall not concern ourselves with the problems of executive-level personnel, which are dealt with in Chapter 22. The problems of lower-level management and the workers are the ones we shall attempt to solve here.

The effectiveness of every organization depends to a great extent on how well its human resources are utilized. Their effective use depends on management's policies and practices. Management of a company's human resources is a shared responsibility. The day-to-day supervision of people on the job is the duty of the operating managers, who must integrate the human, financial, and physical resources into an efficient production system. However, the formulation of policies and procedures for (1) estimation of work force needs, (2) recruitment and selection, (3) training and development, (4) motivation, (5) compensation, (6) discipline, (7) relations with employee associations, and (8) employment termination is generally the responsibility of personnel managers working in cooperation with executives from marketing, production, and finance as well as the firm's lawyers.

The Saint-Gobain minicase at the end of the chapter is an example of a lack or failure of cooperation—and perhaps communication—between financial and personnel management. The personnel people should have been able to warn of the possible adverse labor relations results caused by sudden revelations of previously secret financial information.

PERSONNEL NEEDS, AVAILABILITY, AND LABOR LAWS[1]

☐ Analysis of the Labor Force

Because of the labor force's influence on the choice of plant site, factory design, and production processes, data on the available labor force must be gathered prior to making final decisions in these areas. Labor laws, going wage rates, and the characteristics of workers, such as their skills, work attitudes, and prejudices about gender and caste, as well as their propensity to join labor organizations and to strike, all weigh heavily in these decisions. All too often, failures to obtain such information result in costly mistakes. Managements, attracted by low wage rates, have set up plants only to learn later that the labor costs are considerably higher than expected because of the existence of **fringe benefits,** which are usually government requirements. Such errors could have been avoided by consulting local experts.

fringe benefits benefits for employees over and above base wages, including bonuses, maternity leaves, education leaves, sick leaves, and medical payments

A simple reading of the labor laws by a layman, and particularly a foreign layman, will almost never give a complete or accurate understanding of their exact meaning or of how they are applied and enforced by the authorities. Sometimes laws are enforced very stringently and in surprising ways, but often

they are ignored. In addition, firms frequently pay and give more than the legally required minimums. A study by the American Chamber of Commerce in Mexico showed that 19 percent of the 121 companies surveyed gave punctuality and attendance bonuses averaging 20 percent of monthly wages. Death benefits paid by the firms averaged 15 months' wages for natural deaths and 26 months' wages for accidental death. One company gave a 100-minute coffee break. In all, more than two dozen types of benefits were offered that were not required by law. These extra payments and benefits usually were not due to misreadings of the law; they were meant to increase employee satisfaction and to decrease costly employee turnover.

One potentially costly omission is the failure to ascertain the availability of **skilled labor** or of **unskilled labor** willing to work on an assembly line. Establishing a plant solely because of an abundance of low-cost labor can be a big mistake if the cost and time required to train for necessary skills have not been factored into the cost analyses and start-up plans.

Of course, the employer may try to bring from abroad the skilled personnel who are unavailable locally, but that effort usually meets with host country government hostility and resistance; the host country wants its own people hired and trained. Less host country resistance may be encountered if a labor shortage is due to its people's unwillingness to work on an assembly line or if there is very low unemployment.

Those situations led to the northern European guest worker programs we discussed in Chapter 12. You recall that when unemployment grew among the local people, the guest workers were no longer welcome.

□ Employee Facilities

Another element of personnel planning is that of **employee facilities** on and off the job. For example, will a first-aid dispensary be sufficient, or must a hospital and dental clinic be provided either because the law demands it or because there are no satisfactory facilities nearby? If an appreciable number of foreign workers will be employed, special dietary kitchens and recreation equipment may be needed. When women are employed, provision must be made to care for children; the firm may build a nursery (required by law in some countries) or contract private nurseries to provide the services. In Germany, a number of firms subsidize privately operated day nurseries in exchange for guaranteed numbers of places for their employees' children. Local authorities in Italy provide nurseries financed by part of the employer's social security payments.

In situations where the plant is located some distance from the nearest city, the firm may construct a "company town." However, in extended family-type societies, this may be a trap for the well-intentioned employer. Employee dissatisfaction and unrest may develop as the employee's extended family moves into housing designed for only the immediate family, causing overcrowding and shortages of water, sewage facilities, medical facilities, or schools. Alternatives to the company town are for the employer to provide or subsidize transportation to and from the nearest communities or to subsidize local government housing. Using these alternatives, the workers are less likely to blame their employers for problems that arise with their living quarters.

skilled labor labor that has learned job-useful skills through training and/or experience

unskilled labor labor that has not learned such skills

employee facilities not directly job related, but may be necessary to attract and keep employees; include recreational or medical facilities, child day-care centers, or special dietary kitchens

Because a growing number of workers are faced with caring for elderly parents, some companies are offering intergenerational day-care centers.

Courtesy of Stride Rite Corporation

RECRUITMENT AND SELECTION

◻ Recruitment

Once it has been determined how many of what types of employees will be needed, the personnel department can begin to recruit. Various kinds of labor recruitment sources are available. Suitable candidates may be found within the hiring unit of the company if it is already in operation, within other units of the company, or from the outside.

Internal sources.   The use of internal sources, the company's present employees, can be an effective recruitment method. The cost is relatively low, morale benefits from inside promotions, and each applicant is already known to the employer. Where labor is organized, the company-union contract may require members to be given the first opportunities to apply for vacant positions.

Employees as recruiters—advantages.   The use of a firm's present workers to locate new employees can be efficient and low cost. Such practices can build morale.

Employees as recruiters—disadvantages.   It is human nature that the employees will try to help family and friends. Thus, considerations of family, similar social status, caste, geographic origin, culture, or language are usually more important than qualifications for the vacant position. Such considerations exist in any country, but they are especially prevalent in less developed countries, where an employed member of the extended family is under pressure to help the other members find work. More than one foreign managing director has been shocked to find that the local personnel director has filled the plant with relatives or people from the same hometown. Such a work force can be expected to be more loyal to the personnel director than to the firm.

External sources.   Overseas, ICs tend to employ the same kinds of external recruiting methods and sources as are used in their home countries. These may include (1) newspaper advertising, (2) trade schools, (3) radio advertising, (4) labor unions, and (5) employment agencies. However, there are important differences between their use in the industrialized countries and their use in the developing countries.

Unskilled workers.   Because of high unemployment in most LDCs, the IC subsidiaries there generally have no difficulties in filling jobs calling for little or no skill. Furthermore, such companies usually have a recruiting advantage over indigenous concerns because of the ICs' reputations for on-the-job training, higher wages, and other benefits.

Skilled workers.   The recruitment of skilled workers is more difficult because they are generally in short supply in developing countries. Some walk in, attracted by the knowledge that advancement may be more rapid in foreign-owned firms than in locally owned ones, but managements will try to utilize other methods and sources as well. Newspaper advertisements will not have the effectiveness to which foreign managers are accustomed, because in the LDCs, many workers who learned their skills on the job can neither read nor write. A solution to this difficulty is to announce the jobs on the radio.

Employment agencies are utilized much less in the LDCs than in the industrialized countries. The job applicants frequently cannot afford to pay the agency's fee even if that were legal, which it often is not. In cases where the companies pay the fee, it is not unusual for the agencies to connive with the applicant to split the payment. The applicant takes the job, and the company pays the fee, which the agency splits with the hired applicant, who then quits. The agency and the applicant can repeat this as many times as they can get away with it.

◻ Selection

By means of the selection processes, management chooses those applicants whose qualifications seem most nearly to match the job requirements.

Industrialized countries.   Most companies in the industrialized countries follow rather standard procedures of requesting personal information, including work experience, to be given on an application form and during interviews. In some countries, the worker carries an identification book, which must be presented when seeking employment. The book entries constitute a record of employment, including jobs, wages, and employer comments. If the worker has a prison record, the book will include information about that. The hiring company may give prospective employees a physical examination and aptitude or psychological tests.

Developing countries.   In LDCs, the hiring process is usually less formal. Less testing is done, and when it is done, the results are likely to be used somewhat superficially. As has been mentioned before, family ties, social status, caste, language, and common origin are more likely to be elements of hiring decisions in LDCs than in other countries.

AP/Wide World Photos

One way prospective employers and employees get together.

Recruiting and selecting employees are the initial steps in building an effective work force. Once the workers are hired, they must undergo training and development.

TRAINING AND DEVELOPMENT

Most new employees need to be trained and developed to fit into the employer firm's specific operations. In addition, because of technological or market changes, employees sometimes need to have their skills upgraded or need to be taught new ones. The preparation and supervision of training and development programs, both in-house and off-premises, are normally the responsibility of the personnel department after it ascertains operating department needs.

◻ In-House Programs

in-house training programs training programs developed by the employer on its premises

Firms in both the developed and developing nations offer several kinds of **in-house training programs.** Among these are on-the-job training, apprenticeship training, classroom sessions, conferences, and simulation. The programs frequently overlap.

on-the-job training worker learns by doing the job under the supervision of an experienced employee

On-the-job training.   **On-the-job training** methods make either a supervisor or an experienced operator responsible for training new or promoted employees. Developed countries generally utilize more training aids than LDCs do. The use of audiovisual equipment and simulation training on identical equipment set up in an area away from the actual production space enable the learning workers to master the job more quickly than they could on the production line. Because of the high cost of many training aids and shortages of experienced trainers, these methods have been slow to appear in the less developed nations. However, this is changing as many ICs are transferring the methods to their LDC subsidiaries with excellent results.

One of those results is the recruiting edge that good training gives the IC subsidiaries in attracting needed employees. This works both ways, however, as the locally owned firms regularly hire away workers who have been trained by foreign-owned companies—one of the benefits that LDCs derive from multinational operations within their borders.

> **Managers of IC subsidiaries in Mexico have been heard to complain that "they must be training half the machinists in Mexico."**

Labor trainers in developing nations have found that the people learn industrial skills rapidly. More difficult is teaching new workers who come from farms and villages how to adjust socially and psychologically to factory life. Some of these workers must be taught not only job skills but also the concept of time. They are not accustomed to reporting to work at the same time and place each workday or to meeting production schedules.

They must be introduced to factory teamwork and to an industrial hierarchy. Frequently, the company must compromise and not attempt to change customary farm and village practices too quickly and completely.

> **A Spanish company opened a factory in Guatemala, hired local people, and tried to operate as if it were in Europe. The Spanish management installed work hours and production routines and schedules that had worked efficiently in Spain. They were nearly disastrous at that stage of development in Guatemala.**
>
> *Reactions.* **The people refused to work and became hostile. Guatemalan troops were necessary to protect the factory. Management at last considered local needs and compromised, and mutually satisfactory solutions were found.**
>
> *Solutions.* **The solutions included four-hour breaks between two daily work periods. During the breaks, the male employees took care of their farms and gardens and the female employees attended to household needs and cared for their children. As another part of the solution, the employees were willing to work Saturdays to make up production lost during the breaks.[2]**
>
> **Through compromise and patience, European management, operating in a preindustrial setting, was able to achieve satisfactory production. It studied, negotiated, and adapted to local needs. The alternatives were low production or perhaps even a destroyed factory.**

apprenticeship programs
beginning workers work under the direction of skilled workers for a minimum period of two to five years

Apprenticeship programs.   **Apprenticeship programs** are a special kind of on-the-job training for skilled tradespeople, such as plumbers, electricians, and toolmakers, that has existed for many years. Young workers called apprentices assist experienced craftsmen for periods of two to five years, until the apprentices are capable of doing the job without supervision.

In the more developed nations, the majority of the trades require the apprentices to pass examinations before they are certified as skilled craftspeople. Europe's apprenticeship training is especially good. It is a highly formalized part of a nation's educational system, and it includes classroom instruction as well as on-the-job training.

The combination of classroom and on-the-job training is utilized in the United States by some firms, but the practice has not been incorporated into the national educational system to the extent that it has in Europe. Some vocational schools and community colleges do offer cooperative programs with industry that approach the European system, and many community and city colleges and high schools have a wide variety of vocational and trade courses that workers can take on their own.

Managers coming from countries with formal training programs to a developing nation must be careful when they hire persons claiming to have a skilled trade; the types of training programs with which the manager is familiar are extremely rare in the LDCs. Even if the applicant is truly skilled, the skill may be narrowly limited to what was learned on the job.

◻ Off-Premises Training and Development

Sending workers and supervisors off the company's premises has become an accepted practice in the United States and other developed nations. Personnel managers have learned that training and development by skilled educators working in an educational setting are often less costly and more effective than training and development done in-house with company employees. France has a particularly innovative law that permits workers to apply for a one-year leave of absence to enroll in an approved training program if they have been employed for at least two years. The French government and the employers share the expenses, which include the employees' salaries while they are in training.[3]

off-premises training
sending employees out of the plant to a school or other training site

Off-premises training is far less common in the developing nations, but multinationals' subsidiaries in LDCs are beginning to cooperate with the host governments in inaugurating such programs. In addition, schools and universities in the LDCs, aided by their counterparts from the industrialized countries, are offering training and development programs to local industry.

One of the authors, working with professors of engineering from his university, helped two universities in Thailand establish business and technical training programs during 1989 and 1990. The Thai universities report the programs are making good progress.

MOTIVATION

Regardless of how well employees are selected and trained, they will not perform satisfactorily unless they are properly motivated. Effective personnel management requires an understanding of the motivational processes, including human needs. Without an understanding of those needs, managers cannot determine the kinds of employee motivation needed to induce employees to work toward the organization's goals.

◻ Bonuses, Salaries, and Wages

Not long ago in the United States, the compensation hierarchy was clear cut; executives received bonuses on top of their salaries, middle and lower management were paid salaries only, and the other employees got wages. Those days are gone.

To motivate workers and give them greater incentive to improve productivity and meet international competition, American firms are making sweeping worker compensation changes. For example, many are replacing base wage increases with bonuses or gain-sharing plans to reward improvements in quality or productivity. At other plants, pay-for-knowledge plans reward workers for the job-useful skills they master in addition to paying for the work they perform. Figure 20–1 offers a guide to these **incentive pay plans**. It comments on how they work, how to make them effective, and their advantages and disadvantages.

incentive pay plans forms of worker compensation in addition to basic wages with the purpose of improving quality and productivity

□ Incentive Pay Plans

These plans not only encourage workers to produce more and better, they also hold down fixed wages and wage-related benefits and let compensation costs rise and fall with the company's profits.

Not all such plans succeed. They need a well-defined business strategy, and when installed for no clear reason, they usually fail. Profit is a business objective, but profit-sharing plans for workers may not be effective motivators because most employees have little influence on profits. Too many decisions and forces that are beyond the workers' control affect profit. Such decisions and forces include pricing policy, marketing strategy, assumption of debt or taxes, or market competition.

How to make an incentive plan succeed is the subject of the list below.* It begins with a clear strategy and recognizes that sometimes a plan must be phased out:

1. **Start with a clear strategy.** Think hard about your goals. Focusing just on customer service, for example, could also raise costs.
2. **Focus on jobs that can be measured.** Make sure managers know what constitutes peak performance and how to value it.
3. **Decentralize incentives.** Allow individual business units to tailor reward plans to their specific situations.
4. **Separate incentives from base pay.** Deliver incentive rewards in a lump sum to highlight the link between rewards and performance.
5. **Create a "sunset" provision.** State conditions, such as the introduction of new technology or a change in business plans, under which the program will be modified or terminated.

Is the plan working?   Look again at the business incident, and you can see that Monsanto's plan was succeeding. Costs and customer complaints were down—measurable results. Before such results are in, management should be able to get indications of the plan's progress. Listen to the workers: are they interested and beginning to try it? Talk to the workers: do they understand the plan? Is the listening and talking more effective? In other words, are worker-management communications improving? Are the incentives being paid for the targeted results, and are they being withheld when targets are not hit? And finally, are desired end results being achieved, such as lower costs, better quality, higher productivity, fewer customer complaints, and more profit?[4]

For incentive plans to be successful, they must be reviewed and updated regularly. Conditions change. One company instituted an incentive system for its word processing personnel. They were expected to produce a certain num-

* Source: *Fortune*, December 19, 1988, p. 54. Courtesy of *Fortune*.

□ **FIGURE 20–2**
Quality Circle

Definition:
A small group of people from the same work area who meet on a regular basis to identify, analyze, and solve product quality and other problems in their area.

Participants:
Leader—train, maintain records, motivate, lead, resource.

Facilitator (part- or full-time)—train, resource, group dynamics.

Member—identify problems, contribute ideas, develop solutions, implement solutions when feasible.

Management—obtain ownership support, furnish prompt responses, deal with issues and problems that surface, share information, provide resources.

responsible for meeting quality targets. This helps motivate the workers and permits problems to be tackled early in production.

Jill H. King* suggests the outline of a QC as shown in Figure 20–2. She has identified a number of problems and issues in the QC movement. A few of them are middle-management resistance, unclear goals, little or no union involvement, and inadequate training. Another problem she identified is lack of top-management commitment, which brings us to the subject of company-wide quality control.

□ Companywide Quality Control (CWQC)

Companywide quality control (CWQC) is not a new system or scheme. According to one writer, it is a holistic approach to achieving objectives more effectively for an entire company.[13]

Companywide. With CWQC, quality control begins with the product design in the production process and, equally important, applies to every job in the company. In Japan, all the employees in every aspect of their jobs are thought of as being components of CWQC. In the United States, by contrast, quality control grew out of inspecting the end product to ascertain whether it met engineering specifications. In many American companies, that is still all it means.

Quality. In Japan, quality means user satisfaction. The Japanese believe the American definition of quality as meaning conformance with engineering specifications is too narrow. For the Japanese, the user may be the ultimate customer, but in a multiple-procedure manufacturing process, the user is the next department of the company, and the work done at each production stage must satisfy each succeeding stage. Some American departments regard the next department as a "policeman" or even as an "enemy."

A good comparison between the American and Japanese approaches to quality control can be seen in Figure 20–3, which illustrates the additional stages employed in Japan. Control is approached from more points of view in Japan than in the United States.

Figure 20–4 shows that Japanese manufacturers involve their suppliers in the production process at the product development and design phases. That is much sooner than is the usual American practice, and the American suppliers

* King is manager, personnel training and development, Human Resources, Radar Systems Group, Hughes Aircraft Company.

■ **FIGURE 20-3**
The Buildup of Quality in Seven Stages

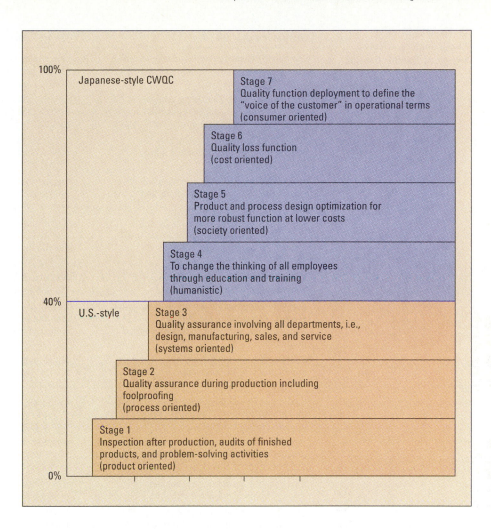

100%

Japanese-style CWQC

Stage 7
Quality function deployment to define the "voice of the customer" in operational terms (consumer oriented)

Stage 6
Quality loss function (cost oriented)

Stage 5
Product and process design optimization for more robust function at lower costs (society oriented)

Stage 4
To change the thinking of all employees through education and training (humanistic)

40%

U.S.-style

Stage 3
Quality assurance involving all departments, i.e., design, manufacturing, sales, and service (systems oriented)

Stage 2
Quality assurance during production including foolproofing (process oriented)

Stage 1
Inspection after production, audits of finished products, and problem-solving activities (product oriented)

0%

■ **FIGURE 20-4**
Quality Effort by Activity

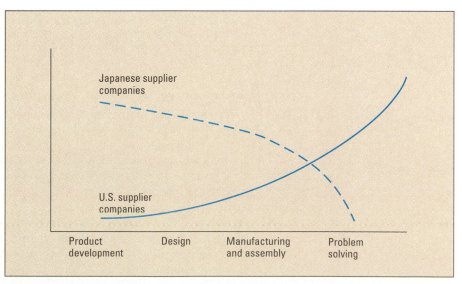

Japanese supplier companies

U.S. supplier companies

Product development   Design   Manufacturing and assembly   Problem solving

Source: *Quality Progress,* May 1986, p. 78.

□ **FIGURE 20–5**
Implementing a New Image of Quality Control

The Old Image of QC	The New Image of QC
Low quality is caused by low performance of people. Automation is the key to higher quality.	Low quality is caused by poor management of people. Respect for people is the key to higher quality.
Loss of work ethic causes poor quality in the United States. The Japanese maintain a quality edge due to their ethical and cultural values.	American workers, when properly managed, are as good as or better than any others, particularly in their commitment to jobs.
Some defects are acceptable. Lots are accepted if they meet minimum quality standards on average.	Zero defects is the goal. There is not a minimum average acceptable quality. All units should be free of defects.
Inspect for product problems regularly, then rework. Rework is done at a later and separate stage.	Inspect for process problems; and fix problems so they do not recur. Any repair work is done on the line with no delay.
Higher quality means higher costs and therefore lower profits. Quality is expensive and a burden for manufacturing.	Higher quality is a means to higher profits. Quality is the goal; it is not the burden for manufacturing.
Quality is inspected into the product. Nonconforming units are continuously discovered, reworked, or scrapped.	Quality is designed and built into the product. A nonconformance is a means for resolving the problems permanently.
A quality control organization, as a separate department, inspects the output of manufacturing and evaluates the quality of production.	Quality is everyone's job. Total quality control includes all functions and individuals and all stages of manufacturing.
Quality is secondary to profits. To maximize profits, the sum of prevention, inspection, and failure costs is minimized.	Initial investment in quality is key to long-term profits. The book value of nonconformances is not simply deducted from profits.
Catch mistakes and fix them. Units are routed to manufacturing and inspection several times to pass the requirements.	Do it right the first time. Quality at the source is the key. Do not make mistakes. Quality is free if produced for the first time.
Suppliers are adversaries and thus suspect. All products must have at least a second source. Order as needed and expedite.	Suppliers are trusted members of our team. Work with a primary source to ensure reliability and quality.
Buy from the lowest bidder. Competition among the suppliers will reduce the total cost.	Buy for quality and reliability. Information and profits may be shared with suppliers.
Quality is a function of manufacturing. The products have high quality if they are manufactured properly.	High quality depends on all stages, from design to shipping, and is reached only if all functions work properly together.

are much more likely to be involved in later problem solving than are their Japanese counterparts.

CWQC and quality circles.   We are brought back to the idea expressed earlier that management—from top to bottom—must be involved for QCs to be truly and lastingly effective. QCs must be only one part of companywide quality control activities.

To envision the top-to-bottom and bottom-to-top nature of CWQC, look again at Figure 20–3. It illustrates that quality control must be the concern of everyone in the company, from the CEO down, with ideas and suggestions for improvement originating at every level.

The lessons of "Old Image–New Image" presented in Figure 20–5 may be summarized as follows: Concerns about a product's quality must begin at the product's design stage. Cooperate with suppliers to ensure the quality of the components coming from them. Quality consciousness is the responsibil-

□ **FIGURE 20–5**
(Concluded)

The Old Image of QC	The New Image of QC
Errors will be caught by the inspectors. Keep the production line moving by keeping a safety stock.	Do not pass on nonconformances. Stop the line if there is a quality problem. A safety stock of work in progress is a waste.
Produce as many units as possible in the shortest possible time to increase efficiency and utilization.	Produce effectively only what is needed and only when it is needed for the quality requirement of the internal or external customers.
Use specialized workers on operations to reduce the time needed for training. Produce units on an assembly line with highly specialized, single-operation–type workers. Do not rotate workers; rotation may reduce efficiency.	Train workers for diversified jobs and high flexibility. Promote cross-training and job sharing among workers.
The quality department is responsible for quality. Problems need not be communicated to and from manufacturing.	Quality consciousness is the responsibility of everyone involved. Suggestions and discussions are particularly welcomed.
Management must discern quality problems and delegate responsibility for improvement. Employees should carry out the plans.	Management depends on employees to identify and solve problems. Management works closely with employees to resolve problems permanently.
The worker is responsible for most quality problems. He should be disciplined and trained to perform properly.	Management systems are the cause of most quality problems. Workers should be allowed to participate in management.
Statistics are an exotic tool for quality engineers. Control charts are used to highlight the problems.	Every employee should have an understanding of statistical quality control, which is used to highlight areas for improvement.
Additional inventory is maintained to keep workers utilized. The workers' idle time is a waste.	Inventory is a waste. The workers may spend their nonproductive time in other productive functions.
Large lot sizes are produced to increase quality and to reduce production cost and average setup time.	Setup should be reduced to allow for lot sizes of one. Lower lot size means lower lead time, higher flexibility, and less rework.

Source: Mehran Sepehri, "Quality Control Circles: A Vehicle for Just-In-Time Implementation," *Quality Progress*, July 1985, p. 23.

ity of every worker, and when a nonconformance is spotted, the production line should be halted and the quality error corrected immediately. Workers should participate in management of their part of the operation, and the executives should work closely with the employees to resolve problems permanently.

One lesson from Figure 20–5 taught by Dr. Deming and learned by his Japanese students is the establishment of close, long-term relationships with the company's suppliers. Such relationships result in understanding and trust between the company and its supplier, and they improve the quality of the materials supplied. This practice, now prevalent in Japan, is attacked by would-be exporters to Japan as a nontariff barrier to trade.[14]

Now some Americans are listening to Dr. Deming. They include Chevron, Ford, Campbell Soup, Hewlett-Packard, Kaiser Tech, Lockheed, and Varian Associates. Stripped of the jargon, Deming's philosophy is threefold: give workers chances to make more decisions, listen carefully to the customer, and use statistical analysis to detect and repair flaws.[15]

ROBOTICS AND CADCAM

robotics the use of machines to help an existing work force improve manufacturing reliability and quality and to replace human labor

Robotics is the industry of machines that work with humanlike skill. Robots are substitutes for human workers, and management has concluded that is must use many more robots to improve productivity. Japan is in the lead in the use of robots. In 1990, about 220,000 industrial robots were flexing their muscles around the clock in Japan; the number in Europe was some 56,000; and there were approximately 37,000 in the United States. In other countries there were about 75,000.

On the subject of robots taking the jobs of human laborers, robotics consultant Vincent M. Altamuro (see the quotation at the beginning of this chapter) makes several points. For one, the cost of robots is going down while the cost of labor is going up. For another, managers consider robots to have an advantage over people in workplaces with dangerous or noxious situations. Employers don't have to worry about a robot being killed, injured, or having its health impaired.[16]

▫ Steel-Collar Migrant Workers

As members of management have been termed *white-collar workers* and members of the labor force have been termed *blue-collar workers,* some writers refer to robots as *steel-collared workers,* and these workers are migrating. Japan's worldwide share of the fast-growing robot market is 57.5 percent, with Western Europe having 14.5 and the United States 9.5 percent.

Japan's major advantages are that workers in automotive, electronics, and other factories are accustomed to and readily accept automation technology; product demand is still strong in the home market; and manufacturers make most of the machines they use so there is little competition from imports.[17]

▫ Computer-Aided Design (CAD), Computer-Aided Manufacturing (CAM)—CADCAM

CADCAM a production process involving computer-aided design and computer-aided manufacturing equipment

The world market for **CADCAM** equipment grew rapidly during the 1980s and was worth $13.9 billion in 1990. It is forecast to rise to $26.2 billion by 1995.

As with robotics, the use of CADCAM is spreading to smaller manufacturing companies, which are finally replacing draftsman's tables with computer-aided design (CAD) systems. Small companies still dominate the CADCAM equipment manufacturing field, with most being U.S. owned. European companies follow, with those of Japan in third place.

There is probably no better way of assessing the industry's prospects than to examine new uses for CADCAM. At Boeing, the introduction of a new generation of CAD tools is aimed at eliminating the risk of design mistakes. The linchpin is Catia, a three-dimensional CAD program supplied by Dassault Systems of France. Linked to a network of IBM workstations and mainframes, Catia will enable Boeing's new 777 commercial jet to be the first designed completely on computer.[18]

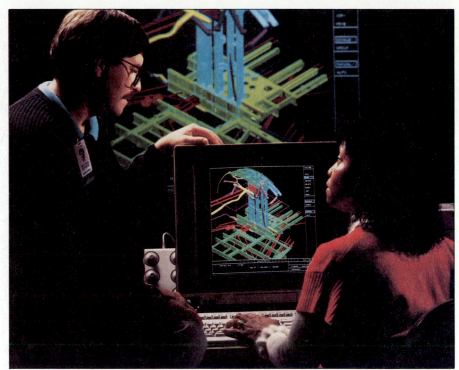

Computer-aided designs afford manufacturers accurate simulations of products and their component parts.

Courtesy of The Boeing Company

□ Factories of the Future

As computers become more powerful and less expensive, they are reshaping the factory. CADCAM, robotic tools, sensors, and improved telecommunications techniques are forging the factory of the future.

Using computers instead of people costs 8,000 times less today than in 1950. Electronic transactions can be made 80 million times faster now than then. Errors occur in modern computers at the rate of 1 in 3 million, compared with 1 in 30 when humans do similar calculations.

New future directions.   Businesses adopting computer-aided management methods may find themselves heading in a variety of new directions. These directions include:

1. *Production disbursement.* Production is moving into even smaller manufacturing units.

2. *Labor costs less important.* As computer-controlled robots become less expensive and more efficient, labor costs will shrink as a percentage of total costs. Manufacturers may become less attracted to low-wage countries.

3. *Engineering centralized.* Characteristic of high-tech engineering is centralized design. Product blueprints are likely to be transmitted from the head office via long-distance telephone lines to CAM plants in the company's principal market regions and countries.

4. *Manufacturing flexibility.* A wider variety of products can be produced at no greater costs. The plants could break even at 30 to 35 percent of capacity, compared to 65 to 70 percent in conventional operations.
5. *Plug-in repairs.* Product faults can usually be diagnosed by plugging the product into a computer. General Motors plans to use computerized diagnostics in its U.S. repair shops.
6. *Economies of scale.* The conventional assembly line economies of scale will be diminished. That could be counteracted by economies in such areas as marketing research and development.
7. *Consultants and contractors.* Small businesses with the latest computer-aided designs and techniques are beginning to sell services to the bigger companies. Some of those companies may decide to subcontract production.

Fears.   Many managers are hesitant to adopt computerized manufacturing systems. Their concerns include potential misuse, reliability, security, difficult maintenance, and cost. Perhaps kicking and screaming, they will probably be forced to go along by competition.[19]

COMPENSATION

Financial compensation is not the only motivator, but it is a pervasive one that affects people at every economic level. In addition to satisfying basic wants, money satisfies social and esteem needs. Personnel managers must formulate compensation plans that combine employee needs satisfaction with incentives to result in satisfactory work performance for the employer.

□ Wages and Salaries

Employees are paid on the basis of productivity, time spent on the job, or a combination of the two unless union contracts or government laws specify otherwise. In the industrialized countries, the time unit for which pay is established is generally the hour, whereas a daily rate is most common in developing countries. The piece rate* pay method is quite common. In some countries, of which Japan is a good example, seniority is an important element in determining employees' pay rates.

When the subsidiaries of multinationals commence operations in a foreign country, they usually set their pay scales at or slightly higher than the prevailing wages paid by indigenous companies. The foreign-owned subsidiary does not want to be accused of exploiting the local workers. Although it might seem that paying wages higher than the going rate would be welcomed by the host government, usually the opposite is true. Local firms are quick to complain that such wages will cause unrest and disruption in the labor force. The foreign manager—even in developed countries—is repeatedly counseled by local managers, "Don't spoil our people."

More and more often, workers are paid by the hour. Even in the developing countries, where daily and piece rates can still be found, payment by the

* Piece rate is payment per unit produced; for example, $1 per basket woven or 25 cents per button sewn on.

☐ **FIGURE 20-6   Working Time Necessary to Buy a Big Mac**

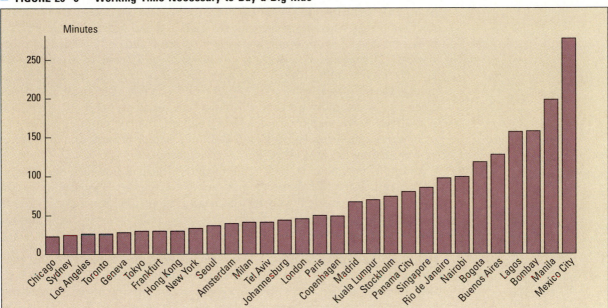

Source: *The Economist,* November 2, 1991, p. 99.

hour is becoming the norm. So, how does the wage they earn by the hour translate into how much they can buy?

You will recall that when we were discussing purchasing power parity of currencies, we used the Big Mac standard developed by *The Economist.* The Union Bank of Switzerland has used the same standard to compare earnings around the world. Figure 20–6 shows how many minutes or hours of labor are needed to buy a Big Mac in 30 cities around the world. By this measure, the best-paid workers are in Chicago, where it takes only 18 minutes to earn the price of a Big Mac.

Compare that with Mexico City, where workers have to labor for almost four hours to earn their bite. Union Bank does not include Moscow, but a correspondent of *The Economist* reports it costs locals almost two days' pay for a Big Mac.

☐ **Benefits**

The types and sizes of the supplementary benefits* that workers receive vary considerably among nations and are frequently higher as a percentage of wages than the U.S. average of 35 percent. A study conducted a few years ago revealed such benefit percentages to be Belgium, 55 percent; France, 70 percent; Germany, 45 percent; Italy, 92 percent; Luxembourg, 41 percent; and the Netherlands, 50 percent. The benefit percentages tend to increase as labor unions negotiate new contracts or as governments legislate more and higher benefits.

---

* Frequently called fringe benefits.

Benefits: contractual or legislated.   In the United States, many—but by no means all—benefits result from labor contracts. The opposite is true of many other countries, where most benefits are legislated and ordered by the governments. In France, for example, the following are mandated by law: (1) profit sharing, (2) year-end bonuses, (3) paid holidays, (4) paid vacations of two days for each month worked, (5) three days' leave for the father when his child is born, (6) severance pay, (7) 70 to 90 percent of medical and dental expenses, (8) disability benefits, (9) retirement insurance, and (10) payments to relatives on the employee's death. In addition, the law requires allowances for maternity, housing, moving, and children. Similar benefits and allowances are required by the laws of all European countries.

Europe is not alone in such requirements. Brazilian law includes most of the benefits listed for Europe, plus an extra one—a grant paid to the dependents of a worker who has been sent to prison. An unusual benefit called for in Mexican law is up to three scholarships for workers or their children.

Additional voluntary benefits.   Some employers grant benefits greater than those required by law. Japanese firms are notable in this regard and typically pay such things as commuting expenses and housing allowances as well as providing resort housing for employee vacation use. Some American banks make low-interest loans to employees to purchase housing or an automobile.

DISCIPLINE

Although an effective personnel program of selection, training, motivation, and compensation is essential for the attainment of the organization's goals, there always will be occasions that require employee discipline. Employees' job performance may be poor, or safety, time, or other rules may be broken. Such rules can be especially difficult to enforce if the employees are unaccustomed to working in an industrial organization.

▫ Less Developed Countries (LDCs)

When managers from industrialized nations start factory operations in developing countries, they frequently encounter different practices, attitudes, and cultures. If the safety shoes hurt the workers' feet, the workers take them off, just as they did on the farm, and if the workers are tired, they rest when they want to and not when the rules permit. Usually they do not set out to break the rules deliberately; they just fail to understand or see any sense in them. This is why, as we have mentioned previously, workers without industrial experience must be taught not only how to do the job but also how to work in an industrial setting.

The extended family encountered in some LDCs can cause discipline problems. Loyalty tends to be more to one another than to the employer, and the member of the family who is the supervisor may hesitate to discipline other members who are workers. Companies have tried to avoid situations of this kind by bringing in young, nonfamily, technical graduates as supervisors. The workers will generally accept the authority of such supervisors unless they regard the new supervisor as belonging to a lower caste or having a lower social status than their own. As we have indicated, such problems exist in certain developing countries.

One other cultural difference leading to disciplinary difficulties in some LDCs is leadership style. Managers from Europe or North America, especially those who practice participative leadership, may view the local supervisor's authoritarian approach as too tough or cruel. However, those managers should change the local supervisor's approach slowly and cautiously—and maybe not at all. In cultures accustomed to a strong father figure, the workers regard a supervisor who attempts participative leadership as weak and indecisive.

With the growth of industry in LDCs and perhaps with a second generation of workers in the factories, the attitudes of workers, including those toward authority, change, and management, must be sufficiently flexible to adapt to these changes. In addition, the managers will be working to create change. Concepts and methods of supervisory training and practices developed in industrialized nations are exportable and should be utilized.

□ Developed Countries

In industrialized nations, management must communicate the rules and expected performance to employees; but, unlike in some LDCs, the employees will likely understand and accept the reasons for them. When they do not, management must take corrective steps, such as (1) clearer explanation of the rules, (2) docking of some pay, (3) demotion, and (4) discharging the worker.

In nonunion plants, management selects the corrective steps, keeping in mind that it wants a productive, efficient work force. Management must select, train, motivate, and compensate well enough to achieve that goal.

In industrialized nations, however, management is quite likely to encounter labor unions. They have great impact on the whys, hows, and whens of discipline but are sufficiently important to be treated separately.

UNION RELATIONSHIPS

Labor unions can be a force for discipline because (1) they should require their worker members to adhere to agreed rules and (2) they establish with management a set of disciplinary procedures through collective bargaining.

□ Collective Bargaining

Of course, disciplinary procedures are not the only subjects of bargaining between labor and management. In the United States, some other subjects of **collective bargaining** are wages, retirement plans, union shop, work rules, and management rights. Elsewhere, as has been pointed out, in both developed and developing countries, many of those subjects and others are legislated or decreed by the government.

collective bargaining the process of negotiations between employers and the labor union(s) representing the employees

□ Labor's Political Influence

Labor has considerable political influence in the United States, as the large unions have powerful lobbying operations in Washington and the state capitals and support friendly candidates in their political campaigns. However, labor in European and other countries is sometimes even more powerful politically, and it sometimes merges with a major political party. One of the two largest political parties in Britain is called the Labour party; and the Histadrut, the general trade union in Israel, has a powerful influence in the formation of Israeli governments.[20]

Even when collective bargaining takes place, the governments in some countries are deeply involved. Their involvement often stems from the fact that large parts of industry are nationalized. For example, at Renault, the French government-owned automobile manufacturer, unions make use of political pressures in their bargaining with managers, who are government employees. The resulting agreement terms then set the standards for other firms.

A number of developing nations require a government official to be present during the bargaining process because they fear that the generally weak unions with relatively uneducated leaders will lack the capacity to bargain with the skilled management representatives. In addition to government help, union negotiators in LDCs sometimes get help from the union that organized the employees of the parent company in its home country.

□ Home Country Assistance

Industrial country labor unions that have organized the parent company occasionally send their negotiators abroad to bargain with its subsidiaries. They may do this to help both the local unions and themselves. A more costly contract will increase the subsidiary's labor expense and thus may impede the transfer of production from the home plant to overseas facilities. This sometimes produces an odd situation, such as the one that occurred at an American subsidiary in the Caribbean. Company negotiators from the home office were surprised to find themselves face to face with the same union officials who had negotiated the union's contract with the parent company in the United States.

Localize labor relations.   Until subsidiary management becomes skilled in labor contract negotiation and union relationships, the IC headquarters should send negotiators and consultants from the home country. However, recognizing that each country presents a unique set of labor conditions, types of unions, attitudes, and laws, most multinational enterprises hold local management of foreign subsidiaries responsible for labor relations in their own country.

In the first place, this is done because the subsidiary's management should be much better informed about conditions and trends in its country than parent company management would be. Second, the subsidiary's management will have to live with its labor agreement, so it should have the authority to negotiate and agree with labor. Without such authority, the prestige of the subsidiary's management would be lowered, and it would have much more difficulty developing and implementing the long-term personnel policies necessary for the subsidiary's successful operation.

Before the home headquarters would entrust subsidiary management with the scope of authority suggested above, headquarters would want to be satisfied that the subsidiary managers are thoroughly trained and capable. The IC should also exercise some coordination.

Coordination of labor relations.   Coordination of labor relations can be important because labor contracts made in one country might provide precedent in other countries. This will be more and more the case as unions develop international cooperation.

If IC headquarters is to carry out its coordinating duties intelligently, it must require a continuing flow of labor relations information from each subsidiary. This gives headquarters' management the facts needed to use labor conditions as one important component in investment or reinvestment decisions. Such facts are also necessary to permit management evaluations among the subsidiaries.

Not only has union activity become international, thus requiring management to coordinate labor policy worldwide, but labor has also entered the boardroom and become a part of management. One name for this process is **codetermination.**

codetermination the participation of labor in the company management up to and including the board of directors

◻ Labor in Management: Codetermination

Like it or not (most managements do not), there is a growing movement toward granting workers some voice in management. Participatory management is required by law in various countries; companies must comply if they wish to do business there. In other countries, management is voluntarily bringing about worker participation. As was mentioned in Chapter 12, in 1980 Chrysler Corporation elected the president of the United Automobile Workers to its board of directors, although the company dropped the union president's spot on its board in 1991.[21]

The oldest legal requirement for codetermination was the 1951 German law calling for a 50–50 management-labor membership on the board of directors of the iron, coal, and steel industries. In 1951, the Germans passed another law calling for a one-third representation for labor on the boards of other German industries of certain sizes. In 1976, the labor representation was increased to 50 percent. Other European countries and Japan have similar legislation.

Most managements have objected and resisted. At least one German firm, Volkswagen, has had difficulties with new investment decisions because of codetermination. On the other hand, some reporters find more labor peace in countries with labor participation in management (sometimes referred to as "industrial democracy") than in those without it.

Some students of international business operations foresee possibilities that intraenterprise cooperative projects could become difficult or impossible because of codetermination. If labor board members of an important subsidiary in Europe believe a parent-ordered project is not in the best interest of the subsidiary's labor force, they can block it. The possibility has been referred to as "mutiny on the multinational."[22]

Management is learning to live with codetermination, industrial democracy, or whatever it is called because, in most cases, it must. Among the measures that management has adopted for this purpose have been opening and improving lines of communication and improving relationships between labor and management board members. There has been some inclination to lessen dependence on a subsidiary that might "mutiny" against the system. One management function that has been complicated by codetermination is the firing of workers.

EMPLOYMENT TERMINATION

As we have mentioned, Volkswagen and other firms have faced delays in decisions to invest in new plants in other countries because of labor fears of job losses in the home country. When labor is represented on a company's board of directors, it has the power to delay or even prevent actions it feels will cause layoffs among the work force. In addition, labor has the power to strike, and labor unions negotiate labor contracts with employers.

▫ Labor Contracts

One subject probably covered in every labor contract is the termination of employment. Standards of work performance are established, and when managers feel that a worker is not performing up to the standards, management must consult with union representatives before firing the worker. The union representatives may agree that the worker is not performing adequately and should be discharged, or they may suggest a transfer to a different job. If management and the union disagree, the contract contains a provision for grievance procedures or arbitration to resolve their differences. In most countries, many aspects of labor relations, including worker discharge, are covered by laws and government regulations.

▫ Labor Laws

A number of countries have laws that oblige firms to give severance pay to terminated employees who have obtained permanent status, usually after a 60- to 90-day trial period. In Mexico, workers who have been employed for even one day after the trial period must be paid three months' wages if they are discharged. That amount is increased by 20 days' wages for each additional year of employment.

Because of laws requiring that sizable sums be paid to permanent workers on discharge, some companies have striven to keep a large part of their work force as temporary workers by firing them one day before the temporary period expires and then rehiring them. Many governments have amended their laws to prevent that sort of practice.

A number of multinationals and other employers have complained of the excessive labor costs imposed by labor laws, and some countries have changed their laws to make employee discharge easier. Peru now requires a worker to be employed for three years instead of 90 days before becoming a permanent employee. Chile has eliminated the requirement that allowed permanent workers to be fired solely for legally recognized causes. Now the firm need give only 30 days' notice or 30 days' severance pay.

▫ Other Termination Conditions

Of course, not all employees are union members, not all companies are organized by unions, and not all countries have laws dealing with employment termination. Under such circumstances, the discharge of employees is at the discretion of the employers, subject to any agreements between the employees as individuals and their employers. The employees' skills and the availability of replacements would affect the relative bargaining positions of the employees and the employers.

SUMMARY

Because of the importance of an adequate labor force, a would-be employer must carefully study how to find it, hire it, train it, and—if necessary—fire it. Who is available, and how do host country laws and practices limit the employer's freedom?

Motivation of workers is important to get productivity and quality products from them. There are a number of incentive pay plans, each with advantages and disadvantages. Pay and incentive practices in the United States have changed considerably in the last few years. Japanese practices—many of which they learned from the American, Deming—are in some ways different and are now being tried in the United States, with mixed results.

Deming advocated quality circles and companywide quality control. Quality is every employee's business, from the floor worker to the CEO.

Computerized robotics are leading to the factories of the future. More and more work will be done by machines and less by laborers. The design draftsmen are being replaced by computer-aided design (CAD) equipment, and production is being accomplished with computer-aided manufacturing (CAM) machines. The combination is called CADCAM.

Discipline of the work force is necessary. It differs somewhat between LDCs and industrialized countries.

The same can be true of company relationships with labor unions. The unions are making efforts to cooperate internationally. Under codetermination laws or practices, labor unions have seats on many companies' boards of directors.

Termination of employment may be governed by the union-company agreement. In some countries, it is covered by law.

QUESTIONS

1. Before making an investment that will involve hiring employees in a foreign country, what are some questions concerning labor in that country to which management should get answers?

2. What are some advantages and disadvantages of using present employees to recruit new employees?

3. Why have many firms begun to utilize off-premises training and development programs?

4. What are quality circles? How do they relate to companywide quality control?

5. Describe and explain changes in American compensation and incentive practices in recent years.

6. What are some common fringe benefits?

7. Discuss the changes in the types of factories and production being brought about by faster, cheaper computers and more efficient robots.

8. What is collective bargaining?

9. Why is it important for a multinational to coordinate labor relations?

10. What is codetermination? What are some contrasting attitudes toward it?

11. The Japanese have opened manufacturing plants in the United States. How well are their personnel practices working?

☐ MINICASE 20-1

Philippine Pesos for a New Plant

The company you work for manufactures a product that is sold in the home market and exported. The manufacturing process calls for semiskilled and skilled labor.

To assure itself of a production facility within the ASEAN market, which your company forecasts will grow and raise trade barriers to outside products, the company has decided to invest in the Philippines. Research and negotiations by your representatives in Manila and elsewhere in the country have led to decisions not to build the plant in Manila but in a rural area on an island near Luzon, where Manila is located.

The chosen area is depressed economically, with high unemployment and low literacy. Most of its people have few industrial skills.

The Philippine government induced the company to locate there by offering an array of enticements. There will be a 10-year tax holiday for the company and for the foreign management and technical personnel it employs. The government will donate the land site chosen by your company for its plant. The government will improve the ferry and air transport and the telephone and telegraph service between the island and Luzon.

The government has other funds available to help your company set up and get into successful operation.

You are the personnel manager for the new Philippine operations. What problems should you anticipate? What solutions should you consider? The government has asked your suggestions as to how it can best spend the funds it has available for helping your company—Philippine pesos only—to assist you in solving personnel problems you foresee. How will you suggest that the pesos be spent?

☐ MINICASE 20–2

Keep It Top Secret*

Management of the French multinational enterprise Saint-Gobain opposed the efforts of another company to acquire control of it. As part of its opposition campaign, the management appealed to Saint-Gobain's stockholders not to sell their stock and revealed to them much of the previously secret financial data about the company. Its profitability (larger than had been publicly admitted previously) and its use of a Swiss holding company to reduce taxes were told to stockholders to induce them to hold their shares.

At that time, Saint-Gobain also had labor relations difficulties with unions in France, Italy, the United States, and West Germany. Of course, the unions got their hands on the previously confidential information.

The unions coordinated their collective bargaining in all four countries. Saint-Gobain was hit by strikes and finally made large concessions to settle. As a result, Saint-Gobain made little profit during the late 1970s.

1. Would you have handled this situation in the same way that Saint-Gobain's management did? Discuss.

2. Now that the damage has been done, what labor relations steps should Saint-Gobain take? Explain.

3. What is your guess as to why management made the revelations?

*Source: David A. Ricks, M. Fu, and Jeffrey S. Arpan, *International Business Blunders* (Columbus: Grid, 1974), pp. 59–60.

SUPPLEMENTARY READINGS

Albano, Debbie. "British Miners Strike—Seek World Support." *Labor Today,* January 1985, p. 1.

Bhatt, Bhal J., and Edwin L. Miller. "Industrial Relations in Foreign and Local Firms in Asia." *Management International Review,* Summer 1984, pp. 62–73.

Busch, G. K. *The Political Role of International Trade Unions.* London: Macmillan, 1983.

Cramer, James, and Patricia Wallace. "Understanding Your Japanese Manager." *The Asian Wall Street Journal,* July 30, 1990, p. 11.

Dreyer, Peter H. "European Unions on the Defense." *Journal of Commerce,* March 12, 1986, p. 4A.

Ebrahimpour, Malig. "An Examination of Quality Management in Japan: Implications for Management in the United States." *Journal of Operations Management,* August 1986, pp. 4–9.

Enderwick, Peter. "Ownership Nationality and Industrial Relations Practices in British Nonmanufacturing Industries." *Industrial Relations Journal,* January 1986, pp. 50–62.

Foreign Labor Trends in a number of separate countries. These are released by the U.S. Department of Labor, Bureau of International Labor Affairs. Each is prepared by the American embassy in the subject country.

Fucini Joseph J., and Suzy Fucini. *Working for the Japanese.* New York: The Free Press, 1991.

Gordon, William I. "Gaining Employee Commitment to Quality." *Supervisory Management,* November 1985, pp. 30–38.

Harnett, Donald C., and L. L. Cummings. *Bargaining Behavior: An International Study.* Houston: Dame Publications, 1980.

Hutchins, Dave. "Quality Is Everybody's Business." *Management Decision,* Winter 1986, pp. 3–10.

Jacoby, S. M. "The Future of Industrial Relations in the United States." *California Management Review,* Summer 1984, pp. 90–94.

"Japanese Management: Good or Bad?" "Disillusioned" Gary J. Katzenstein "Encouraged" Richard O'Neill, *Los Angeles Times,* December 10, 1990, pp. D3 and 20.

Jones, Sam L. "Quality Circles Can Enhance Firm's Communication." *American Metal Market,* September 7, 1984, pp. 6–11.

Kaha, Helen. "Cooperation Is Focus of Labor Study." *Automotive News,* June 23, 1986, p. 1.

Landon, David N., and Steve Moulton. "Quality Circles: What's in Them for Employees?" *Personnel Journal,* June 1986, pp. 23–29.

Main, Jeremy. "How to Win the Baldrige Award." *Fortune,* April 23, 1990, pp. 101–16.

Matsuura, Nanthi. "Japanese Management and Labor Relations in U.S. Subsidiaries." *Industrial Relations Journal,* Winter 1984, pp. 38–44.

Moffat, Susan. "Should You Work for the Japanese?" *Fortune,* December 3, 1990, pp. 107–11.

Poole, Michael. "Industrial Relations in the Future." *Journal of General Management,* August 1985, pp. 38–48.

Reitsperger, Wolf D. "Japanese Management: Coping with British Industrial Relations." *Journal of Management Studies,* January 1986, pp. 72–86.

Siberman, David. "Labor Law Turned Upside Down." *American Federationist,* July 6, 1985, pp. 5–11.

Trever, Malcolm. "Quality Control—Learning from the Japanese." *Long-Range Planning,* October 1986, pp. 46–54.

Zahasin, Gretchan. "Quality Control: It's Money in the Bank." *ABA Banking Journal,* December 1986, pp. 22–27.

ENDNOTES

1. Some experts refer to the subject we shall cover here as human resources planning. However, that appears to us to include all the functions numbered in the introduction, and we wish to limit the material in this section to the analyses of the company's personnel needs, the availability of the needed personnel, and applicable laws.

2. Manning Nash, "The Interplay of Culture and Management in a Guatemalan Textile Plant," in *Culture and Management,* ed. Ross A. Webber (Homewood, Ill.: Richard D. Irwin, 1969), pp. 317–24.

3. Denis Debost, *Summary of French Labor and Social Security Laws* (Paris: French Industrial Development Agency, 1972), p. 7.

4. Nancy J. Perry, "Here Come Richer, Riskier Pay Plans," *Fortune,* December 19, 1988, pp. 50–58. This article gives numerous examples of incentive pay plans in action.

5. Ibid.

6. Louis Kraar, "Japan's Gung-Ho U.S. Car Plants," *Fortune,* January 30, 1989, pp. 97–108.

7. "Battle at Smyrna," *The Economist,* August 8, 1989, p. 27.

8. James Risen, "Japanese Labor Policies Stirring U.S. Rebellion," *Los Angeles Times,* May 20, 1989, pp. A1 and 18.

9. Regina Eisman, "When Cultures Clash," *Incentive,* May 1991, pp. 65–70.

10. Leslie Helm, "The Rule of Work in Japan," *Los Angeles Times,* March 17, 1991, pp. A1 and 23–24.

11. Davida M. Amsden and Robert T. Amsden, "ICQCC Seoul 82," *Quality Circle Journal,* September 1983, pp. 12–14.

12. Richard Koenig, "Quality Circles Are Vulnerable to Union Tests," *The Wall Street Journal,* March 28, 1990, p. B1.

13. Wayne S. Rieker, "QC Circles and Companywide Quality Control," *Quality Progress,* October 1983, pp. 14–17.

14. *The Economist,* November 23, 1985, p. 81.

15. Jeff Pelline, "Hero of Japan Tones Up Chevron," *San Francisco Chronicle,* January 10, 1989, p. C1.

16. George Melloan, "Robots Talk Back to Product Designers," *The Wall Street Journal,* May 26, 1987, p. 29.

17. Lori Vallgra, "Fuzz Logic and Robots Spell Technological Advantage," *Financial Times,* May 14, 1991, p. 4.

18. Andrew Baxter, "CADCAM Market Is Expected to Rise to $26.2 Billion by 1995," *Financial Times,* May 14, 1991, p. 2.

19. For a comprehensive look at American, European, and Japanese approaches to the factory of the future, see Nicholas Valery, "The Challenge," *The Economist,* May 30, 1987, a survey. For more recent views, see "Computers in Manufacturing Survey," *Financial Times,* May 14, 1991, sect. III, pp. 1–6.

20. *Trade and Investment in Israel* (Tel Aviv: Bank Leumi Le Israel, 1978), p. 67.

21. Jesus Sanchez and Donald Woutat, "Chrysler to Drop Union President's Spot on Its Board," *Los Angeles Times,* March 14, 1991, pp. D1 and 4.

22. Robert J. Kuhne, "Statutory Codetermination: Mutiny on the Multinational?" Paper presented at the annual national meeting of the Academy of International Business, Orlando, Florida, August 1977.

Chapter 21

Strategic Planning and Organizational Design

Planning is no panacea. Nor is it necessary to overcomplicate the process, making up those elaborate flow charts with circles and squares going in every direction, which was evident in the 1970s. But good planning is something that we simply cannot do without. Planning in business is not a virtue; it is a necessity. As such, it's the real mother of invention.

J. Tylee Wilson, CEO of R. J. Reynolds

LEARNING OBJECTIVES

In this chapter, you will study:

1. The benefits of global strategic planning.
2. The steps in a global strategic planning process.
3. What a planning staff does.
4. Various examples of corporate mission statements, objectives, quantified goals, and strategies.
5. New directions in strategic planning.
6. Various organizational forms.
7. Some newer organizational forms.
8. The characteristics of the "right" organization.

KEY WORDS AND CONCEPTS

- Watch list
- Mission statement
- Corporate strategy
- Scenario
- Contingency plans
- Top-down planning
- Bottom-up planning
- Iterative planning
- International division
- Hybrid organization
- Matrix organization
- Matrix overlay
- Strategic business unit (SBU)
- Horizontal organization

BUSINESS INCIDENT

A Global Strategic Planner

Minnesota Mining & Manufacturing (3M), known as one of the best-managed and most innovative American international companies, was founded in 1902. However, it was in business for nearly 50 years before it established an international division and began to export. Yet, by 1990, 48 percent of its total sales ($13.0 billion) were coming from foreign markets; $1.2 billion were from U.S. exports. Managers of its overseas subsidiaries operate with a high degree of autonomy and finance their own expansion. But corporate culture is worldwide; in fact, many managers are third-country nationals (citizens of neither the home nor the host country who work in a host country affiliate).

Structured strategic planning was not adopted until 1981, after a new CEO joined the firm. He felt that although cross-functional teams at the product level were doing a good job of decision making, they weren't steering the company. Despite the long-term nature of many of its product developments, the company's planning was essentially short term. The president recognized that 3M could continue to innovate on a large scale only if its technological resources were shared among its units, and he wanted to operate on a planned global strategic basis without losing the autonomous, entrepreneurial ability of the product divisions. The result was a reorganization of the company's 200 organizational units worldwide into 20 strategic business centers (SBCs).

Within each SBC, planning starts with the operating managers of the various subsidiaries, who analyze internal strengths and weaknesses and external forces, such as new technology and government regulatory changes; make a competitor analysis; and determine the company resources they will need to achieve their objectives. Their plans go to the SBCs for review and consultation. SBC plans then go to a strategic planning committee consisting of vice presidents at headquarters who represent the

BUSINESS INCIDENT (concluded)

☐ **FIGURE 21-1   3M Strategic Planning Cycle**

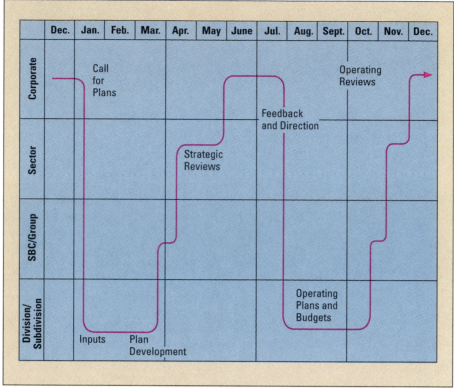

Source: "Planning Global Strategies for 3M," *Long-Range Planning,* February 1988, p. 15.

four sectors into which the 20 SBCs are divided. The plans are reviewed with at least two members of the strategic planning committee present, and results of this review are discussed with SBC managements. Any differences between SBC managements and sector management are reconciled.

Two months later (July), the corporate headquarters' 34-person management committee, to which the 12 strategic planning committee members belong, reviews the plans and votes on spending priorities. Feedback and direction are given to the operating units, who then prepare operating plans and budgets by December and submit them to headquarters. There, they are finalized jointly with corporate worldwide plans.

A few days before the December operating reviews, the management committee holds brainstorming sessions to discuss trends and developments over the coming 15 years. The general manager of each business unit pre-

sents the best picture possible for that industry for the period. The outcome of this meeting is a broad guide for strategic planning. The company's strategic planning cycle is diagrammed in Figure 21-1.

Although planning is done by operating managers, the director and staff of a planning services and development unit provide an analysis of 3M's 20 principal competitors worldwide and any other information the units require. They also try to identify opportunities and new products.

Allen Jacobson, who became CEO in 1986, says, "When you get a new chief executive and strategic planning together, people expect a dramatic change. I'm not the least bit interested in drama, I'm interested in seeing our business progress. Our company is multiproduct, multi-technology, multinational, and multimarket. We probably sell to a greater variety of commercial, industrial, and consumer markets than anybody else. Now with that diversity, you can't make all the important decisions on the

13th or 14th floor [offices of top managements] of this building. You have to have a system that depends on your people, or on the people closest to the job, the technology, and the customer." He admits that there is more headquarters involvement in seeing (1) that business plans are consistent with overall strategy and (2) that the company is exploiting all of the opportunities in an area.

Source: Carol Kennedy, "Planning Global Strategies for 3M," *Long-Range Planning*, August 1988, p. 63; and "U.S. Corporations with the Biggest Foreign Revenues," *Forbes*, July 22, 1991, p. 289.

GLOBAL STRATEGIC PLANNING

◻ Why Plan Globally?

Numerous international firms such as 3M have found it necessary to institute formal global strategic planning to provide a means for top management to identify opportunities and threats from all over the world, formulate strategies to handle them, and stipulate how to finance the strategies' implementation. Global strategic plans not only provide for consistency of action among the firm's managers worldwide but also require the participants to consider the ramifications of their actions on the other geographical and functional areas of the firm.

◻ Standardization and Planning

Historically, more aspects of production than of marketing have been standardized and coordinated worldwide. This is because many top executives believe marketing strategies are best determined locally due to differences among the various foreign environments. Yet, you have seen that there is a growing tendency to standardize not only marketing strategies but also the total product, which leads to their inclusion in the global strategic planning process. Of course, you realize that their standardization can also be the *result* of strategic planning as managements search for ways to lower costs and to present a uniform company image as global producers of quality products. We mentioned in Chapter 19 that many Japanese firms have adopted this strategy. Let us look at the planning process.

◻ Global Strategic Planning Process

Global strategic planning, as you know, is the primary function of managers, and the manager of strategic planning and strategy making is the firm's chief executive officer. The process of strategic planning provides a formal structure in which managers (1) analyze the company's external environments, (2) analyze the company's internal environment, (3) define the company's business and mission, (4) set corporate objectives, (5) quantify goals, (6) formulate strategies, and (7) make tactical plans. For ease of understanding, we present this as a lineal process; but in actuality, there is considerable flexibility in the order in which firms take up these items.

In the meetings that one of the writers attended, if during the analysis of the corporate controllable variables committee members wanted to discuss the corporate objectives they felt were affected by some of those variables, they would do so.

mission statement a broad statement that defines the organization's scope

respect to our present objectives? Have we uncovered any facts that require us to delete goals, alter them, or add new ones? After completing this internal audit, the committee is ready to examine its business and **mission statements.**

Defining the corporate business and mission statements.   These broad statements, communicate to the corporation's stakeholders (employees, stockholders, governments, suppliers, and customers) what the company is and where it is going. Some firms have both statements, whereas others combine them into one. In either case, these statements must be evaluated against changing realities uncovered in the external and internal analyses and then altered when necessary.

Some examples.   Chrysler has extremely short mission and business statements. This is how they appear in the firm's annual report:

Who we are: A car and truck company.

Our mission: To satisfy our customers.[2]

Gerber Products Company gives much more information in its business and mission statements. The company says that it is "a leading provider of food, clothing, and care products for families with children from birth through age three." Its mission statement is the following:

"The human, physical, and financial resources of Gerber Products Company are dedicated toward:

- Establishing Gerber as the premier brand on food, clothing, and care items through age three.
- Giving our customers and consumers what they want all the time, every time, on time.
- Continuously pursuing improvements in all phases of our business.
- Seeking intelligent risks that will build shareholder value.
- Providing long-term shareholders with superior returns.
- Creating opportunities for all associates to achieve their full potential.
- Maintaining the Gerber heritage as the authority in the field of infant and child nutrition and care."[3]

Bausch & Lomb, noted for its contact lens and eye-care products, combines the statements. "Bausch & Lomb is one of America's oldest and most successful companies, with a heritage of technical achievement and product excellence dating back to 1853. The company markets its products on the basis of quality, differentiated benefits, and in many cases the recommendation of healthcare professionals. Its strategic focus is on selected segments of global healthcare and optics markets where it is competitively advantaged with superior technology, low production costs, and established brand names."[4] After defining the business and mission statements, management must then set corporate objectives.

Set corporate objectives.   Objectives direct the firm's course of action, maintain it within the boundaries of the stated mission, and ensure its continuing existence. The Campbell Soup Company says, "We want to outperform our peer companies in the food industry." Also, "management wants to prove that a free-standing management can make the best use of Campbell's assets."[5] But how does Campbell's management know if it is achieving these objectives?

Quantify the objectives.   When objectives can be quantified, they should be. What does Campbell Soup's management believe to be the best use of the company's assets? How will it know if it outperforms other firms in the food industry? The company's annual report states, "Our goals for the next five years are: (1) average a net earnings per share growth rate of at least 20 percent, (2) average a return on equity of at least 20 percent, and (3) average cash return on assets of at least 20 percent."[6]

Despite the strong preference of most top managers for verifiable objectives, they frequently do have nonquantifiable or directional goals. One of PepsiCo's objectives, for example, is to accelerate profitable growth. Although this goal is not quantified, it does set the direction for managers, and requires them to formulate more specific strategies to attain it. Incidentally, objectives do tend to be more quantified as they progress down the organization to the operational level, because, for the most part, strategies at one level become the objectives for the succeeding level. Up to this point, only *what*, *how much*, and *when* have been stipulated. *How* these objectives are to be achieved will be determined in the formulation of strategies.

Formulate the corporate strategies.   Generally, participants in the strategic planning process will formulate alternate **corporate strategies,** or action plans, that seem plausible considering the directions the external environmental forces are taking and corporation's strengths and weaknesses. Suppose (1) their analysis of the external environment convinces them that the Japanese government is making it easier for foreign firms to enter the market and (2) the competitor analysis reveals that a Japanese competitor is preparing to enter the United States (or wherever the home market is). Should the firm adopt a defensive strategy of defending the home market by lowering its price there, or should it attack the competitor in its home market by establishing a subsidiary in Japan? Management may decide to pursue either strategy or both, depending on its interpretation of the situation.

When choosing among strategies, management must consider corporate culture.[7] If it decides to put into effect a quality control system that includes quality circles, and heretofore there has been little employee participation in decision making, the strategy will have to include the cost of and time for training the employees to accept this cultural change.

Strategies may also be general.   At the corporate level, strategies, like objectives, may be rather general. PepsiCo states that to achieve its objective of accelerating growth, it is "executing these strategies of (1) segmenting the market to reach more people with more products, (2) expanding through existing and new distribution channels, (3) staying contemporary to attract new generations of customers, and (4) strengthening and expanding our infrastructure to make us more competitive in existing markets and to reach new markets."[8] You can be sure that the marketing function, which receives these strategies as its objectives, will be required to quantify as many as possible.

Scenarios.   Because of the rapidity of environmental changes, many managements have become dissatisfied with planning for a single set of events and have turned to **scenarios,** descriptions of events apt to occur in the future that bear on the performance of the organization. Commonly, scenarios are made for the worst-case, most likely, and best-case situations. They are intended to raise the managers' awareness and avoid surprises. Often, the "what if"

corporate strategy action plan to enable an organization to reach its objectives

scenario description of a possible future, often most likely, worst, and best cases questions raised reveal weaknesses in present strategies. Some of the more common kinds of subjects for scenarios are large and sudden changes in sales (up or down), sudden increases in price of key raw materials, sudden increases in health-care costs, and changes in the political party in power. Often, scenarios are the basis for preparing standby or contingency plans.

contingency plans plans for the best- or worst-case scenarios or for critical events that could have a severe impact on the firm

Contingency plans.   Most managements prepare **contingency plans** for worst- and best-case scenarios and for critical events as well. Every operator of a nuclear plant has contingency plans, as do most producers of petroleum and hazardous chemicals since such ecological disasters as the Valdez oil spill and the tragic Bhopal gas leak occurred.

Prepare tactical plans.   Because strategic plans are fairly broad, tactical (also called operational) plans are a requisite for spelling out in detail how the objectives will be reached. In other words, very specific, short-term means for achieving the goals are the object of tactical planning. For instance, if the British subsidiary of an American producer of prepared foods has as a quantitative goal a 20 percent increase in sales, its strategy might be to sell 30 percent more to institutional users. The tactical plan could include such points as hiring three new specialized sales representatives, attending four trade shows, and advertising in two industry periodicals every other month next year. This is the kind of specificity found in the tactical plan.

◻ Strategic Plan Features and Implementation Facilitators

Sales forecasts and budgets.   Two prominent features of the strategic plan are *sales forecasts* and *budgets*. The sales forecast not only provides management with an estimate of the revenue to be received and the units to be sold but also serves as the basis for planning in the other functional areas. Without this information, management cannot formulate the production, financial, and procurement plans. Budgets, like sales forecasts, are both a planning and a control technique. During planning, they coordinate all of the functions within the firm and provide management with a detailed statement of future operating results.

Plan implementation facilitators.   Once the plan has been prepared, it must be implemented. Two of the most important plan implementation facilitators that management employs are policies and procedures.

Policies.   Policies are broad guidelines issued by upper management for the purpose of assisting lower-level managers in handling recurring problems. Because policies are broad, they permit discretionary action and interpretation. The object of a policy is to economize managerial time and promote consistency among the various operating units. If the distribution policy states that the firm's policy is to sell through wholesalers, marketing managers throughout the world know that they should normally use wholesalers and avoid selling directly to retailers. The disclosure of the widespread occurrence of bribery prompted company presidents to issue policy statements condemning this practice. Managers were put on notice by these statements that they were not to offer bribes.

Procedures.   Procedures prescribe how certain activities will be carried out, thereby ensuring uniform action on the part of all corporate members. For instance, most corporate headquarters issue a procedure for their subsidiaries to follow in preparing the annual budget. This procedure assures corporate management that all budgets will be prepared using the same format, which will facilitate their comparison.

◻ Kinds of Strategic Plans

Time horizon.   Although strategic plans may be classified as short, medium, or long term, there is little agreement as to the length of these periods. For some, long-range planning may be for a five-year period. For others, this would be the length of a medium-term plan; their long range might cover 15 years or more. Short-range plans are usually for one to three years; however, even long-term plans are subject to review annually or more frequently if a situation requires it. Furthermore, the time horizon will vary according to the age of the firm and the stability of its market. A new venture is extremely difficult to plan for more than three years in advance, but a five- or six-year horizon is probably sufficient for a mature company in a steady market.

Level in the organization.   If the corporation has three organizational levels, as 3M does, there will be three levels of plans, each of which will generally be more specific and for a shorter time frame than it is at the level above. In addition, the functional areas at each level will have plans and sometimes will be subject to the same hierarchy, depending mainly on how the company is organized.

◻ Methods of Planning

top-down planning
planning process that begins at the highest level in the organization and continues downward

Top-down planning.   In **top-down planning,** corporate headquarters develops and provides guidelines that include the definition of the business, the mission statement, company objectives, financial assumptions, the content of the plan, and special issues. If there is an international division, its management may be told that this division is expected to contribute $5 million in profits, for example. The division, in turn, would break this total down among the affiliates under its control. The managing director in Germany would be informed that the German operation is expected to contribute $1 million; Brazil, $300,000; and so on.

Disadvantages of top-down planning are that it restricts initiative at the lower levels and shows some insensitivity to local conditions. Furthermore, especially in an international company, there are so many interrelationships that consultation is necessary. Can top management, for example, decide on rationalization of manufacturing without obtaining the opinions of the local units as to its feasibility?

The advantage of top-down planning is that the home office with its global perspective should be able to formulate plans that ensure the optimal corporatewide use of the firm's scarce resources.

bottom-up planning
planning process that begins at the lowest level in the organization and continues upward

Bottom-up planning.   **Bottom-up planning** operates in the opposite manner. The lowest operating levels inform top management of what they expect to do, and the total becomes the firm's goals. The advantage of bottom-up planning is that the people responsible for attaining the goals are formulating them. Who knows better than the subsidiaries' directors what and how much the subsidiaries can sell? Because the subsidiaries' directors set the goals with no coercion from top management, they feel obligated to make their word good. However, there is also a disadvantage. Each affiliate is free to some extent to pursue the goals it wishes to pursue, and so there is no guarantee that the sum total of all the affiliates' goals will coincide with those of headquarters. When discrepancies occur, extra time must be taken at headquarters to eliminate them.[9] Bottom-up planning is the almost invariable method used by Japanese managements because they strive for a consensus at every level.

iterative planning repetition of the bottom-up or top-down planning process until all differences are reconciled

Iterative planning.   It appears that **iterative planning,** which 3M practices, is becoming more popular, especially in global companies that seek to have a single global plan while operating in many diverse foreign environments. As you saw, iterative planning combines aspects of both top-down and bottom-up planning.

◻ New Directions in Planning

Planning during the 60s and early 70s commonly consisted of a company's CEO and the head of planning getting together to devise a corporate plan, which would then be handed to the operating people for execution. Changes in the business environment, however, caused changes to be made in three areas: (1) who does the planning, (2) how it is done, and (3) the contents of the plan.

Who does it.   By the mid-70s, strategic planners had become dominant figures in their companies. They were accustomed to writing a blueprint for each subsidiary, which they would then present to the management of each operating unit. The planners' power grew and the operating managers' influence waned, and of course there was hostility between the two groups. Roger Smith, former chairman of GM, says, "We got those great plans together, put them on a shelf, and marched off to do what we would be doing anyway."[10]

But a number of factors were acting to upset this pattern. It became clear that world uncertainty made long-range planning in detail impossible, so corporate plans had to be short and simple. With huge, detailed plans no longer as useful as they had been, there was less need for professional planners. Stronger competition made a practical knowledge of the company and the industry an essential input to strategic planning. This brought senior operating managers into the planning process, enabling firms to change the role and reduce the size of their planning staffs. General Electric, for example, reduced its corporate planning group from 58 to 33, and GM decreed that "planning is the responsibility of every line manager. The role of the planner is to be the catalyst for change—not to do the planning for each business unit."[11]

How it is done.   By the 19860s, firms were using computer models and sophisticated forecasting methods to help produce the voluminous plans we mentioned above. These plans were not only huge but also very detailed. As a Texas Instruments executive put it, "The company let its management system, which can track the eye of every sparrow, creep into the planning process, so we were making more and more detailed plans. It became a morale problem because managers knew they couldn't project numbers out five years to two decimal points."[12]

The heavy emphasis on these methods tended to result in a concentration on factors that could be quantified easily. However, the less quantifiable factors relating to sociopolitical developments were becoming increasingly important. Also, the rapid rise in the levels of uncertainty made it clear to top managers that there was no point in using advanced techniques to make detailed five-year forecasts when various crises were exposing the nonsense of many previous forecasts. (Prior to 1973, for example, there had been a great discussion as to whether the price of crude oil would ever go above $2 per barrel.)[13]

Because of these problems, many firms have moved toward a less structured format and a much shorter document. General Electric chairman J. F. Welch says, "A strategy can be summarized in a page or two."[14]

Contents of the plan.   The contents of the plan are also different. Managements of many companies say they are much more concerned now with issues, strategies, and implementation. The planning director of Shell Oil, the British-Dutch transnational, says,

> The Shell approach has swung increasingly away from a mechanistic methodology and centrally set forecasts toward a more conceptual or qualitative analysis of the forces and pressures impinging on the industry. What Shell planners try to do is identify the key elements pertaining to a particular area of decision making—the different competitive, political, economic, social, and technical forces that are likely to have the greatest influence on the overall situation. In a global organization, the higher level of management is likely to be most interested in global scenarios—looking at worldwide developments—while the focus becomes narrower as one proceeds into the more specialized functions, divisions, and business sectors of individual companies.[15]

□ Summary of the Planning Process

Perhaps a good way to summarize the new direction in planning is to quote Frederick W. Gluck, a director of the multinational management consulting firm McKinsey & Co. and a principal architect of its strategic management practice. Gluck says that if major corporations are to develop the flexibility to compete, they must make the following major changes in the way they plan:

1. Top management must assume a more explicit strategic decision-making role, dedicating a large amount of time to deciding how things ought to be instead of listening to analyses of how they are.

2. The nature of planning must undergo a fundamental change from an exercise in forecasting to an exercise in creativity.

3. Planning processes and tools that assume a future much like the past must be replaced by a mind-set that is obsessed with being first to recognize change and turn it into a competitive advantage.

4. The role of the planner must change from being a purveyor of incrementalism to that of a crusader for action and an alter ego to line management.

5. Strategic planning must be restored to the core of line management responsibilities.[16]

ORGANIZATIONAL DESIGN

Organizing normally follows planning because the organization must implement the strategic plan. The planning process itself, because it encompasses an analysis of all the firm's activities, often discloses a need to alter the organization. Changes in strategy may require changes in the organization, but the reverse is also true. A new CEO joins the firm, or an important customer changes its method of operating—adopts a synchronous production process, for example. Planning and organizing are so closely related that normally the structure of the organization is treated by management as an integral part of the planning process.

In designing the organizational structure, management is faced with two concerns: (1) finding the most effective way to departmentalize to take advantage of the efficiencies gained from the specialization of labor and (2) coordinating the firm's activities to enable it to meet its overall objectives. As all managers know, these two concerns run counter to each other; that is, the gain from the increased specialization of labor may sometimes be nullified by the increased costs of greater coordination. It is the constant search for an optimum balance between them that causes firms to make frequent changes in their organizational structures. However, as one critic of this frantic search for the suitable organization points out, "The companies I studied have *not* continually reorganized their operations. Each has retained for years a simple structure built around an **international division**—a form of organization that many management theorists regard as embryonic, appropriate only for companies in the earliest stages of worldwide growth."[17] IBM and Ford are two examples of global firms that have international divisions, although for the most part, firms have abandoned the international structure.[18]

international division
a division in the organization that is at the same level as the domestic division and is responsible for all non-home country activities

▫ Evolution of the Global Company

You will remember reading in Chapter 2 that companies often enter foreign markets first by exporting and then, as sales increase, forming overseas sales companies and eventually setting up production facilities. As the firm's foreign involvement changed, its organization frequently changed. It might first have had *no one* responsible for international business; each domestic product division may have been responsible for filling export orders. Next, an export department might have been created, and, when the company began to invest in various overseas locations, it might have formed an international division to take charge of all overseas involvement. Note that the international division itself is usually organized on a regional (geographical) basis. This is how IBM and Ford organize their international divisions. IBM's corporate organization is shown in Figure 21–3.

Note that although IBM continues to maintain an international division, its role has changed. In the past, IBM's overseas operations were highly centralized under its international division, IBM World Trade Corporation. Now most of the company's foreign operations are organized by regions, which IBM World Trade, as a nonadministrative umbrella, oversees. Generally, there are few global firms that still use the international division form, and those that do usually have made changes to fit the company needs, as have IBM and Ford.[19]

☐ FIGURE 21–3   International Division—IBM Corporate Organization

Corporate Management Board
Board Chairman (A)

Vice Chairman (B) Vice Chairman (C)
6 Senior Vice Presidents (D)
8 Vice Presidents (E)

Management
Committee
A, B, C,
3 Ds

F   G   H   I   J   K

B-Vice Chairman and
President, IBM
World Trade Corp.
C-Vice Chairman

F-Operations
Staff
G-General
Counsel

H-Technology
I-Finance &
Planning

J-Law & External
Relations
K-Personnel

Group Executive,
Information
Systems Group
(C)

Group Executive,
Communications
Group
(D)

Group Executive,
Products Group
(D)

Group Executive,
Storage Group
(C)

Group Executive,
Technology Group
(C)

Group Executive,
IBM World Trade
Americas Group
(B)

Group Executive,
IBM World Trade
Asia/Pacific
Group
(B)

CEO IBM
World Trade/Europe
Middle East/Africa
Group
(B)

IBM Canada
Latin America
Division

IBM Australia
IBM China
IBM Japan
IBM New Zealand
SE Asia Countries

Area Divisions
IBM France
IBM Germany
IBM Italy
IBM United Kingdom

☐ **FIGURE 21–4   Global Corporate Form—Product**

As their overseas operations increased in importance and scope, most managements, with some exceptions, felt the need to eliminate international divisions and establish worldwide organizations based on *product, region,* or *function.* In rarer instances, customer classes are also a top-level dimension. Some service companies and financial institutions are organized this way. At secondary, tertiary, and still lower levels, these four dimensions—plus (1) process, (2) national subsidiary, and (3) international or domestic—provide the basis for subdivisions.

Managements who changed to these types of organizations felt they would (1) be more capable of developing competitive strategies to confront the new global competition, (2) obtain lower production costs by promoting worldwide product standardization and manufacturing rationalization, and (3) enhance technology transfer and the allocation of company resources.

Global corporate form—product.   Frequently, this structure has been a return to preexport department times in that the domestic product division has been given responsibility for global line and staff operations. To be able to operate overseas, each product division generally has regional experts; so, while this organizational form avoids the duplication of product experts common in the company with an international division, it creates a duplication of area experts. Occasionally, to eliminate placing regional specialists in each product division, management will have a group of regional specialists in an international division that advises the product divisions but has no line authority over them (see Figure 21–4).

Although organization by product is most favored by global companies, the organization alone does not guarantee that the firm is a global one. The Worldview on page 744 describes the attempt of Japanese companies organized by product to change from multinational to global companies.

Global corporate form—geographical regions.   Firms in which geographic regions are the primary basis for division put the responsibility for all activities under area managers who report directly to the chief executive officer. This kind of organization simplifies the task of directing worldwide operations, because every country in the world is clearly under the control of someone who is in contact with headquarters (see Figure 21–5).

Of course, this organizational type is used for both multinational (multidomestic) and global companies. Global companies that use it consider the divi-

□ **FIGURE 21–5   Global Corporate Form—Geographic Regions**

sion in which the home country is located as just another division for purposes of resource allocation and a source of management personnel. Some U.S. global companies have created a North American division that includes Canada, Mexico, and Central American countries in addition to the United States, possibly in part to emphasize that the home country is given no preference.

The regionalized organization appears to be popular with companies that manufacture products with a rather low or, at least, stable technological content that require strong marketing ability. It is also favored by firms with diverse products, each having different product requirements, competitive environments, and political risks. Producers of consumer products, such as prepared foods, pharmaceuticals, and household products, employ this type of organization. The disadvantage of an organization divided into geographic regions is that each region must have its own product and functional specialists so that although the duplication of area specialists found in product divisions is eliminated, a duplication of product and functional specialists is necessary.

Production coordination across regions presents difficult problems, as does global product planning. To alleviate these problems managements often place specialized product managers on the headquarters staff. Although these managers have no line authority, they do provide input to corporate decisions concerning products.

Global corporate form—function.   Few firms are organized by function at the top level. Those that are obviously believe worldwide functional expertise is more significant to the firm than product or area knowledge. In this type of organization, those reporting to the CEO might be the senior executives responsible for each functional area (marketing, production, finance, etc.), as in Figure 21–6. The commonality among the users of the functional form is a narrow and highly integrated product mix, such as that of aircraft manufacturers or oil refining companies. For example, Sun Co., a petroleum company that also mines coal, has three group heads reporting to the CEO: (1) refining and marketing, (2) exploration and production, and (3) energy minerals.[20] Because of the presence of the last group, Sun really has a mixed, or hybrid, organization.

☐ **FIGURE 21–6   Global Corporate Form—Function**

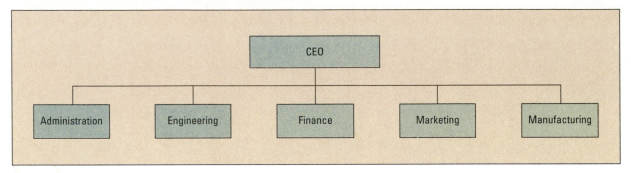

hybrid organization
structure organized by more than one dimension at the top level

Hybrid forms.   In a **hybrid organization,** a mixture of the organizational forms is used at the top level and may or not be present at the lower levels. Figure 21–7 illustrates a simple hybrid form.

Such combinations are often the result of a regionally organized company having introduced a new and different product line that management believes can best be handled by a worldwide product division. An acquired company with distinct products and a functioning marketing network may be incorporated as a product division even though the rest of the firm is organized on a regional basis. Later, after corporate management becomes familiar with the operation, it may be regionalized.

A mixed structure may also result from the firm's selling to a sizable, homogeneous class of customers. Special divisions for handling sales to the military or to original equipment manufacturers are often established at the same level as regional or product divisions.

matrix organization
an organizational structure composed of one or more superimposed organizational structures in an attempt to mesh product, regional, functional, and other expertise

Matrix organizations.   The **matrix organization** has evolved from management's attempt to mesh product, regional, and functional expertise while still maintaining clear lines of authority. It is called a matrix because it superimposes an organization based on one dimension on an organization based on another dimension. In such an organization, both the area and product managers will be at the same level and their responsibilities will overlap. An individual manager—say, a marketing manager in Germany—will have a multiple reporting relationship, being responsible to the area manager and, in some instances, to an international or worldwide marketing manager at headquarters. Figure 21–8 illustrates an extremely simple matrix organization based on two organizational dimensions. Note that the country managers are responsible to both the area and the product line managers.

Ciba-Geigy, the Swiss chemical and pharmaceutical multinational, has an organizational structure based on a matrix of *three* dimensions: (1) product, (2) function, and (3) geographic region. Lines of communication flow both horizontally and vertically across these main dimensions. However, final authority rests with the executive committee, which is the highest executive body in the parent company. The task of this committee is to maintain two-way communication between the home office and the lower units. Committee members are not supermanagers of the divisions.

Problems with the matrix.   Although at one time it seemed that the matrix organizational form would enable firms to have the advantages of the product, regional, and functional forms, the disadvantages of the matrix form

No clear decision making authority

handwritten: product regional functional

☐ **FIGURE 21-7   Hybrid Organizational Form**

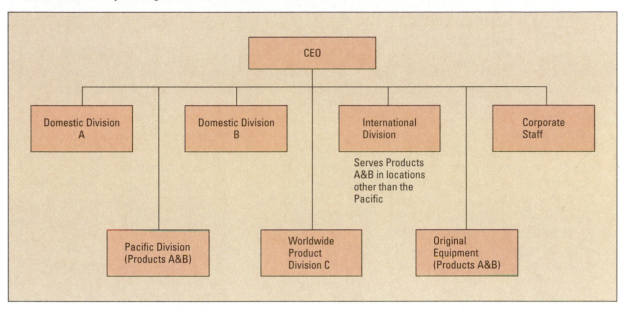

☐ **FIGURE 21-8   Regional-Product Matrix**

WORLDVIEW
Japanese Firms Formulate Global Strategies

Many Japanese firms are striving to become global companies. Although they have had foreign factories and sales offices for decades, their product development, marketing, financing, and investment plans have been directed from Japan; they are Japanese multinationals whose management philosophy is decidedly ethnocentric (home country does it better). Why should long-established firms like Toyota, Matsushita, and Hitachi, all of which are convinced of the superiority of the "Japanese way," change their methods of operating which have been so profitable for so long?

The main reason is that their overseas manufacturing operations are becoming so large and diversified that they are beyond effective centralized control from the home offices. Governments, especially those of EC members, are enacting stricter local-content laws requiring local manufacture, not just assembly. NEC, for example, has formulated a new global strategy of manufacturing in "optimum locations." A network of regional manufacturing operations now does work for each other, with or without support from NEC plants in Japan. Matsushita is rearranging its 69 overseas plants in a "global localization" plan to supply four "major poles"—North America, Europe, Japan, and the rest of Asia. It now has regional headquarters for each area. To get the latest technology needed to remain competitive worldwide,

Japanese companies have established research centers in the United States and Europe. These too are becoming difficult to manage from Japan.

For many Japanese companies accustomed to strict control from headquarters, it is going to be difficult to give responsibility and authority to distant operations and leave it to their local managers to adjust to the cultures, tastes, and business practices of their markets. Also, they are not particularly skilled in dealing with minorities (which they don't have at home), as their records in the United States and other countries show. They have the same problem with unions as well.

The role model for many of the Japanese companies trying to become global is IBM. They are impressed by the more than 30 research facilities IBM has around the world. Of course, IBM's global success is not due solely to a worldwide network of research centers; one of the ingredients of its success is that IBM-Germany is a true German company, as IBM-Japan is a Japanese company. An executive of a large Japanese publisher, when asked which firm had written the software his firm uses for computer translation, said it could only have been a Japanese company—IBM.

Source: "The Multinational, Eastern Style," *The Economist,* June 24, 1989, pp. 63–64.

---

matrix overlay
an organization in which top-level divisions are required to heed input from a staff composed of experts of another organizational dimension in an attempt to avoid the double-reporting difficulty of a matrix organization but still mesh two or more dimensions

have kept most worldwide companies from adopting it. One problem with the matrix is that the two or three managers (if it is a three-dimensional matrix) must agree on a decision. This can lead to less-than-optimum compromises, delayed responses, and power politics where more attention is paid to the process than to the problem. When the managers cannot agree, the problem goes higher in the organization and takes top management away from its duties. Because of these difficulties, many firms have maintained their original organizations based on product, function, region, or international division and built into the structure accountability for the other organizational dimensions, called by some a **matrix overlay.**

Matrix overlay.   The matrix overlay attempts to address the problems of the matrix structure by requiring accountability of all functions in the organization while avoiding the burdensome management stresses of a pure matrix structure. We have already mentioned how a firm organized by product may have regional specialists in a staff function with the requirement that they have input to product decisions. They may even be organized in an international division, as we mentioned previously. Conversely, a regional organization would have product managers on its staff, who provide input to regional decisions.[21]

Other solutions.   Planning is a way to get both product and regional managers involved in decision making. At General Electric, each country executive develops a comprehensive country opportunity plan covering all products and strategies that is then compared with plans of the product groups. Conflicts are identified and solutions proposed.[22] A regionalized organization might follow the same procedure using worldwide product committees. Another solution is to transfer product managers to regional divisions, and vice versa, so they have a better appreciation for the need to coordinate their decisions.

▫ The "Right" Organizational Form

Four facts concerning organizational forms should have become evident from our discussion: (1) there is not one "right" way to organize; (2) generally, organizations are not "pure," but mixed; (3) the greater the specialization of the organization's units, the more difficult it is to coordinate their activities; and (4) organizational structures are never permanent.

▫ Changing Forms

Managements are constantly searching for an organizational form that will be more responsive to the firm's needs. Not only have they mixed the standard forms, but they have conceived some entirely new ones.

strategic business unit (SBU) business entity with a clearly defined market, specific competitors, the ability to carry out its business mission, and a size appropriate for control by a single manager

Strategic business units.   Strategic business units (SBUs), which originated with General Electric, are a relatively new organizational form in which product divisions have been redefined as though they were distinct, independent businesses. An SBU is commonly defined as a business entity with a clearly defined market, specific competitors, the ability to carry out its business mission, and a size appropriate for control by a single manager. Most SBUs are based on product lines, and if a product must be modified to suit different markets, a worldwide product SBU may be divided into a few product/market SBUs serving various countries or groups of countries. Strategic business units do not determine how a company as a whole will organize its internal operations.

Sectors or operating units.   Companies with numerous SBUs (Gillette calls them *product groups*) frequently group them into another unit, called *sector* by 3M and *operating unit* by Gillette. Other firms use other names. The heads of these organizations are just under the CEO and carry such titles as company vice president or, in Gillette's case, vice chairman.

Horizontal organization.   There are some large technology-oriented global firms in highly competitive industries such as electronics and computers that have decided the traditional ways of organizing are not suitable for them. They need flexible organizations so that they can respond quickly to advances in technology and be product innovators. In a *Business International* study of

400 companies worldwide, the two organizational goals most cited by CEOs were (1) enhancing the firm's responsiveness to customers and (2) creating a company that values entrepreneurship and a profit orientation.[23]

Ralph Larsen, CEO of Johnson & Johnson, the health-care giant (1991 sales—$12.4 billion), says that in the 1990s the company is embarking on a philosophical restructuring, where corporations make their businesses more decentralized and give people the freedom to act without going to headquarters for permission.[24] Jack Welch, General Electric's CEO (1991 sales—$60.2 billion), believes most businesses are overmanaged and underled. He thinks that managers should get out of the way of the workers. Welch is determined to change the company's culture and organization into what he calls a "boundary-less company." He wants GE to be a firm where (1) internal divisions blur, (2) suppliers and customers are partners, and (3) there is no separation between domestic and international operations—each GE business is as much at home in Korea as it is in South Carolina.[25]

horizontal organization
a form of organization characterized by lateral decision processes, horizontal networks, and a strong corporatewide business philosophy

These firms have decided that the only way they can accommodate their needs is to adopt a radical system of organizing people and work called **horizontal organization,** or *corporate networking*. In certain industries such as construction, aerospace and automobiles, there are *teams* drawn from different departments to solve a problem or deliver a product.[26]

This organization has been characterized as "anti-organization" because its designers are seeking to remove the constraints imposed by the conventional organizational structures. In a networked firm, employees worldwide create, build, and market the company's products through a carefully cultivated system of interrelationships. Marketers in Great Britain speak directly to production people in Brazil without having to go through the home office in Germany, for example. Proponents of the horizontal organization claim lateral relationships incite innovation and new product development. They also state that the organization "puts greater decision-making responsibility in the hands of middle managers, who are not required to clear every detail and event with higher-ups. The idea is to substitute cooperation and coordination, which are in everyone's interests, for strict control and supervision."[27] Firms that have adopted the horizontal organization have a strong corporatewide business philosophy that binds the employees. IBM and Dow Chemical are examples.[28]

□ Managerial Talent

The managerial talent available to the corporation has been and will continue to be extremely significant both in the choice of organizational form and in the transition from one form to another. Evidently, the lack of global orientation on the part of product managers was a strong factor in Bristol-Myers' decision to revert to an international division after having had a global product organization.

The importance of capable managers cannot be overestimated. They can make a less-than-optimum organization function well. There is less need for a matrix organization, for example, if area managers work well with managers having global responsibility for products. By their personal capabilities, these managers can overcome the problem of other organizational forms in getting the needed cooperation and coordination, which is usually achieved through a matrix. Product managers who are able to generate support and enthusiasm for their product lines do not require a dotted line to be drawn on a chart. In fact, management often formalizes such actions after observing what actually takes place.

◻ Corporate Survival into the 21st Century

Managers will make greater use of the *dynamic network structure* that breaks down the major functions of the firm into small companies coordinated by a small-sized headquarters organization. Business functions such as marketing or accounting may be provided by separate organizations connected by computers to a central office.[29] To attain the optimum level of vertical integration, a firm must focus on its core business. Anything not essential to the business can be done cheaper and faster by outside suppliers.[30] You may remember the discussion in Chapter 13 concerning the hollowing-out of a nation's industry. The athletic footwear firms such as Nike, Reebok, and Adidas are doing just that. Those companies only design and market shoes; all three buy their shoes from the same Indonesian manufacturer.

As American companies prepare for the global battles of the 1990s, we must remember that organizations, like people, have life cycles. In their youth, they're small and fast-growing, but as they age, they often become big, complex, and out of touch with their markets. The firms of tomorrow must learn how to be large and entrepreneurial. As one CEO put it, "Small is not better; focused is better."[31]

SUMMARY

Many global companies have instituted formal worldwide strategic planning to identify opportunities and threats, formulate strategies ot handle them, and stipulate the means to finance those strategies. Global strategic planning provides a formal structure in which managers (1) analyze the company's external environments, (2) analyze the firm's internal environment, (3) define the company's business and mission, (4) set corporate objectives, (5) quantify goals, (6) formulate strategies, and (7) make tactical plans.

Operating managers do the planning; the planning staff assists them primarily by providing information on the environments. Statements of the corporate business and mission communicate to the firm's stakeholders what the company is and where it is going. Its objectives direct its course of action, and its strategies enable management to reach its objectives. Scenarios and contingency plans help management prepare for critical events. Tactical plans are detailed plans for implementing the strategies. Planning may be top-down or bottom-up, but iterative planning, a combination of both, has become more popular. Plans are becoming shorter and more concerned with issues, strategies, and their implementation instead of the voluminous, detailed forecasts of the past.

Organizational design usually follows strategic planning, and, because of the close relationship between the two functions, both are commonly done during the strategic planning process. Companies may (1) have an international division, (2) be organized by product, function, or region, or (3) have a mixture of them (hybrid form). To attain a balance between product and regional expertise, some managements have tried a matrix form of organization. Its disadvantages, however, have caused many managements to put a matrix overlay over the traditional product, regional, or functional form instead of using the matrix. Horizontal organizations (corporate networking), strategic business units (SBUs), and sectors are newer organizational forms that firms are using to become global enterprises. Managerial talent is extremely significant in the choice of organizational form. The firms of tomorrow must know how to be large and entrepreneurial. Small is not better; focused is better.

QUESTIONS

1. Why have many worldwide firms found it necessary to institute global strategic planning?

2. Prepare a watch list for Exxon.

3. Suppose the competitor analysis reveals that the American subsidiary of your firm's German competitor is about to broaden its product mix in the American market by introducing a new line against which your company has not previously had to compete in the home market. The environmental analysis shows that the dollar-mark exchange rate is going to continue to make American exports expensive in Germany. Do you recommend a defensive strategy, or do you attack your competitor in its home market? How will you implement your strategy?

4. You have been employed by the Brazilian subsidiary of an American multinational corporation whose primary interest is in the financial performance of its subsidiaries. A Japanese firm is setting up a Brazilian subsidiary and has offered you a salary that you cannot refuse. What cultural adjustments will you probably have to make in your new job?

5. You are the CEO of the Jones Petrochemical company and have just finished studying next year's plans of your foreign subsidiaries. You are pleased that the Israeli plan is so optimistic because that subsidiary contributes heavily to your company's income. But OPEC is meeting next month. Should you ask your planning committee, which meets tomorrow, to construct some scenarios? If so, about what?

6. The planning perspective should be benefit oriented rather than solution oriented. Please explain the meaning of this statement.

7. Your firm has used bottom-up planning for years, but the subsidiaries' plans differ with respect to approaches to goals and assumptions—even the time frames are different. How can you, the CEO, get them to agree on these points and still get their individual input?

8. Your matrix organization isn't working; decisions are taking too long, and it seems to you that, instead of best solutions, you're getting compromises. What can you, the CEO, do?

9. You are the CEO of Mancon Incorporated, and you have just acquired Pozoli, the Italian small-appliance maker (electric shavers, small household and personal care appliances). It has been in business 30 years and has manufacturing plants in Italy, Mexico, Ireland, and Spain. Its output is sold in more than 100 markets worldwide, including the United States. Your company is now organized into two product groups—shaving, personal care, and an international division at the top level. How are you going to include Pozoli in your organization?

10. It is obvious that in formulating new strategies, management may uncover a need to change its organization. Can you give some situations where the reverse may be true?

11. Can a worldwide company with an international division be a global company?

12. Why has the horizontal organization been characterized as "anti-organization"?

□ MINICASE 21–1

What Organizational Form Should Gillette Have?

The Gillette Company, founded in 1901, is an international consumer products firm engaged in the development, manufacture, and sale of a wide range of products for personal care or use. Major lines include blades and razors, toiletries and cosmetics, stationery products, Braun electric razors and small appliances and Oral-B oral care products. Braun and Oral-B are former independent companies that were acquired by Gillette. It has also acquired Jafra, a California firm that operates in 14 countries—including the United States—with 130,000 independent representatives visiting the homes, as Avon does. Jafra's management has reorganized to emphasize Latin American sales, which are growing rapidly. Its worldwide sales in 1988 were $120 million. Jafra products are made in California and Spain.

Sales of blades and razors amounted to $1.147 billion in 1988 and contributed 60 percent of Gillette's profits. In most major markets worldwide, Gillette blades and razors continue to outsell all competitive brands combined. Although worldwide sales of double-edged blades dropped slightly, the company retained its leadership in this category. Disposable razors registered a substantial sales increase internationally. Since the early 1970s, Gillette has begun blade manufacturing in over a dozen developing countries, including Egypt, China, India, and Pakistan. Companies in these last two countries are joint ventures.

Sales of stationery products (such as Paper Mate, Flexgrip, and Liquid Paper), which amounted to $385 million in 1988, were assisted by sales from Waterman, a French manufacturer of premium pens and pencils acquired in 1987, and Sylvapen, an Argentine manufacturer of coloring sets and writing instruments purchased in 1986. Both product lines are now marketed internationally.

In 1988, sales of toiletries and cosmetics amounted to $1.019 billion. The recent acquisitions of La Toja Cosmeticos, a Spanish maker of bath products (1986); UNISA, a Chilean skin care manufacturer (1987); and Antica Erboristeria, an Italian producer of herbal toiletries (1988) contributed to a 10 percent increase over 1987 sales. Jafra's sales are included in this total. Interestingly, Gillette now has seven different manufacturing plants in Spain, far more than in any other European country.

Braun, a German manufacturer of electric shavers and small household and personal care appliances, was founded in 1921 and acquired by Gillette in 1967. Its household appliances include hand mixers, coffeemakers, juice extractors, and electric alarm clocks; cordless curlers, electric toothbrushes, and water jets are some of its personal care appliances. Its hand mixers are first in sales in the United States, Canada, and most European countries, and its cordless curlers are the top seller worldwide. The company's market share of cord shavers in Japan, where it has had a sales company for 25 years, is 60 percent. Total sales in 1988 were $824 million. Braun has manufacturing facilities in Germany, Mexico, Ireland, and Spain and employs 8,200 people worldwide in production and sales. Its products are sold in more than 100 countries.

The name Gillette does not figure prominently in Braun's advertising.

Gillette acquired Oral-B, another California company, in 1984. It has 1,450 employees worldwide who sell a broad range of oral care products to dentists and consumers in 30 countries. Its most important product, toothbrushes, is the top seller in the United States and several foreign markets. Sales in 1988 were $202 million. Oral-B manufactures in the United States, Ireland, and Australia.

Gillette distributes its products in over 200 countries and territories and has 62 manufacturing facilities in 28 countries. These include 3 plants in the United States for blades and razors, stationery products, and personal care products; 2 plants in Canada for the above-mentioned product lines; and 8 plants of Braun, Oral-B, and Jafra; and 28 plants in the rest of the world, *excluding* Europe. Worldwide, total sales were $3.58 billion in 1988, a 13 percent gain over 1987. Management's goal is sustained profitable growth, which the company achieves by emphasizing strong technical and marketing efforts in existing lines and selective diversification, both internally and through acquisition. The company is known as one of the industry's top innovators and now has an equally important goal of shortening new product development to prevent competitors from rushing to copy a new product that appears in one market and getting their copies in other markets before Gillette. The company is ready for Europe 1992. In 1983, management standardized its European marketing mix.

Due in part to takeover threats, Gillette reorganized its entire organization in 1987 to lower operating costs.

How would you have organized the company?

(*To the instructor:* There is a current chart of the company in your I.M.)

Source: Gillette Company, *Annual Report 1988;* "Braun: Cutting into Japan's Shaver Market," *Journal of Japanese Trade & Industry,* November 2, 1984, p. 45; and "The Innovation Strategy That Keeps Gillette in the Pink," *International Management,* September 1984, p. 90.

□ MINICASE 21-2

Electrex, Incorporated—Must It Reorganize?

Electrex, Inc. manufactures electronic and electrical connectors used on such diverse products as computers, home appliances, telecommunications, and the air bag and antiskid systems of American cars. The company has been in business since 1965. The table on page 750 provides the important financial information for the last five years.

For some time, Electrex had been exporting to the Far East, where its major markets are Japan, Singapore, and Taiwan. When its foreign sales were confined to exports, the company functioned well with an export department whose manager reported to the company's marketing manager. In 1987, however, other American firms tried to enter

Five-Year Financial Highlight Summary (in $ millions)

	1991	1990	1989	1988	1987
Net sales	$353.0	$298.2	$271.9	$257.4	$231.1
Gross profit	134.1	116.3	110.3	106.7	94.9
Selling, general, and administrative expense	70.5	61.2	55.8	51.8	45.1
Income from operations	63.6	55.1	54.5	54.9	49.8
Income taxes	23.9	20.9	20.9	21.8	20.9
Effective tax rate (%)	37.6	37.9	38.3	39.7	42.0
Net income	39.7	34.2	33.6	33.1	28.9

the market, and there were rumors that a Japanese firm was searching for a licensor in the United States to supply it with manufacturing technology. Electrex decided to set up its first foreign plant in Japan. When it did, it hired financial and marketing people with Japanese experience and established an international division at headquarters to oversee the Japanese operation. The president felt that the situation would be repeated in Taiwan, Singapore, and Thailand. These were all good export markets at that time, but it was reasonable to suppose that some competitor would soon set up manufacturing facilities in one or more of them. Having a small international division with some

Far East expertise that is responsible for monitoring these markets would help the firm avoid being surprised by a competitor's move.

After the Japanese Electrex plant was in production, more Japanese firms were willing to do business with the company than when it served the market by exports. In fact, the major portion of the 1991 sales increase was due to improved sales to the Japanese. However, the new customers also brought the company into a new, higher level of competition than it had known before. The Japanese competitors were bringing out new products at a considerably faster rate than Electrex. The president wondered if horizontal linkages across functions, such as the automakers have used to reduce their design time, might help his firm. Also, on his trips to Japan, the marketing people told him things about the market and the competitors that were not being sent to the Electrex home office.

It was obvious to the president that overseas production and growth in overseas sales demanded a reorganization of the firm. Even though the company had only one plant in Japan now, the president was confident that other plants would soon be needed. How should the company be organized to handle the new foreign production facilities? How can Electrex reduce the time needed to bring new designs to market?

SUPPLEMENTARY READINGS

Company Examples

"Companies That Compete Best." *Fortune*, May 22, 1989, pp. 36–44.

Herbert, Ira C. "How Coke Markets to the World." *The Journal of Business Strategy*, September–October 1988, pp. 4–7.

Kennedy, Carol. "Planning Global Strategies for 3M." *Long-Range Planning*, February 1988, p. 9–17.

Pink, Alan I. "Strategic Leadership through Corporate Planning at ICI." *Long-Range Planning*, February 1988, pp. 18–25.

"Survival and Growth in This Age of Global Competition." *Business International*, January 13, 1986, pp. 9–11.

Competitive Strategy Planning

Attanasio, Dominick B. "The Multiple Benefits of Competitor Intelligence." *The Journal of Business Strategy*, May–June 1988, pp. 16–19.

David, Fred R. "A Framework for Conducting an External Strategic Management Audit." *Journal of Business Strategy*, Spring 1986, pp. 22–33.

Porter, Michael, ed. *Competition in Global Industries*. Boston: Harvard Business School, 1986.

Shanks, David C. "Strategic Planning for Global Competition." *The Journal of Business Strategy*, Winter 1985, pp. 80–89.

Issues Analysis

Kharbanda, Om P., and Ernest A. Stallworthy. "Planning for Emergencies—Lessons from the Chemical Industry." *Long-Range Planning*, February 1989, pp. 83–89.

McConkey, Dale D. "Planning for Uncertainty." *Business Horizons*, January–February 1987, pp. 40–45.

Nigh, D., and P. L. Cochran. "Issues Management and the Multinational Enterprise." *Management International Review*, 1987/1, pp. 4–12.

"Planning for Uncertain Futures: Building Commitment through Scenario Planning." *Business Horizons*, May–June 1990, pp. 55–58.

Preble, John F., and Pradeep A. Rau. "Combining Delphi and Multiple Scenario Analysis for Planning Purposes." *Journal of Business Strategy*, Fall 1986, pp. 12–21.

Organization Design

"Are Regional Headquarters Worthwhile?" *Business Europe,* December 21, 1987, pp. 2−5.

"ASEA Brown Boveri Organizes for 1992." *Business Europe,* May 9, 1988, pp. 14−20.

Bartlett, Christopher A. "MNCs: Get Off the Reorganization Merry-Go-Round." *Harvard Business Review,* March−April 1983, pp. 138−46.

Bartlett, Christopher A., and Sumantra Ghoshal. "Organizing for Worldwide Effectiveness: The Transnational Solution." *California Management Review,* Fall 1988, pp. 54−74.

Bush, John B., Jr., and Alan L. Frohman. "Communication in a 'Network' Organization." *Organizational Dynamics,* Autumn 1991, pp. 23−26.

" 'Corporate Networking.' " *Business International,* July 9, 1990, pp. 225−28.

Daft, Richard L. *Organization Theory and Design.* 4th ed. St. Paul, Minn.: West Publishing, 1992.

"Facing Up to the Globalization Challenge." *The McKinsey Quarterly,* Winter 1986, pp. 52−68.

"Global Organization: Square D Managers to Compete Globally." *Business International,* September 21, 1987, pp. 297−302.

Gluck, Federick W. "Strategic Planning in a New Key." *The McKinsey Quarterly,* Winter 1986, pp. 18−41.

"How Decentralization Sparked a Revival for Campbell Canada." *Business International,* January 25, 1988, pp. 20−21.

Kriger, Mark P., and Patrick J. J. Rich. "Strategic Governance: Why and How MNCs Are Using Boards of Directors in Foreign Subsidiaries." *Columbia Journal of World Business,* Winter 1987, pp. 39−45.

New Directions in Multinational Corporate Organization. New York: Business International, 1981.

Restructuring and Turnaround: Experiences in Corporate Renewal. New York: Business International, 1987.

"The Issues Globalists Don't Talk About." *International Management,* September 1987, pp. 37−42.

"The Multinational, Eastern Style." *The Economist,* June 24, 1989, pp. 63−64.

White, Roderick E., and Thomas A. Poynter. "Achieving Worldwide Advantage with the Horizontal Organization." *Business Quarterly,* Autumn 1989, pp. 55−60.

Strategic Planning

Chakravarthy, Balaji S., and Howard V. Perlmutter. "Strategic Planning for a Global Business." *Columbia Journal of World Business,* Summer 1985, pp. 3−10.

"Corporate Strategy for the 1990s." *Fortune,* February 29, 1988, pp. 34−42.

David, Fred R. "How Companies Define Their Mission." *Long-Range Planning,* February 1989, pp. 90−95.

Gluck, Frederick W. "A Fresh Look at Strategic Management." *The Journal of Business Strategy,* Fall 1985, pp. 4−19.

Hamel, Gary, and C. K. Prahalad. "Do You Really Have a Global Strategy?" *The McKinsey Quarterly,* Summer 1986, pp. 34−50.

King, Elizabeth M., Wayne Norvell, and Dan Devine. "Budgeting: A Strategic Managerial Tool." *Journal of Business Strategies,* Fall 1988, pp. 69−75.

Maddox, Nick, William P. Anthony, and Walt Wheatly, Jr. "Creative Strategic Planning Using Imagery." *Long-Range Planning,* October 1987, pp. 118−24.

Mintzberg, Henry. "Strategy-Making in Three Modes." *California Management Review,* Winter 1972, pp. 44−53.

Naylor, Thomas H. "The International Strategy Mix." *Columbia Journal of World Business,* Summer 1985, pp. 11−19.

Porter, Michael. "The State of Strategic Thinking." *The Economist,* May 29, 1987, pp. 17−22.

Reed, Richard, and M. Ronald Buckley. "Strategy in Action—Techniques for Implementing Strategy." *Long-Range Planning,* June 1988, pp. 67−73.

Zabriskie, Noel B., and Allen B. Huellmantel. "Developing Strategic Thinking in Senior Management." *Long-Range Planning,* December 1991, pp. 25−32.

Strategies

Ackerman, Laurence D. "Identify Strategies That Make a Difference." *The Journal of Business Strategy,* May−June 1988, pp. 28−32.

Gilbert, Xavier, and Paul Strebel. "Strategies to Outpace the Competition." *The Journal of Business Strategy,* Summer 1987, pp. 28−36.

Harrison, E. Frank. "Strategic Control at the CEO Level." *Long-Range Planning,* December 1991, pp. 78−87.

Lei, David. "Strategies for Global Competition." *Long-Range Planning,* February 1989, pp. 102−9.

Shrivastava, Paul. "Integrating Strategy Formulation with Organizational Culture." *The Journal of Business Strategy,* Winter 1985, pp. 103−11.

Vernon-Wortzel, Heidi, and Lawrence H. Wortzel. "Globalizing Strategies for Multinationals from Developing Countries." *Columbia Journal of World Business,* Spring 1988, pp. 27−35.

Ward, John L., and Stanley F. Stasch. "How Small-Share Firms Can Uncover Winning Strategies." *The Journal of Business Strategy,* September−October 1988, pp. 26−31.

ENDNOTES

1. Wroe Alderson, *Dynamic Marketing Behavior* (Homewood, Ill.: Richard D. Irwin, 1965), pp. 75–97. In the late 1970s, McCarthy and other writers of "Principles of Marketing" texts discussed the use of transvection as a unit of analysis.

2. Chrysler, *Annual Report,* 1990, inside front cover.

3. Gerber, *Annual Report,* 1991, p. 4 and inside front cover.

4. Bausch & Lomb, *Annual Report,* 1990, inside front cover.

5. Campbell, *Annual Report,* 1990, p. 2.

6. Ibid., p. 4.

7. Paul Shrivastava, "Integrating Strategy Formulation with Organizational Culture," *The Journal of Business Strategy,* Winter 1985, pp. 103–11.

8. PepsiCo, *Annual Report,* 1989, pp. 12–13.

9. "Who Should Be Responsible for Business Strategy?" *The Journal of Business Strategy,* November–December 1988, pp. 40–41.

10. "The New Breed of Strategic Planner," *Business Week,* September 17, 1984, p. 62.

11. Ibid., p. 62.

12. Ibid., p. 64.

13. P. W. Beck, "Corporate Planning for an Uncertain Future," *Long-Range Planning,* August 1982, p. 14.

14. "New Breed of Strategic Planner," p. 66.

15. "Corporate Planning for an Uncertain Future," p. 17.

16. Frederick W. Gluck, "A Fresh Look at Strategic Management," *The Journal of Business Strategy,* Fall 1985, p. 6.

17. Christopher A. Bartlett, "MNCs: Get Off the Reorganization Merry-Go-Round," *Harvard Business Review,* March–April 1983, p. 138.

18. "Building a Competitive Organization for the 1990s," *Business International,* June 11, 1990, p. 190.

19. " 'Corporate Networking' Increases Organizational Choices," *Business International,* July 9, 1990, p. 225.

20. Sun Co., *Annual Report,* 1987, p. 49.

21. "Seven Organizational Alternatives for MNCs in the 1990s," *Business International,* February 13, 1989, p. 46.

22. *New Directions in Multinational Corporate Organization* (New York: Business International, 1981), pp. 1–6.

23. "Building a Competitive Organization for the 1990s," p. 185.

24. "Is Big Still Good?" *Fortune,* April 20, 1992, p. 52.

25. "Jack Welch Reinvents General Electric—Again," *The Economist,* March 30, 1991, p. 59.

26. Daniel Robey, *Designing Organizations* (Homewood, Ill.: Richard D. Irwin, 1991), p. 217.

27. " 'Corporate Networking' Increases Organizational Choices," p. 226.

28. "Achieving Worldwide Advantage with the Horizontal Organization," *Business Quarterly,* Autumn 1989, pp. 55–56.

29. Richard L. Daft, *Organization Theory and Design,* 4th ed. (St. Paul, Minn.: West Publishing, 1992), pp. 226–28.

30. "Is Big Still Good?" p. 52.

31. Ibid., p. 60.

Chapter 22

Control and Staffing

There's no great difference in managing a small or large company. In both cases, it's simply a matter of having more money at the end of the day than when you started in the morning.

> Rune Andresson, managing director of Trelleborg A. B.

How does it work out when there is a woman manager in the family? There is no solution because there is no problem in Japan. Management is for men only.

> William A. Cohen, in a review of Mitsuyuki Masatsugu

As I saw it, here was a sector of the economy crying out for the application of good management skills.

> Sydney Biddle Barrows, descendant of the *Mayflower* pilgrims, describing her decision to create and manage a profitable New York call girl network

As a general matter, we [Americans] pride ourselves on our pioneering traditions. But outside the publicly funded defense area, we underinvest in research and development. Some high-priced managers seem to spend less time developing R&D budgets than they spend reviewing golf scores.

> Richard G. Darman, director, Office of Management and Budget

LEARNING OBJECTIVES

In this chapter you will study:

1. The reasons companies use controls.

2. Where decisions are made in an IC—at the headquarters of the multinational, at the subsidiaries' offices, or cooperatively by the parent and subsidiary companies—and some reasons why certain decisions are made where they are.

3. The methods used to try to control subsidiary companies less than 100 percent owned and joint venture partners when they are entirely independent organizations.

4. The importance of timely, accurate, and complete reports from subsidiaries and joint venture partners on a variety of subjects.

5. The danger that too many reports can result in an information glut and confusion unless they are organized, coded, and computerized.

6. The difficulties of finding qualified executives for multinational companies.

7. The importance of foreign language abilities.

8. Comparisons of home country, host country, and third-country nationals as employees.

9. Some of the complications of creating compensation packages for expatriate employees that permit them and their families to maintain their living standards abroad and reimburse them for hardships and inconveniences without overcompensating them.

KEY WORDS AND CONCEPTS

- Subsidiaries
- Affiliates
- Subsidiary detriments
- Information glut
- Geocentric
- Language trap
- Expatriate
- Allowances
- Bonuses
- International status

BUSINESS INCIDENT

Michel Thomas's foreign language centers in Beverly Hills and New York charge pupils up to $12,000 for 10 days' intensive instruction in French, German, or Spanish. Until recently, his star students were show business celebrities, such as Woody Allen, Ann-Margret, and Donald Sutherland. Today his best customers are executives from Boeing, Chase Manhattan, General Electric, Shearson Lehman Hutton, Westinghouse, and the like. Why the boom? "The answer's simple," says Thomas. "1992."

Source: "Le Defi Is Back," *The Economist,* May 13, 1989, p. 70.

The planning that is the necessary foundation for all aspects of any successful business was dealt with in the preceding chapter. The control activities of which we shall speak here are the efforts to (1) put the plans into effect, (2) learn whether the plans are working as intended (they rarely do), and (3) make whatever corrections seem called for and practicable.

In Chapter 20, we discussed labor relations policies and practices of an international company (IC) with regard to the workers and their supervisors in the operation. To complete the picture, we must examine IC policies and practices covering selecting, training, and compensating executive personnel.

The business incident illustrates one aspect of the training as managers rush to become proficient in other languages. The languages offered by Michel Thomas's schools are European, but equally important for business-people are Asian languages, notably Chinese and Japanese.

CONTROL

Every successful company uses controls to put its plans into effect, evaluate their effectiveness, make desirable corrections, and evaluate and reward or correct executive performance. Matters are more complicated for an international company than for a one-country operation. In earlier chapters, we have brought out the complicating causes. They include different languages, cultures, and attitudes; different taxes and accounting methods; different currencies, labor costs, market sizes; different degrees of political stability and security for personnel and property; and many more. For these reasons, multinational companies need controls even more than do domestic ones.

□ Subsidiaries, 100 Percent Owned

subsidiaries companies controlled by other companies through ownership of enough voting stock to elect board of directors majorities

The words **subsidiaries** and **affiliates** are used interchangeably, and we shall examine first the control of those in which the parent has 100 percent ownership. This avoids for now the additional complications of joint ventures or subsidiaries in which the parent has less than 100 percent ownership. We shall deal with those later in the chapter.

□ Where Are Decisions Made?

affiliates sometimes used interchangeably with "subsidiaries," but more forms exist than just stock ownership

There are three possibilities. Two of them are that all decisions are made at either the IC headquarters or at the subsidiary level. Theoretically, all decisions could be made at one or the other location. As common sense would indicate, they are not; instead, some decisions are made at one place, some are made at the other place, and some are made cooperatively.[1] Many variables determine which decision is made where. Some of the more significant variables are (1) product and equipment, (2) the competence of subsidiary management and reliance on that management by the IC headquarters, (3) the size of the IC and how long it has been one, (4) the detriment of a subsidiary for the benefit of the enterprise, and (5) subsidiary frustration.

Product and equipment.   As to decision location, questions of standardization of product and equipment and second markets can be important.

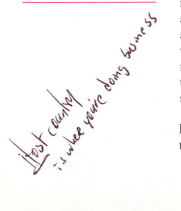
host country -- is where you're doing business

Standardize?   An easily made argument is that the product and the equipment with which to make it should be tailored to fit each national market. The other side is that overall enterprise gains from worldwide uniformity may more than compensate for individual country losses. Standardization of equipment may result in lower purchasing costs of the equipment as well as savings in equipment operation training, maintenance, and spare parts.[2]

As to the product, uniformity gives greater flexibility in its sourcing. For example, if the product is made in two or more countries and such difficulties as strikes, natural disasters, political upheavals, or currency problems affect one country, the product can be delivered from the other.

In determining whether equipment and product should be standardized worldwide or tailored to different national markets, a company should gather opinions from each affected subsidiary. If any subsidiary can demonstrate that the profit potential that can be realized from tailoring to its own market is greater than the profit potential the enterprise will realize from standardization, the subsidiary should be permitted to proceed. Elements of profit potential would include the size of the subsidiary's market, the competition there, and the possibilities for exporting to areas with similar characteristics. Of course, the decision in such a case is cooperative in that the parent has the power to veto or override its subsidiary's decisions.

Second markets.   The parent company may introduce a product in its largest market; by the time that product is offered in smaller markets, the company may have adapted it to eliminate "bugs" or improve performance. The parent would want to ensure that the mistakes already discovered and corrected would not be repeated in later markets. Even though some subsidiaries may wish to alter the product, second-market situations would indicate IC central decision making. Such decision making would be necessary to ensure uniformity of quality and performance as well as market timing and product improvement.

Competence of subsidiary management and reliance on that management by parent headquarters.   Reliance on subsidiary management can depend on how well the executives know one another and how well they know company policies, on whether headquarters management feels that it understands host country conditions, on the distances between the home country and the host countries, and on how big and old the parent company is.

Move the executives around.   Some ICs have a policy of transferring promising management personnel between parent headquarters and subsidiaries and among subsidiaries. Thus, the manager learns firsthand the policies of headquarters and the problems of putting those policies into effect at subsidiary levels.

A result of such transfers, which is difficult to measure but nevertheless important, is a network of intra-IC personal relationships. This tends to increase the confidence of executives in one another and to make communication among executives easier and less subject to error.[3]

Another development is that some ICs have moved their regional executives into headquarters to improve communications and reduce cost.

Does parent headquarters understand host country conditions?   One element in the degree of headquarters' reliance on subsidiary management is the familiarity of headquarters with conditions in the subsidiary's host country.

The less familiar or the more different conditions in the host country are perceived to be, the more likely headquarters is to rely on subsidiary management.

How far away is the host country? Another element in the degree of headquarters' reliance on subsidiary management is the distance of the host country from home headquarters. Thus, an American parent is likely to place more reliance on the management of an Indonesian subsidiary than on the management of a Canadian subsidiary. This would be for two reasons: American management would perceive management conditions in Canada to be more easily understood than conditions in Indonesia, and Indonesia is much farther from the United States than Canada is.[4]

Size of the IC and how long it has been one. As a rule, a large company can afford to hire more specialists, experts, and experienced executives than can a smaller one. The longer a company has been an IC, the more likely it is to have a number of experienced executives who know company policies and who have worked at headquarters and in the field. Successful experience builds confidence.

In most ICs, the top positions are at headquarters, and the ablest and most persistent executives get there in time. Thus, over time, headquarters of a successful company is run by experienced executives who are confident of their knowledge of the business in the home and host countries and in combinations thereof.

It follows that in the larger, older organizations, more decisions are made at headquarters and fewer are delegated to subsidiaries. The smaller company, in business for a shorter period of time, tends to be able to afford fewer internationally experienced executives and will not have had time to develop them internally. The smaller, newer company has no choice but to delegate decisions to subsidiary management.

The generality that the larger, older ICs delegate fewer decisions is subject to exceptions, and there seems to come a point in growth where the centralization trend reverses. Studies by Robbins and Stobaugh show that as ICs become very large and complex, they tend to decentralize. There come to be too many decisions for headquarters to deal with each one. At that point, the companies develop policies and guidelines for the subsidiaries. Headquarters reserves decision authority only for the most important matters and establishes processes to monitor the others.[5]

Decisions that may benefit the enterprise to the detriment of a subsidiary. An IC has opportunities to source raw materials and components, locate factories, allocate orders, and govern intraenterprise pricing that are not available to a non-IC. Such activities may be beneficial to the enterprise yet result in **subsidiary detriments.**

subsidiary detriment a small loss for a subsidiary results in a greater gain for the total IC

Move production factors. For any number of reasons, an IC may decide to move factors of production from one country to another or to expand in one country in preference to another. Tax, labor, market, currency, or political stability are a few possible reasons.

The subsidiary from which factors are being taken would be unenthusiastic. Its management would be slow, at best, to cut the company's capacity. Headquarters would make such decisions.

Which subsidiary gets the order?   Similarly, if an order—say, from an Argentine customer—could be filled from a subsidiary in France or another in South Africa or a third in Brazil, parent headquarters might decide which subsidiary gets the business. Among the considerations in the decision would be transportation costs, production costs, comparative tariff rates, customers' currency restrictions, comparative order backlogs, and taxes. Having such a decision made by IC headquarters avoids price competition among members of the same IC group.

Multicountry production.   Frequently, the size of the market in a single country is too small to permit economies of scale in manufacturing an entire industrial product for that one market. An example is Ford's production of a light vehicle for the Asian market.

In that situation, Ford negotiated with several countries to the end that one country would make one component of the vehicle for all of the countries involved. Thus, one country makes the engine, a second country has the body-stamping plant, a third makes the transmission, and so forth. In this fashion, each operation achieves the efficiency and cost savings of economies of scale.[6] Of course, this kind of multinational production demands a high degree of IC headquarters' control and coordination.

Which subsidiary books the profit?   In certain circumstances, an IC may have some choice of two or more countries in which to declare profits. Such circumstances may arise where two or more units of the IC cooperate in supplying components or services under a contract with a customer unrelated to any part of the multinational. Under these conditions, there may be opportunities to allocate higher prices to one unit or subsidiary and lower prices to another within the global price to the customer.

If the host country of one of the subsidiaries has lower taxes than the other host countries, it would be natural to try to maximize profits in the lower-tax country and minimize them in the higher-tax country. Other differences between host countries could dictate the allocation of profit to or from the subsidiaries located there. Such differences could include currency controls, labor relations, political climate, or social unrest. It is sensible to direct or allocate as much profit as reasonably possible to subsidiaries in countries with the least currency controls, the best labor relations and political climate, and the least social unrest.

The intraenterprise transaction may also give a company choices of profit location. Pricing between members of the same enterprise is referred to as *transfer pricing,* and while IC headquarters could permit undirected, arm's-length negotiations between itself and its subsidiaries, that might not yield the most advantageous results for the enterprise as a whole.[7]

Price and profit allocation decisions like these are usually best made at parent company headquarters, which is supposed to maintain the overall view, looking out for the best interests of the enterprise.[8] Naturally, subsidiary management does not gladly make decisions to accept lower profits, largely because its evaluation may suffer. We shall discuss management evaluation further on in this chapter.

The following two tables illustrate how the total IC enterprise might profit even though one subsidiary makes less. Assume a cooperative contract by which two subsidiaries are selling products and services to an outside customer for a price of $100 million. The host country of IC Alpha levies company income taxes at the rate of 50 percent, whereas IC Beta's host country taxes its income at 20 percent. The customer is in a third country, has agreed to pay $100 million, and is indifferent to how Alpha and Beta share the money. The first table below shows the enterprise's after-tax income if Alpha is paid $60 million and Beta, $40 million.

	Receives (in $ millions)	Tax (in $ millions)	After Tax (in $ millions)
Alpha	$60	$30	$30
Beta	40	8	32
			$62

Thus, after tax, the enterprise realizes $62 million.

The second table shows the after-tax income if Alpha is paid $40 million and Beta, $60 million.

	Receives (in $ millions)	Tax (in $ millions)	After Tax (in $ millions)
Alpha	$40	$20	$20
Beta	60	12	48
			$68

Thus, after tax, the enterprise realizes $68 million.

These simple examples illustrate that the IC would be $6 million better off if it could shift $20 million of the payment from Alpha to Beta, while the customer is no worse off, as it pays $100 million in either case. Alpha, having received $20 million less payment, is $10 million worse off after taxes, but Beta is $16 million better off and the enterprise if $6 million ahead on the same contract. Given the number of countries and tax laws in the world, there are countless combinations of how such savings can be accomplished. Financial management awareness and control are the keys.

We do not mean to leave the impression that the host or home governments are unaware of or indifferent to transfer pricing and profit allocating by ICs operating within their borders. The companies must expect questioning by host and home governments and must be prepared to demonstrate that prices or allocations are "reasonable." This may be done by showing that other companies charge comparable prices for the same or similar items or, if there are no similar items, by showing that costs plus profit have been used reasonably to arrive at the price. As to allocation of profits, the IC in our example would try to prove that the volume or importance of the work done by Beta or the responsibilities assumed by Beta, such as financing, after-sales service, or warranty obligations, justify the higher amount being paid to Beta. Of course, the questioning in this instance would come from the host government of Alpha if it got wind of the possibility of more taxable income for Beta and less for itself.

Subsidiary frustration.   An extremely important consideration for parent company management is that the management of its subsidiaries be motivated and loyal. If all the big decisions are made, or are perceived to be made, at the IC headquarters, the managers of subsidiaries will lose incentive and will lose prestige or face with their employees and the community. They may grow hostile and disloyal.

Therefore, even though there may be reasons for headquarters to make decisions, it should delegate as much as is reasonably possible. Management of each subsidiary should be kept thoroughly informed and should be consulted seriously about decisions, negotiations, and developments in its geographic area.

▫ Joint Ventures and Subsidiaries Less than 100 Percent Owned

A joint venture may be, as defined in Chapter 2, a corporate entity between an IC and local owners or a corporate entity between two or more companies that are foreign to the area where the joint venture is located, or it may involve one company working on a project of limited duration (constructing a dam, for example) in cooperation with one or more other companies. The other companies may be subsidiaries or affiliates, but they may also be entirely independent entities.

All the reasons for making decisions at IC headquarters, at subsidiary headquarters, or cooperatively apply equally in joint venture situations. However, headquarters will almost never have as much freedom of action and flexibility in a joint venture as it has with subsidiaries that are 100 percent owned.

Loss of freedom and flexibility.   The reasons for that loss of freedom and flexibility are easy to see. If shareholders outside the multinational own control of the affiliate, they can block efforts of IC headquarters to move production factors away, to fill an export order from another affiliate or subsidiary, and so forth. Even if outside shareholders are a minority and cannot directly control the affiliate, they can bring legal or political pressures on the IC to prevent it from diminishing the affiliate's profitability for the enterprise's benefit. Likewise, the local partner in a joint venture is highly unlikely to agree with measures that penalize the joint venture for the IC's benefit.

How the Japanese do it.   Japanese companies used the joint venture method abroad earlier and more extensively than did American or European companies. In attempting to control their joint ventures, the Japanese companies use several devices.

The Japanese partner provides and controls the technology and the management expertise. It furnishes key components and parts for the finished product. It tries to put its Japanese personnel into the important executive positions of the joint venture.[9]

As might be expected, the Japanese have encountered resistance to putting Japanese in the important executive positions from their joint venture partners or from host governments. The natural desire of these partners and governments is that their own nationals have at least equality in the important positions and that they get training and experience in the technology and management.[10]

◻ Reporting

For controls to be effective, all operating units of an IC must provide head-quarters with timely, accurate, and complete reports. There are many uses for the information reported. Among the types of reporting required are (1) financial, (2) technological, (3) market opportunity, and (4) political and economic.

Financial.   A surplus of funds in one subsidiary should perhaps be retained there for investment or contingencies. On the other hand, such a surplus might be more useful at the parent company, in which case payment of a dividend is indicated. Or perhaps another subsidiary or affiliate needs capital, and the surplus could be lent or invested there. Obviously, parent headquarters must know the existence and size of a surplus to determine its best use.

Technological.   New technology should be reported. New technology is constantly being developed in different countries, and the subsidiary or affiliated company operating in such a country is likely to learn about it before IC headquarters hundreds or thousands of miles away. If head-quarters finds the new technology potentially valuable, it could gain competitive advantage by being the first to contact the developer for a license to use it.

Market opportunities.   The affiliates in various countries may spot new or growing markets for some product of the enterprise. This could be profitable all around, as the IC sells more of the product while the affiliate earns sales commissions. Of course, if the new market is sufficiently large, the affiliate may begin to assemble or produce the product under license from the parent company or from another affiliate.

Other market-related information that should be reported to IC headquarters includes competitors' activities, price developments, and new products of potential interest to the IC group. Also of importance is information on the subsidiary's market share and whether it is growing or shrinking, together with explanations.

Political and economic.   Not surprisingly, reports on political and economic conditions have multiplied mightily in number and importance over the past 15 or so years as revolutions—some bloody—have toppled and changed governments.[11] Democracies have replaced dictatorships, one dictator has replaced another, countries have broken apart or reunited—changes have been occurring on almost every continent.

One early example of how accurate reporting saved an American company a lot of money involved Citibank in Iran, where the bank had a representative office during the 1970s. Even though some government intelligence services were said to have been surprised when the Ayatollah Khomeini threw out the shah of Iran in 1979, the Citibank Tehran office had become aware of potential danger as early as the summer of 1978. The office first lowered the ceiling on Iranian loans and then froze any new business, even to existing customers, in the autumn of 1978.[12]

◻ Management Evaluation

One important use of reports is to evaluate and compare management performance in every unit of the IC. The raw financial figures are not adequate for this, nor do they give a fair, comparative evaluation.

Parent headquarters' decisions may have awarded an export order to one subsidiary in preference to a second even though the second might have gotten the order if competition had been permitted. Through no skill or fault of theirs, management of the first subsidiary looks good in comparison with management of the second.

Or, in an intraenterprise transaction, a larger profit may be left in a low-tax country and a smaller profit in a high-tax country. This is done for the benefit of the enterprise, and management in the high-tax country should not be penalized in its comparative evaluation because it has been done.

In making evaluations, management should try to factor out conditions beyond its control. These conditions include price controls, currency controls, inflation, political upheaval, terrorism, and changes in currency exchange values.

◻ Information Glut

In 1970, information processing equipment accounted for 11 percent of all the durable equipment bought by private enterprises. In 1989, the figure was 51 percent. A study by Gary Leneman of Harvard concluded that between 1978 and 1984, capital invested in information technology had only a marginal impact—if any—on labor productivity and output.

While productivity in the information services area was stagnant during those years, manufacturing productivity was growing healthily by over 3 percent a year. Thus, it has been said, manufacturers would have done better investing the money they spent for information technology in almost any other part of their businesses.[13]

Many white-collar workers today are given information to process and a computer to process it with, and they're instructed to tell the boss when finished. Frequently, they believe the best way to prove their worth is to generate more information than anyone else. The result is that managers are flooded with more data, some of it superfluous, than they can mentally process.

Although capitalism suffers from an **information glut,** in August 1991 millions celebrated the 10th anniversary of IBM's personal computer. One who did not was Paul Saffo of the Institute for the Future. According to him, "PCs are the last gasp of the old information order rather than the onset of a new revolution," by which he means PCs automate old ways of doing things rather than introduce new ways.[14]

Among others who agree is John Whiteside of Digital Equipment Corporation. When he returned to his office from a three-week assignment, he found over 1,000 electronic messages. His solution to the overload was to code each incoming message by its source. His computer sifts through and assigns high priority to messages from the company president while putting announcements about cafeteria hours at the bottom. Some messages are killed outright, such as those from one individual who sends nothing but bad jokes.

information glut a situation in which more information has been gathered than can be intelligently or efficiently used

Are computers telling us more than we ever wanted to know?

Telegraph Color Library/FPG International

While careers and family commitments consume ever more time, the volume of information people feel they need to absorb is growing. The fear of falling behind has made information join food and exercise as a guilt group.[15]

STAFFING

Finding the right people to manage an organization can be difficult under any circumstances, but it is especially difficult to find good managers of overseas operations. The Business Incident and first pages of Chapter 1 demonstrate the high importance and priority top executives of ICs place on finding and hiring such managers. We recommend you read that material again.

Finding the right people for foreign management positions is difficult because such positions require more and different skills than do purely domestic executive jobs. The right persons need to be bicultural, with knowledge of the business practices in the home country plus understanding of business practices and customs in the host country. The successful manager of a foreign affiliate must be able to operate efficiently in one culture and to explain operations in that culture to executives in another culture. Such managers exist, and they may be found in (1) the home country, (2) the host country, or (3) a third country.

◻ Sources of Managers

Home country.   Most multinationals utilize citizens of their own countries in many foreign management and technical positions even though at first such personnel are usually not knowledgeable about the host country culture and language. Many such expatriates have adapted, learned the language, and become thoroughly accepted in the host country. Of course, it would not be necessary for a host country citizen to undergo all of that adapting, but for a variety of reasons, IC headquarters frequently needs or wants its own nationals in executive or technical positions abroad.

Host country nationals unavailable.   A foreign subsidiary often cannot find suitable host country personnel for management jobs, and in such instances, parent headquarters will send out its people to manage until local personnel can be found and trained. Those are full-time jobs, but other circumstances call for temporary help from headquarters. Labor negotiators, mentioned in Chapter 20, and other specialists may be sent to troubleshoot such problems as product warranty, international contracts, taxes, accounting, or reporting. Teams may be sent from the home country to assist with new plant start-up, and they would probably stay until subsidiary personnel were trained to run and maintain the new facilities.

Training for headquarters.   Another reason for using home country citizens abroad is to broaden their experience in preparation for becoming high-level managers at headquarters. Firms with large parts of their earnings from international sources require top executives who have a worldwide perspective, business and political.[16] It is difficult to impossible to acquire that sort of perspective without living and working abroad for a substantial time.

Headquarters' representatives.   Some firms, although their policy is to employ host country nationals in most positions, want at least one or two home country managers (commonly the general manager or the finance officer) in their foreign subsidiaries. If new technology for the subsidiary is involved, the parent company will probably station at least one of its technologically qualified experts at the subsidiary until its local personnel learn the technology. In this way, the home office can be confident that someone is immediately available to explain headquarters' policies and procedures, see that they are observed, and interpret what is happening locally to the IC's management. Positions that an IC must take or demands that it must make are sometimes not popular with a host government. It can seem unpatriotic for a host country national to do such things, whereas the host government can understand—and sometimes accept—such positions or demands from a foreigner.

> One of the authors remembers the relief expressed by the Argentinean executives of an Argentine subsidiary of an American IC because an American manager was present to press the Argentine government for what seemed to be unusually extensive payment guarantees. The contract was for a product partly manufactured and assembled in Argentina but mostly manufactured in the United States and imported into Argentina from the United States. The Argentine executives feared that the very specific and high-level payment guarantees would antagonize government officials. The subsidiary was an Argentine company, subject to that country's laws and dependent in part for business from government departments and government-owned companies. Its managers were residents and would stay in Argentina, while the American was there only until the signing of this contract and the guarantees. After he flew away, the local people could blame him and the American parent IC, thus deflecting anger and resentment from themselves.

Host country.   When host country nationals are employed, there is no problem of their being unfamiliar with local customs, culture, and language. Furthermore, the first costs of employing them are generally lower (as compared to the costs of employing home country nationals), although considerable training costs are sometimes necessary. If there is a strong feeling of nationalism in the host country, having nationals as managers can make the subsidiary seem less foreign.

The government development plans and laws of some countries demand that employment in all sectors and at all levels reflect the racial composition of the society. In other words, more skilled and managerial slots must be given to the local people. If foreign-owned firms in Indonesia fail to hire enough *pribumi* (indigenous Indonesians), the firms are likely to encounter difficulties with reentry permits for foreign employees as well as with other government licenses and permits that the firms need. Bribery requests have been known to increase until more pribumi were hired and promoted. Malaysia threatens to revoke the operating licenses of foreign-owned firms that fail to have a satisfactory number of *bumiputra* (indigenous Malays) in sufficiently elevated jobs.[17]

A disadvantage of hiring local managers is that they are often unfamiliar with the home country of the IC and with its policies and practices. Differences in attitudes and values, as discussed in Chapter 9, can cause them to act in ways that surprise or displease headquarters. Also, local managers may create their own upward immobility if, because of strong cultural or family ties, they are reluctant to accept promotions that would require them to leave the country to work at parent headquarters or at another subsidiary.

A new problem has developed for foreign-owned companies that hire and train local, host country people. The best of these people may be pirated away by local firms or other IC subsidiaries, as local executive recruiters are constantly on the lookout to make raids.[18]

Finally, there can be a conflict of loyalty between the host country and the employer. For example, the host country national may give preference to a local supplier even though imported products may be less expensive or of better quality. Local managers might oppose headquarters' requests to set low transfer prices in order to lower taxes payable to the host government.

Third country.   The disadvantages often encountered when using employees from the home or host countries can sometimes be avoided by sending nationals from a third country to fill management posts. A Chilean going to Argentina would have little cultural or language difficulty, but IC headquarters should be careful not to rely too heavily on similarities in language as a guide to similarities in other aspects of the cultures. Mexicans, for example, would have to make considerable adjustments if they were transferred to Argentina, and they would find a move to Spain even more difficult. This is because the Mexican culture is far less European than that of either Argentina or Chile. While the latter two cultures are certainly not identical, they do have many similarities. A fair generalization is that after an executive has adapted once to a new culture and language, a second or succeeding adaptation is easier.

An employer should not count on cost savings in using third-country nationals. Although they may come from countries where salary scales are lower, in such countries as Brazil and most of the nations of northwestern Europe, salaries may be higher than American companies are paying at comparable position levels. Furthermore, many multinationals give international status* to both home country nationals and third-country nationals, who then receive the same perquisites and compensation packages for the same job.

◻ Selection and Training

The selection and training of managers varies somewhat, depending on whether the candidate is from the home country, the host country, or a third country.

Home country.   Relatively few recent college graduates are hired for the express purpose of being sent overseas. Usually they spend a number of years in the domestic (parent) company, and they may get into the company's international operations by design and persistence, by luck, or frequently by a combination. Those who make it into the international side may be assigned to the firm's international division, where they handle problems submitted by foreign affiliates and meet overseas personnel who are visiting IC headquarters.

If the company feels that it will likely send home country employees abroad, it will frequently encourage those employees to study the language and culture of the country to which they are going. Such employees will probably be sent on short trips abroad to handle special assignments and to be exposed to foreign surroundings. Newly hired home country nationals with prior overseas experience may undergo similar but shorter training periods.[19]

It is increasingly possible for American ICs to supplement their in-house training for overseas work with courses in American business schools. In recognition of the growing importance of international business, those schools are expanding the number and scope of international business courses. In addition, a number of university-level business schools are now operating in other countries.[20]

One large problem that has plagued employers is caused by the families of executives transferred overseas. Even though the employee may adapt to and enjoy the foreign experience, the family may not, and an unhappy family may sour the employee on the job and split up the marriage. In either event, the company may have to ship the family back home at great expense—seldom less than $25,000. Consequently, many companies try to assess whether the executive's family can adapt to the foreign ambience before assigning the executive abroad.

Host country.   The same general criteria for selecting home country employees apply to host country nationals. Usually, however, the training of host country nationals will differ from that of home country nationals in that host country nationals are more likely to lack knowledge of advanced business techniques and of the company.

Host country nationals hired in the home country.   Many multinationals try to solve the business technique problem by hiring host country students on their graduation from home country business schools. After being hired, these

---

* International status is discussed later in this chapter.

new employees are usually sent to IC headquarters to receive indoctrination in the firm's policies and procedures as well as on-the-job training in a specific function, such as finance, marketing, or production.

Host country nationals hired in the host country.   Because the number of host country citizens graduating from home country universities is limited, multinationals must also recruit locally for their management positions. To impart knowledge of business technique, the company may do one or more things. It may set up in-house training programs in the host country subsidiary, or it may utilize business courses in the host country's universities. The IC may also send new employees to home country business schools or to parent company training programs. In addition, employees who show promise will be sent repeatedly to the parent company headquarters, divisions, and other subsidiaries to observe the various enterprise operations and meet the other executives with whom they will be communicating during their careers. Such visits are also learning experiences for the home office and the other subsidiaries.

Third country.   Hiring personnel who are citizens of neither the home country nor the host country is often advantageous. Third-country nationals may accept lower wages and benefits than will employees from the home country, and they may come from a culture similar to that of the host country. In addition, they may have worked for another unit of the IC and thus be familiar with its policies, procedures, and people.

The use of third-country nationals has become particularly prevalent in the LDCs because of shortages of literate, not to mention skilled, locals. It can be an advantage to get someone already residing in the country who has necessary work permits and knowledge of local languages and customs.

Host country attitudes.   If the host government emphasizes employment of its own citizens, third-country nationals will be no more welcome than home country people. Actually, third-country nationals could face an additional obstacle in obtaining necessary work permits. For example, the host government can understand that the German parent company of a subsidiary would want some German executives to look after its interest in the host country. It may be harder to convince the government that a third-country native is any better for the parent than a local executive would be.

Generalizations difficult.   We must be careful with generalizations about third-country personnel, partly because people achieve that status in different ways. They may be foreigners hired in the home country and sent to a host country subsidiary either because they have had previous experience there or because that country's culture is similar to their own. Third-country nationals may have originally been home country personnel who were sent abroad and became dissatisfied with the job but not with the host country. After leaving the firm that sent them abroad, they take positions with subsidiaries of multinationals from different home countries. Another way in which third-country nationals can be created is by promotion within an IC. For instance, if a Spanish executive of the Spanish subsidiary of an Italian multinational is promoted to be general manager of the Italian firm's Colombian subsidiary, the Spanish executive is then a third-country national.

geocentric to hire and promote based on ability and experience without considering race or other factors

As multinationals increasingly take the **geocentric** view toward promoting (according to ability and not nationality), we can be certain to see greater use of third-country nationals. This development will be accelerated as more and more executives of all nationalities gain experience outside their native lands. Another, and growing, source for third-country nationals is the heterogeneous body of international agencies. As indicated in Chapter 4, these agencies deal with virtually every field of human endeavor, and all member-countries send their nationals as representatives to the headquarters and branch office cities all over the world. Many of those people become available to, or can be hired away by, multinational companies.

Language training.   As the Business Incident indicates, American companies are taking more seriously the language abilities of their employees. But neither they nor most Australian, British, Canadian, and New Zealand firms are sufficiently serious. The English speakers are trapped by their language.

The English language has become the *lingua franca* of the world; it is everybody's second language. The high ground in the modern world is held by people who speak an international language well and have an impenetrable language of their own. Hungary went its own way within the Soviet empire since few Russians had a clue what the Hungarian dissidents were saying. Israel knows what the Arabs are planning in Arabic; most Arabs are flummoxed by Hebrew. The Japanese are wonderfully protected by their language as they move abroad selling and investing with particular gusto in the English-speaking world.

The French have at long last got the message. Suddenly, waiters in obscure bistros insist on speaking English. They are taking the battle to the enemy. Success is not persuading others to speak your language; it is persuading them that it is quite unnecessary to try.

When trying to sell to potential customers, it is much better to speak their language. As English speakers try to sell abroad, it is far more likely their customers will speak English than that the English speakers will be able speak the customers' language. Customers can then hide behind their language during negotiations.

language trap a situation in which a person doing international business can speak only his or her home language

Two of the supplementary readings deal with this **language trap.** They are Charles Batchelor's "Hoist with the English Language Petard" and "Lingua franca, lingua dolorosa."

□ Women

The subject of staffing the executive offices of modern American companies is not completely covered without a look at the growing role of women. About half of the students in American business schools are now women; they have moved into the managements of banks, businesses, and government agencies and have been at least as successful as their male counterparts. Old-girl networks are now in place alongside the old-boy networks, providing role models and helping younger female managers.[21]

Most observers agree that these are positive developments for IC management. They are developments, however, that cannot be transferred intact out of the United States to every other country of the world. As was indicated in Chapter 12, attitudes toward and treatment of women differ vastly from one

WORLDVIEW
Women and Foreign Postings

When Carla Hills was first nominated for her job as U.S. trade representative, some people had doubts.

Philip Grub, a George Washington University professor of multinational management, told a conference that among concerns about Hills herself, he questioned the cultural sensitivity of sending a woman to negotiate with the Japanese. Senator Steven Symms wondered whether she would appear as rigorous as the "tough men, warriors" who preceded her.

Such anxieties go to the heart of the debate over who should be doing America's business overseas. In choosing their emissaries, companies are often daunted by stories of submissive Asian wives, racist remarks by Japanese leaders, and laws barring Saudi women from driving. The result is that women and minorities, although making small gains, are even rarer among managers abroad than they are at home.

But the few women and minority executives who have worked overseas say many companies are clinging to false notions about other cultures. Although the executives acknowledge that hurdles exist, they say misguided attitudes leave companies unreasonably pessimistic about overcoming them.

"It's a classic case of projection," says Lennie Copeland, a producer at Copeland Griggs Productions, Inc., in San Francisco, which makes films on cultural issues in business. "The American company has a problem accepting women, so they assume it's going to be worse overseas."

Women account for only 5 percent of American expatriate managers, although many more are sent on brief assignments, according to a survey by Moran, Stahl & Boyer, Inc., a New York consulting firm. Of the companies polled, 80 percent said there were disadvantages to sending women overseas.

"Clients refuse to do business with female representatives," one company told Moran. Another explained: "The desired expatriate is a 30-ish married man with preschool-age children. This is to project our image as a conservative institution with good moral fiber. . . . Many of our potential female expatriates are single, and a swinging single is not the right image."

A survey of industrial and service companies with international operations revealed that 36% of the companies had no female expatriates. The reasons given:

Women lacked technical qualifications	Local national prejudice	Conflict with spouse's career	Women hadn't applied	Other
33.9%	19.6%	17.9%	16.1%	12.5%

The following shows the geographical breakdown of women assigned overseas:

Europe	Asia/Pacific	Canada	Latin America	Elsewhere
54.4%	24.2%	9.4%	5%	7%

Even some executives with international experience agree that there are practical limits. They cite Saudi Arabia and Pakistan, for example, as places where it doesn't make sense to send a woman.

But Stephen J. Kobrin, a professor of international management at the University of Pennsylvania's Wharton School, contends that many cautionary arguments echo those once made by corporations against hiring women at home. "If you follow this to its logical conclusion," he says, "you're back in 1954."

Women executives who have worked abroad also complain that companies often fail to differentiate among nations in given parts of the world—ruling out, say, all of Asia for women. "People lump all those countries together," says Anna Ball, president of Ball Seed Company in West Chicago, Illinois. Ball adds that while she works comfortably in Japan, she finds South Korea and especially Taiwan much more accepting of businesswomen.

Conversely, many Americans assume England is the closest thing to home outside North America (the Moran survey showed that almost 24 percent of the female expatriates were posted there). But Americans find that many British men are uncomfortable with female managers.

Robert Petzinger, managing director of AT&T's international communications services in London, recently chose an American woman to head a sales force there. He says five of the men she will manage immediately let him know they thought he had "made the wrong choice." Petzinger adds that he has told the woman she faces a challenge.

Even where a culture puts several restraints on its own women, outsiders may be treated differently, notes Nancy Adler, associate professor at McGill University in Montreal. "You are seen as a foreigner first and then as a woman," she says. "The best predictor of success isn't how they treat their own women, but how they treat other Americans."

Pat Burns, director of industrial development for Madison Public Relations Group, Inc., in Washington, D.C., has been doing business in northern Africa and the Mideast since the mid-1970s. On one occasion in Sudan, she was invited into the home of a businessman, who brought her a cushion, served her food, and washed her arms with rose water after the meal—all things a man normally would never do for a woman. After the meeting, Burns asked her local agent how the man could have violated accepted rules of conduct. "Oh, it's no problem," she recalls being told. "Women do not do business; therefore, you are not a woman."

Ironically, many women feel they have an advantage in business overseas for the same reason they have trouble in business at home: their different upbringing. Consultants say women are generally more patient than men and more interested in creating harmony and consensus.

"That's considered wimpy here," says Marlene L. Rossman, a New York marketing consultant, "and considered very appropriate overseas."

As companies address the "glass ceiling" problem at home, more are pushing the boundaries abroad as well. AT&T, for example, last year commissioned a 22-country study by Moran to evaluate how women are received in various places and what barriers they might face. A few of the findings are illustrative: Chinese businessmen seem less threatened by American women than by American men; there is less *machismo* in Argentina than in other Latin countries.

Daniel McCabe, manager of human resources for AT&T's international communications services, says he wanted to have a "defensible study behind us" when encouraging managers to send women farther afield.

Amid such efforts, though, one of the hardest parts of an overseas assignment for women remains: in showing respect and understanding for the local culture, they may have to tolerate attitudes they wouldn't brook at home. Burns says she has gone out of her way in the Mideast to express respect for a business partner's wife or daughter, or to praise women executives and officials. Still, she says, when a Saudi general recently invited her to visit and asked whether she minded using the women's entrance, she replied, "Not at all."

Source: Jolie Solomon, *The Wall Street Journal*, June 2, 1989, p. B1.

Female executives are gaining altitude.

Dennis Hallinan/FPG International

culture or religion to another. A review of material in Chapter 12 could be helpful at this point.

▢ Résumés Can Mislead

The résumés of most job applicants are probably reasonably accurate, although people are taught how to put their best foot forward and present themselves in the best light. Sometimes that light distorts reality.

The case of Friedrich von Braun was reported by the press in 1986. He was the managing director of Commodity Fundsters, a British company that was in financial difficulty.

Von Braun said that his claim to be the third son of a German baron was based on tales his mother had told him. He could not explain why he was brought up in Warrington, England, and was known to the locals as Fred.

His claims to have been educated at Eton were based on a one-day trip to Windsor in the summer of 1955; he said he had learned a lot about history at that time. He did spend two weeks at Oxford—in a squat on the Iffley Road.

As for his listed hobbies (opera and observing art), he admitted that his work had allowed him no time for either in the past 18 years.

He worked not for the famous banking firm Morgan Stanley, as listed in his résumé, but for Stanley Morgan, a Welsh farmer. His "brilliant" banking career was not with the American bank First Interstate but with a Panamanian financial company known to its liquidators as First Into Straits.

Von Braun said that his career details were misleading because of some "insignificant" typographical errors. He maintained that the mistakes were irrelevant to his ability to look after the interests of "wise" investors who entrusted their money to him.

▫ People's Republic of China Different

An American banker sitting in his cramped hotel office in Beijing said, "Foreigners coming to China had better be prepared for the bleakness of Chinese life." China is an especially tough assignment for Western managers; for one thing, Western-style housing is unavailable, so most Western managers must spend their entire stays in a hotel room.

A study was made of the assets that a Westerner needed to succeed in China. Knowledge of Chinese business customs, negotiating style, and social practices was ranked as most important, but not much more so than Chinese language, politics, and culture.

One manager quoted in the study remarked on "a general sense of uncertainty" in his business dealings. He noted the "vagueness of the Chinese system. You think something will be a problem, and it's not, and vice versa." Another stressed that Westerners in China should understand that despite the recent economic reforms, "communism and the bureaucratic system are number one."[22]

▫ Selection Do's and Don'ts

Executives who should know better sometimes assume that all nationalities work within a framework of common cultures and business practices. Instant communication of information, supersonic travel, and the emergence of international financial institutions have created a global economy.

Yet, this economic interdependence does not translate into a common "business culture." Business standards and practices reflect the cultures in which they are rooted. Their nuances very widely by continent, by country, and even by region.

An executive with no cross-cultural experience can, regardless of other professional credentials, unwittingly wreak havoc with corporate plans abroad. The ability of a company to succeed in another country rests heavily on the managers' abilities to function in that country's culture. An executive search firm has drawn up a checklist of do's and don'ts in selecting executives for foreign operations.

Do promote from within. All other things being equal, selecting a known employee reduces risk. The employee knows the company and the company knows the employee's strengths and weaknesses. The weaknesses of a new person may not be evident at first.

Don't promote an insider if the outsider is clearly better qualified. "John's been doing a good job in New York, and he's always liked London" is not good enough. It can be a costly approach.

Don't be blinded by language fluency. Just because a candidate is fluent in the host country's language does not mean he or she is the best person for the job. Unless your business is the local Berlitz franchise, the candidate must have the requisite technical and managerial skills.

Do assess the total person. Functional skills, language proficiency, and knowledge of the international business environment are all important. With regard to international business savvy, third-country nationals are sometimes better qualified than people born in the host country who have not lived and worked abroad. It has been noted that Scandinavians, Dutch, and Swiss are disproportionately represented in international business management positions. They come from small countries with limited markets, so their education and business experience have been geared to the outside world. As a group, these executives have an outlook that is more cosmopolitan than nationalistic.[23]

While there is no denying fundamental differences in cultures, some say good managers share the same skills worldwide. "The skills are the same," says Jane Wilson of Clark Wilson Publishing, which publishes materials that help companies rate managers' skills in clarifying and communicating goals, planning, problem solving, giving feedback, and tending to details. The 3M Company agrees. It rates its managers around the world on a single scale that seeks to gauge what level of responsibility they can handle. They can then be assigned where needed without regard to nationality. For example, in 1991, two of 3M's managers who are Italian were tapped to fill senior slots, one in the United States and the other in Japan.[24]

COMPENSATION

Establishing a compensation plan that is equitable, consistent, and yet does not overcompensate the overseas executive is a challenging, complex task. The method favored by the majority of American ICs has been to pay a base salary equal to that paid to a domestic counterpart and then, in the belief that no one should be worse off for accepting foreign employment, to add a variety of allowances and bonuses.

▫ Salaries

The practice of paying home country nationals the same salaries as their domestic counterparts permits worldwide consistency for this part of the compensation package. Because of the increasing use of third-country nationals, those personnel are generally treated in the same way.

Some firms carry the equal-pay-for-equal-work concept one step further and pay the same base salaries to host country nationals. In countries that legislate yearly bonuses and family allowances for their citizens, a local national may receive what appears to be a higher salary than is paid the **expatriate,** although companies usually make extra payments to prevent expatriates from falling behind in this regard. In Great Britain, it is the practice to pay executives relatively lower salaries and to provide them with expensive perquisites, such as chauffeured automobiles, housing, or club memberships. A number of American companies follow British practices in compensating their executives working in Britain.

expatriate a person living outside of his or her country of citizenship

◻ Allowances

allowances employee compensation payments added to base salaries because of higher expenses encountered when living abroad

Allowances are extra payments made to compensate expatriates for the extra overseas costs they must incur to live as well abroad as they did in the home country. The most common allowances are housing, cost-of-living, tax differentials, education, and moving.

Housing allowances. Housing allowances are designed to permit executives to live in houses as good as those they had at home. Typically, the firm will pay all of the rent that is in excess of 15 percent of the executive's salary.

Cost-of-living allowances. Cost-of-living allowances are based on the differences in the prices paid for food, utilities, transportation, entertainment, clothing, personal services, and medical expenses overseas as compared to the prices paid for these items in the headquarters city. Many ICs use the U.S. Department of State index, which is based on the cost of these items in Washington, D.C., but have found it is not altogether satisfactory. For one thing, critics claim this index is not adjusted often enough to account for either the rapid inflation in some countries or the changes in relative currency values. Another objection is that the index does not include many cities in which the firm operates. As a result, many companies take their own surveys or use data from the United Nations, the World Bank, the International Monetary Fund, or private consulting firms. Figures and comparisons on costs of living, prices, and wages can also be found in private publications. (See Table 22–1.)

Allowances for tax differentials. ICs pay tax differentials when the host country taxes are higher than the taxes that the expatriates would pay on the same compensation and consumption at home. The objective is to ensure that expatriates will not have less after-tax take-home pay in the host country than they would at home. This can create a considerable extra financial burden on an American parent company because, among other things, the U.S. Internal Revenue Code treats tax allowances as additional taxable income. There are other tax disincentives for Americans to work abroad.*

Education allowances. Expatriates are naturally concerned that their children receive educations at least equal to those they would get in their home countries, and many want their children taught in their native language. Primary and secondary schools with teachers from most industrialized home countries are available in many cities around the world, but these are private schools and therefore charge tuition. ICs either pay the tuition or, if there are enough expatriate children, will operate their own schools. For decades, petroleum companies in the Mideast and in Venezuela have maintained schools for their employees' children.

Moving and orientation allowances. Companies generally pay the total costs of transferring their employees overseas. These include transportation for the family, moving household effects, and maintaining the family in a hotel on a full expense account until the household effects arrive. Some firms find it less expensive to send the household effects by air rather than by ship because the reduction in hotel expenses more than compensates for the higher

---

* For more on this subject and other effects of U.S. tax laws on American ICs, see the taxation section of Chapter 11.

□ **TABLE 22–1**
BI's Executive Cost of Living in Major Cities

Ranking/City	BI Index* (N.Y. = 100) September 1991	BI Index* (N.Y. = 100) April 1991	Ranking/City	BI Index* (N.Y. = 100) September 1991	BI Index* (N.Y. = 100) April 1991
1. Tokyo	169	163	11. Milan	117	116
2. Osaka/Kobe	157	152	12. Vienna	114	118
3. Oslo	139	138	13. Copenhagen	113	114
4. Libreville	138	141	Taipei	113	106
5. Abidjan	136	149	14. Geneva	110	113
6. Brazzaville	132	139	15. Barcelona	108	110
7. Helsinki	130	133	16. Madrid	107	108
Stockholm	130	131	17. Tel Aviv	105	104
8. Tripoli	126	129	18. Hong Kong	104	101
9. Dakar	122	132	Rome	104	104
Paris	122	124	Seoul	104	100
Zurich	122	127	19. Frankfurt	103	104
10. Douala	118	na	20. Lomé	102	106
London	118	117	Lyon	102	106

*The weighted index is calculated by comparing average prices from each city with average prices in New York (the base city for this report). Any city can be used as a base—the order of ranking will remain the same, though BI indexes will alter accordingly. All currencies were converted on September 30, 1991.

Source: *Business International,* December 9, 1991, p. 416.

cost of airfreight. It has also been found that moving into a house sooner raises the employee's morale.

Companies may also pay for some orientation of the employees and their families. Companies frequently pay for language instruction, and some will provide the family with guidance on the intricacies of everyday living, such as shopping, hiring domestic help, and sending children to school.

□ **Bonuses**

bonuses expatriate employee compensation payments in addition to base salaries and allowances because of hardship, inconvenience, or danger

Bonuses (or premiums), unlike allowances, are paid by the firm in recognition that expatriates and their families undergo some hardships and inconveniences and make sacrifices while living abroad. Bonuses include overseas premiums, contract termination payments, and home leave reimbursement.

Overseas premiums. Overseas premiums are additional payments to the expatriates and are generally established as a percentage of the base salary. They range from 10 to 25 percent. If the living conditions are extremely disagreeable, the company may pay larger premiums for hardship posts.

Contract termination payments. These payments are made as inducements for employees to stay on their jobs and work out the periods of their overseas contracts. The payments are made at the end of the contract periods only if the employees have worked out their contracts. Such bonuses are used in the construction and petroleum industries or by other firms that have contracts requiring work abroad for a specific period of time or for a specific project. They may also be used if the foreign post is a hardship or not a particularly desirable one.

Home leave.[25]   ICs that post home country—and sometimes third-country—nationals in foreign countries make it a practice to pay for periodic trips back to the home country made by such employees and their families. The reasons for this are twofold. One reason is that the companies do not want the employees and their families to lose touch with the home country and its culture. The other reason is that the companies want to have the employees spend at least a few days at company headquarters to renew relationships with headquarters' personnel and to catch up with new company policies and practices.

Some firms grant three-month home leaves after an employee has been abroad about three years, but it is probably a more common practice to give two to four weeks' leave each year. All transportation costs are paid to and from the executive's hometown, and all expenses are paid during the executive's stay at company headquarters.

◻ Compensation Packages Can Be Complicated

One might think from the discussion to this point that compensation packages, while costly—the "extras" may total 50 percent or more of the base salary—are fairly straightforward in their calculation. Nothing could be further from the truth.

What percentage?   All allowances and a percentage of the base salary are usually paid in the host country currency. What should this percentage be? In practice, it varies from 65 to 75 percent, with the remainder being banked wherever the employee wishes. One reason for these practices is to decrease the local portion of the salary, thereby lowering host country income taxes and giving the appearance to government authorities and local employees that there is less difference between the salaries of local and foreign employees than is actually the case. Another reason is that expatriate employees have various expenses that must be paid in home country currency. Such expenses include professional society memberships, purchases during home leave, or tuition and other costs for children in home country universities.

What exchange rate?   Inasmuch as most of the expatriate's compensation is usually denominated in the host country currency but is usually established in terms of the home country currency to achieve comparable compensation throughout the enterprise, a currency exchange rate must be chosen. In countries whose currencies are freely convertible into other currencies, this presents no serious problem, although the experienced expatriate will argue that an exchange rate covers only international transactions and may not present a true purchasing power parity between the local and home country currencies. For instance, such items as bread and milk are rarely traded internationally, and living costs and inflation rates may be much higher in the host country than in the home country. Multinationals attempt to compensate for such differences in the cost-of-living allowances.

More difficult problems must be solved in countries that have exchange controls and nonconvertible currencies. Without exception, those currencies are overvalued at the official rate, and if the firm uses that rate, the expatriate employees are certain to be shortchanged. Reference may be made to the free market rate for the host country currency in free currency markets in, for example, the United States or Switzerland or to the black market rate in the host country, but these do not give the final answers. In the end, all companies must pay their expatriate employees enough to enable them to live as well as others who have similar positions in other firms, regardless of how the amount is calculated.

A common compensation component at many American companies is a stock plan that provides employees opportunities to acquire the company's stock on favorable terms. Such programs are designed to increase loyalty and productivity, but they sometimes run into problems outside the United States.

Share ownership is unknown or restricted in numerous countries. Pepsi-Co's vice president of compensation and benefits says, "We had to develop a customized approach in every country we operate in." DuPont discovered it could not give stock options in 25 of 53 nations, primarily because laws ban stock options or limit ownership of foreign shares. Reader's Digest Association and Colgate-Palmolive are designing global stock programs, country by country.[26]

◻ Compensation of Third-Country Nationals

Although some companies have different compensation plans for third-country nationals, there is a trend toward treating third-country nationals the same as home country expatriates. In either event, there are areas in which problems can arise. One of these areas is the calculation of income tax differentials when an American expatriate is compared with an expatriate from another country. This results from the unique American government practices of taxing U.S. citizens even though they live and work abroad and of treating tax differential payments made to those citizens as additional taxable income. No other major country taxes its nationals in those ways.

Another possible problem area is the home leave bonus. The two purposes of home leave are to prevent expatriates from losing touch with their native cultures and to have them visit IC headquarters. A third-country national must visit two countries instead of only one to achieve both purposes, and the additional costs can be substantial. Compare the cost of sending an Australian employee home from Mexico with that required to send an American from Mexico to Dallas.

Regardless of problems, the use of third-country nationals is growing in popularity. As businesses race to enlarge their ranks of qualified international managers, third-country nationals are in greater demand. They often win jobs because they speak several languages and know an industry or country well.

The average number of third-country nationals per U.S.–based international company rose to 46 in 1991, from 33 in 1988. For example, the head of Raychem's Italian subsidiary is French, the sales manager in France is Belgian, and the head of the Spanish unit is Cuban.[27]

◻ International Status

international status entitles the expatriate employee to all the allowances and bonuses applicable to the place of residence and employment

In all of this discussion, we have been describing compensation for expatriates who have been granted **international status.** Merely being from another country does not automatically qualify an employee for all of the benefits we have mentioned. A subsidiary may hire home country nationals or third-country nationals and pay them the same as it pays host country employees.

International status has its benefits.

Courtesy of Daily & Associates

However, managements have found that although an American, for example, may agree initially to take a job and be paid on the local scale, sooner or later bad feeling and friction will develop as that person sees fellow Americans enjoying international status perquisites to which he or she is not entitled.

Another use for international status is to promote host country employees to that status even without transferring them abroad. This is a means of rewarding valuable people and of preventing them from leaving the company for better jobs elsewhere.

So international status means being paid some or all the allowances and bonuses we have discussed, and there can be other sorts of payments as individual circumstances and people's imaginations combine to create them. The Philippine Airlines ad shows two sleeping men. The one in the bottom picture is clearly the one with international status. The executives' compensation package is sufficiently important and complicated to have become a specialization in the personnel management field; at one firm, the title is "International Employee Benefits Consultant."[28]

Help is becoming available from outside the IC. For one example, Ernst & Young publish an International Series, pamphlets advising about transfer to specific countries.[29] Some comparisons of pay and buying power in several

☐ **TABLE 22–2   Executives' Gross Pay and Buying Power (In pounds sterling)**

	Junior Manager		Middle Manager		Head of Function		Head of Division	
	Gross Pay	Buying Power	Gross Pay	Buying Power	Gross Pay	Buying Power	Gross Pay	Buying Power
Hong Kong	18,682£	18,267£	29,480£	27,536£	42,635£	39,824£	63,610£	59,415£
United States	25,779	23,048	35,326	29,672	48,888	39,165	68,978	52,736
Switzerland	35,385	22,805	46,885	28,722	65,219	37,420	90,079	48,735
West Germany	28,497	18,800	39,091	25,774	55,463	35,594	82,339	49,176
Canada	22,823	18,806	31,255	24,074	45,095	32,186	60,014	40,570
France	22,084	16,931	30,829	22,773	44,037	30,579	61,846	41,157
Spain	21,938	15,750	31,186	21,466	44,577	28,668	64,659	37,483
Italy	23,216	14,898	32,681	20,115	47,026	27,275	67,708	37,510
United Kingdom	18,758	15,015	25,017	19,603	35,027	26,163	48,280	34,115
Belgium	24,933	16,141	34,983	20,139	49,900	25,532	71,216	32,624
Netherlands	21,775	15,992	30,274	20,302	42,875	25,553	57,775	31,761
Australia	18,545	15,118	25,455	18,928	33,383	22,746	45,980	29,608
South Africa	12,335	12,966	16,366	16,238	22,804	21,336	31,511	28,229
Ireland	18,993	13,275	25,459	16,323	34,182	20,235	45,315	25,229
New Zealand	13,524	10,827	17,988	14,078	24,059	18,498	32,312	24,509
Finland	22,970	12,156	30,202	14,608	40,480	18,041	53,975	21,998
Denmark	25,289	12,149	32,143	13,888	43,302	16,538	64,799	21,641
Greece	11,657	9,678	16,272	12,794	23,906	18,144	32,294	23,546
Norway	18,954	11,669	25,122	14,055	33,627	16,987	43,496	20,390
Sweden	20,151	10,544	27,560	13,294	37,566	17,009	49,695	21,511

Source: Michael Dixon, *Financial Times*, November 22, 1991, p. 1.

countries and at four different ranks of executives in each country can be seen in Table 22–2. First is a junior manager, then a middle manager, upward to the head of a function such as finance or marketing, and finally the head of the whole division.

☐ Perks

These originated in the perquisites of the medieval lords of the manor, whose workers paid parts of their profits or produce to the lords to be allowed to continue working. Today, perks are symbols of rank in the corporate hierarchy and are used to compensate executives while minimizing taxes. Among the most common perks are

Cars, which higher up the organization ladder come with chauffeurs.

Private pension plan.

Retirement payment.

Life insurance.

Health insurance.

Company house or apartment.

Directorship of a foreign subsidiary.

□ FIGURE 22–1   European Holidays

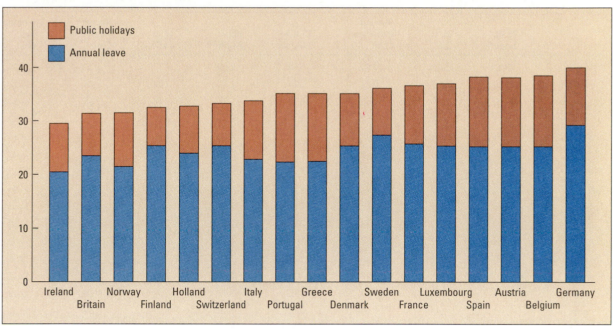

Source: *The Economist,* June 1, 1991, p. 97.

Seminar holiday travel.

Club memberships.

Hidden slush fund (such funds are illegal, but some corporations are said to have them).

□ What's Important to You?

While working abroad as an executive of an American multinational, one of the authors had a colleague who was an American expatriate married to a French woman. They had raised a family in several countries where they had been assigned by the company. Together with some other cosmopolites, they devised a table of items deemed important to at least one of them in choosing a city for location of a company facility that employs foreigners.

The list included the usual items, such as cost of living, safety of personnel, medical facilities, housing, and schools. It also included such other items as availability of good wine at reasonable prices, quality of theater and whether it was live or cinema, number and type of one-star or better *(Michelin Guide)** restaurants, type and accessibility of sports facilities for both participants and viewers, and shopping facilities for fashionable clothes.

The table of items was circulated informally throughout the firm's many locations, and many cities in its network were graded as to each item on a 1-to-10 scale. When the New York headquarters saw the table, there was much mirth and merriment; suggestions—perhaps not all of them serious—

* *The Michelin Guide* rates restaurants and hotels in France and neighboring countries.

☐ **TABLE 22–3   The Price of Overindulgence around the World (In pounds sterling)**

	75 cl. Scotch	75 cl. Gin	Average Indulgence Cost	12 Alka-Seltzers	100 Aspirins	16 oz. Coffee	Average Treatment Cost	Average Full Cost
Helsinki	30.83£	25.12£	27.98£	1.00£	3.66£	2.12£	2.26£	30.24£
Stockholm	30.09	22.47	26.28	0.77	2.99	2.07	1.94	28.22
Copenhagen	27.53	15.58	21.56	0.72	5.37	2.72	2.94	24.50
Singapore	22.87	18.89	20.88	1.20	4.62	2.60	2.81	23.69
Tokyo	18.51	11.65	15.08	—	9.71	6.04	7.88	22.96
Moscow	23.42	7.88	15.65	1.35	6.15	4.95	4.15	19.80
Sydney	17.11	10.14	13.63	1.22	3.21	3.37	2.60	16.23
Vienna	15.25	8.25	11.75	1.61	4.60	2.96	3.06	14.81
London	14.78	9.97	12.38	1.41	2.92	2.43	2.25	14.63
Cairo	14.25	10.90	12.58	0.23	1.96	3.56	1.92	14.50
Hong Kong	12.60	10.12	11.36	1.10	3.80	3.28	2.73	14.09
Amsterdam	11.97	9.02	10.50	1.36	7.42	1.69	3.49	13.99
Frankfurt	11.03	7.53	9.28	1.85	6.83	2.54	3.74	13.02
New York	11.22	9.83	10.53	1.03	3.42	2.32	2.26	12.79
Toronto	12.11	9.77	10.94	1.03	2.12	2.17	1.77	12.71
Brussels	12.54	8.79	10.67	1.07	3.04	1.91	2.01	12.68
Madrid	11.92	6.63	9.28	1.82	5.17	2.04	3.01	12.29
Paris	12.02	8.58	10.30	1.02	3.39	1.21	1.87	12.17
Milan	8.53	5.21	6.87	1.63	8.09	3.04	4.25	11.12

Source: *Financial Times*, December 20, 1991, p. 25.

were made as to additional items about which they would like information when they visited the cities.

However, the mirth and merriment subsided as more and more executives being assigned or reassigned abroad used the table to demand better compensation packages. Some even refused transfers because of the ratings given a city.

Also important to employees may be the number of vacation days they are likely to get from country to country and comparisons of how much it costs to celebrate and then to treat a resulting hangover. As to vacation days, Europeans are well ahead of the Americans and Japanese. The average Japanese is entitled to 15 days a year and usually takes fewer, while the average American takes about 20 days. In the European vacation league, the Germans are tops with 40 days; the Irish are at the bottom with 27 days, but still well ahead of the Americans and Japanese (see Figure 22–1).

As to comparative costs of celebrating and treating hangovers, Table 22–3 shows Helsinki to be the most expensive and Milan the cheapest. The study gave a choice of celebratory beverages—scotch or gin—and three possible treatments—Alka-Seltzer℠, aspirin, or coffee.

SUMMARY

Intraenterprise controls must be effective if an IC is to maximize success and minimize problems. Such controls include guidelines as to where decisions will be made, which may be at the parent company level, at the subsidiary company level, or cooperatively at both levels. Among the factors that affect intraenterprise controls are product and equipment introduction, improvement, and standardization; the competence of subsidiary management; the distance of the host country from the home country and the differences in their cultures; and the size of the IC and how long it has operated multinationally. Guidelines as to where decisions will be made are affected by circumstances in which some detriment to a subsidiary will result in greater benefit for the enterprise as a whole. Such detriment/benefit situations arise in intraenterprise transactions wherein profit can be maximized in lower-tax countries and minimized in higher-tax countries or tariffs can be minimized by intraenterprise transfer price decisions. Also, where a customer order can be filled by more than one unit of an IC, having the parent decide which unit gets the order can avoid intraenterprise competition and can ensure that such considerations as order backlogs, labor problems, and comparative tariffs are taken into account.

It is easier for a parent company to exercise control over a subsidiary if it owns 100 percent of the subsidiary than if it owns less than 100 percent. And control of a joint venture with a separate entity in which the parent company has no ownership is more difficult than control of a subsidiary in which it has less than 100 percent ownership. In such instances, control is sought through control of the capital and technology as well as by holding strategic joint venture executive positions.

For controls to work, all operating IC units must provide headquarters with timely, accurate, and complete reports. These reports should cover such subjects as finance, technology, market opportunities, new products, competitor activities, price changes, market share, and political and economic information.

As companies' expenditures for information processing equipment have grown to over 50 percent of investments in all durable equipment, executives frequently get more information than they can deal with efficiently. They are devising ways to handle this information glut.

A very important use of reports is as a means for evaluating and comparing management performance. For this purpose, the raw figures are inadequate and may be misleading. The parent company must factor in such elements as decisions it made that penalized one subsidiary while benefiting another and conditions beyond the subsidiary management's control, such as inflation or political instability.

It is difficult to locate effective executives for multinational operations. Two or more cultures are involved, and usually two or more languages. The IC may find employees in its home country, the host country, or elsewhere, and the nationalities of those employees may be home country, host country, or third country. The types of training employees should receive and the adaptation they should undergo depend on their nationality and previous experience. The home country national needs to learn about the host country culture and language, while the opposite is true of the host country national. Frequently, third-country nationals are hired because they have experience with both—and sometimes other—cultures and languages.

Many English-speaking businesspeople find themselves in a language trap. A great and growing number of people can understand English, as it has become the world's second language. At the same time, too few English native-tongue speakers speak and understand other languages.

IC headquarters often sends specialists to assist foreign subsidiaries with problems that have multinational ramifications, such as taxes, labor, or product sales contracts. In addition, headquarters usually likes to have one or two of its nationals in such key positions as general manager or financial manager.

Moving employees from country to country among subsidiaries and the IC home operations can develop and mature those employees and provide learning experiences for the subsidiaries and home operations. Such moves can be for temporary duty or longer-term assignments. One result desired from such moves is the formation of personal relationships among IC personnel that will facilitate intraenterprise communication and understanding.

Company loyalties and nationalistic attitudes must be taken into account. Host country employees may place host country interests above those of the company and may be reluctant to press their governments for unpopular concessions even though the company would benefit. However, all countries have rules and limitations on the number of foreign employees that can be brought in.

Most executives sent from their home countries take families, and the difficulties of cultural and linguistic adaptations may be more severe for the families than for the executives. Most companies now make efforts to evaluate whether the families can and will adapt before sending executives abroad. Failure to adapt causes broken families, poor employee morale, and expensive relocation of families back to the home countries.

Expatriate employees are generally paid the same basic salary as their domestic counterparts. However, additional expenses and hardships are frequently encountered abroad, and the expatriates receive additional payments in the forms of allowances and bonuses or premiums. Among the allowances commonly given are those for housing, cost of living, tax differentials, schooling, moving, and orientation. The bonuses include overseas premiums and contract termination payments, which are used if living conditions are difficult or if a specific term or project must be completed. Another bonus is home leave for employees and families, whose purpose is to prevent expatriates from losing touch with their native cultures and to permit them to visit IC headquarters at least periodically.

Compensation packages for expatriates are complicated because there are so many variables to consider. In addition to home country salary levels, the types and levels of compensation of equivalent executives in the host country must be considered. Comparative taxes, costs of living, and inflation rates must be factored in, as must difficulties of living conditions. An additional set of complications can arise from the currencies utilized; some currencies are freely convertible, but most are not, and currencies fluctuate in value in terms of each other.

The expatriate who is paid some or all of the bonuses and allowances we have discussed is said to be on international status. From time to time, firms will promote subsidiary host country nationals to international status. Their motives for doing so may be to reward such employees for meritorious service or to keep them from leaving to work for a competitor.

Women are moving in increasing numbers onto and up corporate executive ladders. With regard to assignment and promotion abroad, they are encountering the same obstacles and glass ceilings they meet at home, although the excuses for not sending and promoting women abroad are sometimes different. The excuses are variations of the theme that the host country cultures do not accept women executives. Nevertheless, women are overcoming the obstacles and moving up.

QUESTIONS

1. In determining whether decisions will be made by the parent company or by its subsidiaries, what are the considerations when equipment and products are standardized worldwide rather than tailored to individual national circumstances and markets?

2. *a.* In an IC, what are some decisions that could result in detriment for a subsidiary but greater benefit for the enterprise?
   b. In such circumstances, where will the decision be made—at IC headquarters or at the affected subsidiary?

3. What measures can be utilized to control subsidiaries that are less than 100 percent owned by the firm or joint venture partners in which the firm has no ownership?

4. What are the roles of reporting in multinational controls?

5. *a.* When subsidiaries report net profits, must parent management look behind the reported numbers to evaluate subsidiary managements fairly?
   b. Explain.

6. When staffing a multinational organization for service outside the IC home country, what are some advantages and disadvantages of hiring home country personnel?

7. What is the English language trap?

8. Why has there been an increasing use of third-country nationals in the foreign operations of ICs?

9. Why are expatriate employees frequently paid more than their colleagues at equivalent job levels in the home office?

10. Why are compensation packages for expatriates more complicated than those for domestic employees?

11. What is international status? Who gets it? Why?

12. Women executives face obstacles to assignment and promotion both in the home country and in host countries. What additional obstacle applies to the latter?

◻ MINICASE 22–1

Female Executives in International Business

For a number of reasons, women are being hired and promoted as executives by American business. The United States is almost alone in this development. Some Western European countries are moving slowly toward more female executive development, but elsewhere in the world, notably Latin American, Africa, Asia, and Eastern Europe, women are given very few executive opportunities.

Suppose you are the chief executive officer (CEO) of an American multinational. On your staff and in the U.S. operating divisions of your company are several bright, able, dedicated female executives. They are also ambitious, and in your company, international experience is a must before an executive can hope to get into top management.

An opening comes up for the position of executive vice president in the company's Mexican subsidiary. One of the women on your staff applies for the position, and she is well qualified for the job, better than anyone else in the company. Would you give her the position? What are the arguments pro and con?

Another position becomes available, this one as treasurer of the Japanese subsidiary. The chief financial officer of the company's California division applies for this job. She has performed to everyone's satisfaction, and she seems thoroughly qualified to become the treasurer in Japan. In addition, she speaks and writes Japanese. She is the daughter of a Japanese mother and an American father, and they encouraged her to become fluent in both English and Japanese.

Would you give her the job? Why or why not?

SUPPLEMENTARY READINGS

"A Better Deal for Women." *Financial Times*, October 29, 1991, p. 20.

Adler, Nancy J. "A Typology of Management Studies Involving Culture." *Journal of International Business Studies*, Fall 1983, pp. 29–48.

Bacchus, I. William. "Staffing for Foreign Affairs: A Personnel System." *Public Personnel Management*, Fall 1985, pp. 315–30.

Batchelor, Charles. "Hoist with the English Language Petard." *The Economist*, April 18, 1989, p. 15.

Bogan, Mary. "Women's Fast Tracks and the Risk of Running into Sidings." *Financial Times*, August 7, 1991, p. 19.

Dymsza, William A., and Anant R. Negandhi. "Introduction to Cross-Cultural Management Issues." *Journal of International Business Studies*, Fall 1983, pp. 15–16.

Gates, Stephen R., and William G. Egelhoff. "Centralization in Headquarters–Subsidiary Relationships." *Journal of International Business Studies*, Summer 1986, pp. 71–92.

Guisinger, S. E., and associates. *Investment Incentives and Performance Requirements*. New York: Praeger Publishers, 1985.

Hagerty, Bob. "Companies in Europe Seeking Executives Who Can Cross Borders in a Single Bound." *The Wall Street Journal*, January 25, 1991, pp. B1 and 2.

Harvey, Michael C. "The Other Side of Foreign Assignments: Dealing with the Repatriation Dilemma." *Columbia Journal of World Business*, Spring 1982, pp. 53–59.

Hill, Ray. "Women-Owned Companies Finally Start Making Their Mark." *International Management*, May 1986, p. 66.

"Japan Learns about Sexual Harassment." *The Wall Street Journal*, October 21, 1991, p. D2.

Kale, S. H., and D. Sudharshan. "A Strategic Approach to International Segmentation." *International Marketing Review* 5, Summer 1987, pp. 60–70.

Lecraw, J. D. "Performance of Transnational Corporations in Less Developed Countries." *Journal of International Business Studies* 14, Spring–Summer 1983, pp. 15–33.

"Lingua franca, lingua dolorosa." *The Economist*, August 24, 1991, p. 16.

Murray, Robin, ed. *Multinationals beyond the Market: Intra-Firm Trade and the Control of Transfer Pricing*. New York: John Wiley & Sons, 1981.

Neff, Robert. "When in Japan, Recruit as the Japanese Do—Aggressively." *Business Week*, June 24, 1991, p. 58.

O'Dwyer, Gerard. "The Fair Sex Gets the Fairest Deal in Scandinavia." *The European*, June 2, 1991, p. 3.

Packard, P., and J. Slater. "Staff Appraisal: A First Step to Effective Leaders." *Journal of Occupational Psychology*, September 1985, p. 261.

Rosener, Judy B. "Ways Women Lead." *Harvard Business Review*, November–December 1990, pp. 119–21.

Tomoda, Shizna. "Measuring Female Labor Activities in Asian Developing Countries: A Time Allocation Approach." *International Labor Review,* November–December 1985, p. 661.

Tully, Shawn. "Where People Live Best." *Fortune,* March 11, 1991, pp. 44–54.

Turbeyz, Peggy. "International Organization Helps Women Overcome Barriers to Obtaining Credit." *American Banker,* September 6, 1985, p. 16.

Weigand, L. T. "Social Cost/Benefit Analysis for MNCs." *Harvard Business Review,* July–August 1983, pp. 146–52.

Weihrich, Heinz, and Diethard Buhler. "Training Managers for the Global Market." *Business,* July–September 1990, pp. 40–42.

ENDNOTES

1. Louise Kehoe, "Radical Change of IBM Format," *Financial Times,* November 21, 1991, p. 27.

2. Richard N. Farmer and Barry M. Richman, *International Business,* 3rd ed. (Bloomington, Ind.: Cedarwood Press, 1980), chap. 12.

3. William K. Brandt and James M. Hulbert, "Patterns of Communications in the Multinational Corporation: An Empirical Study," *Journal of International Business Studies,* Spring 1976, pp. 17–30.

4. Jacques Picard, "How European Companies Control Marketing Decisions Abroad," *Columbia Journal of World Business,* Summer 1977, pp. 113–21.

5. Sidney M. Robbins and Robert B. Stobaugh, *Money in the Multinational Enterprise* (New York: Basic Books, 1973), pp. 140–51; see also Barbara Durr, "ITW: Ultimate Widget Group Fastens on to Bright Ideas," *Financial Times,* August 5, 1991, p. 8.

6. Farmer and Richman, *International Business,* pp. 285–86.

7. Mohammad F. Al-Eryani, Pervaiz Alam, and Syed H. Akhter, "Transfer Pricing Determinants of U.S. Multinationals," *Journal of International Business Studies,* 3rd quarter 1990, pp. 409–425.

8. Itzhak Sharov, "Transfer Pricing: Diversity of Goals and Practice," *Journal of Accountancy,* April 1974, pp. 56–62.

9. Stefan H. Robock and Kenneth Simmonds, *International Business and Multinational Enterprises,* 4th ed. (Homewood, Ill.: Richard D. Irwin, 1989), pp. 526–28.

10. Wendell H. McCulloch, Jr., "Japan's Trade and Investment with the Less-Developed Countries," *The Wall Street Journal,* October 3, 1980, p. 19.

11. Richard Thomas Cupitt, "Foreign Political Risk Assessment," *The International Trade Journal,* Summer 1990, pp. 341–56.

12. Richard F. Janssen, "U.S. Lenders Taking New Looks at Risks from Political, Social Upheavals Abroad," *The Wall Street Journal,* March 13, 1979, p. 7.

13. "Too Many Computers Spoil the Broth," *The Economist,* August 24, 1991, p. 30.

14. Ibid.

15. James S. Hirsch, "Flood of Information Swamps Managers," *The Wall Street Journal,* August 12, 1991, p. B1.

16. Farmer and Richman, *International Business,* chap. 10.

17. *Business International,* July 2, 1983, pp. 209 and 211.

18. *Business International,* July 22, 1983, pp. 228–29.

19. Lisa Wood, "Search for Worldly-Wide Company Executives," *Financial Times,* April 9, 1991, p. 15.

20. Shawn Tully, "Europe: Best Business Schools," *Fortune,* May 23, 1988, pp. 106–10; see also Shawn Tully, "The Hunt for the Global Manager," *Fortune,* May 21, 1990, pp. 140–44.

21. Amanda Bennett, "Women's Job Contacts May Hold Them Back," *The Wall Street Journal,* September 4, 1991, p. B1.

22. John Frankenstein, "Training Experts to Manage in China," *The Asian Wall Street Journal,* August 26, 1985, p. 17.

23. Fortunat F. Mueller-Maerkl, "Do's and Don'ts in Selecting Managers for Foreign Operations," in *U.S.–German Economic Survey* (New York: German/American Chamber of Commerce, 1984), pp. 123–25.

24. Amanda Bennett, "Good Managers Share Same Skills Worldwide," *The Wall Street Journal,* September 4, 1991, p. B1.

25. Some writers regard paid home leave as an allowance, but our experience convinces us that it is a premium, because ICs consistently give more frequent or longer home leaves to employees working in less desirable assignments.

26. Joann S. Lublin, "Employee Stock Plans Run into Foreign Snags," *The Wall Street Journal,* September 16, 1991, p. B1.

27. Joann S. Lublin, "Firms Woo Executives from Third Countries," *The Wall Street Journal,* September 16, 1991, p. B1.

28. G. W. Hallmark and Charles W. Rogers III, "The Challenge of Providing Benefit and Compensation Programs for Third-Country Nationals," in *The International Essays for Business Decision Makers,* vol. 3, ed. Mark W. Winchester (New York: AMACOM for the Center for International Business, 1978).

29. *Handbook for Employees Transferring to France,* Ernst & Whinney, International Series, March 1980; *to the United States,* March 1980; *to Belgium,* April 1980; *to the United Kingdom,* April 1980; *to Italy,* June 1980; *to Hong Kong,* October 1980; *to Luxembourg,* October 1980; *to Denmark,* October 1980; *Abroad,* November 1980; and more. They are updated periodically.

Chapter 23

Trends and New Directions

Arrangements such as the European single market and the Western Hemisphere FTA being negotiated can be building blocks rather than stumbling blocks for the world economy.

> Robert Lawrence, professor,
> Harvard University

There is a joke about buying a huge ship, equipping it with the CAD–CAM automated production capability, and dropping anchor on the shore of whatever country at the moment offers the best currency exchange opportunity.

> Gerrit Jeelof, vice chairman, N.V.
> Philips Gloeilampenfabrieken

It can bring jobs and development to China or anyplace else it locates. And, if a government pushes it around, it can move its computer-aided manufacturing elsewhere. Its real assets are its brains and its access to world money markets.

> Patrick Wang, managing director,
> Johnson Electric Industrial
> Manufactory, Ltd.

LEARNING OBJECTIVES

In this chapter, you will study:

1. A day in the life of tomorrow's manager.
2. Effects on families of changing communications facilities.
3. Changes in home countries.
4. Changing attitudes toward ICs.
5. Changes in sizes and strengths of ICs and banks.
6. Weaknesses of Japanese banks.
7. Growing strength of overseas Chinese.
8. Western Hemisphere free trade area agreements (FTAs).
9. FTAs, EEA, and GATT.
10. How political developments affect business.
11. Trends shaping the world.
12. Effects of privatization.

KEY WORDS AND CONCEPTS

- Two-career couples
- Demographic changes
- 24-hour, seven-day executive
- IC home countries
- Globalization-localization

BUSINESS INCIDENT

A Day in the Life of Tomorrow's Manager: He or She Faces a More Diverse, Quicker Market

6:10 A.M. The year is 2010, and another Monday morning has begun for Peter Smith. The marketing vice president for a home-appliance division of a major U.S. manufacturer is awakened by his computer alarm. He saunters to his terminal to check the weather outlook in Madrid, where he'll fly late tonight, and to send an electronic-voice message to a supplier in Thailand.

Meet the manager of the future.

A different breed from his contemporary counterpart, our fictitious Peter Smith inhabits an international business world shaped by competition, collaboration, and corporate diversity. (For one thing, he's just as likely to be a woman as a man and—with the profound demographic changes ahead—will probably manage a work force comprising mostly women and minorities.)

Comfortable with technology, he's been logging on to computers since he was seven years old. A literature honors student with a joint M.B.A./advanced-communications degree, the 38-year-old joined his current employer four years ago after stints at two other corporations—one abroad—and a marketing consulting firm. Now he oversees offices in a score of countries on four continents.

Tomorrow's manager "will have to know how to operate in an anytime, anyplace universe," says Stanley Davis, a management consultant and author of "Future Perfect," a look at the 21st-century business world.

Adds James Maxmin, chief executive of London-based Thorn EMI PLC's home-electronics division, "We've all come to accept that organizations and managers who aren't cost-conscious and productive won't survive. But in the future, we'll also have to be more flexible, responsive, and smarter. Managers will have to be nurturers and teachers, instead of policemen and watchdogs."

BUSINESS INCIDENT (concluded)

7:20 A.M. Smith and his wife, who heads her own architectural firm, organize the home front before darting to the supertrain. They leave instructions for their personal computer to call the home-cleaning service as well as a gourmet carryout service, which will prepare dinner for eight guests Saturday. And they quickly go over the day's schedules for their three- and six-year-old daughters with their nanny.

On the train during a speedy 20-minute commute from suburb to Manhattan, Smith checks his electronic mailbox and also reads his favorite trade magazine via his laptop computer.

The jury is still out on how dual-career couples will juggle high-pressure work and personal lives. Some consultants and executives predict that the frenetic pace will only quicken. "I joke to managers now that we come in on London time and leave on Tokyo time," says Anthony Terracciano, president of Mellon Bank Corp. in Pittsburgh. He foresees an even more difficult work schedule ahead.

But others believe more creative uses of flexible schedules, as well as technological advances in communications and travel, will allow more balance. "In the past, nobody cared if your staff had heart attacks; but in tomorrow's knowledge-based economy, we'll be judged more on how well we take care of people," contends Robert Kelley, a professor at Carnegie Mellon University's business school.

8:15 A.M. In his high-tech office, which doubles as a conference room, Smith reviews the day's schedule with his executive assistant (traditional secretaries vanished a decade earlier). Then, it's on to his first meeting: a conference via videoscreen between his division's chief production manager in Cincinnati and a supplier near Munich.

The supplier tells them she can deliver a critical component for a new appliance at a 10 percent cost saving if they grab it within a week. Smith and the production manager quickly concur that it's a good deal. Although they'll have to immediately change production schedules, they'll be able to snare a new customer who has been balking about price.

Today's manager spends most of his time conferring with bosses and subordinates within his own company, but tomorrow's manager will be "intimately hooked to suppliers and customers" and well versed in competitors' strategies, says Stanley Davis, the management consultant.

The marketplace will demand customized products and immediate delivery. This will force managers to make swift product-design and marketing decisions, which now often take months and reams of reports. "Instant performance will be expected of them, and it's going to be harder to hide incompetence," says Ann Barry, vice president of research at Handy Associates, Inc., a New York consultant.

10:30 A.M. At a staff meeting, Smith finds himself refereeing two subordinates who disagree vehemently on how to promote a new appliance. One, an Asian manager, suggests that a fresh campaign begin much sooner than initially envisioned. The other, a European, wants to hold off until results of a test market are received later that week.

Smith quickly realizes this is a cultural, not strategic, clash pitting a let's-do-it-now, analyze-it-later approach against a more cautious style. He makes them aware that they're not really far apart, and the European manager agrees to move swiftly.

By 2010, managers will have to handle greater cultural diversity with subtle human relations skills. Managers will have to understand that employees don't think alike about such basics as "handling confrontation or even what it means to do a good day's work," says Jeffrey Sonnenfeld, a Harvard Business School professor.

12:30 P.M. Lunch is in Smith's office today, giving him time to take a video lesson in conversational Chinese. He already speaks Spanish fluently, having learned during a work stint in Argentina, and he wants to master at least two more languages. After 20 minutes, though, he decides to go to his computer to check his company's latest political risk assessment on Spain, where recent student unrest has erupted into riots. The report tells him that the disturbances aren't anti-American, but he decides to have a bodyguard meet him at the Madrid airport anyway.

Technology will give managers easy access to more data than they can possibly use. The challenge will be to "synthesize data to make effective decisions," says Mellon's Terracciano.

2:20 P.M. Two of Smith's top lieutenants complain that they and others on his staff feel a recent bonus payment for a successful project wasn't divided equitably. Bluntly, they note that while Smith received a hefty $20,000 bonus, his 15-member staff had to split $5,000, and they threaten to defect. He quickly calls his boss, who says he'll think about increasing the bonus for staff members.

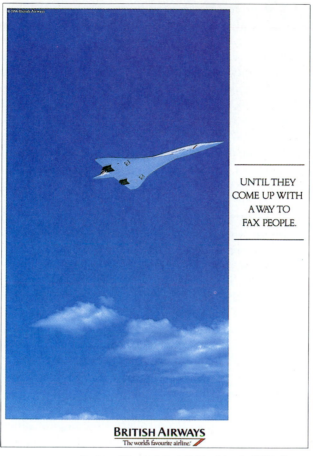

UNTIL THEY
COME UP WITH
A WAY TO
FAX PEOPLE.

BRITISH AIRWAYS
The world's favourite airline.

Super fast and efficient travel now makes it possible to conduct business around the world and still be home for dinner. The debate is still on, though, as to the effect this has on workers' lives.

Courtesy of Saatchi & Saatchi Advertising, for British Airways

With skilled technical and professional employees likely to be in short supply, tomorrow's managers will have to share more authority with subordinates and, in some cases, pay them as much as or more than the managers themselves earn.

While yielding more to their employees, managers in their 30s in the year 2010 may find their own climb up the corporate ladder stalled by superiors. After advancing rapidly in their 20s, this generation "will be locked in a heated fight with older baby-boomers who won't want to retire," says Harvard's Sonnenfeld.

4 P.M. Smith learns from the field that a large retail customer has been approached by a foreign competitor promising to quickly supply him with a best-selling appliance. After conferring with his division's production managers, he phones the customer and suggests that his company could supply the same product but with three slightly different custom designs. They arrange a meeting later in the week.

Despite the globalization of companies and speed of overall change, some things will stay the same. Managers intent on rising to the top will still be judged largely on how well they articulate ideas and work with others.

In addition, different corporate cultures will still encourage and reward divergent qualities. Companies banking on new products, for example, will reward risk takers, while slow-growth industries will stress predictability and caution in their ranks.

6 P.M. Before heading to the airport, Smith uses his videophone to give his daughters a good-night kiss and to talk about the next day's schedule with his wife. Learning that she must take an unexpected trip herself the next evening, he promises to catch the SuperConcorde home in time to put the kids to sleep himself.

Source: Carol Hymowitz, "Day in the Life of Tomorrow's Manager," *The Wall Street Journal,* March 20, 1989, p. B1.

two-career couples household relationships in which both partners work outside the house

24-hour, seven-day executive an executive on call all hours of the day, including weekends and holidays, as a result of today's advances in communications

One thing suggested by the Business Incident is that **two-career couples** will be a continuing and perhaps growing phenomenon in the future. Even for one-career couples, the working spouse/executive will find that the computer and fax will supersede time zones. Such a person will be a **24-hour, seven-day executive,** on call all hours of day and night, including weekends and holidays. Observed holidays are very different from country to country —for example, only the United States observes the Fourth of July—and many executives work on weekends.

The Worldview, "Executives Find They're Always on Call as Computer, Fax Supersede Time Zones," gives a few glimpses at how some executives and their families cope with changing international business demands. As you read it, consider how you might deal with family–business conflicts if they confront you.

International companies (ICs)—including multinational companies, multinational enterprises, globals, or transnationals, as the multicountry banking and business organizations are variously called—are undergoing several types of change. For one thing, many companies with home countries other than the United States have grown more rapidly than U.S.-based companies. For another, the number of companies whose home countries are developing countries is growing.

The companies' relationships with the EC and the UN are changing, and the attitudes and policies of less developed countries (LDCs) as host countries are becoming more hospitable.

Many people are speaking of different sorts of organizations and operations when they refer to multinational companies and globals/transnationals. A number of national laws requiring minimum local-manufactured content and/or investment control are inhibiting the globalization of some ICs. Differing national consumer tastes are also causing some companies to tailor their products, at least partially, to individual markets, and flexible manufacturing systems are making the tailoring faster and less costly.

Some of the organizations are structuring themselves to globalize as much as is profitable under control of a home country headquarters, while maintaining flexibility to tailor for national or regional markets where that approach is more profitable or legally necessary. In the tailoring instances, management in the host countries has more autonomy.

There are those who want and others who fear the creation of trade blocs of countries with free trade within the bloc but protectionism against the rest of the world. Such blocs are forming or are under discussion; whether they will cooperate or compete with each other remains to be seen.

World business is strongly affected by politics. The U.S.S.R. has ceased to exist, and the trading bloc, COMECON, which the U.S.S.R. dominated, has been dissolved. The Eastern European countries that were COMECON members are now struggling to create democracies and convert from centrally planned to market economies. Before the U.S.S.R. collapsed, the Baltic states—Estonia, Latvia, and Lithuania—had declared their independence and been recognized by the West and Russia.

Russia is by far the largest republic of the remaining 12 (there were 15 before the Baltics seceded). Most of the 12 have joined in a Commonwealth of Independent States (CIS), whose powers and functions are still evolving.

The bureaucracies of the old U.S.S.R. and the COMECON countries were corrupt and cumbersome, but Westerners had learned who was who and how to deal with them. Now it's all new as the countries and republics sort out their procedures and different people gain power. It is not only new rules of the game that Westerners must learn; there are entirely different games.

In Tienanmen Square in Beijing, the capital of the People's Republic of China (PRC), thousands of students, intellectuals, and workers demonstrated for days and nights, demanding negotiations with the government for "democracy." In early June 1989, China's People's Liberation Army used tanks and infantry to massacre apparently thousands of demonstrators and clear the square. Such a massacre was denied by the PRC government, although it had been reported by both Chinese and foreign news correspondents and other observers. Not disputed was the subsequent hunt for and arrest of demonstration leaders, some of whom were condemned to death. These developments caused American, European, and Japanese businesses to pull back while the dust settled in the PRC and they reevaluated the political and business climates there. The PRC business activities in the southern coastal areas near Hong Kong hardly blinked an eye and continued to grow, and by the end of 1990, the foreign banks and businesses were again active in the PRC.

There is a new political/military fear. Several of the world's remaining dictatorships are building their armaments, including biological, poison gas, and nuclear weapons. Iraq was caught doing this, and Iran, Libya, North Korea, and Syria are in the process. Other countries such as India, Israel, and Pakistan have or are near having such weapons. With the breakup of the U.S.S.R., some of its armaments, together with the technicians to demonstrate their use, are on the market.

Japanese managers face new realities that their growing capital investments may help them deal with. The Japanese banks whose continuing growth had appeared inevitable have been shown to have feet of clay.

In the Pacific Rim there are many different markets. Globalization must yield to localization there. A Chinese connection is also developing in the area.

We shall touch on trends shaping the world. They include population/global work force, food, energy, environment, science and technology, communications, industry, education and training, world economy, warfare, and international alignments.

Privatization will take new forms. Our politicians, from presidents and prime ministers to dog catchers, may be companies.

With the collapse of the U.S.S.R. and perhaps the communist PRC government, some 80 percent of mankind, about 4 billion people, will be entering the world marketplace. Will there be a golden age of capitalism?

Let us now discuss briefly the trends and new directions we see as they regard those matters. Of course, trends frequently change directions; being proved wrong is a risk the writer of this sort of chapter must accept.

IC HOME COUNTRIES AND BANKS IN DEVELOPED HOME COUNTRIES

IC home countries those nations in which international companies are based

After World War II, U.S. companies got off to a head start with foreign investments that resulted in many U.S.-based ICs. Over the years, companies from every industrial country and many developing countries steadily increased their foreign investments. Now **IC home countries** are found throughout the world.

WORLDVIEW
Executives Find They're Always on Call as Computer, Fax Supersede Time Zones

Joanne de Asis juggles time zones.

At least two nights a week, she talks with CS First Boston's clients in Asia. If she's trying to close a deal, she may not get to sleep until three. Then, in the afternoon, when Asia is still asleep, she may take care of personal business. "Because I put in such odd hours," she says, "I have no qualms about skipping out at three in the afternoon" for a parent-teacher meeting.

But Ms. de Asis, a 40-year-old director, international, complains that it's hard to plan social activities, whether it's dinner with friends or visiting her large family. Recently, she says, she had to close a deal from the ladies' room of the Metropolitan Opera House, where she was watching the Bolshoi.

As more companies go global, their executives have less time to call their own. If they aren't traveling abroad, they're working late or being interrupted at home by calls and faxes from people in other time zones.

While few of these executives would give up their big salaries, they always seem to be on call, much like the family doctor of days gone by. And the change is being felt further down the pecking order as companies dismantle international divisions and shift down the ranks the responsibility of linking up with overseas units.

In international business, "it's almost impossible to separate your work life from your personal life," says Geoffrey M. Heal, an economics professor at the Columbia Business School. "You end up living your work."

Mr. Heal should know. Before he sold his interest last year, he was the New York–based president of Financial Telecommunications Inc., a company that provides computer and communications services to securities firms in New York, London, and Tokyo. He had a direct leased line to the London office installed by his bed as well as a facsimile machine and a personal computer. "I had to deal with people in London very early in the morning and Tokyo very late at night," he says.

Bruce Hoeffel, Minnesota Mining & Manufacturing Co.'s executive director of international human resources, argues that technological advances like faxes and electronic mail have helped managers. "There may

be more time spent at work," he says of 3M managers. "But the speed of communications that we have today has greatly aided the ability of the manager to perform global work without working 24 hours a day."

Still, faxes and electronic mail can't substitute for the personal touch that phone calls and visits provide. Last year, Arthur M. Pappas, the 44-year-old head man for Asia and Latin America at Glaxo PLC, a British pharmaceutical company, spent 43 days in London, 63 in Singapore, 47 in Raleigh, North Carolina, 22 in other U.S. states, and 123 in other countries. Mr. Pappas figures that the 20 managers who report to him around the globe are "on a more intimate discussion basis" with him because of his extensive travel. "There's no intermediary staff to sift through what their opportunities are," he says.

"You cannot use a computer to do critical decision making in a group," says Leonard Liu, president of Taiwanese computer maker Acer Group and chief executive of its U.S. unit in San Jose, California.

Mr. Liu, 49 years old, says he often talks to managers in Europe at 6:30 A.M. from his home in the San Francisco Bay area. In the evenings, he may confer with the Taipei office well into the night, again from his home. His travel schedule leaves him only 10 days a month in San Francisco, where his wife and eight-year old son live. "We are trying to globalize the company and get the people in local areas to work closely with each other," he says. "I basically make myself the bridge."

But Mr. Liu does draw the line. He has refused to install a phone in his car. The 40 minutes it takes him to drive between his home and his office is a "decompression period," he says. He adds that a spouse who can keep a semblance of regularity at home helps a lot. "My wife is the boss," he says. "When I'm not around, things don't wait to be taken care of."

Although most executives determine their own schedules, many concede that they aren't always happy with the outcome. These routines "aren't an incredibly effective and sane way of carrying on," says James Maxmin, 48, the newly appointed chief executive of Laura Ashley Holdings, PLC. They're "just the best of a series of not particularly attractive alternatives."

ARRIVE HOME
READY TO MAKE
THAT IMPORTANT
PRESENTATION.

When you fly British
Airways Club® Class,
you'll enjoy our
renowned British
service that pays
attention to every little
detail. You'll arrive
refreshed and ready
to handle anything
that needs your
personal attention.

CLUB

BRITISH AIRWAYS
The world's favourite airline®

IC executive, bearing gifts, welcomed home.

Courtesy of Saatchi & Saatchi Advertising, for British Airways

Mr. Maxmin, who used to run Thorn EMI PLC's worldwide consumer electronics and appliance rental business, has yet to find a solution to his family's "separation anxiety." While he was at Thorn, Mr. Maxmin's heavy travel schedule included commutes between London, where the company is based and where he has four children in school, and Boston, where he and his wife live. He doesn't expect the situation to change when he takes over at Laura Ashley this September.

To keep in touch while he's away, Mr. Maxmin relies on phone calls, as many as eight a day to his wife and one to his children. The huge phone bills, he says, are "the price you pay."

When he's home, he takes business calls and urgent faxes. That degree of accessibility is necessary to run an international business with few layers of management, he says. But he refuses to talk on the phone at dinner time. "Meals we try to keep sacred," he says. "It's an important time to talk and be with one another."

Mr. Maxmin also finds relief restoring a ramshackle farm in Maine. He has been logging to clear the fields and rebuilding stone walls. Putting up a wall one stone at a time "links you back to reality," he says.

Most executives agree that they have accepted midnight phone calls and computer messages as part and parcel of being in international business. "It's second nature for me," says John E. Davies, 55, who heads Ec- ogen Inc., a biological pesticide start-up based in Lang- horne, Pennsylvania. "I'm as used to it as I would be if I took the bus every morning."

When Baldwin Technology Co., a parts maker for the printing industry, sharply increased its overseas business to 65 percent of revenue, the travel schedule of its chair- man and chief executive jumped, too. Wendell Smith, 55, now spends only a fifth of his time at the executive suite in Rowayton, Connecticut, compared with 50 per- cent five years ago. "When you're growing at the rate we are, you cannot integrate acquisitions or make changes sitting at the home office," Mr. Smith says.

The change came at a good time for Mr. Smith and his wife, though. Their five daughters are grown, so they sold their family house in Rowayton and moved—fax machine in tow—to Bermuda.

As companies have crisscrossed the globe, the firms that serve them have followed. Charles J. Conroy, 37, an international law specialist with the law firm Baker &

McKenzie in New York, advises clients on three conti- nents. He recently crammed five Asian and European cit- ies into a 10-day trip, a schedule he characterizes as "easy."

Mr. Conroy says he tries to segregate his trips into two-week chunks every six weeks, so that he will be home for long stretches of time. He also takes advan- tage of his odd hours of free time. He has gone to his office at 5:30 A.M., for example, so that he can spend a few hours in the afternoon with his daughter before catching an evening plane to Europe.

But sometimes the best-laid plans can go awry. Mr. Conroy recalls being awakened at two in the morning recently by the insistent ringing of his fax machine. An Asian client was sending an 80-page message, and the machine had run out of paper midway.

Source: Lourdes Lee Valeriano, *The Wall Street Journal,* August 8, 1991, p. B1.

ICs Based in Industrial Countries

Among the world's 25 largest public companies, the home country counts in 1986, 1988, and 1991 were as follows. In 1986, U.S.-based ICs led the league with 11, while 10 were based in Japan and 4 in Europe.[1] By 1988, the num- bers had changed, with 17 based in Japan, 5 in the United States, and 3 in Europe.[2] Still another shift occurred by 1991, when there were 11 ICs with U.S. bases, 10 from Japan, and 4 Europeans.[3]

The articles listed in endnotes 1, 2, and 3 provide figures for market val- ues, annual sales, percent change from previous year, and fiscal year profit. The changes from country to country and year to year are caused by stock market price variations and company sales, but also by currency value fluctua- tions, a very important factor. All the figures are in U.S. dollars, so that for all non-U.S. companies, they must be converted from their currencies to dollars.

ICs Based in Other Countries

The only non-American, European, or Japanese IC among the world's 100 largest public companies is Broken Hill of Australia in 75th place.[4] But compa- nies based in numerous developing countries have ventured abroad. Seven very big ones are Hyundai of South Korea, Walsin Lihwa of the Republic of Chi- na, and the state oil companies of Brazil, Kuwait, Mexico, Saudi Arabia, and Venezuela, which have become ICs with factories and other holdings abroad.

As mentioned in Chapter 17, the People's Republic of China is investing in several foreign countries. Many Indian companies operate multinationally, as do companies based in Hong Kong, Singapore, the Philippines, Malaysia, Argentina, and Thailand. Some nonoil Mexican companies are spreading their investment wings abroad. They include Vitro, Cementos Mexicanos, Alfa, and Cydsa.[5]

The motives of ICs based in nonindustrial countries tend to differ somewhat from those based in industrial countries. ICs from advanced countries speak of exploiting experience with high-tech production and using marketing expertise. Those from other countries emphasize diversification of risk, high local return, experience with labor-intensive production, business associates who are relatives or countrymen in the host country, and small home markets.[6]

There are also similarities. Both groups are abroad to get and defend markets.

◻ Biggest Banks: Where Based, Strengths, and Weaknesses

Among the world's 25 largest banks, the home country counts in 1985, 1987, and 1991 were as follows. In 1985, 4 were U.S. based, 12 Japan, and 9 Europe.[7] By 1987, only 1 U.S. bank made the big 25 while there were 17 based in Japan and 7 in Europe.[8] In 1991, there was still only 1 U.S. bank among the largest 25. It was Citicorp, which had been the world's largest in 1985 but had fallen to 8th place in 1987 and 22nd in 1991. The number of Japanese banks in the top 25 in 1991 had fallen to 15 while the European-based banks increased to 9.[9]

Reasons for the greater relative growth of Japanese-based companies and banks are several. Among the most important must be included the single-minded and highly successful export policies of Japanese business and government. They have made deep penetration into North America, Europe, and most other markets—and grown rapidly in the process.

The resulting trade surpluses have provided huge amounts of dollars and other currencies for business expansion and for Japanese banks to lend and grow. At the same time, American and, to a lesser extent, European banks were lending less as they concentrated on collecting the billions they had poured out to Latin American, African, Asian, and East European borrowers during the 1970s and early 80s.

These trends have not reversed. Japan continues to run very large balance-of-trade surpluses. Moreover, as Japan begins to collect interest and profits on its foreign loans and investments, its balance-of-payments surpluses will swell.

Countervailing trends are trade protectionist measures in Europe and North America. In 1988, the United States passed a new trade act, the centerpiece of which is Section 301, which required the Bush administration to name countries that are guilty of "unfair" trade practices against the United States. In June 1989, three countries were identified, and the main target was Japan. If, after 18 months of negotiations, the United States is not satisfied that the unfair practices are ended, the law requires sanctions against imports from the offending country.

◻ Japanese Banks' Foundations Crumbling?

In November 1990, IBCA, the European credit-rating agency, downgraded six Japanese banks due to a drop in their profits following the decline of the Tokyo stock market.[10] In May 1991, the American credit-rating group, Moody's Investor Service, lowered the senior debt ratings of three Japanese banks, saying they were under "greater than average pressures" from financial liberalization in Japan and that their exposure to real estate developers was "significant."[11]

What's going on here? In 1991 it was reported that 14 of the 25 largest banks in the world were Japanese. The truth is that Japan faces a banking crisis far more menacing than the well-publicized one affecting the United States.

This truth has cast its shadow over the Japanese financial market. Those markets, widely perceived as furnishing Japan with a formidable competitive advantage, in fact have become a threat to Japanese competitiveness. The equity market can no longer supply cheap capital to expansive banks and companies. Plummeting real estate and stock prices are producing a record number of bankruptcies. Bad debts abound.

Fundamentally, the Japanese financial market lacks real capital. Asset inflation has provided both collateral for debt (needed in lieu of real capital) and paper profits needed to obscure poor operating profits. In essence, the equity and real estate markets were feeding on each other through cross-holdings and leveraged property transactions that created phantom capital.

The drop in real estate and stock prices is causing an implosion of asset values and beginning to leave its mark on Japanese banks. They lent heavily to stock market and real estate speculators during the 1980s.

Japanese government officials are undoubtedly aware of the dangers. However, they downplay or even deny them as they wish to avoid an international loss of confidence in Japanese banks and markets.[12]

BUSINESS ASIA

The world has grown accustomed to the Japanese. They have built high rises and factories, sold their products, and invested. But, if the 1980s was the decade of the Japanese, the 1990s may well belong to the overseas Chinese, who are quietly emerging as the rising Pacific power. Chinese entrepreneurs have established themselves in American industries, particularly on the West Coast; but unlike the Japanese giants whose logos are emblazoned on skylines, the Chinese presence represents more than an expression of a foreign power. Rather, it is an extension of an elaborate transnational ethnic network from Southeast Asia and the Chinese coastal provinces to the American West Coast.

◻ The Chinese in Asia

Centered in Hong Kong, Singapore, and Taipei, the roughly 50 million overseas Chinese already dominate the economies of most Southeast Asian countries, the world's fastest-growing region. They control the majority of the corporate assets in Indonesia and Thailand and dominate the Malaysian economy. The Chinese are passing the Japanese as the region's largest foreign investors. In the Chinese coastal provinces, their dominance is even more marked.

◻ The Chinese in America

The million-strong Chinese community in California is the largest outside Asia. It increasingly serves as the center for technology, marketing, and design. It is "the starter for the barbecue" says Denny Ko, president of Taiwan Aerospace. "You come up with ideas and heat the coals, and when it is hot, then you move it to another spot and light the starter again with another idea." One Taiwan Aerospace idea in 1991 was to offer $2 billion for 40 percent of the McDonnell-Douglas commercial aircraft operations.

◻ The Chinese in the Pacific Rim: "Spacemen" with Money

Unlike the Japanese, who try to keep higher-value production at home, Ko says the Chinese will be more willing to work with U.S. firms. He and many other of the Chinese businesspeople and engineers live or have lived in the United States. They shuttle back and forth between Asia and the United States as transpacific nomads and have become known in Taiwan as *tai kun fai jen,* or spacemen. Even defining the nationality of these Chinese—American, Australian, Canadian, Hong Kong Chinese, Singaporean, or Taiwanese—is not easy.

Spacemen have money.   Taiwan, the source of Ko's financing, has foreign currency reserves larger than those of any country except Japan. Overseas Chinese in Southeast Asia have an estimated wealth of more than $250 billion, and their savings rates go as high as 35 percent of income, which is more than double the rate of the thrifty Japanese.

They may represent the last readily available horde of capital in the world. Consider the U.S. banks struggling under loads of bad LDC and property debt; consider the European banks trying to finance the immense capital needs of Eastern Europe and the republics of the former U.S.S.R.; consider the fragile conditions of Japanese banks, which we discussed above in this chapter. But the overseas Chinese have lots of money.

Entrepreneurial Chinese.   All around the Pacific Rim, the Chinese have established themselves successfully in all kinds of businesses. Commercial and investment banks, manufacturing of all kinds, fashion design, and garment production are a few.

Perhaps their greatest long-term impact will be in the technology field, where Chinese companies are one of the few expanding presences. Moreover, Chinese from Taiwan and China represent the two largest groups of foreign graduate students in U.S. engineering and science programs.[13]

Spacemen not above the law.   Hong Kong has become a center of international arms traffic, legal and illegal. Henry Fok, a Hong Kong resident and one of the world's richest men with an estimated worth of $1.3 billion, made his money by supplying arms to the PRC during the Korean War. His relationships with the PRC leadership remain close.

In 1992, his son, Thomas, sat in an American jail, held without bail. As a result of a successful sting operation, he was arrested and charged with arms smuggling and money laundering. Before his arrest he had described himself as an agent of the PRC Ministry of Defense and said he had dealt with the Iranian navy, national guard, and missile forces as well as with the Pakistanian army and the Tamil Tigers of Sri Lanka. Thomas Fok's case provides a glimpse of how some of Hong Kong's wealthiest and best-established individuals travel around the world making connections and deals. He has homes in Canada and Hong Kong and was using a Canadian passport when arrested in New York. For more on the Fok story, see the Supplementary Reading by Jim Mann, "Hong Kong Is a Top Gun in Arms Traffic."

CHANGING ATTITUDES TOWARD INTERNATIONAL COMPANIES

In the European Community (EC), at the United Nations (UN), and in the host, less developed countries (LDCs), the ICs are being treated with more respect and given warmer welcomes. One notable and important exception to this has been India. But recently the minority government of P. V. Narasimha Rao has acted boldly in beginning to reduce controls and subsidies. Both the IMF and the World Bank are cooperating and trying to ease the way for India. However, publicly owned enterprises will remain dominant in large parts of the economy, and it remains to be seen how well private companies—particularly foreign-owned ones—will fare.[14]

As the EC moves along with its economic and monetary union, European companies are merging with each other and with firms from outside Europe to achieve sufficient size to compete in the new 320-million-consumer market. Competition is expected from other European companies as well as from American and Japanese firms. The EC Commission is encouraging the mergers.[15]

ICs once seemed fated to succeed colonial powers as the bogeymen of UN agencies and their LDC clients. Now they look nicer than bank loans. Of course, part of the reason for this is that bank loans are much scarcer than they were in the 1970s and 1980s, but there is much more to it than that. Third World governments are coming to appreciate the technology, employment, skills, exports, and import substitutes that ICs deliver.

TREND TOWARD GLOBAL?

Yes and no. As one writer puts it, "There's no place to hide as global companies build, buy, and sell across borders. But why hide? Wealth is multiplying, along with the markets it sustains."[16] Politicians and labor leaders, unlike businesspeople, take a parochial view of global investment, fearing loss of sovereignty and jobs. But foreign-owned companies account for more than 20 percent of German industrial production and more than 50 percent of Canadian. In Brazil, $30 billion of foreign investment is largely responsible for that country's growing automotive, office equipment, farm machinery, and pharmaceutical industries, and foreign investment in the United States is booming. None of these countries has experienced a resulting sovereignty loss. As to jobs, the foreign owners hire locals for all but the very top executive positions—and sometimes for them, too.[17]

"Think globally, act locally" is a frequently heard phrase in business. To maximize global opportunities while being sensitive to national or regional markets or requirements, executives must be both world-wise and knowledgeable about the corporate culture of their own ICs. The companies that are succeeding move executives between parent company and foreign subsidiaries on both long- and short-term assignments. Third-country nationals frequently are high in management.

Of the American motor companies, Ford is the most global, as some of its management assignments demonstrate. The managing director of Ford-Italy is French. A Norwegian runs the Ford sales company in Spain. A Belgian is in charge of the U.K. body and assembly shop. The head of Ford-U.K. is English, but before that assignment he was chief of the Brazilian operations. And so it goes throughout the company, including the movement of Europeans to senior management posts in the United States.

Ford hires M.B.A.s from business schools, who are usually given jobs outside their native countries. For its existing managers, Ford presents an international outlook at its Executive Development Center, where executives from all over the world attend sessions at least once every two years.[18]

Of course, Ford is not alone in its efforts to globalize its managers. Texas Instruments requires managers with global responsibility to meet with their overseas colleagues every quarter to set worldwide strategy.[19]

Many Occidental businesspeople think of the Orient as a homogenous region and speak of Asian people as if there were little to differentiate the Chinese from the Indonesians from the Japanese from the Koreans and so forth. If that were correct, one global approach would suffice to succeed throughout Asia. Yue-Sai Kan states emphatically that is not correct, that international businesspeople must have a **globalization-localization** mind-set. "Globalization means localization," she says, and "businesses are going to have to learn how to localize their business styles to many different markets."

Ms. Kan is hostess and executive producer of the television series, "Asia, Looking East," and "One World." Her four-part series, "Doing Business in Asia," has aired on PBS stations throughout the United States and is available on videocassette. The next Worldview, "Asia and the World," is her survey of different parts of Asia, in which she offers some advice and forecasts.

globalization-localization
the concept that, to become global, a company must tailor, or localize, its business approach to individual countries

TRADE BLOCS/FREE TRADE AREAS

Groups of nations around the world are banding together to increase trade and investment within the group. Other nations are considering beginning negotiations aimed at creating such groups.

In 1985, the United States signed a Free Trade Area (FTA) agreement with Israel that is taking effect gradually over a decade. Under the agreement, all tariffs will be phased out, as will all quotas except on certain agricultural products. Israel agreed to cease subsidizing exports to the United States. Protection of intellectual property rights were reaffirmed, and liberal investment policies have been maintained.[20]

An FTA between Canada and the United States went into effect in 1989. Those countries are each other's largest trading partners, and their two-way trade volume of some $125 billion makes it the world's biggest bilateral trade

WORLDVIEW
Asia and the World

With all the excitement over the economic integration of Europe in 1992, the democratization of Eastern Europe, and the U.S.–Canada Free Trade Agreement and potential pacts with Mexico and Chile, American businesspeople may be wondering why they need to look to the Pacific Rim for international commercial opportunities.

The reason is that practically overnight the economies of the Pacific Rim have become the hottest markets in the world. They are certainly the world's fastest-growing economies. They've been working very hard and, as a result, have become cash rich.

A swing across the Pacific Rim nations will give you an idea of just how much money is around and how much people are spending. Asia has become a very important market for American goods and services, and because Asians are spending money that they've earned—not borrowed as we have—they have a lot of money for external usage. For example, the Japanese are making $120 billion worth of foreign investments this year, and the Hong Kong Chinese and Taiwanese are also investing great amounts.

Globalization Means Localization
Business in the 1990s is not going to be local. To succeed, businesspeople are going to have to look beyond their shores. The byword of the 1990s is globalization, and globalization means localization because American businesses will have to localize their business styles to a lot of different markets. If we do not maintain competitiveness in the 1990s, we are probably going to watch ourselves become a second-class world economic power. In many ways we are already second-class, but it could get even worse.

Americans' most common misperception about Asia is that it is a homogenous whole. All the countries in Asia are distinctly different, with unique characteristics created by unique histories.

In Japan, the type of creativity, mind-set, and methodology is completely different from Hong Kong's. The concept of time is one example. The Japanese are infamous for taking practically forever to make decisions. In Hong Kong, on the other hand, there is a saying: "If you register in the morning, you can make money by the afternoon—and in the evening someone will copy you."

Midsized Firms Drive Taiwan
In Taiwan, the miracle of economic growth has been achieved principally by the 800,000 small and midsized companies which make up about 80 percent of the economy. When you do business in Taiwan, you are probably dealing with the boss. Red tape is cut, products can be produced in smaller quantities, and delivery is faster. Avon ladies in Taiwan, for example, don't mail in their orders once a week: They fax them in once a day, and ship out orders every day.

Conversely, with the Japanese it's rare to get a contract concluded in less than a year, and the average contract takes five years. This is because the key to the Japanese society is consensus and you deal with people who must put their "chops" and approvals on everything. Therefore, you must be willing to allot sufficient time to get a deal done. However, once a contract is signed, execution is very fast because all the layers of the management have already approved it.

The Korean Exception
The stereotypical Asian mind-set doesn't apply in Korea. If there is one characteristic that defines Koreans, it is impatience. They want to be rich today. They want to be successful today.

Even though the big corporations represent the driving force behind the Korean economy (which is dominated by 40 or 50 huge companies), these companies are family businesses that tend to be run by one person. Business is conducted much faster than in Japan where consensus rules. Korea does have consensus, but it's a different type of consensus because the huge Japanese companies are not owned by one person: The man who runs Mitsubishi didn't start Mitsubishi.

Entrepreneurial and Global-Minded
If any characteristics can be said to be common to all Asian peoples, it is that they are all entrepreneurial and global-minded. While American business can't be condemned for a lack of entrepreneurialism, U.S. companies have lacked the global perspective that has made Asian companies the worldwide powerhouses they are today.

American businesses who aspire to success in global markets can learn some lessons from the experience of these Asian companies. When these entrepreneurs entered the U.S. market 20 years ago, they didn't know our language. Asians were still mysterious to most Americans, and Americans were equally mystifying to them.

What they did was—and there was no trick to this—they studied the market; they made mistakes; they tried again; they learned our language; they learned our lifestyles; they modified their products to our likes and dislikes; and, finally, they improved their products to the point where they were better than ours. Not surprisingly, they captured large shares of our market.

This was not achieved overnight. The lessons to learn from the Asians are patience and the value of investing the time to learn a market. You can't expect to walk into a meeting in Asia with a contract in your pocket, and walk out with the contract signed. One of the biggest mistakes Americans make is to charge in like a bulldozer. Many Americans don't seem to realize that they're doing business in a completely different environment. As a result, Americans often end up offending their Asian hosts—unintentionally, yes, but damaging all the same. Perhaps the best advice is: If you have to be successful the first time you go, don't go.

Trust Is Key

In most Asian countries (except possibly Hong Kong) people still need to get to know you, learn to trust you. The key word for doing business in these countries is "personal." American business is far less personal. American business tends to focus exclusively on price and product quality. Personal relationships play a very small part. Asians are legendary for sealing business deals with a handshake but, before this can happen, there has to be trust. This can take time, but after your first contract, the second is virtually automatic because Asians prefer to do business with people they like and know and trust.

Another business area where Asians differ is price. The Japanese will pay for the best quality they can find, whether for cars, luggage, or whiskey. This is not the case in other Pacific Rim countries like the Philippines or Thailand, and the Chinese are obsessed with getting the best deal. In Japan, if the quality is there, price is an afterthought. However, don't expect other Asians to share their cavalier attitudes toward pricing.

The Question of Hong Kong

One event that has raised speculation about the fate of the Pacific Rim in the next decade is the return of Hong Kong to China in 1997. Apprehension has grown since Tienanmen Square. One has to realize that the Chinese consider June 4 an isolated event, an internal affair. And it is immaterial to the Chinese whether you agree with their point of view or not.

Hong Kong is different because China knows it is an international affair. The Chinese government really does intend to keep Hong Kong the way it is. Anyone interested in doing business in Hong Kong over the long term should look at Hong Kong's constitution. It was five years in the making and everything in it indicates that Hong Kong will stay the same: It will remain a free port; it will have its own free currency; it will be left very much to itself, especially in economic areas.

Looking toward the Pacific Rim Century

Only one word can describe the Pacific Rim economies by the turn of the century: huge. Of course the big news right now is Eastern Europe. But the development of Eastern Europe is also very good for Asia, as this gives them more new markets to conquer. However, in regard to investment opportunities, remember that Eastern Europe lacks a decent infrastructure. I was in Dresden several months ago and couldn't even make a phone call. Even the less developed nations (LDNs) of Asia have more advanced infrastructures. You can make direct long-distance calls from many parts of China.

In the coming years, LDNs like Indonesia and Malaysia will become the focal points in the region. They are blessed with resources, huge populations, and very stable governments. These countries will grow very fast.

The Future Has Arrived

The trend of the future has already begun. If a Japanese company wants to manufacture an electronic product and believes it can be produced more cheaply in Taiwan, it may produce the components in Taiwan, and then ship the components to the Philippines or Malaysia where there are tax incentives for assembly operations.

In the next 10 years, Asia will grow to become its own best market. Still, the Pacific Rim countries will always consider the United States a primary market. They can't afford not to, just as U.S. companies can't afford to overlook Japan—the second largest market in the world—and other Pacific Rim markets.

Protectionist threats and the possibility of recession in America concern countries the world over, as their economies are largely influenced by what happens to the U.S. economy. This is particularly true for the Pacific Rim nations. However, in 10 years, as they become more self-sufficient, their dependence is certain to diminish.

Source: Reprinted from *Export Today Magazine*, November–December 1990, by permission of the publisher, Trade Communications, Inc., 733 15th Street, N.W., Washington, D.C. 20005.

relationship. As with the Israeli agreement, the FTA with Canada will be phased in over a 10-year period.

In 1991, negotiations commenced to bring Mexico into the U.S.–Canada FTA. The Mexican leadership was enthusiastic about such an agreement and campaigned in Canada and the United States in favor of it. Many Canadians feel their FTA with the United States is not developing as well for them as they wished and are leery of expanding it to include Mexico. However, it is clear that Mexico and the United States will proceed with negotiations, and Canada wants a place at the negotiating table.

In the United States, there are opponents and proponents of an FTA with Mexico. Organized labor is unanimous in its opposition because it fears loss of jobs as employers move south to take advantage of lower Mexican wage rates. Many environmentalists oppose an agreement because they do not believe Mexico has or will enforce laws to clean up and keep clean the land and streams along the Mexican–U.S. border.

Proponents argue that new foreign investment will create many new jobs in Mexico, bringing up their wage rates. In the meantime, this argument continues, rising Mexican income will create growing markets for U.S. goods, thus saving and creating jobs in the United States.

As to the environment, the Mexican government maintains it will bring its laws and practices up to U.S. standards. American government officials are cooperating with their Mexican counterparts in those efforts.

Still another argument for the Mexican agreement is that the jobs created in Mexico following an agreement would prevent many Mexicans from illegally immigrating into the United States. The alternative, some say, would be an invasion, as millions of unemployed Mexicans poured into the United States in search of work.

□ A Western Hemisphere FTA?

In 1990, President Bush announced an Enterprise for the Americas Initiative to encourage free trade agreements among Western Hemisphere nations. Most of those nations welcomed it enthusiastically. That was certainly the case in Argentina, Brazil, Chile, and Paraguay. One of the authors traveling through those countries after the announcement read favorable comments in the press and heard supportive, optimistic statements by academic, business, and government people with whom he spoke.

While Canada, Mexico, and the United States are busily negotiating in North America, other Western Hemisphere nations are not idle. In June 1991, the United States signed a framework trade agreement with Argentina, Brazil, Paraguay, and Uruguay designed to move the nations toward more liberal trade relations. In addition, the United States has signed bilateral trade agreements with Bolivia, Chile, Colombia, Costa Rica, Ecuador, El Salvador, Honduras, Peru, and Venezuela. It is negotiating similar agreements with Guatemala, Nicaragua, Panama, and a group of 13 Caribbean nations.[21]

Also in 1991, Argentina, Brazil, Paraguay, and Uruguay signed the Treaty of Asunción, creating the Mercosul trade zone. The pact aims to create a free trade zone by the start of 1995. Six months after the signing, Mercosul was showing surprisingly promising results with a large upswing of trade between the member-countries and a rash of accords between governments and private companies for political and economic cooperation.[22]

Chile may reach an FTA with the United States before Mexico does. There are fewer complications and opponents to the Chilean agreement. For one thing, the environmentalists have no fear of pollution from Chile due to its distance from U.S. borders. In addition, U.S. labor seems to worry little about loss of jobs to Chilean production.

Also, if complications slow an agreement with Mexico, establishing one with Chile would demonstrate that agreement is possible. It is hoped that would forestall disillusionment and waning interest in other Latin countries.[23]

In 1992, a group of Andean countries began implementation of a free trade zone. Bolivia, Colombia, Ecuador, Peru, and Venezuela began the process of abolishing trade barriers.[24]

□ Europe

Not to be outdone, the European Community is developing its own bloc, which will result in a market of 320 million relatively—or very—affluent consumers. When the European Free Trade Association joins the EC to create the European Economic Area (EEA), there will be a market of 380 million, even more affluent, consumers. Eastern European countries that were members of the ex-COMECON are lining up to get in. We dealt with these subjects in Chapter 4.

□ FTAs versus EEA?

A potential conflict exists between the current and possible future Western Hemisphere FTAs and the EEA. In other words, they could lower trade and investment barriers among members while maintaining or raising them against outsiders. This would damage all the countries and lower their citizens' standards of living.

That should not and need not happen, but at least one author recommends using FTA leverage to discourage the EEA from becoming a Fortress Europe.[25] Of course, the leverage would work both ways.

□ FTAs and the GATT

The General Agreement on Tariffs and Trade (GATT) has over 90 member-countries, and some argue that GATT would be a better forum for trade liberalization than FTAs. However, there need be no conflict between GATT reforms and FTAs. If FTA members recognize and enjoy the economic benefits of open markets, it makes no sense for them to forgo those benefits because other nations are not as wise.

It has been pointed out that FTAs could help in the GATT process. As the GATT Uruguay Round is dealing with trade problems not touched in earlier rounds, such as subsidies, services, government procurement, and intellectual property, solutions negotiated in an FTA could provide guidance for the GATT solutions.[26]

Latin politicians do not view a successful conclusion to the GATT Uruguay Round talks as a prerequisite for their own free trade aspirations. If those talks fail or end in weak compromises, countries could speed up the Western Hemisphere agreements, if only for self-preservation.[27]

One author, Robert Lawrence, says arrangements such as the EEA and FTAs can be building blocks rather than stumbling blocks for the world economy. He points out that they can boost growth and promote trade with countries outside the blocs and that countries cannot prosper without trade outside their own regions.[28]

POLITICAL DEVELOPMENTS AFFECT BUSINESS

This heading has been rendered a truism by events during the late 1980s and into the 1990s. Most of the former U.S.S.R. republics now compose the Commonwealth of Independent States. Those nations, along with the former Soviet satellite states of Eastern Europe, are groping from centrally controlled economies toward market economies. Most Latin American countries are now democracies and are negotiating toward a Western Hemisphere FTA.

Democratic movements are stirring in a number of African countries, some of which are cooperating with the IMF and the World Bank to develop market economies. In South Africa, apartheid laws have been repealed, and black African leaders have been released from prison and permitted to return from exile. Negotiations are under way to form a democratic government. As a result, Europe, Japan, and the United States have ended or relaxed many of the sanctions against trade with or investment in South Africa.

Tensions and fears stemming from the cold war between NATO and the Warsaw Pact nations have been replaced by a new danger: the proliferation of biological, nuclear, and poison gas weapons and the expertise to build and use them. Although the Soviet Union has collapsed, its thousands of weapons together with the people who built them and know how to use them are still there.

Several rich third world countries, such as Iran, Iraq, Libya, and Syria, would like to buy and hire them. The potentials for disaster are real.[29]

TRENDS SHAPING THE WORLD

The world has moved past the post–World War II era. NATO and the Warsaw Pact are no longer threatening each other with their nuclear and other arsenals. As the Iraq–Kuwait war illustrates, wars are not behind us, but they will be regional, which is not to say they won't be extremely dangerous. Consider the growing number of countries that have or soon will have biological, nuclear, and poison gas weapons.

Investment and trade will be greatest in three geographic blocs of nations—Europe, the Pacific Rim, and the Western Hemisphere. That will leave vast regions of the world, such as Africa, the Indian subcontinent, and Southeast Asia, doomed to poverty largely by their own leaders. Yet even those nations should benefit from the new global structure because in a more prosperous world, the developed countries will be better able to help the less fortunate.

Several trends will shape the world. We have identified 12.

□ Population

The rich get richer; the poor have children. Throughout the industrialized world, workers have retirement programs such as social security. In the developing lands, those too old for labor rely on their children to support them, so they have as many as they can.

Surprisingly, while the richer countries' peoples grow more conscious of personal health, developing countries are adopting unhealthy practices such as smoking, high-fat diets, and sedentary life-styles. Already devastating some LDCs is AIDS. According to the World Health Organization, AIDS will have infected 40 million by the year 2000; sub-Saharan Africa is especially hard hit, and the infection is spreading fast in Southeast Asia.

□ Food

Farmers will continue to harvest more food than the world needs, but inefficient delivery systems will prevent it from reaching the hungry. This will be particularly true in former Iron Curtain countries.

□ Energy

Despite all the calls to develop alternative sources of energy, oil will provide more of the world's power in 2000 than it did in 1990. This is partly because oil prices will be low. A reason for low prices is the low cost to lift oil, which ranges from $1.38 per barrel in Saudi Arabia to $5.00 per barrel in Prudhoe Bay and the North Sea.

In addition, the industrialized nations have some three months of supplies in storage and can hold off buying if OPEC prices get too high. Contributing to this is OPEC's inability to cut back production very effectively when the market is glutted.

Some competition from other energy sources will help hold oil prices down. Natural gas, solar, geothermal, wind-generated, wave-generated, and nuclear energies are possible alternatives.

Windy places can generate their own energy.

Courtesy of Pacific Gas & Electric

◻ Environment

Air pollution and other atmospheric issues will dominate eco-policy discussions for many years. Carbon dioxide is concentrating in the atmosphere, with global warming said to be a result.

The earth's rain forests in Brazil and elsewhere are being destroyed for very temporary economic gain. That will cease as the IMF and World Bank help underwrite alternatives.

Disposal of the world's trash is a growing problem. Recycling is a necessity, and recyclables will become valuable resources by 2000.

◻ Science and Technology

Technology has come to dominate the economy and society in the developed countries. Its central role can only grow. In home and industry, robots will perform more and more tasks.

The technology gap between developed and developing countries will continue to widen. This will aggravate the disparity in income and trade, leaving the LDCs to exporting natural resources and low-tech manufactures.

◻ Communications

The world's communications networks will grow at increasing velocity. A person equipped with a mini-transceiver will be able to send a message anywhere in the world.

Computers and communications are quickly finding their way into information synthesis and decision making. Word processors will be able to transcribe dictation through voice recognition. Computers will translate documents from language to language.

◻ Labor

Low birthrates in developed countries will result in fewer young workers. Higher birthrates in LDCs will offset that to some extent. Table 23−1 shows the aging of the world's work force and population.

Labor union membership is declining in the United States. According to the United Automobile Workers, union members in the work force will fall to 12 percent by 1995 from 17.5 percent in 1986, and will continue down to 10 percent by 2000. Membership in Latin America and the Pacific Rim will remain low, and in the developing world it will be extremely low.

More women will continue to enter the work force. The percentage of women working outside the home or farm differs greatly from country to country, largely because of religious practices and social expectations. Those practices and expectations are changing, and as labor shortages occur, women will emerge to take the unfilled jobs.

◻ Industry

International companies will continue to grow, and many new ones will appear. Demands will grow for industry to increase its social responsibility, and companies increasingly will be judged on how they treat the environment.

◻ Education and Training

Most developed countries have literacy rates of more than 95 percent. The proportion of illiterates among the world's adult population has decreased, although the absolute number has grown. This is particularly true in the developing nations.

Educational rethinking is changing the American schools. In the long run, this will repair the nation's competitive position in the world economy.

◻ World Economy

The world economy will grow at a rapid rate for the foreseeable future, but the gap between the rich and poor countries will widen. The poor countries will fall further and further behind because their populations will continue to grow faster than their incomes.

The world economy will be increasingly integrated. Investment markets will become closely connected. All major currencies will be linked and convertible using a model similar to the EMS's exchange rate mechanism.

□ **TABLE 23–1**
The World's Work Force and Population Are Aging

Country or Region	Share of Work Force under Age 34		Share of Population over Age 65		Labor Force Participation of Workers over Age 65
	1985	2000	1985	2000	1985
World*	**57.1%**	**51.7%**	**5.9%**	**6.8%**	**32.8%**
Developed regions†	**46.9**	**40.7**	**11.2**	**13.3**	**9.0**
United States	50.4	39.5	12.3	12.9	10.3
Japan	33.8	33.9	11.1	15.8	26.0
Germany	45.7	37.4	14.2	16.0	3.2
United Kingdom	43.6	38.8	15.5	15.4	4.6
France	47.0	41.5	13.6	15.6	3.0
Italy	48.0	44.6	14.0	16.7	3.9
Spain	49.9	49.0	9.1	11.5	3.8
Canada	50.9	39.7	11.1	13.1	7.1
Australia	50.7	44.4	10.7	11.6	5.1
Sweden	38.7	36.3	16.9	17.2	5.4
Developing regions†	**60.7**	**54.9**	**4.2**	**5.1**	**26.3**
China	63.7	53.3	5.5	7.3	16.0
India	55.6	52.0	3.4	4.1	40.1
Indonesia	55.7	52.7	2.8	4.2	38.3
Brazil	62.5	42.1	4.0	4.9	17.7
Pakistan	63.3	59.2	4.1	3.9	33.7
Thailand	62.8	55.2	3.9	5.2	27.2
Mexico	61.4	51.9	4.1	4.9	42.1
Turkey	59.6	54.4	4.3	5.2	10.9
Philippines	59.2	54.8	3.3	3.8	44.8
South Korea	54.7	44.2	4.5	5.9	26.5
U.S.S.R.	50.2	42.9	9.3	11.9	4.4

*Totals include some countries not listed in table.
†Developed and developing regions as defined by the International Labour Office.
Source: International Labour Office, *Economically Active Population, 1950–2025;* and *Yearbook of Labour Statistics, 1988.*

Aid to the poorer countries will be money that would have been spent on armaments. The IMF and World Bank will help distribute aid, and developing countries may have to set up population control programs to be eligible.

□ **War**

Iraqi President Saddam Hussein was only the first of many small despots who will try to win by conquest what cannot be achieved by negotiation. Some of the likely wars will be Israel versus the Arab countries, India versus Pakistan, and Northern Ireland versus itself.

In the Middle East, "the enemy of your enemy is your friend." Iran and Iraq will tolerate each other because of their stronger hatred of the West. The United States and Syria will never be friends, but both dislike Iraq. Turkey and Greece will be hard-pressed to overlook their differences about Cyprus but may do so in an effort to counter terrorism.

A. Tannenbaum/SYGMA

Some forms of terrorism will always be with us.

□ International Alignments

The information revolution has enabled many people formerly insulated from outside influences to compare their lives with those of people in other countries. East Germans learned via West German TV; Romanians learned through Hungarian media.

International broadcasting entities such as Voice of America, the British Broadcasting Corporation, and Cable News Network disseminate information around the world, sometimes influencing and inspiring events as they report on them. These trends can only spread as world telecommunications networks become ever more tightly linked.

As people learn more, they break up old alignments and form new ones. Here are some forecasts.

Yugoslavia will split into a loose confederation based on the region's three dominant religions—Greek Orthodoxy, Roman Catholicism, and Islam. Czechoslovakia will loosen the ties between the Czech and Slovak regions. The Communist party and elements of the Soviet armed forces will attempt another coup that will fail, and a commonwealth of 15 largely independent states will evolve.

Quebec will secede from Canada. Shortly thereafter, the four eastern Canadian provinces will join the United States, and the other Canadian provinces will follow suit later.

Hong Kong and Macao will join the PRC, and the Republic of China (Taiwan) will later negotiate its affiliation with the mainland. The two Koreas will reunite during the 1990s.

Cooperation will develop among intelligence and police agencies such as Interpol, the CIA, and the KGB. They will combat terrorism and crime worldwide.

PRIVATIZATION ABOLISHES POLITICIANS

The advantage of privately owned over government-owned enterprises has been stated as follows. Everybody working in private business, from the entrepreneur through the work force, gets more money if the business makes money, or profits. Too many losses, and they go bust. People in public activities learned they got more money if they failed to make money because they could then demand more government financing.[30]

◻ Railways and Highways

As highway traffic jams become less and less bearable, societies will turn to the railways. An electronic attachment on each highway vehicle will be activated whenever it enters an area where it adds to traffic jams. The device will record the distance the vehicle travels and time it spends in that area. The vehicle owner will be billed at discouragingly high rates for the distance and time. More efficient railroad operations will make them profitable, and both they and the highways will be privatized.

◻ Prisons

Prisons are a ridiculous public service with negative gross production. Instead of curing criminals, they create recidivists. A 20-year-old person sent to prison is more likely to become a habitual criminal than one who narrowly escapes being sent there.

Entrepreneurs of private prisons will be paid more if released prisoners do not recommit offenses. The prison company will suffer financially if its graduate is again convicted of a crime.

◻ Lawyers

People will recognize that most of the work of lawyers can be done more quickly by telecommuting into programs that interpret the law. They will answer your specific questions, and cases in noncriminal law will then be settled increasingly by each side putting its case to the computer and agreeing to accept its verdict.

Lawyers will be needed longer in the criminal law system, but even there it is conceivable that criminals will agree to plea bargain after seeing on computer files all the evidence against them and getting the computer's judgment of how little chance they have of getting away with their defense.

This could be a popular option for the criminals if they were offered a choice of not going to prison. It costs some $50,000 a year to keep a person in prison. Private organizations would be paid the $50,000 in return for which they would agree to reform the criminal within the community. Of course, if the reform fails, the reform company would repay some or all the $50,000.

◻ Municipal Services

Companies will compete on state, county, and city ballots for election to provide police, street cleaning, garbage collection, street, sewer repairs, and whatever other services for a stated amount. If they do not satisfy the citizens, they can be thrown out of office at the next election or recalled.

◻ Presidents and Prime Ministers

Competing companies will present cabinets of people who will explain the qualities and types of government they propose to offer. They will set forth the costs they foresee, which will involve little or no new taxes. Be sure to read their lips.

SUMMARY

As worldwide telecommunications and travel become more efficient and rapid, executive families will have to adapt life-styles. That will be equally true for one- or two-career couples.

Political events are affecting business. COMECON, the Soviet-dominated trade bloc, no longer exists, and its former members are trying in varying ways to develop market economies. They want investment from and trade with the West. Although the PRC still has a hard-line communist government, some private businesses are thriving there, particularly in the coastal provinces.

Most ICs are based in Europe, Japan, and North America. However, growing numbers are now calling developing and newly industrialized countries home.

Most of the world's biggest banks are Japanese, but weaknesses have materialized in the Japanese banking system. Much of its lending has been for speculative stock market and real estate investments. As stock and property values tumble, the capital bases of Japanese banks are crumbling.

Overseas Chinese have become a potent business force, particularly in the Pacific Rim. They may represent the world's last readily available hoard of capital.

Attitudes toward ICs have improved in the EC, at the UN, and among LDCs. The ICs are more and more appreciated for the technology, capital, and management expertise they can furnish.

"Think globally, but act locally" is a phrase often heard. ICs are expanding globally but are learning they must be sensitive to local cultures and tastes that differ greatly from country to country even in the same geographic area, for example, Africa, Asia, Europe, and the Americas.

Trade blocs and free trade areas are being negotiated. They involve Asian, European, and Western Hemisphere groups. While some fear they may be protectionist and lead to trade wars, others believe they can complement GATT and stimulate more rather than less trade and investment.

Trends shaping the world are in areas such as population, food, energy, environment, science and technology, communications, labor, industry, education and training, world economy, war, and international alignments.

Finally, it is possible that private businesses may replace politicians. People would elect the companies that offered the best services at the lowest costs to perform practically all of what are now called public services. If the companies promise to keep taxes down, be sure to read their lips.

QUESTIONS

1. Why have Japanese banks grown more rapidly than those based in Europe or the United States?

2. Do Japanese banks now seem as strong as they once appeared? Discuss.

3. What does Section 301 of the 1988 U.S. trade act provide?

4. Why are ICs becoming more popular with the EC, the UN, and LDC host countries?

5. Discuss some differences in the motives of ICs based in industrialized countries as compared to those based in LDCs or newly industrialized countries.

6. Are some products being tailored for national or regional markets? Why?

7. Who are the "spacemen" introduced in this chapter? What are they doing?

8. What are free trade areas (FTAs)?

9. Will FTAs necessarily conflict with GATT processes? Discuss.

10. Will FTAs necessarily conflict with EC 1992? Discuss.

11. a. Read your newspapers and periodicals, and discuss how political events are affecting business in the PRC.

    b. Do the same concerning the former Soviet Union.

    c. Choose some other area of the world and do the same.

12. What changes are occurring in the world labor pool?

13. How can management deal with the changes of available labor?

14. Discuss the concept of privatizing the politicians out of existence.

▫ MINICASE 23–1

Competition within the Multinational

MC is a multinational with subsidiary manufacturing plants in several countries around the world. MC has just won a very large contract to supply locomotives to Paraguay, which is modernizing its entire railway system with financing from the World Bank.

MC's home country is the United States, and it could manufacture parts or all of the locomotives in its U.S. plants. MC subsidiary companies in Spain, Mexico, and Australia could also manufacture parts or all of the locomotives. The managers of all those subsidiaries know about the big new contract, and each is eager to get the work involved in performing it.

A meeting of the subsidiary chief executive officers (CEOs) is called at MC's headquarters in New York to discuss which plant or plants will get the work. The manager of the American locomotive plant is also at the meeting, and she makes a strong case for giving her plant the work.

It has laid off 1,000 workers, and this big job would permit it to recall them. In addition, the American plant has all of the latest technology, some of which has not been supplied to the subsidiary companies.

The subsidiary CEOs each argue that there is unemployment in their countries too, and that as responsible citizens they must hire more local people. Each CEO also points out that hiring local people would reduce hostility toward the subsidiary in the host country and give it defenses against left-wing attacks on foreign-owned companies. One CEO suggests that each plant enter competitive bids and let Paraguayan Railways make the decision.

You are the CEO of MC, and you have the authority and responsibility to allocate parts or all of the work to one or more of the plants. List and explain the considerations that will govern your decisions.

SUPPLEMENTARY READINGS

Bartlett, Christopher A., and Sumantra Ghoshal. "Organizing for Worldwide Effectiveness: The Transnational Solution." *California Management Review*, Fall 1988, pp. 54–74.

Byrne, A. John, and G. David Wallace. "For More and More Foreign Companies, America Isn't Paved with Gold." *Business Week*, February 3, 1986, p. 84.

Cannon, Frederick, Peter Allen, and W. Bruce Wydick. "California, Mexico, and the North American Free Trade Agreement." *Economic & Business Outlook*, Bank of America, September–October 1991, pp. 1–6.

Casson, Mark. *Multinational and World Trade Vertical Integration and the Division of Labor in World Industries.* London: Allen & Unwin, 1986.

Cetron, Marvin, and Owen Davies. "50 Trends Shaping the World." *The Futurist,* September–October 1991, pp. 11–21.

Davidson, W. H., and D. G. McFetridge. "Recent Directions in International Strategies: Production Rationalization or Portfolio Adjustment?" *Columbia Journal of World Business,* Summer 1984, pp. 95–101.

Dornbusch, Rudiger. "If Mexico Propers, So Will We." *The Wall Street Journal,* April 11, 1991, p. 14.

Eaker, R. Mark, and Loan Lenowitz. "Multinational Borrowing Decisions and the Empirical Exchange Rate Evidence." *Management International Review,* Winter 1986, pp. 24–35.

Erdilek, Asim. "Multinationals in Mutual Invaders: Intra-Industry Direct Foreign Investment." *Journal of International Business Studies,* Summer 1986, pp. 182–91.

Fisher, Bart S., and Jeff Turner, eds. *Regulating the Multinational Enterprise: National and International.* New York: Praeger Publishers, 1983.

Flamn, Kenneth. *The Global Factory: Foreign Assembly in International Trade.* Washington, D.C.: Brookings Institution, 1985.

Fraser, Damian. "NAFTA Free Trade Talks Reaching Most Critical Stage." *Financial Times,* October 8, 1991, p. 8.

Ghosh, Pradip K., ed. *Multinational Cooperation and Third World Development.* Westport, Conn.: Greenwood Press, 1984.

Grosse, Robert. "Financial Transfer in the MNE: The Latin American Case." *Management International Review,* Winter 1986, pp. 33–42.

Hall, R. Quane. *Overseas Acquisitions and Mergers: Combining for Profits Abroad.* New York: Praeger Publishers, 1986.

Hennast, Jean. *A Theory of Multinational Enterprise.* Ann Arbor: University of Michigan Press, 1982.

Hladik, Karen F. *International Joint Ventures: An Economic Analysis of U.S.–Foreign Business Partnerships.* Lexington, Mass.: Lexington Books, 1985.

"Japanese Banks: America Cracks Down." *The Economist,* January 18, 1992, pp. 80 and 82.

"Japanese Banks' Bad-Debt Troubles." *The Economist,* September 14, 1991, pp. 97–98.

"Japanese Banks Deep in Bad Debt." *The Economist,* November 2, 1991, pp. 70–72.

Johnston, William B. "Global Work Force 2000: The New World Labor Market." *Harvard Business Review,* March–April 1991, pp. 115–26.

Kester, Carl, and Timothy A. Luehrman. "Why Dollar Bashing Doesn't Work: Effect of Cheapening Currency on Manufacturers." *Fortune,* October 27, 1986, pp. 137–39.

Lachenmayer, Hubert. "The Effect of Currency Exchange Risks on the Cost of Equity Capital of the International and Multinational Firm." *Management International Review,* Spring 1984, pp. 28–36.

Linsberry, Gary. "American Insurance Companies Help Overseas Corporate Subsidiaries to Comply with Pension Legislation." *Barron's,* November 3, 1986, p. 50.

Macrae, Norman. "A Future History of Privatization, 1992–2022." *The Economist,* January 3, 1992, pp. 15–18.

Mann, Jim. "Hong Kong Is a Top Gun in Arms Traffic." *Los Angeles Times,* January 18, 1992, pp. A1 and 14.

McGurn, William. "Freeing Trade." *National Review,* May 13, 1991, pp. 21 and 24.

Pratten, Cliff. "The Importance of Giant Companies." *Lloyds Bank Review,* January 1986, p. 33.

Rapoport, Carla. "Tough Times for Japan's Banks." *Fortune,* July 16, 1990, pp. 66–69.

Simon, Barnard. "Work Starts on Free Zone from Arctic to Acapulco." *Financial Times,* June 12, 1991, p. 2.

"South American Common Market." *Review of the Economic Situation of Mexico,* Banamex, June 1991, pp. 259–63.

Sprinivasan, Venkat, and Yong H. Kim. "Payments Netting in International Cash Management: A Network Optimization Approach." *Journal of International Business Studies,* Summer 1986, pp. 1–11.

Swanson, E. Peggy. "Portfolio Diversification by Currency Denomination: An Approach to International Cash Management with Implications for Foreign Exchange Markets." *Quarterly Review of Economics and Business,* Spring 1986, pp. 95–106.

Szala, Ginger. "How Multinational Firms Use Futures and Options: Currency Trading One Way to Curb Risk." *Futures,* September 1985, pp. 54–61.

Wilson, Elizabeth. "The Impact of the Dollar on High-Tech Multinationals." *Electronic Business,* May 15, 1985, pp. 59–66.

ENDNOTES

1. *Forbes,* July 26, 1986, p. 54 ©Forbes, Inc., 1986.
2. *The Wall Street Journal,* September 23, 1988, p. R18.
3. *The Wall Street Journal,* September 20, 1991, p. R8.
4. Ibid.
5. Damian Fraser, "Vitro Heads Mexico's U.S. Drive," *Financial Times,* August 10–11, 1991, p. 10.
6. Louis T. Well, Jr., *Third World Multinationals: The Risk of Foreign Investment from Developing Countries* (Cambridge, Mass.: MIT Press, 1983).
7. *Worldscope,* 1986.
8. *The Wall Street Journal,* September 23, 1986, p. R19.
9. *The Wall Street Journal,* September 20, 1991, p. R9.
10. Deborah Hargreaves, "Japanese Banks Lose Top IBCA Rating," *Financial Times,* November 5, 1990, p. 19.
11. Robert Thomson, "Moody's Downgrades Three Japanese Banks," *Financial Times,* May 3, 1991, p. 22.
12. Daniel J. Kreps, "The Hidden Crisis: Japan's Banks Pose Threat to Its Economy," *Barron's,* January 6, 1992, pp. 15–25.
13. Joel Kotkin, "The Chinese Connection," *Los Angeles Times,* December 22, 1991, p. M1.
14. "Perestroika in India," *Financial Times,* August 7, 1991, p. 8.
15. John Robinson, "The European Commission: A New-Found Friend of Business," *International Management,* September 1986, pp. 70–74.
16. Richard I. Kirkland, Jr., "Entering a New Age of Boundless Competition," *Fortune,* March 14, 1988, pp. 40–48.
17. Ibid.
18. Michael Skapinker, "Ford's Cosmopolitan Carousel," *Financial Times,* May 12, 1989, p. 9.
19. Andrew Kupfer, "The Long Arm of Jerry Junkins," *Fortune,* March 14, 1988, p. 28.
20. Edward L. Hudgins, "Free Trade Areas: Removing Trade Obstacles and Bucking Protection," *Backgrounder,* no. 587, The Heritage Foundation, June 17, 1987.
21. "U.S. Signs Trade Pacts with Latin Nations," *The Wall Street Journal,* June 21, 1991, p. B4.
22. Christina Lamb, "South America's Mercosul Trade Zone Leaps Ahead," *Financial Times,* October 30, 1991, p. 6.
23. George Holding Taylor, "Chile Can Win on Fast Track," *The Wall Street Journal,* November 1, 1991, p. A15.

"They helped with translators and things like letterheads; they even found us a butcher to supply a party when we left them," says Hartley. Today, Psion operates from smart new offices in Bad Homburg. This enables it to skirt another potential snag—high city rents. Being just outside Frankfurt, its rents are only DM19 a square metre, compared with DM45 in central Frankfurt.

Once out of the Lairco fold, she found the biggest hurdle was the bureaucracy. "I saw it as a challenge. I took it in my stride. All the requirements have got to be adhered to, and it is important to do them correctly. It became a matter of egoism."

Actually establishing the subsidiary—the most common form is the GmbH (Gesellschaft mit beschränkter Haftung), a limited company—is the least of the obstacles. That requires a minimum capital of DM50,000 ($27,000) and can be done, with the necessary lawyers' signatures and official registration, in under two months.

More frustrating are practical matters like telephones, accommodation, furniture, cars, and, not least, staff.

Here Hartley has a few words of warning. Furniture can take up to 10 weeks to arrive, because suppliers work to orders. "So at first, it was a bit sparse here." For cars, too, the German practice can be frustrating. The leasing company insisted on bank guarantees for Psion's first three cars.

Taking on staff may also be a headache. A top bilingual secretary can cost DM5,000 a month. "Just hiring a secretary can be such an important first step," says Alexander Lairo. "Some look for foreign companies because they know how to take advantage of them."

Under strict labor laws, inefficient staff cannot easily be fired. On the other hand, many Germans are skeptical about working for foreign, especially small, companies—wondering how long they will last.

"We employ people at the start of each quarter," says Hartley. This is normal German practice. "In England, people tend to come and go." In Germany, most employees want security and are thinking of their pension rights at a young age. "We wanted to employ one woman as a secretary, and her husband wanted to know all about our parent and its activities." In the end, she decided the job was too risky.

To guard against disappointments on both sides, a probationary period of three months is usual for most staff, with six for managers. Also, employees expect to be paid a 13th month, though this does not necessarily mean the total sum is any different from what they would receive on a 12-month basis.

Germans are also used to better working conditions that those existing in many other countries. Comments John Brennan, head of Access Business Services, a similar operation to Lairco: "Germans expect bigger offices than maybe their chairman would occupy in the United States."

That may be the least of the differences, however. At the German headquarters of Toys "R" Us in Cologne, Joseph Baczko, president of its international division, explains how a raft of objections was thrown up by outsiders when the group considered coming to Germany: "We were told the Germans like wooden toys and are keen on technical things. Well, we sell a lot of plastic, we are self-service, and we sell both technical and nontechnical items."

Some local manufacturers also thought Toys "R" Us would be better advised to go for 5,000 square feet instead of its usual 45,000-square-foot stores. It ignored this.

"We were told we wouldn't get the permission," adds Baczko, "Our management has to come face to face with the conventional wisdom every day and challenge it."

The U.S. concern has done so to the extent that it now has 12 stores in Germany. Its goal is 50.

Because busy young German mothers are used to hypermarkets and supermarkets, says Baczko, they have taken to the all-embracing Toys "R" Us concept, where a host of products is offered all year round and not just at Christmas.

Even the limited shopping hours in Germany are not seen as a hindrance, though Baczko does not regard them as immutable. "We didn't come to Germany just to get market share. We aim to be number one, and we will be. In that way, restrictive trading practices work in our favor. We are the point of convenience for the customer."

To obtain the edge-of-town sites it requires, Toys "R" Us is prepared to argue with local authorities for as long as it takes. "There's not one site yet that we've abandoned." Where sites are not zoned for retailing, the company has to do a lot of badgering, especially where local competitors have strong influence. "We have to fight; we continue to do that every day."

Within the company, Toys "R" Us strives for harmony and informality. All staff have stock options, which is unusual in Germany—"a bit of sweet equity underscores the entrepreneurial drive," says Baczko.

Staff are also encouraged to call each other by first names, definitely a rarity in German operations where titles and surnames are used. "To us, the culture is very important. If they're all going to be entrepreneurs, you can't have that type of hierarchy."

With typical American energy, Toys "R" Us has managed to both work with the German system and implant its own concept onto the retail landscape. "There's been nothing put forward as an obstacle or as a reason for not being here that has not proved to be false," insists Baczko.

Its managers clearly have to be untypical, gung-ho types. Speaking as distant revelers rolled through Cologne's streets, he concluded: "If you're not ready to be here on carnival day in Cologne, you probably don't belong here."

Few newcomers have the resources or the fiercely can-do approach of Toys "R" Us. But all face basically the same problems in Germany. Dieter Glotzel, general manager of Cisi Engineering, part of Cisi Software of France, agrees with Psion that distribution is a major hurdle, especially for specialized products and services. So is finding the right staff, blending both technical and sales expertise. He reckons French engineers are much better educated in information technology than Germans are.

Overcoming many Germans' aversion to risk taking is also not easy. "A lot of people strive for security and would never join a small firm. Others have the pioneer spirit, and those are the ones we want." Cisi is still small in Germany, with turnover of around DM1 million. But like Toys "R" Us at the other end of the scale, it is breaking new ground in a market that can pay handsome dividends if well nurtured.

Source: *The Financial Times*, March 15, 1989, p. 19.

CASE 3
New Government Demands Quick Profit

The postal services of Durbania were not as efficient as they should have been—mail was delayed and sometimes lost—and it was running seven-digit losses, which were increasing. In desperation, the minister for postal services turned to the private sector for a management and organization expert and hired Jason McNab, one of the best. McNab took over as chairman of postal services.

He found the following state of affairs. The equipment was old, out of date, and subject to frequent malfunction. As with all postal services, this one is required to pick up and deliver mail throughout the whole country, including the sparsely populated mountains and rural areas. It cannot shut down those loss-causing services and concentrate on the profitable business and urban customers.

Competition was growing from such profitable, private communications methods as electronic mail, facsimile transmission, and UPS-type services. Durbania's postal service offered none of those services.

After two years in the job, McNab had ended the long history of increasing postal service losses, and they were stable along with the government subsidy necessary to keep services going. He was well along with a multimillion-dollar investment program that was on track to make postal services break even within five years.

At this time, Durbania held elections, and the Reform party won in a landslide over the Labor party, which had governed for eight years. McNab expected a period of uncertainty followed by a cost-saving exercise that would pay lip service to promises to lower inflation and speed up privatization of public services.

To his surprise, the Reformers acted quickly, as the central bank raised discount rates 2 percent as an inflation-fighting measure. That would make the financing for his modernization of the postal service equipment more expensive.

Then, barely a week after the new postal minister's appointment, McNab was summoned to her office. She got straight to the point by announcing to a stunned McNab that his government subsidy would be withdrawn at the end of the next fiscal year, which was only 20 months in the future. "We've got to reduce public spending next year, and I don't think we can afford you. We should see a return on assets—perhaps 2 percent— in three years," she told McNab. Her goal was to privatize the postal service before the end of Reform's four-year term.

McNab explained his schedule, which projected an end of losses and at least a break-even in five years. He pointed out that higher interest rates were already hampering his modernization efforts and how difficult it would be to cut costs sufficiently to offset loss of the subsidy.

"That's your problem," said the minister. "If you don't think you can meet the new government's goals, then I'm sure we'll be able to find someone who can."

Poor McNab rushed back to his office and called a must meeting of the top postal service managers for that night. He had no time to spare. They worked through the night and until noon the next day; when the meeting ended, they were tired but enthusiastic. They had decided on the only strategy bold enough to have any reasonable chance of success.

They decided they must increase revenue and cut unit costs, which are the only ones that reasonably can be cut back given the large fixed-cost base of the postal system. They must maintain output if revenue is to rise.

The revenue increases required to have any chance of profitability in three years must come from the high-income parts of the market. These are premium services for which customers are willing to pay for quality service. The postal service must move into competition with private companies and offer electronic mail, facsimile, and UPS-types of services.

Its fixed assets, which it must maintain to remain a postal service for all the people, will give it excellent bases from which to offer the premium services. They decided they could not afford to cut the investment program. Not only will it increase quality of services, it will also result in a more salable asset at privatization time.

Source: Adapted from "Dilemma & Decision," *International Management*, December 1988, p. 22.

Glossary

absolute advantage   The advantage enjoyed by a country because it can produce a product at a lower cost than can other countries.

accidental exporting   Export business obtained through no effort of the exporter.

accounting exposure   The total net of accounting statement items on which loss could occur because of currency exchange rate changes.

adjustment assistance   Financial and technical assistance to workers, firms, and communities to help them adjust to import competition.

ad valorem tariff or duty   Literally "according to the value." A method in which customs duties or tariffs are established and charged as a percentage of the value of imported goods.

advertising, paid   Nonpersonal presentation of ideas, goods, or services by an identified sponsor.

advising bank   The bank that notifies the beneficiary of the opening of a letter of credit. The advising bank makes no payment commitment.

aesthetics   A culture's sense of beauty and good taste.

affiliated company   May be a subsidiary or a company in which an IC has less than 100 percent ownership.

A.G.   Aktien-Gesellschaft. A joint stock company in Germany.

agency office   An office of a foreign bank in the United States that cannot accept domestic deposits. It seeks business for the bank when U.S. companies operate internationally.

air waybill   For goods shipped by air, performs the functions of a bill of lading in land surface transport or of a marine bill of lading in water transport.

allowance   Extra payments to expatriate employees to meet the higher costs they incur abroad.

American depository receipt (ADR)   Stock of a foreign corporation is deposited at an American bank. The bank issues an ADR, not the corporation's stock certificate, to an American investor who buys shares of that corporation. The stock certificate is kept at the bank.

antiboycott law   An American law against complying with the Arab countries' boycott of Israel.

antitrust laws   Laws to prevent business from engaging in such practices as price-fixing or market sharing.

appreciation   An increase in the value of one asset in terms of another.

apprenticeship program   Enables a person to learn a job skill by working with a skilled worker.

appropriate technology   The technology—advanced, intermediate, or primitive—that most fits the society using it.

arbitrage   The simultaneous purchase and sale of something in two (or more) markets at a time when it is selling (being bought) at different prices in the markets. Profit is the price differential minus the cost.

arbitration   The settlement of a dispute between parties by a third, presumably unbiased, party, not a court of law.

arm's-length transaction   A transaction between two or more unrelated parties. (A transaction between two subsidiaries of an IC would not be an arm's-length transaction.)

associations   Social units based on age, sex, or common interest, not on kinship.

back-to-back letter of credit (L/C)   A paying bank that will pay the exporter opens a back-to-back L/C based on the underlying L/C the exporter's supplier (a manufacturer, for example) may be paid.

back-to-back loans   A unit of one IC lends to a unit of a second IC; and at the same time and in equivalent amounts, another unit of the second IC lends to another unit of the first.

backward vertical integration   Establishing facilities to manufacture inputs used in the production of a firm's final products.

balance of payments (BOP)   A financial statement that compares all reported payments by residents of one country to residents of other countries with payments to domestic residents by foreign residents. If more money has been paid out than received, the BOP is in deficit. If the opposite condition exists, the BOP is in surplus.

banker's acceptance   A draft drawn, for example, by an exporter on an importer's bank. If the bank accepts the draft, the bank has agreed to pay in accordance with its terms.

bank swaps   To avoid currency exchange problems, a bank in a soft-currency country will lend to an IC subsidiary there. The IC or its bank will make hard currency available to the lending bank outside the soft-currency country.

barter   The exchange of goods or services for goods or services. No money is used.

bill of exchange (draft)   An unconditional written order calling on the party to whom it is addressed to pay on demand or at a future date a sum of money to the order of a named party or to the bearer. Examples are acceptances or the commercial bank check.

bill of lading (B/L)   A receipt given by a carrier of goods received and contract for their delivery. Usually a B/L is made to the order of someone and is negotiable. The B/L is also a document of title with which the holder may claim the goods from the carrier.

blocked account   Financial assets that cannot be transferred into another currency or out of the country without the government's permission.

bonded warehouse   Warehouse authorized by customs authorities for storage of goods on which payment of import duties is deferred until the goods are removed.

bonds: (1) Eurobond   A long-term bond marketed internationally in countries other than the country of the currency in which it is denominated. The issue is not subject to national restrictions.

(2) zero-coupon bonds   Pay no periodic interest (hence their name), so the total yield is obtained entirely as capital gain on the final maturity date.

(3) dual-currency bonds   Denominated in one currency but pay interest in another currency at a fixed rate of exchange. Dual-currency bonds can also pay redemption proceeds in a different currency than the currency of denomination.

(4) floating rate bonds   The most commonly issued instrument, the interest coupons on which are adjusted regularly according to the level of some base interest rate plus a fixed spread.

bonuses   Extra payments to expatriates because of hardships and inconveniences encountered in some foreign postings.

boomerang effect   Refers to the fact that technology sold to companies in another nation may be used to produce goods that will then compete with those of the seller of the technology.

bottleneck   Operation in production system whose output sets limit for entire system's output.

bottom-up planning   Planning process that begins at the lowest level in the organization and continues upward.

brain drain   The loss by a country of its most intelligent and best educated people.

branch office   An office or department of a company at a location away from headquarters. It is a part of the company and not a separate legal entity, as is a subsidiary, an affiliate, or a joint venture.

Bretton Woods   A resort in New Hampshire at which bank and treasury officials of the major Allied powers met near the end of World War II. There they established the International Monetary Fund, the World Bank, and an international monetary system.

bribes   Gifts or payments to induce the receiver to do something illegal for the giver.

buffer stock   A supply of a commodity that the executive of a commodity agreement tries to accumulate and hold so that when the price of the commodity begins to rise above desirable levels, sales can be made from that stock to dampen the price rise.

Canadian Shield   A massive land area of bedrock covering one half of Canada's land mass.

capital intensive   Describes processes that require a high concentration of capital relative to labor per unit of output and products produced by such processes. The opposite is labor intensive.

capitalism   All possible activities are performed by private business or persons rather than by a government.

cartel   An organization of suppliers that controls the supply and price of a commodity. To be successful, a cartel should have relatively few members who control most of the export supply of the commodity; the members must observe the cartel rules; and the commodity must be a necessity with a price-inelastic demand.

caste system   An aspect of Hinduism by which the entire society is divided into four groups plus the outcasts, and each is assigned a certain class of work.

central banks   Government institutions with authority over the size and growth of the national monetary stock. Central banks frequently regulate commercial banks and usually act as the government's fiscal agent.

centrally planned economy   Governments plan and direct almost all economic activity and usually own the factors of production.

centrally planned markets   Markets in which there is almost no free market activity and the government owns all major factors of production, controls labor, and tries to plan all activity.

central reserve assets   Gold, SDRs, ECUs, or hard foreign currencies held in a nation's treasury.

certificate of review   Legal document issued by U.S. Department of Commerce that grants immunity from state and federal antitrust prosecution to export trading companies.

chaebols   The large South Korean business conglomerates that have succeeded worldwide in such fields as computers, construction, shipbuilding, textiles, and steel.

CIF (cost, insurance, and freight)   A term used in the delivery of goods from one party to another. The price includes the costs of the goods, the maritime or other appropriate transportation, the insurance premium, and the freight charges to the destination.

climate   The meteorological conditions, including temperature, precipitation, and wind, that prevail in a region.

cluster analysis   Statistical technique dividing objects into groups so that the objects within each group are similar.

COCOM   Voluntary group of most NATO nations that administers a common set of export controls to prevent transfer of sensitive goods to hostile nations.

codetermination   A system in which representatives of labor participate in the management of a company.

collection documents   All documents submitted to a buyer for the purpose of receiving payment for a shipment.

collective bargaining   Bargaining between an employer and a labor union about employee wages and working conditions.

commodity agreement   An agreement between the producers and consumers of a commodity (for example, tin, cocoa, or rubber) to regulate the production, price, and trade of the commodity.

common external tariff   Under an agreement reached by a group of nations, such as the EC, the same level of tariffs is imposed by these nations on all goods imported from other nations.

communism   A theory of a classless society conceived by Marx. Lenin, Stalin, and others developed it differently.

comparative advantage   Unless a country has the same absolute advantage in producing all goods and services, there would be some goods and services in which it had less relative advantage. It would gain by importing those and exporting the ones in which it had an absolute advantage, or the greatest relative advantage.

compensation   A form of countertrade involving payment in goods and cash.

compensatory financing   A program to assist countries in financial difficulties due to drops in export earnings because of natural causes, such as drought, or because of international market price decreases. The IMF and the EC have compensatory financing programs.

compensatory trade   Any transaction that involves asset transfer as a condition of purchase.

competitive alliance   Cooperation between competitors for specific purposes.

competitive analysis   Process in which principal competitors are identified and their objectives, strengths, weaknesses, and product lines are assessed.

competitor intelligence system   Procedure for gathering, analyzing, and disseminating information about a firm's competitors.

compound duty   A form of import duty consisting of an ad valorem duty and a specific duty.

confirm   Act of a correspondent bank in the seller's country by which it agrees to honor the issuing bank's letter of credit.

confirmed letter of credit (L/C)   An L/C confirmed by a bank other than the opening bank. Thus, it is an obligation of more than one bank.

confiscation   Seizure by a government of foreign-owned assets that is not followed by prompt, effective, and adequate compensation.

Confucian work ethic   Same as the Christian work ethic. The term is used in Asian nations where Confucianism is a major religion.

conservative   In American political usage, a conservative advocates minimum government activity.

contingency plan   Plan for the best- or worst-case scenarios or for critical events that could have a severe impact on the firm.

contract manufacturing   Manufacturing of a product or component by one company for another company. The two companies may or may not be related by stock ownership, common parent, or otherwise.

controllable forces   The forces internal to the firm that management administers to adapt to changes in the uncontrollable environmental forces.

convertible currencies   Currencies that may be changed for or converted into other currencies, at least for current account payments, without government permission.

cooperative exporters   Established international manufacturers who export other manufacturers' goods as well as their own.

coproduction   A form of industrial cooperation in which two or more factories produce components for a final product.

corporate strategy   Action plan to enable an organization to reach its objectives.

cottage industry   Production away from a central factory, typically in the worker's own home or cottage.

Workers are paid on a piece-rate basis, or so much for each unit produced.

counterfeiting   Illegal use of a well-known manufacturer's brand name on copies of the firm's merchandise.

countertrade   A transaction in which goods are exchanged for goods. Payment by a purchaser is entirely or partially in goods instead of hard currencies for products or technology from other countries.

countervailing duty   An additional amount of tariff levied on an import that is found to have benefited from an export subsidy.

country risk assessment   Evaluating the risks before lending or investing in a country.

covered investment or interest arbitrage   Investment in a second currency that is "covered" by a forward sale of that currency to protect against exchange rate fluctuations. Profit depends on interest rate differentials minus the discount or plus the premium on a forward sale.

covering   Buying or selling foreign currencies in amounts equivalent to future payments to be made or received. A means of protection against loss due to currency exchange rate fluctuations.

credit or money market hedge   Hedging by borrowing the currency of risk, converting it immediately to the ultimately desired currency, and repaying the loan when payment is received.

cross investment   Foreign direct investment made by oligopolistic firms in each other's home country as a defense measure.

cross rate   The direct exchange rate between two non-U.S. dollar currencies. It is determined by observing the U.S. dollar exchange rate for each of the other two currencies and, from those rates, computing their direct exchange rate.

culture   The benefits, rules, techniques, institutions, and artifacts that characterize human populations.

currency area   The group of countries whose currencies are pegged to any one DC currency. Many LDCs peg the value of their currency to that of their major DC trading partner.

currency exchange controls   A government's controls over how much foreign currency its residents or visitors can have and how much they must pay for it.

currency swap   The exchange of one currency into another at an agreed rate and a reversal of that exchange at the same rate at the end of the swap contract period.

customhouse broker   Independent business that handles import shipments for compensation.

customs union   An arrangement between two or more countries whereby they eliminate tariffs and other import restrictions on one another's goods and establish a common tariff on the goods from all other countries.

debt capital   Money raised by selling bonds, the principal and interest on which must be repaid.

debt default   When a debtor fails or refuses to pay a debt.

debt rescheduling   Defaulted debt is renegotiated, giving the debtor a longer time to pay and/or a lower interest rate.

demonstration effect   The result of having seen others with desirable goods.

demurrage   Charge assessed by a carrier on an exporter or an importer for excess time taken to unload or load a vessel.

depreciation of a currency   A decline in the value of a currency in terms of another currency or in terms of gold. "Depreciation" and "devaluation" are used interchangeably.

devaluation   Depreciation of a currency by official government action.

developed   A classification for all industrialized nations; that is, those that are more developed technically.

developed countries (DCs)   Industrialized countries.

developing   A classification for the world's lower-income nations that are less technically developed.

development banks   Banks that aid less developed countries (LDCs) in economic development. They may lend or invest money and encourage local ownership. They may be worldwide, regional, or national.

direct exporting   The exporting of goods and services by the firm that produces them.

direct investment   Sufficient investment to obtain at least some voice in management. The U.S. government considers 10 percent or more equity in a foreign company to be direct investment.

dirty float   A currency that floats in value in terms of other currencies but is not free of government intervention. Governments intervene to "smooth" or "manage" fluctuations or to maintain desired exchange rates.

discretionary income   The amount of income remaining after paying taxes and making essential purchases.

disposable income   The amount of income remaining after taxes.

distributors   Independent importers who buy for their own account for resale.

district export councils   Groups of volunteer businesspeople in every state that are appointed by the U.S. Department of Commerce to assist exporters.

documentary drafts   Drafts accompanied by such documents as invoices, bills of lading, inspection certificates, and insurance papers.

domestication   Term used to indicate process in which a host government brings pressure to force a foreign owner to turn over partial ownership to the host country government or host country citizens.

domestic environment   All the uncontrollable forces originating in the home country that surround and influence the firm's life and development.

domestic international sales corporation (DISC)   A subsidiary corporation of a U.S. company that is incorporated in a state of the United States for the purpose of exporting from the United States. DISCs are given certain tax advantages. Generally, they have been superseded by foreign sales corporations.

drafts (bills of exchange)   Orders drawn by a drawer that order a second party, the drawee, to pay a sum of money to a payee. The payee may be the same party as the drawer.

drawback   The reimbursement of the tariff paid on an imported component that is later exported. When a component is imported into the United States, a tariff is levied on it and paid by the importer. If that component is later exported, the exporter is entitled to get 99 percent of the tariff amount from U.S. Customs.

drawee   See *drafts*.

drawer   See *drafts*.

dumping   Selling abroad at prices lower than those charged in the home or other markets.

duties (tariffs)   Amounts charged when goods are imported into a country. If such duties are based on the values of the goods, they are called ad valorem. If they are based on the number of items imported, they are called specified.

earned income   Income derived from efforts, labor, sales, or active participation in business. Salaries, wages, bonuses, and commissions are examples. Unearned income is a return on investment of money or time. Examples are interest, dividends, and royalties. The distinction is important for purposes of U.S. taxation of American residents abroad.

East–West trade   Trade between the centrally planned economies of the communist block (East) and the more market-oriented economies of the OECD nations (West). Recent developments, such as the breakup of the Soviet Union and the end of the COMECON trade bloc that it dominated, have reduced the number of avowedly communist countries. Many of those countries are trying to achieve market economies and democracy, but progress is slow and difficult at best.

Edge Act corporation   A subsidiary of a U.S. commercial bank that operates in a foreign country. The Edge subsidiary, operating abroad, is free of restraints of U.S. law and may perform whatever services and functions are legal in the countries where it operates.

employee facilities   Schools, cafeterias, housing, recreation, or other employer-provided facilities.

environment   All the forces surrounding and influencing the life and development of the firm.

environmental scanning   Procedure in which a firm scans the world for changes in the environmental forces that might affect it.

equity capital   Money raised by selling corporate stock that represents ownership of the corporation.

equity-related bonds   Bonds that are convertible at the option of the holder into other securities of the issuer, usually common stock-type equity. Called convertibles in the United States.

escape clause   A legal provision concerning products whose tariffs have been reduced. If, thereafter, imports increase and threaten the domestic producers of those products, the escape clause permits the tariffs to be put back up.

estimation by analogy   Using a market factor that is successful in one market to estimate demand in a similar market.

ethnocentricity   A belief in the superiority of one's own ethnic group.

Eurobonds   Bonds that are issued outside the restriction applying to domestic offerings and are syndicated and traded mostly from London. Most of these bonds are denominated in U.S. dollars.

Eurocurrency   A currency being used or traded outside the country that issued it.

Eurodollar   The U.S. dollar is the most widely used Eurocurrency.

European Currency Unit (ECU)   A currency unit established by the European Monetary System. Its value is determined by reference to the value of a "basket" of currencies. The currencies in the basket are those of the system's member-countries.

European Economic Area   The European Free Trade Area consisting of the EC and EFTA.

European Monetary Cooperation Fund (EMCF)   Lends assistance to EMS member-countries that have difficulties in keeping their currencies within the agreed value relationships.

European Monetary System (EMS)   A system, established in 1979, under which West European countries agreed to keep their currency values within an established range in relation to one another.

exchange rate   The price of one currency stated in another currency.

exchange rate risk   In activities involving two or more currencies, the risk that losses can occur as a result of changes in their relative value.

Eximbank (Export-Import Bank)   Principal federal government agency that aids American exporters by means of loans, guarantees, and insurance programs.

export bill of lading   Contract of carriage between shipper and carrier. Straight bill of lading is nonnegotiable; an endorsed "to-order" bill gives the holder claim on merchandise.

export draft   An unconditional order drawn by the seller on the buyer to pay the draft's amount on presentation (sight draft) or at an agreed future date (time draft) that must be paid before the buyer receives shipping documents.

export incentives   Subsidies or tax rebates paid by governments to companies to encourage them to export.

export licenses   A government document that permits the exporter to export designated goods to certain destinations. In the United States, the export license will be either a General Export License or a Validated Export License.

export management company   A company that acts as the export department for other companies. It performs all export-related services for its customers except supplying the product.

export processing zones   Specific and limited areas into which imported components may be brought for further processing. The finished product must be reexported to avoid payment of import duties.

export trading company   A firm established principally to export domestic goods and services and help unrelated companies export their products.

exposure netting   An open position in two or more currencies whose strengths and weaknesses are thought to balance one another.

expropriation   Seizure by a government of foreign-owned assets. Such seizure is not contrary to international law if it is followed by prompt, adequate, and effective compensation. If not, it is called confiscation.

extended family   Includes relatives beyond the parents and children.

extortion   The demand for payments to keep the receiver from causing harm to the payer.

extraterritorial application of laws   Attempts by a government to apply its laws outside its territorial borders.

factor   A buyer, at a discount, of a company's receivables with short-term maturities of no longer than a year.

factor endowment   A country is or is not endowed with one or more of the factors of production, capital, labor, and natural resources.

factoring   Discounting without recourse an account receivable.

"factory door" cost   The production cost of a good or service to which marketing and general administrative costs have not been added.

firm surveillance   The IMF has the power to monitor the exchange rate policies of member-nations.

fiscal policies   Government policies about the collection and spending of money.

fixed exchange rates   A system under which the values of currencies in terms of other currencies are fixed by intergovernmental agreement and by governmental intervention in the currency exchange markets.

fixed interest rate   An interest rate that is set when a loan is made and remains the same for the life of the loan regardless of whether other interest rates rise or fall.

floating exchange rates   A system in which the values of currencies in terms of other currencies are determined by the supply of and demand for the currencies in currency markets. If governments do not intervene in the markets, the float is said to be "clean." If they do intervene, the float is said to be "dirty."

floating interest rates   A loan situation in which the interest rate set when a loan is made may rise or fall as the interest rates of some reference, such as LIBOR or the prime rate, vary. Sometimes called variable rates.

floating-rate notes or bonds   Debt instruments with floating or variable interest rates. The interest rates are pegged to a fluctuating interest rate, such as the six-month LIBOR rate.

fluctuating exchange rates   See *floating exchange rates.*

Foreign Corrupt Practices Act of 1977   An American law against making questionable payments when American companies do business abroad.

foreign exchange   The exchanges of the currency of one country for that of another country.

foreign exchange rates   Prices of one currency in terms of other currencies.

foreign exchange reserves   Gold, SDRs, U.S. dollars, and other convertible currencies held in a nation's treasury.

foreign financing   Occurs when a foreign company or other borrower comes to a nation's capital market and borrows in the local currency; for example, when an Italian company borrows U.S. dollars in New York or French francs in Paris.

foreign freight forwarder   Independent business that handles export shipments for compensation.

foreign national pricing   Local pricing in another country.

foreign sales corporation (FSC)   A corporation provided for in the Tax Reform Act of 1984. The FSC replaces the domestic international sales corporation (DISC) as a tax incentive for exporters.

foreign tax credit   The credit an American taxpayer may take against American income tax for tax levied on the same income by a foreign government.

foreign trade zone (FTZ)   American version of a free trade zone. In an FTZ, goods may be imported and manufactured or handled and changed in any way. No tariff need be paid unless and until the goods are removed from the FTZ into the country where the FTZ is located.

forfaiting   Has the same purposes and procedures as factoring, which is the sale by an exporter of its accounts receivable for immediate cash. However, there are two important differences: (1) factoring involves credit terms of no more than 180 days, while forfaiting may involve years; (2) factoring does not usually cover political and transfer risks, while forfaiting does.

forward contract   A contract to exchange one currency for another currency at an agreed exchange rate at a future date, usually 30, 90, or 180 days. May be used to hedge. See *forward rate*.

forward rate   The cost today for a commitment by one party to deliver to or take from another party an agreed amount of a currency at a fixed or future date. This rate is established by the forward contract.

Fourth World   The poorest of the world's countries.

franchising   A franchisee pays a franchisor for the right to use the franchisor's logo, procedures, materials, and advertising.

free trade zones   An area designated by the government of a country for duty-free entry of any nonprohibited goods.

friendship, commerce, and navigation (FCN) treaties   The basic agreements between nations about such matters as treatment of each others' citizens or companies.

fringe benefits   Payments or other benefits given to employees over and above base wages.

general export license   Any export license covering export commodities for which a validated license is not required. No formal application is required.

generalized systems of preference (GSP)   An agreement under the auspices of GATT under which many products of developing nations are provided duty-free access to developed nations.

general trading companies   Exist in many countries, including the United States, though the Japanese versions of these companies, called *sogo shosha* in Japanese, are the best known. For many years, the sogo shosha have imported and distributed commodities and products for use by Japanese industries and consumers, sought foreign customers for Japanese companies, and exported to other companies.

geocentric   As used in this book, hiring and promoting employees because of their abilities without reference to their nationality or race.

gilts   Technically, British and Irish government securities, though the term also includes issues of local British authorities.

glasnost   A word popularized by Gorbachev meaning openness of information.

global company   A company that markets a standardized product worldwide and allows only minimum adaptations to local conditions and tastes from country to country. Its financial, marketing, and advertising strategies are global with little differentiation among countries or areas as to product. Other authors, particularly when writing about the automobile industry, mean the company's ability to source parts and components from subsidiaries in several countries for assembly in the market country or area.

GmbH   Gesellschaft mit beschrankter Haftung (organization with limited ability). A German form of business organization.

GNP/capita   The gross national product of a nation divided by its population (an arithmetic mean).

gold exchange standard   The system established at Bretton Woods whereby the value of one currency (the U.S. dollar) was set in terms of gold. The United States held gold and agreed that when another country accumulated U.S. dollars, it could exchange them for gold at the set value.

gold standard   A system under which currency values are set in terms of gold and each country agrees that if a second country accumulates more of a first country's currency than it wants for other purposes, the second country can exchange the first country's currency for that amount of the first country's gold.

gold tranche   The amount of gold paid by a country as its contributed capital in the International Monetary Fund.

gray market   Where goods are sold, that are either legal but unauthorized imports bearing domestic manufacturers' trade names or are exports diverted to the domestic market.

gross domestic product (GDP)   The market value of a country's output attributable to factors of production located in the country's territory. It differs from GNP by the exclusion of net factor income payments, such as interest and dividends received from, or paid to, the rest of the world. See *gross national product (GNP)*.

gross national product (GNP)   The market value of all the final goods and services produced by a national economy over a period of time, usually a year.

Group of 5   The term used for meetings of the finance ministers and central bank governors of France, the Federal Republic of Germany, Japan, the United Kingdom, and the United States.

Group of 7   The Group of 5 plus Canada and Italy.

Group of 10   The Group of 7 plus Belgium, the Netherlands, and Sweden.

Group of 77   Had its origins in the caucus of 75 developing countries that met in 1964 to prepare for UNCTAD. After the first UNCTAD meeting, the caucus grew to 77.

guest workers   Foreign workers who are brought into a country by legal means to perform needed labor.

hard currency   A currency that is freely convertible into other currencies.

hard loans   Loans that must be repaid in a hard currency at market interest rates.

hedging   Selling forward currency exchange, borrowing, or using other means to protect against losses from possible currency exchange rate changes that affect the values of assets and liabilities.

hierarchy   A system in which there are several layers of authority between the lowest rank (say, the peasant or untouchables) to the highest rank (say, king, commissar, or brahmin).

hit list or super 301   Refers to Section 301 of the U.S. 1988 Trade Act, which requires the U.S. trade representative to prepare a list of countries that systematically restrict access of American products to their markets.

hollowing out   Refers to the practice of firms that close their production facilities and become marketing organizations for other producers, mostly foreign.

home country   The country where the parent company's headquarters are located.

host country   The country in which foreign investment is made.

human needs approach   A way to economic development that includes the elimination of poverty and unemployment as well as an increase in income.

hybrid organization   A structure organized by more than one dimension at the top level.

hypermarkets   Huge combination supermarkets and discount stores where soft and hard goods are sold.

import substitution   An industrialization policy followed by some developing nations by which the government encourages the local production of substitutes for imported goods. High import duties protect local producers from import competition.

incentive pay plans   Plans that pay employees more for achieving certain goals.

income distribution   A measure of how a nation's income is apportioned among its people. It is commonly reported as the percentage of income received by population quintiles.

INCOTERMS   A publication of the International Chamber of Commerce setting forth recommended standard definitions for the major trade terms used in international trade.

indexing   Taking into account the effect of inflation on assets and liabilities and adjusting the amounts of these items to preserve their original relationships.

indicative planning   Planning done by governments in collaboration with industry. It is essentially a forecast of the direction the economy is expected to take. The indicative plan does not control economic activity as in the centrally planned economies, and firms are free to make their own decisions.

indirect exporting   The exporting of goods and services through various types of home-based exporters.

industrial cooperation   A long-term relationship with a company in the West in which an LDC produces products for its own market and/or export to the West.

industrial espionage   Stealing trade, process, customer, pricing, or technology secrets from a business.

industrial targeting   Government practice of assisting selected industries to grow.

information glut   There is too much information to absorb or it is not properly classified or organized.

infrastructure   The fundamental underpinnings of an economy—roads, railroads, communications, water supplies, energy supplies, and so forth.

in-house training programs   Programs provided by an employer on its own property.

instability   As used in this book, occurs when a government is likely to be overthrown by a revolution or coup.

insurance certificate   Evidence that marine insurance has been obtained to cover stipulated risks during transit.

interest arbitrage   Lending in another country to take advantage of higher interest rates. Such arbitrage tends to equalize interest rates.

Interest Equalization Tax (IET)   From 1963 to 1974, a tax that U.S. residents were required to pay on the purchase of foreign securities. The IET was a device to combat U.S. BOP deficits.

interest rate swap   A transaction in which two parties exchange interest payment streams of differing character based on an underlying principal amount. The three main types are coupon swaps (fixed rate to floating rate in the same currency), basis swaps (one floating rate index to another floating rate index in the same currency), and cross-currency interest rate swaps (fixed or floating rate in one currency or fixed or floating rate in another currency).

intermediate technology   Production method between capital- and labor-intensive methods.

internalization theory   An extension of the market imperfection theory, which claims that to obtain a higher return on its investment, a firm will transfer its superior knowledge to a foreign subsidiary rather than sell it on the open market.

international division   A division in the organization that is at the same level as the domestic division in the firm and is responsible for all nonhome country activities.

international environment   The interaction between the domestic and foreign environmental forces.

international finance center   A multinational's or global's office that handles the great majority of international money transactions for all the firm's units.

international financing   Occurs when a borrower raises capital in the Eurocurrency or Eurobond markets, outside the restrictions that are applied to domestic or foreign offerings. See *foreign financing*.

international law   A body of principles and practices that have been generally accepted by countries in their relations with other countries and with citizens of other countries.

international management information system   Organized process of gathering, storing, processing, and disseminating information about international operations to managers to assist them in making business decisions.

international monetary system   The agreements, practices, laws, customs, and institutions that deal with money (debts, payments, investments) internationally.

international product life cycle   A theory that helps explain both trade flows and foreign direct investment on the basis of a product's position in the four stages of (1) exports of an industrialized nation, (2) beginning of foreign production, (3) foreign competition in export markets, and (4) import competition in the country where the product was introduced originally.

international status   Confers extra perquisites and privileges on a multinational's top employees.

intervention currency   A currency bought or sold by a country (not necessarily the one issued by it) to influence the value of its own currency.

intraenterprise transaction   A transaction between two or more units of the same IC.

irrevocable letter of credit (L/C)   Refers to a letter of credit that cannot be canceled.

Islam   A religion found primarily in North Africa and the Middle East. Moslems believe the future is ordained by Allah (God). The Koran, a collection of Allah's revelations to Muhammad, the founder of Islam, is accepted as God's eternal word.

iterative planning   Repetition of the bottom-up or top-down planning process until all differences are reconciled.

J curve   A curve illustrating the theory that immediately after a country devalues its currency, its imports become more expensive and its exports cheaper, thus worsening a BOP deficit. As the country's exports increase, it earns more money and the deficit bottoms out and becomes a surplus up the right side of the J.

joint venture   May be (1) a corporate entity between an IC and local owners, (2) a corporate entity between two or more ICs that are foreign to the area where the joint venture is located, or (3) a cooperative undertaking between two or more firms for a limited-duration project.

just-in-time delivery   A balanced system in which there is little or no delay time or inventory.

key currencies   Those held extensively as foreign exchange reserves.

labor force composition   The different sorts of available laborers, differentiated in terms of skill, age, race, or gender.

labor intensive   Describes products whose production requires a relatively large amount of labor and a relatively small amount of capital. Also describes the manufacturing process.

labor market   The labor available in an area.

labor mobility   The movement of labor from one location to another.

labor productivity   How much a labor force produces in a given time period.

labor quality   The skill and industriousness of labor.

labor quantity   The number of available laborers.

labor unions   Organizations of laborers that represent and negotiate for workers.

lags   As used in this book, delaying conversion when payment is to be made in another currency in the belief the other currency will cost less when needed.

landlocked   Refers to a nation bordered on all of its frontiers by land.

LASH   Specially designed oceangoing vessel for carrying barges.

leads   As used in this book, converting immediately when payment is to be made in another currency in the belief the other currency will cost more when needed.

left wing   Extremely liberal, in the American sense of the word.

less developed countries (LDCs)   Countries with low per capita income, low levels of industrialization, high illiteracy, and usually political instability.

letter of credit (L/C)   A letter issued by a bank indicating that the bank will accept drafts (make payments) under specified circumstances.

liberal   In American political usage, a liberal advocates extensive government intervention in business and society.

licensing   A contractual arrangement in which one firm, the licensor, grants access to its patents, trademarks, or technology to another firm, the licensee, for a fee, usually called a royalty.

lingua franca   A foreign language used to communicate among diverse cultures that speak different languages.

linkage   In international marketing, the creation of demand in a second national market by movement of the product and/or the customer into that market.

Lombard rate   The interest rate that a central bank charges other banks on loans secured by government and other selected securities.

Lomé convention   An agreement between 68 African, Caribbean, and Pacific states and the EC by means of which 99.2 percent of the former group's exports are admitted duty-free to the EC.

London Interbank Offered Rate (LIBOR)   The interest rate the most creditworthy banks charge one another for loans of Eurodollars overnight in the London market. LIBOR is a cornerstone in the pricing on money market issues and other short-term debt issues by both government and business borrowers. Interest is often stated to be LIBOR plus a fraction.

long position   The position taken when a party buys something for future delivery. This may be done in the expectation that the item bought will increase in value. It may also be done to hedge a currency risk.

managed float   See *floating exchange rates.* "Managed" is a more decorous word than "dirty."

managed trade   Trade managed in some way(s) by governments.

management contract   An agreement by which a foreign firm provides management in all or specific areas to a local company for a fee.

management information system (MIS)   The computerized system through which multinational or global executives get timely, relevant information about all the company's units.

manufacturers' agents   Independent sales representatives of various noncompeting suppliers.

manufacturing rationalization   Division of production among a number of production units, enabling each to produce components for all of a firm's assembly plants.

maquiladora   Introduced by the Mexican government to create jobs for its people. Plants along the Mexican-American border cooperate, with the plant on the American side doing the capital-intensive work and the Mexican plant doing the labor-intensive production.

market economies   Economies that are characterized by a relatively large, free (nongovernmental) market sector. There is no such thing as a totally free market; all governments regulate, tax, and intervene in various ways.

market factors   Economic data that correlate highly with market demand for a product.

market indicators   Economic data used to measure relative market strengths of countries or geographical areas.

market method to correct BOP deficit   Deflate the economy and devalue the currency.

market screening   A version of environmental scanning in which the firm identifies desirable markets by using the environmental forces to eliminate the less desirable markets.

Marshall Plan   The U.S. aid program that helped European countries reconstruct after World War II. Cooperation among the European countries was a forerunner of the EC.

material culture   Refers to all man-made objects and is concerned with how people make things (technology) and who makes what and why (economics).

matrix organization   An organizational structure composed of one or more organizational structures superimposed over one another in an attempt to mesh product, regional, functional, and other expertise.

matrix overlay   An organization whose top-level divisions are required to heed input from a staff composed of experts of another organizational dimension. It attempts to avoid the double-reporting difficulty of a matrix organization but still mesh two or more dimensions.

mercantilism   The economic philosophy that equates the possession of gold or other international monetary assets with wealth. It also holds that trade activities should be directed or controlled by the government.

merchant banks   Combine long- and short-term financing with the underwriting and distributing of securities.

minorities   As used in this book, a group of people of one race or religion living in an area populated by a larger number of people of a different race or religion.

mission statement   A broad statement defining the organization's scope.

mitbestimmung   German for "codetermination." The Germans pioneered codetermination, and their word for it is frequently used.

monetary policies   Government policies regulating whether the country's money supply grows and, if so, how fast.

money markets   Places where currencies are traded or capital is raised.

monopolistic advantage theory   The idea that foreign direct investment is made by firms in oligopolistic industries that possess technical and other advantages over indigenous firms.

most favored nation (MFN)   The policy of nondiscrimination in international commercial policy, extending to all nations the same customs and tariff treatments as are extended to the most favored nation.

multinational economic union   A group of nations that have reduced barriers to intergroup trade and are cooperating in economic matters.

multinational, multinational company, or multinational enterprise (MNC or MNE)   Terms used by some authors to mean an organization consisting of a parent company in a home country that owns relatively autonomous subsidiaries in various host countries.

national (macro) competition   Ability of a nation's producers to compete successfully in the world markets and with imports in their own domestic markets.

national economic plans   Plans prepared by governments that state their economic goals and means for reaching them for periods of usually up to five years.

nationalism   A strong attachment to and support of one's country.

nationalization   Government takeover of private property.

national tax jurisdiction   Taxation on the basis of nationality regardless of where in the world taxpayer's income is earned or where the activities of the taxpayer take place.

natural resources   Anything supplied by nature on which people depend.

net negative international investment position   Residents of a country have less investments abroad than nonresidents have in the country.

neutralizing the balance sheet   Having the assets in a given currency approximate the liabilities in that currency.

newly industrializing countries (NICs)   A group of middle-income nations with high growth in manufacturing. Much of their production goes to high-income, industrialized nations.

nonmarket economy   The World Bank designation for a communist nation.

nonmarket measures   Use of currency controls, tariffs, or quotas to correct a BOP deficit.

nonrecourse financing   Financing in which the factor assumes the full responsibility and all the risk of collecting from a third party. See *forfaiting*.

nonrevenue tax purpose   Use of a tax to encourage some perceived socially desirable end such as home ownership, or to discourage something undesirable, such as tobacco.

nontariff barriers (NTBs)   Constraints on imports other than import duties, such as quotas, product standards, orderly marketing arrangements, customs and administrative procedures, and government participation in trade.

note issuance facility (NIF)   Medium-term arrangements that enable borrowers to issue paper, typically of three- or six-months' maturity, in their own names. A group of underwriting banks guarantees the availability of funds to the borrower by purchasing any unsold notes or by providing standby credit.

off-premises training   The employer sends workers away from its property to a school or other site to be trained.

offshore banking   The use of banks located in other countries, particularly tax havens like the Caymans and the Bahamas.

offshore funds   Investment funds whose shares are usually denominated in U.S. dollars but located and sold outside the United States. There are tax and securities-registration reasons for such funds.

on-the-job training   Employees learn a job by performing it under supervision.

opening bank   The bank that opens a letter of credit (L/C). This bank will honor (pay) drafts drawn under the L/C if specified conditions are met.

orderly marketing agreements (OMAs)   Compacts negotiated between two or more nations under whose terms the exporting nation or nations agree to limit exports of specified goods to the importing nation. They are sometimes called voluntary export agreements (VEAs).

Overseas Private Insurance Corporation (OPIC)   A U.S. government corporation that offers American investors in developing countries insurance against expropriation, currency inconvertibility, and damages from wars and revolutions.

overvalued currency   A currency whose value is kept higher by government action than it would be in a free market.

paper gold   See *special drawing rights (SDRs)*.

parallel importer   Wholesaler who imports products independently of manufacturer-authorized importers or buys goods for export and diverts them to the domestic market.

parallel importing   The importing of a product by an independent operator that is not part of the manufacturer's channel of distribution. The parallel importer may compete with the authorized importer or with a subsidiary of the foreign manufacturer that produces the product in the local market.

parent company   A company that owns subsidiary companies.

par value   The value that a government, by agreement or regulation, sets on its currency in terms of other currencies. At Bretton Woods, other currencies were assigned par values in terms of the U.S. dollar.

paternalism   A system in which a chief, sheik, or other authority figure cares for all the people as if he were their father.

pegged exchange rate   An exchange rate in which a country's currency is fixed in terms of another country's currency. Frequently, the other country is a major trading partner or a country with which there was a colonial relationship.

perestroika   A word popularized by Gorbachev meaning modernizing the economy and devolving decision power from the central government.

peril point   In U.S. law, a point below which a tariff cannot be lowered without causing or threatening serious injury to U.S. producers of competitive products.

physical product   The basic physical product produced by a firm's production system. It does not include attributes added after production, such as packaging, brand name, service, or financing.

political risks   The risks to a business and its employees that stem from political unrest in an area. As a result of such unrest, the markets or supplies of the business may be disrupted or the business may be nationalized and its employees may lose their jobs or be kidnapped, injured, or even killed.

population density   A measure of the number of inhabitants per area unit (inhabitants per kilometer or mile).

population distribution   A measure of how the inhabitants are distributed over a nation's area.

polymetallic deposits   Deposits that contain a number of metals.

portfolio investment   The purchase of stocks and bonds to obtain a return in the money invested. The investors are not interested in assuming control of the firm.

preindustrial societies   A designation that can signify anything from traditional societies through societies in the early stages of agricultural and industrial organization.

preventive maintenance (planned maintenance)   Maintenance done according to plan, not when a machine breaks down.

price and wage controls   Government limits on prices that may be charged and wages that may be paid.

privatization   When a government transfers ownership and/or operation of a government-owned enterprise to private owners/operators.

product liability   Liability of a product's manufacturer for damage caused by the product.

pro forma invoice   Exporter's formal quotation containing a description of the merchandise, price, delivery time, method of shipping, terms of sale, and points of entry.

programmed-management approach   A middle-ground advertising strategy between globally standardized and entirely local programs.

promotion   All forms of communication between a firm and its publics.

promotional mix   A blend of the promotional methods a firm uses to sell its products.

Protestant work ethic   The duty of Christians to glorify God by hard work and the practice of thrift.

public relations   Various methods of communicating with the firm's publics to secure a favorable impression.

purchasing power parity   The relative ability of one unit of two countries' currencies to purchase similar goods. From this relative ability is derived an indication of what the market exchange rate between the two currencies should be.

quality circles (quality control circles)   Small work groups that meet periodically to discuss ways to improve their functional areas in the firm and the quality of the products.

questionable or dubious payments   Bribes.

quota   (1) A limitation on imports by number or by weight; for example, only so many of a given item or only so many pounds or kilos may be imported. (2) At the IMF, each member-nation has a quota that determines the amount of its subscription and how much it can borrow.

regional dualism   A situation in which some regions of a nation have high productivity and high incomes while other regions of the same country have little economic development and lower incomes.

regression analysis   Statistical technique that utilizes a linear model to establish relationships between independent variables and the dependent variable.

reinvoicing   Centralizing all international invoicing by an IC. The reinvoicing center decides which currencies should be used and where, how, and when.

repatriation   The transfer home of assets held abroad.

representative office   An office of an out-of-state or foreign bank that is not permitted to conduct direct banking functions. The purpose of such an office is to solicit business for its parent bank, where it can conduct such functions.

restrictive trade practices legislation   The European versions of American antitrust laws.

revaluation of a currency   An increase in a currency's value in terms of other currencies. See *devaluation*.

reverse engineering   Also called *benchmarking:* Dismantling a competitor's product to learn everything possible about it.

reverse imports   Products made by a multinational's overseas subsidiaries that are exported to the home country.

revocable letters of credit (L/Cs)   L/Cs that the opening bank may revoke at any time without notice to the beneficiary.

Rhine waterway   A system of rivers and canals that is the main transportation artery of Europe.

right wing   Extremely conservative politically.

robotics   Machines, usually computer controlled, doing work previously done by human workers.

RO–RO   Specially designed oceangoing vessel that permits any equipment on wheels to be rolled on board.

rural-to-urban shift   Describes the movement of a nation's population from rural areas to cities.

S.A.   Société Anonyme, Sociedad Anomina, or Societa Anomina. Joint-stock companies (in French, Spanish, and Italian, respectively).

safe haven   The currency of a country that is politically secure is called a safe haven currency.

sales company   A corporate entity established in a foreign country by the parent company to sell goods or services imported from the parent company and other foreign affiliates.

sales promotion   Selling aids, including displays, premiums, contests, and gifts.

S.A.R.L.   Société à Responsibilité Limitée.

scenario   Description of a possible future. Managers often use most likely, worst, and best cases for the purpose of planning.

securitization   The term is most often used to mean the process by which traditional bank assets, mainly loans or mortgages, are converted into negotiable securities. More broadly, refers to the development of markets for a variety of new negotiable instruments.

self-reference criterion   Unconscious reference to one's own cultural values when judging behavioral actions of others in a new and different environment.

shale   A fissile (capable of being split) rock composed of laminated layers of claylike, fine-grained sediment.

short position   The position of a party when it has sold something it does not own. This is for future delivery in the expectation that the item sold will decrease in price. It is also done to hedge a currency risk.

sight draft   A bill of exchange that is payable immediately on presentation or demand. A bank check is a sight draft.

skilled labor   Employees trained in needed skills.

Smithsonian agreement   New agreements on currency par values, the value of gold, and tariffs reached by the major trading countries at the Smithsonian Institution in Washington, D.C., in December 1971. When the United States closed the "gold window" in August 1971, the world currency exchanges were thrown into turmoil, and such agreements became necessary.

snake   During the 1970s, several West European countries agreed to keep the values of their currencies within established ranges in terms of one another. The currencies would all float in value in terms of other currencies—for example, the U.S. dollar and the Japanese yen.

socialism A theory of society in which the government owns or directs most of the factors of production.

soft currency A currency that is not freely convertible into other currencies. Such a currency is usually subject to national currency controls.

soft loans Loans like those granted by the IDA. These loans may have grace periods during which no payments need be made; they may bear low or no interest; and they may be repayable in a soft currency.

sogo shosha The Japanese term for general trading companies.

sovereign debt The debt of a national government.

sovereign immunity The immunity of a government from lawsuits in the courts of its own country or other countries unless it submits voluntarily. Such immunity is particularly likely to exist if the government limits itself to "governmental" functions as opposed to economic ones.

sovereignty The power of each national government over the land within its border and over the people and organizations within those borders.

special drawing rights (SDRs) Accounting entries at the IMF. SDRs are treated as reserve assets and are credited or debited to member-countries' accounts. Sometimes called paper gold, they permit liquidity to be created by agreement at the IMF rather than having it depend on the U.S. BOP deficit.

specific tariff or duty A method of measuring customs duties or tariffs by number or weight instead of by value. Thus, the amount of the tariff or duty is based on how many units or how many pounds or kilos are imported, regardless of their value. See *ad valorem tariff or duty.*

spot rate or spot quotation The rate of exchange between two currencies for delivery, one for the other within two business days.

stability As used in this book, occurs when a government is not likely to be overturned by a revolution or a coup.

standardization of the marketing mix The utilization of the same pricing, product, distribution, and promotional strategies in all markets where the firm does business.

straight bonds or notes Issues with a fixed (not floating) coupon or interest rate.

strategic business unit (SBU) Business entity with a clearly defined market, specific competitors, the ability to carry out its business mission, and a size appropriate for control by a single manager.

subcontracting Prime manufacturers purchase of components from other suppliers. Used in industrial cooperation.

subsidiaries Companies owned by another company, which is referred to as the parent company.

subsidiary detriment A subsidiary is deprived of a potential advantage so that the multinational as a whole may enjoy a greater advantage.

subsidies, export Financial encouragement to export. Such subsidies can take the form of lower taxes, tax rebates, or direct payments.

superstores Name given to hypermarkets in Japan and in some parts of Europe and the United States.

swaps Are of two basic kinds: interest rate swaps and currency swaps. Interest rate swaps typically exchange fixed-rate for floating-rate payments. Currency swaps are accords to deliver one currency against another currency at certain intervals.

swing In a bilateral trade agreement, the leeway provided for mutual extension of credit.

switch trade A type of countertrade utilized when a country lacks sufficient hard currency to pay for its imports. When it can acquire from a third country products desired by its creditor country, it switches shipment of those products to the creditor country. Its debt to the creditor country is thereby paid.

synchronous production An entire manufacturing process with unbalanced operations. Total system performance is emphasized.

takeoff A phase in the development of an LDC when its infrastructure has been sufficiently developed, enough interacting industries have been established, and domestic capital formation exceeds consumption, so that the country's own momentum carries the development process onward.

tariff quota A tariff that has a lower rate until the end of a specified period or until a specified amount of the commodity has been imported. At that point, the rate increases.

tariffs See *duties.*

tax haven A country that has low or no taxes on income from foreign sources or capital gains.

tax incentives The tax holidays that LDCs sometimes give companies and their managements if they will invest in the country, or that DCs sometimes give them to induce investment in an area of high unemployment or to encourage exports.

tax treaty A treaty between two countries in which each country usually lowers certain taxes on residents who are nationals of the other, and the countries agree to cooperate in tax matters like enforcement.

Taylor's scientific management system   A system based on scientific measurements that prescribes a division of work whereby planning is done by managers and plan execution is left to supervisors and workers.

technological dualism   The presence in a country of industries using modern technology while others employ more primitive methods.

terms of sale   Conditions of a sale that stipulate the point where all costs and risks are borne by the buyer.

terms of trade   The real quantities of exports that are required to pay for a given amount of imports.

territorial tax jurisdiction   The levying of tax on taxpayers while living and working in the territory of the taxing government. Income earned while living and working elsewhere is not taxed or is taxed at a lower rate.

terrorism   The use by nongovernment forces of murder, kidnapping, and destruction to publicize or gain political goals.

third-country nationals   Citizens of neither the home country nor the host country who work in a host country affiliate.

Third World   The Eastern-bloc countries that were dominated by the U.S.S.R. were considered one world. The countries of the West, primarily the OECD countries, were considered another world. All other countries are sometimes referred to as the Third World countries.

tied loans or grants   Loans or grants that the borrower or recipient must spend in the country that made them.

time draft   An unconditional order drawn by the seller on the buyer to pay the draft's amount at an agreed future date.

top-down planning   Planning process that begins at the highest level in the organization and continues downward.

topography   The surface features of a region, such as mountains, deserts, plains, and bodies of water.

total product   What the customer buys; it includes the physical product, brand name, after-sale service, warranty, instructions for use, the company image, and the package.

total quality-control system   A system that integrates the development, maintenance, and improvement of quality among all functional areas of the firm.

trade acceptance   A draft similar to a banker's acceptance, the difference being that no bank is involved. The exporter presents the draft to the importer for its acceptance to pay the amount stated at a fixed future date.

trade bloc   A group of countries with special trading rules among them, such as the EC.

trade deficit/surplus   A trade deficit is an excess of merchandise imports over exports. A trade surplus is the opposite.

trade fair   A large exhibition generally held periodically at the same place and time at which companies maintain booths to promote the sale of their products.

trade mission   Group of businesspeople and/or government officials (state and federal) that visits a foreign market in search of business opportunities.

trading at a discount   When a currency costs less in the forward market than the spot cost.

trading at a premium   When a currency costs more in the forward market than the spot cost.

trading companies   Firms that develop international trade and serve as intermediaries between foreign buyers and domestic sellers, and vice versa.

traditional economy   An area in a most rudimentary state. In such an economy, the people are typically nomadic, agriculture is at a bare subsistence level, and industry is virtually nonexistent.

traditional hostilities   When nations, races, or religions have been in conflict for long periods.

transaction risk   The risk run in international trade that changes in relative currency values will cause losses.

transfer price   The price charged by one unit of an IC for goods or services that it sells to another unit of the same IC.

translation risk   The apparent losses or gains that can result from the restatement of values from one currency into another, even if there are no transactions, when the currencies change in value relative to each other. Translation risks are common with long-term foreign investments as foreign currency values are translated to the investor's financial statements in its home currency.

transnationals   Used by the UN and some others to connote organizations variously called global, multinational, or worldwide companies.

Treaty of Rome   Established the EC.

trend analysis   Statistical technique by which successive observations of a variable at regular time intervals are analyzed for the purpose of establishing regular patterns that are used for establishing future values.

twin plants   Along the Mexican-American border, the plant on the U.S. side does the high-tech, capital-intensive part of production, while the Mexican plant does the labor-intensive part. Also called *maquiladoras*.

unbalanced growth theory   The idea that economic growth can be attained by deliberately creating an imbalance in the economy through investment in an industry that will require further investment in supporting industries to reduce the imbalance.

uncontrollable environmental forces   The external forces in the domestic and foreign environments over which management has no direct control.

underground economy   The part of a nation's income that, underreported or unreported, is not measured by official statistics.

undervalued currency   A currency that has been oversold because of emotional selling, or a currency whose value a government tries to keep below market to make its country's exports less expensive and more competitive.

unit labor costs   The labor cost to produce one unit of output.

unskilled labor   Employees without needed skills.

unspoken language   Nonverbal communication, such as gestures and body language.

untouchables   Lowest-caste Indians. Mahatma Gandhi called them *harijans*, the children of God.

Uruguay Round   The round of GATT negotiations that held its first meeting in Uruguay in 1986.

validated export license   A required document issued by the U.S. government authorizing the export of specified commodities.

value-added tax (VAT)   A tax levied at each stage in the production of a product. The tax is on the value added to the product by that stage.

variable levy   Import duties set at the differences between world market prices and local government-supported prices. Used by the European Community on grain imports to ensure that they have no price advantage over locally grown grains.

vehicle currency   A currency used in international transactions to make quotes and payments. The U.S. dollar is the currency most often used.

venture capital   Money invested, usually in equity, in a new, relatively high-risk undertaking.

vertical mobility   An individual's opportunities to move upward in a society to a higher caste or a higher social status.

voluntary export agreements (VEAs)   See *orderly marketing agreements.*

voluntary export restraints (VERs)   Export quotas imposed by the exporting nation.

watch list   List containing items of interest concerning uncontrollable variables of special interest to the firm.

Webb-Pomerene Act   Exempts from U.S. antitrust laws those associations among business competitors engaged in export trade. They must not restrain trade within the United States or the trade of any other U.S. competitors.

worldwide companies   Used by some authors to connote the organizations referred to by others as globals, multinationals, or transnationals.

zaibatsu   Centralized, family-dominated, monopolistic economic groups that dominated the Japanese economy until the end of World War II, at which time they were broken up. As time passed, however, the units of the old zaibatsu drifted back together, and they now cooperate within the group much as they did before their dissolution.

zero-coupon bonds   Bonds that are issued at a heavy discount and pay no interest but are redeemable at par at a future date.

Name Index

A

Abelson, Alan, 190, 213
Acheson, A., 154n
Ackermann, Josef, 366n
Adams, Stanley, 375, 386n
Adelberg, Arthur, 557n
Adler, Nancy, 771
Akhter, Syed H., 786n
Alam, Pervaiz, 786n
Alden, Vernon R., 480n
Alderson, Wroe, 730
Al-Eryani, Mohammad F., 786n
Alfonze, Perez, 155n
Aliber, Robert Z., 109, 217n
Allen, Robert, 76
Allison, D., 434
Almond, Peter, 366n
Altamura, Vincent M., 694, 714
Altman, Oscar L., 155n
Amsden, Davida M., 725n
Amsden, Robert T., 725n
Amuzegar, Jahangir, 218n
Anderson, Warren, 278
Andresson, Rune, 754
Aoki, Eri, 410
Applegate, Jane, 399n
Aquilano, Nicholas J., 692n
Argentinis, Takis, 632
Armstrong, A., 436
Arnold, Eiting, 154n
Artzt, Edwin L., 510–12
Axtell, Roger E., 333n

B

Baba, M. L., 286
Baker, James, 209
Balassa, B., 155n
Baldrige, Malcolm, 388
Ballance, Robert H., 481n
Ball, Anna, 771
Ball, Donald A., 31n, 155n
Bardon, Alvaro, 77
Barham, John, 366n
Barnard, Bruce, 180
Barnouw, V., 331n
Barrows, Sydney Biddle, 754
Barry, Ann, 790
Bartels, Robert, 283n
Barth, Michael, 121
Bartlett, Christopher A., 752n
Barton, William J., 366n
Bass, James, 120

C

Baumol, William J., 432n
Baxter, Andrew, 725n
Bayer, Friedrich, 10
Beck, P. W., 752n
Becker, Truman, 233
Belassa, Bela, 115n
Bell, Geoffrey, 186n
Bennett, Amanda, 786n
Bering-Jensen, Henrik, 366n
Bernstein, Harry, 433n
Bieber, Owen F., 427
Blasi, Joseph, 427
Boniver, Margherita, 409
Borchard, Edwin, 122
Borge, Victor, 220
Botton, Gilbert de, 61
Boulton, Leyla, 155n, 630n
Bovard, James, 97
Brady, I., 331n
Brandt, William K., 786n
Brittan, Sir Leon, 376
Brown, Weir M., 186n
Brownlie, Ian, 365n
Buckley, P., 116n
Burns, Pat, 771
Bush, George, 150, 558, 804
Butler, Joseph H., 269

Cahill, Laurena, 630n
Campbell, Betsy, 211
Cardin, Pierre, 66
Carrington, Tim, 432n
Carter, Jimmy, 390
Casson, M., 116n
Caves, Richard, 108
Chambers, Al, 592n
Chase, Richard B., 692n
Chesley, Paul, 299n
Chirac, Jacques, 79
Choate, Pat, 155n
Chrystal, K. Alec, 100
Clark, Lindley, Jr., 366n
Clercq, Willy de, 145
Cockburn, Patrick, 399n
Cohen, Stephen S., 660
Cohen, William A., 754
Colbert, Jean-Baptiste, 343
Collor de Mello, Fernando, 212
Connally, John, 167
Conroy, Charles J., 796
Consias, Kimon, 346
Cook, James, 155n
Coombs, Charles, 186n
Copeland, L., 331n

Copeland, Lennie, 770
Coughlin, C. C., 100
Craig, C. Samuel, 506n
Crawford, Leslie, 155n
Crawford-Mason, Clare, 692n
Crespo Velasco, Jorge, 366n
Cresson, Edith, 409
Crozier, Brian, 154n
Culbertson, John, 111–12
Cupitt, Richard Thomas, 786n
Curry, Lynne, 630n
Curzon, Gerard, 155n
Cutler, Lloyd N., 390–91

D

Daft, Richard L., 331n
Dahlburg, John-Thor, 660
Daniels, John L., 22
Darman, Richard, 754
Davidson, Joe, 399n
Davis, John E., 796
Davis, Stanley, 789–90
Dawkins, William, 366n, 631n
de Asis, Joanne, 794
Debost, Denis, 725n
de Gaulle, Charles, 343
Delors, Jacques, 147
Delphos, William A., 592n
Deming, W. Edwards, 664, 708, 713
Deng Ziaoping, 611–14
Denman, Sir Ray, 76
Derby, Roger, 560
Deschampneufs, Henry, 254
DeWitt, R. Peter, 75n
Dixon, Michael, 705
Dobyns, Lloyd, 692n
Donaghue, Hugh P., 623
Donahue, Joseph, 97
Donahue, Thomas R., 402
Donlan, Thomas G., 399n
Douglas, Susan P., 506n
Doz, Yves L., 693n
Dreinin, E., 155n
Dreyfus, Patricia A., 595
Drucker, Peter, 550
Dunkel, Tom, 399n
Dunning, John H., 109

E

Edwards, David, 632
Eells, Richard, 333n

Eisman, Regina, 725n
Ellingsen, Peter, 630n
Elliott, John, 630n
Elliott, Karen, 155n
Endean, Chris, 399n
Estaing, Giscard d', 186n
Estenssero, Victor Paz, 354
Estey, John s., 400n
Evans, John W., 155n
Evans, Richard, 400n

F

Farmer, Richard N., 786n
Fidler, Stephen, 218n
Flanigan, James, 432n
Fok, Henry, 799
Fok, Thomas, 799–800
Foster, G., 331n
Frankel, Larry, 211
Frankenstein, John, 786n
Fraser, Damian, 815n
Fraser, Douglas, 427
Frost, Caroline, 22

G

Galante, Steven P., 399n
Gardner, Richard N., 155n
George, Barbara Crutchfield, 401n
Giles, Martin, 155n
Gluck, Frederick W., 737
Goh, Munechika, 410
Goldberg, Carey, 630n
Goldstein, Henry M., 186n
Goldstein, Mark A., 399n
Golt, Sidney, 155n
Goodrich, Leland M., 155n
Gorbachev, Mikhail, 601–2, 614, 620–21
Gottfredeen, Janet, 663
Gourlay, Richard, 155n
Graham, E. M., 108
Griggs, Lewis, 331n
Grub, Philip, 770
Gumbel, Peter, 631n
Gwyn, Richard, 432n
Gyarmaty, Roger, 653

H

Hall, E. T., 290–91, 293, 333n
Hallmark, G. W., 786n
Hambro, Edward, 155n
Hamilton, Maska, 432n

Company Index

Subect Index